P9-DXT-468

DELIVER US FROM EVIL

DELIVER US *from* EVIL

THE SLAVERY QUESTION IN THE OLD SOUTH

LACY K. FORD

OXFORD UNIVERSITY PRESS

2009

OXFORD
UNIVERSITY PRESS

Oxford University Press, Inc., publishes works that further
Oxford University's objective of excellence
in research, scholarship, and education.

Oxford New York
Auckland Cape Town Dar es Salaam Hong Kong Karachi
Kuala Lumpur Madrid Melbourne Mexico City Nairobi
New Delhi Shanghai Taipei Toronto

With offices in
Argentina Austria Brazil Chile Czech Republic France Greece
Guatemala Hungary Italy Japan Poland Portugal Singapore
South Korea Switzerland Thailand Turkey Ukraine Vietnam

Published by Oxford University Press, Inc.
198 Madison Avenue, New York, NY 10016

www.oup.com

Library of Congress Cataloging-in-Publication Data
Ford, Lacy K.
Deliver us from evil : the slavery question in the old south
/ Lacy K. Ford.
p. cm.
Includes bibliographical references and index.
ISBN 978-0-19-511809-4
1. Slavery—Southern States—History—18th century.
2. Slavery—Southern States—History—19th century.
3. Whites—Southern States—Attitudes—History—18th century.
4. Whites—Southern States—Attitudes—History—19th century. I. Title.

E446.F67 2009 973.7'13–dc22 2008047533

9 8 7 6 5 4 3 2 1

Printed in the United States of America
on acid-free paper

FOR JANET, TRAVIS, AND SONYA

CONTENTS

DELIVER US FROM EVIL

INTRODUCTION

Anticipating Thomas Jefferson's personal travail on the subject of slavery, the British literary critic Samuel Johnson taunted the presumed idealism of the American movement for independence by famously asking why the "loudest yelps for liberty" came from the "drivers of negroes."[1] Johnson's caustic comment merely highlighted a tension already present in the minds of many southern slaveholders during the founding era. The existence of slavery posed a number of troubling questions for the South. Could slavery coexist with the new nation's republican ideals? Did the economic benefits of slavery outweigh the costs? Did slavery expand or limit economic and social opportunities for whites? Was there any other way to generate as much wealth in the South as slavery created? Would the wealth held in slaves survive an effort to change labor systems? Could whites ever be safe in a society with large numbers of slaves? Would the spread of evangelical Christianity challenge the dominant slaveholding ethos? Understanding the ideas and interests that shaped the answers to these and other questions about slavery offers a partial answer to Johnson's sarcastic query. More important, these slavery-related questions—or, when viewed collectively, simply "the slavery question"—and the corresponding search for answers chart the evolution of white attitudes toward the South's peculiar institution during the early national and Jacksonian eras.

Most of the questions about slavery were the same across the entire slaveholding South, but the answers provided by whites from various parts of the South often differed sharply. In particular, the ideas and interests surrounding slavery in the upper South and lower South evolved along very different trajectories, and the respective answers these two identifiable southern regions developed to the slavery question differed significantly—and contradicted each other at times. Nonetheless, taken together, these different and often conflicting answers to the slavery question did much to determine the destiny of the Old South. As a whole, this book explores the white South's twisted and tortured efforts to answer the slavery question from the drafting of the federal constitution in 1787 through the appearance of the abolition mail and petition campaigns in the mid-1830s, and particularly how those answers varied across space and through time. Drawing heavily on primary sources, including newspapers, government documents, legislative records, pamphlets, speeches, and manuscripts, as well as a rich secondary literature, this study attempts to recapture the varied and sometimes contradictory ideas and attitudes held by groups of white southerners as they debated the slavery question among themselves. In particular, it tries to re-create the political, intellectual, economic, and social thought of leading white southerners as they engaged in discussions about the appropriate role and configuration of slavery in southern society.[2]

Across several generations of scholarship, the American Civil War and the reasons for its coming have generated an impressive body of scholarship. The largest share of that vast literature has dealt either with the war itself and how it was fought or with the political developments that led directly to it. Both of these bodies of literature focused on the late antebellum or war years. Even the growing number of studies on the broader social, economic, and ideological dimensions of pre–Civil War southern society and its differences from the North have tended to concentrate on the late antebellum era, helping sustain a popular mythology of the Old South as a timeless society without a creation story.[3] In more recent years, however, a spate of important works on the South of the early republican and Jacksonian eras has signaled that current scholars are rapidly moving beyond their predecessors' preoccupation with analyzing southern society in its late antebellum maturity and attempting to recover the origins of the Old South. Yet despite this evidence of an ongoing shift in the historiography, much of this latest work focuses on communities, subregions, or states, leaving the task of explaining the historical construction of the Old South, with all its rich internal variation, far from complete. By explaining white efforts to answer the slavery question during this era, this study will fill an important portion of that remaining void.[4]

Fleshing out an argument advanced by William Freehling, this examination of the southern search for answers to the slavery question contends that there was not one antebellum South but many, and not one southern white mind-set but several.[5] It maintains that southern white views on the slavery question varied across space and changed over time. The geographic variation of white attitudes was defined chiefly by the correlated variables of racial demography and economic base, though an array of other factors also heightened differences. Foremost among these internal divisions, and the one central to the book's analytical framework, was that between the upper South and the lower South. These two major southern regions differed about many matters related to slavery. These disagreements included, but were not limited to, the desirability of gradual emancipation, the proper role and scope of the slave trade, the purpose and practicality of African colonization, the appropriate response to both threatened and actual slave revolts, the value of paternalism as a method of slave control, the appropriate ideology for the defense of slavery in national forums, and the ultimate future of slavery in the American republic. This study examines the creative tensions these differences generated and the efforts of white southerners to resolve or accommodate these tensions.

In addition to the variation across space, southern white attitudes toward slavery also evolved over time. Historians have traditionally described this as a shift from an acceptance of slavery as a necessary evil in the early republic to the embrace of the institution as a positive good in the late antebellum period. This description contains enough validity to remain viable as a shorthand summary, but it is nonetheless an oversimplification that obscures as much as it explains. My analysis posits that white attitudes toward southern slavery evolved through three identifiable phases between 1787 and 1840. The first phase ran from the founding era (1780s) through the closing of the foreign slave trade in 1808. This phase was characterized by ambivalence and inaction among upper South whites, whose rhetoric called for a gradual end to slavery but whose actions did little to achieve it, and a growing commitment to slavery among lower South whites scrambling to capture a share of the emerging cotton bonanza.

The second phase ran from the end of the foreign slave trade to Nat Turner's rebellion and the rise of immediate abolitionism in the North in the early 1830s. During this phase, whites in both the upper and lower South sought answers to the slavery question and appeared to find them in ideas or policies that the other questioned. Upper South whites, for example, looked to diffuse slavery further south though the interstate slave trade. Lower South whites often proved willing buyers, but at other times they supported state efforts to restrict the interstate trade in attempts to prevent their states from becoming too black. In the lower South especially, the paternalist movement emerged and gained influence, but it also drew persistent and sometimes bitter criticism from those who insisted that force and intimidation were crucial to slave control. This confrontation attained high visibility during the Denmark Vesey scare and its aftermath in the early 1820s and raged intermittently for more than a decade.

The third and final phase began with the Turner insurrection and the immediate abolitionists' attack on slavery during the 1830s. This phase saw both upper South whites and lower South whites finally settle on answers to the slavery question that they would continue to rely on throughout the rest of the antebellum era—but their answers were still in some ways at odds with each other. Even with the abolitionist chorus rising to full voice and the value of a solid South self-evident, solidarity could be achieved only on the narrowest of grounds: opposition to abolition.

THE VARIATION AND DYNAMISM of white southern attitudes toward slavery defy succinct summary. But the following outline of my interpretation of those views and their evolution conveys the essence of a complicated narrative. Between the constitutional convention (1787) and the federal ban on the foreign slave trade (1808), many white southerners, especially those in the upper South, saw slavery as a drag on the region's economy, inimical to the republican values on which the nation was founded, and a threat to the safety of whites in slaveholding areas. Many upper South whites looked for ways to wean their region from slavery, but agreement on practical measures for doing so was hard to conjure. During the same years, however, the cotton revolution of the late 1790s and early 1800s swept through the lower South, drawing staple agriculture and slavery out of its coastal and tidewater enclaves and spreading it across much of the lower South, from the Pee Dee River in South Carolina to the Red River in Louisiana and beyond. This staple boom cemented the lower South's commitment to slavery as a labor system and caused many lower South whites to identify slavery with prosperity and dynamism rather than with stagnation and inefficiency. But the lower South's deepening involvement with slavery brought with it a new set of problems related to the institution's growth and expansion. Among these problems were the need for a large and reliable supply of slaves and a slave trade that could provide them, the rising tensions between whites and slaves as many counties grew much more heavily black, and, perhaps most important, the threat to white security posed by a growing slave population that eventually reached majority status in many lower South counties. The lure of the profits and wealth generated by slave labor, along with the rising value of capital invested in slaves, overwhelmed any concerns about the difficulties of slave control during the region's periodic staple booms. But the cyclical downturns in the staple-driven economy tended to change lower South whites' calculus of consent on these issues, leading to efforts to modulate the region's deepening involvement with slavery.

During the second phase of evolution of white attitudes, beginning around 1808, both the upper and lower South sought answers to the slavery question in their respective regions through an internal reconfiguration of slavery. But, unsurprisingly, the two regions embraced reconfigurations of very different kinds. Upper South whites no longer desired a plan for emancipation, no matter how gradual, but rather aimed for a steady demographic reconfiguration of slavery that involved both diminishing the importance of slave labor to the region's economy and reducing the number and proportion of enslaved and free blacks living in the region. They wanted a "whitening" of the upper South. This whitening would leave the region less burdened by surplus slaves, better poised for economic development through free labor, less vulnerable to slave unrest, and closer to the full realization of still resonant Revolutionary ideals.

But while whites in the upper South agreed on the need to gradually wean the region from its excessive reliance on slave labor and to reduce its free black population, they disagreed sharply among themselves over exactly how this demographic reconfiguration should occur and how dramatic it should be. Ultimately, after much internal wrangling, an uneasy consensus emerged around the ideas of lessening the importance of slavery gradually, primarily through the sale of slaves to other parts of the South (diffusion) and secondarily through private manumission and colonization. To achieve this desired whitening of their region, upper South whites supported the geographic expansion of slavery accompanied by an active interstate slave trade. Moreover, the colonization of willing free blacks promoted private manumission by assuring upper South slaveholders and other whites that, once freed, blacks would be removed from the region. Together, diffusion and colonization constituted the upper South's tentative program for whitening their region and its equally tentative answer to the slavery question.

To a significant degree, however, the upper South's answer to the slavery question left the future of slavery in the upper South in the hands of both whites and slaves in the lower South. With the foreign slave trade banned and the cotton revolution still on the march across the lower South, that region's demand for slave labor could be legally filled only by the importation of slaves from the upper South. Demand for slaves in the domestic market provided an outlet for surplus slaves from the upper South, reduced the enslaved proportion of the upper South population, returned capital to the upper South, and supplied the desired labor for lower South staple growers. But the internal slave trade also generated its share of tension between the upper and lower South. Whites in the lower South resented the outflow of capital to the upper South and often suspected that upper South masters and traders dumped unhealthy, troublesome, and even incendiary slaves on the lower South market. At times of heightened fear of insurrection, lower South whites ascribed rumored unrest to the influence of slave instigators recently purchased from the upper South. Thus, at times lower South states passed legislation either banning the importation of slaves for sale altogether or restricting it significantly. In doing so, they sought to control racial demography, preserve white security, and slow the drain of capital from the region. Laws restricting the internal slave trade often proved difficult if not impossible to enforce, and they were usually repealed when insurrection fears subsided and rising staple prices spiked demand for additional slave labor. Nonetheless, the periodic efforts of lower South legislatures to restrict the interstate slave trade worried upper South slave sellers and posed problems for the upper South's whitening strategy.

In the lower South, the same growing dependence on slave labor that gave rise to efforts to better control the domestic slave trade also increased the region's interest in its own reconfiguration of slavery. But to achieve greater security and peace of mind, lower South whites sought not a demographic reconfiguration but an ideological one, centered on a better rationale for the holding and managing of slaves: the idea of paternalism. Led by a group of unlikely ideological insurgents (Christian ministers and lay leaders), the paternalist movement began in the early 1800s as a small but vocal group eager to "reform" slavery and moved slowly to a position of respectability and eventually one of dominance by the late 1830s. Over the course of these three decades, the ideology of paternalism gradually gained hard-won acceptance among lower South whites as the preferred social ideal for organizing a slaveholding society.[6] Lower South whites who sought an ideological reconfiguration around the notion of paternalism were seeking to render slaveholding consistent with existing republican and emerging humanitarian ideals while accepting the inevitability of the region's dependence on slave labor.

Advocates of paternalism likened the plantation (and even the large farm) to an extended family, in which masters governed their slaves with firmness and benevolence, much as they claimed to manage their own wives and children. But with the authority of a family patriarch also came responsibility. Paternalistic masters were expected to attend to their slaves' spiritual welfare as well as their physical needs, most often by devotedly inculcating Christian doctrine and morality, or at least the masters' version of them, among the enslaved. The paternalistic ideal hardly defined the reality of slaveholder practice in the early-nineteenth-century South, but the end of the African slave trade in 1808 made the paternalist project of "domesticating" slavery plausible in a way that had been unthinkable as long as large numbers of Africans continued to flow into the slave population.[7] Thus the movement's influence grew once the federal ban on the foreign trade took effect.

Yet from its inception, the paternalist movement attracted more than its share of critics, and it remained a controversial and much-challenged movement for more than two decades. Indeed, in 1822, the assumptions of paternalism were badly shaken by real or imagined insurrection plots crafted by Denmark Vesey and his lieutenants in Charleston. The Charleston investigators of the alleged plot denounced paternalism's permissiveness and indicted its encouragement of slave literacy and loosely supervised slave worship for facilitating slave unrest. They contended that paternalism both emboldened slaves and enervated masters. These critics of paternalism argued that slavery could be sustained only through reliance on force and intimidation—that is, by maintaining a degree of terror among slaves. This attack on paternalism succeeded in formally curtailing such paternalist projects as the promotion of slave literacy and the use of slave exhorters to win converts. But, while placed on the defensive by the white reaction to the Vesey scare, paternalists compromised and persevered. As a result, they successfully defended their ideology as the only means of rendering slavery acceptable in the eyes of an increasingly skeptical world. Over time, the ideal of paternalism advanced as a trope through which more and more slaveholders understood themselves and their role as masters.

Whether as a method of slave management or an ideology of slaveholders' self-understanding, paternalism gained influence in the upper South as well. In the upper South, paternalism attracted advocates in the more heavily slave counties, such as those in Southside Virginia, where most slaveholders wanted to blunt internal as well as external efforts to end slavery.[8] But in the upper South as a whole, the balance of white opinion pushed primarily for continuing the demographic reconfiguration of slavery and saw the paternalist project as secondarily useful as a means of mollifying critics of the institution's harshness while the broader demographic reconfiguration proceeded apace. In 1831, Nat Turner's slave rebellion abruptly reminded many upper South whites that the demographic reconfiguration was not occurring rapidly enough, and sparked renewed debate over accelerating the whitening process.

But the demographic reconfiguration desired by upper South whites was itself partially an expression of a South-wide white desire for an even broader type of ideological reconfiguration, one that would make race the chief mark of social distinction in the region. By the early 1830s, a newly coherent ideology of white supremacy arose to replace the elaborate if informal eighteenth-century system of social hierarchy, which tacitly assigned rank using a variety of measures, with a new nineteenth-century dichotomy of white domination and black subordination. By the 1830s, white southerners (and many other white Americans) increasingly defined social difference primarily by race rather than by class, wealth, family, ethnicity, religion, conduct, region, or even property ownership. The ideology of white supremacy replaced an elaborate system of social hierarchy, in which race had been one difference among many, with a simple system centered on race.[9] During the 1830s, this more systematic ideology of white supremacy assigned blacks, free or enslaved, a permanently inferior status and systematically denied them economic and political rights based on skin color.

The triumph of a systematic ideology of white supremacy lent momentum to the embrace of paternalism on the basis of the racial inferiority of the enslaved. But the ideology of white supremacy could justify racial separation or racial exclusion as well as racial slavery, and it could be (and was) used to justify the whitening of the upper South as well as the adoption of paternalism in the lower South. In Tennessee and North Carolina, upper South states where racial lines had not already been firmly drawn in the public sphere, the rise of this ideology generated a fresh determination to reconfigure the boundaries of political and civic life in ways that systematically excluded all blacks, including propertied free blacks, from political rights. In 1834 and 1835, state constitutional conventions in Tennessee and North Carolina, respectively, fully disfranchised free blacks. The flip side of this movement to eliminate blacks from civic and political life was the increasing tendency of white southerners to see their skin color as a source of entitlement to all the rights and privileges of citizenship.

By the mid-1830s, the Old South suddenly faced an unrelenting abolitionist attack given tangible form by the movement's alarming petition and mail campaigns.[10] Under such attack, the ideology of paternalism moved gradually from respectability to hegemony in the lower South. As it did, it figuratively transformed slavery into a "domestic institution," a label Jacksonian-era and late antebellum southerners frequently applied to it. The triumphant paternalist movement in the lower South relied on a mixture of racial, religious, and practical arguments for its explanatory power. Slavery, white defenders of the institution insisted, was particularly well suited to the racial characteristics of blacks, whom white southerners perceived as docile and childlike when properly managed but otherwise savage and degraded. Paternalism, these whites argued, provided the enslaved with the direction, guidance, and benevolent discipline they otherwise would have lacked and, as many lower South whites saw it, rendered the institution valuable to both slave and master.

Yet the prevailing Christian teachings insisted not only that paternalist masters instruct slaves in church doctrine and values but also practice Christianity in their treatment of slaves as in all their other social relations. This twist in paternalist ideology set a high standard of responsibility for slaveholders, one that masters found difficult to meet even when they tried. Thus lower South Protestantism answered the question of whether a Christian could be a slaveholder in the affirmative, thereby supplying much grist for the emerging proslavery argument. But those same teachings, when taken seriously, also made it clear that it was no easy matter for a slaveholder to practice Christianity. With its triumph in the aftermath of the abolition mail and petition campaigns, paternalism became the dominant ideology of slavery in the lower South, as well as in some slaveholding enclaves in the upper South, and it held that position until slavery itself collapsed during the Civil War a quarter century later.

Over time, lower South proslavery theorists also successfully blended the concepts of race and paternalism to position black slavery as a bulwark of white independence. According to these thinkers, the paternalistic relationship between masters and slaves prevented the development of capitalist-style labor strife in the Old South. Slavery mitigated by paternalism allowed the South to avoid many of the class tensions associated with capitalist society. Presumably free from the fear of falling into dependency and subordination, common whites in the lower South increasingly claimed independence and autonomy on the basis of their whiteness rather than ownership of productive property or the possession of productive skills. By positioning black slavery as the foundation of white independence, the mature proslavery ideology depicted the peculiar institution as a protector of cherished republican values rather than as a threat to them. It both reversed the formulation Jefferson and Madison held at the time of the founding, which believed slavery a threat to republican values, and strengthened the value of black slavery to the white plain folk. In the lower South at least, slavery, through an ideological reconfiguration, had become both a foundation for a republican social order and a promoter of democracy for white men.

THE STRUCTURE AND ARGUMENT of the book are more easily understood if a few parameters and definitions are made explicit up front. This book is a study of white attitudes and policies toward slavery in the early national and Jacksonian South. It makes no systematic effort to examine or depict the experiences of the enslaved themselves. For my understanding of those critical issues, I have relied heavily on a generation of scholarship that has achieved a sweeping reinterpretation of American slavery. This body of literature emphasizes slavery's evolution in North America and its regional variation and employs close analysis of slave demography, work, religion, family, culture, and resistance. It also examines how masters struggled with the contradictions of maintaining a brutal and oppressive system of human bondage in a republic founded on the principles of freedom and equality and how the enslaved used those contradictions to resist the slaveholders' search for domination and control.

A few of my categories deserve definition and explanation. When referring to the Old South, I include all of the antebellum slaveholding states, including those upper South states (Maryland, Delaware, Kentucky, and Missouri) that later refused to join the Confederacy. However, any slaveholding areas that were thinly settled or had not gained statehood by the late 1830s, such as Florida, Arkansas, and Texas, are generally not treated in the book. Also, for purposes of clarity, I refer to the slaveholding South as a "section." Its two major divisions, the upper and lower South, are referred to as "regions." For purposes of definition, the lower South includes South Carolina, Georgia, Alabama, Mississippi, and Louisiana. I define the upper South as Virginia, Maryland, Delaware, Kentucky, Missouri, Tennessee, and North Carolina. As states that constituted the middle ground between upper and lower South, Tennessee and North Carolina are at times referred to as the "middle South," but for most purposes these two states are treated as part of the upper South.

In the lower South, slaves accounted for more than 40 percent of the region's population in 1830, while in the upper South as a whole slaves were less than one-third of the total population. Cotton was the major cash crop in every lower South state, but in the upper South, cotton emerged as a profitable cash crop only in portions of North Carolina and Tennessee and in a few Southside Virginia counties. Neither region was homogenous. The upper South had subregions, such as Virginia's Southside, Maryland's lower peninsula, middle Tennessee's heartland, Kentucky's bluegrass region, and others where lower-South-style slave demography and plantation agriculture flourished. The lower South included areas, such as the Georgia and Alabama hill country, the Alabama wiregrass region, and the Mississippi pine barrens, that resembled the upper South in racial demography. Every lower South state seceded from the Union and joined the Confederacy in the winter of 1860–61 following Lincoln's election. No upper South state seceded from the Union until after the Confederate attack on Fort Sumter and President Lincoln's call for volunteers to put down the rebellion, and even then, only three states, Virginia, North Carolina, and Tennessee, chose the Confederacy over the Union.

The book attempts a comprehensive study of white thought on the slavery question, and in general it treats and analyzes every southern state at some point in the narrative. But not all states appear with equal frequency or emphasis. For the most part, decisions about which states deserved the most attention were based on a judgment of which states were most central to the particular subject at hand. Hence a strong focus on Virginia emerges from the book's treatment of the founders' ambivalence toward slavery and the reaction to the discovery of the Gabriel insurrection plot, and the tight focus on South Carolina and Louisiana emerges in the examination of territorial expansion and the reopening of the African slave trade. In the same manner, Virginia and Tennessee are highlighted when exploring the upper South's discussion of emancipation following Nat Turner's revolt, and North Carolina and Tennessee emerge as the focus of my examination of the elimination of free black suffrage by the egalitarian constitutional "reform" movement of the 1830s.

Additionally, throughout the book I have paid special attention to white voices from and events in Virginia and South Carolina, using them, in some sense, as indicative of what I came to understand as the dominant views of whites in the upper and lower South, respectively. By far the most heavily populated state in the South, Virginia had the largest number of slaves of any state in the nation, and in 1800 it had more slaves than all other states of the upper South combined. With its large slave population and its relatively stagnant tobacco economy, Virginia embodied the emerging predicament of the upper South regarding slavery. Politicians in the lower South looked to Virginia, with its large population and political clout, to judge the mood and direction of white sentiment in the upper South. South Carolina, with its emerging slave majority, its early and eager embrace of cotton as a cash crop, its active intellectual and cultural center in Charleston, and its precocious proslavery radicalism, often anticipated the course later followed by other states in the lower South. Upper South politicians may not have viewed South Carolina actions as indicative of current lower South sentiment, but they definitely saw South Carolina as the vanguard of lower South opinion and a possible indicator of the future direction of that opinion on matters related to slavery.

South Carolina also becomes the book's focus during the section on the Denmark Vesey insurrection scare and its aftermath.[11] The Vesey scare produced a pivotal moment in the efforts of lower South whites to decide the future of slavery in their region. By mobilizing the previously inchoate opposition to paternalism, the scare put paternalism, still an insurgent ideology, on the defensive and threatened its future influence. As an alternative, Charleston authorities openly advocated harder-edged methods of slave control, and the potency of this freshly cohered opposition raised the stakes of the debate for defenders of paternalism.

Finally, some discussion of the book's chronological coverage seems appropriate. Starting with the federal constitutional convention seemed logical because the compromises and understandings concerning slavery forged at the convention not only created the republic but also revealed lines of division between upper and lower South that remained salient throughout the early national and Jacksonian eras. Deciding exactly when to bring the story to an end for the purposes of the book proved more difficult, but a consideration of the white southern response to the abolition petition and mail campaigns of the 1830s emerged during my research as the appropriate point to conclude the account. The rise of immediate abolition and that movement's involvement in the mail and petition campaigns of the 1830s generated widespread alarm across the South. These campaigns extended abolition's reached deep into slaveholding country and forced national councils of government to address issues related to slavery on virtually a daily basis. They also convinced many white southerners that radical abolitionists were willing to encourage insurrection and bloodshed to hasten the end of slavery. The white southern reaction to these campaigns brought a hardening of perspectives on the slavery question in both the upper and lower South. Internal differences of opinion about slavery and its future continued to flourish in the South, and debate over the appropriate political strategy for defending slavery remained vigorous down to the coming of Civil War, but after the abolition mail and petition campaigns of the late 1830s, white southerners tacitly agreed that the South should present a united front against the newly militant abolition movement. Thus they began to mute their internal differences on the question of slavery when confronted with outside criticism. Thereafter, internal differences remained, but the public discussion of them centered more on strategic and tactical issues related to the defense of slavery against an increasingly hostile world and less on the viability of plans for reconfiguring slavery internally.

THIS BOOK IS ORGANIZED both chronologically and topically, moving back and forth from upper to lower South as it moves forward through time. Its argument unfolds gradually through a detailed narrative. Part One, "The Upper South's Travail," examines the changing structure and demography of slavery in the early republican upper South. It explores how the decline of the Chesapeake tobacco economy gave masters an incentive to dispose of surplus slaves, just as the rhetoric of the American Revolution gave upper South masters an ideological motivation to put slavery on a slow journey toward extinction. It also looks at how the expansion of slavery across the Appalachians into Kentucky and Tennessee engendered ambivalence toward the institution among whites in the new states. This part also explores the impact of Gabriel's insurrection plot on the upper South's consideration of slavery's future. White authorities in Virginia brutally suppressed the rumored rebellion in peremptory fashion and enacted strong measures to protect white safety. But the longer-term impact of the Gabriel insurrection scare intensified discussion of ways to facilitate colonization, encourage gradual emancipation (through the presumed success of colonization), and, most of all, stimulate the diffusion of slaves to the new cotton lands of the Southwest through the domestic slave trade.

The book's second part, "The Lower South's Embrace," details how the first short-staple cotton boom linked cotton profits, slavery, and territorial expansion in momentous ways. It examines South Carolina's contested decision to reopen the African slave trade to meet the labor demands of the cotton boom and supply slaves to the nation's new purchase, Louisiana. It also explores the anxieties generated in the region by South Carolina's decision to reopen the foreign slave trade, the rapid expansion of slavery into the Old Southwest, and the German Coast slave insurrection in Louisiana in 1811. Finally, this section briefly examines the resistance fomented by a coalition of the British, enslaved blacks, and native Americans during the War of 1812, and Andrew Jackson's concomitant rise as the champion of whites who wanted safe access to land, slaves, and cotton profits.

The third part, "Paternalism Rising," chronicles the emergence of the paternalist movement from its humble late-eighteenth-century origins to become a potent insurgency in the lower South. Paternalism's advocates faced twin challenges: they had to both persuade slaves to accept Christianity and convince whites that paternalism was an effective method of slave control. This part first charts paternalism's rise during the Second Great Awakening and its emergence initially in areas such as the Carolina and Georgia Lowcountry, which had a network of well-established churches. Then it examines the actions of those lower South whites who countered that paternalism was not an effective means of slave control.

Part Four, "Paternalism in Crisis," examines the most significant challenge the paternalist movement faced during its insurgent phase: the Denmark Vesey insurrection scare and the white response to the scare. In a series of three chapters, this section describes the scare itself, examines the analysis of the plot by local whites, who laid much of the blame on the softness of paternalism as a method of slave control, and then explores the refusal of the South Carolina legislature to adopt many of the draconian control measures recommended by Charleston-area leaders in response to the Vesey scare. Lowcountry leaders then reacted to the legislature's moderation with the formation of an aggressive voluntary organization, the South Carolina Association, charged with protecting the interests and safety of white Charlestonians. The association quickly emerged as the vanguard of proslavery radicalism in the lower South and a sworn enemy of the paternalist movement.

Part Five, "Words and Deeds," charts the course of the colonization movement in the South during the 1820s. Interest in colonization spiked across much of the region in the aftermath of the Vesey scare, both as a means of removing free blacks from the region and as a method for facilitating gradual emancipation. The part's first chapter presents the southern debate over colonization as three parallel discussions. One discussion centered on the disagreement within the upper South over whether colonization should be used to encourage gradual emancipation or simply as a means for reducing the region's large free black population. A second discussion revolved around the dispute between the upper South and lower South over whether colonization was a legitimate means for eliminating some problems related to slavery or merely an abolitionist wedge designed to undermine slavery. The third was a debate between southern and northern colonizationists over the ultimate purpose and preferred pace of the movement. This part of the book then turns to an examination of the immediate reaction of upper South whites to the publication of David Walker's *Appeal* and Nat Turner's slave revolt in Virginia. The deep fear and persistent anxiety that the Turner insurrection aroused among upper South whites, and white Virginians especially, is discussed as background to a growing popular interest in accelerating the demographic reconfiguration of slavery in the region.

Part Six examines the upper South's political and policy response to the Turner insurrection, including the epic and bitter Virginia legislative debate over gradual emancipation in 1831–32 as well as Tennessee's equally spirited and more decisive debate on the same subject in 1834. The section also analyzes how these post-Turner discussions of slavery and race led the upper South to embrace "whiteness" as both a justification for the demographic reconfiguration of slavery and a guiding principle of civic life. Toward that end, this part analyzes how Tennessee's decision to eliminate free black suffrage in 1834 and North Carolina's bitterly contested decision to disfranchise all free blacks at its 1835 state constitutional convention both reflected and enhanced the upper South's interest in an ideological whitening of the region.

The book's final part concludes the volume with three chapters on the final challenges to paternalism and its eventual triumph as the dominant ideology of slaveholding in the lower South. This section evaluates the spread of alarm and anxiety across the lower South in the aftermath of the publication of Walker's pamphlet and news of Turner's revolt. In the face of such alarming news, the ongoing contest between paternalists and their critics initially intensified. The paternalists maintained that only their approach could render slavery safe for the lower South, but the movement's opponents launched a fierce offensive, seeking to undermine the paternalist argument in light of open slave violence and aggressive abolitionist threats to slavery from outside the region. Initially, critics of paternalism succeeded in shifting the lower South's focus to the need for tighter control of slaves and free blacks. As a result, they won approval for measures banning the education of slaves and limiting the ability of paternalists to continue their mission to the region's slave population.

The section then details the broader southern reaction to the abolition mail and petition campaigns crafted by the American Anti-slavery Society. Spreading alarm and producing a call for unity and action, particularly in the lower South, the abolition mail campaign struck many whites in the South as nothing short of a terrorist attack on the region, and the mail and petition campaigns together left more white southerners than ever convinced that, at least on the point of abolition, the South had to meet its critics with one voice.

Finally, the third chapter of this part describes and analyzes the fleshing out of the ideological reconfiguration of slavery in the lower South and explains the final rise of the paternalist movement from insurgency to orthodoxy in the region. Despite the initial setback paternalism suffered from the concerns aroused by the Turner insurrection and the abolition mail campaign, ultimately the ideology's triumph in the lower South owed much to the perception that it offered the most effective counter to the emerging humanitarian critique of slavery as an evil that required immediate redress—a line of argument that lay at the core of the new abolitionist crusade. With paternalism safely ensconced at the center of its defense of slavery, the lower South's new proslavery argument also embraced a newly coherent defense of slavery as the most appropriate labor system for a republican social order and generated its own stinging critique of the dependency and degradation that it contended was engendered by free wage labor in the North. In the end, the lower South's ideological reconfiguration of slavery married the virtues of paternalism as a system for managing enslaved blacks to the economic and political imperatives of independence and egalitarianism for white males. The union was sealed with a public vow to make race the central social distinction in southern society.

In sum, by retracing and analyzing the convoluted journey the Old South, in all its internal variation, took to arrive at its mature answers to the slavery question, this study presents white southern views on slavery as the South entered the era of sectional conflict. It was during that era that white southerners offered their most overt political and ideological defense of slavery in national forums. But the road to that position had been long and complicated. The Old South's answers to the slavery question, imperfect and unacceptable as they were, had not been found easily or without conflict. The account that follows will tell that story.

PART ONE

THE UPPER SOUTH'S TRAVAIL

Though deeply indebted to slave labor for no small portion of their wealth, many upper South whites of the founding generation saw slavery as a troublesome legacy from their region's economic past rather than as a key to its future prosperity. Moreover, this generation of whites witnessed the massive flight of upper South slaves toward the British promise of freedom during the Revolutionary War. This experience shattered white confidence in the loyalty and obedience of slaves. In addition to a sluggish economy and heightened concern for white safety, upper South whites of the founding era also had ideological and moral questions about slavery. Their republican ideals, which treasured liberty and despised dependence, raised questions about whether slavery was compatible with the guiding principles of the new nation. During the same era, the spread of evangelical Christianity in the upper South challenged the morality of holding slaves. Hence whites in the upper South revealed degrees of ambiguity about the future of slavery in their region from the republic's founding through the Missouri Compromise and beyond.

Yet despite potent economic and ideological incentives to reduce their reliance on slave labor, continued if diminished profits from staple production, heavy investment in slaves, and the desire to sell surplus slaves to buyers further south combined with the unanswered question of how whites could live peacefully with their former slaves to sustain a powerful if ambivalent attachment to slavery among many upper South whites. Efforts to craft viable plans for gradual emancipation and colonization in the region foundered in the face of this attachment. Only Delaware managed to free most of its slaves by encouraging private manumission, though Virginia and Maryland controlled the size of their slave populations to a degree through the sale of slaves south and liberal private manumission policies. Across the Appalachians, slaveholders settled pockets of fertile land in the Kentucky bluegrass region and in Tennessee's Nashville basin and sought state constitutional protection for their slave property to fend off political and religious criticism of the institution.

The Gabriel insurrection scare of 1800 lent a renewed sense of urgency to upper South whites' search for answers to the slavery question, given the all too apparent dangers of living in a slave society. The state explored colonization options with new vigor but paltry results. But then the first cotton boom swept across the lower South, creating ready markets for large numbers of upper South slaves after Congress banned the foreign slave trade in 1808; this improved prospects for reducing the size of the upper South's slave population through the internal slave trade. By 1820, the upper South, and even Virginia with its largest-in-the-nation slave population, could conceive of controlling its racial demography through the diffusion of slaves to the lower South and continued experimentation with plans for colonization of free blacks.

CHAPTER ONE

OWNING SLAVES, DISOWNING SLAVERY

Writing in 1786, George Washington outlined a position on slavery that quite possibly reflected the center of gravity of Virginia opinion on the question during the Confederation era. The former general of the Continental Army and future president told a fellow Virginian that it was "among his first wishes" to witness the development of a plan "by which slavery in this country may be abolished by slow, sure and imperceptible degrees."[1] Many Virginia slaveholders would not have shared Washington's vision, especially those who resided south of the James River, but the Mount Vernon planter's view was nonetheless a common—perhaps the most common—opinion of slavery in Virginia during the post-Revolutionary era. Slavery should be phased out, surely but slowly, and at little cost to those who held slaves. In hindsight, of course, historians can see Washington's position for exactly what it was: a wish and not a plan, a preference but not a priority. But for at least two generations, if not longer, many Virginians and other upper South slaveholders strained to find near-perfect policies for doing exactly what Washington suggested: phasing slavery out in ways that created minimal disruption for, minimal sacrifice by, and minimal opposition from the very whites who benefited the most from slavery.

At the Constitutional Convention of 1787, the otherwise influential Virginians and other delegates from the Chesapeake and mid-Atlantic states found themselves outflanked by resolute founders from South Carolina and Georgia on the issue of the international slave trade. South Carolina delegates left little doubt about where they stood on the matter. Charles Cotesworth Pinckney, later a prominent Federalist and American diplomat, insisted that "South Carolina and Georgia must have slaves." A second distinguished South Carolina delegate, Revolutionary governor

John Rutledge, warned his fellow delegates that "if the Convention thinks that North Carolina, South Carolina, and Georgia will ever agree to the plan, unless their right to import slaves be untouched, the expectation is vain. The people of these states will never be such fools as to give up so important an interest." Rutledge stated directly what Pinckney implied: that without some protection for the right to import slaves, the southernmost states of the Confederation would not join the new Union.[2] Though a critic of such obstinacy, Virginia's James Madison later confirmed in a letter to Thomas Jefferson that "South Carolina and Georgia were inflexible on the point" of the slave trade.[3] To secure a window of opportunity for reopening the foreign slave trade, South Carolina and Georgia delegates formed a temporary but momentous alliance with New England shipping interests. The lower South delegates agreed to allow Congress to approve navigation laws by a simple majority rather than a two-thirds vote, sacrificing the de facto southern veto over national maritime policy. The right to block such legislation, which the South enjoyed as long as a supermajority was required for approval, long had been held as crucial to the region's agricultural export economy, and such a sacrifice by the lower South revealed the depth of its interest in extending the African slave trade. New England delegates reciprocated by accepting a twenty-year constitutional moratorium on any federal prohibition of the slave trade.[4]

Slaveholders in the upper South joined the commercial interests in the mid-Atlantic region to denounce the Convention's willingness to tolerate the international slave trade and the unholy alliance that sustained the compromise measure. "Twenty years will produce all the mischief that can be apprehended from the liberty to import slaves," James Madison complained, and so "long a term will be more dishonorable to the American character than to say nothing in the Constitution."[5] Fellow Virginian George Mason, though less nationalist than Madison, also recognized that giving the slave trade constitutional protection for so long rendered the expansion of slavery inevitable and threatened the new nation with bloody insurrection. "The Western people are already calling out for slaves for their new lands, and will fill that country with slaves if they can be got thro' S. Carolina and Georgia," Mason complained.[6] The following year, as an opponent of ratification at the Virginia convention, Mason declared that by allowing the "nefarious" slave trade to continue for twenty years, the proposed Constitution "adds daily to our weakness" rather than ensuring "our domestic safety." Mason complained that the document gave more protection to the slave trade than to slavery itself, contrasting the proposed Constitution's solicitude for the slave trade with its failure to include a firm guarantee "that will prevent the northern and eastern states from meddling with our whole property of that kind." Mason conceded that slaves were not "a desirable property," but he argued that ending slavery would "involve us in great difficulties."[7]

Yet despite their opposition to the extension of the international slave trade and their comments on the threat slavery presented to the American experiment in republicanism, upper South leaders, and particularly Virginians, were active in the new republic's earliest efforts to secure slavery, especially in areas where it already existed or might logically expand. In August 1789, the First Congress renewed the Northwest Ordinance, with its ban on slavery in the territory intact and President George Washington signed the bill into law. Later in 1789, when North Carolina agreed to cede its western land (later Tennessee) to the nation, Congress agreed to the state's condition that no law or regulation be placed on the territory that "would tend to emancipate slaves." And in 1790, Congress organized the Southwest Territory along the same general lines as the Northwest Territory, with the exception of the Northwest Territory's ban on slaves.[8] These congressional actions amounted to the informal adoption of the first federal policy toward slavery in the territories. It effectively sectionalized slavery, allowing the institution to flourish south of the Ohio River and east of the Mississippi while banning it in all territory north of the Ohio and allowing all northern states to phase out slavery as they chose. Strikingly, Congress adopted this informal policy with little or no controversy, but its impact was nonetheless dramatic.[9] The sectionalism that ultimately grew out of the policy would generate much controversy in the coming decades.

Upper South whites appeared comfortable with the congressional decisions about the territories, as did lower South whites. But southern whites as a whole showed decidedly less equanimity toward the abolition petitions submitted to the Second Congress by Quaker groups in New York and New Jersey and the Quaker-driven Philadelphia Abolition Society.[10] A petition from the Philadelphia Quakers, signed by the society's president, Benjamin Franklin, labeled slavery as "inconsistent" with "the character of the American people" and urged "the restoration of liberty" to those "groaning in servile subjection."[11] Predictably, lower South congressmen took the lead in demanding the rejection of such petitions on the grounds that they requested unconstitutional actions and that debate might inspire slave insurrection. Charleston's William Loughton Smith, an arch-Federalist, argued that the petitions asked "for a violation of Constitutional rights" and represented an assault on "the virtue and patriotism of the house." South Carolina anti-Federalist Aedanus Burke claimed that the petitioners were trying to "meddle in business with which they had nothing to do." And Thomas Tucker, another South Carolinian, suggested prophetically that while the abolitionists might "expect a general emancipation of slaves by law," the southern states would never submit to such action "without a civil war."[12]

But northern representatives argued that the petitions deserved congressional reception because of citizens' right to seek redress from the government. At least some of these northerners thought slavery was a "monstrous principle" and an "indelible stain" on the American polity.[13] Virginia representatives sought a middle ground between northern defenders of the petitions and lower South opponents. Out of respect for the republican right to petition, James Madison favored receiving the petitions and sending them immediately to a select committee, which he expected to quickly conclude that Congress had no power to interfere with slavery where it existed and no power to ban the slave trade until 1808, though it could recommend levying the $10 head tax on slave imports allowed by the Constitution. In the end, most upper South representatives joined northern representatives in agreeing to send the petitions to a select committee. Eight of ten representatives from Virginia voted for referral to a select committee, while lower South representatives voted overwhelmingly against referral.[14]

The report of the select committee conformed to Madison's expectations. It found that Congress could not interfere with either slavery or, for a time, the slave trade, but it did lament the plight of the "humane objects" of the petitions, prompting another round of outrage from the lower South. "We took each other with our mutual bad habits and respective evils, for better, for worse," William Loughton Smith observed; "the Northern states adopted us with our slaves; and we adopted them with their Quakers."[15] Madison again sought moderation, arguing for publication of the committee report in order to inform the public that Congress could not end slavery or the slave trade. Madison's proposal won narrowly, but a number of Virginia representatives defected to vote with the lower South. After the House action, Madison learned from friends in Virginia that public opinion there applauded the Senate for refusing to take notice of the petitions but found "great fault" with the House for "wasting so much time and Expense" on the matter. The increasingly apparent gravity of the situation moved Madison to work behind the scenes to dissuade antislavery groups from sending petitions to Congress and to persuade Congress to refuse to accept petitions that asked it to take action the body had already decided it had no power to take.[16] On the latter point, he succeeded reasonably well. After 1790, Congress considered only narrowly framed petitions dealing with issues related to regulating the slave trade. At the level of federal policy, the influential Virginians had taken the lead in turning back, and ultimately damping, a challenge to slavery without appearing to defend slavery. It was a gambit they yearned to perfect.[17]

AT THE STATE AND LOCAL LEVELS, however, the concern George Mason expressed at the Constitutional Convention for the domestic safety of whites in a slave society reflected the long-standing fears and anxieties of large numbers of upper South slaveholders. Many of these slaveholders had experienced what historians now view as the greatest slave revolt in American history: the flight and rebellion of tens of thousands of slaves, many of them from Virginia, during the American Revolution. Lord Dunmore's 1774 offer of freedom to all slaves who remained loyal to the Crown had hardened white resolve to fight for independence, but it also raised black hopes for freedom. Estimates suggest that more than thirty thousand slaves either were freed by the British or escaped in the hope of finding protection from the British military. Many of these African American loyalists were either never returned by the British or never recovered by their owners. A great number of these owners carried large debts from slave purchases for which the slaves were their best or only collateral. This unprecedented black Revolutionary flight for freedom proceeded on a large enough scale to shatter any white illusions that upper South slaves were content with their lot. It also raised troubling questions about the security of investment in slave property. But the persistent efforts of upper South whites to secure reparations from the British for their "lost" slaves were as much a balm to the wounded pride of the slaveholders as an attempt to recoup financial losses.

No small number of upper South slaveholders observed the enslaved population's Revolutionary-era record of flight and rebellion and decided that it would be wise to rid themselves of slavery entirely if they could, or partially if they could not fully extricate themselves from this peculiar and volatile institution. Other upper South slaveholders thought the Revolutionary erosion of slavery simply meant that the institution's foundation needed immediate strengthening, even if only for temporary stability rather than for perpetual benefit. To a large degree such views defined the poles of debate among slaveholders in the upper South over policies regarding slavery for several decades.[18]

In the post-Revolutionary upper South, practical doubts about the fundamental vulnerability to unrest of a society with a large proportion of slaves merged with triumphant republican ideals and an emerging Christian morality to raise serious reservations about the future of slavery in the United States, or at least in the upper South. Almost all of the upper South founders expressed a desire to end slavery eventually even if they proved reluctant to take bold steps toward that goal. George Washington, who manumitted his own slaves, often privately voiced sentiments in favor of gradual emancipation and clearly stated that it was "his will and desires" that "all the slaves which I own" shall "receive their freedom."[19] Virginia's Richard Henry Lee, a former president of the Continental Congress, thought slavery a "moral blight."[20] Patrick Henry puzzled over why, "at a time when the rights of humanity are defined and understood with precision, In a country, above all others, fond of liberty," citizens would adopt "a principle as repugnant to humanity as it is inconsistent with the bible, and destructive to liberty?"[21] Henry's anti-Federalist ally George Mason labeled slavery an "Evil" and bemoaned its "ill Effect" on the "Morals and Manners of our People," though Mason warned that it was best not "to expose our Weakness by examining this Subject too freely" in public.[22] Later, Henry and Mason's nationalist nemesis, James Madison, privately admitted that slavery was "unrepublican."[23]

But the most memorable expression by a republican slaveholder of the agony induced by extolling liberty while holding slaves came from Thomas Jefferson in his *Notes on the State of Virginia*. Jefferson's ambiguous views on slavery remain compelling to historians more than two centuries later not so much because they are those of the nation's most brilliant founder or because Jefferson left himself so vulnerable to the charge of hypocrisy but because they embodied in a single capacious mind so many of the contradictions and complexities evident in the collective mind of the early republican upper South.[24] His emotional, even passionate critique of slavery rendered in an often-quoted section of his *Notes* revealed many of the early republican fears about slavery. Jefferson worried about slavery's tendency to corrupt the character of the virtuous (white) republican. "The whole commerce between master and slave is a perpetual exercise of the most boisterous passions, the most unremitting despotism on the one part, and degrading submissions on the other," Jefferson lamented. "The man must be a prodigy who can retain his manners and morals undepraved by such circumstances."[25] Thanks to compelling genetic evidence, informed Americans now know that Jefferson was not such a prodigy. Jefferson fathered at least one child by his slave Sally Hemings, and most historians now concede that Jefferson's reference to the "boisterous passions" encouraged and unleashed by slavery likely includes a measure of first-person confession.[26]

But Jefferson's rather sweeping indictment of slavery as antirepublican contained many of the criticisms that reverberated throughout the upper South for the next fifty years. For Jefferson, slaveholding schooled white Virginians in the most unrepublican character. Not just masters but all whites in a slaveholding society were "daily exercised in tyranny" and transformed into "despots" by the power of mastery and the potential, indeed the inevitability, of its abuse. Nor did slavery promote the spirit of self-sufficiency so admired by republican freeholders. Instead, it destroyed the "industry" of whites. "In a warm climate," Jefferson argued, "no man will labor for himself who can make another labor for him." And Jefferson's observations convinced him that only a "very small proportion" of slaveholders were "ever seen to labor." The Sage of Monticello also worried about white safety. Either "a revolution of the wheel of fortune" or a divine justice that "could not sleep forever" might combine with the "numbers" of slaves in Virginia to unleash a slave rebellion that would ignite a larger civil war between whites and blacks that would end in the slaughter of one race. Jefferson concluded by wishing, "under the auspices of heaven, for a total emancipation" carried out "with the consent of the masters, rather than by their extirpation."[27]

With the exception of his reference to divine justice, however, Jefferson's soliloquy on slavery's incompatibility with republican ideals omitted any reference to the other important moral code that nurtured post-Revolutionary doubts about slavery among whites in the upper South: the growing influence of evangelical Christianity. Arguably, the teachings of evangelical Christianity and the activism of church leaders proved the single most powerful influence spurring upper South whites to question slavery in the late eighteenth century.[28] Beginning with revivals led by the evangelical Presbyterian Samuel Davies in the 1740s, and expanded by the evangelical appeals of Methodists and Baptists to Virginians of both races, evangelical Christianity gained influence in late-eighteenth-century Virginia and in some instances offered serious challenges to the moral and political authority of Virginia's largely Anglican gentry. The new communities of faith created by the evangelical movement included both whites (even prominent and wealthy whites) and blacks (slave and free). In the state's Tidewater region, slaves often constituted the majority of church members. In 1788, Richard Courtney, pastor at Richmond's First Baptist Church, served a "large congregation of Negroes" there. These evangelical churches, which usually allowed only white males to participate in matters of governance, were hardly models of racial egalitarianism, but the practice of worshiping together, sharing faith, and calling members "brother" and "sister," regardless of race or secular status, offered a less hierarchical manner of racial interaction than was found in any other Virginia institution.[29]

Evangelical Christianity not only provided a key point of contact, and at least to some degree shared cultural values, between the races but also mounted a serious critique of slavery based on the religion's foundational teachings and values. Since the evangelical denominations were actively proselytizing in Virginia, this critique had the potential to reach a larger audience than the antislavery messages emanating from the Quakers. In fact, in 1784, just as American Methodists severed their ties with Britain's Anglican church, the newly independent denomination also denounced slavery, ordering local pastors and circuit riders to free their slaves or face expulsion, and issuing a similar warning to the lay members who bought and sold slaves.[30] But the antislavery message of evangelical pastors often failed to find receptive ears among the laity. British-born Methodist evangelist Thomas Coke, a sharp critic of slavery, encountered violent opposition to Methodist antislavery teachings while preaching in Virginia's southern Piedmont. His message, Coke wrote, once prompted many who heard him to "combine together to flog me." A brave local sponsor of Coke's revival saved him from a beating that particular night, but Coke resumed his travels in Virginia and North Carolina with a keen awareness that criticism of slavery might lead to physical danger.[31] Another Virginia Methodist, Jesse Lee, warned Coke that such preaching would fail to encourage manumission among slaveholders, instead producing a white backlash against both slaves and evangelicals.[32] Coke later admitted that he learned to preach against slavery without giving "much offense"—dubious as that virtue might have seemed to antislavery evangelicals—by first preaching to the slaves "on the Duty of Servants to Masters" and then advising masters on their responsibilities, which included looking for appropriate times and circumstances to manumit slaves.[33]

In 1785, the Methodist Conference in Baltimore dropped its demand that lay members manumit their slaves and refrain from buying and selling slaves. This quick reversal of position, Jesse Lee later explained, came because the original Methodist rules were "offensive to most of our southern friends; and were so much opposed by some of our private members, local preachers, and some of the traveling preachers... that they were never afterwards carried into full force."[34] The Methodists, though hardly becoming proslavery, seemed willing to mute their critique of slavery in the interest of opening more doors to their evangelical efforts. But while the Methodists softened the sections of their Book of Discipline that required specific action against slavery, they continued to preach and teach about the inequities of slavery. In a sense, the modification of their discipline was not so much an abandonment of their criticism of slavery as an effort to give their pastors and revivals time to move the laity toward the clergy's position. Over time, however, the preponderance of influence seemed to flow in the opposite direction.[35]

As late as 1790, Virginia Baptists debated the "equity" of slavery at the meeting of their General Committee. Unable to reach a conclusion, the body appointed a subcommittee, including David Barrow and William Fristoe, two critics of slavery, to report on the issue. The subcommittee eventually agreed on a resolution prepared by John Leland, a Baptist pastor and champion of religious liberty, and reported back to the assembly as a whole. The resolution called slavery "a violent deprivation of the rights of nature and inconsistent with republican government" and recommended that all Baptist brethren "make use of every legal measure to extirpate the evil from the land." The Baptist General Committee approved.[36] The phrase "every legal measure," however, proved critical for the interpretation of the resolution. The main legal measure available Virginia in 1790 was the private manumission of slaves. Thus the Baptist resolution appeared to encourage the denomination's slaveholders to manumit their slaves where that practice was legal. But the phrase implied tacit disapproval of any evangelical encouragement of rebellion or running away, and it suggested that Baptists could support gradual emancipation measures as long as they worked through the appropriate legislative channels and abided by legislative outcomes. This made the Baptist position no less an ethical challenge to slavery but rendered the denomination's stance less radical and threatening as a practical matter.

SLAVE UNREST, UNLIKE the evangelical challenge, grew more rather than less threatening during the 1780s and 1790s. Upper South slaveholders became especially anxious about security once news of the rebellion in Saint-Domingue reached the Chesapeake's shores in 1791.[37] Even George Washington reacted to the news with shock. "Lamentable!" President Washington gasped after hearing the news, and he decried the appearance of "such a spirit of revolt among the Blacks." As he puzzled over reports, Washington concluded that it was "difficult to say" where such a revolutionary bid for freedom among the New World's enslaved "would stop."[38] The revolt in Saint-Domingue also conjured horrible premonitions in the active mind of Thomas Jefferson. "I am becoming daily more convinced," Jefferson admitted to James Monroe, "that all the West India islands will remain in the hands of people of colour, and a total expulsion of whites ... will take place." Jefferson thought his fellow Virginians should be able to "foresee the bloody scenes which our children certainly, and possibly ourselves (South of Patowmac) have to wade through, and try to avert them."[39] Indeed, in 1793, rumors fueled by the "example of the West Indies" swept through Virginia's Tidewater and Eastern Shore counties that an insurrectionary force totaling six thousand slaves was prepared to rise and take "full possession of the hole [*sic*] country in a few weeks."[40] John Randolph of Roanoke even claimed that he overheard one of his slaves tout the alleged plot's prospects by reference to "how the blacks has kill'd the whites in the French Island...a little while ago."[41] Later in the decade, with Toussaint L'Ouverture in power in Saint-Domingue, Maryland's Robert Goodloe Harper warned that Toussaint's officers were preparing to invade the southern states with "an army of blacks."[42] Such fears of outside interference with upper South slaves reminded the region's slaveholders of the destabilizing impact the British had had on slavery during the Revolution. In the minds of many upper South whites, a system, however profitable, that provided such a source of vulnerability demanded either reform or elimination, though neither appeared easy to accomplish.

YET IDEOLOGICAL AND RELIGIOUS DOUBTS about slaveholding, and even deep fears for white safety might have been quieted, as they eventually were in the lower South, by a booming economy sustained by slave labor. Instead, during the late eighteenth century, the troubled tobacco economy of the upper South served only to heighten the region's desire to diminish its reliance on slavery, and perhaps even abandon the increasingly peculiar institution altogether. To a large degree, the original upper South states, Virginia, Maryland, and Delaware, were products of the tobacco and slave production culture that emerged in the Chesapeake region during the colonial era.[43] White indentured servants provided the bulk of the labor at first, but after Bacon's Rebellion in the 1670s, landowners gradually shifted toward enslaved blacks as their preferred form of labor. By the 1720s, slavery was well established in the Chesapeake region and generated much wealth for Chesapeake planters.[44] In a sense, upper South tobacco growers "chose" slavery in a way that rice planters in the Carolina Lowcountry, where the slave and staple culture arrived as a whole from Barbados, did not, perhaps giving the Chesapeake slaveholding society a sense of the institution's contingency that the Lowcountry lacked. Over time, tobacco and slaves penetrated further inland, especially in Virginia, but Maryland and Delaware planters were seldom far away from the bay, and the Chesapeake region remained the center of upper South slave society for many decades.[45]

By the late eighteenth and early nineteenth centuries, the tobacco economy of the upper South stagnated, precipitating a gradual, if uneven, shift of land and labor out of tobacco and into the production of foodstuffs. Invigorated demand for foodstuffs from growing cities along the mid-Atlantic seaboard and from Europe triggered the shift, and hence the region's emerging grain-based economy quickly became as deeply enmeshed in the export market as had the area's older tobacco economy. But the labor needs of the new grain-raising economy differed sharply from those of the increasingly ossified tobacco culture due to significant differences in crop culture and production cycles. Grains such as wheat and oats required substantially less labor than tobacco except during harvest. Tobacco production, in which labor-intensive chores dominated the cultivation process throughout the growth cycle, required constant application of labor. Thus slavery, with its high ratio of fixed costs to marginal cost, suited tobacco well. Grains, with their sharp peaks and valleys in the demand for labor, rendered slavery relatively inefficient and called for a flexible labor force with low fixed costs. Thus even though large portions of the upper South continued to grow tobacco and remained heavily dependent on slave labor, the future prospects for the slave-labor portion of the region's economy appeared problematic.[46]

Waning tobacco profits and the comparative economic decline of slavery differentiated the upper South from the lower South, where staple profits exploded in the 1790s. Within the upper South, however, the economic viability of slavery varied greatly from subregion to subregion. While many white farmers in Piedmont Virginia and southern Maryland shifted to grains and hence needed fewer slaves, many planters and farmers in Virginia's Southside either maintained profitability in tobacco or wedged themselves into the periphery of the emerging cotton boom. Yet even in the heyday of the Chesapeake tobacco culture, the three original upper South states hardly participated in the slave and staple economy to the same degree. In 1790, Delaware had just under nine thousand slaves out of a total population of more than seventy-one thousand. With slaves constituting only 13 percent of its population in 1790, Delaware stood as a middle ground between the more northern Middle Atlantic states of Pennsylvania, New Jersey, and New York, where slaves accounted for less than 2 percent of the population, and the other Chesapeake-region states such as Maryland, where slaves were 32 percent of the population, and Virginia, where slaves were 39 percent of the population.[47]

In Delaware, slavery took its strongest hold in the southern portions of the state and grew generally weaker as one traveled north. Only in Sussex, the southernmost of Delaware's three counties, did slaves constitute more than 15 percent of the population, and even in Sussex slaves accounted for only 19 percent of the total population. Further up the peninsula toward Philadelphia, the counties of Kent, which included the state capital at Dover, and New Castle, which included Wilmington, were both less than 15 percent slave. In Kent, free blacks already outnumbered slaves, a portent of things to come in Delaware.[48] In 1790, Maryland looked much more like a state committed to slavery than Delaware. Maryland placed third among all states in terms of numbers of slaves, as its slave population of 103,000 nearly matched the 107,000 slaves in South Carolina, the new Union's blackest state (43 percent) in 1790, and Maryland's 32 percent proportion of slaves was almost the same as that of Georgia. In Maryland, a large majority of the state's slaves lived in the six or seven counties that lay mostly below the fall line, which ran along a curve from the District of Columbia to the uppermost reaches of Chesapeake Bay. Maryland's three black-majority counties lay near the Eastern Shore, wedged between Chesapeake Bay and the Potomac River.[49]

This static glance at upper South demography in 1790 suggests that Maryland was almost as deeply enmeshed in the slave economy as Virginia and South Carolina. But the underlying dynamics of the staple economy were already working to weaken Maryland's commitment to slavery. In the upland or interior counties of northern

Maryland, where slaves were less than 20 percent of the population, the local economy had already begun to move toward the production of foodstuffs as an export crop and a growing involvement with a craft and protoindustrial economy similar to that of Pennsylvania. The labor demands of the emerging northern Maryland economy favored free workers and family farmers, so the dynamics of the area's political economy were moving the region away from slavery and staple production rather than toward them.[50]

In 1790, Virginia held more than 293,000 slaves, more than 42 percent of all slaves in the United States that year. Virginia masters held nearly a third more slaves than South Carolina and Maryland owners combined, and only South Carolina had a larger proportion of slaves than Virginia. In 1790, the Old Dominion was also home to 12,766 free blacks, more than any other southern state, and more than a third of all free blacks living in the South that year. Slaves, of course, were not evenly distributed throughout Virginia, a state that spanned an area from Chesapeake Bay and the Atlantic Ocean in the east across the Tidewater, the Piedmont, the Blue Ridge Mountains, the great valleys, and the Allegheny Mountains to the banks of the Ohio River. If slavery varied across a north-south axis in Maryland and Delaware, it varied along an east-west axis in Virginia. By 1790, slavery had already crossed the fall line separating the Tidewater from the Piedmont and gained a strong foothold in the latter region, running, albeit with diminishing concentrations, to the foot of the Blue Ridge Mountains. West of the Blue Ridge, in the state's valleys and in its trans-Allegheny section, lived very few slaves and fewer slaveholders. Most whites in these areas expressed reluctance at, and sometimes an aversion toward, seeing slavery spread into their portion of the state on a large-scale basis.[51]

Further west still, across the Appalachians in the territories of Kentucky and Tennessee, slaves initially accounted for very small proportions of the population by southern standards. In 1790, five of every six people in the rather sparsely populated Kentucky territory were white. That same year, nearly eleven of every twelve people in Tennessee, which had roughly half the population of Kentucky, were white. Thus slavery remained a marginal institution in these upper South territories, even though they were both populated mainly by settlers from Virginia and North Carolina. During the 1790s, both Kentucky (1792) and Tennessee (1796) became states, and over the next twenty years both experienced rapid population growth, yet both states remained heavily white. Between 1790 and 1810, Kentucky's white population exploded, increasing from just over 60,000 to almost 325,000 in twenty years. The state's slave population also grew rapidly during these years, but in 1810 Kentucky was still just over 80 percent white.

Tennessee's population growth paralleled that of Kentucky during these years, only on a smaller scale. Tennessee's white population increased sevenfold between 1790 and 1810 (increasing from just over 30,000 to almost 215,000), and the state remained over 80 percent white throughout the period. Even in 1810, after the slave population of the two states had grown to nearly 125,000, Kentucky and Tennessee together served as home to only three-fourths as many slaves as North Carolina.[52] If judged by demography alone, early Kentucky and Tennessee appeared to be places where a movement to gradually end slavery might succeed.

In the founding era, republican ideals, Christian morality, fear of slave unrest, and troubling questions about the long-term economic viability of the area's slave economy all pushed upper South whites to question a perpetual commitment to slavery as a labor system. Yet post-Revolutionary southern critics of slavery faced entrenched and obstinate resistance from slaveholding interests as they tried to wean upper South society from its dependence on slavery. The value of slave property, the continued (if stagnant) need for slave labor, and the deep-seated white belief that whites and blacks could never live together in freedom made slavery a difficult institution to weaken or phase out in the absence of intricate plans for how emancipation would occur and how postemancipation society would be organized. Broadly acceptable plans proved extraordinarily difficult, if not impossible, to craft. Nevertheless, during the early national era, efforts to restrict or weaken slavery in some manner emerged in all three original upper South states as well as in the two newly formed states in the trans-Appalachian South.

In all three original Chesapeake states, various options for slowly ending slavery, lessening the region's dependence on slave labor, and reducing the number and proportion of slaves and free blacks in the total population received attention. The gradual emancipation of slaves and the colonization or other removal of the resulting free black population emerged as the preferred alternative. But even most advocates of gradual emancipation and colonization recognized that, at best, it offered a complicated, expensive, and slow method of reducing the importance of slavery in the region. Steady manumission of individual slaves by their masters under terms of state laws provided another option, though one less likely to effect dramatic change in a short period of time. But this alternative avoided many of the bewildering complications and public expense involved in even the most plausible general emancipation schemes. If the importation of additional slaves was banned or sharply restricted, private manumissions would slowly limit the growth of the upper South's slave population and possibly even reduce it, depending on the ratio of slaves sold or taken from the region by emigrating owners to the natural increase of the area's slave population. But without accompanying plans for colonization or removal, manumission threatened to create a large caste of free blacks, a "class" almost universally despised by whites in the upper South. Thus even the simplest methods of weakening slavery had drawbacks.

Efforts to dilute slavery's influence faced less opposition in areas where slavery was less central to economic success and less fundamental to the existing social order.

In Delaware, critics of slavery enjoyed a measure of success in limiting the internal slave trade and encouraging private manumission. Late in the eighteenth century, as the once rich soil along southern Delaware's coastal plain grew depleted from persistent tobacco cultivation, the state's tobacco planters were hurt by competition from newer tobacco-growing areas, and thus began the gradual but profitable switch to wheat and other grains. As slavery declined in importance to the state's economy, Christian moralism married economic self-interest among Delaware merchants and landowners to create support for minimizing the use of slave labor in the state.[53]

During the late 1780s, Quakers (who were comparatively large in number in Delaware), Methodists, and others who objected to slavery on both moral as well as economic grounds forged a coalition that persuaded the Delaware legislature to both tighten regulation of the internal slave trade and ease the path for private manumissions.[54] Beginning in 1787, the Delaware legislature passed a series of laws that pressured the state's slaveholders to reduce their surplus slave population by manumission rather than sale. The Delaware legislature banned the importation of slaves for sale in 1787 and declared that any slaves brought into the state illegally would be declared "free to all intents and purposes." Delaware's 1787 slave code also imposed restrictions on masters trying to sell slaves to out-of-state buyers, requiring any person wishing to sell slaves out of state to receive permission from three justices of the peace.[55] Two years later, the legislature, unhappy that its previous action had failed to slow the sale of slaves as much as expected, stiffened the requirement, mandating that potential slave sellers seek and receive permission of five justices of the peace instead of three.[56] To be sure, slaveholders in southern Delaware often evaded these restrictions by traveling to nearby states to sell slaves. But those who did so endured the aggravation of travel and often suffered a financial loss because of their eagerness to sell their merchandise and return home. At the very least, Federalist-era Delaware succeeded in eliminating active slave markets within the state's borders and in making it difficult for Delaware's slave owners to reduce their holdings by sale.[57]

To complement its regulation of the internal slave trade, Delaware also moved aggressively to encourage private manumission. The same 1787 Delaware code that restricted the internal slave trade also gave masters the right to emancipate all healthy slaves between the ages of eighteen and thirty-five without posting a bond.[58] With the state's prohibition of the out-of-state sale or hiring of slaves limiting their options, Delaware slaveholders found creative ways to reduce their slave holdings at minimal financial sacrifice. The method of choice was the delayed emancipation agreement, an innovative contract that deferred manumission until some distant but carefully specified time (such as the death of the master, upon the slave reaching a certain age, or after a specified number of years of service). Under delayed emancipation agreements, masters continued to profit from their slaves' labor even after providing for their eventual manumission. After entering into delayed emancipation agreements, masters often "hired out" their "term" slaves in Delaware's urban labor markets and received income from the slaves' employer.[59]

Popular with masters, these delayed manumission agreements often shifted the financial sacrifice of emancipation to the heirs of slave owners. Disappointed heirs and eager creditors regularly contested delayed manumission agreements, slowing the already tedious pace of probate court activity to a crawl. In fact, legal disputes over delayed manumission became so common in the state during the 1790s that in 1797 the legislature declared written manumission contracts "necessary for the security of...slaves, whose masters may intend to manumit them," since oral contracts could be "misunderstood or forgotten." The requirement of written contracts ensured that slaves who were promised freedom by their masters were protected from petulant heirs and aggressive creditors.[60] In 1810, at the urging of Governor George Truitt, the Delaware legislature passed a comprehensive statute codifying delayed emancipation. It stipulated that under delayed manumission agreements, blacks who worked for masters or were hired out to other employers remained slaves until their specified term of service had expired, and children born to "term" slave women were themselves slaves until they reached adulthood (age twenty-one), when they automatically received their freedom. As a protection for these slaves who enjoyed either a contractual or statutory expectation of freedom, the legislature barred owners from selling a term slave out of state without permission of the court and subjected violators to a $500 fine.[61]

Delaware's act of 1810 clearly defined deferred emancipation and enhanced the legal protection the state offered slaves under such agreements. With its passage, Delaware committed to a course of encouraging private manumission while taking no direct action to promote general emancipation, no matter how gradual. Yet Delaware's informal endorsement of individual manumission, though a course hardly destined for universal effectiveness across the slaveholding states, proved effective in the context of the state's evolving commercial economy. From 1790 to 1820, individual emancipations in the state proceeded at a steady pace. The absolute number of slaves in Delaware declined from nearly 8,900, or 15 percent of the population, in 1790 to about 4,500, or just over 6 percent of the population, in 1820. Partially due to increased manumission, the free black population in Delaware grew from just under 4,000 in 1790 to over 13,000 by 1820. When Delaware formed its first government under the United States Constitution, more than 70 percent of its black population remained shackled by slavery; less than three decades later, as the recession of 1819 settled hard on the Delaware countryside, nearly three-quarters of Delaware's blacks and mulattoes were free.[62]

Individual manumissions eroded slavery with agonizing slowness, but they offered hope for upper South slaves. More than any other staple-growing state, Delaware whites made progress toward gradually eliminating slavery through private manumission. And they did it without "whitening" the state's population through either expulsion or colonization of free blacks and, even more strikingly, while discouraging the sale of slaves to the lower South. Of course, such progress was facilitated in Delaware because its racial demography resembled that of Middle Atlantic states such as Pennsylvania or New York more than that of Maryland or Virginia.

But racial demography was not everything. Delaware could have chosen to rid itself of blacks by selling its slaves off to the cotton South, especially after 1800. Buyers in the lower South's first cotton belts clearly preferred upper South ("domestic" or "country-born") slaves to African imports, and Delaware slaves would have fetched good prices in the lower Piedmont of South Carolina and Georgia. But Delaware residents increasingly recognized that blacks could both provide skilled labor, working not only in tobacco fields but also as artisans, mechanics, and workers in the shops spawned by protoindustrialization in the state's urban areas, and serve as free laborers on the new grain and truck farms in some rural areas at a lower cost than slaves. Delaware sought to reduce the amount of slave labor within its borders, but not necessarily the amount of black labor. Freeing slaves relieved masters of their year-round cradle-to-grave responsibilities and allowed employers to hire healthy black workers as needed. Delaware's gradual shift to free labor eliminated both the capital investment and high fixed costs associated with slave labor.[63] But Delaware's option was not one that the much blacker states of Maryland and Virginia were likely to choose.

In Maryland, where nearly one-third of the population were slaves and where slavery remained central to the early national-era economy, the gradual and voluntary course of private manumission charted by Delaware nevertheless proved strikingly popular. Maryland had long allowed manumission by deed, and in 1790 the legislative also approved manumission by will.[64] With liberal manumission laws firmly in place and the area's rural tobacco economy in comparative decline, thousands of slaves were freed in Maryland during the early national era. Manumission developed a momentum of its own. As one observer later noted, the "history" of manumission in Maryland revealed that "manumission begets manumission" and "that they increase even in a geometrical proportion."[65] Moreover, delayed emancipation agreements similar to those used in Delaware quickly emerged on a widespread basis, as Maryland masters also allowed slaves to buy their freedom through a variable number of years of faithful and productive service.[66]

Ironically, the practice of delayed manumission, which over time helped slow the growth of the slave population in Maryland, actually stimulated the expansion of slavery in the city of Baltimore during the republic's first two decades. As delayed emancipations grew increasingly common in rural Maryland, an entirely new commodity appeared in the Maryland labor market: the so-called term slave. Term slaves were bought and sold in the labor market at prices considerably lower than those of a life slave of similar age, health, and labor skills. These discount prices made term slaves affordable to merchants, master craftsmen, and industrialists as well as "gentlemen" looking for house servants, who usually found the price of life slaves prohibitive. Hence many rural masters granted delayed manumissions to slaves whose labor they no longer needed and then sold these term slaves to Baltimore buyers as a way of minimizing their financial loss.[67] In 1790, only 1,200 slaves lived in Baltimore, but as delayed manumissions grew common in rural areas and the related purchases of term slaves increased, the city's slave population grew to 2,800 in 1800 and then to 4,700 in 1810. Never again was Baltimore home to as great a number of slaves as it was in 1810, because many term slaves became free blacks over time.[68] Ultimately, growing numbers of manumissions, whether immediate or gradual, fostered the dramatic growth of Maryland's free black population during the republic's early years. In 1790, Maryland's free blacks accounted for 8,000 of the state's overall black population of 111,000 (roughly 7 percent). By 1820, almost 40,000 free blacks called Maryland home (27 percent of the state's total black population).[69]

But the key to Maryland's rapidly changing slave demography was its increasingly active role as an exporter in the emerging domestic slave trade. Maryland had banned the importation of slaves for sale by land or water in 1783, largely because the state had little need for more slaves. A few years later, Maryland considered a Delaware-like ban on the export of slaves for sale. Buoyed by their success in banning the slave trade altogether in Delaware, Quakers urged the 1789 Maryland legislature to prohibit the export of slaves from the state by sale; their efforts failed when a legislative majority insisted that such a ban would not only interfere with the property rights of slaveholders but also prevent the "desirable" exodus of slaves through sale to a "warmer and more congenial climate." Two years later, another Quaker-led effort to block slave exports failed.[70]

Over time, Maryland developed an identity as a slave-exporting state. Indeed, many Maryland planters routinely sold off a portion of their slaves, both to raise ready cash and to eliminate the expense of maintaining unneeded labor. One such planter, Edward Lloyd, the Eastern Shore's largest slaveholder, annually sold off a portion of his workforce, usually teenage males, in an effort to reduce redundant labor on his plantation.[71] Buyers came from all over, but especially from the lower South, to shop for slaves in the active Maryland market. South Carolina planter John Springs, seeking to stock his expanding Upcountry plantation with slaves and looking to resell slaves to other buyers in the lower South market, made frequent trips to Maryland to purchase slaves. Springs later noted that he usually made handsome profits on slaves he resold. On the whole, white Marylanders of the era viewed the slave trade as "an almost universal resource to raise money."[72] And raise money they did. According to Michael Tadman's estimates, Maryland exported more than twenty-two thousand slaves to other states through the domestic slave trade between 1790 and 1800, a number equal to roughly one-fifth of its total slave population.[73]

Together with restrictions on slave imports and an active pace of manumissions, this aggressive exporting strategy dramatically slowed the growth of Maryland's slave population. In absolute terms, the state's slave population increased by only 4,000, from 103,000 to 107,000 in the years from 1790 to 1820. More importantly, as Maryland continued its aggressive program of slave exporting, the proportion of slaves in Maryland's total population shrank from 32 percent in 1790 to only 19 percent in 1820.[74] In just three decades, Maryland had moved from being a state as dependent on slave labor as Georgia to one whose proportion of slaves more closely resembled that of Kentucky.[75]

White Virginians who yearned for a whiter Virginia envied Maryland's success but were unable to imitate it. In 1790, the proportion of slaves in Virginia's total population, 39 percent, was the highest in the upper South, and the absolute number of slaves was the highest in the nation. Yet many, arguably even most, whites thought slavery an "evil" of some sort, though they often disagreed over its proper remedy or could see no practical remedy at all. But they did not, on the whole, deny the evil. However serious post-Revolutionary Virginians were about phasing slavery out altogether, a fairly broad consensus existed that the state should not become any more deeply immersed in slaves than it already was, and that the state's social and economic future lay in reducing the proportion of slaves in the state while protecting the value of existing slave property. Such an approach required a delicate balancing act, and sharp disagreements existed among white Virginians over questions of how far and how fast the state should move away from its dependence on slavery. Some white Virginians, particularly in the state's Southside region, saw no need to move away from slavery at all.

Led by Thomas Jefferson, a post-Revolutionary chorus of slavery's critics tried to map a course that would lead the Old Dominion away from its reliance on slavery, while cautioning that any such movement should be measured and gradual. During the early 1780s, Jefferson crafted a plan of post-nati emancipation, calling for the granting of freedom to all slaves born after December 31, 1800. Jefferson kept his gradual emancipation proposal under wraps until it was published, initially over his objection, as an appendix to the *Notes on the State of Virginia* three years later.[76] By the time Jefferson wrote *Notes*, he had already developed the views on the slavery question that he would hold, with relatively minor modifications, until his death in 1826. He seldom took actions based on those views, but he articulated them privately (usually only when asked) with considerable consistency. Jefferson was convinced that slavery was an evil that must be eliminated. But he believed that it must be eliminated gradually and in an orderly fashion, guided by the very planter elite whose members would have to sacrifice their wealth and patrimony in the process. He realized that public opinion was not ready for a general emancipation, however gradual, and that the political price for advocating it would be higher than he was willing to pay. A general emancipation in Virginia, where the "disease...is incorporated with the system," Jefferson reasoned, called not only for "time, patience and perseverance" but also for a "revolution in public opinion." Jefferson cautioned advocates of emancipation to allow for the "snail-paced gait" at which the "advance of new ideas" would capture "the public mind."[77] But Jefferson also warned slaveholders reluctant to support any plan of emancipation that they must initiate the process sooner rather than later if they expected to control it. "Nothing is written more certainly in the book of fate than that these people are to be free," Jefferson declared. "The South needs to act soon if it is still in our power to direct the process of emancipation peaceably" and "in slow degree."[78]

Jefferson conceded that any program of emancipation, not matter how gradual, stood no chance of gaining popular acceptance unless it was coupled with a plan for removal. He was convinced that "deep rooted prejudices entertained by whites" coupled with "ten thousand recollections, by the blacks, of the injuries they have sustained" would, in the absence of a colonization program, inevitably "produce convulsions which will probably never end but in the extermination of one or the other race." The place of black freedom, Jefferson contended, could not be the former place of slavery. "[I]f a slave can have a country in this world," Jefferson asserted, "it must be any other in preference to that in which he is born to live and labour for another."[79] In Jefferson's mind, because peaceful coexistence of the races remained impossible, the emancipation of slaves also meant a removal of free blacks to another location; so, as the final element of his program, Jefferson counseled patience to champions of gradual emancipation and colonization.[80]

In 1785, two years after Jefferson had drafted his plan for gradual emancipation and colonization but more than a year before it was published, a group of Virginians with an outlook far different from Jefferson's went public with a call to end slavery. The state's Methodists petitioned the Virginia legislature for a gradual emancipation of slaves, arguing that liberty was the birthright of "every rational creature without exception" and that slavery represented a system of "oppression" even more onerous than the slavery Great Britain had tried to impose on the colonies prior to the Revolution. These Methodist petitions, which included no call for colonization or removal, argued that slavery led to a "deep debasement" that "incapacitates" the human mind for the "Reception of the noble and enlarged principles of the Gospel."[81] In a bold gambit to advance their cause, religious leaders tried to persuade George Washington to sign the petition. Daniel Roberdeau, a former member of the Continental Congress and an evangelical Presbyterian, arranged a meeting in Alexandria between Washington and two leading Methodist evangelists, Thomas Coke and Francis Asbury. According to Coke and Asbury, Washington expressed sympathy for the goal of gradual emancipation but declined to sign the petition, vowing instead to make his sentiments known by letter should the legislature begin serious deliberation of the issue.[82] Washington might follow, the Methodists thought, but he would not lead. In all likelihood, Washington was honest about his general desire for gradual emancipation but dissembled about his willingness to speak publicly on its behalf; the Mount Vernon master almost certainly reasoned that the legislature would table the petition immediately and thus release him from any obligation to comment publicly on the matter.

The Methodist petitions sparked their opponents to generate a number of proslavery petitions from Southside Virginia.[83] These petitions expressed vintage republican concern about dangerous and disorderly banditti (free blacks) whom they deemed unfit for citizenship, and associated criticism of slavery with a British plot to undermine the Americans' newfound independence. One Amelia County petition denounced the "Horrors of all the Rapes, Murders and Outrages" against white society at large that would result from the emancipation of "a vast Multitude of unprincipled, unpropertied, revengeful, and remorseless Banditti."[84] Another petition from Lunenburg County attacked emancipation as a "wanton" assault on the very property rights that undergirded a republican social order. The Lunenburg petitioners admitted that they had expected such an attack on their rights by the British but expressed shock and dismay that any white Virginian would advocate a measure (emancipation) that would lead the "Country to inevitable ruin."[85] Aware that the evangelicals' petitions seeking emancipation advanced a Christian critique of slavery, the proslavery petitions from Southside countered with biblical arguments of their own. A petition from Brunswick County joined several others in pointing to Old Testament examples of slavery and claiming that Jesus and his apostles "came into the World and past [*sic*] out of it again" leaving ancient slavery as they had found it.[86] Collectively, these petitions expressed candid and unsentimental expectations that slaves were an angry and dissatisfied lot who would strike back at their oppressors with remorseless revenge if given the opportunity.

Although the Virginia House of Delegates rejected the Methodist petitions praying for a general emancipation unanimously, measures short of a full-scale gradual emancipation retained popularity in Revolutionary Virginia. Following the ideals rather than the practices of its leading Revolutionary statesmen, Virginia led the post-Revolutionary rush to establish laws facilitating private manumission, despite intense opposition from Virginia slaveholders who thought the British had already done more than enough to undermine slavery in the state. In 1782, Virginia eliminated all statutory restrictions on voluntary manumission by masters. The new law gave masters full power to emancipate individual slaves by "written instrument," whether by will or manumission agreement, without any legislative or judicial involvement. The next year, the Virginia Assembly also boosted the state's free black population when it rewarded slaves who had served in the Continental Army with freedom in return for their contributions "toward the establishment of American liberty and independence."[87] The liberalization of the state's manumission laws prompted a doubling of the Old Dominion's free black population within two years, a sixfold increase over the next eighteen years, and a tenfold increase over the next twenty-eight years. As the free black population of Virginia rose from a mere twenty-eight hundred in 1780 to more than thirty thousand by 1810, however, conservative slaveholders from Virginia's Southside complained that the increase would bring "final Ruin" to the state. Southside slaveholders insisted that the liberal manumission laws of 1782 had produced a burgeoning free black population "productive of a very great and growing evil," and urged the legislature to reassert direct control over the manumission process rather than leaving the question up to individual masters. But the legislature rejected such appeals by decisive margins throughout the 1780s, and unrestricted private manumission remained the policy of Virginia.[88] Virginia's continued interest in promoting individual manumission promoted the state's larger goal of limiting the growth of its slave population. But as a means of phasing slavery out in Virginia, private manumission represented the equivalent of emptying Chesapeake Bay with a tin cup.

Virginia authorities had taken decisive measures to end its participation in the African slave trade in 1778, in large part because many Virginia whites felt the state already had more slaves than it needed. Indeed, part of Jefferson's indictment of the British for "forcing" the slave trade on reluctant Americans in his original draft of the Declaration of Independence grew out of colonial Virginia's frustration at its inability to secure imperial approval for ending the importation of slaves before the Revolution. The 1778 ban on the importation of slaves remained in effect with only minor modifications for nearly a quarter century. It not only prohibited the foreign slave trade but also banned the importation of slaves from other states for sale or hire. As an exception to the latter prohibition on domestic imports, the law allowed slaveholders planning to settle permanently in Virginia to bring their slaves with them as long as masters registered their slaves in their county of residence and took an oath pledging that these slaves would not be sold.[89] The Virginia bans on the importation of slaves, both foreign and domestic, arose, as did later ones in other states, as part a calculated effort to keep the state from becoming too black and to protect the market value of existing slave property.

Like their counterparts in Maryland, white Virginians participated actively in the domestic slave trade as sellers of slaves to out-of-state buyers. Between 1790 and 1800, Virginia exported more than twenty-two thousand slaves, a greater number than any other slaveholding state, though a much lower percentage of its total slave population than Maryland exported during the same decade. Together, Virginia's determination to restrict the importation of slaves, its success in making individual manumission a simple process, and its active participation in exporting slaves to other states all worked toward slowing the growth of slavery in the state and perhaps slowly eroding the importance of slavery to the Virginia economy, but they did so without taking any decisive steps toward a general plan of gradual emancipation. At the turn of the eighteenth century, Virginia seemed to embrace choice as its answer to the slavery question. Old Dominion slaveholders could choose to sell, free, or keep their slaves as they saw fit.

IN THE OLDER SLAVEHOLDING AREAS of the Chesapeake region, proponents of a slaveless or less slave-oriented society worked around the institution's margins in an effort to keep open prospects for emancipation, on whatever scale and at whatever pace. At the very least, they attempted to keep slavery from growing stronger until some broadly acceptable and affordable plan for gradual emancipation could be formulated. But in areas west of the Appalachians, where whites were proportionately many and slaves, by any measure, were few, opponents of slavery had an opportunity to attack the institution before it had a chance to consolidate its hold on the region. Indeed, as settlers flowed from Virginia, Maryland, North Carolina, and other nearby states across the mountains into Kentucky and Tennessee during the 1780s and 1790s, whites took their various attitudes toward slavery (and in some cases their slaves) with them into a new and more fluid environment. Sensing that slavery had a foothold but not a stranglehold on the trans-Appalachian upper South, evangelical Christian leaders voiced sharp criticisms of slavery in these areas in an effort to slow the institution's growth there.[90]

In post-Revolutionary Kentucky, land-hungry planters and farmers from Virginia, and to a lesser extent Maryland and North Carolina, wrested the territory away from Daniel Boone's hunter generation of settlers and their Native American nemeses. As part of this process, a gaggle of Virginia-born planters established a foothold for slavery in the Bluegrass region around Lexington.[91] At virtually the same time, an array of evangelicals, also chiefly migrants from the Old Dominion, mounted an effort to prevent slavery from taking permanent root in Kentucky.[92] Presbyterian minister David Rice, a slaveholder who observed the Kentucky land grab firsthand, took the lead in launching the attack on slavery. As "creatures of God," he insisted, "we are, with respect to liberty, all equal." Slavery, Rice contended, "produces idleness" and destroyed the work ethic by reducing labor from a virtue to a "disgrace." Moreover, slavery tended "to sap the foundations" of moral and political virtue and undermined the very republican character on which the American experiment in self-government depended. The pastor concluded that only if slaveholding states resolved "unconditionally to put an end to slavery" could a collapse of the new republican order be averted.[93]

Neither Rice nor the Baptist and Methodist evangelicals who echoed his sentiments actually expected an immediate emancipation of slaves in Kentucky, where just over one-fifth of all households owned slaves in 1790, but they did want an immediate acknowledgment of the problem and progress toward a remedy. To assist in such an effort, evangelical critics of slavery developed an agenda for the 1792 state constitutional convention. They hoped to slow, if not block altogether, the introduction of new slaves into Kentucky, to protect the right of masters to manumit their own slaves without legislative approval and, most importantly, to prevent the convention from adopting any constitutional provision that would prevent future legislatures from passing a general emancipation law.[94]

Other Kentuckians had other ideas for handling the issue of slavery at the convention. Planters from the Bluegrass region, the chief outpost of staple culture in Kentucky, planned to use the convention to secure property rights in land and slaves and to establish a stable, even conservative, republican government for Kentucky. John Breckinridge, a slaveholding Virginian who migrated to Kentucky in the early 1790s and later emerged as a prominent Bluegrass politician, admitted before the convention began that he was "somewhat afraid of the Kentucky politicians with respect to negroes."[95] Worried that the evangelicals and their supporters might try to strike against slavery, the Bluegrass faction wanted a constitutional provision guaranteeing that the legislature could not free slaves without their masters' consent and without providing direct monetary compensation to slaveholders.[96]

In the larger political context, the Kentucky constitutional convention of 1792 reflected the ongoing contest between farmers and squatters who constituted the "popular" or radical faction in state politics and the emerging Kentucky gentry, patterned on the Virginia model, who sought robust checks on the potential excesses of popular democracy. Pre-convention electioneering centered on a dialogue between the popular and gentry positions on various issues, of which slavery was one. Once delegates were elected, Rice and other antislavery evangelical ministers accounted for seven of the forty-two delegates, and they used the convention as a forum to critique slavery.[97] In his convention speeches, Rice again highlighted the debilitating impact of slavery on white work habits and raised questions about internal security. In a slave society, Rice maintained, promising young men of talent and standing often expected to inherit "an independent fortune consisting in land and slaves" and thus succumbed to the temptations of "pleasure and dissipation." But if slavery led heirs of planters astray, its tendency to undermine the work ethic (and indeed the very definition of work) throughout every class of white society troubled the Presbyterian pastor more profoundly. Where "slavery becomes common, industry sinks into disgrace," Rice argued. "To labour, is to slave: to work, is to work like a Negroe." Expressing concern about the threat of slave insurrection, Rice argued that chattel bondage placed every slave in "a state of war with his master." From the slave's perspective, this "war" was both "unprovoked" and "properly defensive," but it was nonetheless "a perpetual war." Unless plans were laid for ending slavery, this undeclared state of war would one day erupt into open conflict, as it recently had in the West Indies, where insurrection wrote the "melancholy effects of this wretched policy [slavery]" with "the blood of thousands." Rice concluded his unsparing critique of slavery with an appeal to Christian morality. "It is quite evident that Slavery is contrary to the spirit and genius of the Christian religion," Rice declared. "It is contrary to that excellent precept laid down by the divine author of the Christian institution...[that] *Whatsoever ye would that men should do to you, do ye even so to them*."[98]

Yet even so bold a critic of slavery as Rice argued for a gradual and prudent policy of emancipation. Rice compared the "evil" of slavery to "a tree that has long been planted, it has been growing many years, it has taken deep root, its trunk is large, and its branches extended wide; should it be cut down suddenly, it might crush all that grew near it; should it be violently eradicated, it might tear up the ground on which it grows, and produce fatal effects." While "slaves have a just claim to be freed instantly," Rice reasoned, their treatment as slaves had "rendered them incapable" of "enjoying" or "using" their freedom responsibly. Thus Rice recommended empowering the Kentucky legislature to "prevent the importation of any more slaves" and to adopt an "expedient" a plan of post-nati emancipation combined with a system of "proper education" to train slaves destined for freedom to become "useful citizens."[99] When offering a specific program for emancipation, the pulpit firebrand Rice began to sound more and more like George Washington, that paragon of dignified reserve, in wanting to eradicate slavery slowly, by "imperceptible degrees." But Rice at least did propose a plan of emancipation at a state constitutional convention.

At a convention where four out of every five delegates (as opposed to just over one in five households in the territory) owned slaves, slavery did not go undefended. Leading the opposition to gradual emancipation was George Nicholas, a member of an old Virginia family and a substantial slaveholder. Nicholas chose to make his case for giving slavery constitutional protection on the grounds of securing property rights. Nicholas claimed that he had never approved of slavery but warned that "the removing of it in a proper manner would be attended with great difficulties." A clause protecting property rights in slaves, the former Virginian argued, would prevent "one part of the community" from being "generous at the expense of the other part." Nicholas played on popular fears of racial amalgamation, predicting that a general emancipation would lead to widespread miscegenation and a general dilution of the white race.[100]

Nicholas, the chief architect of the conservative strategy, and his gentry allies had taken pains to present a series of resolutions at the convention that amounted to an informal draft of a constitution. One of the proposed clauses prohibited legislative emancipation and required that any emancipation plan include monetary compensation for slaveholders. Nicholas had known since well before the convention that protecting slavery depended on attracting the support of the large portion of the community who did not own slaves. To build such a coalition, he proved willing to compromise on questions of primary importance to the state's egalitarians. Long an advocate of freehold suffrage, Nicholas yielded to the democratic faction's insistence that equality meant white manhood suffrage, rationalizing his decision on the grounds that "the wealthy will nineteen times out of twenty be chosen" by the voters anyway. He also knew that such an accommodation with popular democracy would render the egalitarian faction more amenable to the constitutional protection of slavery. The gentry faction's resolutions included other means of checking popular rule, such as life tenure for judges and an indirectly elected state senate, but the conservative concession on a property requirement for voting arguably garnered substantial support for the protection of slavery among some of the convention's more egalitarian delegates, many of whom wanted a democratic constitution but did not share Rice's moral disdain for slavery.[101]

The issue finally came to a head on April 18, 1792, when Sam Taylor, a delegate from Mercer County, moved to deny slavery any constitutional protection and leave all questions related to the institution up to future legislatures by removing Article IX, which included all the draft provisions regarding slavery, from the state constitution. By a vote of twenty-six to sixteen, delegates voted against Taylor's motion. Rice had resigned from the convention before the key vote on slavery, but six of the sixteen votes in favor of removing the clause came from the remaining clergy (three Baptist, two Presbyterian, and one Methodist), and an additional six minority votes came from active Presbyterian laymen. Twelve of the sixteen votes against providing constitutional safeguards for slavery came from slaveholders, but all of the twenty-six votes in favor of constitutional protection of the master's right to hold slaves came from slaveholders.[102]

The convention's critics of slavery failed to prevent the convention from including a guarantee against legislative emancipation into the state's first constitution, though the constitution allowed private manumission. On the question of the slave trade, however, results were mixed. The 1792 constitution banned the importation of slaves from foreign countries and critics almost secured a ban on the interstate slave trade as well. Hubbard Taylor, a defender of Bluegrass interests, admitted that he and several other delegates who voted to protect slavery would have supported an absolute ban on the importation of slaves and would have been willing to set a date certain for the prohibition had it not been for the influence of George Nicholas, a determined opponent of such a ban.[103] Nicholas believed that slaveholders were precisely the kind of "valuable immigrants" the state needed, and that an absolute ban on the importation of slaves would dissuade them from coming to Kentucky. William Lewis, another member of the Bluegrass gentry, agreed, calling a ban on the importation of domestic slaves a "wretched piece of policy." Slaveholders, Lewis claimed, were the "most desirable emigrants, not only on account of the wealth they introduce" but also for the "character" they brought to the state.[104] In the face of such opposition, the convention decided against a constitutional ban on slave imports, but it did grant the legislature the authority to ban the importation of slaves as merchandise if they chose to do so. In its final form, Kentucky's first constitution shied away from any approach toward gradual emancipation except private manumission, embraced the importation of slaves by settlers, and generally placed the slaveholders in control of the future of slavery in the state without actually endorsing slavery as a "good."[105]

Despite their defeat at the 1792 convention, critics of slavery in Kentucky continued undeterred in their efforts to limit slavery's influence. In 1794, the Transylvania Presbytery, which embraced the entire state of Kentucky, instructed all slaveholders to prepare their slaves for the eventual "enjoyment of freedom." But while this official assemblage of Kentucky Presbyterians viewed "with deepest concern" all "vestiges of slavery which may exist in our country," it declined to exclude slaveholders from communion.[106] Though "fully convinced of the great evil of slavery," the Transylvania Presbytery concluded that "the final remedy" for the evil belonged only to "the civil power." And the presbytery again admitted that it did "not think they have sufficient authority from the word of God to make it [slaveholding] a term of church communion." Thus the presbytery left "it to the conscience of the brethren to act as they think proper, earnestly recommending to the people ... to emancipate such of their slaves as they may think fit subjects for liberty." Going further, the Transylvania Presbytery sought to render more and more slaves likely candidates for manumission by urging communicants to "take every possible measure by teaching their young slaves to read" and to "give them such instruction ... to prepare them for the enjoyment of liberty." The presbytery remained hopeful that emancipation "will be accomplished as soon as the nature of things admit."[107]

Animated primarily by the 1792 Kentucky constitution's undemocratic features, including an indirectly elected upper house and the life tenure of judges, a movement emerged to reform the 1792 constitution almost as soon as it took effect. Unsurprisingly, evangelical critics of slavery quickly joined the reform movement.[108] These critics argued that slavery "ought to be abolished as soon as equity and the safety of the state admit."[109] Convinced by continued evangelical rumblings that the issue of slavery might be rejoined when a convention for constitutional reform was called in 1799, Kentucky slaveholders prepared for the election of delegates. John Breckinridge, an expatriate member of the Virginia gentry and an opponent of a second convention, initially offered an emphatic defense of slavery grounded in the idea of property rights. What, Breckinridge demanded to know, "is the difference whether I am robbed of my horse by a highwayman or of my slave by a set of people called Convention"?[110] But George Nicholas, the wily architect of the first Kentucky constitution, advised Breckinridge to take a more conciliatory stance. Nicholas admitted that he opposed a second convention, but he warned Breckinridge that "opposition to it will only increase the fever, and render the opposers personally obnoxious."[111] Conservatives knew that they must again fashion a rationale for the constitutional protection of slavery that appealed to nonslaveholders as well as slaveholders, to reformers as well as conservatives. Seeking to win over all landowners, Breckinridge argued that "if they [opponents of slavery] can by one experiment emancipate our slaves; the same principle...will enable them at a second experiment to extinguish our land titles."[112] In a society where controversy and litigation over the legitimacy of land titles flourished as readily as bluegrass, charges that the critics of slavery had made common cause with those seeking to vacate any number of land titles generated considerable concern among landowners.

One reform candidate not associated with the evangelicals resented the effort to equate criticism of slavery with a threat to property titles generally. Henry Clay, an outspoken supporter of constitutional reform whose early legal career in Lexington revolved around land disputes, replied to Breckinridge's argument. Clay charged that the efforts of conservative slaveholders to link gradual emancipation with the revocation of land titles were either misguided or disingenuous attempts to thwart all reforms by portraying reformers as enemies of property.[113] In an appeal to the voters of Fayette County, the twenty-one-year-old Clay announced his support of removing the constitutional protection from slavery so that a future legislature could pass a plan of gradual emancipation without first amending the state constitution. "All America acknowledges the existence of slavery as an evil," Clay asserted, one that not only deprived the slave of freedom but also "Injures the master" by "laying waste his lands" and "enabling him to live indolently."[114]

Once again, Nicholas, this time assisted by Breckinridge, built a coalition to defend the constitutional protection for slavery by making a concession to the reform faction. Conservatives agreed to support the direct election of state senators, a measure they had long opposed but a major goal of reformers. In the pre-convention canvass, conservatives organized slates of candidates around the principles of direct election of senators and the preservation of a constitutional prohibition on legislative emancipation. Thus the question of removing the protection of slavery was widely debated during the canvass. The results immediately reassured slaveholders and revealed the underlying weakness of emancipation sentiment in Kentucky. Only four outright emancipationists won election to the second convention. Moreover, representation of the antislavery clergy declined from the 1792 convention. Only three ministers served as delegates in 1799, and one of those invoked the Bible in defense of slavery rather than in criticism. In final form, the 1799 constitution preserved the protection of slave property, again prohibiting the emancipation of slaves without the permission of their owners, but also again leaving masters free to manumit slaves on their own authority.[115]

While the Nicholas-Breckinridge strategy of protecting slavery by making concessions to democratic impulses in Kentucky doubtless strengthened the hand of slavery's defenders at the convention, the weakness of emancipation sentiment at Kentucky's 1799 convention also grew from the increased presence of slavery in the state. The proportion of Kentucky households owning slaves had increased from 22 percent in 1790 to just over 25 percent in 1800 and the absolute number of slaves in the state had increased from under fifteen thousand to more than forty thousand, even though slaves as a proportion of the total Kentucky population remained virtually unchanged. Bluegrass planters were learning that they could grow hemp for export profitably, and in Bourbon County, planters learned that their bountiful corn crops made a fine whisky when distilled. These products quickly became new Kentucky staples and heightened the commonwealth's interest in slavery, if only for a time.[116]

Defeated again at the 1799 convention, critics of slavery in Kentucky retreated, at least temporarily, from the political realm. By 1808, the Methodists had softened their stance against slavery in an effort to evangelize slaves. Presbyterians in Kentucky generally followed suit. Kentucky Baptists split by local association. One Baptist association in Kentucky declared that it was "improper for ministers, churches, or Associations to meddle with emancipation from slavery or any other political subject."[117] But in the congregational setting, some Baptist leaders remained outspoken in their opposition. Baptist pastor David Barrow attacked slavery as "odious to all true republicans." One Kentucky Baptist association then expelled Barrow for "preaching the doctrine of emancipation to the harm of the brotherhood." In 1807, Barrow and other Baptists who agreed with his position on slavery organized a separate association, subtitled "Friends of Humanity," but this association never attracted more than three hundred of Kentucky's seventeen thousand Baptists. Barrow and his supporters organized the Kentucky Abolition Society in 1808, and it served as the loudest voice against slavery in the commonwealth for the next fifteen years, but its practical influence was minimal.[118]

A bit further south, in territorial Tennessee, early criticism of slavery emanated from scattered Quaker and Presbyterian churches and eventually took deep root in the hills and hollows of east Tennessee, where the local economy never depended heavily on slave labor.[119] North Carolina's terms for ceding the Tennessee territory to the Union required that slavery be allowed during the territorial phase. Yet the early settlers of Tennessee migrated not from the Chesapeake hearth but from the much whiter Piedmont regions of North and South Carolina and the Holston Valley in southwestern Virginia, and fewer than four thousand slaves lived in the territory in 1790. Local tradition holds that the state's first constitutional convention in 1796 received but ignored petitions bearing more than two thousand signatures urging that slavery be banned from Tennessee after 1864, though no official record of these petitions or the convention's handling of them has survived.[120] The state constitution produced by the convention made no general statement concerning slavery as a matter of policy but imposed a tax on slaves, suggesting that Tennessee's founders expected the institution to exist there. In 1797, slavery critic Thomas Embree, a Quaker from the Knoxville area, organized antislavery societies in two east Tennessee counties. Embree pledged these societies to the goal of using "legal means" to promote the cause of emancipation. Embree proposed liberal manumission and a program of education for slaves to prepare them for eventual emancipation, but his efforts attracted only limited support.[121]

The practice of private manumission appeared common in early Tennessee, but pleas for the state to adopt liberal manumission laws were not entirely successful. From its admission as a state, Tennessee required legislative approval of private manumissions. Complaining that it annually considered too many petitions for private emancipation, the 1801 legislature turned the question of manumission over to the county courts. The law required masters seeking to manumit slaves to explain their motives and intentions to the court and give a bond adequate to cover any expenses the county might incur for care of the ex-slave. Approval of manumission required agreement of six of the nine county court justices. Arguably, this law did little to make manumission more difficult—appearing before the county court was probably no more cumbersome than petitioning the legislature—but the new law did make manumission decisions dependent on the general tenor of county opinion. Evidence suggests, however, that in early national Tennessee, the chief reservation about manumission was the fear that the newly freed blacks would impose a financial burden on local governments. If that objection could be overcome, approval came readily.[122]

By the early 1800s, even east Tennessee critics of slavery such as Embree agreed that gradual emancipation constituted "the only safe and practical method of abolition."[123] Moreover, the negotiation of successful treaties with the Cherokees in 1805 and 1806 helped facilitate the settlement of the more fertile region of middle Tennessee during the first decade of the nineteenth century. The opening of this area to widespread settlement and Tennessee's essentially unregulated participation in the interstate slave trade introduced more and more slaves into the state, though it remained overwhelmingly white in 1810. On balance, Tennessee's connections with the lower South were strong enough that its early leaders appeared more concerned about making sure that Tennessee acquired enough slaves than with finding a way to phase out slavery. Thus Tennessee's early opponents of slavery were easily brushed aside by the state's emerging political leaders. Still, criticism of slavery in Tennessee never entirely abated. Retaining a stronghold in the eastern portion of the state, critics of slavery in Tennessee were heard if not heeded throughout the antebellum era.[124]

In the final analysis, the early evangelical campaign against slavery in the trans-Appalachian South made scant headway. It failed to convince political leaders in either Kentucky or Tennessee to adopt a plan for gradual emancipation or ban the importation of more slaves. For the long term, it left in its wake not a thriving antislavery movement but rather a scattered handful of manumission or abolition societies that made more noise than difference over the coming decades. Arguably the primary achievement of the evangelical movement against slavery lay in extracting concessions from the area's reluctant defenders of slavery that the institution flourished as an evil that defied remedy rather than as a positive good to society. George Nicholas and John Breckinridge could agree with Henry Clay and even David Rice and David Barrow that slavery was an evil. But such ideological concessions did little to hasten slavery's demise and doubtless proved of little solace to the region's tens of thousands of slaves. And if there was much common ground for identifying the evil, there seemed virtually none on the question of finding a remedy. But the upper South's continued rhetorical adherence to the idea that slavery was a temporary evil made significant impressions on the minds of many northerners, who believed that southern leaders viewed slavery as an unfortunate and impermanent institution and were working patiently to eliminate it.[125]

During the 1790s, relatively unrestricted private manumissions by individual slaveholders remained almost the only active means for advancing the cause of emancipation in the upper South. Yet almost all whites in Virginia, regardless of their position on the future of slavery in the region, recognized that this method eroded slavery at a glacial pace if at all. Some of the Old Dominion's critics of slavery were dissatisfied with this pace and advocated alternative measures. James Madison quietly articulated a clear vision of how a program of gradual emancipation accompanied by colonization might nudge slavery toward ultimate extinction in Virginia. Like his friend Jefferson, Madison thought that blacks could never be fully "incorporated" into the white republic, not because of any innate black limitations but because "the prejudices of the Whites, prejudices proceeding principally from the difference of colour, must be considered permanent and insuperable." Thus, Madison argued, "some proper external receptacle" must be located where freed blacks could enjoy freedom and self-government apart from whites. Madison thought the solution to this problem lay in the creation of a large colony of free blacks in Africa. In a private memorandum written to a Philadelphia Quaker friend in 1789, Madison proposed the creation of a colony of ex-slaves in Africa as "the best hope yet presented of putting an end to the slavery in which at least 600,000 unhappy negroes are now involved." Madison believed that manumission without colonization was not only doomed to failure but also likely to spawn a searing white backlash against the very idea of emancipation. Virginia's liberal manumission law had helped foster the growth of the Old Dominion's free black population during the 1780s, and based on his observations of that population, Madison concluded that free blacks retained "the vices and habits of slaves." Such perceptions of free black behavior, Madison thought, would only discourage whites from further support of gradual emancipation. Moreover, the inevitable tensions "inspired by their former relation of oppressors and oppressed" prevented free blacks and whites from cooperating in a biracial republic. Such an experiment could only end in dispute and violence. For Madison, as for Jefferson, the integration of free blacks as citizens into a previously white republic seemed impossible.[126]

During the 1790s, another friend of Jefferson, St. George Tucker, a young professor of law at William and Mary, also laid out a plan for gradual emancipation. Tucker shared Jefferson's interest in gradual and timely emancipation, and in 1795 he began preparation of a formal proposal for general emancipation that he planned to submit to the Virginia legislature.[127] "The introduction of slavery into this country," Tucker declared, "is at this day considered among its greatest misfortunes by a very great majority" of Virginians. Though often "reproached for an evil," Virginians, Tucker insisted, could not have "avoided" slavery any more than "hereditary gout or leprosy." But while exonerating the "present generation" of Virginians from any blame for slavery, Tucker also admitted that prospects for general emancipation were doubtful at best, since many whites in early national Virginia conceded that slavery was an evil but were nevertheless reluctant to give it up. "The malady has proceeded so far," Tucker acknowledged, "as to render it doubtful whether any specific plan can be found to eradicate, or even palliate the disease." Tucker saw this reluctance as the poisonous product of generations of slaveholding experience, arguing that the Virginia legislature had little appetite for general emancipation because "every white man felt himself born to tyrannize" while viewing blacks as "of no more importance than...brute cattle." In his heart of hearts, Tucker knew that overcoming such "deep-rooted, and innate prejudices" might lie "beyond the power of human nature to accomplish."[128]

Yet Tucker remained determined to try. He proposed a very gradual emancipation process, calling for the emancipation of all female slaves once they reached the age of thirty. All males born to these women before the age of thirty would remain slaves for life. By most estimates, Tucker's plan would have taken more than a century to free all slaves. But Tucker saw the agonizing slowness of the process as his proposal's greatest strength, since it guaranteed Virginia landholders access to a sizeable force of male slave labor for generations to come and ensured than emancipation came at a low cost to taxpayers.[129]

Tucker's plan did not mandate the colonization of free blacks. Accepting as fact the common white belief in the "marked physical and intellectual inferiority" of blacks, Tucker hoped free blacks would leave Virginia of their own accord, but he thought that mandatory colonization was incompatible with the spirit of republicanism. In Tucker's proposal, free blacks who chose to remain in Virginia would be forced into a permanent system of forced labor, resembling indentured servitude or apprenticeship, and a permanent status as denizen (which Tucker called "civil slavery"), a status that allowed these recently freed ex-slaves even fewer rights than other free blacks held in Virginia. The avowed purpose of "civil slavery" was to push freed blacks toward leaving the state. Even though he spoke of it as a plan of colonization, Tucker's plan for removal was really one of voluntary migration. Predictably, this idea of dumping free blacks into other states was not well received in the recipient areas, and most Virginians recognized that other states could pass laws to frustrate Tucker's plan of voluntary migration. While Tucker's approach to encouraging migration relieved the state of the financial burden of paying for mandatory colonization, his critics rightly countered that his plan for "removal" failed to guarantee the departure of the blacks freed by his emancipation provisions.[130]

When Tucker finally submitted his detailed plan for general emancipation to the legislature in 1797, his worst fears about Virginia's unwillingness to address the slavery issue were realized. George K. Taylor, a Federalist delegate from Prince George County who had previously agreed to introduce Tucker's letter and plan to the House, reported to his friend that "such is the force of prejudice" against the idea that his efforts on Tucker's behalf would prove futile. Taylor's reckoning of legislative sentiment proved accurate. The lower house of the assembly voted overwhelmingly to table the proposal. In the upper house, a few senators defended Tucker's plan, but the senate as a whole politely ignored it.[131] A chagrined Tucker admitted that he had underestimated the opposition to general emancipation in Virginia. Only "actual suffering" by slaveholders, a concerned Tucker predicted, would open their ears to the "voice of reason."[132]

Just over two years later, white Virginians narrowly missed feeling such "actual suffering" when state and local authorities, acting on tips from slave informants, scotched an alleged insurrection plot of "extensive" proportions in Richmond, one designed to "fight the White People for freedom," in the late summer of 1800.[133]

CHAPTER TWO

REBELLION AND REACTION

Gabriel, a skilled slave blacksmith, possessed both the skills and the opportunity to organize an insurrection.[1] He was literate, and his master, Thomas Prosser, permitted him to travel regularly between Brookfield plantation in southern Henrico County and nearby Richmond, where his master also owned a town home. According to evidence developed by white authorities in the investigation and trials that followed the discovery of an insurrection plot in late summer of 1800, Gabriel's rebellion had been several months in the making, involved a number of skilled slave artisans in Richmond and surrounding areas, and attracted a following estimated by Gabriel himself at between five hundred and six hundred. Gabriel's motives, if any other than a willingness to take a risk in pursuit of freedom, remain a matter of conjecture.[2] A year earlier, in 1799, Gabriel and two other slaves plotted to steal a hog from a white tenant farmer in the Brookfield neighborhood. When the white tenant, a former overseer named Absalom Johnson, caught the three slaves in the act, Gabriel fought him, and bit off a piece of Johnson's ear during the fight. Gabriel's offense, assaulting a white man, was a serious one. It placed him in the hands of white authorities and at risk of hanging. The matter went before the slave court in Henrico County. The court found Gabriel guilty but, through benefit of clergy (which Virginia law allowed slaves as well as whites to claim), his sentence was reduced to thirty-nine lashes. His thumb was then branded, as was the common practice, to indicate to all that he was no longer entitled to invoke benefit of clergy.[3] This severe punishment for hog stealing and assaulting a white man, and the permanent stigma of a branded thumb, doubtless left Gabriel angry, and perhaps gave him special motivation to seek revenge against white authorities.

Over the next year, Gabriel recruited his lieutenants chiefly from the ranks of slave artisans and other skilled slaves he knew in and around southern Henrico County and the city of Richmond. For the most part, the skilled blacksmith showed a reluctance to recruit unskilled plantation slaves, who typically enjoyed less autonomy and freedom of movement than urban slaves and who were also less likely to be able to read and write. Gabriel apparently thought skilled, literate, urban slaves less likely to betray the plan than field slaves or house servants, who often worked more closely with their masters and had less familiarity with the world beyond their local community.[4] Using his ability to travel more or less freely to advance his cause, Gabriel attended church services, community barbecues, and "fish feasts" throughout the Richmond hinterland to recruit potential followers. According to slave trial testimony, after attending church services, Gabriel often invited "Some of the Negroe men to drink grog" with him. Once the men had assembled, he explained his plan to organize a rebellion and throw off the yoke of slavery. He would then ask those gathered who would be willing to fight for their freedom to stand. Gabriel had usually planted one or two committed followers in the crowd to stand first as an inducement for others to join.[5] Gabriel's lieutenants allegedly recruited slaves from as far away as Caroline County and Petersburg using similar techniques.[6]

Though knowledgeable about the Bible and fully aware of the growing influence of Christianity among slaves, Gabriel refrained from making overtly religious appeals for freedom fighters. He recognized the radical potential of Christianity and understood the importance of the exodus story and Old Testament prophecies concerning justice and the fulfillment of the poor. But while aware of the influence these messages had on blacks around Richmond, Gabriel never postured as a religious crusader or a messianic leader. He also refused offers of help from blacks professing expertise in African practices of voodoo and magic. A literate creole himself, Gabriel apparently mistrusted conjurers and healers and thought they encouraged false confidence where sound judgment and thoughtful commitment were needed.[7]

The evidence produced at the trials of the alleged conspirators suggested that the common denominator among slaves who agreed to participate was their hatred of slavery and their desire for freedom. Yet those slaves approached by Gabriel or his lieutenants who either declined to participate in the alleged revolt or who equivocated about their decision also hated slavery and desired freedom. They were less simply willing to take a risk on a plan that was unlikely to succeed and certain to ignite swift and brutal white retribution. Slaves with wives and children often argued that they had too much to lose from joining such a desperate if noble adventure. A few slaves suggested that they had no quarrel with their particular master and no desire to harm the master or his family. A large proportion of slaves contacted by the rebellion's organizers expressed a willingness to join the rebellion if it took place without prior discovery and appeared to have a reasonable chance for success. But they were unwilling to accept a leadership role in the rebellion or participate in the launching of the rebellion out of fear that if the plot failed, they would fall victim to ruthless white reprisals.[8]

Yet the slave artisans and other skilled slaves who loomed large among the alleged conspirators also had a lot to lose. As urban slaves, many of the accused slave rebels had enjoyed a measure of de facto freedom through the privileges granted and autonomy tolerated by their masters in return for their skill or the money their skills earned as well as from the informality of slave management practices in Richmond in 1800. Patrols were on duty irregularly; passes were seldom checked; little effort was made to identify forgeries. Many skilled slaves were hired out by their masters and reported in only irregularly. Traffic between town and countryside was the norm rather than the exception, so the movement of large numbers of slaves throughout the community, especially on a Saturday night, generated little concern among whites.[9]

The later white investigation revealed the alleged details of Gabriel's plot. The rebels would gather in the country, kill whites in the immediate neighborhood with primitive weapons they had forged, then proceed to Richmond, where they would be joined by the urban slave rebels. One group of rebels would start a fire in a warehouse district in the city's southeastern end. When whites hurried to this remote area of the city to put out the fire, another group of rebels would seize weapons from the state arsenal near the capitol and slaughter whites as they returned from the warehouse district. The rebels would then kidnap Governor Monroe and hold him prisoner.[10]

On the point of just how extensive the subsequent slaughter of whites would be, accounts varied. Some reports held that "whites were to be put to death indiscriminately," while others suggested that Gabriel intended to "slay the white males from the cradle upward" but allow the women to live.[11] One account even held that any white might be spared who pledged allegiance to the revolution and was willing to sacrifice one arm as proof of loyalty. Another report insisted that if whites were willing to grant the rebels their freedom and "hoist a white flag," then Gabriel and his fellow rebels would "dine and drink with the merchants of the city." But the most commonly repeated notion of how far the slaughter of whites would go simply held that all whites would be killed except Quakers, Methodists, and Frenchmen, whom Gabriel planned to spare because they had tried to help the slaves win freedom.[12]

The exact nature of Gabriel's plan for the rebellion will never be known. Before the putative rebels could start one fire or shed the first drop of white blood, the rebellion was betrayed by slave informants and thwarted by disruptive summer weather and prompt white intervention.[13] According to the account developed by white authorities through their slave informants, the insurrection was supposed to begin on the night of August 30, 1800, but failed to launch because of what one observer called "the most terrible thunderstorm, accompanied with an enormous rain...ever witnessed in this state."[14] The torrential rains flooded roads and washed out key bridges in the area, making travel and communication between Richmond and the surrounding countryside difficult. Only a few prospective rebels arrived at the proposed meeting place. Gabriel huddled with his closest associates and decided that their numbers were not large enough to proceed. Gabriel reluctantly sent out word that the action would be postponed until the following evening (Sunday night), and urged would-be insurgents to meet at the tobacco house on Thomas Prosser's plantation. Gabriel's rebellion had been postponed by rain.[15]

As the hard rain fell that night, two slaves, Pharoah and Tom, who worked for Mosby Sheppard, a small farmer in the vicinity of Prosser's Brookfield plantation, quietly visited their master in the small "counting room" of his house. At this meeting, they revealed the insurrection plot to Sheppard. Pharoah, age twenty-seven, was a skilled scythe wielder whose services his master valued greatly during the wheat harvest. Pharoah had agreed to join the insurrection a few weeks earlier, but as the hour of reckoning neared, the husband and father of two apparently had second thoughts. Pharoah confided his information and his newfound doubts to Tom, a thirty-three-year-old slave on the Sheppard farm who often tended Sheppard's house when the master was away. Upon hearing of the plot, Tom suggested they both inform Sheppard. And so Sheppard learned that an insurrection was scheduled to begin that very night, and that "Prosser's Gabriel" was the "principal man" behind the plot.[16]

Skeptical, but knowing he could afford to take no chances with such information, Sheppard immediately braved the storm to report his newly acquired information to a neighbor, William Mosby. An alarmed Mosby quickly rode to the house of the local militia captain, planter William Austin. Austin immediately mobilized his own "troop of horse" and ordered others to do likewise. Despite the inclement weather, Austin and Mosby managed to put several small patrols in the field that evening, riding in and around Brookfield plantation, where Gabriel lived. The patrols found nothing. Mosby now doubted the reliability of Sheppard's slave informants. But when he returned home early the next morning, one of his own female house servants approached him and confirmed that an insurrectionary force of "300 or 400, some from town and some from country," were now set to rise on Sunday evening.[17] Only then did Mosby send word to Governor James Monroe in Richmond. Monroe decided to keep the report "secret" until he learned the "extent of it," in an effort to avoid an unnecessary public scare. But the governor nonetheless moved quickly to set the appropriate security measures in motion. He removed the public arms from the state capitol to the penitentiary, where they could be more easily defended, mobilized several regiments of the state militia for several weeks' duty, made preparations for a military defense of Richmond, and launched a relentless search for insurrectionists.[18]

Once authorities were alerted and the militia mobilized, the slave rebels either dispersed, fled, or went into hiding. Many were rounded up and arrested by patrols or the militia. On the day after Monroe ordered the mobilization, white patrols arrested six slaves, and over the coming days whites arrested so many that one Richmond slave complained, albeit with some exaggeration, that a "man can't go out of his house now but he is taken up to be hanged."[19] By September 9, roughly thirty alleged conspirators had been arrested, but whites still had only a partial understanding of the nature and extent of the planned rebellion, nor had they captured all of the ringleaders. At this point, Governor Monroe ordered the trials to begin in order to make "further discoveries" about the plot. Doubtless Monroe also sought to both deter future slave unrest and reassure anxious whites through prompt retributive justice. Gabriel, however, had somehow escaped. He had made his way to a flatboat on the James River and floated downriver to Norfolk, where he was not arrested until two weeks later, after the state put a $300 price on his head.[20]

After the so-called trials that followed the arrests, white authorities executed twenty slaves in Richmond during the fall of 1800. Other putative rebels questioned during the investigation and trials gave additional information to white authorities. Even before Gabriel was captured, as the number of slave executions surged past ten and headed toward twenty, Governor Monroe wondered if the spree of executions had served their purpose and should end. He worried that an excessive number of executions might tarnish Virginia's reputation and bring sharp criticism down on his Republican Party at a time when it desperately needed to win pivotal northern support for Jefferson's presidential bid. On September 15, Monroe asked his political mentor, Jefferson, "When to arrest the hand of the Executioner." Given the number of alleged conspirators already in custody and the number of others not yet captured, a number that included Gabriel and at least two of his top lieutenants, Monroe estimated that the death toll could easily run higher than fifty, and perhaps even reach a hundred, if the executions proceeded unabated. Uncertain whether "mercy or severity" represented "the best policy in this case," Monroe was inclined to think that "when there is cause for doubt, it is best to incline toward the former."[21] When Jefferson's response arrived five days later, the Sage of Monticello supported the governor's inclination. Jefferson reported that "there is strong sentiment that there had been hanging enough." The "other states and the world at large," he cautioned Monroe, "will freely condemn us if we indulge a principle of revenge."[22] Privately, no less an intrepid defender of slaveholders' rights than John Randolph of Roanoke quipped with his usual sarcasm that the whole insurrection "had been quieted without any bloodshed, but that which has streamed from the scaffold."[23] Another critic anonymously questioned the use of the testimony offered by slave co-conspirators hoping to save their skin or gain their freedom by providing authorities with new "discoveries." This writer suggested that such a practice made it "impossible" to know where "this dreadful tragedy will terminate."[24]

Other white Virginians thought the swift, severe, and numerous punishments necessary. Once Fredericksburg resident John Minor learned the alleged scope of the plot, he lamented that the "delusion of the poor Blacks has been much more extensive" than was first believed. "My heart bleeds for them," Minor claimed, "and yet this degree of severity [of punishment] is necessary."[25] As arrests began in majority-black Petersburg, local whites there sent Monroe more draconian recommendations. "My opinion is that where there is any reason to believe that any person is concerned," former Petersburg state senator James Jones declared, "they ought immediately to be hanged, quartered and hung up on trees on every road as a terror for the rest." Jones' parting advice was succinct: "Slay them all."[26]

Neither the trials nor the executions were likely to cease until Gabriel was found. In late September, he was captured in Norfolk and returned to Richmond in irons. On October 10, after his conviction, Gabriel was executed in Richmond in front of a considerable crowd. According to the trial record, Gabriel divulged little about the conspiracy.[27] Of course, that he said little about the planned revolt did not mean that others, who knew far less, were equally reluctant to comment as interrogations persisted. Thus almost all of the white understanding of the scare came from either black testimony given under fear and duress or from preconceived white notions about how and why such plots developed.

The Gabriel insurrection scare, coming during the middle of a heated political campaign, offered politicians a chance to turn the scare to partisan advantage. Monroe and the Republicans in power could do little more than try to handle the insurrection with firmness and dispatch, showing enough severity to convince the community it had deterred other slaves from attempting insurrection but not betraying so much concern about the threat of insurrection that their constituents remained nervous. As Monroe's exchange of letters with Jefferson revealed, this proved a fine calculation. Federalists, on the other hand, enjoyed more latitude with the issue, and, as Republican John Randolph complained, they "endeavoured to make an electioneering engine" of the scare. Federalists had long charged that the Republican affinity for the French and their ideas of "liberty, equality, and fraternity" threatened to spread Jacobinism and Saint-Domingue-style insurrection along the Atlantic coast. Suddenly they had an example to sustain their argument. Federalists in the towns of the Tidewater and along the fall line warned that the French cry of "liberty and equality had been infused into the minds of negroes," encouraging them to revolt. Republican polemicist James Callender countered these charges with even wilder charges of his own, claiming that Alexander Hamilton was the only white man in the United States capable of concocting such a malicious plot. In Philadelphia, the clever Republican press reminded voters that it was the English and not the French who had shown the greatest willingness to tamper with Virginia slaves.[28] But, setting hyperbolic partisan accusations aside, it was perhaps John Randolph of Roanoke who, after attending some of the interrogations of accused slaves, offered the most troubling assessment of Gabriel's rebellion. The aspiring insurrectionists, the Southside planter concluded, "manifested a sense of their rights, and contempt of danger, and a thirst for revenge which portend the most unhappy consequences." The slave rebels, Randolph mused, had "exhibited a spirit, which, if it becomes general, must deluge the Southern country in blood."[29]

THE POPULAR AND OFFICIAL REACTIONS to the Gabriel scare produced both a drive to make slavery safer and more secure through stricter laws controlling the upper South's black population and a reexamination of the possibilities of colonizing free blacks outside the United States. By late fall, the elections were over, and the Republicans could claim a narrow win over the Federalists in the so-called Revolution of 1800. After considerable intraparty wrangling with Aaron Burr in the electoral college, Virginia's Jefferson became the first Republican president. With that goal achieved, Governor Monroe and other Virginia leaders looked to the approaching legislative session as a time to explain the scare to the public and to take action to reduce the danger of such plots in the future. Monroe knew that agreement on appropriate measures would come hard, and other Virginians, less prominent but arguably no less eloquent and perceptive than the governor, also hoped to influence the direction of the legislature's coming deliberations. But Monroe had the best pulpit from which to guide Virginia's debate, and as he prepared a report to present to the legislature in December, he had access to more information about the insurrection than any other white Virginian.

Monroe's report narrated the version of the insurrection that he wanted the public to know. It admitted that Gabriel's plot represented a threat of "considerable extent" to whites and conceded that Gabriel and his lieutenants had recruited a "large" number of followers who, if they had managed to catch Richmond off guard, might have left "the town in flames, its inhabitants butchered, and a scene of horror extending through the country." Monroe also worried that plans for an extensive insurrection "may occur again at any time, with more fatal consequences, unless suitable measures be taken to prevent it." Yet Monroe expressed confidence that the slave insurgents' success could not have lasted long. As soon as the militia mustered and counterattacked, Monroe argued, the whites' advantages in "Numbers, in the knowledge of the use of arms, and indeed in every other species of knowledge" would have quashed the insurrection after no more than a "moment" of success. But the resulting loss of white lives and property would have been significant. Given the seriousness of the Gabriel scare, Monroe urged the sitting legislature to consider taking whatever "prudent precautions" it could to prevent future insurrections and to ensure the quick failure of any rebellions that did occur.[30]

Monroe's message made plain what virtually all thinking white southerners knew in 1800, even if they seldom stated it bluntly: it was impossible to prevent insurrection scares or even insurrections from occurring on occasion. As long as slavery existed, Monroe conceded, whites could not "count with certainty" on slaves being docile and submissive. Unrest and rebellions on some scale and with some frequency were inevitable. But, like so many other white southerners, Monroe believed that the proper vigilance and appropriate public policy measures could "Secure the Country from any calamitous consequences" arising from these scares and revolts.[31] Vigilance, appropriate security measures, superior arms, and superior knowledge, whites believed, could quell any insurrection before it had advanced too far. The true danger of insurrection was that some whites would likely lose their lives and others would see their property destroyed (though none did in the case of Gabriel's aborted plot) before the white militia prevailed. For the loved ones of those whites killed during the early stages of a rebellion, however, there would be little solace in the ultimate success of the white counterattack.

Yet the more fundamental threats to slavery arising from the danger of insurrection, Monroe recognized, were long-term. Too many scares and certainly too many actual rebellions might so frighten the white population that popular pressure would emerge to end slavery. Whites were willing to live with the chronic threat of slave terror, but only as long as it remained just that—a chronic threat that only seldom became an acute event. But white vulnerability to slave terror could ultimately undermine white support for slavery. Most slaveholders believed that such white anxiety represented the most serious internal threat to slavery, and they worked hard to prevent it from building.

Once the legislature met, Monroe's voice was not the only one that lawmakers heard; others offered more specific suggestions about how Virginia should respond to the threat of slave insurrection. Because Monroe and the Virginia Republicans were in office, it was the Federalists and conservatives who advanced alternatives most aggressively. A "Private Citizen" told the *Virginia Gazette* that the motivation of Gabriel and his followers was nothing less than the same desire for freedom and self-government that resided "in the very spirit of our government." Republicanism, with its love of independence and its hatred of despotism, served as a breeder of unrest and insurrection among the enslaved. As such, the writer argued, the state could hardly expect to prevent slaves from wanting freedom; it could sustain slavery only by adopting the tough measures needed to make sure this desire never found successful expression. The writer's list of recommendations included strengthening the executive branch so that it could respond to emergencies without convening the council, strengthening the state's militia, and ending private manumissions. Ending Virginia's policy of virtually unrestricted manumission, the writer felt, would slow the growth of a large class of free blacks that many whites thought contributed to the spread of slave unrest both by word and example. The anonymous citizen even raised the possibility of creating one of the most unrepublican of institutions—a standing army—to better defend the state against slave rebellions.[32]

If "Private Citizen" stopped short of saying that slavery was incompatible with republicanism, a conservative writer in Fredericksburg went the whole way. In a letter to that city's *Virginia Herald*, the anonymous writer declared that only a "fool" would think there could be a "compromise between liberty and slavery." The writer also urged the legislature to take a tougher stance on slave control and enact "those rigorous laws which experience proved necessary" to maintain slavery and protect whites. Slavery, the Fredericksburg writer reasoned, "is a monster—the most horrible of monsters," and hence required tight control. The Fredericksburg conservative also expressed his disdain for egalitarian sentiments in a slaveholding society. The slaveholder, this writer declared, expressing perhaps the worst fear of many upper South whites, "can never be a Democrat."[33]

Taken together, "Private Citizen" and the Federalist writer in Fredericksburg advanced conservative remedies for the problem of slave insurrection. They wanted all the old measures of slave control either reenacted or strengthened and they wanted the state's lenient policy toward private manumission replaced with one that would make manumission far less common. In short, they recommended a crackdown, a get-tough policy, on slaves and free blacks. Yet there was very little evidence that either private manumissions or the presence of free blacks had much to do with the Gabriel scare (since very few, if any, free blacks were involved), though better organization of the patrols and strengthening the state militia, measures also championed by Monroe as well as the conservatives, certainly made sense to Virginia whites of many persuasions. The other implication white Virginians could draw from the Gabriel scare—the notion that the state should hasten its efforts to end slavery, or at least to reduce its dependence upon the institution—also surfaced in the post-scare debate, chiefly in the form of a proposal offered by yet another private citizen, George Tucker of Richmond. A lawyer and a cousin of the better known St. George Tucker, the younger Tucker submitted a recommendation for gradual emancipation and colonization that received considerable attention during the legislative session of 1800–1.[34]

In his proposal, Tucker expressed an Enlightenment confidence that "progress in human affairs" not only was inevitable but also applied to black slaves as well as free whites. As a result, white Virginians would face more attempted insurrections as slaves moved from the "darkest ignorance" into the "dawn of knowledge." Tucker advised the state to embrace its future by slowly extricating itself from slavery through a gradual emancipation and to avoid racial amalgamation by sending the former slaves to a colony designed to receive them. Specifically, Tucker advocated buying land west of the Mississippi for a colony of free blacks, and perhaps unwanted slaves, and he urged the state to use its tax policy to encourage masters to embark on a journey toward voluntary, gradual manumission. As slaves were freed and sent west, Tucker argued, whites would enjoy a whiter and more securely republican Virginia. Virginia could then gradually get out of the business of repression and insurrection prevention and again assume a leading role as an avatar of progress in the young republic.[35] Because of its timing, Tucker's proposal, a "mere skeleton of an argument intended for a thinking few," received more attention than his older cousin's more detailed proposal had a few years earlier, and by March 1801 it was in a second printing.[36]

The 1800–1 legislature, of course, came nowhere close to approving Tucker's recommendation that Virginia commence a program of gradual emancipation, but his idea of a black colony west of the Mississippi caught the fancy of more than a few lawmakers looking for a place to transport free blacks, convicted felons, and unwanted slaves. A committee appointed by the legislature to examine "the subject of the late conspiracy" recommended a set of policy changes that included a mix of the conventional and the bold.[37] Several of its recommendations were aimed at tightening the state's control of its combined slave and free black populations, control that many conservative Virginians thought had grown increasingly tattered and weak since the Revolution. The committee recommended strengthening both the state militia system, the force most needed to prevent or suppress any attempt at insurrection, and the slave patrols, which served as the eyes and ears of the white community by nightly monitoring slave after-hours activity. John Randolph of Roanoke, visiting Richmond at the time of the scare, had complained that the state "only could muster four or five hundred men of whom not more than thirty had muskets" to turn back an insurrection.[38] In mid-January 1801 the legislature readily approved bills designed to bolster both the militia and the patrols. It also approved the purchase and emancipation of the key slave informants, Pharoah and Tom, for their service to the state, making them the only slaves freed by the plot.[39]

The legislature's response to the committee's other recommendations proved more complicated. One recommendation called for the repeal of the state's 1782 statute giving masters virtually unrestricted power to manumit their slaves without legislative permission. The Gabriel scare gave long-standing opponents of private manumission a new opportunity to identify the state's lenient manumission policy as evidence of its inattention to slave control. Yet this recommendation advocated state interference with the authority of the individual slaveholder, which the Virginia legislature generally had been loath to exercise. Moreover, many Virginia slaveholders opposed the recommendation as an infringement of their "liberty"; still other white Virginians thought a reversal of state policy on private manumission would stand as a repudiation of the informal commitment of the state's founders to tilt state policy toward freedom whenever practical. Together, such objections defeated the committee's recommendations for requiring legislative approval of all private manumissions, though the issue would arise repeatedly over the next several years.[40]

The committee's boldest proposal was its recommendation that the slaves currently jailed for a capital offense should be sold on condition of removal from the United States. The idea of selling convicted slaves and transporting them out of the country had been quietly bruited about for weeks as the Virginia political elite's appetite for executions ebbed and the costs of suppressing the insurrection and keeping the peace mounted. Suppressing the Gabriel scare had become an expensive business in Virginia. It involved the expense of compensating owners for executed slaves, the ongoing cost of keeping convicted slaves and free blacks in jail, and the unexpected military expenses associated with thwarting the insurrection and ensuring public safety during the anxious aftermath. This financial burden strained the state's purposely lean budget. The economy-minded Monroe thought that selling the convicted slaves and sending them out of state would provide a needed boon to state finances and help prevent further executions. The legislature approved the committee's recommendation, and within ten days nine slave prisoners (eight of whom were sentenced to die for participation in the Gabriel revolt) were sold to traders and transported to the New Orleans market for sale into the Louisiana territory as that region prepared for the shift from Spanish to French control.[41]

Another of the committee's bold recommendations was likely inspired by preliminary knowledge of George Tucker's proposal, namely, that the state, in conjunction with federal authorities, should seek to purchase land "beyond the borders of the state" where "persons obnoxious to the laws or dangerous to the peace of society" might be sent. To an extent, this recommendation flowed logically out of the committee's support for transporting existing slave criminals to foreign territory. In many respects, it amounted to the creation of a British-style penal colony established to receive Virginia criminals, especially those slaves and free blacks deemed dangerous or threatening. As a first step toward state support for colonization, this proposal was a curious one. Unlike George Tucker's proposal, or even Jefferson's earlier musings, it called for the removal of only slave and free black criminals, not a larger program of gradual emancipation and colonization. Still, the measure was suggestive of underlying interest in the idea of colonization in the state, and precisely because the recommendation was cautious and conservative, the legislature approved it in January 1801, instructing Monroe to consult with federal authorities about identifying an appropriate location and acquiring such a colony.[42]

More than five months later, Monroe wrote President Thomas Jefferson beginning what would become an extensive correspondence on the issue. The governor urged Jefferson to use federal authority to locate and procure land for a colony. Monroe speculated that the legislature's phrase, persons "dangerous to the peace of society," might be construed to embrace blacks not charged with capital offenses, and that if such an "enlarged construction" of the resolution were adopted, then the request brought "vast and interesting objects into view." In making his request, Monroe conceded that slavery was an "evil" and an "embarrassment" to the republic, but he complained of "the extreme difficulty in remedying it."[43]

Jefferson welcomed the request. Like Monroe, he recognized that the question of criminal exile raised the larger possibility that colonization might be gaining traction as the means for ultimately ridding Virginia of free blacks and reducing its slave population. The legislature's request appeared very much like one of the first in a series of small steps that Jefferson had long anticipated would characterize Virginia's difficult journey toward emancipation. In November 1801, he replied with a detailed analysis of possible places of exile. A colony within the United States, Jefferson reasoned, would likely prove unacceptable, either to Virginia or to other states due to its proximity. He also doubted that either the British or the "Indians" would sell land to the United States for such a purpose. Jefferson expressed a desire to avoid a racial "Blot or mixture" in any territory that might one day become part of the new republic by establishing a colony of former slaves within the nation's borders. So Jefferson considered Saint-Domingue as a possible destination for Virginia's black colonists, noting coyly that its "present ruler [Toussaint] might be ... willing to receive ... [those] deemed criminal by us, but meritorious perhaps by him." But lower

South slaveholders objected to Saint-Domingue and other West Indian locations on the grounds that such a colony was likely to emerge as a staging ground for future efforts to incite insurrections in or to plan invasions of the American South. Still, Jefferson expressed optimism about the future of colonization, holding that "Africa would offer a last and undoubted resort" for a black colony.[44] Yet the resolution passed by the Virginia assembly in 1801 left Jefferson confused about exactly what his native state wanted. Whom exactly did the state propose to colonize and where did Virginians want to send them?[45] Jefferson's reply asked the legislature for clarification on these matters. When the Virginia assembly convened again in December 1801, it held a closed-door session to consider its response, and then appointed a committee to handle the matter.[46]

While the committee crafted its report, news of yet another insurrection plot surfaced. In mid-January 1802, Monroe alerted the legislature to "a threatened insurrection among the Slaves" in Nottoway County, two counties away from the state capital. Monroe, and probably many others in Richmond, suspected that this latest scare was somehow a residue of the Gabriel plot, as they assumed that some unapprehended rebel had stirred unrest in another county. The scare, which affected a number of counties along the Appomattox, James, and Roanoke rivers in southeastern Virginia, arose from the discovery of an alleged plan, concocted chiefly by slave boatmen working largely unsupervised on these rivers, designed to take place on Easter weekend.[47] Testimony later extracted from the accused indicated that the putative rebels expected that once the "great Conflagration of houses fodder Stacks, etc" began, "the poor sort that has no blacks" would be "willing to Acknowledge, liberty and Equality" of blacks.[48] As word of the coming uprising spread up and down the rivers of southeastern Virginia, the rebellion plot gained such wide currency that its discovery became almost inevitable.[49] On January 1, 1802, a slave patrol in Nottoway discovered a late-night gathering of slaves. After aggressive interrogation, one of the slaves offered information about a large-scale insurrection in the making. With memories of the Gabriel scare fresh in their minds, white authorities swung into action. The militia and patrols mobilized to prevent any mobilization of black rebels. White investigators uncovered reports and rumors of a geographically extensive plot (though the numbers of slaves involved remained unclear) reaching throughout much of southeastern Virginia and as far as Albemarle Sound in northeastern North Carolina.[50] Trials and punishments began in county courthouses across the area, and the so-called Easter rebellion, like Gabriel's rebellion before it, was quashed before it began. As reports came in from southeast Virginia, Governor Monroe began to doubt the veracity of at least some of the slave testimony given under duress (in some cases, reported torture). Recognizing that there could be no end to the proliferation of charges as accused rebels fingered others in calculated efforts to help themselves, the governor looked to the legislature to find a more comprehensive solution to what appeared to be an increasingly chronic problem of slave unrest.[51]

Whatever the nature and magnitude of the threat revealed by the "discovery" of the alleged Easter insurrection plot, the resulting scare prompted the legislature to consider more seriously the benefits of colonization and additional measures for ensuring white safety. In another closed-door session in January 1802, delegate Abraham Venable presented a two-part committee resolution crafted to clarify the body's original request for the purchase of land for a colony. The first resolution specified that individuals designated for colonization included only those convicted of "Conspiracy, insurgency, treason and rebellion." As to location, the committee urged the federal government to purchase land in Africa or in the Spanish and Portuguese colonies in South America. These locations suggested that the assembly as a whole did not think that Louisiana was far enough away for the colony of felons, rogues, and revolutionaries they had in mind. But the committee, influenced by Monroe's report of a new insurrection scare, went beyond its request of the previous year and asked the president to seek land "to which free negroes or mulattoes, and such negroes or mulattoes as may be emancipated, may be sent or choose to remove as a place of asylum."[52] The committee had quietly extended its recommendation to include colonizing not simply criminals but other free blacks and newly manumitted slaves as well. The committee recommendation passed both the house and senate within a week, without a roll call in either chamber. Nor did either chamber print the resolution in its regular journal, perhaps in deference to Jefferson's request for confidentiality.[53]

The legislature's colonization resolutions clearly opened the door for a process that champions of gradual emancipation had long envisioned. Virginia might ever so slowly free its slaves, whether by private manumission or a state-mandated program of gradual emancipation, upon the condition that the newly freed blacks would be removed to a colony established to serve as their new homeland. A successful small-scale experiment with colonization, visionaries surmised, might encourage private manumissions or even inspire a plan for gradual emancipation. Yet the legislative resolution of 1802 lacked specificity and detail. Apart from convicted criminals, it did not address the issue of whether members of the current free black population would be forced to leave or merely encouraged to leave if they wanted to. Nor were masters manumitting slaves compelled to colonize them. And the resolution certainly offered no promise of compensation to anyone nor any details about how the transportation would be funded or how the colony would be maintained, though it seemed to envision a major federal role in providing financial support for the project. But for all the questions left unanswered, these resolutions expressed a sentiment, one that coalesced in the face of insurrection scares, endorsing colonization as part of Virginia's answer to what its politicians increasingly acknowledged was the question of how to maintain both republican ideals and white security in a social order that was nearly two-fifths enslaved.

MONROE QUICKLY FORWARDED word of the assembly's action to the president, along with a copy of the resolutions and a letter of explanation. For Monroe, the will of the Virginia legislature was now clear. The new legislative resolutions, he explained, "embraced two descriptions of negroes": slaves who had committed certain specified felonies, and existing free blacks and blacks who might be freed in the future. The legislature had recommended locations in Africa or South America for the convicted slave criminals but made no recommendation for the destination of the second group. The legislature's chosen course of action, Monroe believed, represented a "Policy equally wise and humane to ourselves and the people who are the object of it," and he urged Jefferson to "promote" the state's interest in colonization.[54]

At this point, Jefferson appeared enthusiastic about his state's decision and he quickly initiated the diplomatic contacts required to set the process in motion. Jefferson thought the best place for removal was Britain's existing colony in Africa, Sierra Leone, founded in 1791 as a refuge for Chesapeake slaves who had left with the British after the Revolution but found life difficult in Britain, Canada, and other British colonies.[55] Initially, British diplomatic officials welcomed Jefferson's inquiries, but repeated American diplomatic contacts with the private British company that controlled the Sierra Leone colony yielded little enthusiasm. Directors of the colony claimed that the "Idle and disorderly behaviour" of the American ex-slaves who settled in Sierra Leone initially, along with the difficulty of integrating a group of Jamaican maroons who had recently arrived in the colony, had soured the company on accepting more American slaves (or ex-slaves) as colonists. Rufus King, the antislavery New Yorker serving as American minister to Great Britain, decided not to push the issue until he found the colony's directors in a more accommodating mood.[56] When King raised the issue again nearly a year later, the initial response was again encouraging, but soon word of new unrest in Sierra Leone caused the directors to declare the colony "ungovernable" and abandon it to the Crown. The Jefferson administration's negotiations with the British for access to Sierra Leone soon sputtered to a halt.[57]

Moreover, in the summer of 1802, Governor Monroe called Jefferson's attention to what he perceived as a problem with Virginia's legislative resolutions recommending colonization. Monroe argued that many of the destinations pondered by Virginia accepted only free blacks. This meant that Virginia slaves convicted of involvement in insurrection plots would be freed if removed to such a colony. Transportation to Sierra Leone would actually "Put culprits in a better condition" than they enjoyed in Virginia, which might signal that slaves would in fact be rewarded for fomenting insurrection by being granted freedom and colonized. This was a precedent that certainly neither Jefferson and Madison wanted to set. But the legislative resolutions in question suggested separate courses of action, and possibly separate destinations, for the relative handful of slave felons awaiting transportation and the larger number of free blacks Virginia hoped to colonize. Jefferson was clearly able to make such a distinction, and evidence suggests that he continued efforts to locate a colony as the state requested, though less energetically and optimistically once the option of Sierra Leone lost its viability.[58]

The Virginia legislature continued to press the president for information about the acquisition of such a colony.[59] After his administration acquired the Louisiana Territory in 1803, Jefferson thought a portion of that territory might be set aside for a colony for free blacks (though not slave criminals). Virginia had transported several slaves convicted of participation in Gabriel's rebellion there while the territory was still in foreign hands, but Jefferson knew that white settlers would never accept a colony open to slave felons. Moreover, as the months passed, it became increasingly clear that most southern Jeffersonians saw Louisiana as an emerging empire for white settlers and their slaves and not as a colonial refuge for free blacks, so Jefferson again puzzled over an appropriate location for removal. Late in 1804, Jefferson informed the new Virginia governor, John Page, that he was still unable to recommend a "specific asylum" for Virginia's free blacks. Saint-Domingue remained "too unsettled," but Sierra Leone might once again emerge as a possibility once the British government assumed control. Jefferson promised to keep the matter under his "constant attention" as circumstances changed.[60]

To the legislature's frustration, Jefferson never took further action to find land for a colony despite continued pressure from his home state. The documentary record leaves no clear explanation of Jefferson's inaction. Perhaps Jefferson simply decided that the moment for the successful promotion of colonization was not yet at hand. Possibly the difficult task of finding an "asylum" for relatively small numbers of Virginia's free blacks and newly manumitted ex-slaves took a backseat to Jefferson's other pressing concerns, including the purchase of Louisiana, his reelection campaign, securing an end to American participation in the international slave trade, and dealing with growing British and French interference with the United States' international commerce.

Yet the most straightforward logic suggests that Jefferson knew that he faced serious constitutional and diplomatic obstacles in the effort to locate an appropriate colony for the Old Dominion's free blacks. No private entity yet existed in the United States that might manage and support a colony. Also, Jefferson doubtless agreed with Madison, a supporter of colonization, who counseled that acquiring overseas property for the purpose of establishing a colony for free blacks would surely require a constitutional amendment.[61] Sierra Leone was the ideal option; it was the only choice that allowed Jefferson to avoid any ideological and constitutional inconsistency. After 1803, when Jefferson received much criticism for bending his traditional constitutional stance of strict construction for the purpose of acquiring an "empire for liberty," he grew all the more aware that his administration dared not stretch its cloak of constitutional authority too far or too frequently.

Since Jefferson remained engaged in considering options rather than acting on them, the Virginia legislature continued to push for action. In 1805, frustrated with the administration's delay, the Virginia General Assembly formally asked its representatives in Congress to set aside a portion of the Louisiana Territory as a destination for free blacks and slaves who might be deemed threats to public safety.

The Jefferson administration simply ignored the request. Soon, deepening tensions between the young American republic and both of the two major European powers, Britain and France, rendered diplomatic action even more treacherous and delayed Virginia's active pursuit of colonization for more than a decade.[62]

As THE PROSPECTS of finding a location for a colony where free blacks might be relocated faded, conservative Virginians grew increasingly determined to limit the growth of the free black population by barring private manumission. Despite the failure of the state to restrict private manumission in 1801, supporters of banning the practice continued their sharp attacks over the next five years. These conservative critics wanted to return to the pre-1782 law requiring legislative approval to free any slave, a change critics thought would make manumissions rare. Raising the specter of the Gabriel and Easter insurrection plots, Old Dominion conservatives argued that free blacks might one day "furnish the officers and soldiers around whom the slaves will rally" to sustain such a rebellion.[63] One champion of legislative approval clearly drew on the white understanding of Gabriel's plot when he charged that "blacks who are free obtain a knowledge of facts by passing from place to place in society; they can thus organize insurrection."[64]

Defenders of the existing policy of private manumission touted the rights of a master to free his own slaves. Piedmont representative John Love of Fauquier claimed that the "right of property in a slave was the same as that in a horse, or other personal thing."[65] Other defenders of private manumission raised humanitarian issues as well as assertions of property rights. Dabney Minor, a delegate from the western Piedmont, an early center of gradual emancipation sentiment, argued that eliminating private manumission would "shut against this unfortunate race...the only door through which they can enter the sacred ground of liberty," producing a sense of "damnation" and "despair" among otherwise loyal slaves. In Minor's view, such callous action would render these slaves more, rather than less, likely to rebel. As another defender of private manumission pointed out, the "prospect of emancipation" offered slaves a strong "inducement to inform masters" of looming trouble.[66] After all, defenders of manumission reminded lawmakers, slave informants revealed the Gabriel plot.

These annual legislative debates over the state's manumission policy finally ended in a compromise in 1806. Defenders of private manumission prevented conservatives from returning control of individual emancipation to the state legislature, but opponents of private manumission found a way to slow the growth of the state's free black population. In order to reach a compromise, conservatives conceded the masters' right "to dispose of property freely," without state interference, but in turn they gained support for a bill requiring all manumitted slaves to leave the state within twelve months of their emancipation or forfeit their freedom. The "removal" requirement may have dissuaded some masters from manumitting slaves, and doubtless the provision made freedom less attractive to slaves with strong ties to family and community in Virginia. But without state regulation, the practice of private manumission continued in Virginia, and lax enforcement of the removal provision partially mitigated the hardship caused by the new law.[67] Despite the fear generated by the recent insurrection scares, white Virginians were not ready to turn their backs on private manumission as a means of reducing the number of slaves in the state. Instead, they insisted that slaves could not be freed unless they were also removed from the state. Thus the manumission law of 1806 nudged Virginia toward further exploration of colonization as part of the state's answer to its free black question, if not its slavery question.

The mandated expulsion of all newly freed blacks in Virginia produced a prompt and predictable reaction from nearby states. Within a year of the passage of the Old Dominion's removal law, Maryland, Delaware, and Kentucky passed laws forbidding free black immigrants from settling there, an action later followed by a number of other states. Maryland, doubtless expressing sentiments shared by Virginia's other neighbors, groused that the Old Dominion had "vomited" free blacks inside its borders.[68] Along Virginia's southern border, North Carolina, also hoping to prevent Virginia from exporting its problems south, restricted the immigration of free blacks by requiring in-migrants to post a substantial bond with local sheriffs.[69] Thus Virginia discovered quickly that neighboring states resented its efforts to dump unwanted blacks, slave or free, over state borders. But exportation, whether through sale or removal after manumission, remained a potentially effective (and, in the case of sale, profitable) method for the diminution of slavery in the state, which is why white Virginians refused to abandon the idea.

Nor did temporary resolution of the colonization and manumission issues end the post-Gabriel search for answers to the slavery question. Two major insurrection scares in three years intensified white concerns about their safety and pushed the Virginia legislature toward tougher regulation of its black population. Reacting to the scares, planter Charles Pettigrew reluctantly concluded that "slavery and Tyranny must go together."[70] Certainly legislative action suggested that many Virginia whites agreed with Pettigrew's conclusion, especially once the colonization option failed to materialize. In 1804, after considerable discussion, the legislature banned the "common practice" of permitting slaves and free blacks to gather without white supervision "at meeting houses and places of religious worship in the night," because evidence generated by the investigations of both the Gabriel and Easter rebellion plots indicated that such religious gatherings offered prime insurrection-organizing opportunities. The legislative majority declared that such evening religious meetings had been "productive of considerable evil to the community."[71] This ban on meetings held by evangelical denominations after the slave's plantation workday ended drew sharp protests from evangelicals, including some slaveholders. At its 1805 session, the

Virginia General Assembly softened the ban, approving a compromise that allowed evening religious assemblies as long as the master or a member of the master's family was present and as long as the meetings were conducted by a "regularly ordained" white minister. These provisions appeared to satisfy both conservative demands for white control of religious gatherings and the determination of evangelical Christians to hold night meetings to convert and instruct slaves, but the new law certainly left black Christians with less autonomy.[72] White authorities were also concerned over slave literacy, since a disproportionate number of slaves believed recruited by Gabriel could read and write. In 1805, the legislature passed a law warning guardians of young slaves and free blacks against such teaching but stopped short of making it a crime to teach slaves to read or write. Free blacks, however, who attempted to teach other blacks to read risked becoming victims of extralegal justice at the hands of angry whites.[73]

Gabriel's success in recruiting among skilled slaves called renewed attention to the controversial practice of slave hiring. While the practice of slaves "hiring out" on their own time had been officially banned since 1781 (and again in 1792), the ban had been largely ignored since its passage. The need for skilled labor in Virginia's town and cities, especially as white artisans began to move north to avoid slave competition, spurred both white employers and slaves-for-hire to flaunt the law routinely. Masters, of course, were allowed to hire out their slaves as they saw fit, and that practice remained common in Virginia throughout the early national era.[74] But masters often kept only loose track of these skilled slaves' activities, met with the slaves in question only occasionally to collect wages, and either overtly or tacitly allowed these slaves to hire themselves out once their obligation to the master was met. The practice of hiring out skilled slaves was apparently profitable to all concerned, but it allowed these skilled slaves degrees of mobility and autonomy that many whites thought undermined the discipline needed to maintain slavery. One Virginia editor pleaded unsuccessfully for legislation confining slave labor to agricultural pursuits precisely because skilled and mobile slaves, like Gabriel, had the "means, without much exertion," to form "plots and conspiracies."[75] But the Virginia assembly took no action on the question until 1808, when it finally prohibited masters from hiring out slaves. But again, merchants and craftsmen appear to have joined masters in roundly ignoring the law, though they tended to conduct their labor market transactions more discreetly than before.[76]

Without question, fear of insurrection remained vivid in the minds of many white Virginians for years after the alleged Gabriel and Easter plots were thwarted. In the spring of 1808, a British visitor to Richmond observed that the sounding of the city's "Fire Bell" always "produced a Very great alarm in this Country" because of the "apprehension that it may be the signal for, or a Commencement of the rising of the Negroes."[77] That white Virginians feared few things as much as a "fire bell in the night" doubtless inspired Jefferson's famous simile during the Missouri crisis, and suggested the degree to which such fears entered the vernacular of everyday life in a slave society. Also in 1808, rumors of a Christmas day slave rebellion circulated in a number of counties, including Albemarle, Jefferson's home county. Writing from that Piedmont county, Congressman Wilson Cary Nicholas' wife, Peggy, expressed relief that she had "escap'd the horrors of massacre" at the hands of an alleged insurrection plot only by the "mercy of providence." She then urged her husband to move their family to whiter reaches beyond the Blue Ridge. "Gracious God," she pleaded, "what is there in this country to make amends for all this terror?"[78]

In evaluating Virginia's long-term response to the Gabriel and Easter insurrection scares and to the renewed concern over slave unrest generally, it is important to sort through what the state did and what it did not do. It did promptly consider measures that directly enhanced white security, such as militia reform and strengthening the slave patrol. And it took prompt action to execute or transport condemned insurrectionists. Beyond that, the state's actions were deliberate rather than hasty. It began to consider colonization, initially as a means of ridding itself of slaves involved in insurrection plots, but later as a means for reducing the state's free black population. On the questions of private manumissions, conservatives who advocated a ban repeatedly failed to garner enough support to pass restrictive legislation. In the end, a compromise measure left manumission decisions in the hands of masters but mandated that all manumitted slaves must leave the state. The legislature banned nighttime religious gatherings for blacks but then quickly modified the law to allow such gatherings if whites were present and in charge of the service. Lawmakers also expressed disapproval of growing slave literacy but took only weak action to slow its spread. And finally, eight years after the Gabriel scare, the legislature approved a ban on masters hiring out their slaves, but the law proved unenforceable. In the end, Virginia did not turn its public policy toward slavery around on a dime in response to these insurrection scares. To be sure, conservative defenders of slavery argued that both public and private discipline of slaves had grown lax and needed tightening, and they urged a regimen of legislative restrictions to restore a more authoritarian "old order" of slave control. But champions of this strict reactionary regimen did not prevail on a consistent basis in either the legislature or the court of public opinion.

Moreover, a number of harsh restrictions were never even seriously considered in Virginia. No politician engaged in broad-based bashing of the evangelical denominations that had increased slave access to the scriptures and encouraged religious gatherings. Many whites believed that black religious meetings had served as one of several recruiting grounds for the leaders of slave unrest and that biblical texts may have influenced the choices of some slaves, yet they mounted no frontal assault against either white or black evangelicals. Instead, most white Virginians looked to the removal of existing free blacks and newly emancipated ex-slaves as part of a gradual whitening of the state. White Virginians still aimed to eliminate slavery of their own accord and at their own pace.

Yet Virginia's response to the early-nineteenth-century insurrection scares made it clear that the state's whites, whatever their views on the future of slavery, simply could not envision a biracial society that functioned on any basis except that of racial slavery. In this slave society, the free black population, however large or small, constituted a pariah class, one neither trusted by whites nor accepted by slaves, a class neither subject to the discipline of slavery nor allowed the opportunities available to even the poorest whites.[79] Most elite whites in this era remained uncertain whether the observed "degradation" of free blacks resulted from decades of experience living either under slavery or in close proximity to slavery or whether it was a sign of innate racial inferiority. The comparatively open-minded Jefferson suspected that blacks were innately inferior, especially in the "faculties of reason and imagination," but he also admitted that much consideration should be given to the "differences of condition, of education, of conversation, of the sphere" in which blacks, slave and free, lived. Despite his own personal uncertainty, however, Jefferson expressed no doubt that the "Deep-rooted prejudices" against blacks on the basis of color would forever block their inclusion in a white republic.[80] St. George Tucker questioned the idea of innate black inferiority but, like Jefferson, was quick to point to the "deep-rooted" and innate "prejudices" of whites as an ineradicable barrier to the acceptance of blacks as equals in Virginia society. Tucker thought it misguided to impose slavery on people by nature "equally free and independent" simply because they "differ in complexion," but he acknowledged that sentiment in Virginia advocated precisely such a policy.[81] James Madison, usually judicious in all his expressions of opinion, noted that free blacks often retained "the bad qualities of the slaves with whom they continue to associate, without acquiring any of the good ones of the whites." Yet Madison concluded that blacks were excluded from republican society chiefly "by prejudices ag[ainst] their color and other peculiarities" rather than because of innate inferiority.[82] On balance, early republican Virginians remained uncertain whether slavery had rendered blacks "unfit" for freedom or the alleged racial inferiority of blacks had rendered them ready subjects for slavery.

Yet while modest differences of opinion lingered on the subject of racial differences, virtually all whites believed that the color of slaves and free blacks would always serve as a badge preventing their recognition as citizens in a white republic. Whites unwilling to admit their own prejudice on the subject could readily blame policies of subordination and separation on the overweening prejudice against blacks in society at large. Thus no matter the strength of the ideological or economic misgivings about slavery harbored by whites in the upper South, given the absolute size of the region's slave population, most whites could not envision any systematic plan of emancipation, even of the most gradual nature, that was not also accompanied by the removal of blacks from the upper South. Moreover, even those who had little or no desire to end slavery often favored the removal of free blacks as a means of enhancing white safety.

The immediate post-Gabriel explorations of a federally facilitated state colonization program ultimately came to nothing. And as the second Jefferson and first

Madison administrations drifted first into commercial conflict with the major powers of Europe and later into open warfare with Great Britain, any prospect for the creation of a colony beyond the borders of the United States became temporarily impractical. At the same, whites increasingly came to covet American territory too much to allow its use as a colony for free blacks. Lower South whites viewed any American location for such a colony as too close to both white settlements and West Indian influences to be considered safe. But, ironically, the seeming impossibility of creating an overseas colony during these years stimulated the upper South's interest in the idea. A hiatus from the practical frustrations of trying to locate a colony rendered the idea of colonization more compelling. One of the state's leading Federalists, Charles Fenton Mercer, predicted that colonization would wipe "from the character of our institutions the only 'blot' which stains them."[83] And from the opposite end of Virginia's political spectrum, Republican John Taylor of Caroline judged slavery a "misfortune" and endorsed colonization. In his *Arator* essays, Taylor suggested that "if England and America would erect and foster a settlement of free negroes in some fertile part of Africa, it would soon subsist by its own energies," and "slavery might then be gradually reexported, and philanthropy gratified by a slow reanimation of virtue, religion and liberty of the Negroes."[84]

Though very much a war of the so-called Virginia dynasty's making, the War of 1812 brought a reprisal of the Revolutionary War era's slave unrest, albeit on a smaller scale, in the vulnerable Chesapeake region.[85] In April 1812, authorities in Virginia's southern Piedmont arrested a slave named Tom for the murder of his master. In the "interrogation" that followed, Tom maintained that the murder was but a small part of a larger insurrection plot, one that had drawn encouragement from rumors of an impending British invasion. Tom also told the authorities that the Richmond theater fire of 1811, which killed incumbent governor William George Smith and a number of other prominent whites, had been received by blacks as a sign that "God Almighty had sent them a little Hell for the white people" and that worse was still to come.[86] Apparently fearing just that, early in 1813 the Virginia legislature took the unprecedented step of calling for the creation of a state army to defend against slave insurrections. Alarmed that such a precedent might weaken federal control of the war effort, President Madison sent James Monroe to Richmond in an effort to persuade Governor James Barbour and the Virginia legislature to repeal the statute. The legislature ultimately agreed, but only after Monroe promised to send a regiment of federal troops to defend the exposed Norfolk area.[87]

During the war, some three thousand to five thousand slaves in Virginia and Maryland fled from more than seven hundred different masters.[88] In April 1814, British admiral Alexander Cochrane issued a "proclamation," similar to that issued by Dunmore forty years earlier, offering freedom and resettlement to all fugitive slaves.[89] As many as two hundred Chesapeake-area runaways joined British marines and took part in the sacking of the nation's capital. American brigadier general John P. Hungerford complained that these refugee black soldiers' familiarity with Virginia geography gave the British "a great advantage over us in a country where the passes and by-ways through our innumerable necks and swamps are so little known."[90] When the British left the region to take the war to the Gulf Coast, at least some white Virginians questioned anew their commitment to slavery. John Coalter, St. George Tucker's son-in-law, recommended selling off all slaves over the age of fourteen on the grounds that these slaves were "broken and deranged" by the war. Coalter argued for keeping all slaves age fourteen and under "as a stock to begin on after the war," and proposed an intensive training program designed for young slave "Ploughboys and girls."[91] The sack of the nation's capital caused a retired Thomas Jefferson to ponder anew the "power of our present enemy" and the effect the British could have on slavery if "stationed permanently within our country, and offering asylum and arms to the oppressed." Such ruminations inclined Jefferson to encourage, but not to lead, efforts to produce emancipation "through the generous energy of our minds" rather than see it accomplished through "the bloody process of St. Domingo" or "excited and conducted" by the British military.[92]

Once the War of 1812 ended, upper South colonizationists wasted no time pushing their cause anew. They still desired a state-approved and federally assisted program of colonization, but now they also saw the virtue of using one of the early nineteenth century's new and increasingly popular institutions for promoting the public good: the voluntary association. Virginia's Charles Fenton Mercer took the lead in the effort to create such an association dedicated to colonization. A Tidewater-born and Princeton-educated Virginia Federalist, Mercer settled in Loudoun County in Virginia's northern Piedmont and championed a program of state banking, internal improvements, and public education, as well as the colonization of free blacks. He saw the Jeffersonians as bitter political enemies, though some of his favorite measures, including colonization, bridged the partisan divide.[93]

Early in 1816, Mercer was elected a member of Virginia's new Board of Public Works, the entity charged with overseeing the state's dynamic new program of internal improvements. In February, during an evening of heavy drinking in Richmond with his legislative roommates, Mercer heard his fellow Federalist, Philip Doddridge of Ohio County, complain that Thomas Jefferson was a "consummate hypocrite" because he had recommended the colonization of free blacks in his *Notes on the State of Virginia* but had "coldly evaded" repeated requests by the Virginia legislature to assist in the development of a practical plan for colonization in the aftermath of the Gabriel scare. Doddridge, brilliant but prone to excessive drinking, divulged that when he was serving in the state senate such requests were made and that a number of discussions concerning colonization were held behind closed doors during Monroe's governorship. For proof of his account, Doddridge urged Mercer to ask the clerk of the senate to see the records of that body's secret proceedings and the confidential communications between Jefferson and Monroe on the subject.[94] Mercer soon confirmed Doddridge's account and eagerly spread the word about Virginia's once-confidential discussion of colonization, vowing to take up the cause himself at the legislature's next session. In the meantime, Mercer worked for the creation of a national organization committed to colonization. During the summer of 1816, he traveled north and won the support of Maryland Federalist Francis Scott Key, one of the nation's leading lawyers; Elias B. Caldwell, Mercer's former Princeton classmate; and Caldwell's brother-in-law Robert Finley, a Presbyterian minister and head of Princeton Theological Seminary. Together this group used personal contacts and connections to build expanding networks of support for the organization that became the American Colonization Society (ACS) in December 1816.[95]

The motives of the many founders of the ACS proved varied and complex, but on the whole, the driving force behind the colonization movement came from committed clergy in mainstream Christian churches. The same wellspring of humanitarianism that inspired the creation of the Benevolent Empire throughout much of the North also spawned collective voluntary action in favor of colonization. Initially, the formation of the ACS received a reasonably warm reception in the South, where its policy of colonizing only free blacks (whether those long free or those recently manumitted) but not attempting to interfere with slavery attracted strong support from some whites and seemed either marginally useful or innocuous to many others. The new colonization organization found southern support among Presbyterian, Methodist, Baptist, and occasionally Episcopalian clergy and the lay members they most influenced. The movement also attracted support across the partisan divide, attracting both Republicans and former Federalists. Colonization gained an especially strong following in the upper South, where Virginia, Maryland, and Kentucky lent strong support to the formation of the ACS. Indeed, an impressive array of upper South slaveholders attended the American Colonization Society's organizational meeting in December 1816, and prominent Virginians, including James Madison, John Randolph, John Marshall, James Monroe, and John Tyler, appeared on the society's membership rolls.[96] Additionally, a number of prominent upper South politicians offered bountiful rhetorical support, and less bountiful financial support, to the ACS for many years. Local ACS auxiliaries appeared with some frequency in the region, and in 1816, the Virginia legislature quietly endorsed the idea of colonizing free blacks.[97]

In neighboring Maryland, Robert Goodloe Harper wrote a widely circulated public letter pleading the case for colonization. Harper argued that most free blacks lived as paupers "at the expense of the community" while possessing the potential to stir restlessness and resistance among slaves. He argued that colonization would remove "a population for the most part idle and useless, and too often vicious and mischievous." Harper also asserted that the presence of slaves and free blacks in Maryland hindered the formation of a reliable class of free white laborers in the state. Whites, Harper claimed, "saw labour as a badge of slavery" and shunned it, and he asserted that skin color presented an impassable barrier to "social equality" for blacks.[98] He concluded that blacks and whites could never live together in freedom. Harper's pamphlet helped generate strong interest in the colonization movement in the state. Maryland formed a state chapter of the colonization society in 1817, and at both its 1817–18 and 1818–19 sessions, the Maryland legislature unanimously endorsed the principle of colonization. Even North Carolina momentarily showed a measure of enthusiasm for colonization in 1819, when the ACS established a chapter in Raleigh and incumbent governor John Branch agreed to serve as its president.[99]

From its inception, the ACS sought federal money to acquire an African colony. But in the early years, Congress, grappling with the national hardships imposed by the Panic of 1817, politely rebuffed ACS requests, throwing the society back on private philanthropy for its financial sustenance. In 1819, the ACS, led by society member and treasury secretary William Crawford, urged President Monroe to interpret the Slave Trade Act of that year, which empowered the federal government to establish an outpost on the African coast and to use a naval squadron to rescue Africans from the clutches of the international slave trade, as a justification for establishing a colony on the African coast. As was his habit, Monroe took the request to his cabinet. Secretary of State John Quincy Adams objected strenuously. Adams, an outright opponent of slavery who viewed colonization as a temporizing palliative, argued that Monroe lacked the constitutional authority to establish and maintain overseas colonies. Monroe, a colonization supporter, nonetheless remained favorably inclined toward Crawford's proposal. But when Secretary of War John C. Calhoun and Attorney General William Wirt both agreed with Adams, Monroe yielded to collective wisdom for the moment. Later in the year, however, Crawford and ACS leader Francis Scott Key again approached the president seeking a more generous construction of federal power under the Slave Trade Act. This time Wirt responded with a written opinion explicitly denying that the act provided authority for federal aid to the ACS. But after intense lobbying from ACS leaders, and doubtless knowing Monroe's preference, Wirt withdrew his objections. Monroe agreed to send government agents to the coast of Africa to locate territory suitable for an outpost and to use the American navy to provide protection for a colony. Shortly after Monroe's decision to provide aid from the $100,000 already appropriated to enforce the Slave Trade Act, the sour tone of the Missouri debate killed any chance of expanded financial assistance for the ACS until verbal wounds healed. But the society never abandoned its desire to tap federal funds to advance its cause.[100]

The emergence of an active colonization movement in the upper South in the years following the War of 1812, and particularly the ACS' efforts to establish a federally assisted colony in Africa, spawned a countervailing cohort of critics. Most critics focused on the practical difficulties of colonization, including but not limited to finding locations for colonies, raising money to pay for the transportation of free blacks and to subsidize the operation of the colonies in their critical early years, and persuading reluctant free blacks to go voluntarily. In Virginia, states'-rights advocates John Randolph of Roanoke and Littleton Tazewell both dismissed colonization as an "extravagant, or ridiculous project."[101] Advocates of forced colonization faced fierce political opposition, including that of the newly formed ACS itself, to the passage of coercive legislation. And those who favored compensated emancipation and voluntary colonization confronted the daunting task of finding a source of funds to compensate masters for freeing slaves. Upper South colonizationists recognized the scope of these problems but championed the cause nonetheless because they viewed colonization, for all its complications, as essential both to reducing the importance of slavery in the region and to diminishing the threat posed by the area's free black population.[102]

THROUGHOUT THE EARLY NATIONAL PERIOD, the idea of whitening the upper South through colonization remained little more than a vision. Prior to 1820, no actual colonization project had been established under American auspices. So whites committed to whitening the upper South sooner rather than later also articulated support for the idea of "diffusion"—spreading the existing slave population over a larger territory as a means of reducing the proportion of blacks in the region's population. The concept of diffusion rested on the notion that slavery weakened as it expanded. Thus diffusionists advanced the argument that while slavery remained a definite evil, it was an evil whose consequences proved less harmful when the institution was allowed to expand than when it was confined or restricted. Diffusion would allow the Chesapeake region to draw down its slave population profitably through sale. The idea gained popularity as new territories opened, particularly to the extent these new territories were both open to slavery and adaptable to staple production. Hence the post-Revolutionary settlement of Kentucky and Tennessee suggested the possibility of diffusion, but it was the opening of the Mississippi Territory in 1798, just as short-staple cotton was emerging as an important cash crop in the lower South, that galvanized upper South sentiment behind diffusion as a whitening strategy.[103]

During the congressional debate over the expansion of slavery into the Mississippi territory in 1798, Virginian John Nicholas, who publicly labeled slavery the "misfortune" of southern society, argued that allowing slavery to expand westward would "be doing a service not only to them [slaves] but to the whole Union" because it would "open the Western country" and "spread the blacks over a large space, so that in time it might be safe to carry into effect the plan which certain philanthropists have so much at heart," referring to emancipation.[104] Fellow Virginian and Jeffersonian William Branch Giles agreed that diffusion diluted the evils of slavery, though he stopped short of portraying diffusion as a means of facilitating gradual emancipation. Giles argued that the diffusion of the slave population across space would yield an "amelioration" in the overall condition of slaves by "spreading them over a large surface of country." Many of slavery's harsher aspects, Giles contended, resulted from slaves being "crowded together" in only a few states.[105] Kentucky senator John Breckinridge, the conservative architect of that state's 1799 constitution, echoed these sentiments a few years later when Congress debated the expansion of slavery into Louisiana. "I wish our negroes were scattered more equally not only through the United States but through our territories," he observed, "so that their power might be lost." The "power" that Breckinridge feared was that of insurrection, the threat that "our slaves at the South will produce another St. Domingo." Diffusion would serve as a palliative, Breckinridge believed, and would "disperse and weaken the race—and free the southern states from a part of its black population, and of its danger."[106]

Public arguments in favor of diffusion often focused on the advantages it offered slaves in terms of treatment, living conditions, and prospects for future emancipation. But in practice, the policy of diffusion served the interests of the upper South's whites, and especially its slaveholders, by encouraging the westward expansion of slavery. Diffusion ensured a market for the surplus slaves from old tobacco states and provided upper South slave owners with a means of both divesting themselves of expensive labor and recouping the capital they had invested in slaves. It also facilitated the development of promising western lands, where upper South investors often held large speculative interests, and it helped protect, at least for a time, the political clout of slaveholding states in Congress through the creation of additional slave states.[107]

By the time of the Missouri crisis of 1819–21, diffusion had emerged as the upper South's most popular rebuttal to two increasingly common northern complaints: that too little was being done to improve the treatment of slaves and that the South was not doing enough on its own to eliminate the institution. The policy of diffusion, some upper South whites thought, refuted both charges. Virginia congressman Philip P. Barbour argued that the "condition of slaves would be greatly improved by their being spread over a greater surface" because diminishing the density of the slave population lessened fears of insurrection and encouraged slaveholders to adopt less draconian regimens of slave control.[108] Another Old Dominion congressman, future president John Tyler, agreed that through diffusion "you also ameliorate the condition of the black man" by increasing the prospects for emancipation at some later date.[109]

Thomas Jefferson and James Madison gave the idea of beneficent diffusion its most formidable endorsement in their observations on the Missouri crisis. Jefferson wrote that the diffusion of slaves "over a greater surface would make them individually happier," and insisted that diffusion would "proportionally facilitate the accomplishment of their [slaves'] emancipation by dividing the burthen on a greater number of coadjutors."[110] In Jefferson's view, the spreading of slaves across a broad southern space would encourage an eventual emancipation by thinning the concentration of slaves and dispersing the financial sacrifice and social risks ultimately involved in emancipation. Madison endorsed "an uncontrouled dispersion of slaves now in the U.S." as "not only best for the nation, but most favorable to slaves, both as to their prospects for emancipation, and as to their condition in the meantime." Madison defended diffusion as "humane" and argued that since the importation of African slaves had been prohibited in 1808, "a diffusion of those in the Country, tends at once to meliorate their actual condition, and to facilitate their eventual emancipation." Madison had long linked the expansion of slavery to the question of the slave trade. As long as the foreign slave trade remained open, Madison favored limiting the expansion of slavery geographically because the federal government had "no mode" through which it could "check the evil" of slavery except the "indirect one of narrowing the space open for the reception of slaves."[111] After the foreign slave trade was closed in 1808, however, the dynamics of expansion changed. With the growth of the slave population effectively limited, the expansion of slavery into new areas, or "the interior dispersion of slaves," as Madison styled it, emerged as the better policy for ameliorating and weakening slavery.[112]

In several respects, diffusion represented a thoroughly Jeffersonian remedy to the problem of slavery in early national America. By spreading the peculiar institution across time and space, diffusion purchased security for the larger republican vision of Jeffersonians at the expense of the party's ideological purity. Just as the expansion of the white population into the Louisiana Territory nurtured independence through expanding possibilities for yeoman self-sufficiency, diffusion reduced the danger of slave insurrection and promoted humane treatment by dispersing the slaves across a larger area. Defenders of diffusion claimed that it facilitated the emancipation of slaves at some distant future date by ensuring that slaves were a smaller percentage of the overall population in any given state than otherwise would have been the case. Upper South whites came to believe that slave demography held the key to effective emancipation on the northern model. The smaller the slave proportion of the population, diffusionists asserted, the more probable eventual emancipation. Through diffusion, Jeffersonian Republicans could advocate the eventual end of slavery in the American republic while insisting that any steps toward this end, however tentative, be taken under the direction of slaveholders, largely in their interest, and at their preferred pace.

Doubtless some diffusionists were disingenuous and thought the concept simply a way to put a benign face on the expansion of slavery. Yet at least some advocates of diffusion, including Jefferson and Madison, gave every indication of believing that a policy of diffusion would, over time, persuade upper South whites of the practicality as well as the desirability of a general emancipation. Arguably diffusionists of this stripe underestimated the sweeping impact of the cotton boom on the lower South after 1800, and the seemingly insatiable demand for the slaves that boom spawned among white farmers and planters. And perhaps diffusionists also failed to recognize the changing demographic patterns within the slave population, which indicated that even without the importation of slaves from abroad, the size of the slave population could grow at impressive rates. Still, even the best-intentioned diffusionists knew that whatever its overall impact, the expansion of slavery over a larger area left upper South slaveholders in a better position for continued profits from an active internal slave trade and a labor force whose size and flexibility better suited their evolving needs.[113]

The use of the interstate slave trade to whiten the region, an idea later openly endorsed by Thomas Dew, a William and Mary professor and studied opponent of gradual emancipation and colonization, as the best plan for ending slavery in the region, also helps explain why the issue of the slave trade emerged as a pivot point between upper and lower South.[114] The upper South's steady opposition to the importation of foreign slaves centered not only on its desire to slow the growth of its slave population but also on a desire to limit the supply of slaves available to other staple-growing regions, thereby protecting or enhancing the market position of upper South slave sellers. At the same time, the upper South vigorously defended the interstate slave trade as a vital safety valve for venting its burgeoning surplus slave population in a profitable manner and as a key to its emerging whitening strategy. Maryland and Virginia slaveholders participated vigorously in the selling of slaves in the domestic market. From 1790 to 1820, Maryland exported nearly 75,000 slaves, a total representing nearly three-quarters of its 1790 slave population, and during that same period, Virginia exported nearly 140,000 slaves, a total representing just under half of its 1790 slave population. Altogether the roughly 220,000 slaves exported by upper South states during the early national era represented more than 40 percent of the total upper South slave population at the time of the republic's founding.[115]

In sum, whites in the early national upper South considered a variety of approaches to addressing the problem of slavery. The relative weight given to the various methods of minimizing slavery's importance and whitening the region remained a source of serious debate and disagreement in the region throughout the era. Even those individuals most firmly committed to diminishing slavery often disagreed over the best combination of means toward that end. Upper South whites wanted abundant and reliable labor, solid profits, white control of polity and society, and personal and community safety. They feared economic stagnation, racial mixing, a free biracial society, slave violence, and a large free black population. They walked a tightrope balancing their aspirations and anxieties. While they sometimes doubted their ability to afford slavery, they more often conceded that they could not afford emancipation. Moreover, any plan to phase out slavery, no matter what the mechanism, drew sharp dissent from those portions of the upper South where slavery was most firmly entrenched. Slaveholders from Southside Virginia, the Northside tobacco belt of North Carolina, a few plantation counties in southern Maryland and Delaware, and the Bluegrass area of Kentucky remained in no hurry to see slavery end and, arguably, hoped it never would.

Yet, sensing that slavery was incompatible with republicanism, public safety, and sustained economic development in the region, a majority of upper South whites looked for ways to answer the slavery question over the long term. Behind each course of thought, action, or inaction lay the economic, moral, and security interests of the region's whites. Upper South whites usually summarily rejected plans for a northern-style emancipation. Comparatively bold post-nati emancipation plans such as those of Thomas Jefferson and St. George Tucker received only scant attention. More modest efforts to gradually marginalize slavery through a combination of extensive individual manumissions, the colonization of newly freed slaves, and the diffusion of slaves to the South and West by sale and migration became the viable staples of the upper South's political thought regarding slavery.

Over time, a loose and uneasy consensus emerged around the idea of diminishing the importance of slavery in the upper South very gradually through a demographic reconfiguration of the institution. Using individual manumission and colonization along with the sale and forced migration of slaves to other parts of the South, this demographic reconfiguration of slavery would make the upper South whiter by spreading or diffusing slaves across a wider territory or moving them to a foreign colony. In 1820, in the absence of an active program of colonization, the success of this reconfiguration project hinged chiefly on an active interstate slave trade to facilitate the most financially attractive option for reconfiguring slavery in the upper South: the sale of slaves to the cotton South. Ideologically, commitment to this demographic reconfiguration of slavery allowed upper South whites to disown slavery even as they protected their right to own and sell slaves.[116]

PART TWO

THE LOWER SOUTH'S EMBRACE OF SLAVERY

At the same time the upper South struggled to find answers to its questions about slavery, the lower South appeared to embrace slavery unequivocally as the key to its current and future prosperity. As the region rushed headlong into the first cotton boom, it seemed that the only slavery question that engaged lower South whites was how to squeeze the most profit out of the most slaves. But a closer examination reveals that even the lower South's deepening commitment to slavery was not made without reservations. As the lower South grew ever more deeply enmeshed in the slave-driven staple economy and acquired more and more slaves, questions emerged about how white safety could be secured in a society with so many slaves. Yet as fears of slave unrest multiplied in rapidly blackening areas of the lower South, planters, lesser slaveholders, and farmers still demanded more and more slaves as huge fortunes were accumulated from staples. When South Carolina reopened the African slave trade in 1803 (a fitful and divisive decision examined in detail in this section) to supply slaves for the lower South staple boom, it both defied national opinion and threatened the slave-selling interests of the upper South. Even after the closing of the foreign slave trade in 1808, the lower South's need to balance the desire for slave-generated wealth and the concern for white safety by modulating the region's racial demography remained as a recurring public policy conundrum.

The region's worst fears were nearly realized in 1811 when a major slave revolt erupted along the so-called German Coast portion of the Mississippi River in Louisiana, forcefully reminding lower South whites of the danger they lived in. The rebellion was savagely crushed by white authorities, but soon thereafter, British and Native American efforts to stir up slave unrest during the War of 1812 again raised questions about white security. Andrew Jackson's successful wartime exertions against Native Americans and the British appeared to strike a blow for prosperity, white safety, and the future of slavery in the lower South. But these struggles nonetheless served as vivid warnings to lower South whites that to live in a slave society was to live with the threat of unrest, retribution, and rebellion. The profits of slavery came at a price.

CHAPTER THREE

OPENING THE SLAVE TRADE

No issue better revealed the complexity of the slavery question in the Old South or so clearly illustrated the tension between upper and lower South than the issue of the slave trade, both foreign and domestic. Upper South slaveholders preferred closing the foreign slave trade but valued a vigorous internal trade because they wanted to supply the lower South with slaves from their growing surplus; many lower South slaveholders also wanted to protect both the value of their slaves and white safety by slowing the pace of slave imports, but as the cotton boom spread from South Carolina to the Louisiana Territory, whites in the newer staple regions demanded more slaves. These positions led to disagreements over the foreign slave trade both within the lower South and between the lower South and the upper South, and these disagreements open a window into the slavery question as seen in the lower South.

"The Negro Business is a great object with us, both with a View to our Interest individually, and the general prosperity of this State and its commerce," Joseph Clay, a Savannah merchant, told prominent Georgia politician James Jackson in 1784. "It is to the trade of this Country, as Soul to the Body," and the "planter will as far as in his power sacrifice everything to obtain Negroes." While some slaves imported by Georgia merchants came from the West Indies, most arrived directly from Africa. In Clay's estimation, no lower South "business house" could remain financially "stable" without securing a share of the lucrative Atlantic slave trade.[1] Clay's frank portrayal of Confederation-era Savannah highlighted the voracious desire for slave labor exhibited by planters and farmers in the lower South, a desire apparently unchastened by the difficulties with slave control they experienced during the American Revolution.[2] In light of Clay's observations, it is hardly surprising that South Carolina and Georgia delegates to the 1787 Constitutional Convention in Philadelphia made keeping the international slave trade open, at least for a time, a sine qua non for joining the new Union. Given the wealth generated by the international slave trade and the lower South's heavy reliance on slave labor in the production of rice and Sea Island cotton, the region's determination to extend the life of the Atlantic slave trade represented a drive to protect a vital if embattled interest. It is hardly surprising that South Carolina's Charles Cotesworth Pinckney, his younger cousin Charles Pinckney, and their lower South colleagues left Philadelphia well pleased with the compromise they extracted from the convention. This compromise, very much a part of the multitiered bargaining that characterized the convention, secured a constitutional guarantee that the foreign slave trade could remain open for at least twenty years if the individual states chose to permit it.[3]

Yet just two months before delegates convened in Philadelphia for the convention, the state legislature in the Pinckneys' native South Carolina had voted to close that state's international slave trade. Moreover, every member of South Carolina's distinguished delegation to the Philadelphia convention had served in the 1787 legislature and only one of the four future founders, Charles Cotesworth Pinckney, voted to keep the state's slave trade open. The other three, John Rutledge, Charles Pinckney, and Pierce Butler, all voted to close the state's foreign slave trade.[4] Ironically, given later developments in Philadelphia, Thomas Jefferson congratulated the South Carolina legislature for "suspending the importation of slaves, and for the glory you have just acquired by endeavouring to prevent it forever." The "abomination" of the slave trade "must have an end," Jefferson asserted, "and there is a superior bench reserved in heaven for those who hasten it."[5] This apparent contradiction between South Carolina's insistence on a federal constitutional guarantee for the international slave trade at the Philadelphia convention and the state's desire, expressed just a few months prior to the convention, to close the African trade, at least temporarily, suggests an underlying complexity in the issue of the slave trade, and indeed on the issue of slavery itself, not revealed in Clay's remarks on the trade's economic importance or by the lower South delegates' unified and seemingly defiant stance in Philadelphia.[6]

At its March 1787 session, the South Carolina General Assembly debated the slave trade, both foreign and domestic. Advocates of closing the foreign slave trade arrived with circumstances on their side. The economic disarray of the state during the Confederation period, highlighted by the crushing burden of individual indebtedness (often the result of slave purchases) and the social unrest that emerged from the resulting debt crisis, prompted the legislature to prohibit not only the foreign slave trade but also the interstate slave trade in the interest of capital accumulation and creditworthiness.[7] Proponents of these bans argued that closing the trade would raise the value of slaves by restricting supply. The increase in slave values would assist slaveholders in paying down their debts. Closing the trade, Charleston merchant Alexander Gillon predicted, would trigger "negroes" to "rise in value," and allow "the debtor who sold slaves" a "better chance of satisfying his creditors."[8] The voting pattern in the legislature on the final 1787 roll call to close the trade fell along intrastate sectional lines. Lowcountry representatives, who controlled the state's malapportioned assembly, voted 61–17 to close the trade, while representatives from the slave-hungry backcountry, a region still searching for a reliable export staple, voted 29–18 to continue it.[9] Moreover, large slaveholders (those owning more than twenty slaves) serving in the assembly, whether from Lowcountry or backcountry, favored closing the trade by a margin of two to one (33–16) while lesser slaveholders narrowly favored keeping it open (27–25). This voting pattern suggests that large slaveholders cared more about protecting the value of their investment than about the rapid extension of slave-based agriculture to the state's interior. Unsurprisingly, the strongest support for keeping the slave trade open came from small slaveholders in the backcountry, who voted 21–9 against closing the trade.[10]

Just a few months later, Revolutionary-era governor John Rutledge, both Pinckneys, and Pierce Butler, all Lowcountry slaveholders, emphatically insisted on some constitutional protection for the international slave trade, going so far, in James Madison's view, as to make the protection of the trade a prerequisite for union. Presenting a united front and using a lobbying style honed during their colonial negotiations with the British Parliament and Court bureaucracy, South Carolina and other lower South delegates prevailed on the slave trade question through an improbable alliance with New England shipping interests, much to the chagrin of upper South delegates from Virginia and Maryland. Charles C. Pinckney touted the twenty-year window of protection for the slave trade as a ringing victory for southern interests, claiming "we have secured an unlimited importation of negroes for twenty years."[11]

But not all South Carolinians, especially champions of the emerging backcountry, shared the delegates' enthusiasm for twenty years of protection against a federal ban. "Why limit us to 20 years, or rather why limit us at all?" Anti-Federalist Rawlin Lowndes protested, "Without negroes this state would degenerate into one of the most contemptible in the Union."[12] South Carolina's Federalist-controlled ratifying convention approved the constitution, but also tried to reassure anxious backcountry representatives that slaves would eventually be available for their region if desired. Federalists signaled that the 1787 legislature's decision to close the foreign trade was merely a temporary expedient, prompted by heavy indebtedness among the state's planters. The 1787 law closed both the foreign and domestic slave trades for three years; at the same session, the legislature had approved a three-year installment plan for debt payment as part of a debtor relief package. Once the debt crisis passed, these Federalists suggested, the legislature would reconsider opening the slave trade.[13] The question of obtaining constitutional protection for the right to participate in the international slave trade was clearly different from the question of whether any particular state wanted to participate in the trade at any given time.

In 1788, however, the South Carolina legislature reopened the domestic slave trade but agreed to keep the foreign trade closed for at least five more years, suggesting that a ban allegedly initiated out of temporary expediency was hardening into settled policy.[14] In 1791, the South Carolina legislature rejected a renewed effort to close the internal slave trade, but that same year, news of the successful uprising in Saint-Domingue reached South Carolina, raising new concerns about the spread of insurrection through the "common wind" of the slave trade, whether foreign or domestic.[15] Governor Charles Pinckney worried that the Caribbean insurrection might explode into a "flame which will extend to all the neighboring islands, and may eventually prove not a very pleasing or agreeable example to the Southern states."[16] When the legislature considered the slave trade issue again in 1792, the successful slave rebellion in Saint-Domingue weighed heavily on its deliberations, and it extended the ban on the foreign slave trade for two additional years. More strikingly, it also voted to close the domestic slave trade "ever hereafter," in an effort to prevent slaveholders in other states from selling troublesome slaves, including those influenced by insurrectionary ideas from the Caribbean, to South Carolina. As expressed through these votes, concern over the spreading influence of the slave insurrection in Saint-Domingue overwhelmed the interior's yearning for cheaper slaves in the collective mind of a Lowcountry-dominated legislature.[17]

By 1793, Lowcountry whites understood the once-admired French Revolution largely through the lens of the successful 1791 slave rebellion in Saint-Domingue and the French revolutionary government's recognition of the new island government less than two years later. Indeed, as soon as word of the Caribbean slave uprising reached South Carolina, the Lowcountry's rice aristocracy worried about the security of their property and the safety of their little world. After all, the Lowcountry resembled the Caribbean more than any other slaveholding section of the United States, and Charleston resembled a Caribbean port. During the1790s, French refugees, along with their slaves, fled the West Indies and arrived in Charleston by the hundreds, worrying local whites no end. Casting a wary eye toward the West Indies, Ralph Izard, a wealthy Lowcountry rice planter, predicted in 1792 that "the time is at no very great distance when the property in Negroes will be rendered of no value." The "enthusiasm of a considerable part of this country as well as of Europe, on this subject," Izard observed, "cannot fail of producing a convulsion which will be severely felt by the southern states."[18] Two years later, the Federalist Izard's concern about Caribbean unrest expanded to include white immigrants. Turmoil in the West Indies, Izard suggested, "would occasion a prodigious number of the lower order of Frenchmen to come to this Country," and these radical French would "fraternize with our Democratical Clubs & introduce the same horrid tragedies among our Negroes, which have already been so fatally exhibited in the French Islands." Izard puzzled over South Carolina's indifference. "Are the inhabitants of South Carolina ignorant of these things," he mused, "or is it the will of God that the Proprietors of Negroes should themselves be the Instruments of destroying that species of property."[19]

Over time, more and more Lowcountry Carolinians came to share Izard's view. As understanding of the events unfolding in Saint-Domingue spread, so did a general anxiety that slave unrest would spread from the Caribbean to the lower South. To be sure, Federalists fretted more over the French Revolution than Republicans did, and they definitely played on the fear of slave insurrection in their campaigns more than Republicans did, but the Jeffersonian opposition in South Carolina also worried about the export of revolution from Saint-Domingue. Pierce Butler, a Republican planter with substantial backcountry interests, agreed with Izard on the danger emanating from the French islands. "I am very well persuaded," he declared, "that if our state Legislature do not pass some laws to prevent the importation of slaves from the West Indies...our property in Carolina is held by a slender tye."[20] After 1793, the legislature not only kept the foreign slave trade closed but prohibited the importation of slaves from other states. The backcountry's repeated pleas for the reopening of the slave trade seldom generated any legislative response. Despite growing signs of a prodigious cotton boom in the interior, fear of the unfolding drama in Saint-Domingue and the desire to protect Lowcountry investment in slaves combined with the malapportionment of the legislature to keep the slave trade, both foreign and domestic, closed.[21]

Yet not even the continued bans on both slave trades allayed the Lowcountry's concern about potential slave unrest during the late 1790s. Throughout the decade, South Carolinians always kept at least one eye on developments in Saint-Domingue. In 1797, most white Charlestonians attributed an alleged insurrection plot in their city to the recently arrived "French negroes" and believed it was "to be executed by them alone."[22] The rumors proved exaggerated, if not altogether unfounded, and no open insurrection appeared. That same year, Robert Goodloe Harper, a Charleston lawyer who speculated heavily in Upcountry land, pondered the possibility of a black invasion from the West Indies. "Anyone well-acquainted with the seacoast," he maintained, "would know that the black population is very great...and the terrain ideal for guerilla activities." He fretted that "Victor Hugues and Toussaint have each of them considerable force," which they might send to the southern coast of the United States. "[I]f they were to get possession of Savannah or Charleston, they might do immense mischief before they could be dislodged," Harper worried. Always an advocate of federal power, Harper warned that if the national government could not protect whites in the South Carolina Lowcountry, the region's "confidence in the Union" would diminish.[23] By 1798, Charles Pinckney, again serving as governor, mobilized the state for possible war against France and urged more vigilant slave patrols and more limited use of slave passes. He warned planters that "in the present uncertain and eventful state of things," no matter relating to "security and Protection" should be taken for granted.[24] Fear that slave unrest might be imported from the Caribbean even reached the far Upcountry when a slave plot was discovered on John Ewing Colhoun's Pendleton District plantation.[25] Just across the Savannah River, neighboring Georgia, the state that had joined South Carolina in intransigent defense of the foreign trade in Philadelphia a decade earlier, banned the foreign slave trade in its state constitution of 1798. That same year, the Georgia legislature also banned the interstate slave trade, suggesting that Federalist-era Georgians also worried about the influence on the lower South of slave rebellion in the Caribbean.[26] In sum, concern over potential insurrection ebbed and flowed during the volatile 1790s, with rumors of slave insurrection sweeping through the lower South most feverishly, as Mark Kaplanoff suggested, "whenever Saint Domingo was in the news" or "the Federalists were trying to win an election."[27]

FEAR AGAIN SWEPT THROUGH the lower South in the immediate aftermath of Gabriel's Rebellion in Virginia in 1800. Though the Charleston press suppressed the details of the Virginia insurrection scare, South Carolinians were kept apprised of developments in Virginia in broad terms. Governor John Drayton, annoyed that he had received no official communication from Virginia about the incident, wrote James Monroe in late September asking for details. South Carolina, Drayton explained, felt "prudent apprehensions" that the "mischief" might spread "even so far as our state."[28] As he awaited Monroe's reply, the governor tightened security. He ordered the slave patrols on alert. He encouraged these patrols to search "negro homes" for weapons and ammunition, to break up all large gatherings of blacks "at any time or place" unless white people were present, and to detain slaves who "tread from home" without proper passes. Upon learning that a white overseer had been murdered in the rural Lowcountry in early October, Drayton sent two units of militia into the countryside to investigate, not only to capture perpetrators but also to ferret out any insurrection plans percolating in the swamps. After extensive operations, the militia commanders reported no success in apprehending the killers of the overseer, and they also reported finding no evidence of larger dangers.[29] When Monroe finally replied to Drayton, the Virginia governor conceded that the insurrection might have proved a "formidable" threat to Virginia but that he had "no reason" to think it "extended to any state south of us."[30] Later in the year, in his public statement to the legislature, Drayton acknowledged that the "insurrection which had nearly taken place in Virginia" triggered "some uneasiness" in the minds of white Carolinians, though his actions earlier in the fall suggested a greater level of anxiety.[31]

Reliable reports of white evangelical opposition to slavery in the Palmetto State worried Drayton as much as, if not more than, news of the quashed insurrection plot in Richmond. Well before information about the Gabriel scare reached South Carolina, United States senator Jacob Read, a Charleston Federalist, alerted the governor that a Methodist pamphlet seeking to "promote . . . emancipation" and thus "highly incompatible with the rights of all the Southern States" was circulating together with a companion antislavery petition, which its authors hoped to present to the state's General Assembly during its 1800 session.[32] Read's July letter to Drayton bordered on the apoplectic. Evangelical criticism of slavery, Read dramatically declared, made it "the duty of every man who regards his own life and the lives of his family and friends to be on guard, to warn others, and to exert himself to prevent the expected dangers."[33]

Reacting to the Methodist statement against slavery with a fervor that matched that of evangelical pastors in the pulpit, Read accused the "Quakers and the Methodists" of mounting a concerted campaign aimed at "sapping" the strength of the southern states. The Quakers, Read averred, were generally "harmless" because they "have no organized institutions and but few active instruments." But the aggressively evangelical Methodists were a different matter. The Methodists, Read noted, had a strong church hierarchy and a multitude of preachers who "were vastly more dangerous" than the Quakers. Moreover, the Methodists had long engaged in missions to the slaves and hence built relationships with the enslaved. In Read's jaundiced view, as the first emancipation movement gained momentum in the North, the denomination's "Pious Pastors" were using "every endeavour" to advance the cause. Noting that several of the pastors who signed the Methodist statement, including the tireless Francis Asbury, had regularly visited South Carolina, the excited South Carolina senator argued that while previous Methodist "attempts" to free slaves in South Carolina had been "scant and silent and addressed to their own silly followers," the denomination, heady with the success of gradual emancipation elsewhere, would now attempt to "lay the firebrand to our houses and the dagger to our throats."[34]

Drayton examined the Methodist proclamation Read enclosed and pronounced it "highly incompatible with the rights of all Southern States." Its contents, Drayton agreed, promoted "emancipation."[35] In fact, the Methodist statement, adopted at the church's General Conference in Baltimore in May 1800, denounced slavery as "repugnant to the inalienable rights of mankind and the very essence of civil liberty" and claimed that slavery ran counter to the "whole spirit of the New Testament" because it exposed the enslaved to the "arbitrary will and almost uncontrollable power" of their masters. Looking to "give a blow to the root of this enormous evil," the Methodist General Conference urged each local conference to use its "most respectable" members, including elders, deacons, and "traveling preachers," to draw up and secure signatures on petitions to state legislatures seeking the gradual emancipation of slaves. The process of mounting pro-emancipation petition campaigns, the Methodists urged, should continue annually until their request was fulfilled.[36]

According to Drayton, the Methodist statement had "already been distributed" and petitions in favor of emancipation circulated "in some parts of this state."[37] In response, the governor issued "some instructions regarding better government of negroes" in an effort to prevent the "mischiefs" Read feared. But, despite his concern, Drayton proved reluctant to interfere with white religious activities, including the mission to slaves, without palpable evidence of mischievous intent. The governor's restrained approach and concern for white civil liberties frustrated hard-liners such as Read, who advocated more forceful measures against the Methodist petitioners. Read suggested that if any of the pastors who signed the Methodist statement visited South Carolina, they should be arrested and their papers confiscated "for our own safety." The senator also suggested that anyone found distributing the Methodist address should be arrested and "any Committees and Societies also found" disrupted and banned. The evangelical challenge represented "no common danger," Read insisted, and "ought to be met with rigorous measures."[38] Drayton defended his unwillingness to interfere with the work of white evangelicals in the state, even those who circulated pro-emancipation petitions among whites, claiming that he "never had any information lodged with me against any white person accused of fomenting disturbances among negroes."[39] But Read wanted a purge: "I wish with all my heart that magistrates across the state could be induced to arrest...all those ignorant vagabonds calling themselves preachers who are overrunning our Country imposing on the weak and credulous and bring infinite mischief on Society," the senator complained angrily.[40]

By the time the legislature met in late November, it was clear that the Methodist activity in the state coupled with reports of Gabriel's failed insurrection plot had exposed a raw nerve in the security-conscious Lowcountry. A concerned legislature proved willing to go well beyond Drayton in its efforts to reassure slaveholders who harbored suspicions that evangelical Christianity might prove slavery's undoing in the lower South. During its 1800 session, the legislature approved a rigid ban on all secret or "behind-closed-doors" gatherings (including religious ones) that included slaves and free blacks and were held "for the purpose of mental instruction," even if the meetings were held during daylight hours and whites were present at them. Additionally, the new law banned all gatherings held between sundown and sunup, regardless of the circumstances of the assembly. The law allowed sheriffs, patrols, local police, and the militia to "disperse" such meetings, and it subjected slaves and free blacks who were arrested at such meetings to punishments of as many as twenty lashes. These dramatic new restrictions, which in practice fell mainly on black religious gatherings, stymied the efforts of Protestant denominations, especially the Methodists and Baptists, to proselytize slaves. The instructional meetings held by the evangelical denominations had often taken place at night, after the slaves' plantation and other work was done, and to a lesser extent even daylight religious gatherings were often held behind doors that closed once the service or instruction began, to avoid profane interference with sacred proceedings. If enforced, the new restrictions fell just short of constituting a total ban on the evangelical outreach to slaves and free blacks.[41]

In addition to addressing white fears of growing white evangelical activism on behalf of slaves, Governor Drayton urged the legislature to strengthen the so-called Negro Acts, legislation that regulated "the government of our slaves."[42] Eagerly embracing Drayton's recommendation, legislators quickly turned the focus of the 1800 session to tightening white control of the state's slave and free black population. By the end of the session, the legislature had approved a draconian new black code. In addition to limiting the rights of slaves and free blacks to assemble, it also included tough new laws concerning three other critical matters: the regulation of the interstate slave trade, the strengthening of the slave patrol system, and limitations on a master's ability to voluntarily free his or her own slaves.[43]

Feeling surrounded by insurrectionary tendencies, first in the Caribbean and then in Virginia, Palmetto State legislators believed that the importation of slaves from these troubled areas introduced erstwhile rebels into the state. The interstate slave trade had been closed since 1792, and the prevailing statute banned the importation of slaves as merchandise for sale or hire but allowed slaveholders who intended to settle in the state to bring in an unlimited number of slaves without subjecting these arriving masters (or their slaves) to any special restrictions or regulation. As part of its 1800 crackdown, the legislature required slaveholders seeking residence in the state to present proof to a magistrate that they had owned the slaves accompanying them for at least two years and to pledge that for an additional two years they would sell none of the slaves who migrated with them. Moreover, masters who wanted to bring more than ten slaves with them had to seek special legislative permission for their slaves to enter the state. Both the prospect of appearances before magistrates and the necessity of petitioning the legislature to bring larger numbers of slaves into the state loomed as a deterrent to slaveholders looking to settle in South Carolina.[44]

The legislature also put sharp new enforcement teeth in its regulation of the slave trade. The 1800 law subjected local tax collectors who failed to report illegal slave imports to stiff fines, and put the burden of proof in slave-smuggling cases on the accused smugglers. Further, the new legislation authorized the state militia to assist in policing slave smuggling and gave the militia the same authority to "attack, wound and kill" when they encountered smugglers that they had long enjoyed when acting to quell an insurrection. On the whole, the revised ban on the interstate slave trade made it much more difficult for slaveholders or slave traders to circumvent the law and much less appealing for slaveholders to migrate to South Carolina with their slaves.[45]

During the same session, the legislature moved to codify the responsibility of masters for the general safety of the white community. In the fall of 1800, the two militia captains dispatched by Governor Drayton to investigate the murder of an overseer in the Lowcountry complained bitterly about the inadequacy of the existing slave patrol system. The "inefficiency" of the patrol in the rural areas outside Charleston, Captain William Hayne told Governor Drayton, left him unable to find more than twenty whites able to perform patrol duty in an area with seventy-eight plantations and in all likelihood more than two thousand slaves. Hayne urged Drayton to seek legislation requiring every plantation owner to either perform patrol duty or to hire an overseer capable of serving in the owner's place. The other captain, Paul Hamilton, claimed that too many wealthy planters ignored patrol duty and easily paid the small fines imposed on those who neglected it. In response, Drayton sought changes in the patrol law, and the new black code of 1800 required masters residing on plantations with at least "ten working negroes" to either swear that they were resident on their plantations or hire a white overseer capable of performing patrol duty if they were not. This provision of the code defined the large slaveholder's responsibility for protecting white safety by ensuring adequate personnel for slave patrols.[46]

More strikingly, however, the new slave code limited the slaveholder's traditional prerogative to manumit slaves. Complaining that it had "been a practice for many years" in South Carolina for masters to emancipate slaves "of bad character, or, from age and infirmity, incapable of gaining their livelihood by honest means," the legislature required all masters seeking to free slaves to appear before a local magistrate and a jury of five local freeholders to prove that any slaves they planned to free were of good character and could support themselves.[47] This measure protected the larger white community against the danger and expense of a growing, dependent free black population, but it may also have been motivated in part, as were similar measures in Virginia, by fears that the Methodist petition campaign, while likely to encounter steadfast opposition from the state legislature, might persuade many evangelical slaveholders to manumit their own slaves. The new restrictions on manumission constituted a dramatic departure from South Carolina's usual policy of refusing to interfere with a master's authority over slaves. Breaking with tradition, the new law limited the master's control over his property in the interest of white safety. Taken as a whole, the legislature's rigorous new black code, and especially its willingness to interfere with religious practices and to limit masters' previously sacrosanct prerogatives over their slaves, revealed mounting white anxiety over slave unrest.

EVEN WITH THE TOUGH NEW LAWS regulating slaves and free blacks on the statute books, suggestions that the ongoing turmoil in the West Indies was generating ripple effects along the Atlantic coast prompted South Carolina whites to look assiduously for insurrection plots in their midst. The most ominous of these insurrection scares occurred in the Georgetown area late in the summer of 1802. The scare had its origins in reports circulated by New York City mayor Edward Livingston that some black prisoners from Saint-Domingue had escaped from the French frigates that brought them into the port of New York. The rumor mill soon processed this news into reports that the French planned to release incendiary black "brigands" up and down the Atlantic coast. These reports generated something of a general alarm in southern port cities and other vulnerable coastal areas. General James Jackson organized a response in the city of Savannah and alerted militia units in that state's coastal counties.[48] In South Carolina, Governor Drayton put the state militia on alert and organized a network of lookouts along the coast. In this state of heightened anxiety, one of the lookouts near Georgetown sighted an unidentified ship (possibly a ship involved in the increasingly active illegal slave trade) in the waters outside Winyah Bay. This sighting spawned rumors that a West Indian expeditionary force was preparing to land and lead a slave rebellion in the Lowcountry. With the heavily black Georgetown District on the razor's edge of alarm, the sighting of a single black man, allegedly of French background, traveling without a pass on a Saturday evening prompted the rapid spread of reports that an armed brigade of French-speaking Caribbean insurrectionists had finally come ashore at Georgetown.[49]

A local militia unit investigated the complaint with alacrity and found nothing to corroborate the alarm, but poor communication among militia leaders led Brigadier General Peter Horry, a wealthy Georgetown planter, to mobilize the state militia to defend against an invasion that never materialized. Once Horry personally arrived in All Saints Parish, conversations with prominent rice planter and state legislator Joseph Alston convinced the militia commander that all reports of impending danger had been unwarranted. Embarrassed by launching a full-scale mobilization based on inaccurate information, Peter Horry decried the false alarm as a problem of "great consequence." An experienced military officer who had served ably with Francis Marion during the Revolution, Horry judged it "shameful to sport with the feelings of so many men...and to occasion distress to their families." He promptly initiated disciplinary proceedings against Captain John Joshua Ward, a popular local militia officer, for his failure to properly vet the rumors in time to prevent mobilization and fright among the Lowcountry's white population.[50] Claiming that he had been "cautious" in his investigation of the rumors, Ward expressed dismay that false reports of an invasion of All Saints Parish had reached Georgetown and insisted that he had issued no orders containing such a claim. Ward's version was supported by two noncommissioned officers, and Horry dropped his complaint. Governor Drayton defended his own hasty overreaction, citing the fear of the reported arrival of "French Brigands Incendiary prisoners of colour" and the danger of delay as his reasons for mobilizing the state militia on scant information.[51]

The whole Georgetown scare, with its false alarms and finger-pointing by prominent men, revealed just how precarious a balance South Carolina leaders had to maintain between internal security and social peace. With fears of a Caribbean-style rebellion by the Lowcountry's large slave majority running high, any alarm triggered an immediate and overwhelming response. Yet, even more than in the whiter upper South, false alarms weakened security by alarming white families unnecessarily, wrenching white males away from home and hearthside in the dark of night for no purpose. Such unnecessary mobilizations rendered whites skeptical of all future alarms. Moreover, repeated scares, whether justified or unjustified, heightened fear and uncertainty among whites. The scares that proved false alarms created doubt about the competence of local and state authorities; those that proved justified necessarily suggested that slaves were capable of ghastly deeds. Thus scares undermined the public's confidence in its own security in the face of potential slave unrest. White confidence in public safety remained a sine qua non for slaveholding societies, even ones as overwhelmingly dependent on slave labor as the South Carolina Lowcountry. Any loss of confidence in the ability of political and military leaders to safely manage the area's slave population threatened to undermine support for slavery itself in the long run. Whites demanded vigilance from their militia and patrol leaders, but they also expected these leaders to avoid crying wolf too often.

DESPITE LINGERING WHITE FEAR of slave unrest, the draconian slave control measures approved by the legislature in 1800 triggered a significant popular backlash. The first, and initially most potent, protest came from evangelical Christians angered by restrictions on their efforts to provide religious instruction to slaves. As soon as the law took effect, the state's evangelical community actively sought repeal or revision of the law. In 1801, Richard Furman, pastor of Charleston's First Baptist Church, leader of the state's Regular Baptist denomination and long active in the effort to offer Christian instruction to slaves, persuaded the Charleston Baptist Association to petition the legislature asking for the removal of the new restrictions on assemblies including slaves and free blacks.[52] When the legislature denied the petition, Furman, a slaveholder himself, garnered an even larger number of signatures on a similar petition sent to the legislature the next year. Methodists, who also frequently had used nighttime meetings for the religious instruction of slaves, expressed strong disapproval of the existing law as well, but since the opprobrium attached to the Methodist denomination in the Lowcountry had helped inspire the restrictions, they were inclined to let the Baptists and Presbyterians take the lead in the protest.

In 1802, citizens of the Upcountry district of Chester, home to large numbers of Presbyterians and Associated Reformed Presbyterians (ARPs), joined the protest by petitioning for repeal of the restrictions on religious gatherings.[53] These petitions, one signed by an impressive array of Baptist ministers and the other by a large number of Chester District citizens, complained bitterly that the restrictions grew out of the mistaken assumption that such instruction was "intended to infuse the mass of domestics [slaves] with sentiments unfriendly to subordination and peace." In fact, the petitioners countered, "it is certain that the plain doctrines and positive precepts of Christianity, as professed and supported by the body of our citizens, have a direct contrary tendency," and instead encouraged obedience and loyalty among slaves. The petitions reminded legislators that many of the ministers who had signed the Charleston Association's petition "had long been in the habit of giving religious instruction to slaves," including lessons about the Christian duty of remaining "subject to Authority." These evangelists used the slaves' fidelity to that teaching as a "test of their sincerity in religion." Furman and other white evangelists claimed that "from the most careful observation" made during their mission efforts toward slaves, they had gleaned "very satisfactory evidence that the principles so inculcated have been conscientiously imbibed by the body of those Negroes who have attended on their ministry," and that these principles "have governed their conduct" in a proper manner. The petitioners also warned the legislature that the severe restrictions approved in 1800 could easily "have a strong indirect tendency to produce the evil it was designed to prevent" by causing slave and free black Christians, "that class of negroes who value religious privileges," to lash out in anger and resentment against the fresh denial of privileges formerly enjoyed.[54] Acknowledging that the "situation" in South Carolina was "delicate" due to the size of the state's black population (though the state had a white majority in 1800), the petitioners insisted that the state should make a "proper discrimination" based on "known principles and conduct" between "innocent" gatherings for religious worship and instruction and meetings where evidence proved a desire to "destroy the foundations of peace and social order."[55]

Again in 1802, the legislature received the evangelical petitions but granted the petitioners no relief. By then, the evangelical movement was rapidly gaining influence in the state, particularly in the Upcountry, as the Great Revival ignited religious enthusiasm across the South.[56] Thus, in 1803, the evangelical protest, again orchestrated by Furman and other Protestant clergy, succeeded in prompting a reconsideration of the law. The proposed revisions allowed religious gatherings of slaves and free blacks if they were held before nine o'clock in the evening and if the majority of attendees were white. The legislature, noting the petitions of "certain religious societies in this State" urging such a change, ultimately approved the modification of the 1800 law. Yet the concessions did not come easily. In the House, the revisions passed on a 50–45 vote because of strong support from Piedmont representatives, who favored revision by a 21–8 margin.[57]

In the end, South Carolina evangelicals had persuaded a legislature still controlled by the Lowcountry elite to relax restrictions on slave worship and the religious instruction of slaves, despite the elite's lingering fear that religious enthusiasm inspired slave unrest. Yet even though the revised statute was heralded as a victory for the evangelicals, the new law left in place significant limitations on the ability of blacks to gather, even for religious purposes. In the Upcountry, the condition that all gatherings had to include white majorities loomed as an imposition, but it was a requirement that could often be met. But in the black-majority Lowcountry, where blacks outnumbered by whites by large proportions in most areas, almost all religious assemblies had consisted of large black majorities, so the new law offered little relief there. Over time, however, some latitude was allowed in the enforcement of the 1803 law. Religious gatherings generally proceeded unimpeded as long as whites were present, whether or not they constituted a majority, and evening meetings were often allowed to continue past nine o'clock as long as they had begun earlier in the evening and involved no suspicious activity. Oral tradition among white evangelical families maintained that blacks were often allowed to hold religious services of their own, separate from white services, with few if any whites present, in clear violation of the law. At times, whites "not in sympathy with the church" would "interfere" with these services, but these hostile whites would usually, but not always, "desist" if the slave congregants could present passes signed by their masters.[58]

The rigid new ban on the introduction of slaves imposed by the South Carolina legislature also generated popular protest. Even with fear of insurrection running high, residents of the interior cotton belt railed against the new restrictions on the importation of slaves. In March 1802, an Edgefield District grand jury, speaking from the heart of the emerging upland cotton region, complained that the law stood as an "insurmountable Bar in the way of men of Property moving into this state." In "this way the Value of our Landed property is Reduced and the growing wealth and population of the upper Country obstructed."[59] Three months later, another Edgefield grand jury also urged repeal of the ban, arguing that the "utter and compleat prevention of persons coming from our sister states into this State (with Negroes)" remained "highly disadvantageous to the prosperity of the district and the back Country generally."[60] In the fall of 1802, residents of neighboring Abbeville District, home of the Calhoun family plantations, petitioned the legislature to repeal the ban, calling it a "direct bar to the increase of wealth and population in the upper and middle districts." They explained that the "upper Districts" were "populated heavily" by settlers from "the back parts of the middle and northern states" who had a "habit of removing to the upper parts of this State with their negroes and other property to settle amongst us." But the "Operation of that Law," the petitioners argued, forced prospective settlers with slaves into North Carolina, Georgia, or Tennessee, depriving South Carolina of "population and wealth and of a number of honest respectable settlers."[61] The legislature granted the petitioners no relief from existing restrictions in 1802, but backcountry restlessness on the subject suggested that the matter would be revisited as the first short-staple cotton boom extended its reach.

THE COTTON BOOM had begun to flourish in the lower South as soon as Eli Whitney and others discovered how to clean large quantities of the short-staple cotton craved by the British textile industry. By 1800, interior planters such as Wade Hampton I and Thomas Taylor of Richland District annually produced huge cotton crops. South Carolina's cotton exports increased from 93,540 pounds in 1793, the year Whitney made his first gin, to more than 8 million pounds in 1801.[62] Charleston physician and historian David Ramsey captured the impact of the cotton boom on the Palmetto State economy when he observed that during the first decade of the nineteenth century, cotton "trebled the price of land suitable to its growth" and "doubled" the annual income of growers. The "clear profits on one crop planted in cotton . . . will purchase the fee simple of the land," Ramsey claimed. "Two, three or four will in like manner pay for the negroes who make it."[63] Governor John Drayton's widely circulated *A View of South Carolina*, published in 1802, also emphasized the transforming effect of short-staple cotton on the state's interior. Drayton proclaimed it a matter of "National Joy" that a "staple so valuable as cotton is now added to the produce of the state . . . [and] increases annually both in the lower and upper country."[64] The Upcountry's James Spratt, a Catawba River planter who was among "the first to plant cotton on a vast acreage," joined others in the region to form a generation of cotton planters who by "exploiting the fertility of the virgin land and the fecundity of the virgin slave produced a wealth and established a culture" in the upland South.[65]

Played out on a regional scale over nearly a quarter century, the first cotton boom transformed the lower South, slavery, and even the larger American economy in significant ways. It drew large-scale commercial (plantation) agriculture out of its tidewater (rice), coastal (Sea Island cotton), and river bottom (sugarcane) confines and spread it across as much of the lower South as could provide an adequate frost-to-frost growing season. It also lured many small farmers into staple production since cotton production required a much smaller capital outlay than rice or sugar. Precisely because it spread large-scale commercial agriculture across a vast expanse of the lower South, the first cotton boom also thrust slavery out of its old staple-growing enclaves (chiefly the tidewater regions of Virginia and Maryland and northeastern North Carolina, where tobacco had been grown since the 1620s; the rice- and Sea Island cotton-growing regions of South Carolina and Georgia; and the more recently established sugarcane-growing areas of the lower Mississippi Valley and around Mobile) and made slavery a truly regional institution. The cotton boom of the late 1790s and early 1800s created the first cotton belt in the southern interior. Buckled in or around Augusta, Georgia, at the fall line of the Savannah River, the belt stretched outward in two directions, reaching into the non-tidewater Lowcountry and the lower Piedmont regions of both South Carolina and Georgia. Many emigrants soon departed from the first belt with their slaves to relocate on even more fertile black and brown loam soils found in portions of north Florida, Alabama, Mississippi, Louisiana, and eventually east Texas.[66] From this cotton-driven migration emerged the large, newly rich, heavily slave, and often politically conservative black belt of the Old South. An ancillary cotton boom emerged along the lower Mississippi River in the Natchez area, where local farmers insisted as early as 1797 that "the farms in this District would be of little more value to the present occupiers than an equal quantity of waste land" without the labor "performed by slaves."[67] When Congress, pressured by politicians from both upper and lower South, permitted the domestic slave trade in the Mississippi Territory in 1798, the slave population in the territory increased from just under thirty-five hundred in 1801 to nearly seventeen thousand by 1810, and cotton production reached ten thousand bales by 1801. By 1803 cotton plantations lined both sides of the Mississippi from Natchez to Baton Rouge.[68]

The consequences of this cotton revolution were profound and far-reaching. In the expansion of slavery across the lower South, the previously separate slave cultures of the Chesapeake, Lowcountry, and Gulf Coast commingled through the tens of thousands of slaves who moved with the cotton boom. As Ira Berlin has argued, out of this forced migration and subsequent interaction emerged a single, varied, but identifiable African American culture, the culture of the migration generation of slaves.[69] Moreover, as cotton gradually but inexorably became the great southern staple, its presence encouraged the development of a domestic textile industry in New England even as it cemented the South's commercial ties with Great Britain. Thus the transatlantic political economy that shaped so many antebellum political calculations began to emerge. Within the slaveholding states, the first cotton boom created a new set of economic and political dynamics. It broadened the scope and scale of the potential market for slaves from the upper South, where slave-based agriculture seemed at best mature and slow-growing and at worst on the wane. The upper South thus found an increasingly valuable commerce in supplying the lower South with slaves. These interests came together to create a truly regional market in slavcs. The slave-selling upper South needed lower South buyers and a political climate that frustrated state-level tendencies to regulate or ban the interstate slave trade. At times, however, lower South state legislatures had different ideas about the value of a rapidly growing slave population and took action to regulate or restrict the interstate slave trade.[70]

In South Carolina, pleas from the lower Piedmont heartland of the first upland cotton boom highlighted the internal tensions arising from South Carolina's existing prohibition of both the external and internal slave trades. Counties and districts in the upland or lower Piedmont regions of South Carolina and Georgia, areas previously relegated to the margins of the staple economy, believed that restrictions on the slave trade prevented them from acquiring the labor they needed to take full advantage of the cotton boom. They blamed both Lowcountry greed (the desire to increase the value of their own slaves) and fear (of insurrection) for the bans. With both bans in effect, the upland cotton boom in South Carolina and Georgia brought with it a revival of the illegal slave trade, which previously had been effectively damped by Saint-Domingue-related fears. Some contemporary estimates placed the number of slaves illegally imported (chiefly from Africa) between 1800 and 1803 at ten thousand, a total equal to perhaps half the number of imports a legal trade would have brought in during the same years. More carefully calibrated modern estimates suggest that at least three thousand slaves entered South Carolina illegally from 1800 through 1803.[71] Regardless of the precise number of illegally acquired slaves, the cotton boom revived slave smuggling on a fairly large scale. In time, this increase in the illegal slave trade, and the complicity of so many white Carolinians in it, emerged as a potent argument for reopening the legal slave trade, whether foreign or domestic.

Despite the profits flowing from the first cotton boom, a wary South Carolina legislature turned a deaf ear to the backcountry's plea for more slaves by an overwhelming margin in 1802. That year's legislature soundly defeated a proposal to reopen the foreign slave trade, 86–11 in the state house of representatives and by voice vote in the state senate.[72] In weighing the balance between fear of a larger slave population and the related possibility of declining slave values, on one hand, and the ambitions of interior cotton growers, on the other, a legislature still dominated by Lowcountry interests decided to keep the slave trade closed. Denied the labor of legally imported slaves, the cotton revolution nonetheless proceeded apace, and the balance of fear and greed against ambition and opportunity shifted dramatically during 1803, when a coincidence of diplomatic luck and Jeffersonian vision brought the Louisiana Territory into American possession.[73]

TO THE SURPRISE of many political observers, in late November 1803, just one year after its desultory rejection of inland cotton growers' pleas for a reopened slave trade, the South Carolina legislature suddenly began a serious reconsideration of the issue, undoubtedly prompted by both persistent backcountry pressure and the prospect of supplying legions of slaves to the lower Louisiana Territory for handsome profits.[74] While under Spanish control in the 1790s, Louisiana had closed its own flourishing slave trade with the Caribbean due to a growing fear that insurrection sentiment would spread from Saint-Domingue to the mainland. But neither South Carolina slaveholders and traders nor Louisiana authorities failed to notice the opportunities for the continued expansion of slavery in the New Orleans hinterland once Louisiana became American property. South Carolina politicians welcomed the controversial Louisiana Purchase with rare bipartisan enthusiasm. For the most part, South Carolina Federalists, still strong in the state's overrepresented Lowcountry and usually more than willing to excoriate the Republican Jefferson, not only refrained from criticizing the president on the Louisiana issue but affirmatively supported the acquisition. The Federalist-leaning Charleston *Courier* hailed the purchase and praised Louisiana as a "greater treasure to the western part of the US than a mountain of gold." Republican Thomas Sumter Jr. reported that among Federalists "many of the moderates...approve of the acquisition," while only "a few mad-dog federalists" opposed it. And early in its 1803 session, the South Carolina legislature applauded the "wise measures adopted and pursued by the executive of these States [Jefferson] to obtain the sovereignty and possession of Louisiana."[75]

In his opening message to that same legislature, South Carolina's newly elected governor, James B. Richardson, a planter who previously had opposed the foreign slave trade, reversed his position and urged the legislature to consider reopening the trade. Richardson, a resident of the interior cotton-growing district of Clarendon, publicly offered two reasons for his change in position. First, Richardson claimed, recent experience had shown that, despite the application of "all possible vigilance," enforcement of the existing ban remained virtually impossible. Richardson maintained that "the interest of the citizens [of South Carolina] is so interwoven with the species of property [slaves]" that it left them unwilling to assist the efforts of state authorities to enforce the ban. Thus the continued importation of slaves remained "beyond the possibility of prevention." Richardson's second objection to the prohibition grew logically out of his first. Since it was impossible to prevent successful smuggling of slaves along the coast, the existing ban operated very unevenly on different parts of the state. In "the present state of things," Richardson explained, the "seacoast districts" managed to "accumulate this property [through the illegal trade] without the possibility of being detected," while "those of the interior and middle districts only experience the operation of the law." Thus, Richardson argued, the existing ban proved "oppressive" to Upcountry districts, where landowners "held it an object of desire, to augment their capital in the accumulation of such property." Richardson concluded by demanding the law's repeal.[76] No mention was made of the acquisition of Louisiana.

When the 1803 legislature took up the question of reopening the foreign slave trade, debate over the issue was anything but desultory. The combined political force of interior demand for slaves and the prospect of supplying Louisiana with slaves drove the state senate to move quickly toward consideration of reopening the African slave trade. Debate over the question in the usually collegial senate proved heated. Federalist Robert Barnwell, a Revolutionary veteran once held as a prisoner of war by the British, led the senate opposition to the trade. The widely respected Barnwell warned that a reopened slave trade would quickly lessen the value of all slave property, and "negroes would soon not be worth one half of what they now sold for." Additionally, Barnwell, a successful rice planter who owned more than 150 slaves, feared "ruinous speculation" and a rapid drain of capital from the state. "Every one would purchase negroes," the Beaufort rice planter predicted, because it was "well known that those who deal in this property would sell it at a very long credit." South Carolinians, Barnwell worried, "would purchase at all hazards, and trust to fortunate crops and favorable markets for making their payments." Within a few years, "if this trade is continued open," South Carolina would "be in the same situation of debt...as at the conclusion of the revolutionary war." That debt burden, Barnwell reminded his listeners, had prompted economic difficulty and debtor-driven social unrest in the state during the Confederation era. Barnwell also offered a "still more cogent and impressive" argument that reopening the African slave trade threatened the state's domestic security, though the press declined to print his full argument on this point. In a state periodically gripped by fear of insurrection, arguments about threats to white safety likely carried considerable weight. William Smith of York, an entrepreneurial Upcountry cotton planter who emerged as the leading champion of reopening the overseas slave trade, replied to Barnwell, but he limited his public justification for reopening the trade to highlighting the proven inability of the state to stop the illegal importation of slaves, an enforcement task Smith labeled "impossible."[77] Remarkably, the senate, which had kept the trade closed on a voice vote in 1802, opened it on a similar vote in 1803, and sent a bill to the house for its approval on December 6.[78]

The house, however, initially displayed decidedly less enthusiasm for reopening the foreign slave trade than the senate. In fact, during the early days of its 1803 session, the house seemed more interested in tightening the existing ban than in legalizing the slave trade. The house initially appointed a committee to close loopholes in the laws prohibiting the slave trade, and a few days later the house referred Richardson's request for reopening to the same committee.[79] The arrival of the senate bill on December 6 complicated matters, but the house agreed to consider both the senate bill and the pending committee report while sitting as a "Committee of the Whole." On December 10, 1803, Henry Deas, representing the house committee, told the larger body that the committee had concluded that "the laws prohibiting the importation" of slaves could be amended "so as to prevent their [slaves] introduction amongst us" and recommended that a committee be appointed to draft such a bill.[80] A five-person committee, dominated by known opponents of the slave trade, was selected for that purpose, and the house delayed further action. On December 12, 1803, Representative William Falconer of Chesterfield, reporting on behalf of the drafting committee, introduced a bill to "prevent" the importation of slaves. A motion to postpone debate on this bill indefinitely failed by a large margin.

On December 14, 1803, the house considered the proposal tightening the ban on both the foreign and domestic slave trades. A motion was made to amend the bill to allow the interstate slave trade while keeping the foreign trade closed. But the amendment to reopen the domestic slave trade only was defeated handily, 66–36, on a highly sectional vote. This one-sided vote revealed much about legislative sentiment concerning the slave trade. Representatives from interior districts overwhelmingly favored reopening the interstate slave trade and supported the amendment by a margin of 36–10. Representatives from the Upcountry, those districts lying on and above the fall line, favored reopening the domestic slave trade even more emphatically, 28–5. But Lowcountry representatives easily killed the amendment, voting unanimously, 56–0, against reopening only the domestic slave trade.[81]

No other single vote on the slave trade so readily revealed the differing interests of the Lowcountry and Upcountry on the issue of the slave trade. Interior districts, and particularly the Upcountry districts, had in the late eighteenth century been the destination for a large white in-migration down the Great Piedmont road from Pennsylvania and Virginia. Many of these recently settled Upcountry families still had extended family in Virginia, North Carolina, and Georgia. As active participants in the short-staple cotton boom, these Upcountry whites wanted to buy slaves from other states, where they could find significant quantities of either American-born slaves or slaves long resident in North America for reasonable prices. As long as both the foreign and domestic trades were closed, Lowcountry sellers enjoyed a monopoly on slaves sold to the interior market, a monopoly that held slave prices, and hence the profits of slave sellers, artificially high. This policy had helped Lowcountry landowners gradually escape their post-Revolutionary debt and brought a measure of stability to the state's economy and tax base, but it had done so at the expense of Upcountry opportunity and ambition. Lowcountry legislators saw little reason to sacrifice their advantage lightly.

Moreover, those Lowcountry interests seeking to resume the foreign slave trade in order to supply Mississippi and Louisiana as well as the South Carolina interior with African slaves knew that they would likely need Upcountry support to do so. They wanted any consideration of reopening the domestic trade tied to the question of reopening the foreign trade as well. Following the defeat of the amendment proposing the reopening of the domestic slave trade, the House voted on the toughened prohibition measure offered by the special committee. In a dramatic reversal of the position it had taken just a year earlier, the House defeated the bill to continue the prohibition of both the foreign and domestic slaves trades on a 58–45 vote. Again, the vote carried strong sectional overtones. Lowcountry representatives voted 33–19 in favor of continuing the prohibition of both slave trades, while interior members opposed continuing both bans by a margin of more than three to one (39–12). Again, representatives from those districts lying on or above the fall line opposed the continued prohibitions even more decisively, 32–5, than the interior as a whole. But the house bill to keep both the foreign and domestic slave trades closed failed because the unanimity of the Lowcountry opposition had eroded. Anything approaching unanimous support from the Lowcountry would have preserved the ban, but more than a third of Lowcountry representatives voted to defeat the continued prohibition. For the first time in more than a decade, inland proponents of reopening the slave trade found a number of allies in Lowcountry delegations. But Upcountry advocates of importing more slaves also knew that gaining Lowcountry support for the renewed importation of slaves required reopening the foreign slave trade and not simply the interstate slave trade. The success of any proposal to allow the renewed importation of slaves into South Carolina required an intrastate sectional coalition, and that coalition hinged on reopening both the foreign and domestic slave trades.[82]

Once it defeated the attempts to extend and tighten the existing bans on the foreign and domestic slave trades, the House turned immediately to action on the Senate bill reopening both trades. The vote to reopen both the foreign and the domestic slave trades proved quite close. On December 17, 1803, session-long legislative maneuvering culminated in a 55–47 vote in favor of reopening the foreign slave trade as well as the domestic trade.[83] A four-vote shift in the House would have changed the outcome. Interior representatives voted solidly but not overwhelmingly, 29–22, in favor of reopening both trades. Interior support for reopening the foreign as well as domestic slave trades was decidedly less overwhelming than for reopening the domestic slave trade alone. The margin in favor of reopening among interior representatives fell from twenty-six to seven when resumption of the foreign trade was added to the mix. Inland legislators clearly felt that African slaves presented a greater threat to white security than domestic slaves, but they still provided the reopening bill with more than half of the votes it needed to pass—and virtually all of its margin of victory. Lowcountry representatives favored reopening both trades by only one vote, 26–25. Yet the twenty-six Lowcountry votes in favor of reopening represented a sharp change of opinion in the area. Moreover, since the Lowcountry controlled South Carolina's badly malapportioned legislature, the bill could not have passed without substantial Lowcountry support. Had the roughly one-half of Lowcountry representatives who had previously opposed reopening by overwhelming margins not broken ranks and supported the reopening of both the foreign and domestic slave trades, the ban would have remained in place despite persistent Upcountry interest in reopening the slave trade.[84]

Close analysis of the final vote on the slave trade bill in the House, however, suggests revealing voting patterns within the state's two major sections and the possible lines of the cross-sectional coalition that secured passage of the bill. In the interior, support for reopening both slave trades was strongest in those areas just moving into the vortex of the cotton economy. Representatives from districts lying on or above the fall line voted in favor of reopening the overseas and interstate slave trades by seven votes, 22–15, providing all of the bill's margin of victory among interior representatives and all but one vote of the bill's margin in the House. But Upcountry support for reopening both the foreign and domestic slave trades lay mostly in the lower Piedmont, where cotton production was expanding most rapidly. Lower Piedmont representatives cast seventeen votes in favor of reopening and only ten against. Upper Piedmont legislators, representing hill-country districts still largely isolated from the cotton economy, split evenly on the reopening proposal, as did representatives from districts in the lower reaches of the state's interior, where plantations were already well stocked with slaves. Strikingly, the area of the state most overwhelmingly in favor of reopening the foreign and domestic slave trades was not the short-staple-cotton-producing lower Piedmont but the portion of the Lowcountry lying between Charleston and the Georgia border. In the parishes south of Charleston and around Beaufort, an area near the Georgia border where Sea Island cotton flourished, the bill to reopen the slave trade received support from fifteen house members and opposition from only two. More than the seven-vote margin for reopening in the lower Piedmont, this thirteen-vote margin in the southernmost Lowcountry parishes emerged as the key to reopening the slave trade in South Carolina. The rest of the Lowcountry, including the Charleston and Georgetown areas devoted almost exclusively to rice production, opposed reopening the trade. Representatives from these areas voted 23–13 against the bill. Together, the districts of the lower Piedmont and the Lowcountry parishes south of Charleston voted for reopening both the foreign and domestic slave trades by a margin of twenty votes. The rest of the state voted against the proposal by a margin of twelve.[85]

This vote represented a dramatic about-face on the slave trade issue in one year. No single factor fully explains the sudden shift in legislative sentiment on the foreign slave trade. A multiplicity of motives prevailed among the Lowcountry legislators who supported reopening the African slave trade. Some wanted cheaper slaves for the flourishing Sea Island cotton culture and the expansion of short-staple cotton production in parts of the Lowcountry that lay beyond the reach of the tidal rice culture. Still more Lowcountry legislators favored reopening because they hoped their families, friends, and constituents could profit from the slave trade itself, which had built many fortunes across several generations in eighteenth-century Charleston. Indeed, the wealth of Charleston during the city's late-eighteenth-century golden age, the so-called Age of the Pinckneys, rested heavily on wealth accumulated through the slave trade. Upcountry demand for more slaves to work cotton during the heady years of the first boom clearly explains why determined interior legislators persisted in their efforts to open the trade and later to keep it open. Interior senators and representatives who supported reviving the slave trade sought to increase the supply and thus lower the purchase price of slaves needed to work the ever-expanding cotton fields of the South Carolina interior. They would have been satisfied with the reopening of the interstate slave trade alone but needed Lowcountry support, which they could gain only by supporting the reopening of the foreign trade as well.

Yet neither the demand for more slaves from the emerging cotton belt nor the avarice of would-be business partners in the slave trade can entirely explain the suddenness or the timing of South Carolina's stunning reversal of a decade-old policy. Instead, the sudden appearance of a golden opportunity to supply the newly acquired Louisiana Territory's voracious appetite for African slaves through the port of Charleston changed the landscape of political support for the international slave trade in short order in 1803.[86] South Carolina congressman Thomas Lowndes, a Georgetown rice planter who opposed reopening the slave trade, conceded that demand for slaves would be enhanced "by the immense accession of territory to the United States by the new cessation of Louisiana," suggesting that South Carolinians were well aware of the possibilities of the Gulf Coast market when they reopened the trade.[87]

In the end, South Carolina's decision to reopen the trade depended on the formation of an ad hoc coalition rather than on a concerted strategy. Legislative support for reopening the slave trade emerged through cautious coalition building, and the pro-reopening coalition contained groups with rather different motives. Again, the most clear-cut line of demarcation within the pro-slave-trade coalition lay in the differing motives of Upcountry and Lowcountry supporters. The inland districts, whose citizens preferred to purchase creole slaves from Virginia or Maryland, wanted the domestic trade reopened. Lowcountry support for a revived slave trade hinged almost entirely on the prospect of importing African slaves and the profits that Lowcountry merchants and traders might derive from such traffic. It took a coalition of the two groups to pass any reopening legislation at all. The pattern of legislative voting during the 1803 session revealed the outlines of prior conflict within the ultimate pro-reopening coalition. Neither Upcountry nor Lowcountry could achieve its preferred version of the slave trade without help from the other. By tying the reopening of the foreign and interstate trades together, supporters of each found enough votes to pass, albeit narrowly, a bill reopening both. Arguably, both parts of this pro-slave-trade coalition saw advantages in positioning South Carolina to nurture the expansion of slavery in Louisiana, but almost certainly the inland majority for reopening was more concerned with its own pressing need for affordable slave labor than with securing a larger empire for slavery.[88]

Moreover, as lucrative as the possibility of providing Louisiana with slaves appeared, reopening the foreign slave trade in anticipation of serving this market involved considerable risk. The United States Congress enjoyed clear constitutional authority to control the slave trade in the Louisiana Territory after its acquisition in 1803, and given the approaching end of the constitutional protection of a state's right to reopen the foreign trade, some restrictions on Louisiana's participation in the slave trade, if not an outright prohibition, loomed as a real possibility. Buyers in the loosely governed Mississippi Territory next door to Louisiana arguably appeared more reliable customers for reexports from South Carolina. Congress had allowed the interstate slave trade (but rejected the international) in Mississippi in 1798, and the Natchez region quickly joined the South Carolina and Georgia interiors in the early phase of the first cotton boom. Yet prior to the American acquisition of Louisiana in 1803, slave owners and aspiring slave owners in the Natchez hinterland worried about the presence of a foreign power just across the Mississippi and recognized that foreign control of the port of New Orleans represented a potential problem for marketing their crop. Mississippi slaveholders seemed far less likely to purchase African slaves than domestic ones given competitive prices, but once New Orleans and the rest of Louisiana were safely in American hands and the uncertainty caused by foreign control of the port removed, Natchez-area planters appeared a reliable market for slaves reexported from South Carolina. Moreover, given its recent sanction of the interstate slave trade there, the federal government seemed less likely to interfere with the slave trade in Mississippi than in the newly acquired Louisiana Territory, where all the issues of territorial governance remained undetermined. The prospect of reexporting slaves imported from Africa to eager buyers in Louisiana played a role in South Carolina's decision, and more specifically the timing of the decision, to reopen the African slave trade, but it was only one factor among several.[89]

Shortly after the United States purchased Louisiana in 1803, President Thomas Jefferson appointed Isaac Briggs as government surveyor for an area that included the newly acquired territory around New Orleans. "[T]he number of slaves in this territory is already great," Briggs, a Quaker who disapproved of slavery, observed with concern upon his arrival, "and the infatuated inhabitants are in the habit of increasing it, by large importations." The surveyor reported that Louisiana slaves were already "discontented" and "disposed" to rebel. The scenes of Saint-Domingue might replay themselves in Louisiana, he mused. God and nature had made Louisiana a "Paradise," Briggs declared. "But man has converted it into a Pandemonium."[90]

Louisiana planters had long balanced their desire for slave labor against their fear of slave unrest, but they found the balance difficult to maintain. During its earlier history as both a French and Spanish colony, Louisiana had struggled with the issue of the overseas slave trade. Spanish territorial policy encouraged the importation of slaves. Even after the 1791 rebellion in Saint-Domingue prompted Spanish colonial authorities to ban slave imports from the West Indies, the importation of African slaves continued with uninterrupted vigor for four years. However, after a bloody uprising at Point Coupee in 1795, Spanish Louisiana officially closed the foreign slave trade in 1796 to prevent further importation of revolutionary ideas and rebellious slaves from Saint-Domingue, despite strenuous objections from south Louisiana sugar planters. But in 1800, not long before Spain ceded control of the region to France, Spanish authorities in Louisiana reopened the African trade (but continued the prohibition against West Indian slaves) to accommodate the ongoing demand from local planters. The reopening of the African trade in 1800 made it even more difficult to prevent slaves from the West Indies from being imported illegally into Louisiana. When the territory was acquired by the United States in 1803, Louisiana was an active but anxious participant in the foreign slave trade.[91]

Louisianians wanted more slaves during the 1790s, as both cotton and sugar emerged as huge moneymakers. Planters along the western bank of the Mississippi across the river from Natchez participated eagerly in the same cotton boom that transformed the lower Piedmont regions of Georgia and South Carolina, but the sugar boom taking place simultaneously in southern Louisiana rendered the magnitude of the staple bonanza in Louisiana largely unmatched elsewhere in the South. The lower Louisiana sugar boom ignited when the world's most productive sugar plantations, those in Saint-Domingue, were thrown into disarray by slave revolution. Markets opened by the decline of Caribbean production and the migration of sugar expertise from the islands to Louisiana fueled the boom in sugar in the Orleans Territory. After American possession, territorial governor William Claiborne, a Virginia-born Republican with experience as governor of the Mississippi Territory, marveled at the wealth generated by planters in Louisiana's newly molded sugar bowl. "The facility with which the sugar planters amass wealth is almost incredible," Claiborne reported, "It is not uncommon with 20 working hands to make from 10 to 14 thousand Dollars, and there are several Planters whose field negroes do not exceed forty who make more than 20,000 Dollars each year."[92] Claiborne, who thought the African slave trade "barbarous," moved quickly to keep West Indian slaves out of Louisiana for security reasons. But, Claiborne conceded that with staple profits high, the people of the territory "seem impressed with the opinion that a great, very great, supply of slaves is essential to the prosperity of Louisiana."[93]

WASHINGTON POLITICIANS of virtually all persuasions assumed that South Carolina had reopened the African slave trade in order to supply the Louisiana

Territory with slaves, and many of these lawmakers were determined to thwart South Carolina's ambition. Petitions from North Carolina, Tennessee, and Virginia joined those from northern states in expressing outrage at renegade South Carolina's decision to reopen the overseas trade. The petitioners implored Congress to impose a tax of $10 per slave (the maximum allowed by the Constitution) on the new trade to punish the Palmetto State. The U.S. House of Representatives wasted no time before taking up just such a measure in January 1804, and members used the debate over the tax proposal as an opportunity to chastise South Carolina for reopening the foreign slave trade. The ensuing House debate revealed the depth and breadth of hostility toward South Carolina's decision. Northern representatives almost uniformly denounced the decision to reopen the trade, though most conceded its constitutionality. Pennsylvania Republican David Bard, a Princeton-educated Presbyterian minister, called the slave trade a "horrid traffic," and Rhode Island Republican Joseph Stanton claimed that South Carolina's decision to reopen the trade not only shook "the pillars of public security" but also "tarnished the American character."[94]

Members of South Carolina's own House delegation, though unanimous in their opposition to the proposed tax on slave imports, refused to defend their state's decision to reopen the African slave trade beyond the mere assertion of its constitutionality. Lowcountry congressman Thomas Lowndes acknowledged the "dissatisfaction and resentment" triggered by his state's action and explained that South Carolina had reopened the trade in part because, lacking federal help, the state had been unable to enforce the existing prohibition. Lowndes admitted that the "interests" of his state no longer "required" the trade, and he thought that "an end should be put to it." However, he recognized that not all southerners shared his views. "When I say that I myself am unfriendly to it," Lowndes observed, "...I do not mean to convey the idea that the people of the Southern States are universally opposed to it." In fact, "many of the people in the Southern States feel an interest in it and will yield it with reluctance."[95] Georgetown's Benjamin Huger declared that "he had always been hostile to the importation of slaves" and told the House that if he had held a seat in the state legislature, he would have voted against reopening the trade. But Huger advised Congress against taking any action to stymie the trade. Such federal intervention, Huger warned with troubling prescience, "must excite jealousy and a spirit of resistance."[96] Upcountry Republican Thomas Moore, a planter from Spartanburg District, also judged the slave trade a "horrid traffic," but he too advised Congress that southerners were so committed to buying more slaves that a $10 head tax (which he opposed) would "not prevent the importation of a single person."[97]

While the House debated the imposition of a head tax on slave imports and flogged South Carolina for reopening the trade, news that the United States Congress might place restrictions on South Carolina's ability to reexport African slaves to Louisiana prompted some South Carolinians to urge the state legislature to reverse its course. In early February 1804, South Carolina representative Baylis Earle interrupted heated House debate over the taxation of imported slaves and urged postponement of any action until the South Carolina legislature had a chance to reconsider its position. Earle, an Upcountry slaveholder and ironworks operator, claimed that he had received reliable information from South Carolina that the legislature would hold a special session in April to consider repealing the 1803 statute reopening the trade.[98] Pennsylvania's Andrew Gregg joined Earle in urging Congress not to fasten a stigma on South Carolina until the state had ample opportunity to repeal the law, and the House adjourned debate. The congressional reporter recording the debate took the highly unusual step of inserting a note in the official record insisting that "not a single voice was raised" in the House "in defense of the act of the legislature of South Carolina allowing the importation of slaves"; on the contrary, all speakers "deprecated" the trade. Even those who voted to postpone action on the tax simply wanted "to give the Legislature of South Carolina an opportunity" to repeal the act and not to show any hint of approval for South Carolina's actions.[99]

Meanwhile, in the United States Senate, debate ranged broadly over the larger question of how territorial Louisiana should be governed. This debate not only revealed partisan disagreement over westward expansion but also complicated sectional disagreements over the future of slavery in the United States and its territories. In broad ideological terms, most New Englanders and many other northerners wanted to restrict the expansion of slavery, preparing the way for a future time at which the nation's republican experiment in self-government would free itself of the stain of slavery. At the same time, most lower South congressmen favored expanding slavery's reach, and hence its influence, because they viewed slave labor as essential to the region's prosperity. Upper South politicians often claimed to stand with northern restrictionists in their desire to first restrain and then diminish slavery's influence on the republic, but their mechanism for weakening slavery's grip, diffusion, sought to diminish slavery's influence by extending its demographic reach. Occupying a middle ground between restriction and expansion, upper South diffusionists argued that the diffusion of slaves from existing slaveholding states and territories would satisfy Louisiana's demand for slaves, lessen the danger posed by large slave populations in long-settled areas, and ultimately weaken the attachment to the peculiar institution that existed in many of the older slaveholding states.

Arguably the best case for diffusion advanced in 1804 came not from an upper South senator but from New Orleans sheriff Lewis Kerr. Kerr vehemently opposed continuing Louisiana's foreign slave trade because he recognized that "a considerable share" of slaves imported from overseas would "be derived from the french islands" and "consist principally of such negroes as cannot be retained there with safety to their owners or the public peace." Access to the domestic slave trade, however, would allow Louisianians "to draw off the slaves now in the western states, and thereby at least extenuate the general evil." Opening the domestic slave trade in Louisiana, Kerr believed, would render an "essential service" to other slaveholding states by opening an "advantageous" market for their surplus slaves while providing Louisiana with "a race of servants already acquainted with our habits and attached to our country."[100]

Such logic hardly convinced northern critics who saw diffusion as ill-disguised hypocrisy, a way of proclaiming slavery an evil while expanding its influence in the interest of protecting the value of the upper South's slave property. New Hampshire senator William Plumer insisted that "the zeal displayed by the Senators from the Slave States, to prohibit the foreign importation of Slaves into Louisiana, proceeds from the motive to raise the price of their own slaves in the market" as well as to preserve "the means of dispersing of those who are most turbulent and dangerous to them."[101] Lower South politicians also viewed the upper South's diffusionist stance with a measure of cynicism, but they recognized that expansion could proceed under the disguise of diffusion. They were thus willing to cooperate with diffusionists, provided the terms of cooperation were satisfactory. In turn, upper South lawmakers were willing to cooperate with northern restrictionists if the terms of cooperation facilitated diffusion rather than an absolute prohibition or an unfettered slave trade.

These broad ideological contours were further confused by the particulars of the Louisiana question. In deciding the future of slavery and the slave trade for Louisiana, Congress faced a situation where the African slave trade had flourished under colonial rule and continued unabated under American authorities. Interim governor Claiborne had done nothing to slow the African trade except attempt to prevent the illegal importation of slaves from Saint-Domingue. Moreover, South Carolina's decision to reopen the African slave trade allowed prospective slave buyers in Louisiana to purchase recently imported African slaves indirectly through the Palmetto State. Thus a ban on the African slave trade only facilitated the success of South Carolina's transparent effort to corner the Louisiana slave market. No state, north or south, wanted to reward South Carolina by granting it a de facto monopoly on the Louisiana trade. Finally, those with the greatest interest in keeping the direct African slave trade open, the Francophone Louisiana merchants and farmers who had long trafficked in African slaves, were not represented directly in the debate, so they had to depend on others to plead for a continuation.

Thus alignments in the congressional debates over slavery in Louisiana were complicated. Sparks flew in every direction during the Senate debate, and not strictly along sectional lines. Most northern senators reluctantly conceded the inevitability of slavery in Louisiana, just as they had six years earlier regarding Mississippi. But many of these northern senators were eager to condemn slavery as a national evil and to limit its influence and future expansion. "Negroes are rapidly encreasing in this country," complained Connecticut senator James Hillhouse. "I consider slavery an evil, and wish to check it wherever I have the authority."[102] These limiting efforts focused on preventing Louisiana from participating in the African slave trade, a trade most northerners, and certainly almost all New Englanders, felt would be permanently closed by Congress as soon as the Constitution allowed (1808). Lower

South senators generally favored the idea of allowing Louisiana to supply itself fulsomely with slaves but they disagreed among themselves over the best means of doing so. Georgia senators preferred allowing Louisiana to continue its African trade for a few years. South Carolina senators, regardless of their original opinion on their state's reopening of the African slave trade, preferred closing the African slave trade to Louisiana in favor of the domestic slave trade so that their state could supply the territory with recently imported slaves from Africa.

Under most circumstances, the upper South's preference for diffusion would have been well served by banning the foreign slave trade but allowing domestic trade. But since South Carolina had reopened the African trade, upper South senators knew that Louisiana slave buyers could purchase recent African imports indirectly through South Carolina. Thus opening the domestic trade to Louisiana was more likely to slow and even stymie diffusion than to encourage it. Still, much of the most vehement opposition to Louisiana's direct participation in the foreign slave trade came from the upper South. Upper South rhetoric focused on the danger of exposing the South to additional West Indian influence, a subject given greater salience by the "discovery" of insurrection plots in Virginia in 1800 and 1802. Kentucky senator John Breckinridge expressed concern that "our slaves in the south will produce another St. Domingo" unless foreign imports were banned. Delaware's Samuel White reminded senators that "Nothing but the intervention of Heaven, an unusual thunder-storm, prevented the slaves, only two years since, from destroying Richmond in Virginia." Every slaveholding state, White maintained, made "severe and expensive provisions" to "guard the lives of masters and their families against the violence of slaves" and to "avoid the fate of St. Domingo."[103]

The leading Senate voice favoring the importation of foreign slaves into Louisiana came from the venerable Georgia Republican James Jackson, a coastal rice planter. Jackson, who claimed that he had little fear of insurrection, argued that "slaves must be admitted" into Louisiana, because "it cannot be cultivated without them." Men "from the north and the east do not know that the white man cannot endure the heat of a vertical sun," Jackson insisted, and "they cannot cultivate and raise a crop of rice—negroes are necessary for that country." A few northern senators joined with those from the lower South to agree that Louisiana could scarcely develop if it was denied slaves. New Jersey Federalist Jonathan Dayton, a former Speaker of the House and a recent visitor to Louisiana, argued that "slavery must be tolerated, it must be established in that country [Louisiana], or it can never be inhabited. White men can not cultivate it."[104]

Dayton's views were not shared by most northerners. Ohio's John Smith denied the claim that Louisiana could not be cultivated by whites. "I have traversed many of the settlements in that country," Smith reported. "I know that white men labour there—they are capable of cultivating it." Delaware's Samuel White claimed that if "white men became accustomed to the culture of that country [Louisiana]," they would "by long habit, be brought to bear the heat and fatigue" as well as blacks. "We boast of liberty and yet... establish slavery by law," White complained. But the leading opponent of allowing Louisiana unfettered access to African slaves was James Hillhouse, the Federalist senator from Connecticut. To support his position, Hillhouse cited not only the inherent evil of slavery but also the institution's tendency to produce dangerous rebellions. "Increase the number of slaves in Louisiana, [and] they will in due time rebel," Hillhouse insisted. "Why add fuel to this tinder box, which when it takes fire will assuredly extend to some of your states." Ohio's John Smith agreed with Hillhouse on the latter point, claiming that with the introduction of additional foreign slaves into Louisiana, the area's slave population would "soon become so numerous as to endanger the government and ruin that country."[105] After considerable debate, on January 26, 1804, the Senate voted 21–6 to ban participation by Louisiana in the foreign slave trade. Georgia's two senators cast votes against the ban, as did four New Englanders, though the New Englanders were casting protest votes against the Senate's decision to allow slavery in Louisiana at all rather than expressing support for the foreign slave trade.[106]

Thus the contours of a possible compromise satisfactory to both upper and lower South remained elusive. The logical coalition of upper South diffusionists and lower South expansionists foundered on the rocks of South Carolina's reopening of the African trade. As long as South Carolina imported slaves from Africa, any law allowing the domestic slave trade would effectively circumvent a ban on the foreign slave trade. This back-door opening of the foreign trade for Louisiana, and the profits it promised to the pariah state, weakened political support in the upper South and in the North for allowing Louisiana to participate in the domestic slave trade. Vermont's Israel Smith explained the problem. Opening the domestic slave trade in Louisiana, Smith contended, "will operate as an encouragement to South Carolina to import slaves" and effectively "rather encrease than prevent slavery" in the territory. With the cause of diffusion seemingly frustrated by South Carolina's actions, North Carolina's Jesse Franklin professed a willingness to solve the problem by sending "a frigate to Charleston to prevent the landing of slaves from Africa imported by South Carolina—and frittering those nefarious traders to pieces."[107]

Yet with the foreign slave trade easily defeated, diffusionists again patiently made their case to the Senate, looking for allies wherever they could find them. Kentucky's John Breckinridge took the lead in arguing the case for diffusion, declaring that it was "good policy to permit slaves to be there [Louisiana] from the United States," because it would "disperse and weaken" slavery and "free the southern states from a part of its black population, and of its danger." Full prohibition of both the foreign and domestic slave trade in Louisiana, Breckinridge argued, would prevent "men of wealth from the southern States" from settling in the new territory.[108] But to succeed in 1804, diffusionists had to forge a different coalition, one that attracted northerners willing to accept the managed growth of slavery in Louisiana rather than lower South politicians willing to sacrifice the foreign trade. Ohio's John Smith noted that he would favor allowing the domestic slave trade because "slaves are already there" and the government could not effectively "prevent slaves going there [Louisiana] from the United States." "I know this is an evil," Smith declared, "but it is an evil they will have."[109] Robert Wright of Maryland, who had supported the effort to ban the foreign slave trade, suggested promising grounds for compromise. He proposed allowing slave owners, but only owners, to take their slaves to Louisiana if they intended to settle there permanently. A coalition began to take shape. To accommodate northern senators willing to accept diffusion but unwilling to allow South Carolina to reexport African slaves to Louisiana, a number of upper South senators decided to support restrictions on the domestic slave trade that would allow slaves to enter Louisiana only if their masters took up residence there.[110]

In a complex series of maneuvers beginning on January 30, 1804, and spilling over into the next day, the United States Senate tentatively forged its first policy toward slavery in lower Louisiana. First, Connecticut's Hillhouse introduced a motion to free all slaves taken to Louisiana when they reached the age of twenty-one, which was defeated 17–11.[111] With his obligatory attempt at emancipation formally defeated, Hillhouse then introduced a compromise measure that called for an absolute ban on the importation of any slaves from abroad and a ban on the importation of slaves from within the territory of the United States unless those slaves were taken into Louisiana by American citizens who intended to settle there. And even those slaves could accompany their masters into Louisiana only if they were born in the United States or had been imported prior to 1798 (the year Georgia had closed the foreign slave trade). The proposal placed tighter restrictions on the introduction of new slaves into Louisiana than most southerners wanted, but Kentucky's John Breckinridge persuaded enough diffusionists to support Hillhouse's compromise proposal to carry it by an 18–11 margin.[112]

A look at the final vote on the Hillhouse bill revealed the restrictionist nature of the bill. South Carolina's availability as a reexporter of African slaves had forced diffusionists to grudgingly accept a very limited flow of slaves to Louisiana in order to avoid an outright ban on slave importation.[113] All seven of the votes in favor of the measure from slaveholding states came from the upper South (two from Kentucky, two from Maryland, and one each from Delaware, Tennessee, and North Carolina). Eleven of the eighteen votes in favor came from nonslaveholding states, whose senators thought the Hillhouse bill would produce the least possible increase in Louisiana's slave population consistent with the economic health of the territory. That included yes votes from Hillhouse himself and from other antislavery northern senators such as New Hampshire's Simeon Olcott and William Plumer. The eleven no votes against Hillhouse's bill came from an awkward coalition of senators who thought the restrictions were too severe, including six senators from slaveholding states (two from Georgia, two from Virginia, and one from Tennessee and North Carolina), as well as votes from New Jersey's two senators, who also favored a more liberal importation policy, and three northern senators who thought the restrictions were not strict enough.[114]

Even though it passed, the Hillhouse compromise attracted more than its share of criticism. The approved bill allowed Louisiana to increase its slave population only through the in-migration of slaveholders from other states. Lower South expansionists naturally excoriated the narrow scope of the bill. Recalling the large-scale smuggling recently carried out by illicit traders and furtive buyers in South Carolina and Georgia between 1800 and 1804, Georgia's James Jackson complained that the congressional restrictions were so draconian that it would be "as impossible to prevent the importation" of slaves into Louisiana "as to move the sun into the moon." Virginia's Wilson Cary Nicholas, a close political ally of President Jefferson, voiced the frustration of the disgruntled portion of diffusionists who thought the restrictions too severe, arguing that the people of the Louisiana Territory should make their own decision about domestic imports. Ironically, Vermont's Israel Smith, an avowed opponent of slavery, agreed with Jackson and Nicholas. Smith predicted that the law restricting the slave trade would prove "useless" in practice. "If a law was made to prohibit the use of cyder in New England, where it is now used in every family," Smith asked his Senate colleagues, "could you carry it into effect?" Moreover, Smith rightly surmised, the passage of such severe restrictions on slave imports at the beginning of American occupation would "estrange" Louisianians, especially French Louisianians, from the United States Government at the very moment American authorities in the territory were seeking to gain the support.[115]

The Senate-approved measures limiting the importation of slaves into Louisiana to those accompanying residents and in-migrants also had to gain House approval and await agreement on all other aspects of setting up territorial government in Louisiana. After weeks of maneuvering, the larger bill for organizing the Louisiana Territory finally became law on March 26, 1804. The Senate version concerning the slave trade survived the tortured legislative journey largely intact. The final legislation held that "no slave or slaves shall directly or indirectly be introduced" into Louisiana except by an owner who was "a citizen of the United States, removing to said territory for actual settlement," and that any slave or slaves brought to Louisiana by owners must have been imported into the United States prior to May 1798.[116] The bill could not have been drawn more precisely to prevent South Carolina from reexporting slaves from Africa to Louisiana, and the South Carolinians who had engineered the reopening of the foreign slave trade found themselves under political fire at home. Upper South diffusionists and northern restrictionists felt they had gained as much as they could have hoped from the congressional decision. Soon, however, Congress would discover that reaction to the new law would reveal that what American politicians in Washington thought best for Louisiana and what both francophone and English-speaking Louisiana planters wanted were two quite different things.

CHAPTER FOUR

EXTENDING SLAVERY

In December 1803, the United States officially took possession of Louisiana. The two commissioners named by President Jefferson to represent American authority in its new possession—William C. C. Claiborne, the incumbent territorial governor of Mississippi and now Jefferson's choice to head the American administration in Louisiana, and General James Wilkinson, commander of the nation's western forces—rode into New Orleans to receive the territory from France. Claiborne, a Jeffersonian prodigy of sorts, was not yet thirty years old when the president chose him to serve as the head of civil authority in Louisiana. Educated in the schools of his native Virginia, Claiborne moved to eastern Tennessee as a young man and established a law practice in mountainous Sullivan County. He served in the Tennessee state constitutional convention of 1796 at the age of twenty-one. In August 1797 he was elected to Congress to fill Andrew Jackson's unexpired term. The next year, Claiborne was reelected in his own right even though he was under the constitutional minimum age for representatives. In Congress, Claiborne quickly became part of an alliance of pro-Jefferson representatives from Virginia, Kentucky, and Tennessee. In 1800, he was among the congressmen who withheld Tennessee's vote from Aaron Burr to elect Thomas Jefferson president, apparently earning the Sage of Monticello's lasting gratitude. In 1801, as part of his effort to replace all Federalist territorial governors with loyal Republicans, Jefferson named this young Republican loyalist governor of the Mississippi Territory, a position Claiborne held until Jefferson made him territorial governor of Louisiana in March 1804. Claiborne served as territorial governor until Louisiana became a state in 1812. During his years as territorial governor, Claiborne proved a man of sound judgment and steady character who did more to shape the development of Louisiana than any other single individual.[1]

Though Claiborne was guarded about publicly expressing his full opinion in Louisiana, Congress' tight restrictions on the introduction of additional slaves into Louisiana suited him. Claiborne had long abhorred the foreign slave trade, and during his early months in Louisiana he worried that too many slaves were being imported. Claiborne believed that a large number of slaves from Saint-Domingue entered Louisiana despite a standing prohibition against importing slaves from that hotbed of revolution. Yet during the winter of 1803–4, in the months before Congress adopted a policy, Claiborne recognized that any prohibition of the slave trade, domestic or foreign, would make it difficult to reconcile French Louisianians to the new American government. "The continuation of the slave trade for a few years is viewed by the inhabitants as essential to the Welfare of this Province," Claiborne warned Secretary of State James Madison. "No act of Congress would excite more discontent than an immediate Prohibition."[2]

Evidence supporting Claiborne's assessment mounted during the early months of 1804 as Louisianians impatiently awaited word of the congressional decision concerning the slave trade and other important matters of territorial governance. To all who would listen, white Louisianians expressed their sentiments favoring a wide-open trade. After touring lower Louisiana as a special agent for Claiborne in February, New Orleans resident Dr. John Watkins reported, "No subject seems to be so interesting to the minds of the inhabitants...as the importation of brute Negroes from Africa." Louisiana planters and farmers "appear only to claim it [the slave trade] for a few years," observed Watkins, a trilingual Virginia native who had won respect among the French-speaking population, but "without it, they pretend that they must abandon the culture of both Sugar and Cotton" because white laborers "can not be had in this unhealthy climate." So intense was white Louisianians' opinion, Watkins advised, that the elimination of all restrictions on the slave trade would "better reconcile them [Louisianians] to the Government of the United States, than any other privilege that could be extended to the Country."[3] Despite his personal opposition to the trade, Claiborne understood the position of Louisiana planters and merchants. "The African trade has hitherto been lucrative," Claiborne explained to Madison, "and the farmers are desirous of increasing the numbers of their slaves."[4]

During the weeks of uncertainty during the winter of 1804, few white Louisianians expected a total ban on the importation of slaves for sale. Instead, they appeared most concerned that Congress would ban their direct trade with Africa, forcing Louisianians to buy African slaves through South Carolina. The "admission of Negroes into the State of South Carolina has served to increase the discontent here," Claiborne explained. Louisianians "generally can not be made to understand the present power of the State Authorities with regard to the importation of slaves," and "they suppose that Congress must connive at the importation into South Carolina," which many Louisianians believed was "done with a view to make South Carolina the sole importer for Louisiana."[5] Of course, at the very time suspicion mounted in Louisiana that Congress was in league with South Carolina, Congress was actually working as hard as it could to craft a policy that would prevent South Carolina from profiting from its decision to reopen the trade.[6]

News concerning the congressional debate over the future of the slave trade in Louisiana filtered into the territory slowly, and unofficial reports from Washington suggested that the final shape of the bill remained uncertain. Anxious to be heard on the subject, merchants and planters from the New Orleans area held a meeting on Monday evening, March 12, to consider sending a commissioner to Congress to present the "grievances" of Louisiana. The meeting was organized and attended primarily by French-speaking merchants and sugar planters intent on highlighting "the desire of the inhabitants for the continuation of the slave trade." One francophone planter urged that a series of public meetings be held throughout the province to express Louisiana's discontent with any restriction on the foreign slave trade. Such a mobilization of Louisiana's still predominately francophone planters worried Claiborne. To counter this movement, Dr. John Watkins, working closely with the governor, delivered remarks in both French and English that persuaded the assembled interests to avoid "public agitation" until they saw the final shape of congressional legislation. The meeting appointed three attendees, led by Watkins, to draft a list of grievances, but set no date for the committee to issue the report. Claiborne expected no further action on the petition. But the cautious governor knew that outright prohibition of the slave trade would prompt another public outcry that might not be so easily contained.[7]

Claiborne was not wrong. As soon as news of Congress' handiwork on the question of the slave trade reached Louisiana in late March 1804, it became "a source of great dissatisfaction" in the territory. Claiborne quickly alerted Madison that the "people" were preparing a memorial to Congress on the subject.[8] For French residents of Louisiana, the American legislation, which not only banned both the foreign and domestic slave trades but also limited the importation of slaves by prospective residents to those who were United States citizens, amounted to a virtually complete prohibition. The predictable results of such a draconian policy were bitter protest against the policy, a flurry of active slave buying in the months before the new ban took effect, and, over the longer term, the resurgence of an active illegal slave trade. The citizens of Louisiana, a hard-pressed Governor Claiborne told Madison, believed that "a great, very great supply of Slaves is essential to the prosperity of Louisiana" and they would not fail to import as many slaves as possible for as long as possible. A nervous Claiborne predicted that in months before the congressional ban took effect in October 1804, "thousands of African negroes will be imported into this province."[9]

Bitter protest came quickly. White Louisianians, and especially French-speakers, pleaded with the American government for concessions to the province's dominant pro-slave-trade sentiment. Planter Joseph Dubreuil warned President Jefferson that prohibiting the importation of African slaves would leave Louisiana a "vast swamp unfit for any creatures outside of fishes, reptiles, and insects."[10] In New Orleans, a large group of citizens, led by recent arrival Edward Livingston, a former mayor of New York who had taken up practice as an attorney in New Orleans, prepared a formal remonstrance urging Congress to reopen the trade. The remonstrance insisted that the "natural constitutions and habits of labor" among African slaves "enable them to resist the combined efforts of a deleterious moisture, and a degree of heat intolerable to whites." The need for coerced labor to perform the arduous and deadly work of maintaining the levees that "restrain the waters of the Mississippi," the New Orleans memorialists insisted, "is all important to the very existence of our country." If the slave trade is "justifiable anywhere, it is surely in this province," the remonstrance concluded; without it, "cultivation must cease and the improvements of a century destroyed," leaving the Mississippi River to "resume its empire over our ruined fields and demolished habitations."[11]

In a mid-April report to President Jefferson, Claiborne again emphasized that "prohibiting the Importation of Slaves into Louisiana" was viewed by the citizens as "a great Grievance." Much "irritation is manifested" on the subject, Claiborne continued, "and the general opinion seems to be that the Territory cannot prosper without a great encrease of Negros." The governor's report also warned the administration that the expected Americanization of Louisiana would do little to damp enthusiasm for the slave trade. Recent American arrivals to Louisiana were generally as "clamorous in favor of the traffic" as francophones, Claiborne noted, and they "inveigh against a prohibition." Claiborne defended his futile efforts to shape public opinion, explaining that he had "offered such reasons against the African Trade as I thought best calculated to reconcile the Inhabitants to its abolition." In his efforts, the governor referred frequently to "the Horrors of St. Domingo" and the "apprehension of similar horrors in this Province at some future Day." Claiborne admitted that his efforts had changed few minds and banefully concluded that "nothing will satisfy" local white opinion except "an uninterrupted Trade to Africa for three or four years."[12]

The Jefferson administration hoped time would reconcile white Louisianians to the restrictions, but the coming of the hot and humid Louisiana summer did little to abate local resentment of the ban. In early summer, Claiborne reported that the "great body of the people have only one objection" to American policy, "and that relates to the prohibition of the African trade."[13] In midsummer, Claiborne reported the further passage of time had failed to soften Louisiana's opposition to the restrictions on the slave trade. "I find an almost universal sentiment exist[s] in Louisiana in favor of the African trade," Claiborne advised the State Department.[14] Moreover, white Louisianians' desire for more slaves persisted in the face of the real and present dangers of slave unrest. Claiborne's warnings about a rebellion in Louisiana similar to the cataclysm in Saint-Domingue were hardly unfounded. American control of the republic's newest possession remained tenuous, and in 1804 the Louisiana Territory was still a very dangerous place. Slaves and free blacks outnumbered whites in many areas of the territory, and in New Orleans most estimates placed the black majority there at nearly three to one. Given the area's racial demography and its proximity to the Caribbean, the threat of a Saint-Domingue-style revolution from below loomed as a matter of grave concern.[15] In February, Watkins informed Claiborne that "a Vessel having on Board twelve Negroes" rumored to be "Brigands from the Island of St. Domingo" had passed up the Mississippi River far enough to alarm planters along the so-called German Coast west of New Orleans. According to Watkins, the blacks on board the vessel frequently went ashore and "in the French language made use of many insults and menacing expression to the inhabitants," spreading fear by "boasting of what they had done in the horrors of St. Domingo."[16] New Orleans mayor Étienne de Boré complained to Claiborne that American authorities had not done enough to apprehend this vessel and others like it. In reply, Claiborne insisted that he was making every effort to preserve "the peace and safety of the country."[17] Such incidents reinforced the governor's underlying concern that Louisiana could turn into another Saint-Domingue. "[A]t some future period, this quarter of the Union must (I fear) experience in some degree the Misfortunes of St. Domingo," Claiborne lamented, and that period would be hastened "if the people should be indulged by congress with a continuation of the African trade."[18] In the meantime, Claiborne did as much as he could with the resources at his disposal to guarantee white security.[19]

As fall approached, an insurrection scare gripped New Orleans and threatened to fulfill Claiborne's prediction of a reprise of the Saint-Domingue revolt in Louisiana. On September 17, 1804, a group of New Orleans residents informed Claiborne of an incident at the home of Michael Fortier, a merchant and member of the city council, that gave inhabitants "every reason to apprehend the existence of a plot . . . by the Slaves of this city, and perhaps those of the province." The plot, these local whites believed, threatened the "individual Safety of all The Inhabitants" and provoked a "Fear that they will see Their country a prey to the same Events which have laid waste the French colonies & Particularly the Proud and rich Colony of San Domingo."[20] The scare, as it was explained to Claiborne, arose from "several Negro's having been found traveling By Night with Arms in their hands" near Fortier's house and "some menacing expressions" emanating from two of the armed slaves. These observations, combined with "a general Spirit of Insubordination which of late has been manifested," left whites in the city fearful "that they are in eminent Danger."[21]

The predominately French-speaking New Orleans whites alerted Claiborne to the threat and urged the governor to use "all possible means to uncover the plot" and to punish all insurrectionists "[w]ithout any compassion." Only "prompt and Severe Justice," these citizens claimed, would serve as an "Example to those having evil intentions, and arrest the evil in Its Inception."[22] Recognizing that public confidence in American authority was at stake, Claiborne promptly took "every measure" of precaution. He increased patrols at night, placed the city militia and armed volunteers on ready alert, made munitions from the city magazine available to these security forces, and vowed that if "the Danger should increase," he would "put a public Musket in the hands of every White man in the City." Privately, however, Claiborne expressed doubt to both Jefferson and Madison "that there are good grounds for the Alarm."[23] Apparently either Claiborne's security measures were effective or his hunch that the scare lacked "good grounds" was correct. Nothing further came of the alleged insurrection plot that fall.

Strikingly, this incident and recurring reports of the infiltration of Louisiana by slaves from Saint-Domingue did nothing to diminish the enthusiasm of white Louisianians for the foreign slave trade. The same francophone planters who were quick to alert Claiborne to the rumors of slave unrest or the appearance of "brigands" in the territory remained the most vocal champions of importing slaves, and especially slaves from Africa. But these Louisiana French had plenty of support from more recent American arrivals who also wanted to keep slaves flowing into Louisiana. In nearly every report Claiborne made to Washington during the fall of 1804, and in virtually every other assessment of Louisiana's unhappiness with American rule advanced during those months, the impending bans on both the foreign and domestic slave trades were identified as the single most important factor in white Louisianians' dissatisfaction with American governance. Much like their counterparts in other parts of the lower South, Louisiana planters offered no remedy for the problem of insurrection other than quick discovery and brutal punishment. The idea that closing the slave trade, even just the African slave trade, might diminish the danger of rebellion held little appeal. The balance of greed and fear in territorial Louisiana tilted heavily toward the former. By November, Claiborne had grown plaintive on the subject, worrying that the ban on the slave trade might permanently jeopardize American ability to win the loyalty of white Louisianians. "The Searcher of all hearts knows how little I desire to see another of that wretched race set his foot on the shores of America," Claiborne pleaded. "But, on this point, the people here [Louisiana] are united as one man. There seems to be but one sentiment throughout the province. They must import more slaves, or the country was ruined forever." Even the "most respectable characters" in Louisiana, Claiborne reported, could scarcely "suppress the agitation of their temper" when any "check to that trade was suggested."[24] Nothing about Washington's control of Louisiana during its first territorial phase, not even the quick introduction of English as the official language, bothered white Louisianians as much as congressional restrictions on the slave trade. Even the often-expressed desire of some Louisianians for immediate statehood appeared rooted not so much in a desire for equality as in the belief that as a state, Louisiana could open and maintain the African slave trade on its own until 1808. So great was the desire of white Louisianians for more slaves that nothing—not reports of bloodshed from Saint-Domingue, frequent insurrection scares, sightings of alleged Caribbean brigands, nor the constant admonitions of a level-headed territorial governor—could persuade them that restrictions on the slave trade were necessary for white security.

South Carolina's Consternation over the congressional ban on Louisiana's participation in both the foreign and domestic slave trades was second only to that of Louisiana. The decision of Congress to effectively ban Louisiana's participation in the domestic slave trade (allowing the importation only of slaves accompanying owners who intended to become legal residents) as well as the foreign trade caught most South Carolina champions of reopening the African slave trade by surprise. As Congress intended, the ban temporarily thwarted South Carolina's effort to serve as the chief supplier of slaves to Louisiana's booming plantation regions. This lost opportunity may not have mattered to the Palmetto State's inland planters and farmers seeking to purchase more and cheaper slaves to grow cotton, but it dealt a significant blow to those Lowcountry interests that had supported reopening the African slave trade in hopes of sharing in its commercial bounty. As a result, the initial congressional restrictions on the importation of slaves into Louisiana weakened the political coalition between Upcountry staple growers and Lowcountry commercial interests that had succeeded in reopening the slave trade in 1803, and generated a strong movement to close the African trade in 1804.[25]

South Carolina's biennial legislative campaigns in October 1804 revealed that the state's decision to reopen the African slave trade looked increasingly unwise to most Lowcountry voters. When the results of the legislative canvass were tabulated, fourteen of the twenty-six Lowcountry representatives who had voted for the trade were not returned to the legislature. With voter backlash evident, at least in the Lowcountry, the new legislature reconsidered the foreign slave trade question when it convened in late November 1804. Clearly a solid majority in the South Carolina house now wanted to close the foreign slave trade. On the key vote, a procedural maneuver by defenders of the trade to delay debate on the bill, the house refused to delay by a vote of 54–31. Of the twelve Lowcountry representatives who favored reopening the trade in 1803 and survived the election of 1804, seven abstained from voting, four switched positions and voted against the slave trade, and only one maintained his support for the African trade. Of the fourteen new representatives who had defeated or replaced slave trade supporters, thirteen favored closing the trade and only one favored keeping the trade open. With the option to reexport Africans to Louisiana at least temporarily blocked and voters angry, Lowcountry support for the foreign slave trade nearly evaporated in the South Carolina house.[26]

Yet before the house could take final action on its bill, the South Carolina senate voted 17–16 to reject closing the African slave trade, rendering house action moot. In the senate's roll call, intrastate sectional voting patterns appeared even more clear than in the 1803 house vote reopening the trade. Six Lowcountry senators joined eleven senators from the interior to keep the African slave trade legal. Only five interior senators joined the eleven Lowcountry senators who voted to close the trade. Thus eleven of the sixteen senators representing interior districts favored keeping the trade open. In contrast, nearly two-thirds of all Lowcountry senators were ready to close the trade. Lowcountry support for the African slave trade had nearly disappeared in the house, whose members faced the voters every two years, but in the senate, where only half of the body faced reelection in any given election cycle, the African trade retained just enough support among Lowcountry senators to remain open. Four of the six parish votes against closing the trade came from the same coastal area between Charleston and Beaufort that had tended to support opening the African trade in 1803, but these defenders of the trade picked up the support of two senators from the Georgetown area, giving the slave trade at least some support from each of the state's three port cities, Charleston, Georgetown, and Beaufort. Together, support from the interior and port-area senators sustained South Carolina's involvement in the African slave trade in the face of intense opposition, but only by the narrowest of margins.[27]

With this vote, the South Carolina legislature disappointed its congressional delegation and others who hoped it would act quickly to close the African slave trade at its 1804 session. The legislature's refusal to reverse course on the African slave trade left the state open to further condemnation from other states. It also complicated the pressing national question of how to regulate Louisiana's desire to import more slaves.

In December 1804, just weeks before Congress convened to consider the status of Louisiana once again, Governor Claiborne again reminded Secretary of State Madison that a "great anxiety" existed in Louisiana over its future governance and that "the importation of Negroes continues to be a favorite subject with the Louisianians."[28] Ultimately, such pressure nudged Congress to quietly modify its territorial legislation in March 1805, elevating the "Territory of Orleans" to the "second stage" of territorial governance. Louisiana authorities, including Claiborne, interpreted the revised status as giving Louisiana the same right enjoyed by the Mississippi Territory: to import slaves from any of the states or territories, though not from overseas.[29] Louisiana's planters and merchants were at least partially satisfied with the opening of the domestic trade since they could import African slaves indirectly through South Carolina rather than having to purchase English-speaking slaves from the upper South or the lower South's first cotton belt. Claiborne, whose experience as territorial governor of Mississippi prepared him to oversee the domestic slave trade, was doubtless pleased that this fundamental source of French Louisiana's discontent with American rule had been removed.

The new legislation, though passed in March, did not take effect until October 1, 1805, leaving six more months of frustration for eager slave buyers in Louisiana and, if anything, encouraging an even more active illegal trade in the interim. John Watkins, now mayor of New Orleans and an emerging political rival of Claiborne, was concerned about the delayed implementation of the new law. Watkins acknowledged that a ban on the "importation of native Africans" enhanced white security, but he worried that "public opinion" desiring "more slaves" would encourage an active illegal trade despite the government's best efforts to prevent it. Even the "Best organized Government on Earth," Watkins argued, would find itself helpless to prevent the "Introduction of more slaves" from overseas in the face of overwhelming public determination to do so. Ironically, Watkins maintained, the forthcoming ban put Louisiana in danger of being "overrun with the wretches of St. Domingo, Martinique and Jamaica instead of the harmless African" because there was less risk involved in smuggling slaves from the Caribbean than from Africa.[30]

In a larger sense, Watkins worried that Louisiana simply lacked the ability to defend itself against slave unrest without increased assistance from the federal government. Because of its "contiguity to the West India Islands" and "the great number of slaves and free people of color as well as bad disposed white people now among us who have been conversant with the crimes that have disgraced and the innocent blood which has encrimsoned the plains of St. Domingo," Watkins contended, Louisiana would live "in danger" of slave insurrection as long as the protection offered by the United States remained "so feeble." The Louisiana militia would "never be worth much," Watkins believed, because "our numbers are so few and scattered over such an extensive country." According to the New Orleans mayor, the solution lay in an American policy that encouraged the immigration of "Americans" who owned slaves and by stationing large numbers of federal troops in the territory. In the mayor's estimation, the enlarged presence of federal troops would "ultimately and permanently" encourage "the migration of native Americans to this Country." In "a country of slaves," Watkins reasoned, traditional republican (and Republican) misgivings about standing armies had to yield to a practical recognition that a sizeable military presence was needed to guarantee public safety. Without such a presence, Watkins held, "I defy all the vigilance of man to prevent the introduction of [foreign] slaves by some means or another. The people ask for new Negroes, you refuse them, they say they must have Slaves of some kind and will and do procure such as they can get."[31] The popular and perceptive Watkins argued that the American government should grant Louisiana a legal slave trade because otherwise area residents would participate eagerly in a more dangerous illegal one, and that the Jefferson administration needed to abandon any idea that Louisiana could prosper and develop without a large federal presence there. If the administration could bend constitutional scruples to purchase Louisiana, Watkins believed, it could also discard ideological shibboleths in its efforts to govern the territory.

As the legalization of the domestic slave trade neared in Louisiana, public enthusiasm for acquiring more slaves became palpable. The newly appointed United States attorney for the Orleans District, James Brown, a Virginia native who had built an impressive legal practice in Lexington, Kentucky, before migrating to New Orleans, observed that during the fall of 1805, the "prevailing anxiety for the importation of slaves" prompted "every man capable of reading the Acts of Congress to examine the regulations in force on that subject." Upon doing so, Louisiana lawyers had "unanimously expressed an opinion that the prohibitions against the importation of Slaves contained in the Act of 1804...are repealed," Brown reported, and as a result, "our citizens possess the right of importing into this country any Slaves legally introduced into any of the States."[32]

Finally, in October 1805, after more than eighteen months of uncertainty, turmoil, and protest, quiet legislation and generous interpretation by a territorial administration freed Louisiana to participate as vigorously as it wanted in the domestic slave trade. Through South Carolina, where the African slave trade remained open, Louisiana could now import recently arrived Africans indirectly. And Louisianians did so vigorously. From 1805 until 1807, while the African trade remained open in South Carolina, the reexport trade to the Gulf Coast boomed. Louisiana imported at least five thousand slaves from the Palmetto State, a total equal to more than a third of Louisiana's existing slave population, during these years.[33]

THROUGHOUT THE FIRST NINE MONTHS of 1805, while Louisiana waited for the domestic slave trade to open in October, criticisms of the African slave trade multiplied in South Carolina. Lowcountry planters and professionals lamented the overall economic impact the slave trade was having on the state. Their complaints indicated that while the slave trade itself was booming, it was doing so at the expense of regular business in Charleston and solvency across the state. Henry William DeSaussure, one of the state's most respected lawyers, reported to a friend in 1805, "The State of our Market is dreadful. There is a perfect Stagnation of everything, but the importation and Sale of new Negroes, which continues in full activity." DeSaussure worried that unless the trade was closed quickly, the state's slave population would be "immensely increased" and "new and enormous debts contracted."[34] Ebenezer Thomas, a Charleston bookseller, later recalled that once the slave trade opened, "vessels were fitted out in numbers, for the coast of Africa, and as fast as they returned, the slaves were bought up with avidity, not only consuming the large funds that had been accumulating, but all that could be procured, and finally exhausting credit, and mortgaging slaves for payment."[35]

In the face of such disruption of normal trade and the explosion of indebtedness in the Palmetto State, the 1805 legislative session gave South Carolina opponents of the foreign slave trade yet another chance to end the trade in advance of the expected congressional ban. In the annual gubernatorial message, new governor Paul Hamilton, an Edisto Island rice planter, called for an "an immediate stop to this traffic." Hamilton agreed with the observations of DeSaussure and Thomas, arguing that the foreign slave trade was "draining us of our specie, thereby embarrassing our commercial men, and materially lessening the sale of our produce." Hamilton also warned that the trade remained a threat to public safety. "In proportion as you add to the number of Slaves," Hamilton maintained, "you prevent the influx of men who would increase the means of defense and security."[36]

Governor Hamilton believed he had reason to worry about security in 1805, as rumors of insurrection swept through Columbia while the legislature was in session, prompting the deployment of militia units to guard the state's legislative chambers. As insurrection rumors flew wildly, New England visitor Edward Hooker reported that an innocent black was shot by white patrols during the scare. After that incident, Hooker observed, the "town negroes" all lived in "dreadful consternation...fearing I suppose that they will be butchered by one party or the other."[37] Fears of a blacker and more debt-ridden state ran deep throughout the Lowcountry.

In the midst of the scare, which never advanced beyond the rumor stage, the state house of representatives considered a bill that proposed closing the trade, declaring that "the importation of slaves is repugnant to the true interests of this State, and dangerous to its tranquility and safety."[38] During the extended house debate that ensued, Keating Simons, a Charleston lawyer and Berkeley Parish planter who owned more than eighty slaves, attacked both the inhumanity of the African trade and "the danger to be feared from the number of blacks in the country." Georgetown's Joseph Alston, a Republican who often worked to reduce tensions between Upcountry and Lowcountry, also urged his colleagues to put "justice" and "humanity" ahead of "sordid interest" and end the importation of African slaves. But James Miles, a Lowcountry planter from Prince William Parish, countered that closing the trade would deny the Upcountry "equal privileges" with the Lowcountry. If "now, when they are fast becoming rich enough to buy slaves, they are prevented" from importing slaves, Miles reasoned, the interior districts had reason to complain of inequity. Echoing Miles' sentiments, John Taylor, representing the Upcountry district of Pendleton, urged the legislature to "give the upper country planters an opportunity, by purchasing more slaves, to be on a more equal footing with their fellow citizens in the lower country."[39] After heated debate, the South Carolina house voted 56–28 in favor of closing the African slave trade.

But in the state senate, Upcountry senators, led by the forceful and pragmatic William Smith of York, fought to keep the African slave trade open. After watching Smith from the senate gallery, Edward Hooker, a keen political observer, described Smith as a legislative leader whose floor speeches were neither "fluent" nor replete with "the handsomest language," but the New Englander conceded that "in the course of his argument" Smith "gets out considerable that is to his purpose." Smith's leadership helped defeat the house bill closing the trade by a 16–15 vote. The final senate vote that kept the slave trade open triggered a rare celebration in the senate chambers. Senators who supported the trade "reached across tables and over chairs to shake hands with each other," while supporters of the trade from the house who had come to watch greeted the vote with "a great deal of smiling." Unsettled by the decision, the Federalist visitor Hooker privately denounced the senate vote as a "Horrid exhibition of Horrid Republicanism."[40]

The final senate vote in 1805 revealed persistent sectional voting patterns. Eleven of the fifteen senate votes to close the African slave trade came from the Lowcountry parishes, while ten of the sixteen votes to keep the trade open came from senators representing the interior. Nine of twelve senators from above the fall line favored keeping the trade open. But nearly three-fourths of all Lowcountry senators wanted it closed, as much to protect the value of their own slaves as out of concern for public safety or a looming debt crisis.[41] Robert Marion, a Republican state senator from St. John's-Berkeley Parish and owner of more than a hundred slaves, joined the Lowcountry majority in voting to close the trade, acknowledging that he "uniformly opposed the importation of slaves" because the greater "restriction imposed on the importation, the more it would raise the value of those he possessed."[42] Despite this clear sectional pattern, a modicum of Lowcountry support for the trade remained crucial to keeping it open.

In 1806, outgoing governor Paul Hamilton used his last message to the legislature to plead once again for the closing of the foreign slave trade. He declared that the trade was "draining our country of specie" to the point of "pecuniary distress" due to the "eagerness of purchasers" to buy slaves even if they incurred heavy indebtedness. Such an appetite for slaves without due regard for accumulating debt rendered the trade "every day more mischievous." Hamilton reminded the legislature that South Carolina's refusal to close the trade had earned the state the disapproval of the rest of the Union. "Let us, therefore, remove temptation from the eyes of our citizens," Hamilton urged, and "cease to practice what every other state in the union discountenances." In the house, a bill closing the African slave trade passed just two votes shy of unanimity, but the *Charleston Courier* legislative correspondent predicted that the bill "will be put to sleep in the Senate, as I think there will be a majority of two against it."[43]

The senate vote keeping the trade open was even closer than the *Courier* correspondent predicted. The senate killed the closing of the trade with a 16–16 tie vote, though the tie may have reflected a prior arrangement among legislative leaders to allow the trade's supporters to cast no more votes in its favor than absolutely necessary to keep it open. In any event, the senate vote in 1806 had a markedly less sectional character than earlier votes on the African slave trade. Interior senators voted against closing the African slave trade by a margin of only nine to seven, and for the first time senators from above the fall line split evenly, six against six, on the issue.[44] But the trade gained support among parish senators, who cast seven votes in favor of keeping the trade open and only nine to close it. The reason for the modest resurgence in parish support for the African slave trade lay in the fact that the reexport trade to Louisiana had been proceeding full bore since October 1, 1805, finally bringing large profits to Lowcountry merchants and investors involved in the commercial end of the trade, a boon that all senators recognized would end a year later when Congress closed the overseas slave trade. Interior support for the trade had eroded slightly because the region had already imported enough slaves for its own use and interior planters and farmers were less involved in the commercial end of the slave trade than Lowcountry merchants and planters. However, York's William Smith, now president of the senate, remained the trade's staunchest advocate in the legislature. But in 1806, Starling Tucker, a senator from the Upcountry district of Laurens who was normally associated with Smith's emerging political faction, split with the York senator to vote against the trade. Joseph Calhoun of Abbeville and Samuel Mays of Edgefield, who served areas lying at the heart of the first upland cotton boom, also voted to close the trade in 1806, as did the senators from the hill-country districts of Spartanburg, Greenville, and Pendleton.[45]

After reopening it in 1803, South Carolina maintained the African slave trade for four years, not only despite serious internal divisions but also in the face of stinging external criticism. Such criticism emanated not only from northern opponents of the institution but from other slaveholding states as well, particularly those in the upper South. Late in 1805, the Tennessee General Assembly, with the support of the state's congressional delegation, passed a resolution, later transmitted to the South Carolina legislature, urging an end to "the further importation of slaves from any of the West Indies and from the coast of Africa." The legislatures of North Carolina and Maryland joined that of Tennessee in calling for a constitutional amendment that would allow Congress to ban the African slave trade immediately rather than wait until 1808.[46] In 1806, a leading North Carolina newspaper, the *Raleigh Register*, denounced South Carolina's decision to keep the overseas slave trade open as "a detested, short-sighted policy, which in order to increase the wealth of a few can impose upon the State the greatest calamity with which any nation has ever been afflicted."[47] Over time, however, these criticisms of South Carolina's policy proved counterproductive and, as members of its congressional delegation had warned in 1804, fueled resentment of outside interference with the state's business. The *Charleston Courier*, which had opposed the reopening of the trade as "repugnant to the principles of sound policy," expressed its "utmost indignation" at the "scandalous and scurrilous" indictments of the slave trade published by northern newspapers. The benefits to the state from "more labor," the *Courier* observed, did not merely flow to "private interest" but also filled the "public coffers of the nation." Local merchants "who embark in this trade," the newspaper insisted, "do no more than carry the intentions and wishes of the government of their country into operation." Northern cries of "humanity! humanity! humanity" rang hollow, the *Courier* claimed, when they came from states whose merchants and shippers financed the trade and transported the slaves, and it was "a fact known to every citizen of Charleston, that where there is one ship belonging to this port employed in the slave trade, there are three vessels from northern states."[48] Outside criticism of a South Carolina decision concerning slavery, even a decision made with no small amount of internal conflict, caused even the most reasonable people in the state to dig in their heels and defend the state's prerogatives.

South Carolina political leaders on all sides of the slave trade issue, along with most politicians throughout the region, fully expected the United States

Congress to prohibit the importation of slaves from overseas as soon as constitutional protection of the trade expired in 1808. Moving quickly to see that their expectations were fulfilled, President Thomas Jefferson urged Congress late in 1806 to prepare in advance for the expiration of the constitutional protection by passing a federal statute banning the importation of slaves from foreign nations effective on January 1, 1808. Annoyed at Jefferson's eagerness to close the trade, John Randolph of Roanoke expressed constitutional reservations about any congressional action on the subject prior to 1808, but Jefferson wanted the government poised to close the trade as soon as the Constitution allowed. Ending the overseas slave trade would, in Jefferson's view, remove the people of the United States "from all further participation in those violations of human rights which have so long continued on the unoffending inhabitants of Africa, and which morality, the reputation, and the best interests of the country have long been eager to proscribe."[49] Coming from the pen of the same author who fastened blame for American participation in the slave trade on the British king in his draft of the Declaration of Independence, such sentiments hardly seemed surprising. A bit more surprisingly, however, no southerner in Congress at the time proved willing to defend the international slave trade as a national policy, and few doubted that the importation of slaves from overseas would be banned as soon as the Constitution allowed.

Yet if unwilling to defend American participation in the Atlantic slave trade, southern congressmen worried about specific provisions in the proposed legislation banning the trade. During congressional discussion over ending foreign slave trade, southern members expressed persistent concern over three key issues: the disposition of slaves brought into the United States illegally, the severity of punishment imposed on violators of the federal ban, and the question of government regulation of the domestic seaborne slave trade.[50] Each of these issues sparked sharp congressional debates with audible sectional overtones. Many northern members wanted to grant freedom to illegally imported slaves. Southern members preferred having illegally imported slaves seized as contraband, with their ultimate fate decided by the individual states in which they were held. Northerners objected to the notion that the government could confiscate human beings. Massachusetts representative Barnabas Bidwell complained that the idea of confiscation rested on the "false principle" that "a property may be had in human beings." Georgia representative Peter Early, a Virginia native and Princeton graduate who had moved to the Georgia frontier, took the lead in presenting a hard-edged southern position. Sentiments such as Bidwell's, Early warned, threatened "nine-tenths of the property of the Southern States, and might in its effects strike at all property held in slaves." Southern politicians also vehemently opposed the idea of freeing illegally imported slaves, fearing that it would inundate the southern states with free blacks (since slaves freed under this proposed provision likely would have been seized in southern ports). Nathaniel Macon labeled the proposal to free illegal imports "deplorable." The more voluble Early argued that to "have among us any considerable quantity" of free blacks "is an evil far greater than slavery," claiming the proposal would "turn loose, in the bosom of the country, firebrands that would consume them."[51] After much debate, the House fashioned a measure that, after tweaking by the Senate and a conference committee, agreed that any illegally imported slaves would be placed at the discretion of the state in which they were discovered. This provision satisfied the South more than the North, but southern congressmen achieved the compromise only through crucial cooperation from thirteen northern representatives who voted with forty-seven southerners and Speaker Macon to push the bill through the House.[52]

Congress also satisfied southern sentiments by rejecting a proposal calling for the death penalty for violators of the slave trade ban, settling instead for a punishment consisting of a $100,000 fine and four years' imprisonment. Southern congressmen, however, found less to like in Congress' final decision on the seaborne domestic trade. Though it refused to ban such trade altogether, as some antislavery congressmen suggested, Congress nevertheless prohibited ships weighing less than forty tons, precisely the type of vessels normally used, from participating in the coastal slave trade. Because it limited a slaveholder's ability to transport slaves from state to state by sea, John Randolph claimed with his usual hyperbole that such a restriction touched not only the right of slaveholders to move from state to state but also the "right of private property" and could "be made the pretext of universal emancipation."[53] The always caustic Randolph demanded that northern representatives "disclaim and disavow" any constitutional authority to interfere with "the right of property of masters of slaves" imported prior to the ban, and unless northern members were willing to offer such a pledge, Randolph insisted, southern members should "secede and go home."[54]

Few other southern senators expressed as much ideological fervor over the issue as Randolph, but several did manifest a touchy sensibility on the subject of the slave trade, apparently feeling that closing the slave trade attached a stigma to slavery that they preferred to minimize. In addition to their opposition to congressional interference with the seaborne domestic slave trade, southerners in Congress also bridled at northern rhetoric used at various points during the debate. In particular, northern charges that the trade was tantamount to "man-stealing" aroused the ire of southern members. In the South, Georgia's Peter Early insisted, citizens "might deprecate slavery as an evil; as a political evil, but not as a crime." Early contended that even though the slave trade was outlawed by the Georgia Constitution of 1798 and was arguably an unwise practice, it was not perceived in the lower South as "an offense which nature revolts at."[55] Nor did southern members appreciate Connecticut's Benjamin Tallmadge's quotation from Exodus pronouncing capital punishment for man-stealers. North Carolina's James Holland noted that if "that good old book [the Bible] is brought in [to the debate]... Slavery appears to be tolerated there."[56] Despite such rhetorical sectional skirmishes, Congress, in the end, banned the foreign slave trade, effective January 1, 1808, in a manner generally acceptable to southerners in Congress.[57]

AS SOUTH CAROLINA's foreign slave trade headed toward its final closing at the end of 1807, the state's most successful upland cotton planter, Wade Hampton I of the Richland District, evaluated its impact, agreeing in the main with the concerns often expressed in earlier years by Lowcountry critics of the trade. "[T]he African trade has stripped the planting interests, pretty generally, of their resources," Hampton observed, "and involved many of them in debt."[58] Overall, South Carolina's reopening of the slave trade allowed it to import more than fifty thousand African slaves in four years, or roughly one-tenth of all African slaves imported into North America during the entire overseas slave trade. Probably no more than fifteen thousand of those African imports remained in South Carolina as slaves, while more than 60 percent were reexported to other parts of the lower South, including significant numbers to the Mississippi and Louisiana territories. Whatever the intent of those South Carolina legislators who reopened the African slave trade and kept it open for four years, the reopening of the trade not only cemented the Palmetto backcountry's commitment to slaveholding as a way of life but also indisputably expanded and strengthened the presence of slavery in Mississippi and Louisiana. Thus the last stage of the legal foreign slave trade in the United States both sustained the cotton revolution and intensified the lower South's commitment to slavery during the same decades that the first round of emancipations in the North guaranteed a gradual end to slavery there.[59]

The temporary reopening of the African slave trade also permanently changed the nature and distribution of the slave population in the lower South. South Carolinians, and seemingly most lower South slaveholders, came to prefer American creoles or "country-born" slaves, born and nurtured on North American soil, to African or Caribbean imports. Activity in the slave markets during the years of the African trade clearly reflected these preferences. Reports from the era indicated that country-born slaves often brought twice the price of African imports in South Carolina. For example, in 1805, slave Charles Ball found himself part of a coffle of fifty-one slaves being driven from Maryland to Georgia as part of the internal slave trade. During a prolonged stop near Columbia, Ball overheard one South Carolina slaveholder state his firm preference for "domestic" slaves over the recently legalized African imports. "[B]y going to Charleston," the prospective buyer could "buy as many Guinea negroes as I please for two hundred dollars each," but instead he willingly offered twice as much for the American-born Ball. "I like this fellow [Ball]," the buyer told the slave trader, and "I will give you four hundred dollars."[60] This price differential between African imports and creole slaves cut two ways, both revealing the cotton planters' preference for African Americans over Africans and also suggesting how the reopening of the foreign trade lowered prices for slave buyers. On the whole, white southerners perceived Africans, who often retained tribal scars, filed teeth, and other overt signs of their history as warriors, as savage and uncivilized. To white eyes at least, the physical appearance of country-born slaves revealed their American nativity and a "domestic" countenance that reassured skittish whites of their presumed obedience and docility. In this matter, as with many others related to slavery, lower South whites manifested a remarkable capacity for self-deception. Historical analysis of the hard evidence suggests that, in fact, creole slaves provided every bit as much resistance, every bit as much potential for insurrection, as African imports. But southern slaveholders nevertheless clearly preferred the imagined familiarity of African American slaves over the exotic dangers they described as "African savagery." Recalling the days of the South Carolina slave trade during the congressional debates over Missouri in 1820–21, both William Smith and Charles Pinckney spoke in sharp racist tones about the inhumanity of Africans but with paternalistic fondness about American-born slaves. Even newspaper sketches of runaways reflected the perceived difference, often picturing Africans as robust warriors but describing country-born runaways as deceptive itinerants and vagabonds.[61]

Louisiana slaveholders, however, remained noteworthy exceptions to the lower South's preference for domestic slaves. Still predominately French during the first decade of the nineteenth century, slaveholders in the Louisiana Territory preferred African slaves to American-born slaves obtained from other parts of the United States.[62] Quite logically, the area's francophone slaveholders saw little advantage in buying slaves who could communicate in English, especially since creole slaves carried a premium price. African and especially Caribbean slaves were more likely to have been exposed to the French language, and even if they had not, their linguistic capacity often remained uncluttered by English. But Louisiana slaveholders developed a preference for African slaves that went beyond a straightforward favoritism based on language skills. Over time, Louisiana slaveholders had come to think that the "uncivilized" African slaves were less tainted with ideas of resistance and rebellion than American (not to mention West Indian) slaves. Governor Claiborne noted these local preferences, explaining that "African Negroes are thought not to be dangerous," while American-born slaves were seen as "indolent, vicious, and debauched." Another Louisiana observer explained that Africans were perceived as "more robust, more laborious," and "more adapted to the labors of the field" than American slaves, who many Louisiana slaveholders believed were more intelligent but also less industrious than recently arrived Africans.[63] Ironically, Maryland senator Samuel Smith agreed with Louisiana slaveholders on this point. "American" slaves, as opposed to imported Africans, Smith warned, "will prove adders that will sting" Louisianians "to the heart."[64] Thus, as African slaves flowed into Louisiana through South Carolina from late 1805 through 1807, supplying the demand generated by sugar and cotton planters, their background matched the preferences of Louisiana buyers well.

Nevertheless, the influx of ever more slaves into Louisiana heightened persistent white fears of slave insurrection, especially among territorial authorities charged with protecting the existing population. White fear peaked in 1809 when a third and final wave of refugees from the revolution in Saint-Domingue sought to enter Louisiana. The first wave had arrived in 1793 shortly after slave unrest began on the islands. The second wave left Saint-Domingue in 1803 when island blacks defeated the French. Some of these refugees came to Louisiana, but more settled in Cuba. The third wave of French refugees to seek safe harbor in Louisiana were those who had earlier settled in Cuba but were now fleeing that island once Napoleon's invasion of Spain turned their Cuban hosts into enemies. After leaving Cuba, many of these third-wave refugees sought residence in lower Louisiana, where they found the French language and the sugar plantations familiar. But the arrival of these francophone refugees and their slaves presented a dilemma to territorial authorities.[65]

The cautious Governor Claiborne characterized the slaveholding refugees as "persons of good character" but worried that their slaves' experience in the Caribbean would serve as a source of future unrest.[66] Moreover, both the 1804 Governance Act of Louisiana and the subsequent 1808 federal ban on the foreign slave trade loomed as legal obstacles to the importation of slaves from Cuba, even if they arrived with white refugees. In mid-May, Claiborne asked the State Department for advice about how to handle the problem. At the same time, he instructed civil and military authorities to stop incoming vessels carrying slaves originally from Saint-Domingue. In June 1809, responding to pleas from Louisiana and elsewhere that special leniency be shown to these refugees, Congress passed a law allowing both the refugees and their slaves to enter the country. But even before news of congressional action reached the territory, Claiborne had begun to allow refugees with slaves to enter on his own authority. The governor made at least a symbolic effort to screen out slaves known to have been close to previous rebellions. As time passed, however, Claiborne pled with diplomats throughout the Caribbean to encourage refugees to "seek Asylum elsewhere than in the Territory of Orleans."[67] Working largely on his own, Claiborne nervously crafted a pragmatic policy that strengthened ties between American authorities and the Louisiana French. He also worked to highlight American determination to become a reliable protector of the rights of slaveholders, arguably the single most important item on the political agenda of both French- and English-speaking white Louisianians.

Yet, as a whole, Americans in Louisiana remained uneasy about the influx of French-speaking immigrants from the Caribbean, and especially about the arrival of slaves who might have had contact with the rebellion and ongoing turmoil in Saint-Domingue. One American complained in June 1809 that Louisiana was being "over run with french people & Negroes from St. Yago, Havana and other posts in Cuba."[68] But French-speaking Louisianians strongly favored providing a safe harbor to fellow francophones fleeing Caribbean unrest. Claiborne admitted that opinion on the question divided sharply along ethnic lines. "The foreign Frenchmen residing among us . . . take great interest in favour of their country men, and the sympathies of the Creoles of the Country (the descendants of the French) seem also to be much excited," Claiborne observed, but the "English part of our society on the contrary (with some few exceptions) appear to be prejudiced against these Strangers, and express great dissatisfaction that an Asylum in this territory was afforded them."[69] Roughly two-thirds of the nearly four thousand migrants to Louisiana between 1806 and the summer of 1809 were refugees from the West Indies. But in summer of 1809, the third-wave immigration of Saint-Domingue refugees via Cuba poured more than nine thousand French-speakers (2,731 whites, 3,102 free people of color, and 3,226 slaves) into the territory in a single year.[70] The Louisiana French occasionally expressed concern about the "contamination" of these slaves by Haitian influences but generally welcomed the new Caribbean immigration because it gave new strength, political and cultural, to the French community. Anglophone Louisianans worried that the new French immigration would slow or even reverse the growing Americanization of the territory. Even Governor Claiborne's secretary, William B. Robertson, lamented the influx of French refugees, complaining that it would "rivet upon us a decided and irresistible preponderance of French influence—and thus prevent us for many years to come from considering this... as an American country."[71]

In the opening days of 1811, Claiborne's long-standing fears of a Caribbean-style uprising in Louisiana were partially realized as the largest slave insurrection ever to take place within the borders of the United States erupted from the center of Louisiana's wealthy sugar bowl. In the so-called German Coast parishes of St. John the Baptist and St. Charles, heavily black areas up the Mississippi River from New Orleans, more than two hundred slaves participated in a rebellion launched on or about January 8, 1811.[72] The insurrectionists killed the son of prominent planter Manuel Andry and seized a stash of public weapons stored at Andry's plantation before heading not toward the Texas borderlands and possible escape but toward New Orleans, with a plan to "go to the city and kill the whites." After leaving Andry's plantation, the buoyant rebel force burned three plantations and killed planter Jean-François Trepagnier before stopping for rest and revelry at Michael Fortier's sugar plantation. In the meantime, a revenge-minded Andry, who had not only lost his son but been wounded by an axe-wielding rebel during the initial attack, gathered a posse of eighty men and pursued the rebels.[73]

When news of the insurrection reached New Orleans, the "whole city was convulsed." Captain John Shaw, the newly appointed naval commander for New Orleans, reported that "I have never before been witness to such general confusion and disarray."[74] Concerned that the local militia might fail to quell such a large rebellion, Governor Claiborne approached General Wade Hampton, the American military commander for the Southwest who had been sent to the region to help secure American control of newly acquired West Florida, at midday on January 9 and asked him to lead a combination of regular soldiers and volunteer militia upriver to the German Coast to suppress the rebellion.[75] Hampton, an experienced commander, learned from Claiborne that "a formidable insurrection had commenced among the blacks, on the left bank of the river, about forty miles north of this city [New Orleans]," and was "advancing rapidly" toward New Orleans, leaving "fire, Murder & pillage" in its wake. Hampton agreed with Shaw that "the confusion" in New Orleans "was great beyond consideration," owing largely to the facts that the number of federal troops in the city was "inconsiderable" and "nothing like an organized militia" existed.[76]

Hampton intended to bring order out of confusion. By early evening, the general had organized a small contingent of thirty regular army soldiers, two companies of volunteer militia, and a company of seamen on loan from Captain Shaw. This hastily assembled force slogged its way "six leagues" upriver "through roads half a leg deep in mud" to a plantation where the rebels held fortified positions.[77] Before dawn on January 10, Hampton moved to encircle the insurrectionists, but a premature attack by local volunteers alerted the rebels to the presence of Hampton's gathering force. The rebels fled quietly in the early dawn light to avoid a direct confrontation with Hampton, only to encounter Andry's volunteer force on Bernard Bernoudy's nearby plantation the next morning. There the rebels made their stand. At Bernoudy's, Andry's men confronted the insurrectionists, whom the planter described as waiting with "colors displayed and full of arrogance."[78] Andry and his men launched a furious attack against the insurrectionists and quickly routed the rebels. With victory in hand, Andry's posse massacred the insurrectionists before federal troops arrived to take control of the situation. Andry boasted that his men "made considerable slaughter," killing at least fifteen rebels and wounding many more. Concluding that the planters in the area of insurrection were now "equal to the protection of their own property," Hampton deployed his troops in a series of follow-up operations designed to round up rebels who had fled the rout at Bernoudy's and also pacify "Every Settlement of Consequence" in the German Coast area.[79] Hampton felt that though his "means were slender," his "movement" had "the effect of giving the first check to a flame which might have inflicted more human misery than ever has been felt within the United States."[80]

Back in New Orleans, Claiborne had taken immediate steps to provide as much security for the city as he could. He ordered the city's ramshackle militia on alert and called for patrols by "day and night." At Claiborne's urging, the city council turned out a far larger city guard than normal. Claiborne even called out an elite unit of free colored militia to defend the city.[81] By January 12, reports from the German Coast convinced Claiborne that "we have nothing further to apprehend (for the present) from the brigands," and two days later he assured United States secretary of state Robert Smith that the insurrection had been "quelled" and "nearly the whole of the Insurgents killed or taken."[82] Claiborne immediately began distributing kudos to those who had quashed the rebellion and defended New Orleans. He congratulated Andry and other German Coast planters for their "brave and firm conduct" and praised Hampton for his "prompt and judicious" action. The citizens of New Orleans later held a festive dinner in Hampton's honor.[83] Claiborne even thanked the free colored militia unit for the "patriotism and bravery" it showed during the crisis. Yet the insurrection persuaded Claiborne to take the unusual step of putting public guns and public ammunition in private hands because, in his judgment, "late events" rendered it "surely of importance that the Militia should be armed." To reassure residents of St. Charles Parish, Claiborne distributed both "the public muskets" and the "public powder" among "the freemen of the parish."[84]

As Louisiana whites celebrated the quick end of the rebellion, local authorities, with the avowed intent of deterring future revolts, went about the gruesome business of meting out punishment. Claiborne told planters in the German Coast area that it was "absolutely essential to our future safety that a proper and great example should be made of the guilty."[85] And even before the rebellion was fully defeated, Andry, one of its first victims, declared that authorities "must make a GREAT EXAMPLE" in destroying the insurrection.[86] On this point, Louisiana authorities did not disappoint the injured and grief-stricken German Coast planter. The brutal suppression of the German Coast insurrection and the subsequent trials of alleged participants took a heavy toll on the German Coast black population. Overall, at least 115 slaves were killed or executed in the suppression and punishment of the rebellion.[87] As many as sixty-six slave rebels were killed by regular troops, territorial militia, or Andre's posse either in the fighting that eventually crushed the insurrection or during the impromptu and unrestrained flurry of retribution that immediately followed in the fields and woods along the German Coast.[88] Another twenty-seven rebels were missing and presumed "dead in the woods."[89] Two sets of public "trials" followed the insurrection, resulting in the conviction and execution of more than two dozen additional slaves, including any survivors identified as leaders or instigators of the rebellion. On Jean Noel Destrehan's plantation in St. Charles Parish, Judge Pierre St. Martin and five prominent planters convened a "court" that held three days of proceedings. Judge St. Martin's "court" convicted twenty-one slaves and sentenced them to death.[90] The "court" in St. Charles Parish sentenced the guilty slaves to be shot on their home plantations and to have their heads placed on stakes "as a terrible example to all who would disturb public tranquility in the future."[91] The parish court subjected the insurrection's alleged ringleader, Charles Deslondes, to special torture. According to one source, they chopped his hands off and shot him in both legs and in the body, and then burned him alive in a "bundle of straw."[92]

In New Orleans, another set of "trials" were held before a tribunal of five prominent planters, including the pioneering sugar entrepreneur and former New Orleans mayor Étienne de Boré. These proceedings led to the execution of at least four slaves.[93] The death sentences handed down by the New Orleans "court" were carried out by "hanging and beheading" and proceeded on a one-execution-per-day basis. One observer of the executions reported that the convicted slaves "were hung for the sake of their heads, which decorate our levee—They look like crows sitting on long poles."[94] Edward Palfrey, a young visitor from Massachusetts, had watched the brutal process unfold. He recounted seeing New Orleans authorities hang the rebels and then "cut off their heads and stick it in a pole and set it up in the street."[95] News of such cruelty disturbed some Americans, including former New Orleans naval commander John Porter, who declared himself "shocked at the barbarity of the planters."[96] A full three months later, a flour trader on the Mississippi river reported seeing "a number of Negro heads sticking in poles on the levee" as he approached New Orleans.[97] White authorities orchestrated such visible and grisly punishments with a large slave and free black audience in mind, as "a warning to others."[98]

The German Coast slave revolt of 1811 remains at best partially explained. The two parishes in which the rebellion centered, St. Charles and St. Martin, were roughly 60 percent black in 1810. The absolute size of the population in this area had nearly doubled (from thirty-two hundred to sixty-two hundred) over the previous two decades, but the proportion of slaves in the total population had remained roughly the same. These wealthy sugar parishes were attracting more settlers with slaves, but they were not in the process of becoming suddenly blacker at the time of the rebellion. But the narrow strip of land along the eastern bank of the Mississippi River where the rebellion actually unfolded, the German Coast itself, was even more heavily black than the parishes as a whole. According to Adam Rothman's calculations, this plantation area had 274 whites but nearly five times that many slaves (1,480) as well as 89 free people of color in 1810. Moreover, more than 86 percent of all household heads along the German Coast owned slaves and the average number of slaves held in the area was forty-three.[99] The overwhelming black majority along the German Coast, one that rivaled that of rice districts of the Carolina Lowcountry in its proportion, could have given slaves a measure of confidence about their prospects for success, especially if they did not know that the United States Army loomed nearby to assist the local militia in their efforts to put down the rebellion.[100] Evidence also indicates that at the time of the rebellion, male slaves far outnumbered female slaves in the German Coast region, suggesting an underdeveloped family structure in the area that may have left many German Coast slaves with less to risk than slaves in areas where strong networks of slave families had developed. But demographic factors alone can scarcely explain an insurrection. Large black majorities prevailed in other parts of the South, particularly along the Atlantic rice coast, and significant gender imbalances often characterized life in newer slaveholding areas, creating situations presumably conducive to rebellion but not spawning an actual insurrection unless special leaders appeared or special circumstances emerged.[101]

Accounts either left by whites or extracted from slaves under duress suggest that Charles Paquet, a local free person of color, may have allowed the planning of the rebellion to occur at his home, and at least one accused rebel blamed an otherwise unknown leader, "Joe the Spaniard," of recruiting rebels in front of Paquet's home.[102] Paquet had a history of getting in trouble with whites for harboring runaway slaves, but little is known about the mysterious "Joe the Spaniard," if such a person even existed, except that one accused slave fingered him as a ringleader.

Both contemporaries and historians have identified Charles Deslondes, a mulatto slave who was working on the Andry plantation when the rebellion erupted, as the primary leader of the revolt. Rumors held that Charles, owned by the widow of planter Jean-Baptiste Deslondes, was a native of Saint-Domingue. By singling out Charles as a probable leader of the revolt, white Louisianians revealed their suspicion that the uprising was somehow linked with the rebellious spirit imported from the Caribbean.[103] But there remains scant evidence to support the claim that Charles hailed from Saint-Domingue, and other than the identification of Charles as a leader, there is little evidence to suggest that slaves from the Caribbean were either a strong presence among or exerted a disproportionate influence on the insurrectionists. According to estimates, more than half of all German Coast slaves had been born outside Louisiana, and almost all of those slaves came from various parts of Africa, though a few came from the Caribbean or other southern states. But most of the slaves who were executed for their leadership roles in the rebellion were creoles and mulattoes, and many of the rebels were either skilled slaves or domestics. But if creoles played a disproportionate role in the rebellion's presumed leadership, a number of recently imported Africans also appeared in the rebel ranks. No consistent pattern of slave ethnicity or nativity among slave rebels appears to explain the German Coast rebellion. If anything, the prosopography of slave rebels along the German Coast proved that "a diverse group of enslaved people could join together in an effort to liberate themselves by force of arms." But the diversity of the insurrectionists does little to explain either the origins of the rebellion or its timing.[104]

The German Coast rebellion occurred during a period of unusual political instability, even by the standards of the Louisiana Territory. Just four months before the rebellion, Catholic priest Miguel Hidalgo led a populist revolt in New Spain. After achieving an impressive victory at Guanajuato, the Hidalgo revolutionaries advocated the abolition of slavery in New Spain and threatened to execute all slaveholders who refused to emancipate their slaves. News of the Hidalgo insurgency spread rapidly though Texas and reached Louisiana. Such reports might have influenced aspiring slave rebels to strike for freedom.[105] On Louisiana's other border, closer to the German Coast, recent instability in West Florida, and, perhaps more importantly the American preoccupation with establishing control of West Florida, may have convinced German Coast slaves that distractions elsewhere made the time right for rebellion. The American takeover of West Florida had pleased white Louisianians generally, but it had raised concerns among slaveholders that either the accompanying uncertainty or retributive Spanish instigation might encourage slave unrest.[106] General Wade Hampton always believed, as a military man assigned to defend the region from the Spanish and those making mischief under Spanish influence, that the rebellion was "unquestionably of Spanish origin" and reflected "extensive combination" on the part of the rebels. Even after the presumed leaders of the insurrection were captured, Hampton still suspected Spanish intrigue. "[W]ithout Doubt," Hampton asserted, there "were others behind the Curtain Still More formidable."[107]

Yet despite Hampton's suspicions, no evidence ever surfaced linking the rebellion to the activity of Spanish provocateurs. Given the communication networks developed by Gulf Coast slaves by this time, networks as complex as those developed by slave boatmen on the Mississippi or as simple as eavesdropping on a master's conversation, it is difficult to imagine that the slave communities along the German Coast were unaware of political developments, at least at some level, in Mexico and West Florida during the fall of 1810. But if German Coast slave rebels took their cue from the liberty-seeking actions of either Mexican revolutionaries or American nationalists in West Florida, or if they were incited by Spanish agents, there is little evidence in the surviving record to prove it.

In the end, most white Louisianians spent less time analyzing the causes of the insurrection than in congratulating themselves on the thoroughness with which the rebellion had been quashed. On balance, both Louisiana authorities and local slaveholders felt the rebellion had been crushed with an efficiency and a brutality adequate to deter future efforts. Governor Claiborne lauded the conduct of Hampton and his troops, noting that "the ardor and firmness of the Militia have made an impression upon the Blacks that will not (I suspect) for a length of time be effaced."[108] Claiborne also told the territorial legislature that the insurrection plot was not of "extensive combination" and was instead "the result of previous concert between the slaves of a few neighboring plantations." The "example" made of the "principals in this Insurrection" will "produce the desired effect." Claiborne hoped the insurrection would persuade the legislature "to give us a more energetic Militia system" and provide "some check to that indiscriminate importation of Slaves from the southern States."[109] Louisiana's legislative council agreed with half of the governor's assessment, announcing itself convinced of the necessity for a strong and well-disciplined militia. The Louisiana house, after noting that the insurrection was "feeble" and "its suppression immediate," also concurred on the need for an improved militia. The "Blacks have been taught an important lesson—their weakness," the house noted, "and we have learned that our Security depends on the order and discipline of the Militia."[110] But no political body in Louisiana showed any inclination to limit the domestic slave trade in any meaningful way. While the scope of the German Coast rebellion hardly could have escaped people as familiar with fears of slave revolt as white Louisianians, the gruesome sight of the heads of executed slaves mounted on poles atop levees, at plantation gates, and at road crossings up and down the Mississippi River seems to have somehow reassured Louisiana whites that their ultimate control remained safely intact.

Indeed, the conduct of South Carolina's Hampton, a man with virtually unsurpassed firsthand knowledge of the rebellion, seemed to affirm local optimism. With the rebellion suppressed, Hampton resumed buying both land and slaves in Louisiana. Shortly after the insurrection, he purchased more than thirty-eight thousand acres of land and 285 slaves at a price of over $300,000, establishing his combined planting operations in South Carolina, Louisiana, and elsewhere as among the most extensive in the entire South.[111] Just three months after the rebellion, Hampton's aide-de-camp wrote that the general, known as a "prudent, discriminating man," remained "convinced" that Louisiana "is the paradise of the new world."[112] By the late 1820s, Hampton had become the leading producer of sugar and molasses in Louisiana and revenues from his three Louisiana plantations were estimated at $100,000 per year.[113] North Carolina native and future Louisiana planter William Hamilton shared Hampton's ebullience on the subject of Louisiana as he pitched Louisiana's virtues to his own family back in North Carolina. "An acre of ground well prepared," Hamilton argued, could yield two thousand pounds of sugar. A "good Planter," he believed, "possessed of a hundred French acres and forty negroes" could produce $14,000 worth of sugar, molasses, and related products in a given year. Louisiana was a cotton bonanza as well. "One good Negroe can make 5 bales of Cotton," worth $500, Hamilton claimed, and forty prime field hands could tend two hundred acres and produce $10,000 worth of cotton annually. To affirm his point, Hamilton insisted that his reports were based on "Fact, indisputable fact."[114]

Throughout the lower South, where the cotton economy expanded westward at a furious pace, slavery provided the labor essential to sustained economic growth in the region. At the same time, the growth of the region's slave population, whether through natural increase, importation from overseas, or emigration and sale from the upper South, heightened white anxiety about the dangers of living in a slave society, including but not limited to insurrection. Thus, as staple profits rolled in and slave majorities emerged in many counties, lower South whites found the perennial tension between greed and fear a compelling dilemma, especially at moments when specific insurrection scares gripped southern communities. Fear of insurrection —and, indeed, occasional confirmation of such fears by rebellions such as the one along Louisiana's German Coast—remained part of life in the slaveholding South throughout the antebellum era, despite the recurring efforts of white southerners to reassure themselves that slaves in their locale were happy, docile, and unlikely to cause trouble unless provoked by incendiary outsiders. The Southwest region's divided mind balanced recurring fears of the unthinkable horrors of insurrection against the promise of quick staple wealth tied to the use of slave labor in the region. But if minds were divided, they were not unable to resolve the tension. The promise of staple wealth usually prevailed over fears of a Saint-Domingue style bloodbath. Once scares receded into memory, the drive for profit and economic security usually prevailed, and the region grew ever more deeply enmeshed in the slave economy.[115]

Back in South Carolina, fears of a repeat of Saint-Domingue never receded far from the minds of Lowcountry planters, but Upcountry leaders generally downplayed such fears. In December 1811, as a young War Hawk attempting to prepare the southern mind for a war to defend export staples, first-term Upcountry congressman John C. Calhoun expressed doubt that "the disorganizing effects of

French principles" had much impact on the southern slave population. "I cannot think our ignorant blacks have felt much of their baneful influence," Calhoun opined in December 1811, apparently nonplussed by the recent German Coast rebellion. "I dare say not more than one-half of them ever heard of the French Revolution."[116] Whether the few score whites living in South Carolina's black-majority parishes found Calhoun's claim reassuring remains unknown, but throughout the early national era, the lower South remained convinced of the benefits of slavery while keeping itself perpetually alert for the first sign of insurrection.

Given the overall level of disruption and danger generated by the War of 1812, Calhoun's prediction that the lower South could survive a war essentially unscathed by slave rebellion proved problematic. The lower South did survive the war without the eruption of a major slave rebellion that took the lives of a large number of whites, but the region's collective nerve was rattled repeatedly by the threat of insurrection. Rumors of insurrection plots and insurrection scares abounded throughout the duration of the war, particularly in the Southwest, where the threat of conflict with the region's native population loomed large as well.

To a considerable extent, the United States fought this second war against Great Britain in order to preserve the unfettered right to export its valuable slave-cultivated staples as it saw fit, without threat of harassment by the powerful British navy or interference from Parliament's foreign policy. Early republican nationalists such as Calhoun, Henry Clay, William Lowndes, and, more reluctantly, President James Madison supported the war precisely because it was fought on behalf of export staples. New England interests, for the same reason, looked upon the conflict with askance. But if the War of 1812 was fought to defend the Jeffersonian vision of an expanding republic producing staples for export, the short-term impact of the war was to cripple the development of the lower South's burgeoning new cotton economy, a result of insurrection scares, depressed prices, war mobilization, and actual fighting.[117] As the war proceeded, in the lower South the conflict evolved into a war against hostile native Americans, runaway and maroon slaves, and the British, with the threat of slave insurrection always looming. And it was precisely this threatening environment that called forth a leader seemingly undaunted by such danger: Andrew Jackson.[118]

Once the War of 1812 began, the vision of lower South expansion that took hold was that of Andrew Jackson rather than Thomas Jefferson. It was not so much a vision of an "empire for liberty" where slavery might expand in order to die eventually as that of a kingdom for cotton, slaveholders, and aspiring slaveholders, where white staple growers might thrive unbothered by indigenous enemies or foreign powers. Jackson saw the war as an opportunity to expel the British, the bulk of the remaining Native American population, and any runaway or maroon slave communities from the potential cotton lands of the lower South, to make room for the settlement of white families and their slaves. Jackson told Claiborne that he yearned to plant "American eagles on the ramparts" all along the Gulf Coast, from Pensacola to Mobile to New Orleans. "British influence must be destroyed," Jackson insisted, "or we will have the whole Southern tribe of Indians to fight and insurrections to quell in all Southern states."[119]

Andrew Jackson certainly brought his lingering Revolutionary resentment of the British to this assessment of dangers facing the South, but the general's opinions were not uncommon among whites in the lower South. Fear ran deep in the region that a British invasion, or even the threat of one, would arouse both hostile Indians and restive slaves to collective action against an encroaching white staple culture. Thus, among residents of the lower South, the war renewed the tension between white desire to support the war and their persistent concern about slave insurrection. In the heart of the new Mississippi cotton belt, whites endorsed Madison's war policy in July 1812, declaring it "essential to the sovereignty and Independence of our Country" to resist the "Unjust pretensions and aggressions of the British government."[120] But at virtually the same moment, Natchez-area overseer James Moore reported that local authorities had arrested "the heads" of an alleged insurrection plot and were holding them in "separate confinement."[121] White southerners remained on alert for any sign of slave insurrection or Indian hostility throughout the war. Mississippi's territorial governor, David Holmes, sought additional arms for the underprepared local militia because "In Slave Countries the Danger of Insurrection" always exists "and the Inhabitants should be prepared to meet the event."[122] Confirming Holmes' judgment, an overseer in Mississippi's Second Creek region reported that "the Negroes were making every preparation a few Days ago to Rise and Destroy the white inhabitants of this territory, Women and Children Excepted."[123] In neighboring Louisiana, New Orleans authorities executed several slaves for plotting an insurrection in 1812, and rumors of additional plots circulated throughout the duration of the war. In 1814, Mississippi's James Moore again reported rumors of slave unrest as the threat of the British invasion of New Orleans emboldened the slaveholding regime's "many internal enemies."[124]

In the meantime, General Jackson struggled to secure the region against all foes. But even after his hard-fought victory over the Red Sticks, a dissident Creek faction, at the Battle of Horseshoe Bend, Jackson worried that the British planned to arm the Indians of Florida and encourage slave insurrection across the lower South. Jackson warned that the British would strike against either Mobile or New Orleans and would "attempt to incite the black population to insurrection and massacre."[125] In August 1814, Claiborne informed Jackson in the wake of the British march through Washington that "Louisiana has at the moment much to fear from Domestic Insurrection," arguing that "the enemy has been intriguing with our slaves, and, we have much cause to suspect that they, on their part, meditate mischief."[126] In mid-October 1814, Louisiana militia leader Jacques Villeré admitted that the state had much "to fear about the 'domestic enemy,'" because the "agents of the English Government found everywhere" were "by the most infamous methods incite our slaves to revolt, murder, pilfering ..."[127] Following the approach that had so distracted the American military during the Revolution, the British had indeed promised freedom to all slaves who would aid the redcoat cause. By the time General Andrew Jackson arrived in New Orleans to defend the city against British invasion in December 1814, Villeré and his state militia were spending much of their energy capturing and returning slaves who had run away in response to the British offer.[128]

Upon his arrival, Jackson quickly mustered every resource available to defend the city. His cobbled-together force included Creeks and Cherokees loyal to the American cause, and much to the consternation of Louisiana whites, he organized two battalions of free black militia in New Orleans.[129] This affront to some local racial sensibilities produced considerable objection from area whites, including that of one militia paymaster who questioned paying free black troops. An impatient Jackson curtly ordered the paymaster to pay everyone on the roster without concern for "whether the troops are black, white or tea."[130] In a pitched battle against the British on February 8, 1815, Jackson won a stunning victory over British regulars commanded by Major General Sir Edward Packenham, a veteran of the Napoleonic Wars. The British, who stormed an entrenched American position, suffered staggering casualties, including more than thirteen hundred killed or wounded and another five hundred missing or captured out of a total attack force of five thousand. The Americans lost only thirteen killed and fifty-eight missing.[131] But even Jackson's overwhelming victory over the British failed to quell fear of slave insurrection in heavily black portions of the Louisiana countryside. In Attakapas Parish, state legislators urged Jackson to leave the state militia in their area after the defeat of the British because the "great disproportion between the white and Black population" left "serious apprehension" in a parish where "there is scarcely white Men enough sufficient at any time to form the necessary patrols to keep the blacks in order."[132]

Lower South whites suffered many hardships during the war, but the threat of slave insurrection produced more concern than casualties. In reality, a small number of slaves helped the ill-fated Red Sticks in their war against the emerging cotton economy and other slaves sought protection from and assisted the British in hopes of gaining their freedom, but the nearly constant threat of insurrection during the war was hardly matched by actual rebellion. Still, Calhoun had been wrong to cavalierly suggest that few slaves would consider insurrection, and even more wrong that whites had little to fear, even though no major insurrection actually occurred during the war. Yet, despite an otherwise wretched war effort, the lower South escaped what its inhabitants most feared: the ravages of a major slave insurrection.

At the same time, General Andrew Jackson's hard-won series of victories over the Creeks and the British, and his constant vigilance against slave revolt, did much to make large stretches of the lower South safe for slavery and staple agriculture. Shortly after the Battle of New Orleans, Jackson himself declared the victory one that would "always be hailed by every true american."[133] Certainly Jackson's victories over the Creeks and his more famous victory over the British secured the popularity of the "Old Hero" (his nickname prior to "Old Hickory"). Lower South whites credited Jackson with driving dangerous Indians off potentially productive cotton lands and bestowed upon the Old Hero their eternal gratitude. It took a series of postwar military maneuvers and treaty negotiations over two decades to fully complete the Jacksonian triumph in the lower South, but grateful white voters gave Jackson a chance to finish the job of Indian removal later in his political career. He did not disappoint his followers, and more than 175 years later, statues of General Jackson stand as tribute throughout the region: on the riverfront in Jacksonville, Florida; on the statehouse grounds in Mississippi's capital city; and on a popular square named in his honor in New Orleans, the region's longtime cultural and economic center.

Still, despite Jackson's success and the prevention of a major wartime insurrection, the German Coast rebellion of 1811 and the perils that compounded the military defense of the lower South during the War of 1812 made preventing insurrections a lingering concern, bordering on preoccupation, among whites in the region in the war's aftermath. The heroics of Jackson and his men may have made the lower South safer for slavery than before, but safer did not mean safe. There was no such thing as a safe slave society. In the lower South, slavery stood the old Jeffersonian wisdom on its head. Eternal vigilance became the price of slavery.

At times, lower South whites seemed eager to pay, whatever the cost. At other times, they were stingier in their assessment and sought to qualify, control, and even slow their deepening commitment to slavery as a social system. They wanted slavery, but they wanted it on their own terms. As the cotton belt extended across the lower South, finding the appropriate balance between economic prosperity and white safety became the chief question concerning slavery in the region. An answer that allowed whites to have as much of both as possible remained elusive.

PART THREE

PATERNALISM RISING

As lower South whites increasingly found themselves contending with the daily dangers of living among large numbers of slaves while depending on the profits from slave labor to drive their region's economic vitality, they looked for ways to both limit the danger and live more comfortably among slaves. Measures for better control of slaves were a hardy perennial; other ideas for reducing the dangers were an innovation. The most important such innovation was the emergence of a historically specific and ideologically distinct brand of paternalism during the first two decades of the nineteenth century. Cobbling together a coherent body of ideas from Christian theology and teaching about moral stewardship, family responsibility, and evangelism, and drawing on a pool of able leadership provided by the Protestant clergy and active lay leaders, the emerging paternalist insurgency challenged existing notions of the master-slave relationship, including norms of slave management, discipline, and instruction, without challenging the morality of slavery itself. The paternalist insurgency built credibility by achieving success, albeit modest at first, in converting both masters and slaves to Christianity and incorporating large numbers of slaves into active congregations. As they did, they convinced some initially skeptical whites that paternalism could lead to a more orderly and productive mode of daily life in a slave economy while also saving souls.

Yet convincing a preponderance of whites in the lower South that paternalism was an effective method of slave control proved a slow, difficult, and contested task. The paternalist insurgency encountered entrenched opposition from older notions of slave management based on regular shows of force and intimidation, which retained popularity among slaveholders who thought that paternalism required too much coddling of slaves. More importantly, the Christian mission to the slaves, with its emphasis on black worship participation, the use of approved blacks in leadership roles, and the evangelical determination to teach slaves to read, became a lightning rod for the planters' and civil establishment's criticism of the movement. When incidents of slave resistance or autonomy, such as the aborted Camden insurrection in South Carolina in 1816 or the creation of an independent "African" congregation in Charleston the next year, were attributed to the leadership of literate black Christians, establishment fears that the paternalist mission to the slaves was fraught with danger appeared confirmed. White interest in a broad array of control measures, including regulation of the internal slave trade, bans on free black immigration, and more restrictive manumission policies, was rekindled. Some lower South whites concluded that paternalism posed a mortal threat to the slaveholding social order of the Old South, yet as outside attacks on slavery arose during the Missouri debates, others began to see paternalism as a shield against harsh external critiques of slavery.

CHAPTER FIVE

PATERNALISM EMERGES

During the first two decades of the nineteenth century, the lower South's new cotton economy expanded inland and westward at a furious pace, spreading with it slavery, which provided the labor that sustained the region's economic boom. At the same time, the growth of the region's slave population heightened white anxiety about the dangers of living in a slave society. As staple profits rolled in and new slave majorities and larger slave minorities emerged in more and more cotton counties, lower South whites found the perennial southern tension between greed and fear a compelling dilemma, especially at moments when occasional insurrection scares gripped southern communities. But as scares passed, the drive for profit and economic gain usually prevailed, and the region grew ever more deeply enmeshed in the slave economy.[1] As slavery expanded, lower South leaders worked to secure the institution against emerging external threats (hostile northern politicians) and recurrent internal ones (insurrections, insurrection scares, and the reaction of a fearful public to insurrections and scares). Securing slavery against these threats, from both without and within, proved no easy task. Increasingly, a portion of the region's intellectual, moral, and political leadership realized the need to smooth out the institution's rough edges, to render it more ideologically defensible—perhaps not a positive good, but a social system in which the morality of masters could be easily defended, the treatment of slaves justified, and the safety of whites guaranteed.[2] Such a task required nothing less than a reconfiguring of slavery. In the upper South, the relative stagnation of the tobacco economy and the federal ban on the importation of foreign slaves spurred the region to seek a demographic reconfiguration of slavery through manumission, colonization, and diffusion. In the lower South, the exploding cotton economy combined with the closing of the foreign slave trade to accelerate the region's interest in a very different but equally fundamental reconfiguration of slavery. The reconfiguration sought by lower South whites was not a demographic reconfiguration but an ideological one aimed at changing the way masters and other whites conceived of the institution, rendering slaveholding consistent with existing republican and emerging humanitarian ideals while accepting and even embracing the region's growing dependence on slave labor.[3]

The dramatic and contested ideological reconfiguration of slavery that occurred in the minds of a growing phalanx of white southerners between 1790 and 1820 centered on the transformation of southern slavery into a truly "domestic" institution. As historian Willie Lee Rose has suggested, during the first three decades of the nineteenth century white southerners were "engaged in a process of rationalizing slavery" by "domesticating" it. This involved inculcating familial values into the attitudes and practices of masters (and other whites) as well as slaves. Thus the domestication of southern slavery depended heavily on the emergence of the ideology of paternalism as the prism through which both masters and slaves understood slavery. In Rose's view, for slavery to become a domestic institution, the master had to "preside" as benevolent patriarch (or, when men were absent, as matriarch) over "three interlocking domesticities—his blood family, the slave families, and the plantation community family." Thus the domesticating of slavery required not only treating slaves "well" (as if they were family) but also understanding slavery fundamentally in familial terms. Hence both the practical and the ideological progress of domesticating slavery depended on the full embrace of the paternalist ideology by slaveholders. White southerners had to accept paternalism as a way of understanding slavery, and they had to try to convince slaves to accept paternalism as a means of making the best of their fate.[4]

In an important work expanding on Rose's provocative insights, Jeffrey Young maintained that between 1800 and 1815, southern slave owners "established an ideological foundation for the defense of slavery," a foundation that rested on the notion that slavery as it existed in the South was a thoroughly domestic institution. The process of domesticating slavery called for the "social subordination of women and slaves" to protect and enhance "the liberties of white men." Arguing that slaveholders adapted such an ideology from religious and literary sources, Young suggested that it provided a "blueprint for moral mastery" that called for slaveholders to internalize the notion that "masters should maintain highly personalized, affectionate relations with their slaves."[5] Thus the rise of paternalism in the lower South and the attempt to domesticate slavery were part and parcel of the same endeavor. The effort to domesticate slavery hinged on the spread of a paternalist ideology, and the growing acceptance of an ideology of paternalism among lower South masters proved a powerful agent for the perceived domestication of slaves.

This new ideology of paternalism emerged in the early-nineteenth-century South partially in response to specific historical developments that occurred early in the first decade of the nineteenth century and prompted some whites to reconfigure slavery. Thus the emphasis on domesticity and paternalism represented new departures in thinking about slavery, departures inspired by new circumstances rather than the continuation of long-term trends. In her initial essay on the subject, Rose insisted that eighteenth-century planters had remained "more concerned with the state of their crops than with paternal relations with their chattels," and that slaveholding founders had operated under "no illusion" about the "essentially exploitative nature" of slavery. Moreover, Rose argued, the "very frequency and casual nature" of the abuse of slaves prior to 1800 suggested that "pervasive brutality and suffering" characterized the pre-paternalist era of slavery.[6]

That said, there is no question that the early-nineteenth-century effort to domesticate slavery built on a foundation laid during the latter half of the eighteenth century. A significant body of scholarship, exemplified by Joyce Chaplin's work on humanitarianism, rightly suggests that lower South slaveholders, or at least those in the South Carolina and Georgia Lowcountry, began a "reassessment" of their assumptions about slaves and slavery sometime during the third quarter of the eighteenth century.[7] It was during these years that at least some slaveholders began to see their slaves as humans rather than purely as property. Out of this belated but critical recognition of the basic humanity of slaves emerged a logic supporting a different style of slave management and a different conceptualization of resident slaveholders' role in a slave society. This late colonial humanitarianism owed its appearance in the lower South not only to the suggestive intellectual influences of the early Scottish Enlightenment but also to the growing prevalence of creole or country-born slaves in the slave population and from the moral message advanced by the evangelists of the First Great Awakening and the institutional churches they helped create.[8] Humanitarianism first appeared in slaveholder ideology when the "plantation generation" of slaves grew dominant in Lowcountry slave communities and as the evangelists of the first awakening made headway in the lower South, suggesting an evangelical moral code to masters and aspiring masters.[9]

The later paternalist movement certainly benefited from the inroads previously made by humanitarianism, and the later movement relied significantly on the institutional and personal foundations (scattered evangelical churches and rudimentary denominational structures, plus core groups of Christian pastors, masters and slaves in particular) developed by the earlier movement. However, as important as the first humanitarian movement was, there were marked limits to its influence. First, much of the interior region later enveloped by the cotton boom of the late 1790s and early 1800s were only lightly touched by the first awakening.[10] Second and more important, during the American War for Independence and its economically depressed aftermath, a restless and even rebellious Revolutionary generation of slaves replaced the plantation generation as the dominant cohort of the region's slave population, and Lowcountry slaves' wartime resistance, the large numbers of slaves who absconded as runaways and refugees, and slave aid to the British cause disabused lower South masters of notions that their slaves had become malleable and quiescent.[11] The plantation equilibrium of the 1760s had been dramatically disturbed.[12] Moreover, by 1799, the Lowcountry evangelical movement had long since lost its momentum, and Charleston Baptist leader Richard Furman openly lamented the "languishing state" of religion in the entire region.[13]

Thus the origins of the paternalist movement may date to the mid-eighteenth century but its active and mature phases were clearly nineteenth-century phenomena. The first humanitarian movement had established a beachhead in the lower South during the late colonial era, a beachhead it held under considerable duress at times. This beachhead served as a valuable training ground and staging area for the later paternalist movement, but the ideals of paternalism and domesticity were unable to advance significantly across the broader, and broadening, field of slave society until a second religious awakening again expanded the humanitarian impulse in the region and the closing of the foreign slave trade guaranteed the eventual emergence of a predominately American-born slave labor force.[14] In fact, as historian Mark Kaplanoff argued, during most of the eighteenth century the plantation society of the South Carolina Lowcountry "in many ways approximated a West Indian model with absentee planters, looser supervision of work routines, limited black acculturation and savage discipline." But in the early nineteenth century, Lowcountry planters began to cultivate the image of "being country gentlemen," and as the "cotton boom spread smaller, more closely supervised plantations through the interior," the region developed signs of "a growing paternalist style among the planters and of a well understood accommodation between planters and slaves about the conditions of life and labor."[15] Agreeing with Kaplanoff, Jeffrey Young has also argued convincingly that the idea of master-slave relations characterized by paternalism "had been foreign to the vast majority of eighteenth century planters," who had both "despised and feared" their slaves. Eighteenth-century slaveholders in Georgia and South Carolina, in Young's view, never viewed the ideal of plantation domesticity as a safe or satisfactory ideological mooring for their society.[16] Even more recently, Robert Olwell, a historian of eighteenth-century southern slavery, described the slaveholders' embrace of paternalism and domesticity as a post-eighteenth-century development, at least in the Lowcountry. According to Olwell, patriarchal ideas influenced late colonial and Revolutionary-era masters, but in the postcolonial era, masters "no longer described themselves as monarchs and their plantations as little kingdoms." Instead, masters became heads of "households" rather than principalities and slaves became "children" rather than "subjects." The "distance, autonomy and violence of patriarchy," Olwell contended, gradually gave way to "the closer and more controlling, if less overtly brutal, language of 'paternalism.'"[17]

The paternalism of the early nineteenth century, though shaped by its forerunners, was a new set of ideas at work in the social order, and it emerged from a very specific set of historical forces and for a very specific purpose.[18] Students of paternalism differ over the relative importance of the specific historical precipitants that shaped its rise, but almost all agree about which matters to include on the list: the need to find slave management techniques that encouraged productivity and minimized resistance, the closing of the foreign slave trade (which enhanced the importance of increasing the productivity of existing slaves), the need for slave management practices that encouraged the future increase of slaves, the increase in the proportion of slaves who were country-born, the expansion of the short-staple cotton boom into new areas of the lower South, the expanded role of evangelical religion in the region, and the slaveholders' desire to portray slavery to the larger world as a just and humane institution in response to the chatter of antislavery criticism that was beginning to reach their ears.[19] The mix, timing, and relative importance of these factors mattered, however, and in the following narrative, I will present my own views of when, how, and how much each contributed to the emergence of paternalism in the lower South.

The particular set of ideas and assumptions grouped here under the rubric of "paternalism" consisted of four main ideological propositions. First, slaves must be recognized as human beings, regardless of the degree of their alleged inferiority, white perceptions of the uncivilized or savage nature of their society in Africa, and any supposed limitations on their potential. Thus it was incumbent upon whites, and especially upon Christian whites, to recognize the humanity of slaves and treat them accordingly. Second, based on the common humanity of master and slave, the day-to-day governance of a slave population should be conducted similarly to how male household heads governed their white families, that is, with a combination of fairness and firmness, a balance of affection and discipline. This familial treatment would produce the master's preferred form of subordination among slaves, willing obedience. Paternalism would render slaves more manageable, slave labor more efficient, and slave unrest less common. Third, paternalism required stewardship on the part of the master. Strictly speaking, masters could embrace and practice paternalism without being Christian, but overwhelmingly the advocates of paternalism professed Christianity and the movement bore their stamp. Thus stewardship most often took a Christian form, which demanded not only practicing the Golden Rule in the treatment of slaves but also regular and systematic efforts to teach slaves Christianity. Finally, paternalism required the paternalist to show some larger scope of humanitarian concern not simply in the daily treatment and provisioning of slaves or even in the nurture of slave families and religion, but also in the acceptance of a broader social responsibility for making slave society work humanely as well as profitably. The paternalistic slaveholder had to accept a measure of responsibility not only for his or her neighbor but also for his or her neighbor's slaves and his or her neighbor's treatment of slaves. Now, it goes without saying that virtually no slaveholder succeeded in fulfilling the paternalist ideal, and probably few tried with a high degree of consistency, but the ideal was touted from church pulpits, society hall lecterns, and courthouse steps and published in plantation management handbooks, religious tracts, and occasional pamphlets throughout the region as the preferred ideal.[20]

Among the factors that encouraged the emergence of paternalism were the practical necessities of managing slaves in a manner that encouraged cooperation and productivity. As Eugene Genovese and others have argued, the pattern of resistance and accommodation, and resistance to accommodation and still further accommodation to resistance, that characterized the day-to-day reality of the master-slave relationship encouraged the development of a paternalistic understanding of slavery. These daily, ongoing negotiations between masters and slaves took place in the context of uneven power and even terror, but they were nonetheless compelled by both the master's thirst for profit and the slaves' desire to play some role in shaping their everyday existence. These negotiations created room for maneuver on the part of slaves and the need for some measure of accommodation on the part of masters.[21]

As early as 1800, William Moultrie, a Lowcountry planter, Revolutionary war hero, two-time governor of South Carolina, and active member of Charleston society, stated the emerging case for practical paternalism succinctly. In "the part of the country where I live," he claimed, "there is great moderation & [i]ndulgence given to slaves." At the time of his death in 1805 Moultrie owned nearly nine thousand acres scattered over two states, but his main residential plantations lay in the rice- and cotton-growing parish of St. John's-Berkeley, just northwest of Charleston. In advancing his case for "moderation and indulgence" among slaveholders in the Cooper River basin parishes, Moultrie argued for the existence of paternalism in one of the South's oldest and most heavily black slaveholding subregions. Moultrie argued that such paternalism was "for the best in the end" because it rendered slavery "[m]ore satisfactory and profitable." "[W]hat you may think you lose in making small crops you amply make up for by the [i]ncrease and long life of your slaves," Moultrie contended. No better rationale for paternalism was required. Moreover, Moultrie favorably contrasted the paternalistic slave management practices common by 1800 with the harsh treatment of slaves a generation earlier. Moultrie recalled that in previous decades slaves had often received as many as fifty lashes "for not doing what was called their task…when it was perhaps impossible for them to do it."[22]

But daily negotiations between master and slave did not necessarily lead to the emergence of the paternalist ideology (as opposed to the mere practice of accommodation by some masters) unless other factors were also present. If the practice of a self-interested paternalism somehow emerged inevitably from the harsh logic dictated by a daily dependence on slave labor and the desire of the enslaved to carve out a measure of autonomy for themselves until more direct paths to freedom could be cut, the self-conscious self-definition of the slaveholder as a paternalist depended heavily on two separate and distinct developments: the closing of the foreign slave trade in 1808 and the dramatic spread of evangelical Christianity through the South during the Second Great Awakening. Together, the closing of the foreign slave trade and the period of sweeping religious revival shaped and accelerated the emerging reconfiguration of slavery as a paternalistic or domestic institution.[23]

As William Freehling has pointed out, the closing of the African slave trade dramatically reshaped the institution of slavery in the American South in ways that gave momentum to the paternalist argument. The end of the foreign slave trade limited forever the size of the slave population in the American South. From 1808 forward, the natural increase of the slave population and the scope of slave smuggling would determine the number of slaves available to cultivate southern staples. Hence, regardless of the slave management practices used by earlier generations, after 1808 southern slaveholders knew that only practices that effectively encouraged slave reproduction could ensure the continued growth of the region's slave population.[24]

Once the federal ban on slave imports took effect, few lower South slaveholders doubted that the need to cultivate a family atmosphere encouraging longevity and reproduction among slaves held the key to the future of the slave economy. In 1815, William Johnson, a United States Supreme Court justice and a South Carolinian, summed up these views well in a public address in Charleston, telling his audience that the end of the slave trade would accelerate their prospects of enjoying capital gains from the ownership of slave property. With the foreign trade banned, Johnson opined, "the value of this [slave] property must therefore advance." Johnson flattered his listeners that "none who hear me need the incentive of interest to prompt their benevolent exertions," but he argued that if anyone needed an extra reason for benevolence, "they too will see in the propagation of their slaves the only resource for future wealth." His rhetorical pandering aside, the erudite but worldly jurist knew well that many in his audience and more across the South needed every possible incentive to employ "benevolent exertions" in their management of slaves. Thus Johnson emphasized that with the closing of the external slave trade, self-interest presented a powerful inducement to paternalism as a practice as well as an ideal. Both "humanity and self-interest require of us the care of our slaves," Johnson observed. The Jefferson-appointed justice explained that the "interest of the owner is to obtain from his slaves labor and increase" and maintained that intelligent owners knew that neither could "be expected without due attention to their health and comfort, or without bestowing upon their offspring the care which infancy and childhood" required.[25]

Moreover, the permanent closing of the African slave trade also helped redefine the composition of the southern slave population. Over time, with the foreign trade officially outlawed, southern slave communities inevitably would become more and more dominated by American creoles and African Americans and less and less influenced by new slave imports from Africa or the Caribbean. Though hardly welcomed by Louisiana slaveholders, who expressed a continued preference for slaves fresh from Africa, the shift in the composition of the South's slave population suited the predilections of most other southern slaveholders, who preferred acculturated country-born slaves to natives of Africa or the rebellion-tainted Caribbean. The end of the foreign slave trade also meant that slaveholder efforts to make slaves more loyal and compliant (such as efforts to Christianize slaves) promised greater benefits to whites because it reduced country-born slaves' exposure to new and direct African and Caribbean cultural influences that could undermine white efforts to cultivate domesticity among slaves.[26] Toward that end, William Johnson advised Lowcountry slaveholders that providing "sufficient food and clothing" was essential to effective labor, but advised that truly wise masters went further, offering "just treatment, a kind word, and a little extra indulgence or gratification." Such paternalistic practices, Johnson concluded, "produce wonderful effects." The "return of affection and fidelity" from slaves, Johnson reasoned, "often goes far beyond the benefit conferred."[27] By encouraging such paternalism, the closing of the foreign slave trade not only domesticated the slave trade but contributed to the domestication of slavery as well.[28]

But the emerging paternalist ideal drew perhaps its greatest sustenance from the rapidly spreading teachings of an aggressively evangelical version of Reformed Christianity in the South during the late eighteenth and early nineteenth centuries. While the daily functioning of slavery as a labor system, with its seemingly inevitable patterns of accommodation and resistance, generated the practices masters touted as paternalism, and the closing of the foreign slave trade helped render the slave population more domestic in both the literal and figurative meanings of the term, the larger public articulation of paternalism as the slaveholding ideal owed much more to the spread of evangelical Christianity through the South during the days of the Second Great Awakening than to any other factor. As evangelical religion spread its influence, the articulated ethos of paternalism exerted steadily greater influence among slaveholders.[29] While in some areas the religious awakening briefly offered a serious challenge to slavery, in the lower South the denominations that drew strength from the awakening soon dropped their challenge to slavery in order to win converts among whites and to gain the opportunity to preach Christianity to the region's large slave population. Out of these expanding evangelical efforts emerged a coherent portrait of slavery as an institution that could be rendered consistent with Christian teachings if characterized by domesticity and paternalism. Over time, the message of evangelical ministers increasingly focused on the mutual obligations and duties of masters and slaves within the confines of paternalism. These messages insisted that both masters and slaves work to domesticate slavery.[30]

Justice William Johnson, an active member of Charleston's Circular Congregational Church, a church known by 1815 for its energetic work among slaves, knew better than most that under a well-implemented regimen of paternalism "the Christian ... will often see more to be envied in the life of the slave than in that of the master." Johnson readily admitted that all masters were imperfect paternalists, flawed by a "too frequent readiness to yield ourselves up in passion in our treatment" of slaves, and in need of God's grace for their shortcomings. But he credited slaves with a special endurance, one that often led them to water the "fresh grave of a master with the bitterest tears." Johnson believed that masters should "address ourselves more to their [slaves'] affections" and "bestow more liberally ... our confidence." Johnson cautioned that "a favorable result ought not to be hastily expected, for their [slaves'] uncultivated natures must be gradually wrought upon." Johnson thought it "absurd" to expect in slaves the same "elevation of the soul" that "characterized the freeman." But he argued that paternalism, if properly practiced, would nonetheless tend to render slaves faithful. The justice never doubted that the paternalist "experiment" was worth the effort.[31]

Like many other Christian ministers, evangelists, and lay people during the early nineteenth century, Georgetown Baptist pastor Edmund Botsford had committed his life to Johnson's proposition. Botsford, an evangelical preacher who converted many slaves during the first decade of the nineteenth century, applauded the paternalism that he believed was rapidly gaining ground among slaveholders. Critics of slavery, Botsford believed, often presented the institution "as much worse than it is." He conceded the harshness of eighteenth-century slavery but pointed to the meliorating effect of Christian paternalism on early-nineteenth-century slavery. "I grant it [slavery] was much worse forty or fifty years ago than at the present time," he wrote in 1812, but insisted that the increased piety of both masters and slaves had mitigated the worst features of the institution. "Of late years," he argued, "a great number of slaves have become serious and are united with religious societies & and many of them are to all appearance truly pious." Pious slaves, Botsford thought, served as a "restraint" on other slaves "of a bad character." The task system in the rice fields, Botsford explained, imposed a work routine that was "by no means excessive," and he argued (though apparently without firsthand knowledge) that slaves in the Upcountry, who often worked on smaller farms and alongside their owners, fared even "better" than Lowcountry slaves in terms of food and clothing. Under the influence of paternalism, the conditions of slave life were improving.[32]

Thus, during the first two decades of the nineteenth century paternalism as a social ideal gained increasing currency among slaveholding whites in the South. To be sure, the paternalistic ideal was hardly the reality of plantation and farm life across the slaveholding South. Especially in the lower South, the cotton boom and the rapid expansion of slavery produced as much cruelty, as much if not more disruption of slave family and community life, and as much tension between masters and slaves as ever, but as the ideal of paternalism advanced, southern slaveholders conceived of themselves and explained themselves to the rest of the world through the prism of paternalism and domesticity. The precepts of paternalism may have been honored mainly in their breach, but as Young pointed out, between 1800 and 1815 southern "slaveowners established an ideological defense of slavery" that centered on the domestication of the South's peculiar institution.[33] The end of the foreign slave trade and the emergence of humanitarian concerns generated by the expanding influence of Christianity in the region spawned paternalism as an ideology and helped transform slavery into a domestic institution, at least in the minds of most whites. Jacksonian-era and late-antebellum white southerners frequently and casually styled slavery as a domestic institution. In the minds of these whites, domesticity became enshrined as the core of the region's self-justification for slaveholding, and paternalism offered an explanation of why slavery was just and humane. Thus paternalist ideology not only empowered the white male slaveholder, making him master of exterior worlds large or small, depending on the scope of his property holdings, but more emphatically the master of his own household, where white dependents, including spouses, children, and extended families, looked to the master, the head of the household, for both protection and comfort in return for loyalty and obedience. The eventual triumph of paternalism and domesticity as ideals of a slaveholding society linked a traditional and often defensive cultural worldview firmly to the idea of the household as the primary social unit and the male as the household head, creating a social grounding for cultural conservatism in the American South that proved difficult to dislodge over many generations.[34]

Yet the early paternalist arguments advanced by Moultrie, Johnson, and Botsford between 1800 and 1815 represented merely a first distillation of fuller and more rounded explications of paternalism and slavery as a domestic institution that would be articulated during the Missouri debates of 1820–21, in famously succinct form by Richard Furman in 1822, and later by John C. Calhoun in 1837. During the Missouri debates, Georgia senator Freeman Walker declared that southern slaves were "well clothed" and "well fed." Kentucky senator Richard Johnson asserted that every master stood as the "guardian" of his or her slaves. And South Carolina senator William Smith invoked paternalism when he declared that "the whole commerce between master and slave is patriarchal."[35] Richard Furman, writing from an overwrought Charleston in the aftermath of the Denmark Vesey scare, maintained that where paternalism was practiced, slaves "become part of his [the master's] family (the whole, forming under him a little community), and the care of ordering it, and of providing for its welfare, devolves on him." The authority of the master was an extension of the authority of the parent, and the master's responsibility for exercising that authority well and wisely was as great in the case of slaves as in the case of children. Furman made his case from the Bible, especially in the patriarchy seemingly endorsed by the Old Testament, and he rooted slavery's legitimacy in the evangelical sense of a perfect creation corrupted by sin into a broken world.[36]

Fifteen years after the publication of Furman's pamphlet, Calhoun invoked a very similar and memorable domestic metaphor during a congressional debate over abolition petitions. Predictably, Calhoun, who kept his religious views private, made his stand on the ground of political economy rather than religious piety. "Every plantation is a little community," Calhoun explained to the United States Senate in 1837, "with the master at its head, who concentrates in himself the united interests of capital and labor, of which he is the common representative." Calhoun's brief description of southern slavery made no reference to spiritual responsibility or to bonds of personal affection (though he spoke of the latter on other occasions), but his portrait of a slaveholding community was a domestic one, with the responsibilities of the community leader resting with the master.[37]

BUT FOR EARLY paternalists such as Botsford and Johnson, these large and confident claims for paternalism lay a few years in the future. In 1815, the champions of paternalism still fought hard to claim contested ground. In its own way, paternalism was, prior to 1815 and arguably much longer, an insurgent ideology, one seeking both the embrace of the elite and acceptance by the downtrodden. Its spokesmen often assumed the tone of insurgents rather than of an establishment, of the challenger rather than the incumbent. Like Botsford, Furman knew the story of the evangelical insurgency well. He was its product. Born in New York in 1755, Furman moved to South Carolina with his family as an infant. In 1770, Furman's parents left Charleston for the High Hills of Santee. In 1771, influenced by middle-country evangelist Joseph Reese, Furman abandoned his Anglican upbringing for immersion as a Separate Baptist. Self-taught in Latin and Greek, Furman was ordained as a Baptist minister in 1774. Shortly thereafter Governor John Rutledge asked the young Baptist pastor to plead the cause of revolution to reluctant rebels and outright Loyalists in the bitterly divided western Upcountry. Over the following decades, Furman worked to disestablish the Anglican Church in the state (a goal achieved in 1790), to unify South Carolina's often contentious Baptist sects, and to establish an effective organization of ecclesiastical governance for Baptists. In the early years of his ministry, Furman spoke against slavery, but over time he muted his moral opposition to slavery and instead insisted on the necessity of carrying the Christian mission to the slaves. During the first two decades of the nineteenth century, Furman worked closely with Botsford and other Baptists in South Carolina, encouraging their evangelical efforts and giving special approval for their mission to the slaves. In a sense, Furman led the evangelical insurgency in South Carolina, and even if he generally guided it in a moderate direction, he knew its oppositional character well.[38] Calhoun, a full generation younger than Furman and Botsford, could, by the 1830s, speak about paternalism with the confidence of one who believed the issue largely settled. For Moultrie, Johnson, Botsford, and even Furman in 1822, no such assumption was warranted. It took the religious awakening of 1790–1820 to establish a firm base of Christians from which to propagate paternalism, and it took champions of paternalism time to persuade others to embrace it. The triumph of an insurgency required time, effort, and—perhaps most important—an institutional base, the last of which the movement found in the region's evangelical churches and denominations.

In the 1760s, when John C. Calhoun's father, Patrick, sought to establish a Presbyterian church in the upper Savannah River valley, the elder Calhoun could accurately claim that in the backcountry, "many people had never seen a church or heard a sermon."[39] But during the last third of the eighteenth century, Christian denominations gained a foothold in the state, and from the beginning, the conversion of slaves emerged as a major concern of the evangelical denominations, particularly in the slave-rich Lowcountry. Above the fall line, Presbyterian churches appeared in rural areas with the arrival of the Scots-Irish (like Patrick Calhoun) from the 1760s through the 1780s. Baptists made headway in the upper Piedmont and in South

Carolina's northeastern or Pee Dee section. As early as the 1770s, a Massachusetts-born Baptist, Elhanan Winchester, a minister of strong if sometimes muted anti-slavery views, built a strong congregation with a huge slave component at the Welsh Neck Baptist Church in the Pee Dee region of South Carolina. Winchester held revivals and used his magnetic personality to bring at least 130 blacks into the congregation by 1779. At that point, Winchester encouraged the creation of a separate black congregation, and church records indicate that in 1779, "the negroes were constituted into a Church by themselves."[40] In 1782, Edmund Botsford replaced the heterodox and controversial Winchester at the Welsh Neck church, and in time the Calvinist Botsford curtailed the independence of Welsh Neck's black communicants, but he did not end Baptist efforts to win black converts at Welsh Neck.[41] Eight years later, in 1790, a Baptist minister from the Welsh Neck area claimed that he "preached to 300 [blacks] at a time."[42] In 1784, the first Methodist Conference held on American soil, meeting in Baltimore, sent three revivalists to South Carolina, including Francis Asbury, later a well-known bishop. Asbury preached in Charleston and the surrounding Lowcountry throughout the late 1780s and into the 1790s, often drawing crowds of several hundred listeners, groups usually characterized by their large black majorities. In the heavily black rice capital of Georgetown, Asbury drew an audience of four hundred, which included only twenty whites. In 1794, Asbury lamented the "superficial state of religion among the white people who are called Methodists" but noted approvingly that "the women and Africans attend our meetings."[43]

But if evangelical denominations established a foothold in South Carolina in the second half of the eighteenth century, it took the Great Revival of 1802–5 and the subsequent sustained awakening that swept across the South to secure and expand the influence of evangelical Christianity in the region. The awakening both kindled religious sentiments in people previously uninfluenced by religion and rekindled dormant religious sentiments in many others.[44] Moreover, as Donald Mathews has argued, existing churches and denominational structures moved quickly to consolidate gains made at the revivals by bringing recent converts onto the membership rolls of specific churches.[45] In South Carolina, the Great Revival movement appeared first in the form of a large revival in the Waxhaw region of Lancaster District, near the North Carolina line. The Waxhaw meeting, organized by local Presbyterians and held in late May 1802, lasted for five days and attracted more than twenty ministers and more than three thousand seekers. At the Waxhaw camp meeting, these seekers heard Baptist and Methodist as well as Presbyterian sermons. Reports from the revival suggested that it won more than a hundred converts to the faith.[46] Intrigued by reports, Richard Furman traveled to Waxhaw to observe the revival firsthand. He concluded that listeners "seemed to be seriously concerned for the salvation of souls" and the "preaching" seemed "well-calculated to inspire right sentiments and make right impressions."[47] From Waxhaw, the revival movement spread rapidly throughout the state and continued for at least a decade.

As the revival movement swept through South Carolina, Methodists were the most aggressive participants in the new evangelical efforts. Revivals were often led by the Methodists, who were better positioned than other denominations by doctrine and liturgy to lead the revivals and make converts, whether black or white. In the Lowcountry, the Methodists proved the most successful of the evangelical denominations, converting both whites and blacks in larger numbers than others.[48]

The Methodist message that salvation was open to all, not just some, appealed to Lowcountry slaves, but early Methodism's opposition to slavery appealed even more. The founding Methodist Conference in the United States, held in Baltimore in 1784, declared that slavery violated the Golden Rule and should be eradicated, though perhaps gradually, from Christian society. The conference insisted that Methodist circuit riders not hold slaves. Given the insurgent nature of Methodism during the 1780s, few itinerant ministers owned any slaves to give up, but the ban on slave ownership among them gave the denomination credentials as an antislavery church. Moreover, Methodist preachers often spoke against slavery from the pulpit and in their devotionals, at once alarming many southern slaveholders and driving them away from the denomination but heightening its appeal to slaves.[49] Ironically, some of the strongest testimony to the power of the Methodists' appeal and their special success with blacks came from the carping pens of envious Baptist rivals. Baptist unifier Richard Furman welcomed the evangelical revivals, but he distanced himself from two distinctly Methodist practices: the offering of general communion and the enthusiastic worship liturgy.[50] Furman's friend and fellow Baptist Edmund Botsford agreed, complaining that camp meetings, especially when led by Methodists, quickly became "a place of confusion & not of order." Botsford decried the Methodists' "vociferous manner of conducting worship, in which they seem to glory," and averred that he could not "submit to general communion." Nevertheless, Botsford noted with some envy that in the early nineteenth century Lowcountry, the Methodists "seem to carry all before them."[51]

But the Baptists hardly conceded the field of slave conversion to the Methodists, even if they enjoyed marginally less success in their endeavors. In August 1802, after hearing reports of large-scale camp meetings in the Waxhaw section of the lower Piedmont and along the Little River near the coast, the cautious Botsford assessed the revival movement and concluded that "much good has been done" at such meetings. Even though "some irregularities" occurred at these vast outdoor encampments, the cautious Botsford concluded, "God is certainly bringing many souls out of darkness into light, & from the bondage of sin into the glorious liberty of the sons of God" at these proliferating revivals. "I do not approve of the irregularities," Botsford continued, but in a land "overrun with infidelity," something "extraordinary" was required "to arouse people from such a state."[52] After attending an interior camp meeting in November 1802, Botsford praised the multidenominational gathering for its "good sound preaching, pathetic exhortations & fervent prayers" and reported approvingly that he saw "no irregularity, no disorder, no claping [*sic*] of hands, no raving, nor stamping."[53] Richard Furman also pronounced a general blessing on the revivals, calling them "a blessed visitation from God," and claiming that in the back country, "Baptists decidedly take the lead in the revival."[54] Furman did not "fully approve of the encampments on acc[oun]t of the bad use made by some of the night meetings, etc," nor did he "approve of the general communion—or of those who make so much noise." But Furman concluded that, their excesses not withstanding, the revivals produced "a great and good work of God in the land."[55]

In the Lowcountry, Baptists, like the Methodists, enjoyed far more success in reaching blacks than whites. In October 1808, Botsford noted that he felt "no excitement among any of the white people" in the Georgetown area but boasted that the "poor blacks appear very attentive & some I trust converted, greater numbers still attend."[56] A few years later, Botsford exalted that "the Lord seems at work among the poor black people. Many are attending worship & appear to be very attentive. Last Sabbath morning I baptized 18."[57] In 1816, Furman confirmed Botsford's observation that blacks showed more interest in the evangelical Baptist message than whites. "We continue in Charleston to have some additions," Furman observed, "but chiefly Negroes." And while visiting Georgetown four years later, Furman again noted that he had baptized thirty-two people, "all Negroes, but one."[58] Botsford used the inherent drama of the sacrament to seek more converts. "At my coming out of the water," Botsford reported, "I addressed them [blacks] on the necessity of repentance faith." Botsford decided that the spiritual theater of baptism by total immersion helped level the playing field with the more enthusiastic Methodists in terms of attracting blacks. "I find the Methodists don't like this baptizing often," Botsford claimed, "to but poor negroes. The administration of the ordinance somehow makes strange impressions on many." Reports confirming Botsford's impressions of black preference for immersion bolstered his confidence: "A lady of respectability told me yesterday that she had heard several say that immersion was undoubtedly the right mode [of baptism], & that they liked to see it performed, it made very different impressions on the mind than seeing an infant sprinkled." In a Baptist jab at rival denominations, Botsford added, "No wonder, one is an ordinance of Jesus Christ, the other an invention of man."[59]

As the second awakening matured across South Carolina, churches grew apace as they integrated recent converts into their congregations. In the Upcountry, York District's Bethesda Presbyterian Church grew from 60 members in 1802 to more than 300 by 1805, largely as a result of revivals; Fairforest Baptist in Greenville added 216 new members between 1802 and 1804, and Bethel Baptist of Spartanburg added 247 in the same period.[60] A few years later, in 1809, a series of revivals in Edgefield added nearly a thousand new members to church rolls in the district and drew praise from Edmund Botsford for their solemn tone and the absence of "any noise or falling down."[61] In the white-majority South Carolina Upcountry, the awakening appealed to whites as well as blacks. Church membership grew from 8 percent of all Upcountry whites in 1799 to 23 percent in 1820 and expanded significantly over the next two decades.[62] Moreover, Richard Furman claimed that for every actual church member there were at least six others who accepted Christian teachings but never joined a specific church.[63] Furman likely overstated his claim, but Christians, and especially evangelical Christians, unquestionably enjoyed an even larger following across South Carolina than church membership rolls indicated. Indeed, the impact of the Second Great Awakening on the lower South as a whole and on South Carolina in particular during the first two decades of the nineteenth century can hardly be overstated. Neither evangelical Christianity nor the ideology of paternalism it encouraged achieved hegemony during this awakening, but the years between 1800 and 1820 served as a critical leg of the lower South's journey toward its reputation as the Bible Belt.

As SIGNIFICANT NUMBERS of whites and blacks entered the evangelical fold, whether guided by Methodists, Baptists, Presbyterians, or even Episcopalians, efforts to teach and preach the ideology of paternalism to both masters and slaves became commonplace. In later antebellum years, such studied efforts to defend slavery as Christian, explain the Christianity of slaveholders to a skeptical world, and boast of white efforts to Christianize the slaves flowered into an extensive literature that constituted a significant portion of what historians have rather crudely lumped together as the "proslavery argument."[64] But these earlier messages were generally delivered and heard as sermons or teachings at class meetings or as addresses at agricultural society meetings rather than through pamphlets and essays. Typical, however, of the message expressed in these early efforts to convince slaveholders of the advantages of paternalism and domesticity, and hence of the value of allowing clergy to evangelize slaves, was a tract, *Sambo and Toney: A Dialogue in Three Parts*, written by Edmund Botsford and first published in 1808.[65]

Botsford planned his work with some care, seeking advice from fellow Baptist ministers, including Richard Furman, about both writing and marketing the tract. Acknowledging his strategic decision to focus on the evangelical message rather than character development or entertaining plot, Botsford explained, "My aim is instruction & not to take off characters." The pastor envisioned two audiences for his work. One consisted of skeptical whites, chiefly slaveholders, in whom he hoped the tract, aided by the work of the Holy Spirit, would effect an appreciation for the role Christianity could play in "domesticating" slaves. Botsford believed his tract would be "useful" because the "master will see our [evangelical Christian] intention of communicating nothing that can have a tendency to make his servants worse." At best the evangelical message could make slaves more obediently domestic; at worst it would do no harm. Botsford also hoped churches and philanthropists would purchase his pamphlet for distribution "among the Negroes," a purpose that tacitly revealed Botsford's understanding that literacy was widespread among slaves despite white misgivings about teaching slaves to read. "I think, if I know my heart,"

Botsford confided to Furman with revealing candor, "my views are for the benefit of that class of our poor bedeviled fellow creatures [slaves] who are too little attended by all of us." Hoping to recover the printing costs but planning to keep no additional compensation from the sale of the work, Botsford ordered an initial printing of a thousand copies and planned to sell them at five cents per copy.[66]

Overall, Botsford's *Sambo and Toney* fared well in the market, running through at least three printings. In February 1809, a pleased Botsford informed Furman that he had already enjoyed "pretty good success with Sambo & Toney," having received payments for books sold and orders for another three hundred, to leave him just seven dollars short of recouping the costs of his first printing. Botsford sought to market the book through Georgia Baptist leaders in 1809 because "there are a great many Negroes in and about Savannah," but expressed disappointment that no books had been ordered from Charleston "to dispose among the black people."[67] Later that same year, Botsford received reports that five hundred copies of his pamphlet had been reprinted in Norfolk and that pastors in Hartford, Connecticut, were discussing plans for reprinting it there.[68] *Sambo and Toney* was reprinted again in 1814, and, according to Richard Furman, copies from this later printing sold feverishly in Charleston for many months. Botsford even allowed himself a moment of self-satisfaction when he learned that a ship's captain had reported seeing a copy of *Sambo and Toney* in London.[69]

In many respects, Botsford's popular allegory presented a rather standard Baptist conversion story. Sambo, a slave sold from the Lowcountry to an inland cotton plantation after the death of a kind master, found both Christianity and a second "good" master in the interior. In the tract's first conversation, the recently converted Sambo, returning to the Lowcountry with a load of cotton for sale, encountered an old Lowcountry friend, Toney. Sambo quickly discovered that Toney remained unchurched despite the emergence of an active Christian life around his plantation home in the rice country. Putting his new evangelical faith into practice, Sambo proceeded to proselytize Toney. At first, Toney resisted politely, telling the newly zealous Sambo, "I hope you no one of them religious sort a-praying negroes." Toney reported to Sambo that "we have praying and singing, exhorting and preaching all round us...but I like none on it. I think I'm as good as them that make such a noise...they be hypocrites." Toney insisted that his vices consisted only of a little swearing and a little stealing from his master and a good bit of "dancing and frolicing." Admitting that he wanted to enjoy life while still a young man, Toney promised that he would think seriously about his prospects for the hereafter as he grew older. "[T]ime enough, by and by, when I an old man" served as Toney's refrain concerning religion. Comments such as this by Toney opened the door for one of Sambo's most potent evangelical arguments. Sambo warned Toney that no person was promised a long life, or even tomorrow, and pleaded with Toney to realize that if he died before accepting Christ, his soul might be lost for eternity. As Sambo hurried off to tend his boatload of cotton, his heartfelt concern moved Toney toward a round of soul-searching, in which the faithless slave pondered the frightening possibility of early death and eternal damnation.[70]

At one level, the fact that both the Christian and the unbeliever in Botsford's tale appeared as slaves seems merely incidental to the story. The same story line and dialogue, if not the same dialect, would have fit two whites in the same situation equally well. But as Sambo's efforts to convert Toney proceeded, the issue of slavery impinged more directly on the unfolding narrative, revealing by degrees Botsford's intent as author. As Sambo pleaded with Toney not to risk dying with his sins unforgiven, Toney expressed doubts that reflected his status as a slave. "This religion for white men, not for negro," Toney complained to Sambo, citing a white overseer's declaration that "all black people will go to the devil." Toney also insisted that "the minister never say anything" to "we black people." Sambo disagreed, replying that "the minister preach to every body" and that "the word of the Lord speak to every body alike, white people, black people, rich man, poor man, old man, and young man," and urged them all to repent. Though Sambo's first visit to the Lowcountry ended with Toney still outside the evangelical fold, his proselytizing had at least persuaded the reluctant Toney to grapple with the likely fate of his soul. After the premature death of a young friend and conversations with Davy, a black Christian class leader near his plantation, Toney attended meetings where a white evangelist preached about human sin and divine forgiveness. Toney finally converted, much to the delight of his wife, Fanny, who also joined the church, and his master, a religious man who encouraged Toney in his faith.[71]

On Sambo's next trip to Charleston, he met with Toney again and learned of his conversion. "Blessed be God for his goodness," Sambo exclaimed, praising Toney's willingness to serve as one of "Christ's soldiers." While seemingly overjoyed, Sambo, ever the Baptist, also insisted on testing Toney's faith with two questions. The second question, which focused on Toney's understanding that he could be saved not by his works but only through God's grace, emerged logically from Baptist theology, but the first question Botsford's Sambo posed rooted the conversion squarely in the context of slavery. "[D]o you now think it no harm to steal from your master?" Sambo asked. Toney replied that he would no longer steal from anyone, whether master or stranger, but Sambo reiterated his point anyway, insisting that the "Christian man no thief." Reassured of Toney's true faith, Sambo promised to visit Toney on his home plantation when possible.[72]

On his promised later visit to Toney's plantation, Sambo met Davy and Toney's wife, Fanny. They shared Christian fellowship, celebrating their growth in faith, and explored, largely through Davy's experienced guidance, the future challenges they were likely to face on their spiritual journey. But in this dialogue, where his characters pondered the practical impact of their Christianity on their daily lives, Botsford inserted strong passages designed to convince his white readership of the advantages that the Christianization of slaves and the practice of Christian stewardship by masters offered to a slaveholding society. In short, he made his case for Christian paternalism as a means of social control and community security through the dialogue of his slave characters. Reminding whites of the ongoing need to offer financial support for the mission to the slaves, Botsford had Toney, Fanny, and Davy all tout the success of the local white missionary in his ministry to slaves. "Our minister has been one good man for sure," Fanny declared, "all the black people love him too much, he talk so plain we poor black people understand most every word he say." Toney agreed, noting that the minister was "one very good man and love teach we black people." Nor was the broader impact of the mission efforts understated. Davy remembered that when he was a boy "there was hardly any such thing [as the gospel] among black people." Davy proclaimed himself "thankful to God" that now "most every plantation hear the word of the Lord." Davy also believed that his master "would be glad if all we black people was converted."[73]

But even more important to Botsford than highlighting the importance of evangelical ministers and Christian masters as instruments of conversion was the desire to emphasize the practical results of these conversion efforts on the overall character and conduct of slaves. Having praised God and white masters for the spread of Christianity, Botsford's Davy went on to explain the responsibilities of Christian slaves. The word of the Lord, Davy related to his brothers and sisters of faith, instructed believers "to do our duty to God and master, it tell us how to be content and not murmur, and be honest, and how we should love our wives and take care of our children, and try to live in peace with one another, and as much as we can with everybody." Davy taught the idea of domesticity as well as the gospel of Salvation. A life of peaceful witness, Davy insisted, served God better than "to wrangle and quarrel and murmur." Sambo agreed, and before leaving to return upcountry, he admonished his fellow Christian slaves to "let your whole conduct be sober and steady as becoming men professing godliness. Learn to be content with what you have, and guard against a murmuring, discontented spirit.... Mind your master's business, and be obedient to him in all things, pray daily for him and his family." Slaves who lived in faith, Sambo exulted, would one day be received into the "world of joy and peace, where sin and sorrow cease," and where, "with all redeemed of the Lord," the faithful "will sing the song of Moses and the Lamb." Only in a reference to the afterlife did one of Botsford's slave characters mention Moses, the emancipator of Hebrew slaves from Egyptian bondage.[74]

Lurking just beneath the powerful conversion story, where the fear of hell joined the love of God in winning another slave for the Baptists, lay a not-too-subtle story of the domestication of slavery. Told entirely from the perspective of black slaves, *Sambo and Toney* represented an elaborate effort by Botsford to convince the white portion of his audience that missionary efforts directed toward slaves not only saved souls but also rendered bondsmen more domestic—more receptive to paternalism, more accepting of their status in southern society as they anticipated their eternal reward. In Botsford's account, the once indifferent Toney not only renounced his sinful (and slightly disruptive) ways but also embraced paternalism, as had Sambo and Davy before him. In doing so, they not only received Christ as savior but also accepted the earthly authority of the master, the sanctity of family life, and the notion that their conduct as slaves should reflect their "godliness." Moreover, Toney, the freshly converted slave, openly embraced a new concept of domesticity for life in his own household. "I have always loved my wife, and now I love her more than ever," he declared to Sambo after his conversion.[75]

As a whole, Botsford's tract attempted to convince whites they should support efforts to Christianize slaves as a means of making slavery work more smoothly by rendering slaves more faithful and obedient to their earthly masters. As Botsford portrayed it, paternalism strengthened slavery by making the institution depend less on coercion and more on acceptance and cooperation. Toward that end, Botsford's prepublication consultations had focused on how to use language to convey the virtues of Christian domesticity to both slaveholders and slaves. In particular, Botsford pondered the appropriate dialect in which to write his black voices. After receiving advice from Furman and others, Botsford decided to let the three chief slave protagonists, Sambo and Toney, and Toney's wife, Fanny, all either recent converts or still unbelievers, speak "something more in the Negro stile [*sic*]," while Botsford presented Davy, a longer-term Christian and a class leader, as "one who can read and having conversed frequently with the minister," speaking with a less distinct black dialect. To be sure, Botsford also thought that his choices would allow the pamphlet to reach a larger audience because his language would "suit the whole state at large better than strictly the low country lingo."[76] But it is also clear that Botsford's decision to have the slave Davy, the mature Christian, speak in a voice that sounded less like that of the unconverted and recently converted slaves strongly suggested to readers the role Christianity could play in domesticating slaves, in rendering them less African and more American, less rebellious and more obedient, and less threatening and more familiar.

As activists in an insurgent movement, Botsford and paternalism's other early advocates knew the limits of its influence, but they remained confident that its influence was expanding rather than contracting. In an unpublished essay, "On Slavery," written around 1812, Botsford lamented that the practices of slave management too often fell far short of the prescribed paternalist ideal. Slave punishments were too often severe, Botsford conceded. Indeed, for all his effort to spread paternalism and for all his work instructing Christian slaves to obey their masters, Botsford hardly emerged as a defender of slavery, even when the system's worst excesses were eliminated by paternalism. "Upon the whole," Botsford concluded, "Slavery is attended with many evils & I wish not to defend it." After all, "slavery in its best state is a very great evil." He believed, however, that the triumph of Christian paternalism "would continue to meliorate" the treatment and condition of slaves until "some way and means shall be fallen on for their emancipation," a project Botsford thought "must be a work of time." Though Botsford was an evangelist for paternalism, his views appeared more like those of a gradual emancipationist from the upper South than those of the handful of Lowcountry rice planters who regularly listened to his sermons in Georgetown. By conceding that slavery remained an evil and looking toward a carefully calibrated emancipation at some unspecified future date, Botsford remained more critical of slavery than the bulk of his white Lowcountry parishioners. His underlying reservations about slavery established his kinship with many others in the evangelical movement, including the young Richard Furman, Methodist bishop Francis Asbury, and at least a half dozen Presbyterian pastors in the Upcounty who challenged their congregations on the subject of slavery before deciding to mute their concerns and concentrate their energies on the religious instruction of slaves. But, despite his lingering conviction that slavery was an evil, the body of Botsford's writings on slavery echoed the arguments of Johnson and Moultrie that the treatment and condition of slaves were steadily improving under the application of Christian paternalism.

A key paternalist selling point to masters was that Christian slaves, when managed properly, were hardworking, obedient, and well behaved. Appealing to slaveholders' account ledgers as well as to their consciences, Christian paternalists told masters that the best way to ensure a loyal and easily managed slave labor force lay in supporting the religious instruction of slaves. But paternalists did not hesitate to challenge masters about their own stewardship obligations, which included fair treatment, adequate provisions, respect for family, and the nurturing of Christianity among slaves. Masters, paternalists insisted, had a compelling moral obligation as well as a secular interest to treat slaves as if they were part of an extended family.[77]

However imperfectly the paternalist ideal touted by Moultrie, Johnson, Botsford, Furman, and many other southern champions of paternalism was implemented or how hypocritically this ideal was embraced by masters, the ideology of paternalism clearly gained adherents and influence in the lower South during the first two decades of the nineteenth century. Over time, paternalism gradually became the dominant trope by which slaveholders understood their position and responsibilities and through which they justified their position to the larger world.[78]

But during the first two decades of the nineteenth century, the paternalist ideal and the conception of slavery as a domestic institution remained insurgent ideals in a region where slavery had flourished for generations. As Jeffrey Young has noted, "dissenting conceptions about the master-slave relationship persisted" even as the evangelical enlightenment taught the ideals of paternalism and domesticity to southern society.[79] These conflicting views of slavery and slaveholding confronted paternalism at virtually every point of its rise. In its insurgent years, the argument for paternalism received a lukewarm and even skeptical reception from substantial segments of the southern slaveholding community. Thus the emergence of paternalism as an articulated social ideal proved contested and tentative during the first quarter of the nineteenth century, and perhaps longer, as earlier conceptions of slavery and competing ideas of slaveholder values and proper slave management retained significant influence among white southerners.[80]

THE CONCEPTIONS OF SLAVERY that flourished in the lower South before the emergence of paternalism hardly constituted a coherent ideology, but rather consisted of loose and sometimes contradictory sets of notions, practices, and traditions, often based on particular local needs and experiences. If they shared a central tenet, however, it was a belief that coercion lay at the heart of successful slave management and should be used as frequently and forcefully as needed to render the slaves' obedience complete.[81] The pre-paternalist emphasis on coercion as the foundation of slavery grew in part from the eighteenth-century white fear of African slaves as robust warriors. The same discernment that prompted South Carolina slaveholders to view creole or country-born slaves as more manageable than African imports led slaveholders in the lower South to conclude that recently imported African slaves respected only superior force.[82] Reliance on coercion as the best means of slave management was also rooted in eighteenth-century experience, in which the Stono Rebellion, along with memories and myths growing from it, news of unrest and rebellion in the Caribbean slave colonies, and the restlessness, rebellion, and flight of slaves during the American Revolution, efforts now described as the "largest slave rebellion in American history," affirmed white perceptions that slavery could be maintained only through the iron fist of force. Thus late-eighteenth-century slaveholders still deemed severe and even draconian punishments as central to slave control, and they saw overweening displays of slaveholder power as the best means of intimidating slaves into line. The slaveholding elite in the lower South made few apologies for the severity of its regime.[83]

Yet as a practical matter, eighteenth-century masters often found that relying heavily on coercion as their chief of slave management proved counterproductive. Thus the actual practice of slavery in many parts of the lower South conceded slaves considerable autonomy over their own work routines and off-time activities (whether work or leisure) and even significant freedom of movement. Such calculated leniency helped the institution function economically, as slaves not only produced but transported and sold goods for their owners while at the same time providing for their own subsistence and engaging in informal market activity for their own benefit.[84] Indeed, in some parts of the lower South, especially in the port cities of Charleston and Savannah and the nearby tidewater rice plantations, a well-documented looseness characterized the day-to-day operation of slavery. In Charleston and Savannah, slave artisans and mechanics routinely "hired out" from their masters, often worked for extra money on their own time, and commonly worked and sometimes lived with minimal white supervision. Other slaves, and especially slave women, served as vendors in the city markets, and house slaves often enjoyed considerable freedom of movement and association in the cities.[85] On the nearby tidewater rice plantations, the prevailing task system often allowed slaves time to garden for themselves and even to market their produce. Task slaves usually worked with a minimum of supervision. Some plantations were at times controlled almost entirely by black drivers, and masters were usually absent for several months out of every year. The goods slaves produced and the jobs they did for whites as part of their involvement in informal gray-market economies rendered life more convenient for whites while giving at least some slaves a modicum of autonomy.[86] This looseness of slavery as a working institution, particularly in urban areas, might be termed the "old accommodation," an informal understanding in which slaveholders who were committed ideologically to the maintenance of slavery through coercion and overwhelming force tacitly agreed in practice to a laxity of discipline and control that allowed some slaves privileges within the larger confines of a very brutal institution. Slaveholders made this accommodation precisely because such flexibility made them richer and their lives more convenient. Yet such calculated leniency in the slaveholding regimen necessarily coexisted uneasily with the pre-paternalist belief that the security of white society depended on the ability of slaveholders to strike fear into the hearts of slaves.

The draconian eighteenth-century view of slave discipline and the looseness of the "old accommodation" were separate parts of the same self-contradictory whole.[87] The tension between the need for forceful control of slaves and the flexibility required for optimal economic return from slave labor that characterized the "old accommodation" remained a central contradiction in pre-paternalist slavery. Champions of paternalism argued for smoothing out the contradictions of slavery, both in ideology and practice, and rendering these part of a coherent, domestic whole, creating a labor and social system based on the model of the patriarchal family. They saw an opportunity to replace the ideological inconsistencies of pre-paternalist slavery with the ideological coherence of paternalism. Paternalists maintained that excessive reliance on coercion as a means of slave control not only failed to produce efficient labor from slaves but also left southern slaveholders exposed to outside criticism of their peculiar institution for its brutality. These advocates of domesticating slavery saw the need for melioration of the conditions of slave life and considered paternalism the means. At the same time, paternalists often worried that the "old accommodation" encouraged moral laxity among loosely supervised slaves. Paternalists saw themselves as champions of morality and discipline and sought to render slavery more domestic by giving it a sense of order and discipline as well as a sense of kindness and reciprocal affection.

The principal conflict between paternalists and their critics remained the hoary pre-paternalist maxim that slavery must be maintained primarily through force. Even though pre-paternalist slaveholders accepted accommodations with slaves that diminished the frequency with which they resorted to physical coercion, they continued to insist that overweening power served as the key to effective slave control. Adherents to pre-paternalist attitudes worried about the growing influence of evangelical Christianity generally and especially feared the dissemination of evangelical ideas among slaves. Some slaveholders were concerned that the influence of evangelicalism, with its teachings of love and forgiveness, might render masters too kind or too soft to discipline slaves appropriately. Paternalists, in turn, worked hard, publicly and privately, to counter this indictment by insisting that firm discipline stood as a central paternalist obligation.[88] In 1816, while away from Charleston tending to affairs on his plantation in the High Hills of Santee, Richard Furman learned from his wife at home that she was having "much Trouble and vexation from the bad conduct" of "unfaithful servants." The pious clergyman immediately vowed to "do something effectual toward removing the Evil" when he returned to Charleston.[89] A year earlier, Charleston's William Johnson explicitly denied that paternalism countenanced "misplaced" lenience or "unsteady government." To the contrary, Johnson argued, a paternalist's "model government of slaves" ought to be "that of a well-disciplined army." Johnson knew that in order to win adherents among legions of skeptical slaveholders, paternalism must be seen as an effective method of slave control. Paternalism required that a slave be held to a standard of "rigid obedience," but in return he or she was to receive "every thing necessary to primary wants, and every comfort that his condition admits of." The "fear of the lash," Johnson explained, could compel only "reluctant services," but paternalism could nurture a "generous motive for obedience" among slaves and inspire work performed with "alacrity and affection." The paternalist ideal found fulfillment, Johnson explained, where the slave "is treated indeed as a bondsman but still as a man—where, whilst respect and a faithful discharge of the duties assigned him are exacted in the one hand, on the other he is treated with kindness, humanity and encouraging benevolence."[90]

While allowing for the measured "correction" and corporal punishment of disobedient or dangerous slaves, southern paternalists nevertheless maintained that the idea of domestic slavery rested primarily on a sense of mutual respect and obligation, with coercion and force only as a last resort. Paternalists urged not merely the wisdom but the moral necessity of restraint in meting out corporal punishment and taught masters to use kindness and persuasion rather than threats and punishments in their governance of slaves. To be sure, the paternalist teachings of religious leaders went roundly ignored on many farms and plantations, and even some masters who were members in good standing of Christian churches repeatedly failed to live the values they professed, though they risked sanction by their churches for their backsliding. Yet while the fear that evangelical slaveholders might not prove tough enough to maintain discipline on farms and plantations proved largely unfounded in practice, it nonetheless flourished among skeptical slaveholders for many years.[91]

If many slaveholders worried that paternalists failed to discipline their slaves effectively, even more slaveholders doubted that the religious instruction of slaves was prudent. They feared that it filled slaves with the idea of Jubilee and redemption and threatened to encourage ideas of rebellion and noble sacrifice. Too much encouragement of religious instruction and religious thinking among slaves, skeptics of paternalism reasoned, inevitably promoted dissatisfaction and rebellion. This long-standing prejudice against religious instruction of slaves grew in part from the openly antislavery stance taken first by Quakers and then by many Methodists in the last quarter of the eighteenth century. The secular slaveholder suspicion of religion emerged from the simple logic that instruction in Christianity led slaves to a belief that they enjoyed equality with whites in the eyes of God. In particular, the Old Testament story of Moses, in which a divinely anointed leader heroically led Hebrew slaves out of bondage, offered nineteenth-century black slaves in the South a powerful biblical example of successful rebellion blessed by the Almighty. If such heroic and messianic visions tempted slaves toward unrest and rebellion, slaveholders reasoned, the whole venture of Christianizing slaves became problematic.

But the biggest fear among slaveholders centered on the evangelicals' insistence on teaching slaves to read. In the minds of paternalism's opponents, teaching slaves to read not only enhanced the possibility that slaves would focus on biblical passages that whites wanted slaves to ignore, but also provided slaves with a skill they could use for other purposes—forging passes, sending notes, keeping up with the news, and much more. Nothing about the effort to domesticate slavery threatened the pre-paternalist slaveholding order as much as the desire of evangelical paternalists to teach slaves to read.[92] Yet in the face of intense criticism on this point, evangelical leaders, including clergy such as Richard Furman and Edmund Botsford, insisted that any Christian should be able to read Holy Scripture for him- or herself. In arguably the paternalist insurgency's darkest hour, Furman argued that the "Scriptures are given to Man (*without respect of persons*) to make him wise unto Salvation" and thus "all are required, by Divine Authority to read them, because they contain the Words of Eternal Life" (emphasis added). Because all were required by God to read the Word, evangelicals believed, slaves must be taught to read.[93] This belief not only cost evangelicals support in some quarters but also led them into conflict with civil authorities where white safety depended on the tight control of slaves.

Skepticism of efforts to convert slaves to Christianity and the related concern over teaching slaves to read remained especially strong among both Anglican and unchurched planters in the black majority regions of South Carolina and Georgia. As late as 1807, the ever-vigilant Jacob Read, who had warned South Carolina governor John Drayton about insurgent Methodist literature in 1800, still viewed the continued exertions of evangelicals who sought to spread the gospel among slaves with alarm. "It is vain to conceal from ourselves," Read maintained, "the fact that there are spread every where through the state [South Carolina] the religious and other enthusiasts who are preaching very dangerous doctrines and inciting in our black population sentiments that must lead to fatal results." Nothing "but their want of a common head & someone daring enough to make the attempt and in a degree capable of directing their measures," Read concluded, "prevents their carrying into a most sanguinary execution." Read's fears were twofold. He worried about the possible antislavery views of the religious enthusiasts who spread the gospel in the lower South, and he worried that, even without pastoral encouragement, slaves who could read would eventually seek a black Moses to led an effort to reprise the Exodus saga on Lowcountry soil.[94] Other slaveholders offered additional reasons for disliking the paternalist message. Contradicting paternalist claims that converted slaves made good plantation workers, Read's fellow Federalist Ralph Izard believed that Christian slaves worked less hard than others.[95] A few years later, Hugh McCauley, overseer on one of Isaac Ball's Lowcountry plantations, made the same judgment. The overseer reported that he had improved the work habits of Ball's slaves by "putting a stop to this pretended religion." Once he banned nighttime religious meetings on the plantation, McCauley claimed, "the negrows git theare rest at nights & don't give half the trouble by lying up and pretending to be sick when nothing but the want of rest was the matter."[96] In 1810, the aging founder Charles Cotesworth Pinckney admitted that his efforts to organize a Bible society in Charleston faced strenuous opposition from Lowcountry planters wary of the penchant of such societies for making Bibles available to literate slaves. Pinckney personally discounted the swirling concern about giving Bibles to slaves, but his "opponents," the Federalist elder statesman claimed, "are apprehensive...that it [a Bible society] will have a tendency to excite disturbances among our domestics."[97]

Nor were the fears of Read, Izard, Ball's overseer, and Pinckney's opponents and other Lowcountry slaveholders completely unfounded. Evangelical appeals captured the attention of many South Carolina blacks, slave and free, during the second awakening, and many evangelical leaders were unrelenting in their effort to teach converted slaves to read. By 1810, the sheer number and proportion of slave and free black evangelicals in the South Carolina Lowcountry gave both concerned slaveholders and civil authorities pause. The copious records kept by the regional Methodist conferences in South Carolina confirmed the growing importance of Methodism as a religion of slaves and free blacks, especially in the Lowcountry. In 1790, only 16 percent of all members of Lowcountry Methodist churches were black, but black membership rose rapidly to 37 percent by 1800, more than 53 percent in 1810, and more than 60 percent in 1815. As a rule, Baptist scribes and clerks failed to break their congregations down by race in church records prior to the 1830s, but scattered impressionistic evidence and suggestive statistics from later decades (especially the 1830s) indicate that blacks constituted substantial proportions, and often majorities, of growing Baptist churches in the Lowcountry and significant minorities in the congregations of the smaller but more numerous Baptist churches of the whiter Upcountry during this era.[98] In 1827, just two years after Richard Furman died, his former church, First Baptist of Charleston, had more than eight hundred members, three-fourths of whom were black.[99] At Edmund Botsford's old church, Georgetown Baptist, a racial breakdown of membership showed blacks outnumbering whites twelve to one. In the same era, at Congaree Baptist, located in a rich plantation area just east of Columbia, blacks outnumbered whites ten to one, and at Columbia's First Baptist, a nullification-era census of members showed 60 whites and 240 blacks.[100] Doubtless these black membership proportions from the late 1820s and 1830s reflected heavier proportions of black members that would have counts taken in 1810 or 1815, but the pattern was clear. Evangelicals enjoyed remarkable success in winning slave converts, especially in the Lowcountry, where slaves constituted a large proportion of the overall population.[101]

The numbers and proportions of black evangelicals alone justified the concerns expressed by skeptical slaveholders about the evangelical mission to the slaves. But the mode of church organization and the strategy employed to advance the evangelical effort gave such critics even more substantial grounds for complaint. Even though the denominations, and with a few exceptions individual churches, remained under white control, their aggressive efforts to win slave converts led both Baptists and Methodists to actively involve blacks in their teaching and preaching efforts. Ultimately, both denominations allowed their black congregants a much greater measure of autonomy than many masters and civil authorities considered acceptable. As early as the 1790s, Bishop Asbury often designated black class leaders to teach and "minister" to groups of black Methodists in the Lowcountry.[102] Charleston Methodist pastor William Hammett devised an elaborate system for sending trusted black "exhorters" from his Charleston church into the surrounding countryside to win slave converts as early as 1793.[103] In 1800, Methodist bishops in the lower South received permission from the General Conference "to ordain local deacons of our African brethren" in "places where they built a house or houses for the worship of God." The Methodists' ability to ordain black deacons remained contingent on having "qualified" individuals, that is, members who could obtain a two-thirds vote of the male members of his association and a recommendation from the minister of the local circuit.[104] Many of these black Methodist deacons immediately began work on their own plantations and in nearby communities seeking slave converts and furthering the religious instruction of those already converted. In the Georgetown circuit, Asbury won many black converts and allowed them to conduct independent class meetings. In 1811, William Capers, a leader of the Methodist mission to slaves in South Carolina and later an influential bishop, deployed a group of black Christians he called "extraordinary colored men" into the countryside surrounding Charleston to carry the evangelical message to the slave majority on Lowcountry farms and plantations.[105] By 1814, the more than four thousand black Methodists in the Charleston area had their own preachers, elders, and class leaders, conducted their own worship, held their own disciplinary actions, raised their own money, and even held separate Quarterly Meetings.[106] Just a few years later, Trinity Methodist in Charleston had forty-two hundred blacks on its membership rolls and allowed these blacks to organize into more than seventy classes, which often were conducted by a black leader.[107] Even in the more heavily white Upcountry, Asbury generally organized black Methodists into separate classes from white converts and allowed the blacks considerable autonomy.[108]

Again, Lowcountry Baptists followed the Methodist lead, with Baptist evangelists often preaching to slaves with little if any white supervision, selecting leaders from black converts, and using these converts to teach and exhort their slave brethren. In

1790, a Baptist minister in Welsh Neck reported that "God hath done great things" for "blacks in the area" and that he had preached to as many as three hundred blacks at a time, with "not one white present but myself." Moreover, the Pee Dee Baptist pastor continued, "we have several [blacks] in our church who go to the plantations, and preacher to their own color on Lord's day evenings and at other times when we have no service at the meeting house."[109] In 1807, at rural Philadelphia Baptist church in Upcountry Spartanburg, blacks were allowed to attend meetings run by slave preachers and black deacons, but because "the laws of our land forbid negroes assembling without white people being with them," the church appointed whites to attend. By 1823, another small Upcountry church, Big Creek Baptist in the Anderson district, approved the use of black exhorters, who were sometimes allowed to travel outside the county to carry the evangelical message.[110]

But it was in the black-majority Lowcountry that the Baptists, like the Methodists, depended most heavily on black leaders. "Among the poor blacks I have good help," Edmund Botsford boasted from Georgetown in 1812, including "some 3 or 4 who are leading characters in the church are in good esteem by their owners and the world at large; this is a very great help, so far as concerns the black people."[111] By 1819 the role of these black messengers in Baptist evangelical efforts had become so protean that Charleston's First Baptist Church, the church served by Richard Furman, published a complex set of rules and of regulations for black Baptist lay leaders. Baptists scrutinized the claims of blacks, slave and free, who wanted to "exercise their gifts" carefully, as they did similar claims from whites, and they approved roughly the same percentage of black requests as they did those of whites.[112] Throughout the expanse of the Lowcountry, from Mechanicsville just outside Charleston to Cheraw on the Pee Dee near the North Carolina border, Baptist churches allowed their black members to meet separately virtually every Sunday and to function as nearly independent churches, with the Mechanicsville church just cautious enough to insist the meeting be held during daylight, as state law required.[113]

The idea of black revivalists and exhorters traveling around the slave-majority Lowcountry, preaching to slaves and holding impromptu worship services at night or during the slaves' off-times, and doing all this with a minimum of direct white supervision embodied the concerns of paternalism's opponents about mischievous itinerants and roving incendiaries seeking to undermine slavery. The idea of blacks holding their own classes and sometimes even separate worship services with the blessing of established churches nominally controlled by whites, and even the idea of a white revivalist preaching to an all-black audience, proved only marginally less disconcerting to worried slaveholders. And the idea that out of all this religious activity a new and comparatively large cohort of literate of slaves would emerge simply topped off white alarm at the evangelical paternalist movement.

Thus white ministers, revivalists, and lay leaders of the active evangelical denominations knew that they must counter such traditionalist fears of evangelical inclusiveness and its subversive potential. When he wrote *Sambo and Toney* in 1808, Edmund

Botsford understood that views such as those of Jacob Read and other opponents of evangelical paternalism, as well as the caution of Episcopalian clergy, still carried weight. Thus he carefully advanced his case for both the Christian mission to the slaves and the embrace of paternalism as the foundation of the master-slave relationship before venturing on to his most controversial point: his insistence that slaves should be taught to read. On this point, Botsford challenged a conventional taboo of pre-paternalist slavery, albeit one long violated routinely by self-interested masters. South Carolina had passed statutes making it illegal to teach slaves to write shortly after the Stono Rebellion in 1740, but the statute said nothing directly about reading, though elite white opinion in the lower South frowned on teaching slaves to read. Nevertheless, masters interested in using slaves to help procure supplies and market their crops often violated this prohibition and taught selected slaves to write with apparent impunity. Thus masters interested in teaching religion or simply bettering the lives of their slaves frequently flaunted prevailing white opinion and allowed, or even encouraged, the teaching of slaves to read. But the statute remained on the books and public opinion supported the notion that an unlettered slave population remained a key to preventing slave insurrection and limiting servile unrest.[114] In the final pages of his tract, Botsford explained the importance of slave literacy through the characters of Sambo, the converted slave, and Davy, the experienced slave teacher of Christianity. Shortly after Toney's conversion, Sambo admonished him, "Toney, you must learn to read, then you will understand these things more better." Later, Davy reported to Sambo that "Toney and his wife are both learning and will soon be able to read the word of the Lord." Davy also insisted that no one was "too old to learn" to read. Literate slaves could nurture their own faith and help bring others to Christ through reading scripture.[115]

Botsford carefully placed his encouragement of slave literacy near the end of *Sambo and Toney* because he understood the controversial nature of that portion of his message. But Botsford's elaborate advance preparation for writing also revealed his desire to push the cause of slave literacy. In his conscientious efforts to choose the appropriate dialect for his slave characters, Botsford concluded that he should not go too far in the direction of authenticity. Thus he decided against using the unique "Low country lingo" (Gullah) that slaves from the region inhabited by the fictitious Toney and Sambo would have used. He made this decision in an effort to gain the largest possible black readership. "[W]ith the Negroes there is a great diversity in their manner of expressing themselves," Botsford explained, but slaves "who can read learn to read by our own common spelling & would be at a loss to read their own lingo as we could spell it."[116] Again, Botsford's strategic writing decisions revealed much about the slaveholding world in which he lived, or at least about his informed perceptions of that world. First, Botsford knew that despite the best efforts of men such as Jacob Read and others to discourage the practice, many slaves had been taught to read, no small number by religious instructors, whether white or black. He knew that the language these slaves read differed in significant ways from the one they spoke and that the spoken word varied much more widely than the written word. To reach slave readers, an author needed to write not in the dialect(s) spoken by blacks but in the language in which the literate black minority had been taught to read. If Botsford had thought there was an insignificant or unimportant number of slave readers, he hardly would have given the issue as much prayerful consideration as he did.[117] Botsford's studied eagerness to reach slaves who could read, and his choice of a dialect that he felt would be most accessible to slave and free black readers, indicated that he and other evangelicals, though well aware of the intolerance of many planters on the subject, still saw slave illiteracy as a problem for evangelical efforts. They intended to quietly encourage reading and writing among slaves, especially those who showed a penchant for serving as leaders in the church.

Botsford also recognized that opportunities to teach and preach to black slaves would become much more abundant if slaveholders understood the impact of Christianity on slaves as one of domestication. In his mind, there were two ways for slaveholders to reach such an understanding of evangelical Christianity's impact. The most direct way was for slaveholders and other whites to become evangelicals themselves and embrace the evangelical vision as their own. The other way, and perhaps the more probable given the indifference of Georgetown-area whites to Botsford's evangelical appeals, was for whites to notice the improved behavior and countenance among slaves who professed Christianity. On one occasion, after overhearing a white person observe that "the Baptist negroes behaved well," Botsford claimed that he experienced "no greater joy than to hear that my children [slave converts] walk in truth."[118] In Botsford's view and that of many other evangelicals, Christianity offered salvation for slaves and the way to the domestication of slaves for masters. To be sure, Botsford's motives, notwithstanding his sincere zeal for winning black converts, hardly countenanced the messianic or millenarian expectations some slaves ultimately derived from evangelical Christianity. But even if the evangelical churches did not advocate emancipation, their emphasis on conversion and the role literacy played in the nourishment of the evangelical faith certainly made them institutions that troubled the dominant slaveholding culture.

DESPITE ITS GROWING INFLUENCE, paternalism in the lower South still regularly confronted formidable opposition rooted in dissenting conceptions of the proper master-slave relationship. Such opposition posed a serious threat to the success of paternalism in the first two decades of the nineteenth century and beyond. Champions of paternalism still had to convince skeptical and even hostile slaveholders that their notion of stewardship would prove tough enough to maintain slave discipline and prevent insurrection. Both religious skeptics and liturgical Christians doubted that the new paternalism, with its evangelical outreach to slaves and its emphasis on stewardship, offered effective prescriptions for slave control. In particular, the paternalists' apparent support for teaching slaves to read and allowing black Christians a degree of autonomy in worship attracted sharp criticism from those who saw literacy and autonomy as key building blocks for resistance movements. Paternalism and the idea of "domesticating" domestic slavery gained much ground between 1800 and 1815, but postwar developments reminded paternalists that virtually all ground, including that which they appeared to hold, remained contested terrain. It would take still more time before paternalism would establish itself as the "dominant social ideology" of the lower South.[119] The events of the next decade did little to assuage, and much to alarm, skeptics of paternalism, and they kept its champions scrambling feverishly for the ideological high ground.

CHAPTER SIX

PATERNALISM CONTESTED

The timing of paternalism's emergence proved problematic. The evangelical awakening of the early 1800s and the federal closing of the foreign slave trade in 1808 provided the paternalist movement with needed momentum, perhaps even with its raison d'être. But paternalism also emerged just as a variety of contingencies conspired against its success. The massive migration of whites, and the concomitant forced migration of slaves, to the fresh cotton lands of western Georgia, Alabama, Mississippi, and Louisiana generated a need for strict slave discipline in rapidly developing areas that played against the paternalist message of familial treatment of slaves. The constant tension punctuated by open conflict between the whites who settled the lower South and the Native American population that had long called the region home also encouraged whites to see military and paramilitary force as essential to their survival. And open warfare with Great Britain and the increased fear of slave insurrection that accompanied it worked against the thrust of paternalist ideology by generating a popular taste for force and coercion. Moreover, postwar developments quickly brought two core paternalist projects, the Christian mission to the slaves and the concomitant interest in teaching slaves to read, under direct attack. For paternalism as an ideology of slave control to prosper in this hostile environment, its adherents had to negotiate difficult terrain. They had to prove paternalism a flexible and well-rounded set of ideas capable of handling a variety of contingencies.

THE WAR OF 1812 failed to spawn a deadly slave revolt in the lower South, but repeated rumors of insurrection during the war years wore the nerves of the region's whites raw. As a result, the same postwar nationalist movement that insisted on the need for a stronger, better-integrated Union also generated renewed interest in tighter control of slaves in the lower South.[1] In South Carolina especially, prominent military figures such as David R. Williams, James Hamilton Jr., and Joel Poinsett returned from the war eager to apply quasi-military principles of organization and discipline to the problems of social organization in a slave society.[2] In their view, the lower South's domestic institution, just like the endangered young republic, cried out for better government, improved social organization, and enhanced discipline. To an extent, the need for "better government" of slaves comported well with the paternalists' desire to improve order through the melioration of slave living conditions. But the postwar era's heightened concern over the question of slave control also presented advocates of paternalism with fresh public doubts to assuage, and unexpected developments soon brought such doubts into sharp focus.

The peace was still relatively young when news of two incidents of slave unrest in Calhoun's supposedly tranquil South Carolina challenged both the substance of the emerging ideology of paternalism and the mettle of its champions.[3] During the early months of 1816, South Carolina leaders grew increasingly concerned when the long-standing nuisance of "petty plundering" by a maroon community of runaway slaves, who successfully concealed "themselves in the swamps and marshes contiguous to the Combahee and Ashepoo rivers" outside Charleston, evolved into raids against "the planters in open day" and attacks on "the inland coasting trade" as well. These raiding parties, consisting chiefly of runaway slaves, repeatedly escaped "without leaving a trace of their movements by which they could be pursued" along the Lowcountry's "many creeks and water courses." Earlier efforts by local authorities to capture these raiders had been turned away by the maroon force and thus emboldened the marauders. As these plundering raids increased in frequency and boldness, Governor David R. Williams found both the numbers of the maroon marauders and the arms and ammunition they possessed alarming. The governor feared that continuation of the maroon activity could lead to open insurrection, perhaps on the scale of Saint-Domingue, in the Lowcountry. To end the depredations and prevent further problems with the growing maroon community, Williams mobilized the state militia to locate and destroy the furtive swamp community. The militia's action, which Williams deemed successful, either "captured or dispersed the whole body of the community" and dampened, at least momentarily, white fear of maroon activity. But the very need to call out the state militia to stamp out maroon raiding suggested that white control of slaves in the Lowcountry was precarious.[4]

That same year, South Carolina whites discovered and thwarted a slave insurrection conspiracy in the cotton-market town of Camden, on the fall line of the Wateree River. During the summer of 1816, Camden-area whites learned of plans for an alleged insurrection when a "favorite and confidential slave" informed his master of a plot being discussed among local slaves. According to the slave informant, the execution of the plot was scheduled for the Fourth of July, a day whites traditionally gathered to celebrate American independence. After igniting the local powder magazine as a distraction, the slaves and free blacks would gather in another part of town to seize arms from the arsenal. The rebels would then "massacre whites and burn the rest of town."[5] Believing the report plausible, the master of the informant contacted Governor Williams, a native of the Pee Dee region and a brigadier general in the United States Army during the War of 1812. Williams promptly asked the master in question, James Chesnut, a planter and a militia colonel, to investigate. Later described by his gifted daughter-in-law Mary Boykin Chesnut as "[p]artly patriarch, partly grand seigneur" and "a man of great shrewdness," the fabulously wealthy and politically well-connected Chesnut proved the right man for his assignment, and he eventually received primary credit for both discovering and quelling the revolt.[6] Chesnut's investigation, characterized by Governor Williams as "a counter-plot," consisted primarily of asking his trusted slave to join the plot, attend the organizational meetings, and return secretly to his master with reports of the conspirators' identity and plans. The slave agreed. Chesnut then turned over the information he obtained to the Camden town council for action.[7]

On July 2, the Camden town council, led by intendant Abram Blanding, organized a posse under the guise of a fox hunt. The posse seized at least six different slaves in six different places at approximately the same time to avoid revealing the discovery of the plot to potential rebels in time for them to escape. Subsequent interrogations, under conditions that unquestionably involved torture, appeared to reveal that the planned rebellion, possibly in the works for at least six months, involved luring the local white home guard to a fire at one end of town while slaves and free blacks took advantage of the diversion to seize weapons from the city arsenal at the other end. According to rumors reported by one contemporary, after seizing arms and ammunition, the putative slave and free black rebels planned to "murder the Men but the women they intended to have reserved for their own purposes."[8]

The investigation led to the arrest and "trial" of these seventeen alleged slave rebels in the Magistrates and Freeholders Court. Slaves suspected of involvement were confined in the Camden jail, where they were held "on their backs on the bare floor" and restrained so that they could "scarcely move their heads." With these and other hardships imposed on slave suspects, the council's investigation predictably extracted "ample testimony to convict the principals" at trial. Local whites accepted these statements and "confessions" made under duress by suspected insurrectionists as hard evidence of a well-planned rebellion. During these "trials," every slave "who was most deeply implicated" initially pleaded innocent, but "upon conviction," all acknowledged involvement in the insurrection plan. To the minds of white observers, none of the convicted rebels demonstrated even "the smallest compunction for having conceived and matured the design."[9]

According to the surviving records, a slave named March, belonging to Camden lawyer Chapman Levy, and Jack, a slave belonging to planter Thomas Lang, "attempted and conspired to raise an insurrection." When the state and local authorities arrested March and Jack, a Magistrates and Freeholders Court was summoned for July 3, with five local freeholders joining the existing Kershaw justices of the peace as court members. Previously, on July 2, the town council of Camden examined several witnesses. During the examinations, Sam, a slave of William Lang, reported that he had indeed been approached two weeks earlier by Jack, who, Sam alleged, had asked him to join an effort "to raise an army to fight the white people." Sam reported that Jack had promised that the assembled slave force would be armed with guns "but did not tell him where they were to be got." Sam told his examiners that he refused to join. Other slaves testified that prospective rebels told them that "the black people below wanted to rise against the white people," asked them to join "to fight this country," and warned that the rebels would "kill" the "black people" who "would not join."[10] The accused leaders replied that they "never engaged in any plan for rising," and one accused rebel admitted that he had told recruiters that the proposed insurrection "would be a good scheme if they could get through with it" but that "negroes were so deceitful that it would not do." Ultimately, the court proceedings resulted in the conviction of March and Jack, the two alleged ringleaders, and three other slaves. They were executed by hanging on July 5. The state legislature rewarded the slave informant by purchasing his freedom and providing him a guaranteed income of $50 per year for life.[11]

As news of the alleged insurrection spread across the state, a Charleston newspaper termed it a threat of a "dangerous nature" that had been "suddenly discovered and arrested." The newspaper recommended that all "concerned" with the aborted insurrection "receive summary punishment for their folly and wickedness."[12] By July 10, "compendious reports" of the "attrocious" [*sic*] Camden incident reached the Lowcountry, where anxious observers noted with relief that the "infatuated wretched" slaves who hatched the alleged plot had "confessed their guilt," but worried that "there are probably a number concerned who have not been arrested." Thus, a Charleston newspaper warned, "VIGILANCE *should be the watch-word*."[13]

Throughout July, Camden suffered from "great confusion owing to the fear of an insurrection of the Blacks," as local whites expressed surprise and dismay at the apparent bloodthirstiness of the insurrection plan. According to investigators, the plot called for the murder of an aging white preacher, a nonslaveholder, who had long ministered to slaves and was widely known for his kindness and compassion. Camden's white community pronounced themselves satisfied that the slave insurrectionists had been "tried before a respectable court" and shown "every indulgence" possible "under the existing circumstances." Yet white fears and resentments lingered. Rachel Blanding, the wife of prominent local physician William Blanding and sister-in-law of the town intendant, expressed thinly veiled contempt for the "two or three [alleged slave conspirators who] confessed…and died like heroes." But Blanding reserved her deepest contempt for one rebel "who was a professor of religion" and who claimed that "he had only one sin to answer for": that "he had set down to the communion Table with the white people when he knew he was going to cut their throats as soon as convenient."[14]

Following the execution of the alleged ringleaders of the insurrection plot, however, white Camden residents gradually grew more composed, though many girded themselves for anticipated slave resistance to the stern new disciplinary measures promised by local plantation owners and other masters. Rachel Blanding predicted that slaves in the Camden area would be treated "with more severity than ever" and feared future "trouble" as a result of the harshness of the new regimen. By late July, the aborted insurrection had kindled "such a disgust to Slavery" in Rachel and William Blanding that they pondered moving to a free state. "I think it is time for us to leave a Country that we cannot go to bed in safety," Rachel mused.[15] By late November, however, Governor Williams advanced a different view, praising the actions of Chesnut and other local authorities as "successful" and "judicious." Williams declared that all such insurrection plots would "ultimately" prove "certain of failure," but conceded that white lives often hung precariously in the balance while such plots were discovered and quelled.[16]

During the Camden scare, five slaves were executed for plotting an insurrection, at least a couple of others were punished severely, and the slave informant was both freed and given a guaranteed income for life. No white lives were lost; no record survives suggesting that any whites were even injured. But fresh grounds for a counterattack on evangelical efforts to convert slaves had been generated. In the postscare analysis, the central role allegedly played by slave "professors" of Christianity in the Camden insurrection plot triggered a new round of heightened concern about the evangelical mission to slaves across South Carolina. One wary white Charlestonian, doubtless concerned by the news of unrest in Camden, complained publicly in mid-July 1816 about the nightly religious meetings in his city, attended chiefly by blacks. "Almost every night there is a meeting of these noisy, fanatic worshipers,'" the complainant noted, "Midnight! Is that the season for religious convocation?" Answering his own question, this anxious white, who identified himself only as "H.F.F.," declared, "That the meeting of numerous black people to hear scripture expounded by an ignorant and (too frequently) vicious person of their own color can be of no benefit either to themselves or the community is certain; that it may be attended with many evils is...obvious to every reflecting mind."[17] One Camden resident later recalled his feeling of bitterness when he learned that "faithful servants" of "hitherto unexceptional character" had been identified as leaders of the rebellion plot. A few slaves, he noted, "appear to have been actuated solely by the instinct of the most brutal licentiousness and by the lust of plunder," but most of the putative rebels, he believed, were inspired by "wild and fanatical ideas of the rights of man, and the misconceived injunctions and examples of Holy writ."[18]

In Camden, the local newspaper, the *Gazette*, joined Governor Williams in praising the "vigilance and promptitude" of state and local authorities in preventing the insurrection, but the newspaper blamed the insurrection squarely on efforts by white evangelicals to Christianize South Carolina's slave population. Through its editorial column, the Camden newspaper launched a full-scale attack on the notion that Christian slaves and paternalistic masters reduced the likelihood of slave uprising. "It is Melancholy to reflect that those who were most active in the conspiracy occupied a respectable standing in one of our churches," *Gazette* editor William Langley, a member of the town council who heard the testimony of the accused slaves, opined. Highlighting the participation of black Christians in the alleged insurrection, Langley suggested that such an example of "Ethiopian depravity" should deter all future efforts to evangelize slaves. Evangelicals exercised their "laudable zeal" in "vain," since it was impossible to "inculcate" the "sacred principles of our religion without enlightening the savage mind." Once slaves were so enlightened, the newspaper contended, masters and other whites could not "repress" the "spirit of liberty" that necessarily followed the "acceptance of sacred truths" by slaves. All efforts to provide slaves "an acquaintance with the gospel," the newspaper claimed, had failed to produce the "smallest reformation" of character among slaves. "Chicanery, debauchery, incest, and theft are generally the concomitants of their profession [of faith]," the editor maintained.[19] In the eyes of some Camden-area whites, the Christian mission to the slaves had achieved little in the way of making slaves more honest or obedient.

Moreover, evangelical mission efforts elicited further vilification when it was revealed that two of the slaves charged with plotting the Camden insurrection could read and write. Since Christian leaders often advocated teaching slaves to read so that they could study the Bible and nurture their faith on their own, evangelicals shouldered the blame when literate slaves played prominent roles in fomenting slave unrest.[20] While Edmund Botsford's fictitious slaves pondered salvation, praised familial love, and learned to read in order to receive the gospel, the Camden scare suggested to many whites that slaves actually met to plot rebellion and to ponder the revenge they would enjoy in killing all white males and from "the more brutal sacrifice of the female."[21] The *Gazette* recommended a prompt end to mission efforts. "Receive them [slaves] no longer into our religious fellowship," the newspaper thundered in its concluding statement, "it is incompatible with our interest."[22]

Such frontal assault on efforts to Christianize the slaves ran the risk of overstatement and internal contradiction. Langley attributed a powerful influence to religious instruction when he argued that slaves exposed to the radical potential of a faith that exalted freedom in Christ would no longer accept subordination to earthly masters. But the *Gazette* editor also suggested that Christian instruction had minimal impact on slave morality when he argued that Christianity had done little to remedy the dishonest, mischievous, and lascivious behavior that he believed defined the slaves' collective character. For Langley and others who shared his view, Christianity both so transformed the spirit of slaves as to render then unfit for continued bondage and failed abjectly to mitigate the depravity whites saw in enslaved people of African descent. Despite its internal contradictions, however, the *Gazette*'s indictment of the

Christian mission to slaves and its identification of that mission as a primary cause of the recent insurrection plot revealed the persistent power of the internal southern critique of paternalism on the grounds that it was an ineffective, and ultimately unsafe, method of managing slaves.[23]

CLEARLY THE PRESENCE of slaves who had joined Christian churches among the leaders of the alleged Camden insurrection plot left some whites suspicious of, and others openly hostile toward, African American religious activity. These whites remained unconvinced by the evangelical clergy and lay leaders who argued that the mission to the slaves and the inculcation of the paternalist ethos in masters would eventually produce a more docile, obedient, and even grateful slave population. Thus the involvement of Christian slaves in such plots raised serious questions for evangelical champions of paternalist ideology. Paternalism hinged on the assumption that the triumph of the domestic ideal within slavery was best realized by Christian masters owning and caring for Christian slaves. In and of itself, the Camden insurrection scare hardly reversed the growing influence of evangelical Christianity and the paternalist ethos on either masters or slaves in the lower South. But such examples of slave rebellion seemingly rooted in Christian religious fervor and inadvertently nurtured by paternalist masters raised enough questions about the paternalist strategy to slow its advance and leave it vulnerable to continued attack.

The insurrection scare in the South Carolina interior heightened an emerging uneasiness over the nature and direction of religious activity among slaves and free blacks in both the Upcountry and the Lowcountry. During the second decade of the nineteenth century, slave patrols and biracial gatherings of evangelical Christians met in a series of tense encounters across the state. Acting under the terms of the 1803 law empowering patrols to disperse nocturnal meetings, including religious ones, involving slaves unless whites were in the majority at the meeting, patrols frequently disrupted religious meetings held in the evenings, a popular time for such gatherings because slaves had generally completed their daily work responsibilities by sundown.[24] In some cases, the disruption of nighttime religious meetings occurred frequently enough to constitute a pattern of harassment. Methodist class leaders recalled that unsympathetic whites often went beyond the law and tried to disrupt all religious meetings that featured the instruction of slaves or slave testimony, even those held in broad daylight on Sunday afternoons. Patrols, though perhaps skeptical of the evangelical mission to the slaves, usually ended their interference if the slaves present could produce valid passes and the white evangelicals present could demonstrate control of the meeting.[25]

But in some cases, the patrols embodying the underlying white suspicion of the evangelical ministry to the slaves proceeded recklessly. In Fairfield County, an emerging cotton plantation county just above the fall line, an aggressive slave patrol disrupted daytime meetings of whites and blacks at the Shady Grove Methodist church so often that intimidated ministers refused to schedule services there. Shady Grove class leaders kept the meetings going, only to be disrupted again by an overzealous patrol that whipped one slave, threatened others, and scattered everyone in attendance without checking for written passes. Dempsey Graham, the white Methodist class leader at Shady Grove, tried to bring criminal charges against the patrol commander, John Bell, for the illegal disruption of a religious meeting. But a Fairfield district grand jury refused to indict the beat captain, who promptly brought a civil suit against Graham for damages arising from false imprisonment. In the Fairfield Court of Common Pleas, a local jury ignored the trial judge's instructions and returned a verdict for Bell, the beat commander, ordering the class leader Graham to pay just over $56 in damages. Judging from the actions of the grand jury and the trial jury, local white opinion in Fairfield clearly seemed on the side of the patrol and its suspicion of biracial evangelical gatherings. At the grassroots level, whites, and especially whites in areas with rapidly growing slave populations, showed a willingness to grant slave patrols wide latitude in dispersing religious meetings attended by slaves, regardless of the presence of whites and the prior approval by masters of their slaves' participation in these meetings.[26]

But local white opinion in Fairfield did not prove the final arbiter of the matter. The Methodist class leader appealed the verdict, and South Carolina's highest court, the Court of Appeals, reversed the trial jury's decision and found in favor of Graham. The court vacated the jury award granted to the beat commander, emphasizing that the patrol had not gathered the evidence necessary to show the religious meeting in violation of the state's 1803 law. According to the state's highest court, it was "impossible to ascertain" from the evidence presented whether or not a majority of those attending the meeting were white. Without a clear violation of the 1803 law proven, the patrol had no legitimate grounds on which to disrupt the meeting. The right to worship, the court declared, remained "inalienable" as long as all state laws were honored. This 1818 decision by South Carolina's high court weakened many of the existing provisions limiting biracial religious meetings by requiring carefully documented proof that laws had been broken. In a sense, the court's decision affirmed an informal presumption of innocence for religious meetings. It placed the burden of proving open flaunting of the law on the shoulders of the patrol, whose members repeatedly showed themselves more adept at meting out summary punishments than at systematic collection of evidence. While the law against nocturnal gatherings and meetings with black majorities remained on the books and all future efforts to liberalize South Carolina laws regarding religious assemblies involving slaves failed, in practice patrols and other local authorities generally ceased to harass or disrupt such meetings as long as all slaves had passes, some whites were present at the meetings, the meetings were in no way secretive, and there was no independent evidence of malicious or mischievous intent on the part of those attending.[27]

Such ongoing skepticism about the nature of the evangelical outreach to slaves was hardly confined to the South Carolina interior. After the War of 1812, scrutiny of slave and free black Christians escalated in the heavily black Lowcountry. In 1815, the Methodist Church in South Carolina, aware that the autonomy it allowed its black members fostered continued distrust among whites, altered a number of its practices in order to enhance white control of church activities. The Methodists abandoned their long-standing practice of holding separate quarterly conferences for "colored" Methodists, and white stewards assumed direct control over African American donations (received chiefly from free blacks who owned property or businesses) that previously had been managed by black lay leaders. The Methodists' actions in 1815 appeared to grow out of white concern over the use of church funds. That year, the Reverend Anthony Senter discovered what he believed was a discrepancy in the financial records of the quarterly conference of "colored" members. Senter and other white Methodists feared that black Methodists were using church collections to buy freedom for some of their fellow members without white knowledge. Thus the Methodists ended the practice of separate quarterly conferences and also required that any "church trials" previously conducted in front of black members only must be now conducted in the presence of a white minister. Separate class meetings directed by African American class leaders were allowed to continue, though these remained a subject of some controversy among white Methodists. Overall, the new Methodist regulations restricted black autonomy within the church and, according to leading Methodists, prompted "quite an agitation" among the denomination's large African American membership.[28]

In Charleston, the city's free black Methodists, who had liberally supported the church financially, deeply resented the denomination's new assertion of control over black tithes and offerings. Representatives of the disaffected free black Methodists traveled to Philadelphia to visit Bishop Richard Allen's new African Methodist Episcopal church, the first independent African American denomination in the United States. By 1817, growing black dissatisfaction with the white-controlled Methodist conference led to the withdrawal of more than forty-three hundred African Americans, slave and free, or about four-fifths of the church's total membership, from the Lowcountry Methodist diocese in Charleston. Led by free black Methodist lay leader Morris Brown, a significant portion of these departing black members, both slave and free, formed an autonomous African American church, the Zion African Methodist Episcopal Church, in Charleston that same year.[29] Brown, who remained in occasional contact with Allen and the AME church in Philadelphia, apparently organized the Charleston church in a local hearse house, where it held its earliest services.[30]

The African Methodist church in Charleston held services regularly by late 1817, apparently with the forbearance if not the approval of at least some whites in the Charleston religious community. But civil authorities in Charleston almost immediately initiated a pattern of harassment. In December 1817, Charleston's white authorities labeled the AME services "a nuisance" and arrested more than 460 African Americans during worship. The next year, free blacks and slaves who worshiped at AME services found themselves involved in a series of confrontations with Charleston authorities. Sometime in May 1818, white authorities arrested an entire black congregation that had gathered to hear preaching by individuals whom Charleston whites called "Blacks constituted as Bishops and Preachers in one of the Northern cities." These black preachers had apparently intended to "hold meetings of black congregations exclusively." Upon arrest, they were held overnight and then "dismissed personally by the City Magistrates, who explained the law [against all-black assemblies] and admonished them individually to abstain from a repetition of a like breach of the laws." The visiting African American religious leaders approached the Charleston city council and sought a special dispensation to hold their meetings as they preferred, but their request was denied. In early June, these same black pastors defied city and state authorities and held a "large and unlawful assemblage of Free People of Color and Slaves, as they had done before," in "a house in the suburbs of the City." The city guard broke up this meeting and arrested more than 140 members of the African church, including Morris Brown, who accepted a sentence of one month in jail rather than leave the state, and four other ministers.[31] In the face of such harassment, official disapproval, and public suspicion, Charleston's African Methodists continued their worship and other activities, which were tolerated (albeit with suspicion and animosity) for more than four years. Elder-in-charge Brown, a native South Carolinian, led a congregation of more than fourteen hundred with the help of two other preachers, Henry Drayton and Charles Corr, and at least eight deacons. An AME historian with firsthand knowledge of the Charleston congregation remembered that the church suffered persecution at the hands of whites and was often forced to operate under the most severe restrictions.[32]

In 1820, an impressive effort on the part of the AME church to build a house of worship in the Charleston suburbs attracted determined opposition from Lowcountry whites. Using funds provided by free black donors, the AME church acquired a tract of land in the Hampstead section of Charleston Neck for the construction of a sanctuary where its expanding membership could worship.[33] But area whites bitterly opposed to the independent African church used their clout to prevent the opening of the new sanctuary. A group of Edisto Island planters complained to the state legislature that "a spacious building" had been erected for "exclusive worship" by free blacks and slaves. The Edisto Island petitioners denounced such worship as "highly impolitic and dangerous" and urged the state to banish from the state anyone caught worshiping at the new facility. These Lowcountry whites claimed that "missionaries from the eastern states" had been found "assembling our Slaves and preaching doctrines little short of exciting Insurrection."[34] At the same time, a petition from a large number of white citizens from the city of Charleston proper also complained about the independent African church. Again, the Charleston citizens wrote of a "spacious" building constructed for "the exclusive worship of Negroes and coloured people." These Charleston petitioners declared that the building funds had been supplied from "Abolition Societies" in "the Eastern States." They also assured the legislature that white-controlled Charleston churches had plenty of room to accommodate the slaves and free blacks who were served by the African church.[35]

Aware that they faced strong opposition from some Lowcountry whites, free black church leaders petitioned the legislature for permission to worship in their new building. In an effort to assure whites that the AME church represented no threat to the existing social order, the petitioners promised that "the door of the church" would "remain open always," that all services would be conducted during daylight hours, that white ministers and guests would "always be welcome," that the church would admit no slave to membership "without the approbation of his or her owner," and that "no minister of color who does not reside in this state shall officiate for said congregation." Moreover, the leaders of the Zion AME church pledged to "preserve the utmost order and decorum in the said congregation" and to "inform" against "evilly assigned persons of color." The AME petition enjoyed the support of prominent members of the Charleston clergy. It was signed by Benjamin Palmer, pastor of the Circular Congregational Church and an officer in the Charleston Bible Society, and the pastors of all the leading Presbyterian churches in the Charleston area: Artemis Boies, newly ordained pastor at Second Presbyterian; George Reid, pastor of First (Scots) Presbyterian; A. W. Leland, of James Island Presbyterian; and John Buchan, of St. Andrew's Presbyterian, along with several other white pastors in the city.[36] Additionally, the AME church's leadership believed that its personal connections had secured the approval of Governor John Geddes, a former intendant of Charleston and a member of First (Scots) Presbyterian, for their request.[37]

Despite visible support from prominent white clergymen and tacit gubernatorial assurances, the Charleston legislative delegation recommended rejection of the AME petition, arguing that blacks could find "sufficient room" and would be welcome to worship at a large number of churches in Charleston. The delegation declared that it "cannot approve" of blacks gathering "under their own teachers for religious worship." African American Christians, Charleston legislators insisted, "would be better instructed by well-educated and pious divines in the Churches" of Charleston than "by ignorant and fanatical preachers of their own color."[38] Despite the denial of its request for an approved place of worship, the African church continued to hold services in the Hampstead community for another year and a half, and two additional AME congregations formed, one meeting on Anson Street and the other in Cow Alley.[39]

Though hardly unexpected, the argument of the Charleston delegation against the Zion AME church revealed the circular logic of many lower South whites on the subject of the Christian education of slaves. Lower South whites had repeatedly argued that blacks could not serve as religious leaders or teachers because they lacked the necessary education and training, yet these same whites steadfastly opposed allowing slaves to learn to read and write. The controversy over the independent

AME congregation again revealed the hostility of many Lowcountry whites toward efforts to educate blacks, especially when such efforts were in any way connected with the local AME congregation. In 1820, Edisto Island whites complained bitterly of the existence of "schools for negroes" that were "organized and conducted not only by Negroes and coloured people and other persons of this state" but also by "several Missionary school masters from the Eastern States." Given what Edisto Island whites saw as the "systematick and settled hostility" of "many distinguished characters, the many abolition societies, & the clergy" of the eastern states toward slavery and the "unrestrained sentiments and declarations" made by easterners on the subject, the Edisto petitioners argued that "all such intruders" should be viewed as "spies" who should be "arrested and banished" from the state.[40] City whites also declared schools that "taught reading and writing" to blacks, slave and free, an "evil" of "the greatest magnitude." These schools, white Charlestonians claimed, were "organized and conducted not only by negroes and coloured people" but also "in some instances by white persons of this State." Moreover, the Charleston petitioners complained, during the winter of 1819–20 it became "well-known" that "several missionary-school masters or teachers arrived in Charleston from Philadelphia amply furnished with pecuniary means by the abolition societies of that State for the avowed purpose of educating our negroes." The Charleston petitioners urged the legislature to tighten state laws against teaching slaves to read and write. Teaching slaves to read, Charleston whites insisted, was "mischievous and impolitick and at variance with slavery."[41] To wary Lowcountry whites, an educated slave, even a slave who could read a little, loomed as dangerous, and the fight to keep the lid on the reading genie's bottle appeared a noble, if losing, cause.

For Charleston-area whites, especially Christian leaders, the presence of an active AME church operating largely beyond the control of the white religious community represented a significant practical and ideological problem. For many white Charlestonians, the problems raised by the active AME congregations in their midst highlighted the dangers presented by free blacks. Free blacks had clearly provided the leadership needed to start the church; provided the offerings necessary to fund the church's activity; traveled out of state to find institutional, educational, and perhaps financial support for the new church; and, as the petition to the legislature suggested, provided the church with a civil presence.

At the same time, white evangelicals in the South tended to applaud the success of all Christian witness and church development efforts, and for the most part Charleston's newly organized AME church gave every outward indication of respecting white authority. The endorsement of the AME petition by Benjamin Palmer, an impressive array of Charleston-area Presbyterian ministers, and a handful of other white clerics suggested that some of the most erudite white Christians in the Lowcountry at least accepted the idea of an independent black congregation in the city. Yet these same white Christians accepted the notion that what they termed "a proper understanding" of the gospel required careful white guidance and instruction. They also knew that the future of the entire mission to the slaves depended on maintaining the support of skeptical civil authorities who worried that slaves instructed in the gospel often became slaves unlikely to accept permanent subordination. One Charleston minister, who was not unsympathetic to the position of black Christians, admitted to the religious press that "the jealously of the people against religious meetings, consisting entirely of blacks, and particularly where the worship is to be conducted by them," remained intense. Whites feared such meetings, the pastor explained, because "most of the incipient schemes of insurrection ... that have been detected [a likely reference to the Camden scare], have taken place at professedly religious meetings."[42] Professing white Christians in the South Carolina Lowcountry realized that evidence of rebellious or insubordinate behavior from members of the AME church, slave or free, would endanger the entire evangelical effort to reach the slave population and even threaten the expected triumph of paternalism in the region.

THE THREAT THE EVANGELICAL MISSION to the slaves presented to white security was hardly confined to South Carolina. The evangelical denominations had established a foothold in Mississippi well before the territory gained statehood, and one historian has estimated that by 1817 about one in twenty Mississippi residents belonged to a church. Both Mississippi Methodists and Baptists paid special attention to the mission to slaves.[43] By 1820, there were three Baptist associations in Mississippi and each of them included at least one African church. Moreover, Mississippi's Union Baptist Association's largest church, which accounted for nearly one-fifth of all the association's members, was an African church. And both the Pearl River Baptist Association and the Mississippi Baptist Association also included at least one African church. Black preachers preached to both mixed and exclusively black audiences in Mississippi, and as Randy Sparks pointed out, the independent African churches "attracted more members than did the biracial churches."[44]

The success of the evangelical mission to the slaves and the evangelicals' apparent tolerance of exclusively black African churches as well as biracial churches led some Mississippi whites to conclude that black and biracial religious gatherings needed tighter regulation. In 1822, a revision of Mississippi's code of laws championed by popular governor George Poindexter, a former attorney general, placed severe new restrictions on the slaves' established worship practices. It required that all religious services with blacks in attendance be conducted by a white pastor and prohibited all religious gatherings attended only by slaves.[45] Such regulations were decidedly at odds with the common practice in Mississippi, where a few independent black congregations flourished and blacks routinely attended worship services led by black preachers. Mississippi Methodist leader William Winans complained that the new law represented "a wanton curtailment of the religious privileges of Slaves" and argued that the law had aroused "very general and strong feelings of opposition in all Christian Communities in the State."[46] Sensing popular resentment of the new restrictions, even among white church members, the white evangelical clergy immediately mobilized a political campaign for modification of the law. Winans took the lead, criticizing the restrictive new code at camp meetings and placing the blame for the law squarely on the large shoulders of Poindexter, who was making a run for Congress in 1822.[47]

Though usually exceedingly popular among Mississippi voters, the talented Poindexter offered evangelicals an easy target for criticism. A Virginia native and son of a Baptist minister, Poindexter arrived in Natchez in 1799 and subsequently cut a wide swath through early Mississippi politics, emerging as an "idol of the people" and becoming "closely and prominently connected" with "everything that occurred in the Mississippi territory."[48] A man of unquestioned intellect and insight, Poindexter also developed a well-deserved reputation as a man with an undisguised appetite for excess—in drinking, gambling, and other forms of dissipation. Poindexter stood accused of having fired prematurely in a duel and falsifying charges of infidelity against his wife to obtain a divorce in 1815.[49] Doubtless some of these charges were exaggerated by Poindexter's long-frustrated political opponents, and even the evangelical Winans judged Poindexter as "one of the greatest men I ever knew." But Winans insisted that Poindexter's "tragedy" lay in refusing to allow "moral principles" to exercise "control over his actions."[50]

Poindexter's weaknesses left him open to evangelical criticism in 1822. Both the Pearl River and Mississippi Baptist associations joined Winans and the Methodists in the fight to repeal the new restrictions on slave religion.[51] This concerted evangelical opposition defeated Poindexter's congressional bid, and at its next session the Mississippi legislature modified the law to allow slave religious meetings led by black preachers, provided that services "be conducted by a regularly ordained or licensed white minister" or attended by at least two whites who were members of an established church or religious society.[52] Poindexter immediately expressed mortification at the political strength of the evangelical movement in Mississippi, but even the amended law still left black religion subject to considerable white oversight. The revised law forced independent black congregations to seek affiliation with white churches, and over time, the concessions Winans' campaign won from the legislature encouraged biracial religious activity at the expense of independent black worship. But white Baptists in Mississippi continued to denounce masters who "look upon slaves with no more respect than a dumb beast," insisting that "however sable their hue and however degraded their condition in this life," slaves possessed "rational and immortal souls."[53]

The position of the evangelicals on the cotton frontier of Mississippi in the early 1820s resembled the one they had enjoyed in the South Carolina Upcountry two decades earlier when evangelicals there helped soften a set of worship restrictions favored by Lowcountry planters.[54] Arguably the Mississippi evangelicals enjoyed more success than their counterparts in South Carolina, suggesting that institutionalized opposition to the evangelicals, whether in the form of an entrenched Anglican clergy and laity, a Federalist Party skeptical of any democratic movement in or out of politics, or a wealthy and interconnected planter elite whose influence dated back two or three generations, was much more firmly entrenched in the Lowcountry than along the Pearl River or even in the Natchez hinterland. Yet elite white alarm at the nature of the evangelical mission to slaves in Mississippi as well as in South Carolina indicates that such concern, to varying degrees, stretched across the lower South.

AMID CONCERN ABOUT WHAT ROLE paternalism and the Christian mission to slaves might play in nurturing slave unrest and even rebellion, the postwar problem of slave control extended well beyond questions about appropriate religious instruction of slaves and the degree of autonomy given to black worship. Indeed, fresh postwar examples of slave unrest, highlighted by the Camden insurrection scare of 1816, also accentuated the threat to white safety inherent in the dramatic increase in the number and proportion of slaves in the lower South's population during the first two decades of the nineteenth century. Even though cotton growers in the lower South steadily demanded more slaves, whites in the region nonetheless worried about the region's propensity to grow blacker. Across the lower South, either the ratio of slaves to whites, the absolute number of slaves, or both increased dramatically between 1800 and 1820.

In the older states of South Carolina and Georgia, the slave population grew dramatically in both size and proportion. In 1800, South Carolina was almost 57 percent white, and Palmetto State whites outnumbered slaves by more than 50,000. By 1820, the state had a slave majority of more than 20,000, and only 47 percent of the state's population was white. Moreover, the absolute size of the South Carolina slave population had grown by more than 100,000, from 146,000 to over 258,000, in twenty years. During the same years, Georgia's slave population grew by 150 percent, from just over 60,000 to almost 150,000, and the state's white majority shrank from nearly 63 percent to less than 56 percent. In the newer states of Louisiana and Mississippi, the proportion of whites in the total population fell only slightly during this era, from 59 to 56 percent in Mississippi and from 49 to 48 percent in Louisiana, but by 1820 the absolute number of slaves in both states had increased dramatically since the turn of the century. Estimates place the 1800 slave population of what later became Mississippi at roughly 3,500, while the state's 1820 slave population totaled nearly 33,000. In Louisiana, the number of slaves increased from just under 13,000 in its pre-1803 colonial days to almost 70,000 in 1820. By 1820, only the newest lower South state, Alabama, had a white majority of more than 60 percent. Just one year after becoming a state in 1819, whites in Alabama outnumbered slaves by well over 40,000, with whites accounting for nearly two-thirds of Alabama's total population, a proportion that stood as something of a golden mean in the minds of many whites.[55] White concern over the rapidly growing size and proportion of the lower South's black population revived interest in measures that improved white security by controlling the growth of the region's black population, slave and free. Since individual slaveholders usually desired and facilitated slave reproduction to increase the value of their personal property, lower South states with rising proportions of slaves turned to the regulation of the internal slave trade as a means of slowing the growth of the slave population.

In 1816, just a few months after the discovery of the alleged insurrection plot in Camden, support for an outright ban on the importation of slaves from other states gained strength in portions of the South Carolina interior previously committed to growing cotton and acquiring slaves against all obstacles. Through the fall of 1816, Upcountry grand juries complained pointedly about the dangers posed by the active trade in slaves, even though the identified leaders of the alleged Camden plot were not recent arrivals to the state. The greatest concern emerged in districts along the Catawba-Wateree river system in the eastern Upcountry, an area that was part of Camden's rural hinterland. A York District grand jury complained that "the unparalleled ingress" of slaves from further north represented a "grievance of no inconsiderable magnitude," whether "considered in a moral point of view" or "as a political evil fraught with dangerous consequences."[56] In Fairfield, a cotton-growing district just across the Wateree River from Camden, the grand jury called "the introduction of Negro slaves" into the state "truly distressing." In addition to declaring a paramount concern for the safety of white citizens, the Fairfield grand jury also declared that the importation of slaves threatened the "purity of our Republican institutions" and was "no less afflicting to Humanity and Religion."[57] In Richland, another district neighboring Camden, a grand jury, with planter Thomas Taylor as foreman, decried the "importation of slaves...from other states of the Union" as a "traffic which we think detrimental to the interests and dangerous to the safety of the state."[58] And just across the Congaree River from Richland, a Lexington grand jury presented the internal slave trade as a "grievance." The Lexington grand jury blamed the "dangerous system of Speculation and Negro trading" for the rapid increase in the state's slave population and warned that the trade might have "fatal" consequences for the "welfare, preservation, and existence of our republic."[59] Further upcountry, a Spartanburg grand jury found the domestic slave trade "lamentable" and branded it "dangerous to the Safety of the State."[60]

Predictably, the greatest concern about the internal slave trade emerged in Kershaw District, where Camden was the courthouse town. In mid-November, just over four months after the scare, the Kershaw grand jury, with *Camden Gazette* editor William Langley as foreman, called for an end to "the pernicious tendency of introducing into our state the slaves of another." The Kershaw grand jury pointed to "the evil arising from an overgrown black population in the West Indies or some of our sister states as alarming precedents," and argued that the state had been furnished "abundant proof" of problems emerging from "so dangerous a traffic." The "affair of the 4th July last" in Camden, the Kershaw grand jury insisted, "ought to convince every reflecting mind" of the need to ban the importation of slaves.[61] All of the grand juries that indicted the importation of slaves called for either an outright ban on the trade or the imposition of a prohibitive tax on it. When the South Carolina legislature convened in November 1816, Governor David R. Williams, who had worked closely with Camden authorities to uncover the plot, urged the body to stop the "remorseless, merciless traffic which brings among us slaves of all descriptions from other states" and which stood as "a reproach to our morals and an outrage to our feelings." Though fully aware of the recent insurrection scare, Williams focused his critique on humanitarian concerns. He denounced the "ceaseless cupidity of the trade," with its "crowds of suffering victims" transported and sold at the behest of "insatiable avarice." The "lights of humanity—a wise policy—and the prayers of the just," the governor contended, all required a prompt end to the domestic slave trade.[62]

Pressed by public anxiety over the Camden insurrection scare to respond to Williams' plea, the 1816 legislature banned the importation of slaves from other states without leaving a roll call vote on the subject. A healthy majority of legislators from the heavily black Lowcountry had long been willing to ban slave imports, both to enhance white safety and to increase the value of slaveholder assets, so the passage of the ban emerged from the shift of Upcountry legislators previously committed to keeping the interstate slave trade open. The penalties for violating the new ban were severe and included the seizure and sale of illegally imported slaves, with half the revenue from all the sales of intercepted slaves going to reward informants. District tax collectors were empowered to require slave owners to swear oaths that they had not purchased any slaves in a manner contrary to the law.[63] South Carolina, the only state in the Union to legally participate in the foreign slave trade in the nineteenth century, closed the interstate slave trade less than a decade after the final enslaved African entered the port of Charleston. Different moments and different constellations of interests produced different public policies toward the slave trade.

Though pleased that the legislature banned the importation of slaves, *Camden Gazette* editor William Langley wondered if lawmakers had gone far enough. In a pessimistic December editorial, Langley fretted openly over the peculiar institution's unique capacity to corrupt and degrade the region's white population. The "influence of slavery extinguishes the spark of religious fervor [among whites] and produces cruelty to which is super-added its pernicious effects in a political point of view," the editor lamented. Echoing Jefferson's concerns from the Revolutionary era, Langley conceded that slavery "begets idleness, voluptuousness, and a thirst for power" among whites; worse, it "endangers our safety and destroys our domestic tranquility." Langley emphatically denied rumors that he was "an advocate for emancipation," but he admitted regret that "the policy of our country has not been to remove, instead of introduce, domestic enemies." Langley approved of closing the interstate slave trade, and he mused that colonization might be an idea worthy of consideration.[64]

Few white South Carolinians joined Langley in pondering the merits of colonization as a means of reducing the state's risk of slave insurrection. In fact, within a year, many whites complained bitterly about the state's new ban on the importation of slaves. A Spartanburg grand jury reversed the position expressed by the body a year earlier, presenting as a grievance the fact that South Carolina citizens were "not allowed to purchase Negro property from the adjoining states." The 1817 South Carolina legislature received several dozen petitions from slaveholders seeking exceptions to the law.[65] Critics of the ban on slave imports generated enough support for repeal that at the beginning of the legislative session in November 1817, the new governor, Andrew Pickens, an Upcountry planter from Edgefield, claimed that the "general interest loudly calls" for modification or repeal of the law. On the basis of the state's year of experience with the law, Pickens argued that the "agricultural prosperity" of the state depended "so much upon persons of this description"—that is, slaves—that the ban had damaged the state's economy. The new governor, the first Palmetto chief executive from above the fall line, maintained that the existing law prevented people "who wish to become residents among us" from "bringing with them their slaves, to whom they are attached, not only because they are instruments of wealth and Comfort, but often because they have descended to them from revered and respectable ancestors." Pickens contended that the ban on importing slaves from other states forced South Carolina to "leave their land uncultivated" and deprived the state of prospective citizens of "character, usefulness, enterprise, and wealth."[66]

Throughout the 1817 session, legislators wrestled with the issue of the 1816 ban on slave imports. Neither the House nor the Senate proved willing to heed Pickens' urging to repeal the ban outright. Instead, both chambers considered bills creating specific but limited exceptions to the general prohibition.[67] The House and Senate tentatively approved differing drafts of legislation allowing citizens to import slaves acquired by inheritance or marriage from decedents or spouses in other states and permitting slaveholders to bring slaves they owned in other states into South Carolina without interference. A conference committee composed of members from each chamber had difficulty resolving the differences between the two bills, but on December 18, 1817, the legislature finally agreed on a statute that approved very limited exceptions to the 1816 ban. The new law created a system of special licenses, approved by the county courts, that allowed residents of the state to bring in slaves from other states if they could prove they had owned those slaves before the ban was passed in 1816 or if they had acquired those slaves through inheritance or marriage. This law required applicants to provide extensive documentation (such as wills, marriage certificates, or some other "satisfactory evidence") in order to acquire a license to bring slaves into the state. Such cumbersome legal requirements, as well as the stiff penalties for violators, were included to prevent abuse of the statute by traders.[68]

Undeterred by their failure in 1817, however, advocates of repealing the ban on slave imports pressed their case again in 1818. Fear of insurrection waned as the Camden incident faded in citizens' minds, and emerging Upcountry cotton districts regained their appetite for importing slaves, with some districts overtly reversing their position from two years earlier. In October 1818, a York grand jury complained that the ban was "unequal and unjust" in its operation and demanded either an outright repeal or a modification allowing residents to import slaves "for their own use." A Chester District grand jury claimed that the ban was unfair and "particularly detrimental" to "the interests of the upper country."[69] Governor Pickens again attacked the prohibition of the importation of slaves in his 1818 message to the legislature, terming the ban "repugnant to the interests of many of our citizens." The ban, Pickens claimed, prevented the immigration of "prudent and conscientious men, who would be valuable acquisitions to our society," while it did little to prevent the illegal importation of slaves. Pickens argued that despite the severe penalties imposed and strong enforcement provisions specified by the 1816 law, the ban had grown so unpopular in many areas that it was "violated in many instances with impunity, as no one will incur the odium attached to the character of an informer."[70]

Pickens' call for repeal sparked "eloquent and animated debates" in the 1818 legislature.[71] In the state house of representatives, inland cotton planters, led by John Witherspoon of Marion and George McDuffie of Abbeville, championed reopening the interstate trade. Charlestonians, including state house Speaker and future nullifier Robert Y. Hayne, future Unionist Daniel Huger, and aging Federalist Keating Simons, a leading opponent of the reopening the foreign slave trade fifteen years earlier, vigorously opposed reopening the state to imports.[72] After extended debate, the 1818 legislature voted to repeal the 1816 ban on slave imports. The House approved the final reading of the bill by a large majority, 73–39. The House vote to repeal reflected the continued sectional division on the issue. More than three-quarters of the votes in favor of repeal came from the interior districts, while three-quarters of the votes against repeal came from the Lowcountry parishes. Eight of every nine interior delegates voted in favor of repeal. Two of every three parish representatives voted against repeal.[73] Additionally, Senate votes on reopening the state to slave imports followed a pattern similar to votes concerning the international slave trade during the 1803–7 era. On the key state senate vote on December 2, advocates of repealing the ban on the importation of slaves prevailed narrowly, 22–19. The traditional division between the interior cotton districts and the Lowcountry parishes shaped the outcome. Senators from interior districts favored reopening the interstate trade by a margin of 15–9. Camden's Chapman Levy, the senator from Kershaw District and owner of two of the slaves executed as leaders of the Camden insurrection, joined the Upcountry majority voting to reopen the trade. Yet senators Robert Clendenin of York and John McCreary of Chester voted against repeal, in defiance of grand jury sentiment in their districts. Senators from the Lowcountry parishes voted against repeal, but only by a 7–10 margin. Charleston maintained its hard-core opposition to reopening the interstate trade, with all ten senators representing Charleston and the surrounding parishes voting against repealing the existing ban. However, lawmakers from the Beaufort area joined inland senators in favor of reopening the domestic slave trade, reviving the alliance that had renewed South Carolina's involvement in the international slave trade fifteen years earlier. All six senators representing parishes in the Beaufort judicial district voted in favor of reopening the domestic slave trade, as did one senator from the Georgetown area. With both legislative chambers approving a bill repealing the 1816 ban, South Carolina resumed participation in the interstate slave trade in 1819 after a contentious two-year hiatus.[74]

South Carolina's reopening of the trade doubtless proved popular in the state's interior, where staple agriculture continued its expansion and slaveholders and nonslaveholders alike sought a ready supply of slaves. But doubts lingered in the Lowcountry. During the 1818 session of the state legislature, Senator Thomas Bennett, a successful Charleston merchant and rice miller, cast one of the ten Lowcountry votes against repealing the prohibition on the importation of slaves. Three years later, another legislature elected the ambitious and talented Charleston businessman governor of the state. In his first message to the legislature (1821), the new governor urged the legislature to consider closing the internal trade once again. Bennett decried "the continuation of that inhuman traffic for slaves with our sister states." Through the domestic slave trade, Bennett lamented, "human misery is made to swell the coffers of eager avarice" in violation of both "the calls of patriotism and the mild precepts of Christian charity." The governor urged the legislature to "arrest this enormous evil" and "check a vice whose rapid growth threatens the peace of society." Bennett's passionate appeal went unheeded. But his effort to revive the debate revealed the ongoing concern over the internal slave trade in the South Carolina Lowcountry, where fear of slave unrest remained persistent.[75]

Renewed debate over the trade-off between the potential dangers of the domestic slave trade and the supposed need for additional slave labor also surfaced in neighboring Georgia. Late in 1816, the Georgia legislature approved a tough ban on the importation of slaves for sale or hire. Doubtless influenced by the recent insurrection scare in South Carolina and its own burgeoning slave population, Georgia's new statute levied heavy fines against violators and permitted the confiscation and sale of illegally imported slaves. But, unlike the South Carolina ban of the same year, the Georgia law also allowed residents to import slaves for personal use and permitted emigrants settling in Georgia to bring slaves with them.[76] Even with its loopholes, the new Georgia law still proved difficult, if not impossible, to enforce. Sources suggest that more than eight thousand slaves were illegally imported into Georgia during 1817 alone. In December 1817, the Georgia legislature responded to the continued influx of slaves by banning the importation of slaves altogether, a ban that included slaves owned by prospective in-migrants.[77] Despite the tougher new restrictions, a Putnam County grand jury complained that the ban was widely ignored. It claimed that more than twenty thousand slaves entered Georgia illegally between 1816 and 1818.[78]

In his 1818 legislative message, Georgia governor William Rabun called for stricter enforcement of the ban, complaining that violations had grown "every day more common." Yet Rabun recognized that enforcement languished because the restrictions remained wildly unpopular in many quarters. "[I]t is lamentable fact," the governor explained, "that this abominable trade has so many advocates among us, that an informer, or even an officer...attempting to enforce the law, is by many considered an officious meddler and treated with derision and contempt."[79] The 1818 Georgia legislature added an enforcement incentive by allowing whites who seized illegally imported slaves to retain one-tenth of the net proceeds from their sale at public auction.[80] But the new incentive also proved of little avail. The parallels with nearby South Carolina were striking. Putting laws on the books restricting the importation of slaves, and even writing strong enforcement provisions into those laws, proved possible when citizens were reminded of the threat posed by wayward slaves. But actually sustaining public support for laws that hindered an active trade in the Old South's most valuable commodity and ran counter to the economic interests of slave buyers as well as slave sellers proved well-nigh impossible. Citizens effectively repealed bans and restrictions on the domestic slave trade through both their refusal to comply with these laws and their refusal to inform on others. The Georgia ban remained on the books until 1824, but enforcement always proved difficult, sporadic, and ultimately ineffective.[81]

Further to the southwest, where slaves were still flowing onto the latest cotton frontier in large numbers, concern about the growing size of the slave population existed, but the popular desire for slave labor limited state interference with the active interstate slave trade. In 1818, a year after Mississippi entered the Union, the Mississippi legislature denounced slavery as "condemned by reason and the laws of nature." That same year, Mississippi's leading politician, George Poindexter, told Congress that in his heart he felt a "solicitude to expel from our country, whenever practicable, anything like slavery." But Poindexter added a quick disclaimer. "[I]t is not with us a matter of choice whether we will have slaves or not; we found them here, and we are obliged to maintain and employ them," the Mississippi congressman explained. "It would be a blessing, could we get rid of them; but the wisest and best men among us have not been able to devise a plan for doing it."[82]

Devising a plan to get rid of slavery was one thing, but drafting legislation to limit the growth of the state's slave population through the interstate slave trade was another. The state's original (1817) constitution, crafted at a convention heavily influenced by Natchez-area interests, gave the legislature "full power to prevent slaves from being brought into this State as merchandise," but guaranteed immigrants the right to bring slaves they owned with them when they came to settle. Yet Mississippi lawmakers enacted no restrictions on the domestic slave trade until after the Denmark Vesey scare startled the state in 1822.[83] In neighboring Louisiana, the slave population grew from just under thirty-five thousand in 1810 to roughly sixty-nine thousand a decade later, largely though forced immigration and the domestic slave trade. In 1817, a year after the Camden scare, Louisiana decided that, given the volume of slaves coming into the state, it needed to take decisive action to prevent dangerous and undesirable slaves from being sold into the state. That year, the legislature passed a law barring the importation of slaves who had committed serious crimes. The legislation required the importer to meet the burden of proof that slaves coming into the state had committed no crimes, and the law required as proof a certificate from the clerk of the court in the county from which the slave came. Both owners and traders who attempted to import slaves in violation of the law were subject to stiff fines. Little evidence survives concerning the effectiveness of Louisiana's attempt to ban the importation of slaves with criminal records, but such a limited ban arguably represented the least interference with the valuable trade that a state could attempt and still try to placate whites worried about slave unrest.[84]

Across the lower South, legislative flip-flops and inaction produced erratic and incoherent policies that hardly lessened the region's anxiety over the wisdom and safety of the interstate slave trade. On one hand, the scales were heavily weighted with the love of profits earned either by working slaves in the cultivation of staples or by the sale of surplus slaves to eager planters and farmers in fertile new areas further to the southwest. These considerations were balanced against gnawing fears for personal and family safety in a society where slaves constituted an ever larger proportion of the population and showed an occasional penchant for concerted rebellion. States that were already net slave exporters, such as Georgia and South Carolina, could try placing serious restrictions on slave imports because many citizens already had enough slaves, while in the net slave-importing states of Mississippi and Louisiana, politicians showed comparatively little interest in placing meaningful restrictions on slave imports until stronger signs of slave unrest surfaced. But even in the newest cotton states public concern over the importation of troublesome slaves prompted the adoption of measures designed to enhance white security.

Free blacks offered an easier target than the interstate slave trade for politicians eager to enhance white security. In 1820, the entire free black population of the lower South numbered only slightly over twenty thousand, less than 2 percent of the region's total population of nearly 1.2 million. Most of this small free black population was urban, living in port cities such as New Orleans, Charleston, Mobile, and Savannah, with smaller, scattered clusters of free blacks residing in inland trading centers such as Natchez, Augusta, and Columbia. Largely because of the urban nature of the lower South's free black population, more than three-fourths of all the region's free blacks lived in either Louisiana (New Orleans), which served as home to more than half the region's free blacks (nearly 10,500) in 1820, or South Carolina (Charleston), home to another third of the free black population (just under 7,000). Alabama, Mississippi, and Georgia each had free black populations totaling less than 1 percent of their total population, and even in South Carolina, free blacks were less than 2 percent of the population. Only in Louisiana, where free blacks accounted for roughly 7 percent of the population in 1820, did the free black proportion of the total population exceed 2 percent.[85]

Yet despite the relatively small size and proportion of free blacks in the lower South, white leaders across the region worried that free blacks represented both a practical problem for slave control and a troubling ideological inconsistency in the emerging racial argument for slavery. Local authorities worried that the free blacks' ease of movement, their access to information, and the very example of their freedom put them in a position to encourage slave unrest and insurrection by both word and deed. Evidence from the Caribbean and earlier insurrections and scares in the United States lent credence to such fears. Moreover, as white society in the lower South moved toward fashioning a coherent defense of slavery based on race, the presence of a significant free black population, and especially the small cohort of economically successful free blacks, emerged as a troubling anomaly for slavery's defenders. The presence of a small but visible cadre of successful free blacks challenged the very foundations of racially based slavery and paternalism because it suggested that, under some circumstances, blacks could take care of themselves quite well, better even than many whites. Some whites discounted these concerns, arguing that members of the free black elite served as a useful intermediate class that provided a check against undiscovered unrest among slaves. But more whites saw the tangible success of a small minority of free blacks as a nagging inconsistency, if not a dangerous flaw, in the racial justification for slavery.[86] These concerns sparked a post–War of 1812 drive for either tighter control of free blacks in the lower South or their removal.

The postwar drive for more systematic control over the free black population appeared most emphatically in Georgia and South Carolina, where efforts to slow the growth of the states' burgeoning free black population gained momentum after 1815. Despite its relatively small proportion of free blacks (about 0.5 percent of the population), Georgia passed draconian new laws aimed at blocking the growth of its free black population in the postwar years. Earlier, after watching its tiny free black population triple during the 1790s, the Georgia legislature in 1801 had ended the practice of allowing masters to manumit slaves without its approval, and in 1810 Georgia became the first southern state to invite all free blacks to place themselves under the supervision of white guardians.[87] The centerpiece of Georgia's postwar crackdown was a more comprehensive law, enacted in 1818, that dramatically increased the fines imposed on masters who manumitted slaves without the legislature's approval, repealed an earlier law allowing masters to free slaves in their last will and testament, and, perhaps most important of all, approved an outright ban on the immigration of free blacks to Georgia.[88]

In South Carolina, where the size of the state's free black population more than tripled in the first three decades of the new nation's existence, growing from just over eighteen hundred in 1790 to nearly seven thousand thirty years later, escalating concern over the presence of free blacks led Governor John Geddes to urge the state's legislature to prohibit free black immigration and impose tighter restrictions on voluntary manumissions in South Carolina in 1820. Geddes recommended "the adoption of the strongest measures" to stop black in-migration because "a number of free persons of color have emigrated and are daily emigrating to and settling in this state," and the state had "a duty to oppose at the threshold everything likely in its consequences to disturb our domestic tranquility."[89] The arrival of free black teachers from the North, perceived by many area whites to be emissaries from either the AME Church or abolition societies, fueled the movement to ban free black immigration. The South Carolina legislature heeded the governor's advice and prohibited the immigration of free blacks into the state under penalty of stiff fines and immediate deportation during its 1820 session.[90]

The South Carolina legislature also decided to limit the growth of its free black population by tightening the state's manumission policy. Prior to 1800, manumission in South Carolina required only the consent of the master and a certificate of freedom for the manumitted slave's future use. In 1800, however, the legislature, noting that "it has been a practice for many years" for some slaveholders to manumit slaves of "bad or depraved character, or from age and infirmity, incapable of gaining their livelihood from honest men," required masters wishing to free a slave to appear before a magistrate and five freeholders for approval. At the hearing, the master carried the burden of showing that the slave had demonstrated good character and could earn a living on his or her own.[91] The court's monitoring of the manumission process assured the local white community that the slave recommended for freedom would prove neither a burden nor a threat. Yet the inclusion of the Magistrates and Freeholders Court in the process did little to reduce the number of manumissions in South Carolina over the next two decades. Thus, in a dramatic departure from state's traditional policy of keeping restrictions on the prerogatives of slave owners to a minimum, the 1820 legislature passed a bill requiring direct legislative approval for all manumissions.[92]

Initially, the new policy of legislative manumission had nearly the same effect as an absolute ban. In the first year of the law's operation, the legislature referred to committee all of the more than forty petitions for manumission it received. There legislators initially considered approving those petitions in cases where the master could give "security" that the manumitted slave would leave the state. Governor Geddes, who proposed the stricter manumission legislation, conceded that the tougher "restrictions on emancipation might be dispensed with if persons emancipated should be obliged to depart the state." But, despite the governor's concession, the 1821 legislature took no final action on any of the petitions. Not a single slave was manumitted during the first year of the legislative petition system. Over time, the legislature reviewed petitions for manumission annually but usually approved only those requests that provided for the freed slave's certain and immediate removal from the state.[93] Together, the ban on free black immigration and the restrictions on voluntary emancipations reflected the state's growing antipathy toward free blacks as a class. These new policies effectively slowed the growth of the free black population in South Carolina from nearly 50 percent between 1810 and 1820 to only 16 percent between 1820 and 1830.

By 1820, Louisiana had an even larger free black population than South Carolina. But when the Americans assumed administration of the territory in 1803, there were only seventeen hundred free blacks in Louisiana. Due to its French and Spanish colonial past, Louisiana's social and legal customs concerning free people of color differed significantly from those in other states, though its patterns and practices hardly seemed unusual by the larger standards of the non-English-speaking Atlantic world. A significant proportion of Louisiana's free "colored" population at the time of acquisition consisted of people of mixed race, the product of interracial unions between white soldiers, government officials, traders, and adventurers and slave women and free women of color during the state's colonial era. The Creole culture of Louisiana whites attached little or no stigma to these interracial relationships and assignations, and white Creoles openly acknowledged both their relationships with and progeny by their "colored" paramours. Such latitudinarian views of race ran counter to the more draconian attitudes of American territorial officials toward miscegenation, but at least for a time after the Louisiana Purchase, the culture and custom of Louisiana, and especially New Orleans, remained Creole.[94]

Shortly after Americans took control of Louisiana, the same flow of refugees from the West Indies that raised concern about the in-migration of slaves exposed to revolution also brought a wave of French-speaking free people of color from the West Indies.[95] Concerned about this influx, the American territorial government tried to control the immigration of free blacks from the Caribbean. First, the government authorized the New Orleans city council to require all free people of color entering the city to register with municipal officials in an effort to screen out undesirable immigrants. But the city's anglophone mayor admitted that the process allowed "many worthless free people of color" to enter the territory and that authorities were unable to "drive them away after they have come."[96] Moreover, in 1806, an informant reported to the territorial governor, Claiborne, that a number of free blacks in New Orleans had joined a plot to help the Spanish recapture Louisiana.[97] Claiborne and the territorial legislature quickly enacted a law banning the immigration of free blacks from the West Indies (with the exception of women and young children). Free blacks already in Louisiana were required to offer proof of their freedom or be classified as fugitive slaves. In 1807, the territorial legislature extended the ban on in-migrants to include free blacks from any part of the world and strengthened the punishments for violators. The restrictive legislation of 1807 also included a provision limiting manumissions in the territory. Masters could free only slaves over the age of thirty who were able to support themselves and who had no record of bad conduct, and they could do this only if the community did not object and a superior court judge approved. The 1807 immigration law proved difficult to enforce, however, given the indifference if not the outright hostility of much of the territory's French-speaking white population to the ban.[98]

Largely due to the influx of refugees from the West Indies, the free black population of Louisiana doubled between 1804 and 1808. In 1809, the exodus of

French-speaking free blacks from Spanish-controlled Cuba brought more than thirty-one hundred more Caribbean free blacks to Louisiana.[99] Governor Claiborne reluctantly agreed to ignore the ban on immigration from the Caribbean out of humanitarian concern for refugees fleeing actual or feared slave revolts, and because he knew he did not have the resources necessary to enforce the ban effectively even if he tried.[100] Still, Claiborne yearned to stem the tide of West Indian immigration. He asked other West Indian colonies not to send additional émigrés to Louisiana and complained that the territory already had a larger free black population than "comports with our interest."[101] An American regime determined to reduce the free colored population of Louisiana had instead overseen a period of dramatic increase, as the Louisiana free black population had increased by more than 330 percent between 1803 and 1810, with just over half of the new free black population arriving from Cuba in a period of little more than a year.[102]

Louisiana's burgeoning population of *gens de couleur libre* soon found that the ongoing Americanization of Louisiana brought a chronic diminution of their rights. As early as 1805, the city council of territorial New Orleans formalized colonial practice by limiting voting rights to the "free and white."[103] Upon Louisiana's admission to statehood in 1812, the state's first constitution also explicitly limited political rights to whites, excluding even the lightest-skinned, most affluent, and most respected free people of color from the political process.[104] Americans were also uncomfortable with the colonial practice of allowing free people of color to carry guns and organize their own militia units, and they complained mightily about it to Louisiana authorities.[105] The need to defend New Orleans from the British led General Andrew Jackson to encourage the organization of free colored militia units during the War of 1812 using promises of enhanced rights under American postwar rule as an inducement.[106] Yet the defeat of the British at New Orleans brought neither citizenship nor enhanced rights to Louisiana's free colored elite. In all likelihood, however, their loyalty to the United States during the war helped them preserve their unique status as a third caste in the face of an American view of race that was more dichotomous than that of the earlier ruling regimes.[107] After the War of 1812, American-born whites in Louisiana pushed for tighter restrictions on free people of color, but their efforts yielded comparatively meager results: an 1817 legislative ban on the immigration of domestic free blacks with a criminal record, a ban far less restrictive than those approved by other lower South states.[108]

In nearby Mississippi, home to fewer than five hundred free blacks, white authorities tended to see Louisiana's growing free black "problem" as theirs as well. From the moment it gained statehood in 1817, Mississippi worried about the possible spillover of Caribbean-born free blacks. Between 1810 and 1820, the small Mississippi free black population increased by 90 percent, a rate that troubled whites in the Natchez region and southwest Mississippi, where virtually all of the state's free blacks lived. Moreover, as a state involved in heavy river commerce, Mississippi worried about becoming an avenue of escape for slaves as well as a breeding ground for insurrection. Thus, in an effort to monitor its free black population closely, the state required free blacks to carry a "certificate of freedom," for which they paid an annual fee. Employers were subject to significant penalties for hiring free people of color who lacked the proper documentation. But it was not until 1822, in the months immediately after the Denmark Vesey insurrection scare in South Carolina, that the Mississippi legislature, largely controlled by Natchez-area lawmakers, passed legislation banning the immigration of free blacks and prohibiting manumission without legislative approval.[109]

TAKEN AS A whole, the lower South's postwar effort to assert firmer control over its black population, slave and free, reflected not only its increasing commitment to slavery as a lasting economic system but also its awareness that the region existed as part of a larger and rather unstable slaveholding world whose ills threatened to infect their region. From the south, the region feared the contagion of Caribbean slave unrest and insurrection. The long-unfolding Haitian Revolution (1791–1804), which featured slave insurrection, and the Cuban unrest of 1809 generated deep fears that revolution-minded slaves and free blacks could make their way into the lower South. They might arrive directly with refugees or indirectly through less vigilant upper South states. Lower South states feared that upper South states interested in reducing their dependence on slave labor and reducing the size of their black population would dump unhealthy, lazy, troublesome, and even incendiary slaves into the lower South as part of the regular domestic slave trade. They also worried that upper South manumission laws requiring newly freed blacks to leave the state would send a dangerous trickle of free blacks southward. Lower South states, no matter how committed to slavery, also worried about their own internal racial demographics quite apart from their concerns about Caribbean influences and upper South motives. They wanted more slaves but were wary of the rise of either state or local black majorities. The sum of these concerns led to a concerted effort among lower South states to control the growth of their black population through regulation of the domestic slave trade and sharp restrictions on free black immigration and manumission, and to seek better control over both slaves and free blacks already residing in the lower South through tighter laws, improved slave patrols, and better-trained state militias.

The post–War of 1812 search for white security in the lower South both sustained the emergence of paternalism and challenged it. To a degree, the tougher postwar restrictions on slaves and free blacks in the lower South comported well with the emerging ideology of paternalism. Closer scrutiny of slaves and free blacks could enhance masters' control over their presumed "dependents" without making discipline more severe or capricious. The regulatory state could become the paternalistic master's most valuable ally. At the same time, however, the tightening of public regulation of slaves and free blacks ran counter to the central thrust of paternalism: that the master's measured familial treatment of slaves as domestic dependents would of itself gradually bring order and efficiency to the institution. In that sense, the need for tighter regulation of slaves and free blacks both served as a rebuke to the excesses of the "old accommodation" and revealed a lingering skepticism of paternalism's effectiveness as a means of slave control. Even more threatening to paternalism was the hostility to slave religion and slave literacy that emerged in the postwar era. In practice, of course, champions of paternalism knew that they needed support from appropriate state authorities if their efforts were to succeed, and they accepted appropriate state regulation. Above all, whites recognized that governmental regulation of slaves and free blacks was essential to protect white society against insurrection. Prevailing white opinion still believed that a governmental iron fist was needed to fill out paternalism's velvet glove.

DESPITE THE CONTINUING PROBLEMS paternalism encountered in its efforts to persuade slaveholders and other white southerners of its effectiveness as a method of slave control, southern politicians quickly grasped paternalism's utility as a defense of slavery against outside criticism. The use of paternalism as a justification of slaveholder conduct was purposely unveiled to a watchful nation during the Missouri debates of 1820 and 1821. In fact, the rhetoric of paternalism readily leaped off the tongues of lower South politicians when congressional debate over the admission of Missouri erupted. During these debates, southern senators and representatives offered an affirmative defense of the slaveholder as paternalist in response to the northern condemnation of slavery. They pulled up short of calling slavery per se a positive good. But they had already grown adept at the language and argument of paternalism, and they did not hesitate to characterize the master-slave relationship in paternalistic terms. To be sure, the political use of the ideology of paternalism as a defense for slavery did not reflect a consensus among slaveholders around the paternalist ideal. But it did reveal the growing centrality of paternalism to the slaveholders' understanding of how they could best present themselves to an increasingly skeptical world.

During the debates, Georgia senator Freeman Walker insisted that the "slaveholding states...yield to none on the practice of benevolence and humanity." Far "from being in that state of intolerable vassalage which some gentlemen seem to believe," Walker maintained, slaves in the southern states were "treated with kindness and humanity." To Walker's eyes, slaves appeared "cheerful and happy."[110] North Carolina senator Nathaniel Macon, the laconic Old Republican, defended slavery as a cultivator of domesticity. Macon urged northern senators to "go home with me, or some other Southern member, and witness the meeting between the slaves and their owner, and see the glad faces and hearty shaking of hands." Older slaves, Macon contended, "are better taken care of than any poor in the world, and treated with decent respect by all their white acquaintances."[111] The upper South's

Richard Johnson also evoked the paternalist ideal in his defense of the conduct of slaveholders. Under slavery, the Kentucky senator argued, slaves "were trained to industry" and compensated by "kindness and humanity." The slave enjoyed "the rights of conscience" and worshiped God "as he chooses." As proof of the latter proposition, Johnson claimed that "quite as great a proportion of them become believers...and are admitted into the communion of the Christian church" as whites. Growing Christian sentiment in slaveholding communities offered slaves protection from the cruelty of the occasional harsh master. "No man among us can be cruel to his slave," Johnson avowed, "without incurring the execration of the whole community."[112] Both Walker and Johnson remained careful not to claim that slavery was anything other than a long-standing problem that white southerners tried their best to meliorate to the extent circumstances permitted. The "evil [slavery], if it be one, already exists," Walker argued. "It has taken deep root in our soil, and I know of no means of extirpating it." Johnson denied that southerners were trying to "justify the abstract principle of slavery," claiming instead that they merely sought to defend their honor as slaveholders saddled with the responsibility of managing a necessary evil.[113]

In the House of Representatives, South Carolina's Charles Pinckney, the only member of Congress in 1820 who had served as a delegate to the Philadelphia convention in 1787, also used claims of paternalism to defend the conduct of southern slaveholders. A "great deal," Pinckney lamented, "has been said on the subject of slavery—that it is an infamous stain and blot on the States that hold them, not only degrading the slave but the master, and making him unfit for republican government; that it is contrary to religion and the law of God; and that Congress ought to do everything in their power to prevent its extension among the new States." In a narrow compass, Pinckney refuted these criticisms point by point. "Is there a single line in Old or New Testament, either censuring or forbidding it [slavery]?" Pinckney asked rhetorically. Jews, Greeks, and Romans, Pinckney contended, had held slaves in the biblical world. Apart from England, the Charlestonian noted, the notion of liberty languished throughout the early-nineteenth-century world, and the lower classes were found "half-starved, half-naked, and in the most wretched state of human degradation." Even in England, Pinckney contended, "the comforts" of the lower classes "are far inferior to those of our slaves." In New York and Philadelphia, the South Carolina founder continued, the streets were "crowded with idle, drunken negroes at every corner," proving to his mind that "freedom is one of the greatest curses you can inflict on [blacks]." By contrast, the aging Charlestonian claimed, in the plantation South, "every slave has a comfortable house, is well fed clothed and taken care of; he has his family about him, and in sickness has the same medical aid as his master, and has a sure and comfortable retreat in old age." The "mild treatment" accorded southern slaves, Pinckney maintained, upheld the region's honor. For "slavery to exist, there must be discipline," the founder conceded, but the "discipline ought to be mild."[114]

But not even Pinckney sounded as aggressive a tone as South Carolina's senator William Smith, the Upcountry's redoubtable champion of reopening the African slave trade nearly two decades earlier. A York District planter-lawyer approaching sixty years of age in 1820, Smith had emerged as one of the South's most outspoken strict constructionists. In a variety of speeches to the Senate during the Missouri controversy, Smith moved, albeit tentatively, away from the assumption, explicit in Richard Johnson's remarks, that slavery remained a "necessary evil."[115] Smith directed his attention to refuting the famous denunciation of slavery offered by the young nation's leading apostle of liberty, Thomas Jefferson. Reversing Jefferson's much-quoted assertion from *Notes on the State of Virginia* that "the whole commerce between master and slave is a perpetual exercise of the most boisterous passions," Smith countered that "the whole commerce between master and slave is patriarchal." The paternalistic slave owner, Smith contended, "had no motive" for "boisterous hostility" because such ill will was both "at war with his interest" and "at war with his comfort." In fact, Smith argued, southern slaves were "so domesticated, so kindly treated by their masters," that southerners worried little about insurrection. Rather than living in a state of "constant alarm" or "constant danger," Smith maintained, southerners knew that abolitionists could not "excite one among twenty [slaves] to insurrection." Smith contended that most southern slaves were "well fed, well clothed, and supremely happy." Indeed, Smith claimed that slaves on the whole were so well treated in the South that there was "no class of laboring people upon the globe, except in the United States," that was "better clothed, better fed, or more cheerful." Nor, in Smith's view, did the observation of slavery during childhood breed arrogance and despotism in young whites, as Jefferson feared. With black children as "constant associates," Smith suggested, young whites developed so much affection for young slaves that "in thousands of instances there is nothing but the shadow of slavery left" when whites and their youthful slave companions reached adulthood.[116]

Smith's sweeping contradiction of Jefferson's contention that slavery was unrepublican shocked his northern listeners, who heard the South Carolinian's remarks, whether accurately or not, as a bold departure from previous southern defenses of slavery as a necessary evil. Smith certainly never explicitly called slavery a positive good, and his confrontational style may have shaped northern perceptions of his speeches as much as the substance of his comments did. But even if Smith stopped short of arguing for slavery as a positive good, he nonetheless offered an aggressive defense of paternalism, of a "patriarchal" commerce between master and slave, as an ideal and practice that rendered southern slavery compatible with Christianity and republicanism. Smith's account replaced Jefferson's "boisterous passions" with the tender mercies of domesticity.[117] A robust application of paternalism, Smith contended, effectively meliorated whatever evil rested inherently in slavery. In fact, paternalism meliorated the evils of slavery so effectively that often only the "shadow of slavery" remained. Smith's argument for the slaveholder as paternalist and slavery as a domestic institution grew naturally out of emerging self-perceptions among the region's slaveholders, but it sounded unfamiliar and incredible to many of his northern colleagues.

By 1820, lower South whites were seeking to embrace slavery (albeit on their own terms) rather than puzzling over how to extricate themselves from it. In so doing, they were beginning to fashion an ideological reconfiguration of slavery. This reconfiguration insisted that when governed by paternalism, slavery became a domestic institution that recognized the humanity of slaves and treated them accordingly. Since the end of the war in 1815, the lower South had experienced a significant insurrection scare, felt renewed anxiety over the dangers imported through the interstate slave trade, grown increasingly concerned about the nettlesome presence of free blacks, endured persistent division over the desirability of converting slaves to Christianity (especially if that conversion involved teaching slaves to read and write), and witnessed slavery bitterly denounced in national councils.

Against this backdrop, a drama began to unfold in Charleston that threatened to stop the progress of paternalism dead in its tracks. From its beginning in late May 1822, this drama occupied the minds of Charleston residents through a tumultuous summer and fall and brought terrible tragedy to Charleston's black community. Growing out of a major insurrection scare, one driven inexorably if erratically forward by rumor, innuendo, coerced confessions, rumblings about the role of black Christians in the alleged plot, and controversy among members of the state's political elite, the drama provoked alarm and anxiety of unprecedented proportions among whites and blacks in Charleston and the surrounding Lowcountry during the fateful summer of 1822.

PART FOUR

PATERNALISM IN CRISIS

In 1822, Charleston, though home to many dissenting points of view, stood as the central staging ground and ideological epicenter of the paternalist insurgency. With the evangelical denominations well established in the city, with paternalists Richard Furman and Benjamin Palmer both holding pastorates there, with the city's influential Episcopalian clergy at least nominally supportive of the movement, and with significant lay champions, such as Justice William Johnson, as residents, the paternalist movement had built an impressive leadership cadre and presence in the city. The collapse of the insurgency in Charleston could well have meant its collapse everywhere. At the same time, nowhere was the movement better equipped to defend itself than in Charleston. Given the nature of the attack on paternalism that came as part of the public reaction to the discovery of the Denmark Vesey insurrection plot during the summer of 1822, the movement needed all the strength it could muster to stand its ground.

The Denmark Vesey insurrection scare and the alarming reports by white authorities of its scope and danger terrified local whites. The reaction of local whites to the Vesey scare threatened the paternalist insurgency with the imposition of a Carthaginian peace that could have dealt the movement a death blow. Charleston authorities, led by city intendant James Hamilton Jr., indicted paternalism for its encouragement of slave literacy, for its use of black religious leaders, and for nurturing "lenient" treatment of slaves. These critics of paternalism touted more muscular methods of slave control, culminating in the formation of the South Carolina Association, an extralegal body charged with policing slaves in Charleston. By mobilizing opposition to paternalism, the Charleston authorities nearly discredited the movement and threatened its viability as an ideology of slaveholding in the lower South. Only a skillful response and a knack for accommodation on the part of Charleston paternalists allowed the insurgency to avoid permanent damage.

CHAPTER SEVEN

THE SCARE

It began with hearsay.[1] On Saturday, May 25, 1822, Peter, a slave of John Prioleau, told his owner's wife and son that he had heard a rumor about a slave insurrection. Peter reported that William Paul, a slave owned by two Charleston grocers, had heard about plans for a large-scale insurrection during a visit to a busy wharf along East Bay Street. Paul later told Peter what he had heard. The Prioleau family's information was at best thirdhand, but it is still striking that they kept the information to themselves for five days, with the wife and son informing husband and father John Prioleau only after he returned to Charleston from his rural plantation on Thursday, May 30. Doubtless concerned about the delay, John Prioleau immediately notified the Charleston intendant, James Hamilton, who promptly convened a special meeting of the city council to consider the information. Hamilton also asked Governor Thomas Bennett, who had authority to mobilize the state militia, to attend.[2]

Prioleau's slave Peter testified that William Paul had "accosted" him on the wharf near the fish market and spoke to him "with considerable earnestness" about a plan in the works among slaves "determined to shake off our bondage." Peter told the authorities that he told William that he "would have nothing to do with the business" because he was "grateful" to his "master for his kindness and wished no change."[3] Even before hearing Peter's testimony, city officials quickly arrested William Paul and questioned him late that Thursday evening. At first, William Paul admitted having a conversation with Peter near the fish market but denied that its substance concerned an insurrection plot. A worried council confined Paul overnight in the city guardhouse before moving him the next morning to the notorious "black hole" of the Charleston workhouse. Paul was questioned again on Friday morning and gave a statement implicating two other slaves, Peter Poyas, an artisan who hired out, and Mingo Harth, as leaders of an impending insurrection. Authorities promptly arrested and examined Poyas and Harth and searched their belongings, but released them shortly thereafter. Later, the court that investigated the insurrection plot claimed that Poyas and Harth conducted themselves with so much "composure and coolness" and treated the charges against them with "such levity" that the authorities were "completely deceived" by their performance, though the subsequent movements of Poyas and Harth were carefully watched with the hope of learning more about the alleged plot.[4] Additional "measures of precaution" were taken to protect the city. In the meantime, William Paul remained confined to the workhouse for further questioning. On June 8, after spending a week in solitary confinement and apparently growing increasingly fearful that he would soon be executed, Paul "confessed" that he had knowledge of an "extensive" plot seeking "an indiscriminate massacre of the whites" and led by a slave who carried "a charm which rendered him invulnerable."[5]

With the second confession of William Paul in hand, Hamilton and the city council appointed an ad hoc investigative body, known as the Committee of Vigilance, which quietly continued the investigation. Following the example of Colonel James Chesnut's investigation of rumors of insurrection in Camden in 1816, the strategy of the city investigators (led by Hamilton) centered on infiltrating the alleged conspiracy with a loyal domestic slave who enjoyed the full confidence of his fellow slaves and free blacks. George, a slave of John Lyde Wilson and reportedly a class leader in Benjamin Palmer's Congregational church, agreed to spy on his fellow slaves and church members. On Friday, June 14, George, known by his owners for his "uncommon intelligence," reported that one of his church friends told him that an insurrection was scheduled for Sunday, June 16, and that this plot involved "some of the colored members" of Palmer's church.[6] According to authorities, George Wilson's information comported closely with William Paul's earlier statements, and implicated Rolla Bennett, Governor Bennett's house servant, as a leader in the plot. John Wilson alerted Hamilton, who informed Bennett. The governor mobilized the militia, Hamilton called out the city guard, and whites feverishly prepared to defend the city. Bennett placed the troops under the command of Robert Y. Hayne, the state attorney general, a friend of Hamilton's and, like the ambitious young Charleston intendant, a rising star of Lowcountry politics.[7]

The hour of the expected apocalypse came and went without incident. The only commotion in Charleston that Sunday evening emerged from the activities of whites defending the city. But Hasell Wilson, an eleven-year-old boy at the time, later recalled the evening as one marked by rumors of danger and the "passing of patrols on the street" throughout the night, rendering "every slight noise" a matter of so much concern that "no one, not even the children, ventured to retire" that evening. The next morning, a quiet dawn brought Charleston a "general feeling of relief," but the underlying "anxiety and suspense" lingered for "some time."[8] Charleston authorities later concluded that by late that Sunday afternoon, the conspiracy's putative leader, a free black carpenter named Denmark Vesey, realized that his plan had been discovered and postponed action. On the night of their planned attack, local authorities believed, the would-be rebels found "the whole town surrounded by the most vigilant guards" and thus they "dared not show themselves."[9] Apparently state and city authorities had mobilized their defenses just in the nick of time. Lacking the element of surprise, the putative rebels deferred action. Charleston remained quiet.

But talk of looming insurrection persisted, and Charleston remained in a heightened state of paramilitary preparedness for nearly a month. Moreover, the public received comparatively little hard information about the scare for nearly two weeks after the Sunday mobilization of the city guard and state militia.[10] But if official word was relatively slow in coming, rumors abounded. White and black grapevines worked overtime during the scare, producing high levels of anxiety throughout the city as unofficial leaks, informal reports, and both informed and uninformed speculation made the rounds through the city in late June and early July. Certainly no resident of Charleston, white or black, failed to recognize the mobilization of state troops and local guards as signs of an insurrection scare, and observant Charlestonians noticed the arrest and confinement of a number of blacks in the city's workhouse, and perhaps even the frequent gatherings of leading white citizens there. Indeed, Hasell Wilson remembered that rumors of a possible insurrection, confirmed by the city's visible and noisy state of mobilization, created a "feeling of alarm and anxiety that pervaded the whole community, from the time the danger became known until all the risks appeared to be over."[11] As late as mid-July, Charleston milliner E. M. Starr reported delaying a planned vacation from Charleston's summer heat until the scare had passed so that he could be sure his store and its contents were safe.[12] Few understood exactly what was going on in the center of Charleston that summer, but virtually everyone knew something was afoot.[13]

Meanwhile, city authorities, led by Hamilton, pursued their investigation with single-minded determination. On Monday, June 17, the day after the expected revolt failed to materialize, Hamilton and the city council called for the formation of a special Magistrates and Freeholders Court to investigate "the causes and character of the existing disturbance" and to bring "to light and punishment the suspected and guilty."[14] Privately, Governor Bennett strenuously objected to the formation of the impromptu city court, urging instead a special state-led investigation and the handling of any resulting criminal charges through the regular state courts. But the strong-willed intendant Hamilton and other city officials ignored Bennett's objections and convened the Magistrates and Freeholders Court anyway.[15]

In 1822, the ambitious and energetic James Hamilton, age thirty-six, stood near the beginning of a long, colorful, and controversial political career. He had already served in the state legislature, where he orchestrated a presidential campaign for fellow Lowcountryman William Lowndes, former Speaker of the U.S. House, against the wishes of Vice President Calhoun's supporters. Hamilton's ambition and talent would eventually take him to the United States Congress during the 1820s and to the governorship of South Carolina in 1830, and it would establish him as the chief political mobilizer for the Nullification Party in South Carolina in 1831–33. Hamilton played the latter role with considerable aplomb, and many observers attributed the ultimate success of the Nullifiers at the polls more to Hamilton's skill at political mobilization than to the persuasive force of Calhoun's argument. Despite holding the position of city intendant at the time of the 1822 insurrection scare, Hamilton had only recently resumed residence in Charleston after a lengthy absence. He moved his residence to the city from his wife's Beaufort District plantation in 1819, ostensibly to assume an established law practice, but also to enjoy the vitality of the bustling port's active social and political life.[16]

Born in 1786 at Rice Hope plantation along the Santee River north of Charleston, Hamilton was the son of James Hamilton Sr., a Pennsylvanian who had come south with the Continental Army, and Elizabeth Lynch, a rice heiress whose family had been deeply involved in Revolutionary-era South Carolina politics.[17] As a youth, Hamilton split his time between the Santee plantation, summers and schooling in Newport, Rhode Island, the early republic's resort for the rich and famous, and stints at his family's Charleston residence on the corner of East Bay and Society. As an adolescent, Hamilton went north for his education in Newport and stayed to study law in Dedham, Massachusetts. Returning south in 1810, Hamilton, age twenty-four, practiced law briefly with William Drayton, a prominent Charleston attorney with impeccable family connections. In 1811, Henry Middleton, another prominent Charlestonian, was elected governor and asked Hamilton to serve as his personal secretary. Hamilton eagerly accepted this invitation to enter the political world. But with the outbreak of the War of 1812, Hamilton quickly resigned his position with Middleton and entered military service, rising to the rank of major while serving as deputy inspector general for yet another prominent Charlestonian, General George Izard. Hamilton found little chance to distinguish himself militarily as an inspector under the cautious Izard, but during the war he cemented his ties to the Lowcountry's putative aristocracy by marrying into the fabulously rich Heyward family. His fiancée, Elizabeth Heyward, brought three plantations and 250 slaves to Hamilton through their marriage in 1813.[18]

When he was discharged from the army in June 1815, Hamilton and his bride returned to South Carolina and settled at one of Elizabeth's plantations, Callawassie, near Beaufort. Successful but bored as a rural rice planter, Hamilton eagerly returned to Charleston in 1819 when a retiring Drayton asked him to assume his law practice. With Drayton's approval, Hamilton soon asked James Louis Petigru, who later emerged as antebellum South Carolina's most distinguished attorney, to become his partner. Petigru brought a keen knowledge of the law and a steady work ethic to the partnership. Hamilton brought it personality, a public face, and the energy and connections needed to attract clients. In November 1819, after living in the city for less than a year, Hamilton was elected to the first of three consecutive terms in the state house of representatives, where he earned a reputation as an ardent champion of banking interests and judicial reform. Late in 1821, Hamilton was elected intendant of Charleston.[19] For a young politician with talent, wealth, and connections, Hamilton's selection as intendant of Charleston seemed more a matter of doing the things necessary to advance than a rendezvous with political destiny. After all, the office had served as a stepping-stone to the governor's chair for other Charlestonians (including the incumbent Bennett and his predecessor John Geddes), but its normal duties ran toward the mundane. But James Hamilton Jr., a man judged by supporters and opponents alike as a politician whose talent and charm were exceeded only by his ambition and opportunism, missed few chances to find and ride a political hobby, no matter how unexpected its appearance.

When the Vesey insurrection scare occurred on his watch as intendant, Hamilton moved aggressively to turn problem into opportunity. He threw his prodigious energy first into thwarting the alleged rebellion and then to turning the entire incident to his political advantage. The court called by Hamilton and the city council in defiance of the governor's wishes included Lionel Kennedy and Thomas Parker, two Charleston lawyers who served as the presiding magistrates, and five prominent freeholders, Nathaniel Heyward, Julius R. Pringle, James Legare, Robert J. Turnbull, and Colonel William Drayton. All of these men were recommended by Hamilton, approved by the city council, and officially summoned by Kennedy and Parker. The freeholders recommended by Hamilton for the service on the court hardly could have been a more distinguished group. By 1822, the sixty-six-year old Nathaniel Heyward, a scion of a wealthy rice-planting family who married into the almost equally wealthy Manigault family in 1788, had established himself as one of the richest planters in the entire South, operating several large Lowcountry plantations, including the thirty-five-hundred-acre Silk Hope on the Cooper River. Over the course of his life, Heyward resided mainly at the Bluff, a plantation on the Combahee River, and in his Charleston town home at 118 East Bay. He was also the great-uncle of James Hamilton's wife, Elizabeth Heyward Hamilton. Julius Reid Pringle, named collector for the port of Charleston by President Monroe in 1819, had served as president of the South Carolina state senate, and his family held extensive wealth in both Charleston and Beaufort districts. James Legare had served in the Continental Army during the Revolution and survived confinement as a prisoner of war. After the Revolution, Legare served two terms in the state legislature, developed extensive plantation interests in St. John's Parish, and served as a director of a major Charleston bank. William Drayton, once Hamilton's mentor at law, hailed from one of the Lowcountry's most prominent and politically active families, and before closing his practice stood as one of the city's most respected lawyers. Robert J. Turnbull, a future states' rights champion, also established an extensive legal practice in Charleston before exchanging it for a second profitable career as a Sea Island planter. The court's five freeholders, though differing from each other in some respects, all trusted Hamilton, and in 1822 they still shared Hamilton's faith in measured nationalism. Drayton, Heyward, and Turnbull all had strong ties to the old Federalist Party (the party of Hamilton's father), Legare's sentiments were strongly national, and Pringle, like Hamilton, belonged to the so-called nationalist wing of the Republican Party and held a major patronage post in a Republican administration.[20]

On June 18, the two magistrates formally called into session the court that included these distinguished freeholders. After some deliberation, the court decided to conduct its business privately, and began its proceedings. Existing sources suggest that the interrogation of suspects, and the physical punishment that likely accompanied it, was carried out in the Charleston workhouse. The court also held its sessions in the workhouse, emphasizing the site's advantages as an area of privacy and security. Between June 19 and 27, the court, together with the Committee on Vigilance, heard and compelled statements from a number of "witnesses," including some informants who claimed to have evidence against the supposed ringleaders of the alleged insurrection. The court later claimed that it received its first break in the investigation on June 19, and arrests began shortly thereafter. Statements given to the Committee on Vigilance and the "testimony" of witnesses before the court during this period identified, to the satisfaction of authorities, Denmark Vesey as the principal leader of the insurrection. After a search lasting several days, authorities arrested Vesey in the home of his wife on June 22. To the shock and apparent dismay of those close to the investigation, the court also identified not one but three trusted slaves of incumbent South Carolina governor Thomas Bennett as active allies of Vesey.[21]

During this first phase of its activity, the court took statements, arrested suspects, and imposed sentences but, as far as the best surviving primary source evidence indicates, conducted nothing that remotely resembled a trial. By June 27, the court had heard enough "evidence" against Vesey and five of his alleged slave co-conspirators, including the three Bennett slaves Rolla, Ned, and Batteau, as well as Peter Poyas and Jesse Blackwood (who allegedly had been given the assignment of recruiting slave rebels from the countryside), to convict the six men and sentence them to death by public hanging for fomenting an insurrection that never materialized. With the sentences pronounced, the court recessed.[22] And, as publicly announced, on July 2, the executions of Denmark Vesey, Peter Poyas, Jesse Blackwood, Rolla Bennett, Ned Bennett, and Batteau Bennett proceeded as scheduled, providing visual confirmation to both white and black Charlestonians of the seriousness with which white authorities were treating the ongoing scare. Writing on the day after the execution of the Vesey Six, James Hamilton privately declared that the condemned men "met their fate with the heroic fortitude of martyrs."[23] The weight of the historical evidence suggests that these first executions led to hope among whites that the scare was almost over and to fear among blacks that the carnage had just begun.

PRIOR TO HIS ARREST as the alleged leader of the 1822 insurrection plot, the historical record contains remarkably little hard information about Denmark Vesey. Nevertheless, according to extant sources, when Charleston authorities arrested and convicted Denmark Vesey and sentenced him to the gallows for organizing a slave insurrection in the summer of 1822, he had lived in Charleston for more than forty years without leaving a record of a single incident of conflict with local white authorities. Denmark Vesey came to Charleston as the property of John Vesey, a ship captain and a slave trader who resided in Charleston. While on a regular slave-buying trip to St. Thomas in 1781, Captain Vesey noticed the uncommon "intelligence" of a fourteen-year-old boy named Telemaque. The captain purchased Telemaque but sold him a few weeks later in Saint Domingue. On Vesey's next visit to the island, however, Telemaque's new owner returned the boy as "unsound," claiming he was "subject to epileptic fits." Compelled by local authorities to accept the return of Telemaque and refund the money, Captain Vesey kept the young man as his own slave. According to Hamilton, Telemaque served Vesey as "a faithful slave" for nearly twenty years, and during that period the local community's dialect changed the pronunciation of Telemaque to Denmark. In 1800, Denmark Vesey won a $1,500 prize in the East Bay lottery. He used $600 of his prize to purchase his freedom from Captain John Vesey for less than market value. Hamilton judged Denmark Vesey, who earned a good living as a carpenter and accumulated an estate estimated at $8,000 by a local newspaper in 1822, as "distinguished for great strength and activity." Other records indicated that Vesey, who could read and write and enjoyed the run of the city and surrounding countryside, joined the Second Presbyterian Church in 1817, and testimony given during the investigation indicated that Vesey had become a member of the African church by 1822. Hamilton described Vesey's personality as "impetuous and domineering," and indicated that Vesey had often displayed "haughty and capricious cruelty" toward his "numerous wives and children." Yet Hamilton also maintained that, as a community, Charleston blacks looked up to the prosperous, independent Vesey "with awe and respect." Hamilton judged Vesey as "ambitious" and "despotic"; other whites in Charleston apparently viewed Vesey as an arrogant free black who harassed and intimidated other blacks while showing carefully calibrated signs of defiance toward whites.[24]

Charleston newspapers published the court's first announcement of the pending executions on June 29, breaking the Charleston authorities' long official silence on the investigation. But by that time the white rumor mill in the city was working overtime.[25] Despite later claims that the investigation and the court kept their proceedings a "profound secret," court members clearly discussed those proceedings with a number of private individuals. In late June and again in early July,

John Potter, a prominent Charlestonian, wrote Langdon Cheves, a Charleston native living in Philadelphia while serving as president of the Bank of the United States, informing him of the insurrection scare and the upcoming execution of "six wretches" and revealing a knowledge of details known only through a thorough acquaintance with the court's supposedly confidential proceedings. Citing information obtained from "a member of the court," Potter reported with disgust that Rolla Bennett, the governor's trusted carriage driver, intended to kill his master and take the governor's daughter as his prize, a thought that made Potter's blood "recoil in my veins." Potter characterized the plot as one that was "deeply laid" with a "cunning" that "would surprise the community." He reported with alarm that the plan "was that all the males were to be cut off—!" and he claimed as early as June 29 that all the rebels' organizational meetings were "held under the perfidious cover of religion," aided, Potter believed, by black missionaries from Philadelphia.[26] Later statements from black witnesses suggested that Charleston's black grapevine hummed with activity during June and July as well, as some slaves and free blacks disappeared into the workhouse while others gave statements and remained at large. For example, one black witness, Edwin Paul, later testified that "every body even the women" were puzzled that "Monday Gell & Denmark Vesey were not taken" when the first suspects were arrested.[27]

YET BY JUNE 21, the day before Vesey was arrested, and with public anxiety running high in the city, the court found itself already enmeshed in two separate but related controversies, one public and the other largely private (for the moment). On that Friday, the conservative, business-oriented *Charleston Courier*, the city's leading newspaper, published an unsigned essay entitled "Melancholy Effect of Popular Excitement," which offered city residents a cautionary tale concerning rumors of slave unrest.[28] It recounted an incident that had occurred in Edgefield District more than a decade earlier. According to the story, in 1810 or 1811, the governors of both South Carolina and Georgia, acting on oral reports and purported written evidence that a slave insurrection was afoot in the Augusta area, mobilized state militias to defend against impending attack. A Charleston resident visiting the Augusta area asked to review the evidence, and upon so doing promptly informed both governors that the alleged plot was a hoax. According to the essay, Georgia's governor refused to accept the "mortifying discovery of his having been duped" and left the militia on alert. As restless troops patrolled the region, a drunken cavalry trumpeter sounded his bugle for amusement. But the idle amusement of one member confused the rest of the militia, which promptly embarked on a frenzied search for a slave trumpeter, who, whites feared, had signaled the onset of the expected rebellion. The militia cavalry, for all its riding, found only a "poor half-witted Negro," who was blindfolded, threatened with "instant death from a sabre," and "whipped severely to extort a confession" before he identified a nearby slave named Billy as the owner of a horn. The militia discovered Billy, a trusted blacksmith, "quietly sleeping" in "a degree of comfort very unusual for a slave," but they also found a boatman's horn in his home and thus seized Billy for trial. As the author described it, "The Court of Magistrates and Freeholders was selected from men of the first respectability in the neighborhood; yet in fact, although no evidence was given whatever as a motive for sounding the horn, and the horn was actually found covered with cobwebs, they condemned that man to die the next day!" Billy's owner, "one of the worthiest men in all that country," urged a further review of the evidence, but the court held firm. As a result of the governor's stubbornness and the court's recalcitrance, Billy was "hung amidst crowds of execrating spectators"; "such appeared to be the popular demand for a victim, that it is not certain a pardon could have saved him."[29]

The essay told an intriguing story of unfounded rumors credited, slight truths exaggerated, rational concerns mushrooming into irrational fears, a local gentry carried away with emotion and ambition and playing to the fears of the people, a hastily convened court seeking popular favor rather than justice, an anxious public finding an insurrection where only rumor existed, and a slave executed, even murdered, to satisfy popular need for action. Given the timing of its publication, the essay appeared to invite the Charleston public to compare the conduct of the recently convened court in Charleston with the earlier one in Edgefield. At the time of publication, only *Courier* editor A. S. Willington knew the identity of its author. But during the week after the appearance of the anonymous essay, irate members of the Vesey court inquired and discovered the author's identity (probably because Willington, sensing the possible "damage" done to the court by his decision to publish, revealed it). The author of the unsigned essay was United States Supreme Court justice William Johnson, a brother-in-law of incumbent governor Thomas Bennett and a formidable figure in the political and intellectual life of Charleston. If, as he later claimed, Johnson simply published the essay in an effort to calm the hysteria sweeping Charleston in late June of 1822, his effort not only failed miserably but drew such a negative response from both the Magistrates and Freeholders Court and the court of public opinion that his effort actually exacerbated the existing crisis.[30]

Upon learning that Johnson was the author of "Melancholy," members of the court privately demanded a public statement from Johnson declaring that he "did not mean to imply anything disrespectful towards the court." When such a statement was not immediately forthcoming from the headstrong justice, on Saturday, June 29 the members of the court issued a public notice expressing outrage at Johnson's publication. The court claimed the anonymous essay "injured and defamed" it by insinuating that "under the influence of popular prejudice," it "was capable of committing perjury and murder."[31] Johnson's initial reply to the court, also published on the twenty-ninth, labeled the attack against him "one of the most groundless and unprovoked attacks" ever made on a public figure. The justice asked the public to withhold its judgment on the matter until he could explain his actions at length.[32]

On July 6, still under intense pressure to issue a statement denying any intent to impugn the court's conduct, Johnson published a sixteen-page pamphlet explaining his actions.[33] Johnson maintained that he submitted his original essay for publication purely as "a solemn warning to the fabricators of alarming rumours" and as a "precaution to the weaker sex against suffering their fears to be alarmed by every aggravated rumour that reached them."[34] Johnson claimed that he had no knowledge of the local court's existence, much less its activity, when he wrote the essay, presumably on Monday, June 17, or even when he delivered the essay to the newspaper on Thursday, June 20. Johnson also claimed that the court had pressured him almost daily for a retraction during the week of June 21 to 28, and that his brief publication on June 29 reflected his frustration with the court's heavy-handed tactics.[35] Johnson characterized the court's demand for a statement from him disavowing any intent to defame its members as an imperious "command" offered not "in the language of my natural political and social equals, but that of dictators." As such, these demands constituted an "attack on my republican sensibilities."[36]

In advancing the argument that the rumors of insurrection exposed the "weaker sex" to unwarranted fear and anxiety. Johnson doubtless had in mind his own daughter Anna, who grew distraught as the threat of insurrection gripped in the city. Writing from her father's home in Charleston on June 23, Anna told her cousin in North Carolina that "our city is now in the most fearful state." Through her uncle, Governor Bennett, and her father, Anna Johnson had access to considerable information concerning the ongoing investigation. Investigators led by Hamilton, Anna Johnson reported, had overheard "scenes of rapine and murder talked of with the coolness of demons." Anna wrote that once the insurrection began, "the men and Black women were to have been indiscriminately murdered—& we poor devils were to have been reserved to fill their harams—horrible." Anna also believed that her "beautiful young cousin," Governor Bennett's daughter, was "set apart for the wife or more properly 'the light of the Haram' of one of their Chiefs," Rolla Bennett. And, despite her father's skepticism, Anna Johnson apparently credited reports estimating the number of rebels involved in the alleged plot at three thousand.[37]

Justice William Johnson clearly failed to calm his own daughter's nerves, and instead of tempering the public's anxiety and prodding the court toward restraint in its investigation, his public foray on behalf of restraint and calm ignited further controversy. Not only did Johnson's cautionary tale fall on deaf ears, but it called forth widespread public support for the court and its actions, even though most Charlestonians knew only the broad outlines of its activities. *Courier* editor Willington quickly expressed regret that his newspaper had published the original essay, and he offered a hearty endorsement of the "character and conduct of the gentlemen who compose the Court."[38] During the first week of July, the members of the court tendered their resignation, but the Charleston press and public praised their efforts profusely and urged them to remain on the job.[39] On July 1, a letter to the *Courier* praised the court's "sacrifice of time, of feeling, and of personal considerations" and pleaded with the court to "reflect upon the all important nature of the subject" and the "progress which has been made" before resigning. The court, according to the writer, enjoyed the "unbounded and unequivocal confidence" of the community. The letter also claimed that no tribunal had ever "united in a higher degree, integrity, talents, firmness, humanity and all those qualities which are calculated to ensure justice to the accused and security to the public." Thus, "the citizens of Charleston and its vicinity, cannot refrain from expressing an anxious wish that the gentlemen who compose the present Court would continue their services until the causes and extent of the excitement which now pervades our community shall be thoroughly explored." The writer claimed that the "whole of our citizens will unquestionably accord" with the "sentiments" of his communication and that "thousands of them would, if necessary" sign the request that the court remain on duty.[40] "A Citizen of Charleston" told the editor of the *Southern Patriot* that "the gentlemen composing the Court" enjoyed the appreciation of "the whole community" for "their unwearied labors and calm and discriminating investigation" of the "painful and distressing" business before them. The writer concluded that the "combination of talents, respectability and integrity" of the men of the court "reconciles every man to the awful examples" they were making of slaves deemed guilty of plotting insurrection. "Citizen" also noted that James Hamilton was "due the undivided thanks and approbation of his Fellow Citizens" for "his able, faithful and zealous discharge" of his duties as intendant.[41]

Evidence of the popular support the court enjoyed during the controversy appeared in private correspondence as well as in the public press. In early July, Charleston native and state equity chancellor Henry William DeSaussure offered an assessment of the court, its members, and the contretemps that swirled around it in a letter to Charleston congressman Joel Poinsett. The chancellor praised Hamilton and the city council for acting with "discretion & Firmness" and thus earning the "thanks of the country." DeSaussure also praised the court, which he judged as "wisely selected from the best informed, most reasonable & firm of the Community." The court, in DeSaussure's view, consisted of "men neither to be misled by violent popular rumors, nor deterred from the performance of a painful duty by a false humanity." The chancellor expressed disappointment that Judge Johnson "had been drawn into an unpleasant controversy" and deemed the justice's public writings well-intentioned but "indiscreet."[42] During the same week, Charleston native Martha Richardson told her nephew that Johnson's reply to the court was "very lame" and pronounced the justice "humbled" by the exchange. Richardson reasoned that "delicacy should have kept him [Johnson] silent," since three of the first six blacks convicted by the court belonged to his brother-in-law (Bennett). She thought the judge's motive arose not only from a desire to protect Bennett's property but also from "a vanity to appear more wise and resolute than his neighbors" in the face of crisis.[43] And Hamilton himself confided to friends that "our friend judge Johnson" had "involved himself in an unpleasant controversy with public authorities and the court" by offering an admonition to both that the intendant judged "very unreasonable and unnecessary."

But Johnson's involvement, Hamilton concluded with a measure of satisfaction, had only produced "a great ferment excited against him."[44]

WHILE JUSTICE WILLIAM JOHNSON played the loser's hand in a very public confrontation with Hamilton and the court, his brother-in-law, Governor Thomas Bennett, was also engaged in a heated, but initially unpublicized, dispute with Hamilton and the court over the probable scope and severity of the alleged insurrection and the legality of the court and its procedures. Elected governor of South Carolina in 1820 at age thirty-nine, Thomas Bennett had enjoyed a meteoric rise in early-nineteenth-century Charleston politics. In partnership with his father, Bennett owned and operated perhaps the largest rice and lumber milling operations in Charleston and emerged as a leading city booster while still a young man. Embracing the Jeffersonian Republican cause as the era of Federalist domination in Charleston politics waned, Bennett first won election to the state house of representatives in 1804 at age twenty-three, and he served almost continually in the legislature over the next fifteen years. From 1814 to 1817, Bennett served as Speaker of the house, and in 1819 he won a seat in the state senate in a special election; he was reelected to a full term in the senate in 1820, but resigned when his legislative colleagues elected him governor in late November 1820. Like a number of other prominent South Carolina Republicans of the post–War of 1812 era, including established leaders such as Calhoun, Langdon Cheves, and William Lowndes, and promising newcomers such as Hamilton, Hayne, and Joel Poinsett, Bennett mixed his Republicanism with a penchant for aggressive government action. As a state legislator, he vigorously championed internal improvements, and favored the creation of the state-controlled Bank of the State of South Carolina and served on its first board of directors. In addition to his legislative experience, Bennett had served one term as intendant of Charleston during 1812–13. Thus, prior to the insurrection conspiracy of 1822 and the controversy surrounding it, Bennett had demonstrated remarkable political skill.[45]

Nothing in his ascendancy to the office of governor suggested that Bennett was anything less than a political prodigy who might have expected further political preferment from his state, if he chose to seek it, after his term as governor ended. But during the final six months of his term, Bennett became embroiled in a series of political controversies over the alleged insurrection conspiracy that shaped the rest of his political life decisively and adversely. When the insurrection scare gripped Charleston in mid-June, Bennett objected vigorously to the formation of the Magistrates and Freeholders Court, preferring instead to initiate a special state-controlled investigative committee charged with the systematic gathering of evidence. Under Bennett's plan, the state investigating committee would collect evidence and then turn any prosecutions over to the regular state criminal court system. Bennett discussed the matter with Hamilton before the city intendant called the Magistrates and Freeholders Court into session, but found Hamilton determined to keep the matter under city control.[46]

Bennett's dissatisfaction with the court and its procedures only grew once its proceedings began. Bennett disapproved of the procedures adopted by the court, especially its decision to conduct its business in secret and to pronounce sentence on the accused without allowing them to hear and possibly counter the testimony against them. Because the court's inquiry touched Governor Bennett's household early, bringing three of his trusted household servants under quick suspicion, Bennett knew firsthand that masters were sometimes denied the opportunity to visit their own accused slaves. Bennett also believed that his slaves had been tried on the basis of testimony of dubious reliability and sentenced to death when such an extreme punishment was not justified. On July 1, the day before the first round of executions, Bennett urged the court to review the sentence of his slave Batteau "with a view to the mitigation" of his "punishment." The court claimed that it reviewed its verdict and even reexamined two witnesses against Batteau, but the process reaffirmed the initial sentence. This incident only served to increase Bennett's frustration with the court.[47]

Bennett also revealed his disdain for the court's proceedings through his reaction to a personal visit from St. John's Parish planter James Ferguson. Hamilton's Committee on Vigilance had informed Ferguson that two of his slaves had been implicated in the insurrection plot by the confession of Jesse Blackwood, the member of the Vesey Six responsible for spreading the word among plantation slaves outside Charleston. After hearing Blackwood's account in person, Ferguson pronounced himself "satisfied" with the truth of the accused's statements, and on June 28, Ferguson visited Bennett in Charleston to offer the governor assistance in the capture of his two slaves since his plantation lay outside the jurisdiction of the court. Ferguson recalled that Bennett replied that "it would be a great pity" if "those poor wretches should suffer upon slight evidence." Ferguson thought the evidence against his slaves more impressive than did Bennett, who refused to arrest the suspected slaves and instead referred Ferguson to the Magistrates and Freeholders Court. Ferguson recalled that Bennett "expressed some regret" over his ongoing involvement in a "misunderstanding with the Court," but the governor clearly remained unconvinced that the alleged insurrection plot involved more than a few slaves and free blacks. Bennett's indifference to the news about possible slave conspirators in the heavily black countryside left Ferguson perplexed, and the incident, though later recounted by the court as a means of embarrassing the governor, indicated that, even in late June, Bennett already believed that an overeager court was blowing the alleged insurrection conspiracy out of proportion and crediting charges that lacked credibility.[48]

Undeterred by his initial failure to influence Hamilton and the court, Bennett continued his private efforts to stop or alter the court's proceedings. On July 1, the governor wrote state attorney general Robert Y. Hayne to call the constitutionality of the local court into question. Bennett asked if the so-called trials being held by the court met state constitutional standards. "Can a Court of Justice...be held behind closed doors?" Bennett asked. "Can a prisoner be legally tried and convicted without being confronted by his witnesses and every one of them? Can a corporation legally organize a court for the trial of felons?" In the letter, Bennett readily volunteered his own answer to the questions he posed. Bennett argued that the "the negative of each [question he posed]" stood "as the immutable rules of Courts exercising criminal jurisdiction."[49] On July 4, Hayne replied to the governor, taking a position in opposition to Bennett's on every issue. Hayne opined that the Magistrates and Freeholders Court convened in Charleston was perfectly legal in every way. "If I had been asked whether a free white man could be tried by a Court sitting behind closed doors and without being confronted with his witnesses," he wrote, "I should have had little difficulty in giving the answer....But nothing can be clearer than that slaves are not entitled to these rights." The question concerning free black defendants appeared different on its face, but, Hayne concluded, free blacks "are treated by laws in all respects in the like manner of slaves." Hayne admitted that "in general" it was "very just and proper that a Court of Freeholders sit with open doors, but circumstances may exist to justify and even recommend" closed sessions. "As far as I am acquainted with the facts," Hayne concluded, "such circumstances have recently existed and probably now exist." In essence, Hayne maintained that the constitutional safeguards alluded to by Bennett applied only to whites. The talented and ambitious attorney general viewed the actions of the Charleston court as justified on the grounds of white self-preservation. Hayne went on to caution the governor against further challenges to the court's authority. Hayne reminded Bennett that the "executive is not bound to examine Judicial errors." Going further, the attorney general advised the governor that "however your judgment may disapprove" of the court's actions, the governor had no official responsibility for them.[50] In simple terms, Hayne warned Bennett to leave the court alone.

Frustrated by his failure to either influence or invalidate the court, Bennett generally kept his own counsel until after all executions had been carried out (August 9), but his antipathy toward the court and its mode of operation in no way diminished. Together, the brothers in-law, Johnson and Bennett, one a United States Supreme Court justice and the other the incumbent governor of South Carolina, and both highly respected Charlestonians, tangled with city intendant James Hamilton and the court and lost. They failed miserably in their efforts to challenge the legal and extralegal processes used to thwart the alleged insurrection plot and mete out the prescribed punishments, and in all likelihood their efforts served only to spur the court into more far-reaching action. Once their respective roles as critics of the investigation and the court became known to the public, both Bennett and Johnson emerged from their contretemps with Hamilton and the court with diminished reputations and a sharp drop in their popularity. At the end of the day, they had little to show for their sacrifice of political capital except having inadvertently contributed to sending an already high-handed court lurching further out of control.

Even as Hamilton fended off criticism from Johnson and Bennett and cultivated popular favor with great aplomb during the court's early July recess, his own personal views on the insurrection plot had clearly taken firm shape. The popular intendant outlined these views in a letter to the mayor of Savannah written on July 3, the day after the execution of the Vesey Six.[51] Hamilton claimed that the plot had been long in the making and that the rebellion was scheduled to begin on Sunday, June 16. Charleston's black rebels were to have formed three columns. One column would have attacked the guardhouse and arsenal to seize arms. The newly armed rebels later would have met the two additional columns in the city center. The rebel plans called for setting the city ablaze with no fewer than forty fires and "the householders murdered at their doors on coming out." The "conflagration," Hamilton believed, would have signaled "negroes from the country to flock in & join their associates in arms in the city." That Charleston whites were spared this fate, Hamilton argued, owed almost entirely to "the fidelity of a favorite slave to his master."[52]

This early July letter also revealed that Hamilton had already convinced himself that the "plot had its origins among the Black class leaders of some of the different religious associations of this city—and altho its cause may in some degree be referable to the temporal inconveniences and suffering unavoidably incident to a state of slavery there are mainly attributable to religious fanaticism." The "ring leaders of the conspiracy," Hamilton claimed, "were all of them class Leaders or Deacons." Nor did Hamilton hesitate to praise his own investigation as one of "great activity and perseverance," and he asserted that "no excesses of popular feelings & prejudices have disgraced the character of our city—& that a remarkably respectable court has conducted its deliberations with humanity to the accused but with great energy as it regards the public safety."[53] Upon hearing Hamilton's preliminary private account, Martha Richardson expressed relief that the Savannah area had experienced "no cause for alarm," but she surmised that blacks in the Savannah area "knew of this business long before it was known by us."[54]

Back at the workhouse, the investigation continued despite the court's twelve-day recess, from June 27 to July 10. Five arrests of slaves later identified as "ringleaders" were made during the recess. Those arrested included Monday Gell (arrested on June 27, the day the court recessed); Charles Drayton, arrested on July 2; Harry Haig, confined on July 3; and Gullah Jack Pritchard and John Horry, arrested on July 5. Moreover, surviving manuscript records reveal that between July 2 and July 9, while officially in recess, the Committee of Vigilance and perhaps the court itself continued to take statements, some of which the court later labeled "confessions" from suspects, and gathered information later called "testimony" from other witnesses, many of whom were confined in the workhouse.[55]

The court, buoyed and perhaps even emboldened by strong signs of popular approval, returned to session on July 10 and remained at work for the next two and a half weeks.[56] But upon resuming business following the recess, the court apparently changed its mode of operation significantly. According to the evidence left in its own manuscript record of proceedings, the court, during its July session, abandoned its earlier practice of taking statements, determining guilt or innocence, and pronouncing judgments, substituting a new and somewhat trial-like procedure of bringing witnesses to testify against a particular defendant accused of specific crimes. It also heard on occasion from the accused, represented by their masters or attorneys hired by the masters. The accused may also have been present when testimony was offered against them, though there is no hard evidence to prove that they were. Whether or not these changes represented quiet responses to criticism from Johnson and Bennett and a resulting fear that their previous procedures might not receive public approval if they became widely known remains unclear. What is clear is that once the court reconvened, the scope of the investigation had widened considerably as a result of the "statements" taken during its supposed recess.[57] Immediately after reconvening, the court tried Gullah Jack Pritchard, Monday Gell, Charles Drayton, Harry Haig, and John Horry, all arrested since the court recessed on June 27 and charged with serving as key co-conspirators with Vesey, and sentenced them to death. The court scheduled the executions for July 12, less than a week after the arrest of two of the condemned, Gullah Jack Pritchard and John Horry.[58]

But even the conviction of another five alleged ringleaders scarcely slowed the investigation (though authorities later reported that they had hoped these sentences would bring the matter to a close). The investigation's new momentum came from the emergence of new star witnesses from the ranks of the condemned. These witnesses claimed to have inside knowledge of a much more extensive and intricate plot than the court had yet discovered. While in custody between his arrest on July 2 and scheduled execution on July 12, Charles Drayton, slave of popular former governor John Drayton, became "overwhelmed with terror and guilt" and sank into "a state of panic and depression" driven by "fear of death and the consequences of an hereafter, if he went out of the world without revealing all he knew." On July 9, the night before the court reconvened, Drayton asked to see Hamilton, who apparently visited Drayton early on the morning of the tenth. Hamilton claimed that he promised Drayton no mercy or reduction in sentence—no deal for testimony, in modern parlance—but Drayton nonetheless provided the intendant with "many particulars" that suggested a "much wider diffusion of the plot than ... was imagined."

Drayton told authorities that Monday Gell, whom Drayton blamed for landing him in such "a miserable and perilous condition," knew far more about the scale and scope of the insurrection plot than he had yet revealed. Drayton implied that he could get more information from Gell if allowed to converse further with the condemned harness maker, and the court complied, putting them in the same cell alone for twenty-four hours while adopting what the court later termed "some little stratagem to divert the suspicions of Monday, that Charles was confined with him merely for the purpose of getting information out of him." Moreover, after hearing Drayton's new information, the court postponed the executions of Drayton, Gell, and Harry Haig for first one week and then another, but Gullah Jack and John Horry were hanged as scheduled on July 12.[59] The delay of the announced executions of three convicted insurrectionists signaled the public that new developments were afoot in the investigation. Nor were these new developments a mystery to elite Charlestonians with close ties to the court. John Potter reported to Langdon Cheves on July 10 that the court's new investigations revealed "with every step" that "the Conspiracy had spread wider and wider." In the court's second session, Potter observed, confessions "were made more freely" and "a vast number of slaves were taken up" by authorities.[60]

On July 13, Drayton testified concerning the new information he had obtained from Monday Gell. When the court confronted Gell with Dayton's alleged testimony, the artisan, after more than two weeks of confinement in the workhouse, "confessed his own guilt." Not only did Gell offer a statement or "confession" outlining an extensive and well-planned black conspiracy, but he also agreed to testify against many of the blacks he implicated in his newly expansive account of the intended insurrection.[61] Over the next two weeks, Gell named thirty-five co-conspirators, testified against numerous defendants, sometimes offering details omitted or denied in his first confession, and eventually, sometime before July 27, offered a second confession, which detailed the most sweeping account of the insurrection yet. Planned and led by Denmark Vesey, the rebellion drew on lists of those who had agreed to participate, locations of weapons available for rebel use, slaves recruited from the countryside, the possibility of communications with Saint Domingue, and a decision, largely dictated by Vesey, to "kill both women and children" as well as men.[62]

Together, the testimony of Gell, Drayton, and four other star witnesses hoping for commutation of their sentences helped send at least twenty-five additional blacks to the gallows and many others into exile, and convinced Charleston authorities that they had quelled a rebellion of staggering proportions. According to Michael P. Johnson's calculations, three superstar witnesses, Monday Gell, Charles Drayton, and Perault Strohecker, provided roughly 75 percent of the testimony against the convicted rebels. At least one of the three superstar witnesses testified in all but five proceedings in which the accused were convicted, and at least one superstar witness testified in every trial that ended in the conviction and execution of the accused. Thus, driven largely by Monday Gell's evolving testimony, and the testimony of others such as Charles Drayton and Perault Strohecker, whose very lives in all likelihood depended on producing convictions, the Charleston massacre of 1822 proceeded without additional public dissent. In its July session alone, the court tried forty-nine men and convicted forty-four; twenty-six men were sentenced to death by hanging, and eighteen were sentenced to exile outside the United States.[63]

By July 24, the court had grown so pleased with its handiwork and the effective testimony of Gell, Drayton, and Haig that it asked Governor Bennett to commute the sentences of its three star witnesses from death to exile. According to the court, Gell, Drayton, and Haig were "unquestionably guilty of the offenses with which they have been charged; but under the impressions that they would ultimately have their lives spared, they have made to us disclosures not only important in the detection of the general plan of the conspiracy, but enabling the Court to convict a number of the principal offenders." The court claimed that under the circumstances, execution of its star witnesses would amount "almost to treachery." Moreover, the court argued, commutation of the sentences would show Charleston-area slaves and free blacks that "even their principal advisors and ringleaders cannot be confided in, and that under temptation of exemption from capital punishment they will betray the common cause." Bennett declined the request the next day, tersely telling the court that it had "cloaked" itself with all the authority necessary to commute the sentences independent of the governor's power of pardon. The court promptly fulfilled the terms of the informal plea bargain it had offered its three key slave witnesses and reduced the sentences of Gell, Drayton, and Haig from death to exile. On July 26, believing the bulk of its business done, the Magistrates and Freeholders Court adjourned sine die.[64]

Once the court adjourned, it received the "grateful thanks of their fellow citizens for their labors." The *Charleston Mercury* praised the court's "humanity," "wisdom," and "perseverance" and claimed that the court had "secured the safety of the city, and the lasting gratitude of its inhabitants."[65] Three weeks later, a public letter signed "Many Citizens" thanked the members of the court for "their zeal, their vigilance, their firmness" and vowed to "protect from aspersion the characters of those who have acted in our behalf."[66]

By the time the court finished its work, its members believed they had uncovered not only one massive insurrection plot but two additional contingency plans crafted by slaves and free blacks remaining at large after the first arrests were made. In the court's view, the original conspiracy had been primarily the work of Denmark Vesey and nine slave ringleaders: Peter Poyas, Monday Gell, Gullah Jack Pritchard, Rolla Bennett, Ned Bennett, Batteau Bennett, John Horry, Jesse Blackwood, and Charles Drayton.[67] According to evidence later presented by the court, the Vesey conspiracy involved not only a large-scale uprising of city blacks but also the arrival of slaves from the countryside to join the insurrection, and perhaps even the appearance of ships from Saint Domingue, sent either to carry the rebels to freedom or loaded with troops to assist in the killing of Lowcountry whites, possibly both. The court believed that Vesey had carefully organized the would-be insurgents, assigning able and trusted lieutenants to lead specific groups of rebels in accomplishing very specific tasks. Vesey's plan appeared elegant but complicated. Its success demanded courage, careful execution, good timing, cohesion and loyalty among rebels, white incompetence, and luck. Testimony suggested that Vesey intended to kill as many whites as possible, including women and children; other convicted slaves claimed that the rebels intended to kill all the men, and once that was done, they "would know what to do with the women." The second alleged insurrection, planned for June 29 or 30, was supposedly designed to rescue Denmark Vesey and his five lieutenants who were scheduled to hang on July 2. The third plan, allegedly orchestrated by Gullah Jack, was scheduled for July 6 to avenge the execution of the Vesey Six, but the plot was thwarted by the timely arrest of its purported leader, Gullah Jack, on July 5. The court insisted that it had discovered and thwarted a vast conspiracy responsible for at least three related insurrection plots.[68]

On August 1, another Magistrates and Freeholders Court, and again one composed of distinguished members of the Charleston polity, including Joel R. Poinsett, Robert Y. Hayne, and Charles M. Furman, was organized.[69] It was only when this second court convened that, after a "free interchange of sentiments," the members of the court "unanimously" decided that "with respect to capital punishments, enough had been done by way of example in relation to this conspiracy," and that the court would use "banishment" as its most severe punishment unless the accused was a "leader" in the putative rebellion or his case was "distinguished by very peculiar circumstances."[70] After the Vesey scare was revealed, it took six weeks and the execution of thirty-four blacks before white Charlestonians would conclude, as Jefferson and Monroe had after the Gabriel scare, that there had been "hanging enough." The first court had done the heavy lifting, but the second court conducted fourteen trials in two days between August 3 and 8. In its first trial, the second court sentenced one slave, William Garner, accused of being a chief recruiter among black draymen, to the gallows. Garner had escaped to Columbia using a legitimate pass from his mistress before charges were lodged against him, but Governor Bennett quickly notified Columbia authorities, who found Garner, arrested him, and held him until he could be safely returned to Charleston for trial. In the thirteen other cases, seven defendants were convicted and sentenced to transportation beyond the borders of the United States; the other six were acquitted. The second court adjourned on August 8. When Garner was executed on August 9, 1822, the trials and punishments connected with the alleged Denmark Vesey insurrection scare were officially over.[71]

THE VESEY INVESTIGATION resulted in the execution of thirty-five blacks, slave and free, and the deportation of thirty-two others. The guilt of those convicted, even if judged according to the standards whites typically used to determine the guilt of slaves and free blacks during the 1820s, much less when judged by the standards of modern jurisprudence, remains almost impossible for historians to determine with any degree of certainty. As the trials and resulting punishments wound toward their tragic conclusion, city, state, and court authorities all scrambled to shape the public's understanding of the scare, to paint the picture of thwarted insurrection that they wanted the public, and posterity, to see. The court, recognizing that the public remained eager for a full explanation of affairs, and knowing also that Governor Thomas Bennett remained critical of its activity and was unlikely to leave his ink in the well for long, prepared to tell its story in two forms. James Hamilton, the political impresario of the investigation, penned a brief account for quick publication, and the court's two presiding magistrates, Lionel Kennedy and Thomas Parker, prepared a lengthier official report for release later in the fall.

In the meantime, as the public awaited official publications, private conversations and correspondence produced an informal narrative that circulated pretty extensively among the Charleston elite. This informal narrative was shaped chiefly by leaks from Hamilton and the court and hence anticipated their later reports in important ways. Anna Johnson remained concerned about insurrection well into July, her father's pleas to the contrary notwithstanding, writing her cousin on July 18 that "nothing but the merciful interposition of God has saved us from horror equal if not superior to the scenes acted in St. Domingo." By mid-July, Anna had gained enough perspective on the plot to admit that she had heard rumors of "circumstances real and imaginary," and she promised to repeat only information "I know of that Bears the stamp of truth." Nonetheless, Anna's correspondence presented a disconcerting summary of the rebels' plan. The rebels, she reported, intended "to take the city and keep it as long as possible and then carry us & the common negroes to St. D there to be sold as slaves with as much plunder as they could find." Charleston, she concluded, "would have been a complete scene of desolation."[72]

None of Anna Johnson's July letters even hinted that city authorities exaggerated the threat posed by the insurrection or that the court got carried away with its own authority, as her father and uncle had charged. Instead, during the investigation's early stages, Anna judged Hamilton and the court as the "most impartial and honourable men of our city," and even more than a month into the investigation, she declared that she had "never heard in my life more deep laid plots or plots more likely to succeed."[73] She accepted the verdict that the accused rebels, scheduled for execution, "are guilty most certainly" even though it made her "blood curdle" to think of how many executions the city carried out.[74]

Also in mid-July, John Potter reported that the plot involved setting fires across the city, and as the "white males were to appear—even before they could leave their own doors, the indiscriminate massacre was to take place." With the males dead, Potter declared, "the females were to be reserved for worse than death." Local authorities believed that Vesey planned to rob the banks and carry off "as much plunder as he could to St. Domingo" while leaving behind "his Blind agents" to "perish for their crimes."[75] The insurrection "scheme," Potter advised Langdon Cheves, was "cunningly devised," and "had the execution been as well supported, many of us this day would not have been left to tell the tale."[76] Perhaps the most cunning aspect of the alleged plot, in Potter's view at least, emerged from the testimony of Harry Haig, a condemned slave of Dr. Henry Haig, who claimed that Gullah Jack had pressured him "to poison his master's well." Haig claimed that he refused Gullah Jack on this point, even though he admitted joining the insurrection. Potter believed that a general poisoning of Charleston wells was an intended part of the foiled plot, and he reported that Hamilton, shortly after learning of the poisoning plan, estimated that "50 or 60 more" blacks "will have to be tried for their lives." "Good God, what have we come to," Potter exclaimed.[77]

In early August, Martha Richardson wrote an account consistent with the earlier ones by Anna Johnson and John Potter. Richardson weathered the Vesey scare from the presumed safety of Savannah, where she resided with her brother-in-law John Screven and received regular reports on the scare from family and friends, including Charles Harris, the mayor of Savannah. She declared that the accused insurrectionists were "true warriors" and that "not a single woman knew a word of their plans." Richardson believed that the plot had been four years in the making but that the plans were so "secret" that "no suspicion" was derived from the "conduct" of the slaves or free blacks. She noted that "two negroes belonging to the same master —both working in the same mill— were ignorant that either was engaged in the plot until they met in jail." Moreover, she predicted that life would prove "dreadful" in Charleston in the aftermath of the scare. "[A]ll confidence is lost in our servants," she declared. As proof of her points, Richardson told the chilling story of the arrest and trial of Elias Horry's trusted personal servant, John Horry. When the constables arrived in Elias' yard to "take up his waiting man," the master assured the authorities they were "mistaken." Elias then accompanied his trusted slave to trial, "convinced still he could not be guilty." After hearing the evidence presented, Horry asked his trusted slave directly, "Tell me, are you guilty, for I cannot believe unless I hear you say so." John Horry replied yes. When asked what he had intended to do to aid the plot, John told his master that he had planned "to kill you, rip open your belly & throw your guts in your face." On the whole, Martha Richardson observed, the insurrection plot reeked not only of the treachery of trusted domestics but also "of the wildest plans engendered by religious enthusiasm and wrong conception of the Bible." Given the prominence of religious slaves among the accused insurrectionists, Richardson concluded that "a little learning is a dangerous thing."[78]

In different levels of detail, the accounts of Anna Johnson, John Potter, and Martha Richardson presented consistent informal accounts of the insurrection plot. The similarity of their accounts suggests several significant points about the information circulating in Charleston during the month of July. First, detailed, if not necessarily accurate, information circulated widely among members of the city's well-connected elite despite the investigation's avowed need for, and claims of, secrecy. Second, the leaks, if they can be called that given how freely they flowed, revealed that the court had become convinced of many of the alleged insurrection plot's particulars early in the investigation, and certainly well before the details were fleshed out in the effusive "confessions" of Monday Gell and Charles Drayton in mid-July. The fact that Hamilton and the court had developed a coherent interpretation of the alleged plot by early July gives credence to the notion that later slave "confessions" may have been calculated by the convicted to fit the preconceptions and prejudices of white authorities. Moreover, the leaked accounts also worked to shape public perceptions in a manner conducive to the court's position long before the intendant's account of the incident appeared in August, and well before the court issued its official report in late October. Third, these private accounts indicated how certain elements of the insurrection story gained a sense of familiarity, and even "a stamp of truth," in the public mind well before published accounts circulated, and that the stories usually originated in information shared by Hamilton or members of the court with friends and acquaintances.[79]

THE BATTLE TO SHAPE the public's lasting impressions of the Vesey insurrection scare reached a fever pitch in August 1822. The first extensive public commentary on the Charleston insurrection scare of 1822 by someone with official knowledge of its details appeared in a circular letter written by Governor Thomas Bennett, who won an apparent race with Hamilton to publish the first summary of the scare. Bennett distributed his letter on August 10, only one day after the last execution of a condemned slave, suggesting that he had prepared his account in advance and was ready to issue it at the earliest appropriate moment. The *Charleston Courier* published Bennett's circular on August 23, and one of the republic's leading political newspapers, the *National Intelligencer*, obtained the circular and published it on August 24.[80] The *Intelligencer* editors claimed they had acquired the letter "accidentally," but because the subject was of "so pervading an interest," they decided not to withhold it from publication.

In the letter, clearly prepared for national as well as local consumption, Bennett conveyed the message to audiences outside South Carolina that Charleston had experienced an insurrection scare, that the scare unfortunately had been blown out of proportion by some local authorities, that the real threat presented by a handful of calculating slave and free black incendiaries had been easily discovered and thwarted, and that the port city was once again busy exporting valuable southern staples and supplying the plantations and farms that grew those staples. In a frank and detailed account of the matter, Bennett again suggested that the court had exaggerated fears needlessly and given weight to incredible rumors. He argued that the court had levied excessive punishments against many of those convicted, and though the potential dangers arising from the plot were serious enough on their merits, the court had inflated them entirely out of proportion. Bennett worried that because of the court's exaggeration of the plot and the needless severity of the punishments it meted out, "the reputation of the state must suffer abroad." Bennett feared that such a blot on the state's image in the eyes of the world might trigger "a rapid deterioration of property values" in South Carolina by spreading the impression that neither people nor property was safe there.[81]

To prevent such an unfortunate turn of events, Bennett offered an explanation of the Vesey conspiracy that blamed the court as much as the black insurrectionists for the midsummer tragedy in Charleston. The public mind, Bennett insisted, "was agitated by a variety of rumors, calculated to produce great excitement and alarm." The court's actions encouraged a "general impression...of a very extensive conspiracy," and "greatly magnified" the threat of an immature plot, which, "as soon as discovered...ceased to be dangerous." In particular, Bennett expressed disappointment that the court's insistence on handing down the "severest punishment, beyond any former example," thus creating the impression of a larger and more dangerous slave insurrection plot than actually existed.[82]

Despite his criticisms, Bennett credited the investigation for its "zeal" and recounted some of its findings to his readers. Though the governor did not see eye to eye with the court on much, he agreed concerning Monday Gell's active role. In fact, Bennett went even further than the court in laying responsibility for the insurrection plot at Gell's feet, identifying the literate slave artisan as "the most daring and active" of the conspirators. Gell, Bennett explained, "could read and write with facility" and thus exerted "an extraordinary and dangerous influence over his fellows." As a slave allowed by his owner to "occupy a house in a central part of the city," Gell enjoyed "hourly opportunities" for the "exercise of his skill on those who were attracted to his shop by business or favor." It was in Gell's shop, Bennett suggested, "that his artful and insidious delusions were kept in perpetual exercise."[83] In his account, the governor scrupulously avoided any mention of the alleged involvement of his own household slaves or of their conviction and subsequent execution. Bennett concluded his letter by pronouncing South Carolina and its authorities equal to the challenge of any conceivable revolt, and argued that no large-scale rebellion could possibly succeed before one or more of the conspirators betrayed the plan. In summing up the incident, Bennett insisted that "the scheme has not been general nor alarmingly extensive." Moreover, the governor found it "a cause for much satisfaction" that even though "religion, superstition, fear, and almost every passion that sways the human mind" had been "artfully used' by leaders of the insurrection, "so few [blacks] have been seduced from a course of propriety and obedience."[84] Bennett's account concluded that an insurrection plot had been formed, but that it also had been quickly discovered and easily foiled.

Bennett's account offered the most detailed account of the insurrection scare yet offered to the public when it first appeared, but the governor's efforts to shape public perceptions of the scare were easily trumped by James Hamilton's publication, just a few days later, of his own account of the investigation and its findings.[85] Once Hamilton's forty-eight-page pamphlet appeared, the popular intendant's account quickly captured the public imagination in Charleston and its surrounding environs. Its contents soon evolved into the core of received truth about the scare in the memory of white Charlestonians. In his pamphlet, Hamilton argued that Vesey's planned rebellion produced a period of "great and uninterrupted excitement" in which "justice has been blended with enlightened humanity." No "cruel or barbarous modes of punishment have been resorted to," Hamilton insisted, and the trials, in his view, proved noteworthy for "the wisdom, impartiality, and moderation that governed them." The trial procedures, Hamilton claimed, in clear contradiction of the surviving primary evidence, were "even superior to those which the ordinary modes of judicature would have afforded ourselves." The court decided before trials began, Hamilton claimed, "that the testimony should be regulated by those established rules of evidence which are elsewhere found so important in the exposition of truth; that no slave should be tried but in the presence of his Master or his Attorney; that the testimony of one witness, unsupported by circumstances, should lead to no conviction involving capital punishment; and that the statement of the party himself should be heard in examination of such particulars as seemed most inculpatory." The court, Hamilton grandiloquently concluded, would humbly "submit our conduct to the award of posterity, and ourselves to the protection of the Supreme Ruler of events."[86]

Hamilton's bold statements about the fairness of the court's procedures are directly contradicted by much of the surviving evidence, including Bennett's complaint to Hayne and the manuscript version of the trial report, which suggest both that such claims were blatantly false and that Hamilton knew they were false when he made them. Indeed, Hamilton was aware, even if the bulk of Charleston's white population was not, that Governor Bennett had forcefully if futilely complained about the court's procedures as early as late June, and that he had eventually taken his complaints to the state attorney general. But the secrecy of the proceedings, which Hamilton defended, provided the talented intendant an opportunity to shape the public understanding of the alleged conspiracy he claimed to have unraveled and punished, and to do so while basking in the praise of the Charleston press for his bold and decisive action.[87]

After defending the court's conduct in his introduction, Hamilton presented the Charleston public with its first overview of the insurrection scare other than Bennett's brief version. The intendant painted a picture of a bloodbath narrowly avoided, of bold and timely action by city and state authorities, and of a relentless investigation that carefully sorted out all charges before punishing the leading black insurrectionists with swift severity. By Hamilton's count, 130 slaves and free blacks were arrested. Thirty-five, including all "ringleaders" save Monday Gell, received the death penalty, and thirty-seven, including Gell, were ultimately banished from the state. The "most important object in uprooting a conspiracy," Hamilton maintained, "we have fully accomplished by bringing to punishment the whole of the ringleaders."[88] But Hamilton included the most important message of his account in the brief notice, "To the Public," that introduced the pamphlet and explained his reasons for publishing it despite "the difficulties and embarrassments necessarily incident to the subject." The account, Hamilton observed, could ensure the "salutary inculcation of one lesson among a certain portion of our population," and that lesson was "that there is nothing you are bad enough to do, that we are not powerful enough to punish."[89]

Hamilton's account not only defended the court's conduct and briefly sketched key particulars of the alleged insurrection plot but also attempted to "take some notice of the causes of this conspiracy" in order to lay a foundation for public policy changes he considered necessary to prevent the creation of future plots. Hamilton thought Vesey, a successful free black carpenter, was motivated primarily by a "malignant hatred of whites" and an "inordinate lust for power and booty." After "laying our city in ashes, and moistening its cinders in blood," Vesey planned to "pillage our banks" and depart for "San Domingo," leaving his "deluded followers" behind to face the inevitable retribution of South Carolina's white militia aided, if necessary, by federal troops. In assessing the alleged architect and general of the proposed rebellion, Hamilton portrayed Vesey as a man of extraordinary ability, an evil genius, a man of uncommon courage, vision, imagination, determination, flexibility, charisma, and organization, a commander who knew his enemy well and anticipated almost every contingency. As presented by Hamilton, Vesey's mean brilliance rendered the plot he masterminded all the more dangerous (and hence Hamilton's feat in discovering and thwarting it all the more impressive). But when evaluating Vesey's motives, Hamilton could see Vesey only as a terrorist driven by the pursuit of money, revenge, power, and perhaps fame, and never as a disciplined black revolutionary interested in freeing slaves and expropriating the ill-gotten gains of the slaveholding rice aristocracy for the benefit of that hard-pressed experiment in black self-government, Haiti.[90]

In assaying the motives of Vesey's alleged slave lieutenants, Hamilton's speculation centered on matters of controversy familiar to all Charlestonians, and most white South Carolinians, by the early 1820s. His commentary focused on two perceived problems: a growing leniency in the treatment of slaves, and the role played by slave literacy and black Christianity in mobilizing the insurgency. Hamilton did not hesitate to berate masters he perceived as responsible for these problems. He called lenient treatment of slaves "misguided benevolence" rather than paternalism. He insisted that all of the slaves identified as "ringleaders" in the conspiracy "had no individual hardship to complain of," but rather ranked among the "most humanely treated negroes in our city." Indeed, Hamilton pointed out with dismay, the "facilities for combining and confederating in such a scheme" were "amply afforded" by "the extreme indulgence and kindness, which characterizes the domestic treatment of our slaves." The intendant thought this benevolence was largely the product of paternalistic attitudes among Christian masters. Even more specifically, Hamilton and many other members of the Charleston elite blamed what they perceived as the dangerous increase in slave literacy on Christian interest in converting slaves, and the confident intendant reserved his sharpest rebuke for those who supported teaching slaves to read and write. Hamilton complained that many masters, "not satisfied with ministering to the wants of their domestics, by all the comforts of abundant food and excellent clothing," had not only "permitted their instruction [in reading and writing], but lent to such efforts their approbation and applause."[91]

For the most part, of course, masters who encouraged slave literacy had been influenced to one degree or by the evangelical awakening of the early nineteenth century. The trend that James Hamilton lamented, and even linked with insurrection plots, was the trend that Edmund Botsford, Richard Furman, and scores of other evangelical ministers and their dedicated followers worked tirelessly to sustain. When painted in bold relief, it was a war of two cultures, pitting profit- and security-minded slaveholders against soul-saving and hardship-mitigating evangelicals (who were often also slaveholders). Put another way, the conflict pitted Christian paternalists against wizened masters bad enough to do whatever it took to sustain slavery. At least in his report, Hamilton stopped short of launching a full-blown assault on the evangelical mission to the slaves that had produced so many black Christians in Charleston, but he certainly fingered improperly supervised black Christianity as the chief motivating force behind the alleged insurrection.[92] "Religious fanaticism has not been without its effect on this project," Hamilton asserted, calling the independent African church a "hotbed, in which the germ [of insurrection] might well be expected to spring into life and vigour." Among "the conspirators," Hamilton noted, "a majority of them belonged to the African church, and among those executed were several who had been class leaders." The African church was broken up, "voluntarily," as Hamilton described it, immediately after the Vesey scare, with its property confiscated or destroyed, its leader, Morris Brown, eventually forced to leave the state (probably with special assistance from Hamilton), and many of its loyal members returning to religious fellowship among Charleston's white Methodists, Presbyterians, Congregationalists, and Baptists.[93]

Hamilton's indictment of the African church, and unsupervised black religious gatherings generally, suggested the need for new restrictions on the religious instruction of slaves and a sharp curtailment of religious autonomy among both slaves and free blacks. Other white Charlestonians went even further than Hamilton in blaming efforts to Christianize the slaves for the creating the environment which spawned the Vesey plot. Nor did Hamilton ignore the question of other religious influences on the alleged insurrection. While he singled out the treachery of black Christians and their white facilitators for special opprobrium, largely because the ongoing effort to Christianize the slaves enjoyed such significant white support and encouragement, he also emphasized the role of traditional African beliefs in convincing slaves to participate in the insurrection. According to Hamilton, Vesey, leaving "no engines of power unessayed," approached the Angola-born conjurer known as Gullah Jack, a man Hamilton described as "fifteen or twenty years in this country" and yet seemingly "untouched by the influences of civilized life," and asked him to recruit a company of African-born slaves for the rebellion. Vesey, Hamilton postulated, "turned his eye to this Necromancer, aware of his influence with his own countrymen [Angolan-born slaves and free blacks], who are distinguished both for their credulous superstition and clannish sympathies." Even "those negroes who were born in this country," Hamilton lamented, often spoke sincerely of Jack's "charmed invincibility."[94] When Martha Richardson, still in Savannah, read Hamilton's account of the plot, she called it a "history of the wildest plans—engendered by superstition and ignorance," but she agreed with the persuasive intendant's conclusions, insisting that "most of the ringleaders were of the Gullah tribe mechanics and draymen—of the Methodist religion."[95]

Hamilton's brief account of the scare appeared in August, immediately and effectively countering Bennett's controversial narrative. But Hamilton's account was relatively brief. He had other matters to tend in the fall of 1822, including campaigns for reelection to the state legislature and as city intendant, as well as a Bank of the United States stockholders meeting in Philadelphia. So the members of the Vesey court had asked the presiding magistrates, Kennedy and Parker, to draft an official report detailing the investigation and trials. Nearly two months later, in late October 1822, Kennedy and Parker secured the endorsement of the entire court and submitted their *Official Report* to the local district court.[96] The *Official Report* included an explanation of court procedures, a narrative of the "Conspiracy and Intended Insurrection," and, as its longest section, a supposed transcript of the trials. The narrative provided the fullest account of what the court believed it had uncovered, or at least the account the court wanted the public and posterity to believe, about the Denmark Vesey insurrection scare. For some purposes at least, the most important fact about the report was (and remains) that it tells the story the court wanted told. It shaped public perception of events, and it was certainly intended to do just that. As such, it makes important points about the Vesey court's agenda, regardless of the historical truth of its claims.[97]

Predictably, given the timing of its release (after the publication of Bennett's August letter but before the governor's much-anticipated November message to the legislature), the report, in the manner of Hamilton's account, began with an aggressive defense of the court's rules and procedures. The report claimed that from its inception the court agreed to five basic and inviolable rules of procedure: no slave would be tried except in the presence of his owner or appropriate legal counsel; no defendant would be convicted of a capital offense on the uncorroborated testimony of only one witness; the accused would be allowed to confront witnesses against them (unless anonymity had been granted the witness for reasons of personal safety); defendants could be represented by counsel if requested by masters; and, finally, the "accused should be heard" and allowed to examine witnesses. The report claimed that after "mature deliberation," the court decided to close its doors to the public to protect the identity of certain witnesses and to prevent court proceedings from impeding the investigation. The report, however, admitted that before the court "proceeded to any trial," it had been "engaged [for] some time in examining all the testimony they could obtain" in an effort to determine "how far a conspiracy had really been formed." Only after being convinced "of the existence of a plot" did the court formulate its alleged rules of procedure.[98]

As Michael P. Johnson's meticulous scrutiny of the court's own manuscript record of its proceedings revealed, the *Official Report*'s claims on behalf of the court's procedures fundamentally misrepresented its actual conduct. Johnson's analysis of the court's manuscript record suggests that many of the accused apparently never saw their accusers, and that even when the accused had counsel they were often unable to cross-examine witnesses. Other evidence suggests that masters were apparently often excluded from the court's proceedings, and an impressive array of evidence suggests that collaboration among witnesses for the court rendered the safeguard of requiring two witnesses for conviction of a capital offense meaningless. Thus many of the assertions made by the *Official Report* were either known to be false by the report's authors at the time or represented palpable distortions of the truth likely intended to mislead the public about the court's actual procedures.[99]

On its face, however, the court's official report also included the most detailed account of the investigation and the alleged insurrection conspiracy available to the public. In its account, the court insisted that Denmark Vesey, a free black carpenter, stood "at the head of the conspiracy" and that "with him the idea doubtless originated." According to the report, Vesey used a plethora of methods to arouse discontent among Charleston-area slaves. Well acquainted with the teachings of Christianity, Vesey, the court claimed, "rendered himself perfectly familiar with all those parts of Scriptures which he thought he could pervert to his purpose." Allegedly, Vesey chastised slaves who displayed respect or deference to whites, drew heavily on antislavery arguments used in the Missouri debates, and "sought every opportunity of entering into conversations with white persons that could be overheard by Negroes" in order to "artfully introduce some bold remark on slavery."[100] In sum, the court presented Vesey as a calculating and intelligent troublemaker who steadily sowed seeds of discord among Charleston blacks. While the court suspected that Vesey had been spreading discontent for up to four years, they also concluded that the actual planning of the rebellion began in December 1821. At that time, Vesey contacted Rolla and Ned Bennett, slaves of Thomas Bennett, and Peter Poyas, a skilled slave artisan, promising them leadership roles in the rebellion; shortly thereafter he recruited Gullah Jack. He also enlisted a number of lesser officers, to some of whom he delegated the task of lining up support from plantation slaves living in the countryside around Charleston. Vesey told recruits he expected help from Haiti and Africa; he threatened retribution against blacks who refused to join the revolt. In short, Vesey used any appeal that might prove effective in helping him raise a rebellion in the heart of slave country.[101]

The court claimed that by Friday, June 14, city authorities knew enough about the likelihood of an insurrection scheduled for the evening of Sunday the sixteenth to take highly visible and effective preventive measures. Noting the presence of a "strong guard" on patrol on the sixteenth, Vesey decided to delay action. Soon thereafter, Vesey and several other "ringleaders" were arrested, scotching the original insurrection plot once and for all. Yet, according to the court, even with Vesey and five of his top lieutenants in custody, other leaders still at large contrived a plan to launch the insurrection on July 2, "immediately after the nightly Guard and

Patrols had been discharged from duty," in an effort to rescue Vesey and the five slave accomplices sentenced to die with him. But two of the rebel leaders were arrested on July 2 and their plan was foiled. The court also believed that Gullah Jack planned to make yet a third try to raise an insurrection on July 6, as he "resolved to rise and attack at day dawn" to avenge the execution of the Vesey Six, but the arrest of Gullah Jack on July 5 and the continued activity of the guard "effectually stopped" this plan of rebellion. Once Gullah Jack and John Horry were arrested (July 5) and sentenced to die on July 12 alongside Monday Gell, Charles Drayton, and Harry Haig, the court felt "some prospect of the investigation closing." But when Gell and Drayton "confessed," their statements and subsequent testimony lent incredible new energy to the investigation, which gained momentum as it roared off in pursuit of new leads offered by its star witnesses.[102]

Thus the court's description of the alleged insurrection conspiracy as wide-ranging, meticulously planned, and capable of at least some initial success appeared to justify the court's swift action, sweeping investigation, and draconian punishments. "By the timely discovery of the plot," the *Official Report* concluded, "South Carolina has been rescued from the most horrible catastrophe with which it has been threatened since it has been an independent state." The report claimed that the revolt "could not possibly" have succeeded over the long term, but "before [the slave rebels'] suppression, Charleston would probably have been wrapped in flames—many valuable lives have been sacrificed and an immense loss of property sustained by the citizens." Moreover, the court's report maintained that the impact of the insurrection would have reached beyond the city limits and deep into the countryside, where "plantations in the lower country would have been disorganized, and the agricultural interests would have sustained an enormous loss."[103]

While the *Official Report*'s analysis of the causes of the insurrection conspiracy paralleled those Hamilton outlined in August, it offered more extensive commentary on many points. Testimony suggesting that the insurrection had been discussed for at least four years prompted the court to note that this dissatisfaction among blacks appeared "about the time the African congregation...was formed." The report also observed that "a decided majority of the insurgents, either did or had belonged to the African congregation, among whom the enlistments were principally and successfully carried on." The "African congregation...," the report continued, "was not only composed altogether of colored persons, but their Ministers were also colored....The influence which such men and class leaders must necessarily acquire of the minds of ignorant blacks is evident." In such settings, "perverted religion and fanaticism" taught that slaves should seek "the freedom and privileges enjoyed by the whites." The court noted that it "was also about this time [of the formation of the African church], that class meetings of the colored people had become so common as they now are; each class having a colored preacher or leader." These meetings, the court lamented, were "held usually at night...avowedly for religious instruction and worship," and "no white person attended." That "inflammatory and insurrectionary doctrines...were inculcated at these meetings or some of them, was positively proved," the court claimed, and it believed that black class meetings were "used as places of rendezvous and rallying points" as the alleged insurrectionists planned their revolt for the summer of 1822. Clearly the court deliberately presented a forceful argument that the spread of Christianity among blacks, when unaccompanied by proper white supervision and control, created an environment where slaves and free blacks spawned and incubated insurrection plots. The *Official Report* maintained that the "great impropriety of allowing meetings of any kind to be held solely by slaves...must forcibly strike every reflecting mind."[104]

The court's *Official Report* also highlighted the "melancholy truth" that all the leaders of the alleged insurrection, except Gullah Jack, enjoyed "not only the unlimited confidence of their owners" but also "had been indulged in every comfort, and allowed every privilege compatible with their situation in the community." As a free black, the report noted, Vesey owned "a considerable estate," conducted "a good business as a carpenter," and "enjoyed so much confidence of the whites" that the community "discredited" charges against him until "proof of his guilt" became "too strong" to ignore. The report also emphasized that Vesey and his "ringleaders" confined their recruiting efforts "to Negroes who hired or worked, such as carters, draymen, sawyers, porters, laborers, stevedores, mechanics, and those employed in lumber yards," those "who had certain allotted hours at their disposal." Following Hamilton's lead, the court's *Official Report* also emphasized the unique characteristics of the "ringleaders." A "slave of great value," Peter Poyas enjoyed the "confidence of his master" and had earned a reputation for being "a first rate ship carpenter." Rolla Bennett, the "confidential servant of his master," often guarded Thomas Bennett's family when the governor was away. Ned Bennett also served the governor as a "confidential servant" known for "general good conduct." Known as a "most excellent harness maker," Monday Gell "kept a shop on his own on Meeting street" and lived with "his time and a large proportion of the profits of his labor...at his own disposal."[105] In the minds of many whites, the fact that the putative leaders of the alleged insurrection came from the ranks of Charleston's most comfortable and autonomous slaves, slaves some whites referred to as privileged, did not suggest that extending slaves more comforts and privileges promised to make them more loyal and obedient.

When fall arrived in Charleston and the surrounding Lowcountry in 1822, it ended a summer of anxiety and terror. Both races lived amid confusion throughout most of June and July, as most whites and blacks knew little about what was happening or what might happen next except what they heard on the urban grapevine. Whites lived nervously with partial knowledge of a looming and lingering insurrection scare and noticed security measures and grisly punishments that suggested a scare of some magnitude. Once the investigation began, Charleston-area blacks, slave and free, lived in fear about their future. Neither the guilty nor the innocent knew if or when they might be taken up for questioning or even fingered as a participant by one of the accused. Whites believed themselves the intended victims of a terrorist plot, yet no black insurgent spilled one drop of white blood that summer. Blacks, on the other hand, saw prominent members of their community first arrested and then executed or deported in significant numbers without public trials or explanation. To them, the investigation and subsequent punishments appeared as a reign of white terror. When Anna Hayes Johnson privately lamented that the insurrection scare, investigation, trials, and punishment left "a look of horror on almost every countenance" in Charleston, her observation applied to black faces as well as white ones.[106]

However broad and serious the insurrection plot of 1822, its discovery and subsequent investigation had far-reaching implications. The alleged plot and the very real white reaction to it affected nothing less than the future of slavery in the lower South. With the publication of the court's official report in late October, the public war of insurrection accounts entered a hiatus. But the public discussion and analysis of the events of the summer of 1822 and their causes continued unabated. Keen interest in preventing such plots from developing in the future produced a sweeping reexamination of existing policies and attitudes toward both slaves and free blacks. This informal reexamination of the state's public policy toward slavery proceeded with considerable vigor until the legislature finally met in late November. During the late summer and fall of 1822, white Charlestonians and their parish country neighbors debated how to make slavery safe for whites in the black-majority Lowcountry and other black-belt regions of the lower South.[107]

CHAPTER EIGHT

ANALYZING THE SCARE

Recent scholarship arguing that no uprising of the coherence or magnitude of the insurrection plot (or plots) Charleston authorities claimed to have uncovered and thwarted was actually planned for the city in the summer of 1822 suggests with considerable plausibility that the scope and sophistication of these plots were greatly exaggerated by authorities who interpolated evidence from statements made by witnesses who were intimidated, threatened, and even tortured. For the purposes of my analysis, however, the salient issue is the white reaction to the reported Vesey plot. This reaction emerged from the information the Charleston public received at the time and the resulting widespread acceptance of the idea that the dangerous plot described in reports issued by Charleston's official investigators had, in fact, matured in Charleston that summer. Whites who defended an alternative version of the scare during the summer and fall of 1822 quickly lost credibility with the Lowcountry public.[1]

As Lowcountry whites contemplated the implications of a successful insurrection their midst, their leaders debated the appropriate means of making sure that no future plot could come to fruition. As part of this debate, whites of various persuasions offered both their diagnoses of the scare and proposals to prevent future plots. This public discussion over causes and preventative measures quickly revealed the sharp conflict that emerged between local authorities and the paternalist movement that escalated as the scare and the ensuing reaction unfolded.

Even while the Vesey court was still meeting in July, and long before Governor Bennett and Intendant Hamilton published their dueling accounts in August, there appeared public and private commentary on the causes of the Vesey plot and recommendations for preventing future insurrections. As early as July 19, one Charleston white called publicly for "new regulations for the government of our servants," specifically recommending the tighter regulation of dram shops and slaves who hired out.[2] In the weeks and months that followed, a series of public meetings, letters to the editor, newspaper editorials, grand jury presentments, pamphlets, petitions, and memorials allowed an alarmed public to present its own piecemeal analysis of the aborted insurrection and to recommend appropriate remedial action. Thus, both during and after the Vesey scare, the Charleston press teemed with suggestions for preventing future insurrection threats, but the commentators did not always agree on exactly what type of remedy was needed.[3]

In the course of this impromptu public analysis, white Charlestonians quickly arraigned all the usual suspects, sometimes regardless of the evidence at hand. With the first court still deeply engaged in its work in early July, equity chancellor Henry William DeSaussure identified the "great intercourse" that slaves in the port city enjoyed with the West Indies as the primary cause of unrest. Such contact, the judge opined, "must introduce among our people" many persons "who have been engaged in Scenes of blood" and who would inevitably "beguile our Slaves into rebellion with false hopes and idle expectations."[4] Other whites blamed slaves who hired out. This common urban practice effectively removed these slaves from the watchful eyes of their masters.[5] In August, following the last execution, Congressman Joel Poinsett attributed the actions of the "miserable deluded conspirators" to the "discussion of the Missouri question at Washington." The Missouri debate, Poinsett advised President James Monroe, "was considered by the unfortunate half-instructed people as one of emancipation."[6] Other whites blamed slaves imported from other states through the active interstate slave trade, even though there was scant evidence that any slaves recently arrived from other states played a significant role in the alleged plot.[7] The carelessness of the existing slave patrols came under attack, as did the perceived "uppityness" of privileged slaves who enjoyed the run of the city.[8] One observer called for an increase in parish patrols, funded by the state, and urged that on Sundays the patrols routinely "visit every place of worship in the parish."[9] Another citizen called for the state to quarter a "standing army" in a newly-constructed "Citadel," which could also serve as a "refuge" for citizens in times of danger.[10] One Charleston grand jury specifically complained that the "expensive dress" worn by some "persons of colour" proved "subversive of that subordination" required by slavery and white supremacy.[11] Private citizens joined Charleston grand juries to complain repeatedly about dram shops that sold spirits to slaves and often served as gathering places for free blacks, slaves, and whites of "dissipated" character. Denmark Vesey and other accused insurrection leaders allegedly had frequented such shops.[12] A grand jury headed by court member Robert Turnbull complained about free black artisans and mechanics taking jobs from whites and about the "number of schools" in the city run by free blacks.[13] Other citizens identified the mere presence of free blacks in a society committed to racial slavery as a dangerous inconsistency.[14] One writer went so far as to recommend that the legislature "allow no free persons of color to remain in the state."[15]

SUCH ACTIVE PUBLIC COMMENTARY on the Vesey unrest continued until the legislature met in late November. Citizens of all kinds proposed a variety of remedial measures. Prominent citizens not directly tied to the court or the investigation offered extended analyses of the scare and suggested systematic programs to prevent future revolts. Usually appearing in pamphlet or serial form, these analyses emerged as talking points for public discussion of the Vesey crisis as it entered a second phase, the phase between initial public reaction and legislative decision making.

During the fall, two generations of Charleston's Federalist leadership weighed in on the crisis. Thomas Pinckney, a Revolutionary War hero, and Henry William DeSaussure, the respected equity chancellor and Pinckney protégé, both produced extended analyses of the conditions that created the Vesey crisis and offered detailed recommendations for reducing the risk of future insurrections. The seventy-two-year-old Pinckney, the Federalist candidate for vice president in 1796, came from the first family of Lowcountry politics. His older brother Charles Cotesworth Pinckney and his cousin Charles Pinckney both attended the federal constitutional convention, and Thomas himself chaired the South Carolina ratifying convention in 1788. Before the Revolution, Thomas had received the best British education available, graduating from Oxford University and studying law at London's prestigious Inner Temple before beginning the practice of law in Charleston in 1774. During the Revolution, Pinckney rose to the rank of major in the Continental Army, serving with distinction under General Benjamin Lincoln. Wounded at the Battle of Camden, Pinckney emerged from the war with hero status. After losing his vice presidential bid in 1796, Pinckney served two terms as a Federalist congressman from Charleston. He then retired to his law practice and plantation life in the wake of the post-1800 Jeffersonian ascendancy. As an aging war veteran, Thomas Pinckney again served his country during the War of 1812, rising to the rank of major general and reviving his reputation as a military hero of the founding generation.[16]

In his sweeping analysis of the context of the Vesey scare, published in early November 1822, Pinckney identified a broad array of problems that he believed facilitated the insurrection plot. Pinckney concluded that ongoing events in Saint Domingue (and contact between Charleston and the Caribbean) as well as growing anti-slavery sentiment in the North nurtured unrest among Lowcountry slaves, but he admitted that these problems lay beyond the city's or state's power to control. In Pinckney's view, attempts to isolate Charleston and its hinterland from such sources of antislavery sentiment inevitably would prove futile. The former Revolutionary leader also blamed slave literacy for the increased the risk of rebellion, but he likewise despaired of slowing the growth of literacy among slaves. The "particular way of thinking and weakness of many proprietors," Pinckney reasoned, coupled with the fact that "the dangerous instrument" of learning "was already so widespread among slaves" and so "easily communicated" from slave to slave, rendered it unlikely that the rise of literacy among slaves could be checked effectively. Pinckney strongly disapproved of the "indulgences" shown favored slaves as the ideology of paternalism increased its sway in the lower South, but he again recognized that it would be difficult to curtail "privileges" enjoyed by urban slave artisans without incurring a painful backlash of some sort. In a sense, Pinckney's analysis both indicted paternalism as a cause of the Vesey insurrection scare yet conceded that paternalism had advanced to such an extent that its continued practice, at least in some instances, appeared inevitable.[17]

But if broader abolitionist trends lay beyond southern restraint, and if the "problem" of slave literacy had already expanded beyond effective means of control, Pinckney joined a rising chorus of voices seeking a remedy for the threat posed by slave and free black artisans who enjoyed the run of the city. In October, a Columbia grand jury had seconded Charleston's complaint about slave artisans and mechanics who hired out. The Columbia grand jury cited the "serious and alarming consequences arising from owners permitting their slaves to hire their own time." The practice of slaves hiring out, the Columbia jury claimed, not only produced "demoralizing" effects on the slaves by giving them too much freedom and allowing them to earn excessive spending money, but also allowed them to "monopolize" occupations in "various mechanical trades" at the expense of the "free white population of the same employments." The Columbia grand jury noted that the recent insurrection scare in Charleston "originated and was matured" by the "machinations" of slave and free black artisans.[18] While doubtless motivated in part by the self-interest of white artisans and mechanics hoping to rid themselves of pesky slave competition, these complaints about skilled slaves hiring out on their own time seemed on point, given the prominence of slave artisans among the Vesey insurrection's alleged organizers.

Agreeing with the Columbia grand jury, Pinckney recognized that the Charleston city economy depended heavily on the skills of slave and free black artisans, but he argued that if blacks, slave and free, were banned from all mechanical pursuits, skilled white labor would flow in, probably from overseas, to fill the void. This tide of white immigration, in Pinckney's view, would carry a double benefit. First and foremost, the influx of whites would help reverse the city's demographic trend toward larger and larger black majorities. Pinckney estimated that replacing all slave mechanics, artisans, and shopkeepers with skilled white labor would reduce the city's black population by nearly half while adding "5000 [white] men to our muster rolls." Moreover, Pinckney judged the "excess" of kind treatment he thought characterized master-slave relations deleterious in the busy but intimate city environment, but he thought planters could treat their rural plantation slaves, distant from urban temptations, with such kindness with less risk. Thus Pinckney recommended transferring urban slaves to the countryside, where they could be profitably employed away from the many temptations, abundant information, and ready communication of city life, and at only a small financial sacrifice to their owners.[19]

This "whitening" of Charleston would not only enhance the city's security, Pinckney maintained, but eventually improve the quality of its labor force. Pinckney thought white mechanics superior to slaves in "natural ingenuity," and argued that they would bring more skill and expertise to artisanal occupations. While "good imitators may be found among the blacks," Pinckney asserted, "it is rare to find one who can plan or invent." Pinckney's dream of "whitening" Charleston also involved a desire to replace slave domestics, who, the retired general believed, posed the most dangerous threat to white society because of their daily proximity to white families and their intimate knowledge of family habits. But in yet another concession to reality, Pinckney admitted that ridding Charleston of black domestics presented a more complicated problem than replacing black artisans because whites disdained being placed "so nearly on a level with the slave."[20]

On the whole, Pinckney sought to limit the damage done by paternalism's excesses by removing the black majority from city to country, where he believed no amount of paternalism and no degree of demographic imbalance could render slaves as dangerous as they had proven in the city. But Pinckney's proposed whitening was decidedly narrow in its compass. He sought only to whiten the city of Charleston, creating a white-majority fortress at the center of a heavily black hinterland, which his proposal would make even blacker. Pinckney took what passed as a regionalist strategy for gradually ending slavery in the upper South and contorted it into a localist strategy designed to make slavery safe for the South Carolina Lowcountry.[21]

But there was also a decided note of resignation in Pinckney's argument. He knew that the risk of insurrection could be reduced but never eliminated. He openly conceded that some sources of slave unrest lay beyond white control. Contact with the Caribbean and the larger Atlantic world, the expanding reach of Christianity among slaves (and the potential radicalism of that message), spreading slave literacy, and the desire of affluent urban whites for domestic servants all represented genies that could hardly be returned to their bottles. Pinckney accepted these risks as ones a slaveholding society had to run. He eschewed apocalyptic rhetoric and urged tightening the system where it could be tightened and enduring the rest—with proper vigilance.

According to the announcement that accompanied the release of Pinckney's pamphlet, the aging hero composed it while on an "excursion into the interior," undertaken in the late summer of 1822.[22] If Pinckney made it as far into the interior as Columbia, he likely visited his younger friend Henry William DeSaussure with news of events from Charleston. DeSaussure, who served briefly as an aide-de-camp to General Pinckney in the military mobilization following the Chesapeake affair, was the son of a successful Lowcountry merchant and Revolutionary war veteran,

Daniel DeSaussure, of Huguenot descent. Henry himself had joined the Revolutionary war effort to defend Charleston at age sixteen and was quickly captured by the British but paroled to Philadelphia. After acquiring a legal education in Philadelphia, DeSaussure was admitted to the Charleston bar in 1785. He enjoyed a measure of political success in Federalist Charleston, serving as city intendant in 1799 and as a member of the legislature for two terms. The young DeSaussure had emerged as one of the leading figures of the Charleston bar before his election to the chancery court in 1808. He even mentored a young John C. Calhoun at law in 1805.[23] As equity chancellor, DeSaussure proved prolific, writing nearly half of all the equity decrees published in the state over a twenty-year period. While serving on the equity bench, DeSaussure moved his family to Columbia in 1812, where he stood at the center of the small capital city's social life. In the aftermath of the Vesey crisis, DeSaussure wrote a series of anonymous articles in September and October for a Columbia newspaper, the *South Carolina State Gazette*, and these essays were quickly republished in pamphlet form.[24]

The learned chancellor, persistent in his conservative Federalist sympathies, agreed with his mentor Pinckney that slaves should be "confined as much as possible to agriculture." Agricultural slaves, DeSaussure believed, "are found to be the most orderly and obedient of slaves." For DeSaussure, the appropriate reaction to the Vesey scare was clear. "There should be no black mechanics or artisans," he argued, "at least in the cities." The problem, according to the chancellor, lay in the separation slave artisans and mechanics enjoyed "from the eye and inspection of their masters." Working largely on their own, slave artisans "acquire vicious habits injurious to themselves" and "set an evil example to other slaves." Particularly dangerous, DeSaussure believed, were the interactions between slave artisans and the "many worthless and idle strangers from the West India Islands." Such "bad company" tended to "infuse false notions and delusive hopes" in the minds of Charleston slaves, rendering them "dissatisfied with their condition" and vulnerable "for plots and mischief." So DeSaussure not only called for the end of slave hiring but also the banning of slaves from all artisanal and mechanical positions in the Charleston economy.[25]

DeSaussure also issued an emphatic denunciation of teaching slaves to read and write. Despite his own well-known piety, the chancellor urged that the Christian mission to the slaves proceed with great caution and only under close and constant white supervision. The chancellor declared it as "trite as it is true that knowledge is power." In DeSaussure's view, "education [of slaves] therefore should in no account be admitted." The chancellor admitted that it pained him to "close the book of knowledge on the human mind, and shut it out from the delights of learning," and he knew that many whites found such a prohibition a "hard measure," but he argued that it was a "favour" to slaves to keep them "in ignorance." A lack of education kept slaves contented "with their lot." DeSaussure also insisted that slaves "should have no separate place of worship," as they had in the African church and sometimes enjoyed in the Baptist and Methodist denominations with a minimum of white supervision. He advocated a "Station" for blacks "in every place of worship used by whites," a place where they "should be able to see and to hear" (but definitely not read) biblical and Christian principles taught and preached. These services should instruct slaves "to be obedient, and to serve industriously." DeSaussure, active in the Congregational church when he lived in Charleston, added with equal firmness that the church should also teach the master that he was "bound to treat his slaves with gentleness and kindness and to provide for their comfort, in sickness as well as in health, in infancy, and old age, as well as in the vigor of useful life."[26]

On the latter points, DeSaussure sounded like a stern paternalist, one willing to impose harsh restrictions on slave learning and slave religious practices, but in return for the severity of these restrictions, he pushed masters toward the appropriate treatment of slaves. Slaves, he argued, were entitled to "kind treatment and complete protection" from their masters, but both individual masters and state authorities had an obligation to ensure "the proper subordinations of the slaves."[27] DeSaussure pronounced himself committed to the continued melioration in the conditions of slave life, but he also sounded like a master increasingly committed to something approaching perpetual slavery, defined on the basis of race. But even DeSaussure hinted at a willingness to reach a different conclusion about racial inferiority (though not about slavery), provided that a series of highly improbable conditions were met. If slaves were confined to agricultural pursuits in the countryside, treated over a prolonged period with the proper mix of discipline and kindness by their masters, and shielded, as they were by the closing of the foreign slave trade, "from the leaven of barbarism" that had long been "continually infused" by the "foreign admixture of native Africans" into the "mass" of Lowcountry slaves, DeSaussure mused, then it was possible that "there may be a reasonable hope" that domestic slaves "born and bred in the country" might eventually emerge as a "Docile, and in some degree a civilized people." But, DeSaussure insisted, even if slaves became "in some degree a civilized people," they could not be converted "with safety" into "free men." Thus DeSaussure advanced a vigorous argument against any form of emancipation because emancipation would inevitably end in a war of the races.[28]

Taken together, these pamphlets penned by two Federalist friends not only touched on many of the same themes but also sounded the same tones in their analysis. They attacked abolition, lamented the influence of Caribbean unrest, and blamed the activities of "outsiders" for trouble among otherwise compliant southern slaves. But Pinckney and DeSaussure also placed much of the blame for the recent insurrection scare on problematic practices originating much closer to home. Like Hamilton and the Magistrates and Freeholders Court, they indicted free blacks and slaves who hired out because these blacks had the unsupervised time and resources to collectively plan and finance a rebellion. The writers bitterly denounced the education of slaves and whites who supported such education. Pinckney and DeSaussure insisted that an educated slave was a dangerous slave. They also complained about slave Christianity, especially when the religious instruction of slaves proceeded without white supervision as it had in Charleston's African church, or with too little white supervision, as Pinckney and DeSaussure thought occurred in some of the evangelical denominations. In sum, Pinckney and DeSaussure complained about a system of slavery that has become too indulgent, too lenient, too concerned with "elevating" the slave—a system, in short, that yielded too many concessions to slaves. In essence, Pinckney and DeSaussure complained about paternalism. DeSaussure even joined Hamilton and the court in asserting that only force could maintain slavery, and that whites had to remain willing to use it. Our "examples have been written in Blood," DeSaussure admitted, "but policy and perhaps humanity rendered them indispensable—& will deter similar efforts for 20 or 30 years."[29]

In a very real sense, Pinckney and DeSaussure offered a nostalgic Federalist lament over how slavery had grown more troublesome and less safe since the golden "Age of the Pinckneys." In this remembered golden age, Pinckney and DeSaussure believed, whites had been in charge and knew it; they had seen no need to extend privileges to slaves and certainly no need to educate them as part of the effort to make them Christian. In the view of these Lowcountry Federalists, this decline of slavery was hardly monocausal, but its primary cause was the emergence of a pious new paternalism among slaveholders and the consequent extension of excessive kindness and dangerous privileges to slaves. Both churchmen themselves (Pinckney an Episcopalian and DeSaussure a Congregationalist), these pamphleteers embraced a form of humanitarianism, one centered in the responsibility of the master to take care of his dependents, but Pinckney and DeSaussure objected to the new paternalism, articulated by evangelicals, that emphasized teaching slaves to read and allowing them a meaningful worship liturgy. Instead, they advocated a more muscular paternalism, one based on an aristocratic sense of class obligation rather than in a spirit of evangelical stewardship.[30]

Weighted with Federalist overtones, the indictments of paternalism offered by Pinckney and DeSaussure were also decidedly localistic in nature. Writing from Charleston and Columbia, respectively, Pinckney and DeSaussure wrote trenchant critiques of urban slavery—slavery in places where substantial numbers of slave artisans ranged freely and prospered while only loosely accountable to their masters, where free blacks were relatively numerous, where religious assemblies were large and frequent, where slave education projects flourished in significant numbers, where masters often "indulged" favored domestic slaves, and where a learned clergy held some influence.[31] In other words, they indicted slavery in Charleston on the eve of the Vesey scare. They both seemed willing to consider that slave artisans might be safely employed in the countryside and that "indulgent" or paternalistic treatment of slaves on comparatively isolated rural plantations might not prove as problematic to the overall safety of slave society as when practiced in a fluid and volatile urban setting.[32] But while focused on the peculiar vulnerabilities of slavery in the cities, the indictment of paternalism as a mode of slave management offered by Pinckney and

DeSaussure nevertheless added volume to the rising criticism of paternalism triggered by the Vesey scare.

THIS POST-VESEY INDICTMENT of paternalist efforts to foster black Christianity drew considerable strength from what passed as hard evidence collected during the Vesey trials. The court's investigation found that the ability of key "ringleaders" to read and write played an important role in the organization and planning of the revolt. Both Denmark Vesey and Monday Gell could read and write well, as could Peter Poyas, and if any of the court-reported testimony can be accepted as accurate, they used their literacy to read scripture passages, pamphlets, and local newspaper material related to slavery to potential insurrectionists. Vesey and Gell allegedly showed skill in interpreting, or misinterpreting, these sources to encourage slave participation in the rebellion. Additionally, the ability to communicate plans, instructions, and warnings in writing, to forge passes to facilitate travel, to write letters to Saint Domingue seeking assistance, and even to keep rosters of prospective rebels or lists of possible weapons emerged from the court's report as integral parts of the alleged conspiracy. While some masters, in order to make better use of selected slaves on business errands, had long ignored 1740 laws prohibiting teaching slaves to write, it had been evangelical ministers and lay leaders who quietly but forcefully urged the cause of slave literacy in the interest of promoting a better understanding of scripture, a more rapid dissemination of the Word, and more meaningful faith development among slaves. To be sure, evangelical efforts in this regard had attracted criticism long before the Vesey insurrection brought the issue to the fore with renewed force and urgency.[33] But after Vesey, critics sought either a stronger prohibition on teaching slaves to read or much reinvigorated enforcement of the existing ban.[34]

In an even larger sense, post-Vesey analysis suggested that paternalism and the Christian insistence on the religious instruction of slaves weakened white control and threatened white security, as critics of paternalism increased their calls for "reforms" to make slavery safe for the Lowcountry. Charleston newspaperman Edwin Holland, editor of the *Charleston Times,* blamed both the aborted Camden insurrection of 1816 and the Vesey insurrection conspiracy chiefly on relaxed discipline of slaves practiced by paternalistic masters and on the spread of heterodox religious ideas among slaves. Like virtually every other commentator, Holland fingered the "religious itinerants" who "excited among our Negroes such a spirit of dissatisfaction and revolt" as the chief source of subversive ideas among slaves. "How blasphemously the word of God was tortured, in order to sanction the unholy butchery that was contemplated," Holland complained, noting that the insurrection "was put into operation by the dispersion among our Negroes of religious magazines, newspaper paragraphs and insulated text of scripture."[35] One of Holland's correspondents, Benjamin N. Elliott, agreed that assemblies permitted for the "religious instruction" of slaves only loosely supervised by whites were instead used as "occasions to instill sentiments of ferocity, by falsifying the Bible."[36]

Vesey court member Robert Turnbull agreed that the growth of paternalism in the Lowcountry had prepared the ground for the planned revolt. Turnbull argued that the "condition of our slaves, within the last thirty years, has been considerably ameliorated," explaining that while the labor required of slaves had "not been diminished," they "have been treated with more indulgence and have had more attention paid to their comfort and accommodation than formerly." Turnbull saw much to decry and little to applaud in this expansion of "paternalism." Slave behavior, in Turnbull's view, had deteriorated significantly, "owing to a relaxation in discipline which experience abundantly proves has been almost always carried too far." The flaw in paternalism as an ideology of slave management, Turnbull believed, was that regulations that might prove effective incentives or deterrents for shaping white behavior "entirely fail when applied to the government of slaves." Turnbull sounded individually the same emphatic note sounded collectively by the October report of the Vesey court, on which he served, saying of slaves: "The only principle upon which any authority over them can be maintained is fear," Turnbull insisted, "and he who denies this has but little knowledge of them."[37]

After evaluating all factors contributing to the insurrection scare, Holland concluded, "The Crisis through which we have so recently and providentially passed" grew inevitably from "a general spirit of insubordination among our slaves and free negroes." That spirit, the editor argued, sprang directly "from the relaxation of discipline on the part of the whites," a trend that "had long been discernible." This relaxation of discipline, as Holland (and his correspondents) identified, had been much encouraged, if not entirely caused, by the spread of Christian paternalist ideology among Lowcountry slaveholders and its injudicious application by them. Holland thought that teaching slaves to read scripture and allowing slave Christians relative autonomy in their worship undermined the very nature of the master-slave relationship, which required absolute control by the master and enforced subordination on the part of the slave. Carrying his argument to its logical conclusion, Holland explicitly rejected the notion that Christian trusteeship on the part of masters and other whites might meliorate potential antagonisms between free whites and black slaves. The editor instead endorsed an older conception of slaveholding that depicted whites and blacks as permanent antagonists locked in a perpetual struggle for domination and even survival. For Holland, the defining metaphor for slavery was not the nurturing patriarch attending to his extended household of dependents but that of a Roman patrician, in the later days of empire, enjoying his sophistication and prosperity while he exploited its subjects and held the "barbarians" at bay. The "Negroes are truly the Jacobins of the country," Holland warned his fellow whites in the Lowcountry, "they are anarchists and the domestic enemy; the common enemy of civilized society and the barbarians [who] would, if they could, become the destroyers of our race."[38]

A lengthy fall memorial from the citizens of Charleston to the legislature summed up popular sentiment in the aftermath of the summer scare well and offered a litany of legislative recommendations to address the concerns raised. The memorial called for the expulsion "of every free person of color" from the state, tough new restrictions on slaves who hired out, legislation banning blacks from the "mechanical arts" unless these slave mechanics worked under the direct supervision of their masters, the reorganization of the city guard, the end of importation of slaves from the upper South (where masters, white Charlestonians believed, too often decided to dump troublesome or rebellious slaves into the lower South), capital punishment for whites involved in planning an insurrection, and "severe penalties" for anyone who taught slaves or free blacks to read or write.[39] The memorialists argued that unless these causes from which the insurrection emerged were addressed, they would produce "a series of the most appalling distresses."[40]

The expulsion of free blacks, the memorialists argued, would free the Lowcountry from the dangers posed by this curious "third class," which enjoyed "more privileges than the slaves" yet possessed but "few rights of the master." Because they were at liberty, free blacks moved "unrestrained over every part of the state," amassed "wealth to an unlimited extent," procured "information on every subject," and united in "association or societies." With freedom of movement, money, knowledge, and the right to gather together, free blacks stood well positioned to lead revolts. And since they were "deprived of all political rights" and "subjected equally with slaves to the police regulations for persons of color," they had reason to combine with slaves for the purpose of insurrection. Free blacks, the memorialists concluded, "have sufficient liberty to appreciate the blessings of freedom" but remained "sufficiently shackled to be sensible that they enjoy comparatively few of those blessings." From such a class, people free but not equal, revolutionary leaders were sure to emerge. In 1822, white Charlestonians were still close enough to the Revolution they announced in 1776 to understand the power of that logic. Moreover, the very presence of free blacks in a slave society, the memorial continued, was "pregnant with evils" because of the impact that presence had on slaves. The freedom of some blacks, no matter how imperfect, "excites discontent among our slaves," who "pant after liberty" upon seeing free blacks "going whither they please" and "expending their money how they please." The memorial acknowledged that "very few of the free people of color were engaged" in the alleged Vesey plot, but the insurrection's leader, Denmark Vesey, had used his freedom to "communicate so extensively with the slaves in the country" to produce a plot of the magnitude "exposed" by the court.

Restrictions on slaves hiring out were also needed, the memorial maintained, because "negroes who work out are released in considerable degree from the controul of their masters" and were informally permitted to "regulate their own conduct." This de facto freedom allowed these slaves to "assemble together whenever they wish[,] and having their time at their own disposal," they had the opportunity to "originate, prepare and mature their own plans for insurrection." The same logic applied, memorialists insisted, to "negro mechanics," who, "having a stated portion of labor to perform," often completed that labor early and enjoyed much free time, especially "in the evenings and on the Sabbath," available for "forming combinations and devising schemes." With a very few exceptions, the memorial reminded legislators, "the negroes engaged in that conspiracy [the Vesey plot] were mechanics or persons working out." Autonomous hands, it seems, were the hands of aspiring insurrectionists. The memorial also demanded that the legislature either ban or severely limit the interstate slave trade. Memorialists argued that the trade dumped a "degraded and villainous body of negroes" on the state and claimed that "these most worthless and abandoned characters" contaminated the minds "of our most valuable domestics."

But for all its specific recommendations, the overarching argument advanced by this carefully crafted citizens' memorial consisted of nothing less than a full-fledged critique of paternalism as a failed ideology of slave control. The memorial noted the rapid rise of paternalism, conceded its growing acceptance among significant portions of the population, and acknowledged the promise it held for many, but then insisted that the discovery of the Vesey plot indicted paternalism as a misanthropic failure. "Under the influence of mild and generous feelings," the memorialists explained, "the owners of slaves in our state were rearing up a system which extended many privileges to our negroes; afforded them greater protection; relieved them from numerous restraints, enabled them to assemble without the presence of a white person for the purpose of social intercourse or religious worship, yielding to them the facilities of acquiring most of the comforts and many of the luxuries of improved society; and what is of more importance, affording them the means of enlarging their minds and extending their information." The Charleston memorialists admitted that these new ideas of slaveholding had "met with the approbation of by far the greater number of our citizens" and that "many good and pious persons cherished the expectation that our negroes would be influenced in their conduct toward their owners by sentiments of affection and gratitude." Even signers of the memorial admitted that the new paternalism had produced "tranquility and good order" for a time and led many in the community to "regard the extension of privileges in a favorable light." Many in the community, if not the community as a whole, had grown hopeful that as slaves "were more indulged, they would become more satisfied with their condition and more attached to whites." But the Vesey scare had exploded all such false hope and left the misguided optimism of the "good and pious" in ruins. Despite "promising appearances," slaves were "plotting the destruction" of whites just as the latter held "the utmost confidence in the fidelity of the negroes." The Vesey plot had exposed beyond all doubt, the memorialists insisted, that lenience and advantages had failed to produce reciprocal "satisfaction and affection" among slaves. Whites had been repaid for their kindness with the creation of an insurrection plot "comparable to the worst West Indian atrocities." In the minds of memorialists, the Denmark Vesey insurrection scare had proved paternalism's skeptics right.[41]

Thus, in very tangible ways, the white response to the Vesey scare put paternalism on the defensive as never before. To be sure, paternalists had been challenged by skeptics from the moment they began to make their case for a Christian-centered paternalism, but no event or incident, not even the Camden insurrection scare of 1816, had given critics of paternalism as much ammunition as the Vesey scare did. The visibility of slave Christians as alleged leaders of the thwarted rebellion, the number of alleged insurrectionists identified as having an association with the African church, and the newly energized opposition to slave literacy threatened to slow, weaken, or even destroy the evangelical effort to Christianize slaves. To Christian leaders in the South Carolina Lowcountry, these attacks, surfacing just six years after slave "professors of religion" had been identified as the leaders of the aborted Camden insurrection plot, represented nothing less than a fundamental challenge to the expanding evangelical influence on southern society and to the emerging understanding of slavery as a paternalistic or domestic institution. Thus the alleged insurrection conspiracy of 1822 generated, among other things, a full-fledged crisis for paternalism as an ideology of slaveholding, at least in the South Carolina Lowcountry.

SUCH A CHALLENGE could not go unanswered by leaders of the paternalist movement, and much depended on the persuasiveness of the answer they provided. Fortunately for their cause, the Lowcountry's Christian community proved willing and able to defend itself. The Charleston clergy of the era consisted of a number of religious leaders whose reputations extended beyond their region and whose achievements would earn them lasting recognition as denominational leaders. At the head of the Vesey-era Charleston clergy stood Richard Furman, pastor of the city's First Baptist church and the preeminent southern Baptist of his generation. The learned Furman, a skilled church diplomat, enjoyed national prominence in his denomination, having served twice as president of the national Triennial Baptist Convention, and beyond.[42] Close to Furman in public affection stood Congregationalist Benjamin Morgan Palmer, pastor of the Circular Church in Charleston and the leading Congregationalist in the South. Known for his personal kindness, Palmer earned respect and influence through the "great charm of his character" and the "transparent simplicity" of his faith.[43] The insurrection scare had touched Palmer personally: Billy Palmer, a slave of Palmer's father and a longtime member of his church, had been identified as a prominent member of the insurrection plot. Palmer was grief-stricken when he learned of the charges against "his confidential class leader," who had "received a Communion of the Lord's Supper" from the pastor's hand only "a week or two before his just conviction."[44] Episcopal pastors at St. Philip's and St. Michael's churches, standing in the heart of the city, held at least nominal sway over the heavily Anglican planter elite of the area.[45] Local Presbyterian leaders of the era lacked the stature and influence James Henley Thornwell would later enjoy, but Arthur Buist at First (Scots) Presbyterian had strong ties to the local elite.[46]

John Bachman, the young pastor of the Charleston Lutheran church at the time, later emerged as one of the leading Lutheran clergyman of the of the nineteenth century.[47] The city's young Catholic priest, John England, would later gain respect as one of the nation's leading bishops.[48] It was an erudite, generally collegial, and comparably influential clergy. Some of these religious leaders contributed directly to the emerging defense of paternalism and the religious instruction of slaves, and some assisted only indirectly, if at all. But seldom had one southern city's clergy been as well equipped for the task at hand than that of Charleston in the late summer and fall of 1822.

The Vesey conspiracy trapped these and other Lowcountry Christian leaders in an awkward double bind. They had to explain both how slaveholders could be Christians and how Christians could be slaveholders. More and more, southern religious leaders heard their northern brethren charge that holding slaves was inherently unchristian, yet at the same time, increasingly vocal groups of white southerners complained that Christians were too "humane," too gentle in their treatment of slaves, and too reluctant to resort to coercion—too effusive in their application of paternalism, simply too "soft"—to remain effective masters. To be sure, few southern skeptics expressed their doubts in such bald terms, but the implications of Hamilton's summary, the court's *Official Report,* Pinckney's critique, and Holland's complaint were unmistakable. An excess of paternalism, especially when lavished on favored domestic or skilled slaves working in an urban environment, too much education of slaves, and too much "humanity" on the part of masters failed to keep slaves properly subordinate and intimidated.

Recognizing that sharp criticism of their mission to the slaves by popular and respected civic leaders posed a serious threat to their work, white Christian leaders in Charleston quickly fashioned their own interpretation of the Vesey conspiracy and advanced their own suggestions for preventing the recurrence of such plots. The initial response to public criticism of the Christian ministry to the slaves came, albeit cautiously, from Charleston's religious press. In late August 1822, the Charleston *Southern Intelligencer*, a religious newspaper that regularly discussed questions related to the future of slavery in the South, cautiously took issue with Intendant Hamilton's published account of the crushed insurrection.[49] Aware of the popular disfavor that tended to fall on those who engaged in public tussles with the personable Hamilton, the newspaper's editors went out of their way to acknowledge that the Lowcountry remained "under great obligation" to Hamilton, the city council, and the court for their "industry and vigilance" in discovering the plot and their "unwearied patience" during the difficult investigation that followed. Moreover, the editors showed no reluctance in praising not only the "rectitude and legality" but also the "mildness and humanity" of the court's decisions. But, publishing an extract from Hamilton's report as evidence, the editors nevertheless pointed out that Hamilton laid much of the blame for the insurrection on the putrid fruits of Christian efforts to convert slaves. The Presbyterian-controlled newspaper gingerly accused Hamilton of failing to distinguish between the "good" inherent in evangelism and the corruption of that good that surfaced during the investigation of the alleged insurrection plot. In the editors' view, the intendant's report mistakenly identified Christianity's "pure and holy influence" with the "wicked and corrupt conduct" that produced the insurrection scare. By casting such aspersions on the work of the churches, the editors claimed, Hamilton had wounded the feelings of much of the city's Christian community. Many Lowcountry Christians perceived Hamilton's criticism "as calculated to make an impression unfavorable to religion" and thwart the church's important efforts to evangelize slaves in the area.[50]

In mid-September, Benjamin Palmer, known for his spiritual integrity and his active work among slaves, preached a sermon at the Circular Church on "the case of servants." Predictably, given the lingering tensions from the insurrection scare and the large black congregation Palmer's services often attracted, his sermon drew on the words of the Apostle Paul admonishing slaves to "obey in all things your masters according to the flesh." Palmer recounted the story of Philemon and Onesimus to support the notion that shared Christianity still left one man a master and the other a slave. But Palmer's sermon also included criticism of those authorities who used the insurrection scare to mount an attack against the Christian mission to the slaves and the cause of paternalism generally. "[I]f those who have uttered their vociferations most loudly and issued their rage and blasphemy against religion, its professors and its ministers, most copiously during the late disturbances," Palmer boldly proclaimed from the pulpit, "would employ but half their noise and half their strength and zeal in tracing out the source and drying up the streams of moral corruption in the midst of us...there would be much less occasion for religion to be blamed and abused for things, with which it has nothing to do."[51] Palmer's sermon required courage. He had not only called out the city's many critics of Christian paternalism but even dared suggest that the "streams of moral corruption" had their source in slavery. White prophets were as few as profits were abundant in the slaveholding South, and even Palmer often came up short, but it was not common for southern ministers, including those who disliked slavery and prodded masters to better attend their spiritual responsibilities toward slaves, to refer to slavery as a source of "moral corruption" in southern society. Palmer's message commanded attention if not agreement. If Lowcountry leaders would support colonization and consider a gradual emancipation, Palmer implied from his pulpit, then the city would also gradually be freed from insurrection scares and the excesses of insurrection investigations and punishments. Worried parishioner Mary Beach credited Palmer with standing "as fearless in the pulpit as [Martin] Luther."[52]

Later in the fall, the *Southern Intelligencer* departed from its August caution and took a bold stand, openly taking issue with DeSaussure's essays on slavery. In an article entitled "Emancipation," likely written by Palmer, the newspaper defended colonization against DeSaussure's emphatic dismissal of the idea in his essays. "Emancipation" argued that a serious effort to colonize the city's free blacks would likely minimize the danger of future insurrections in Charleston. An "immediate emancipation," the author conceded, would be "inconsistent with the safety of society and the constitutional rights of the people," but the South should never completely dismiss the idea of "removing gradually" its black population, including slaves, as a means of ensuring white safety and maintaining an appropriate racial balance in the region. The essayist insisted that any viable plan for gradual emancipation must also include a plan for colonization of former slaves that included a specific location for the colony and a reliable source of funding for the relocation effort. If those conditions could be met and the gradual emancipation process made voluntary, then, the author predicted, such a plan would "receive the warm approbation of every southern planter." The *Southern Intelligencer* insisted that a gradual approach to emancipation and colonization would have the effect of lessening many of the lower South's most pressing problems. "We are not called to work miracles," the author asserted, "but we are called to do what we can." It would be a "great thing to open a door for the gradual removal of an evil; if but little is effected, we at least have the satisfaction of knowing that we have done all we can."[53]

In assaying the continued public reaction to the Vesey scare and the various ad hoc prescriptions for preventing future rebellions the crisis generated, church leaders grew rightly concerned that demands for tougher regulation of efforts to Christianize slaves, and especially for stiffer penalties for those who taught slaves to read (as evangelical ministers and their class leaders often did), stood near the center of the proposed remedial legislation being readied for the upcoming legislative session. Church leaders mobilized to defend their existing practices. Their first major collective effort developed under the auspices of the redoubtable Charleston Bible Society, which sent a private letter to Governor Thomas Bennett in late September 1822 seeking his help in preventing such restrictive legislation.[54]

Founded in 1810, largely through the efforts of prominent Episcopal lay leader Charles Cotesworth Pinckney, delegate to the federal convention of 1787 and once the Federalist nominee for the presidency, and his close friend Richard Furman, the Charleston Bible Society joined its sister societies across the republic in an effort to place Bibles in the hands of as many individuals as possible, slave and free.[55] More active in the North than in the South, Bible societies worried many southerners precisely because they encouraged slaves to read scripture. North Carolina Jeffersonian Nathaniel Macon considered these Bible societies as little more than disguised abolitionist cells. Such was emphatically not the case in Charleston, where at least some large slaveholders supported the organization with enthusiasm. In 1822, an aging Charles C. Pinckney served as president of the society, but its board included a number of prominent Charleston clergymen and Christian lay leaders. Furman served on the board, as did the outspoken Congregationalist Palmer, who was a close friend of both Pinckney and Furman. Palmer's family had moved from Massachusetts to Charleston during the American Revolution. The young Benjamin Palmer was educated at the College of Charleston and at Princeton, where he studied under Samuel

Stanhope Smith. He became a Congregationalist minister in 1803 and served a parish in Beaufort before coming to the Circular Church in Charleston as co-pastor in 1814. Joining Furman and Pinckney in the city, Palmer brought renewed energy to the Bible society and he became Charleston's leading champion of benevolent societies in general. Such open support for benevolent societies raised more than a few eyebrows in Charleston, but even Palmer's opponents conceded his "moral courage." Presbyterians Arthur Buist, of First Scots, and Artemis Boies, minister at Second Presbyterian, were also board members. Buist, the son of popular and long-time First Scots pastor George Buist, accepted a call to the pulpit at his father's old church in April 1821. A Charleston native educated at Princeton and Edinburgh, the young Buist's education and family connections gave him an influence beyond that expected from a young minister so new to his Charleston pulpit. Moreover, both Buist and his deceased father were close friends of Richard Furman, who performed the younger Buist's marriage ceremony.[56] Buist was joined on the society's board by talented young lawyer Thomas Smith Grimké, who had serious reservations about slavery, and James Legare, a prominent area planter who also served on the first Vesey court.[57]

Dated September 23, 1822, the society's letter to the embattled Governor Bennett was sent over the name of President Charles C. Pinckney on behalf of the society's board. But without question, the communication was chiefly the literary and intellectual handiwork of Richard Furman, whose style and views it clearly bore.[58] The letter made two requests, one official but relatively mundane and the other unofficial but controversial. First, on behalf of the society, and aided by the support of a petition published earlier in the city's religious press, the board asked the governor to declare an official day of thanksgiving to thank divine providence for delivering the state from the "execution of a Ferocious, diabolical design," the Vesey plot.[59] Second, the Bible society sought Bennett's support for its efforts to discourage any additional legislative restrictions on the society's work of making scripture available to slaves.

In making the society's case for both requests, Furman revealed much about the board's perceptions of the alleged insurrection plot. Such perceptions were informed by a variety of events and experiences. During the investigation and trials of June and July, members of the Charleston clergy, including Bible society board members Furman and Palmer, as well as Catholic bishop John England, a Methodist pastor named D. Hall, and perhaps others, visited the Charleston workhouse regularly and, according to surviving accounts, held at least some pastoral conversations with accused insurrectionists.[60] Legare, of course, was not a minister, but as a member of the first Vesey court, he heard much of the testimony and knew the interior workings of the court better than all but a handful of people. At the same time, Furman and the board were also aware of the broader political dynamics at work that summer. Writing after Bennett's circular letter was published in August, they certainly knew that the governor held a different reading of the evidence than did Hamilton and the court. They knew that he had been openly critical of the intendant's and court's handling of the investigation and trials. They also knew that Hamilton had aggressively defended his actions in public (and in private as well). By September, they well knew that those who had publicly disagreed with Hamilton had inevitably lost public favor. Doubtless this array of strategic considerations as well as its deeply held convictions and opinions shaped the board's communication with Bennett.

The board's letter to the governor did not hesitate to advance a different estimation of the aborted rebellion's scope and significance than that earlier presented by the governor. Furman labeled the governor's judgment that "the conspiracy was confined to a few, & the Evil, therefore, to be considered of no great magnitude, as to its Extent, & the Probability of success" as a "problematical" conclusion. The board noted that many of the city's "discerning Citizens, not in the habit of indulging suspicion," had observed "the spirit of Conspiracy & revolt…or the Effects of Guilt" operating "extensively" among area slaves. Having taken issue with Bennett's view of the planned rebellion, the board proceeded to request an official day of thanksgiving, which it argued would remind slaves both of the swift and decisive governmental action that foiled the rebellion and that some of the insurrection's leaders apparently had been ready to flee to the Caribbean with as much plunder as they could manage while leaving their abandoned followers to face the deadly repercussions.[61]

But the more important issue for Furman and the board was the looming legislative threat to their efforts to evangelize slaves. The board expressed its "apprehension" that the "claims laid to a religious Character by several of those who ranked as Leaders in the nefarious scheme" had turned many citizens against "the Use of Bible among the Negroes." Such opposition, Furman continued, would manifest itself in legislative proposals designed to prevent slaves from learning to read or use the Bible freely. Furman insisted that the Bible sanctioned slavery, despite claims to the contrary by "some very worthy men." To be sure, Furman conceded, the teachings of the Bible had been abused by some, but "to argue against its use, from the abuse it has suffered," Furman continued, was not "logical, just or pious." The "Scriptures are given to Man (without respect of persons) to make him wise unto Salvation," and "all are required, by Divine Authority to read them, because they contain the Words of Eternal Life." Thus any prohibition on the reading of the Bible tended to "contradict and oppose the Divine Authority." To suppose that scripture inspired insurrection, as critics did, bordered on blasphemy, in the board's view.[62]

The board then turned to what would prove white Christians' chief line of defense against the anti-instruction sentiment that emerged with force after the Vesey plot. The letter admitted that "a considerable number of the Persons who were concerned in the late Conspiracy professed to be of a religious character." But, Furman insisted, "it is also true that the most leading characters among them, and the chief of the rest, were members of an irregular Association, which called itself the African church, & was intimately connected with a similar body in Philadelphia, from which their sentiments & directions in Matters of religion were chiefly Derived." These principles, Furman allowed, included a "Scheme of general emancipation, for which they are zealous advocates," a scheme they supported with a "misconstruction" of scripture. At the same time, blacks who composed the "well-known, regular & esteemed members of Churches" had "not been impeached." In fact, Furman argued, the conspirators apparently were afraid to "trust" these black members of regular churches. "Nothing that we can discover," Furman insisted, indicated that "the meetings of the religious Negroes approved by the churches to which they belong, for reading the scriptures, learning their Catechisms, and the general purpose of Devotion and religious Improvement, have been in any way Instrumental in producing or advancing the late horrid Design." Furman concluded that operations of the Vesey plot revealed what many Christians had long believed, that "one of the best securities we have to the domestic Peace and safety of the state is found in the sentiments...of the religious Negroes, which they derive from the Bible." Hence, "instead of taking the Bible away from them & abridging the truly religious Privileges they have been used to enjoy," it would make more sense to adopt measures allowing them to study the Bible under the kind of "regulation the least liable to abuse." The society concluded by asking the governor to use his "influence" to discourage legislation that would make it more difficult to offer biblical instruction to slaves.[63]

Bennett pondered the Bible society's requests. Just over a week later, on October 1, he replied, politely but firmly rejecting the society's request for an official day of thanksgiving but pledging his support for the society's position on the religious instruction of slaves. Bennett's reply, written over a month after his August circular and about six weeks before his message to the legislature, revealed his continued disagreement with the actions and conclusions of Hamilton and the court. He rejected the idea of an official day of thanksgiving largely because he thought the celebration of the holiday would do too much to expand slave knowledge of the rebellion and thus deepen their appreciation for the degree of fear it had spread throughout the Lowcountry. Bennett also thought a day of thanksgiving sent the wrong signals to the rest of the nation, signals suggesting that, contrary to emerging slaveholder claims across the lower South, most of the region's slaves were not content with their condition and that lower South whites did indeed live in chronic fear of rebellion. Defenses of slaveholder benevolence and expressions of their confidence in the loyalty of their slaves were rendered less convincing, Bennett argued, if the state officially thanked divine providence for delivering masters from the hands of rebellious slaves.[64]

In Bennett's view, the less seriously South Carolina appeared to take the Vesey scare, the better. If Hamilton and his supporters exaggerated the area's vulnerability to advance their anti-paternalist cause, Bennett thought admitting vulnerability was a strategic mistake. What Bennett and Hamilton shared was an assumption that they were preparing for a long battle with critics of slavery. Hamilton wanted to prepare for that battle by making sure slaves were effectively subdued and that whites adhered to the same line of defense. Bennett preferred turning away the challenge with an air of confidence and a posture of humanitarianism designed to disarm critics and reassure allies. To the governor, Hamilton's exertions only highlighted the region's vulnerability. To Hamilton, Governor Bennett's veneer of confidence cavalierly ignored real threats to white security.

Bennett also used his response to the Bible society as yet another occasion to air his own views on the Vesey plot. He discounted the idea that leading rebels expected help from Africa, the West Indies, or Great Britain, and he dismissed reports that "all the negroes between this [Charleston] and Columbia were engaged" or "that all the wells were to be poisoned." Bennett believed that the insurrection's black organizers touted such grand prospects in their recruiting efforts but doubted they ever intended to act on such plans. "All of these things," Bennett reasoned, "no doubt may have been employed by the conspirators as a means of seduction," but they were "certainly not entitled to belief." Without question, Bennett admitted, "professors of religion were seduced" by the plot's organizers, but it was "not the religion of these men that they invoked; it was the passions which were unsubdued by [Christianity's] mild precepts" that insurrectionists played on. To suppose that the putative rebels had grown more vulnerable to the "wicked machinations or evil devices" of rebel leaders because they "had received some religious instruction," Bennett concluded, "is to estimate human nature beyond the standard which human actions indicate." Bennett thought that the Bible society's board exaggerated the existing degree of public hostility toward the continued religious instruction of slaves. But he nonetheless pledged to "use the little influence which I possess" to "avert that which so justly excites the deep concern you have expressed."[65]

Doubtless the Charleston Bible Society was pleased to have Bennett's help in opposing legislation hostile to the religious instruction of slaves, but the society was not ready to abandon its request for an official day of thanksgiving. The resourceful Furman regrouped and took a new approach to the issue. Furman presented the question to his own denomination's governing body, the newly formed South Carolina Baptist Convention, which quickly gave Furman's draft resolution its hearty approval. The convention urged the governor to declare a day of thanksgiving to thank God for delivering the state from both the aborted insurrection and the fierce hurricane that struck the coast near Georgetown in the fall of 1822. The convention also promised to make a fuller statement of its views on slavery available to the governor at a later date. Armed with this endorsement, Furman waited until John Lyde Wilson replaced Bennett as governor late in the 1822 legislative session and, having obtained prior assurances that Wilson would approve such a request, submitted the proposal to the new governor in writing. Wilson promptly approved it.[66]

A second communication to the governor fulfilled the Baptist convention's promise and included a significantly expanded version of the Bible society's September letter to Bennett.[67] Approved by the convention, the letter was unquestionably the work of Furman, who signed it on behalf of South Carolina Baptists.[68] The letter, quickly published in pamphlet form with Furman identified as author, outlined the position of the state Baptist convention on the "lawfulness of holding slaves" from a "moral and religious point of view."[69] Furman, long a slaveholder, used the opportunity both to defend Christian slaveholders from the increasingly scathing criticisms voiced by antislavery Christians in the North and to defend Christian paternalism as a model for slaveholding against the increasingly formidable criticisms from secular and civil authorities in the lower South.

Furman's pamphlet quickly dispatched the argument that holding slaves was inherently unchristian, and he distanced South Carolina Baptists from those antislavery advocates who based their arguments for emancipation on Christian theology and teaching. Furman acknowledged that some Christian writers, almost exclusively from outside the South, had advanced arguments "very unfriendly to the principle and practice of holding slaves," and conceded that a few of these writers sought to "produce insurrection and rebellion" among slaves. No matter how "benevolent their intentions," Furman admitted, advocates of a "scheme of general emancipation" who pursued their ideal with "intemperate zeal" became the "means of producing in this country, scenes of anarchy and blood." Personally, Furman doubted that slaves were ready for freedom. "While men remain in the chains of ignorance and error, and under the domain of tyrant lusts and passions," he observed, "they cannot be free." But should "a time arrive, when the Africans in our country might be found qualified to enjoy freedom," Furman mused, the state Baptist convention "would be happy in setting them free."[70]

Doubtless many Lowcountry planters looked warily upon Furman's mention of a possible future emancipation predicated simply on a finding that slaves were "qualified to enjoy freedom." The question of precisely who would make such a determination—a determination that alarmed slaveholders thought Denmark Vesey and his followers had recently tried to make for themselves, and one growing numbers of antislavery northerners felt fully justified in making—remained explosive. But the possibility of a conditional end to slavery at some future date remained an important article of faith for Furman and other evangelicals even in the aftermath of the Vesey scare. Until the appropriate time for emancipation revealed itself, however, the "right of holding slaves is clearly established in the Holy Scripture, both by precept and example," Furman insisted. To illustrate his point, Furman pointed to the holding of slaves by Old Testament Israelites and reminded readers that only Hebrew slaves, not gentile slaves, were freed on the biblical day of Jubilee. In the New Testament, Furman continued, both Greeks and Romans held slaves, yet many of these masters, along with their slaves, accepted Christianity as taught by Paul and other early Christian apostles. In "things spiritual," Furman reasoned, New Testament slaves and masters "enjoyed equal privileges," but "their relationship as master and slave was not dissolved." Rather, masters were instructed to give their slaves "the things that are just and equal." Furman conceded that "Christian nations have not done all they might...for the civilization and conversion of the Africans," and he admitted that "much cruelty has been practiced in the slave trade" and that the "religious interests" of slaves had been "too much neglected." But "the fullest proof of these facts," Furman argued, "will not also prove, that holding men in subjection, as slaves, is a moral evil and inconsistent with Christianity."[71] Masters may have fallen short of Christian ideals in their actions, Furman reasoned, but the spiritual infirmity of masters hardly stood as a moral or spiritual condemnation of slavery as an institution.

But while Furman refused to concede biblical ground to antislavery Christians, he proved just as unwilling to yield ground to slaveholding and secular critics of the mission to the slaves and the paternalist ideal. Furman decried the growing post-Vesey sentiments calculated to "deprive slaves of religious privileges" by "awakening in the minds of masters a fear that acquaintance with the Scriptures, and the enjoyment of those privileges" would necessarily lead to unrest and rebellion. Furman firmly told these proslavery critics of the church that while slavery was justified by scripture, the responsibilities of masters were specified as well. The "religious interests of the Negroes," Furman insisted, must be "seriously considered by all our Citizens." For "though they are slaves, they are also men," Furman declared, "and are with ourselves accountable creatures; having immortal souls, and being destined to future eternal reward." Thus the slaves' claim on their masters for religious instruction was "of the most serious nature." Furman conceded that the duty of white Christians to nurture the religious life of slaves had been "neglected and disregarded by many" even though he argued that, as a rule, the "various Christian denominations among us do conscientiously regard this duty."[72]

Furman regretted the emergence of an "erroneous view" in the public mind equating the spread of Christianity among slaves with an enhanced desire among slaves to seek an early end to their bondage. At this point, Furman countered head-on the criticism of the evangelical ministry to slaves that had emerged from the Vesey insurrection scare. In the "late projected scheme for producing an insurrection among us," the "considerable number" who "laid claim to a religious character," Furman insisted, repeating nearly verbatim the argument he had advanced in his earlier letter to Bennett, "were members of an irregular body, which called itself the African church." The African church "had intimate connection and intercourse with a similar body of men in a Northern city, among whom the supposed right to emancipation is strenuously advocated." On the other hand, Furman insisted, "very few" participants in the conspiracy were "members attached to regular churches."[73]

In other words, it was false Christianity and not "right teaching," the independent African church and not regular biracial churches, that slaveholding society had to fear. Thus the public should direct its concern toward limiting the abuse of Christianity, not restricting its proper practice. It was the duty of masters to protect their slaves and provide "such necessaries and conveniences of life as are proper to their condition as servants" on "just and rational principles." But it was also the "positive duty of servants" to "reverence their master, to be obedient, industrious ... [and] faithful." Masters, in turn, were responsible for giving slaves "religious instruction;

or at least afford them opportunities, under proper regulations, to obtain it." If slaves received their instruction "from right sources," Furman argued, "they will not be in danger of having their minds corrupted by sentiments unfriendly to the domestic and civil peace of the community." Furman conceded that laws to prevent and punish insurrection were necessary in a slave society, but added that "on the other hand, laws, also, to prevent them [slaves] from being oppressed and injured by unreasonable, cruel masters, and others" and protect their free exercise of religion "under proper regulations" were needed. Furman urged an alarmed state "not to interdict," as "some have supposed necessary," in areas where "reason, the conscience, the genius of Christianity are concerned" on "account of the bad conduct of others."[74] He urged the legislature and other civil authorities to avoid any further interference with the Christian mission to the slaves.

Furman also defended the broader concept of a paternalistic relationship between masters and slaves against critics from both inside and outside slaveholding society. A master, Furman claimed, "may, in an important sense, be the guardian and even father of his slaves." Treated with "justice and humanity," Furman contended, slaves "become part of his family (the whole, forming under him a little community) and the care of ordering it, and of providing for its welfare, devolves on him." Thus, Furman explained, "what is effected, and often at a great public expense, in a free community, by taxes, benevolent institutions, bettering houses, and penitentiaries, lies here on the master."[75] In a few sentences, Furman had given the paternalistic master the role as primary agent for social improvement played in the North by a proliferating array of benevolent institutions, from Sunday school associations to temperance societies. But while serving as a one-person benevolent empire, the master who abused his authority or took his responsibility too lightly "must answer for it at the Divine tribunal," and perhaps, in the most flagrant instances, to civil authority as well. In conclusion, Furman insisted that slavery could be a beneficent institution and that in the South it had been "the means of [slaves'] mental and religious improvement, and so of obtaining salvation" and that a "just and humane master, who rules his slaves and provides for them, according to Christian principles," should "rest satisfied that he is not in holding them, chargeable with moral evil, nor with acting . . . contrary to the genius of Christianity."[76]

Taking the lead in defending the evangelical position on the proper relationship between Christianity and slavery, Furman articulated the most carefully reasoned rebuttal of religion-based criticism of slavery that the slaveholding states had yet produced. Ironically, this rebuttal emerged chiefly from an effort to defend the religious instruction of slaves against increasingly potent attacks launched by other white Southerners. Though brief by the standards of later defenses of slavery, Furman's essay grounded his defense of the morality of slaveholding in scripture. But perhaps even more important, Furman forged one of the earliest and most coherent statements on paternalism as the proper model for master-slave relationships. Furman rooted the master's authority and responsibility firmly in his (and it was usually a man's) role as head of the household, with slaves as well as free white dependents forming the family or community around the presumably benevolent patriarch. He defended the authority of the master as being as legitimate as the authority of the parent. Furman, of course, recognized that with the authority of a household head came serious secular and spiritual responsibilities. He acknowledged that too many masters fell short of adequately fulfilling those responsibilities. With this argument, Furman laid the foundation for future religious arguments defending slavery, arguments that often lacked the restraint Furman demonstrated in his 1822 pamphlet.

In sum, Furman's pamphlet argued that slaveholding was not inherently inconsistent with the profession of Christianity and that the profession of the Christian faith was not inherently incompatible with being an effective master. He ventured no argument for slavery in the abstract, instead offering a particularistic analysis of slavery based on the specific historical contingencies of his time and locale. Doubtless he even startled some of his readers with his contention that South Carolina Baptists would readily support a general emancipation when slaves had proven a fitness for freedom that satisfied the evangelical mind, though the rest of his essay suggested that such an eventuality remained so distant and improbable that Furman risked little with his suggestion. Still, with critics of religious instruction of slaves in full voice in the immediate aftermath of the Vesey scare, Furman's letter constituted a bold defense of Christian paternalism in the face of mounting local opposition. The prominent Baptist defended Christian efforts to convert slaves and the practice of paternalism against internal criticism that grew more vociferous after evidence from the Vesey investigation confirmed critics' worst fears. But Furman also recognized that as he defended evangelical outreach to slaves he also must justify slaveholding to Christians outside the region, not only because opinion outside the South ran increasingly against the institution but because evangelicals needed the internal legitimacy that came from defending the community against aspersions cast on it by outsiders.

If Furman presented the evangelical case for the compatibility of slavery and Christianity with boldness and a measure of courage given his time and place, Episcopal clergyman Frederick Dalcho, assistant pastor at the prestigious St. Michael's church in Charleston, soon advanced the liturgical version of the same argument.[77] A successful physician and editor, the scholarly Dalcho had turned to the ministry as a third career in 1813. Born in London in 1770 to Prussian parents, Dalcho migrated to Baltimore, where he earned a medical degree. His service as a United States Army surgeon took him to Savannah. Upon leaving the army he moved to Charleston and established a profitable medical practice. Though successful as a physician, Dalcho joined the local Federalist newspaper, the *Charleston Courier*, as coeditor in 1806. He retained that position until 1813, when he began serious study for the ministry. A rural Episcopal church in the Charleston area, St. Philip's-Stono, asked Dalcho to join them as lay reader in 1814. By 1817 Dalcho had begun serving St. Michael's in Charleston on as-needed basis. In 1818, the rector of St. Michael's, Nathaniel Bowen, was named bishop of South Carolina, and Dalcho joined St. Michael's as a full-time assistant pastor, remaining there until 1833.[78] During a career marked by journeys from healer to intellectual, from physician to editor, from pastor to polemicist and, ultimately, to amateur church historian, Dalcho felt a duty to serve God's people, but his combative intellect served him better as newspaper editor and pamphlet writer, and perhaps even as historian, than as parish minister.

In his pamphlet, Dalcho echoed Furman in advancing the argument that slavery and Christianity could coexist in southern society. The ownership of slaves violated no moral precepts of Christianity as long as masters provided sufficiently for the slaves' physical and spiritual needs. Nor did Christian treatment of slaves or teaching slaves to read undermine the discipline necessary to maintain the institution, as long as masters modulated their kindness with firmness and the teaching of scripture done under appropriate white supervision. Slaveholders could be good Christians, and Christian masters could run profitable and well-disciplined plantations and farms. Dalcho admitted the "difficulty and delicacy" of discussing the subject of slavery publicly so soon after the Vesey scare, but the Anglican divine declared himself "constrained by a sense of duty" to call the attention of slaveholders to his subject: according to "the Scriptures of the Old and New Testament, that Slavery is not forbidden by Divine Law, and, at the same time to prove, the necessity of giving religious instruction to our Negroes."[79]

Dalcho maintained that "slavery is found not to be contrary to the laws of God, so it is left to our own judgment whether to hold slaves or not," but he joined Furman in insisting that "the same God who permits slavery, has required of us, in his holy word, their religious instruction." Christians could hardly "claim the authority of God, in one case" and yet "reject it in another." So Christians who held slaves also shouldered a special responsibility. "If we are the owners of slaves," Dalcho declared, "our duty to God, to our country, and to ourselves, all urge the necessity of affording them instruction in the Gospel of Jesus Christ, the Savior of the souls of men."[80]

Dalcho also followed Furman's example in avoiding any argument for slavery in the abstract, advancing an even more localist defense of slaveholding in the Lowcountry than his Baptist counterpart. In Dalcho's account, the virtues of slavery lay almost entirely in the institution's ability to work profitably the swamps and marshes of South Carolina's disease-infested parish country. The Lowcountry "could not be cultivated by white people," Dalcho maintained, because the "Swamps would send thousands to their graves in the first summer."[81] Echoing the argument advanced by almost all advocates of paternalism, Dalcho believed that Lowcountry slavery had grown more benevolent over time, and the Episcopal rector joined the evangelical Furman in arguing that slaves in South Carolina "are treated with more humanity and kindness than millions of white people in other parts of the world." Slaves were "but lightly worked, their pregnant women are treated with indulgence and care;

they are well clothed, well fed, and well nursed when they are sick." Such treatment of slaves, Dalcho acknowledged, emerged in part from enlightened self-interest and had produced the "natural increase of the slave population after 1810." But the cleric nonetheless called the evolution in treatment "no mean compliment to the humanity of American slaveholders."[82]

Dalcho joined Furman in sketching a portrait of a social system defined by paternalism, with the patriarchal master serving as the legal and moral head of an extended household full of unequal people, dependents, who required the master's protection and supervision and who were expected to return obedience and labor. Under Christianity, Dalcho insisted, "masters will become more kind, and slaves more obedient." Dalcho's explanation of the authority and responsibilities of masters also paralleled Furman's. Just as God stood as "moral governor of the Universe," Dalcho declared, "the fathers of families" and the "owners of slaves, each in their respective spheres," all stood as "the head of a moral government." Masters, "invested" with "this moral control" by virtue of their slave ownership, shall "be held accountable for its use." In return for their stewardship, Dalcho argued, masters earned the right to expect "obedient and orderly behaviour" from slaves. Obedience "rendered through fear," Dalcho argued, "will never be sincere," but obedience that grew out of "a proper sense of moral obligation" would "always be faithful." Dalcho insisted that Christianity required "obedience, submission, and subjection" from slaves even if they had a bad master. There was "nothing in the law of God, which can, in the slightest manner, justify the disobedience and revolt of slaves," Dalcho assured skeptical slaveholders.[83]

Dalcho argued that the chief lesson of the Vesey scare was not that the religious instruction of slaves was inherently subversive but that the "leading doctrines of the Bible" should be taught only by "regular, judicious clergymen." Dalcho reminded readers that "none of the Negroes belonging to the Protestant Episcopal Church was concerned in the late [Vesey] conspiracy." He attributed the absence of Episcopalian slaves among those accused of insurrection to the denomination's "sober, rational, sublime, and evangelical worship." On this point, Dalcho indirectly chided his brothers and sisters in the evangelical denominations, though he explicitly cited Methodist rather than Baptist excesses. Because the "sober" Episcopalian liturgy did not permit the extemporaneous prayers that constituted such an important part of Methodist meetings, Dalcho contended, "nothing [existed in the Anglican liturgy] to inflame the passions of the ignorant enthusiast, nothing left to the crude, undigested ideas of illiterate black class leaders." The Vesey rebellion, Dalcho insisted, had its "origin and seat in the African Church, which was entirely composed of negroes, under preachers of their own color."[84] Only "injudicious instruction," not the general catechizing of slaves, posed a danger, Dalcho contended. "It is ignorance, superstition, fanaticism and a false representation of their condition" that led slaves astray.[85]

Dalcho believed that the key to the proper religious instruction of slaves lay in having them "attend the regularly settled places of worship." Slaves should not be "be allowed to hold separate meetings of their own, under teachers of their own color, as ignorant, as superstitious as themselves; who will expound the Scriptures according to their own views, or excite the malignant passions of their deluded hearers, by perhaps, an unintentional, if not a designed, misconstruction of the sacred page."[86] The background and training of the clergy charged with the mission to the slaves loomed as a matter of great importance. Dalcho argued that the "peculiar character" of slaveholding societies required that only men "acquainted with the real character of Negroes" and "their capacity for attaining moral and religious instruction" should be allowed to teach and preach to slaves. These religious leaders needed the "prudence which is necessary" to improve the "moral and spiritual condition" of slaves "without deranging the existing order of society." Dalcho dismissed "persons born and educated in all the prejudices of non-slaveholding countries" and "mere itinerants here for a few winter months" as "unfit" for the instruction of slaves. Such teachers, Dalcho complained, too often possessed "speculative notions of personal liberty" that threatened the southern social order. "There is a chain which bonds together the various orders of our community," Dalcho asserted, "which must not be broken." Dalcho's chain extended vertically, defining a social hierarchy, rather than horizontally, which would have been a metaphor for an interdependent, egalitarian social order. Yet every denomination, Dalcho conceded, possessed clergymen of "sufficient learning" and seriousness to meet his requirements. Thus if "Masters of slaves will unite in the great Christian scheme of conversion," the means and personnel to effectively undertake a well-planned ministry to the slaves would be found readily.[87]

In contrast to Furman, however, Dalcho articulated a starkly limited paternalism that valued the piety of masters far more than the spiritual potential of slaves. Unlike Furman, Dalcho remained deeply skeptical about slaves' capacity for moral development. He thought that the Vesey rebellion plot revealed that "little confidence could be placed in the religious profession of negroes," since they apparently felt "little real devotion" to the faith even after conversion.[88] Dalcho's pessimistic view of the slaves' capacity for moral and intellectual improvement colored his argument for paternalism. He expected slaves to greet paternalism with a measure of calculated resistance and twist paternalism's intentions to their own purposes. "Gratitude is not one of their virtues," Dalcho observed with reference to slaves. "What they receive they consider their due, and indulgence too often leads them to practice imposition." Thus, despite the wise application of paternalism by many slaveholders, the "severest" master, Dalcho conceded, "will always have the most orderly slaves." Whatever the results, however, the duty of masters was clear. They must treat slaves "with Christian kindness in every respect" but "make them perform their duty." Like children, slaves "were to be corrected" when "they will not do what is right." Dalcho argued that the mission to slaves would do at least some good, and that masters were morally obliged to try to bring the Word to their slaves regardless of outcome. Dalcho supported the effort to Christianize slaves more because it was required for the salvation of masters than because he expected Christian paternalism to render slaves more moral or more readily controlled.

Dalcho's paternalism held a harder edge than Furman's. Masters must be respectful but firm with their slaves. Stern correction must follow slave misdeeds. Even paternalists should not lose sight of the benefits of severity in slave management. In return for their kindness, Dalcho warned, slaveholders must expect ingratitude. Slaves would try to take advantage of a master's kindness and impose on his generosity. The slaveholders' reward, Dalcho believed, would come from a triune God who expected his servants to serve faithfully, not from increasingly productive and well-behaved slaves. Moreover, Dalcho's blunt assertions about slaves' lack of capacity for learning suggested a racial view markedly different from Furman's. Dalcho's paternalist masters loomed not so much as surrogates for benevolent associations as colonial viceroys doing a thankless duty as they reaped a harvest of spoils. Dalcho viewed the negative characteristics of black slaves, which he saw as ingratitude, disloyalty, laziness, and insincerity, as innate racial characteristics, and he doubted that the slaves' conversion to Christianity would meliorate these innate character tendencies very much, even though he insisted whites were obligated to try. Slaves, Dalcho admitted, were men, and thus had souls in need of salvation. But unlike Furman, who leaned toward seeing slavery as a school from which graduation might ultimately be possible but not anytime soon, not only did the notion of equality never emerge from Dalcho's pen, but he never suggested that black slaves would ever be fit for freedom in the American South. Dalcho's muscular paternalism stood a better chance of appealing to fabulously wealthy rice and Sea Island cotton magnates who rented and purchased pews at Lowcountry Episcopal churches than did Furman's more egalitarian version. These Episcopalian masters generally admired the idea of a hierarchical social order and were willing to seek it in their relations with other whites as well as in their relationships with slaves and free blacks. They embraced paternalism with one arm, keeping the other hand free for the lash. They accepted the responsibilities of power and place, but they also expected to use the whip as well as the Word in managing slaves.

Yet, like Furman, Dalcho pulled up well short of a full-blown proslavery argument. Slavery as an abstract principle, the Episcopal pastor admitted, "is not in accordance with all our feelings. We deprecate the evil which attends it.... We would most willingly apply the remedy if we knew what it was." Dalcho, perhaps to the shock of his slaveholding parishioners, set a more precise, if equally improbable, condition for ending slavery in the South Carolina Lowcountry than Furman did. If, Dalcho argued, "the non-slaveholding states will purchase our plantations and slaves, and send the latter to Africa, under the patronage of the Colonization Society...I do not in my conscience believe there would be many Planters in South Carolina who would hesitate one moment to get rid of both, even at something below their value." But "as to parting with them without an equivalent, [it] is out of the question; for our servants are our money."[89] Instead of asking antislavery advocates for patience, as

Furman had, so that the fullness of time could eradicate existing inequalities between races, Dalcho sought a fully compensated emancipation accompanied by African colonization. He defined full compensation as payment for damages to land values as well as for the loss of slaves, and included the cost of the immediate colonization of former slaves in his demand as well. Of course, Dalcho knew that neither the national government nor any benevolent society could afford to call his bluff. Thus he would not have to test his parishioners to see if they would, in fact, approve a general emancipation even on such generous terms. Dalcho did not make an improved level of civilization among slaves a precondition for emancipation because, unlike Furman, he did not believe such improvement possible.

Both Dalcho and Furman clearly saw race as the critical component in slavery as the institution existed in the lower South. For both clergymen, the logic of slavery lay in the labor needs generated by a subtropical climate capable of producing staples of enormous value and the availability of African and African American laborers, largely non-Christians drawn from traditional civilizations easily categorized as "inferior" by post-Enlightenment Americans. Yet in his justification for maintaining black slavery Furman focused precisely on the possibility of changing "uncivilized" traits. Furman even suggested that once the process of "civilizing" slaves, a process enhanced by Christianization, reached a certain point, southern Baptists would readily consider the efficacy of emancipation. To be sure, the tone of Furman's remarks suggests that he expected this process of civilization to be long and arduous, far slower than even thousands of total immersions welcoming slaves to the Baptist faith. Still, Furman insisted on the spiritual equality of slaves and other blacks and seemed to view their moral and spiritual condition as a matter of progress along a continuum of civilization, not as an inherent or immutable condition. Furman perceived blacks as inferior, but he blamed that inferiority on their condition, their environment, and their background, and he believed that as those circumstances changed, so too would the social and cultural attainments of blacks, even as slaves.

From the Charleston clergy's response to this crisis of paternalism emerged an embryonic southern argument that defended slaveholding as consistent with the tradition, faith, and practice of Christianity, but this response did not offer a sweeping argument styling slavery as a positive good. In fact, these early religious pamphlets on slavery written by prominent members of the Charleston clergy were not so much defenses of the peculiar institution as they were assertions that slaveholders could be good Christians and that Christians could be good masters. The assertions of influential clergy enjoyed wide currency, but they were in their origin almost entirely local and tactical in nature, written in response to post-Vesey criticisms of Christian paternalism and the movement to provide religious instruction to the slaves. They defended the church's mission to the slaves and the evangelical insistence that slaves be taught to read scripture. They assured skeptics that leading Christians were willing to defend the slaveholding social order as long as that order was maintained in accordance with Christian tenets. In a larger sense (as we shall see in the next chapter), these tracts were part of an intense but provincial debate, one conducted in and around Charleston, over how to make slavery safe for the Lowcountry. In virtually every document a strong measure of Lowcountry particularism appeared. There was virtually no claim advanced by these clergy that slavery might prove a great leveler among whites or that it served as the foundation for a model republican social order.

On balance, the Lowcountry religious community, despite some internal differences, met the post-Vesey assault on paternalism and the Christian mission to slaves with considerable energy and firmness as well as with some tact. They conceded that the church was guilty of some excesses in its zeal to encourage slave Christianity, and especially in the acceptance, and even encouragement by some, of the independent African church, but they argued that no movement should be judged solely by its excesses. The mission to the slaves and the ideology of paternalism it exuded, church leaders insisted, deserved the continued support of the community for the good the mission had done, was doing, and ultimately would do. In return, the church promised to monitor the instruction and worship of slaves more carefully. On the question of teaching slaves to read for the purpose of giving them direct access to the Bible, the evangelical denominations made no concessions, even in the face of intense planter opposition. Moreover, the arguments of Palmer, the actions of the Charleston Bible Society, and the writings of Furman and Dalcho tacitly proffered a tentative accommodation to paternalism's Lowcountry critics. The white church would agree with civil authorities that the local reaction to the Vesey scare was fully justified by the evidence collected by the court and that the doctrines espoused by and the plans laid in the independent African church lay at the heart of the insurrection's origins. The white church would accept, even applaud, the forced closing of the African church and monitor the religious instruction of slaves and free blacks more diligently than in the past. In return, white Christian leaders wanted state and local civil authorities to refrain from tightening the regulation of the religious instruction of blacks and hoped that the avowed critics of paternalism would mute their voices in the spirit of giving paternalism a chance to prove itself.

Yet Charleston's civil authorities and many Lowcountry planters remained skeptical of both the promise of paternalism as an ideology and the promises of church leaders, and especially from the evangelical denominations, concerning the religious instruction of slaves. Still uncertain was whether the positions the defenders of paternalism had staked out could hold politically. Their first test would be the 1822 session of the state legislature, where crucial decisions about the white security would be made.

October elections determined the composition of the new General Assembly, which convened annually in late November and usually remained in session for just under a month. James Hamilton, elected to the house from Charleston, planned to lead the legislative charge for his preferred slave control agenda. Governor Thomas

Bennett prepared his much-anticipated message to the legislature. Legislators from the interior packed to head for Columbia and learn more about the previous summer's insurrection scare. As preparations began for this pivotal legislative session, Justice William Johnson privately vented his lingering anger over Charleston's response to the alleged Vesey plot in a letter to Thomas Jefferson. "This last summer has furnished but too much cause for shame and anguish," Johnson told Jefferson, "I have lived to see what I never believed it possible I should see,—courts held with closed doors, and men dying by scores who had never seen the faces nor heard the voices of their accusers." Johnson assured Jefferson that the actual danger from the insurrection plot "was nothing in comparison with what it was magnified to," and proceeded to list the "Incalculable evils" resulting from the "exaggerated accounts circulated" concerning the alleged plot. "Our property is reduced to nothing," Johnson claimed, "strangers are alarmed at coming near us; our slaves are rendered uneasy; the confidence between us and our domestics destroyed—and all because of a trifling cabal of a few pennyless unarmed uncombined fanatics ... which certainly would have blown over without an explosion had it never come to light."[90]

CHAPTER NINE

REACTING TO THE SCARE

During the fall of 1822, James Hamilton, burnishing his new reputation as the leader who crushed the Vesey revolt, emerged as the political impresario of the South Carolina Lowcountry. The ambitious Hamilton had thrown some sharp elbows to retain control of the Vesey investigation, and he made the most of the opportunity he created. Early in October 1822, Hamilton left the state to attend a Bank of the United States stockholders meeting in Philadelphia and visit New York.[1] While traveling in the North, Hamilton won reelection both as intendant of Charleston and as a member of the state legislature. In the race for intendant, Hamilton trounced former intendant John Geddes, long a formidable vote getter in the city.[2] In his bid for the legislature, the popular intendant led the Charleston ticket even though he was out of the state during the campaign.[3] Clearly the credit white Charlestonians gave Hamilton for ferreting out and squelching the Vesey plot paid off handsomely in both these races.

Moreover, Hamilton had barely received news of his reelection as both intendant and state representative when he decided to throw his hat into a special congressional race in South Carolina's Second District, which embraced the rural districts of Beaufort and Colleton but not the city of Charleston. The Second District congressional seat came open due to the illness, retirement, and eventual death of influential national Republican William Lowndes, whom Hamilton considered a political mentor.[4] Eager to put his talent on the national stage, Hamilton had earlier considered a race for Congress from the Charleston district. But that seat was held by a Hamilton friend and ally, Joel Poinsett, a formidable political figure in his own right. The unexpected vacancy in the rural parish country south of Charleston, a district that included within its boundaries the Callawassie plantation on which Hamilton had resided before moving to Charleston, proved too tempting to pass up.[5]

Returning from his northern swing, Hamilton announced his candidacy in the special election on November 19 and accepted the daunting challenge of reintroducing himself to Beaufort and Colleton voters, and refuting charges that he was an absentee candidate, all in less than two weeks.[6] Prior to Hamilton's announcement, the apparent front-runner for the seat was Beaufort planter and physician Richard Screven, whose Republican leanings made him more popular than the other announced candidate, a Beaufort planter and city intendant of Federalist lineage, William Elliott. After an abbreviated campaign, Hamilton won the seat with an outright majority, garnering 57 percent of the vote in a three-way race.[7]

Possessing considerable political skill, much personal charm, abundant energy, and extraordinary ambition, James Hamilton proved a master at the political art of identifying a popular hobby, enhancing the hobby's importance, mobilizing support for the hobby, and then riding the hobby to prominence and power, where he would sometimes use his clout to pursue an agenda only loosely related to the hobby that carried him to power. As a political mobilizer and rider of hobbies, Hamilton had few peers.[8] Historians are indeed remiss if they fail to appreciate Hamilton's political talent, but they are also remiss if they fail to note his unbridled ambition and his willingness to use any and every opportunity to enhance his own prestige and standing. That Hamilton might exaggerate the magnitude of the threat emanating from the alleged Vesey conspiracy in order to magnify his own accomplishment in crushing it lies more in the realm of the probable than that of the merely possible. Regardless of the extent of the slave insurrection planned during the summer of 1822, and regardless of how close that plot came to implementation, there can be no question that the discovery and suppression of it provided James Hamilton with valuable political capital, which he proved eager to use.

Determined to set the legislative agenda on issues of white security and slave control, Hamilton arrived in Columbia in late November 1822 ready to personally lead the Charleston delegation's efforts to toughen the state's so-called black codes, despite his involvement in the Lowcountry congressional campaign. Moreover, unlike his nemesis Governor Bennett, Hamilton came armed not only with ideas but also with popularity among his Lowcountry colleagues and constituents.[9] But before Hamilton could present his sweeping slave control agenda to the legislature—his program aimed at making the state safe for slavery by making slavery safe for the state—he had to watch the incumbent governor, Bennett, use his annual message to make one last effort to shift the terms of debate over the Vesey crisis. Though ultimately unsuccessful, the embattled Bennett's efforts showed more of the political acumen for which the governor had been known before the crisis than had his awkward midsummer efforts to call the actions of Hamilton and the Vesey court into question.[10]

In his first legislative message of the year, written on November 26, Governor Bennett set forth an ambitious legislative agenda but made only passing reference to the Vesey plot, noting that "insurrectionary designs" formed "by a few of our domestics" had produced "unusual excitement" in Charleston the preceding summer. Bennett noted that the plot was "promptly met and arrested" and that "exemplary punishment" had been inflicted "on some of the instigators." In this initial message, Bennett's reference to the plot as one formed by "a few slaves" and his characterization of the scare as one affecting only the city of Charleston rankled Lowcountry legislators. The Charleston delegation, which included Hamilton, believed the plot had involved hundreds if not thousands of slaves and reached beyond Charleston into the rural parish country. Otherwise Bennett's brief mention of the Vesey scare drew little public comment. Bennett, however, promised that "a detailed account" of the entire incident would be provided to the legislature "without delay."[11]

Just two days later, Bennett presented a lengthy and controversial report on the Vesey plot to the legislature.[12] In broad terms, Bennett's unusual but much-anticipated second message had five major points: that vigilance, good fortune, and slave loyalty had indeed foiled an insurrection plot in Charleston during the previous summer and that some new security measures were needed to make sure that any future plot failed as miserably as Vesey's; that both the Charleston investigating committee and the Vesey court had overstepped the bounds of their legitimate authority; that they had justified their grab for power by exaggerating the scope and danger of the insurrection plot; that the state needed to adopt statutes clearly delineating the authority of such bodies to prevent such abuse in the future; and, most important, that the legislature should not overreact to the Vesey scare in a manner that undermined the paternalism that increasingly characterized the master-slave relationship and represented the best chance for whites to enjoy safety in a slaveholding society.

Bennett advanced his opinions and recommendations in calm and reasoned tones. He questioned the judgment rather than the motives of those he criticized. He took pains to offer praise for intendant Hamilton and the Charleston city council when he felt it possible to do so. But Bennett's message nevertheless reasserted with specificity his controversial charges that city authorities had usurped state jurisdiction by setting up a court that interrupted his own plans for a thorough state-led investigation. He again blasted the Vesey court for holding secret sessions and refusing to allow the accused to confront their accusers. When the court decided to "close its doors upon the community," Bennett argued, it "shut out those rays which occasionally illuminate the obscurity in which innocence and guilt are indistinguishable." The governor also criticized the court for uncritically accepting testimony that was transparently "the offspring of treachery or revenge" and had clearly been proffered with "the hope of immunity." Bennett also argued that the number of executions resulting from the court's proceedings far exceeded that necessary to "produce a salutary terror" among Charleston's black population. The nature and scope of the investigation and the court's proceedings aroused public fears unnecessarily by crediting "assertions of an alarming, extensive and deeply concerted plan" of insurrection when such assertions were not readily corroborated by other evidence. Bennett also faulted the court's heavy reliance during its July session on testimony offered by Monday Gell and Charles Drayton. In the case of Gell, Bennett argued, a "stratagem had been employed" to extract from Gell the testimony the court desired. Bennett claimed that the Committee of Vigilance used the confession of another alleged conspirator to "relate" to Monday Gell "a tissue of facts which were assented to and eventually produced his confession." Charles Drayton, Bennett asserted, "predicated his chances of survival on the number of convictions he could make" through his testimony. "Nothing could exceed the chilling depravity of this man," Bennett insisted.[13] In sum, Bennett accused Hamilton and the court with conducting extralegal proceedings, with crediting dubious and desperate testimony, and even with manufacturing testimony it knew to be unsubstantiated, all in an effort to cast the "proper" interpretation on the alleged plot.

For all his criticism of the investigation and the court's proceedings, Bennett acknowledged that a potentially dangerous insurrection plot had been afoot in Charleston during the spring and summer of 1822, and that the "standing and respectability of character of a few who countenanced the plan gave an imposing effect to the enterprise." Like Hamilton, the court, and all other observers, Bennett lamented the "influence of several wicked men who professed religion and were leaders of religious associations" who used "delusions" to recruit or intimidate potential followers. But Bennett also reminded the legislature that the even the conspirators recognized that the "fidelity" of many slaves to their masters constituted a real obstacle to the rebel plan. After all, Bennett pointed out, alleged ringleader Peter Poyas advised his recruiters to "take care and don't mention it [the planned insurrection] to those waiting men who receive presents of old coats from their masters" in order to avoid betrayal of the plot by loyal house servants. In the end, the very "fidelity" that Poyas feared and Bennett praised had led, in the governor's view, to the discovery of the plot.

Bennett claimed that the loyalty of faithful slaves offered the best defense against successful insurrection; such loyalty could hardly prevent invidious plots from being formed, but it ensured their timely betrayal and discovery. Noting that whites owed "the present and all previous discoveries" of insurrection plots to slave informants, Bennett urged that no remedial measures be taken that might "rebuke or destroy by unnecessary rigour" such fidelity between slave and master. Bennett recognized that additional "measures of prevention" must be considered by the legislature, but he urged that body to "attentively guard against" adopting any measures "which may produce excessive coercion." Bennett insisted that "successful rebellion cannot occur" in South Carolina precisely because of the "liberal and enlightened humanity" that guided the treatment of slaves in the state and produced "many attachments that operate as checks on the spirit of insubordination." Still, Bennett admitted that the state must fashion policies to diminish the number of incidents "limited in extent and duration" that would inevitably arise.[14]

Bennett's message proceeded to offer a thorough and thoughtful analysis of the state's existing laws related to the "government" of slaves and free blacks along with his carefully reasoned suggestions for improving these laws. On balance, Bennett's review of South Carolina's informal black code found the existing legislation "intelligent," and he recommended minor tweaking rather than wholesale revision. In several instances, Bennett argued that better enforcement of existing statutes rather than new legislation provided the best protection against future insurrection. In particular, Bennett endorsed existing laws limiting the right of slaves to assemble "beyond a very limited number...without the presence of a white person" and praised restrictions on slaves receiving "instruction beyond what is requisite for their spiritual and eternal welfare." He argued that if such regulations were "rigidly observed" it would become "wholly impossible" for "dangerous combinations," like those believed responsible for the summer conspiracy in Charleston, to form. But Bennett conceded that enforcement of these regulations had been lax, in no small part because "it has been regarded the duty of every individual in society" to enforce the laws. In Bennett's view, matters that were everyone's duty easily became no one's duty.

As a remedy, Bennett made a sweeping and radical proposal of his own. He recommended the creation of a state-staffed enforcement board in every district and parish, vesting primary law enforcement responsibilities in a cadre of "state officers" empowered to "inspect generally" the "conduct and dwellings" of slaves to ensure compliance with the law. The state's laws, Bennett had concluded, needed minimal revision, but the enforcement of those laws needed a radical overhaul. Absent additional evidence, it is difficult to know how seriously Bennett expected either the legislature or public to take his recommendation for a sprawling state constabulary. As a logical means of ensuring enforcement of the provisions of state's ever-evolving black code, the recommendation made perfect sense. The call for a state police force, organized by district, also held promise of accomplishing what Bennett had been unable to do in the Vesey incident: keep law enforcement and the criminal justice process in the hands of state officials rather than local authorities. Yet the creation of a large standing police force, in effect a permanent state-run slave patrol, represented a dramatically expanded presence of state government in South Carolina, a presence expanded at the sacrifice of local control, and an added expense for taxpayers to bear. Moreover, the new state police force, which would regularly patrol the slave quarters and yards in the parishes and districts, would likely intrude on the prerogatives of masters concerning matters of slave management, and hence put the state in a new and expanded role as mediator of master-slave relations. Any one of these considerations—the expansion of state power, the loss of local control, the additional cost to taxpayers, and state interference with masters' governance of slaves—might have violated the state's ideological sensibilities enough to defeat Bennett's plan, but taken together they surely doomed the proposal from its inception.

Yet, as Bennett well knew, any serious effort to prevent whites from teaching slaves to read, for instance, would have required such a police force, and one that operated aggressively. Perhaps Bennett, still stung by what he perceived as the usurpation of state power by local authorities in Charleston, wanted to formally extend state authority and the state's organizational presence into every district in a meaningful and visible way in an effort to stymie aggressive local cabals. At the same time, however, Bennett's proposal alerted white South Carolinians to just how difficult and expensive a meaningful crackdown on slave and free black activities would be. The disruption of common practice and the extension of state power required to enforce draconian new laws would all come at a price for whites, whether in terms of money or convenience. Thus, to an extent, Bennett's proposal for a state slave police appears calculated as much to caution legislators against an overreaction to the Vesey crisis as to actually fashion an enlarged state role in maintaining slave discipline. Whatever Bennett's intentions, legislators from interior districts certainly recognized that enforcing rigid discipline on slaves and free blacks involved the creation of a bigger, more active, more intrusive state government, and they approached such reform proposals warily.[15]

Bennett also claimed that problems with slave discipline often originated on plantations whose absentee owners failed to "employ overseers" and thus deprived their plantations of "the vigilance essential to the preservation of order." As a remedy, Bennett recommended legislation requiring the presence of a white proprietor or overseer on every slaveholding unit regardless of size, and one overseer employed for every fifty slaves on large plantations. Again, Bennett must have known that such a requirement would prove unpopular with and expensive for Lowcountry planters with second homes in Charleston or the mountains, who typically spent at least two seasons of the year away from their plantations, often leaving behind less white supervision than Bennett's proposal required. Again, Bennett's nettlesome remedy had little chance of legislative success, calling as it did for expanded state regulation of plantation life, but it exposed the cost and sacrifice that a genuine effort to make the state safe from insurrection would require. Taken together, these recommendations by Bennett represented less the tighter regulation of slaves than the tighter regulation of masters through an expansion of state power.[16] It seems likely that Bennett's proposals were designed as much to remind legislators of the sacrifices tighter slave control would require and to reveal the shallow and symbolic nature of Hamilton's still-veiled reform proposals.

Following conventional wisdom, Bennett joined the chorus urging the legislature to ban slaves from artisanal or "mechanical" pursuits, pointing out that slave artisans in Charleston enjoyed the "time and means for exciting discontent" while at the same time driving the city's white artisans into poverty or out of the state. Bennett also joined the consensus lamenting the "rapid increase of the free colored population" in Charleston, blaming the increase on the expulsion laws of "states contiguous to us," so he recommended stricter enforcement of existing laws prohibiting the in-migration of free blacks. He also called for the state to expel all free blacks who had arrived as the result of restrictive legislation in other states. Once actions controlling the in-migration of free blacks from out of state had taken hold, Bennett maintained, "little danger may be apprehended" from free blacks who were South Carolina natives or long-term residents.[17]

Predictably, given his simmering feud with the Charleston court, Bennett's most controversial recommendation to the legislature involved his request that lawmakers clarify the powers and responsibilities granted to the Magistrates and Freeholders Courts. "If it is your object...to establish tribunals which shall exercise the power of life and death and the absolute control over an immense and valuable property, unlimited by those rules which ordinarily govern judicial inquiry, unrestrained by any regulations but such as these courts may adopt or reject," Bennett told the legislature, then "an unequivocal and full avowal should distinctly manifest that will." In other words, if the legislature wanted the Magistrates and Freeholders Courts to have unlimited powers and a free hand in investigating and punishing suspected slave insurrections, it should explicitly grant such power. This thinly veiled rebuke of the Charleston court constituted both Bennett's most direct indictment of the court and his parting shot to it.[18]

Bennett concluded his message with a frank and largely unsentimental assessment of slavery. He advanced an aggressive defense of the proposition that slavery in the lower South had evolved into a necessary, and likely perpetual, evil. Given the slaveholding states' vital economic and security interests, decisions about slavery should remain an entirely southern matter. "Slavery abstractly considered," Bennett observed, "will perhaps lead every man to the same conclusion, but the period has long passed by when a corrective may have been applied. The treasures of learning, the gifts of ingenuity, and the stores of experience have been exhausted in the fruitless search for a practicable remedy. The institution is established; the evil is entailed, and we can now do no more than steadily pursue that course indicated by stern necessity." As part of that stern necessity, Bennett urged the state to "frown indignantly on every project of partial and general emancipation as destructive of [slaves'] happiness and subversive of our own." With regard to the slave population, Bennett declared, "we must be true to ourselves and just to them; watch over their welfare with kind solicitude, but tenaciously protect our own." Such a course, Bennett predicted with unjustified confidence, would lead "the world [to] cease to chide us for evils we did not originate and cannot remedy" and encourage "the reflecting and virtuous of every community" to "sympathize with us."[19]

Bennett's message stunned legislators. When the message was read in the house chamber, legislators listened in "profound silence."[20] After its quiet initial reception, the message sparked "much excitement" in the chamber because it was perceived as "touching harshly upon the citizens of Charleston, and especially upon the characters of the gentlemen of the Court."[21] The Charleston *Gazette* claimed that the "language" of the message and the "opposition" it expressed toward the "acts and publications" of the court "gave great offense" not only to members of the court who served in the legislature but also to the "body generally." The house of representatives, which included Hamilton as a member, refused to approve the routine publication of the message because members believed it "reflected unworthily" on the "honourable Court." The message expressed opinions "unsupported by the feelings and opinions of the house." In fact, the house felt that Bennett's message presented a view of the Vesey investigation and trials "not borne out by either the law or the evidence."[22] Taking an unusual step, the legislature ultimately expressed its disapproval by voting, 80–35, to postpone indefinitely action on the governor's controversial message.[23] With this action, the house delivered yet another sharp rebuke to Bennett's conduct. In the arena of public opinion, Bennett lost yet another battle to Hamilton.

ONCE THE LEGISLATURE began business in earnest, Hamilton presented the Charleston agenda to the legislature with his usual aggressiveness. He asked the General Assembly to ban the importation of slaves from other states for sale or hire, to banish all free black males who had entered the state during the past five years, to prevent masters from allowing slaves to hire out on their own time, and to tighten the "regulation and government" of free blacks generally. Though broad in scope, Hamilton's proposals reflected a measure of restraint that he had not demonstrated during his investigation or in his published account of the investigation. Strikingly, Hamilton asked for no legislation hindering the Christian mission to the slaves and no additional legislation limiting slave literacy. Though Hamilton was doubtless influenced by his calculation of what was possible politically, his shift away from the overt criticism of the religious instruction of slaves he had ventured earlier suggests that Furman and the Charleston Bible Society had perhaps made persuasive overtures to Hamilton (as well as Bennett) the previous fall.[24]

The legislature's response to Hamilton's proposals proved decidedly mixed. In fact, Hamilton's proposal to close the internal slave trade caught some observers by surprise, since little if any evidence from the Vesey investigation linked the alleged plot to the internal slave trade. And that decision proved a political miscalculation. On December 9, on the second reading of Hamilton's bill in the house, a test vote on the proposed closing of the interstate slave trade revealed extensive opposition to the measure. The clause setting stiff fines for citizens who imported slaves in violation of the proposed ban failed on a vote of 52–61. The vote revealed sharp sectional divisions on the issue, as parish representatives voted overwhelmingly, 38–4, in favor of the penalties needed to enforce an outright ban on the interstate slave trade, with the Charleston delegation (St. Philip's and St. Michael's parishes) alone providing fifteen votes in favor of the measure and no votes against it. Representatives from the interior districts, where expanding cotton production still generated demand for more slaves, opposed the clause by a margin of 57–14, with delegations from the

Upcountry districts of Edgefield, Laurens, Newberry, Union, Spartanburg, and York voting unanimously against the provision.[25]

The house vote kept South Carolina active in the interstate slave trade and gutted the signature piece of Hamilton's proposed reform agenda. It also signaled trouble for the several other provisions of the bill crafted by the energetic and intriguing Charleston intendant, who immediately regrouped. A motion to reconsider the vote keeping the slave trade open prompted the house, with Hamilton's encouragement, to appoint a special committee to revise the bill and present a new version at a later date. Newberry's John Belton O'Neall, later a distinguished jurist on the state's Court of Appeals, chaired the seven-member committee, which included not only Hamilton but two other members of the Charleston delegation: Lionel H. Kennedy, one of the magistrates who had served on the Vesey court, and Henry Laurens Pinckney, a close political ally of Hamilton. Ironically, even though the house had defeated the proposal to close the interstate slave trade, the special committee included five legislators who had voted in favor of closing the trade and only two representatives who had opposed the ban.[26] Five days later, on December 13, the special committee presented its revised bill to the house. The new version included a provision, supported by Hamilton, that attempted to slow the internal slave trade by requiring any citizen who wanted to import slaves from out of state to first seek permission from the legislature.

But Hamilton's second angle of attack on the domestic slave trade, the idea of prior legislative approval of slave imports, fared no better than his first. The house voted 67–52 to strike the legislative permission requirement from the bill. Once again, the house vote fell largely along sectional lines. Lowcountry parish representatives opposed striking the requirement by a margin of 35–11, while the interior districts favored removing the restriction on the internal slave trade from the bill, 56–17. When considered in tandem with the December 9 vote to keep slave trade open, the deep sectional divisions appeared in stark form. Forty-six inland representatives voted to keep the interstate slave trade open in both instances, providing over two-thirds of the votes needed to defeat both efforts to close the trade. At the same time, thirty-three parish delegates voted to either end or severely restrict the Palmetto State's involvement in the interstate slave trade on both occasions, supplying the core legislative support for closing the internal slave trade.[27] The Vesey scare may have made white security the paramount concern in the Lowcountry, but Upcountry legislators, representing an area still deepening its involvement in the cotton economy, were hardly ready to sacrifice the opportunity to purchase slaves from other states to heightened Lowcountry fears of insurrection.

Later the same day, other parts of Hamilton's bill for "better government" of slaves and free blacks also encountered tough legislative sledding. The house soundly defeated Hamilton's proposal to deport all non-native free people of color who had not lived in South Carolina for five years, on a 68–46 vote. Again, the interior districts provided more than 80 percent of the votes against mandatory deportation. Conversely, parish representatives supported the idea of banishing recently arrived free blacks from the state by a better than three-to-one margin. The house also defeated Hamilton's effort to impose a prohibitive tax of $50 per year on every non-native free person of color who had not lived in the state more than five years, although this measure failed by a very narrow margin, 56–54. While the proposal to heavily tax all free blacks garnered a modicum of additional support from the interior, it nevertheless failed because of overwhelming opposition from the inland cotton districts. Representatives from interior districts opposed the clause 17–49, while parish members approved of it, 37–7. The Upcountry districts of Chester, Edgefield, Lancaster, Laurens, Pendleton, Spartanburg, and York all voted unanimously against the exorbitant head tax, and representatives from above the fall line opposed the measure 7–36. Thus, when the house adjourned for the day on December 13, Hamilton's proposals lay in momentary disarray, defeated by strong opposition from representatives of interior districts, and especially by an Upcountry consensus against such sweeping changes in the state's informal black code.[28]

But when the house resumed business the next morning, the indefatigable Hamilton had regrouped yet again. Dropping his efforts to ban the interstate slave trade, Hamilton substituted a plan to regulate the internal trade by imposing a tax on all slave imports, and the house accepted the shift to taxation without a recorded vote. Additionally, Hamilton narrowed his plan to force free black newcomers out of the state through heavy taxation to include only free black males between the ages of fifteen and fifty rather than all free blacks. Free black males in that age cohort posed the greatest risk of rebellion, Lowcountry supporters of the tax argued, yet they also seemed most able to afford the tax if they owned property and possessed special labor skills. The more narrowly targeted tax on free black male newcomers of prime working age passed the house with comparative ease, 74–38, as the parishes approved the clause 42–5, while inland districts split nearly evenly, 32–33, on the question.[29]

Still, when the watered-down version of Hamilton's original bill came before the house for a final reading on December 17, its fate remained uncertain. Representatives from the interior districts generally persisted in their firm opposition to taxing the interstate slave trade and remained lukewarm about a tougher policy toward free blacks. On a vote of 64–51, however, the bill to tax slave imports, limit the autonomy of slave artisans, tax free black men who had recently arrived in the state, and tighten regulation of free blacks passed the house. A shift of a mere seven votes would have defeated the bill, however, and pronounced sectional patterns of voting remained evident. Hamilton succeeded admirably in whipping Lowcountry members into line. Parish representatives voted almost unanimously, 41–1, in favor of the bill, providing just under two-thirds of the votes needed for passage. Legislators from interior districts still opposed the final bill by a margin of slightly more than two to one, voting 23–50 against passage. Core opposition persisted in the Upcountry districts of Chester, Edgefield, Fairfield, Lancaster, Laurens, Spartanburg, Union, and York, whose delegations voted solidly against the bill. Since interior members had split pretty evenly on the question of taxing free black male newcomers of working (and rebelling) age, the spirited inland opposition clearly arose primarily from dislike of the tax on imported slaves.[30]

After its third reading, the house-approved bill went to the senate. In the state senate, even the watered-down compromise bill approved by the house encountered serious opposition. By December 20, the senate, long a bastion of Upcountry opposition to any interference with the interstate slave trade, rejected the idea of taxing all slaves imported for sale or hire on a voice vote and quickly changed the title of the bill to emphasize its newly narrowed focus on the regulation of free blacks and slaves. On December 21, the senate approved the truncated bill; the house agreed to the senate version, omitting any tax on the slave trade, and the measure became law without any additional restrictions on the interstate slave trade.[31] In the end, overwhelming opposition from an Upcountry decidedly less worried about the Vesey scare than the Lowcountry defeated Hamilton's effort to ban the importation of slaves into South Carolina. Upcountry numbers thus achieved what the social standing and reasoned arguments of Governor Bennett and Associate Justice William Johnson could not: they stopped Hamilton from getting his way.

Despite its reluctance to interfere with the interstate slave trade, and its internal division over how to best regulate the state's free black population, the 1822 South Carolina legislature nevertheless passed sweeping new laws governing slaves and free blacks in South Carolina. Yet even in the aftermath of the worst insurrection scare in the state's history, the South Carolina legislature showed a measure of restraint in its action regarding slaves. In the face of Hamilton's political savvy and influence, strong opposition from inland legislators defeated proposals to either ban the interstate slave trade or impose a tax on it. The 1822 legislature did approve strict legislation banning the traditional practice of allowing slaves to hire out on their own time, but from the moment of its passage the law was enforced only sporadically, and most slave artisans resumed business as usual in 1823. The legislature also proved willing to continue its recent pattern of passing increasingly restrictive legislation concerning free blacks. It levied a prohibitive tax of $50 per year on all free black males of prime working age who had arrived during the preceding five years, approved a statute preventing free blacks from reentering the state if they left, and, in an action with significant long-term consequences, decreed that by June 1, 1823, all free blacks must have procured white guardians or face expulsion from the state.

Still more dramatically, the legislature enacted what became known as the Negro Seaman's Act, which allowed local authorities to imprison free black sailors or ship employees arriving in South Carolina ports until their ships were ready to depart. The provocative Seaman's Act, which had passed with little discussion, soon ignited international controversy and drew South Carolina into an early and prolonged confrontation with the federal government.[32] On balance, the legislative session produced a vigorous but, with the exception of the Seaman's Act, restrained response, certainly one less sweeping and draconian than the Hamilton-led Charleston delegation sought to the insurrection scare of the previous summer.

By the standard of James Hamilton's success in other Vesey-related matters, his performance in pushing the Charleston delegation's agenda through the legislature was plagued by political miscalculations. In seeking to ban or limit the importation of slaves into South Carolina in 1822, Hamilton overreached. His decision to use a ban on the importation of slaves as a political hobby in the fall of 1822 remains puzzling. To be sure, the idea of prohibiting or significantly restricting the importation of slaves from other states had long been popular throughout much of the Lowcountry. Limiting slave imports not only slowed the blackening of the already heavily black Lowcountry but also protected the value of the region's extensive investment in slave property. Serving such a localized self-interest enhanced Hamilton's standing with his Lowcountry base, but, as votes in the 1822 legislature revealed, it did little to win him the support of interior politicians. Moreover, given the "evidence" developed by his own investigation and the testimony taken by the Vesey court, as well as the general thrust of public commentary during the fall of 1822, Hamilton lacked any new or fresh basis for touting an end to slave importation. Little of the evidence uncovered by the city's investigation suggested that slaves recently imported from other states played any significant role in the alleged plot. Indeed, none of the so-called ringleaders or key witnesses were identified as slaves recently arrived via the domestic trade. Moreover, in the commentary afterward, ending the trade was mentioned less frequently than limiting the religious instruction given to slaves and prohibiting the teaching of slaves to read.

Tellingly, Hamilton failed to include either of these last two measures in his fall legislative agenda, even though he had identified them as major problems in his own public report on the insurrection. Perhaps by joining Hamilton and the Vesey court in portraying the independent black church as a breeding ground for the plot, the formidable Charleston clergy had succeeded in persuading Hamilton to limit the scope of his crusade against the religious instruction of slaves to the closing and destruction of Charleston's once active AME church (what was called the "African church"), cleverly defended the mainstream churches' mission to the slaves, and deflected restrictive measures aimed at limiting efforts to teach slaves to read. In doing so, the Lowcountry clergy tacitly accepted stricter regulation of slaves and free blacks as long as those regulations did not undermine the ideology of paternalism, which the clergy now defended with full voice.[33]

Apart from his miscalculation on the question of the interstate slave trade, however, Hamilton proved a master of this emerging politics of slavery during the Vesey scare. Hamilton, and other Lowcountry politicians who shared his views, used public reaction to the Vesey scare to push preexisting and partially related political agendas. In this sense, Hamilton and his allies practiced an early but already sophisticated version of the politics of slavery.[34] One clique, faction, or party would accuse the other of being somehow "soft" in its defense of slavery. The alleged softness could fall into many different categories: reluctance to respond to slave unrest with sufficient force and vigilance, unwillingness to defend slavery aggressively enough against outside criticism, insufficient vigor in pushing for a better fugitive slave law, or timidity in defending the "rights of slaveholders" in national councils. In a very real sense, the immediate post-Vesey political debate in the Lowcountry had as much to do with posturing on the politics of slavery as with any serious effort to identify the causes of the Vesey unrest and use this understanding to find ways to prevent future rebellion. Political posturing masqueraded as insurrection analysis.

On the whole, South Carolina authorities responded to the Vesey incident in rather confused and contradictory fashion. Charleston's white investigators, public officials, and other observers identified the whole range of customary villains (free blacks, slave artisans, tavern keepers, black religious leaders, members of the African church, sailors, etc.) as possible instigators of the revolt. These white guardians of public safety then accused all these "usual suspects" with either creating the atmosphere in which an insurrection could occur or taking leadership positions in the plot itself. As critics such as Thomas Bennett and William Johnson noted at the time, Charleston authorities punished with unprecedented severity and speed blacks convicted of being part of the alleged conspiracy. The number of executions and deportations carried out in response to a revolt that never occurred and never spilled a single drop of white blood spoke volumes about the level of white panic in Charleston during the summer of 1822. It also said much about local white determination to deter future plots and, perhaps even more significant, about the need of white political leaders to respond with ferocity and dispatch to insurrection scares in order to retain public confidence.

Yet, largely as a result of Upcountry reluctance to embrace excessively punitive measures, post-Vesey state legislation tacked along a generally moderate rather than radical course. It targeted those blacks who enjoyed some freedom of movement: all free blacks (who were required to enlist white guardians) and especially recently arrived free black males (who were also taxed heavily), as well as slave artisans (who were forbidden to hire out their own time). This round of restrictive legislation certainly tightened, on paper, regulation of free blacks and slave artisans, but the strictness or laxity of enforcement of these statutory provisions depended largely on the discretion of local sheriffs and the wishes of the local population. Laws on the books empowered whites to clamp down on free blacks and slaves artisans with full legal authority, but these same laws did not change longstanding attitudes of accommodation. The peculiar agony of free blacks and slave artisans in post-Vesey South Carolina lay not so much in the yoke of increased regulation and diminished autonomy as in the uncertainty over what white authorities might do and when they might do it. Beyond Charleston and its hinterland, popular indifference often made enforcement of draconian slave regulations difficult if not impossible.

Yet a critical portion of the South Carolina Lowcountry's political leadership still chafed at the interior's moderation, at Bennett's nonconformist stand, and at the clergy's insistence on the continued application of paternalism to the "problems" of slavery. The leadership insisted on dramatic action designed as much to demonstrate their bold stand for white security as to effectively enhance the physical security of Charleston and its hinterland. Thus, while much of South Carolina's post-Vesey legislation seeking tighter state control over the activity of slave artisans and free blacks produced only relatively minor changes in the day-to-day lives of the state's black majority, the state's decision to pass and enforce the Negro Seaman's Act produced at least two years of dramatic controversy between South Carolina and federal authorities. In these controversies, the Hamilton faction remained aggressive in its assertion that state and local authorities retained the power to make all essential decisions regarding slavery and white security, and its leaders remained dismissive of those who did not share their zeal for provincial autonomy. In these confrontations over the enforcement of the Seaman's Act, if not in remedial post-Vesey legislation, the emerging radicalism of the Lowcountry's politics of slavery revealed itself—and with substantial flair.

Beginning in January 1823, the Charleston sheriff initiated enforcement of the Seaman's Act, seizing free black sailors from ships docked in Charleston harbor and holding them in custody until the ships were ready to leave port. American ship captains took the matter to state courts, but first a local trial court and later the South Carolina Court of Appeals upheld the Seaman's Act and offered neither captains nor their sailors any relief.[35] But when free blacks from British ships were detained, Stratford Channing, the British consul in Washington, took a written complaint, dated February 15, to Secretary of State John Quincy Adams. Before replying, Adams consulted with the South Carolina Lowcountry's delegation to the United States House of Representatives, seeking their assistance in finding a mutually acceptable solution to the problem. Adams first discussed the issue with the voluble first-term congressman Hamilton, who read the British minister's letter and immediately labeled it "objectionable." Hamilton told Adams that the language of the British letter failed to respect South Carolina's position as an "Independent State." But Joel Poinsett, the congressman who represented Charleston and maintained close ties to the Monroe administration, assured Adams that he would work quietly to remedy the problem. Accepting Poinsett's assurance, Adams delayed for four months and then informed the British that future difficulties of this kind could be avoided.[36] Precisely how Poinsett intended to fulfill his promise to Adams remains unclear, but during the late spring and early summer, Charleston authorities allowed enforcement of the Negro Seaman's Act to lapse. For a number of weeks, free black seamen from the West Indies and elsewhere again walked the streets of Charleston.[37]

But a large cohort of Lowcountry slaveholders reacted to the relaxed enforcement of the Seaman's Act with a determination to restore vigilance. In late July 1823, prominent Charleston area planters, lawyers, merchants, and political leaders met in the city to form the South Carolina Association, a citizen's organization devoted to ensuring aggressive enforcement of the laws for the "better government" of slaves and free blacks passed by the legislature in 1822.[38] The association's membership list crossed factional and occupational lines but included a disproportionate number of James Hamilton's allies and others who had played an active role in either foiling the Vesey insurrection and punishing its alleged conspirators or securing reform legislation from a divided legislature. The association's leadership featured Henry Laurens Pinckney, a state legislator and future congressman who had consistently supported Hamilton's legislative agenda in 1822; Robert J. Turnbull, a member of the Vesey court and a sharp critic of federal power; Henry Deas, a Charleston lawyer and planter who served on the first Vesey court; Keating Simons, a longtime opponent of South Carolina's participation in both the African and interstate slave trade; aging Revolutionary veteran and post-Vesey pamphleteer Thomas Pinckney; Isaac Holmes, a rising eminence in the Charleston bar and a future congressman; Nathaniel Heyward, Hamilton's brother-in-law and a wealthy rice planter who owned more than a thousand slaves in South Carolina; Joseph Manigault, a wealthy rice planter; Stephen Elliott, president of the Bank of the State of South Carolina; and many of Charleston's other prominent and influential citizens.[39] In the Charleston of 1823, an association that included not one Pinckney but two, the patriarch of the Heyward rice planting empire, and at least two members of the respected Vesey court, and which enjoyed the support of the popular Hamilton, constituted a formidable presence in the city. Once formed, the South Carolina Association served both as "an eternal watchdog over the slaves and as a fertile source of southern radicalism."[40]

While a few citizens questioned the potential for abuse of power by such an extralegal association, the body quickly became quite popular in Charleston.[41] The press generally praised the association for helping law enforcement "in carrying into effect, the many wholesome statutes in force relative to our coloured population," and the organization sought to become "the repository of all information" regarding possible infractions against the prevailing laws regulating slaves and free blacks.[42] One member of the new organization, clearly not worried about overstatement, called the association "perhaps the most important association that ever has been, or ever can be formed, in the Southern States." Complaining of the "daily violation or evasion of the laws, made to regulate the conduct of our colored population," this founding member of the association blamed the Vesey conspiracy on the "laxity in the whole of our system" and feared that such indifference would lead to the state's "ruin." Formed to "uphold at every hazard, the policy upon which is built our security," the association was composed of "well-informed citizens" who were combining not for "party purposes or political influence" but who stood "ready to bow with reverence to the supremacy of the laws." Toward the latter end, the association intended to use its "ample means" to "aid the execution of the laws founded on the local and peculiar policy of South Carolina" by providing the "earliest possible information" of possible violations of existing laws to civil authorities.[43]

This public explanation of the association's purpose attempted to allay scattered public fears that the voluntary association intended to mete out extralegal justice, as mobs and cabals had been known to do on occasion in South Carolina. Instead, the association would be the eyes, ears, and perhaps feet of civil authorities in the Charleston area, alerting the proper authorities to violations of various portions of the state's newly revised black codes. In practice, the association pressured authorities into acting promptly on matters that otherwise they might have moved against slowly or ignored altogether.

The formation of an auxiliary of the South Carolina Association on nearby Edisto Island produced less reassuring rhetoric from its founding members. With radical Whitemarsh Seabrook as one of its organizers, the auxiliary lamented that "the period is rapidly approaching when the sober dictates of reason on the subject of slavery" appeared destined to "yield to the hypocritical feeling of a misguided Philanthropy." Thus the Edisto Island organizers felt it necessary to "crush the spirit of insubordination and revolt" through the "zealous" commitment of private citizens. The Vesey plot, Edisto Island whites argued, revealed that the "mid-night incendiary has escaped with impugnity" and "the assassin perfected his schemes of horror." Independent of all other considerations, the auxiliary's organizers argued that the simple fact that roughly three thousand slaves and only two hundred whites resided on Edisto Island demanded special organization on the part of the island's whites. This demographic "fact speaks volumes," auxiliary leaders insisted, and demanded the "urgent necessity of extreme circumspection" to prevent "demagogues from infusing into the bosoms of our credulous and superstitious coloured population the most dangerous and revolting doctrines." The Edisto Island auxiliary spoke the hyperbolic language of the emerging anti-antislavery radicalism as well as the language of the anxiety felt by whites who lived in areas with black supermajorities. It was not the language of "reverence to the supremacy of the laws."[44]

Predictably, the recently neglected enforcement of the Seaman's Act became the immediate focus of the South Carolina Association's attention. Free blacks employed on commercial vessels visiting Charleston had ample opportunity "for introducing among our slaves" the "moral contagion" of "free principles." Such communication, the association warned, threatened to "invite new attempts at insurrection." By late July, the association had created a standing committee that assisted local authorities in enforcing the Seaman's Act through "incessant information and prosecutions."[45] In August 1823, the Charleston sheriff, pressured by the association, boarded the British vessel *Homer* in Charleston harbor. Once on board, he seized and detained a free black Jamaican, Henry Elkison, who was also a British subject. Presenting written evidence of Secretary of State Adams' assurance that the Seaman's Act would not be enforced, the British consul in Charleston sought relief from the federal court in the city, where, following the custom of the day, Supreme Court Justice William Johnson, the bitter critic of city actions during the Vesey scare, presided on the federal bench in his home circuit.[46]

In arguments before the justice, Elkison's lawyer argued that the Seaman's Act violated a commercial treaty of 1815 between Great Britain and the United States, and that the federal government's treaty-making power stood paramount to any state laws. The South Carolina Association, rather than the state, supplied attorneys to defend the Seaman's Act. The association's solicitor, Isaac Holmes, joined Benjamin F. Hunt, a prominent member of the Charleston bar, in defending the act. Hunt advanced the argument that the federal courts lacked jurisdiction to provide relief from a state law, but he also argued that South Carolina was a sovereign state with full power to "prohibit the entry of foreigners" and to "set the terms on which they might remain." Hunt characterized the Seaman's Act as a "mere police regulation" amounting to little more than a quarantine against disease. The association-provided co-counsels argued that such laws were "founded upon the right of self-preservation, and it is quite immaterial whether destruction is threatened by disease or bloodshed." Going beyond Hunt's careful arguments about jurisdiction, association attorney Isaac Holmes argued that rather than see the state surrender its power of self-preservation to federal treaty-making authority or the supremacy of the Constitution's commerce clause, he would prefer a dissolution of the Union.[47] As Justice Johnson later recalled the moment when he heard Holmes' suggestion of disunion voiced in open court before the hundreds of witnesses assembled to see the high-profile case argued, he had to "lay down my pen, raise my eyes from my notes, and fix them on the speaker's face." But Holmes proceeded, Johnson recalled, "in a style which bore evidence of preparation and study."[48]

After hearing arguments, Justice Johnson denied Elkison's request for release, reluctantly agreeing with Hunt's argument that a federal court had no power to grant a writ of habeas corpus to free a state prisoner. Johnson concluded that he did have the power to issue a civil writ requiring the release of Elkison, but he noted that such a writ would not be enforceable against the sheriff, who, as an agent of the state, was protected from such action by the Eleventh Amendment. But before acknowledging that he had no ready remedy to offer the plaintiff, Johnson issued a powerful obiter dictum. In this section of his decision, he boldly refuted the association's arguments on the constitutional points in question. Johnson found that United States Constitution rendered "the right of the general government to regulate commerce with the sister states and foreign nations" a "paramount and exclusive right." He also found that the Constitution established Congress' treaty-making authority, which, when exercised within its proper limits, created "the supreme law of the land," not to be altered by state legislation. Johnson rejected the association counsel's plea urging the necessity of the Seaman's Act and the right of "the state alone" to judge such necessity. "Is it not asserting the right in each state to throw off the federal constitution at its will and pleasure?" Johnson asked. If so, he concluded, the Union, "like the old confederation... [,] becomes a rope of sand."[49]

The state sovereignty arguments advanced by Holmes and Hunt troubled Johnson so much that immediately after the release of his decision, the justice wrote former president Jefferson to alert his longtime patron to the radicalism of the South Carolina Association. "That greatest of Evils, Disunion, appears to be losing its Terrors," Johnson told Jefferson. "My Ears are shocked at Times by Expressions that I hear on this subject." Johnson retained hope that "there may be temperate men enough" among the radicals "to control them and the furious Passions and false Policy which govern most of them."[50] Defenders of the association were equally troubled by Johnson's assertion of federal primacy in the matter. In Washington, Secretary of State John Quincy Adams observed that South Carolina senator Robert Y. Hayne, a close friend of Hamilton, reacted with "so much excitement and temper" when Johnson's decision was mentioned that his dinner companions found it "painful" and "necessary to change the subject."[51]

In Charleston, Johnson's ruling created an uproar, and his numerous critics in the city showed no interest in changing the subject. The leading papers refused to print Johnson's decision, so the justice quickly published it in the form of a pamphlet, which ignited a war of newspaper columns pitting leading members of the South Carolina Association against Johnson in a battle of pseudonymous essays that filled the Charleston papers from August to October 1823.[52] Critics of Johnson's opinion defended the right of an individual state to protect itself against internal and external threats. Johnson's replies appealed to the spirit of Union, loyalty to the Constitution, and the federal government's clear right to regulate commerce as bedrock values in the American experiment in republicanism. Perhaps the most biting attack on Johnson and his decision came from a series of essays written under the pseudonym Caroliniensis by Robert Turnbull and Isaac Holmes, both leading members of the South Carolina Association. In broad terms, the Caroliniensis essays emphasized state sovereignty and attacked Johnson's denial of the right of an individual state to void federal laws and treaties.[53] The association-inspired criticism of Johnson revealed the city's preoccupation with home rule, or local sovereignty, as the key to sealing off slaveholding society from outside threats. The greatest danger South Carolina faced, Caroliniensis insisted, came from "the free and uninterrupted ingress of a colored population into the State, from the North and elsewhere, with their known habits, feelings and principles, animated and emboldened as they are, by the philanthropy of the day, and by the events, which Europe in its throes and convulsions casts upon mankind." Thus Justice Johnson's denial of the right of self-preservation to South Carolina stripped the state of "that first undeniable attribute which is the foundation of sovereignty."[54]

Johnson replied to these and other attacks under the pseudonym Philonimus, countering that the states "are unknown to foreign nations, and their sovereignty exists only with relation to each other and the general government."[55] Concerning internal security issues, Johnson felt that the Madisonian notion of divided sovereignty left the states plenty of power to protect themselves. He saw arguments in favor of undiminished state sovereignty as little more than veiled threats of disunion. The doctrine of undivided state sovereignty, Johnson warned, reduced "our noble Constitution, the delight of our eyes, the ark of our salvation, the admiration of nations," to "a mere letter of attorney" similar to those sold for a penny "at any printer's counter."[56]

In the end, neither Johnson's constitutional arguments nor his appeals to the love of Union shifted public opinion in Charleston. Throughout the final five months of 1823, the enforcement of the Seaman's Act proceeded unabated in Charleston in open defiance of the opinion offered by a United States Supreme Court justice. Under intensified pressure from the South Carolina Association, Charleston authorities resumed the practice of confining free black sailors who came into the local port. By October 1823, the association claimed that it had caused action against 154 individuals under the terms of the Seaman's Act. In November 1823, the association enjoyed enough public popularity to secure more than three hundred signatures in support of a legislative petition seeking state recognition of the association as a legal corporation.[57] As detention of black sailors continued despite his ruling, Justice Johnson conceded that he lacked any means of enforcing his decision. "I would have nobody to call upon," Johnson complained, "since the District Attorney is himself a member of the Association." The association "trampled on" the Constitution, Johnson believed, "as much influenced by the Pleasure of bringing its Functionaries into contempt by exposing their impotence as by any other consideration whatever."[58] Johnson might have expected his chief justice, the nationalist John Marshall, to appreciate his decision to stand boldly on qualified national ground in the face of withering states' rights sentiment, but Marshall thought the Republican Johnson should have refused to hear the case on jurisdictional grounds to avoid "butting against a wall in sport."[59]

Toward the end of 1823, the British again appealed their cause to Secretary of State Adams, urging him to take "immediate measures" to protect British seamen from confinement at the hands of South Carolina authorities. Adams asked the British to wait to see if the South Carolina legislature might provide relief through modification or even outright repeal of the Seaman's Act at its December session.[60] At that session, South Carolina lawmakers took only modestly conciliatory action, repealing the provision of the 1822 law that called for the enslavement of any free black sailors who did not leave port with their ships. Additionally, free people of color serving on foreign warships (but not commercial vessels) were exempted from confinement as long as they declined shore leave and remained on board ship. But a recalcitrant legislature would go no further, leaving the rest of the law, including its provision for temporary detainment of black sailors, intact.[61]

Exasperated British diplomats continued their protests, demanding not only repeal of the "obnoxious law" but also "redress and reparation." Secretary of State Adams conferred with President Monroe, and Monroe then asked United States Attorney General William Wirt for a formal opinion.[62] On May 8, 1824, Wirt released an opinion holding that the United States Constitution conferred on Congress the exclusive power to regulate commerce and gave the national government final treaty-making authority, and that those powers had not prohibited the use of free colored seamen; thus any South Carolina laws interfering with these free colored seamen violated federal law. Wirt concluded that the Negro Seaman's Act was void because it violated the Constitution, international treaties, and statutes of the United States.[63]

Word of Wirt's forceful opinion reached South Carolina governor John L. Wilson in July 1824. Wilson informed the legislature when it met in November, writing a lengthy letter to the state senate elaborating his own view that South Carolina had the right to control entrance and exit from her ports in order to safeguard the "peace and tranquility" of the state, just as it had the right to quarantine people with infectious disease in the interest of public health.[64] In a second message on the subject, Wilson urged the legislature to show a "firm determination" to protect the state's "sovereignty and independence." The governor claimed that there was "more glory in forming a rampart with our bodies on the confines of our territory, than to be the victims of a successful rebellion, or the slaves of a consolidated government."[65] Echoing Wilson, Sea Island cotton planter Whitemarsh Seabrook decried the positions of Monroe and Wirt for upholding the "alarming doctrine" that "South Carolina possesses no right to enact laws guarding against the corruption and consequent insubordination of her slaves."[66]

Both houses of the South Carolina legislature quickly moved the issue to the top of their agenda. Each chamber drafted separate resolutions defending the Seaman's Act as modified in 1823. The senate voted 36–6 to denounce the federal government's "unconstitutional interference" with state sovereignty and to declare that a state's right to defend against insurrection was "paramount to all laws, all treaties, all constitutions."[67] The senate resolution bristled with such defiant language that even United States Senator Robert Y. Hayne, a staunch defender of the Seaman's Act and no stranger to political confrontation, worried that the body had adopted an excessively hostile tone.[68] The house approved a resolution similar in substance but decidedly less confrontational in tone. The two chambers were unable to reconcile their competing resolutions on the issue, so the 1824 General Assembly never formally approved a resolution.[69] Nevertheless, since no local or state court would rule against the state, South Carolina continued to enforce the Seaman's Act for decades, much to the consternation of the national government and foreign powers, who continued to protest intermittently, albeit to little avail. The apparent inability of the federal government to enforce its laws in South Carolina, despite federal court decisions and the attorney general's opinions upholding the constitutionality of federal laws and treaties and declaring the Seaman's Act void, annoyed the British and other foreign nations but emboldened South Carolinians eager to use states' rights as a mechanism to defend slavery.[70]

Thus, in one of the state's first contests with the federal government over issues related to slavery, the South Carolina Association had demonstrated that a vigorous defense of state authority proved an effective shield against federal intervention, at least as long as federal authorities remained unwilling to escalate the confrontation.[71] Ardent states' rights advocate Whitemarsh Seabrook defended South Carolina's resistance as "an act of necessity, grounded in the immutable principles of self-preservation." Without the Seaman's Act, Seabrook argued, South Carolina would be asked to "put to hazard our dearest privileges, rather than impair the self-styled liberties of a Hindoo, or a Malay." South Carolina's "determined opposition," Seabrook insisted, had induced the "constituted authorities" of the nation to "pause and reflect."[72]

But as the grip of fear associated with the Vesey scare weakened, not every major interest in the Lowcountry agreed with Seabrook's radical interpretation. In particular, potent Charleston commercial interests grew disillusioned with the Seaman's Act, if not with the activities of the South Carolina Association. As early as 1826 (and again in 1830), the Charleston Chamber of Commerce petitioned the legislature for either a repeal of the 1823 Seaman's Act or a lessening of the punishments associated with its violation.[73] The laws constituting the Seaman's Act, the chamber's memorial asserted, "proved extremely detrimental to the commerce of Charleston and of the state at large." The restrictions on the use of black seaman, especially as cooks and stewards, positions in which blacks predominated in the Atlantic maritime industry of the era, drove "vessels from our ports" and imposed the "very heavy expense" of "employing white cooks and stewards in the place of blacks" on South Carolina–owned merchant marine vessels. The cumulative impact of these restrictions, the chamber claimed, was that "numerous vessels which would have otherwise come to Charleston...have, rather than submit to our laws, gone on to the port of Savannah or to some other port in which no such interdictions are enforced." The Charleston Chamber of Commerce conceded that if a uniform system of restrictions existed throughout all Southern states, the restrictive legislation would not be an impediment to the state's commerce, but no such uniform system existed. Instead, under the existing mix of state laws, shippers found "strong inducements" to give "preference to other Southern States over Charleston." Thus, in the chamber's view, the Seaman's Act had done little but "depress the commerce of South Carolina and to establish on its ruins the trade and prosperity of a rival port."[74]

The chamber's memorial also argued that the Seaman's Act weakened the state's influence on national policy, not because of its states' rights character, but because South Carolina's "relative rank and importance" on the "scale of the Union" depended on the health of its commerce. Moreover, the severity of the punishments prescribed by the Seaman's Act inevitably led to evasion of the law. The "humanity of our Juries," the Charleston chamber claimed, "revolted" against the severe penalties attached to the laws, explaining that a local grand jury had refused to indict accused violators in every case brought by local prosecutors except one, and in that case, the court directed the petit jury to acquit the accused.[75] Thus, in the chamber's view, the draconian laws on the books dissuaded commercial vessels from using the port of Charleston, and yet the harsh penalties rendered the laws impossible to enforce, depriving the city of the security benefits the laws promised.

But if the Charleston Chamber of Commerce saw the Seaman's Act as a major drag on commerce and urged its repeal, it nevertheless praised the South Carolina Association for its vigilance and organization. The chamber argued that "the unfortunate occurrence" that had given rise to the Seaman's Act had also spawned a "highly respectable and very numerous association" that had assumed "the sole and exclusive purpose of detecting attempts at disturbance" and "preserving order and good government among our slaves." The association's vigilance, the chamber argued, had rendered it "impossible for a seditious movement to remain a moment undiscovered" and had superseded the "necessity of the laws in question." The chamber's position was at first glance a curious one, appearing to argue that formal laws against black seamen were damaging to the port's economy but endorsing extralegal action against black seamen. In fact, the chamber's argument suggested that generic laws against black seamen, which were expensive for shipping interests and difficult to enforce on a consistent basis, were a drag on Charleston's commerce, but the presence of the association, which had the ability (arguably extralegal) to quarantine blacks identified as incendiary on a selective basis preserved public safety at minimum expense to local taxpayers and the port's commerce. Following an increasingly common Lowcountry bent, the Charleston Chamber deemed laws blunt and cumbersome but found selective extralegal activities an appropriate sword of justice in a slaveholding society.[76]

But as it applauded the effectiveness of the association, the Charleston Chamber of Commerce lamented that the Seaman's Act remained a source of "great division of sentiment" in Charleston. The community was badly divided over both the "constitutionality" and the "expedience" of the act. The chamber demurred on the constitutionality question, though it pointed out that "many of our best and most enlightened men" considered the law a direct violation of the provision giving Congress the exclusive power to regulate commerce. But the chamber emphatically found the Seaman's Act inexpedient and a hindrance to Lowcountry prosperity. Other questions aside, the chamber concluded that the laws tended to "drive away commerce and impoverish our City."[77]

Despite such bitter protest from the Charleston commercial community, the Negro Seaman's Act, as modified in 1823, remained on the books and at least nominally in force until 1835, when the South Carolina legislature toughened the law still further in response to intensified abolitionist activity. The South Carolina Association remained periodically active over the years, energizing itself when it thought lax enforcement of the black codes or a related political issue threatened the state's ability to manage its slave majority. In 1828, the association sought a formal corporate charter from the legislature, boasting that it had "in a great measure restrained the coloured population of other states from mingling with and contaminating our own slaves." It even claimed that it had "discovered the first openings of insurrectionary schemes, and without creating any alarm among the citizens, have been enabled to crush those schemes before they had fully developed themselves and poured out all their horrors over an unsuspecting community." An appreciative legislature apparently agreed, incorporating the South Carolina Association "for the purpose of aiding in the execution of the laws in relation to Negroes and other persons of color, and taking all lawful means for the prevention of disturbance or insurrection among them."[78] The extralegal association had been granted corporate standing and legislative approval. In post-Vesey South Carolina, vigilante activity could sometimes gain official as well as popular sanction.

JUSTICE WILLIAM JOHNSON, arguably the leading critic of the state's defiant stance on the Seaman's Act, saw the Lowcountry's radicalism as arising more from preexisting political jealousies than from an emerging strain of radicalism designed to defend slavery against coming assaults. The combative judge understood the politics of the Vesey scare and the controversy over the Seaman's Act through the fading partisan dynamics of the defunct First Party System. These partisan dynamics had propelled him into prominence as a Jeffersonian Republican and ultimately facilitated his nomination to the Supreme Court by Jefferson. They led Johnson to interpret the Vesey scare and its aftermath in terms of residual partisanship left over from the tough battles between once-dominant Federalists and insurgent Republicans in the port city. Johnson was not alone in seeing the politics of the early 1820s through eyes wary of lingering Federalist conspiracies. Jefferson interpreted the Missouri crisis almost entirely as a Federalist gambit to regain political relevance, and Johnson's view of Charleston politics in the Vesey era mirrored Jefferson's assumptions about the Missouri controversy. Johnson's reasoning was undoubtedly shaped by lingering tensions between the judge and the city's elite, which had at one time been heavily Federalist, and from the judge's sense that the old elite struggled to retain effective control over the city rather than yield to leaders of less distinguished lineage. When Johnson viewed the leadership of the Vesey court and the South Carolina Association, he saw Pinckneys of Federalist party fame. When he saw James Hamilton in action, he thought not so much of the nationalist Republican the young intendant professed to be as of the wealthy family of Federalist background, and Hamilton's connections to the Lynchs, Heywards, and Pinckneys. Johnson revealed his perspective clearly when he complained to Jefferson in August 1823 that the very Federalists who had "made such an Outcry against self-created societies" when Democratic-Republican clubs were gaining influence in Charleston during the 1790s "are now Heading a most formidable one in this Place."[79] To be sure, it took a significant degree of political presbyopia to see the South Carolina Association as a Federalist plot, but that was how Johnson saw it, and he reasoned and reacted accordingly.

Mindful of the Hartford Convention, Johnson had come to associate disunion sentiment with disgruntled Federalists scheming for partisan revival. In turn, he identified Republicans with the protection of the Union, that cherished ark of republican liberty. Well before the Elkison case came to his courtroom, Johnson had outlined his position to a skeptical Jefferson. Johnson claimed that the acquisition of Louisiana had defeated Federalist designs for both monarchy and consolidation. The "extent of our territory and the scope given to...that class of men who never can be yoked to the car of despotism," Johnson maintained, had convinced Federalists that their old pet antirepublican projects were "ludicrous." Believing consolidation vanquished, Johnson saw a new plan, "a plan as pregnant of evil as either of the others—a separation of the states," as the Federalist ploy for regaining power.[80] Jefferson remained unconvinced. He cautioned Johnson pointedly that "there is no danger I apprehend so much as the consolidation of our government by the noiseless, and therefore unalarming, instrumentality of the Supreme Court. This is the form in which federalism now arrays itself."[81] Johnson respected Jefferson's opinion, but he sounded the theme of divided sovereignty when he reminded his friend and patron that "the distinguishing characteristic of the Republican Party was to check the intemperance of both Democrats and Federalists and administer the government agreeably to the true views of the Constitution, equally uninfluenced by the pretensions of the states or the United States."[82]

Johnson viewed the activities of the South Carolina Association and its vigorous assertions of state sovereignty as a new Federalist foray against Republicanism and the Madisonian division of sovereignty on which republican constitutional theory rested. His emotions on the subject ran close to the surface. "I fear nothing so much as the persecuting spirit that is abroad in this place," Johnson told Jefferson. "Should it spread thro the state & produce a systematic policy founded on the ridiculous but prevalent notion that it is a struggle for life or death, there are no excesses we might not look for—whatever their effect upon the Union." Above all, Johnson saw the South Carolina Association's new claims for undivided state sovereignty and their use of disunion as a tool of political argument as any Jeffersonian would have seen a Federalist hobby: as a well-disguised bid for a return to aristocratic rule. Recalling earlier Federalist taunts of Democratic-Republicans Societies as Jacobin clubs, Johnson noted with sarcasm, "They now pronounce the Negroes the real Jacobins of this country, and in doing so shew what they meant when they honored us with the same epithet."[83]

But in his assessment of events in Charleston during the early 1820s, the politically minded Johnson seemed strangely unable to sense the political ground shifting under his feet.[84] He failed to recognize that a new and intensely localist faction was emerging, one led by Hamilton but drawing support from many of the area's leading politicians, who, regardless of their prior stance on the boundaries of states' rights and federal authority, now stood ready to assert state sovereignty, in its most radical forms if necessary. This new radicalism emerged as part of a concerted effort to protect their slaveholding society from both outside interference and internal unrest. This new, decidedly activist states' rights faction hardly embraced limited government in the abstract; they were willing to use the power of government, and particularly state and local government, aggressively in defense of white security and local control over slavery. They saw, or at least claimed to see, the ability to maintain maximum control over their admittedly "peculiar and local" society as a matter of survival.[85] Former Federalists and national Republicans joined longtime states' rights Republicans to forge an assertive new coalition committed to defending the slaveholding society of the Carolina Lowcountry against all threats. This movement, embodied in the South Carolina Association, represented a counterrevolution of sorts, driven by the politics of slavery. In 1823, however, this counterrevolution, though it generated faint echoes of support from black-belt enclaves scattered across the lower South, held sway only in the heavily black South Carolina Lowcountry, a region recently alarmed by an insurrection scare that had been presented to the public as one of previously unimagined proportions.

Johnson believed that grudges held against him for his role in questioning the propriety of the Vesey investigation and trials had as much to do with the association's vigor in enforcing and defending the Negro Seaman's Act as did concern that West Indian sailors might encourage slave unrest. While Johnson was undoubtedly right to see a connection between his criticism of official Charleston's swift and severe response to reports of a slave insurrection plot and South Carolina's defiant defense of the Negro Seaman's Act, he failed to fully grasp that Charleston's response to the Vesey scare had unleashed a new and potent politics of slavery in the Palmetto State, a politics that had the potential to forever redefine the state's federal relations, and perhaps reshape its internal political landscape as well. The Vesey incident together with the controversy over the Seaman's Act revealed the power of the politics of slavery to galvanize otherwise disparate factions behind a consensus in favor of whatever measures promised to best protect white security.

In the five years after the Vesey scare, politics in Charleston and the Lowcountry took on an increasingly radical tone. Together, the Vesey scare, the federal opposition to the Seaman's Act, and the American Colonization Society's increasingly aggressive efforts to seek federal aid for their cause drove Lowcountry leaders into fierce opposition to federal power. Lowcountry concerns about the safety and security of slavery were compounded by the presidential election of 1824. While the frontier hero Jackson was hardly the political darling of the Charleston rice and Sea Island cotton planter elite, the House of Representatives' ultimate choice of John Quincy Adams, a New Englander who had actively sought to dismantle the Seaman's Act, as president over the slaveholding leader of the popular and electoral vote worried opponents of federal power. Adams' election placed lower South congressional delegations on guard against new assertions of nationalism in Washington. In the hypersensitive Lowcountry, politicians increasingly insisted that the imperatives of living as slaveholders in a society with a large slave majority demanded that the region retain control over all important questions related to slavery. To ensure such control, the South Carolina Lowcountry assumed a militant posture toward any outside "interference" with slavery. In the years immediately following the Vesey scare, Charleston's combative political temperament and its vibrant intellectual community produced an ideological anti-antislavery offensive of sorts, one replete with harsh invective for those who criticized slavery.[86]

DESPITE THE RAPID EMERGENCE of radicalism in the South Carolina Lowcountry in the immediate aftermath of the Vesey plot, the scare had remarkably little impact across the rest of the South. Rather than precipitating a wave of draconian measures tightening white control over slaves and free blacks across the South, the Vesey scare initiated a period of calm state-by-state reappraisal of public policy related to white security and racial control. As a general rule, the policies reconsidered in light of the Vesey scare were those addressing issues that allegedly played a role in the formation of the Vesey plot, according to the reckoning of Charleston authorities. The issues included the in-migration of free blacks, ease of manumission, slave literacy, unsupervised assemblies of slaves and free blacks, reliance on slaves and free blacks as artisans and mechanics, and the interstate slave trade. Outside of South Carolina, legislative reexamination of laws on these subjects in the aftermath of the Vesey scare produced only modest changes in existing policy, not a full-scale reaction tightening white control over slaves and free blacks.

Throughout the upper South, the Vesey scare had a negligible impact on state policy. Virginia had reacted aggressively to the Gabriel plot two decades earlier and, along with most upper South states, had long since settled on a policy of banning slave imports as part of a deliberate effort to keep the region from becoming too black. Virginia's general policy toward free blacks also changed little in the aftermath of Vesey. The Old Dominion continued its liberal manumission policies and looked to reduce the region's large free black population through colonization.[87] In North Carolina, the Vesey rebellion generated concern among slaveholders in heavily black tobacco-growing areas in the northeastern portion of the state, but the legislature took no dramatic action in the aftermath of the scare. This pattern of "leniency" toward slaves and free blacks in the old North State continued uninterrupted until 1829, when nervous white reaction to David Walker's *Appeal* triggered a round of increased legislative regulation.[88]

If the upper South remained nonplused by the Vesey scare, the lower South reacted with studied caution. The scare prompted almost every state in the lower South to reevaluate its policies on matters related to the control of their slave and free black populations, but these reevaluations produced only scattered and minor changes in state law. Georgia, though worried about Vesey-style rebellions in its heavily black rice swamps and older cotton-growing regions, actually repealed its existing ban on the importation of slaves in 1824, just two years after the Vesey scare, because of continued difficulties in enforcing the prohibition. In 1826, Georgia mandated that all newly manumitted slaves be removed from the state, but that decision owed more to a desire to assist emerging efforts to colonize free blacks than to the Vesey scare. Moreover, despite widespread popular support for the state's tight restrictions on private emancipation, Georgia slave owners regularly skirted the law to free small numbers of slaves. Plagued by meager resources, Georgia authorities found it difficult to enforce the removal section of the manumission law against contrary local opinion. In practice, Georgia's policy toward manumission amounted to an extralegal local option approach. It tolerated owners freeing slaves of their choice as long as local opinion supported manumission.[89] The Vesey scare did nothing to change this ad hoc approach to manumission.

In the newer cotton states, Alabama responded to news of the Vesey plot by tightening its regulation of free blacks, especially regarding their interaction with slaves. Late in 1822, the Alabama legislature banned free black ownership and operation of taverns, venues repeatedly identified by Charleston authorities as places where Vesey had allegedly spread dissatisfaction. Of course, such locations often had been labeled a nuisance by local grand juries well before reports of the Vesey plot added new evidence that such establishments housed conclaves dedicated to subversive communication. The 1822 Alabama legislature took no other action related to control of slaves and free blacks, but the state's original constitution, written in 1819, had already placed a number of significant restrictions on slaves and free blacks. Alabama also had an existing law prohibiting the education of slaves that encompassed free blacks as well. This ban on the education of slaves and free blacks represented a self-conscious attempt by Alabama lawmakers to limit black literacy. The Alabama constitution also required legislative approval of all manumissions as well as the consent of the master and proof that the slave(s) in question possessed "good character." But the otherwise stringent Alabama constitution placed no restrictions on the in-migration of free blacks. The Vesey rebellion scare failed to prompt any shift in this policy, and through a mix of legislative manumission and in-migration, Alabama's free black population increased steadily during the 1820s. It was not until after the Nat Turner rebellion that Alabama prohibited the in-migration of free blacks.[90]

In Louisiana, where the sugar-growing parishes had long relied heavily on slave labor, the increase in the slave population sparked by the Red River cotton boom raised scattered alarms about the size and proportion of the state's slave population during the 1820s. But Louisiana's concerns had less to do with post-Vesey fears of insurrection (Louisiana knew a bit about insurrection firsthand) than with the staggering debts incurred by Louisiana planters enlarging their holdings. In 1826, four years after news of the Vesey scare circulated, the state prohibited the importation of slaves from other states (with exceptions for residents and immigrants) for a period of two years in an effort to slow the outflow of private capital from the state as well as to control the growth of the state's slave population. But the legislature repealed the restriction on slave importation a year early.[91] Across the river in Mississippi, the 1822 legislature, influenced by reports of the Vesey scare, adopted a "character test" for imported slaves. The statute required either the slave traders or prospective buyers to procure character references for the slaves in question from two freeholders in the slaves' previous area of residence. Designed to prevent the dumping of troublesome or rebellious slaves from other parts of the South and slow the work of slave traders, this regulation did not apply to either Mississippi residents or immigrants who intended to settle permanently in Mississippi. Moreover, in 1822, the Mississippi legislature, dominated by lawmakers from the Natchez area, passed legislation prohibiting manumission without legislative approval and requiring all slaves freed by their owners to leave Mississippi immediately. While the latter provision proved difficult if not impossible to enforce, for the rest of the decade the legislature regularly and routinely rejected more petitions for manumission than it approved.[92]

Thus, outside of the South Carolina Lowcountry, no sweeping or draconian shift in either white attitudes or state policies toward slaves and free blacks followed the Denmark Vesey insurrection scare. No siege mentality seized the region immediately. Apart from South Carolina, no state set up a garrison to fend off outside threats. To be sure, the Vesey scare prompted a review of policies and attitudes related to control of slaves and free blacks, but this reconsideration generated a myriad of piecemeal and generally reasonable state responses, such as restricting the interstate slave trade and limiting the growth of the free black population, rather than a single pattern of bold reaction. For the moment at least, fear and defiance prevailed only in the South Carolina Lowcountry.

Apart from South Carolina, no state in either the upper or lower South reacted dramatically to news of the Vesey scare, a stark contrast to the regionwide panic that would follow the Nat Turner rebellion just under a decade later. Despite legitimate concerns about white security in the face of slave unrest, the foiled Vesey rebellion failed to convince the South as a whole that it was under siege. Upper South whites continued their efforts to whiten their region through the interstate slave trade, liberal manumission policy, and colonization. Lower South whites continued to monitor the interstate slave trade, perhaps viewing it more warily after the Vesey scare than before, and gave renewed attention to the idea of reducing the region's free black population through colonization. In an ironic twist, an improbable moment for cooperation between upper and lower South behind the idea of colonization appeared at hand, at least if warnings from South Carolina that colonization was abolition in disguise could be ignored.

PART FIVE

WORDS AND DEEDS

Across the South, the Denmark Vesey scare triggered a new round of interest in the colonization movement as an answer to the slavery question. In the lower South, it increased white interest in colonizing free blacks and troublesome slaves as a means of enhancing white security. In the upper South, colonization remained a key component in any practical plan for gradual emancipation, since virtually all whites agreed that the two races could not live together in freedom. With the founding of the politically well-connected American Colonization Society in 1816, it seemed possible that the post-Vesey environment might inspire cooperation between the upper and lower South on the issue and give colonization a more central role in each region's efforts to answer the slavery question. But the lingering sectional tensions over the Missouri controversy, a new spirit of antiabolition radicalism in South Carolina and other black-belt areas, and internal disagreements among southerners about the appropriate nature and scope of colonization hindered the movement's progress throughout the decade. Still, the vigorous discourse about colonization among white southerners of differing persuasions on the issue served as a window into evolving southern attitudes about slavery and its future.

The terms of debate over the slavery question both broadened and sharpened in powerful ways with the 1829 publication of David Walker's pamphlet calling for slaves to rise against their oppressors, which caused more consternation across the South than any previous incident, and with the 1831 Nat Turner insurrection, which took more white lives than any other North American slave insurrection. The level of public fear aroused by the Turner insurrection among upper South whites not only led to the savage repression of the rebellion but also kindled keen interest in tighter measures for the control of slaves and free blacks in the short term. Over the long term, the concerns raised by the Turner rebellion heightened interest among upper South whites in making their region safer by making it whiter, whether through diffusion or through gradual emancipation and colonization. The greater the danger whites perceived from slave unrest, the greater the popular interest in accelerating the whitening of their region.

CHAPTER TEN

DISCOURSES OF COLONIZATION

Initially, the upper South emerged from the Missouri debates inclined to believe that the best answer to the slavery question lay in demographic reconfiguration of the institution that would ameliorate the institution's worst evils. Moreover, the methods for such a reconfiguration were beginning to come together. The congressional compromise allowing slavery to expand into Missouri further facilitated the process of diffusion, a process already under way through the sale and migration of slaves to Kentucky, Tennessee, Alabama, Mississippi, and Louisiana. The early success of the ACS in procuring federal help in establishing a colony in Liberia buoyed hopes that free blacks and newly manumitted ex-slaves could be removed from the upper South and safely colonized in Africa. A minority of upper South slaveholders, generally concentrated in Southside Virginia, opposed colonization altogether and favored a more overt defense of slavery, but these opponents of colonization appeared on the defensive during the early 1820s. The efforts of many lower South states to regulate the interstate slave trade loomed as a potential problem for diffusionists, and gradual emancipationists in the region remained concerned about the glacial pace of "whitening" generated by colonization and diffusion alone. But on the whole, the prospects for whitening the upper South through a demographic reconfiguration of slavery seemed promising in the early 1820s, and both diffusion and colonization appeared to be effective mechanisms for whitening the upper South.

The lower South, however, remained of two distinct minds about the appropriate answer to the slavery question in the region. Neither of the two "answers" most commonly advanced involved emancipation. One significant group of lower South whites sought a melioration of the perceived evils associated with slavery through an ideological reconfiguration that would render slavery a truly "domestic" institution. The ideology and practice of paternalism, these lower South whites reasoned, extended the protection of the household to slaves, and, over time, created a set of domestic relations that, as William Smith put it, left only the "shadow of slavery" visible. Yet during the 1820s, paternalists in the lower South were still insurgents struggling against both indifference and active opposition. Moreover, paternalist insurgents had been placed on the defensive, at least in the South Carolina and Georgia Lowcountry and other southern black-belt areas, by the Denmark Vesey insurrection scare. The Vesey investigation and other perceived threats to white safety fueled the reemergence of an older approach to managing slave society, one that called for strict control of the slave population through force, intimidation, and vigilance. This neotraditional mode of slaveholding, which emphasized the undiminished power of the master and the absolute subordination of the slave, depended little on the internalized values of either masters or slaves. Instead, its proponents argued that the answer to the slavery question in the lower South lay in recognizing the danger that a coddled and loosely managed slave population posed to white society. The neotraditional approach was often embraced by avatars of the new political radicalism, devotees of an extreme states' rights creed based less on the old republican fear of centralized power than on the need for slaveholders to keep power in safe (read state and local) hands. This new states' rights radicalism was designed not so much to disperse power in defense of liberty as to concentrate power in the hands of slaveholders in order to protect slavery.

Ultimately, these two modes of defending slaveholding, the paternalist and the neotraditional, would reach an accommodation, but during the 1820s they remained separate and often antagonistic approaches. Yet both paternalists and neotraditionalists in the lower South recognized that their region's dependence on slave labor placed it beyond the reach of a demographic reconfiguration like that sought by upper South whites. Indeed, in the lower South that reconfiguration ran in the other direction, toward the region growing blacker and more dependent on slave labor, as more and more slaves flowed into the ever-expanding cotton belts. And, ironically, any hope that upper South whites had for a successful demographic reconfiguration that would whiten their region depended heavily on continued demand for large numbers of additional slaves to work the staple crops of the lower South.

As a result, the events of the early 1820s, particularly the Missouri debates, the Vesey scare, and the determined efforts of the ACS to gain federal assistance for its colonization efforts, brought these different approaches to "solving" the problem of slavery into sharper contrast. The initial point of contention between the regions was colonization. In the years immediately after the Vesey scare, lower South opinion of the colonization movement soured. By 1825, the new radical defenders of slavery in the lower South launched a sharp and expansive attack on the colonization movement, a key element of the upper South's plans for a demographic reconfiguration of slavery. This lower South attack generated in turn an active defense of colonization by upper South whites eager to use the movement as a means of whitening their region. The friction generated by this ideological rub ignited a polemical firestorm that largely pitted politicians and thinkers from the lower South against their counterparts in the upper South. At the same time, this fierce debate over colonization also revealed and deepened internal tensions within each region. In the upper South, champions of demographic reconfiguration found their apparent hegemony challenged by internal opponents of colonization. In the lower South, proponents of ideological reconfiguration found their efforts to persuade slaveholders of the virtues of paternalism vigorously disputed by those who thought paternalism lacked the strength and toughness to keep slaves under control.

Thus, during the decade of the 1820s, a lively discourse over colonization erupted in the American South. More precisely, the decade witnessed the appearance of a series of related southern discourses about colonization. The formative discourse was between upper South colonizationists who saw the movement as crucial to the demographic reconfiguration of slavery in the region and increasingly skeptical lower South planters and intellectuals who saw colonization as nothing less than the leading edge of a growing abolition movement. To these lower South skeptics, the colonization movement appeared to encourage the federal government to interfere with slavery in the southern states. Such interference might be indirect and innocuous at first, involving only the use of federal funds to transport free blacks to a colony in Africa, but lower South critics of the ACS predicted that such activity would nudge the South down a slippery slope toward an overt federal effort to assist in the emancipation of slaves. Subsidiary to this central line of discourse between upper and lower South lay at least two related discussions. The first was a debate within the upper South between those whites who supported colonization, arguably the dominant strain in the region as a whole, and a vocal set of Tidewater and eastern Piedmont planter conservatives who increasingly shared the lower South's determination to turn back all attempts to interfere with slavery at the threshold. The upper South's internal critics of colonization tried to generate lower-South-style hostility toward colonization among upper South whites committed to states' rights political doctrines, and hence to weaken support for colonization in the region. This approach enjoyed measured success, especially as Andrew Jackson's popularity surged among common whites in the region. The second subsidiary discourse centered on a disagreement between southern supporters of colonization (mostly from the upper South) and the colonization movement's national leaders over how hard to press the cause in a South disturbed by the tenor of the Missouri debates, alarmed by the Vesey scare, and increasingly wary of federal action. In particular, many upper South colonizationists urged the ACS to delay its request for federal funds in light of southern opposition. In the post-Vesey climate, these southern colonizationists cautioned, such a request was unnecessarily polarizing. Their advice was largely ignored by the ACS national leadership, which nonetheless touted the conservatism and caution of the society's approach. The swirl of these three related discourses of colonization often left the discussion convoluted and confused, and it is difficult to tease apart their strands, but, taken together, the three discourses reveal the growing distance between upper and lower South over the issue of colonization in particular, and over how to answer the slavery question in general.[1]

PRIOR TO THE MISSOURI DEBATES and the Vesey scare, the colonization movement had enjoyed relatively broad tolerance, as a concept if not as a practice, among whites in both the upper and lower South. At its inception in late 1816, the American Colonization Society enjoyed a significant measure of support in the lower South. With its announced intention to colonize only free blacks who voluntarily chose to leave the country, it brought together a broad if shallow coalition of support across the South. Clearly gradual emancipationists thought that colonization might encourage masters who disliked slavery to free their slaves voluntarily. The promise of the removal of these recently freed blacks from the community, some colonizationists believed, would convince masters that manumission would not lead to increased problems with free blacks in their local community. Slaveholders looking toward gradual emancipation, a type of slaveholder not uncommon in the upper South, saw colonization as an essential mechanism for bringing their ultimate plans to fruition, since virtually no slaveholder could envision the peaceful coexistence of the races under conditions of freedom. From the other end of the spectrum, the prospect of removing the despised and dangerous free black population appealed to slaveholders who had little or no interest in emancipation, no matter how gradual. Regardless of one's position on the future of slavery in the young American republic, the colonization movement offered the prospect of some improvement in the social organization of slavery to almost all whites by offering a means of reducing the size of the region's free black population.[2]

Such inclusiveness was not cynically calculated by the ACS or leading colonizationists generally. In many respects, the colonizationists' approach mimicked that of the founders: seeking to weaken slavery where they could, accommodating it out of political necessity where they could not weaken it, and leaving the institution's future in the hands of time and events. Overwhelmingly, leading colonizationists were sincere philanthropists. They thought the ACS offered an active but prudent approach to meliorating two of the great problems gripping the young republic: the presence of slavery and the coexistence of races highly unequal in power and, in the minds of many whites, ability.[3] Belief in black inferiority, whether innate or conditional, infected the overwhelming majority of white minds, and certainly racism and notions of white supremacy suffused the colonization movement. Other than from blacks themselves, little dissent emerged along these lines during the 1820s.[4] Where free, however, blacks immediately expressed opposition to the ACS and blasted its racist assumptions. In 1817, for example, James Forten and the Reverend Richard Allen led a three-thousand-person protest against the movement in Philadelphia, and prominent free blacks in the North emerged as the colonization's movement most persistent critics.[5] Nevertheless, among southern whites, the Jeffersonian despair of the future of a biracial republic remained dominant throughout the 1820s, and grew more entrenched and unyielding in its position, and arguably coarser and more threatening in its expression, as the years passed.[6]

After the Vesey scare, slaveholders in the lower South turned a newly skeptical eye toward the activities of the American Colonization Society. As one conservative slaveholder later explained, the "establishment of a self-created society at the seat of government, which society numbers in the lists of its members many of the most distinguished officers and agents of the government itself, and which extends its influence through the Union by means of affiliated associations formed in different states" constituted a cause for concern.[7] This growing southern sensitivity to northern "agitation" on the slavery issue manifest itself in intensified opposition to continuing ACS efforts to secure federal aid. Indeed, in 1823 and 1824, even upper South supporters of the ACS warned the organization that it should delay any attempt to obtain federal funds until the newly adverse political climate improved. In February 1824, Virginia's Charles Fenton Mercer, ACS founder and unflinching supporter of the movement, advised the society against seeking federal aid and urged it to proceed with the "utmost prudence and caution" in promoting its cause within the South.[8] Yet despite these warnings, the ACS forged ahead with efforts to gain additional federal assistance.

To complicate matters even further, in 1824 the ACS sought state endorsements of its plan to seek federal money as a means of prodding Congress to support its request.[9] The 1824 Ohio state legislature offered such an endorsement, branding slavery a national evil and calling on Congress and other states to use the colonization movement as a means of ending slavery "with the consent of the slaveholding states." Echoing an idea floated privately by an aging Thomas Jefferson that same year, the Ohio proposal recommended freeing all slave children once they reached the age of twenty-one, provided that they could be colonized. Connecticut quickly joined Ohio in endorsing the proposal and denouncing slavery as "a great national evil." New Jersey applauded colonization as a method to "effect the entire emancipation of the slaves in our country" as well as providing an overseas "asylum" for free blacks destined for second-class citizenship within the United States.[10] Coming from the North and expressing some hostility toward slavery, these endorsements arguably did the colonization movement in the South more harm than good. Evidence of sympathy for emancipation also surfaced among colonizationists in the upper South, a development that disturbed lower South critics of colonization even more than the northern resolutions branding slavery a national evil. Delaware praised colonization as "one of the grandest schemes of philanthropy" ever considered by Americans, and Kentucky, rather than denouncing the Ohio resolutions as lower South skeptics expected, urged southern respect for the ACS, claiming that "no jealousies ought to exist, on the part of this or any other slaveholding States," concerning the idea of colonization.[11]

In the lower South, the northern states' endorsement of colonization as a means of a general, if voluntary, emancipation sparked immediate opposition. South Carolina promptly denounced the Ohio resolution in bold terms. Georgia, Louisiana, and Alabama all quickly concurred in the denunciation. And slavery's less apologetic defenders in the upper South also rose to assail the colonization movement's aggressive new bent. Missouri immediately denounced the resolutions, and one Virginian called the colonization movement an "insidious" attack on slavery.[12] In 1825, New York's Rufus King further stoked the fires of southern discontent by proposing that funds from the sale of public lands be used to finance an aggressive colonization effort that would promote the idea of general emancipation as well as accelerate the removal of free blacks.[13]

King's proposal, coming fast on the heels of federal efforts to supersede the Negro Seaman's Act in South Carolina, immediately drew spirited denunciations from the lower South. In the United States Senate, South Carolina's Robert Y. Hayne condemned King's proposal as one designed to permanently "disturb the peace and harmony of the Union." Congress, Hayne insisted, "had no power to appropriate the public land" to provide financial assistance to a private philanthropy such as the ACS.[14] Georgia governor George Troop, normally an ally of the pro-ACS William Crawford, blasted the bill as "impertinent intermeddling with our domestic concerns." Troop claimed the proposal put the power of the federal government in the hands of "a combination of fanatics" bent on "the destruction of everything valuable in the southern country."[15]

As southerners in Congress worked vigorously to block federal aid to the colonization movement, denunciations of the colonization movement erupted outside legislative chambers, especially from the newly minted radical faction in the Carolina Lowcountry. Not surprisingly, the sharpest rebuke of colonization, and the ACS in particular, spewed from the vitriolic pen of South Carolina Sea Island cotton planter Whitemarsh Seabrook. Seabrook, age thirty-two, owned more than fifty slaves in 1824. Despite his youth, the combative Seabrook had already emerged as a political leader in the Lowcountry. Prior to the Vesey scare, Seabrook had joined his handful of white neighbors on Edisto Island to complain about the white mission to the slaves and the teaching of slaves to read and write. In 1823, he participated actively in the formation of the controversial South Carolina Association and quickly became one of the new organization's officers. Late in 1825, Seabrook produced a strident pamphlet that revealed the tidewater South's fear that the colonization movement served chiefly as an entering wedge for abolition.[16]

The radical Lowcountry planter argued that recent northern actions on the subject of slavery, such as the Ohio resolution and King's proposal to sell public land to finance colonization, signaled slaveholders that "the tenure by which we hold our slaves is becoming daily less secure." Seabrook contended that colonizationists portrayed slavery in "false and revolting colors," by maintaining that "slavery contradicts the primary principles of our government; that our slaves are wretched, and their wretchedness ought to be alleviated; that they are dangerous to the community and this danger ought to be removed; and that if the evils attendant on the circumstances of our black population are not speedily eradicated, God, in his righteous judgment, will raise up a Toussaint, or a Spartacus, or an African Tecumseh, to demand by what authority we hold them in subjugation." Seabrook viewed such characterizations as slander against the slaveholding South and a form of sectional demagoguery designed to inflame northern opinion against slaveholders. He took special aim at the ACS for its alleged role in initiating the latest round of antislavery activity, not only through its decision to seek federal aid but also through the rhetoric it used to promote colonization. Under its "specious plan" for "aiding the cause of the free colored population," Seabrook claimed, the ACS had rallied "the pulpit and the bar, the press and the legislative hall" behind a disguised crusade to end slavery sooner rather than later.[17] Why, Seabrook asked, "is the subject of slavery agitated at all" by the ACS if its primary emphasis was "the simple question of transporting free negroes to Africa?"[18]

Seabrook believed he knew the answer. The ACS request for federal support suggested that the society harbored more sweeping ambitions than simply the colonization of existing free blacks or those comparatively small numbers of slaves annually manumitted by willing masters. The amount of federal aid the ACS sought suggested, at least to wary slaveholders such as Seabrook, that the society contemplated a broader plan of emancipation and colonization than the lower South could accept. A sweeping plan for large-scale emancipation, however gradual, followed by colonization of the freedpeople, Seabrook insisted, would necessarily undermine the discipline and loyalty of those who remained enslaved. Could anyone believe, Seabrook asked, "that our slaves could witness the removal of their brethren, without an effort on their part to participate in the imaginary benefits of the congressional statute?" The practical impact of a federal law financing a large-scale colonization effort, Seabrook maintained, would be the "extinguishment of the relations between master and servant," and this process would be "the work of a day."[19]

The legacy of the Denmark Vesey scare, as interpreted by James Hamilton, the Vesey court, and the South Carolina Association, shaped Seabrook's critique of colonization. Seabrook saw the Vesey plot as evidence that southern slaves were extraordinarily responsive to any suggestion that manumission or a general emancipation might be in the offing. Any encouragement that slavery was anything but permanent and inevitable, Seabrook believed, inspired slave resistance and undermined white control over slaves. In black-majority areas such as the Carolina and Georgia Lowcountry, the tiny white minority had to meet every potential danger at the threshold and maintain tight control over slaves.

Behind Seabrook's argument against the ACS decision to seek federal aid lay his opposition to any national discussion of colonization, no matter how the issue was framed. Recalling the "inflammatory speeches" of the Missouri controversy and their alleged impact on fomenters of the Vesey plot, Seabrook contended that "the question of slavery" could never "be canvassed without the most malevolent and serious excitement." Such a debate would "engender animosities" and foster "sectional divisions." Seabrook knew that abolitionists could not "immediately" prevail in a congressional discussion of slavery. But the mere discussion of the issue might have other potentially fatal side effects. Seabrook believed that a national debate over the future of slavery would trigger increased slave resistance and rebellion, forcing many white southerners to live under a quasi-permanent state of siege. Thus by its very occurrence, Seabrook believed, a national discussion of slavery undermined the institution. Again recalling the Vesey plot, Seabrook argued, "Our history has verified the melancholy truth that one educated slave, one colored freeman, with an insinuating address, is capable of infusing the poison of insubordination into the whole body of the black population." Aspiring black leaders, in fact, often "intentionally misrepresent facts, and draw with a deeper colouring the lineaments of those baneful pictures" with which the Missouri debates provided them. "Was this not done by the leaders of...contemplated risings of the negroes in at Camden in 1816 and in Charleston in 1822?" Seabrook asked defiantly. "Did not the unreflecting zeal of the North and East and the injudicious speeches on the Missouri question animate Vesey in his Hellish efforts?"[20]

Seabrook remained a sharp critic of paternalism. He acknowledged that slaves would push hard, perhaps even strike violently, for freedom once emancipation on any substantial scale flourished under congressional sanction. Thus, despite the growing challenge of the paternalist ethos in the South Carolina Lowcountry and the claims of paternalist rhetoric in published pamphlets and speeches, Seabrook's reasoning suggested that slaveholders in heavily black subregions of the South remained unconvinced that paternalism could render slave society secure as long as talk of colonization and possible emancipation peppered political conversations and filled the public press. Indeed, Seabrook's rhetoric suggested that the slaveholders' control had grown so fragile that even faint echoes of talk about ending slavery, or merely reducing its extent, might bring the whole institution down violently in "the work of day."[21]

Seabrook's scathing attack on colonization forcefully expressed the growing hostility of whites in the black-majority South Carolina Lowcountry to any outside "interference" with the institution of slavery. Over the next several years, the vibrant intellectual community in Charleston and the city's combative political temperament produced a number of essays attacking the critics of slavery, generating an anti-antislavery offensive.[22] Early in 1826, Charlestonian Edward Brown joined Seabrook with a denunciation of northern antislavery sentiment, a denunciation that included the colonization movement. In his pamphlet *On the Origins and Necessity of Slavery*, Brown echoed Seabrook's argument, accusing antislavery organizations of "endeavouring by every secret art in their power" to "mar" the "prosperity" of the slaveholding states and "finally to destroy the property" of their citizens. Brown argued that the failure of slaveholders to rebut systematically the "libels" advanced against them "on the general question of slavery" had produced "a serious injury to their characters, their property, and their cause." Slavery as it existed in the South had been "grossly misrepresented," Brown asserted, by both abolitionists and colonizationists, who used isolated "facts at which humanity shudders" to "represent the general treatment of slaves." The "aspersions" cast "on the characters of the people of the slaveholding states" regarding the "treatment of their negroes" demanded prompt and effective rebuttal.[23]

Brown maintained that the material condition of slaves in the South "has been proved to be equal, if not superior, to the condition of the poor in Great Britain." The moral condition of southern slaves compared favorably with that of free blacks in the North, who, Brown claimed, had "plunged" into "moral misery" under the "specious philanthropy" that flourished in the so-called free states. For comparative purposes, Brown estimated that "there are as many slaves in the Southern states who attend public worship, and are members of Christian churches, as negroes in the Northern states and the poorer classes in Europe, in proportion to their respective numbers." Thus Brown concluded that "weakening the power and influence of the master over the slave" would entail a great moral and physical evil on blacks as well as whites. Allowing a freed slave to "stalk forth into the community as a free vagabond, whose colour and caste [are] preventing him from rising to a respectable grade in society," Brown argued, "leaves him an easy prey for the temptor's snare, whatever the temptation may be."[24] Brown's argument was not so much an overt embrace of paternalism as it was a tirade against northern antislavery advocates and the false premises he insisted they used in their arguments. But his pamphlet was a sign that even southern defenders of slavery whose primary focus lay elsewhere could find embedded in the paternalist argument material needed to rebut critics of slavery.

Still, during the 1820s, tracts defending slavery remained highly localized in their origins, emanating chiefly from the South Carolina Lowcountry, a region rendered acutely sensitive to criticism of slavery by its demography and the aftereffects of the Vesey scare. Above all, the essays of Seabrook and Brown testified to the distrust of colonization that gripped Charleston and its hinterland, and the area's growing tendency to equate colonization with abolition. Charleston Congregationalist pastor Benjamin Palmer, a colonizationist, privately denounced the "base representations" of the movement "constantly made" in Charleston's "public prints." Palmer insisted that such radicalism, though virulent, remained a highly localized sentiment. The minister reported that he had "reason to believe" that such "fiery, inflammable feelings" remained "in a great degree confined to Charleston and the lower country." He was "persuaded" that such radical sentiment "does not much, if at all, effect the interior and upper parts of this state nor do I believe it a prevalent feeling in either Georgia or North Carolina."[25]

But such anticolonization sentiment was not quite as geographically confined as Palmer believed. Though decidedly less strident than their lower South counterparts, upper South conservatives eagerly joined Seabrook in balking at the ACS request for federal aid. Beginning in August 1825 and continuing for more than ten months, John White Nash, a member of the Virginia House of Delegates from Amelia County, a slave-majority county in the state's eastern Piedmont, published a series of anticolonization essays in the Richmond *Enquirer* under the pseudonym Caius Gracchus.[26] A conservative opponent of constitutional reform in Virginia politics, Nash fit the emerging profile of upper South critics of colonization. A prominent planter and politician, he lived in a black-belt area and maintained a generally conservative stance on state political issues at a time when pressures for a broad democratization of the Virginia constitution, hinging on a shift of the basis of representation in the state legislature to the white basis, loomed large. The specific irritant that pushed Nash to take his case against the ACS public was the organization of a local auxiliary in nearby Powhatan County, but the society's newfound willingness to enlist federal patronage to advance its cause served as the focus of his wrath. The ACS request for congressional aid, Nash argued, stretched the construction of the "common defense" and "general welfare" clauses of the Constitution well beyond the point advocated by "even the wildest of latitudinarians." Nash denounced the ACS as a "repository of all the fanatical spirits in the country," and warned that it harbored a "viper" within "whose sting is to poison every source of domestic quietude."[27]

In his sustained attack on the ACS, Nash restated the popular understanding that the Constitution represented a series of sectional compromises over the issue of slavery. The key compromises within the larger package involved linking of the issues of representation and taxation, the adoption of the three-fifths clause, and securing an extension of the foreign slave trade by conceding majority control of maritime policy. Such sectional compromises had endured the strains of nearly three decades. But, Nash suggested, the ACS efforts to involve the federal government in the financing of colonization threatened the historic constitutional bargain by undermining the crucial agreement that placed slavery beyond the reach of federal interference. Moreover, Nash contended, ACS agitation on the colonization question generated discontent among southern slaves themselves. Expressing a growing concern among many black-belt slaveholders, Nash worried that slaves, when "goaded up to [a] state of frenzy" by the ACS' "fanatical inspirations," might seek to "throw the whole country in a flame." The "ravages" of that "conflagration," Nash reminded his fellow Virginian, would reach "our fields, our kitchens, and even the sacred retreat of our chambers."[28]

Paging through the annual reports of the ACS, Nash found abundant evidence to support his charge that the true aim of the society was not merely the colonization of free blacks but full-scale emancipation of all slaves. A movement for general emancipation required nothing less than a crusade to change the hearts and minds of white southerners—an attempt, Nash warned, "to revolutionize the whole character and habits of the people of the South." Such a crusade, Nash believed, would undermine the emerging system of paternalism that white southerners were coming to believe characterized southern slavery. Nash claimed that this paternalism expressed itself in the peculiar "love which most masters entertain for their slaves," who often "had been raised with us in all the pastimes and amusements of youth" and shared "every delicacy that parental kindness could lavish" upon them.[29]

Nash also denied the charge made by many colonizationists that slavery presented a threat to republican government. In fact, Nash argued, the "ownership of slaves had a great tendency to produce" a "peculiar cast of character" among white southerners that rendered them exemplars of republican citizenship. "Proud, high-spirited, and independent," white southerners, Nash claimed, displayed a "love of freedom" and "a jealousy of any invasion of their rights, either individually or politically," that left them well suited for republican citizenship. As eyewitnesses to the ongoing enslavement of blacks, southern whites remained zealous defenders of their own freedom, their vigilance enhanced by the visible bondage around them. Citing the independence of white southerners and their sensitivity to inequality among whites as republican virtues nurtured by slavery, Nash suggested that the plain folk of the South compared favorably as citizens to workers of the North, who "in their intercourse with their employers are almost as servile as the Southern slave" yet in politics "are admitted...to an equality of rights." Free labor, Nash declared, produced the "real aristocracy in Society, founded upon the possession of wealth, the most odious of all distinctions." By contrast, Nash contended that slavery, "as it respects the white population," had "a natural tendency to produce a greater degree of equality than exists in States where slavery is unknown."[30] In making this argument, the otherwise conservative Nash placed himself in the forefront of those who argued not only that the paternalism of southern slaveholders mitigated the potential harshness of slavery for the slaves but that slavery as a labor system generated a political benefit: an independent white population unusually vigilant in defense of their own liberty even as they maintained a system of slavery for others. In doing so, Nash suggested that paternalism, the lower's South's agent of ideological reconfiguration, could be used in an indictment of colonization, a key component of the upper South's plan for a demographic reconfiguration.

Alarmed that upper South conservatives had joined lower South planters in bashing the ACS, Virginia colonizationists wasted no time in responding to Nash. The initial burden of response fell to William Fitzhugh of Fairfax, the national vice president of the ACS. Writing in the *Enquirer* under the pseudonym Opimius, Fitzhugh denied that the ACS had played any role in creating the Missouri crisis. He explained that the various petitions from northern states urging Congress to fund the ACS endorsed emancipation only under terms and conditions acceptable to the slaveholding states. He defended the ACS decision to seek federal appropriations as fully justified by the circumstances and fully consistent with the "common defense" and "general welfare" clauses of the Constitution. Fitzhugh also emphasized the advantages for slaveholders inherent in ACS efforts to colonize free blacks, who stood as "an intermediate class" whose presence exercised a "paralyzing influence over the physical energies of the nation," one both degrading to free white labor and disruptive to slaves. In sum, Fitzhugh insisted that the ACS had no intention of disrupting the "domestic tranquility" of the slaveholding South with reckless plans for a general emancipation. Identifying slavery as the primary cause of the state's "languishing agriculture, our deserted farms, our decayed fortunes, our decreasing population," Fitzhugh urged any Virginian to "cast up in his own ledger his profit and loss for the last fifteen or twenty years, and then let him say whether or not slave labor is not a curse on the land." Gradual and voluntary emancipation combined with colonization, Fitzhugh argued, remained the best method to save Virginia from "progressive debility and premature decay."[31]

Recognizing Nash's drift away from a long-shared assumption that slavery was inherently an evil, Fitzhugh also took exception to the Amelia representative's characterization of slavery as a benign, paternalistic institution. "Slavery, even its mildest form," the ACS supporter reminded his fellow Virginians, "is an evil of the darkest character; cruel and unnatural in its origin." Slavery represented such a blight on republican society that "no plea can be urged in justification of its continuance but the plea of necessity." That "plea of necessity" rested not on the master's need for labor or desire for wealth, or even on society's respect for property rights, but solely on the basis that no remedy existed that did not presage evils even greater than those attached to slavery. To defend slavery as a "necessary evil," Fitzhugh insisted, a high standard for "necessary" must be met. Fitzhugh noted that Nash, despite the latter's paeans to the virtues of paternalism, had nonetheless described the slave population as "dissolute and abandoned in their moral character" and as possessing "passions and feelings of the most lawless and brutal kind," admissions that suggested either the failure or the absence of the paternalism Nash and other apologists for slavery increasingly lauded.[32]

Careful to balance his presentation, Fitzhugh, after rejecting the paternalist apology for holding slaves, also distanced the colonization movement from abolitionists, who, "guided by a blind and mistaken enthusiasm," called for "the immediate and unqualified emancipations of our slaves" without considering the social outcome of such a sudden and radical measure. But the Virginia colonizationist also emphatically rejected the notion that slavery was of "divine origin" and thus beyond the interference of man. Those slaveholders and other southerners who acknowledged "no term" to the existence of slavery and threw "every obstacle in the way" of "gradual and voluntary emancipation," Fitzhugh charged, shirked the duty of all Americans, as Christians and republicans, to remove the evil of slavery from the nation's bosom as soon as it was possible to do so in an orderly and humane fashion.[33]

Despite Fitzhugh's rebuttal, by late 1826, lower South critics of colonization and their cohort of upper South allies had the ACS on the defensive. The ACS leadership knew, based on reports received from members of local auxiliaries in the upper South, that the organization's support was collapsing in much of eastern Virginia. Norfolk's John French, a society supporter, advised ACS secretary Gurley that "opposition and indifference [to the society] prevail generally" in eastern Virginia. The articles by Nash and others criticizing the ACS had taken their toll, French reported, and "the state of the publick mind" prohibited "anything like pressing the subject." Whites in Tidewater Virginia, French noted, viewed slavery with a "very jealous eye," and "after all of the talk" of gradual emancipation and colonization, "there is scarcely a willingness to give up the sable race." "There is, to be sure," French continued, "a great desire to get rid of the free ones," but he conceded a lack of universal commitment even on that issue. Eastern Virginians, French judged, "wanted [free blacks] taken from near their vicinity," but they remained reluctant to finance a removal of free blacks from all over the state.[34]

The appearance of anticolonization polemics written by upper South politicians alerted ACS leaders to the need to buoy their support among upper South slaveholders, and while the organization recognized that reassurances from the society's national officers, including Fitzhugh, might calm the waters a bit, similar reassurances from local colonization activists might prove even more convincing. Thus the ACS encouraged its upper South members to rally in its defense. The eloquent young Lynchburg lawyer Jesse Burton Harrison, the Harvard-educated son of a successful tobacco merchant, did just that in an April 1827 address to a meeting of his hometown colonization auxiliary. Harrison, who had impeccable political connections (he was a cousin of Henry Clay), tried to convince the area's slaveholders that the ACS would do them no harm and meant them no disrespect. The ACS, Harrison insisted, was no abolition society. The young lawyer took pains to distance the society from the "few fanatics" who "would urge us on to the sudden and total abolition of slavery." The ACS, he continued, offered no criticism of masters and "disavows with horror the idea of offering temptations to any slave." Declaring that he would be "a slaveholder today without scruple," Harrison admitted that he was nonetheless unwilling to rest "contented" with the idea of perpetual slavery in the United States. To Harrison, the idea of "slavery in the abstract" seemed "detestable." But until the time arrived for the completion of emancipation, "no one shall upbraid a humane master" and "not a whisper of sedition be suffered to reach the slave." The society even rejected the idea that the "General Government have any power to emancipate." Instead, Harrison reminded his audience, the ACS recognized "that the States have exclusively the right to regulate the whole subject of slavery." The ACS deserved the full support of southern slaveholders, Harrison contended, because the "removal of every single free black in America" would be "productive of nothing but safety to the slaveholder."[35]

To counter the criticism of colonization that was spewing from South Carolina, Harrison jabbed at the moral obtuseness of white South Carolinians on the slavery issue, quipping that colonization seemed like a plague only to "the people of South Carolina," the same citizenry that alone had proven difficult to "convince of the wickedness of the slave trade." Harrison noted with pride that Virginia "stands in no close alliance to Carolina on this head." Showing a measure of independence from the parent organization, the Lynchburg attorney opposed the ACS request for federal funds, urging the ACS to seek funding from state legislatures and not the United States Congress, out of deference to the prevailing states' rights sentiments in the South.[36]

Despite repeated and articulate assurances from ACS supporters in the upper South that the organization had no intention of supporting a general or involuntary emancipation, lower South leaders remained wary of, if not alarmed at, the society's actions. Whatever else they may have thought about slavery prior to the ACS campaign for congressional funding in 1825, a preponderance of white southerners believed that the North and the national government would leave all final decisions concerning the disposition of slavery in the hands of the slaveholding states. After the appearance of the ACS initiatives, however, many southern whites doubted that the North remained deferential to southern opinions on the subject. White southerners not only came to question exactly how honorable northern intentions concerning slavery were, they also detected more than a hint of moral disdain in northern criticisms of slavery. Northerners no longer stopped at complaints about the general evil of slavery, but began to suggest that the imperatives of Christian teachings and humanitarian morality required at least some evidence of progress toward emancipation. In southern eyes, such talk represented not only a verbal assault on southern wealth and property but also an attack on southern honor and piety.

In the upper South, the society's defenders had to fight doggedly to hold the support it had previously enjoyed. In addition to the ACS' troubles in Virginia, the debates of the 1820s slowed the growth of colonization sentiment in Kentucky even though that state's favorite political son, Henry Clay, emerged as a strong supporter of the ACS. In 1823, the Presbyterian Synod of Kentucky had endorsed colonization, but by 1829 only five local chapters had been organized in the commonwealth, in part because of opposition from the state's politically powerful Bluegrass region.[37] In the lower South, the equation of colonization with abolition had driven the ACS to the brink of oblivion. Soon after the Lowcountry radicals launched their offensive against the ACS, whites across the rest of the lower South began to share the Lowcountry's suspicions of the colonization movement. They increasingly saw it as a veiled threat to slavery rather than simply as a mechanism for removing free blacks. In the Pearl River cotton belt of southwestern Mississippi, where the colonization of free blacks once enjoyed substantial support, planters complained by the late 1820s that ACS efforts to obtain financial assistance from Congress ran counter to the states' rights sentiments that were popular in the state, and predicted that if Congress established a precedent by legislating on a matter so closely related to slavery, it would soon consider calls for a general emancipation.[38] Similarly, colonization made little headway in the new cotton-growing regions of Alabama, despite the energetic efforts of James G. Birney, a Kentucky native who moved to Huntsville to start a colonization newspaper. After months of effort, the usually indomitable Birney conceded a "deadness to the subject of African Colonization" in Alabama. Birney blamed his lack of success on pandemic white fears that the ACS might interfere with slavery rather than focus solely on the colonization of free blacks.[39] As the Georgia legislature explained in a retrospective view of colonization, whatever support the ACS had initially enjoyed in the lower South emerged "from the general impression in the Southern states" that its object "was limited to removal" of the "free people of color and their descendants and none other."[40] Once talk of using the colonization of free blacks to encourage gradual emancipation reached Georgia ears, support for the ACS evaporated rapidly.

Worse still for the ACS, support for the society slipped further when advocacy for colonization began to take on a partisan or factional cast. During its formative years, the ACS had attracted support from Federalists and Republicans alike. To an extent, the movement held the political center, critiqued on one hand by those southerners most concerned about maintaining slavery into the distant future and on the other hand by those northerners who wanted to take more decisive action to end slavery quickly. But after the election of 1824, a clearer factional dimension entered the colonization equation. The stroke that helped derail Crawford's 1824 presidential campaign also forced him to play a much less visible role in the ACS. Moreover, Crawford, who had always seen the deportation of the existing free black population as the ACS' first priority, began to entertain doubts about the society's overall value as avowed proemancipation sentiment grew in the North. Doubtless the strong-willed Georgian thought he needed to hold his states' rights base in the lower South to remain a viable force in national politics. During these same years, Henry Clay, a loyal champion of the colonization cause, informally assumed the position formerly held by Crawford as the society's leading southern politician. Contemporary political observers judged Clay's commitment to colonization as sincere. But the same observers also viewed Clay's active role in the society as a part of a calculated effort to build a national political coalition that might help carry him to the presidency. Seeing colonization as a viable middle way between support for emancipation and a defense of slavery, Clay, ever the savvy politician, knew that the society could help sustain his popularity in the upper South and among northerners who disliked slavery and abolition with roughly equal fervor. Clay included the ACS plea for federal financial aid as a part of his "American System" of moral and material uplift sustained by federal funds.[41]

But Clay's identification with the colonization movement generally and the ACS in particular hurt the colonization cause in some quarters. In the lower South, Clay's defense of gradual emancipation and colonization lessened slaveholders' already diminishing level of comfort with the ACS still further. In the upper South, Clay's active involvement with the ACS after the election of 1824 led supporters of Andrew Jackson to see the society as little more than a "political engine" for the Kentuckian. Loyal Tennessee supporters of Jackson charged Clay with "making use" of the ACS for "political purposes—for gaining popularity in the North." As one ACS loyalist lamented, Clay's involvement with the society prompted many Jackson "partizans" to "view us with some suspicion." Other ACS supporters worried that Clay "had been helping himself to a ride on our shoulders," but judged the Kentuckian's "service to the Society worth the burden."[42] Thus, at least in the upper South, the southern debate over colonization began to parallel factional bickering within the increasingly unwieldy Jeffersonian Republican Party. With important exceptions, supporters of Jackson and the emerging Democratic-Republican faction tended to oppose ACS requests for federal aid and took a dim view of colonization generally. Southern supporters of Clay and the "national Republicans" remained decidedly more likely to support colonization and to favor the ACS requests for federal funds, though they were hardly unanimous on the latter question. The introduction of a partisan dimension into debate over colonization further complicated an already complicated matter.

As a result of the emerging Jacksonian suspicion and increasing lower South hostility, some political strategists urged the ACS not to seek federal aid again until after the presidential election of 1828, when the intrepid General Jackson appeared destined to avenge the "corrupt bargain" between Adams and Clay. Petersburg colonization supporter William Atkinson advised ACS president R. R. Gurley in July 1827 that "the overwhelming majority" of eastern Virginians, "believe that Congress have no power" to appropriate funds for the ACS.[43] But at its national meeting in 1827, the ACS membership decided to forge ahead with its request for federal aid to assist in its efforts to colonize free blacks. The ACS board appealed for the "immediate and effectual interposition of the Government" on behalf of colonization, as the society again insisted that its "real and only" design was the colonization of free blacks.[44]

Despite its conservative wrapping, the new ACS appeal for federal aid spurred yet another round of denunciations from the lower South. An outraged Georgia legislature blasted the idea of colonization as "wild and fanatical and destructive." Georgia lawmakers argued that opponents of slavery within the ACS were "preparing a mine" that "once exploded will lay our much-loved country in one common ruin." They rebuked all nonslaveholding states for their "cold-blooded selfishness" in seeking "an interference with our local concerns and domestic relations." At "the first establishment of the Colonization society," the legislature recalled, "the general impression in the Southern states" was that the society's aim "was limited to the removal beyond the U. States of the then free people of color and their descendants, and none others." Auxiliary societies were formed in Georgia on that assumption, and their "influence and resources" had "daily increased." More recent actions of the ACS, however, convinced the legislature that "this impression was false" and that the society was committed to ending slavery and removing all blacks from the United

States. Such a removal, the legislature predicted, would prove "especially ruinous to the prosperity, importance, and political strength of the Southern states." Outside "interference" with slavery violated the legislature's belief that the institution must remain a "local concern," and was thus both unconstitutional and intolerable.[45] Even Georgia's friends of colonization recognized the emergence of intense popular hostility to the movement. In the state's hilly upper Piedmont, the active Jackson County ACS auxiliary complained that the movement suffered "great discouragements" arising "out of ill-founded jealousies and fears of the South relative to the ultimate designs of the North."[46]

South Carolina radicals heaped even more venom on the ACS. On the floor of the United States Senate, South Carolina's Robert Y. Hayne again asserted that the federal government had no right to appropriate money for the purpose of African colonization, calling such an appropriation unconstitutional as well an "entire departure" from "the fundamental principles and settled policy of the country." Predictably, the South Carolinian scored the ACS for its attempt to involve the federal government in questions of slavery and manumission previously considered the constitutional prerogative of the states. Colonization, Hayne argued, "not only relates to a subject with which the Federal Government can have nothing to do, but which it will be extremely dangerous for them to meddle with." Hayne warned the Senate of the "danger of touching a subject with which the feelings and interests of a large portion of the Union are so closely connected." Of all the "extravagant schemes" that had been devised to interfere with slavery, Hayne contended, the idea of African colonization represented the most "wild, impractical, and mischievous."[47] South Carolina's other senator, William Smith, long a rival of Hayne in Palmetto State politics, also denounced colonization, claiming that "free blacks...would be better where they were, than to send them to Africa." Moreover, Smith contended that if the ACS estimates were taken at face value, the cost of colonizing six thousand free blacks annually would run to more than $1 million. With its persistent requests for federal funds, Smith concluded, the ACS had devolved into an "entering wedge" for abolition.[48]

While Hayne and Smith disparaged the ACS and its plea for funds in Washington, back home in South Carolina, Hayne's fellow veteran of the Vesey investigation, planter-lawyer Robert J. Turnbull, produced a vituperative pamphlet, *The Crisis*, linking colonization with high tariffs, federal aid to internal improvements, and all other measures designed to prostrate states' rights on the altar of a "consolidated national government."[49] The ACS, Turnbull warned, constituted a "midnight assassin" plotting to do the will of the abolitionists. Turnbull denounced the ACS' organ, the *African Repository*, for emphasizing the "cruelty" of masters toward slaves and praising "those silly mortals who sacrificed their wealth upon the altars of a moral enthusiasm; who think they aggrandize their country by manumitting their slaves, and thus letting loose beings, neither fitted, by education, or by habit, for freedom, and who must be a walking pestilence wherever they go." All ACS publications, in

Turnbull's view, sought to "make the slave dissatisfied with his condition and the master doubtful whether he can hold in subjection his slave." The Charlestonian urged South Carolinians in Congress to meet the issue at the threshold. Echoing the argument Whitemarsh Seabrook had advanced more than two years earlier, Turnbull claimed that mere discussion of the issue was "equivalent to an act of emancipation" because such discussion "would universally inspire amongst the slaves" the hope of freedom, and lead to increased slave resistance, including insurrection plots.[50] In the rhetoric of the Carolina Lowcountry, colonizationists had become assassins, slaveholders who freed their own slaves had become fools, and, most striking, the mere discussion of colonization had become an act of emancipation. Such apoplexy on the subject was hard to reason with, but at the urging of the ACS leadership, upper South colonizationists tried.

The ACS had long known that few lower South slaveholders could be numbered among those who considered manumission, but the collective impact of denunciations of the ACS from Seabrook, Brown, Hayne, Smith, Turnbull, Troop, and the Georgia legislature fostered concern throughout the organization's leadership. Virginia's supporters of colonization worried that the movement was "losing ground in the Southeast."[51] Observers in North Carolina reported that "everything connected with emancipation and colonization is unpopular in the state."[52] From points around the South, society supporters urged the leadership to respond to the mounting criticism.[53]

In an effort to buoy colonizationists in the upper South and reassure those willing to listen in the lower South, editor Robert Gurley and the *African Repository* missed few opportunities to plead their case to the growing number of southern skeptics. Gurley defended the society's request for funds, insisting that the society "promulgates no new or dangerous doctrine" and that it certainly had not fallen victim to an "ungovernable spirit of fanaticism." The *African Repository* also regularly ran brief extracts from the society's correspondence with the handful of South Carolinians, usually clergy, who supported colonization. The *Repository* also focused on the willingness of scattered lower South slaveholders to manumit slaves on the condition of colonization. One South Carolinian, a planter from the Cheraw area, expressed an eagerness to free twenty-five slaves, "all native Africans and their children," who were "willing and even anxious" to go to Liberia. The Cheraw planter volunteered to deliver his slaves to Georgetown provided that the society could arrange for their transportation from there.[54] The loss of these slaves, the *African Repository* claimed, and would leave the owner with but "a bare competency" to live on. Similarly, late in 1827, Secretary Gurley explained the motives and policies of the ACS to the Jackson County auxiliary in Georgia's upper Piedmont in an effort to reassure wavering Georgia colonizationists that the society did not serve as a front for the abolition movement. The Jackson auxiliary replied, pledging its continued loyalty to the ACS and praising the society as "one of the greatest national and Christian enterprises" attempted in the young republic.[55]

Upper South colonizationists also urged Gurley to aggressively disseminate the "Virginia point of view of our association" in a concerted effort to "throw a great light into the public opinion in the South." Many southern colonizationists mistakenly thought a thorough exposition of this so-called Virginia point of view, that of emphasizing the colonization of blacks already free and slaves voluntarily manumitted and saying little about colonization as an integral part of a plan of gradual emancipation, would rally faltering support for the society by exposing the overstatements of its opponents. Lynchburg's Jesse Burton Harrison agreed that the "arguments of South Carolina and Georgia must be conquered" and again volunteered to write an essay countering lower South critics.[56]

Harrison called Turnbull's charge that the ACS harbored "a rooted design" to abolish slavery "manifestly unfounded." The young Virginia native pointed out that Massachusetts colonizationist Edward Everett, hardly a friend of slavery, had publicly vowed that if and when a slave insurrection threatened, he and his fellow Massachusetts citizens "would be the first to take down their knapsack and the musket" and march to "fight" beside the slaveholders.[57] Though he identified himself with the "community of slaveholders," Harrison disagreed with Turnbull's assertion that slavery had become "so interwoven with [the South's] prosperity" that it could not be ended, even gradually, without bringing utter social and economic ruin to the region. Doubtless underestimating the strength of proslavery sentiment in his native state, Harrison claimed that there were not a "hundred men in Virginia" who would defend the idea of perpetual slavery. Instead, most Virginians, and even most Virginia slaveholders, Harrison argued, hoped that one day their posterity might find a way "to relieve themselves of the curse." If the rich cotton and swampy rice lands of Carolina could be cultivated only by slave labor, Harrison predicted, the Palmetto State's interest in perpetual slavery would construct a permanent "barrier between the interests" of South Carolina and Virginia. The Old Dominion, Harrison believed, would be better off as a "flourishing commonwealth of homogeneous freemen" than as a permanent part of a stagnant slaveholding social order.[58]

Yet Harrison reserved his sharpest rebuke for Turnbull's insistence that it was wrong for the ACS to "speak of slavery at all." Virginians, from the founding generation forward, had never "dreaded the bare hinting at slavery as an evil," and instead sought the "amelioration of slavery" while it existed. Harrison expressed disdain for Turnbull's boast that South Carolina had "set its face against all emancipation." Naming the evil of slavery, working for its melioration, and looking toward its ultimate termination, Harrison insisted, had long constituted the Virginia position on slavery and would continue to do so.[59] Acknowledging that his own Lynchburg auxiliary believed it "doubtful" that Congress had the constitutional authority to provide financial assistance to the ACS, Harrison joined many upper South colonizationists in urging the society to abandon its controversial annual petitions for federal assistance and seek aid from state treasuries instead. Harrison also urged the colonization movement to add "to our benevolence no small quantity of self-interest" by focusing for a time on the broadly popular project of removing existing free blacks, while waiting to push the cause of gradual and voluntary emancipation only when prevailing economic conditions and public opinion warranted.[60]

Harrison's reply to Turnbull suggested that avid colonizationists in the upper South had begun to abandon their commitment to a common southern front on the issue of slavery. Harrison had certainly lost hope of converting South Carolina to the colonization cause and may have felt that other portions of the lower South were drifting toward a Palmetto-style obstinacy. Another upper South colonizationist, replying to Hayne in the *National Intelligencer* under the pseudonym Virginius, chided South Carolina for its instinctive opposition to any discussion of slavery, lamenting that "the subject of domestic slavery can scarcely be mentioned, south of a certain line, without quickening into activity, feelings which all men must find unpleasant."[61] Increasingly, upper South colonizationists who called for an accelerated pace of removal and argued the case for gradual emancipation faced an unrelenting barrage of criticism from self-interested defenders of slavery in the rice and cotton South. The logic behind lower South intransigence was not hard to conjure. "Gratification of selfishness in the pursuit of personal gain is a prevailing trait in our quarter," one frustrated colonization sympathizer reported from the cotton frontier in middle Tennessee, and "there could be no part of the world where [slave] property is sought with greater avidity."[62]

As the lower South appeared headed toward a lasting embrace of slavery, upper South champions of free labor, including Harrison, saw the need for decisive action on behalf of colonization. Slowing the pace of emancipation and colonization in the upper South in an attempt to placate a lower South that refused to be placated only sacrificed the interests of an economically stagnant upper South to those of its truculent but flourishing lower South neighbors. Yet talk of an accelerated pace of voluntary emancipation and colonization angered many conservative slaveholders in Virginia's Tidewater and Southside areas, where colonization sentiment survived only from a desire to remove the sizeable existing free black population. Thus disagreement within the upper South prevented the debate over colonization from reducing to a dialogue between upper and lower South. Still, lower South critics of the colonization movement, and especially hard-liners such as Seabrook and Turnbull who equated colonization with abolition, saw the wavering of the upper South on the issue as yet another reason to insist that all decisions related to slavery remain the preserve of the individual states. The fate of South Carolina slaveholders, they reasoned, must remain in safe hands, and by the late 1820s, even the hands of Virginia slaveholders hardly seemed safe.

DESPITE THE ACS' concerted efforts to deny radical intentions, conservative opponents of colonization struck hard at the society's ongoing efforts to procure federal funding with vigorous state's right arguments. In April 1828, United States Senator

Littleton Waller Tazewell, a leading strict constructionist from Virginia, pushed a report through the Senate Foreign Relations Committee that held that the federal government lacked the constitutional authority to establish colonies overseas. In a forceful denunciation of the entire colonization project, Tazewell's report concluded that the United States government had no authority to acquire territory from a sovereign power except when justified by a declaration of war or by the authority of a formal treaty ceding territory from a foreign nation to the United States. The establishment of an empire, Tazewell claimed, ran contrary to the "genius" of the young nation's republican origins and Constitution. Moreover, the conservative Virginian noted, the "framers of the Constitution" had wisely "abstained from bestowing upon the [national] government...any power whatever over the coloured population of the United States, as such, whether this population was bond or free." Indeed, any attempt to endow the federal government with such a power, the report noted, would have "defeated the great objects of the patriot statesmen" who drafted the Constitution. Thus control of slaves and free blacks had been intentionally "left to the control of the States respectively" by the founders, Tazewell argued. Congress should hardly venture onto ground where the founders had feared to tread. The federal government "cannot assist" and "ought not to countenance" the plans of the ACS, Tazewell concluded, instead leaving all such questions to "be dealt with by the several state sovereignties."[63]

Yet Tazewell's report ranged well beyond the issue of constitutionality to examine the feasibility of the colonization effort. Using estimates that sparked controversy, Tazewell claimed that in a nation of nearly 2 million slaves and roughly 380,000 free blacks, the cost of transporting free blacks to an African colony, which he estimated at $20 per head, would by itself cost $50 million. And Tazewell's estimate included no funds either for establishing and maintaining colonies in Africa or for compensating slaveholders who freed their slaves. Moreover, Tazewell argued, during the long transition period created by the colonization of free blacks, chaos and confusion at home would undermine slavery. The gradual loss of free black labor, Tazewell argued, would disrupt the slave economy by creating a large class of fugitive slaves running away to seek employment in towns and cities as replacements for the departed free blacks. Tazewell also painted an ominous picture of the ACS itself. When a presumably benevolent society sought, in Tazewell's words, "to establish colonies; to erect governments, nay, to found empires independent of the United States, the example of such an association can not be productive of any benefit."[64]

For many critics of colonization, Tazewell's report answered the constitutional question once and for all. Born in Williamsburg in 1774, Tazewell attended William and Mary and later became one of Norfolk's most prominent lawyers. An Episcopalian, he served in the Virginia House of Delegates for more than twenty years before his election to the United States Senate in 1816. Though mentored early in life by John Marshall, Tazewell matured into a Jeffersonian politician who supported the Virginia and Kentucky Resolutions in 1798–99. Later, Tazewell absorbed and followed many of John Taylor of Caroline's states' rights theories and gave them practical expression in the political arena. A staunch conservative in the state constitutional debate that raged in Virginia by 1828, Tazewell believed that the "protection of interests" stood as the chief "object of government" and that interests should not be calculated "in proportion to noses."[65] Known widely as a man of ability, Tazewell's words carried influence in the states' rights camp and merited respect everywhere.

Tazewell's 1828 report fashioned a constitutional argument for federal noninterference with slavery. His argument rested not only on a strict construction of the Constitution that limited the scope of federal power but also on a legacy from the founding that held that the Constitution emerged from a sectional bargain that ensured federal quietude on the issue of slavery as a precondition for Union. In advancing these arguments, Tazewell's report sounded the themes of states' rights, strict construction, and constitutional protection that would echo loudly through the various debates over slavery and slavery-related issues throughout the rest of the antebellum era. But his report on colonization also anticipated the political logic of Andrew Jackson, whose presidential candidacy he aggressively supported in 1828, more than the constitutional logic of John C. Calhoun. Tazewell's stirring conclusion portrayed the ACS as a voluntary association bent on empire building and subsidized meddling in state matters, subverting the republican vision of the founders. Tazewell's denunciation of the unrepublican association suggested an angle of attack used to great effect by Jackson in his veto of the "monster" bank four years later.

Few informed observers doubted that Tazewell's critique of the ACS would find a ready audience among southerners skeptical of colonization. One concerned colonizationist lamented that Tazewell's report put the "apparent head of the Virginia political corps with the splendid talents attributed to him" firmly on record against colonization, and rightly predicted that the report would possess "the charm of oracles in the South."[66] And in the months that followed Tazewell's report, discouraging news from all over the South poured into ACS headquarters. In eastern Virginia, William Atkinson reported from Petersburg, home of a once robust local auxiliary, that another petition to Congress for assistance would "destroy our hopes of success in the Southside of James River, and I think, in the State." Atkinson reported that he personally doubted that Congress had the authority to aid colonization, but even if it did, another request from the ACS would be "neither politic or well-timed." If "the Society . . . perseveres in making application to Congress," the Southside lawyer predicted, it will risk "alienating all their friends in the Southern Atlantic States."[67] Atkinson surmised that the delegations from southern states would all vote against an appropriation, and he doubted that other congressmen would "venture to pass a law, affecting our coloured population, against the will of southern members." If Congress did act in the face of united southern opposition, Atkinson warned, it would "kindle the embers of opposition among the southern people into a consuming flame."[68] From Norfolk, an active ACS supporter reported that opposition to the ACS request prevailed there. Across the Old Dominion, other friends of the colonization movement advised that it would be wise for Virginia colonizationists to remain quiet until the popular fury against the appeal for federal aid had subsided. In 1828, eastern Virginia's suspicion of colonization increased to the point that the flourishing Richmond ACS auxiliary declared independence from the ACS and reorganized as the Colonization Society of the State of Virginia. Even under its new name, the state-centered society remained essentially inactive for the next two years.[69]

Outside Virginia, scattered field observers also filed troubling reports. In North Carolina's western Piedmont, a supportive minister admitted that "considerable" local opposition frustrated colonization efforts. From middle Tennessee, Lyman Brewster reported that those formerly friendly to the society now voiced dissatisfaction with its course and that many citizens openly disapproved of the society altogether. To further accentuate the popularity of slavery in his area, Brewster noted that while an emancipation society existed in his county (Maury), it consisted of "only three men," all brothers who "own no slaves," and the brothers were "very unpopular on account of the society."[70]

In the lower South, support for colonization sank to new lows following the Tazewell report. From South Carolina, an isolated procolonization minister reported that he encountered "violent" opposition to the ACS in Beaufort and that the society remained "exceedingly unpopular" in Charleston. Congregationalist Benjamin M. Palmer attributed this lack of popularity to "malignant misrepresentations" emanating from enemies of the society.[71] A Mississippi colonizationist admitted that public opinion in that state had turned "not generally favorable."[72] But perhaps the most discouraging report came from Georgia's Jackson County, where a local auxiliary had long enjoyed substantial support. In July 1829, the head of the auxiliary reported that the "influential leaders" of the local colonization movement had "left the county," leaving the auxiliary with little money and less support. Worse still, the Jackson auxiliary announced its own demise, canceling its subscription to the *Repository* and concluding that "we despair of being able to effect anything further in the shape of a society."[73]

Recognizing the impact of Tazewell's report, Gurley and the *African Repository* replied to Tazewell, defending colonization as constitutional under the "general welfare" clause. The ACS, Gurley pleaded, merely sought means sufficient to accomplish its ambitious ends. No private association, Gurley admitted, could "alone consummate the proposed design." But congressional support could make all things possible. "The object is national," Gurley maintained, "it demands national means." The ACS charged that "prejudice and interest" related to the question of slavery had combined to lead southerners to "cavil at the exercise of the simplest and most obvious powers of the General Government." If the United States could negotiate territory away from Native Americans and purchase Louisiana from France, it could purchase land from African nations. The ACS asked merely for assistance in defraying the expense of maintaining an African colony, Gurley insisted, and Congress certainly had power over federal appropriations. Gurley also emphasized the voluntary nature of the society's approach to colonization. The ACS offered to remove only slaves voluntarily and legally freed by their masters and to colonize only those free blacks who wanted to leave the United States. In seeking federal aid, Gurley argued, neither the ACS or any of its friends sought the "exercise of any power calculated to interfere, in the smallest degree, with either individual rights or state authority—we seek the removal of no free person of color without his consent, and of no slave without the consent of his master, and of neither, without the consent and cooperation of the state in which he lives." In other words, Gurley argued that the ACS merely sought federal money to assist in consensual, not forced, colonization.[74]

As suspicion of the ACS as an entering wedge of abolitionism grew in black-belt areas of both upper and lower South, the colonization movement struggled to hold onto a modicum of support in otherwise hostile areas by emphasizing its role in the removal of free blacks from southern society. Writing from the cradle of hostility toward the colonization movement, Charleston's Palmer saw a future for the society if it could unite "both friends and foes of slavery" behind a common goal: the removal of free blacks.[75] Similarly, a speaker at an ACS auxiliary meeting in Washington County, North Carolina, an eastern county with a large slave population and a large proportion of free blacks, emphasized the value of colonization as a mechanism for removing dangerous free blacks from the community. The "slavery of other nations," the speaker reminded his audience, "has been that of men of the same complexion with the free." Thus, as soon as those slaves were released, they could "mingle and lose themselves in the general community of the country, undistinguished by any stamp of nature." But such was not the case in the American South, where slavery was defined by race, and race largely defined by color. The speaker conceded that a few free blacks were "upright and industrious," but he argued that the "greater portion" were "a source of malignant depravity to the slaves on the one hand, and of corrupt habits to many of our white population on the other." Thus removing all free blacks would "improve the moral character of those who remain in servitude."[76]

In Virginia, the same Powhatan auxiliary that had so worried Judge Nash drafted a legislative memorial seeking the removal of all free blacks from the commonwealth. The Powhatan auxiliary praised the ACS for its refusal to interfere with the "delicate subject of slavery" but hailed its efforts to remove free blacks, who, it believed, exerted a "pernicious and dangerous influence" over slaves and constituted an "evil of immense magnitude" in the tidewater community."[77] Further inland, in an address to the Lynchburg Colonization Society, William Rives, a future United States senator, also urged the removal of "this unprofitable and baneful class," a caste, "degraded, depraved and contaminating all within contact," that filled "the master's mind with distrust and the slave's with impatience of bondage."[78] In 1829, a Virginia legislative committee assigned to report on the memorials petitioning the legislature to support colonization labeled the free black population an "evil, whose presence and magnitude is acknowledged, and whose future increase is dreaded by all." The committee recommended the creation of a limited but permanent state fund to help consenting free blacks migrate to Africa. It noted that such a fund could hardly lead to the "entire extinction of slavery," but "it will at least open a drain for our coloured population...to an extent amply sufficient for all purposes of public security."[79]

Support for colonization as a means of opening a "drain" for free blacks to flow out of the region still found many champions in the upper South, especially in its white-majority areas. In heavily white eastern Tennessee, John A. McKinney, a Presbyterian, explained to a local colonization auxiliary that "the object of the American Colonization Society...is neither more nor less, than to furnish the ways and means of transporting to Africa, with their own consent, the free people of colour who are scattered throughout the United States." The society, McKinney continued, "promises to benefit the free people of color by providing them a home, and raising their present degraded state."[80] McKinney proceeded to lay out a forceful indictment of the position of free blacks in American society, laying much blame for their plight on free blacks themselves but not sparing whites from a share. "If there is in the world, a more wretched class of human beings than the free people of colour in this country, I do not know where they are to be found," McKinney asserted. "They have no home, no country, no kindred, no friends." He conceded the truth of the stereotype of free blacks as "lazy and indolent," but he argued that they had "no motives to prompt them to be industrious." If "they acquire property," he explained, "they hold it by the courtesy of every vagabond in the country, and sooner or later are sure to have it filched from them." McKinney argued that free blacks in the slaveholding states, aware of their plight, frequently fled to free states "as fast as they could get away," hoping "to better their condition." But even in the free states, he maintained, "they find no rest for the soles of their feet." Perceived by whites virtually everywhere in the nation as a "curse to any community," free blacks often found themselves barred from entering states, free and slave, and they faced discrimination wherever they lived. Once returned to Africa, McKinney predicted, blacks "will rise from their present condition to respectability" and the United States would have freed itself from one of its "sorest evils."[81]

But even the ACS' focus on the colonization of blacks who were already free failed to soften opposition among most lower South slaveholders. Instead, in 1829, Charlestonian Charles C. Pinckney, nephew of the founder of the same name, renewed the Palmetto State's attack on the ACS, charging that the movement had proven "particularly injurious" to the recently freed slaves and other free blacks it pledged to help. "Sad experience," Pinckney maintained, "had already exposed the absurdity and cruelty of African colonization." Citing the tragic loss of black lives in and around Liberia, Pinckney argued that instead of creating an "asylum for the free blacks of the United States," colonization efforts had landed the unfortunate free people of color in "another charnel house...under the appellation of Liberia."

Accustomed to the "comparatively healthy climate" of the southern states, Pinckney maintained, black colonists in Liberia fell "prey to African diseases as readily as whites." Moreover, Pinckney judged it "a greater probability" that the colonists would "return to the superstitions of their fathers" and revert to "the prevailing creeds of the multitudes around them" than that they would convert native Africans to Christianity. Pinckney believed that blacks, whether free or slave, lived "better in America" than in Liberia.[82]

Pinckney, a moderate by Lowcountry standards, calmly articulated the deep suspicions lower South slaveholders harbored concerning the ACS. Whatever impact colonization societies in Britain and America made in ending the international slave trade, Pinckney conceded, "entitles them to the thanks of humanity," but, the Charlestonian continued, "their present design, hostile to the Southern states, and the permanence of the Union; and particularly injurious to those whose welfare it pretends to promote by rendering them discontented subjects, or suspected traitors" forced South Carolinians "to watch their proceedings with an eye that never slumbers."[83]

The ACS had long recognized South Carolina as the hotbed of outright hostility to colonization. "Doubtless, the opinions [of Pinckney]...prevail to a very considerable extent among the well-educated and enlightened citizens of South Carolina," the *African Repository* lamented, again emphasizing that the society had never endorsed "immediate and universal emancipation." On this point, the ACS would always respect the "master's rightful dominion over the slave." But the society denied Pinckney's charge that colonization had proven a "sad experiment," instead claiming for its efforts "a measure of success, unparalleled in the history of similar enterprises." The society had acquired a "fertile territory" and placed "1400 souls" on it, where they were "contented, happy and prosperous" and at work "exerting a benign influence upon native tribes, and strengthening the foundations of a free and Christian Society." Given the "difficulties encountered by the Society, and its scant resources," the *Repository* "gladly" submitted the ACS' record to "the tribunal of public opinion" for review.[84]

The judgment of that tribunal might not have been favorable, however. Certainly it would not have been favorable in either the black-belt South or abolitionist enclaves in the North. And in 1829 it remained unclear how moderates across the nation perceived the actual operation of the ACS, as opposed to the idea of colonization. Clearly the ACS' view of conditions in Liberia suffered from a degree of wishful thinking, if not willful self-deception. Moreover, the society apparently genuinely believed its own exaggerated estimate that "a large majority of slave-holders, especially in Virginia and Maryland," shared colonization sentiments. However overstated that claim, any chance the colonization movement had for survival depended on its support in the upper South. The ACS needed a measure of southern support to maintain its credibility in the North, and to maintain any public support in the South, the movement needed the support of slaveholding voices speaking with familiar southern accents. And most slaveholders willing to espouse colonization lived in the upper South. By the late 1820s, the future of the embattled American colonization movement appeared to depend on the political influence and persuasive powers of its advocates in the upper South.[85]

Fortunately for the colonization movement, the ACS had a number of defenders in the upper South, and some of those supporters still saw the removal of all free blacks as a stepping-stone toward gradual emancipation.[86] James McDowell, a rising young political star from Rockbridge County in the Valley of Virginia, spoke for many white-belt Virginians when he endorsed colonization as way to "accelerate" the end of slavery through gradual emancipation rather than "await it in the bloody process of St. Domingo."[87] A Princeton-educated prodigy who had privately worked for the colonization cause since 1825, McDowell, unlike many skittish slaveholders, endorsed the society's efforts to convince masters of the desirability of emancipation as well as to persuade free blacks of the virtues of colonization. He even advocated a program of education that would lead to "the progressive improvement in the condition of the slave" as a means of preparing slaves for freedom—and colonization. As "soon as they are prepared for the event," McDowell argued, free blacks removed to Africa could make their own laws and engage in the "sole management of their own affairs," rather than remain in the United States, where they would always be denied political rights on the basis of race.[88]

McDowell, a leader in the democratic reform movement in Virginia, also maintained that gradual emancipation and colonization offered the added benefit of enhancing white opportunity and white independence. Unless colonization succeeded in removing a substantial number of free blacks from the Old Dominion, McDowell continued, blacks, whether slave or free, might soon crowd whites out of Virginia, cheapening labor so much that skilled white artisans and mechanics might be forced to choose between poverty and migration to a free state. The pragmatic McDowell conceded that even a highly successful colonization effort would leave a "residue" of black labor, free and slave, in Virginia, which would continue to influence the state's labor market and complicate his desired transition to free white labor. But if colonization proceeded successfully, McDowell predicted, every family of blacks removed could be replaced by a family of whites, thus whitening Virginia at a gradual but perceptible pace.[89]

McDowell saw colonization as a way of squaring upper South reality with Jeffersonian rhetoric, a way of ending slavery gradually while removing blacks from upper South society. But McDowell joined the ACS in its condemnation of immediate emancipation. "Instantaneous emancipation would be madness not humanity," McDowell reasoned, "worse to its subjects even than to ourselves."[90] As evidence for his argument, McDowell cited the "wretched condition" of most free blacks throughout the United States. He emphasized that the ACS countenanced "no intermeddling with property in slaves" and held that "rights of masters are to remain sacred in the eyes of the Society." Emancipation, he argued, must be "a work of time and care" and one contingent on "a revolution insensibly produced in our habits and opinions."[91]

Other upper South colonizationists, however, reminded upper South slaveholders that this "work of time" needed to be done in a timely fashion. Maryland's Francis Scott Key joined McDowell in the defense of colonization as a moderate alternative to "abolition on the one hand and disunion on the other." Key cautioned southerners eager to protect slavery that other "schemes more alarming to their interests than Colonization" were rapidly gaining strength in the North, and that these plans would, in all likelihood, surge in popularity if the colonization movement faltered. The altruistic Key, a onetime Federalist, had gained prominence as one of the federal district's leading attorneys, frequently arguing cases before the Supreme Court, and for his work in Christian benevolent associations. For twenty-five years, Key served as vice president of the American Sunday School Union and was an active member of the American Bible Society. He was also a founding member of the ACS. His fame as author of "The Star-Spangled Banner" came later. As a champion of colonization, the Marylander argued that consensual colonization offered the nation its best chance for a compromise solution to the related problems of slavery and race. On one hand, Key urged abolitionists to recognize that their plans for general emancipation without colonization only served to deepen already troubling sectional divisions. On the other hand, Key urged slaveholders and other white southerners to recognize that, if nothing else, ACS activity represented a "preventive of greater evils. The slaveholding states, Key argued, should follow a logic very familiar to them and support colonization as a lesser but necessary evil.[92]

The ACS depended heavily on the most influential colonizationist from the upper South, Kentucky's Henry Clay, to rally support for the society not only in the upper South but in the nation as a whole. Certainly no upper South colonizationist had staked more on the cause than Clay. In an effort to seize the political center, Clay consistently touted colonization as the moderate solution to the divisive issue of slavery. In an address to the society's Kentucky chapter, Clay praised the ACS for its ability to resist the growing pull of extremism on the slavery issue. Clay pointed out that from the moment of its founding the ACS had received "taunts and scoffs" from "both extremes—the partizan of perpetual slavery, and the friend of unqualified, immediate and universal emancipation." As a presidential aspirant, Clay issued clarion calls for continued moderation. "If the question were submitted whether there should be either immediate or gradual emancipation of all the slaves in the United States without their removal or colonization," Clay averred, "painful as it is to express this opinion, I have no doubt that it would be unwise to emancipate them." The "aggregate evils" that would follow a general emancipation, Clay maintained, "would be greater than all the evils of slavery, great as they unquestionably are."[93]

But while Clay accepted slavery as a necessary and temporary evil, one justified by the absence of solutions to the "problems" emancipation would create, he rejected any suggestion that slavery should remain permanently as the foundation of southern society. "Must we endure perpetually, all the undoubted mischiefs of a state of slavery as it affects both the free and bond populations of these States?" Clay asked rhetorically. His answer, of course, was an emphatic no. Clay saw a remedy for the evil of slavery in gradual and voluntary emancipation and voluntary colonization. Clay accepted the position that the sole power to emancipate remained with states, but he cited the formation of state auxiliary societies in Kentucky and Virginia as his evidence that moderation could flourish in slaveholding states despite the harsh polemics of South Carolina pamphleteers.[94]

Clay made perhaps the most forceful case against perpetual slavery of any southern politician with national influence (and ambition), and he also challenged the emerging paternalist movement in the lower South without casting aspersions on either the morality or honor of slaveholders. Clay saw the slaveholding South as very much part of the humanitarian movement that swept the nation in the aftermath of the religious awakenings of the early nineteenth century, and, ever the politician, he acknowledged the potential for benevolence among southern slaveholders. Clay conceded that the "humanity" of slaveholders had "prompted them greatly to meliorate the condition of the slaves." But, countering the paternalist depiction of southern slavery as a world of benevolent masters and contented slaves, Clay maintained that, whatever the motives and feelings of masters, the actual relationship between master and slave necessarily remained one of tension and suspicion. As "rational beings like ourselves," Clay observed, slaves knew well "the wrongs which their ancestors suffered at the hands of our ancestors. And the wrongs they continue to endure." Thus slaves and masters inevitably stood as enemies of each other; slaves could be "kept in subjugation only by the superior intelligence and superior power of the predominant race." Paternalism could never define the master-slave relationship because slaves would always resist rather than accept the fundamental degradation caused by their lack of freedom, no matter how well they were treated. In Clay's view, slavery remained an inherently confrontational system sustained by power and force rather than paternalism. Slavery might prove amenable to a demographic reconfiguration, if whites could agree on the details, but it could never be rendered a "shadow" of itself by ideological rationalization or rhetorical legerdemain.[95]

Overall, Clay's remarks did more to accentuate the differences between upper South and lower South over the question of colonization than to narrow them. Clay defined an upper South position of refusing to accept arguments for perpetual slavery while conceding that slavery must be allowed to exist for an unspecified period of time as a necessary and temporary evil. Clay acknowledged the morality of slaveholders but saw paternalism only as a useful technique for the temporary amelioration of the condition of slaves in the short term and not as a defining ideological reconfiguration of slavery that transformed the institution from an essentially confrontational and explosive relationship between unequals into a domestic relationship where only the "shadow" of oppression and coercion remained. At the same time, Clay touted the idea of a demographic reconfiguration of slavery, partially through gradual emancipation and colonization, and argued that the steady reduction of the South's free black population promoted industry and public safety.

Lynchburg's Jesse Burton Harrison had doubtless overstated the case when he asserted that almost "all masters in Virginia assent to the proposition that when the slaves can be liberated without danger to ourselves, and to their own advantage, it ought to be done," yet he nonetheless expressed a sentiment common enough in the upper South to raise deep fears among whites in the lower South by 1830.[96] Certainly by 1830, lower South slaveholders had grown wary of the colonization movement, and most whites in the lower South opposed any plan to eliminate slavery, no matter how gradual and "voluntary" the process. Taken together, the ACS decision to seek federal funding, growing condemnations of slavery from northern states, the South Carolina campaign to equate colonization with abolition, the emerging Jacksonian suspicion of consolidated federal power (when not in Jackson's hands), and the enhanced concern for white security that appeared after the Denmark Vesey scare left the colonization movement fighting for survival in the lower South. Indeed, support for colonization as a means of gradually lessening the region's dependence on slave labor virtually disappeared in the lower South during the 1820s. With the promise of cotton profits driving their calculations, many lower South whites decided their region would flourish with slave labor and suffer without it. Colonization retained a modicum of support in some portions of the lower South, but only as a mechanism for removing the free black population. And in South Carolina at least, many slaveholders remained so convinced that colonization served merely as a harbinger for abolition that they preferred to accept the problems associated with free blacks rather than encourage colonization on any scale.

As the lower South grew ever more interested in protecting slavery, however, the upper South remained interested in plotting slavery's gradual geographic reconfiguration, if not its ultimate demise. The lower South increasingly saw colonization as at best a nuisance and at worst a meaningful threat to slavery. The upper South valued colonization as one means of diminishing slavery's importance, a means they wanted to keep viable until the course of slavery's future, and that of the region, emerged with more definition.

CHAPTER ELEVEN

RUMORS AND INSURRECTION

During the late summer of 1829, as preparations were under way for the long-awaited Virginia constitutional convention, the Old Dominion's colonizationists pondered the wisdom of raising the issue of gradual emancipation and colonization at the convention. Fredericksburg colonizationist William Blackfoord counseled the American Colonization Society to avoid the issue. Eastern Virginia conservatives, Blackfoord reported, already feared that if the white basis for representation was adopted, western Virginians could place a heavy tax on slaveholders or even emancipate slaves outright "if the majority think it proper." Such reasoning had generated "much real & more affected alarm" among eastern slaveholders and left the "public mind" of the state "too much agitated for the cool examination of this question."[1]

Not all Virginia colonizationists shared Blackfoord's caution (or prudence). They prepared memorials urging the convention to support gradual emancipation and colonization. One such memorial came from the valley's Augusta County. It advocated "ultimately the entire abolition of slavery" in Virginia.[2] Such petitions drew the predictable response from easterners. Norfolk's Hugh Grigsby, the youthful confidant of Littleton Tazewell, complained that colonization petitions asked for nothing less than an "intermingling of government" with "religious abolition societies."[3] John Tazewell, Littleton's brother, agreed with Grigsby, blaming the ACS for the "rank and rapid growth of fanaticism" and denouncing the society as a "poison" improperly labeled "philanthropy."[4]

In late August 1829, in a state half excited and half pensive about the upcoming convention, rumors circulated widely about possible slave insurrections in the upper South, further irritating already frayed nerves in the Old Dominion. Benjamin Brand, Richmond colonizationist and editor, surmised that these rumors of impending insurrection had arisen "probably without any sufficient cause." Just three weeks later, however, reports from Raleigh, North Carolina, brought fresh word of "an alarm" concerning a slave insurrection plot, one allegedly "counseled and drilled by one of the most intelligent Free blacks" in the Tar Heel state. Both Brand and the ACS's North Carolina correspondent agreed that insurrection scares would ultimately "quicken" the work of colonization by reminding whites of the dangers of living in a slaveholding society.[5] In the short term, however, such alarms tended to intensify conservative opposition to colonization.

Ironically, if Brand was correct in his judgment that insurrection scares ultimately boosted the colonization cause, then the fate of the movement lay not with its supporters but in the hands of slaves themselves, a conclusion virtually all whites would have been loath to accept. In the late summer of 1829, with the colonization movement at a low ebb, predictions that insurrection scares might revive the movement seemed far-fetched. Just two years later, as slaveholders evaluated the first reports of Nat Turner's rebellion in Southampton and contemplated their response, Brand's vision seemed prophetic.

LATE IN 1829 and early in 1830, the discovery of the circulation of David Walker's *Appeal* among slaves and free blacks across the South prompted considerable consternation in the slaveholding states and spawned rumors of impending revolts. More than fifty years ago, John Hope Franklin observed that Walker's four-part pamphlet "created more fear in the hearts of Southern slaveholders than any insurrection had done in previous years."[6] At the distance of more than a half century from his writing, a review of empirical data suggests that Franklin's assessment was accurate. The Gabriel's Rebellion scare of 1800, Louisiana's German Coast insurrection in 1811, the Camden insurrection scare of 1816 and the Denmark Vesey scare of 1822 in Charleston ignited deep local fears and spawned regionwide murmurs about the dangers of living in a slave society. But none of these insurrections and insurrection scares generated the breadth of alarm that followed the circulation of David Walker's *Appeal* in 1829 and 1830.[7] Moreover, in terms of measures adopted to prevent future plots, each of the insurrections and insurrection scares of the early national period had generated a remarkably localized reaction from whites. The South as a whole had never reacted with any uniformity across state or subregional boundaries to these scares and insurrections, but Walker's appeal, with its emphasis on slaves and free blacks rising to throw off the chains of slavery, struck raw nerves on a broader scale.[8]

David Walker, a free black born in Wilmington, North Carolina, who later migrated to Massachusetts and opened a secondhand clothing store in Boston, first published and distributed his pamphlet in September 1829. In it, he spared no one his scorn. He disparaged Thomas Jefferson as a white supremacist while calling on the nation to honor the literal wording of the Declaration of Independence by applying it to blacks as well as whites. Walker challenged whites to "compare your own language...extracted from the Declaration of Independence, with your cruelties and murders inflicted...on us."[9] Professing prophetic Christianity himself, Walker expressed disdain for those American Christians who accepted and even championed slavery. Showing an awareness of the latest stock in proslavery arguments, Walker mocked white pretenses to paternalism. Whites "chain and handcuff us...drive us around the country like brutes and go into the House of the God of Justice to return him thanks for having aided them in their infernal cruelties inflicted upon us," Walker ridiculed.[10] He despised the colonization movement, declaring that "America is more our country than it is the whites—we have enriched it with our blood and tears," but he warned that the colonizationists "will drive us from our property and homes, which we have earned with our blood."[11] Walker encouraged blacks, including slaves, to seek education and religion (despite the perversion of the latter by the slaveholding interest), but he repeatedly scored blacks for being "too servile." He openly questioned how whites maintained control of slaves in areas where slaves outnumbered whites by margins of two or three to one. In his *Appeal*, Walker predicted that a strong leader would soon appear to lead slaves in rebellion. Once such an insurrection began, Walker advised, slaves should fight to the death; they must "kill or be killed." Walker argued that, if well armed for battle, twelve black men "will kill and put flight to fifty whites."[12] And, Walker warned in a manner reminiscent of Jefferson, a God of justice might also be a God of vengeance. But it was when Walker spoke of Haiti as an example of God's justice that he alarmed whites the most.

The story of Walker's early life is sketchy and uncertain, and documenting it is complicated by the fact that a mythology grew up around Walker once his pamphlet appeared. As is often the case, it has proven almost impossible for historians to nail down the facts of Walker's career with much specificity. Walker was apparently born to a slave father and a free black mother in eastern North Carolina sometime between 1785 and 1796. Peter Hinks' account of Walker's life holds that he was likely trained in the Christian faith at an AME church and that he almost certainly lived in Charleston at the time of the Denmark Vesey insurrection scare. Soon after the scare, Walker made his way north to Boston, and by 1825 he had thrown himself into the active civic life of free black Boston. He attended the May Street AME Church, held an office in the Prince Hall Masonic Lodge, and was active in the Massachusetts General Coloured Association. He was also a correspondent for the antislavery publication *Freedom's Journal*. Immersed by his own choice in the combative world of antislavery activism and political pamphleteering, Walker penned his stunning *Appeal in Four Articles*, with its withering indictment of slavery and slaveholders and its impassioned plea for slave and free black resistance, in 1829. By the end of the next year, Walker's friends urged him to move to Canada for safety, but the determined free black radical refused.[13] In early August 1830, Walker died in his home under what many of his contemporaries considered mysterious circumstances. Rumors abounded that he had been poisoned, but no conclusive evidence has been found that he died from other than natural causes.[14] Walker's method for distributing his pamphlet, which appeared in three editions in 1829 and 1830, also remains at least partially a mystery. Walker apparently sent a number of copies on consignment to individuals he knew to be sympathetic to his cause, but, as Sean Wilentz points out, he apparently smuggled many copies into the South using "friendly sailors and ship's stewards, black and white," who disseminated copies to the blacks they encountered in various southern ports.[15]

Both the rhetoric of the pamphlet and its furtive appearance in scattered locales across the coastal and fall-line South alarmed and mobilized white authorities. Pamphlets were discovered in Georgia, South Carolina, Louisiana, North Carolina, and Virginia, often having found their way into the hands of local free blacks, some of whom turned copies over to local authorities to stay out of trouble. The discovery of these pamphlets prompted the consideration, and in most cases the adoption, of draconian "white security" legislation in almost every southern state where the pamphlets were discovered. Across the region, state legislatures convened, in some instances in secret session, to discuss ways to keep Walker's pamphlet and others like it from stirring unrest and inciting rebellion among slaves.[16]

WALKER'S PAMPHLET APPEARED first in the lower South. Savannah authorities discovered it in that port city in early December 1829 when a white ship steward gave sixty copies to a local black minister for distribution.[17] Savannah authorities immediately took action to block its further circulation. Moreover, the city's mayor, William T. Williams, quickly corresponded with Boston mayor Harrison Gray Otis requesting that Walker be arrested and punished for distributing such "a highly inflammatory work." Sympathetic to Savannah's predicament, Otis took pains to distance himself from the "bad and inflammatory tendency" of the pamphlet, but he explained that Walker had broken "no Massachusetts law" and could not be arrested.[18] Frustrated, Williams informed Georgia governor George Gilmer of the discovery of the incendiary documents and urged prompt state action. Gilmer received the mayor's missive on December 20, 1829, one day before the state's regular legislative session was scheduled to end. The governor immediately called for a special session and urged the legislature to pass a comprehensive set of measures designed to minimize future dangers from efforts to distribute similar pamphlets.[19]

The Georgia legislature responded by enacting a series of laws they deemed "highly essential to the welfare and safety" of the white people of the state. Georgia lawmakers passed their own version of South Carolina's Seaman's Act, banning black seamen from coming ashore in Georgia ports or having any contact with the state's free blacks and slaves. Black seamen who violated the quarantine law and came ashore anyway would be jailed. The legislature also made it punishable by death for slaves and free blacks to assist in the circulation of any written material that might incite "insurrection, conspiracy or resistance" among the state's blacks, slave or free. The state's reinvigorated black code also banned free blacks from entering the state, and added teeth to an existing statute making it illegal to teach slaves or free blacks to read or write. The Georgia legislature also approved a new ban on the importation of slaves. Patterned after a ban on slave imports passed in 1817 but repealed in 1824, the 1830 law regulating the internal slave trade made it illegal for traders to bring slaves into the state for the purpose of sale, though individuals could still bring slaves in for their own use.[20]

Less than six months after the approval of these stern new measures, white Georgians were again alarmed when copies of the third edition of Walker's pamphlet appeared in the state's post offices. Newspapers urged postmasters and other civil authorities to remain "on the alert" for these "insidious publications" and encouraged efforts to "bring to justice the cut-throats who are engaged in this business."[21] And only nine months after the passage of the new black code, Governor George Gilmer worried that Georgia's recent wave of restrictive legislation had not gone far enough. Gilmer believed that the state needed more protection against the "danger of having the slave population in the State disproportionately great to the free." In particular, Gilmer contended that the renewed ban on the importation of slaves, which applied to traders only and not individuals, would produce "no benefit." It had proven impossible to enforce, Gilmer maintained, because "of the impossibility of distinguishing the trader for profit from the citizen buying for his own use." As an alternative, Gilmer proposed making it a crime to introduce slaves into Georgia for either sale or use, and making the penalty for the law's violation the forfeiting of the slaves in question. Gilmer believed that an absolute ban on the importation of slaves could be easily enforced and argued that the "future prosperity of the state" depended on the adoption of such a measure. The legislature, however, refused to pass Gilmer's radical proposal and left the existing partial ban in place.[22] But despite the Georgia legislature's unwillingness to restrict the internal slave trade as completely as Gilmer recommended, the seriousness with which the distribution of incendiary literature was taken in Georgia was well expressed by the Milledgeville *Federal Union* when it maintained that Walker's pamphlet was "different from other political questions." The "right to tamper *with this species of property* belongs to no *man*, and no *body* of men, but their *owners*," the newspaper grimly asserted. "It is the point of delicacy, and the *sanctum sanctorum* of Southern feeling."[23]

South Carolina's experience with Walker's pamphlet paralleled that of Georgia, though the Palmetto State had already fortified itself against precisely these kinds of incendiary imports from the free states with its post-Vesey legislation, including the successive iterations of the Seaman's Act and the formation of the South Carolina Association as an enforcement arm in Charleston. Nevertheless, in late

March 1830, less than three months after the discovery of the pamphlet in Savannah, the Charleston police arrested Edward Smith, a white ship steward working aboard the Boston-registered *Colombo*, for distributing copies of Walker's *Appeal* to blacks in Charleston. Interrogated at the city guardhouse, and confronted with seemingly irrefutable evidence collected by an investigator who overheard Smith's conversations, the accused steward quickly confessed.[24] Smith admitted that he had been asked by a "genteelly dressed coloured man" in Boston to bring the pamphlets to Charleston and distribute them to blacks in the city without letting "any white person know anything about it." Claiming that he felt a sense of obligation to the black Bostonian but admitting no emotional or ideological interest in the pamphlet itself, Smith gave the pamphlets to blacks who boarded his ship to unload cargo. On May 11, a Charleston grand jury indicted Smith, and six days later he was tried and found guilty of "seditious libel." The jury recommended leniency. Smith was fined $1,000 and sentenced to one year in prison.[25]

Nowhere did the appearance of Walker's *Appeal* arouse more concern or trigger more controversy than in Louisiana, where the free colored population numbered almost seventeen thousand, or about 8 percent of the state's total population. In Louisiana, the legislature reacted quickly to New Orleans authorities' arrest of a free black merchant for circulating a copy of Walker's "dangerous and revolutionary pamphlet" in early March 1830.[26] Reversing a long pattern of de facto tolerance of free people of color in the state, the next legislature prohibited the immigration of free people of color into the state and made all recent free black immigrants subject to deportation. Following the pattern it had earlier established in regulating the internal slave trade, the legislature permitted all free blacks who arrived between 1812 and 1825 to remain in the state provided they could prove their good character before a parish judge. The legislature also made it illegal for black seamen to remain in Louisiana ports for more than thirty days.[27]

Yet Louisiana's rash initial reaction to the David Walker pamphlet scare proved difficult to sustain. The new Louisiana law was sporadically enforced at best, and the state's general tolerance of free blacks reemerged once the immediate concern over Walker's pamphlet passed. When a group of respected free blacks in Baton Rouge protested the 1830 law, one local editor assured the city's free blacks that the new law would be enforced only against "suspicious and arrogant" free blacks who were non-natives.[28] Moreover, within a year, Louisiana governor Jacques Dupre judged the 1830 law ineffective and recommended the passage of a more lenient statute that protected the rights of all free blacks who either owned property or were "gainfully employed."[29] But by July 1831, the return of such leniency aroused concern among New Orleans whites, more than three hundred of whom complained as a group that local officials regularly failed to enforce existing laws against free black immigrants. Their petition argued that strict enforcement of the 1830 law would make it easy to prevent additional free blacks from entering Louisiana. Before New Orleans officials could formally react to the petition, however, public attention was diverted from the issue of free black immigration when the first reports of the Nat Turner insurrection reached the state.[30]

In neighboring Mississippi, the circulation of Walker's pamphlet in New Orleans gave unexpected impetus to the state's embryonic colonization movement. Mississippi's free black population numbered just over five hundred in 1830, a number tiny in comparison to Louisiana's seventeen thousand, and arguably this small free black population appeared much easier to control than Louisiana's much larger one. But Mississippi had long considered its free black population, concentrated as it was in the Natchez region and with its proximity to the large Louisiana free black population, as a "problem." Almost half of the state's free blacks lived in Adams County, where Natchez was the major city, and the slave population in southwestern Mississippi outnumbered the white population by at least two to one. In the older cotton-growing areas near Natchez, response to the circulation of Walker's *Appeal* took an ironic turn. Mississippi colonizationists used the pamphlet's appearance to promote their long-standing desire to create a local ACS auxiliary. As early as 1827, a letter to the conservative *Woodville Republican* declared that "the sable African who has acquired his freedom" exerts "a most pernicious influence on the slave population."[31] William Winans, an activist Methodist minister, emerged as the leading colonizationist in Mississippi. He lined up subscribers to the *African Repository* and communicated regularly with Gurley and the ACS about prospects for a chapter in Mississippi.[32]

News of Walker's *Appeal* broadened sympathy for the idea of removing all of the state's free blacks through colonization. In September 1830, the *Natchez*, an organ of Natchez's planter and mercantile elite, urged Mississippians to take "a dispassionate view of the design of the colonization system" and to "prepare" for the creation of a colonization society in Mississippi.[33] Finally, in June 1831, two months before the Turner insurrection, the Mississippi State Colonization Society was organized with the support of many of the state's leading Protestant ministers and prominent planters from the Natchez region. The Natchez planter elite's support for colonization hinged entirely on the notion of ridding the region of its free black population. In a letter written at the time of the Mississippi Colonization Society's founding, prominent Natchez planter John Ker observed that "the free colored people are more injurious to society than the same number of slaves, and their removal must therefore confer a greater benefit."[34] Yet Natchez planters required regular reassurance that the ACS in no way called for a broader emancipation. Just a few months later, news of Nat Turner's insurrection lent new urgency to the Mississippi State Colonization Society's task of removing free blacks from the state.

Walker's pamphlet apparently did not reach his native North Carolina until the publication of its third edition, but, as John Hope Franklin has so carefully documented, reaction to Walker's *Appeal* in North Carolina was swift and severe once it arrived.[35] One newspaper reported the discovery of Walker's pamphlet near Wilmington. Rumors of insurrection soon swirled through that port city and

Fayetteville, a fall-line town up the Cape Fear River from Wilmington, and through other areas in the eastern portion of the state. Those same areas also reported that free blacks were playing a significant role in distributing Walker's pamphlets and were encouraging insurrection. The *North Carolina Journal* recommended that "any resident Black or white" found in possession of the pamphlet "ought to be punished with the extremist severity of the law." The same newspaper traced the scare emanating from the circulation of Walker's *Appeal* to local efforts to teach slaves and free blacks to read and write. "What kind of charity or policy is that which leads some of our white citizens to take pains to instruct colored people how to read," the editors asked. "The thing is wrong. It is demanded by neither by religion or common sense. It is forbidden by every dictate of prudence and self-preservation."[36]

North Carolina governor John Owen's next message to the legislature blamed free blacks for the circulation of Walker's pamphlet and urged corrective measures.[37] During the 1830 session of the North Carolina legislature, a joint legislative committee reviewed the governor's message on slaves and free Negroes and drafted a full-fledged code circumscribing the rights of the state's free blacks in a number of important ways. The state legislature not only made it unlawful to circulate "seditious publications" but also banned the teaching of slaves to read and write, though instruction in elementary mathematics remained legal. Any free person of color who violated this law was subject to fine, imprisonment, or a whipping consisting of "not less than 20 lashes." New legislation also prevented free blacks from "gaming" with slaves and from selling or peddling goods outside of the county in which they resided. North Carolina's efforts to construct a restrictive legal code for free people of color also included a ban on reentry for free blacks who left the state for more than ninety days. Perhaps most notably, the legislature passed a law, similar to South Carolina's controversial Negro Seaman's Act, quarantining black sailors who arrived in North Carolina ports.[38]

Taken as a whole, the North Carolina legislature constructed an additional set of legal restrictions for free blacks that limited their contact with influences from the free states and reduced the legal range of their formal and informal contact with slaves. Within a year, however, the state's press complained that the quarantine law kept vessels out of the port of Wilmington because few white sailors could be found to serve as cooks or stewards. The wharves of Wilmington lacked the vessels needed to carry away goods. Thus the new quarantine law hindered trade and damaged the prosperity of the state. The *Raleigh Register* urged the legislature to reverse its course and admit that "slavery is a curse to the Southern states." It would be better "to think of some means of getting rid of it [slavery], rather than fly in the face of humanity and the Constitution."[39]

In Virginia, rumors of insurrection plots had surfaced in the summer and fall of 1829, even before Walker's pamphlet circulated. As early as August, Benjamin Brand reported that a "panic respecting an insurrection of the slaves has lately prevailed over a greater part of the state."[40] Thus, when the circulation of Walker's pamphlet in

Richmond was discovered in late December 1829 or early January 1830, the public mind was predisposed toward suspicion and panic. During the Christmas season, the mayor of Richmond learned that Walker had mailed thirty copies of his pamphlet to Thomas Lewis, a free black in the Virginia capital. Quick action by the mayor and other local Richmond authorities captured twenty pamphlets but left the remaining ten at large. The mayor promptly forwarded this troubling news to Governor William Branch Giles. Giles urged the sitting legislature to consider taking quick action to limit the circulation of "insurrectionary pamphlets and speeches amongst the people of color."[41] Despite criticism from the Richmond *Constitutional Whig* and the national press for its secrecy, the Virginia legislature met behind closed doors to consider the problem.[42] During that session, bills prescribing severe penalties for the circulation of seditious pamphlets and making it illegal to teach slaves to read or write passed the lower house but were defeated in the state senate. The next year, however, the legislature again pondered revised bills along the same lines. In April 1831, three months before the Turner insurrection terrorized the commonwealth, the legislature decided to ban all classes designed to teach free blacks to read and write "under whatever pretext." Free blacks who attempted to teach others to read were subject to thirty-nine lashes and white teachers were subject to a $50 fine.[43] Soon, however, the Virginia legislature was forced to confront more dramatic questions about slave resistance and white safety.

Domestic security concerns had troubled white southerners since the origins of slavery in the colonial era. These concerns ebbed and flowed with circumstances and events. Gabriel's Rebellion, successful slave revolts in the Caribbean, the Denmark Vesey scare, the Missouri debates, and like events brought such concerns to the fore. High cotton and rice prices, fabulous sugar profits, and occasional upswings in the tobacco market joined ideas such as whitening, colonization, and paternalism to drive them back to the margins. Still, the intensifying efforts of antislavery advocates in the northern states kept the governments of southern states on their toes. But the security furor triggered by the appearance of David Walker's pamphlet was without precedent—at least in some respects. To be sure, it did not produce as much white consternation and reaction as the Gabriel scare did in Virginia or the Vesey plot did in South Carolina, nor did it foster the emergence of new political arguments defending slavery as the Missouri debates did in some parts of the South. But in those portions of the South with large proportions of slaves, it prompted a more truly regional response. It caused additional states to craft South Carolina–style black seaman's laws, prompted fresh drives to either force all free blacks to leave or severely circumscribe their sphere of autonomy, and revived interest in regulation of the internal slave trade. Moreover, with its obvious appeal to literate blacks, free and slave, the pamphlet did much to regionalize a concern that had long been a hobby of South Carolina radicals: the need to limit slave literacy in the interest of white safety regardless of the impact such restrictions might have on the Christian mission to the slaves and the larger paternalist impulse.

The appearance of Walker's *Appeal* had such a dramatic impact for several reasons. Most important, the pamphlet's publication and circulation were not merely local phenomena, as all of the previous insurrections and insurrection scares had been. Instead, the pamphlet appeared all across the region at roughly the same time (varying only on the issue of which edition of the pamphlet found its way into a given area). Widespread alarms and rising ire across much of the coastal South within a year's time magnified the pamphlet's impact. The enhanced threat posed by the possibility that such incendiary literature could be distributed on a regional basis raised fears across the white South. And the capacity for such a pamphlet to send much of the slaveholding South into a state of frenzy did not escape the notice of antislavery activists outside the region. Finally, the pamphlet generated such a reaction because of its own boldness. The pamphlet was a spirited call to resistance. It hit white apologists for slavery with familiar charges of inequality and cruelty, and it also disparaged new white defenses of slavery, mocking paternalism as a false Christianity rather than a new ideology of harmony and uplift. It suggested that a republicanism based on slavery was not republicanism at all but a form of tyranny, and it insisted that colonization was nothing more than a clever ploy to rob slaves and free blacks of their American birthright.

But no image from Walker's pamphlet haunted white southerners, and especially those who lived in black-belt areas, more than the image of a messianic black leader, a black Moses, who Walker predicted would soon emerge to lead slaves to freedom and revenge. Radicals such as Whitemarsh Seabrook had plied their brand of the politics of slavery with such images of terror since the Vesey scare. To read a southern-born free black's prediction of such the appearance of such a leader lent additional credence to such fears. The question of white security no longer seemed acute and episodic. It appeared chronic and inescapable. Few white southerners worried that a slave insurrection could ultimately prevail, but many worried about their personal safety in the hours before the militia arrived. As Tomlinson Fort, a Georgia physician and newspaper editor, observed at the time of the Walker pamphlet scare, "No southern Man doubts our ability to put down any servile war which can happen amongst us.... The Blood it will cost is the only dread."[44] And cost blood it soon did.

LATE IN THE EVENING of August 21, 1831, Nat Turner, a slave who lived and worked on the farm of Joseph Travis, a carriage maker, in the Cross Keys section of Southampton County, Virginia, met with six accomplices to make their final plans for an insurrection that killed more whites than any other slave rebellion in the American South.[45] Turner and his band of followers took at least fifty-five white lives during a seventy-two-hour rampage before their insurrection was broken up by hastily assembled local patrols and militia units. Descriptions of Turner's personal appearance emphasized his rather commonplace size and visage. Approaching his thirty-first birthday at the time of the rebellion, Turner was described as black and "brightly colored," but definitely not mulatto, a man of average height and facial appearance. At five feet six inches and roughly 160 pounds, he was strong but not an imposing figure.[46] Those who knew or met Turner described him as intelligent. His parents had taught him to read and write in childhood, skills Turner embraced eagerly. Turner claimed that he never drank and generally avoided the company of those who did. In his alleged "confession" to a white lawyer, Thomas R. Gray, offered after his capture, Turner attributed his bloody insurgency to a series of moving religious experiences, which began in childhood. These experiences convinced Turner that God had chosen him for a great work, a destiny revealed to him through continued revelations arranged by the Holy Spirit. Ultimately, Turner understood these revelations as instructing him that his destiny lay in leading a slave rebellion.[47]

Southampton was a Southside county in the cotton-growing area located just west of the Dismal Swamp and on the North Carolina border. In 1831, Southampton was a predominantly rural, agricultural county that sported only a few small villages. Even the county seat, Jerusalem, had a population of only 175, and the two nearest population centers of any size, Richmond and Norfolk, lay more than eighty miles away. Blacks outnumbered whites in the county by a margin of three to two. Slaves outnumbered whites 7,756 to 6,573, and Southampton was also home to more than 1,700 free blacks (more than in the entire state of Alabama and three times as many as resided in Mississippi). The county's comparatively large free black population (11 percent of the total population) offered quiet but visible testimony to the decline of the older tobacco economy in the region. Together, slaves and free blacks outnumbered whites in Southampton by almost three thousand.[48]

During the summer of 1831, Turner began refining his plans for rebellion in the comparatively isolated, black-majority county. He recruited a small band of loyal followers, insurgents who were generally both courageous and ruthless but neither as disciplined nor as abstemious as their leader. According to information gathered by the post-insurrection investigation, Turner originally hoped to launch his rebellion on July 4, 1831, but he fell ill, and he interpreted his illness as a sign that the time for revolt was not at hand. So Turner delayed the launch of his revolt, awaiting a more propitious moment to begin. In August, Turner convinced himself that God sent a lunar eclipse as a sign for him to begin his enterprise and fulfill his destiny. He arranged for his six top lieutenants, a group of six slaves, including at least two Methodist "exhorters" (and perhaps as many as four black preachers or exhorters), to meet with him at Cabin Pond near the Travis farm on Sunday evening, August 21. In addition to Turner, the small band included Henry Porter and Will Francis, both identified as Methodist exhorters, Hark Travis (also known as Hark Moore), identified in at least one source as a Baptist lay preacher, Jack Reese, Sam Francis, and Nelson Williams. They agreed to launch their rebellion later that evening, killing whites, seizing weapons, and recruiting new slave followers as they proceeded.[49]

For Nat Turner, rebellion began at home. Turner and his small band of rebels planned to surprise his master's family in the dark of night and kill them in their sleep, and then seize the Travises' arms, ammunition, and horses to further their work in the neighborhood.[50] Both contemporaries and historians have disagreed over whether Turner had a plan beyond unleashing murder and mayhem in his home community and, if he did, exactly what that plan was. It appears certain that Turner and his initial band of six believed that the ranks of their insurgent force would swell as they performed their lethal work on local farms and plantations and neighborhood slaves saw the revolt in action or heard reports of its progress. The number of Turner's followers did increase as his revolt proceeded, but with agonizing slowness. Turner's force probably never exceeded fifty at full strength.[51]

At about three in the morning on Monday, August 22, Turner and his band approached the Travis house under cover of darkness. Turner used a ladder to climb into the house and let the other rebels in. Nat Turner and Will Francis entered the Travises' bedroom, where Nat's first hatchet blow against Joseph Travis glanced off Travis' head, but his accomplice Will quickly killed both Travis and his wife, Sally, with two blows of his axe. Other whites in the artisan household, including the twelve-year-old Putnam Moore, Nat's legal owner, were killed by other rebels. The rebels found a few guns and some ammunition, as well as hoes and axes suitable for use as weapons. Once in possession of firearms from the Travis homestead, Turner drilled his troops briefly (while many of them drank hard cider), and they then proceeded to nearby farms. Shortly after leaving the Travis farmstead, the rebels realized that they had left Travis' infant son, Joseph, alive, so Turner sent Will Francis and Henry Porter back to kill the boy, which they did.[52] Turner's band then killed Salathiel Francis on a nearby farm. Around six o'clock the next morning, Turner's marauders visited their fourth farm, that of Wiley Francis, who was apparently forewarned, and who, along with his slaves, offered a bit of armed resistance before Nat and his followers decided to move on.[53] Over the next several hours, Turner and his men, sometimes divided into at least two groups, attacked at least a half dozen white households and killed more than twenty whites while suffering no casualties themselves. But they had also attracted relatively few additional recruits (the force totaled about sixteen men at this point) and moved toward no particular destination. By ten-thirty that morning, Turner and his followers had reached the farm of Levi Waller, who had offered his home as protection to neighborhood teacher William Crocker and his students (a group that included two of Waller's children) as word of Turner's spree of terror spread locally. Still intent on carrying "terror and devastation wherever we went," Turner and his men found Waller working outside as they approached. To escape death, Waller fled into the woods and hid. At the Waller farm, Turner's rebels committed the worst slaughter of the rebellion, killing not only Mrs. Waller but also the eleven schoolchildren. Crocker, the teacher, made his escape with the help of a young student, who was killed for her efforts.[54] Only after the rebels had engaged in much of this deadly but aimless marauding did Turner turn his messianic face toward Jerusalem, the Southampton county seat and the alleged location of a major cache of weapons stored there for use by the local white militia, some ten miles to the north.[55]

By the time Turner began making his way toward Jerusalem, white authorities were already making preparations to quash the rebellion. Couriers left Jerusalem and Cross Keys early on Monday, August 22, to take news of the slave rebellion and requests for assistance to Norfolk, Petersburg, and especially Richmond. By midday on Monday, local authorities in Southampton were mobilizing in response to reports of Turner's actions, sending out patrols and local militia as quickly as they could muster them. Ultimately, these units, in haphazard but brutal fashion, crushed the rebellion. In Richmond, Governor John Floyd received news of the revolt in Southampton early on Tuesday morning and promptly made preparations to suppress it, but the governor had to await approval from the state's Executive Council, which he could not procure until early afternoon. By late afternoon on the twenty-third, two Richmond militia units were on their way to the scene of the rebellion, where they would join units from counties neighboring Southampton to assist local authorities, but the state militia did not arrive until August 25, well after the rebel force had been dispersed by the local militia and patrols.[56]

Turner and his freedom fighters advanced less than half of the distance to Jerusalem before they encountered their first organized white resistance. Early in the afternoon of August 22, Turner and his men were intercepted by a small band of armed whites, led by influential local attorney William C. Parker, a veteran of the War of 1812, near James Parker's farm, where a portion of Turner's men had ventured to recruit more rebels. Seeing the approaching whites, Turner used his advantage in numbers and charged Parker's patrol, wounding two whites and knocking several others off their horses before the whites retreated to safer ground. For a moment, Turner and his insurgents appeared to have the upper hand. But as Turner and his "troops" pursued the outnumbered white patrol, they quickly encountered a second and larger patrol. In the brief skirmish that followed, four slave rebels were killed and several others were captured by the better-armed whites. Turner led an orderly retreat, taking a number of wounded followers with him.[57] But with only twenty men left in his band, Turner knew his force was both depleted and demoralized. By evening of the rebellion's first full day, the battered remnant of Turner's wandering brigade of rebels, finding bridges and many farmsteads now well guarded, stopped to spend the evening in the woods near the Ridley plantation, which itself was well fortified with local militia. Fearing a white attack while they rested, some of Turner's men woke the sleeping Turner to urge additional movement.[58]

But Turner waited until daybreak and led his remaining force to the house of Dr. Simon Blunt, where Turner hoped to entice many of Blunt's slaves to join the rebellion. As Turner's group crashed Blunt's front gate and attacked, Blunt and his friends fired back, turning the rebel force away in short order.[59] While moving away from Blunt's plantation, Turner and his rebels ran into another white patrol that killed several insurgents, including Turner's best soldier and chief executioner, Will Francis, whose axe had taken at least six white lives. Nat Turner and the other survivors scattered into the woods and hid, waiting to reconvene under the cover of darkness to plan their next move. Ordering his remaining followers to disperse in search of reinforcements from nearby farms and plantations, Turner headed back to Cabin Pond, hoping against all odds for a rendezvous with other rebels later on. Alone at Cabin Pond, Turner soon became aware that the roads and woods were full of armed whites. By morning, he used a dull saber to dig a cave under some fence rails and hid there, no longer so much the leader of a dangerous rebellion as a lonely fugitive from white justice.[60]

By Thursday, August 25, nearly three thousand white troops had arrived in Southampton. That same day, Brigadier General Richard Eppes, one of the state militia leaders sent to the area to quell the rebellion, reported to Governor Floyd that adequate troops and supplies were on hand to stop the insurrection. Indeed, by the time the state militia arrived in force, they served more to restrain local whites from committing further atrocities against those suspected of aiding Turner than in putting down the insurrection. On August 28, Eppes reported with confidence that the time of danger had passed. Turner remained at large, but all of his followers were either executed or imprisoned. Eppes assured Floyd that there was no convincing evidence of a widespread plan for slave rebellion crossing either county or state lines. Despite frequent reports to the contrary, slaves in neighboring counties remained quiet.[61]

But even with the Turner insurrection apparently quelled, the bloodshed had only just begun in Southampton. Before the additional militia units from other counties mobilized by Governor Floyd could arrive, a frenzied white reign of terror against blacks began. Within the first six days after the rebellion broke out, whites killed at least thirty-nine blacks, many of whom had little or no connection to the insurrection. In Cross Keys, a Southampton town teeming with more than fifteen hundred refugees from the surrounding countryside, a militia unit arriving from Hertford County, North Carolina, found whites showing a "strong disposition" to take revenge on blacks.[62] Nathaniel Francis tied a slave who had tried to kill his wife during the rebellion to a tree in Cross Keys and shot her. But then Francis could do nothing but watch while a mob murdered the slave who had saved his wife's life.[63] A Southampton militia unit shot a slave they encountered near Waller's farm, the scene of the insurrection's greatest slaughter, without knowing whether the slave was involved in the rebellion. In all, seven slaves were killed near the Waller farm by white militiamen, and the "heads of these negroes were stuck up on poles, a warning to all who should undertake a similar plot."[64] Also at Cross Keys, whites brutalized Henry Porter, a leading Turner lieutenant, by cutting his hamstrings, cutting off his nose and ears, and burning him with hot irons. After this torture, whites stuck Porter "like a hog," cut his head off, and spiked it to a whipping post as "a spectacle to other negroes."[65]

In a series of reports from Southampton, John Hampden Pleasants, editor of the Richmond *Constitutional Whig*, openly deplored the conduct of whites. While Pleasants understood that local whites were, "naturally enough, wound up to a high pitch of rage," he nonetheless denounced the indiscriminate killing of prisoners that he witnessed. Some of the scenes are "hardly inferior in barbarity to the atrocities of the insurgents," Pleasants reported, "and it is to be feared that a spirit of vindictive ferocity has been excited, which may be productive of further outrage, and prove discreditable to the country." The "slaughter of many blacks, without trial and under circumstances of great barbarity," Pleasants admitted with dismay, threatened to disgrace Virginia. He estimated that twenty-five to forty slaves, and possibly even more, had been executed. Only the presence of troops from Richmond and Norfolk prevented such "retaliation from being carried much further."[66]

Not all outside militia units acted with restraint, either. Norfolk militia men took heads from murdered slaves back to the port city as evidence of their triumph. Other heads of summarily executed slaves were placed atop posts at crossroads along the way. Richmond troops allegedly treated captured slave rebels "like so many wolves," shooting them down in the road. One northern visitor described seeing slaves "with the flesh of their cheeks cut off" and their jaws broken. As late as September 2, a full ten days after the insurrection had collapsed, a militia unit brutalized a slave by cutting his ears off, rubbing sand in the wounds, tying the victim to a horse, and turning the horse loose in the woods. As one troop of Richmond militia approached the scene of the insurrection, they reportedly asked a slave if they had indeed reached Southampton. When told they had, they promptly killed the slave on the spot.[67] Ultimately outside authorities assisted the cooler heads among local leaders in curtailing the violence, more by pointing out that the retributive bloodbath was killing important witnesses before authorities investigating the insurrection had a full sense of its scope and direction than by appealing to the locals' sense of humanity. Historian Thomas Parramore, who has studied the insurrection as carefully as anyone, estimated that "in the ten days of rebellion and retribution, at least 100 blacks, and possibly several times that figure, were killed, though no more than a handful had taken any part in the uprising."[68]

With Turner in hiding, fifty or more slaves and free blacks were held in four cells of the Jerusalem jail in Southampton County. Just nine days after the insurrection began, the accused rebels who were in custody were assigned counsel and given trials of sorts in a hothouse postinsurrection atmosphere that virtually ensured their conviction. Nevertheless, the testimony of the arrested slave rebels given at the Southampton trials disturbed whites. The slaves on trial referred to Turner as "General Nat" and their testimony suggested that some slaves in other counties knew of their plan even if they were not included in it. Moreover, these slaves on trial for their lives showed little remorse, declaring that they should have killed all the whites "long ago." Over a period of several weeks, eighteen blacks were convicted and hanged; fourteen were convicted and transported out of state. More than thirty prisoners were either acquitted or freed without trial.[69] But even as his followers faced capture and brutal punishment, Nat Turner remained at large. And as long as Turner eluded authorities, area whites remained on edge.

To complicate matters further, on the third day of Turner's rebellion evidence had surfaced from a slave informant suggesting that the insurrection conspiracy may have extended into neighboring Sussex County.[70] Ultimately, fifteen slaves accused by the informant stood trial in Southampton and Sussex counties. The state's star witness in these trials was a young female slave, described in the official record as a "young slave girl," probably somewhere between the ages of twelve and fifteen, named Beck. Beck was a fledgling domestic servant on a plantation that straddled the border between Sussex and Southampton counties. As soon as word of Turner's insurrection reached her household, the young Beck came forward, claiming that she "had heard the thing spoken of by a number of negroes for eighteen months, but she did not believe they were in earnest." But when news of Turner's insurgency reached her ears, she quickly informed her mistress.[71]

Panicked authorities arrested fifteen slaves, eight from Sussex and seven from Southampton, in some cases on little more than Beck's word. In multiple trials in each county, Beck appeared as the chief witness for the prosecution. She testified that at the May 1831 meeting at the Raccoon Swamp Baptist Church, she heard two slaves tell a "party of negroes," numbering at least six, that they were "going to join the black people to murder the white people." Another slave agreed to join, because "God damn the white people, they had been reigning long enough." Beck also alleged that two other slaves present warned her that "if she told the white people about it," they would "shoot her down like a squirrel and would not bury her," and that later other slaves in the group repeated the warning. Beck also testified that roughly two months later, "on the Saturday night and the Monday night of the last Southampton election," she had heard "conversation among the negroes about rising" and heard the plot "spoken of more boldly."[72] Throughout the trials, defense lawyers aggressively attacked Beck's credibility during cross-examination, and her testimony initially held up better in Sussex, where it typically was backed up by a character reference from her master, than in Southampton, where a number of defendants she testified against were acquitted.[73] William C. Parker, who later represented Turner, reported to the *Richmond Enquirer* that no testimony beyond Beck's showed any evidence of a conspiracy, but "if her tale was true," Parker worried, "the plot was more extensive than we had previously believed."[74]

Clearly, for weeks after white authorities quelled the insurrection, many questions about the scope and intent of the insurrection troubled whites. Even with the rebellion suppressed and more than thirty rebels either executed or exiled, fear maintained its grip on many local whites. Security precautions remained the order of the day in eastern Virginia. The city of Norfolk had as many as four hundred men on guard duty each night; in Southampton, women and children continued to gather in the village of Jerusalem while the men of the households remained on patrol.[75] Local militia leaders continued to ask the governor for additional troops, arguing that the mere presence of a local black majority rendered the whole Southside region vulnerable to slave revolt. Three counties west of Southampton, Mecklenburg's William Goode claimed that the situation remained "critical if not perilous" in a county that was over three-fifths black.[76] From Pittsylvania, a county west of Southampton but also on the border with North Carolina, Benjamin Cabell reported that rumors of a widespread insurrection in northeastern North Carolina created the impression that "the Southampton insurrection was a branch only to a plan long since laid," a plot that carried "extensive ramifications."[77] In another nearby county, white leaders reported that slaves there had been "apprised of the insurrection which developed in Southampton" but that the actual rebellion "commenced too soon by eight days," frustrating any concert of action with slaves in other areas.[78]

Moreover, Turner's bloody rampage across a small swath of Virginia's lower Tidewater spread fear, rumor, recrimination, and just plain horror across the state. From the safe distance of the Piedmont, Jane Randolph, wife of Thomas Jefferson Randolph, fretted that her "most torturing imagination had never conjured up anything so terrific as the unpitying and horrible slaughter."[79] Other white Virginians also recoiled in horror. Richmond area slaveholder Robert Waller complained that he could no longer even look as slaves without conjuring mental images of "treachery, murder, and bloodshed."[80] Privately, some white Virginians shuddered at the terror of the white retribution as well as the black insurrection. When prominent Richmond lawyer John Rutherford bemoaned the "shocking butcheries" in Southampton, he was referring to the white retribution as well as Turner's carnage.[81] And even Waller feared that an "involuntary" white lust for revenge would lead to a "scheme of indiscriminate Butchery" against "innocent and harmless slaves and free blacks."[82] George Mumford admitted that in light of "the late melancholy insurrection," many Virginians would doubtless "be infinitely happier without [slaves]," and he vowed that "if any scheme could be devised for their entire emancipation & for freeing the country of their presence I for one would cheerfully part with all I possess without a murmur."[83]

White questions about the nature and scope of the insurrection questions could never be answered with certainty, but the best evidence concerning many of them remained in the mind of Nat Turner, who was still at large. Turner had been identified in press reports as the leader of the insurrection as early as August 27, when John Pleasants referred to him as "Nat—a preacher and prophet" among slaves. After identifying Turner as the leader, Pleasants concluded, based on the interrogation of some of his followers, that he "had no ulterior purpose" but "was stimulated exclusively by fanatical revenge."[84] Despite an intense manhunt, Turner eluded capture for over two months, hiding first on the outer reaches of the Travis farm and later on the Nathaniel Francis farm, both of which he knew well. Finally on

October 30, 1831, a local nonslaveholder surprised Turner in his ad hoc hiding place. Armed with a gun, Benjamin Phipps took Turner, who, carrying only the dull sword he had used as a club and shovel, surrendered without a fight.[85]

Once Turner was finally in custody in Jerusalem, whites eagerly sought the rebel leader's own account of motives and events. Turner, doubtless aware of the importance attached to his explanations, discussed his revolt with local whites for the first time on October 31, when Southampton magistrates James Trezvant and James W. Parker questioned him at length about his actions. A small audience of whites and at least one free black watched Turner's interrogation.[86] One observer felt that Nat's answers revealed "much schrewdness [*sic*] of intellect" as well as an absence of "prevarication." Turner told his questioners that he had been under the "the influence of fanaticism" and felt "destined by a Superior power to perform the part which he did." He even admitted that his actions had been "wrong."[87] Trezvant and Parker appeared to take Turner at his word. But other white interrogators felt differently. Isaac Pipkin of Murfreesboro, a small town just across the North Carolina border, found Nat's answers evasive. Pipkin wrote that Turner spoke of "the signs he saw, the spirits he conversed with, of his prayers, fastings and watchings, and of his supernatural powers, in curing diseases." But Pipkin complained that he "could not get him [Turner] to explain in a manner at all satisfactory" the connections between the signs and the insurrection.[88]

On November 1, with the court's permission, Nat discussed his plans for the conspiracy with a local white lawyer, Thomas Ruffin Gray, who later presented them in pamphlet form as Turner's "confessions." Historian Thomas Parramore has argued that Nat "recognized at once that the young attorney was a God-sent medium for his own purposes" and that Gray "may have fulfilled Nat's primary aim for inciting the revolt," that of telling the story of the courageous but oppressed chattel slave to an increasingly sympathetic world.[89] Gray, the son of a once wealthy local planter and horse breeder, had squandered his portion of the family fortune and was effectively disinherited by his father. Forced to practice law in Southampton County for a living, Gray was thirty-one at the time of the insurrection and had begun a law practice in Jerusalem only a year earlier. When news of Turner's rebellion arrived by messenger, he rode into the countryside with one of the first bands of militia that rallied to suppress the rebellion, and he played an active role in the investigations and trials that followed. The evidence suggests that Gray hoped to write a popular account of the insurrection in an effort to recoup a measure of the fortune he had lost.

Gray interviewed Nat for three days. He had probably attended the earlier interrogation of Turner by Trezvant and Parker, and he had access to the September trial records as well as the testimony of surviving white witnesses to prepare him for his interview with the rebel leader.[90] In addition, the Southampton County court had designated Gray as defense counsel for three of the most important defendants (Sam Francis, Jack Reese, and Moses Moore), each of whom had provided valuable information to the prosecution during the trial process. Evidence gained from his "representation" of these clients certainly helped Gray prepare for his sessions with Turner, and probably gave him access to some information that even Turner did not have.[91]

Gray was also the probable author of the most comprehensive account of the insurrection written before the appearance of the *Confessions*, a lengthy piece that appeared in the Richmond *Constitutional Whig* early in the fall. In this account, Gray had constructed a remarkably accurate narrative of Turner's rebellion before he had talked with Turner. As published by the *Constitutional Whig*, Gray's first account anticipated Turner's *Confessions* in its detailed account of the insurrection and provided an early clue that Gray was systematically compiling evidence for a full account of the rebellion. In the newspaper account, Gray drew on the testimony at the trials, other information circulated in Jerusalem during the investigation, his own experience in the field at the time of the insurrection, and evidence regarding Turner he acquired from people in the community. The account revealed that Gray had come to understand Turner as a religious fanatic well before meeting him. Armed only with accounts of other witnesses, Gray described Turner as a man who had "acquired the reputation of a prophet" in his home neighborhood. The young attorney believed that Turner had pondered the idea of insurrection for nearly three years (based on writings Turner's wife turned over to authorities after a whipping) before deciding to act.[92]

In his later interview with Turner, Gray learned that the accused rebel leader apparently had planned a surprise attack, which would proceed speedily from house to house, spreading "additional horror," and drawing new recruits to the insurgency in significant numbers. Gray explained that Turner's aim was one of "freeing himself and [his] race from bondage." Turner's ultimate objective was "freedom," Gray claimed, and "indiscriminate carnage was his watchword." Gray's account estimated that Turner's insurgency attracted no more than forty active supporters at its peak, and the attorney remained skeptical that any concert of action existed among the larger community of slaves despite continued rumors to that effect. Gray reported that, despite his best efforts to catch Turner in a lie or trip him up over an inconsistency, his cross-examination revealed no discrepancies in Turner's testimony. Gray accepted Turner's insistence that he knew of no larger insurrection plot.[93]

Gray concluded that Turner either was "a complete fanatic" or "plays his part most admirably." He conceded that Turner was a man with "an uncommon share of intelligence, with a mind capable of attaining any thing," but Gray also insisted that Turner's mind was "warped and perverted by the influence of early impressions." Those early impressions, in Gray's view, had chiefly to do with religion. In fact, the *Confessions* presented Turner as a religious fanatic who believed God had called him to a divine mission. Turner began his interview with Gray by explaining that his mother, who was very religious, and his father had told him he was "intended for some greater purpose." That impression was enhanced by his master, also a religious man, and the many church visitors he saw at his master's house or at evening prayers during his childhood, who, noting his unusual intelligence, suggested that his mind should be "directed to religion" rather than to the usual occupations of a slave. Gray conceded Turner's intelligence, and even his charisma, but concluded that the sincerity of his religious views readily hardened into fanaticism. Gray also found the "calm, deliberate composure" with which Turner discussed his violent and deadly rebellion and "his daring to raise his manacled hands to heaven with a spirit soaring above the attributes of man" as proof that the fanatic was in fact a horrible threat to slavery. "I looked on him," Gray confessed, "and my blood curdled in my veins."[94]

In broad terms at least, Turner affirmed the truth of his "confessions" at his "trial."[95] A defiant and unrepentant Turner compared his impending execution with Christ's death on the cross at Calvary. On November 11, 1831, Turner was hung in Jerusalem before a large crowd. According to observers, Turner faced execution with perfect calm, scarcely moving a muscle.[96] Turner's sense of divine mission closely paralleled the emergence of a charismatic black Moses to lead slaves in rebellion outlined in David Walker's pamphlet.[97] But while Turner's ability to avoid capture for two months and face death calmly and without apology drew a grudging respect from white authorities who encountered him in the aftermath of the rebellion, the general emphasis of reports on Turner ran opposite of those publicized nine years earlier during the Denmark Vesey scare. For the most part, Vesey was portrayed as a man of unusual ability and standing, one who had long displayed a measure of defiance of the social norms of early-nineteenth-century Charleston. Whites generally portrayed Turner as distressingly ordinary—a man of ordinary size and appearance, yet considerable intelligence and self-discipline, but no apparent penchant for radical leadership before his bloody rebellion began. Whites portrayed Vesey as cold and calculating; Turner emerged in white accounts as an impulsive visionary.

The local investigation of Turner led to the conclusion that the original plot went no further than Turner and his six initial slave allies, who then recruited additional followers as their marauding proceeded. Testimony suggested some knowledge of the plan in other counties but confirmed that no general slave uprising was planned. Moreover, even Turner appeared to have no plan beyond killing whites and proceeding to Jerusalem to seize additional arms. There were no accounts of networks of communication running far across the countryside, no reliance on possible assistance from the Caribbean, no suggestion of a large plan to link up with other forces. Gray's presentation of Turner's account reinforced the emerging position of local authorities: that Turner's rebellion, bloody and deadly as it was, remained a limited local conspiracy.[98] Ironically, Gray used the harshness of slavery as the linchpin of his argument. The young Southampton lawyer maintained that people "so debased and degraded" as Virginia slaves could never manage "to concert effective measures" for a widespread war against slavery. He supported his contention by noting that the rebels lacked not only guns but any systematic plan of attack other than using the element of surprise in the initial stages of the revolt.[99]

Gray's account and the conclusions of local authorities were doubtless intended to calm rather than heighten local fears. They told their white audiences what they needed to hear. In the upper South, almost any other understanding of the insurrection—any interpretation that suggested a broader conspiracy among slaves in southeastern Virginia and northeastern North Carolina, any official suggestion that the rebellion quietly commanded the support of most slaves in the region or that the revolt was led by a typical slave rather than a religious prophet or charismatic fanatic—would have raised far greater concerns about the safety and stability of a slaveholding society. Thus the strongest defenders of slavery had the most to gain from convincing the white public that Turner's insurrection was entirely local in nature and originated in the fanaticism of a charismatic leader.

As Michael Wayne has pointed out in a different context, whites, and especially slaveholders, often worked hard to control the way slave behavior was presented and explained to the larger public.[100] Slaveholders' efforts to control the presentation of slavery certainly involved sending messages to the slaves about the futility of violent action, but the presentation was also aimed at the white community. This was especially true in places where significant opposition to or doubts about slavery as an institution existed, or where fears about white safety ran deep. In the Virginia of the early 1830s, the idea of the gradual emancipation and subsequent colonization of a large number of blacks still commanded support among at least a significant portion of the state's white population, and eastern Virginia slaveholders, as their behavior at the state's recent constitutional convention amply demonstrated, feared that white-majority regions of the Old Dominion lacked the resolve needed to sustain slavery in the face of pervasive danger.[101]

The contrast between the interpretations developed on the scene by local authorities in the Vesey scare and in the Turner insurrection illustrates the significance and possible influence of the presentation issue. In Charleston during the Vesey scare, in which not a drop of white blood was shed by slave rebels, local white authorities emphasized the breadth of the plot and the wide-ranging plans the rebel leadership had for laying waste to Charleston and freeing large numbers of Lowcountry slaves. They included a possible escape to Haiti and even intervention by black troops from the West Indies as part of the alleged insurrection plan. In Southampton, after a bloody rebellion that killed over fifty whites, local authorities eventually dismissed the possibility of a larger plot and portrayed Turner as a dreamer incapable of crafting a comprehensive plan for black freedom. Clearly one explanation for the disparate interpretations offered by local authorities from the two locales is simply that Southampton authorities needed to calm local fears of a community shocked by the known atrocities perpetrated by Turner and his fellow insurgents. In Charleston during the Vesey scare, white authorities wanted to impress on the local population the nature and scope of the danger averted, if for no other reason than to ensure future vigilance.

But another plausible interpretation, one based on the political dynamics of the two states at the time of the two crises, also suggests itself. In South Carolina in

1822, the planter and civic elite in the heavily slave Lowcountry was fitfully coming to terms with both the northern criticism of slavery and the indigenous paternalist insurgency. The latter's argument for more benign treatment of slaves and ministering to their spiritual needs appeared to many members of the Lowcountry elite as an ideology too lenient to control so vast a slave population. Enlarging the threat posed by Vesey allowed the Lowcountry elite to disband the thriving AME church in Charleston and launch a full-fledged, if ultimately unsuccessful, counterattack against the paternalist insurgency. And the local elite's interpretation of Vesey prepared the state for a politics centered on the defense of slavery, reinforcing tendencies toward consensus that were latent in the Palmetto State's body politic but which were easily mobilized by perceived threats against slavery. The political dynamics of Nat Turner's Virginia were quite different. The Old Dominion was just emerging from a difficult and divisive state constitutional convention in which eastern Virginians had done their best to stymie democratic reform proposals advanced by western egalitarians. The efforts of eastern conservatives to retain as much power as possible in Virginia politics was motivated to a significant degree by their desire to keep slavery beyond the reach of westerners, who, in addition to having the power to impose a tax and a desire to whiten the state, were less committed to the protection of the peculiar institution over the long term. The Southside slaveholders' motive was to portray the Turner rebellion, awful as it undeniably was, as narrow in scope and ambition and easily put down once discovered. Otherwise, they feared, the rebellion would give new impetus to the forces of gradual emancipation and colonization.

But the respective white investigations of the two incidents did identify a common source of inspiration for the two conspiracies: the religious convictions and practices of the leaders of the two plots. Vesey and other purported leaders in the 1822 Charleston plot had been identified by some informants as leaders and active members in the city's controversial African church. White authorities in Charleston certainly credited those charges. White renderings of Turner's motives, based largely on his alleged confession, centered on religious motivation: a sense of divine calling, perhaps even by direct revelation from God. Moreover, just as the literacy of slave and free black leaders of Vesey's alleged plot had loomed large in white accounts of the plot, all sources indicated that Turner was adept at reading and writing, and Turner himself spoke with pride about the felicity with which he had learned to read. Slave religion and slave literacy emerged as issues in both instances.[102]

In fact, in Virginia in 1831, white observers complained bitterly about black religious activity and black literacy and linked the two directly to slave unrest. Just a few days after the Turner rebellion had been defeated, an anonymous group of Richmond citizens warned state authorities that "a numerous meeting of the blacks from this place & the surrounding country" was being held outside the city for the alleged purpose "of Religious worship." The petitioners questioned the "propriety" of "countenancing" such a gathering in light of recent events.[103] From near Norfolk, an anxious Mary Lee also claimed that slaves used their "religious assemblies" to plan the bloody rebellions.[104] And N. E. Sutton, writing from a county near Southampton, claimed that slave informants in his area reported that "large meetings of slaves were held in his neighborhood for the purpose of concerting and effecting the best course...to get clear of the whites," and suggested that such large meetings of slaves could occur only under the disguise of religion. Sutton demanded state legislation requiring any preacher to provide "sufficient evidence that he has been regularly ordained and of his moral worth and standing" before being allowed to preach to slaves in Virginia. Slaves, Sutton insisted, "should not be permitted to preach at any time."[105]

Nor did the religious connection elude Governor John Floyd, who hailed from west of the Blue Ridge and disliked slavery. Despite the conclusions drawn by most local authorities in Southampton, Floyd remained convinced that the scope of the rebellion was wider than assumed. In fact, believing that the rebellion had its origin in the cultivation of religion among slaves, Floyd convinced himself that "every black preacher in the whole country east of the Blue Ridge" knew Turner's secret in advance and was in on the plot. Allowing blacks to assemble in large numbers for religious purposes, Floyd complained, led to black preachers telling "the blacks God was no respecter of persons—the black was as good as the white—that all men were born free and equal—that they cannot serve two masters." Floyd believed that "the preachers" were "very assiduous in operating on our [slave] population—day and night—they were at work." Thus "religion became, and is, the fashion of the times." As Christianity became all the rage, Floyd contended, "our females and most of the respectable were Persuaded that it was piety to teach negros to read and to write—to the end that they might read Scriptures." Over time, many women "became tutoresses in Sunday schools and pious distributors of tracts." Also over time, white vigilance slackened and "large assemblages of negroes were suffered to take place for religious purposes." Once such gatherings became common, "then commenced the efforts of the black preachers." This all occurred, Floyd believed, while whites rested in "apathetic security" until rudely awakened when rebellion erupted in Southampton.[106]

Floyd even went to the trouble of collecting tracts and pamphlets that he believed "were circulated, read and commented upon" at black religious meetings. His collection included issues of Garrison's *Liberator*, minutes of the annual meeting of the Philadelphia Convention of Free People of Color, copies of *The Genius of Universal Emancipation* by Benjamin Lundy, radical northern newspapers, and David Walker's *Appeal*.[107] "I feel fully justified to myself," Floyd concluded, "in believing the Northern incendiaries, tracts, Sunday schools, religion and reading and writing has accomplished this end," that is, the slave insurrection. Floyd's opinion about the influence of slave religion and literacy on the prospects for slave rebellion doubtless met the approval of the recipient of his account, the incumbent governor of South Carolina—arch-nullifier, lead Vesey investigator, and longtime critic of slave religion and literacy, James Hamilton. Among other bold new security measures, Floyd told Hamilton that in his next message to the legislature he would seek legislation to "prohibit all negroes from preaching."[108] Much like Hamilton and the Vesey court nearly a decade earlier, Floyd indicted the Christian mission to the slaves, including the slave literacy it encouraged and the paternalist leniency it nurtured, as the causes of Nat Turner's rebellion. Floyd even placed much of the blame for the bloodshed on white Virginians who had embraced the logic of the Christian mission to the slaves, helped teach slaves to read and write, tolerated large religious gatherings of slaves, and failed to keep a watchful for eye for slave unrest.

Nat Turner's rebellion proved especially difficult for whites to explain because it constituted a domestic attack on domestic slavery. Unlike the Vesey scare, which threatened the destruction and takeover of civil authority in a major southern city, Turner's rebellion began, and ended as well, as an attack on isolated rural households where most victims were known to the slave rebels.[109] The domestic danger signaled by Turner's rebellion did not escape white Virginians. Referring chiefly to Virginia's Southside region, *Constitutional Whig* editor John Pleasants predicted early on that "it will be long before the people of this country can get over the horror of the late scenes, or feel safe in their homes. Many will probably emigrate."[110] Six weeks later, Pleasants' journalistic and political rival Thomas Ritchie, the influential editor of the *Richmond Enquirer*, offered a balanced preliminary assessment of the insurrection's impact. Ritchie explained that Turner's rebellion "has given rise to many fears among the weak, and to much reflection among the wise." Sorting through the information at his disposal in the fall of 1831, Ritchie persuaded himself (as Pleasants had earlier) that "there was no general concert among the blacks of the lower country." But the editor also reported privately that "being continually exposed to such an outbreaking has caused our best thinking politicians to turn their attention to the means of preventing insurrections."[111] Robert Pollard, a friend of William Rives, reflected poignantly on the fears of Virginia's slaveholders. "Every family that have slaves are in the power of those slaves," Pollard wrote; "they sleep in our houses—they in this way have the power of cutting our throats or knocking our brains out while we sleep."[112] Whites in the state's heavily white Valley region, far from Southampton County, also voiced fears of attacks by domestic slaves. Writing from Lexington, constituents told colonization champion and state representative James McDowell, "We feel here that [the elimination of slavery] is a matter of life and death" and "are ready to a man to go to any length in the bounds of prudence and reason to effect a relief from this overwhelming evil."[113] McDowell, long an outspoken supporter of gradual emancipation, judged the Turner uprising a "bloody and shocking tragedy" and conceded that virtually all Virginians harbored "the suspicion that there was a Nat Turner lurking in every family—that the same horrible event could be acted over and over again and at any place."[114]

If nothing else, these ominous musings about the possible treachery of any Virginia slave in the home of any slaveholding family personalized the risk of owning slaves. Within days of the rebellion's bloody beginning, the Virginia militia had routed the Turner insurrection and delivered violent retribution so savage that it discomfited some Virginia slaveholders, who thought the white authorities were responsible for as much terror as the black insurgents. The insurrection never reached more than twenty miles away from its point of origin. Within two months, white authorities had captured the rebellion's resourceful leader. But most white Virginians and other white southerners found only cold comfort in the ultimate suppression of the Turner rebellion because they could not be sure that they would not be among the unlucky early victims whose throats were slashed or heads were bashed as they slept. In Southampton, more than fifty white men, women, and children lay dead as part of the cost of maintaining slavery. A decade or so earlier, many whites in the upper South had found "eternal vigilance" too a high a price to pay for slavery. Nat Turner's rebellion had upped the ante to include human sacrifice. Turner's brief rampage gave whites much more to think about than ever before.

DOUBTS AND DISILLUSIONMENT continued to fester in the Southampton and Sussex areas for many months after Nat Turner's execution. In the face of Beck's accusations, whites at the Raccoon Swamp Baptist Church admitted their suspicion of all black members and launched an inquiry into the "general course" pursued by black members as "professors of Godlyness" at "the time of Horrid Insurrection." The inquiry continued well into the spring of 1832. At the end of May, the Raccoon Swamp Church reported to the Portsmouth Baptist Association that its congregation, still shaken by allegations that some of its black members had supported the insurrection, and troubled that its church grounds may have been used to further the conspiracy, had undertaken a yearlong process of checking on its roll of black members. Despite its year of self-examination, the church still declared itself "in a very dissatisfied condition on account of their colored members." In fact, white church members complained of "an entire loss of confidence" in the "religious feeling" of the church's black communicants.[115]

Other churches in the Portsmouth Association, which included both Sussex and Southampton as well as other southeastern Virginia counties, complained of similar problems. The Mill Swamp Baptist church sought "advice" from the association because since "the insurrection in Southampton, which occurred in their neighborhood, their colored members had become exceedingly refractory and ungovernable, refusing, in many instances, the rule of the Church and disobeying the injunctions of the Gospel." According to Portsmouth Association records, "several" other churches reported "a similar state of affairs among them." The association appointed a committee to examine the situation and report back. The committee advised all churches, and especially Mill Swamp, to give all black members "instruction in relation to Church Government and their duty to their owners"; "in case they refuse the instruction and government of the Church," the association advised, they should be expelled. Additionally, the Portsmouth Association formally advised all churches to "refuse license to coloured persons to preach, and to interdict their holding meetings" as part of the white effort to control black Christians. The association voted unanimously to accept the special committee's report and published it as the official "advice of the Association."[116]

The reaction of white evangelicals in the Southside area to the Turner insurrection and news that religious inspiration and church fellowship may have played a large role in the rebellion's planning and organization was predictable. Whites in Southside Virginia, like whites in other communities where insurrections or insurrection scares occurred, simply lost confidence in the Christian professions of their slave and free black brothers and sisters in the face of abundant evidence suggesting that many black Christians were willing to rise in bloody revolt against whites. Under such circumstances, frightened and alienated whites doubtless responded in ways that infringed on the customary religious autonomy of black members in an effort to reassert white control, not merely of the churches but of the religious message alive in the community generally. Whites restricted black participation in and leadership of worship, refused to license black preachers, and monitored black religious observances in intrusive fashion.

What the otherwise revealing church records leave a mystery, however, are the reasons behind the alleged black recalcitrance and unruliness in Southside Virginia churches in 1832. It is possible, though perhaps unlikely given the Carthaginian peace imposed on the local slave community in the aftermath of Turner's defeat, that many black Christians in the area still harbored the view that the millennium was at hand, that another black Moses would quickly arise to deliver them from the ruthless legion of white Pharaohs who exploited them. Southside blacks might have remained defiant and even militant because they nurtured hope that a new charismatic leader would soon appear to continue and finish the work Nat Turner had begun. Such an explanation for black intransigence is possible, and it is even probable that some Southside slaves held precisely such views.

Yet it seems more plausible to assume that the dissatisfaction of most black Christians with their biracial churches emerged less from radical or visionary perceptions about the potential of prophetic Christianity and more from the practical problems they encountered. It is certainly reasonable for historians to conclude, based on limited direct evidence and more voluminous indirect evidence, that black members in Southside churches recoiled in horror at the savage white reaction to the rebellion. For days whites threatened, brutalized, and killed slaves and free blacks who had no known connection to the rebellion, exercised summary justice against some of those who appeared involved, and generally responded to the insurrection with a reign of terror of their own. This period of wanton white violence doubtless produced not only the fear it was calculated to produce in the local black community but also profound distrust and alienation among black Christians. A few weeks of brutal repression belied years of paternalistic professions from Southside whites. This betrayal could well have driven some black Christians to conclude that their white fellow communicants were the ones unfit for sacrament and service and produced the tension with the churches of the Portsmouth Association. At the very least, the new levels of white control, which blacks saw as interference, over black religious activity in the post-Turner months alienated blacks. They could no longer gather freely to worship, hear preachers of their own color, or teach other blacks to read the gospel. Such imposition of white authority drove yet another wedge between white and black Christians, making reconciliation difficult.

But in their own mysterious and imperfect way, these churches were about the work of reconciliation. If nothing else, the passage of time lessened tensions and blurred memories. Blacks remained members at Raccoon Swamp Baptist, accounting for all but about 40 of the church's 140 members in 1833.[117] By 1834, reconciliation appears to have occurred at Raccoon Swamp. The church reported that "Ethiopia is stretching out her hand" and that thirteen "colored persons" had been received by baptism. The Mill Swamp church still complained that "the word preached seems to profit but little the ungodly" and reported no baptisms, but in 1835, Raccoon Swamp again reported an increase in membership and declared to the Portsmouth Association that "the set time to favor our church has come."[118] At the same association meeting, an African church in Petersburg reported itself "at peace one towards another" and expressed gratitude to the town's white-controlled Market Street Church for its assistance.[119] Even in Southampton and Sussex counties, a new social peace between masters and slaves seemed to hold by 1835.

Indeed, at least some whites in the area seemed eager to put the balance of terror that accompanied the Turner insurrection behind them with overt acts of reconciliation and reversal. Boson, a slave defendant sentenced to death in Sussex on the basis of Beck's testimony, had escaped from the Suffolk jail while awaiting execution, and he evaded recapture for more than three years. But in 1834, he was captured in Norfolk and returned to Sussex, where the county court upheld his death sentence. Stunningly, however, the court immediately asked Governor Littleton Tazewell to commute the sentence.[120] The court's request was supported by Boson's original defense counsel, James S. French, who informed the governor that he had never thought "the charge made out against" Boson, and in the intervening years "many conversations with persons who live in his immediate neighborhood tend to confirm me more strongly in my belief."[121] French argued that many who had once accepted Boson's guilt now doubted it, and pointed out that Boson's trial "came immediately after the Insurrection in this county" and that Boson plus eleven others were convicted on "a naked charge, unsupported by corroborating circumstances, and proffered by a single witness—and that a slave." While a fugitive, Boson had "sought several conversations with respectable gentlemen" in which he "protested his innocence and professed himself ready to deliver up at any time that he could be assured he would not be hung." French concluded his plea to Tazewell by reiterating that he believed "implicitly in his [Boson's] innocence" and urged the Governor to commute the sentence.[122]

Additionally, a group of eighteen Sussex residents, including George Blow, a judge on the original court that convicted Boson, and, less surprisingly, Boson's former owner William Peters, an elder at the Raccoon Swamp Baptist Church, petitioned the governor for clemency. These petitioners admitted that the insurrection's "extreme excitement" had prejudiced their judgment in 1831. The petitioners argued that they "considered themselves the intended victims of the Massacre," but "Time has mellowed our feeling and given full exercise to our reason." The petitioners contended that they "would not screen a participator in that Bloody deed," but they could not see anyone "suffer the penalty of death who we believe not to have been a participant in it." The petitioners admitted that Boson (or "Boatswain," as the petitioners more accurately referred to him) was "perhaps a discontented spirit, and perhaps a refractory Slave." They also admitted that the accused "might have indulged in threats amongst his fellow slaves against the Whites—that he might have been tempted to join the murderers had they, for a time, proved successful and continued embodied carrying on the work of carnage." But such admissions, the petitioners insisted, centered on "probabilities not facts," and there was "not one tittle of evidence to prove that he did commit any such crime."[123]

The Sussex County petitioners, however, did not confine themselves to seeking leniency for Boson; they also ventured a mature judgment on the whole Turner uprising. According to the petitioners, "all the evidence given at the trials in Southampton left the mind convinced that it was not an affair of premeditation but suddenly gotten up by a fanatic who had to use religious delusion and force to induce a very few desperadoes to commence it with him; after a revel, when they became excited by liquor, heightened by the inflammatory declamation of their Leader." Such a narrative of Turner's rebellion led the petitioners to believe that any "threatening conversation at the May meeting at Raccoon Swamp had no connection whatever with the massacre in Southampton."[124] In Richmond, the state's powerful Executive Council recommended in favor of commuting Boson's sentence to transportation out of state, and in early March 1835, conservative governor Littleton W. Tazewell accepted the council's recommendation.[125] A fragile truce in the reign of terror held at last.

North American slavery had always rested on a concept modern Americans might see as the antebellum equivalent of the balance of terror that characterized the Cold War between the United States and the Soviet Union during the second half of the twentieth century. Slaves feared the swift, severe, and sometimes capricious punishments their masters could administer on an as-desired basis; they feared the punishments (including sale) they and their families might be subjected to, not only as a result of their own actions but also because of the actions of other slaves. Slaves generally refrained from open revolt for fear of the reign of white terror that insurrection or even the rumor of insurrection seemed to always bring down on black families and communities. Historian Kenneth Stampp's description of the slaveholder's determination to make his slaves "stand in fear" remains apt. At the same time, however, the white population in the South never could put the idea of a violent slave uprising entirely out of its mind. Fear of a violent reprisal against a master by an individual slave also remained prevalent. At the same time, fear of random violence at the hands of a slave protesting hardship or seeking revenge against a perceived wrong, combined with fears of the ultimate horror, an organized slave rebellion, and remained in the hearts and minds of southern whites. To be sure, Virginia whites, like whites across the South, learned to live with these fears. Perhaps they engaged in a number of self-deceptions, such as believing that their slaves, who were treated well, were far less likely to rebel or resort to violence than slaves generally. The less deceptive rationalization involved the idea that no slave insurrection could ultimately succeed because of the superior organization and firepower of the white population. Southern whites appeared, both publicly and privately, confident of that. But privately they also admitted that no white relished the prospect of his or her head being one of those lopped off by slave rebels before the saving patrol or militia unit could arrive. Other whites reasoned that trusted slaves and clever free blacks would always betray an insurrection plot before it had proceeded too far, and the racist assumptions of many whites led them to believe that no black-generated plot could succeed. Insurrections could materialize and do extensive damage, some whites reasoned, only if they enjoyed white support. While there were serious holes in white reasoning on these points, many white assumptions, including the dubious ones, held often enough to sustain the misconception. They were relatively few slave insurrections. None was more successful that Nat Turner's. Most alleged plots were scotched before even one white life was taken; indeed, the severity of the white response to the insurrections, and even rumors of insurrection, led some southern slaveholders to fear the brutal and often indiscriminate white response to rumors of insurrection (and the resulting loss of slave property) as much as insurrection itself.

Yet, as William Freehling has rightly argued, what slave owners feared most about slave rebellion was not that an insurrection would succeed on a large scale, yielding the much talked-about race war, but rather the erosion of political and social support for slavery as a result of the constant agitation of white fears and anxieties by repeated rumors of insurrection, the occasional full-blown insurrection scare, or even an insurrection itself. Such repeated stress frayed the southern social fabric. How long would white society remain steadfast in support of slavery when constant patrols, women and children becoming refugees in their own communities, lengthy investigations and trials, gruesome public punishments, summary executions, and torture remained visible facts of life in southern communities? How long would whites tolerate such insecurity? An occasional response to perceived threats from slaves might remind white southerners that the price of slavery was eternal vigilance. Frequent mobilization against scares might cause whites to lose patience with the peculiar institution and seek to chart its gradual demise. This, in the end, loomed as Nat Turner's real challenge to slavery, and virtually the entire South, each state in its own way, grappled with exactly how to meet it.

PART SIX

THE UPPER SOUTH RESPONDS

The concerns aroused by Nat Turner's insurrection brought the states of the upper South closer to a moment of decision on the slavery question. Could they continue as they had, content to see slavery erode around the edges? Could they simply slowly decrease its importance to their economy or gradually shrink the proportion of slaves in their state's population? Or must they take some decisive action on the question? Beyond agreement on the need for enhanced security measures of the most fundamental sort, the citizens of upper South states seemingly agreed only on the broad concept that—up to a point—a whiter state was a safer state. But if the whitening of the upper South was a popular notion, how much, how fast, and by what methods it should occur were questions that proved difficult to find agreement on.

As a result, the Turner insurrection spawned heated legislative debates over gradual emancipation and the colonization of free blacks in Virginia in 1831–32 and triggered Maryland's surprising 1832 contretemps over the use of manumission and colonization as a means of whitening the state. It prompted Kentucky, a state that was only one-fifth slave in 1830, to ban slave imports in an effort to prevent itself from becoming substantially blacker. The scare also precipitated Tennessee's extensive and revealing debates over emancipation and colonization at its constitutional convention of 1834 and influenced North Carolina's decision to disfranchise propertied free blacks at its limited 1835 state constitutional convention.

After the post-Turner debates, the uppermost states of the upper South, including Virginia, still saw the answer to the slavery question in a demographic reconfiguration of the institution that would leave the region whiter and less tied to slave labor. Further south in Tennessee and North Carolina, however, the post-Turner rationale for a demographic reconfiguration was less compelling, and the debates in these middle South states were of a somewhat different nature. Less concerned about racial demography, Tennessee and North Carolina whitened their political cultures, heeding the popular demands of white egalitarianism in the Jacksonian South. While the post-Turner discussion of slavery in the upper South revealed that many whites in the region were unwilling to abandon slavery, most upper South whites still saw slavery as an evil for which they had no remedy consistent with the best interest of whites. They had little use for emerging notions, ones gaining ground in the lower South, that slavery was a positive good. The demographic reconfiguration of slavery and the whitening of the upper South's political culture seemed effective answers to the slavery question, provided that rebellious slaves could be deterred and outside critics of the institution muted.

CHAPTER TWELVE

THE UPPER SOUTH DEBATES SLAVERY AND COLONIZATION

In the pensive months following Nat Turner's rebellion, Virginia formally reconsidered its official policy toward both slavery as an institution and the free black population within its borders. Few prominent individuals from any part of the state or on any side of the question doubted that changes must be made. Proslavery planters from Virginia's Southside region advocated tough new measures to enhance white security, including tighter control over the free black population and greater vigilance over the institution of slavery itself. But with the state's tobacco plantations in relative decline and the comparative return on slave labor diminished, many Old Dominion leaders wanted to use the sense of urgency spawned by the Turner insurrection to take bolder steps toward addressing the problem of slavery. Longtime advocates of gradual emancipation and colonization found full voice. Virginia's John Marshall, the venerable chief justice of the United States Supreme Court, expressed a fervent hope that the 1831–32 state legislature would seize on "the excitement produced by the late insurrection" and use the "favorable moment" to pass sweeping legislation facilitating colonization of free blacks. A staunch supporter of the American Colonization Society, Marshall believed that the "removal of our free colored population" was a "common object" in post-insurrection Virginia, and he thought the national government should use money raised by the sale of public lands to finance colonization. But even the loose-constructionist Federalist chief justice doubted a direct federal subsidy of the ACS would pass constitutional muster without an amendment.[1] Marshall's longtime political rival, James Madison, used the postinsurrection discussion to reiterate his view that "slavery was a dreadful calamity" that, after Turner's brief reign of terror, filled "many with dreadful despair."

The aging Madison also favored using funds generated by the sale of public lands to finance a large-scale colonization effort, but the ever scrupulous father of the Constitution demanded a constitutional amendment to authorize such expenditures.[2] Old Federalist Charles Fenton Mercer ridiculed the caution of Marshall and Madison, arguing that unyielding opposition from the cotton states of the lower South would always make impossible the supermajority needed for an amendment. Eager to remove free blacks from Virginia, Mercer insisted that funding a colonization plan required only congressional approval.[3]

William C. Rives, a devoted Madison protégé and consistent advocate of both gradual emancipation and colonization, acknowledged the "delicacy & difficulties" of addressing the slavery question, but he urged the legislature to "look steadily to the ultimate and complete eradication of the evil." The "emancipation of the after-born with suitable provision for the colonization of those who are or may become free," Rives reasoned, "seems...to be the true policy." "Whether or not the public mind will bear it," Rives admitted, "I have no data for judging," but if "something be not done now," he concluded, "we must abandon the great and glorious work [of emancipation] as a hopeless dream of sages and patriots."[4] Richmond lawyer John Rutherford also denounced slavery as "the greatest curse that ever blighted the prospects of any people," and called on the Virginia legislature to address the problem "of our colored population," including both slaves and free blacks. "I admit that this evil, increasing as it does so rapidly and so awfully, requires some prompt and energetic remedy," Rutherford declared. *Richmond Enquirer* editor and political kingmaker Thomas Ritchie felt confident that "our best thinking politicians" will "turn their attention to preventing Insurrections," but the editor hoped that Old Dominion lawmakers would go further and consider a "more radical remedy," in the form of "an energetic system of manumission followed by a removal to Africa."[5]

Late in the fall of 1831, Virginia governor John Floyd, a western Virginian and an advocate of gradual emancipation, prepared for the upcoming legislative session. Floyd wanted the legislature to consider not only the removal of free blacks and the imposition of tighter restrictions on the mobility and religious activities of slaves but also plans for gradual emancipation. Floyd shared his tentative list of legislative proposals with South Carolina governor James Hamilton Jr., the Palmetto State's firebrand of nullification. Floyd proposed confining all slaves to the estates of their masters, prohibiting all black preaching, and expelling all free blacks from the state. Impractical as these measures likely would have proven, they must certainly have been less disturbing to South Carolina's Hamilton than Floyd's final idea: that Virginia use its surplus revenue to finance colonization as a "first step to emancipation." Floyd assured Hamilton that "the last point will of course be tenderly and cautiously managed and will be urged or delayed as your State and Georgia may be disposed to cooperate."[6] Just two days after his letter to Hamilton, Floyd confided to his diary, "Before I leave this government, I will have contrived to have a law passed gradually abolishing slavery in this State." If he failed to do so, Floyd vowed, he would at least "begin the work by prohibiting slavery on the West side of the Blue Ridge mountains."[7]

No record survives of the indomitable Hamilton's probable effort to dissuade Floyd, but the ambitious Virginia governor must have come to understand that South Carolina and Georgia were hardly "disposed to cooperate" with any proposal leading to gradual emancipation.[8] In his annual message to the legislature, Floyd took a decidedly more cautious approach than the one he outlined in his private letter to Hamilton. Floyd's message avoided any mention of gradual emancipation; instead, he recommended a ban on "negro preachers," who, in the governor's view, were "the most active among ourselves, in stirring up the spirit of revolt," and the removal of free blacks from the Old Dominion.[9] Yet despite his public reticence on the subject of emancipation, Floyd remained privately committed to ending slavery in Virginia. In late December 1831, the governor again confided to his diary that would try to "influence" his friends in the legislature to initiate debate on the subject of "gradual abolition." And he promised his diary that he would not "rest" until "slavery is abolished in Virginia."[10] Floyd's reticence in his legislative message drew the ire of at least one Tidewater newspaper, which blasted the governor for not advancing "some recommendation for the gradual extinction of slavery by however slow a process." There "is nothing more sickening to us as a native Virginian," the editor explained, "than the idea that our noble state is forever saddled with the incubus of slavery."[11] Despite the caution of Floyd's message, the weeks after his vow to spark a debate over slavery ultimately produced the most extensive public discussion of emancipation ever held in a southern state.

THE PARAMETERS OF THIS DEBATE had been shaped to a large degree by the legislative apportionment decisions made by Virginia's long and contentious state constitutional convention of 1829–30, held roughly a year and a half before Nat Turner's uprising. This convention, called after years of pressure from western reformers who wanted to democratize the Old Dominion's existing constitution, painted in bold relief some of the most fundamental tensions in the polity of antebellum Virginia.[12] Pitting egalitarian republicans from the state's heavily white western regions (the Valley and the trans-Allegheny) against more conservative republicans from the East (Tidewater and Piedmont), where the slave population was larger, the convention brought contentious questions regarding the relationship of slavery, republican values, and raw political power into sharp relief. The western egalitarians' chief demands were for the elimination of the freehold requirement for voting and a reapportionment of the legislature on the basis of white population. Eastern conservatives wanted above all to keep political power concentrated east of the Blue Ridge by retaining property requirements for voting and using a legislative apportionment formula that included either property or slave population.[13]

The convention battle had as much to do with the demography of the state as with ideology. Virginia's slave population was large and its proportion of the total population high by upper South standards. At the time the convention met, just over 1.2 million people lived in the Old Dominion. Fifty-seven percent were white, nearly 39 percent were black slaves, and just over 3 percent were free blacks. The state's slave population numbered almost 470,000, over 140,000 more than the slave population of black-majority South Carolina and more than the slave populations of Georgia, Alabama, and Louisiana combined. In 1830, Virginia slaveholders held one-fourth of all slaves in the states of the future Confederacy. But, as in every slave-holding state, racial demography varied considerably from region to region. Over 85 percent of Virginia's black population lived east of the Blue Ridge, while only 54 percent of the state's white population did. The eastern population was 50 percent slave, nearly 5 percent free black, and only 45 percent white. Western Virginia was more thinly populated generally, but some 90 percent of westerners were white, and the region contained only 11 percent of the state's slave population. As a result, ending the freehold suffrage requirement had a potential constituency in all portions of the state, but adopting the so-called white basis for representation was primarily a western measure.

After much wrangling, the Virginia Constitutional Convention of 1829–30 produced only relatively minor adjustments to the status quo, largely because easterners had controlled the apportionment of seats at the convention. The new constitution reduced the property requirement for suffrage, but even the reduced requirement disfranchised nearly one-third of all adult white males. The convention adopted the white population as specified in the 1820 census as the permanent basis of legislative apportionment, fixing the representation of the four major regions and ensuring perpetual control by the Tidewater and Piedmont at the expense of the Valley and the trans-Appalachian west. The convention approved the new frame of government on a 55–40 vote, with fifty-four of the yes votes coming from east of the Blue Ridge.[14]

Eastern Virginia delegates had accepted the least reform they could in order to guarantee eastern control for the foreseeable future. Under the new constitution, the Piedmont gained the most, controlling over 31 percent of all seats in the newly apportioned legislature. The Tidewater retained control of 27 percent. Together these two eastern regions, which held roughly 54 percent of the state's white population, controlled 58 percent of the all legislative seats and enjoyed the benefit of a constitution that did not call for reapportionment as population shifted. The 45 percent of whites who lived west of the Blue Ridge controlled only 42 percent of all seats in the newly apportioned legislature, and the lack of a mandated reapportionment of the legislature prevented the West from gaining representation as its population increased. Even though convention delegates could not have known the issue would erupt so soon, the plan of apportionment adopted in 1830 would have a major, perhaps even decisive, impact on the outcome of the legislative debates over emancipation and colonization that occurred less than two years later.[15]

AS VIRGINIA STOOD poised to debate slavery in the aftermath of the Turner rebellion, the tensions between east and west expressed at the constitutional convention remained raw. The white-majority West could prevail on any slavery-related issue only by remaining unified and attracting allies from the East, either from counties in the western Piedmont whose racial demography resembled that of the Valley, from members of the Piedmont or Tidewater elite who still looked to end slavery in Virginia from a sense of Jeffersonian idealism, or from among newly frightened easterners willing to cooperate with the West as a result of the Turner insurrection. As the legislature prepared to meet in the winter of 1831–32, prospects for forging a coalition to support gradual emancipation looked difficult but not impossible.

Both the process of legislative deliberation and the content of the argument mattered in the so-called Virginia slave debates that occurred during the 1831–32 session. The process through which the debates unfolded revealed the determination of Southside conservatives to prevent any discussion of emancipation if at all possible. These conservatives had increasingly come to accept the South Carolina view that any public discussion of slavery weakened the institution by either inspiring slave unrest, revealing white dissension over the question, or both. Thus Virginia conservatives wanted to avoid discussion of the issue altogether, especially given the strain the violence at Southampton had put on public support for the institution in Virginia. But conservative efforts to limit or silence debate only served to enhance the determination of supporters of gradual emancipation and colonization to force a serious discussion of ways to reduce slavery's presence in Virginia. The desire to push for emancipation, though perhaps grounded in moral or ideological qualms about slavery or a belief that the institution was proving a drag on the state's economy, had been heightened by the white security crisis that had emerged as news of Nat Turner's rampage spread across the state. In the view of these reformers, the time for discussion of ending slavery was at hand.

When the legislative session opened in early December 1831, the Speaker of the House of Delegates appointed a special committee on "slaves and free Negroes," which met behind closed doors to study measures designed to prevent future insurrections and insurrection scares through stricter regulation of slaves and free blacks. William Henry Brodnax, one of the two militia generals who had helped restore calm in Southampton after the Turner rebellion and a delegate from a black-majority county in the southern Piedmont, chaired the special committee. Of the committee's thirteen delegates, ten hailed from either the Tidewater or the Piedmont, while only three represented either Valley or trans-Allegheny counties. Clearly the Speaker intended for delegates from slaveholding areas to take the lead in crafting any legislation concerning the future of slaves and free blacks in the Old Dominion.

On the floor of the assembly, members introduced petitions calling for the colonization of all free blacks and restricting the mechanical trades to whites only, and such petitions were routinely referred to the special committee. But on December 14, roughly a week after the special committee began its secret deliberations, the routine was disrupted. William Henry Roane, a delegate from Hanover County and a staunch defender of slavery, presented two petitions to the house. One was a petition from Hanover calling for the removal of all free blacks, but the other was a petition from the Society of Friends that labeled slavery as unjust, inhumane, and a violation of "the first principle of our republican institutions." The Quaker petition urged the passage of a post-nati plan of emancipation followed by immediate colonization as part of an effort to protect the safety and happiness of white Virginians.[16] Defenders of slavery, no matter how guarded in their expression, fully recognized the gravity and explosiveness of the matter at hand. Eastern Virginia defenders of slavery opposed sending the Quaker petition to the special committee because it called for the emancipation of slaves; they argued that any discussion of emancipation went well beyond the scope of the special committee's charge.

This early gambit to short-circuit the discussion of gradual emancipation drew the first attack from opponents of slavery. Rockbridge's Samuel McDowell Moore, an older cousin of colonizationist James McDowell, countered that if "it were possible to devise any plan for the ultimate extinction of slavery," the legislature ought to consider it.[17] More surprisingly, Philip Bolling, a slaveholder from Buckingham, a southern Piedmont county, joined Moore in opposing efforts to block any discussion of emancipation. Slavery had proved the "bane of our happiness," Bolling declared, and caused the "lamentable depression of Eastern Virginia." Every "intelligent individual," he asserted, knew that "slavery is the most pernicious of all evils with which a body politic can be afflicted."[18] Means of removing the evil, he believed, must be discussed. Special committee chair Brodnax, a Southside slaveholder who owned more than sixty slaves, agreed with Moore and Bolling on the narrow point that his committee had jurisdiction over all proposals affecting slaves and free blacks and should consider them regardless of their nature. Brodnax thought that the "evil" of slavery must be discussed in order to "restore confidence and security" to a Virginia society in which many families "locked their doors at night" and greeted their "servants" in the morning "with pistols in their hands." Moreover, Brodnax asked, "is there one man in Virginia who does not lament that there was ever a slave in the state?" Following Brodnax' lead, the chamber voted 93–27 to refer the Friends' memorial to the special committee, where it joined all other petitions addressing the subjects of slavery and free blacks.[19] The bulk of the twenty-seven votes against referring the Friends' petition to Brodnax' committee came from Southside delegates, but the legislators from the rest of the state overwhelmingly supported referring the petition. Many eastern representatives who would later oppose gradual emancipation and colonization agreed that all options should be considered, especially by a committee meeting behind closed doors and controlled by eastern slaveholders.[20]

The initial foray by some conservatives to limit Virginia's post-Turner discussion of slavery had failed. Governor Floyd grew encouraged at the broadened scope of the committee's deliberations, and both of the leading Richmond newspapers again urged the legislature to take bold action. Ritchie's *Richmond Enquirer* noted that "when this dark population is growing upon us...and when our whites are moving westwardly in greater numbers than we like to hear of," some plan of gradual emancipation must be developed to reduce, if not eliminate, the "greatest evil" facing Virginia.[21] The Richmond *Constitutional Whig* agreed with its longtime journalistic rival, calling gradual emancipation a "holy cause." The *Constitutional Whig* hastened to add that it loathed the "sickly philanthropy" of northern critics of slavery who "weep" at what they "do not understand," but its editors endorsed gradual emancipation because of the advantages it offered "the whites and the country."[22]

Despite this flurry of press attention, the Brodnax committee continued its work in secrecy for over three weeks. At the *Enquirer*, editor Ritchie worried about the silence. "Are we forever to suffer the greatest evil, which can scourge our land, not only to remain, but to increase in its dimensions," he implored. "Our wisest men can not give too much of their attention to this subject—nor can they give it too soon."[23] Defenders of slavery also grew impatient with the slow process of committee deliberation. Finally, on January 10, 1832, conservative William Goode, worried by the press endorsements of gradual emancipation, asked the special committee for a progress report. Committee chair Brodnax reported that the committee was engaged in active consideration of two questions: first, the development of a plan for removing free blacks, a question that had taken most of the committee's time, and second, the question of whether to recommend a plan of gradual emancipation. The complicated nature of these issues, Brodnax averred, made agreement on remedies difficult. He indicated that the committee would issue its report within a week.[24]

Hearing Brodnax' answer on the question of gradual emancipation, a frustrated and impatient Goode asked the House to terminate the special committee, arguing that the legislature could not pass an emancipation plan because it lacked the power to "confiscate private property," and it could not initiate the colonization of free blacks because the state lacked the financial resources necessary to fund removal. Moreover, even the mere discussion of emancipation would create "great anxiety" among white Virginians and threaten private property rights. It was "impossible to touch this subject, without impairing the value of the property of slaveholders," Goode insisted.[25] But the Mecklenburg delegate's attempt to muzzle critics of slavery in a state still emotionally raw from the impact of Turner's deadly rampage backfired. Critics of slavery immediately seized the floor, not merely to denounce Goode's effort to disband the special committee and gag the critics of slavery but also to advance specific proposals for the gradual abolition of slavery in the Old Dominion. Thus, in mid-January of 1832, the debate that had smoldered "out-of-doors" since reports of the Southampton insurrection first appeared raged anew inside the Virginia House of Delegates, and in plain public view.[26]

Piedmont delegate Thomas Jefferson Randolph, grandson of Thomas Jefferson, initiated the substantive debate when he offered a proposal to hold a referendum on post-nati emancipation in Virginia. Under Randolph's plan, all slaves born on or after July 4, 1840, would become the property of the state when they reached the age of majority (twenty-one for men, eighteen for women), and their labor hired out to raise money to pay for their removal "beyond the limits of the United States." Randolph's plan freed no slave for at least a quarter century, and slaves would be forced to work to pay for their own involuntary colonization, sparing the state expense but extending the time required to initiate the colonization process. Also, under Randolph's plan, slaveholders could retain their capital by selling their slaves to other slaveholding states as they awaited either the beginning of gradual emancipation process in 1840 or until the individual slaves slated for emancipation reached the age of freedom. The plan guaranteed that the number of slaves in Virginia would dwindle dramatically during the second half of the nineteenth century, but it also appeared to guarantee that at least some slaves would call Virginia home in the early twentieth century.[27]

As plans for gradual emancipation went, the Randolph plan was neither excruciatingly slow nor unusually rapid. Unlike other proposals that were bandied about, Randolph's plan did not involve a heavy investment of public funds but rather envisioned that "each slave pays for his own removal with his own hire." This provision, Randolph argued, made gradual emancipation possible without imposing a huge burden on state taxpayers or involving federal assistance. He also expected most slaveholders to profit from selling their slaves south at good prices to eager buyers in flourishing sections of the cotton South. In short, Randolph offered an affordable plan of gradual emancipation. And his plan was very much a plan to end slavery in Virginia rather than in the South as a whole. The continued drain of Virginia slaves to the cotton South loomed large in Randolph's plan, rendering the plan less objectionable in the eyes of many slaveholders than it would otherwise have been. Yet Randolph's proposal included no compensation for slaveholders, except for sparing them the burden of paying taxes to finance the forced colonization of their former slaves.

This lack of a compensation provision gave defenders of slavery the opening they needed to counterattack. And counterattack they did, charging that the plan represented an unconstitutional and unrepublican confiscation of property without compensation. Conservative Walter Holladay argued that Randolph's post-nati plan violated property rights explicitly guaranteed by the Constitution. "He who imagines that property of the amount of nearly one hundred millions of dollars can be taken from the people of Virginia by the Legerdemain of legislation without a convulsion terrible in its consequences knows nothing of human nature," he maintained, adding that "there is not a place upon the whole earth where we could dispose of more than a half a million human beings in any short period of time without having them perish." The "whole scheme of abolition by purchase and deportation," he concluded, was "a work too great for the power of man."[28] But whatever the reaction to his proposal, Randolph had used conservative efforts to gag critics of slavery as an opportunity to put a plan for gradual emancipation on the floor of the house for debate. Governor Floyd sensed the possibilities immediately. "The slave party have produced the very debate they wished to avoid," he chortled, "and too, have entered upon it with open doors."[29]

Goode quickly tried to repair the damage, insisting that debating slavery would encourage slave insurrection. Slaves were "not an ignorant herd of Africans," Goode declared, but rather an "active and intelligent class" who were aware of legislative proceedings. The spirit of Whitemarsh Seabrook had made its way into Southside Virginia's Goode. But Randolph would have none of such talk. The Nat Turner insurrection had forced Virginians to admit that the "hour of eradication of the evil is advancing," he warned, "Whether it is effected by the energy of own minds, or the bloody scenes of Southampton and St. Domingo, is a tale for future history."[30] Bloody Southampton had suddenly gained equal billing with Saint Domingue in the imagination of white Virginians.

Valley delegate Samuel McDowell Moore followed with a full-blown attack on slavery. Moore blamed slavery for the loose morals, ignorance, and lack of industry that he believed characterized too much of the state's white population. Among landless white Virginians, Moore asserted, "labor was seen as a mask of servitude, and consequently as degrading and disreputable." The presence of slavery created an "indisposition" among the "free population to cultivate the soil" and hence undermined the very foundation of Virginia prosperity.[31] Buckingham's Philip Bolling agreed with Moore about the impact of slavery on the work ethic of white Virginians. Slavery "drives from us the laboring man," Bolling argued, and discouraged the "small freeholders" who face a "hard struggle" for "bare necessities of life—to say nothing of its luxuries." Thus slavery put "an effectual extinguisher upon all the humble aspirations" of common whites in Virginia. The drain and demoralization of free white labor, Bolling insisted, constituted the greatest "evil growing out of our present system of slavery."[32] Later in the debate, Valley delegate Charles J. Faulkner echoed Moore and Bolling, explaining that whites in western Virginia feared seeing the region's vitality converted "into desolation and barrenness by the withering footstep of slavery." The "independent yeomanry" west of the Blue Ridge demanded protection from the curse of slavery, Faulkner claimed, because that peculiar institution "banishes free white labor—it exterminates the mechanic—the artisan—the manufacturer."[33] Slaveholder Thomas Marshall, son of Chief Justice John Marshall, reiterated that reformers' main objection to slavery was not that it was immoral but that it proved "ruinous to whites" by retarding economic improvement, rooting "out an industrious population," and pushing "the yeomanry of the country" to emigrate. Worse still, Marshall predicted with some hyperbole, slavery in Virginia would likely increase "until the whole country will be inundated by one black wave, covering its whole extent, with a few white faces here and there floating on the surface."[34]

Slavery's defenders were not reluctant to respond such criticism, even if they replied by changing the subject from the economic impact of slavery to the conditions of slave life. Southside delegate James Gholson of Brunswick declined to defend slavery "in the abstract" but eagerly defended the treatment of slaves in Virginia. Virginia's slaves, Gholson argued, "are as happy a labouring class as exists upon the habitable globe." They "are content to-day and have no care or anxiety for tomorrow," Gholson noted, and "Cruel treatment of them is discountenanced by Society," though the Turner rebellion triggered public cries for stricter discipline. Perhaps more strikingly, Gholson argued that slaves were not only a contented population but also a "peaceful and harmless one." Gholson dismissed the Turner insurrection as the product of an "ignorant, religious fanatic" who initially enticed only four or five slaves from "his immediate neighborhood" to join his rebellion. For Gholson, "bloody Southampton" was not Haiti, but rather a "solitary occurrence of insubordination," one hardly typical of slave conduct in Virginia.[35] Reformer William Rives countered that the "public mind appeared to be coming to the conclusion that something must be done," because census data showed that "blacks were progressively increasing in number, and the whites steadily declining," as the "drain" of blacks to the cotton South had slowed due to restrictive legislation enacted by states in the lower South.[36]

On the third day of the debate, special committee chair William Brodnax addressed the house. Brodnax conceded that no reasonable person could "doubt or deny" that "slavery in Virginia is an evil, and a transcendent evil." But the Southside planter emphatically defended the property rights of slaveholders against Randolph's "monstrous" post-nati emancipation plan, which Brodnax thought robbed slaveholders of nearly half their property. Brodnax admitted that white Virginians wanted something done about slavery, but he warned delegates that voters "have not called on you to tear all their property away from them; or manumit their slaves without indemnity or compensation." Any proposal for emancipation, he argued, must not only plan effectively for the "immediate removal" of all slaves who were freed but also provide adequate compensation to their former masters.[37] Brodnax then outlined a set of principles that he thought must govern legislative action on the subject of slavery. First, any plan for emancipation must be followed by the immediate removal of the newly freed ex-slaves. Second, any plan must neither weaken the "security of private property" nor "affect its value." Finally, no slave could be freed without either the master's consent or adequate compensation. Brodnax' principles appeared to set a high bar for any plan of gradual emancipation—a bar so high that it could not be cleared. Most delegates who heard his conditions thought their application would prevent the passage of any gradual emancipation bill.[38]

Yet Brodnax knew that white Virginians expected something to be done to improve white security, so he advanced a proposal that met his own stringent conditions. In doing so, Brodnax joined the chorus of diverse voices urging the removal of the state's existing free black population while edging toward a very gradual acceptance of a very gradual emancipation. The Southside planter recommended committing funds ceded to the state by the federal government from the sale of public lands along with the proceeds from the imposition of an annual thirty-cent head tax on whites (a tax he insisted could be paid by "abstinence from two or three glasses of toddy at the courthouse") to support the removal of all free blacks from the state. Using ACS estimates, Brodnax concluded that the money from his two sources could finance the removal of roughly six thousand free blacks per year. At that pace, Virginia could remove all its free blacks within ten years. Once that removal was accomplished, Brodnax argued, the state could begin the gradual emancipation of six thousand to ten thousand slaves per year. Under Brodnax' plan, the state would purchase these slaves from their masters at a "fair price" and quickly colonize them, as they had free blacks in earlier years, in Liberia. This plan, Brodnax insisted, promoted "the interests of all, without violating the rights of any."[39] Thomas Ritchie and the *Richmond Enquirer* quickly endorsed the Brodnax proposal, hailing it as one that held not merely "the middle ground" between abolition and the status quo but the "true ground" on the question of slavery and emancipation.[40]

But not even Brodnax' ever-so-gradual plan for colonizing free blacks and initiating a modest program of gradual emancipation once the state's ability to colonize free blacks had been demonstrated met the approval of eastern defenders of slavery. The Tidewater's Robert Powell doubted that there existed "a solitary gentleman in this house who will not readily admit that slavery is an evil, and that its removal, if practicable would be a consummation most devoutly to be wished," but the Spotsylvania delegate deemed legislative action in support of emancipation ill-advised.[41] Finally, on January 16, Goochland's Archibald Bryce moved that the House of Delegates hear the long-awaited report of the special committee. Brodnax, reporting for the committee, announced that it had concluded that "it is inexpedient for the present legislature to make any legislative enactment for the abolition of slavery"—inexpedient, apparently, to advance even an emancipation plan as cautious as Brodnax' own.[42] In the end, the eastern-dominated committee presented a report that did nothing but suggest the maintenance of the status quo regarding slavery. In a coordinated move, after Brodnax' announcement, Bryce offered a preamble to the committee report calling for the immediate colonization of free blacks, including recently manumitted slaves, as a first step toward the eventual adoption of a plan of gradual emancipation. Virginia must move, the preamble suggested, step by step toward the final abolition of slavery as soon as public opinion would allow, but it could take no direct action against slavery at the present time.[43]

Almost immediately, western delegate William B. Preston, nephew of Governor Floyd and an advocate of gradual emancipation, offered an amendment to the committee report that called for dropping the word *inexpedient* from the report and replacing it with the word *expedient*. Preston's motion would have changed the report to call for the gradual abolition of slavery in Virginia and guaranteed that the Virginia's debate over slavery would continue for a while longer.[44] In response to Preston's provocative amendment, conservative William H. Roane, grandson of Patrick Henry and son of prominent Jeffersonian jurist Spencer Roane, defended slavery openly, arguing that "free white people, free blacks, and slave blacks cannot and ought not constitute one and the same society." Thus Roane urged the removal of free blacks in an effort to stabilize the ratio of free blacks to slaves and whites in the Old Dominion. Trying to establish a racial justification for slavery, Roane denied that "the flat-nosed, wooly-headed black native of the deserts of Africa is equal to the straight haired white man of Europe," and asserted that "slavery as much a correlative of liberty as cold is of heat." "History," Roane concluded, "taught me that the torch of liberty has ever burnt brightest when surrounded by the dark and filthy, yet nutritious atmosphere of slavery."[45] Southside delegate Alexander Knox joined Roane in denying that slavery was an evil. Instead, echoing an argument heard often in the cotton South, Knox insisted that slavery was an "indispensable requisite" in the struggle to preserve "a republican government."[46]

John Thompson Brown offered a more moderate defense of slavery, maintaining that it was a "far greater evil to abolish slavery" than to tolerate it. A native of Lynchburg in the western Piedmont, Brown had first moved west to Clarksburg in the trans-Allegheny and represented Harrison County in the legislature as a democratic reformer on state constitutional issues. In 1830, however, Brown moved east to Petersburg and married into a prominent family. Once Brown was established in Petersburg, his politics took a conservative turn. Based on his experience in Clarksburg, however, Brown claimed to understand western Virginia's desire for a "cordon sanitaire" to protect the region from the expansion of slavery. But, Brown argued, the "fixed and unalterable laws of nature" protected lands west of the Blue Ridge better than "legislative art" could. Though hardly an advocate for slavery in the abstract, Brown advanced a brief paternalist defense of slavery in Virginia. Through the protection offered by Christian masters, Brown argued, slaves in the Old Dominion were better off than "four-fifths of the human family" and "happier than they would be in any other situation. They are happier than their fathers were, and might be happier still if incendiary fanatics would let them alone." Brown favored controlling the influence of slavery by encouraging the "drain of slaves" to the lower South, and predicted that the cotton states would soon facilitate the departure of slaves from Virginia by repealing any laws restricting the importation of slaves from other states.[47] Even ardent Southside conservative William Goode conceded that time would move slavery further south. "The labor of the slave like everything else...will meet the most effectual demand," Goode maintained, adding that it "was the operation of this principle that slavery was banished from the Northern States" and "will be the cure of slavery here."[48]

After hearing these conservative ripostes in defense of leaving slavery alone for the time being, westerners wondered if Goode's cure would come before the disease had done its worst. George Summers of Kanawha pointed out that slavery bred the "embryo tyrant of its little domain" rather than a virtuous republican citizen. Moreover, Summers insisted that no matter how precious property rights were under republican theory, they remained subordinate to rights of self-protection and community safety.[49] Eastern slaveholders cringed when Henry Berry of Jefferson dismissed the protection of slave property and the value of slave wealth as "mere trash" when "weighed against the public safety."[50] James McDowell, representing the Valley county of Rockbridge, maintained that merely branding slavery an evil offered whites no protection from its "deleterious" effects. The "labor of a free white man, in the temperate latitude of Virginia," McDowell insisted, "is more productive than that of a slave."[51] Agreeing with McDowell that slavery attached a false odium to labor, Philip Bolling called for "total eradication" of slavery "for the good of the Old Dominion."[52]

On January 20, Thomas Jefferson Randolph again advanced his proposal for a public referendum on gradual, post-nati emancipation. Even if the measure was approved by voters, Randolph explained, no slave in Virginia would be freed for twenty-eight years, giving slaveholders nearly three decades to plan for emancipation, selling their slaves to the lower South if they chose. And all ex-slaves would be immediately deported to preventing future racial problems in the Old Dominion. Slavery "degraded" honest labor, Randolph claimed; worse, slaves would eventually overwhelm whites in Virginia unless some corrective action was taken.[53] Renegade Southsider Philip Bolling delivered the parting shot to conservatives when he called slavery a "blighting, withering curse" that was "drying up the very lifeblood" of Virginia's "wealth, honor and prosperity."[54]

On January 25, after two full weeks of legislative debate over the evils of slavery and the need for gradual emancipation, a debate that was itself the worst nightmare of radical proslavery South Carolinians such as Seabrook and Turnbull, Virginia's conservative defenders of the status quo again attempted to end debate. A Southside delegate moved to indefinitely postpone further consideration of both the committee report and William B. Preston's amendment, triggering a series of votes that defined the legislature's position on the several issues at hand. Advocates of gradual emancipation and those moderates who wanted a plan for the colonization of free blacks combined forces to defeat the effort of antiemancipation conservatives to postpone action on all bills by a margin of 71–60. Eastern delegates voted 56–20 in favor of postponement (25–10 among Tidewater delegates and 31–10 among Piedmont delegates). In contrast, western delegates voted 51–4 to block postponement (20–4 in the Piedmont and 31–0 in the trans-Allegheny).[55] So the conservative effort to end all discussion and all possibility of state action in 1832 failed due to overwhelming western opposition aided by significant defections from the conservative cause among Tidewater and Piedmont delegates. Yet shortly afterward, another vote rejected Preston's call for the adoption of some plan of emancipation. In an even more sectionalized vote, proslavery conservatives rallied cautious moderates behind efforts to defeat Preston's proposal by a margin of 73–58. Eastern delegates voted overwhelmingly, 67–9, against endorsing gradual emancipation. Western delegates supported the Preston amendment, 49–6.[56] The support of eastern swing delegates had allowed the debate to rage, and these delegates declared themselves opponents of slavery, but they proved utterly unwilling to support any decisive legislative action to weaken the institution.

These crucial test votes revealed that, as with the division between reformers and conservatives at the Constitutional Convention of 1829–30, neither the reformers who wanted to set Virginia slavery on the road to extinction nor the conservatives who opposed any state action on the question of slavery had enough votes to prevail in the legislature in 1832. The balance of voting power lay with a group of swing delegates who seemed unwilling to muzzle debate but even more reluctant to begin even the most cautious journey toward emancipation unless a perfect plan could be agreed on. Inaction through legislative deadlock doubtless seemed satisfactory to many conservatives. But it was grating to reformers who championed gradual emancipation.

As Alison Goodyear Freehling concluded in her fine study of the debate, the legislative voting patterns closely followed the reform-conservative split at the Virginia Constitutional Convention two years earlier. On the whole, eastern members remained determined to maintain slavery as it existed, but representatives from eastern counties that contained significant towns or industrial enterprises often cast dissenting votes.[57] Valley representatives tended to vote with the trans-Allegheny West, but support for the eastern defense of the status quo emerged in Valley counties with larger slave populations. Racial demography influenced voting patterns. Fifty-three of the fifty-eight votes in favor of gradual emancipation (in the form of the Preston amendment) came from delegates who represented counties where slaves were less than 30 percent of the population, and sixty-nine of the seventy-three delegates who opposed gradual emancipation came from counties where slaves accounted for more than 30 percent of the population. Simply put, delegates who represented areas where slaves were a relatively small minority favored gradually phasing out the institution; representatives from areas where slavery provided a large portion of the labor force tended to favor maintaining the status quo. The more possible the eventual whitening of a county appeared, the more popular gradual emancipation was; the less probable a successful removal of a county's blacks, slave and free, and the more dependent a county on slave labor, the less eager delegates were to set in motion any process that might weaken slavery or diminish the number of slaves in Virginia.[58]

Unable to muster a majority in favor of the Preston amendment declaring emancipation "expedient," reformers rallied behind the cautious Bryce preamble, which at least declared slavery an evil and endorsed a move toward gradual emancipation at some future time. On the other hand, conservatives, buoyed by their apparent defeat of any legislative plan for gradual emancipation at the 1832 session, now opposed endorsing gradual emancipation in principle. In the end, enough swing voters agreed with western proemancipation supporters to pass the Bryce preamble, 67–60. Virginia's legislators collectively placed the House on record as favoring the abolition of slavery but required the state to take no action on the matter for the foreseeable future, except perhaps watching the flow of slaves to the cotton South through the interstate slave trade. The Virginia house had refused to endorse slavery but refused to take any measures against it, either.

Bryce, the preamble's author, praised the vote as a "first step" toward the ultimate "abolition" of slavery in the commonwealth.[59] Thomas Jefferson Randolph concluded, in an obvious overstatement, that "friends of abolition have gained all that they asked." He reported optimistically to his wife that "a revolution has commenced which cannot go backward."[60] The same press that had encouraged the debate also approved the compromise result. The Richmond *Constitutional Whig* judged the action "favorable to the cause of abolition." The debate, the newspaper opined, revealed that "public opinion was not sufficiently prepared" for emancipation, no matter how gradual, but the vote on the Bryce preamble indicated that "when public opinion is more developed," Virginia would not hesitate to begin a plan of gradual emancipation.[61] In reality, the approval of Bryce's preamble left Virginia in the same position it had assumed since the Revolution, pledging itself to the gradual abolition of slavery but doing nothing to begin the process.

Private reaction to the legislative debates proved mixed. Conservatives generally expressed more frustration with the debate than satisfaction with the resulting inaction, and advocates of gradual emancipation were privately less pleased than their public comments indicated. Richmond's Lawrence Dade warned that the positions taken by westerners during the debates confirmed eastern suspicions that the West intended to "attack" the East's property in slaves if they gained the political power to do so.[62] Thomas Smith, a conservative delegate from the black-majority district of Gloucester on the Chesapeake's western shore, also complained that the tone adopted by advocates of gradual emancipation led him to worry that Virginia slaveholders' "right to our property" would have "a very precarious tenure" if western reformers gained additional political clout.[63] Robert Pollard approved of the legislature's hypercautious approach, maintaining that to "free our blacks without regard to the rights of property would be beyond the ability of the State," and to "make a partial manumission would make the great body restless and disgruntled...and might drive them to desperate efforts to shake off their yoke." Pollard favored revising laws to ensure the "subjugation" of blacks and waiting for a "more propitious time for steps leading to the abolition of slavery."[64] Conservative Walter Holladay expressed "deep mortification" that the debates had even been held, and his friend Robert Powell considered the prospect of another open legislative debate along the lines of the one that had just occurred as the "most unfortunate event that could possibly happen."[65] Some reformers found reason for optimism. Devoted colonizationist John Rutherford judged the legislative debate an important step toward "finally eradicating the greatest curse that has ever blighted the prospects of any people."[66] But Thomas Ritchie, despite his editorial praise for the legislature's decision, emerged from the debates less sanguine than before. "The great and sorry evil of slavery is deep-seated," Ritchie confessed privately, "almost beyond the actual cautery or the knife."[67]

WITH THE ISSUE OF GRADUAL EMANCIPATION settled for the 1832 session, legislators turned their attention to the issue of the colonization of free blacks. On the surface it seemed that almost everyone involved in the Virginia debate over slavery favored colonization in some shape or form. Champions of gradual emancipation always coupled their proposals with plans for the removal (colonization) of blacks as soon as they were freed, and eastern opponents of all plans for gradual emancipation usually favored the colonization of free blacks in the interest of white security and public morals. Moderates on the question of emancipation also favored colonization of existing free blacks, seeing the measure as a step toward the whitening of Virginia. But by the time the House of Delegates took up the issue of colonizing free blacks in 1832, frayed tempers and hard feelings left over from the debate over gradual emancipation meant that both critics and defenders of slavery were eager to frustrate their opponents and reluctant to compromise. Thus agreement on a specific removal policy proved hard to find.

On January 27, 1832, the special legislative committee on slaves and free blacks reported on colonization. The Brodnax committee proposed a plan of colonization that was partly voluntary and partly coercive. As long as "sufficient numbers" of free blacks were willing to leave Virginia voluntarily, colonization would proceed on a voluntary basis. If volunteers failed to materialize, forced colonization would begin. Once all free blacks willing to leave voluntarily had been removed, black males between ages sixteen and twenty-five and females between fourteen and twenty-three would be deported first, and the coercive process would work its way forward from there, but no free black over the age of forty-five would be forced to leave the state. Colonization would be mandatory for all slaves manumitted in the future. The committee proposed to finance the colonization project with a $100,000 legislative appropriation in 1833 and a $200,000 annual appropriation thereafter, an appropriation funded by a head tax on whites.

Disagreements among those who generally favored colonization erupted immediately. The Richmond *Constitutional Whig,* long an advocate of colonization, bitterly denounced the coercive elements of the committee proposal. A forced deportation of free blacks, the newspaper complained, would "stain the statute book of Republican Virginia with a law which would disgrace Turkey."[68] The *Lynchburg Virginian*, published in a town with an active colonization auxiliary, also denounced coerced colonization as "oppressive, tyrannical and unjust."[69] Active ACS members in Virginia warned that the society could not support mandatory colonization because it violated the organization's founding principle of voluntary removal. Even committee member Charles Carter, a Tidewater resident and ACS supporter, admitted that coercion was "a painful part of the subject," but he expressed his hope that enough free black volunteers would appear to effect colonization without resort to coercion.[70]

When debate on the committee's colonization proposal began in earnest on February 6, 1832, Brodnax defended the committee's plan aggressively, contending that no plan for colonization that did not include coercion could work because few free blacks wanted to leave the state of their own accord. Other delegates countered that free blacks enjoyed a "vested right" to remain in Virginia if they chose to do so. As the debate proceeded, Goochland's Archibald Bryce again offered a compromise. Under Bryce's plan, blacks freed in the future would be subject to mandatory colonization, as would all resident blacks freed after 1806 because they had remained in the state in violation of a statute that required them to leave. Blacks who had been free residents of Virginia prior to 1806 would not be forced to leave. Trans-Allegheny delegate John Campbell agreed that all blacks freed in the future should be forced to leave but insisted that any black already free should be colonized only if willing to go voluntarily. After a short debate, the house rejected both the Brodnax committee's proposal and the Bryce amendment in favor of Campbell's proposal to keep colonization voluntary for all blacks already free and require mandatory colonization only for slaves manumitted in future years. The Campbell proposal passed the House by a margin of 71–54. The trans-Allegheny West voted overwhelmingly in favor of voluntary colonization, as did three-fourths of all Valley delegates. Among eastern delegates, Piedmont representatives split almost evenly on Campbell's proposal. By a two-to-one margin, Tidewater delegates opposed making colonization purely voluntary for blacks already free. In broad terms, supporters of gradual emancipation tended to oppose coerced colonization, while conservatives who blocked all efforts to pass an emancipation measure tended to favor forced colonization of free blacks.[71]

Once the House approved Campbell's plan and the accompanying state funding, the bill went to the state senate, where it encountered still more difficulty. Conservative Southside senators, in a clever effort to kill the bill, proposed that each county finance the removal of its own free blacks. This proposal, which eliminated the state appropriation for colonizing free blacks, proved a "poison pill" that ultimately derailed the measure. The local-funding approach was anathema to many easterners, who knew that some 93 percent of all the state's free blacks lived in the Tidewater and Piedmont. For the same reason, the new funding approach cemented support for the bill among western senators, who favored voluntary colonization but had resisted having their constituents taxed to finance the colonization of free blacks, most of whom lived in the eastern part of the state. With support for the house bill crumbling, advocates of state-financed colonization moved for postponement of the bill. After more than two months of consideration by the Virginia legislature, colonization under legislative auspices was delayed yet again.[72]

But at the next legislative session, the ACS encouraged William Brodnax, whose conservative credentials lent credibility to his colonization efforts, to propose that the legislature appropriate a substantial sum of state money for colonization. The legislature ultimately approved a state-funded colonization measure but appropriated only $18,000 a year for five years, a sum far less than that contemplated a year earlier, to sustain the process. In the end, Virginia endorsed voluntary colonization of free blacks (and the mandatory removal of any newly manumitted slaves) but only provided enough state money to finance a modest effort.[73] State-supported colonization of free blacks became law in Virginia, but the practical impact would remain slight unless or until funding was increased.

Though far less controversial than the debate over gradual emancipation, the discussion of colonizing free blacks nonetheless proceeded with some rancor. Both supporters of gradual emancipation and staunch defenders of slavery generally agreed that the colonization of free blacks was a good idea, but beneath the surface they disagreed over motive, tactics, and, more important, the scope of the project. Proponents of gradual emancipation favored the colonization of free blacks as a means of encouraging gradual emancipation. Slaveholding conservatives supported the colonization of free blacks as a means of removing a potentially incendiary population and rendering an ideological consistency to Virginia's emerging racial argument for slavery. Champions of gradual emancipation saw colonization as a way of weakening slavery with a view toward its eventual elimination; slaveholding conservatives saw colonization as a way of strengthening slavery by eliminating a troublesome intermediate caste. The common ground held by both proponents of gradual emancipation and slaveholding conservatives who favored colonization of free blacks was a desire to whiten Virginia, either a little (slaveholding conservatives) or a lot (supporters of gradual emancipation). If a political center of gravity could be located in the divided and bitter Virginia of the early 1830s, it was found in the idea that a whiter Virginia was a better Virginia. Southside conservatives dissented, but closer to the political center disagreements arose chiefly over how much whiter Virginia should be or how rapidly the state should move in that direction.

LONG AFTER LAWMAKERS decided on inaction, the Virginia debates over slavery and colonization continued through a series of highly publicized pamphlets that arguably presented the three dominant Virginia views of slavery as they cohered in 1832. Conservative Benjamin Watkins Leigh, who had fought hard to prevent the democratization of the Virginia constitution in 1829–30, penned a trenchant critique of the legislative debates.[74] Leigh presented a systematic, if indirect and mildly apologetic, case for perpetual slavery. The author agreed with other white Virginians that Southampton had gained infamy as "the scene of an atrocious crime," but the Tidewater conservative felt that Virginia's political reaction to the Turner insurrection, including editorial comment in the Richmond press and the legislative debates over the future of slavery, had been "the direct reverse of what common reason would have anticipated." Who could have anticipated, Leigh asked, "that the bloody horrors of the Southampton massacre, instead of suggesting plans for stricter discipline, would give birth to schemes of emancipation?" These fresh appeals for emancipation and colonization, Leigh noted with scorn, grew not from a sense of "justice" or "policy" but from "our fears," fears he denounced as "unmanly" and unjustified, since the investigation of the Turner uprising revealed "no general insurrection plot."[75]

As his response to Turner's rebellion, Leigh focused on measures designed to make any future insurrection more difficult. He urged "stricter discipline" among slave patrols and called on the legislature to provide patrols with sufficient "arms and ammunition" to defend against insurrection. He also pleaded with whites to stop the "impudent indulgence" of slaves, and above all, he warned white Virginians that public discussions of slavery-related issues were as threatening as "a volcano in the immediate neighborhood of our dwellings."[76] Leigh also detailed his opposition to Randolph's plan of gradual emancipation, which, he asserted, would leave slaveholders with all the expense of supporting elderly slaves and slave children but would deprive them of the labor of the vigorous adult slaves needed to make the institution profitable. Under this scenario, masters would become "slaves to their slaves."[77] Such a policy, Leigh predicted, would lead to a massive exodus of slaveholders from Virginia and deprive the state of much of its capital and talent. He also posited that gradual emancipation would create a "desire for freedom" among those still enslaved that would produce insurrection and perhaps even a "general servile war," which, Leigh calculated, would end in the "destruction of the negro race." Moreover, Leigh disavowed the reformers' idea that a shift to free labor would prove a panacea for Virginia's economic woes. He doubted that free white labor would come to Virginia because such immigrants would "encounter all the numberless and nameless dangers, which the process of abolition and deportation cannot fail to engender."[78]

Leigh also blasted the Bryce preamble for leaving the prospect of future emancipation in the hands of public opinion. He insisted that the state legislature had no power to free slaves, no matter how sophisticated a legal argument emancipation advocates might make. "All our institutions are founded on the principle, that every man's private property is absolutely his own," Leigh maintained, "and that he holds it independently of the power of the legislature and the will of the majority; and when that principle shall be abandoned, republican government must be destroyed with it."[79] For Leigh, the "scheme of the colonization society" was only slightly less menacing than Randolph's plan for gradual emancipation. Colonization plans were hugely expensive and threatened to place onerous tax burdens on slaveholders. Moreover, arguments advanced by colonizationists tended to "agitate" a "public mind" already "alarmed" by insurrection and thus "lay the ground work" for future "schemes of abolition." In this denunciation of all proposed "schemes of abolition and colonization," Leigh offered his tentative acceptance of perpetual slavery. "I am convinced that no plan for the abolition of slavery and the deportation of slaves is possible," he argued. "I have given my mind to the subject over and over again——I have examined all schemes...with a willingness and earnest desire to be convinced, until I found them all hopeless."[80]

Leigh offered the conservative case, the Southside view, for preserving the status quo regarding slavery in Virginia, and the case that came the closest to endorsing perpetual slavery. In an even more thorough review of the 1831–32 legislative debates, however, Thomas Roderick Dew, a young professor at the College of William and Mary previously best known for his support for internal improvements and his contempt for tariffs, also made a strong case against government action to encourage emancipation or colonization but pulled up well short of suggesting that slavery was a positive good that should be made perpetual.[81] Instead, Dew's essay offered a restrained localist critique of gradual emancipation and colonization. The young political economist explicitly declined to defend "slavery in the abstract," instead presenting caustic criticism of the gradual emancipation and colonization plans discussed by "reformers" in the recent Virginia debates. Dew insisted that he was not opposed to either the elimination of slavery from Virginia or the removal of all free people of color from the state, but rather that he preferred radically different means for achieving those ends instead of those touted in the debates. Dew pioneered not the first "positive good" argument for slavery but a reasoned defense of the "ultimate extinction" of slavery in Virginia through a steady, market-driven flow of upper South slaves to the newer plantation states of the cotton South.[82]

Dew blamed the Southampton uprising for triggering unprecedented levels of "consternation and dismay" among the state's white population. The insurrection, he claimed, had destroyed "for a time all feeling of security and confidence" among whites because the "ghastly horrors of the Southampton tragedy could not be banished from the mind." But whatever slavery's danger, Dew cautioned, "every plan of emancipation and deportation which we can possibly conceive, is utterly impracticable."[83] The essay rehashed in detail the usual arguments against colonization: it violated the property rights of masters (either by illegally seizing property or by unfairly reducing its value); the costs of both just compensation for masters and the colonizing effort were far too high for Virginia's resources (which were held disproportionately by slaveholders) to bear; neither Liberia nor any other proposed colony could receive the number of slaves contemplated in an orderly and humane fashion; and neither slaves nor free blacks would embrace colonization voluntarily once they fully understood its impact. Moreover, since "slave labour gives value" to Virginia's "soil and inhabitants," ending slavery "would pull down the Atlas which upholds the whole system." Dew doubted that free white labor would rush to the exhausted and eroded soil of Virginia when abundant western lands were available at $1.25 an acre. "Eject from the state the whole slave population," he predicted, and "the worn soils of Virginia will not bear the paltry price of government land in the West."[84]

Emancipation without colonization was unthinkable, Dew maintained, because "the emancipated black carries a mark which no time can erase; he forever wears the indelible symbol of his inferior condition: the Ethiopian can not change his skin, nor the Leopard his spots."[85] Moreover, free blacks were "the very drones and pests of our society," among whom "the principle of idleness triumphs over that of accumulation." Thus free blacks "will work nowhere except by compulsion." The young professor also disputed contentions, including those drawn from Jefferson's denunciation of slavery in his *Notes*, that "slavery is unfavourable to a republican spirit." To the contrary, Dew maintained, slavery in Virginia had brought whites "to one common level" as "nearly as can be expected or even desired in this world." With the "menial and low offices all performed by the blacks," Dew noted, "there is at once taken away the greatest cause of distinction and separation" among whites. Hence, in the South, "no white man feels such inferiority of rank as to be unworthy of association with those around him," and this "spirit of equality" among whites "is both the generator and preserver of the genuine spirit of liberty."[86]

Yet for all of Dew's insistence on the virtues of slavery and the folly of all schemes of emancipation and colonization, the young Tidewater professor did not argue that a slave-labor economy was superior to one driven by free white labor, or that Virginia should always retain its slave-labor economy. Instead, Dew hoped for an economic renaissance in Virginia, one driven by transportation improvements, the growth of towns and manufacturing along transportation routes, and, most notably, the attracting of "capitalists and free labourers of the North." This gradual and largely market-driven revolution in the Virginia economy—and Dew indeed saw it as a revolution—would accomplish the work of emancipation naturally, by "increasing the prosperity of Virginia," and diminishing the importance of slavery "without those impoverishing effects which all other schemes must necessarily have." On this point, Dew noted the role of the predominately free-labor city of Baltimore as a "mighty agent" that was "fast-making Maryland a non-slaveholding state." Dew hoped that Richmond, Petersburg, and Norfolk might gradually do the same for Virginia. At the same time, Dew believed that Alabama, Mississippi, and Louisiana, despite their repeated efforts to restrict or even ban the importation of slaves, would necessarily open their borders to additional slave labor and willingly serve as the "absorbent" for Virginia's "excess" slave population. Through a very gradual process, guided by the market's invisible hand, Dew preferred to see the benefits of slavery (and slaves themselves) flow to the lower South so that the Old Dominion could become more like the free-labor North.[87]

Former president James Madison, still a keen commentator on public affairs, read Dew's essay at the young scholar's request, and penned a thoughtful response to it. Madison conceded that the implementation of gradual emancipation and colonization involved overcoming great difficulties, but, unlike Dew, he saw none of these difficulties as "insuperable." Madison chided Dew for attributing "the depressed condition of Virginia" too "much to the tariff laws" and "too little to the existence of slavery" and the impact of the "rapid settlement of the Southwest." Indeed, Madison thought competition from the Southwest even more important than the deleterious effects of slavery in explaining the "actual and prospective depression of Virginia." The "great and adequate cause" of Virginia's decline, Madison contended, was that the "great staples of Virginia have but a limited market which is easily glutted," while "the more Southern staples of Cotton and Rice" continued to prosper. But, unlike Dew, Madison was unwilling to wait on the market to accomplish the ultimate termination of slavery in Virginia. The state's existing economic stagnation was reason enough to accelerate the whitening of the state. The fact that the process of whitening, which Madison believed should involve gradual emancipation and colonization as well as the work of the internal slave trade, would be "slow" and "attended with much inconvenience" and "not even certain in its result," did not mean that it was not preferable to a "torpid acquiescence in a perpetuation of slavery, or an extinguishment of it by convulsions more disastrous in their character & consequences than slavery."[88]

Also disturbed by Dew's critique of colonization, the American Colonization Society encouraged advocates of colonization to reply.[89] Their predictable choice for such a response was the reliable Virginia defender of colonization Jesse Burton Harrison. Acting on the advice of his cousin Henry Clay, Harrison had recently moved to New Orleans to further his career in law and assist Clay in building a political following there, but the Lynchburg native nonetheless agreed to respond, and he wrote a sweeping reply to both Dew and Leigh. In this reply, Harrison sketched the advantages of a whiter Virginia. He endorsed the goal of "ridding Virginia of the evil of slavery in our generation, in that of our children, or of our grandchildren."[90] Paralleling Dew, Harrison confined his critique of slavery to Virginia, carefully avoiding any indictment of slavery in the cotton South, and he admitted that his concerns about slavery were "founded but little on the miseries of the blacks" but instead were addressed "almost exclusively to the injuries slavery inflicts on the whites." Slavery degraded labor, Harrison maintained, and created among whites "a disposition to look on all manual labor as menial and degrading." The attorney argued that whites found it "irksome" to "perform hard work by the side of a slave" and that slavery discouraged manufacturing by retarding the "rearing of a large class of skillful mechanics." Slavery also discouraged immigration. Harrison conceded that staple-growing areas might prosper with slave labor but argued that much of Virginia had graduated from its staple-growing era. He acknowledged that Virginia earned profits and increased its capital through the sale of slaves to states in the Deep South, where demand remained high, but he doubted that the sale of slaves to the lower South benefited the Old Dominion enough in the long run to prevent comparative economic decline. National wealth and population growth were passing Virginia by, Harrison insisted, and he feared that as Virginia grew blacker such backwardness would only worsen.[91]

Harrison agreed that a general emancipation without colonization would "engender evils...greater than all the evils of slavery," but he supported an approach to colonization that would at least stabilize Virginia's population ratio and perhaps start the state on a slow journey toward the elimination of slavery.[92] Moreover, he argued that if measures were initiated to "take the whole labour of the state out of the hands of slaves," Virginia would hold "a thousand temptations" for "different sorts of immigrants, for capitalists, for free labourers, and for her own sons who meditate emigration." Harrison recognized that "the tide of free labour would not instantly begin to flow in" as "each slave is withdrawn," but he believed that once the removal of black labor reached "an irrevocable tendency," then "an adequate supply of free labor would be at hand." In the contest for immigrants between Virginia and the West, Harrison argued, the advantages of markets, churches, schools, ports, mills, shops, and "the blessings of human community" lay with Virginia. Since Virginians "cannot, will not say" that "slavery is not an evil," Harrison concluded, "will they say a remedy is impossible?"[93]

To a large degree, Harrison's goal was not that different from Dew's: a Virginia animated by free white labor, enterprising capitalists, and commercial entrepreneurs largely unhindered by the "scourge" of slavery and free blacks. Both men wanted to whiten Virginia over the long term. But Dew and Harrison disagreed sharply about means and timing. Harrison wanted to accelerate the whitening process through government action. And he wanted the government action to begin right away. Colonization was not only a practical but crucial part of the remedy in Harrison's view, and colonization required government sanction and support. Dew left the pace and volume of the desired drain of slaves from Virginia to the market—specifically to the southern regional market in slaves. Under Dew's scenario, Virginia slaveholders would sell slaves to buyers in the cotton South in return for the capital needed to reinvent Virginia in the image of Pennsylvania. Until that long and uncharted process worked itself out, at a market-driven pace, slave labor was needed to sustain the Old Dominion's agricultural economy.[94]

In many respects, the positions staked out by Leigh, Dew, and Harrison in the months after Virginia's legislative debates over slavery reflected the post-Turner state of Virginia's divided mind on the slavery question. In his critique of gradual emancipation and colonization, the conservative Leigh revealed the strength of the Virginia black belt's commitment to slavery. In Southside Virginia in particular, whites displayed little interest in forcing or even accepting a demographic reconfiguration of slavery. Instead, through a battle of ideas comparable to that occurring in the lower South, these black-belt conservatives pondered whether their slaveholding regime could both embrace paternalism, as many Virginia slaveholders urged, and yet remain tough and vigilant enough to maintain white safety. Like South Carolina's James Hamilton, Leigh wanted a tough-minded slaveholder's regime that kept slaves under control, and like John C. Calhoun, Leigh wanted overt political protection for slavery as one of society's unique interests. Such special interests, in Leigh's view, required protection from the whims of popular majorities, not vice versa, as the emerging Jacksonian wisdom held. This was a slaveholders' worldview that was moving toward, if it had not already arrived at, an ideological acceptance of slavery as a positive good that must be defended.

Thomas Dew articulated a very different critique of gradual emancipation and colonization, one that scarcely touted the virtues of slavery as much as it highlighted the impossible difficulties posed by the prospect of emancipation. It was a version, grounded in political economy and what Dew saw as hard facts, of Virginia's long-standing but uneasy accommodation with slavery as a great evil (especially for whites) for which no adequate remedy could be found. Traditionally, Virginia defenders of this accommodation, a long list that included Jefferson and Madison, sought refuge in the passage of time, which they hoped would reform public opinion and open new strategic opportunities to move against slavery. The Bryce preamble had recently reasserted this stance. Dew's approach to a slaveless Virginia depended heavily on time as well, but it depended even more heavily on the market, which Dew believed would gradually drain slaves further South on the basis of comparative economic advantage. Dew's approach to whitening Virginia drew less opposition from Southside slaveholders than other approaches did because it scrupulously avoided what they were coming to fear most: government intervention to accelerate the whitening process.

Harrison's defense of colonization encapsulated the logic of the Old Dominion's champions of gradual emancipation. These Virginians were willing not only to call slavery an evil, to remind audiences of slavery's unrepublican tendency to concentrate power and create special interests defiant of the public good, and to denounce slavery as the source of the state's comparative economic decline, but also to actually propose aggressive measures, short of immediate emancipation, to lessen the state's reliance on slave labor. A program of government intervention to initiate gradual emancipation and to colonize all free blacks (current and future) and to help fund these efforts seemed not only appropriate but necessary to these reformers. Many colonizationists, including Harrison, remained more comfortable with state funding than with federal support. They were perfectly willing to accept help from Dew's invisible hand in the drawing of slaves south through sale and forced migration, but they had no aversion to government action if it weakened slavery's grip on Virginia. On the whole, these Virginia critics of slavery were comfortable with gradualism as long as action began soon. But Harrison's defense of gradual emancipation and colonization emphasized the new sense of urgency prompted by Turner's rebellion. It also reflected the growing consensus in white-majority areas of Virginia that the state should be whitened and that the whitening should start immediately. Harrison articulated these reformers' desire for a demographic reconfiguration of slavery that should be accelerated by collective action whenever possible rather than one paced entirely, as Dew preferred, by the market's invisible hand.

OTHER STATES IN THE UPPER SOUTH, with smaller proportions of slaves than Virginia and greater distance from the carnage in Southampton, also grappled with exactly what Turner's rebellion meant for them. In Delaware, the state's long-standing policy of encouraging private manumission and allowing free blacks to remain for absorption into the state's growing free-labor economy had eroded slavery to the point that slaves accounted for only a little more than 4 percent of the population by 1830.[95] Yet reports of the Nat Turner rebellion hardened white racial sentiment in Delaware momentarily, turning white attention to the problem of how to control the state's burgeoning free black population, which constituted just over one-fifth of the state's total population.[96] Concern peaked in October 1831 when rumors circulated that a group of armed blacks was planning to take control of a town in Sussex County, the southernmost and most heavily black Delaware county, on the upcoming election day. These rumors, given credibility by the recent Turner insurrection, sparked public demands that Delaware lawmakers take decisive action to prevent a "catastrophe" like the one that had "recently transpired in Virginia."[97] Petitions for tighter restrictions on free blacks flooded the legislature. Petitions from Sussex and New Castle counties demanded the disarming of the state's free blacks; others called for a ban on additional free blacks entering the state and restrictions on the activities of free black preachers.[98] At its 1832 session, the Delaware legislature approved a ban on free black ownership of firearms (unless five white citizens approved an exception) and required all free black preachers entering the state to receive the endorsement of five white citizens plus a justice of the peace before receiving permission to preach. Free blacks were also barred from assembling in groups of more than twelve after midnight.[99] Delaware's free blacks protested vigorously that these new restrictions were "entirely without foundation" and that the new restrictions on religious activity exposed them "to all the horrors of perpetual slavery for the act of worshiping their Creator, according to the dictates of their consciences."[100] Overall, while these restrictions were mild in comparison with those imposed on free blacks in other states in the aftermath of Southampton, Delaware's reaction proved that not even the whitest of slaveholding states could ignore the implications of Nat Turner's rebellion.

News of the Turner insurrection also prompted increased white anxiety in Kentucky, where the diffusion of slaves to the Southwest through sale and migration was emerging as an increasingly popular means of keeping the state as white as its citizens preferred. The intensified post-Turner concern for white security generated renewed efforts to limit slave imports in order to prevent the in-migration of dangerous or troublesome slaves.[101] The state's original 1792 constitution allowed the state legislature to prohibit the importation of slaves, and laws were passed for that purpose in 1794 and 1815, but these statutes contained so many loopholes that they proved impossible to enforce. Beginning in 1827 and continuing for the next five years, Kentucky colonizationists pushed anew for a legislative ban on the importation of slaves, but their efforts proved futile. Moreover, a hostile public reaction to these efforts forced one colonizationist, Robert J. Breckinridge, an outspoken Presbyterian minister who was the son of John Breckinridge, to resign his seat in the legislature after publishing an essay endorsing gradual emancipation.[102]

In February 1833, however, increased public concern about white safety in reaction to the Turner insurrection helped supporters win legislative approval for a ban. That year, Kentucky banned the importation of slaves except by in-migrants coming to take up permanent residence in the state and bringing slaves with them. Even residents were not allowed to purchase and import slaves unless those slaves were part of an inheritance or a marriage gift. The penalty for violation of the ban was forfeiture of the slave(s) in question plus a $600 fine. Enforcement of the statute was placed in the hands of county attorneys, who would receive 20 percent of the value of forfeited slaves.[103] Two years later, proslavery forces led by wealthy Bluegrass planter

Robert Wickliffe, Kentucky's most determined defender of slavery, fought for repeal of the ban. This repeal effort passed the senate but failed in the house, and the ban remained in effect until 1849, when a repeal was approved as part of the political bargaining surrounding the calling of a state constitutional convention.[104]

The Turner insurrection also focused new attention on colonization in Kentucky. The state's Presbyterian Synod had endorsed colonization as early as 1823, and in 1829, the five extant chapters of the Kentucky Colonization Society finally affiliated with the ACS.[105] In 1830, the ACS leadership argued that "[p]robably in no state of the Union has the scheme of African Colonization found more decided friends or met with more general approbation than in Kentucky," and by 1831, some thirty-one local colonization auxiliaries flourished in the commonwealth.[106] Still, even in Kentucky, the ACS found it easier to win rhetorical support than financial assistance. In 1832, the Louisville chapter, the most active of Kentucky colonization auxiliaries, could raise only $800 in support of the cause.[107] But in 1833, Richard Bibb, a Logan County slaveholder, freed fifty-one of his slaves and helped outfit the first cohort of newly freed blacks shipped directly from Kentucky to Liberia, via New Orleans.[108] Colonization publicist James Birney returned to Kentucky in 1833, sensing that the state offered fertile ground for the colonization cause. Birney quickly grew frustrated with Kentucky's reluctance to embrace gradual emancipation as a matter of state policy, however, and these frustrations turned him into an abolitionist and member of the radical American Anti-Slavery Society by 1835. Kentucky's interest in colonization continued, but after the Bibb-led expedition in 1833, Kentucky mounted no further shipments to Liberia over the next five years, and it was not until the 1840s that the idea of Kentucky establishing its own colony for free blacks in Africa, the "Kentucky in Liberia" movement, gained momentum in the state.[109]

Underlying attitudes concerning slavery in Kentucky paralleled those in Virginia. Whites in the urban areas, the mountains, and much of the northern and western portions of the state, where the slave population was small, tended to support the gradual phasing out of slavery. A strong contingent of Bluegrass planters, headed by Robert Wickliffe, clung to slavery almost as tenaciously as Southside Virginia planters did. At the very least, these Bluegrass slaveholders wanted the fate of slavery in Kentucky to remain in their hands, and, as a result, they fought hard to hold the reins of state government. The state's political moderates, who included a modest number of patrician planters and professionals from the Bluegrass, looked to whiten the state, and to varying degrees they were willing to use gradual emancipation and colonization to accomplish this end. In practice, however, these moderates were cautious. Colonization of free blacks was hardly imperative in a state where free blacks numbered fewer than five thousand (less than 1 percent of the total population) in 1830 and could readily move to a free state simply by crossing the Ohio River. By the mid-1830s, moderates knew that Kentucky was selling slaves to the lower South at a healthy pace. They could foresee the state whitening itself almost inevitably. The rest was a matter of pace and means.

Well before Turner's insurrection frightened upper South whites anew, Maryland had informally decided to reduce its dependence on slavery through private manumission and the sale of slaves to the lower South. But, despite some state encouragement of colonization, the decline of slavery had increased Maryland's free black population from just under twenty thousand in 1800 to almost fifty-three thousand in 1830.[110] Thus in 1832, spurred by the bloodshed at Southampton, Maryland had its own debate over slavery. White Marylanders of various persuasions petitioned the legislature for a reconsideration of the state's policy toward slavery and free blacks, and the 1832 legislature referred all petitions to a joint legislative committee controlled by slaveholders. Six of the seven members of the committee were from southern Maryland, where support for slavery was strongest, and all seven were slaveholders. The committee was chaired by Henry Brawner, who owned fifty-eight slaves and represented black-majority Charles County in southern Maryland.[111] In creating this committee and referring all petitions to it, the Maryland legislature knew that it was placing the state's reconsideration of slavery under the initial aegis of slaveholders.

But Brawner's slaveholder-controlled committee produced a surprising report. It denounced slavery as an "admitted and awful evil," and called it a "blighting curse" on the Maryland economy because it discouraged whites from migrating to the state. As a remedy, the Brawner report called for Maryland to encourage gradual emancipation and mandate colonization of free blacks. Brawner thought encouraging gradual emancipation would be easy, since "slavery in our state has been wearing itself out," and he estimated that Maryland masters had already manumitted almost one-third of their slaves. But for Brawner and his committee, emancipation without colonization only made a bad situation worse. Thus the committee urged the state to finance the mandatory removal of free blacks.[112]

Southern Maryland legislators quickly rallied behind the Brawner report, but northern Maryland solons opposed it, preferring to continue the process of emancipation without the removal of free blacks that they had practiced for decades. Because southern Maryland dominated the state's malapportioned legislature, Brawner's plan nevertheless won approval easily, 37–23. Southern Maryland lawmakers voted for it by a margin of 31–6; northern Maryland lawmakers voted against it 16–6.[113] The legislature approved $200,000 of funding, appropriated over twenty years, with a maximum of $20,000 in any given year, for colonization. Additionally, the legislature also used its post-Turner reconsideration of slavery to enact tough new restrictions on the state's rapidly increasing free black population. It banned free blacks from voting, serving on juries, and holding office, passed tough new vagrancy laws allowing the state to force free blacks with no visible means of support to hire out for a year, and if the free black in question was again unemployed after a year of hiring out, then the state could sell the individual as a slave for a year.[114]

But Maryland's tough new mandatory removal law quickly proved a failure. Brawner and his supporters had included enforcement provisions in the legislation.

County clerks of court were required to report any manumissions within five days, and they were subject to a $10 fine for failure to report. All slaves manumitted after passage of the law were required to leave the state. A county judge could make an exception on the grounds "of good conduct and character" if the judge was willing to issue the recently freed black a license to stay.[115] But these provisions provided northern Marylanders with loopholes for evading the law, and they used those loopholes freely. Clerks of court in northern Maryland often failed to report manumissions and county judges in northern Maryland issued licenses liberally. Northern Maryland's clever recalcitrance undermined the state's official policy of mandatory removal.[116]

Brawner and his southern Maryland allies made no effort to stiffen penalties or otherwise compel compliance from northern Maryland. Their hesitation on this point might suggest, as William Freehling has suggested, that Brawner and southern Maryland slaveholders themselves had qualms about enforcing coerced colonization across the board, especially against those free blacks who were, in Brawner's words, "family friends."[117] But it is also possible that the failure of lawmakers from southern Maryland to seek full compliance with the law suggests they had envisioned all along approving a state mandate that could be interpreted as a local-option measure. Slaveholding politicians who left enforcement in the hands of county judges and clerks must have expected some local variation in levels of compliance. Arguably Brawner and his allies were satisfied with establishing a state-funded mechanism for colonizing free blacks from southern Maryland and allowing whites in northern Maryland to chart their own course.

If forced colonization foundered, at least in northern Maryland, the state nevertheless did much to promote voluntary colonization. Founded a few months before Turner's rebellion in 1831, the Maryland Colonization Society worked hard to create a new colony, "Maryland in Africa," located near the existing ACS colony in Liberia.[118] The state spent most of the $200,000 it appropriated for removal to construct and assist this new colony. Having placed draconian new restrictions on free blacks who remained in Maryland, the legislature sweetened the temptation to leave by offering prospective colonists free passage to the colony, rent and board for six months, and five acres to farm for life.[119] But if northern Maryland whites frustrated southern Maryland whites' law requiring mandatory colonization, free blacks frustrated the dreams of Maryland colonizationists even more, refusing to accept the state's incentives to migrate to Africa. Over the first two decades of its existence, the Maryland Colonization Society colonized only about one thousand free blacks, while during the same period, the state's free black population grew by nearly 20 percent per decade.[120]

THE NAT TURNER INSURRECTION produced a heated but ultimately indecisive debate on the slavery question in the upper South. On other questions, such as the status of free blacks and the desire to whiten the upper South, varying but more conclusive answers emerged. In places such as Delaware and Maryland, where slavery was decaying under the weight of its own diminishing profitability, post-Turner debates actually focused on the position of free blacks in economies trying to transition from slave labor to free labor. In Delaware, the protoindustrial economy spreading out of Philadelphia seemed able to absorb healthy quantities of free black labor, rendering the question not so much one of whitening Delaware as one of how best to control its proportionately large (nearly 21 percent in 1830) free black population. Maryland proved divided over how to handle its growing free black population. Apparently agreeing with Delaware, the whiter northern portion of the state thought second-class citizenship and absorption in the free-labor economy in and around Baltimore would work well enough. In blacker southern Maryland, whites preferred whitening the state through the forced deportation (colonization) of free blacks, especially as slavery continued to erode. In Kentucky, where slavery remained robust in key areas of the state but the overall proportion of slaves in the state held at relatively unthreatening levels (25 percent or less), debate focused on public safety and the question of keeping a small free black population small. Diffusion, with some help from colonization and the flight of free blacks to free states, appeared sufficient to keep Kentucky white enough to suit most white Kentuckians.

Virginia, where the Turner rebellion struck the deepest emotional chords, produced the most inconclusive debates. The Old Dominion's huge slave population (pushing ever closer to a half million), its proportion of slaves (edging toward 40 percent), and its free black population (second-largest in the South in 1830) presented by far the most difficult whitening challenge in the upper South. And slaveholders in at least one portion of the state (the Southside) seemed determined to fight whitening with lower-South-style tenacity. In the end, the great Virginia debate over slavery and colonization did more to reveal lines of fissure and the depth of the chasms among whites in the state than to resolve problems. Yet for all the state's inability to find a way to emancipate slaves, or even to colonize a significant number of free blacks, the political center of gravity in the Old Dominion still declared slavery an evil and still sought the whitening of the state, even if the state's "indecisive decision" on slavery and colonization meant that whitening would come chiefly through the sale and forced migration of slaves south. And, if nothing else, Virginia diffused slaves, through sale and forced migration, in prolific fashion. During the three decades following Turner's rebellion, Virginia "exported" roughly three hundred thousand slaves, a number nearly equal to South Carolina's entire 1830 slave population. This thirty-year diffusion lessened the proportion of slaves in Virginia from over 38 percent to 31 percent. Apart from free-labor Delaware, the upper portion of the upper South remained committed to the idea of whitening the region, though no consensus emerged concerning means. In the absence of such a consensus, Thomas Dew's highly visible invisible hand of slave sales and coerced migration did most of the work. For much of the upper South, the practical answer to the slavery question was to let their slaves become the lower South's problem.

CHAPTER THIRTEEN

TENNESSEE DEBATES SLAVERY

In the middle South, that lower tier of the upper South where the proportions and numbers of slaves and free blacks were smaller than Virginia's, the post-Turner crisis also raised questions about the future of slavery and the position of free blacks in a slaveholding society. But in the middle South, these issues were debated not in the aftermath of a divisive state constitutional convention, as was the case in Virginia, but as Tennessee and North Carolina moved haltingly but inexorably toward state constitutional conventions of their own (1834 and 1835, respectively). These constitutional reform movements were driven by the pressure from white egalitarians eager to democratize state politics as thoroughly as possible despite entrenched conservative opposition. Thus, in the middle South, the debates over slavery and free blacks occurred within the cauldron of a white egalitarian crusade for constitutional revision.

TENNESSEE, WITH ITS SLAVE POPULATION hovering around 20 percent of the state's total population, half of its counties having slave populations of less than 13 percent, no black-majority counties, only three counties having slave populations of more than 40 percent, and no black-belt area comparable to Southside Virginia, nevertheless had enough slaves and enough ties to the Old Dominion to react quickly to the news of the Nat Turner insurrection. The insurrection and the scare that followed produced an abrupt turn in many of Tennessee's policies toward slaves and free blacks.[1] Tennessee's post-Turner crackdown covered a broad range of issues but focused on preventing slave unrest. At an active legislative session held in December 1831, the reward for returning a runaway slave was increased, magistrates were given power to appoint patrols if militia captains failed to do so in a timely fashion, and patrols were required to perform daylight duty as well as evening watches and empowered "to arrest all slaves found off their master's plantation without a pass in the daytime as heretofore in the night."[2] Tennessee's 1831 legislature also banned free blacks from entering the state under the penalty of fine or imprisonment.[3]

Yet perhaps the most controversial change in Tennessee law regarding slavery after the Turner rebellion lay in its policy toward manumission. In 1801, Tennessee had ceded control of manumission from the legislature to the county courts, which gained the authority to grant requests by owners to free individual slaves on the condition that masters seeking to manumit slaves provide the county adequate resources to support the newly freed black. But in December 1831, Tennessee reversed its course, prohibiting individual manumission except in cases where the freed person would be immediately removed from the state. Any owner wishing to effect emancipation and removal was required to give a bond equal to the value of the slave to aid in the removal process.[4]

However, after just a year with the new restrictions in effect, enough dissatisfaction with the removal provision existed to prompt a legislative debate over its repeal. The dissatisfaction centered in eastern Tennessee, the portion of the state with the fewest slaves and the home of most of the state's proemancipation sentiment. In September 1833, James W. Wyly, a state senator from eastern Tennessee, proposed eliminating the requirement that slaves manumitted be forced to leave the state immediately at the master's expense. Wyly argued that a return to the law of 1801 would save the legislature time and money by allowing it to focus on major issues, trusting the county courts to provide adequate safeguards for the security of the community, as they had during the previous thirty years. Wyly rested his case on the notion that masters should have the right to treat their property as they saw fit as long as it produced no injury to the community at large. The 1831 law, he pointed out, even prohibited masters from freeing slaves who saved the master's life or exposed planned insurrections. It also prevented heirs from granting deathbed wishes. Yet the "danger of discord or domestic insurrection," feared by opponents of repeal, flourished "only in the imagination." Restrictions on the power of the individual slaveholder represented the triumph of "despotism," in Wyly's view. "We may indeed retain the name of freedom, but it will be the freedom of the slave."[5]

Wyly's proposal for liberalizing the state's recently tightened manumission laws drew vigorous opposition. Leonard H. Sims of Franklin led the opposition. Senator Sims, who had emancipated many of his slaves in 1830, had been criticized during his campaign as "dangerous to our institutions," but in the debate over repeal of the restriction on manumission, Sims emerged as a vigorous defender of the 1831 law. Sims attributed interest in a more convenient and generous manumission policy not to the burden of handling requests placed on the legislature's time but to falling cotton prices, which led masters to free slaves in order to avoid the expense of their upkeep. If a greater number of slaves were freed and "turned loose on society," Sims predicted, they "will mingle with our slaves and corrupt them, and form an association with a degraded set of white persons, and the country would soon be filled with a race of free negroes, mulattoes and quarterroons, who will be a pest and degradation on society." Sims argued that Tennessee slaves, "when well-fed and clothed," were generally "much more contented and happy than the free blacks." The living condition of Tennessee slaves as a class, he maintained, compared favorably with that of workers Sims had seen on his travels to Ohio, where "in their large manufactories whole families, men, women and children, compelled to toil for support," live "in a more hapless condition that the slave." Sims even claimed that "if I had my choice of situations, I would prefer being a slave in this State...than to be in the situation of a laborer in one those Ohio woolen factories."[6]

Sims also argued that the problems associated with a growing free black population should not be taken lightly. He attributed "the horrid massacre committed by the negroes" in Virginia to "permitting the free black and the slave to associate together." Sims judged that there was not an honest free black in his district, and he claimed that personal experience had taught him that "free blacks become the agents or commission merchants for the purpose of receiving and vending the property slaves steal from their masters." Sims vowed his support for private manumissions, but only when followed by colonization. It was imperative "not to permit the liberated negroes to reside among us," he urged, "let them go to Africa...where they can enjoy their freedom."[7]

Maury County's Edward B. Littlefield joined Sims in opposing the repeal of the removal clause. Littlefield claimed that "he was not an advocate of slavery as an abstract principle," and maintained that he "would do anything in the compass of my power to abolish slavery; but it can not be done." Moreover, Littlefield added that, "I would go as far as any man to put a stop to that inhuman traffic in slaves in which is going on in our country." But despite his reservations about slavery and his disdain for the internal slave trade, Littlefield worried about the "mawkish sentimentality prevailing about the condition of our slaves" that had begun in the North and East but "has found its way into Tennessee." Such sentiment was misguided, he argued, because the "Catholic Irish, and the operators of woolen factories of England," live in "a more degraded state than the slaves on our plantations." Moreover, Littlefield complained, outside philanthropy "has for its ultimate object a general emancipation—to interfere with relationships between master and slave, and to deprive the slaveholder of his property without paying him one cent as an equivalent therefore." The bill allowing manumission without removal was not a proposal for general emancipation, Littlefield admitted, but it represented "one step," the infamous entering wedge, toward "universal emancipation." Its success, Littlefield believed, would fuel the "spirit of fanaticism" that was abroad on the subject.[8]

Ultimately, Littlefield moved to a racial justification of slavery. The South's peculiar institution, he contended, differed from slavery in earlier times because southern slaves were "different of colour" from their masters, a fact that would "forever preclude the African from residing among us on terms of equality." Littlefield called these attitudes an "honest and honorable prejudice on the part of the whites, which none of us wish to see done away." Littlefield thought the "place" for free blacks had been provided in "Liberia, under the patronage of the Colonization Society." The ACS, Littlefield declared, promised a great service to the "African race" unless its progress was interrupted by the screeds of abolitionists such as William Lloyd Garrison and Benjamin Lundy. The emancipation-without-removal bill, Littlefield concluded, stood as "an entering wedge of further emancipation measures, which, if successful are to bring on scenes of St. Domingo and Southampton" in Tennessee. "The free negroes, in a slaveholding section, are a curse to society," he proclaimed; "they are a degraded, debased race. They are too lazy to work, and in general get their living by dishonest means....I, for one, am unwilling, in any way, to increase the facilities for emancipation, except on the condition of colonization."[9] The 1833 legislature refused to modify the tough new 1831 manumission law.[10]

These brief legislative skirmishes between eastern Tennessee critics of slavery and state legislators who saw greater evils emerging from emancipation than slavery anticipated more dramatic confrontations on the subject in the near future. In 1830, the proportion of slaves in Tennessee was roughly the same as in Kentucky—about one-fifth of the total population. But slavery was on a different trajectory in Tennessee than in Kentucky. Tennessee's most rapidly growing areas were in its western region, which was hospitable to plantation agriculture. The rapid expansion of slavery into the western valley of the Tennessee River and the highly fertile plateau of west Tennessee lying between the western valley and the Mississippi River made cotton and slavery seem a part of Tennessee's future prosperity rather than a source of stagnation and decline. As a result, slaves as a proportion of Tennessee's population remained roughly the same through the late antebellum decades, while in Kentucky the slave population declined to only 16 percent by 1860.[11]

Still, because of its very white eastern region, where in most counties slaves accounted for less than 10 percent of the total population, Tennessee had long nurtured active manumission and colonization movements, often led by people who considered themselves antislavery.[12] In its early days, the emancipation movement in Tennessee was overwhelmingly religious in nature, drawing the bulk of its support from Quakers and their allies among the Protestant clergy and the latter's dedicated lay followers. As early as 1814, a group of eight east Tennesseans gathered at the home of Elihu Swain in Jefferson County, northeast of Knoxville, and formed a temporary Tennessee Manumission Society. The next year, a larger group of Friends gathered to approve a constitution for the "Tennessee Society for Manumission of Slaves" because "Freedom is the natural right of all men." The society pledged itself to stand for "True Republican principles" and vowed to vote only for politicians who favored emancipation.[13] Similar organizations were quickly formed in seven other east Tennessee counties. In November 1815, the first state convention of these manumission societies was held at the Friends' meetinghouse in Greene County, with Quaker minister Charles Osburn leading the meeting and Presbyterian pastor John Rankin assisting.[14]

The Manumission Society orchestrated the presentation of memorials and petitions to the Tennessee legislature urging that a plan of gradual emancipation be approved. In 1819, thirty-five petitions bearing nearly two thousand signatures inundated Tennessee lawmakers. The legislative committee that received the petitions reported that they "regret the occasion which gave rise to the introduction of slavery in the United States," but since slavery was established, the legislature had no right to tamper with the property rights of slaveholders. Even gradual emancipation, the committee argued, lessened the value of slave property and the "power to lessen the value of a man's property is necessarily the power to render that property of no value whatever." The committee, however, vowed to add no additional restrictions to the voluntary manumission process.[15]

East Tennessee also became a home for the proemancipation press in the South. In 1819, Elihu Embree launched the *Manumission Intelligencer* in east Tennessee, with the support of the Tennessee Manumission Society. Embree, a slaveholding Quaker, claimed that too many southern slaveholders treated slaves like "mules and asses" by "beating, driving, starving and buying and selling them as if they were brutes in reality."[16] When Embree died unexpectedly, emancipation supporters in east Tennessee urged Benjamin Lundy to move his *Genius of Universal Emancipation* from Ohio to east Tennessee. Lundy remained in Tennessee for two years before moving on to Baltimore, but his brief presence in the region raised the profile of emancipation sentiment in the state.[17] In 1823, the Tennessee Manumission Society endorsed colonization as a logical complement to plans for gradual emancipation. The society encouraged masters to educate their slaves "as far as practicable" but urged members not to assist slaves in running away from their masters.[18] In 1827, manumission advocate Thomas Dean labeled slavery a "volcano in disguise" and "dangerous to the safety and happiness of any government on earth where it is tolerated."[19]

As important as the antislavery press and the manumission societies were in keeping emancipation sentiment alive in east Tennessee, rank-and-file activists played a significant role. In an important recent article that refocuses scholarly attention on the persistence of emancipation sentiment in Tennessee, historian Caitlin Fitz found that between 1816 and 1825, more than forty-five hundred signatures appeared on petitions favoring emancipation.[20] In asking the legislature to end slavery, these petitions generally focused on its unchristian nature and charged that the institution contradicted the principles of the Declaration of Independence. Fitz's analysis of petitions from the 1820s found that in east Tennessee 16 to 18 percent of adult white males in Greene, Jefferson, and Washington counties signed emancipation petitions. Yet only eleven counties, all but one located in east Tennessee, had more than 3 percent of all adult white males sign such petitions, while fifty-one counties had less than 3 percent sign. In thirty counties, less than

1 percent of adult white males signed. In twenty-six of those counties, not a single white male signed an emancipation petition. This pattern of petition signatures reveals a thin smattering of emancipation sentiment in middle Tennessee and a paucity of such sentiment in the state's western region, compared to significant support for gradual emancipation in the east.[21] Thus the petitions to the Tennessee legislature during the 1820s indicated a sectionalization of emancipation sentiment in Tennessee. Moreover, by the late 1820s, the manumission movement appeared in decline in Tennessee. The number of manumission societies began to shrink, and petitions to the legislature slowed, perhaps as sheer frustration with legislative dismissal mounted. Advocates of manumission in Tennessee looked either for a new strategy, a new burst of enthusiasm, or a new opportunity.[22] After Nat Turner's insurrection, the threat to white safety posed by slavery spawned at least a modicum of new interest in gradual emancipation, and the public agitation during the early 1830s for a state constitutional convention opened a new venue for advocates of gradual emancipation to argue their case.

A broad array of nagging issues rather than a single compelling one animated calls for a constitutional convention in Tennessee during the early 1830s. In many respects, the state constitutional controversy in Tennessee looked like a less volatile version of Virginia's constitutional crisis. Tennessee's white egalitarians demanded a series of democratic reforms that would eliminate property requirements for voting and office holding, apportion the state legislature on the "white basis," restructure an inefficient judiciary, and revamp a property tax system that taxed land by acreage rather than value.[23] In 1831, Tennessee voters rejected a call for a convention by a margin of just over two thousand votes, but two years later, voters approved a convention scheduled to begin in March 1834.[24] The call for a constitutional convention combined with the anxiety generated among whites by the Turner rebellion to give Tennessee's critics of slavery a new sense of opportunity.[25] During the canvass for the election of delegates to the 1834 convention, critics of slavery revived their moribund petition campaign in an effort to nudge a state recently frightened by slave insurrection and freshly aroused by rhetoric of republican equality closer toward the adoption of a plan for gradual emancipation.

But, as Fitz's analysis of this new round of petitions criticizing slavery emphasizes, the post-Turner round of legislative petitions also shifted the argument against slavery in Tennessee rather dramatically. The new petitions continued to brand slavery as an institution that violated every tenet of Christian morality and corrupted the morals of free people who lived in slaveholding areas, but in these post-Turner, convention-era petitions, the moral evils of slavery took a backseat to warnings about slavery as a threat to, rather than a promoter of, white equality, as well as a danger to white safety.[26] Petitioners complained that slaveholders enjoyed "exclusive" privileges under the terms of the state's 1796 constitution (in terms of voting, representation, and taxes).[27] Hence Tennessee whites lived under the "name" of a "republican institution" when in fact the "most odious features of aristockracy [*sic*]" had invaded the system.[28]

Petitioners also complained that slavery threatened the "future peace" of the state. Calling for the mandatory colonization of all slaves emancipated in the state, these post-Turner petitions insisted that "scenes which recently passed in a neighboring state" warned of "anarchy, ruin and Blood shed" if the state failed to remain appropriately white.[29] In practical terms, many of the post-Turner petitions urged the convention to give the legislature power to approve a plan of gradual emancipation and colonization, if and when it chose to do so, without having to amend the state constitution. Clearly Tennessee's critics of slavery hoped to tap into broader egalitarian reform sentiments concerning republican equality and white safety to advance the cause of gradual emancipation and colonization at a time when the state's fundamental law was in flux.

THE CANVASS FOR CALLING A CONVENTION and electing delegates worried some Tennessee slaveholders. William B. Campbell of Sparta, whose western Virginia kin were strong egalitarian reformers, conceded that Tennessee's tax system was "unfair" and its judiciary "defective," but he worried that the convention would be "rife with demagogues" who would "bring everything down to the simplest democracy," because Tennessee lacked a truly conservative region, like Virginia's Tidewater, to ensure balance.[30] The election results did little to assuage conservative fears about the dangers of democratic excess. Campbell judged the elected delegates "an ordinary body."[31] But once the convention began its work, which lasted for fourteen weeks, its operations surprised its critics. Though its quiet deliberations on the question of slavery hardly drew the attention that Virginia's month of contretemps had two years earlier, Tennessee's constitutional convention of 1834 confronted the issues of emancipation and the status of free blacks early in its proceedings, and the controversy continued throughout the convention.[32]

Memorials offered by antislavery societies from various locales around the state, especially from east Tennessee, prompted consideration of the question of emancipation. None of these memorials asked for immediate emancipation, but they did challenge the morality of slavery, proclaimed its inconsistency with the ideals of the Declaration of Independence, argued its apparent contradiction of the basic principles of republicanism, and warned that it threatened white safety. The memorials also offered a variety of proposals for the eventual elimination of slavery in the Volunteer State, usually ones favoring long waiting periods before emancipation actually began and often coupling emancipation with a condition that newly freed blacks be required to leave the state. One proposal called for the emancipation of all slaves in 1855 contingent upon their removal from Tennessee once freed. Another proposal postponed the day of emancipation until 1866 and expressed the hope that the freed blacks could be colonized promptly. The memorial seeking the earliest action called simply for the emancipation of all children born to slaves after 1835. All of these proposals, while far more radical than a majority of convention delegates were willing to consider, would have allowed Tennesseans to postpone the day of reckoning with slavery for at least a generation.[33]

The bulk of the memorials came from east Tennessee, where slaves accounted for less than 10 percent of the population and where the early antislavery and colonization societies had flourished. Of the thirty memorials in favor of later emancipation, twenty-five came from east Tennessee, while only five came from middle Tennessee, a region that included many Highland Rim counties with few slaves as well as the slave-rich Nashville basin. No memorials calling for an end to slavery came from west Tennessee, an area where the slave economy was growing rapidly. In fact, forty-two of the state's sixty-two counties produced no memorials criticizing slavery, and according to one scholar of slavery in Tennessee, the 105 slaveholders who signed proemancipation memorials together owned fewer than five hundred slaves.[34] Still, the mere arrival of over two dozen memorials seeking emancipation at a sovereign convention in Tennessee triggered intriguing maneuvers on the issue.

On May 24, 1834, the convention referred the memorials to the convention's committee on propositions and grievances rather than permit a lively public convention debate over them.[35] But since memorials were still read on the floor when introduced, delegates considered a variety of additional approaches for handling the issues of slavery and emancipation raised in the petitions. Former governor Willie Blount, a middle Tennessee delegate representing one of the most heavily slave districts in the state, proposed the creation of a twenty-six-member committee charged with writing a provision for the new constitution on "slavery and emancipation" that would "once and for all put these subjects at rest, never to be interfered with by the Legislature in any circumstances." But Washington County's Matthew Stevenson, an east Tennessee delegate and an outspoken defender of the memorials, mocked Blount's proposal by calling for the creation of a committee charged with "designating some future period from which slavery will not be tolerated in this state."[36] On June 6, John M'Gaughey, who represented five districts in east Tennessee with small slave populations, moved for the adoption of Stevenson's earlier motion, initiating nearly a full day of debate and procedural maneuvering at the convention.[37]

East Tennessee delegate John McKinney, an influential member of the convention, countered with the idea of a committee of three, composed of one delegate from each of Tennessee's grand divisions, and instructed by the whole body "to report the reasons why this Convention can have nothing to do with these memorials." McKinney, who represented a county where slaves were less than 8 percent of the population, expressed regret that some delegates chose to "distract ourselves" with the question of emancipation while the long-awaited democratic reforms that spurred the calling of the convention remained unfinished. Noting that even if Tennessee abolished slavery, its slaves would merely be "sold off South" with their "hope of emancipation further removed," McKinney urged the convention to "not meddle with this business."[38]

Middle Tennessee reformer Terry Cahal agreed, maintaining that he "knew nine-tenths of the people would sanction" McKinney's position. Aware of the vigorous debate that had erupted in the Virginia legislature in 1832 and the widespread publicity that accompanied it, Cahal worried that a public debate over emancipation at the Tennessee convention would both undermine already fragile public confidence in the convention and give unintended succor to northern abolitionists. "The eyes of the south, yes, and the north too, were upon us," Cahal reminded the convention. Styling himself the "master of no man," Cahal cautioned delegates against seeking to remedy "the wrongs of the black man" by inflicting "an irreparable injury" on the whites through discussion of "impracticable" plans freighted with "pernicious consequences." Cahal believed, as did many other egalitarian reformers in the convention, that the cause of democratic reform would be doomed if it became entangled with the cause of gradual emancipation. Yet some eastern delegates supported both causes and believed that they were largely inseparable.[39] Thus white egalitarians outside of east Tennessee, and even some east Tennessee reformers, moved to distance themselves from advocates of emancipation, making common cause with conservatives on the issue of slavery.

Delegate Bradley Kimbrough from Monroe, an eastern county along the North Carolina border, urged the adoption of Stevenson's proposed committee of thirteen as "more respectful" to the petitioners, but Davidson County's Francis Fogg countered that a three-person committee was "less unwieldy" and "more likely to make a report that should settle the principle of non-interference" by the convention on the subject of slavery. East Tennessee's Richard Bradshaw, a defender of the memorialists, supported Stevenson's plan and urged the convention to confront the issue of slavery directly. Western Tennessee delegate Adam Huntsman sharply denounced the antislavery memorialists, claiming that "no fanatic" or "enthusiast" preaching "impracticable schemes of emancipation" had ever found a way to square such proposals with the private property rights so clearly protected by the United States Constitution. The staggering cost of the "just compensation" due the owners of slave property rendered emancipation schemes visionary rather than practical. The convention, Huntsman argued, "had no more authority to regulate or disturb the rights of property" in slaves than to confiscate any other kind of property. Yet even Huntsman, an adamant opponent of the memorialists, professed that he was "favorably disposed towards the Colonization Society and all other modes which can . . . be designed of transporting people of color to Liberia," and he stood ready to "provide aid" to "any person who will voluntarily choose to emancipate his or her slaves." Huntsman favored finding blacks "some country where they could have enjoyed rational liberty and republican government." But he vigorously opposed freedom and equality for blacks, whether slave or free, in Tennessee or anywhere in the United States, which Huntsman saw as a white man's country.[40]

Huntsman concluded his blistering critique of the memorials with a motion urging that the convention immediately table all such memorials. Cumberland Plateau delegate William Senter favored Huntsman's motion on tabling, and John J. White also supported tabling the memorials, noting that the convention "already had topics enough before it already, of a sufficiently exciting character without this firebrand being thrown into our proceedings." The convention, he urged, should "set this matter to rest" immediately. After extended debate, the convention approved the Huntsman motion to table the memorials by a vote of 38–20.[41]

In broad terms, this vote represented the first test of strength for proemancipation forces at the Tennessee convention. A few delegates who opposed the emancipation memorials thought they deserved discussion by the convention and voted against Huntsman's gag motion for that reason alone, but the broad contours of the vote nonetheless revealed the key lines of division among delegates over the questions of slavery and gradual emancipation. A vote in favor of Huntsman's motion to table represented a reluctance to even discuss the issue of slavery at the convention, much less take any action that might nudge the state toward gradual emancipation. A vote against the motion generally reflected a desire to have a debate over slavery in Tennessee at the convention with the hope of establishing some plan for future emancipation. Thirteen of the twenty votes against the motion came from east Tennessee. As a cohort, east Tennessee delegates voted 13–7 against the motion. In contrast, middle Tennessee delegates voted 20–7 in favor of the motion to table. Moreover, four of the seven middle Tennessee votes against tabling came from delegates representing Highland Rim and Cumberland Plateau counties with few slaves. Perhaps even more notably, delegates from west Tennessee voted solidly, 12–0, in favor of tabling the memorials. Thus, unlike Virginia, where the less developed western portion of the state expected integration into the free-labor economy of the Ohio Valley, the rich, flat alluvial lands of west Tennessee expected fuller integration into the slave-based staple economy of the lower Mississippi Valley, and hence strongly favored the continuation of slavery.[42]

The passage of the Huntsman motion appeared to have quieted the emancipation issue. But at the afternoon session on that same day, Nelson Hess, a western delegate emboldened by the convention's decision to table the memorials, submitted a series of resolutions defining the centrality of slavery to Tennessee society to the convention. At first glance, Hess' resolutions appeared designed to strengthen slavery by limiting the power of the state legislature over the institution. According to Hess, the legislature should possess "no power to pass laws for the emancipation of slaves without the consent of the owner" and without full compensation to the owners. He also argued that the legislature should have "no power" to prevent emigrants "from bringing slaves with them to Tennessee," and should pass laws prohibiting masters from manumitting their slaves unless provisions were made to remove them from the state once they gained freedom. Yet Hess also wanted to explicitly grant the legislature authority to regulate some matters related to slavery. He argued that the legislature should be granted power to block the importation of slaves for sale, pass statutes requiring masters to treat slaves with "humanity," and prevent free blacks from emigrating to and settling in Tennessee. In essence, Hess proposed a new constitutional "slave code" for Tennessee, one that would outline with some precision exactly how what power the legislature should have over slavery. Rather than defending the principle of legislative noninterference with slavery articulated earlier in the debate, Hess wanted the new constitution to prescribe exactly how and when the legislature might "interfere" with slavery—though generally in the interest of protecting it. Moreover, Hess' proposal, with its provisions for allowing masters to control emancipation, protecting the right of residents to import slaves, and mandating the humane treatment of slaves, arguably would have moved the state toward the acceptance of slavery as a permanent institution governed by paternalism.[43]

Suggesting that Hess' resolutions went too far toward the endorsement of perpetual slavery, and recognizing that they opened a Pandora's box of questions about where the master's power should end and the legislature's begin on matters related to slavery, middle Tennessee delegate Robert Allen presented a resolution calling for the implementation of McKinney's earlier proposal for the creation of a three-person committee, composed of one delegate from each of the state's three grand divisions, to draft a resolution explaining the reasons governing the convention's refusal to "act on the memorials on the subject of slavery." The convention adopted the Allen proposal without a roll call, and convention president William B. Carter of east Tennessee quickly appointed fellow east Tennessean McKinney to chair the committee, with Robert Allen from middle Tennessee and Adam Huntsman from west Tennessee serving as members. Carter's choice of committee members ensured that the final report would bear the careful reasoning and craftsmanship of McKinney, one of the most able men at the convention, and his selections also ensured that the report would advise the convention against taking any action on the emancipation memorials but stop short of judging slavery as anything but a problem that defied solution.[44]

IN THE TENNESSEE CONVENTION's debates prior to the creation of the McKinney committee, a majority of delegates had shown a strong inclination to limit debate over the question of emancipation, with the core of the sentiment coming from western egalitarian reformers. Some strident critics of emancipation wanted not merely to stifle debate on the subject but actually to create strong constitutional protections for slavery that would make it difficult for any future legislature to implement a plan of gradual emancipation. But these delegates seeking constitutional protection for slavery found it hard to forge a majority. A majority of eastern delegates supported a fulsome discussion of plans for gradual emancipation even though it seemed clear that such plans would be rejected by the convention as a whole. Still, advocates of gradual emancipation wanted to be heard.

After more than a week of work, the special committee, chaired by McKinney, submitted its report to the convention. Largely the handiwork of McKinney, the report defended the convention's earlier decision to "refuse to enter upon a lengthy discussion of the perplexing question." Convinced of the "utter impracticability" of all emancipation and expatriation plans, the committee concluded that such a debate would end in "the destruction of that harmony among members...so necessary...for the great work the people of Tennessee sent the convention here to perform." The committee conceded the "rectitude of the intentions" of the memorialists and acknowledged that proving slavery "a great evil" was "an easy task." But it added that "to tell how that evil can be removed is the question that the wisest heads and most benevolent hearts have not been able to answer."[45]

The McKinney committee grounded its opposition to emancipation firmly in the question of racial differences. Where the slave and master were of the "same race and wore the same complexion," the committee observed, slavery had "long ago been extinguished," and following their emancipation, former slaves successfully "mingled with the mass of the community." But, in the American South, McKinney wrote, "the African slave stands in a different attitude—he bears upon his forehead a mark of separation which distinguishes him from the white man—as much after he is a free man as while he was a slave." According to the committee, "complexion" marked "every one of the African race, so long as he remains among white men, as a person doomed to dwell in the suburbs of society, after he is free as much as when he was a slave." Thus the free black was "just as effectually barred" from enjoying "the privileges of membership with the rest of the community after he becomes a nominal free man" as was the slave.[46]

In what proved the most controversial section of the report, the committee went on to claim that because " a free man of colour" inevitably remained surrounded "by persons of a different cast and complexion," free blacks were "despised and trampled by the rest of the community." Judging the condition of free blacks in Tennessee as "the most forlorn and wretched that can be imagined," the committee doubted that freeing slaves to become denizens of a biracial society dominated by whites represented a viable solution to the problem of slavery. Forever stigmatized by the identifying mark of race, the committee insisted, the condition of the free man of color in the midst of a community of white men with whom he had "no common interest, no fellow feeling, no equality," proved "worse" than that of slaves.[47]

Placing the state at odds with much of the upper South, however, McKinney's committee doubted the wisdom of whitening Tennessee by allowing its slaves to be sold further south. The steady flow of slaves to a handful of states in the lower South, the committee contended, could hardly alleviate, and might actually worsen, the overall plight of southern slaves. In Tennessee, McKinney insisted, "slaves are treated with as much humanity as in any part of the world where slavery exists." Tennessee slaves, he contended, "are well clothed and fed," and they "are not prohibited from attending public worship on Sundays," where they were "frequently taught to read at Sunday schools and they have access to religious instruction and the means of grace in common with the rest of the community." The drain of these purportedly well-treated Tennessee slaves "from this State to the states south and west of us," the reported maintained, would likely render slaves "much more uncomfortable." The report argued that slaves would be exposed to more "sickness and death by reason of the unhealthiness of the climate" in the lower South than in Tennessee, giving as an example "the ravages of cholera among the slave population in Louisiana." McKinney's committee concluded slaves would not "enjoy the comforts of life in the same abundance they do now" if sold further south. Most slaves, the report contended, were in "general attached to the homes they now have," and many waited for news about the convention's decision with "trembling anxiety," fearing their forced removal from the state.[48]

In rejecting the idea of draining slaves off to the lower South, McKinney and his committee once again framed the concept of diffusion as Jeffersonians had originally used it, as a means of spreading slaves more evenly over space in an effort to dilute slavery's deleterious effects, rather than its Jacksonian-era usage as a euphemism for whitening the upper South by blackening the lower South. In doing so, the committee echoed many of the original diffusionist themes. As long as slavery existed in the United States, the committee believed, "the benefit of both the slave and the free man" hinged on the principle that "slaves should be distributed over as large a territory as possible," because "thereby the slave receives better treatment and the free man is rendered more secure." Diffusing slaves over a broader space encouraged humane treatment of slaves and promoted the safety of whites, the committee maintained, while draining slaves into a handful of lower South states simply pushed slaves toward harsher living and working conditions and exposed whites to the increased dangers posed by a concentrated and poorly treated slave population. "Let the slaves in the Unites States...be congregated together within the bounds of three or four states, so that they can ascertain by their own numbers and strength, concert plans among themselves, and co-operate with each other," the McKinney committee reasoned, "then what is to prevent a servile war?" Thus the special committee endorsed "diffusion" rather than "draining" as the best policy for protecting whites from the dangers concomitant with slavery.[49]

The committee also discounted the idea of a state-funded program of large-scale colonization recommended by many memorials because the petitioners had failed to fully count "the cost of such an enterprise." The money could not be raised, the report held, and even if it could, many free blacks in Tennessee would not voluntarily leave the state, and McKinney's committee did not think the state could legally compel free people to leave without specific cause. If slaves were freed without colonization, the committee argued, a "constant collision" would occur between whites and free blacks. "Free people of color," the report maintained, "would be motivated" by "envy and hate" and "would have at their command a portion of physical strength that might...be wielded to the worst of purposes." It did not require "the gift of prophecy" to predict that such tension would endanger the peace, prosperity, and even "existence" of the state. "Are the bloody scenes of St. Domingo forgotten," the committee asked; "would not the same horrible tragedy be acted over again in our country, at our firesides, and in our bed chambers"? Any "meddling" with the institution of slavery by the convention, the committee concluded, would accomplish "no possible good" but might produce "evils beyond the power of calculation."[50]

But while the McKinney committee rejected the idea of whitening Tennessee through the drain of slaves to the lower South and denied the feasibility of large-scale, state-financed colonization, it embraced the idea of ultimately whitening the state, and even of weaning it away from slavery, through a properly, and very slowly, implemented plan of voluntary colonization. It commended the American Colonization Society's relocation efforts precisely because the society required the consent of the former slave or free black. The "friends of humanity need not despair," the committee declared, because "Providence has already opened a door of hope, which is every day growing wider and wider" in the form of the Liberian colony, where "the sons and daughters of Africa, made free by the consent of their masters, and transported by funds furnished by the benevolent," can lay the "foundation of a mighty empire." In the committee's view, voluntary colonization, privately financed, could cultivate the goodwill of the community and would grow stronger as the "ministers of our holy religion" knock "at the door of the hearts of our owners of slaves, telling every one of them to let his bondmen and his bondwomen go free." Through the process of voluntary manumission and colonization, the committee predicted, "slavery will yet be extinguished in a way that will work no evil to the white man, while it produces the happiest effect on the whole African race."[51]

Taken as a whole, the McKinney committee's report recommended against the consideration of the emancipation memorials but took considerable pains to distance itself from the idea that "slavery will be perpetual" in Tennessee. Yet as a brief for gradual emancipation accompanied by privately funded, voluntary colonization, the McKinney report contained even more wishful thinking than Virginia's Bryce preamble with its call for emancipation once public opinion evolved to support it. The report also questioned the idea of a demographic reconfiguration of slavery of the kind favored by the upper South, perhaps because, at 80 percent white, Tennessee already seemed white enough.

THE CONVENTION RECEIVED the report and scheduled debate on it for the following Tuesday, June 24.[52] When the debate began, the initial criticism of the McKinney report came not from a defender of the emancipation memorials but from a middle Tennessee delegate who had voted in favor of tabling those memorials, Bedford's Joseph Kincaid. Kincaid objected not to the report's criticism of emancipation but to its harsh depiction of free black life in Tennessee. Kincaid contended that "the free black was not in the degraded situation" described by the McKinney report. At the least, Kincaid noted, free blacks, unlike slaves, enjoyed the freedom to leave the state if they chose. McKinney countered that free blacks who left Tennessee faced decidedly limited opportunities elsewhere. He knew of "no earthly elysium" where free blacks "might go without the stigma of caste upon him and be received to all the rights and immunities of equality, suffrage and freedom." Despite McKinney's retort, Kincaid moved to strike the portions of the report that compared the condition of free blacks unfavorably with that of slaves.[53] Middle Tennessee's Newton Cannon, who emerged as one of the leading figures at the convention, endorsed the McKinney report, claiming that it "spoke his mind on the subject," and opposed striking any portion of the report.[54]

Eastern Tennessee delegates, led by Matthew Stevenson and Bradley Kimbrough, used Kincaid's motion as an opening to criticize the report on broader grounds. Stevenson, who represented Washington, an eastern county that was less than 5 percent slave, declared his opposition to the entire report. Kimbrough, who represented a county that was less than 8 percent slave, went further, suggesting that the convention should at least discuss the issue of slavery because such a discussion might "open the way for the action of the public mind" upon the subject. Kimbrough argued that such openness might help the state get past the notion that there "was something in the word 'slavery' that chilled the blood." Another east Tennessean, Richard Bradshaw, denounced the McKinney report because it branded the petitioners as "fanatics" and "impugned" their motives. Bradshaw, who represented a tier of four counties where slaves constituted less than 10 percent of the population, likened the petitioners to Jefferson and the "other patriots" who had signed the Declaration of Independence and endorsed the idea that "all men are created equal," the very same language used by the Tennessee petitioners for emancipation of slaves. Bradshaw vowed to vote against the whole report.[55]

Maury County's Terry Cahal declared his intention to vote in favor of the McKinney report in its entirety. The middle Tennessee delegate, who represented a county where slaves were roughly one-third of the population, reminded the convention that it had hoped to minimize discussion of slavery issue and warned that "it would be of no use to release the slaves of Tennessee unless you first purified their morals."[56] Cahal, a supporter of colonization, professed his regret "that domestic slavery ever found a home in our country," but he dismissed emancipation without colonization as absurd because of racial difference. Could the emancipator, Cahal asked, "change the African's skin, and elevate his feelings and his mental capacity to the dignity and honor of the white man's?" Cahal insisted that "God has made the difference" between "the races," and it could not be changed by man. "Are not the African's mental capacity, his grade of sensibility, and his color as immutably fixed as the foundation on which rest 'the everlasting hills'?" Cahal argued that he could not think "without horror" of "the wretched and degraded state of society that must be formed in this country if you were to liberate and turn loose on the community our 142,000 slaves amounting to one of every four white men." The founders of the nation, Cahal insisted, never meditated such a "revolution in the social system."[57] Western Tennessee's G. W. L. Marr expressed a willingness to strike the section on free blacks to make the report more palatable to all, but he was also willing to vote for the report in its entirety. Robert Allen, who represented two Nashville Basin counties where slaves were more than 25 percent of the population, opposed striking any portion of the report, and seconded the report's contention that emancipation of Tennessee slaves would merely "place the unfortunate descendants of Africa in a worse condition than the state of slavery."[58]

The convention rejected Kincaid's motion to strike the section on free blacks from the special committee's report by a margin of 42–12.[59] Two-thirds of the dozen votes to strike came from east Tennessee delegates, while three came from middle Tennessee delegates and one came from Marr, a western delegate seeking broad consensus on the overall report. After the defeat of Kincaid's motion, the convention took up the larger issue of adopting the McKinney report, and delegates voted overwhelmingly, 42–10, in favor of its adoption. Eight of the ten negative votes came from east Tennessee delegates, who got help only from Hugh Armstrong, a representative of Highland Rim counties where slaves were less than 10 percent of the population, and Kincaid, who voted against the entire report because he wanted to strike the section on free blacks.[60]

Two days after the convention adopted the McKinney report, however, four delegates, all from east Tennessee, presented an official protest against the adoption of the McKinney report, denouncing it as "a kind of apology" for slavery. The four eastern delegates, Matthew Stephenson, Richard Bradshaw, James Gillespy, and John M'Gaughey, claimed the report rested on premises "subversive of the true principles of republicanism" and flaunted "public opinion" in Tennessee. The protestors invoked the Golden Rule and other biblical arguments against slavery and insisted that if the special committee truly believed that slavery was a "curse and evil," as it stated, then the convention must seek a "remedy" with or without the committee's recommendation. Taking up cudgels against the racial arguments so forcefully advanced by McKinney, the eastern protesters argued that skin color was not "a good reason for denying" blacks "the common rights of man." While conceding that "nature has placed on the man of color a mark of distinction which neither time nor circumstance can obliterate," the protesting delegates nevertheless argued that "God has made of one blood all nations that dwell upon the earth." The protesting delegates noted pointedly that despite the "benefits" and "blessings" of slavery described in the McKinney report, whites had "not fallen quite so much in love with it as to desire it for ourselves."[61]

The convention's decision to publish the minority report in the pages of its official journal prompted a decision to allow the McKinney committee to reply to its critics, and on July 9, the special committee issued a supplemental report aggressively defending itself against the criticism leveled by the four eastern delegates.[62] The committee's supplemental report argued that a close examination of the emancipation memorials revealed that they had been signed by only a small proportion of Tennessee citizens, and, contrary to the claim of the minority delegates, by the owners of very few slaves. To the extent that the memorialists did own slaves, the McKinney supplement suggested that those slaveholders should "begin the benevolent work you have so much at heart, by emancipating your own slaves and sending them to the land of their ancestors." Memorialists, the supplement report continued, "cannot reasonably ask other people to be at the expense of colonizing your slaves." The committee professed no doubt that "the precepts of the Gospel apply to every man's own conscience on the subject of slavery," but declared that there was no precept that required the Christian to "compel your neighbor to do whatever you think right." According to the committee report, the Gospel failed to denounce slavery. Moreover, the apostle Paul, after converting the runaway slave Onesimus to Christianity, sent him home to his master, Philemon, with a letter in which Paul rejected the "self-righteous language of the proud Pharisee" and refrained from calling Philemon a "wicked man." Instead, Paul urged Philemon to receive the converted runaway as something "more than a servant." The Gospel, the committee insisted, has "caused many a master to ameliorate the condition of the slave, by better treatment or making him altogether free." The adoption of any general emancipation measure would "sap the very foundation of republican government," the second McKinney report contended, because slaves could not be emancipated "without endangering the peace and destroying the happiness of the community" and the "State has not the means of removing the emancipated beyond its limits or colonizing them abroad." Finally, the supplemental report concluded that "great mischief may be done by raising expectations in any class of the community, which are not to be, and which can not be, realized."[63]

Eastern delegate James Gillespy attacked the supplemental report, calling it "an apology for slavery if ever there was one extant." He expressed special displeasure with the section of the report "which related to Scriptural proofs of the unrebuked existence of slavery in the days of Christ and the Apostles." Joseph Mabry, who represented the Knoxville area and had signed the protest against the first committee report, mocked the supplemental report's claim that slavery enjoyed a biblical blessing. He sarcastically referred to the report's "brilliant new discovery" that "slavery was perfectly right and the high authority of the apostle Paul quoted as proof of the same." He chided "some ministers of the gospel now on the floor of this convention" whom he had heard "proclaiming from the pulpit against slavery" but who had now "recorded their votes in favor of the report." Bradshaw criticized the special committee's efforts to "attach odium to the few who did sign the protest." Kimbrough also promised to vote against the supplemental report, calling the right of protest a "sacred right of the minority." He also referred the convention to the example of the enslaved Hebrews in Egypt who were delivered through the "remarkable interference of Providence" as an example of biblical criticism of slavery, and he concluded by noting that the "whole drift of the gospel was to relieve oppression and alleviate misery." James Gillespy told the convention that "providence" had "opened the way" for him to emancipate his own slaves the week before he left to attend the convention, but he did not believe this act "relieved him from the guilt of slavery." He recalled viewing the slave market in Nashville and seeing the tears cried by slaves being sold, scenes that he would never forget. Gillespy confessed that he "could not witness human misery without feeling somehow or another wrong about the heart." He also feared future retribution against a slaveholding society, not only before God at the ultimate judgment, but perhaps through an earlier "earthly retribution" as well.[64]

Terry Cahal defended both the original report and the supplement and urged the convention not to waste time debating "theological questions." Western delegate Adam Huntsman added that history showed slavery a part of "every nation almost" and predicted "that it would probably ever be so."[65] But the most fulsome defense of the supplemental report came from McKinney himself. In a speech to the convention, McKinney reminded the delegates that rather than craft an affirmative defense of the peculiar institution, the committee's initial report had "admitted slavery to be an evil, a great evil," and "a thing that all wise and good men devoutly and ardently wished to get rid of," and that the report had applauded colonization as a "providential manner" of helping slaves. He also reminded delegates that the report had urged "ministers of the Gospel" to "appeal to the hearts and consciences of slaveholders" and tell them to manumit their slaves and send them to the "land of their fathers." McKinney expressed concern that Tennessee slaves would learn of the convention debate. What effect, he asked, might a "protest" lodged by a handful of delegates have "on the slave population" when "they assemble out in an old field, as they sometimes do on Sundays, and at other times and places?" "Will it not make them discontented and stir up their minds to deeds of desperation, to be told, and by members of the convention too, that the convention of Tennessee are violators, and enemies of republican government because they would not forthwith emancipate all the slaves in the State? Can anything be more calculated to stir up their minds to act over again the bloody scenes of Southampton?"[66]

McKinney closed by turning the example of the Good Samaritan against the signers of the protest. The Good Samaritan, McKinney noted, acted himself, "He did not call on others to do it—he did not run after the Priest and the Levite and revile them for their inhumanity. He did not stop to tell them they were violating the precepts of their religion by refusing to aid a fellow being in distress." Instead, the Samaritan "went to work himself" and helped the injured man with his own time and resources. "This is the spirit of the Gospel as I understand it," McKinney concluded, "and its mandate to every member in the community is to go and do likewise in all cases, including the relation of masters and servants as well as in all other relations in which one human being can stand to another."[67] When the debate ended, the convention voted by a margin of 47–9 to approve the supplemental report of the special committee, with all nine votes against the adoption of the report coming from east Tennessee delegates who had also voted against the initial report.[68] The convention appeared to have rendered its overwhelming endorsement of the central claim of the McKinney committee's two reports: that slavery was an evil but emancipation under existing circumstances was an even greater one.

But on July 20, three of the four delegates who had filed the formal protest against the initial report of the McKinney committee offered a reply to the supplemental report for the convention journal. Matthew Stevenson, Richard Bradshaw, and John M'Gaughey, all from east Tennessee, explained why they had voted against the committee's second report. The bulk of the minority reply was devoted to the charge that the McKinney committee had taken positions that ran contrary to both Christianity and republicanism.[69] Stevenson, Bradshaw, and M'Gaughey insisted that the Holy Scriptures did not "give countenance to slavery in its worst form," as they believed the McKinney committee contended, but that the "precepts and maxims of the gospel, when carried into full operation and practice," would "banish slavery from the face of the earth." These three proemancipation delegates also explicated the letter from Paul to Philemon very differently than the special committee had, pointing out that Paul told Philemon to treat Onesimus "not now as servant, but above a servant, as a brother beloved." This second protest closed with a scriptural message from the prophet Micah in reference to what the three believed God required of all people: "in all times to do justice, to love mercy, and to walk humbly before God."[70]

EVEN AFTER THE APPROVAL of the select committee's supplemental report, the convention still faced the challenge of deciding whether or not to include a provision concerning the future of slavery in Tennessee in the new state constitution. Many of slavery's more vigorous defenders thought some constitutional bar against future schemes of emancipation essential, while not only the eastern delegates who defended the emancipation memorials but also other delegates who thought slavery an evil (even if it defied all available remedies) and wanted to keep the option of emancipation at some future day available opposed writing a prohibition into the constitution. Early in the convention proceedings, western delegate Nelson Hess had proposed a clause that both prohibited emancipation without the master's consent and required that masters be compensated for any slaves freed.[71] But by the time Hess' proposal reached the floor of the convention for final consideration in late July, the compensation provision had been dropped. The proposed clause considered by the convention on July 30 declared that "the General Assembly shall have no power to pass laws for emancipation of slaves without the consent of their owner or owners." With little recorded public deliberation, the convention approved this Kentucky-style protection of slavery by a very narrow margin, 30–27.[72] The shift of a mere two votes would have changed the outcome, removing the kind of constitutional guarantee that made slaveholders in Kentucky and other states feel insulated from internal opposition to slavery.

The constitutional protection provision prevailed because of its expected strength in middle Tennessee, whose delegates gave it nineteen votes, and western

Tennessee, whose delegates supplied eight votes in favor of the clause out of eleven cast. Predictably, only three eastern delegates voted in favor of the provision, but without those three votes the clause would have been defeated. The constitutional protection for slavery enjoyed the support of two of the most influential delegates at the convention, former governor Willie Blount, who represented a county where slaves accounted for 40 percent of the population, and Newton Cannon, a rising star in Tennessee politics who also represented a county where slaves were nearly 40 percent of the population. Moreover, the most active delegates from western Tennessee, Adam Huntsman, G. W. L. Marr, and William Loving, all supported the provision.[73]

Yet opponents of the constitutional restriction on future emancipation efforts mounted a surprisingly strong coalition against the clause. To be sure, more than half (fourteen) of the twenty-seven votes against the clause came from east Tennessee, the region where gradual emancipation enjoyed the most support, but ten votes against the provision came from middle Tennessee delegates. Support for leaving the question of emancipation up to the state legislature was weak only in western Tennessee, where only three delegates voted against giving slavery constitutional protection. Moreover, the coalition that opposed limiting the ability of future legislatures to free slaves demonstrated much greater voting strength than the much smaller voting blocs that had rallied to defend the emancipation memorials or attack the McKinney reports. Even the fourteen votes from east Tennessee exceeded the level of support generated in the region by supporters of manumission petitions, and the ten votes against constitutional protection from middle Tennessee far exceeded the number of votes from the region against the two McKinney reports. Even more strikingly, the coalition of opponents of the constitutional protection included John McKinney, the author of the earlier reports urging the convention to keep its hands off the slavery issue, and Terry Cahal, who had vigorously supported both McKinney reports and criticized all plans for emancipation. The strength of the minority coalition opposing the constitutional protection of slavery emerged from the reluctance of many delegates to shift control of slavery's future in Tennessee from the state legislature to the hands of slaveholders.[74]

A closer analysis of the convention vote on the constitutional protection issue reveals that the desire to keep the legislature's options open concerning the future of slavery was strongest in the state's whiter counties, while the yearning to give slaveholders as much security as possible was strongest in those counties with higher proportions of slaves. Twenty-three of the twenty-seven votes against the protection clause came from delegates representing counties where the proportion of slaves to the total population was lower than the statewide figure of 20 percent, and a full two-thirds of the votes against the constitutional provision protecting slavery from legislative emancipation were cast by delegates representing counties with slave populations of 15 percent or less. Moreover, seventeen of the twenty-two delegates who represented counties with only 12 percent or fewer slaves voted against the constitutional protection. Conversely, three-fifths (eighteen) of the votes in favor of the constitutional provision were cast by delegates representing districts where slaves accounted for more than 20 percent of the population; perhaps more tellingly, half of all votes in favor of the clause came from delegates who represented counties where the proportion of slaves was over 30 percent. Only three of the thirty votes in favor of the provision came from delegates whose counties had a slave population of less than 10 percent. Even within the battleground region of middle Tennessee, the centrality of slave demography to delegate voting was clear. Middle Tennessee delegates supported the constitutional protection provision by a margin of 19–10, but the bulk of this support came from middle Tennessee districts where slaves accounted for over 27 percent of the population.[75]

Exceptions existed, but the overall pattern was clear. Votes on the constitutional protection of slavery were closely tied to the slave demography of the county they represented. Following the pattern already revealed in Virginia, the whiter the county, the more its representatives favored leaving the question of emancipation in the hands of the legislature. The higher the proportion of slaves in a county, the more likely its delegates were to favor giving slavery explicit constitutional protection. The approval of the protection provision ensured that no future legislature could enact a plan of gradual emancipation and colonization without either gaining the approval of slaveholders or amending the state constitution. The narrow margin by which this provision passed revealed that white Tennesseans in 1834 remained deeply divided over the depth of the state's commitment to slavery. Earlier votes and actions by the convention indicated that delegates were strongly opposed to any action concerning emancipation, no matter how gradual. But on the question of whether slavery should be secured by the state constitution against virtually all future emancipation efforts or left in the hands of future legislators who might choose to move Tennessee away from slavery through gradual emancipation and colonization, they were much more evenly divided. White Tennesseans were unwilling to endorse emancipation as a concept in 1834, much less embark upon any specific plan of emancipation, no matter how gradual or delayed in its implementation, but neither were they united behind the idea of nudging Tennessee closer to an open endorsement of perpetual slavery.

But even with the question of constitutional protection settled, the convention was still unable to put the issue of slavery behind it. On August 5, middle Tennessee delegate Joseph Kincaid, angered by the approval of constitutional protection for slavery, produced a lengthy attack on both McKinney reports. Kincaid claimed that "perhaps a large majority of the people of the state of Tennessee" shared his view that slavery was "a great moral and political evil" that at some point "will be removed from this country," but he recognized that such a removal could only occur at "a very distant day." Thus Kincaid conceded that for the convention to have acted on requests for gradual emancipation would have been "altogether inexpedient." Slavery was an evil, he admitted, but one for which he saw no immediate or foreseeable remedy.[76] Kincaid's complaint against the McKinney committee grew out of his disagreement with the committee's characterization of the condition of free blacks. "It would seem that they [the McKinney committee] hold slavery to be a more enviable situation than freedom," Kincaid claimed. If that were true, he reasoned, then it would logically follow "that these colored people who are now free should be subjected to slavery in order to better their condition—and that slavery should be rendered perpetual." Specifically, Kincaid contended that the severe punishment of slaves was not merely a theoretical proposition but a practice all too common in the Volunteer State. He acknowledged that "many slaveholders in Tennessee" treated "their servants humanely," but, contradicting the claims of most antiemancipation delegates, he doubted that such paternalism applied "as a general rule to the majority." The convention allowed Kincaid's remarks to be published in the journal but took no further action on his complaint.[77]

However politicians viewed the condition of free blacks compared to that of slaves, Tennessee's free black population hardly seemed like either a large or a growing problem during the 1830s. In 1830, the state's free black population was small, just over forty-five hundred, and constituted less than 1 percent of the state's total population. While the absolute size of the state's free black population had increased by 67 percent during the 1820s, its proportion of the total population had remained essentially the same.[78] But the political rhetoric of the era and the amount of convention debate devoted to the status of free blacks suggested that, despite their small numbers, the presence of free blacks was increasingly seen by many white Tennesseans as an ideological, if not practical, problem.

Hardening attitudes toward free blacks among white Tennesseans had been revealed in the 1833 legislative session. A proposal in the state senate by future state attorney general Jacob Yerger of Nashville to make it easier for free black property owners to collect debts from whites attracted fierce criticism from legislators who thought the measure constituted "one step towards placing the free negro on a footing with the white man." When Yerger challenged his critics to defend a system that allowed whites to practice fraud just because the "African has not a skin colored like our own," one rural senator replied that the people of his district "hold the colored race in general as slaves," and he vowed to "vote for no law calculated to put them on a higher footing" or that would "make the situation of the free negro more comfortable than it is." The senate overwhelmingly rejected Yerger's proposal. But more important, rhetoric insisting that whites thought of all blacks as slaves suggested that the upcoming constitutional convention might well place additional restrictions on the already limited autonomy of free blacks.[79]

Beginning early in its proceedings, Tennessee's 1834 convention reviewed the status of free blacks in Tennessee with an eye to making sure the restrictions placed on the state's free blacks ensured racial control and protected white safety, and more than a few delegates expressed strong interest in drawing the lines of inequality between whites and free blacks more sharply than before. But at the heart of the convention's effort to redefine the status of free blacks in Tennessee lay its interest in eliminating free black voting.[80] Tennessee's original 1796 constitution gave the right of suffrage to all "freemen" who met modest freehold, taxpaying, or residency requirements. This provision permitted a rather small number of free blacks who were freeholders or longtime residents of a particular county to vote.[81] As interest in disfranchising all free blacks gained currency at the convention, disagreement arose over whether the failure of the 1796 convention to limit voting rights to whites was an oversight or an intentional decision. Western delegate G. W. L. Marr, speaking on behalf of the venerable former governor Willie Blount, whose older half brother William had attended the convention of 1796, insisted that "free persons of color...were not parties to the political compact," and that the failure of the Tennessee framers to explicitly exclude them was an oversight.[82] But Isaac Walton of Sumner County, the only 1834 delegate who had actually served in the 1796 convention, opposed the disfranchisement of free blacks because he saw it as a rebuke to the state's framers. Walton's view carried the authority of an eyewitness.[83]

Whatever its origins, the phrasing of the 1796 suffrage clause had allowed a number of propertied free blacks in Tennessee to vote for almost forty years, but the mere idea of free black voting attracted sharp criticism at the convention. The question of free black suffrage inevitably became entangled with white egalitarian efforts to eliminate the state's taxpaying requirement for voting altogether. White egalitarians who wanted to move the state away from freehold or taxpaying requirements and toward white manhood suffrage complained mightily about the contradictions involved in a slaveholding society allowing some free black men, who were otherwise considered "outside the social compact," to vote, while denying the same right to many adult white males. Defenders of voting rights for free black property holders usually countered with cautious arguments for the continuation of limited free black voting. Some defended only the practice of allowing free blacks who had voted since 1796 to continue voting; others delegates were willing to allow all black male freeholders to vote; no one favored allowing all free black men to vote.

Controversy over the issue produced a good deal of wrangling at the convention. As early as May 27, middle Tennessee delegate William Ledbetter submitted a resolution recommending that "the right of suffrage be taken from free colored persons" and that, in turn, free blacks be "exempted from military service." But Ledbetter's resolution sparked no discussion for several weeks.[84] At the end of June, however, when the convention finally turned its attention to the larger issue of suffrage, the question of free black suffrage reappeared. Over a three-day period, the convention spent a good deal of time in serious debate over the issue. On June 26, middle Tennessee delegate Thomas Porter moved for consideration of a ban on free black voting. Porter's motion was quickly defeated on an unrecorded vote. Rutherford's Henry Ridley, also from middle Tennessee, quickly offered an amendment to Porter's motion allowing free blacks already entitled to vote under the constitution of 1796 to continue voting but prohibiting all other free blacks from voting while extending suffrage to all free white males over the age of twenty-one.

Moderate reformer Terry Cahal of Maury County, a champion of white manhood suffrage, supported Ridley's motion. Cahal expressed a willingness to let already enfranchised free blacks continue to vote as a matter of courtesy, but he feared that allowing any additional free blacks to vote offered an "invitation" to free blacks in other states to migrate to Tennessee. Since other states, North and South, employed policies designed to encourage free blacks to leave their states, the possibility of obtaining voting rights in Tennessee would make the state attractive, in Cahal's view, to the worst kind of immigrants. The continuation of free black voting in Tennessee, Cahal contended, would quickly make the state "the asylum for free Negroes and the harbour for runaway slaves." Despite Cahal's endorsement, the convention rejected Ridley's amendment. East Tennessee's John McKinney then offered an amendment proposing that suffrage be opened to all free male citizens of the United States who were over the age of twenty-one and met certain residency requirements. McKinney's proposal amounted to an implicit ban on free black voters because most delegates thought free blacks were not considered citizens of the United States. But McKinney's amendment failed as well, and the convention adjourned for the day without reaching any resolution of the issue.[85]

The next day, June 27, William Carter, an eastern delegate and president of the convention, offered a resolution limiting suffrage to white males only. Middle Tennessee delegate Robert Allen, representing a county that was 35 percent slave, spoke against Carter's proposal. Allen admitted that propertied free blacks in Tennessee enjoyed suffrage as a "boon not a right" but pointed out that limiting suffrage to white males would "exclude a description of persons" who had "exercised [suffrage] for thirty-eight years...without ever any evil growing out of it." Allen recommended "letting the matter remain as it is," lest the convention leave the impression that "northern fanaticism have made an impression among us." Allen favored letting free blacks who "have been in the habit of voting" continue to do so, as long as "their numbers and influence remain too inconsiderable to be felt."[86] But, after some procedural wrangling, Carter's proposal passed. James Gray of middle Tennessee quickly moved to strike the word *white* from Carter's proposal, opening suffrage again to black male freeholders, but Gray's motion failed. Carter then proposed his own amendment, one restoring the right to vote to those free blacks who had lived in the state of Tennessee when its first state constitution was drafted in 1796, but the convention rejected Carter's amendment as well. John Purdy of Henderson, a middle Tennessee delegate, proposed allowing free blacks who owned a minimum of $200 in property to vote, but the convention quickly rejected Purdy's proposal. At the end of the day, the convention approved a vaguely worded resolution, also offered by William Carter, allowing free blacks to vote in county elections only, and then adjourned for the day.[87]

On Saturday, June 28, the convention returned to the issue of free black suffrage for the third straight day. Western delegate G. W. L. Marr asked permission to introduce a set of resolutions drafted, according to Marr, by former governor Willie Blount. In his introductory remarks, Marr contended that these resolutions "present the true view of the relation or want of relation between the colored population of the country and its political institutions." The resolutions maintained that free blacks were not "recognized by our political fabric" or as "subjects of our naturalization laws" and thus their "supposed claim to exercise the great right of free suffrage, is, and shall be ... prohibited." The Marr-Blount resolutions also called for the enfranchisement of all free white males.[88] Once Marr's resolutions were introduced, the convention suspended its custom of forcing all such resolutions to lie on the table for a day, and debate resumed.[89]

Arguing that white Tennesseans "reprobate and abhor" black voting, Marr insisted that the "political fabrics of Tennessee denied citizenship to all people of color, slave or free," and hence all free blacks should be disfranchised.[90] Supporting Marr, another western delegate, W. H. Loving, bitterly reproved the convention for refusing to lower the voting age for whites from twenty-one to eighteen while preserving the right of free blacks to vote. Free blacks could not "possibly have a deeper interest in the welfare of the government than white male citizens over the age of 18," Loving, a nonslaveholder, claimed. Loving's arguments rested ultimately on race. He branded free blacks as the "corrupt link between the debased of our own color and the slave," and argued that free black voting served as "an evil example" to Tennessee slaves. "The slave can see no difference between himself and the free Negro," Loving maintained, and thus free black suffrage might "excite feelings in the breast of slaves," leading to "the overthrow or total extinction of the white race" as in the "ill-fated Island of St. Domingo."[91]

In its broad outlines, the rhetorical sparring in June over free black voting revealed white egalitarians' sense that, as champions of white democracy they must advocate firm new racial distinctions to replace older traditions that tolerated looser racial definitions and even tacit privileges for respected free blacks. White egalitarians perceived this older pattern of looseness on some matters of race (generally in cases where certain class and character conditions were met) as part of an elitist republican or even faintly aristocratic political order. Terry Cahal noted tactfully that the defenders of free black voting were delegates of "high moral worth" who spoke with the "patriarchal voice of venerable gentlemen," while many advocates of eliminating all free black voting and extending voting rights to all whites were "younger men."[92] Western egalitarian Loving was more blunt. He claimed astonishment and regret that the "old grey headed gentlemen" of the convention would "argue in favor of allowing free Negroes and mulattoes the highest right and privilege in a free government" without showing the same enthusiasm for white manhood suffrage.[93] The debate over free black suffrage was hardly a mere generational conflict, but it did reflect efforts of white reformers to advance an egalitarian republican agenda at the expense of an older, more conservative set of republican assumptions that characterized the 1796 constitution.

After the debate on June 28, work on the suffrage clause was done by the Committee of the Whole, whose deliberations were closed and hence not reported by the press. In late July, the Committee of the Whole publicly presented a full draft of the amended constitution to the convention. The suffrage provision that emerged from the committee looked different from the one recommended by the convention in late June.[94] The draft's voting rights clause extended suffrage to "every free man" above the age of twenty-one who was "a citizen of the United States" and a resident of a county six months before a given election. This phrasing was similar to that offered by John McKinney but rejected by the convention during the late June debates. The language concerning voters being citizens of the United States suggested that the clause could be used to disfranchise all free black men, or perhaps just some free black men, but in any case it left the issue a matter of interpretation. White egalitarians had little use for such ambiguity. Over the next several days, the convention worked through the articles of the proposed constitution one by one, and on Thursday, July 31, the delegates took up the draft's suffrage provision. As soon as the clause was read, Nashville's Robert Weakly moved to insert the word *white* in front of *free males*, a clear effort to disfranchise all free blacks. Weakly's motion passed by a vote of 33–23. Proemancipation delegate Matthew Stevenson quickly introduced an amendment that would have allowed free blacks currently eligible to vote to continue voting for their lifetime, but the amendment failed, 22–34. The convention had abolished free black voting in Tennessee.[95]

Weakly's successful motion to disfranchise all free blacks won majority approval from each of the state's three grand divisions. But the vote was quite close among delegates from east and middle Tennessee. Nine east Tennessee delegates voted in favor of restricting suffrage to whites only, while eight voted against the amendment. Among delegates from middle Tennessee, sixteen voted in favor of Weakly's amendment, while thirteen voted against it. Western Tennessee delegates voted more solidly, by a margin of 8–2, in favor of restricting suffrage to whites only, and provided over half of the motion's margin of victory. Similarly, Stevenson's motion to allow those free black property holders who were eligible to vote before the convention assembled to continue voting under the new whites-only clause was rejected by delegates from all three sections of the state. But, again, the vote was close among east and middle Tennessee convention delegates and decidedly more one-sided among western delegates. Stevenson's motion lost, 7–9, among eastern delegates and 13–16 among Middle Tennessee delegates. But western delegates again voted solidly, 9–2, against Stevenson's motion, again supplying over half of the margin needed to defeat it. The convention then completed its effort to define free blacks out of the body politic by excluding them from militia service and excusing them from paying the poll tax required of whites, perhaps seeing the easing of these perceived burdens as gestures to mollify newly disfranchised free black property owners as well as to render the new constitution consistent on the question of citizenship.[96]

White egalitarians were unapologetic about their efforts to define suffrage strictly along racial lines. Middle Tennessee's Terry Cahal insisted that it was not only proper but essential to draw bright political lines on the basis of race. Cahal claimed that by championing white manhood suffrage and opposing voting rights for black freeholders he was "guarding and defending the rights of poor white men." He maintained that nature had elevated "poor white men" above "the free negroes" and that where "God had made a distinction" it was "as absurd as was impossible to abolish it."[97] Nothing "could convince the white man that he was not superior to the negro," Cahal contended, and with that "feeling implanted in his bosom," only "God, who could change the African skin, could extinguish the sentiment." This "feeling," Cahal declared, "pervaded the society and was as strongly impressed in the bosom of the poor man as the rich."[98] Westerner William Loving maintained that the "Almighty" had fixed upon the "Negro" race, "a color of indelible hue and pronounced the curse of Ham upon him," creating an "impassable gulph" between the races.[99] Western egalitarian G. W. L. Marr explained how Loving's "impassable gulph" worked in the political realm. Marr's defense of white supremacy went so far as to insist that the United States Constitution's phrase "We, the people" meant "we the free white people of the United States and the free white people only." Marr argued that free people of color had "never at any time been received into our political family." Racial differences, Marr held, highlighted by "the indelible marks of nature," served to "render all familiar and social intercourse abhorrent to our feelings." Since "the white man and the black man cannot live together on terms of perfect equality;" Marr maintained, "they must separate, or one must rule." And white egalitarians had no doubt about which one that should be.[100]

The suffrage clause, as amended by Weakly's motion, was included in the proposed constitution and upon ratification became the supreme law of Tennessee in 1835. For white males, even minimal freeholds were no longer required for voting, and no free black males, not even those possessing a freehold or substantial other property, were given relief from racial exclusion. Merely by inserting the word *white*, the convention of 1834 ended nearly forty years of voting by free black property owners and established the principle of herrenvolk democracy as the rule of voting rights in Tennessee.[101]

In the end, white egalitarian reformers enjoyed sweeping success at Tennessee's constitutional convention of 1834. The convention eliminated all freehold or taxpaying requirements for suffrage and extended the right to vote to all white males over the age of twenty-one. It eliminated all property requirements for holding office, apportioned the state legislature on the basis of eligible voters (white males) rather than "taxable inhabitants" (a designation that included slaves), and abolished the unpopular county court system in favor of a system of elected justices of the peace. But the Tennessee convention of 1834 enhanced the cause of white democracy not only by extending political rights to all whites but also by drawing lines of racial subordination and exclusion more clearly. By rejecting emancipation in any form and eliminating even limited free black voting rights at its 1834 constitutional convention, Tennessee took major steps toward defining itself as a white man's democracy.[102]

Increasingly, egalitarianism in a slaveholding society became defined in starkly racial terms. Previously acceptable distinctions based on property ownership, character, and length of residence collapsed among whites, but at the same time free blacks lost all claims to status based on those same characteristics. The new egalitarian order brought an insistence that all whites be considered equal in the public realm, but it also brought a parallel directive that all blacks be excluded from it. Free blacks were defined out of the public realm altogether, regardless of property ownership, character, or local reputation. The political flattening of class distinctions among whites brought the formal hardening of racial lines.[103]

The new politics of racial difference fit comfortably with both the emerging appeal of paternalism in the lower South and the cause of "whitening" in the upper South.[104] But at its 1834 constitutional convention, Tennessee declined to seek demographic whitening by supporting colonization or encouraging the sale of slaves to the lower South; instead, it thoroughly whitened its politics, bringing all white men into the electorate and expelling all black men from it. It also explicitly endorsed racial justifications for both maintaining slavery and defining even propertied free blacks out of the body politic. Thus Tennessee, a middle South state, chose an ideological whitening of its body politic over a demographic whitening of its society.

Yet for all its ideological whitening, Tennessee stopped well short of endorsing slavery as a positive good. The thrust of the argument at the convention was far more antiemancipation than proslavery, and in the early 1840s a leading Nashville newspaper maintained, "We have nothing to say in favor of negro slavery....We would gladly be freed of them if we knew how." But, seeing emancipation and removal as impossible, the newspaper vowed that as long as blacks were in Tennessee, "ownership is indispensable, and in the meantime we make their condition as comfortable as their situation will permit."[105] Poised between the upper and lower South, Tennessee found its whitening not in conjuring vast demographic shifts but in the embrace of herrenvolk republicanism, an ideology it deemed consistent with holding slaves. But Tennessee still saw paternalism as an alternative to blackening the lower South and not as a justification for doing so, and it had not yet reconciled itself to the idea that slavery was a positive good.

CHAPTER FOURTEEN

ENDING FREE BLACK SUFFRAGE IN NORTH CAROLINA

Only Virginia felt the psychological and emotional impact of the Nat Turner rebellion more forcefully than North Carolina. North Carolina militia units rushed across the border into neighboring Southampton County to help quell the revolt. News about the insurrection spread rapidly, first down the Roanoke River, then throughout eastern North Carolina, and finally reverberating back into the eastern Piedmont. There, as a student at Hillsborough Academy in 1831, William Pettigrew, scion of a prominent eastern family, heard that "the negroes have been rising down in South Hampton, and killed seventy familys." He quickly prayed that "God will keep us in his ways forever."[1] Rumors of impending revolts abounded throughout the eastern portion of the state. Phantom insurrections haunted eastern North Carolina's major towns, and palpable fear gripped the region. False reports circulated that Wilmington was in flames and an insurrection was under way in Fayetteville, heightening fears still further. Conspicuous among the multitude of swirling insurrection rumors were those suggesting impending rebellion in Duplin and Sampson, two rural counties lying almost due east of Fayetteville with 40 and 33 percent slaves, respectively.[2] Prompt action by Fayetteville-area authorities, who dispatched the local militia in impressive numbers, deterred any intended insurrection in these counties, if, in fact, any such action had been planned. Fayetteville merchant John Latta engaged in a hint of self-congratulation about his city's preparedness. "I think it no harm to be prepared for danger," Latta observed, "even if it should not come."[3] Still, fear of slave unrest remained pervasive throughout the eastern portion of North Carolina during the fall of 1831. No fewer than eighteen black lives were taken by white authorities, often on thin evidence, as a sacrifice offered to placate white fears and calm the white imagination.[4]

In terms of shaping public policy, however, the protean fear generated by news of the Turner rebellion had a less dramatic impact on North Carolina lawmakers than on those in several other slaveholding states, in large part because the Tar Heel State had already toughened its black code a year earlier in response to the circulation of David Walker's *Appeal*. The 1830 North Carolina legislature had removed manumission decisions from the county courts to the state legislature, passed a law banning the teaching of slaves to read and write, and instituted a quarantine law that stood as the Tar Heel counterpart to South Carolina's Negro Seaman's Act. Thus, after the Turner rebellion, the North Carolina legislature found that it had already enacted most of the white security measures taken elsewhere in reaction to news of Turner's revolt.

At its 1831 session, the legislature rounded out its new black code as best it could. It approved new laws regulating slave patrols and making sure that public arms could be quickly distributed in the event of an insurrection scare, and perhaps most significantly, the legislature banned black preaching on the basis of intelligence that Turner was a black exhorter. But even if North Carolina had tough laws for the prevention of insurrection on the books in 1831, the proximity of Southampton to North Carolina's northeastern black belt highlighted the state's vulnerability to slave resistance and its need for vigilance.[5] At least one western North Carolina congressman was moved to Virginia-style considerations. "[S]omething ought to be done on the subject of slavery," Lewis Williams told North Carolina supreme court justice William Gaston; "we cannot any longer view it as a distant evil." Williams, a resident of Surry County, a western Piedmont county with a slave population of less than 15 percent, recommended the removal of all free blacks through colonization. Williams was even willing to support a ten-cent-per-slave tax on slaveholders to help finance the colonization, and he expected generous support from Congress as well. Once free blacks were removed, Williams reasoned, the state could "regulate and control the evil of slavery as it exits among us" more effectively.[6]

At the time of the Turner rebellion, North Carolina stood somewhere between Virginia and Tennessee in terms of its racial demography. About one-third of the state's population was enslaved, compared with one-fifth of the population in Tennessee and nearly two-fifths in Virginia. Moreover, roughly two-thirds of all the state's slaves were concentrated in eastern, coastal plain counties, where slaves comprised about 45 percent of the total population. Moreover, roughly one-third of all white households in the East owned slaves during the 1830s. While not as heavily slave as Virginia's Tidewater region, much less the South Carolina Lowcountry, the eastern portion of North Carolina definitely constituted a slaveholding region. Fifteen of the state's sixty-four counties had a black majority in 1830, and perhaps more important, in twenty-seven counties, blacks, slave and free, accounted for more than 40 percent of the population. All of these counties lay in the eastern portion of the state. Slaves accounted for smaller proportions of the population in the rest of the state, roughly 25 percent in the Piedmont and closer to 10 percent in the mountain region. But the percentage of white households that owned slaves had reached significant levels in the rest of the state by the 1830s. The frequency of slave ownership in the Piedmont reached 25 percent of all households in the 1830s, a figure equivalent to that of the South as a whole on the eve of secession in 1860, and even in the mountains roughly one of every ten white families owned slaves. North Carolina's free blacks numbered about 19,500, or only 2.7 percent of the state's total population, a figure that was only about two-fifths the size of Virginia's, but more than four times larger than Tennessee's. Like the state's slaves, North Carolina's free blacks were concentrated in the eastern portion of the state. Every county with a free black population of more than 3 percent lay between Raleigh (Wake County) and the coast. In sum, North Carolina grew whiter as one moved west from the coastal plain to the broad Piedmont and across the eastern continental divide into the mountain region.[7]

Unlike western Virginia's large white majority, which wanted closer ties to the burgeoning free-labor economy of Pennsylvania and Ohio more than better connections with the struggling Tidewater economy, whites in western North Carolina, and especially those in the Piedmont, which lay east of the continental divide, sought improved access to the Tar Heel State's fall line and coastal markets rather than closer connections to an east Tennessee economy that itself hardly shared in the staple bounty that drove southern prosperity. Hence western North Carolina whites felt little desire to attack slavery per se, but they did want a penurious legislature controlled by eastern slaveholders to help finance transportation improvements. Thus slavery never emerged as a central issue in the long campaign for constitutional reform, at least in the minds of western reformers. And eastern North Carolina conservatives never accused western reformers of being abolitionists in disguise, or even of pushing impractical plans for gradual emancipation, charges that flew routinely during Virginia's constitutional controversy. But eastern slaveholders were both determined to retain a system of legislative apportionment that granted some representation based on their property (slaves) and concerned that taxes levied to pay for expensive internal improvements would fall heavily on slaveholders. Having the power under the 1776 state constitution to defend their interests in the legislature, easterners did so with some vigor.[8]

A year further removed from the bloodshed of Turner's insurrection than the Tennessee convention of 1834, North Carolina's constitutional convention of 1835 refrained from addressing the issue of slavery directly, and the convention records reveal no vigorous debates over the future of the peculiar institution in North Carolina, but the question of voting rights for free blacks sparked some of the most contentious debates at the convention and produced some of the sharpest divisions among delegates. The use of the term *freeman* (rather than *free whites*, as used in eighteenth-century constitutions in Virginia and South Carolina) in the suffrage clause of North Carolina's 1776 constitution had opened the door to voting rights for free blacks who met the other constitutional qualifications (freehold or taxpaying requirements), and substantial evidence indicates that free blacks who met these requirements voted regularly and with comparatively little controversy in most counties in North Carolina during the first three decades of the nineteenth century.[9]

In eastern North Carolina, home to the vast majority of the state's free blacks, free black voting played a significant role in some local elections. Reports from eastern counties claimed that "opposing candidates, for the nonce oblivious of social distinction and intent only on catching votes, hobnobbed with the [free black] men and swung corners all with dusky damsels at election balls."[10] In 1831–32, citizens from the coastal town of New Bern, on Pamlico Sound, petitioned the legislature, complaining bitterly that "permitting free Negroes to vote at elections contributes to excite...a spirit of discontent and disorder among the slaves." During "the heat of party contests," these petitioners claimed, free blacks "are courted and caressed by both parties and treated apparently with respect and attention." This campaigning for free black votes created an impression among slaves that free blacks occupied a position of strategic importance in the eyes of prominent whites, the New Bern petitioners insisted. Such impressions undermined the "discipline and subordination" required to render a slave society safe and secure.[11] Also in 1831, Lewis Henry of Cumberland denounced free Negro suffrage for the most personal of reasons: the free Negro vote in his district could "sometime swing elections," and had apparently swung Henry's own in favor of his opponent.[12] In 1832, incipient North Carolina Whig John Bryan advised his brother-in-law Ebenezer Pettigrew that any local candidate who was "violently opposed" by the free blacks probably faced defeat. In other instances, overt support from free blacks tended to stigmatize white candidates who welcomed their support. In any event, in some counties the open courting of free black votes became an accepted if controversial custom.[13]

Thus, in North Carolina more than Tennessee, the debate over free black suffrage contained a practical political component. In a few eastern North Carolina counties at least, where first personal, then factional, and later partisan loyalties divided whites more or less evenly, there were enough free black voters to influence election outcomes on occasion. In such counties, some white politicians found the free black vote worth courting. This practical angle rendered the free black suffrage question less a purely ideological one than it had been in Tennessee. As a result, the push for disfranchisement of free blacks in North Carolina was led not only by white egalitarians seeking ideological consistency but also by some conservatives eager to free their election districts from the influence of free black voters. These conservatives, who generally opposed constitutional reform, couched their public arguments against free black suffrage in terms of drawing a bright line between white citizens and black denizens much as egalitarians did, though conservatives also expressed the more elitist notion that black disfranchisement would free their election districts from the "corruption" and tendency to mobocracy they associated with free black voting. Thus, in North Carolina, the convention votes on the issue of free black disfranchisement hardly reflected a simple split between egalitarians and conservatives. So, in order to understand the ideas and voting patterns in evidence at North Carolina's 1835 convention, it is necessary to understand the larger movement for constitutional reform in the state and the nature of the conservative opposition to the movement that provided the convention stage for the debates over free black suffrage.

THE CONSTITUTIONAL REFORM MOVEMENT in North Carolina drew its support chiefly from westerners who wanted to replace the Revolutionary-era state constitution, which gave control of the state legislature to the eastern portion of the state, with a new constitution that would give the western portion of the state a voice in the legislature commensurate with its rapidly growing population. However, since the constitution of 1776 contained no provision for either periodic legislative reapportionment or a formal constitutional amendment process, the existing legislative apportionment scheme seemed virtually set in stone. The west had to seek redress of its grievances from a recalcitrant eastern legislative majority that declined to yield power. After the close of the War of 1812, the question of constitutional reform reemerged as a regular legislative issue. Postwar reformers pointed out that the majority of the state's white population lived west of Raleigh, while the existing constitution's system of equal representation for each county regardless of population gave the eastern counties firm control of both the state senate and the House of Commons.[14]

As eastern recalcitrance persisted, frustration mounted west of Raleigh, and western reformers soon adopted a more militant posture. In 1820, the Salisbury *Western Carolinian* denounced North Carolina's state government as a "complete aristocracy" that allowed the "few to govern the many." The new Piedmont newspaper advocated the calling of a convention without legislative approval if necessary.[15] In 1822, a group of reform-minded western legislators launched precisely such an effort, calling for a constitutional convention to be held in Raleigh sometime within the next year. Led by Charles Fisher of Salisbury, a self-made Piedmont merchant first elected to Congress in the early 1820s, and Caswell County's Bartlett Yancey, a War Hawk Republican and protégé of Henry Clay, these reformers, chiefly based in the rapidly growing Piedmont, organized political committees of correspondence in western counties to build support for the convention and guide the election of delegates to it. They based their reform appeal on the still-influential republican ideological heritage, demanding reforms consistent with the egalitarian principles of majority rule and equal rights. The reformers denounced the existing constitution as "anti-republican, unjust, and oppressive" and urged reforms that would give "every freeman" an "equality of privileges and influence in the government." The continued legislative dominance of the eastern minority, these egalitarian reformers reminded the public, contradicted the basic principle that "in republican governments the will of the majority...must and ought to prevail."[16]

The self-appointed reform convention met in Raleigh in November 1823. Forty-seven delegates attended, representing twenty-four counties, all located in the western portion of the state. Over a six-day period, the reform convention endorsed a series of proposed constitutional amendments addressing the region's long-standing grievances. As the centerpiece of its reform agenda, the convention proposed apportioning both houses of the legislature according to each county's "federal" population (white population plus three-fifths of its slave population) in order to enhance western power in the state legislature. But as its next session, the eastern-dominated legislature ignored the amendments proposed by the reform convention.[17]

After the failure of the 1823 convention to trigger legislative action, the constitutional reform movement fell dormant for seven years, a casualty not only of its own repeated failures but also of the fresh contretemps arising from the divisive presidential election of 1824. The multicandidate presidential contest of 1824 splintered the previously solid western reform alliance in North Carolina just as it fractured the Republican Party nationally. Some western reformers defended the caucus nomination of William Crawford, while others gravitated toward the war hero Andrew Jackson. Both factions sought allies among Republicans in the East, where previously moribund Federalist enclaves mobilized behind John Quincy Adams. But agitation of the highly sectional constitutional reform question threatened to stymie efforts to build statewide coalitions for the presidential contest.[18] A correspondent for the *Western Carolinian*, a reform organ, noted that the "high excitement on the subject of the presidential election" had divided the reform party in the western portion of the state, and, as reform leader Charles Fisher later observed, "local parties will always be merged into great national parties" because "Federal politics, like Aaron's serpent, will swallow up the rest."[19]

In 1830, however, the appearance of new census data revived agitation for constitutional reform. The new census information showed that the total population of the western part of the state, white and black, exceeded that of the east for the first time. But efforts by western representatives on behalf of a convention made little headway in the legislature.[20] Eastern conservatives praised the existing constitution, labeling it as "as good...as the wisdom of man can make."[21] Moreover, eastern opponents of reform warned their constituents that if western representation in the legislature increased, then "in all probability, you would, in a few years, see every dollar voted out of the Treasury, towards wild and unprofitable schemes of internal improvement and an onerous system of taxation resorted to."[22] Eastern moderate William Gaston explained the reformers' predicament clearly in his analysis of a state "rent asunder by factions." The anticonvention bloc in the east was the legislature's largest faction, but "not quite a majority," he maintained, and thus "nothing less than union of all others can overpower them."[23]

By the 1830s, however, concern that North Carolina was falling behind other seaboard states in the race of internal improvements intensified. The notion that the state had become the nation's "Rip Van Winkle" in the realm of economic development gained traction among some political leaders, including some politicians representing fall-line and coastal towns in the east.[24] Both proimprovement politicians and the concerned portion of the public laid much of the blame for the state's lagging interest in internal improvements at the feet of the eastern-dominated legislature, where politicians from rural eastern counties, which generally enjoyed good river transportation to the coast, proved reluctant to spend tax money (raised to a significant degree through a tax on slaves) on improvement projects. But scattered locales throughout the east (the towns along the coast and the fall line) saw economic benefits flowing from internal improvements. Politicians in these towns saw an advantage in making common cause with the west to promote internal improvements in conjunction with constitutional reform. With the tempting prospect of relatively new railroad technology opening the west to trade, town-based easterners, and especially those in Raleigh, Fayetteville, and Wilmington, began to work with western constitutional reformers to fashion a reform coalition that might revise the state constitution sufficiently to break the eastern stranglehold on the legislature. Breaking this stranglehold, internal improvement advocates and constitutional reformers agreed, held the key to winning legislative approval for both substantial state investments in internal improvement projects and progress on the constitutional reform agenda.[25]

In early January 1833, a Raleigh meeting of reformers designated William Haywood, a talented young Democratic lawyer from Wake County and a promoter of internal improvements, to draft a letter calling for a constitutional convention. Haywood urged county sheriffs to poll voters in every county on the convention issue. In this nonbinding sheriff's poll held in August 1833, nearly thirty thousand westerners cast their ballots in favor of a convention, but easterners generally boycotted the process. Governor David Swain, a reformer from Asheville, used his annual message to urge legislative action on the convention issue at the assembly's 1833–34 session, and during that session, debate over constitutional reform gripped the legislature. For the first time, a measure calling for a convention actually passed the state senate by five votes, but it failed in the House of Commons by four votes.[26] Following this narrow defeat, reformers caucused quickly, formed an executive committee, and made preparations to press the issue again during the 1834 legislative elections. The executive committee consisted of three easterners, Weston Gales, William Haywood, and James Seawell, and two westerners, future United States Senator William Graham and Romulus Saunders. Gales, Graham, and Seawell had emerged as incipient Whigs, while Haywood and Saunders remained leading supporters of the Jackson administration.[27] Thus the reform coalition's executive committee, its brain trust, represented a bisectional, bipartisan coalition. But such accommodation did not percolate downward through either regions or parties. Apart from pro-internal-improvement leaders from the region's leading towns, easterners remained generally hostile to constitutional reform. North Carolina Democrats, stronger in the east than in the improvement-hungry west, showed little enthusiasm for constitutional reform. The emerging North Carolina Whig Party, sensing that reform was a winning issue among its western base, generally supported the calling of a convention, and as a result, most of the western and Whig press pushed reform enthusiastically.[28] The state's leading Whig organ, the *Raleigh Register*, summed up the proconvention argument well when it told voters that until the "all-important matter of reforming the state Constitution" was accomplished, "no one of the other great interests of the State can be thoroughly secured."[29]

For eastern North Carolina, the state's Democratic stronghold, the idea of a constitutional convention was a hard sell. Eastern conservatives feared a "dangerous jealousy against anything like wealth and character," and demanded some check against the "wild career" of the "popular voice."[30] Haywood, as a pro-internal-improvement Democrat, pushed the idea of a convention to wary easterners by arguing that strategic wisdom suggested they should accept a constitutional convention now, which they could limit and influence, rather than continue an obstructionist course likely to result in either civil unrest or the drafting of a more radically egalitarian constitution, or both, within a few years. Simple "common sense," Haywood argued, suggested that eastern North Carolina should accept a convention while it was still "in our Power" to "moderate and control" the extent of reform. Haywood advocated a convention of limited scope empowered "to alter the Constitution as little as possible."[31] As the legislative elections approached, the proreform faction flooded the state with letters, pamphlets, and speeches and recruited proreform candidates to run in swing districts and in key eastern districts where reformers faced an uphill fight. In the end, the reform campaign of 1834 succeeded well enough, electing to the legislature approximately twenty easterners sympathetic to reform.[32]

With a small but crucial bloc of eastern reformers in a position to assist, prospects for success at the 1834–35 legislative session seemed promising after many years of frustration. Western reformers decided to ask only for an "equal" representation in the legislature for their section on the basis of the federal ratio, rather than the predominance that a reapportionment based on white population would have ensured. In a lengthy proconvention essay, William Graham, William Haywood, Romulus Sanders, James Seawell, William Hargrove, and Weston Gales endorsed the called for a constitutional convention because "the will of the majority ought to be supreme," but at the same time they assured voters that they were not "advocates of Licentiousness."[33] The *Raleigh Register* praised the reform faction's growing tendency toward "concession and compromise."[34] When the legislature convened in November 1834, Governor David Swain, who grew up in humble circumstances in Buncombe County but had emerged as the leading figure in western politics and an important cultivator of cross-sectional alliances with easterners, again expressed his full support for both internal improvements and constitutional reform. Swain, who tested his message with eastern reformers before he delivered it, focused on the point that the equal representation of counties "subjects the majority to the rule of the minority." Swain identified "a radical change in representation" as the "great object to be attained" from a convention, but the western-born governor held out an olive branch to conservatives by suggesting that the legislature could "prescribe" specific issues for the proposed convention to consider.[35] Still, even with momentum on the reformers' side, the problem of fashioning an appropriate convention bill, one that would include enough egalitarian provisions to satisfy western reformers but limit the convention's reform reach sufficiently to placate enough eastern legislators to win approval, remained daunting.

Toward this end, eastern reformers in the legislature took the lead in crafting a moderate convention bill that reformers might steer through the House and Senate over the determined opposition of skeptical eastern conservatives. This bill limited the issues that the convention could consider, and it defined the parameters of the crucial apportionment question. In a sense, these legislative instructions limited the convention's range of actions, making the calling of a convention more palatable to some easterners. In late December, the *Register* reported that the bill to call a convention had been committed to a select committee comprising one delegate from each congressional district, giving supporters hope for success even though the bill passed its second reading in the house by only two votes. The *Register* admitted that the convention bill remained an "agitating topic" for legislators, and it judged that the "future prosperity" of North Carolina hinged on the outcome.[36] Finally, on December 31, 1834, the house passed a convention bill drafted by Haywood and his allies by four votes, 66–62. Three days later, the convention bill survived its senate test by a single vote.[37]

The convention bill approved by the legislature in January 1835 not only limited the scope of the convention but also circumscribed its options on the pivotal question of legislative reapportionment. The bill ensured that while the new constitution would enhance western North Carolina's influence in the state legislature, the east would nevertheless retain levels of representation in both house and senate not warranted by its white population.[38] Yet even this compromise bill, which significantly diluted the original egalitarian agenda, had polarized the legislature. Legislative leaders had reached a considered accommodation on the bill, but rank-and-file eastern legislators balked. In fact, the moderate convention bill, with all its safeguards against an excessively egalitarian convention, was rejected by 77 percent of eastern representatives in the House of Commons and 83 percent of easterners in the senate. Western legislators, on the other hand, were almost unanimous in their support of the bill, with 96 percent of western representatives and senators approving the measure.[39] A cohesive reform coalition pushed a decidedly moderate reform bill through a reluctant legislature by very narrow margins. This hardly constituted a legislative embrace of sweeping egalitarian reform. In fact, it represented an effort by the east to concede as little power to the west as was necessary to enable state financing of internal improvements and maintain a modicum of sectional harmony in the state. But, despite the restrictions included in the bill, the North Carolina legislature had finally called a constitutional convention.

Once the legislature adjourned, the proreform *Register* noted that the convention bill conceded "much less to the West" than "they have uniformly contended for," but added that easterners now had a chance to display a spirit of compromise that would allow them to share power more generously with the west.[40] The Whig organ argued that the old constitution had deprived the west of its "just political influence and power."[41] Other Whig-leaning papers around the state also praised the bill. From the northern Piedmont, the Oxford *Examiner* thought the convention bill gave North Carolina a chance to shed its reputation as the "Rip Van Winkle" of the Union, and it urged "magnanimity" from the east in yielding to the "just demands" from the west.[42] The state's Democratic press responded more cautiously. Once the convention bill passed, the *North Carolina Standard* expressed hope that the bill's advocates "will realize all they have anticipated" and that those long "strenuously opposed" to reform would find "their fears more imaginary than real."[43] The *Standard* admitted that for many years the controversy over constitutional reform had "exercised a baleful influence on the legislation of the state." In Person County, a Democratic-leaning district on the eastern edge of the Piedmont, citizens approved a resolution urging support for the convention because "the state is so divided on the subject of a Convention that no general action can be had on so many other subjects of importance and general interest."[44]

In the popular referendum on the convention question held in April 1835, the convention issue polarized voters by section just as it had divided legislators along the same lines three months earlier. Overall, Tar Heel voters approved the convention by more than five thousand votes, 27,550 to 21,694, but the popular vote broke down along sectional lines. Every eastern county except one voted against the convention, while all but two western counties voted in favor of it. The vote was close in only a few counties.[45] When the convention assembled in Raleigh in early June, however, the *North Carolina Standard* conceded that it embodied "as great a proportion of talent and personal respectability as any body emanating directly from the people heretofore assembled in this state." As a result, the Democratic newspaper predicted "harmonious action."[46] The proreform *Register* expressed similarly optimistic sentiments and counseled delegates to approach the convention's work with the "elevated and expanded dignity" which the project deserved.[47] The key to the decision to call the convention of 1835 was that enough easterners, including some key eastern Democrats, wanted a program of internal improvements that they could not get without constitutional reform. Their decision to join the reform cause did not reflect widespread support for reform in the east, but their leadership gave the reform movement just enough eastern support, both in the legislature and at the polls, to help it eke out a victory in 1834 after more than thirty tears of failure. And one of the issues the legislative instructions encouraged the convention to consider was that of ending free black voting in North Carolina.

THE SCOPE OF THE NORTH CAROLINA CONVENTION of 1835 had been limited in crucial respects by legislative instruction. Since the 1834 legislature had arranged the terms of compromise on the most controversial issue on the reform agenda—the apportionment of the state legislature—the convention found itself free to spend more time on issues that would have drawn less attention if the representation controversy had absorbed more of the convention's time. The legislative instructions permitted (though they did not require) the convention to consider the issue of free black suffrage, though very little of the preconvention discussion focused on the issue.[48] But if preconvention discussion of free black voting had been limited, early convention conversations revealed that many North Carolina politicians, clearly worried about remaining the only slaveholding state to allow free black voting, wanted to follow Tennessee's example and eliminate free black voting altogether. On June 12, 1835, a week into the convention, with the distinguished jurist William Gaston in the chair, the North Carolina convention, sitting as a Committee of the Whole, took up the fourth resolution of the call for a convention, the resolution allowing the "abrogation or restriction of the right of free negroes or mulattoes to vote." The ensuing debate stretched over two days and proved lively and revealing.[49]

Judge Joseph John Daniel of Halifax immediately proposed to restrict suffrage to those free blacks who held a freehold worth at least $250.[50] The county, Halifax, that Daniel represented at the convention loomed as central to the debate over free black suffrage in North Carolina. In no North Carolina county was free black voting more common or more important. No county had as many free black voters as Halifax, and since the county's white population was relatively small, these black voters constituted an important swing vote. Halifax was an eastern county just below the fall line of the Roanoke River and just a few miles south of the Virginia border. It was North Carolina's blackest county (67 percent) in 1830, and its free black population of more than two thousand was not only the largest in the state but nearly twice as large as the free black population in the county (Pasquotank) with the state's second largest free black population. The town of Halifax, the county seat, was an active fall-line market town on the Roanoke River and it sported more than its share of mercantile firms and tanneries during the early national period. But apart from the town of Halifax, which lay on the county's northern border, Jacksonian-era Halifax County was an overwhelmingly rural, agricultural county of the sort that rarely supported large free black populations in the antebellum era.[51]

The presence of such a proportionately large free black population in Halifax was something of a historical accident. During the second half of the eighteenth century, when its northern neighbor, Virginia, experienced its most active phase of manumission, Halifax represented the southernmost frontier of the upper South's eastern tobacco belt. As they were freed in Virginia, ex-slaves frequently moved to this frontier, to the edge of the region with which they were familiar, to enjoy their freedom with as little scrutiny by former masters as possible without sacrificing all contact with their former communities. Land for small farms or work at fall-line grinding mills and tanneries was readily available in Halifax, and the county became the recipient of blacks freed under early national Virginia's comparatively lenient manumission laws and pushed out by the Tidewater's stagnant tobacco economy. As the locus of tobacco production shifted to Southside Virginia and a tier of northern coastal plain and Piedmont counties in North Carolina, Halifax emerged as a thriving tobacco-producing county itself, relying heavily on slave labor. By 1830, over 12 percent of Halifax's population were free blacks and over 55 percent were slaves.[52]

Halifax delegate Daniel declared that his proposal to limit suffrage to free blacks who possessed a substantial freehold "was intended as an incentive to this class of persons to use exertions to raise themselves in the public estimation." Daniel, an accomplished lawyer who studied under prominent North Carolina Federalist William R. Davie, was elected to the state supreme court in 1832, where he served with two other distinguished judges, William Gaston and Thomas Ruffin. At the convention, Daniel wanted "to leave the door open to all colored men of good character and industrious habits" to vote. The judge conceded that many free blacks in North Carolina "are worthless in character," and he added that he was more than willing to deny voting rights to "persons of this description." But, Daniel suggested, a provision that allowed propertied free blacks to vote "would have a tendency to conciliate the most respectable portion of the colored population, and thereby give them a standing distinct from the slave population." Given the history of slave insurrections in the West Indies and elsewhere, Daniel argued, "the policy of cultivating a good understanding with the most respectable portion of our free persons of color" might encourage them to "be very serviceable to us in case of any combination for evil purposes among their brethren in bondage."[53] Weldon Edwards, a delegate from Warren County and a nephew of Nathaniel Macon, interrupted to ask Daniel if denying free black taxpayers who did not own a $250 freehold the right to vote violated the North Carolina Bill of Rights or the constitutional guarantee against taxation without representation.[54] Daniel replied that the Bill of Rights "did not apply to men of color" but "embraced only free white men." Daniel explained that while he was willing to allow "colored men of property and standing to vote" as a privilege earned through hard work and good behavior, but he had no intention of implying that they were covered by the state's Bill of Rights generally.[55]

In response to Daniel's proposal, James Bryan of Carteret County initiated the drive for the total disfranchisement of free blacks. Bryan, a Whig lawyer from New Bern, came from a wealthy eastern family of old Federalist loyalties. He was a classmate and brother-in-law of William Gaston, who favored allowing propertied free backs to vote. Despite his Whig politics and his friendship with Gaston, Bryan took an impassioned stand in favor of complete disfranchisement of free blacks. He criticized North Carolina as "the only Southern state" that permitted free blacks "to enjoy the privilege" of suffrage, and argued that "her interests have not been promoted by the concession of the privilege." Bryan claimed that while free blacks were entitled to their "freedom" in a technical sense, he believed they should remain in a condition he termed "civil slavery," arguing that the United States was "a nation of white people" of which free blacks could not be an equal part.[56]

Based on information supplied by Nathaniel Macon, Bryan contended that the interpretation of the word *freeman* in the 1776 constitution that allowed free black suffrage represented a fundamental misunderstanding of the intent of the document's framers. Before that constitution, Bryan maintained, "a free negro was never known to vote." He maintained that limited free black suffrage had existed in North Carolina through "a long and silent acquiescence" that had created "a violent presumption" in favor of continuing the practice. But, in Bryan's view, "the nature of our Government and the institutions of the country never contemplated" that free blacks "should be placed on equality with the free white man." Free blacks, he maintained, were "not freemen in the meaning of our Constitution." When enfranchised, Bryan claimed, free blacks simply became "the tool of the ambitious and designing demagogue," thus increasing the "sources of corruption" for whites "without conferring any benefit on the free Negro." Declaring himself opposed to any "amalgamation of colors," Bryan boldly contended that the United States was "a nation of white people—its offices, honors, dignities, and privileges, are alone open to, and to be enjoyed by, the white people," and thus he objected to "any equality between the white man and the free Negro in the enjoyment of political rights."[57]

Contrary to the expectations of some other delegates, Bryan predicted that the disfranchisement of free blacks would produce little protest from that community because several eastern counties had long informally excluded free blacks from the polls and the victims of this exclusion "have acquiesced in this determination with cheerfulness and contentment." Bryan admitted that "many of this unfortunate race" deserved "a better political fate" than disfranchisement, but he argued that "the interest of the few must yield to the public good." Moreover, most free blacks, Bryan maintained in an exposition of the era's classic stereotype, focused chiefly on the "temporary gratification of the enjoyments of the muster ground and election, and their patriotism is limited to the little selfish feeling of self-importance which these occasions give them." North Carolina, Bryan concluded, "is surrounded by States that have taken away from [free blacks] all the privileges of freemen, except those of a social character." If North Carolina did not do the same, "our good old State will become the asylum of free negroes; they will come in crowds...and we shall be overrun by a miserable and worthless population."[58]

Nathaniel Macon, the venerable president of the North Carolina convention and a former Speaker of the United States House, threw his considerable political weight behind the complete disfranchisement of free blacks. One of the few surviving Revolutionary veterans at the convention, Macon, representing Warren County, where he was part of the Roanoke River planter gentry, admitted that his views on the subject of free black suffrage were more uncompromising than those of most delegates. Macon argued that the practice of free black voting in North Carolina rested on a mistaken interpretation of the Revolutionary-era state constitution. He insisted that free blacks were "no part of the then political family" in 1776. Africans, imported as "merchandise," Macon recalled, were not considered citizens at the time of the Revolution. He admitted that free blacks had voted often in his part of North Carolina, but he added that they had never served on juries nor had their testimony against whites been accepted in court. Insisting that "half-citizens are unknown," Macon urged complete disfranchisement. He also criticized Daniel's proposal for a freehold requirement for free blacks, maintaining that he knew "respectable families of free negroes who had no property," but denying that respectability represented a proper standard for voting. "None of them," Macon reiterated with reference to free blacks, "had any right to vote." He noted that the South, unlike northern states, had a large number of free blacks and no mass exodus was likely. "They are among us—we have no Moses to undertake their cause," Macon argued. The South would forever depend on black labor, slave and free, Macon argued, because "it is doubtful whether our Southern country can ever be cultivated by white men, or that the vast quantity of our Swamp lands can ever be drained; or Internal Improvements be made without them." "It is proper that the colored people, whether free or in bondage," Macon concluded, "should be well treated," but he opposed allowing any free black, regardless of property ownership or character, "the right of suffrage."[59]

In an effort to offset the weight of Macon, John Branch, Daniel's fellow delegate from Halifax, joined the debate in defense of limited free black suffrage. Branch, a former three-term governor, United States senator, and secretary of the navy in Jackson's original cabinet, stood as one of the most distinguished delegates at the convention. Branch's father had been a Revolutionary hero, and the younger Branch, a wealthy patrician given to lavish entertainment, enjoyed great popularity among political leaders in the state. A staunch supporter of Jackson in 1824 and 1828, Branch nonetheless championed internal improvements and favored free public schools. Long concerned about the large free black population in his home county of Halifax, he served as president of the North Carolina chapter of the American Colonization Society. Branch joined Daniel in supporting the vote for free blacks who could meet a $250 freehold requirement. Daniel's proposal, Branch pointed out, would disfranchise the overwhelming majority of free blacks in the state but would keep "the door open to the most intelligent and deserving of the free men of color." Branch admitted that no one had been more "annoyed' by free blacks than he, living in a county where they were numerous, but he argued that under "our present Constitution, free blacks always have been considered as entitled to vote; and such has been the universal and undisputed practice." Branch, who favored the freehold as a general principal of suffrage because "it gives a voter a fixed interest in the country," concluded that free blacks who held property "ought to be represented." Moreover,

Branch noted that Halifax County had nearly three hundred free black voters, who would not receive the news of total disfranchisement calmly.[60]

Jesse Wilson of Perquimons, an Albemarle Sound county that was over 40 percent black, objected to any plan calculated, as Daniel's was, to elevate free blacks. "However much colored persons might be elevated," Wilson argued, "their color alone would prove a barrier to keep them in a degraded state." Moreover, according to Wilson, "the moment a free mulatto obtains a little property, and is a little favored by being admitted to vote, he will not be satisfied with a black wife. He will soon connect himself with a white woman."[61] Jesse Cooper of Martin County, another eastern county that was more than 40 percent black, agreed with Macon and Wilson that no free black, regardless of property ownership, should vote under any circumstances. Cooper declared that any extension of the privilege of suffrage to free persons of color would have a "bad tendency," illustrating for slaves yet another tangible advantage of freedom. Jesse Speight of Greene County, an eastern county that was over 45 percent black, also opposed allowing even substantial free black freeholders to vote. He agreed with Macon that North Carolina's founders had not intended to grant black freeholders suffrage.[62]

Another easterner, Owen Holmes, who represented the port city of Wilmington and a county that was more than 50 percent black, defended limited free black voting. Holmes admitted that he knew many free blacks who lived in a "degraded and corrupt state," but he offered the controversial argument that "the white people were as much to blame" as blacks for the degradation. Whites, Holmes asserted, were "principally the corruptors of the morals of these people." Free blacks who "possess property, and are of good standing," ought to be "distinguished from those ... who are vicious and disorderly." Such a distinction, in Holmes view, "would be the means of conciliating the most worthy men" among the free black population, and that such men "might, in any case of difficulty with the slaves, prove serviceable to the white inhabitants by discovering to them any symptoms of discontent" that "might arise among slaves."[63] As the first day of debate wound down, the voices heard on both sides of the issue had all been from the eastern portion of the state and belonged to delegates representing counties with large black populations where white voters had opposed calling the convention in the first place. At the end of the day, Jesse Wilson's proposal barring all free blacks from voting regardless of property ownership passed the Committee of the Whole narrowly, 61–58, with the margin suggesting that the question of whether to include a complete elimination of free black voting in the new constitution or simply limit suffrage to substantial free black property- holders hung on a mere handful of swing votes. The Committee of the Whole then reported the result to the convention, which received the report and then recessed for the evening.[64]

The next day, the convention considered the report of the Committee of the Whole on the question of free black suffrage, and debate over the issue resumed. New voices were heard, chiefly voices from the Piedmont, where reform sentiment ran high and free black populations were small, but Piedmont voices spoke on both sides of the issue. Emmanuel Shober of Stokes, a north-central Piedmont county where slaves were less than 15 percent of the population, addressed the convention. An active Moravian church leader, merchant and postmaster in Salem, and state senator, Shober had strongly supported constitutional reform. He contended that since free blacks were both "free agents" and "human beings who paid taxes," they were "fit" for voting rights. He urged that free blacks "ought not to be cast off and thrown into the ranks of the slaves of our country" but rather cultivated as possible allies in the ongoing effort to prevent slave insurrection. Shober maintained that an enfranchised free black elite would be a valuable "class of persons standing between the whites and the slave population." To the extent, Shober argued, that "we raise [free blacks] above the slaves, by allowing them certain privileges, they will become our safeguard from any evil designs." But "if...we force the free negro into the ranks of the slaves," Shober continued, "we can expect no friendly aid from them."[65] Shober moved that all free blacks who possessed a freehold valued at $100 be allowed to vote, reducing the property requirement recommended by Judge Daniel of Halifax the preceding day. Craven's William Gaston, arguably the best-known member of the convention other than Macon and Branch and a defender of free black rights, briefly interjected to recommend that the convention restrict itself to consideration of the principle of free black voting rather than parsing the exact levels of the expected property requirement. As a result, Shober withdrew his motion.[66]

Another Piedmont delegate, Rowan's John Giles, agreed with Shober. Giles argued that "expediency" dictated that propertied free blacks should continue to enjoy voting rights. Insisting that he knew of no "evil" that had been produced by free black voting under the old constitution, Giles maintained that if free black votes had been bought, as champions of disfranchisement argued, white politicians were as much to blame as free black voters. Echoing Owen Holmes' sentiments, Giles pointed out that "the vote of a negro was never offered in the market until he knew there was a purchaser," and the purchaser was always a "white man." The Rowan delegate then urged the convention to use its "power" to "devise some mode of raising" free blacks out of their "present degradation." For too long, he maintained, the Old North State's legislature "had acted on a principle of enmity" toward free blacks when they should have pursued avenues of uplift. It "would not be good policy," Giles argued, "to deprive the respectable class of free colored people amongst us from voting." Such a policy would "drive them [free blacks] back into the ranks of the slaves," where they might conspire to foment trouble, Giles feared, rather than "attach them[selves] to the white population." By contrast, limited access to the vote, Giles concluded, "held out a motive" to free blacks "to become industrious and respectable, and to acquire property sufficient to qualify them to exercise the elective franchise."[67]

Josiah Cradup of Granville, a northern Piedmont tobacco county that was more than 50 percent black, countered that voting rights could not elevate free blacks as a population. Free blacks, Cradup insisted, remained "from their color, a separate class." While conceding that some free blacks "were virtuous and exemplary in conduct," he wanted to draw no line of distinction among the black population. Rather than divide the free black population into classes of privileged and unprivileged, Cradup preferred to keep racial lines clear and deny the privileges of citizenship to all, leaving the "division as nature made it."[68] But it was Hugh McQueen of Chatham, a county lying at the eastern edge of the Piedmont, who spearheaded the disfranchisement argument on the second day of debate. McQueen, scion of a prominent planter family from the Deep River area, served in the state House of Commons from 1830 to 1834 and was elected to the more prestigious state senate in 1834, and during his years in the legislature he earned a reputation as one of the state's most eloquent and persuasive orators. McQueen advocated the complete disfranchisement of free blacks regardless of property ownership or other qualifications.[69] He admitted that such a draconian restriction would work a hardship on a few people of "meritorious and exemplary conduct," but he maintained that it would be an "impolitic species of legislation to release the operations of general principle for the benefit of a few individuals." McQueen argued that when granting freedom to certain blacks, the public had "never contemplated" that these free blacks would "enjoy the benefit of a full political or social communion with the whites." The "nature of our condition, and the cast of public sentiment in this country," he argued, "raises an impassable barrier to any such state of things as this." McQueen then disputed Giles' notion that using suffrage to serve as a "stimulus to virtue and merit" constituted wise public policy. If "we once commence the work of holding out to them political privileges as an incitement to virtue," McQueen maintained, "we might as well insert some clause in the constitution making the highest offices of the country accessible to them." The Chatham orator then asked the delegates, "Is there any gentleman on the floor, who would be willing to see the right of suffrage extended to free persons of color if they were likely to constitute a majority of voters in the State?" If not, McQueen queried rhetorically, why then did some delegates propose "to invest the free negroes with the most important privilege which is exercised by the white population of the country?" Free blacks, he insisted, had no claim to "this equality of privilege."[70]

Moreover, McQueen continued, regardless of his own or any other delegate's personal views on the issue, white opinion in the state ran overwhelmingly against free black political participation. "The public sentiment of this country does not admit them to the enjoyment of any office or honor or profit," McQueen insisted. A "broad partition separated blacks from the suffrage," he asserted, since "the white portion of the population of this country constitutes the proper depository of political power." With the "circle of respectable society closed against him," McQueen contended, the free black stood forever "condemned" by whites and "despised" by slaves and could never develop any "attachment to the community."[71]

Jesse Wilson of Perquimons, the eastern delegate who had championed the white egalitarian argument against voting rights for propertied free blacks on the previous day, agreed with McQueen. Wilson maintained that free blacks lacked the "intelligence" and the "integrity" needed to vote. But Wilson went further than any other opponent of free black suffrage had, complaining that too much of the debate over free black suffrage appeared to rest on the assumption that slavery remained a "great evil." To the contrary, Wilson insisted, "it is a great blessing, in the South," where "our system of Agriculture could not be carried on" without it. North Carolina, Wilson claimed, "might as well attempt to build a railroad to the moon as to cultivate our swamp lands without slaves."[72]

As the first round of debate wound toward conclusion, William Gaston, an eastern Whig of Federalist lineage and a widely respected state supreme court justice, reminded the convention that the question at hand was not one of "granting" free blacks the right of suffrage but "whether we should take it away." He acknowledged that if free blacks had never previously voted, the convention likely would not consider extending suffrage to them. But many delegates, Gaston believed, wanted to avoid the "hardship" of "depriving" deserving free blacks of a privilege they had long enjoyed. Gaston conceded his willingness to exclude some free blacks from voting, but he maintained that any free black who "possessed a freehold, was an honest man, and perhaps a Christian" should not "be politically excommunicated, and have an additional mark of degradation fixed upon him, solely on account of his color." The New Bern jurist wanted to cultivate the loyalty of free blacks of property and character as a check on any rebellious tendency among slaves. "Let them [free blacks] know they are part of the body politic," Gaston contended, "and they will feel an attachment to the form of government, and have a fixed interest in the prosperity of the community, and will exercise an important influence over the slaves."[73] Orange County's John Morehead, a leading Whig and a champion of railroad development agreed, arguing, "If we close the door entirely against this unfortunate class of our population. Then we may light up the torch of commotion amongst our slaves."[74] After a passionate last-minute plea against disfranchisement by Cumberland's J. D. Toomer, who charged that to "abrogate" the "right of every free man" to vote "would be tyranny," the convention voted 64–61 eliminate free black suffrage.[75]

Under close analysis, this crucial vote to completely end free black voting in North Carolina revealed complicated but discernible patterns. Certainly all sections of the state and both emerging political parties (Democrat and Whig), as well as those delegates not closely affiliated with either party, were divided over the question. But the vote revealed a distinct split between eastern and western delegates over the issue of free black voting. Eastern delegates gave strong support to total disfranchisement, voting 49–27 in favor. At the same time, western delegates opposed total disfranchisement by a margin of 34–15. Within the west's two major subregions, both Piedmont and mountain delegates contributed to this nineteen-vote western margin against total disfranchisement. Piedmont delegates voted 23–11 against disfranchisement, while mountain delegates voted 11–4 against the measure.[76]

A discernible partisan difference also emerged in the convention vote on free black suffrage, but those were decidedly less clear-cut than the sectional divisions. The margin for approving the complete ban on free black voting came from Democrats, as Democratic-leaning delegates favored total disfranchisement by a vote of 22–16. Eastern Democrats constituted the strongest bloc of delegates supporting total disfranchisement, voting 17–6 in favor, while western Democrats actually opposed disfranchisement 10–5. By very narrow margins, Whigs and independents opposed the complete disfranchisement of free blacks. Whig delegates voted 30–28 against the ban and unaligned delegates voted 15–14 against the ban. Again, sectional distinctions within the parties loomed large. Whigs from western counties voted nearly two to one, 17–9, against total disfranchisement, while eastern Whigs supported disfranchisement, 19–13. More than two-thirds of the Whig delegates who favored complete disfranchisement came from the east, though eastern Whig support for disfranchisement remained less emphatic than that of eastern Democrats. In sum, while neither sectional nor partisan allegiance alone can fully explain the convention votes on free black suffrage, both played a role in the outcome of the vote. Easterners overwhelmingly and Democrats solidly favored the total elimination of free black voting, with eastern Democrats most heavily of all in favor of the ban. Western delegates overwhelmingly and Whig delegates narrowly opposed the total ban. Independents or nonaligned delegates opposed a total ban by a very narrow margin.[77]

The issue of free black voting surfaced again in July when the convention's select committee for drafting all the new amendments reported its penultimate draft to the convention. Once the proposed article barring all free blacks from voting was read to the convention, William Gaston, known at the convention as the "'oil pourer' on troubled waters," suggested that since only a small majority had favored the total abrogation of free black suffrage in the original vote, the issue deserved reconsideration. In an effort to dispel what he termed "misapprehensions" on the subject, Gaston traced the history of free black voting in the Tar Heel State for the convention. He contended that at the time of the Revolution, the majority of free blacks in the state were the mulatto children of free white women. Many of these free blacks had taken the state's Revolutionary-era oath of allegiance, symbolic of state citizenship in 1778. Given the state's long-standing practice of allowing qualified free blacks to vote, Gaston worried that depriving respectable free blacks of the right would alienate them from the white population. Free blacks would resent such a deprivation, Gaston maintained, "not only on account of its value" but because it would be regarded as an indication of a "disposition to force them down yet lower in the scale of degradation, and encourage ill-disposed white men to trample on and abuse them as beings without a political existence, and scarcely different from slaves." Gaston offered an amendment allowing free blacks who owned $500 in property to vote.[78]

Defenders of limited free black suffrage rose to support (or modify) Gaston's amendment. Wilmington's Owen Holmes agreed with Gaston, arguing that allowing propertied free blacks to vote would help to enlist their vigilance against slave insurrection. He warned the convention against throwing respectable free blacks "into the ranks of slaves" when they had proved of "signal service in disclosing plots" and preventing "scenes of desolation and distress."[79] Charles Fisher of Rowan agreed that free blacks of "good standing" should be allowed to vote and "not forced into the class of slaves." Fisher even declared that Gaston's $500 property requirement set the bar too high. "We ought to open a door for such of them [free blacks], as are respectable and worthy," the longtime champion of constitutional reform insisted.[80] Piedmont delegate Samuel King of Iredell explained bluntly that the failure of the state constitution, any subsequent legislation, or the United States Constitution to use the term *free white men* allowed free black men who met other qualifications to vote. Both free blacks who were children of white mothers and free blacks manumitted "for meritorious" services clearly, in King's view, deserved to vote, and hence he planned to "vote against an entire extinction of the right as exercised by people of color at present."[81]

Knowing their working margin was small, advocates of total disfranchisement replied. Jesse Wilson of Perquimons worried that even the discussion free black voting rights would arouse "considerable excitement" among the state's slave population. It would not escape the notice of both slaves and critics of slavery, Wilson argued, that "a respectable portion" of the convention favored free black voting, even if on a very limited basis. Wilson again professed himself "altogether opposed to allowing this privilege to men of color."[82] Disfranchisement advocate Hugh McQueen reiterated that free blacks had "no right" to vote and that "good policy" dictated that "the privilege should be withheld from them."[83] Samuel Carson of Burke, a former congressman, became the first mountain delegate to speak on either side of the subject when he insisted that free blacks should not vote because they were "not citizens." Free blacks, Carson insisted, represented a "separate caste," which "could not be respected" as citizens or voters.[84] New Hanover's Owen Holmes countered that a North Carolina supreme court decision accepted free blacks as citizens, but Carson retorted that "the God of nature had put his mark upon the negro as a separate caste, and in that caste he wished to keep him."[85]

William Gaston, drawing on his status as a state supreme court justice, explained two matters of law to the convention. First, he countered the argument, often advanced by advocates of total disfranchisement, that free blacks should not be allowed to vote because they were not allowed to testify in court. Gaston explained, as many delegates doubtless knew, that the exclusion of free black testimony was not absolute: free blacks were barred from testifying against whites, as sons and fathers were often barred from testifying against each other by civil law, but free black testimony was welcomed in other circumstances. Second, he pointed out that the case referred to earlier by Owen Holmes in his brief exchange with Samuel Carson as affirming free black citizenship had emerged from a situation in which the state supreme court had upheld the rights of a free black to hold slaves and to seek proper remedies in court when his rights as a slaveholder were violated.[86] Gaston's remarks appeared to counter an assertion made by Nathaniel Macon earlier in the convention that the concept of "half-citizens" was not known. Alfred Dockery, an emerging Whig leader and delegate from Richmond County in the eastern Piedmont, favored voting rights for free blacks with property, but he preferred a $250 property requirement rather than several lower ones proposed by some delegates or the higher $500 requirement proposed by Gaston. John Kelly of Moore, another eastern Piedmont county, called total disfranchisement a "rank injustice" and argued that all taxpayers should vote, regardless of color.[87]

Ultimately, after a series of unrecorded votes rejecting a variety of other amendments, the convention affirmed its earlier decision to disfranchise all free blacks by defeating the Gaston amendment by ten votes, 64–54.[88] Fewer votes were recorded on the Gaston amendment than on the original constitutional provision, and Gaston's amendment lost some support from defenders of free black voting who thought the property requirement he used ($500) was too high. Still, despite the fact that the issue was framed in a slightly different fashion than it had been in June, the vote to defeat Gaston's amendment revealed divisions within the convention very similar to those apparent in the earlier vote on disfranchisement, with the margin in favor of total disfranchisement of free blacks increasing slightly.[89] By defeating the Gaston amendment, the convention wrote the "total abrogation" of free black suffrage into North Carolina's amended constitution.

Apart from the total ban on free black voting, the convention, following the terms of the prior legislative authorization, pieced together a moderate reform constitution that contained more egalitarian features than its Revolutionary-era predecessor but retained many of the conservative features common among seaboard state constitutions of the Jacksonian era. The convention followed its legislative mandate and reapportioned the House of Commons according to the so-called federal ratio, a reform formula that ceded control of that body to the western section of the state but gave western counties less representation than they would have gained through the adoption of the so-called white basis. The new amendments also apportioned the state senate on the basis of taxes paid, thus enhancing eastern representation based on its slave wealth and thereby allowing the east to retain effective control of the Senate.[90] In this regard, North Carolina's 1835 constitution resembled South Carolina's after its amendment in 1808. That state's so-called Compromise of 1808 gave nominal control of the lower house to the whiter, interior portion of the state, but not by the margin that an apportionment on the basis of white population alone would have produced, and it left control of the state senate in the hands of those whites who lived in the state's blacker Lowcountry.[91] The North Carolina convention also provided for the popular election of a governor for a two-year term, eliminated borough representation in the state legislature, and replaced a constitutional requirement that holders of high office swear an oath to the truth of the Protestant religion with one that required only acceptance of the truth of the "Christian" religion. Each of these measures, with the exception of the elimination of borough representation, passed with overwhelming support from egalitarian reformers at the convention.[92] The convention adjourned on July 15, 1835, and submitted the new frame of government to voters for final approval in a fall ballot.

On the whole, the reform coalition pronounced itself pleased with the body's work. The Whig press especially praised the convention and the amended constitution. The Charlotte *Journal* thought the "Constitution approached as near perfection as any similar instrument in the country." The *Western Carolinian* called the proposed constitution "one of the best, if not the best, in all the Union." From the east, the New Bern *Spectator* evaluated the proposed constitution in detail and, after some "hesitation," determined that "the best interests of the State will be promoted" by approving the constitution, not because it was "unexceptionable" but because it was "better than any we are likely to get hereafter."[93] The state's leading Democratic newspaper, the *North Carolina Standard,* pronounced itself "better satisfied with the result" of the convention than "had been anticipated."[94]

But the decision to disfranchise all free blacks drew little applause from the press. The *Raleigh Register*, the state's leading Whig organ, openly lamented the disfranchisement of free blacks. "That the right of suffrage, on the part of the free people of color, was totally abrogated," the newspaper complained, "is a source of regret to us. We had hoped that it would have been continued to those of this class who have an interest at stake in the country, and a character to entitle them to the privilege."[95] In the eastern portion of the state, Fayetteville's Whiggish *Carolina Observer* expressed "the general feeling of regret in the community" over the "total disfranchisement of the free coloured people." There were a few free blacks in Fayetteville, the *Observer* declared, who possessed "every qualification of intelligence, respectability, usefulness, and property to entitle them, fairly, to exercise this high privilege."[96] The editor of the New Bern *Spectator* also lamented the total disfranchisement of free blacks, but the *Spectator* acknowledged that the question of free black suffrage had proven "undoubtedly one of delicacy and difficulty" at the convention and decided not to withhold its endorsement of the constitution simply because it was unhappy about the elimination of free black voting.[97] In its evaluation of the new constitution, the *North Carolina Standard* simply did not comment on the exclusion of free blacks.[98]

The popular vote on ratification again revealed the state's deep sectional divisions over constitutional reform at the grassroots level. Tar Heel voters approved the new reform constitution easily enough (by 5,165 votes), but the voting patterns closely followed the patterns of the earlier vote authorizing the call of the convention. The new constitution received overwhelming support in the West, and more than 90 percent of all votes cast in favor of the new frame of government came from western counties. On the other hand, easterners remained steadfastly opposed to constitutional reform, and a full 88 percent of all votes cast against the new constitution came from the East.[99] Privately, eastern delegate James Bryan expressed a sentiment common in the region when he complained that he saw the actions of the convention as "a perfect surrender of all power to the West." But, unlike most of his eastern colleagues, Bryan, a supporter of internal improvements, confessed that "I verily believe they will use it to a much greater advantage for the welfare and prosperity of the State." Still, the New Bern lawyer admitted that he could "not avoid regretting" the east's loss of power.[100] With the ratification of the amendments, North Carolina became the last slaveholding state to ban free black voting. Nonwhites, regardless of wealth or character or community respect were systematically excluded in every slaveholding state. A few restrictions on white voting remained, but more and more all white males over the age of twenty-one who were not criminals could vote.[101] Across the South, voting rights were increasingly becoming a privilege of whiteness.

THE 1835 CONVENTION'S DECISION to disfranchise all free blacks in North Carolina remained a matter of public discussion for a number of years after the constitution was ratified. More strikingly, the decision became a matter of a much clearer partisan divide after ratification than before. As John Hope Franklin pointed out years ago, the total disfranchisement of free blacks in 1835 hardly ended discussion of the matter but rather triggered the use of free black voting rights as a wedge issue in North Carolina politics.[102] As party competition intensified in 1836 and through later years, the ideology of racial exclusion became more well-defined and took on a sharper partisan edge than it had at the 1835 convention. In these postconvention political campaigns, the partisan press often used a candidate's position on free black suffrage in 1835 as a litmus test of acceptability for office. Ironically, given the support Piedmont Whigs had shown at the convention for allowing propertied free blacks to vote, the first use of support for free black suffrage as a partisan smear emerged at a Whig rally in Rowan County in July 1835, just as the convention was winding down. According to Democratic observers attending the Whig rally, Rowan Whigs labeled Martin Van Buren's vote in favor of free black voting at the New York constitutional convention an effort to "place free negroes...on an equal footing with white men." Thus they branded Van Buren unfit for the presidency because his "principles" might be "fatal" to the "rights and safety" of the slaveholding states. Democrats noted that the motion to condemn Van Buren's support for free black suffrage passed unanimously at a rally attended by both of Rowan's delegates to the constitutional convention, Charles Fisher and John Giles. At the convention, both Fisher and Giles not only had voted to preserve voting rights for propertied free blacks but had made floor speeches defending their position in forceful terms. In its coverage of the event, the Democratic *North Carolina Standard* taunted the Rowan Whigs, crying, "Oh, consistency, where is thy virtue? Oh shame, where is thy blush?"[103] The quasi-official Whig press replied promptly but defensively. It simply noted that the incumbent Whig governor, David Swain, another supporter of free black voting rights, was not present at the rally as the Democratic press claimed, and that Van Buren had supported unrestricted fee black suffrage in New York while Fisher and Giles had only supported limiting voting rights to free blacks of property and respectability.[104]

But if Whigs were the first to taunt Democrats for support of free black voting, the longer-term pattern became that of North Carolina Democrats taunting the state's Whigs for supporting free black suffrage in 1835. In the bitterly contested gubernatorial race of 1840 between Democrat Romulus Saunders, a Caswell native and Nathaniel Macon protégé who emerged as a leader of the states' rights wing of his party, and Whig John Morehead, a leading constitutional reformer who became a champion of education and railroad development, prominent Democrat William Haywood blasted Morehead for his support of free black voting at the 1835 convention. Morehead won the election anyway. Once the returns were in with news of Morehead's victory, Democrats complained that local authorities in Whig-leaning Piedmont and mountain counties had allowed free blacks to vote in defiance of the new constitutional prohibition. Democratic observers in Wilkes County claimed that election officials (judges of the county court) "did permit free Negroes to vote." Democrats urged an investigation, claiming that the majority for Morehead in Wilkes, a western Piedmont county with fewer than two hundred free blacks, would have diminished if the unconstitutional free black voting had been disallowed.[105] Such complaints revealed more about partisan bickering in North Carolina during the years of the Second Party System that they did about the possibility that some free blacks may have been allowed to vote in defiance of the constitutional ban. But they also revealed that North Carolina politicians and party strategists increasingly saw past support for free black suffrage as a political liability.

Even as late as 1854 the issue of free black voting surfaced in North Carolina campaigns. In the hotly contested governor's race that year, the Whigs nominated Richmond County's Albert Dockery, a longtime party leader, who had served six terms in the state senate and was elected to Congress in 1846. Born into a family of small farmers, Dockery received little formal education. He remained plainspoken and a loyal Baptist lay leader throughout his life, but he also rose from his humble origins to become a substantial slaveholder and cotton grower. Dockery's formidable political skills carried him to a seat in the state's House of Commons at the callow age of twenty-five, and once in Raleigh, he quickly gained influence as a champion of constitutional reform and state-financed internal improvements. Over time, Dockery parlayed his political connections and his Baptist witness into a series of important positions in the state's growing religious establishment. He served as longtime president of the North Carolina Baptist Convention, a trustee at Wake Forest College, and treasurer of the North Carolina Bible Society.[106] As the gubernatorial race grew heated, the Democratic-leaning *Asheville News* accused Dockery of devoting "all his time and energy at the 1835 convention to putting free negroes on an equality with white men" through his support for free black voting. Dockery's 1835 support for free black suffrage, Democrats contended, would have extended "greater privileges to free negroes than that class exercised in any abolition state."[107] An ally of fellow Whig William Gaston, Dockery had voted against Jesse Wilson's call for total disfranchisement of free blacks and for Gaston's failed amendment to allow free blacks who owned substantial property to continue voting, as had just under half of all delegates. But, in fact, Dockery had spoken only briefly in the debate, and then to suggest a $250 property qualification for free blacks rather than a $100 minimum. With "thousands of acres of vacant land available" in North Carolina, Dockery had argued, "it would be an easy matter to get fifty acres of this land, put a cabin on it, and declare it to be worth $100."[108] Such were hardly the sentiments of a man working day and night to elevate free blacks to parity with whites. Yet the Democratic press charged that Dockery's service at the convention revealed "very plainly that he thinks a free negro ought to exercise all the privileges that a white man does." The Democratic press also repeated their claim that Whig elections officials in western counties allowed free blacks to vote in violation of the state constitution. Dockery's platform of "Negro equality" would "run well" in western counties such as Burke and McDowell, one Democratic newspaper claimed, because in those counties "a great many worthless and trifling free negroes" would "stick to him like a brother, on account of his friendship for them at the convention."[109]

Whigs defended Dockery by arguing that his support of voting rights for free black property owners represented a defense of the principle that "taxation without representation was tyranny."[110] Dockery lost his bid for the governor's office to Northampton's Thomas Bragg, a loyal Democratic foot soldier who reversed his party's traditional stand by strongly endorsing state funding for railroad development. After Dockery's defeat at the hands of a largely unknown Democrat who had successfully stolen a longtime Whig issue, an embattled Tar Heel Whig party criticized Democrats for branding Dockery as the "Free Negro candidate" for governor while at the same time supporting Martin County's Asa Biggs, who had also supported free black suffrage at the 1835 convention, as their candidate for United States Senate.[111] Biggs, long a Democratic favorite, shared Dockery's comparatively modest origins and his Baptist faith but experienced a more tortured political evolution. Biggs' father had been a merchant and Primitive Baptist preacher in Williamston, a small town in the inner coastal plain's plantation belt. Initially educated largely at his father's knee, Biggs became a merchant as a teenager but read law and earned admission to the bar in 1831 at age twenty. Though initially a supporter of the popular hero Andrew Jackson, Biggs and the rest of his family followed their mercantile interests and emerged as Whigs once Jackson's Bank War escalated. In 1840, a twenty-nine-year-old Biggs was first elected to the House of Commons as a Whig. In 1842, however, Biggs left the Whig party and joined the Democrats, apparently because he grew concerned that the national Whig program posed a threat to slavery. Backing away from his earlier commitment to internal improvements, Biggs advocated a program of states' rights, support for slavery, and strict economy in government. By the time of his Senate bid in 1854, Biggs had developed a reputation as a strong southern rights Democrat and a very able lawyer. He won his United States Senate bid in 1854 and was appointed to the federal bench by President James Buchanan in 1858.[112] As a young man at the constitutional convention in 1835, Biggs' record was decidedly mixed. Generally, despite his early Whig leanings, he voted with conservative, antireform eastern delegates, reflecting the preference of his Martin County constituents for the terms of the existing constitution. However, on the issue of free black suffrage, he first voted (on June 10) against the proposal for total disfranchisement. But when the issue reemerged in July, Biggs voted against Gaston's amendment to protect the voting privileges of propertied free blacks. In any case, his initial vote against total disfranchisement apparently gave Democrats no pause in advancing Biggs as a candidate even as they traduced Dockery, the Whigs' gubernatorial nominee, for casting an identical vote.[113] As John Hope Franklin concluded, "votes in the convention of 1835" on the subject of free black voting "haunted every aspirant to public office from that time on," though the results of these smear tactics were mixed.[114]

In many respects, tarring candidates with their past support for free black suffrage proved popular because the ideological terms of the free black suffrage debate became much clearer after the practical issue had been resolved. If the voting patterns and interests of the delegates who made the decision at the 1835 convention were varied and complex, the long-term popular understanding of the convention's decision proved much less ambiguous. Put differently, the public memory of black disfranchisement was much less complicated than its actual history. Once disfranchised, free blacks, including those of "property and standing," found few champions. Moreover, the years after disfranchisement brought an ideological coherence to the disfranchisement movement that the actual process had lacked. Democrats, now embracing racial modernism, mocked the older notion that wealth, property or character mattered to citizenship as elitist and heretical, and they scolded Whigs, the party of moral as well as material uplift, for their alleged concern about providing a means of improvement for the state's free black population. Styling themselves as white egalitarians, Democrats insisted that race mattered, and that little else did.

The convention's disfranchisement of free blacks had determined once and for all that political participation was the exclusive domain, not of all freemen, but of free white males, and that the effort to democratize the political structure of the Jacksonian republic made no pretense of including even propertied and respectable free blacks in the body politic. Indeed, even though opponents of free black suffrage offered little in the way of documented "mischief" caused by free black voters prior to 1835, the convention followed Tennessee's lead toward the final elimination of free black suffrage in the South. Indeed, in 1843, the North Carolina judicial system reaffirmed and codified the convention's new racial definition of citizenship when it declared that by disfranchising free blacks in 1835, a sovereign convention, called by the people and representing the state's "highest authority," had determined that "free persons of color cannot be considered as citizens in the largest sense of the term."[115]

THIS STATE SUPREME COURT DECISION expressed in clear if formal terms the new race-based definition of citizenship that emerged with ever greater clarity across the South during the state constitutional conventions of the Jacksonian era. Egalitarian reforms in state constitutions across the region pared away various property-holding, taxpaying, and military service requirements for white voters, leaving white males entitled to vote on the basis of whiteness alone. At the same time, free blacks were excluded from any of the privileges of citizenship regardless of their wealth, property ownership, character, or even services rendered to the white community, in order to maintain the appropriate racial division. More than narrow legal or constitutional reasoning, the emergence of this new conception of citizenship reflected the triumph of a broad popular view that the defense of the southern social order depended on the existence of a well-defined racial divide, one that granted privilege to whiteness and recognized few distinctions among blacks. Across the South, these ascendancy of these attitudes represented the triumph of a southern variant of racial modernity, which insisted on elevating whites by holding free blacks as well as slaves in clearly subordinate positions.

For southern whites, the preferred position of slaves was clearly a subordinate one; the challenge was holding them there and preserving white safety. With free blacks, the challenge was clearly defining their subordinate position and preventing the free black caste from becoming a menace to slavery. The concept of racial modernism insisted on using race rather than property or character or other considerations to assign status. So free blacks had to be excluded as far as possible from civic (and therefore white) pursuits. The new ideology of racial modernity did not deny that the moral uplift of the black population, slave or free, was an important responsibility of whites.[116] But it insisted that while mutual elevation was the goal, there must always be an appropriate distance between the races. Whites must always be dominant and superior, blacks always subordinate and excluded from the rights and privileges of republican society.

At the North Carolina convention of 1835, many Whigs and some Democrats espoused paternalism as the appropriate relation between the races. These delegates wanted, though on a very limited scale, to recognize achievement, property, character, and religion as indices of full membership in the existing social order. This bit of partially self-interested magnanimity extended only to free blacks (certainly not to slaves), and then not to all free blacks but only those who had made exceptional attainment under adversity and who might emerge as allies of whites during times of slave unrest. In North Carolina, these champions of uplift mustered considerable support in defense of the voting rights of free blacks who owned significant amounts of property. But this position lost, albeit by narrow margins, to an ideology that wanted to establish the "mark of nature" of "the distinction of color" as the incontrovertible qualification for participation in the full rights of citizenship in the North Carolina social order.[117] Harsh toward free blacks, the ideology of racial modernism, with its bright-line distinctions drawn on the basis of race and nothing else, appealed to whites across class lines. It established whiteness as the dominant mode of securing privilege in antebellum southern society. It obviously did not erase all class differences among whites, of course, nor did it undermine the ideology of paternalism and uplift, but it did define racial difference as the key to the southern social order. If southern whites, especially in the upper South, were still awkward in their defense of slavery, a majority were increasingly committed to the ideas of white egalitarianism characteristic of the Jacksonian era.

Joining its middle South neighbor Tennessee, North Carolina struggled less to whiten itself through colonization or the sale and forced migration of slaves further south (though both states did a little of the former and a lot of the latter) than to whiten itself ideologically by disfranchising all free blacks and defining a more subordinate status for the free black population generally. In some instances, this ideological whitening may have made some practical difference to whites (in those North Carolina counties where a significant number of free blacks voted), but for the most part it made chiefly an ideological difference, removing an inconsistency in the racial defense of slavery and establishing whiteness as the basis of citizenship. Such ideological whitening comported well with the desire for white equality, or herrenvolk egalitarianism, advocated by most constitutional reformers in both states.[118]

This hardening of racial lines not only appealed to the popular prejudices of the day, establishing white equality on the basis of pervasive black inequality, but it prepared the region for the confrontation to come: the battle to defend slavery, an institution over which much disagreement remained within the South, against attacks from outside the region. When faced with an increasingly vigorous and hostile outside attack on slavery—an attack that came, like a random poison, through the federal mail, as well as through petitions to Congress seeking redress of grievances of related to slavery—white southerners set aside other differences, including differences of opinion regarding slavery, to defend against the attack. And from this rallying round the cause emerged a South determined to stifle debate, to meet outside criticism at the threshold, and willing to defend the institution of slavery against all foes, and, in the mind of some, at any sacrifice.

PART SEVEN

THE LOWER SOUTH RESPONDS

During the early 1830s, whites in the Old South believed that slavery was under attack. The circulation of David Walker's pamphlet, Nat Turner's slave insurrection, and the rise of northern sentiment favoring immediate abolition alarmed many whites. The corresponding formation of the American Antislavery Society in 1833 and the implementation of the AAS' mail and petition campaigns in 1835 confirmed this growing sense that slavery was under siege. Clearly, the slavery question demanded answers—and soon.

As explained in the previous section, the upper South's response to these attacks consisted of a contested reaffirmation of the idea that the answer lay in arranging the proper configuration of slave demography to ensure white safety and economic improvement. The upper South's clearest answer to the slavery question—the diffusion of slaves to the lower South by sale—held troubling implications for the lower South, where regulation of the interstate slave trade was a perennial concern and the idea of growing blacker as a region lay at the center of concerns about slavery.

In the slave-heavy lower South, the sustained attack on slavery generated even more consternation, and pushed the region to answer its own slavery questions. As part of the region's initial response to the emerging crisis, critics of paternalism reiterated their long-standing claims that the upstart ideology lacked the toughness to maintain slavery when the institution was under constant attack. By giving visibility to the role slave religion, slave literacy, and charismatic slave religious leaders played in slave resistance, the Turner rebellion provided fodder for criticism of the paternalist movement. Thus paternalism's critics pushed hard for new bans on teaching slaves and free blacks to read and write, on the use of black preachers and teachers in the paternalist mission to the slaves, and for tighter control over the circumstances of black worship. They also pushed for tighter control of slaves, the internal slave trade, and free blacks. Initially, critics of paternalism enjoyed a substantial measure of success in their efforts.

The AAS' mail campaign in 1835 proved the pivotal moment in the lower South's ongoing consideration of the slavery question. The distribution of large quantities of abolition literature into southern cities and rural crossroads by means of the United States mail struck many lower South whites as an effort to use the newly improved federal postal system to terrify the South by encouraging slave unrest. The mail campaign mobilized grassroots enthusiasm for a defense of slavery and a counterattack on abolition on a scale the region had not previously seen. In its early stages, the popular mobilization against abolition kept the paternalist project on the defensive.

Over the longer term, however, the ideological attack on slavery, delivered through abolitionist mail and petitions to Congress, pushed the lower South toward acceptance of paternalism as the dominant ideology of slaveholding in the region. The paternalist cause ultimately prevailed in the lower South not simply because of the strategic and indefatigable work of its champions but because paternalism offered the region its best rebuttal to the moral and humanitarian nature of abolitionist charges. With its triumph, paternalism joined an increasingly firm belief in white racial superiority, and a growing confidence that slavery sustained white egalitarianism to complete the successful ideological reconfiguration of slavery in the lower South.

CHAPTER FIFTEEN

REACTION IN THE LOWER SOUTH

Occurring as they did in fairly rapid succession, the circulation of David Walker's *Appeal* and Nat Turner's bloody but unsuccessful slave rebellion had their impact on the lower South as well as the upper South. But given the evolving demographic and economic differences between the two major subregions of the Old South, the focal points of the reaction were quite different. Unlike Virginia and Tennessee, or even Maryland, no state in the lower South responded to the Turner insurrection and its aftermath with a serious debate over emancipation, no matter how conditional or gradual. And while the position of free blacks in the social order of the lower South proved very much a matter of debate and discussion after Walker and Turner, all lower South states had long since limited voting rights to whites only, so free black suffrage was not an issue.

Instead, the post-Walker/Turner discourses in the lower South focused on the internal security crisis facing the lower South. The debates focused on how to control the region's ever-blackening racial demographics, whether or not to regulate the domestic slave trade, the future of paternalism and the religious instruction of slaves, and what set of polices best prevented free blacks from emerging as leaders of slave unrest and even rebellion. The lower South's discussions of slavery in the early 1830s reflected the region's tacit recognition that its destiny for the foreseeable future was tied to slavery and its desire to render its slaveholding society as safe and secure as possible in the face of palpable threats. Thus, when lower South whites discussed slavery during the 1830s, there was less disagreement over ends than over means. In the first few years after Turner, tougher policies concerning slaves, free blacks, and the instruction of slaves often prevailed. The paternalist project again faced formidable opposition.

AS DISCUSSED EARLIER, the first signs of chronic jitters in the lower South appeared as a result of the circulation of David Walker's pamphlet and intensified when reports of the Turner rebellion circulated less than two years later. Along the Gulf Coast, panic spread throughout Louisiana in March 1830 when Robert Smith, a free black merchant in New Orleans, was found in possession of a copy of David Walker's *Appeal*.[1] The discovery of Walker's pamphlet in New Orleans followed closely on the heels of a Christmas 1829 insurrection scare, when an alleged rebellion had been foiled after a slave woman informed on the black conspirators. The Christmas scare had already frayed white nerves in a state where, by 1830, people of color (slave and free) outnumbered whites roughly three to two, and the free colored population numbered almost seventeen thousand, or about 8 percent of the state's total population.[2]

Fearing a large-scale slave revolt guided by free black leadership, a revolt of the kind whites believed Walker's pamphlet encouraged, the Louisiana General Assembly swung into action in 1830, taking a variety of actions to assert greater control over the state's black population, slave and free, in an effort to improve white security. They passed a law prohibiting teaching slaves to read and write and making the publication and distribution of all literature that might "produce discontent among the free colored population" (such as Walker's pamphlet) or trigger "insurrection among the slaves" a capital offense. Going further, the legislature also banned the immigration of free blacks and ordered all free blacks who had entered the state between 1812 and 1825 to register with a parish judge and offer proof of good character in order to avoid deportation.[3] The 1830 legislature also moved to slow the growth of the state's free black population by making manumission more difficult. A new set of post-Walker legislative restrictions required any master who wanted to free a slave to post a $1,000 bond to underwrite the deportation of the manumitted slave beyond Louisiana's borders within thirty days of the emancipation.

Even before the fear spawned by the recent insurrection scare and discovery of the Walker pamphlet began to subside, however, white Louisianians began to find their draconian new laws for controlling free blacks impractical and inconvenient. A Baton Rouge editor openly urged that the tough new laws be selectively enforced, and recommended that enforcement target only "suspicious and arrogant" free blacks along with those who had recently arrived from other states.[4] Less than a year after the passage of the new round of strict regulations, Louisiana governor Jacques Dupre suggested the passage of more lenient statutes that might be more readily enforced. Toward that end, he recommended exempting from threat of deportation those free blacks who owned property or could show reliable proof of employment from the existing laws.[5] The Louisiana legislature decided to drop the stiff bond requirement for manumissions provided that the local parish police approved of the manumissions in question, and it revised the statute to allow recently freed ex-slaves to remain in the state if three-fourths of the parish police voted in favor of retention at two successive meetings. The revision of the restrictive law turned Louisiana's manumission policy into a local-option matter decided by the parish police. Local authorities, who presumably knew the situation best, could be as strict or as lenient as they preferred. Evidence suggests that in practice decisions on manumission varied widely from parish to parish; ironically, parishes with a history of insurrection, such as Point Coupee and St. John the Baptist, often showed the greatest leniency to manumitted slaves.[6]

But before this return to leniency received a full trial, news of Nat Turner's insurrection reached Louisiana in the fall of 1831, igniting a new wave of panic throughout the state. In October 1831, Rachel O'Connor, alarmed by news of Turner's violent rampage, heard disturbing reports about a rebellion on the nearby Barrow plantation. But when a quickly summoned patrol arrived at the Barrow place, they found "the overseer and the Negroes very busy at work gathering crops, as peaceable as lambs, and not one word of truth in the report."[7] Such false alarms and the genuine fears that produced them led the new governor, A. B. Roman, to call for a special session of the legislature to respond to the Turner insurrection. Roman, elected with the active support of Henry Clay, urged the legislature to pass stronger legislation to protect against possible slave rebellions and enhance white security generally. Given the scope of such measures already adopted after the 1829 scare and the discovery of Walker's pamphlet, activity at the special Turner-induced session of the Louisiana legislature in 1831 focused on chiefly on one issue: the regulation of the interstate slave trade.[8]

Louisiana politicians had long worried that the penchant of the state's whites for purchasing slaves both drained the state of valuable capital and increased the state's vulnerability to insurrection. In a state that was three-fifths black, the latter fear loomed especially large in the aftermath of Turner's rebellion. But experience had proven that effective regulation of the internal slave trade was difficult. In 1826, the Louisiana Assembly had banned the introduction of slaves for sale for a period of two years, in an effort to slow both the blackening of the state and the flow of Louisiana capital to upper South states striving to slowly transfer their slaves southward. The law remained in effect for only a little more than a year before popular pressure led to a repeal of the ban before its expected expiration in 1828. But even after repeal, Louisiana politicians worried about the dangers the internal slave trade posed for the state. In 1829 the legislature passed a law requiring all slaves imported to provide two letters testifying to their good character signed by freeholders in their former place of residence and certified by the county clerk there.[9]

But the appetite of white Louisianians for slave labor, despite elite fears of a financial drain and popular fears of black revolt, made any regulation of the internal slave trade problematic. A year before Turner's insurrection, planter E. G. W. Butler noted that in Louisiana a "desire to continually purchase land and Negroes appears to be a characteristic of planters."[10] As another Louisianan wrote in 1830, the "situation of the Country" being "one in which we have to depend altogether on the labour of the Slaves for a support" disposed many to believe it "impracticable" to ban their introduction into the state.[11] Louisiana planter Alexander Barrow went even further, denouncing such a ban as both "unconstitutional and impolitic." Barrow acknowledged that the "the wealth and property" of the state rested "fair and fully upon the labor of slaves." Moreover, he contended, every "man acquainted with the nature of our agricultural labour, & the destructive influence of our climate upon the white population, must acknowledge that without Negroes we should be 'poor indeed.'" Barrow rightly doubted restrictions on slave imports could long survive the opposition of Louisiana landowners not yet satisfied by the available supply of slave labor.[12]

Yet after the Turner insurrection and a bad crop year in the fall of 1831, white opinion momentarily shifted. The 1831 Louisiana legislature once again banned the activity of professional slave traders, allowing only existing residents and immigrants who intended to settle permanently in Louisiana to bring slaves into the state, and it required these residents and immigrants to appear before parish judges to explain their intentions in detail. Even residents were banned from bringing slaves from neighboring states (Alabama, Mississippi, and Arkansas) in an effort to prevent slave traders from setting up shop just outside the state's borders. The law also banned the sale of all slaves imported during the previous five years.[13] Planter J. S. Johnston applauded Louisiana's new restrictions, explaining that the state was "every year drained of our Capital for the purchase of mere Negroes." The new restrictions on the activity of slave traders, Johnston believed, ensured that slaves would "now be brought by actual settlers and our money returned to the country." Johnston even predicted that Virginia would "feel the difference between selling slaves for money and having them carried away by her own people." The impact, Johnston gloated, "will be as beneficial to us as it will be injurious to her." Johnston emphasized that the new law required aggressive enforcement to minimize "evasion," but he believed that if the slave trade was effectively "suppressed for a time," Virginians and other slaveholders in the upper South would "be obliged to emigrate." The prospect of ending the transfer of Louisiana capital through the creation of an increased flow of Virginia's population toward Louisiana pleased Johnston.[14]

For a time at least, Louisiana's new restrictions apparently slowed the activity of slave traders in the state. Reports from nearby Natchez indicated that the market there was inundated with slaves originally intended for Louisiana. But clever slave buyers eventually found ways to circumvent Louisiana's latest round of restrictions. Residents and their legal agents made long journeys out of state to buy slaves, and in 1832 the legislature had to add Tennessee, Kentucky, and Missouri to the list of states from which imports were banned in order to prevent the law from being rendered moot. But the more stringent the regulations became, the more unpopular they grew. In 1833, the legislature loosened the restrictions on slave imports a bit, and by 1834, just over two years after the Turner revolt, all Louisiana's restrictions on the interstate slave trade were repealed.[15] As one observer of the booming cotton economy in the fertile Red River Valley noted, "slaves were introduced into the country by the thousands...[as] farms were extended as if by the hand of magic, [and] people were generally so absorbed in making money that they seemed to be infatuated."[16]

Nor did Mississippi, though far away from the violence in Southside Virginia, go untouched by Nat Turner's rebellion. A Natchez newspaper correspondent used news of Turner's rebellion to upbraid Mississippi slave patrols for their laxness, worrying that it would take "the repetition on our shores of the scenes of Southampton" to "awaken our citizens" to a "sense" of the danger.[17] Privately, Natchez's Stephen Duncan, one of the richest men in the state, urged silent vigilance in his county (Adams), where blacks outnumbered whites five to one. Duncan estimated that there were twenty-two hundred able-bodied male slaves within a four-hour march of Natchez and knew all too well that the heavily black Natchez region was vulnerable to a slave rebellion. "I do not credit the story of an extension of the Virginia insurrection" into Mississippi, Duncan candidly admitted in early September 1831, "tho I do have apprehension that we will one day have our throats cut in this county."[18] The Vicksburg *Advocate and Register*'s public commentary agreed with Duncan's private admission. The editors urged every citizen to work for "a strict and energetic police, and an efficient organization of the militia, especially in those counties where the combustible population predominates." The "events in Virginia should operate as a potent warning to the people of this country," the newspaper opined. "We repose on a volcano."[19]

The idea of being surrounded by a "combustible" population or reposing atop a volcano left white Mississippians alarmed if not panicked by Turner's rebellion. In an effort to calm these fears, at its 1831 session the Mississippi legislature considered a number of measures designed to prevent exactly the kind of concerted black violence that concerned Mississippi whites the most. The session ultimately approved an omnibus statute designed to give the state better control over both its slave and free black population. The statute outlawed the sale of liquor to a slave without the permission of the slave's master or overseer and banned the employment of slaves and free blacks as "hawkers" and traders. In a sharp reversal from traditional practice in Mississippi, the legislation also made it illegal "for any slave, free negro or mulatto to exercise the function of a Minister of the Gospel." Violators were subject to a punishment of thirty-nine lashes. A master could allow one of his own slaves (but no others) to "preach on his own premises" as long as no "slaves other than his own" were allowed to attend.[20] After receiving a petition from the citizens of Adams County, where more than half of all the free blacks in the state lived, asking for the "absolute and unconditional removal of free negroes from the state," the legislature included in the bill a provision requiring all free blacks between the ages of sixteen and fifty to leave the state within ninety days or risk being sold into slavery for five years. Free blacks could avoid expulsion if they could prove to the probate court in their county of residence that they were of "good character and honest deportment" and in turn receive from the court a license to remain in the state. But the statute also gave the courts the right to revoke the license at any time for cause.[21]

Conspicuous by their absence from the omnibus statute of 1831 were restrictions on Mississippi's participation in the interstate slave trade. The legislature had actively considered such restrictions throughout the 1831 session. One proposal sought a ban on the importation of all slaves over the age of fifteen as merchandise unless the slave or slaves imported could produce certificates of good character and behavior "from three respectable permanent citizens and freeholders" who lived in the vicinity of the slave's previous residence.[22] The proposal was amended to prohibit the importation as merchandise of all slaves over the age of twenty who could not produce at least one certificate of good behavior. This provision passed the house and was included in the omnibus bill regulating slaves and free blacks that went to the state senate.[23] On a second reading in the senate, the slave trade provision generated debate in the Committee of the Whole, which postponed action on the bill and referred it to a select committee for further study. The report of the select committee recommended approval of the omnibus bill once all the restrictions on the domestic slave trade were removed. The senate concurred and the omnibus bill became law, but no restrictions on the interstate slave trade were included in the final statute.[24] The reasons the slave trade restrictions were eliminated from the omnibus bill remain uncertain, but restrictions on the internal slave trade were controversial and doubtless endangered the passage of the entire bill. Moreover, the legislature likely decided that it could easily defer to the state's upcoming constitutional convention on the issue of the domestic slave trade.

Both Mississippi legislators in 1831 and the delegates who assembled to draft a new constitution for the state in 1832 knew that the state had long been concerned about the regulations and control of the interstate slave trade and that state action had produced very mixed results. Mississippi's original state constitution, ratified in 1817, gave the legislature the "full power to prevent slaves from being brought into this State as merchandise" but guaranteed immigrants the right to bring slaves with them when they came to settle. Yet, despite holding the prerogative to ban the importation of slaves for sale, the Mississippi legislature had chosen to regulate the interstate trade rather than prohibit it during the years after 1817. Reviving a lapsed territorial practice, the 1822 Mississippi legislature approved a "character test" for imported slaves. The character test statute required either the traders or prospective buyers to procure character references for the slaves being sold from two freeholders in the slaves' previous area of residence. Designed to slow the work of slave traders and improve white safety, this regulation did not apply to either Mississippi residents or immigrants who intended to settle permanently in Mississippi. In 1825, the legislature attempted to both regulate the slave trade and raise revenue with a tax of 2.5 percent on all slaves purchased at auction. But, in response to public outcry, the legislature lowered the tax to 1 percent the following year.[25]

Still, despite taxes and regulation, as new lands in central and northern Mississippi opened for settlement, the demand for slaves grew. In 1828, well before the controversy over Walker's pamphlet and the Turner scare, Mississippi governor Gerard

Brandon complained that Mississippi had become a "receptacle for the surplus black population of the Middle States." The large number of slaves being imported into Mississippi every year, Brandon contended, "excited uneasiness in the minds of many of our fellow-citizens." Yet despite Brandon's recommendation for restrictions on slave imports, backed by similar concerns expressed by members of the powerful Natchez elite, the state legislature paid Brandon's argument little heed.[26] Cotton profits overcame white fears. As one observer from the rich cotton lands near the Pearl River commented in June 1831, "raising cotton absorbs all their politics and meditations." Neighbors greeted neighbors with the salutation "How does your cotton look?"[27]

But in 1832, with slaves pouring into the state and concerns about the Southampton insurrection running high, the Mississippi constitutional convention of that year, a convention called to draft a more democratic state constitution, also considered appropriate actions to enhance white security. Ultimately, an unlikely coalition of Natchez area planters and piney woods whites placed a provision in the proposed constitution prohibiting the introduction for slaves "as Merchandise" after March 1, 1833.[28] Mississippi citizens and immigrants were guaranteed the right to import slaves for their own use until at least 1845. This constitutional ban on the activity of interstate slave traders emerged almost entirely from a desire to prevent the dumping of troublesome and even rebellious slaves from the upper South into Mississippi's rapidly expanding cotton economy.[29] The assumption prevailed that slaves who accompanied masters and those brought into the state by Mississippi slaveholders were of better character and less likely to incite rebellion than those introduced by professional slave traders. Yet by diminishing the supply of slaves, the constitutional provisions also rendered the capital of Natchez-area planters more valuable and gave these planters a protected market in which to sell their own surplus slaves, facts not lost on slaveholders and aspiring slaveholders in other parts of Mississippi. Largely isolated from staple agriculture, piney woods yeomen simply sought to prevent the blackening of the state while protecting the value of their own labor from an infusion of slaves.[30]

Displeasure with the new constitutional restriction on the interstate slave trade surfaced immediately as demand for slave labor in the newly opened Choctaw and Chickasaw lands of northern and central Mississippi intensified. Instead of fleshing out the constitutional prohibition on the slave trade with detailed statutory provisions, as the convention majority expected, the 1833 Mississippi legislature addressed the slave trade issue by giving the required two-thirds approval of both houses to a proposed constitutional amendment repealing the prohibition on the importation of slaves for sale. By March 1833, the legislature had submitted the amendment to the people for their approval at the upcoming fall elections.

Popular support for the amendment seemed evident, and supporters of the 1832 ban were resigned to defeat. Though formerly an advocate of "the interdiction of this trade," the conservative *Natchez Courier* switched positions and endorsed the amendment because the newspaper held "no hopes" that the legislature could draft an "effective" law that would be "respected" by citizens. A similar ban on the interstate slave trade in neighboring Louisiana, the *Courier* noted, was "either evaded or openly violated." Moreover, the ban on activity of professional slave traders meant simply that "the rich may still import" slaves while "the poorer class," who could not afford to travel, "must either submit to the extortions of the wealthy or rest content with what they have." The newly enacted constitutional prohibition had increased the price of slaves, the newspaper claimed, a development through which "the rich are benefitted at the expense of the poor."[31]

On the eve of the popular vote on the amendment, the *Courier* again endorsed repeal, judging the ban "unequal in operation on the poor and the rich" and calling the interstate slave trade the best means for yeomen and small slaveholders to acquire slaves. Along with other political observers in Mississippi, the *Natchez Courier* felt that a "large majority favored the amendment." The votes cast on the amendment in November 1833 confirmed these impressions, as proamendment forces prevailed by a four-to-one margin (4,531 in favor of the amendment and 1,093 against), with only one river county, Jefferson, casting a majority of its votes against the amendment. But while the amendment won a healthy plurality of those voting on the question, it failed to receive the required majority of all eligible voters needed for ratification, at least partially because voters were required to write either "amendment" or "no amendment" on their ballots. Since the actual number of votes cast in favor of the amendment appeared to fall short of 50 percent of all votes cast for members of the legislature, the amendment had apparently failed to capture the votes needed for ratification. The whole question was complicated by the fact that the failure of local sheriffs to report an official number of votes cast left state officials uncertain about whether to certify the passage of the amendment or not. After a period of indecision, the legislature decided that the amendment had not been ratified.[32]

The unexpected failure of the amendment left state policy toward the interstate slave trade confused and uncertain. In the next session of the legislature, a similar amendment crafted to eliminate the constitutional restriction on the importation of slaves again passed the state senate but failed to win the necessary two-thirds approval in the house. In the face of the constitutional prohibition of the slave trade, the same legislature that had failed to approve a new amendment repealing the constitutional ban revived the old policy of taxing slave purchases, approving a 2.5 percent levy on the gross sale price. Thus while the supreme law of Mississippi prohibited the importation of slaves as merchandise after March 1, 1833, the legislature not only approved no penalties or sanctions for violators but instead taxed what appeared to be an unconstitutional trade.[33]

In face of such contradictory actions, surviving evidence suggests that the constitutional provision against the slave trade was honored mainly in the breach. Between 1833 and 1837, slaves poured into Mississippi in record numbers. From 1830 to 1840, the slave population in Mississippi increased from roughly 65,000 to over

195,000, and one contemporary estimate placed the growth of the slave population between 1830 and 1837 at 74,000, a substantial portion of which entered Mississippi through the activity of slave traders. The same estimate placed the debts incurred by Mississippi planters to traders and other sellers between 1832 and 1837 at over $3 million. Finally, in 1837, the Mississippi legislature gave the ban on the activities of slave traders prescribed by the Mississippi constitution of 1832 statutory backing when it passed a bill imposing a system of fines and penalties for those who sold or purchased slaves imported solely for the purpose of sale or hire.[34]

During the Panic of 1837, however, the financial distress that plagued the Mississippi cotton economy precipitated a minor constitutional crisis over the interstate slave trade. Financially embarrassed and overextended slaveholders sought temporary relief from heavy debts arising from slave purchases by arguing that these debts were invalid because the purchases had been banned by Mississippi's 1832 constitution. In a series of sometimes inconsistent decisions, results-oriented state courts in Mississippi tended to void debts planters owed slave traders but upheld debts that purchasers of slaves owed indigenous Mississippi slaveholders. Eventually slave traders, often citizens of other states who transacted business in several states, sought relief in federal court. These cases, centered on the legality of debts incurred in the interstate slave trade between the effective date of the Mississippi constitutional prohibition in 1833 and the passage of enforcement statutes in 1837, wound its way to the United States Supreme Court as *Groves v. Slaughter*. In a narrowly reasoned decision that avoided the issue of whether a provision such as that of Mississippi's constitution violated the federal Constitution's authority over interstate commerce, the United States Supreme Court ruled the debts valid on grounds that Mississippi's constitutional ban took effect only after the state legislature passed the requisite enabling legislation in 1837. This decision supported creditors' rights but avoided the larger and more explosive question of the conflict between federal and state constitutions.[35]

By 1844, however, as financial distress receded, demand for slaves prompted the Mississippi legislature to again attempt to remove the ban on the importation of slaves for sale with an amendment that restored the legislature's power to ban or regulate the slave trade as it saw fit. The fall election campaign produced very little discussion of the issue. Rejecting the argument that reopening the domestic slave trade would allow Kentucky and other upper South states to dump slaves in Mississippi, a leading Whig newspaper argued that it remained "in favor of permitting the planter to increase the wealth and agricultural productions of our State by importing just as many slaves as he pleases." When such a practice became unprofitable, the editor argued, "it will be stopped voluntarily, without the trouble of constitutional clauses or legislative enactments." A prominent Democratic newspaper also endorsed the amendment. At the ballot box, the amendment received overwhelming approval, winning 25,994 to 3,815. Only three piney woods counties voted against the amendment, and even in the river counties, home to much sentiment in favor of restricting the trade a decade earlier, the amendment won easily. The amendment became part of the state constitution in 1846, and the 1846 Mississippi legislature promptly repealed the 1837 statute that prohibited the importation of slaves as merchandise. Mississippi soon resumed the unrestricted importation of slaves.[36]

The prolonged controversy over the slave trade, however, had revealed the fundamental contradictions and concerns of Mississippi society during the Jacksonian era. Even as many white Mississippians yearned for enough slaves to bring cotton riches to themselves and their fellow citizens, they also fretted over the drain of capital to the upper South and, more important, the dangers of a large black population. As a result, they experimented with ways to balance the need for labor against the fear of the state growing too black. Such modulation of the state's racial demography proved next to impossible.

Like Mississippi and Louisiana but with even less resolve, Alabama had also tried to regulate the interstate slave trade well before the Turner insurrection highlighted the threat to white safety. Throughout the 1820s, Alabama residents or legal immigrants could import slaves for their own use, but popular pressure to regulate the activity of slave traders produced annual legislative initiatives to ban the importation of slaves for sale. Crafted primarily to prevent the importation of "undesirable or troublesome" slaves from the upper South by unscrupulous slave sellers, these bills also sought to protect the investments of existing slaveholders and keep the state from growing too black. Finally, late in 1826, the Alabama legislature passed an outright ban on the importation of slaves for sale or hire and included stiff penalties for violators. But Alabama repealed its ban in 1829. Then, as part of the state's legislative response to the Turner insurrection, Alabama reimposed it again early in 1832. Public pressure again forced an almost immediate legislative about face, and in early December 1832, the teeth were removed from the ban passed earlier in the year. Traders were back in business in Alabama, and, despite occasional complaints from heavy slaveholding areas in the state's western black belt during the 1840s and 1850s, the internal slave trade flourished with little governmental interference for the rest of the antebellum era.[37]

Alabama's post-Turner efforts to enhance white safety also focused on adopting a tougher stance toward free blacks. The state's free black population, though small, had increased steadily under the terms of manumission provided in the state's 1819 constitution. But in 1832, to prevent the growth of the free black population though in-migration as well as manumission, Alabama passed a tough new law prohibiting free blacks from coming into the state under penalty of reenslavement. Two years later, the legislature required all manumitted slaves to leave the state upon gaining their freedom. Despite these new measures to slow the growth of Alabama's free black population, Governor Clement Clay still fretted over the state's seemingly lax regulation of free blacks as late as 1835. Labeling the state's patrol system "ineffectual" and judging many free persons of color as "idle and vicious," Clay noted the "pernicious effects of their bad habits and example upon slaves, and the corrupting tendency of their intercourse." As a remedy, Clay recommended legislation requiring the detention of free blacks who lacked "regular employment."[38] Yet despite Alabama's post-Turner concern about its free black population, the colonization movement made no headway in the state. Even the relocation of the energetic James G. Birney to Huntsville to promote the cause failed to persuade Alabama critics of colonization that the movement would not interfere with slavery. By the end of 1832, the usually optimistic Birney reported a "deadness to the subject of African Colonization" in Alabama.[39]

News of the Turner rebellion raised white anxieties in Georgia, just as did across the rest of the South. The "bloody tragedy in Virginia," the Milledgeville *Southern Recorder* reported, triggered "reports of servile insurrection" from "almost every part of the Southern country." A "plausible" rumor circulated concerning an alleged uprising in a county near Milledgeville. The seemingly credible rumor prompted a "considerable bustle of preparation" in the antebellum Georgia capital and aroused "much alarm" among the city's "women and children." The report turned out to be false, lacking "even a shadow of truth for its support." Such false alarms, the newspaper contended, "do much mischief independent of the temporary inconvenience."[40] Georgia opinion makers were quick to blame the Turner insurrection on outside agitators and incendiary publications, such as William Lloyd Garrison and the *Liberator*. In late November 1831, the Georgia legislature offered a $5,000 reward for the apprehension and conviction of the publisher of the *Liberator*, not as a practical measure but as a signal of the state's outrage at the role it believed this publication played in fostering slave unrest.[41] The Milledgeville *Federal Union* castigated the new abolition publication for its "enthusiastic devotion" to "the abstract doctrines of universal liberty." Publications such as the *Liberator* could foment "insurrections and massacres" by appealing to the emotions of discontented slaves, but they could not prevent the inevitable "severe and direful retribution" by whites. "No servile rebellion could succeed," the *Federal Union* concluded, "for the numbers, the superior concert and intelligence, courage and other resources" lay with the white population. A war of black terror met with retaliatory white terror, the editors complained, would only hinder the gradual movement toward that day so "ardently desired" by many whites (the editors claimed) "in which the African race will be gradually released from their present degraded condition."[42]

But despite its anxiety, Georgia changed its state policy regarding slaves and free blacks less dramatically than other lower South states. On the issue of the interstate slave trade, Georgia's state policy had changed frequently since the state had prohibited the importation of slaves for sale in 1817. The ban was lifted in 1824, only to be partially reinstated again in 1829. In 1830, Governor George Gilmer recommended the elimination of the importation of slaves for use as well as sale. Gilmer argued that a law that "prohibits the introduction of slaves by negro traders, but permits every citizen to bring them into the State for his own use," simply invited all Georgia whites to become small-time slave traders. In 1833, Georgia legislature again tightened its restrictions on the slave trade, but the new law still permitted residents to import slaves for their own use.[43]

Ironically, the news of Turner's rebellion and the southern response to it inspired a brief new round of debate over colonization in Georgia. ACS founder and agent Robert Finlay appeared in Augusta early in 1832 and succeeded in organizing a local auxiliary as well as a female colonization society, both of which included some of that fall-line town's "most worthy citizens."[44] Yet at the same time, the Turner insurrection and the Virginia legislative debates stirred opposition to colonization. "The full and open debate in the Virginia Legislature has alarmed the people of the South," noted a Georgia minister who supported colonization, "and I think for the present operated against the colonization cause here." Another Georgia colonizationist concurred, noting that "many false impressions" of the society and its objects flourished in Georgia in the aftermath of Turner's rebellion.[45]

In South Carolina, the timing of the discovery of Walker's pamphlet early in 1830 and Turner's insurrection during the late summer of 1831 coincided with that state's prolonged and volatile nullification crisis, a passionate controversy that divided the state into hostile camps of nullifiers and Unionists and threatened to drive the state as well as the nation to the brink of civil war. But precisely because of South Carolina's preoccupation with nullification, the significance of new black resistance to the slaveholding regime quickly captured the attention of whites in the black-majority state. There was never any hard evidence that any South Carolina blacks, slave or free, were associated in any way with or had prior knowledge of the Turner revolt, but white anxieties nonetheless ran high in South Carolina once news of the bloody revolt reached the state. In the fall of 1831, rumors circulated widely that a slave rebellion was imminent in Camden. In Columbia, a local vigilance association offered a $1,500 reward for the capture of anyone distributing incendiary pamphlets. Charleston leaders sought state funding for a stronger and better-equipped home guard.[46]

Moreover, the post-Turner anxiety ran rampant through the white-majority Upcountry as well as the black-majority Lowcountry. Fears of slave unrest had penetrated the Upcountry during earlier crises, but it was not until the aftermath of Turner's insurrection that fear of insurrection ran just as deep in the predominantly white interior as in the slave-majority Lowcountry. Rumors of insurrection reverberated through the Upcountry during the final months of 1831. Whites in the Upcountry districts of Greenville, Abbeville, Newberry, Laurens, and York hunkered down under rumors of impending insurrection. In Laurens District, two slaves were arrested simply for saying they would join an insurrection if a Nat Turner appeared among them to lead one. In neighboring Union County, a number of slaves were arrested while white women and children were herded into a secure village location just in case trouble erupted. In early October, Abbeville District planter and newspaper editor Samuel Townes told his brother George that "our community is very much excited by reason of an apprehension of a negro insurrection." The editor explained that members of respected planter families who had recently traveled across the Upcountry reported rumors of slave unrest in York, Newberry, and Laurens. These reports, Townes noted, had "nearly scared" Abbeville women "into a cocked hat." For himself, Townes dismissed such reports as mere rumors utterly lacking in foundation, and he also deprecated an "insurrection alarm" in Greenville as the "most supremely ridiculous thing" that he "had ever heard." In a more serious vein, Townes contended that the "foolish fear" generated by the insurrection scares was "highly reprehensible and well calculated to produce the very thing from which it shrinks with so much horror."[47]

Throughout the fall of 1831, public complaints surfaced in South Carolina about disturbing levels of autonomy enjoyed by some blacks and the number of opportunities such autonomy gave both slaves and free blacks to plan and implement rebellion. A Fairfield County grand jury complained about slave mechanics, whose masters often allowed them to "travel about the country in quest of work." These slave mechanics, the grand jury noted, roamed about "without restraint" and enjoyed a "great facility for plotting mischief & maturing plans for disturbing the peace of the community." Moreover, the autonomy slave mechanics enjoyed had an "injurious effect" on efforts to discipline "the slave population generally."[48] A Kershaw District grand jury echoed the Fairfield complaint, calling the work of slave and free black mechanics "a growing evil" and recommending a gradual end to the use of slave mechanics in favor of whites.[49] A Richland district grand jury felt the same way about peddlers, black and white, who were allowed to roam the country selling goods of various descriptions. Through such peddlers, "Incendiary Pamphlets and Letters are circulated with impunity and facility endangering the safety and peace of the state," the Richland jurors argued.[50] A Georgetown grand jury joined its Richland counterpart in raising the issue of incendiary pamphlets. The mayor of Georgetown, A. W. Dozier, sent copies of antislavery publications he had received to the state legislature. Dozier branded such publications as "fanaticism" and worried that this literature might circulate among his district's large black population. Their design, Dozier argued, was nothing less than "to scatter the firebrands of discontent and excite the spirit of Insurrection among the colored people of the South." The Georgetown grand jury, with prominent slaveholder Henry Middleton as foreman, agreed with the mayor, asserting that the "distribution of papers leading to insurrectionary movement among our slave population" was an "evil" that was "daily spreading."[51]

The Turner insurrection also brought popular calls for increased restriction on South Carolina's free black population. South Carolina had already blocked the immigration of free blacks, placed control of private manumission in the hands of the state legislature, imposed serious restrictions on the activities of free blacks, and forced them to obtain a white guardian, all in the aftermath of the Vesey scare. Some of the state's laws regulating free blacks may have been sporadically enforced, but tough restrictive provisions were already on the books. As a result, the 1831 legislature rebuffed calls for additional restrictions on free blacks. Indeed, in December 1831, just three months after Turner's insurrection, the legislature's Committee on the Colored Population rejected imposing additional "Harsh and severe legislation" on the state's free blacks as long as they "conduct themselves" with a "proper appreciation and submission to the status assigned them." Instead, the committee recommended extending "favor and encouragement" to free blacks rather than resorting to "oppression and expulsion."[52] Nor did South Carolina, a substantial slave-exporting state by the early 1830s, consider renewed efforts to regulate the interstate slave trade. During the 1820s South Carolina had exported 20,500 more slaves than it had imported, making it the largest net exporter of slaves in the lower South, and during the following decade, the state's net slave exports would exceed 56,000, making the Palmetto State the largest net exporter of slaves in the entire South, except for Virginia.[53] Thus the state had little interest in interfering with the domestic slave trade.

Yet the popular furor over Turner's insurrection, the publication of Garrison's *Liberator*, the efforts to circulate Walker's pamphlet in South Carolina, and the internal division aroused by the nullification controversy galvanized legislative attention around the issue of slave control. Conditions appeared favorable for the passage of draconian new restrictions on South Carolina slaves and free blacks, particularly in relation to two matters whites had come to associate with slave unrest: slave religion and slave literacy.

Virginia governor John Floyd's fall 1831 letter to South Carolina governor James Hamilton alerted state leaders to the fact that the Virginia governor, a Calhoun ally, blamed the Turner insurrection on slave religion and the distribution of abolitionist writings among literate slaves and free blacks in Virginia.[54] Indeed, in the Palmetto State, the chief thrust of public complaints arising from the Turner insurrection took the form of assaults on the Christian mission to the slaves, particularly to the extent this mission had encouraged the emergence of black preachers, the holding of religious meetings at which blacks often proved a majority, and the education of slaves. The tension between white security and the paternalist effort to Christianize and educate slaves, a process generally aimed at giving slave Christians direct access to scripture, dated back to the Vesey crisis, when bitter criticism of slave religion and slave literacy had emerged from James Hamilton and members of the Vesey court. Only an aggressive defense of the Christian mission to the slaves and the broader concept of paternalism by members of the Charleston clergy had succeeded in limiting the legislative and intellectual impact of this attack.

Despite Lowcountry religious leaders' ability to turn aside this Vesey-era antipaternalist foray, however, many Lowcountry whites, including much of the leadership of the strident South Carolina Association, harbored deep suspicions of the emerging paternalist insurgency. In particular, the association, Charleston's extralegal enforcement arm of the white security movement, believed that additional legislation was needed to control the religious instruction of slaves and the teaching of slaves to read. The 1822 failure of Vesey investigators and their legislative allies to secure legislation prohibiting the teaching of slaves to read left the ineffectual 1740 law against teaching slaves to write as the state's only statutory restriction on black education. In 1829, a Sumter District grand jury expressed this lingering sentiment when it complained that "the liberty which is allowed to owners of teaching their slaves to read, a practice which is generally encouraged, will lead to consequences of the most serious and alarming nature."[55]

In the aftermath of the Turner insurrection, petitions to the South Carolina legislature again brought the issue of slave religion to the fore. In late October 1831, a Richland District grand jury labeled the "frequent assemblies of numerous congregations of people of color for the professed object of worship" as "a great and growing evil in this community." Based on "real events in a Sister State," the grand jurors concluded that these religious assemblies had "a tendency to endanger the Peace and safety of the Citizens of this state by...affording an opportunity of concerting plans inimical to public safety and tranquility."[56] An 1831 Kershaw grand jury also complained of the "practice of Ministers of the gospel of any denomination whatever granting licenses to Negroes as commissioned to espouse the gospel to the Black population of this state." The grand jury insisted that it had no desire to "interfere in the slightest degree with the freedom of conscience or the free exercise of religious worship" provided that "neither involve the danger of the community." But the grand jury was "nevertheless satisfied that the licensing of black preachers" constituted "a fit subject for legislative consideration and prohibition." The licensing of black preachers, the grand jury believed, disturbed "the harmony and security of the people...whether white or black." Recent events in Virginia and North Carolina, the jury claimed, had "brought this subject forcibly to the minds" of Kershaw whites.[57]

The first post-Turner session of the South Carolina legislature, which began in late November 1831, witnessed the beginnings of a fresh new assault on slave literacy and slave preaching and even on the religious instruction of slaves generally. It was an unrelenting assault led by one of the paternalist movement's severest critics, Whitemarsh Seabrook, the wealthy Edisto Island cotton planter and founding member of the radical South Carolina Association. Seabrook had emerged by 1830 as not only a fervent critic of northern "interference" with slavery but also a staunch critic of what he perceived as the southern refusal to meet antislavery criticism with ample firmness. The Seabrook-led assault on Christian efforts to bring religious instruction to the slaves, and on paternalism more generally, continued in the legislature over the course of at least four years.[58]

At the 1831 session of the legislature, Seabrook and other Palmetto critics of paternalism joined legislators who were simply alarmed by the recent Turner insurrection to propose an aggressive set of new regulations concerning slaves and free blacks. The proposed bill would have banned the teaching of slaves to read and write, prohibited the use of black preachers or exhorters under any circumstances, tightened enforcement of existing laws restricting the conditions under which blacks could legally assemble for religious (or any other) purposes, prohibited the employment of slaves as clerks, made it illegal to teach free blacks to read or write, and prohibited blacks, slave or free, from serving as peddlers or hawkers. The Senate Judiciary Committee, chaired by Senator James Gregg of Richland, one of the petitioning districts, recommended the "passage of a Law declaring all assemblies of persons of colour under the pretense of Public worship, even in the daytime unlawful unless six slaveholders were present" and imposing a prohibitive $500 license fee on all "hawkers and peddlers." The bill, which included stringent new measures limiting educational and religious opportunities for slaves, passed two readings in the state senate with ease before being sent to the state house of representatives for consideration.

Initially, the house referred the bill to its judiciary committee for review, and finally on December 17, 1831, the house took action on the senate proposal. Under the leadership of Henry Laurens Pinckney, an arch-nullifier, the house informed the senate that it would accept the bill if and only if the senate agreed to strike the provisions that banned free blacks from being taught to read or write or being employed as clerks and the ban on slave preachers and exhorters. Strikingly, the senate quickly agreed to the remove the portions of the law that the house found objectionable, without further negotiation. Thus South Carolina's 1831 statute relating to slaves focused almost entirely on banning slaves and free blacks from producing, selling, or sharing intoxicating liquor with anyone, slave or free. In addition, the legislature appropriated money to support a one-hundred-person cavalry unit, known as the Charleston Horse Guard, to protect against Turner-like uprisings in the port city, and approved a few other measures to improve patrols and enhance white security. Thus, after bold beginnings, the 1831 South Carolina legislature did little to increase the state's regulation of slaves or free blacks.

The house's seemingly easy gutting of the original senate bill's potent attack on paternalism, with its strict measures to limit slave literacy and tighten state regulation of slave religious activity, and the senate's even more surprising acceptance of the house's demands likely reflect the legislative leadership's preoccupation with a looming matter of larger concern: fashioning the two-thirds majority needed to call a convention for the nullification of federal tariff laws. The nullifiers had held a majority in the legislature since the 1830 elections but did not enjoy the two-thirds majority that Calhoun and other leading nullifiers deemed necessary for the calling of a sovereign convention. Speaker Pinckney and senate president Henry Deas were both close allies of the state's pro-nullification governor, James Hamilton. The attack on slave literacy and the religious instruction of slaves remained inherently controversial, attracting the opposition of a strong minority of legislators, and they were also issues that divided both the nullifier and Unionist camps. These measures were also much less popular in the Upcountry, where the battle over nullification was hotly contested in several districts, than in the Lowcountry. Moreover, Pinckney, while an ardent nullifier, was also a member of Benjamin Palmer's Circular Congregational

Church. Palmer was an avid defender of the religious instruction of slaves in general and of teaching slaves to read in particular. On these issues, Palmer's sympathies lay far more in favor of paternalism than did those of his congregation, but through his connection with Palmer, Pinckney was no doubt well aware of intensity of the state's religious community's opposition to the proposed restrictions.[59] Thus the sudden weakening of the original bill likely owed much to the need of the nullifiers to build a consensus behind their cause and to the prominent role Pinckney played in managing the legislation.

The attack on religious efforts to teach slaves to read, however, continued the following year during the legislature's so-called nullification session of 1832. In the house, prominent nullifier Robert Barnwell Smith (later Rhett) introduced a bill making it illegal to teach slaves to read. The measure passed a first reading in the house without a recorded vote. In the senate, however, a companion bill was referred to the judiciary committee after a first reading, and the judiciary committee judged it "inexpedient" to pass either the house or senate version of the bill. The committee gave no reason for its recommendation, but again it is plausible that the need to unify the legislature behind the idea of calling a nullification convention may have rendered it "inexpedient" to proceed with the attack on the practice of teaching slaves to read, deferring the pitched legislative battle on the issue for another year.[60]

IRONICALLY, THE POST-TURNER LEGISLATIVE ASSAULT on paternalism in South Carolina coincided with an increasingly vocal call from the lower South's religious leadership for aggressive new efforts to take religious instruction to the slaves. In November 1831, the Presbyterian Synod of South Carolina and Georgia held its regular meeting in Columbia, a city still on edge with post-Turner insurrection fears and alive with the rhetoric of the nullification crisis. Among those attending was the young Georgia Presbyterian Charles Colcock Jones, the man who was fast earning a reputation as the lower South's leading "Apostle to the Slaves." Jones, heir to a huge rice fortune in the Georgia Lowcountry and son of a local Revolutionary War hero, had gone north for his education before returning home to Liberty County, a rice- and cotton-producing county in the Georgia Lowcountry, where he urged his fellow Presbyterians to try his method for the moral improvement of slavery in microcosm, expanding the religious instruction of slaves one plantation at a time if necessary. At the synod meeting in 1831, Jones and fellow Presbyterian Benjamin Gildersleeve, the Charleston-based editor of the *Charleston Observer*, an influential religious newspaper in the South, placed a resolution before the synod calling on the church to put new emphasis on its religious mission to the slaves.[61] Well aware of serious and perhaps growing political opposition to the existing religious instruction of slaves emerging in the region, Jones defended the resolution in a speech to the synod. In his remarks, Jones questioned why "the majority...of our citizens" who believe "slavery sanctioned by the Bible" feared having "the Bible, the whole Bible, and nothing but the Bible preached to their servants." If, for any reason, "emancipation would prove the result of the preaching of the Gospel," Jones argued, then "happy are we in believing that it could not come in a more gradual, in an easier, nor in a safer way." It would, Jones boldly concluded, "be the work of the Almighty, the effect of the Divine principles of his Word...and thus may the Glory of the removal of an evil be laid at the foot of the Cross." Ultimately the synod gave its initial approval to the proposed resolution and called for its publication in Gildersleeve's *Charleston Observer*.[62]

Jones' presentation at the synod meeting marked his first large-sale public presentation and it almost immediately attracted regionwide notice. Some two years later, in 1833, a young South Carolina Presbyterian, Alexander Dromgoole Sims, who disagreed with Jones' characterization of slavery as an "evil" and who called slaves "the happiest people on earth," nonetheless joined the Georgia evangelist in insisting that slaves should have access to religious instruction because it was through such instruction that white Christians could improve the moral habits of slaves. And masters, Sims cautioned, should practice Christian stewardship in the administration of their daily duties. Sims wanted unduly severe punishment banned, work regimens kept reasonable, and slave health and comfort attended to.[63] Also in 1833, Presbyterian planter Thomas Clay attracted attention with his presentation at a presbytery meeting in south Georgia of a plan of religious instruction already under way on his plantation in Bryan County, Georgia, a county in which slaves outnumbered whites more than three to one. Clay, who owned some two hundred slaves on his impressive plantation, Richmond-on-Ogeechee, argued that the "moral improvement" of slaves deserved the consistent attention of masters "throughout the Southern Country" but often had failed to receive such attention. Like Charles Jones, Clay emphasized the importance of Sunday schools and evening meetings on plantations. Clay argued that such evening meetings should be held every weekday and include hymns, scripture reading, and a Bible lesson. Such meetings, led by whites, were already being held at several plantations in his community, explained Clay, an elder at Bryan Neck Presbyterian Church, and slave behavior on these plantations was much improved. Slaves, Clay also argued, needed proper food, clothing, shelter, and medical care when they were sick. Christian masters, Clay insisted, must attend to the physical as well as spiritual needs of their slaves, including the recognition of slave marriages.[64]

At the same meeting of the Georgia presbytery, Charles Jones delivered an address, "On the Moral and Religious Condition of Our Coloured Population." In many respects, Jones, though impressed with Thomas Clay and his proposal, painted a bleak picture of the moral and spiritual condition (though not the capacity) of slaves on southern plantations and indicted masters for their excessive materialism. "It is a solemn fact which we must not conceal," Jones contended, "that [slaves'] public and private religious instruction forms no part of the aim of owners generally." Instead, Jones complained, "the great and absorbing aim is to work them profitably." To make matters worse, Jones continued, slaves were "governed too much...by fear of corporeal punishment," and the punishment consisted of "the mere pain inflicted." Jones acknowledged that physical punishment probably had a place in slave management, but he also argued that such punishment had a negative rather than a positive influence on moral character. "I maintain, therefore," Jones explained, "that our government [of slaves], dependent for its support almost entirely...on the principle of fear, will not only be attended with trouble, but will exert a most unfavorable influence on their [slaves] moral character." Moreover, Jones concluded, the "evils" of relying chiefly on physical punishment "degraded" masters as well as slaves. Masters, Jones insisted, must feel a "personal responsibility to God" on the matter of the slaves' "salvation."[65] The plans and speeches and Jones and Clay and others of similar inclination proved that Christian paternalists were at work to change both the dominant mode of slave management in the South and the central paradigm for understanding it. And they worked hard even when the post-Turner atmosphere enhanced popular suspicion of their cause.

THE ENERGETIC WORK of Jones, Clay, and other evangelists to the slaves worried paternalism's opponents. Seabrook and other critics of the religious instruction of slaves hardly found comfort in Jones' claim that if the religious instruction of slaves ended in emancipation, it would merely be a reflection of the inevitable triumph of "the Almighty" over "an evil." It was precisely such talk that opponents of religious instruction wanted to keep slaves from hearing, much less learning to read about in print. Toward those ends, the Richland District grand jury urged the legislature in the fall of 1833 to pass laws that "may effectively put a stop to the teaching of Negroes to read or write" and end the "assembling of negroes under the pretext of religious instruction or for any mental instruction whatever."[66] And also from the state capital, the Columbia town council considered a proposed ordinance to "effectually prevent the teaching of slaves to Read or Write under any pretext whatever." After some deliberation, the town council decided that it lacked the "authority" to pass such an ordinance and could only enforce the provision of the state's existing laws "on the same subject." Thus, instead of approving the proposed ordinance, the Columbia town council asked the city intendant, M. H. DeLeon, to petition the legislature on behalf of the council, seeking the enactment of a statute to "effectually put a stop to a practice which if continued must eventuate...ultimately in discord."[67]

When the South Carolina legislature met again in late November 1833, the nullification crisis was over, and the field was now clear for Seabrook and others to push their attacks on slave literacy and the religious instruction of slaves without regard to party division once again. In 1833, Seabrook introduced a bill in the state senate that would ban the teaching of slaves to read and write, prohibit the use of black preachers, and make it illegal to employ slaves as clerks. Seabrook's friend and ally, Edward Laurens, introduced a similar bill in the house. The senate version passed two readings, one by a vote of 38–2, before the bill was sent to the house for consideration.[68]

Moreover, the bill the senate sent to the house included a ban on teaching free blacks as well slaves to read. On the bill's second reading in the house, representative Thomas H. Nixon of Edgefield offered an amendment to make it unlawful for any "person of color to preach, lecture or give religious instruction on any occasion to coloured persons" unless five "respectable" whites were present. But Nixon's amendment was defeated, 33–64. The entire house, which two years earlier had stripped bare a bold senate bill crafted along the same lines, then readily approved the senate bill by a comfortable margin, 51–34, and returned the bill to the senate for final approval. Seabrook and his antipaternalist allies again appeared poised on the brink of success.[69]

But when the senate, which had earlier approved very similar versions of the bill by large margins, took up the bill by special order on December 18, 1833, Low-country senator Samuel Warren moved to postpone the bill until after January 1.[70] Since the legislature always adjourned before Christmas, the move to postpone until January would effectively kill the bill for the 1833 legislative session. Thus the vote on the Warren motion would determine the fate of the proposal until after the 1834 elections. By 1833, Samuel Warren, the seventy-two-year-old senator from St. James Santee who moved for the postponement, was the grand old man of the state senate. Three times president of the senate earlier in his career, Warren was a veteran of the Continental Army who had lost a leg defending Savannah during the Revolution. As a delegate to the South Carolina state ratifying convention in 1788, Warren had voted in favor of the new federal constitution. By 1832, however, Warren, the owner of more than a hundred slaves, had emerged as a leading nullifier in his parish.[71] The decision of opponents of Seabrook's restrictive bill to choose Warren to move for postponement represented an effort to place the weight of tradition and state history against the bill.

Warren's motion to postpone was approved narrowly, 20–17. The sectional tilt of the senate vote on Warren's motion was clear. The motion to kill attracted thirteen votes from the state's interior (or upper division), including nine from districts lying on or above the fall line, and only six from the Lowcountry parishes. Opponents of the motion to postpone (advocates of the bill) mustered ten votes from the parishes but only seven from the interior and a mere four from above the fall line. The voting coalitions transcended the nullification-era factional alignments. A number of staunch nullifiers, including not only Warren but Georgetown's Robert F. W. Allston, Edgefield's Andrew Pickens Butler, and Richland's James Gregg, joined Unionists such as Charleston's Alfred Huger and Abbeville's Joseph Black to kill the bill. In addition to Allston, Butler, and Warren, a number of the senate's largest planters, including the interior's James Chesnut (Camden), Richard I. Manning (Sumter), and Austin Peay (Fairfield), voted to kill the bill. In essence, the weight and wealth of the senate had supported killing the bill, but succeeded in doing so by only a narrow margin.[72] Seabrook attributed the defeat of the bill to a belief among a narrow majority of the senators that the restrictions on teaching slaves and free blacks to read and write "violated" the traditional "policy of the state."[73] Paternalists and their allies had turned back yet another radical, "infidel" assault, but only by the narrowest of margins after careful coalition building.

Seabrook took it as his personal charge to rally the votes to pass a similar bill at the legislature's next session. Thus, in 1834, Seabrook produced a widely circulated pamphlet defending his hard-line stance against all but the most minimal religious instruction for slaves and his staunch opposition to improving slave literacy.[74] Seabrook crafted his pamphlet partially as an attack on northern abolitionists, partially as a response to the work of Thomas Clay, Charles Jones, and the resolution on the religious instruction of slaves approved by the Presbyterian Synod of South Carolina and Georgia finally published in 1833, and partially in an effort to build legislative support for restrictions on the religious instruction of slaves. He attacked the synod resolution for suggesting that "slavery is unlawful," and blasted the report as a "melancholy delineation" of slavery similar to the ominous portrait that had emerged from the "graphic pencil of Jefferson" during the 1780s. The mere idea that if slaveholders "are to obey the Savior" they "must preach the Gospel to servants," Seabrook declared, was an "unfortunate declaration." The volatile Sea Island planter thought such sentiments could emanate only from those with a desire for emancipation. Seabrook openly worried that preachers were not worldly enough to understand the necessities of slave control or to make trustworthy judgments about protecting the institution of slavery over the long term. "No Christian will deny the importance of religious instruction to slaves," Seabrook admitted, acknowledging that "on this head there is no difference of opinion," but differences quickly arose when the question shifted to "how they ought to be taught, and to what extent." "Is it advisable," Seabrook asked rhetorically, "to make them acquainted with the whole Bible, or to teach them every doctrine...that one book inculcates? In a word, do considerations, predicated on the spiritual welfare of the blacks, demand, that...their religious knowledge should be co-extensive with that of their owners." Seabrook's emphatic answer to his own rhetorical question was an unhesitating no. "The enforcement of such a project [of religious instruction]," Seabrook ranted, "would entitle its friends to a room in the Lunatic Asylum."[75]

Seabrook dismissed notions, such as those systematically developed by Charles Jones, of Christianizing three hundred thousand slaves as "one of those fairy sketches" emerging from "the exuberance of an erratic fancy." He even objected to tailoring sermons or portions of sermons and adapting hymns to allow slave participation because such joint participation promoted the notion of equality among whites and slaves. Seabrook's own preferences were clear. "Let the slave be informed on the points essential to his salvation, and the whole duty of the instructor is fulfilled." Slaves, Seabrook insisted, "were not prepared for the refinement and subtleties" that the "evangelical school" wanted to teach them, and could not grasp "principles" that required "the exercise of a cultivated intellect." Teaching such refined religious principles to slaves, Seabrook insisted, would serve only to turn the docile slave into a "wild and restless fanatic" who would prove "useless, if not dangerous to his master."[76]

Moreover, Seabrook contended that the "safety" of both whites and slaves precluded "an indulgence" like the "education" of slaves. He attacked the idea that the slaveholder and his family should act as "teachers to their own people" as "palpably objectionable" and as a "sophistical and illusory" scheme. Whether the slaveholder's family should teach slaves as many as three times a day, as Thomas Clay recommended, or once per week, as the synod report suggested, Seabrook thought such instruction would begin the "reign of fanaticism and misrule" in the South. Seabrook strenuously objected to the idea of using blacks, whether slave or free, as catechists, repeating the familiar contention that a number of slaves incriminated in the Vesey scare were catechists in their respective churches. "Coloured preachers, lecturers, and catechists have been the instruments of positive evils to society," Seabrook insisted. By attempting to do too much, Seabrook contended, those advocating enhanced religious instruction to slaves threatened to "raze the very citadel of our feelings, associations and prejudices." The Christian impulse to evangelize, Seabrook contended, must be balanced against the "dangers resulting from such efforts" to convert slaves. Calling Thomas Clay's plan of religious instruction the work of a "Tappanist," Seabrook denounced the Georgia Presbytery's instruction regimen as a "wild and fanatical project" that proposed to "rule our slaves by perpetual prayer and exhortation instead of by the exercise of the master's authority."[77]

WHILE SEABROOK USED HIS PAMPHLET to lobby for the passage of tough new laws against teaching slaves to read and write and regulating slave assemblies, the Charleston clergy was actively working to convince state leaders that excessive restrictions on the Christian ministry to the slaves were counterproductive. Meeting privately, Charleston's distinguished composite of clergy agreed on an indirect approach. They decided to seek relaxed enforcement of state laws against religious assemblies that were held at night or were more than 50 percent black rather than criticizing the legislative effort to prohibit the teaching of slaves to read and write, an issue on which the various Christian denominations disagreed sharply among themselves. The Episcopalians, the most influential denomination among Lowcountry planters, generally saw no need to teach slaves to read and write, and the Presbyterians, despite the emphasis their denomination placed on the value of education, were often willing to compromise on the issue of teaching slaves to read in order to gain access to slaves for the purpose of systematic oral instruction. Baptists and Methodists were generally uncompromising in their insistence that slaves should be taught to read so that they could have direct access to the scriptures, and the state's small Associate Reformed Presbyterian denomination was steadfast in its determination to educate slaves. Charleston's Catholic leadership was also unabashed in its desire to educate slaves, although the Protestant need for every believer to have personal access to the Bible was not an important part of the Catholic justification.

During the fall of 1834, an informal meeting of the Charleston clergy at the city's First Presbyterian Church selected a committee to meet with the city council about the ability of slaves and free blacks to assemble for religious purposes. The committee conferred with the council and procured agreement from city authorities to enforce state laws on religious assemblies as the council deemed necessary, provided that the legislature would allow local authorities such discretion on the issues. The Charleston city council agreed to "cheerfully assume the discharge of any duties which the state Legislature in their wisdom may prescribe in relation to the regulations of religious assemblies of Negroes and Persons of Color" within the Charleston city limits. On November 26, 1834, just before the year's legislative session began, another meeting was held at the Methodist parsonage in the city to learn the results of their committee's efforts and prepare the appropriate memorial to the state legislature. Episcopal pastor Christopher Gadsden was called to the chair and Unitarian Samuel Gilman served as clerk. They heard the encouraging report from their committee and drafted a petition.[78]

The memorial to the legislature prepared by the Charleston clergy complained that under existing laws slaves and free blacks of their "respective congregations" could not "be assembled for religious instruction" after sundown "unless a greater number of whites be assembled with them." In Charleston District, where slaves and free blacks made up nearly 75 percent of the total population, holding a meeting with a white majority was virtually "impossible," the memorialists claimed. "During the hours of the day," the petitioners argued, slaves and free blacks were "so universally engaged in their duties...as nearly to preclude their assemblage for the purpose of instruction." Moreover, "at all times," the "instruction imparted must be of such a character as would be uninteresting to white persons." The "number [of whites] requisite to legalize the assembly could scarcely ever be collected," the Charleston clergy complained.[79]

Moreover, the Charleston clergy claimed that the state's laws regulating such assemblies were generally the product of "some special emergency" in the state's history and throughout most of the state were enforced only on "particular occasions" when vigilance was deemed necessary by local authorities. As a result, the petitioners claimed, these laws had become "virtually obsolete in every part of the state." For thirty years, blacks in Charleston had been "indulged with the privilege of religious instruction and worship after sunset with less than a majority of white persons present," unless local authorities thought larger circumstances temporarily dictated strict enforcement of state laws. Expressing a view very much at odds with Seabrook, Laurens, and other radicals, the Charleston pastors claimed that not "the least mischief of any kind" had arisen from such meetings. To the contrary, the petitioners argued, the religious instruction of slaves at such meetings "have contributed, more than any other cause, to the formation of a faithful, valuable, subordinate, and well-affected body of servants." But "recently," the clergy complained, with an intentional lack of specificity, such leniency had been withdrawn in favor of strict enforcement of state laws, and "the coloured people of the city are suddenly left in a condition which nearly precludes...the possibility of religious instruction," while in "other parts of the state" a "greater latitude" in enforcement of the laws remained in effect.[80]

Thus the clergy urged the revision of the laws of 1800 and 1803 so "that the religious meetings of the coloured people of Charleston may be held in such a manner and according to such restrictions as shall be prescribed by the City Council, who have consented to undertake the charge." Such a change, the petitioning clergy argued, would place the regulation of slave assemblies for religious purposes in the hands of those whose "local knowledge, personal interest, and immediate responsibility" would allow them to "secure all desirable vigilance and efficiency in the execution of the laws on its subject." The meeting decided that all willing Charleston ministers would sign the petition in order of their seniority of service in Charleston. The list was as impressive as it was varied. It began with Nathaniel Bowen, rector of St. Michael's Episcopal church and bishop of the South Carolina diocese, followed by Benjamin Morgan Palmer of the Congregational church, Christopher Gadsden, rector of St. Philip's Episcopal, Samuel Gilman of the "Independent" or Unitarian church, Benjamin Gildersleeve, the Presbyterian editor, Basil Manly, who had succeeded Richard Furman at First Baptist, the young Thomas Smyth from Second Presbyterian, Arthur Buist from First Scots Presbyterian, and John Bachman from the Lutheran Church.[81]

ALL THE CLERGY'S CAREFUL WORK on the issue, however, proved to be of little avail. When the state legislature convened in late November 1834, the South Carolina senate took up a bill to restrict various slave activities once again. Early in the session, the legislature showed its respect for Seabrook by electing him lieutenant governor, leaving Charleston representative Edward Laurens to navigate the bill through the legislative straits. Early in the session, the state senate referred the proposal to its judiciary committee to ascertain whether it was "proper & expedient to prevent by law the preaching and instruction of slaves & free persons of color in public to their fellows." Later in the session, the bill was reported out of committee, read for the third time, and approved without a roll call vote on December 16, 1834.[82] The bill also sailed through the house without either objection or roll call vote. In its final form, the 1834 law made it illegal to "teach any slave to read or write," to assist in teaching any slave to read and write, or to hire anyone to teach slaves to read and write. The ban applied only to slaves and not to free blacks, as Seabrook and Laurens had initially hoped. However, both free blacks and slaves found guilty of teaching slaves to read and write were subject to punishments of up to fifty lashes, and any free person of color who kept a school was also subject to the same fines. The statute also outlawed the employment of slaves and free blacks as clerks or salesmen and stiffened penalties for whites and blacks who trafficked in liquor or gambled with slaves. Contrary to Seabrook's wishes, the new law did not explicitly ban the use of black preachers, exhorters, or class leaders. Nor did it toughen the restrictions the state had placed on black attendance at religious gatherings, but with the 1800 and 1803 laws being rigidly enforced in the Charleston area, additional restrictions would have seemed moot.[83]

The reasons for the 1834 legislature's willingness to approve this legislation after three years of rejecting similar measures remain a matter of conjecture. The elections of 1834 had produced a new legislature, though it is difficult to discern any clear pattern in the election results or find expressions of public opinion on the subject during the canvass. However, during the campaign, candidates may have detected an increased public willingness to see such restrictions enacted in the interest of white security. The restrictive measures almost certainly gained a few votes in the legislature once the proposed ban on teaching free blacks to read and write was dropped. Additionally, the delicate matter of building supermajority coalitions on nullification-related issues no longer hindered efforts to forge a simple voting majority to enact the restrictive legislation. Yet perhaps the most persuasive hypothesis is that by late 1834 the legislature certainly would have been aware that almost every other slaveholding state had already imposed or tightened a ban on teaching slaves to read and write in the aftermath of the Turner incident, and South Carolina's failure to do so suggested an unexpected lack of vigilance on the part of the Palmetto State. In any event, the 1834 legislation was a major victory for Seabrook and other South Carolina radicals, and a stinging defeat for the paternalists and their project.

In the short term, the new ban was felt most directly in Charleston, where Catholic bishop John England was quickly forced to abandon his efforts to establish a school for black children in the city.[84] Free black Daniel Payne, a man widely respected for his intellectual prowess and religious sincerity and a close friend of Lutheran pastor John Bachman, was advised by his white friends to close a school for blacks he had been running for years.[85] But the law's short-term repercussions were hardly limited to Charleston. Shortly after the law was passed, Abbeville lawyer David Wardlaw contacted his friends in the large Associate Reformed Presbyterian community at Due West, a community known for its determination to teach slaves to read, to close their school for slaves in light of the new restrictions.[86] The Due West community, roughly 750 strong, was full of Ulster Scots who clung to the "seceder" tradition, which had broken away from the Church of Scotland in the 1730s. These ARPs, perhaps more largely concentrated in the South Carolina Upcountry than anywhere else in the United States, were most easily identified by their practice of singing only biblical psalms. Central to the religious practice of ARPs was the idea of daily family devotionals, which usually involved the reading and discussion of scripture. When, as paternalism suggested, the concept of family was expanded to include slaves, the ARPs expected slaves should be included in the observance of the family devotional. Hence ARPs routinely held classes teaching slaves to read, even though this central element in the ARP discipline attracted criticism from secular authorities.[87] Across the state, the 1834 law either stopped efforts to teach slaves to read or forced them underground.

EDWARD LAURENS QUICKLY PUBLISHED a tract defending the legislature's actions on the subject. The Charleston representative, Seabrook's point man in the house, remained skeptical of paternalism generally, blaming "the organization of new Societies" aimed at ameliorating slavery for encouraging insurrections. Literacy, Laurens declared, rendered the slave "dissatisfied with his lot, and thus invited insubordination." Laurens claimed that he was not opposed to the religious mission to the slaves, but the Charleston legislator insisted that the mission was "not to be furthered by teaching them to read, for where one would draw the pure waters of life from the fountain of inspiration, hundreds would follow after false prophets, to their disquiet here, and their perdition hereafter." The Lowcountry representative also defended the statutory provision banning free blacks from serving as clerks and salesmen, arguing that all "danger of any insurrectionary movement arises from the toleration of this intermediate class [free blacks]—who...must always be the ring-leaders in any concerted scheme—the leader must be a free man who can command his own time, or not even the first preliminaries can be arranged."[88]

Though arguably relieved that the legislature had not extended its restriction of the religious instruction of slaves beyond the ban on teaching reading and writing, defenders of the religious instruction of slaves and champions of paternalism generally could not let the aggressive new critique of the Christian mission to the slaves pass unchallenged. Early in 1835, Episcopal bishop Nathaniel Bowen, acting at the request of the convention of the South Carolina Episcopal Diocese, prepared a pastoral letter to clergy and laity on the subject of the religious instruction of slaves. Bowen's letter was an attempt to blunt the attack launched against the Christian mission to the slaves by taking a middle ground on the issue. Bowen insisted on the need for the religious instruction of slaves but at the same time agreed that such instruction should be carefully controlled by whites and need not extend to the practice of teaching slaves to read and write.[89] The latter practice had become much distrusted by many of the Lowcountry planters who paid for pews in Episcopal churches. The South Carolina Episcopal Convention, however, insisted that the "subject of the religious instruction of our slave population is one of deep and vital interest." Since Episcopalians formed a "large majority of the slaveholders in the low country," they "more than other denominations" were "bound" to provide "instruction" to the slaves sufficient to "make them wise unto salvation." It was imperative, Bowen claimed on the convention's behalf, that slaveholders must quickly "begin the good work," so they could "give an account of our stewardship" on judgment day. Such an outreach to the slaves, Bowen asserted, remained the "indispensable duty of the father and master...to have his household, of whomsoever it may consist...kept in the fear and knowledge of the Lord."[90]

Having established the importance of the religious instruction of slaves, Bowen went on to outline the suggestions of the state convention on how such instruction should take place. The Episcopal plan was similar in many respects to those developed by Presbyterians Charles Jones and Thomas Clay just a few years earlier, plans publicly ridiculed by Seabrook and Laurens. The recommended approach involved weekly preaching to slaves and whites in "unison" by ordained Episcopal ministers plus additional Sunday schools and oral instruction run by the white ministers and their assistants. When possible, the Episcopal clergy, and especially those with rural parishes, were encouraged to catechize and instruct slaves on plantations in the evenings, a practice vigorously denounced by Seabrook. Bowen admitted that the scope and intensity of such labors often required energy and exertion beyond what parish pastors could muster given their other duties, so the bishop recommended the use of well-trained lay catechists, as long as those catechists were white. Bowen also hoped that some Episcopal ministers, and especially young members of the clergy, would dedicate their ministry entirely to the mission to the slaves. But he acknowledged that a shortage of pastors prevented many such assignments from being made in 1835. Since the church lacked pastors, Bowen and the state convention suggested that slaveholding families themselves play a central role in the religious instruction of slaves on family plantations.[91] Bowen argued that such instruction was a part of the slaveholder's Christian duty. To bolster his overall argument concerning the importance of the Christian mission to the slaves, Bowen recounted the conclusion of longtime Charleston Baptist Richard Furman that his "long experience and observations of his Ministry" revealed that "the practical influences of Christian profession and communion" were just as great among slaves as among whites.[92] Taken as a whole, Bowen's pastoral letter, expressing the will of the state's Episcopal convention, recommended a rigorous system of religious instruction for slaves, but one that did not involve the use of black Christians in instructing other blacks or include the teaching of slaves to read.[93]

Ultimately, as much as producing a practical plan for the religious instruction of slaves, Bowen's pastoral letter represented the guarded embrace of the ideology of paternalism by the South Carolina denomination with the closest ties to the state's great planters, while at the same time accepting the radical criticism of paternalism's most controversial tenets: the teaching of slaves to read and the use of black leaders. In this sense, it represented a proposed accommodation between moderate paternalists and the movement's harshest critics. The movement's mission to the slaves would continue, but with more vigilant white supervision and without teaching slaves to read and write. In order to continue paternalism's journey from insurgency to acceptance, some of its champions were willing to make concessions to a hostile political climate. Liturgical denominations were generally willing to accept such an accommodation; the more evangelical denominations often were not.

How far this acceptance of a modified paternalism by the Anglican establishment reached down through the laity remains doubtful, and there is certainly evidence that many Episcopal slaveholders did not share their leadership's enthusiasm for the practice of paternalism at all. And even Bowen and the other Episcopal leaders who commissioned the pastoral letter doubted that the other denominations, and especially the evangelical ones, took the care with paternalism and the religious instruction of slaves that their denomination did. But the mere fact that Bowen and the Episcopal establishment of the Lowcountry had taken a position advancing a paternalist argument against what they perceived as an "infidel" party in their midst suggested that the cause of paternalism and the Christian stewardship of slaves was moving away from dangerous insurgency toward respectability, even in the blackest part of the lower South. At the same time, the necessity of accepting a liturgical accommodation that abandoned the idea of teaching slave Christians to read not only rankled many paternalists but also suggested that their movement still confronted formidable opponents capable of forcing major concessions. In 1835, paternalism had gained influence in its efforts to shape an ideological reconfiguration of slavery in the lower South, but its continued progress seemed to hinge on the need for accommodation and concessions.

As IT HAPPENED, arguably the lower South's leading paternalist, and certainly its most active white minister to the slaves, Charles Colcock Jones, visited Charleston during the fall of 1835 as the political controversy over religious instruction of slaves lingered in the city. Moreover, the new controversy over the distribution of abolitionist literature through the federal mail had raised tensions in the city to a fever pitch. By any measure, Charles Jones was an unusual white southerner, and part of his uniqueness was his unwavering commitment of time and energy to the religious instruction of slaves. Jones rejected the genteel life of a young planter scion for the rigors of a northern education and a turn at seminary. After his confirmation at the Medway Presbyterian Church in Liberty County at age seventeen, Jones left the South to study at Phillips Academy and at the Princeton seminary. Unlike many sons of planters who went north for education, Jones liked and admired the region. He respected what he perceived as northern values: self-discipline, hard work, frugality, thrift, orderliness, and a strong sense of community. He recognized these values as the visible manifestations of Christian piety. Jones contrasted these values with the dissipation and debauchery he knew were too common among whites and blacks who lived under the sprawling live oaks surrounding his boyhood home in the Georgia Lowcountry.[94]

While living in the North, Jones grew sympathetic to criticism of slavery. The more closely he studied slavery "the more enormous does it appear," the young Charles admitted to his cousin and future wife, Mary Jones. Slavery, Jones concluded, was a "violation of all the laws of God and man at once. A complete annihilation of justice. An inhuman abuse of power."[95] When he finished seminary in 1830, Jones considered remaining in the North to assist the American Colonization Society, whose efforts he called "a noble design," and at times Jones' thoughts about the future of slavery ran well beyond colonization. He argued that it was "high time our country was taking some serious measures...whose ultimate tendency shall be the emancipation of the nearly three million men, women and children who are held in the grossest bondage."[96] As he pondered his choice of vocation, Jones balanced his distaste for slavery against his love of home and Mary, the beauty of the Lowcountry, and the appeal of enjoying local influence. He confided to Mary that he was "undecided whether I ought to continue to hold slaves." Could one be a Christian and a slaveholder? Jones mused. If one could, what were the responsibilities of the Christian slaveholder? And if not, what were the responsibilities of a Christian emancipator? Jones concluded, "As to the principle of slavery, it is wrong. It is unjust, contrary to nature and religion to hold men enslaved." But, Jones worried, "would the general interests of the slaves and community at large with reference to the slaves, be promoted best, by emancipation?" Could he "do more for the ultimate good of the slave population by holding or emancipating what I own"?[97] Mary Jones, remaining behind in Georgia, knew how she felt and what she wanted for her future husband. She agreed with Charles about the need for more energetic efforts for the religious instruction of slaves, but she rejected any suggestion that slaves were "ready for freedom." Mary told Charles that it would not "promote the slave's interest to be liberated in his present degraded state...I am sure I know not a dozen [slaves] that I could unhesitatingly say that I thought capable of self-government." Ultimately Jones decided to return to Liberty County, where slaves outnumbered whites three to one, and launch a ministry to the slaves of unprecedented proportion in an effort to "do what I can for them."[98]

Rejecting the idea of emancipating his slaves or even remaining in the North and working for colonization as an absentee planter, Charles Jones returned to the South and quickly initiated what would ultimately become the most impressive mission to the slaves in the entire South in the dense and populous slave settlements of Georgia's Liberty County. A form of Christian cultural imperialism, or paternalism writ large, joined a genuine desire to preach salvation to the black masses to drive Jones to his work. And once back in Liberty County, Jones threw himself into the work with both enthusiasm and care. Christian teaching taken seriously, Jones thought, required that masters not only provide religious instruction for slaves but also treat slaves according to Christian precepts. He knew that many masters fell short on both counts, and Jones planned to address both issues in his ministry. The practice of paternalism, Jones contended, "must be universal; it must have respect to the Negro himself, his family, his house, his food, his clothing, his labour, his correction, his every interest, soul and body, for time and eternity."[99] Painfully aware that evangelical efforts to instruct slaves had run afoul of slaveholder opposition to the teaching of slaves to read, an education that many evangelicals thought essential to giving slaves personal access to the scriptures, Jones crafted a plan for sidestepping the issue by giving slaves systematic oral instruction. Jones worked hard on effective methods for orally catechizing slaves that avoided the slave literacy controversy, and he developed an impressive catechism of his own for precisely that purpose.

Jones' method of instructing slaves was certainly labor-intensive. On his own and surrounding plantations in Liberty County, Jones and other leaders he trained not only preached and catechized slaves on Sundays but went deep into the slave settlements on weeknights for continued instruction at stations he had constructed across the county. On these nighttime visits to the settlements, Jones allowed slaves to share their witness with him, and he listened. However much slaves held back from Jones, they poured out much for his consideration. As cultural imperialists went, Charles Jones proved remarkably willing to listen and learn.[100]

Jones interpreted his calling not only as preaching salvation to the unbeliever but as uplifting the slaves, bringing them out of degradation and immorality, "civilizing" them. When Jones made his choice in 1830, he saw himself as a reformer joining an insurgent movement, the paternalist effort to remake slavery in the Old South. Jones sincerely believed his approach to reforming slavery could be replicated, soul by soul, plantation by plantation, county by county, across the South, bringing slaves to Christianity until both salvation and Christian morality had been widely disseminated among southern slaves.

Jones fully expected to confront a skeptical class of slaveholders whose inclination was to beat paternalism back in favor of older models of slave management that saw force, coercion, and intimidation as more effective methods of slave control, and on that front he was not disappointed.[101] Liberty County was, as a rule, the calm eye of the storm. But when Jones visited Charleston in 1835 he found himself at the center of the controversy. Jones had come to Charleston to visit his family and friends, including his prominent cousin, South Carolina Judge Charles Colcock, on his way to the state capital in Columbia to attend a meeting of the trustees of Columbia Theological Seminary.[102] At the time, Charles was preparing to propose a large-scale, regionwide Presbyterian initiative for the religious instruction of slaves, and he was anxious to sample opinion on the subject in South Carolina. During the summer of 1834, Jones had corresponded with William Plumer, a Virginia Presbyterian who also yearned for an ambitious program of religious instruction for slaves. "The religious instruction of the Negroes," Jones told Plumer, "is the foundation of permanent improvement in intelligence and morals in the slave-holding states." Jones argued that a plan for religious instruction must begin quickly because white "salvation" from "divine judgements depends on it." In his private letter to Plumer, Jones admitted that the religious instruction of slaves stood as "the only entering wedge to the great and appalling subject of slavery." Jones had concluded that the religious instruction of slaves loomed as the "only sun" that could "shed down pure and holy light" and prepare the nation for a gradual and peaceful abandonment of slavery.[103]

White South Carolinians, however, took a dim view of "entering wedges" on the subject of slavery, and ironically, it was skeptics of religious instruction such as Seabrook who most agreed with Jones that such instruction could serve as just such an entering wedge against slavery. Seabrook's tirade against advocates of the religious instruction of slaves was only a year old when Jones arrived at Adger's Wharf in the fall of 1835, and it inevitably proved the subject of many conversations during his visit to Charleston. Episcopal bishop Nathaniel Bowen's wife visited with Jones, as did Thomas Smyth, the impressive intellectual and pastor of the city's Second Presbyterian Church. Smyth and Jones viewed Seabrook and his supporters with disdain.[104] During his conversations with friends and fellow clergy in Charleston in the fall of 1835, Jones grimly concluded that "there is strong opposition to the religious instruction of slaves in this state with many."[105] Henry Laurens Pinckney, formerly an arch-nullifier and Speaker of the house when the ban on teaching slaves to read passed, visited with Charles Jones to offer him the pastorate of the Circular Congregational Church, of which Pinckney was president of the congregation. But during his extended visit with Jones, Pinckney, who had only shortly before experienced a deepening of his religious convictions, admitted that recent public events had undermined local support for religious instruction of the slaves. After visiting in the city for a few days, Jones agreed with Pinckney's contention that the people of Charleston "tended to run into extremes." From Pinckney and others, Jones learned that Methodist missionaries had encountered objections to their work and found "Some Plantations closed against them." Indeed, Jones concluded, "the whole community" in the Lowcountry "will bear on the subject nothing but the most delicate touches." "Nothing," Jones concluded, "can be attempted here until the fever cools."[106]

Worse, in Jones' view, the recent arrival of abolition pamphlets in the mail had pushed Lowcountry defenders of slavery into bolder and more affirmative defenses of slavery, with some going so far "as to justify it *in the abstract*, and to say that there is no moral evil, no curse" to slavery but that the institution was an "*absolute blessing*" and "*must be perpetual*."[107] As Jones' biographer Erskine Clarke has pointed out, the Georgia pastor had run headlong into an emerging proslavery radicalism and quickly recognized the threat it posed to the religious paternalism that he was making his life's work.[108] "The truth is, as Mr. Pinckney and others say," Charles reported to his wife, "the state is divided into two parties the Religious and the Infidel." The "infidel Party," Jones continued, "are opposed to religion in every form," though "many of them pretend to approve" of it in order to maintain credibility with the voters.[109] Henry Laurens Pinckney had told Jones that there had been a movement in the legislature to "prohibit every kind of instruction of the Negroes —even *Religious instruction*!" But the legislature as a whole was not willing to go that far. In Jones' estimation, such radical attacks on the religious instruction of slaves represented efforts by the "infidels" to use the "present state of excitement" to "take a stab at religion." Well traveled in the North as a young man, Jones reckoned that such proslavery radicalism would not only "produce division in the South" but, worse, "convert thousands of northern men now with us, into immediate Abolitionists."[110]

Still, despite an underlying faith in the strength of Christian paternalism, Jones took to heart Pinckney's warning that "every man who was interested in and engaged in doing anything for negroes was in a 'ticklish' situation." Jones defended his own actions by claiming that he had never been accused of "rashness in my operations" but admitted that "it was best in periods of excitement to yield to the storm." As Jones prepared to leave Charleston for his board meeting in Columbia, he concluded that "I now know how matters stand." Discouraged, but resolved to continue the insurgency, Charles Jones turned down the prestigious pulpit of the Circular Congregational Church in the intellectual capital of the South to return for a season to his labors among the slaves in Liberty County, comforted by his belief that time was on the side of the paternalist campaign and his faith that "God reigns."[111]

CHAPTER SIXTEEN

ABOLITION POISON AND SOUTHERN ANTIDOTES

Nothing stirred the already swirling pot of the slavery controversy quite like the abolitionist mail campaign launched against the peculiar institution during the summer 1835. The campaign, part of a concerted strategy developed by the American Anti-slavery Society, sought to swing public opinion behind the abolition movement through propaganda. Taking advantage of a newly efficient postal system and a treasure chest provided by the Tappan brothers and a handful of other wealthy northerners, the AAS sent tens of thousands of antislavery pamphlets and tracts to southern destinations through the United States mail.[1] In the short term at least, the abolition mail campaign generated far more controversy than converts. Initially, even northern reaction to these mass mailings was harshly critical and sometimes violent. Encouraged by respected community leaders, antiabolition mobs appeared in a number of northern cities, attempting to intimidate slavery's severest critics. In some instances, printing presses were destroyed as "gentlemen of property and standing" in the North tried to suppress radical sentiment in their region.[2] In August 1835, a "public meeting" in New York noted that the "conduct of the Abolitionists" was "highly prejudicial to the peace and good order of the slaveholding states" and "dangerous to the perpetuity of the Union." The assembled gentlemen admitted that slavery was an "evil" but concluded that it was one of such "magnitude" that it defied even the "most sagacious" plan for emancipation. The dissemination of abolitionist pamphlets in the South, the meeting concluded, "created a discontented and insurrectionary spirit" among slaves. Reports of antiabolition meetings in places such as New York, Boston, and Philadelphia trickled south and reminded southern slaveholders that they had allies in the free states, but, on balance, this news failed to reassure white southerners that their peculiar institution remained safe from outside interference.[3]

In the South, reaction to the abolition mail campaign bordered on apoplexy. The "abolition crisis" became a household phrase in the South during 1835. An unprecedented flurry of public meetings across the South denounced the incendiary mail campaign in vitriolic terms. Vigilance committees were formed in many communities to protect whites by identifying abolitionist agents at work in the South and watching out for slave unrest, and vigilante justice often punished those accused of distributing abolitionist literature or "interfering" with the slave population. In many respects, the southern reaction to the abolition mail campaign made majoritarian tyranny palpable in the region, as an overwhelming majority of southern whites sought to suppress any antislavery sentiment in the region, justifying their extralegal actions on the grounds of self-preservation and the protection of white safety. Across much of the South, whites, and especially slaveholders, saw the abolition mail campaign of 1835 as nothing short of a terrorist attack, the sending of a dangerous poison through the mail with the hope of causing the destruction of its recipients. In the minds of southern whites, it was an attack that justified almost any countermeasure, including summary justice and restrictions on civil liberties.[4]

Of course, the abolition mail campaign stirred the pot first and most furiously in South Carolina. On July 29, 1835, the steamboat *Columbia*, a cargo vessel from New York, arrived routinely in Charleston harbor, delivering the mail from the New York post office. The regular postal delivery proved "not merely laden but overburthened with abolitionist tracts."[5] Some of the tracts were delivered to area clergy and prominent citizens who promptly returned them to the post office, where Charleston postmaster Alfred Huger immediately sorted the rest of the mail to prevent further dissemination of the pamphlets.[6] Intended recipients included not only the local clergy but also the editors of the *Charleston Mercury*, a leading nullification newspaper. Huger, a slaveholder, a cautious Unionist, and a dedicated federal employee, quickly resolved to keep the inflammatory mail under lock and key until he could decide how to handle the situation. He promptly wrote interim United States Postmaster Amos Kendall and asked for instructions on how to proceed. With the "attention of the Whole Town" focused on the mail being held at the post office, Huger knew that efforts would be made to seize and destroy the abolitionist tracts. Early in the afternoon of the day the controversial literature arrived, the "most respectable men of all parties" gathered outside the post office and demanded that Huger turn over the publications or, as Huger put it, "they would be taken from me." Huger bravely declined but consulted the United States attorney, the local customs collector, and "others of the most distinguished citizens" before charting a course of action. All agreed that the mail, laden as it was with abolition literature, could not be moved safely through the streets. But Huger, aware of his duty to the federal government, steadfastly declined to turn over the mail. Instead, the besieged Charleston postmaster informed the radical South Carolina Association of his intent to retain all potentially offensive mail in the post office until he received further instructions from Kendall.

Fearful that another effort would be made to seize the mail by force, Huger placed all the offensive tracts and pamphlets in a single, separate, and well-labeled bag in order to protect the "substantial sums" of negotiable paper included in the regular business mail of the day. Early that evening, a mob composed of more than two hundred men approached the post office and again demanded that Huger turn over the abolitionist mail. The mob was dissuaded by the presence of the city guard. Later that evening, however, sometime after ten o'clock, a smaller and more radical group referring to themselves as the "Lynch men" assembled at the Exchange Building, marched to the post office, forced entry though a window, and removed the carefully separated bag of mail, including all the abolitionist literature but no other mail, from the post office. The next evening, the Lynch men held a public bonfire, burning that bag of mail as well as other abolitionist literature and effigies of several abolitionists, including Garrison and the Tappan brothers, before a crowd that exceeded two thousand.[7]

On August 1, the fourth day of the crisis, Huger wrote New York postmaster Samuel Gouverneur, asking him to hold all potentially inflammatory mail in New York since it was "impossible to restrain the universal indignation which pervades all classes in Charleston" against the provocative mail without resort to a "military force greater than the Undivided population of Charleston." Huger explained that the mail shipment aboard the *Columbia* had "literally filled our office with thousands of pamphlets upon the question which this community is too Sensitive to admit of any Compromise—the Emancipation of the Southern slave." The Charleston postmaster remained committed to defending the mail until he was "overpowered," but he also resolved not to distribute any of the abolition material until he received further word from Kendall. If Gouverneur did not want to hold the abolition mail until Kendall made a decision, Huger urged the New York postmaster to pack all future abolitionist mail into bags labeled "suspicious" to help prevent interference with what the Charlestonian deemed the regular mail. In his pleas to Gouverneur, Huger repeatedly emphasized the unity of all white Charlestonians against receiving and distributing the abolitionist mail. He described a "disposition to commit violence" manifested by "by those of every Grade in Society from Highest to Lowest," and noted that the "whole civil authority" favored seizing the mail, with "Nullifiers and Union men, Jackson men and Clay men, Van Buren [m]en and [Hugh Lawson] White [men] who differ on all other points" agreeing that the mail campaign must be stopped in its tracks.[8]

The panic that swept Charleston and the vicinity in the aftermath of the seizure of the abolitionist mail surpassed even that of the Denmark Vesey insurrection scare. On August 1, as Huger sought Gouverneur's cooperation, the Charleston city council called a public meeting to address the crisis. The meeting appointed an extralegal Committee of Five to govern the city during the time of crisis. Former governor and United States senator Robert Y. Hayne led the Committee of Five, which included the jurists Henry W. DeSaussure and Judge Charles Colcock. The committee generally struck a more moderate tone than the hotheads who burglarized the post office, and all of the five thought the post office break-in rash and premature. The committee quickly worked out an arrangement with Huger for meeting the mail at the dock, escorting it to the post office to make sure that no literature was disseminated before it reached the post office, and then allowing Huger to detain all controversial publications there until his orders from Kendall arrived. In addition to managing the mail, the committee also suspended all schools for free blacks and temporarily halted all religious classes for blacks in the city. It also subjected strangers in the city to close scrutiny and ordered constant street patrols. Two days later, on August 3, the committee organized a public meeting at which a number of prominent local citizens denounced the abolitionists and demanded that the North recognize that slavery was purely a "domestic Question" which the South alone must handle. A Committee of Twenty-One was formed to petition the citizens of the northern states to put down the radical and provocative abolition societies on their own.[9]

By August 6, Huger had grown comfortable with the temporary arrangements for handling the mail, but he knew that if Kendall ordered him to distribute the pamphlets, "they will unquestionably be arrested in the Streets by the Civil authority of the state and destroyed." Any effort to enforce the law would require a military force "strong enough to subdue South Carolina." The post office break-in, Huger explained, was now "almost universally disapproved," but only because "the community think it wrong to do clandestinely what they have a right to do openly." The continuation of the mail campaign, Huger told New York postmaster Gouverneur, would eventually end "Commercial intercourse" between Charleston and New York. "I do not believe that greater indignation would be felt," Huger maintained, "if the Mail were used to convey a deadly pestilence among us." Moreover, Huger contended, the mail campaign threatened the safety of the very slave community it intended to help by heightening white anxiety to the point of irrationality. The arrival of the incendiary mail, the embattled postmaster explained, had placed the white population so much on edge that a "Single movement at this moment" might kill more than a hundred blacks who were "perfectly innocent." The "fate of the Slave cannot be mitigated by these means," he concluded. Again Huger insisted that there are "no politics in this affair." Men "who hate each other cooperate now," Huger explained, "the most ultra Nullifier and the most confirmed Unionist will go Shoulder to Shoulder—and for once the whole Nation will see the spectacle of a whole state: unanimous."[10]

In the short term, Huger's arrangements with the Committee of Five and his plea for instructions from Kendall eased tensions in the city slightly. Gouverneur agreed to hold all abolitionist mail in New York unless forced to distribute it by Kendall. In the meantime, Kendall took the matter up with President Jackson, who disparaged the abolition mail campaign as a "wicked plan of exciting the negroes to insurrection and to massacre." Jackson told Kendall that the post office should send such "inflammatory papers" to no one except "those who demand them as subscribers."[11] Kendall then told Huger that federal authorities would not try to force the delivery of any portion of the mail that local "circumstances" suggested required "detention."[12] Once Kendall's position became known, Charleston's Committee of Five disbanded and the city returned to its normal form of government. But the city's white population remained livid at the abolitionists' latest gambit.

Vigilance committees remained active throughout the state, and public meetings denouncing abolition were held throughout the fall of 1835. At the end of August 1835, Upcountry planter Robert Gage informed his brother, who was out of the country, that the "daring and ingenious measures of the abolitionists begin to raise a storm in the South—the people are holding meetings in every section & expressing their determination to use every exertion to punish those who would interfere with their property." Several men accused of overt interference with slaves, Gage reported, "have been tried before Judge Lynch [and] condemned & hung without a word."[13] In its coverage of Charleston's response to the abolition mail campaign, the *Charleston Mercury* claimed that it had never witnessed such an "overwhelming expression of public opinion in the city."[14] And Charleston was a city where the public had never been hesitant about expressing its opinion. After a temporary calm settled on Charleston, the temperamentally conservative Huger denounced the "quixotic benevolence" of the abolitionists. The "deplorable consequences" of their "unHoly crusade," Huger predicted, would "make any Man shudder." Such "Fanaticism (mis-called Humanity)," Huger feared, would eventually cause the "Sword to be drawn against our own property" and the "war will be one…of utter desolation and annihilation."[15]

In the case of the postal campaign, with antislavery literature flooding into southern post offices, the energetic and hostile public reaction was not confined to the Carolina Lowcountry but also occurred across as much of the South as enjoyed good postal service. From the Georgia state capital in Milledgeville, the *Southern Recorder* urged the public to a high state of vigilance because "our enemies from without are assailing us by every means within their power; inundating every post office with vile incendiary pamphlets and newspapers." This abolitionist literature, the newspaper insisted, had been mailed by "miscreants" whose intent was to "instruct our servile people in the art of butchering." The *Southern Recorder*, emerging as a leading Whig organ, called for a rigorous patrol system to look for the "agents of our enemies" and suggested that if any were caught "at their infernal work," they should be subjected to the "same justice as the mad dog." Such "villains" would receive their due punishment in Georgia as long as "there are plough lines on our farms and trees in our forests."[16] In North Carolina, the state's leading Democratic newspaper, the *North Carolina*

Standard, reported the arrival of abolition pamphlets through the mail in Raleigh in early August 1835. Denouncing the "Northern fanatical publications" mailed for the purpose of raising "insurrection among the slaves of the south," the pro-Jackson organ explained that the Raleigh postmaster, like Huger in Charleston, held the publications at the post office until clarifying orders were received from Washington. The newspaper labeled it "criminal" that such publications had been "scattered like firebrands through out the country."[17] In Virginia, the anti-Jackson Richmond *Whig* insisted that the new abolitionist offensive required the opposition of "every man, woman and child south of Pennsylvania." The proadministration Richmond *Enquirer* initially saw the evil hand of nullification at work in hyping the crisis and thus issued a double denunciation. Editor Thomas Ritchie, Vice President Van Buren's voice in the South, claimed that the South faced two enemies, the "Northern fanatics" who were "attempting to flood the country with their incendiary publications" and the "factious politicians of the South" who were "availing themselves of the movements of the fanatics to play their political card or sap the Union." The "fanatics are striving to raise the slaves against the South," the *Enquirer* explained, "the Factions to raise the South against the North."[18] In Tennessee, the state's leading newspaper, the *Nashville Republican*, was unequivocal in its expression of contempt for the mail campaign. On August 4, the editors called "the people of the slaveholding states" to "alert." Antislavery "fanatics," the newspaper claimed, "emboldened by the support they have received from a few men of wealth and respectability in Boston and New York," were "constantly at work." Abolition societies, the *Nashville Republican* claimed, had published 122,000 copies of various abolitionist pamphlets and tracts with the intent of distributing them in the slaveholding states. The newspaper called such efforts the "Blind fanaticism and mistaken philanthropy" of people willing to "plunge their country into all the horrors of servile war." The Nashville newspaper urged the South to "let meetings be held in all the slaveholding states ... and let them make known their opinions of these mad schemes of the Abolitionists."[19]

Across most of the South where the abolition mail had been received, the white citizens of the South did just that. More than 150 grassroots antiabolition meetings were held across the South, with some in every slaveholding state except Kentucky and Delaware, during the last five months of 1835. These public meetings represented arguably the most active grassroots mobilization yet to occur in the Old South. Public meetings were held most often in black belt counties where the danger of slave insurrection was perceived as great and the economic stake in slavery high, but meetings occurred in counties with large white majorities as well.[20] In Virginia, at a meeting in Northampton County, whites refused to "condescend" to discuss slavery with its northern critics, insisting that abolitionists needed to accept the fact that slavery was constitutional. Antiabolition meetings were common throughout Virginia's slave-rich Southside. A meeting in Powhatan County denounced the mail campaign as "wanton, mischievous and impertinent." In Richmond, a public meeting in late August decried the recent "mad attempts and designs of the abolitionists," and even *Enquirer* editor Thomas Ritchie had come to express high dudgeon on the subject, urging the South to be vigilant against the threat of abolitionist "emissaries" and insisting that the mail be "quarantined."[21] In North Carolina, an August meeting held in the port city of Wilmington expressed the "Indignation and abhorrence which pervades the southern country against the reckless fanatics enrolled as "Anti-Slavery Societies."[22] A similar meeting in Halifax, a fall-line county near the Virginia border, denounced the "dangerous tendency of the incendiary measures which have been insidiously practiced by a portion of our northern brethren." To the extent northern opinion "countenanced" the "disorganizing and diabolical schemes of the abolitionists," Halifax residents claimed the "right to protect our property and our firesides" by "all means."[23] In Warren County, a tobacco-growing area along the Virginia border that was once part of Nathaniel Macon's congressional district, a large public meeting passed resolutions declaring that the South would defend slavery at "every peril and to the last extremity of life." The Warren County meeting also declared slavery "as it exists" a "benefit and a blessing" to the South. Slaves, the meeting insisted, were "better protected and better provided for" than any other laboring class in the world. Interference with slaves for the purpose of inciting "incendiary and insurrectionary movements" was "criminal," so Warren citizens formed vigilance committees for self-protection.[24] In the cotton-growing area of the Tar Heel State's southern Piedmont, a public meeting in Charlotte discussed the new "danger which threatened the South." At the Charlotte meeting, Mecklenburg County Whigs and Democrats came together to denounce the "wicked projects of northern fanatics." The bipartisan meeting attacked those favoring immediate abolition for circulating "inflammatory and incendiary" literature aimed at exciting "insurrection." Resolutions approved unanimously by the Mecklenburg meeting declared that abolition pamphlets should be returned to their senders, and warned the orchestrators of the mail campaign that such exertions by "Northern fanatics" were likely to make the conditions and treatment of slaves worse rather than better.[25]

In Georgia, a public meeting in Jasper County insisted that slavery was a "domestic question" and called the abolitionists "incendiaries and assassins." The Jasper meeting approved resolutions urging the federal government to prevent the use of the mails for distributing abolitionist literature.[26] Another antiabolition meeting in Gwinnett, a Piedmont county, declared that the South must meet the new abolitionist strategy with "one voice, one universal and unequivocal expression of disapprobation."[27] A public meeting at Sparta, in Hancock County, demanded that a "certain group of misguided fanatics of the North whose pretended philanthropy" led them to support immediate abolition stop their "interference" with and misrepresentation of the "condition of our slaves and the character of their masters." Such "dangerous fanaticism" could not be tolerated, Hancock citizens concluded.[28] In Lincoln County, citizens held "one of the largest meetings ever held by citizens of the county on any occasion," and those assembled displayed determination to make "common cause" against their external critics.[29] A Washington County public rally demanded that the South be "let alone" and spared the North's "insult and dictation." And the Washington meeting applauded the seizure of abolition pamphlets and other literature intended to "destroy the lives of our whole white population...and lay waste the county."[30]

Of course, nowhere were public antiabolition meetings more common than in South Carolina, where one was held in almost every district. At a late summer antiabolition rally in Barnwell, an interior Lowcountry district where slaves constituted nearly two-thirds of the population, former nullifier Edmund Bellinger assessed the threat posed by the abolition mail campaign and proposed the "united wisdom and united power of the Southern States" as a remedy. Toward that end, Bellinger downplayed the divisive nullification controversy and pledged to avoid the "Serbian bog" of states' rights." Bellinger condemned the abolitionist efforts to flood the mails with incendiary publications. He urged northern anti-antislavery forces to silence the voices and stop the presses of those favoring immediate abolition. Above all, he insisted that all white southerners must stand together for "Southern rights and Southern interests."[31] Some public meetings focused on particular local problems. A public meeting in Prince William Parish urged strict enforcement of a new state law requiring all absentee owners of plantations with ten or more slaves to hire an overseer, and in St. James Parish, just outside Charleston, a public meeting condemned the use of black preachers because they tended to "produce the very evil the abolitionists are trying to create."[32] Other meetings addressed the abolitionist challenge more systematically. At an antiabolition meeting in the white-majority Upcountry district of Lancaster, Presbyterian pastor James H. Thornwell presented a formal scriptural justification of slaveholding.[33] In Pendleton district, home to Calhoun's Fort Hill plantation, a large public meeting considered and adopted a substantial set of antiabolition resolutions likely drafted by Calhoun himself.[34]

The antiabolition rally at Pendleton, called by the leading men of the area for the purpose of "taking into consideration the proceeding of the Northern Abolitionists and adopting such measures as might be deemed necessary and expedient" to counter those movements, met at Farmer's Hall in Pendleton village on September 9, 1835. It elected area planter Robert Anderson as chair. The meeting selected a twenty-member committee to prepare a report and resolutions for the meeting's consideration. The committee included John C. Calhoun, Pendleton *Messenger* editor Frederick W. Symmes, former Bank of the United States president Langdon Cheves, former congressional candidate Joseph Whitner, and several area ministers. After an hour or so of work, the committee returned and presented its report and resolutions.

The Pendleton report referred to the mail campaign as the work of "moral incendiaries" who did not shy away from the "Atrocity and wickedness of mad, ignorant and fanatical enthusiasm" that threatened to "excite a War" upon masters that might well culminate in the "misery and annihilation of the slave." It urged the northern press to use prudence and restraint in publishing abolition materials for distribution in the South and insisted that "the liberty of the press implies no privilege to disturb by seditious libel the peace of any community" or "to throw firebrands amidst a peaceful and unoffending people." The report also requested that the federal government provide the "most ample security" in its power to protect the South from the distribution of abolitionist materials through the federal mail. The report concluded by emphasizing the "impropriety" of "mixing up this subject in any manner with the party controversies and political disputes of the day." The nation, and even the South, the Pendleton report admitted, were "divided" on a variety of political questions, but on the question of immediate abolition "there is but one voice, one opinion, one sentiment."[35]

The Pendleton meeting then considered a series of nine resolutions, ranging from positions on constitutional issues to the method postmasters should use in dealing with the mail campaign and the assigned duties of the vigilance committees created by the meeting. The resolutions denounced the "attacks of the fanatics of the North" as "a manifest interference on their part with the domestic institutions of the South" and as a "subversion of the constitutional compact." They urged northern states to "suppress these outrageous attacks" being launched from within their borders. They warned Congress that any interference with slavery in the District of Columbia would be interpreted by the South as giving "countenance" to the abolitionists' "lawless, unconstitutional and incendiary course," and they called on all local postmasters to first detain incendiary mailings and then allow vigilance committees to destroy them. The resolutions also organized vigilance committees to serve as a home guard against such the distribution of such literature and to prevent abolitionist emissaries from "spreading disaffection" among area slaves. After the submission of these resolutions to those attending, both the report and accompanying resolutions were "adopted without a dissenting voice."[36]

IN THE OLD SOUTHWEST, the abolition mail campaign further alarmed a region already frightened to the core by an insurrection scare, centered in southwest Mississippi, that swept through the region in early July 1835, several weeks before the abolition mail began arriving in southern post offices. During the early summer, rumors of slave insurrection began to circulate in the old Southwest. Whites who credited the rumors attributed the planning of the alleged insurrection to a white named John A. Murrell (often spelled Murel or Morel), an outlaw often referred to as the "great western land pirate." Murrell purportedly led a band of thieves whose depredations were both feared and despised up and down the lower Mississippi River during the early 1830s. Murrell apparently made crime pay chiefly by stealing slaves, often with the complicity of the slaves involved. Murrell would steal a few slaves, sell those slaves to unsuspecting buyers for handsome sums, and then multiply his ill-gotten gains by stealing, selling, stealing, and reselling these same slaves again and again. Authorities later claimed that Murrell sometimes murdered his slave accomplices once he thought he could no longer use them in his scams. Murrell's reputed involvement with slaves enhanced public alarm over his activities.[37]

Over time, the activity of Murrell and his followers grew into the stuff of legend in the lower Mississippi region. Rumors circulated that Murrell was the leader of a large and well-organized gang that planned mischief through western Mississippi and eastern Louisiana. But, in 1834, Murrell's notorious career seemingly came to an end when he was captured by Virgil Stewart, a Georgia native who had first joined Murrell's gang and then turned the feared outlaw over to Tennessee authorities, who tried him for slave stealing and sentenced him to ten years in a Nashville prison. In the spring of 1835, Stewart, considered a hero by many for bringing the outlaw to his comeuppance, wrote a for-profit account of his capture of Murrell. This exposé of the activities and composition of the feared Murrell gang claimed that before Murrell was taken into custody, the outlaw and his gang had planned and organized a large-scale slave insurrection slated to involve the entire South. The rebellion was scheduled to begin on Christmas Day, 1835. Stewart also published a list of names associated with Murrell's gang, including nearly four dozen white men who lived in Mississippi.[38]

Stewart's insinuation that the Murrell gang might still be at work fomenting insurrection even with its leader behind bars troubled many white Mississippians during the late spring and early summer of 1835. Within just a few weeks after the publication of Stewart's account, "various circumstances excited some suspicion in the minds of a few of the respectable citizens of Madison county" that slaves in the Beatty's Bluff community on the Yazoo River were planning an insurrection for July 4. Madison County was a rapidly growing cotton plantation area located between the Yazoo and Pearl rivers in southwestern Mississippi.[39] A visitor to the region in 1834 noted that in Madison County "immense bodies of rich land are all being converted into cotton fields and negro quarters." Madison was also a county with many absentee owners who lived "in the older settled parts" of the state, such as Natchez, leaving relatively few whites, other than overseers, in the rural portions of the county.[40] The county appeared vulnerable to insurrection—and was certainly vulnerable to insurrection scares. Once rumors of insurrection surfaced in the county, the local white population mobilized. At the small town of Livingston, near Beatty's Bluff, area whites assembled on June 30 and questioned a group of slaves suspected of being involved in the alleged insurrection plot. Under the interrogation of the lash, several slaves claimed that an insurrection had indeed been planned for July 4, and these slaves implicated several whites as well as a number of additional slaves in the insurrection plot.[41]

On July 2, an angry Madison mob not only executed several accused slaves but also arrested two whites implicated by the slave informants for involvement in the "nefarious scheme." These two whites, Joshua Cotton and William Saunders, were both Thomsonian "steam doctors," men who practiced a version of alternative medicine in the region. Upon the arrest of Cotton and Saunders, Madison County whites created a committee of "thirteen of the most respectable citizens" and clothed them with "ample authority" to investigate and provide "Speedy Justice" in all matters related to the alleged insurrection plot. That such authority was extralegal no one doubted, and few cared. The extralegal committee was created so that slave testimony could informally be used against white men in ways that it could not in regular court proceedings. The investigation in Madison County and surrounding areas centered on "itinerant preachers, clock pedlars, gamblers and steam doctors." Of the two "steam doctors" already charged, Saunders maintained his innocence throughout, but Cotton offered a confession in which he claimed that he was in fact a member of Murrell's gang. Cotton also implicated a number of whites in Madison, Hinds, and Warren counties, and claimed that the insurrection plot "embraced the whole slave region from Maryland to Louisiana and contemplated the total destruction of the white population of all the States." Closer to home, Cotton informed his inquisitors, the local arm of the conspiracy planned to start in Madison and march first to Natchez and then on to New Orleans, "Murdering all the white men and ugly women" while "making wives" of the "handsome women."[42] Another version of the alleged plot held that Madison rebels planned to march toward Vicksburg, and insisted that "the whole country on the riverbank was to be ravaged and inundated with the blood of men, women and children." The committee sentenced the two steam doctors to death by hanging on July 4. Even with Cotton and Saunders the victims of extralegal justice, Madison whites remained in a state of near panic. Over the course of the next three weeks, a mini-reign of counterterror swept Mississippi. At least a dozen whites and many more slaves died at the hands of "Judge Lynch," and most white Mississippians appeared to approve.[43]

During the summer of 1835, most Mississippi whites saw Virgil Stewart as a "great public benefactor" and chose not to question either his motives or his information. Over time, however, a number of antebellum Mississippi's most prominent men came, retrospectively, to see his claim of impending insurrection in 1835 for what it almost certainly was: a fantastic account designed to make money for Stewart at the expense of public peace. As future United States senator Henry S. Foote later recalled, those who "dared even to question the actual existence of the dangers" depicted by Stewart were accused of ignoring the "supposed perils of the hour" or, worse, denounced as "traitors to the slaveholding interests of the South."[44] J. F. C. Claiborne, a candidate for Congress in 1835 who later emerged as nineteenth-century Mississippi's leading historian, also conceded in later years that Stewart's "whole story was a fabrication." In Claiborne's view, Murrell was nothing but a "thief and a counterfeiter," and Stewart was a rogue "subordinate" who turned on his boss and devised a plot to "avenge and enrich himself" at Murrell's expense. Claiborne concluded that the "whole plot and its tragical consequences may now be regarded as one of the most extraordinary and lamentable hallucinations of our times."[45]

But in the summer of 1835, the Mississippi insurrection scare, though likely a "hallucination," prepared the ground for the state's reception of the abolition mail a few weeks later. When such mail appeared, a newspaper in the state capital, Jackson, called on the "fanatics" who distributed the literature to consider the "late proceedings in our state," referring to the insurrection scare, before continuing the campaign that was generating such intense and emotional opposition across the South.[46] When the postmaster at Clinton received several copies of an abolitionist periodical, the citizens of Hinds County met and formed a citizens' committee that replied with an open letter to the publisher of the periodical, *Human Rights*. The citizens' committee urged the editor to send "your Tappans" and "your Garrisons" rather than simply "pitiful caricatures on inanimate paper" to Mississippi. Such famous abolitionists, the committee observed sarcastically, might convince the South to "lay down our weapons of rebellion under the influence of the mighty preaching of such philanthropists!" "Send them, sir," the Hinds committee pleaded; "our sister state of Kentucky annually supplies us with the article of hemp, and it shall be at the service of your emissaries who are apt to be seized with croup on entering into our State."[47]

In Louisiana, fears growing out of the insurrection scare in neighboring Mississippi also shaped the state's response to the abolition mail campaign. There had never been any hard evidence suggesting that there was an imminent danger of slave insurrection in Louisiana during the summer of 1835, but rumors of rebellion associated with the activity of remnants of the Murrell gang circulated up and down the river counties in Louisiana as well as Mississippi.[48] In Jefferson Parish, white patrols were ordered to visit all the slave quarters in the parish and search for weapons. A plantation mistress in Feliciana Parish reported that the parish "gentlemen" had raised money "to hire a company of men to ride day and night as guard over all the parish." Indeed, whites in the parish were so "afraid of all strangers" that they would not "employ them as overseers" out of fear that they were fugitives from the Murrell gang. In many instances, white strangers were "taken up" by Louisiana patrols and "whip'd like dogs" as "Lintch's law" ruled the country. One Louisiana woman quipped that "if they continue hangings as they have for some time past, we should be careful of the children, otherwise the world would be left without people."[49]

After abolition literature was found in the mail, the New Orleans city council issued a report on the postal campaign, entitled *Report on the Conspiracy to Incite a Rebellion Throughout the Slave States*. In the report, city investigators decried the "exertions of a set of fanatical abolitionists" whose "numerous presses ... under the affected garb of benevolence, are perpetually endeavouring to excite our slaves to insubordination and rebellion." The report also denounced the Morrell gang and its remnants as an "organized horde of reckless and bloodthirsty barbarians, who prowl through our own communities" making "incendiary appeals to all the worst passions of our slaves" as part of an effort to raise "a general insurrection." The report claimed that the gang approached only the "most vicious and wicked disposed" slaves and poisoned their minds with talk of "freedom" and oppression. The report recommended the creation of vigilance committees to combat the work of these "misguided fanatics" from the North who infiltrated the southern countryside and the possible efforts of Murrell's "murderous banditti."[50]

Even in Alabama, the reaction to the abolition postal campaign was accentuated by its chronological association with the insurrection scare emanating from Mississippi.[51] Reports that the insurrection plans of the Morrell gang included fomenting rebellion in Alabama reached the state in late July 1835, just a week or so before news circulated of the arrival of abolition mailings in the port of Mobile.[52] The confluence of the two reports left whites in Alabama in a state of compound alarm. A 1835 Tuscaloosa grand jury indicted the editor of the *Emancipator* in absentia for sending incendiary publications into the state. In Madison County, lying at the heart of Alabama's first cotton belt, a large public meeting was held on August 19 at the Huntsville courthouse to determine what actions might be "expedient and necessary" to meet the twin challenges of an insurrection scare and an abolitionist mail attack. At the Huntsville meeting, whites from all sections of Madison County appointed a Committee of Twenty to fashion a response to the challenges. The meeting put special emphasis on presenting a unified front, choosing former governor Theodore Bibb and state supreme court justice Arthur Hopkins to give weight to the committee, and including both prominent Jacksonians and opponents of the administration on the committee in roughly equal numbers. In late August, the Committee of Twenty sponsored an antiabolition meeting at the Methodist church in Huntsville. By the end of the evening, the "vast assembly" present resolved that the abolitionists had launched an "unhallowed warfare" likely to result in "appalling consequences" for "our domestic peace." The Huntsville resolutions challenged the northern states not to stand idly by and watch "Fanaticism deluge our land with the blood of our brethren."[53]

Over the following weeks, Madison's Committee of Twenty created an organizational structure to support its extralegal governance of the county. By late August, the committee had organized a larger "Grand Committee" that consisted of 160 men representing sixteen geographically distinct sections of the county. These ad hoc vigilance committees policed and patrolled the county throughout the fall of 1835. While the county remained on edge for months, and rumors of insurrection and unrest circulated from time to time, these vigilance committees uncovered little, arresting only an unsuccessful womanizer and horse thief whom they whipped before sending him to a nearby county to stand trial.[54]

NOR WAS THE RESPONSE to the abolition mail campaign simply a grassroots affair leading to reigns of vigilante terror sanctioned by local white majorities. The public outcry voiced at scores upon scores of public meetings across the South was heard in legislative halls and governors' offices across the region. For example, excitement spread throughout Alabama when the *Warsaw* entered the port of Mobile carrying not only a batch of abolition pamphlets but also a handful of free blacks seeking to enter the state illegally. Public reaction to this threat led the Alabama legislature to adopt its own version of South Carolina's Negro Seaman's Act, which allowed the state to control who entered Mobile.[55] In neighboring Georgia, Governor Wilson Lumpkin used his November 1835 address to the legislature to call on the northern people to stop the "vile incendiaries who are laboring to stir up insurrection and rebellion in the Southern States." These abolitionists, Lumpkin declared, were "marked by the most vile, bold, dirty spirit that ever disgraced the American name." Slavery was a subject that the South "can not suffer a stranger to intermeddle," the governor explained as he asked the legislature to create a special committee to report on the question.[56] The committee's report blamed northern propagandists for attempting the "violation of the domestic peace" and risking all the horrors of "civil Commotion." With such people, the report declared, there could be "no discussion, no compromise, no doubt." The committee resolved that freedom of the press and freedom of speech are "sacred and inalienable," but when these rights had been "prostituted" to the "vile purpose" of destroying the Union, limits on those freedoms were necessary. Toward that end, the committee urged Congress to "modify the laws of the post office" so that an entity "created for the convenience of the people shall not be converted into the means of spreading servile war and civil strife."[57]

North Carolina's Whig governor David Swain used his November 1835 address to denounce the "spirit of fanaticism" that had "recently been manifested" by the abolition mail campaign. It "becomes us in common with the people of every Southern State," Swain urged, "to speak with a voice which will command attention and respect." The "public safety requires the suppression of these wicked and mischievous publications," he declared. "Upon this question there is no division of interest, and can be no difference of opinion." The "entire South will unite," Swain contended, behind "any measures" necessary to suppress the incendiary publications.[58] In early December, the North Carolina legislative committee appointed to study the question defended the state's "undoubted right to regulate slavery amoungst ourselves." "Left to themselves, we believe, our slaves are a labouring class as little dangerous to society as any in the world," the legislative committee declared. North Carolina was asking not for help in putting down insurrections but only "that our slaves and ourselves may be relieved of outside interference." Again, the state resolved to make "common cause" with its sister slaveholding states on the issue.[59]

When the South Carolina legislature met in late November 1835, a special Joint Committee on Federal Relations considered Governor George McDuffie's suggestion that the state formally ask northern state governments to somehow ban all agitation on the slavery issue.[60] Ultimately, the legislature adopted committee language urging the northern states to "suppress" all "Abolition Societies" and adopt severe punishments for publishing and distributing abolitionist literature designed to "excite the slaves of the southern states to insurrection and revolt." However unlikely or unable the individual northern states were to enact such legislation, the Palmetto State's request was urgent but restrained. The true passions aroused in the state by the abolition mail campaign were more visible in the preamble the legislature attached to the resolutions. In the preamble, South Carolina asserted that through "an efficient police" and "judicious internal legislation" the state was capable of preventing insurrection and that it intended to "arrest" the "torrent of pamphlets and tracts which the Abolition presses of the North are pouring forth with an inexhaustible completeness." But despite its capacity for protecting itself, the state would not tolerate remaining under constant attack. "No people can live under constant excitement and apprehension," the preamble declared, "although real danger can be long deferred." South Carolina, the preamble suggested, would "not suffer under a perpetual panic."[61] It would find a remedy instead. It would consider disunion rather than live in a state of siege or tolerate a ceaseless attack on its internal social arrangements.

THE PROBLEM SOUTHERN LEGISLATURES faced, of course, in dealing with the abolition mail campaign was that it proved hard to find a state solution to a national problem. Southern states could pass internal security legislation, and most states in the lower South did pass such legislation during the 1830s, but with that done, they were left with the alternatives of either urging northern states to gag or at least mute the abolitionists or seeking federal legislation along the same lines. Neither states' rights nor local self-sufficiency, two popular southern political staples, was in itself capable of providing a remedy to the abolition challenge. Some kind of southern regional unity, if only on the narrow issue of abolition, seemed necessary, but such unity had proven elusive since the earliest days of the republic.

Even before the Charleston post office break-in brought the challenge of the abolition mail campaign to the fore, South Carolina's John C. Calhoun had worried privately about the threat the larger abolition movement posed to southern society. He thought the movement threatened not only the region's "liberty and prosperity" but "our existence as a people," and he believed it "certain" that "without our most strenuous & united efforts," white southerners "will be compelled to abandon the South & leave it exclusively to the black race."[62] He hoped the latest abolitionist gambit would alert the South to the growing danger.

So the crisis of 1835 raised Calhoun's hopes as well as his fears. Ten days before he attended the public antiabolition meeting in Pendleton in late August 1835, Calhoun had written Duff Green, a national editor and political ally, that as a result of the abolition mail campaign, "excitement in relation to Northern fanaticks" had "very greatly increased" in the South. He also reported that all "indications" suggested that "the South will be unanimous in their resistance" and that the resistance would extend "even to the extent of disunion, if that should be necessary to arrest the evil." But South Carolina's political impresario expressed sincere optimism that the "evil" of abolition could be "arrested far short of that extremity."[63]

Calhoun's impression of southern unanimity in the face of the abolition campaign was supported by his own experience in the Upcountry, by reports of the antiabolition rallies that occurred across the South in August and September 1835, and by state legislative actions in late fall and early winter. These meetings, resolutions, and legislation reflected the sentiment of an overwhelming majority of southern whites, and particularly lower South whites, that abolition terror must be checked firmly. Upon that point, little disagreement appeared to exist in the South. White southerners appeared willing to put partisan loyalties and other political differences aside to make that point. They insisted on the need to speak with one voice. But when southern representatives gathered in Washington for the winter congressional session, all manner of tactical, strategic, and other political considerations were projected back into the mix, and these representatives, though still steadfast in their desire to check abolition, were forced to choose from a menu of different approaches to achieving the desired ends. With southern politicians facing a variety of options and confronted with the need to attract northern cooperation, differences and disagreements among them reemerged pretty quickly, though a common southern resolve to find an effective check on the new abolition campaign remained strong.

When Congress began its winter session in 1835, there was little question that the new abolition mail and petition campaigns would dominate discussion until some kind of resolution could be achieved. Moreover, Andrew Jackson, a southern slaveholder, was still president and still had a large say in the matter. Without any question, Jackson loathed the abolitionists, and he placed the blame for the existing crisis squarely on them, declaring that the architects of the abolition postal campaign were "guilty" of nothing less than an "attempt to stir up" the "horrors of servile war" in the South. The president proposed a very characteristic solution to the problem: a law that would "prohibit, under severe penalties, the circulation, in the Southern states, through the mail of incendiary publications intended to instigate the slaves to insurrection."[64] Jackson's proposal was bold, it was clear, it was a national solution, and it was intended to strengthen the Union through decisive action against a divisive enemy—the abolitionists. Jackson's proposal was also of dubious constitutionality, perceived by some as a threat to the Bill of Rights, inconsistent enough with states' rights principles to worry many of his southern supporters, and so much a proslavery measure that some northern Democrats were uneasy about supporting it. But it was what Jackson wanted. And Andrew Jackson often got what he wanted.

Jackson's proposal was emphatically not what South Carolina's John C. Calhoun wanted, even though it might have achieved his desired end of stopping the abolition mail campaign in its tracks. Calhoun, the chastened nullifier, remained painfully aware of Jackson's popularity, but he also knew that a law passed by a congressional majority and signed by a president was vulnerable to repeal by another congressional majority with the approval of a less proslavery president a few years later.[65] Jackson's proposal, though intended to terminate the abolition mail campaign, would actually "clothe Congress with the power to abolish slavery," Calhoun contended. Any federal government strong enough to stymie abolition was also strong enough to promote it. Calhoun did not fear the circulation of abolition pamphlets as much as he did the emergence of a future antislavery majority—a future he thought certain to arrive if the antislavery forces continued to get the best of the propaganda war. "The incessant action of hundreds of societies, and a vast printing establishment, throwing out, daily, thousands of artful and inflammatory publications, must make in time, a deep impression on the section of the Union, where they freely circulate," Calhoun argued. "The well-informed and thoughtful may hold them in contempt, but the young, the inexperienced, the ignorant and the thoughtless, will receive the poison." In "the process of time," Calhoun continued, "the artful and the profligate...will unite with the fanatics...and seek advancement by diffusing, as widely as possible, hatred against the slaveholding states." Since "hatred begets hatred and animosity begets animosity, Calhoun predicted, "these feelings would become reciprocal, till every vestige of attachment would cease to exist between the two sections" and the "Union and the Constitution...would forever perish." "Such is the danger," Calhoun concluded, "to which the movements of the abolitionists expose the country."[66]

Acting on his logic, Calhoun maneuvered to have Jackson's proposal referred to a special committee, which the South Carolinian would chair. After much deliberation and disagreement, Calhoun's committee shoved Jackson's proposal aside and reported out a bill giving every state the power to refuse to deliver any mail that ran contrary to the laws of the individual state. Under the terms of this law, a state could effectively quarantine mail that it deemed a threat to its safety and security. The committee bill replaced Jackson's nationalist approach to censoring the mail to a states' rights approach. After debating Calhoun's proposal off and on until June, the Senate rejected it on a 25–19 vote, chiefly because many northern senators, however disdainful of the abolition mail campaign, could not bring themselves to accept such a measure, whether because it was so inimical to freedom of the press and speech or because they worried that their constituents would think them too cozy with the arch-nullifier Calhoun. As congressional debate proceeded, northern politicians increasingly explained that while their constituents had little use for the abolition mail campaign, they had a greater fear of yielding too many freedoms, including the freedom of expression, to the political clout of slaveholders. The terms of debate began to shift, and in July 1836 Congress approved a major post office reform bill. Rather than make overt concessions to the South, as originally discussed, the final bill declared that the federal government would protect the inviolability of the mail. On its face, this new legislation rejected both Jackson's and Calhoun's approach to the abolition mail in favor of protecting freedom of expression and civil liberties. But in practice the new postal law was never fully enforced in the South. Instead, local postmasters in the region continued to act under Postmaster General Amos Kendall's instructions allowing them to detain rather than deliver mail they deemed incendiary. Thus, when postmasters such as Charleston's Huger censored the mail, federal authorities took no action against them, suggesting that an informal understanding along these lines had smoothed the way for passage of a bill that made few overt concessions to the South.[67] Such a wink-and-nod approach to managing the mail clearly left southerners such as Calhoun dissatisfied, but all of Jackson's antebellum successors followed his practice of refusing to take action against southern censorship of the mail. As historian Sean Wilentz concluded, "Postmasters did as they pleased, with the tacit assumption that federal authority over the mails ended at the post office door."[68] But as William Freehling pointed out, a president who allowed the mail to be stopped could also order that the mail be delivered.[69] The failure of Calhoun's bill and the success of Kendall's informal policy seemed to put the future of the South in the hands of every incumbent president. This fact raised the stakes of the presidential contest to new heights in the minds of white southerners, and southern interest in the contest became and remained almost obsessive. Not the least danger Abraham Lincoln posed to the slaveholding states when elected president in 1860 was the possibility that he might simply declare that the mail must go through.

Over time, as southern postmasters refused to deliver abolition mail and federal authorities tolerated the postmasters' decisions not to distribute such mail, abolitionists abandoned the mail campaign as a waste of time and money. But they had made their point. The South had reacted aggressively to the mail campaign by insisting that slavery was more important than the Bill of Rights or the right of any individual to receive the mail he was sent. The willingness of southern slaveholders to slight the fundamental civil liberties of white citizens in defense of slavery hardly failed to escape northern attention, even if most white northerners had little sympathy with the abolitionist efforts to distribute incendiary mail. But apparently most white northerners agreed with the New York *Evening Post*'s assertion that the South "can not trample on the charter of our national freedom to assist the slaveholder in his warfare with fanaticism."[70] On balance, the mail campaign did little to move mainstream opinion in the North closer to radical abolition, but the southern reaction to the mail campaign conjured the existence of a southern "Slave Power" willing to bend the rules of liberty in its defense of slavery. President Jackson himself grew worried about the tactics of the antiabolition forces, telling Amos Kendall that the "spirit of mob law is becoming too common and must be checked or ere long it will become as great an evil as a servile war."[71] Apparently even Andrew Jackson had a limited tolerance for summary justice—at least in those cases in which he was not the summary judge.

In a revealing reflection on the significance of the abolition mail campaign and ongoing antislavery petition campaigns, Calhoun explained why white southerners could have no tolerance for abolitionist speech. Calhoun characterized the abolition mail and petition campaigns as a "war" waged against the South, not with arms but "in the most dangerous manner," with words. The "war the abolitionists wage against us is of a very different character," Calhoun contended. "It is a war of religious and political fanaticism . . . waged not against our lives, but our character. The object is to humble and debase us in our estimation, and that of the world in general, to blast our reputation, while they overthrow our domestic institutions." In a war of this kind, Calhoun insisted, "we must meet the enemy at the frontier . . . it is our Thermopylae." The South could not, Calhoun insisted, stand exposed to "endless attacks on our rights, our character, and our institutions."[72] "Of all questions which have been agitated under our government, abolition is that in which we of the South have the deepest concern," Calhoun told a Georgia audience. "It strikes directly and fatally, not only at our prosperity, but our existence as a people. Should it succeed, our fate would be worse . . . than the Slaves we command. It is a question which admits of neither concession or compromise."

Moreover, Calhoun argued, in the struggle against abolition, the South could look "to ourselves and ourselves only for safety" because the dynamics of party competition in the North rendered otherwise sympathetic northerners unreliable allies. The South Carolina planter acknowledged that "the great body of enlightened citizens in all parties in the North" were opposed to the "wicked and dangerous schemes of the abolitionists," but he believed that the two parties "which divide and distract all the non-slaveholding states" were so intent on "retaining power" that "neither will directly oppose the abolitionists . . . from the fear that by incurring their displeasure they might lose their ascendancy in their respective states or defeat their prospect of rising to power." As "strong as may be their regard for us," Calhoun argued, "their regard for their party at home is still stronger." The South needed "harmony and concert among ourselves" to protect itself.[73]

At the grassroots level, the abolition mail campaign galvanized southern support for slavery in a manner that nothing else had. The mail campaign did not eradicate all differences among white southerners over the issue of slavery in a flash; not even secession a quarter century later would do that. In fact, the mail campaign highlighted some differences, such as those over the issue of teaching slaves to read. But the mail campaign did convince most white southerners that they had to put their differences aside on occasion to present a solid front against the abolitionist attack. The search for such common ground was a hallmark of the public antiabolition rallies, and though the unity of these rallies was superficial at times, papering over lingering differences over slavery that continued to flourish for years to come, it did represent an expression of solidarity against outside critics and a recognition that internal disagreements had to be put aside at times so that the South could speak to outside critics with one voice.

In contrast with the mail campaign, the simultaneous abolition petition campaign, launched to inundate Congress with petitions related to slavery, never stirred the same kind of grassroots rebellion that the mail campaign did, but together with the postal campaign, the petition campaign certainly engaged the full energies of southern politicians in Washington. The petition campaign was older than the mail campaign. Critics of slavery had petitioned Congress on matters related to slavery since the inception of the republic. What changed in 1835, however, was the new American Anti-slavery Society's decision to increase the sheer number of such petitions in an effort to force Congress to take some action on them. The orchestrated increase in the number of petitions led to the decision of at least a handful of southern congressmen to force a showdown with the petitioners. Many of the petitions that were brought to Congress focused on the idea of banning either slavery or the slave trade in Washington, D.C., where the constitution appeared to give Congress full authority to act. Collectively, Congress had no desire to grant any of the petitioners' prayers, but differences emerged over exactly how the petitions should be handled.[74]

In December 1835, South Carolina representative James Henry Hammond, a prominent nullifier doubtless spurred to action by the grassroots reaction to the abolition mail campaign, surprised the House of Representatives by moving to refuse to receive an abolitionist petition rather than follow the usual procedure of receiving and tabling the petitions. Hammond proposed his "gag rule," a refusal to even receive abolition petitions, as a way of putting a "more decided seal of disapprobation" on them.[75] Hammond's fellow South Carolinian, Congressman Francis Pickens, also a Calhoun lieutenant, agreed that Hammond's proposal offered a better way for the slaveholding states to meet the abolitionist challenge "at the threshold," and perhaps scotch the growth of the abolition movement before it gained further momentum.[76] Despite Hammond's ties to Calhoun, evidence suggests that the young Columbia representative, also a prize pupil of the radical Thomas Cooper, made the decision to propose a tough gag rule on his own. Back in Columbia, editor E. W. Johnston, a Cooper protégé who "steadily cursed" Calhoun for his moderation, applauded Hammond's zeal. Johnston maintained that the abolition movement "does not give our people half the alarm it should," and he thought Hammond's bold stand against receiving the petitions might galvanize public attention.[77]

Whatever his role in Hammond's earlier stand in the House, in January 1836 Calhoun, seeing a chance to unify the South behind the antiabolition cause in a way that nullification had failed to do, presented his own gag rule proposal in the Senate. Paralleling Hammond's proposal in the House, Calhoun wanted the Senate to refuse reception of abolition petitions. Calhoun reasoned that since Congress possessed no power to abolish slavery, it had no reason to even imply such authority by receiving the petitions.[78] Most northerners in Congress were only slightly less eager to gag the abolition petitions than were southerners. But they disagreed as much over means as much as they agreed on ends. Insisting that Congress had to respect the citizens' right to petition, Pennsylvania's James Buchanan proposed that the Senate receive the petitions and immediately reject them. Henry Clay, still an advocate of colonization but an outspoken opponent of immediate emancipation, preferred that the petitions be received, referred to committee, and reported back out with a recommendation to deny on grounds of inexpediency rather than unconstitutionality.[79]

In the end, the Senate rejected both Calhoun's bid to meet "the enemy at the frontier" and Clay's more elaborate reception, referral, report, and rejection plan in favor of Buchanan's proposal for receiving but then immediately rejecting the petitions. The key vote in favor of Buchanan's proposal was overwhelming, 34–6, with all southern senators except Calhoun (who abstained) voting in favor of the measure.[80] Even South Carolina senator William Preston praised the Buchanan gag as "the next strongest condemnation of the abolitionists."[81] As a practical matter, Buchanan's method gagged the abolitionist petitions as effectively as Calhoun's. But in the mind of the South Carolina senator, Buchanan's gag rule implied that Congress had power over the decision to emancipate slaves—a concession Calhoun thought dangerous to make.

In the House, James Hammond's bold bid for a strict gag rule ran afoul of the unexpected moderation of another former nullifier, Henry Laurens Pinckney of Charleston. During the nullification crisis, Pinckney had served as the editor of the *Charleston Mercury* and emerged as one of the movement's leading rhetoricians. Pinckney's gag proposal involved referring abolition petitions to a select committee, which would then report that Congress could not interfere with slavery. From the beginning, both political friends and foes rightly suspected that Pinckney's proposal reflected the political preference of the national Democratic Party and its presidential candidate, Martin Van Buren. As the abolition mail and petition campaigns proceeded, Van Buren and his advisors quickly recognized that the vice president would have little chance at the presidency unless he could placate southern opinion on the abolition issue without alienating his northern support. Georgia congressman George Owens detected a "coolness" among northern representatives toward gagging petitioners and warned Van Buren that he must use "every exertion" to bring "the weak—the timid and the doubtful up to scratch" or face the deterioration of his candidacy in the South.[82] Jackson's secretary of state, John Forsyth, even urged Van Buren to encourage "a little more mob discipline of white incendiaries" in the North. "A portion of the magician's skill is required in the matter," Forsyth advised Van Buren, "and the sooner you set the imps to work the better."[83]

Van Buren's political predicament, of course, was more complicated than Forsyth's advice suggested. He had to not only move quickly to prevent further erosion of his support in the lower South, where his opponents regularly pounded him with the charge that he had supported free black voting rights in New York and was weak on slavery generally, but also assure his northern support that he was neither the political handmaiden of the southern slaveholders nor a closet friend of abolition. Van Buren quipped that he must find a way to put a "quietus" on the "abolition question" for "the harmony of our happy Union," but the astute New Yorker knew he needed a solution for the benefit of his presidential prospects.[84] The vice president thought the Pinckney proposal, coming as it did from a South Carolinian and ex-nullifier, would do the trick. Debate and disagreement over various gag rule proposals raged for months. Northern Democrats preferred to call abolitionist interference with slavery "inexpedient"; many southern representatives insisted that it was unconstitutional. A majority of southern representatives wanted the strongest possible gag short of Hammond's proposal to refuse reception of the petitions; most northern Democrats wanted a gag rule that constituted the least infringement of petition rights possible. Both groups of politicians looked to placate nervous regional constituencies—one eager to see its politicians stand firm against the abolition movement and the other interested in seeing its politicians to refuse to make too many concessions to the slaveholding states while still providing some check on radical abolition. As the legislative maneuvering unfolded, Pinckney's proposal was toughened to call for the immediate tabling of abolition petitions rather than burying these petitions in committee. The receiving and immediate tabling of the petitions still fell short of what Hammond, Calhoun, and other hard-liners wanted, but it promised an effective gag on abolitionist petitioners. Finally, in late May 1836, the House voted 117–68 to approve the toughened version of Pinckney's proposal. The measure ultimately attracted a broad base of support. Four-fifths of all northern Democrats and nine of ten all southern representatives of all persuasions voted in favor of Pinckney's plan. The abolitionists had been gagged, not tightly enough to satisfy Calhoun or Hammond, but well enough that Congress could return to business as almost usual. The South had largely united behind a gag rule, but it was behind Pinckney's moderate one rather than Calhoun's hard-line version.[85]

The reasons for Pinckney's apostasy from Carolina orthodoxy at this crucial moment remain a matter of speculation. Henry Laurens Pinckney, the editorialist and rhetorician of nullification, a member of Charleston's first family, a Lowcountry politician formerly closely aligned with Calhoun, seemed an unlikely champion of moderation during the gag rule crisis. Despite his distinguished lineage and considerable influence in Charleston, however, Pinckney remained a second-level politician in South Carolina. He clearly ranked behind Calhoun and William Preston, South Carolina's other senator, and even in Charleston he clearly enjoyed less influence than James Hamilton or Robert Hayne, and perhaps no more than Whitemarsh Seabrook, whom he increasingly came to distrust if not despise.[86] Calhoun always saw Pinckney's surprise defection as a matter of political opportunism. He thought Pinckney sided with Vice President Van Buren to attain pride of place among the ranks of Van Buren supporters in the lower South. Such a gambit, if it worked, would elevate a second-level South Carolina politician to a position of national influence, and perhaps even a chance at the vice presidency, through Andrew Jackson's anointed successor. Calhoun felt Pinckney's betrayal keenly because the Charleston congressman's advocacy of a weaker version of the gag rule frustrated yet another opportunity for South Carolina to take the lead in forging the southern unity that Calhoun thought necessary both to fight abolition and to advance his own claims to high office.[87] James Hammond identified Pinckney's motives as those of vainglory, attributing the Charleston congressman's break with the state delegation to Pinckney's "being flattered with the idea of being a second Clay to save the Union."[88]

Other contemporaries, including men personally closer to Pinckney, believed that his newfound moderation grew from his recent religious conversion. The conversion, Robert Hayne argued, rendered Pinckney "strangely self-willed and erratic." In fact, Hayne had advised Hammond and other South Carolina congressmen "that it would not be an easy matter" to keep Pinckney "straight" after his conversion. Since "he has become a saint," Hayne lamented, Pinckney had shown increasing political unpredictability.[89] Pinckney himself explained his decision as a matter of practicality. The former editor felt that Calhoun's attempt to refuse reception of the abolition petitions united "the whole North" behind a defense of "the right of petition," while it divided the South over the question of whether such a draconian gag on petitions was necessary. By rallying the North behind the right to petition, Calhoun's proposal, in Pinckney's view, obscured the true contest in the North between abolition "fanatics" and the "great body of the people." The South could easily put itself on the winning side of the latter battle but risked losing all if it insisted on making the question into a contest over the right of petition.[90] In South Carolina and in other radical enclaves across the South, opinion turned vehemently against Pinckney, who was immediately denounced as a traitor to the southern cause. He became the object of much political opprobrium in his native Charleston, and Calhoun orchestrated the successful campaign of former Unionist Hugh Legare to unseat Pinckney in the district's 1836 congressional race.[91]

WITHOUT QUESTION, the new abolitionist "war" against slavery, especially when coupled with reports of a large-scale slave insurrection plot in the old Southwest, created an internal security crisis in the lower South and momentarily put the region's paternalists on the defensive. Because the abolition mail campaign involved the distribution of incendiary literature inside the South, it necessarily put defenders of teaching slaves to read on the defensive. The post-Turner, post-Garrison campaign to ban the teaching of reading and writing to slaves seemed vindicated by the new effort to distribute abolitionist literature in the South. Mississippi Presbyterian James Smylie, though not an opponent of slave literacy per se, blamed southern opposition to educating slaves squarely on the threat posed by the abolition mail campaign.[92] Increasingly, paternalists across the South contented themselves with emphasizing the oral instruction of slaves instead, at least for the time being.

In Liberty County, Georgia, Charles Jones' Association for the Religious Instruction of Slaves responded to the abolition crisis by declaring, "As a community we have been but of one mind touching the fanatical and incendiary movements which have occasioned the excitement." Yet, "true to the religion we profess," the association held, "we have maintained our interest in the Best good of the Negroes, as well as our confidence in the means of promoting that good." The association insisted that white southerners should protect themselves "by Law, as far as possible, from the Circulation of Incendiary publications, and from the teachings of incendiary agents," but it also insisted that whites should "look at home, and enter upon our discharge of our Duty to the negroes, as will meet the approbation of God and our consciences, and commend ourselves to the consciences of other men." The association thought it wise "to leave the Abolitionists" to "the judicious and enlightened of the North" in the hope that "their false principles and improper measures will be exposed and put down."[93]

The hand and voice of Charles Jones were clearly evident in the association's words. Jones had returned to Liberty County in late 1835 to ride out the storm of the abolition mail campaign in the relative security of the area where his mission to the slaves was so well established. He sought not protection for himself and his family from slave unrest but a refuge for his cause, the Christian paternalist mission to the slaves, from the winds of antiabolition reaction and mob violence so much discussed during his recent visit to Charleston and practiced throughout the South during the fall of 1835. Through his association, which had long committed itself to the oral instruction of slaves, Jones not only counseled patience but practiced it. He believed the "excitement" would pass. He continued work in Liberty County as he had before the mail and petition campaigns stirred up so much excitement across the region, and he looked to a day when he could again promote his paternalist project on a regionwide basis. Jones proved a disciplined paternalist; he did not have to wait long for his moment.[94]

CHAPTER SEVENTEEN

THE IDEOLOGICAL RECONFIGURATION OF SLAVERY IN THE LOWER SOUTH

For slaveholders in the lower South, developments in the first half of the 1830s had ranged from discomfiting to outright alarming. Threats to slavery, some new and some perennial, appeared from all directions. Traditional defenses, such as vigilance and political clout, hardly seemed adequate any longer. Bold new approaches had struggled to gain traction. South Carolina's doctrine of nullification, an aggressive new political weapon that could defend slavery, had failed to win widespread support, even among slaveholders. The paternalist project had gained ground among slaveholders and southern politicians, but its detractors remained numerous and powerful. At the same time, the abolition movement in the North had proven innovative in both ideas and tactics, upper South states openly debated the future of slavery in their region, and tangible signs of slave unrest appeared in the heart of staple country. In addressing the problem of slavery, the institution's opponents had seized the initiative; its various defenders, knocked back on their heels, lacked a coherent strategy.

Thus, taken together, the appearance of David Walker's pamphlet, the emergence of the new abolition doctrine of immediatism and its regular articulation in Garrison's the *Liberator*, Nat Turner's bloody insurrection in Virginia, and the abolition mail and petition campaigns launched in 1835 forced a reconsideration of prevailing ideas, attitudes, and positions about slavery in the South, especially in the lower South, the region most dependent on slavery and most vulnerable to slave revolt. Over time, the verbal assault by abolitionists, the physical attack by slave rebels, and the repeated threats of such attack did much to reshape southern thinking about and answers to the slavery question.

But the outcome of this reconsideration of slavery and the ultimate form of the reshaping of lower South thought regarding slavery remained very much in question for a number of years. Even among the opinion-shaping political and intellectual elite in the region, different white southerners reacted to these challenges to slavery in very different ways. Ultimately, however, as described in the two previous chapters, the abolitionist attack and the threat of slave insurrection reshaped the lower South's stance on slavery in two rather indistinct and overlapping stages. First, Walker's pamphlet, Turner's rebellion, and the newly aggressive nature of abolition propaganda campaigns initially put advocates of paternalism on the defensive. Walker's pamphlet and the postal campaign cast paternalist efforts to educate slaves in very dark hues because they suggested that slaves who could read and write could easily learn about freedom and justice and spread plans of revolt among their fellow slaves. Turner's insurrection and the related reports that Turner was a slave preacher inspired by a Christian millennial vision also suggested that paternalist efforts to Christianize slaves were fraught with peril. Paternalist advocates of the religious mission to the slaves often either endorsed or tolerated blacks (including slaves) in the roles of "watchmen" or teachers and, in some instances, as preachers. Slave preachers, ordained or not, certainly had a pulpit from which to foment unrest and plan insurrection unless their white minders were ever vigilant. Moreover, in the short term, the abolition mail campaign, with its emphasis on circulating antislavery literature inside the South, galvanized white southern sentiment behind the notion that a literate slave population would inevitably prove a danger to the social order.

The longer-term impact of the abolition petition and mail campaigns, however, with their promise of an unending moral war on slavery, moved the South, and especially the lower South, toward an ideological reconfiguration of slavery that embraced paternalism and placed it at the center of the South's efforts to explain and defend slavery to the outside world. The new abolition campaign attacked slaveholders on humanitarian grounds. Its insistence that slavery was a sin, and that slaveholders' unwillingness to repent by freeing their slaves indicated an unrepentant evil in their hearts, assaulted the character and morality of slaveholders and all who supported and sustained them. This line of abolitionist attack engendered far more bitterness and resentment among white southerners than had earlier criticisms of slavery focusing on the more general social evils of the institution or the disproportionate political power slaves gave the South through the three-fifths compromise.[1] Southerners had fended off this earlier criticism through professions that the South intended to phase out the institution over the long term and, in the meantime, intended to ameliorate the acknowledged evils as best it could. The new attack by those promoting immediate abolition offended many southerners, striking them as slander and libel, and even as the rhetoric of those willing to use terror to achieve their desired ends. As such, the new abolition assault on southern character required a systematic and sustained reply. Indeed, in important respects, the chief difference between the newly invigorated abolitionist criticism of slavery and earlier political crises that spawned criticism of slavery was that the earlier crises were episodic. The round of criticism associated with each of these episodes promised to wane once the particular issue at hand was resolved. The new line of attack by the immediatists was ongoing, and the attackers pledged to sustain the offensive until slavery was abolished. The crisis appeared chronic rather than acute. In sum, southern slaveholders understood the new abolitionist attack as an assault on the humanitarianism of the South and felt that it demanded an answer on those terms.[2]

The result of this pressing need to offer a sustained and effective rebuttal to the abolitionist attack, I argue, was nothing less than an ideological reconfiguration of slavery. The reconfiguration triumphed most thoroughly in the lower South, where it became the dominant mode of understanding slavery and the society it sustained. The ideological reconfiguration also made considerable gains in the upper South, especially in those areas where slavery remained economically robust. But in the upper South as a whole, the ideological reconfiguration of slavery confronted ideas about rendering slavery less vital and less threatening through a demographic reconfiguration of the institution, and many upper South leaders still maintained that slavery should be phased down and then out whenever appropriate methods for so doing presented themselves.

The timing and nature of the lower South's ideological reconfiguration of slavery in the Jacksonian era are easier for historians to reconstruct than they were for contemporaries to discern, but a number of contemporaries did comment on the changing nature of southern attitudes toward slavery during the 1830s. One southern clergyman dated the shift to the "massacre at Southampton," which he maintained "opened the eyes of the South to views of truth and duty in relation to slavery," a duty that centered on "elevating" the "moral character" of slaves. Gag rule advocate James Henry Hammond argued that before the "abolition agitation" began, it had been "common sentiment" in the South "that it was desirable to get rid of slavery," but the new abolitionist attack on slavery spurred a reexamination. As abolitionists used "vile calumnies" and "unmitigated abuse" in their criticism of slaveholders, Hammond contended, fewer southern whites saw slavery as a social evil that merely begged a practical remedy and more saw "Domestic slavery" as the producer of "the highest toned, the purest, best organization of society that has ever existed on the face of the earth."[3] In 1838, John C. Calhoun credited the sustained abolitionist assault on southern character and prosperity with producing "one happy effect at least," that of encouraging the ideological reconfiguration of slavery in the minds of white southerners. The abolition movement, Calhoun claimed, had "compelled the South to look at the nature and character" of slavery and "correct many of the false impressions that even we had entertained in relation to it." "Many in the South," Calhoun admitted, "once believed that [slavery] was a moral and political evil," but after the abolitionists found full voice in the mail and petition campaigns, such "folly and delusion" were gone, as white southerners increasingly saw slavery as "the most safe and stable basis for free institutions in the world."[4]

The ideological reconfiguration of slavery that cohered during the late 1830s combined three key elements, one involving simply a reification of existing thought and prejudice in the region and the other two elements traceable to specific and highly visible historical trends of the era. One key element of the reconfiguration was an insistence that slavery as it existed in the South was justified by racial differences. A small proportion of masters were not white, but all slaves were of the "black" or "negro" race as defined by whites. Racial difference had long been a staple of southern apologies and justifications of slavery, as Jefferson's earliest writings on the subject readily revealed. Yet racial justifications of slavery advanced during the post-immediatism ideological reconfiguration of slavery reached new levels of frequency and presumed sophistication. More and more southern defenders of slavery argued that the inferiority of blacks was permanent and independent of environmental influence or sociological position. Racial differences were increasingly assumed to be a matter of heredity or divine intention. Moreover, for practical purposes, race was defined by white southerners almost entirely by skin color. Color, white southerners repeatedly asserted, identified race in a highly visible and incontrovertible manner.

The second and most original aspect of the ideological configuration, an aspect anticipated by earlier defenses of slavery but one developed in detail primarily after the abolitionists unveiled their immediatist doctrine, contended that slavery protected the independence of whites by preventing the development of a dependent white working class in the region. This claim gained greater salience as the progress of the market and capitalist revolutions created larger free working classes in other parts of the world, including the American North. Through this argument, defenders of slavery presented the institution as the best foundation for liberty and democracy among whites.

Finally, the third element of the reconfiguration, and the key to white southerners' defense of their humanitarianism against the mounting abolitionist attack, was a full embrace of paternalism both as the ideology of slaveholding and as the best practice for slave management. During the decade following the abolitionists' postal and petition campaigns, paternalism moved from an insurgent ideology to a nearly hegemonic one, triumphing over its critics and outright opponents, at least at the level of ideology, with remarkable rapidity given the intense opposition the paternalist insurgency had attracted since it emerged after 1808. Paternalism, the ideology of domestic slavery, became the southern counterpoint to northern arguments that slavery violated foundational maxims of Christian and humanitarian teaching.

In addition to the emergence of its three chief features, the Jacksonian-era ideological reconfiguration of slavery was accompanied by a series of related developments that both shaped the new ideological defense of slavery and were shaped by it. As Mitchell Snay has pointed out, religious leaders played an increasingly assertive role in the defense of slavery during this era. This new role for pastors led, of course, to sectional tensions within the mainline denominations and eventually to the split of the Methodist and Baptist denominations in 1844.[5] Second, the number of pamphlets and tracts devoted entirely to the defense of slavery proliferated as the South's war of words with the abolitionists reached a fever pitch. For the first time, the debate over slavery took on a life of its own in American print. It now transcended specific issues such as the Missouri crisis or the Vesey scare.[6] Finally, a variety of so-called proslavery arguments emerged, emphasizing different points and different justifications and hence often disagreeing with one another in some matters of detail and occasionally disagreeing on more fundamental matters. Thus internal differences over slavery within the South, whether between lower and upper South or within those subregions, hardly disappeared even as the ideological reconfiguration of slavery proceeded. But these differences seldom involved the three key points in the reconfiguration and all disagreements were almost entirely subordinated to the need to present a united front against the aggressive new abolition attack. In a sense, white southerners agreed on the need for unity in defense of slavery but for the most part found such unity easer to advocate than to achieve, largely because everyone wanted unity on their preferred terms.[7]

THE RACIAL NATURE of American slavery had long been a part of southern justifications and defenses of slavery. Thus the centrality of race to the Old South's ideological reconfiguration of slavery marked not so much a departure from previous thought about slavery as it did a change in emphasis. The flattening of other social distinctions by the democratic impulse of the Jacksonian era, arguably expressed most clearly in the state constitutional reform movements of the era, highlighted race as virtually the only difference among men in the Jacksonian world.[8] In the state-of-the-art science of the era, definitions and classifications by race became more detailed and elaborate, and one line of so-called scholarship in the era even argued that the races were the product of separate creations or beginnings. So by the middle of the 1830s, defenders of slavery spoke of race as a justification with increasing confidence and certainty, and with increasing determination that white supremacy must be maintained as the society's central social distinction, not just one distinction among many.[9]

In 1835, South Carolina's Edmund Bellinger claimed that slavery could not be wrong because the "negro is from his intellectual and moral organization incapable of being civilized or enjoying freedom; utterly incompetent to become a citizen of a civilized community." Indeed, Bellinger contended, blacks not only could never "participate in the rights and privileges of white citizens," but, if free, would "corrupt the principles of one half of our population and drag them down—down to their own depraved, degraded and disgusting condition." "All history," Bellinger continued, "shows that the same country cannot contain free races of men too distinct and different to amalgamate." The "contest" between the races "would lead to a fierce and desperate struggle for supremacy," Bellinger concluded, "ending in the extermination of one, or the other, or both!"[10]

On the national stage, prominent southern politicians called attention to the role of racial difference in underpinning slavery. James Hammond claimed that two races could not exist in close proximity under any condition approaching equality because "color draws an indelible and insuperable line of separation between them." South Carolina equity chancellor William Harper asserted that the belief that "the African negro is an inferior variety of the human race is, I think, now generally admitted."[11] In 1838, John C. Calhoun explained the racial basis of southern slavery on the floor of the United States Senate. A "mysterious Providence had brought together two races, from different portions of the globe, and placed them in nearly equal numbers in the Southern portion of this Union," Calhoun asserted, and there they "were inseparably united, beyond the possibility of separation." Under slavery, Calhoun argued, the "inferior" race had "improved" and "attained a degree of civilization never before attained by the black race in any age or country." Calhoun's characterization both bluntly embraced white supremacy and swept away any justification for colonization all in a simple declaration. In Calhoun's view, the superiority of whites made them the agents of civilizing slaves—a process that he believed had come a long way but had a long way to go—and thus made any removal of slaves from the presence of whites a step toward retrogression rather than a means of mutual fulfillment. For Calhoun, slavery had solved the race problem by establishing the proper relationship of black subordination and white responsibility and putting it at the heart of the region's social system.[12] Some years later, J. Henry Lumpkin, a Georgia judge, expressed a harsher but increasingly typical southern white view when he maintained that all efforts to "inculcate care and industry upon the sons of Ham is to preach to the idle winds. To be the 'servants of servants' is the judicial curse pronounced upon their race. And this Divine degree is irreversible."[13]

Southern religious leaders also became increasingly explicit in attributing capacity to race rather than environment, social background, or condition. Mississippi Presbyterian James Smylie argued of blacks that "a flat nose, a curled head, and a black skin, has heretofore, and is likely ever hereafter, to keep them in bondage." Regardless of their genius or morality, Smylie argued, "the African blood flows through their veins, rests like an incubus upon them—pressing them down to the dust."[14] Charleston Congregationalist pastor Daniel Whitaker agreed, contending that slavery brought "humanity to the slave—a being upon whom nature has stamped the badge of mental and physical inferiority, in marks not to be mistaken or eradicated while the world stands." Africans, Whitaker contended, are "a people upon whom God has placed an everlasting badge of inferiority." Blacks were "Imbecile and unreflecting to the last degree," Whitaker maintained, and would "never be able to elevate to the position of the white man." The "African race," Whitaker contended, "has found its level in slavery." The slaves had no right to enter "into social relations on a footing of equality with white citizens, because his skin is black, and because he is of a different and inferior race."[15]

Other southern clergymen approached the racial issue more cautiously. Mississippi Methodist Thomas Thornton accepted the notion that blacks were inferior to some extent, but maintained that the "intelligence of the southern negro extends to and equals all the business operations of a farm, and all the horticultural and other duties of domestic life. In all these, he is his master's adviser, his master's planter, his master's manager." Thornton even contended that the mental condition of slaves was "superior to that of the serfs and peasantry of some European states," suggesting that the Methodist pastor hardly accepted a general argument for racial inferiority. But even Thornton, who was cautious about disparaging black capacity, could not resist taunting abolitionists by asking if they would approve of their daughters marrying a "broad-footed, flat-nosed, coal black, curly-headed strong-scented negro."[16]

The second important aspect of the ideological reconfiguration of slavery embraced by the lower South during the late 1830s was the notion that racial slavery prevented common whites from falling into debilitating and unrepublican dependency by ensuring that the truly dependent laboring class in southern society would be slaves of another race. Such arguments asserting that slavery served as a guarantor of white independence had surfaced from time to time among southern politicians and thinkers since the earliest days of the republic, but it became a much more consistent and integral part of the ideological defense of slavery once the market revolution had created new working classes in other parts of the world and spawned realistic new fears of dependency among the Old South's white plain folk.[17] Following the logic that slavery for blacks undergirded the independence of whites, Lowcountry congressman Robert Barnwell Rhett told his constituents in 1838 that because of slavery, "every white man is a privileged being." Rhett's sometime ally James H. Hammond endorsed "without reserve" the claim of South Carolina governor George McDuffie that "slavery is the corner-stone of our republican edifice" and argued that under racial slavery the "poorest and most ignorant" people, the bane of most republican societies, have no political influence, while a large proportion of southern whites "are . . . Independent in their circumstances" and hence "more deeply interested in preserving a stable and well-ordered government" than their counterparts elsewhere.[18]

The value of independence among the yeomanry and other common whites in the South appeared in bold relief when compared to the dangerous "unrepublican" dependence experienced by free workers elsewhere. In the North, Hammond contended, free labor had found a ruthless master in the "modern artificial money power system," under which "all are subjected to the dominion of capital—a monster without heart."[19] Increasingly, the comparative status of slaves and free workers in other societies emerged as a staple of these discussions of how slavery protected common whites from degradation and dependence. In 1836, Theophilus Fisk, a Universalist minister in Charleston, challenged abolitionists to look at the problems of northern labor as well as southern slaves. "Are there no slaves north of the Potomac?" Fisk asked. "Are there no white laborers at the North bending under a load of poverty and the fetters of ignorance....Look at the cotton mills of New England—half a million females—most of them young and tender." Fisk went on to assert "that there are more slaves in Lowell and Nashua alone than can be found South of the Potomac." In the South, Fisk continued, "between Master and slave, there is mutual dependence, and a mutual interest, at the North, all the interest is all on one side, and all the dependence upon the other. While the white slave is profitable to the master, he is employed; but let sickness or old age lay upon him a palsying hand, and he is kicked into the gutter to starve, or sent to the alms house to die."[20] Alabama Baptist Basil Manly insisted that "there can be no doubt" that southern slaves were "less worked" and no less "well fed and clothed" than European peasants and English workers or "the Laborer in the Northern States of America."[21] Mississippi's Thomas Thornton compared treatment of slaves in the South favorably with the "insolent lewdness in the treatment of poor factory girls" in the North.[22]

In 1839, Abel Upshur, a Calhoun ally from Virginia's eastern shore, fleshed out the argument for slavery as the foundation for white independence and civic equality. In the South, where the "slave is black," Upshur explained, the "white man is never a slave." The southern slave system drew a visible distinction designed to ensure that "the humblest white man" enjoyed "a high sense of his own comparative dignity and importance." Racial slavery served as an "impassable barrier" that "every white man, however proud his condition, is interested to preserve unbroken." Upshur maintained that slavery produced "throughout the southern states" a "remarkable independence, freedom, and equality among all classes of whites." In the South, Upshur contended, "no white man feels such an inferiority of rank as to be unworthy of association with those around him. Color alone here is the badge of distinction, the true mark of aristocracy, and all who are white, are equal, in spite of variety of occupation."[23]

Moreover, Upshur also argued that slavery prevented dependency among whites by ensuring a widespread distribution of property. In Upshur's view, the widespread distribution of property ownership in the South not only ensured the independence of the white plain folk but also damped "the jealousies of the different classes into which societies are usually divided." "Equal in our rank, the spirit of leveling sees nothing to envy," Upshur maintained, "equal in our fortune, the spirit of agrarianism sees nothing to attack." Thus slaveholding society contrasted nicely with the "natural jealousy between labor and capital" that existed in free societies. In a slave society, "labor and capital unite in the same person," Upshur maintained. "The laborer is the slave, and the capitalist is the owner of the slave. Capital has a direct interest to see that labor be not oppressed, and labor has nothing to hope from an attack on capital." Finally, Upshur explained, slavery made the white plain folk good republican citizens because in "our slaveholding communities, the white man, whatever be his condition, is accustomed to exercise absolute authority over the negro....This single fact is enough to...render him extremely jealous of any encroachments upon his own rights...he cannot easily be persuaded to yield the proud distinction of a master, by becoming himself a slave." It was "not an easy thing," Upshur concluded, "to make political slaves of men who are admonished every hour, not only that they are personally free, but that their freedom confers upon them at once, rank, dignity, and power."[24]

The connection between white republicanism and slavery also united infidel with saint. South Carolina College president Thomas Cooper, who was both heralded as a states' rights radical and loathed as a skeptic and infidel, articulated a compelling argument for slavery as the guarantor of white democracy. According to Cooper, the South could accept "universal suffrage" among whites without fear of empowering lower-class enemies of property. The autonomy of common whites in the South, Cooper maintained, contrasted favorably with the dependent position of workers at Lowell and Waltham, who, Cooper claimed, "were compelled to give their votes on printed calico" so that "their masters might be sure they voted according to order" during the election of 1828.[25] Cooper's thinly camouflaged religious skepticism drew the ire of James Thornwell. But Thornwell, though neither democrat nor Democrat, also defended slavery as a guarantor of white freedom and republican liberty, albeit on conservative grounds. Thornwell depicted the struggle for republican liberty between abolitionists and slaveholders as one that pitted "atheists, socialists, communists, red republicans, jacobins, on the one side, and the friends of order and regulated freedom on the other." The theologian credited slavery with protecting "the principles of regulated liberty...resisting alike the social anarchy of communism and the political anarchy of licentiousness." The South, Thornwell contended, stood in support of "representative, republican government against the despotism of the masses on the one hand, and the supremacy of a single will on the other."[26]

The asserted connection between white independence and black slavery grew stronger as the ideological reconfiguration of slavery took firm hold in the late antebellum decades. During the 1850s, W. L. Hudgen, a slaveholder from Upcountry South Carolina, declared that "African slavery" was "of heaven appointment" because it was the system "best adapted to the freedom and equality of the white."[27] In the same region, a Chester District resident claimed that because of black slavery "those invidious distinctions [among whites] which prevail in all free-soil states must be to a very considerable extent unknown" in the South.[28] Another Upcountry planter, Edgefield's Arthur Simkins, held that slavery united the "commonest cottager" with the "planter" as "master within his own domain," where a man of independence "jostles no one and no one jostles him."[29]

The argument that black slavery secured white independence also found expression in the southern critique of "wage slavery" that emerged with some vigor in the late antebellum era. Upcountry South Carolina lawyer William King Easley noted that northern "workshops" were "crowded with withered forms and haggard faces" working "amid the din of the looms and the roar of the spindles and wheels in their giant factories," where observers could hear "the smothering cough of consumptive and starving operatives."[30] Another Upcountry planter called on northern philanthropists to emancipate their own slaves—"slaves that were of their own color, now everywhere reduced by the progress of their manufacturing system to a condition of toil and abject submission to their Master's will even more debasing than that of the Southern slave."[31] Common whites in the South understood, South Carolina planter Benjamin Herndon Rice declared, "that...where Capital rules, where there are no black slaves, there must be white ones."[32]

Arguably, no one understood the concept of wage slavery better than Lowcountry planter and Charleston banker William Henry Trescot. Trescot argued that "wherever the political theory of government recognizes the equality of labor and capital," social reality would often reveal "the one in hopeless and heartless dependence on the other," producing a "constant jealousy and a bitter strife" between the propertied and working classes that divided society and left "the weaker demanding its rights with impotent cursing or enforcing them with revolutionary fierceness." Slavery, Trescot concluded, had proven "the dream of political philosophers" by solving for the South the "most dangerous of social questions," that of class conflict; by becoming the "great leveller, not by dragging down, but by raising up, it has made a society of equals."[33]

With slavery for blacks justified by race and slavery defended as a proper foundation for republican government through its ability to mute class conflict among whites, the question that remained was how slavery could be squared with the safety of whites and the humanity of the slaveholders. Toward that end, the third, final, and arguably most critical, aspect of the lower South's ideological reconfiguration of slavery involved the final triumph of paternalism as the dominant ideology of slaveholding in the Old South. The triumph of paternalism was a slow and contested one, fought for over more than a generation by a cohort of slaveholders, clergy, and other white southerners committed to paternalism as an ideology of slavery and a method of slave management against other slaveholders and white southerners who were in varying proportions indifferent, skeptical, and even hostile toward the paternalist cause.

The triumph of paternalism as the dominant ideology of slaveholding in the Old South was the triumph of a specific and identifiable ideology within a discrete historical setting. It was neither part of a universal tendency toward noblesse oblige among wealthy elites nor the inevitable outcome of day-to-day struggles between masters and slaves, though both of these phenomena, and especially the latter, played a role in shaping both the ideology and the practice. Instead, the rise of paternalism in the Old South was influenced by a number of impinging historical contingencies, some of which threatened its rise and others that advanced its cause. Differently put, the triumph of the paternalist insurgency was historically specific but hardly inevitable. For example, times looked dark for paternalism in the immediate aftermath of Nat Turner's rebellion, as waves of legislation across the lower South created laws either inimical to or difficult to square with paternalism. When Charles Jones visited

Charleston in the fall of 1835, all the wise local voices cautioned against any further advocacy of the paternalist cause, especially as it centered on the religious instruction of slaves, because public suspicion and hostility rendered the question too delicate for further agitation.[34]

But as the South geared up to respond to the substantive charges leveled by the abolitionists in the petition and mail campaigns of 1835 rather than simply the nature of the campaigns themselves, and as effective if temporary remedies were applied to stop the flow of abolition pamphlets into the South and sidetrack the petitions submitted to Congress, the need to effectively combat the abolitionist critics on humanitarian grounds eventually struck many slaveholders and other white southerners as the key to effectively rebuffing the latest antislavery ideology. And they saw it as both essential and urgent. The ideology of paternalism, with its argument about the domestication of slavery and the broad social benefits its proponents claimed not only could but did flow from paternalism as a social system, provided the perfect counter to abolition charges that holding slaves violated all reasonable humanitarian sensibilities. As paternalism gained currency as an ideology for justifying slavery, longtime advocates of paternalism remained determined to make sure that theirs was not a hollow triumph. They insisted on an active religious mission to the slaves and that masters provide better treatment of slaves. These paternalists wanted not only a rhetorical defense of slavery that centered on a paternalist ideology but a system of slavery actually characterized by paternalist practices—at least to the extent possible in a large and diverse region.

The contest over the scope of paternalism's influence in the region was decided emphatically in favor of the paternalist insurgency in the decade after 1835. Expressions of lower South whites' acceptance of paternalism as the dominant ideology of slavery in their region multiplied during this era. Such acceptance of paternalism revealed itself in references to slavery as a paternalistic or patriarchal or domestic institution, or in references to familial bonds or paternal responsibilities, or even in references to kind or benevolent feelings on the part of masters and slaves and the loyalty of one to another. Such sentiments were expressed at the antiabolition meeting in Calhoun's home district of Pendleton in September 1835, when the ad hoc committee's report declared that slavery as it existed in the South "resembles in a great measure a happy patriarchal state in which the benevolence and kindness of the master, and the fidelity and affection of the slave" work together in a "harmonious manner." The "whole subject of Master and Slave," the report insisted, "is one grossly misunderstood, and still more grossly misrepresented out of the States where the Institution prevails."[35] Several years later, James Henry Hammond argued that the South's "patriarchal scheme of domestic servitude is indeed well calculated to awaken the higher and finer feelings." Hammond contended that the South's "patriarchal" system of slavery was "the sacred and natural system" because it placed the laborer "under the personal control of a fellow-being endowed with sentiments and sympathies of humanity." The secular Hammond even touted the religious instruction of slaves as proof of southern paternalism, emphasizing that slaves were a majority of Baptist and Methodist communicants in South and that slaves heard the gospel preached regularly. Slavery in the South, Hammond concluded, was not merely "an inexorable necessity for the present" but "a moral and humane institution," one "productive" of important "political and social advantages."[36]

The advantages of paternalism received even more systematic explication from the clergy than from politicians. In 1837, South Carolina Presbyterian William Rufus Bailey argued that the South sought the moral and intellectual elevation of slaves and to "prepare them for a better world." Bailey conceded that slaves were not likely to find that "better world" until they reached the hereafter, but he claimed that through religious instruction the "evils of slavery have been rapidly diminishing," the "tyranny and oppression of the powerful over the weak exchanged for a paternal care," and "slaves admitted to a place in the regard and attentions of masters and members of his family." Though cruel masters existed, Bailey maintained that slaves were generally treated with "kindness and protection," and he argued that the "personal attachments" between master and slave in South had grown "generally very strong" since the importation of slaves from overseas was banned in 1808. To support his argument about the value of religious instruction, Bailey estimated that two-thirds of South Carolina's thirty thousand Methodists, twenty thousand of the state's thirty-six thousand Baptists, and three thousand of South Carolina's eight thousand Presbyterians were black.[37] Baptist pastor Richard Fuller also touted the introduction of Christianity among slaves as the best means of "elevating the negro in the scale of being, and educating his mind and heart for purposes as yet concealed from us by an inscrutable Providence." Fuller argued that under the effect of Christian paternalism the "condition of the African has been vastly improved, physically, intellectually, morally, and religiously by his transportation to these shores."[38] The most authoritative religious voice in the antebellum South, that of Presbyterian theologian James Henley Thornwell, also spoke on behalf of paternalism. Thornwell attacked the "narrow expediency" often expressed by opponents of paternalism who suggested "that our safety depended upon the depression and still lower degradation of the black race." Instead, Thornwell argued, "time will show" that Christian paternalism would "prove a stronger fortress against insubordination and rebellion than weapons of brass or iron."[39]

Paternalism's journey from insurgency to orthodoxy was hardly confined to the South Atlantic seaboard, where it had gotten its start and arguably faced its toughest challenges. By the late 1830s, paternalism had also become the lingua franca of slavery in the newer cotton states of the Old Southwest. The triumph of paternalism in the states along the Gulf Coast followed the same general trajectory as the ideology's triumph in the South Atlantic region, though some of vectors shaping the path were different. In the older states of the lower South, paternalism faced entrenched opposition from slaveholders with long-established ideas about slave management and control. And the paternalism of evangelical Christians confronted some recalcitrance not only from religious skeptics but also from the Episcopal establishment, where some of the clergy and much of the laity doubted the wisdom of the evangelical enthusiasm for proselytizing slaves and questioned some of the methods the evangelicals used in the endeavor. In the newer cotton states of the Southwest, paternalism faced less opposition from established planters and cautious Episcopalians, if only because there were fewer Episcopalian planters in the region, and those who were there generally enjoyed less influence. But at the same time, paternalism in the old Southwest attracted some opposition from egalitarian evangelicals who persisted in thinking that slavery was wrong and should be phased out over time. These evangelicals were more interested in promoting colonization than in finding ways to render slavery more consistent with Christian teachings, and they were arguably slower to make concessions to the emerging slaveholding order than their counterparts in the South Atlantic region. But despite facing different obstacles in the newer portions of the lower South than in the older portions, paternalism had staked out a formidable position in the newer cotton states by the middle of the 1830s and would gain hegemony there within the next decade.[40]

In 1836, Mississippi Presbyterian James Smylie penned a systematic biblical defense of slavery in response to an abolitionist communication sent by an Ohio presbytery. In his reply, Smylie pledged a willingness to "ameliorate the condition of the colored race," but noted that it "is doubtful...whether there be in the Amite or Mississippi Presbyteries [virtually the whole of Mississippi], an individual member, who is fully convinced that to abolish the relation of master and slave is the scriptural mode of removing the evils of slavery." The influential Smylie denied the abolitionist contention that "slavery is a sin," arguing instead that a careful examination of scripture led him to the conviction "that slavery, itself, is not sinful." The "evils of slavery, like the evils of matrimony," Smylie contended, "may be traced to the neglect of the duties incumbent upon the individuals sustaining the relation" but not to the institution itself.[41] Another Mississippi Presbyterian argued that "the true Scriptural idea of slavery is that of patriarchal relations." Masters, this Presbyterian maintained, stood as "essentially the head of the household in all relations—the head of the wife—the head over his children—and the head over his servants."[42] In Alabama, Baptist pastor and university president Basil Manly declared that slavery was "a kind of Patriarchal Government." God, Manly told slaveholders, "has made you their masters—placed them under your protection" and "made you their guardians, the conservators of their lives and happiness."[43] Mississippi Methodist Thomas C. Thornton maintained that masters accepted slaves as "a trust, placed by the Providence of God in the hands of southerners, and every master is called to discharge his duties with forbearance, patience, and fidelity."[44]

That the triumph of paternalism in the old Southwest occurred after the abolition mail campaign of 1835 is strongly indicated by "before-and-after" reports from the region. Louisiana pastor Tim Flint, who traveled extensively through the old Southwest, later recalled that prior to the abolition attack of the 1830s, most of the planters in the region "admitted that slavery was an evil" but insisted that "the evil must go off as it came on, by a slow and gradual method."[45] Mississippi Methodist pastor John Jones shared Flint's assessment of pre-1835 white opinion in the region, noting that before 1830, most Mississippi evangelicals judged slavery a "great social, political and religious evil" and reasoned that while "it had to be endured for the present," it "ought, as soon as possible[,] be removed."[46]

Jones' own evolution on the issue reflected that of the region. Before his conversion to the evangelical cause, Jones harbored no reservations about slavery. Before he embraced religion, Jones recalled, he "thought it was right for us to have as many of them [slaves] as we could get." Jones admitted that he "took a pleasure in the government of them, even when I had to use some violence to keep them in subjection." When he converted to Methodism, however, Jones began "to look on slavery as a great moral evil," and he wrote and spoke of the "curse of negro slavery." Jones went so far as to claim that "few professors of Christianity," whether from the "laity or clergy," ever even thought "of attempting the justification of African Slavery...from Holy Scripture" prior to the 1830s. During the 1830s, however, the terms of debate with opponents of slavery changed. Jones familiarized himself with Smylie's defense of slavery, and in 1840 Jones wrote in his journal, "More mature experience and a more thorough examination of the whole subject ha[ve] greatly modified my views on slavery."[47]

Another evangelical Methodist, William Winans, the religious leader of the colonization movement in Mississippi, followed a similar path in his views on slavery. Before his evangelical conversion, the Pennsylvania-born Winans considered blacks "an inferior race of human beings." After his conversion, Winans arrived in the Mississippi Territory in 1810 and quickly became one of the most effective evangelical preachers in the area. Early in his career, Winans' views ran strongly toward egalitarian positions, and he demonstrated a willingness to chastise masters who mistreated their slaves. God, Winans decided, was "no respecter of persons or color or condition." Winans responded to this insight by throwing himself aggressively into a ministry to slaves in southwestern Mississippi. During this ministry, Winans observed firsthand the "deep and ardent" piety of many slaves, whom the evangelist confidently declared "children of God by faith, and heirs to the promise of life eternal through Christ Jesus." Late in the 1820s, Winans emerged as the most active champion of colonization in Mississippi, and he ultimately became one of the key organizers of a modestly successful colonization society centered in Natchez. Winans remained a champion of colonization well into the 1830s, even after the new abolitionist attack on slaveholders destroyed most of whatever support the colonization movement had enjoyed in Mississippi. Yet in an 1838 exchange of letters with abolitionist Gerrit Smith, a frustrated Winans complained bitterly that "by disgusting the white man against every measure" that advanced the cause of gradual emancipation, the radical abolitionists had actually strengthened slavery in the region. Winans finally endorsed slavery openly in the early 1840s in the face of growing public hostility toward colonization.[48]

Alabama's Basil Manly had also changed his views on slavery over time. As a young man in 1821, the North Carolina native had referred to slavery as an "evil" under which the nation had "long groaned," and he urged serious consideration of colonization as a gradual remedy.[49] Educated with the slaveholding gentry at South Carolina College, where he finished at the top of his class, Manly was ordained as a Baptist minister soon after his graduation, and he quickly accepted a congregation in Edgefield, where he ignited a successful revival. His work there attracted the attention of an aging Richard Furman, who recommended Manly as his successor at First Baptist in Charleston. In 1826, Manly followed Furman as senior pastor of First Baptist, where he served for eleven years before assuming the presidency of the University of Alabama in 1837. Over time, Manly abandoned his insistence that slavery was an evil and his sympathy for colonization diminished as he emerged as a staunch advocate of paternalism, including Charles Jones' plans for the systematic religious instruction of slaves, in both Charleston and Alabama. Late in his career Manly became a strong advocate of secession.[50]

The circumstances surrounding James Smylie's development of an avowedly proslavery argument during the 1830s also revealed much about the process of the ideological reconfiguration of slavery in the old Southwest. Born in North Carolina and educated at David Caldwell's log college in the Piedmont, Smylie moved to the Mississippi Territory in 1806. By 1809, the Presbyterian minister had put down roots in Amite, a cotton-growing county in southwestern Mississippi. Over time, Smylie emerged as one of the most influential pastors in the region, founding Bible and literary societies, establishing a school for the children of the wealthy Natchez elite, and being courted by prominent politicians eager for a sign of favor. From his "weight of character" and knowledge of the Bible and church law, one biographer claimed, Smylie exerted "magisterial" influence over the southwestern portion of Mississippi. Moreover, Smylie enjoyed material success as well as professional acclaim. By 1830, Smylie owned thirteen slaves and a substantial cotton farm, and by 1840 he owned thirty slaves, establishing himself as a successful planter as well as a forceful preacher.[51]

During the early 1830s, many Mississippi clergy still favored gradual emancipation and colonization, but Smylie undertook a lengthy study of the Bible in an effort to fathom its instruction on the subject of slavery. As a result of that study, Smylie crafted a sermon defending slavery as justified by scripture. He decided to give the sermon at the affluent Presbyterian church in the cotton market town of Port Gibson, but even at an elite church in the heart of Mississippi's first cotton belt, Smylie's sermon went further toward calling slavery a biblically sanctioned positive good than the congregation had expected to hear, and it received mixed reviews initially. In fact, Smylie's sermon "gave great offense" to some in attendance, and many of his fellow pastors urged him "to preach that sermon no more."[52] But when Ohio's Chillicothe Presbytery challenged the Mississippi Presbytery by sending it an abolition petition in 1835, Smylie quickly revised his much-criticized sermon into a systematic response to the Chillicothe petition. The Mississippi presbytery still found Smylie's response too strong in its defense of slavery as a scriptural institution and refused to adopt it as the presbytery's official response. Undeterred, Smylie published the response privately in pamphlet form in 1836, expecting further criticism from his fellow Christians in the region. Indeed, as he awaited publication of the pamphlet, Smylie predicted that he would "be kicked out of the synagogue of Presbyterians, Baptists, Methodists and Episcopalians so soon as it makes its appearance."[53] Once the pamphlet appeared, however, it quickly gained widespread acclaim in the lower South. The religious press hailed the pamphlet, reporting that it enjoyed "an almost unbounded popularity wherever it is read." "The south," the *Christian Herald* maintained, "can do no less than take up Mr. Smylie's latest edition without delay." Smylie embraced the unexpected warmth of the reception.[54] "Contrary to my fears," Smylie reported, "my Methodist, Presbyterian, Episcopalian and Baptist brethren, (so far as I have heard), cordially approve of the doctrines of the pamphlet."[55]

The abolition petition and mail campaigns of 1835 had paved the way for a very different response to Smylie's pamphlet than the author expected. Soon after the pamphlet appeared and received kudos, the Baptist and Methodist press and clergy joined Smylie in defending slavery against the bold new abolitionist attack. Even William Winans defended the meliorative capacity of paternalism against abolitionists, whom he denounced as "incendiaries, cutthroats" and "hydra-headed monsters of inhumanity." A Methodist circuit rider in Mississippi endorsed the biblical defense of slavery, declaring that "slavery as it now exists in the South" (that is, slavery characterized by paternalism) was "not a sin." One devout evangelical layman in Mississippi, who recognized that the clergy had increasingly taken the lead in configuring the South's new defense of slavery, found himself pressured to leave his church by other members of the congregation because he still held the view that "slavery is a great evil."[56] The dramatic shift in clerical opinion, James Smylie believed, had a "prodigious" impact on larger social attitudes in the region, because the pulpit was "like the lever and fulcrum of the ancient Archemedes—it is competent to move the world."[57]

The clergy was certainly well positioned to shape public opinion on slavery in the lower South, and by the late 1840s the shift had proceeded so far that one white Mississippian complained that too much hegemony had been achieved in the state. In 1848, Meadville's Jonathan P. Stewart told a friend that local opinion judged "every man" an "abolitionist who would not agree...that slavery was initiated by our Creator for the benefit of the African, that by slavery the African was civilized and Christianized, [and] that the African race is inferior to the white in intellect and...designed by their Creator for slaves." Stewart demurred from the new consensus. He still considered slavery an "evil" but considered it "a greater evil to free them and leave them amongst us." Stewart thought that the "races cannot exist together as equal, one must be subservient to the other," and admitted that "of course I am in favor of mine maintaining the ascendancy."[58]

All across the lower South, champions of paternalism paired their defense of the ideology and its practice as a means of meliorating the evils of slavery with a complementary insistence that masters take their duties as paternalists seriously. The southern clergy assumed a prominent role in holding slaveholders' feet to the fire on the matter of fulfilling the paternalist's obligations. Mississippi Methodist Thomas Thornton maintained that it was the responsibility of the master and the master's community to work tirelessly for the amelioration of the harsh conditions of slavery just as it was the duty of the slave to work tirelessly for the master's profit. South Carolina Baptist Richard Fuller believed that it was an important part of his calling as a pastor to slaveholders "to excite masters to a sense of their fearful responsibilities, and to the discharge of their solemn duties." Fuller insisted that Christian stewardship placed a heavy responsibility on masters, and he explicitly analogized the responsibilities of masters with those of parents. The "possession of power is, in itself, neither good nor evil," Fuller claimed, though he rebuked masters for the "frequent and shameful abuse" of their power. Fuller reminded masters that they also had a master in Heaven. But despite his ready admission that too many masters abused their power, Fuller nonetheless believed that "God sees here the sincerest friends of the African race," who would never "stint our benevolence" toward slaves. Alabama Baptist Basil Manly admonished slaveholders to make "proper regulations" with regard to slave work, to ensure that slave discipline displayed a "due mixture of firmness and gentleness," and to provide their slaves with an opportunity to "receive religious instruction" and to worship.[59]

From the liturgical side of the clerical divide, Episcopal rector George Freeman of North Carolina reminded masters that they had a tremendous personal responsibility to Christianize their slaves because slaveholders also "have a master in heaven." Freeman sharply chastised masters for not paying enough attention to the spiritual well-being of slaves. Since slaves were so dependent on whites, Freeman argued, masters must be made "more directly responsible for their moral and religious improvement." Freeman urged masters to become just as attentive to the religious instruction of their slaves as of their children. "And are we not," Freeman asked, "God's schoolmasters, employed to rule over and instruct our respective families and households, charged with the high duty of training up children for his kingdom?" He also challenged masters to treat their slaves as "Christian parents" would treat their children, urging them to employ a "mild and merciful discipline" of slaves and telling them that slaves should not be "unduly" or "immoderately" punished. The North Carolina Episcopalian warned that "cruelty, selfishness and even indifference toward them will be visited by Almighty justice with exact and unsparing vengeance." As a rule, advocates of paternalism, and especially members of the clergy, expected paternalism to prevail in practice as well as in theory. They saw paternalism as a way of life and not merely an ideological shield.[60]

A shared commitment to paternalism as an ideology of slaveholding brought together many white southerners who otherwise differed on important religious and political questions. In fact, an embrace of paternalism as an ideology did not even require agreement on all matters closely related to slavery. Many paternalists still thought slavery an evil, if a necessary one, while others came to see it as a positive good. Some thought paternalism smoothed the way for perpetual slavery; others thought paternalism simply the best meliorative course to take on the long, slow road to a distant emancipation. James Hammond, who would later declare the world a servant to King Cotton, conceded as late as 1845, "If you were to ask me whether I am an advocate of Slavery in the abstract, I should probably answer that I am not."[61] Presbyterian Rufus Bailey was more emphatic. He believed slavery in the "abstract" to be "wrong," and even after the abolition mail campaign soured the southern mood in 1835, Bailey maintained that "most Christians would require a distinction to be made between the right of slavery in the abstract and the 'right' as applied to the circumstances in which they are now placed, and would answer differently between the two cases." Bailey conceded that South Carolina governor George McDuffie and former governor Stephen Miller considered slavery "a social blessing," and he recognized that there was "a large class" in the South "who think it justifiable on political, social and religious grounds, [and] necessary to the prosperity of the country, and thus it must be perpetuated." But the Palmetto Presbyterian did not share this view and did not believe it a view that was "extensively entertained" across the South. Bailey contended that "there is also a numerous class, who would be glad to see the system terminated," and "who have been anxiously looking for some practicable scheme of emancipation, in which the real good of the slave and the safety of the country, should be consulted." Bailey argued that the "reflecting" part of the white community in the South remained sympathetic to the idea of colonizing free blacks but would support freeing and colonizing slaves only if masters were compensated. But, in Bailey's view, while many southern whites still saw slavery as an "evil," few saw it as a personal sin that demanded immediate renunciation by slaveholders. "The consciences of the holders are entirely at ease," Bailey asserted. "Bible Christians" in the South, he concluded, encountered little "difficulty on that point."[62] Baptist Richard Fuller, who considered himself a reluctant "apologist" for "an institution transmitted to us by former generations," lamented the existence of slavery and pledged that he was "willing to make greater sacrifices than any abolitionist" for the "extinction" of slavery "if the true cause of humanity would be thus advanced." But for all his expressed reservations about slavery, Fuller concluded that slavery would be perpetual because prospects for emancipation were "surrounded and encumbered with peculiar difficulties" and because slaves in the South were of a "distinct race."[63]

Barnwell planter Edmund Bellinger reasoned his way to the conclusion that, whether or not slavery was wrong, it must be "perpetual." He acknowledged that southern opinion on slavery, including South Carolina opinion, remained too divided to speak with one voice on the subject. He recognized that "some" southerners still considered slavery "an evil, though a necessary evil," and as a "wrong though an unavoidable wrong." But the former nullifier endorsed perpetual slavery because he saw no way to end slavery consistent with the safety and prosperity of the region's whites. He dismissed colonization as the "splendid scheme of fanaticism." The loss of slave labor, Bellinger maintained, would prove "utter ruin to our staple commodity." Moreover, the Barnwell planter argued, colonization would gradually weaken the South politically by reducing its representation in Congress. If colonization was an impractical scheme, Bellinger judged compensated emancipation too expensive. "What treasury on earth could compensate the planter of the South for slave labor?" Bellinger asked. If blacks could not be colonized or freed with full compensation to their owners, Bellinger reasoned, they must remain enslaved. Yet as he spoke and wrote to an anxious public in 1835, Bellinger recognized that his argument for perpetual slavery would catch many listeners and readers by surprise. While the North as a whole opposed the idea of immediate emancipation, Bellinger reasoned, most northerners took it for granted that "Emancipation is an object as much desired by the South as the North provided it be gradual." But Bellinger had personally decided that "slavery is too deeply rooted to be eradicated," and he believed that more and more southerners were beginning to reach the same conclusion.[64]

Presbyterian James Thornwell expressed a more balanced view. He conceded that slavery "is inconsistent with a perfect state." That slavery "is not absolutely a good—a blessing," Thornwell contended, even "the most strenuous defender of slavery ought not permit himself to deny." Instead, the Old South's leading theological defender of slavery came close to conceding one of the immediate abolitionists' most basic points. "Slavery is part of the curse which sin has introduced into the world," Thornwell explained. It existed as a "badge" of the "fallen world," one visited upon humans by the power of evil as a result of the "fall." But slavery "must cease to exist," Thornwell contended, only when all sin had been perfected. Thus he concluded "that there will be no bondage in heaven."[65] Thornwell saw slavery as not so perpetual as to extend into eternity, but he appeared to doubt it could end before the Day of Judgment. Later, Benjamin Morgan Palmer Jr., a Thornwell protégé and prominent Presbyterian pastor, reported that on the eve of the Civil War Thornwell had confided to him that the South should begin to end slavery with a program of gradual emancipation, but Thornwell never aired that view to the public.[66]

But however they felt about slavery in a larger sense, champions of paternalism uniformly agreed that the radical abolitionist assault on slavery was malicious and that southerners needed to stand united in the face of the assault. Bailey contended that no one in the South advocated immediate abolition, and he warned northerners that white southerners would oppose immediate abolition at the threshold and to the last man. He noted that abolitionists had destroyed the old divisions between Unionists and nullifiers in South Carolina. The nullification campaign had left South Carolina bitterly divided, Bailey maintained, but by 1835 unanimity existed in opposition to the abolitionists. Southern support for freedom of speech evaporated, Bailey argued, only when the South was faced with terrorists using free speech to encourage insurrection in the region. Anticipating Justice Oliver

Wendell Holmes' argument that no one had a right to yell "fire" in a crowded theater, Bailey asserted that abolitionists had no right to cry "insurrection" in a community of slaves.[67] Richard Fuller focused on the malevolent consequences of abolitionist success, arguing that "immediate and unconditional abolition would be a revolution involving the entire South in ruin; breaking up all social order and safety; and...inflicting on the slaves themselves irreparable mischief." Emancipation, the South Carolina Baptist claimed, would convert slaves "from a contented and cheerful peasantry, into a horde of outlaws, a multitude of paupers...degraded and outcast from the kindred and privileges of the superior caste."[68] In 1841, Mississippi's Thomas Thornton announced that "if abolitionism is to thrust its blazing torches, fire-brands and death into our midst, This Union of the States is dissolved as sure as there is a God in heaven."[69] More than a decade after the abolition mail campaign began, Presbyterian James Thornwell blasted the abolitionists for their unrestrained assault on the South. Radical abolitionists, the Presbyterian theologian maintained, "shunned" southern society "as scrupulously as if the taint of leprosy adhered to Us." The "insane fury of philanthropy," he continued, had even "aimed at stirring up insurrection in our midst." Paternalism promoted the cause of unity against the abolitionists just as radical abolition had enhanced the appeal of paternalism among southern slaveholders.[70]

As THE LOWER SOUTH'S JOURNEY toward a full ideological reconfiguration of slavery gained momentum, South Carolina's John C. Calhoun articulated an especially coherent version of the new proslavery argument in the nation's capital.[71] In a speech to Congress in 1838, Calhoun stunned the Senate by praising slavery unequivocally as "a great political institution, essential to the peace and existence of one-half this Union." Calhoun's aggressive defense of slavery was grounded in racial difference. When he called slavery a "a great good," Calhoun qualified his assertion by insisting that he had not "pronounced slavery in the abstract a good" but rather judged slavery a good where "a civilized race and a race of a different description are brought together."[72] But, while grounding his ideological defense of slavery in race, Calhoun went on to explain both why slavery served to guarantee republican independence and equality among whites and how paternalism gave slavery a humanitarian foundation.

"Every plantation is a little community with the master at its head," Calhoun told the Senate, "who concentrates in himself the united interests of capital and labor, of which he is the common representative." Calhoun's prototypical plantation stood not merely as an extended household but as a "little community." The master served not simply as head of the household but as steward of the larger community. As a rural patriarch or local notable, the master bore primary responsibility for household and community. As the "common representative" of all household dependents, the slaveholder provided the economic, moral, and familial organization that held the "little community" together. While Calhoun's particular variant of paternalism included no overt reference to spiritual responsibility or bonds of piety, his portrait of a slaveholding community was a domestic one. The responsibilities of the family patriarch or community elder rested with the slave master.

With his metaphor of plantations as "little communities," Calhoun tied the defense of slavery to the emerging concept of "domesticity." The concept of domesticity gained degrees of acceptance in both North and South during the market revolution as a means of protecting the republican household from the strains and depredations imposed by the market economy. Historian John Ashworth has argued that in the North the concept of the family as a haven in a heartless world gained ground directly in proportion to the spread of wage labor in the region. The emergence of wage labor both removed production from the household and forced household members to sell their labor power in the market as a commodity, exposing wage workers to the vulnerability of market fluctuations. Republican theorists had long held that wage labor fostered dangerous dependencies among republican citizens. Domesticity, however, offered a means of damping the negative effects of wage labor. A nurturing family could rekindle or restore virtues eroded by the workplace grind or market competition. The household served as a respite from and reinforcement against the corruptions of the market as well as the temptations of the tavern and bawdy house. Thus the free-labor ideology gradually gained popularity in the North during the late antebellum era precisely because it portrayed slavery, and particularly the family-separating slave trade, as the enemy of domesticity.[73]

Calhoun's ideological reconfiguration of slavery stretched beyond religious sentiments valuing the family to place the role of a domestic labor system at the center of the justification for slavery. In Calhoun's model of domesticity, paternalism became a vital compound lubricating the fulcrum of master-slave relations, replacing the tension between labor and capital that existed in free-labor societies. Thus slavery meliorated by paternalism provided the entire society with a domestic refuge from capitalist class conflict. Extending his model further, Calhoun portrayed the entire South as an aggregate of these little communities. Calhoun's South stood as a loosely knit collection of independent communities serving as extended households. Collectively, these extended households effectively domesticated not only slavery but the entire South. These "small communities aggregated," Calhoun maintained, "make the State in all, whose action, labor and capital is equally represented and perfectly harmonized." Slavery, if properly understood, served as a bastion of domestic defense against both labor strife and capitalist depredation, a large gain, in Calhoun's view, when purchased at the small price of vigilance against slave revolt.[74]

Thus, in the lower South, advocates of paternalism gradually fashioned a justification of slavery that rendered it as a domestic institution, one largely defined and managed within the household and governed (in theory if not in practice) by a familial ethos. Slavery, in Calhoun's view, kept the potentially volatile management of labor inside the paternalistic household, making it a subject of domestic rather than public concern. Thus Calhoun saw domestic slavery both as a paternalistic institution and as a bulwark for republican liberty. It protected not only common whites but the entire South against the growing strife between labor and capital. Calhoun thought domestic values progressed in inverse proportion to a society's reliance on wage labor. Slavery, an institution dating to antiquity and resting on racial difference, offered a solution not only to the ancient republican anxiety, dependence, but also to the most modern of social problems, class conflict.[75]

But even in the late 1830s, such affirmative defenses of slavery still alarmed whites in large portions of the upper South. There, at least outside of Southside Virginia and a few other areas with proportionately large slave populations, the venerable tradition of apologetic defenses of slavery as a necessary evil yielded only gradually, if at all, to bold assertions that slavery was a positive good or a "great political institution." These persistent tensions between upper and lower South were revealed in capsule form by an incident on the floor of the United States Senate in 1837. In an impromptu exchange, Virginia senator William Cabell Rives, a self-styled Madisonian and carrier of the upper South tradition, challenged Calhoun, the self-appointed political strategist for the lower South, and his new ideological justification of slavery. During a debate over the handling of the abolition petitions, Rives averred that while he accepted slavery as an "existing institution," he differed from Calhoun over the issue of "slavery in the abstract." Calhoun quickly interrupted, denying that he had ever "pronounced slavery in the abstract a good," but rather claiming that he defended it as "a good where a civilized race and a race of a different description are brought together."[76] Calhoun countered by asking Rives if he considered slavery a "good." The Virginian replied that he believed slavery "a misfortune and an evil in all circumstances, though in some, it might be the lesser evil." In his larger argument, Rives denounced Calhoun's argument as a "new school" of proslavery. Rives insisted that "it never entered" the minds of the founders to contend that "domestic slavery was a positive good—a great good," and because Rives had worked closely with both Jefferson and Madison, his opinion on the matter carried some weight. Claiming the great tradition of "Washington, Jefferson, Madison, Marshall, the brightest names of my own state" in "lamenting the existence of slavery as a misfortune and evil to the country," Rives ridiculed Calhoun's contention "that slavery is a positive good; that it is inseparable from the condition of man,...and that it is even an essential ingredient in republican government."[77]

Rives stood in 1837 as a latter-day exemplar of the upper South's legitimate if truncated antislavery tradition, which declined to defend slavery as anything but the least of many evils even as it did comparatively little to find a way to remedy the evil. Calhoun's defense of slavery as a positive good alarmed upper South moderates, including Rives, who continued to hope that their region could gradually whiten itself through manumission, colonization, and the sale of slaves to the lower South. In contrast, Calhoun articulated an emerging lower South belief that racially defined slavery for blacks, slavery rendered humane by paternalism, served as the best guarantor of democracy and opportunity among whites. Like the many similar proslavery arguments that followed, Calhoun reversed the Jeffersonian formulation of slavery as a threat to republican values.[78] Jefferson, and others following in his footsteps, had seen racial separation, which he thought could be achieved in North America through colonization, as the key to self-rule for both races. Whites could enjoy republican government on the new American continent and repatriated blacks could help establish self-government for blacks on African soil.[79] Calhoun, speaking more than a decade after Jefferson's death and with a longer and closer view of the impact of the cotton revolution on the lower South, saw the enslavement of blacks as the lasting foundation for the white freedom. For Calhoun, and for much of the lower South, racial slavery replaced racial separation as the key to the future of republican liberty. Moreover, where Jefferson thought slavery corrupted the republican character by imbuing whites with a penchant for aristocratic mastery, Calhoun believed that domestic slavery protected republican society by freeing common whites from the fear of the abject dependency generated by free-labor capitalism, and it insulated propertied whites, yeoman as well as planter, from the threat of proletarian revolution and reprisal.

By the end of the 1830s, the ideological reconfiguration of slavery in the lower South was nearing completion. Once seen as the root of corruption and hypocrisy in republican society, racial slavery, properly mitigated by paternalism, was acclaimed the surest foundation of an egalitarian republicanism crafted for whites only. And, according to theory, if paternalism was properly and thoroughly applied, this was accomplished with minimum threat to white safety.[80]

THE FULLNESS OF PATERNALISM'S TRIUMPH, and an important measure of the success of the lower South's ideological reconfiguration of slavery, is perhaps best revealed by a meeting called by the planter and religious elite of the South Carolina Lowcountry in May 1845 for the purpose of exchanging views on the religious instruction of slaves. The "considerable number of gentlemen" invited to the meeting were chosen for their "long continued personal exertions" in this particular "department of benevolence."[81] The great planters and prominent clergy of the Carolina Lowcountry who organized the meeting invited only two "gentlemen" from beyond the state's borders, Charles Jones and Thomas Clay, the two Georgians denounced a decade earlier by Whitemarsh Seabrook and other opponents of paternalism for their keen interest in the religious instruction of slaves. Clay and Jones decided to attend, and William McWhir, an eighty-six-year-old Presbyterian pastor who had once been Charles Jones' teacher, accompanied them at Jones' request. Their Charleston hosts were an impressive lot, a who's who of the Lowcountry's planter and clerical elite. Among the clergy who attended the meeting were Stephen Elliott, the well-liked Episcopal bishop, William Barnwell, pastor of St. Peter's Episcopal church,

Beaufort Baptist pastor Richard Fuller, Presbyterians Thomas Smyth of Charleston's Second Presbyterian Church and *Charleston Observer* editor Benjamin Gildersleeve, along with William Capers, the Methodist bishop who had taken the lead in that denomination's extensive mission to the slaves. The politicians in attendance were of equal prominence. The political cohort included United States senator Daniel Huger and former secretary of war Joel Poinsett (both nullification-era Unionists), former nullifier and secession radical Robert Barnwell Rhett, a James Island planter, Rhett's more cautious cousin Robert Barnwell, the president of South Carolina College, Christopher Memminger, a Charleston lawyer and future Confederate secretary of the treasury, and others. Joining them were a number of prominent planters and Christian lay leaders, including Thomas P. Alston, Thomas Grimké, Charles Lowndes, Charles Cotesworth Pinckney, and Daniel Ravenel.[82]

The group met for three full days, May 13–15, 1845, at the Depository on Chalmers Street, just a few blocks away from the city's active slave market. On the first day of the meeting, Daniel Huger, Robert Barnwell Rhett, Robert Barnwell, William Barnwell, Episcopal pastors Stuart Hanckel and John Clarkson, botanist Daniel Ravenel, and J. Dyson participated in an "animated discussion" on the religious instruction of slaves. That evening N. R. Middleton, Robert Barnwell Rhett, and others spoke about their extensive efforts, modeled after those of Georgia planter Thomas Clay, to instruct slaves on their plantations. On the second day, after a forceful introduction by Daniel Huger, Richard Fuller and Charles Jones spoke about the religious instruction of slaves.[83] Reports termed Jones' remarks an "impressive" address that reaffirmed his reputation as the leader of the mission to the slaves. In the *Charleston Observer*, Basil Gildersleeve declared that Jones' opinions on the religious instruction of slaves carry "more weight" than anyone else's "with the entire Christian community of every denomination."[84]

Through a circular letter, the meeting's organizers had solicited letters from clergymen and prominent planters around South Carolina and the South. The letter asked pastors and planters for extensive information about the religious instruction of slaves in their area, about the number of slaves who worshiped, about ministers and teachers involved with the instruction of slaves, about the methods of such instruction, and about the impact of such instruction on slave behavior and on "the discipline of plantations." In return, they received some forty-four replies from twenty different districts in South Carolina and seventeen letters from eight different slaveholding states, as well as notices from various leading ecclesiastical bodies of various denominations. Partially as a tribute to Jones, the meeting designated the Georgia pastor to prepare the official report of the proceedings, a report that would chronicle the triumph of paternalism in the lower South. In July 1845, a standing committee of ten designated by the meeting's participants approved the report drafted by Jones and published it in pamphlet form.[85]

The final report, the standing committee thought, revealed "the concern" for "the religious and moral improvement of our coloured population," a concern rising from "religious sentiment" that had become "deeply and extensively felt." The movement had attracted the support and cooperation of "many persons far distant from each other" and "enlisted the efforts of Christians of various denominations." The committee believed that it had "good ground for confidence that the work will prosper" and become "more and more extended." The importance of the religious instruction of slaves, the report held, grew out of the "intimate connection" of such efforts "with the soundness of that public opinion" which in slaveholding states mattered as much as law in influencing the relations between master and slave. Laws had little effect on "the minutiae of plantation management," the report admitted, and hence failed "to secure to the slave that which is just and equal" or to "embrace the various good which the master's position enables and inclines him to dispose."[86]

Slavery, the report contended, was an institution that was largely "patriarchal in character." Proper management of slaves sometimes demanded "firmness of authority" but "oftener claims the exercise of the higher and milder virtues of Christian kindness." Out of this relationship emerged a prevailing public opinion, "a common law of sentiment," which, the committee argued, "influences and controls" the "general management of our negro population." In other words, the Christian paternalists who gathered in Charleston in May 1845 recognized that they had been, and to some extent still were, in a struggle for hegemony with other ideologies of slaveholding and other systems of slave management. They recognized the dominant public opinion, which they cleverly labeled the "common law of sentiment," as the best measure of the influence of any given set of ideas. Once accepted by the "common law of sentiment" as the prevailing ethos, Christian paternalism would extend its influence across space and over time.[87]

Moreover, these paternalists were willing to seek dominance one heart and one soul at a time. "A good man makes a valuable contribution to society in the mere influence of character," the report from the Charleston meeting asserted. "He is the center of kind affections which glow around him, and warm into life the latent sympathies of others." The key was to increase the number of such men. "In proportions as such men are multiplied," the report argued, "will their modes of thinking and acting be infused into general sentiment."[88]

The report also held that economic matters should not be separated from spiritual ones and that "wise management" of slaves must "combine kindness with discipline" with the "aim of making labour effective and the labourer happy." By seeking the "reform" of the "moral being" of both slave and master, the report claimed, Christian paternalism could produce a "mild, regular and beneficial" discipline "to master and slave" which might "so change the character of persons thus taught" as to yield "a change for the better in the government or discipline" of slaves. Ultimately the influence of a Gospel-based paternalism might be that end so desired by all: a "tendency to supercede [*sic*] the law without us by substituting a law within us."[89] The substance of the letters received by the committee in response to its circular tended to confirm the energy and activity with which the Christian mission to the slaves was being conducted in the 1840s. To be sure, all the responses were from either pastors known to be interested in the work of religious instruction or slaveholders who were active laymen in various denominations. As a result, the responses were likely to applaud the work and perhaps even exaggerate its success. Nonetheless, the replies were remarkable for their virtual unanimity on certain points. Almost all responders agreed that they encountered virtually no opposition in their efforts to take religious instruction to the slaves. Almost all slaveholders allowed local clergy access to their slaves; most plantations were open to evening instruction; many even offered stations or chapels for that purpose. Virtually no respondent mentioned any interference or harassment from local authorities. In only a decade, the hostile and suspicious mood of 1835 had evaporated. The opposition to paternalism was now on the defensive; the movement's champions were on the march.[90]

Of all the information gathered from responses to the circular letter, arguably the most crucial in terms of gauging how paternalism, with its emphasis on the religious instruction of slaves, was faring, and might fare in the near future, with the "common law of sentiment" in the lower South lay in the answers to the queries about how the religious instruction of slaves had affected slave behavior and slave discipline. From the South Carolina Upcountry, Greenville's Thomas Brockman noted a "marked difference between those who are religiously brought up and those that are not," adding that "the preaching of the gospel to negroes" was "of incalculable value to them." Spartanburg Methodist James Edward Henry praised the "beneficial effects" of "religious instruction on the hearts and minds of the blacks," asserting that it had rendered them "more honest, truthful, moral and well behaved" as well as more "devoted to their master's interests" than before. Moreover, Henry claimed that there was as "little hypocrisy" among slave Christians as "among the same number of whites." From the eastern Upcountry, York District Presbyterian John Blair reported that "for the last ten or twelve years there had been a remarkable improvement in the moral and religious character of our negroes." The benefits of religious training were especially evident in the town of Yorkville, Blair claimed, where blacks "who have received instruction in reading and religious training from their masters and mistresses" had become "qualified" to lead family worship. An ARP pastor from Chester reported that nearly two dozen black church members could read and that many others were learning, suggesting that the 1834 ban on teaching slaves to read had become a dead letter in some parts of the state. Abbeville Presbyterian James Gilliam, himself a slave owner, declared that the "deeper the piety of the slave, the more valuable is he in every sense of the word."[91]

From the Pee Dee region, a Marlboro District report held that plantations "under religious instruction are more easily governed than those that are not." Similarly, a Darlington District report claimed that over "ten or fifteen years the standard of our negro character has been much elevated—from the influence of religion on the character of both master and servant." The "truth is," the report claimed, the slaves' "nature is as susceptible of improvement as our own." Also from Marlboro,

Methodist Nathan Ware reported that there had been an "astonishing improvement within ten years past" in the behavior of slaves in the district. "We have few runaways," Ware claimed, "and corporeal [*sic*] punishment is but seldom resorted to."[92]

In the Lowcountry, Georgetown planter John Tucker, who invited both Episcopal and Methodist services on his plantation, observed that both "Experience and observation" had "fully taught me the very great benefit of the religious training and instruction of the negroes." From St. Andrew's parish, Episcopal pastor N. R. Middleton reported that religious instruction had "weakened" the "vicious habits" of slaves and "awakened" their "moral sense." Middleton held that "negroes are not what some would make them out to be; they are capable of good feelings, and being influenced by good principles." From James Island, planter John Rivers reported that the "most orderly negroes" are "those connected with the church." Rivers had no doubt that "religious instruction promotes the discipline and subordination on plantations." Charleston planter J. Grimké Drayton complained that those who disparaged the "piety of our negroes" as nothing more than "Psalm-singing and animal excitement" were simply dead wrong. Drayton insisted that he had "never seen clearer examples of undoubting faith" than among his slaves. Presbyterian Edward Palmer reported from Walterboro that after the work of some fourteen years "the practicability of moral elevation and spiritual improvement on the part of the slave is . . . beyond question."[93]

Though fewer in number and less fulsome in detail, reports from other states affirmed the responses from around South Carolina. A letter from Virginia reported that those slaves "who have made the greatest progress in the knowledge of the Scriptures, are, in the same proportion, the best servants." Thomas Clay, reporting on conditions in Bryan County, Georgia, held that his work had been rewarded with improved behavior by slaves but argued that for the system to have "truly and permanently beneficial" effects on plantation life, masters "must not only provide that his people be religiously instructed, but he must manage them on those very principles he wishes them to govern themselves by." Charles Jones reported in detail on his work in Liberty County and declared that slaves in his county had grown more easily managed, more "steadfast in their married relations," and "more careful of character." Reports from Alabama were also encouraging, touting Sabbath school activity there, explaining that Basil Manly had proven a sincere friend to the movement, giving "three discourses" of "great effect" on the subject within a matter of months."[94]

Based on the information received in response to the circular letter, the committee concluded that the responses "breathe a devotion to the cause" in South Carolina and Georgia, and they reasoned that the "same devotion and activity" probably existed throughout the South. If all voices were heard, the committee concluded, the voices "would sound of many waters, and their multitude and their labors would exceed our most sanguine expectations." In "looking back over fifteen years," the committee proclaimed, "we rejoice with gratitude at the progress which the work has made." The "truth is not to be disguised," the committee exulted. "The leaven hid in three measures of meal has been silently and powerfully pervading the mass. From Maryland to Texas, and from the Atlantic to the Ohio,...the great duty is urged and acknowledged; and feeling lives in action." All Christian denominations were "entering the field," which was "wide enough for all." Moreover, Charles Jones and the reporting committee concluded that the religious instruction of slaves, which they saw as "THE GREAT DUTY," had become established as the "THE FIXED, THE SETTLED POLICY OF THE SOUTH" (emphasis in original). The committee believed that "God has so moved (and will continue to move) upon both the understanding and consciences of our Christian citizens, and so opened the door of access to the negroes, and so demonstrated by his blessing his regard for the work, that we can never go back. The Flood had fairly set in...the stream will rise higher and higher and flow with a current that must sweep everything away before it."[95]

Yet almost as important as the actions of the 1845 gathering or the details of its report was the mere holding of the meeting. It was, after all, a great conference of Lowcountry paternalists with a focus on the religious instruction of slaves. Such a meeting would have been unthinkable a decade earlier. The city that was formerly the home of fierce opposition to the religious instruction of slaves had apparently been won over to the paternalist cause. By the mid-1840s, slaveholding Charleston saw the triumph of Protestant Christianity and the ideology of paternalism it espoused as a realist's justification of slavery and not as a softhearted reformer's threat to it. Paternalism was no longer an insurgent ideology but the slaveholders' orthodoxy. Its triumph affirmed and completed the ideological reconfiguration of slavery in the lower South.

THE TRIUMPH OF PATERNALISM as the dominant ideology of slaveholders completed the third and final leg of the ideological reconfiguration of slavery in the lower South. The success of this reconfiguration established racial difference, egalitarianism (for whites only), and paternalism as ideological staples of the Old South, and these staples flourished, albeit in different form, not only through the remaining antebellum years but after emancipation and the collapse of the Confederacy as well.

White southerners had leaned heavily on race to explain much about southern slavery since the early colonial era, but the ideological reconfiguration of the 1830s insisted that race was the key difference among all others, marking a significant turning point in white attitudes in the region. Race mattered; little else did. This singular emphasis on racial difference not only established race as the primary basis for social distinction, shoving character, wealth, education, and property ownership into the background, but it also became a vehicle for denigrating black potential in ways that suggested black subordination should be perpetual. This denigration of black potential, and the certainty with which it was often pronounced, stood in marked contrast to earlier ambivalent and uncertain white assessments of such potential. Moreover, in the realm of public ideology, the Jacksonian flattening of other social and economic differences among white men in favor of a single racial divide rendered the imperatives and prerogatives of whiteness clear and compelling, and gave a harder, uglier, and more permanent edge to the idea of racial difference.

The new ideological configuration's emphasis on white independence and egalitarianism harnessed the great political movement of the age, democracy (at least for white men), to the proslavery cause by explaining how slavery protected white independence and equality by preventing the "fall" of a broad section of independent whites, such as members of the yeomanry, into dependent status and by reminding everyone daily that the social difference that mattered was race. The notion that slavery sustained white independence and equality also had the concomitant virtue of allowing southern defenders of slavery to launch a stinging counterattack against the so-called wage slavery that flourished in the free-labor North. Together, the combined emphasis on race and egalitarianism rendered whiteness a source of entitlement and privilege and made advocacy of white egalitarianism critical to success in the political realm, no matter how many reservations about white equality flourished in planter drawing rooms and mercantile houses across the region.

Finally, the triumph of paternalism gave slaveholders and other committed white southerners a response to abolition criticism that rested on moral and humanitarian grounds, and one that had the blessing of a large portion of the region's clergy. In doing so, paternalism both shored up southern whites' confidence in their own stance on the morality of slaveholding, a matter of concern during the mail and petition campaigns, and gave white southerners a platform from which to defend themselves to the larger world. Moreover, apart from its use to justify slavery, paternalism became a social ideology through which equally independent white men could identify women, children, and others who were not heads of households as their dependents. As a result, in the Old South, one measure of a man's independence became holding sway over dependents. Independence became linked with mastery. White men in the Old South were virtually obsessed with the notion of not becoming slaves, even in a political or metaphorical sense. Yet no more than a few of them shared Lincoln's commensurate aversion to becoming a master. Paternalism had resolved the threat mastery once posed to republican sensibility.

Of course, as sweeping as the triumph of the paternalist reconfiguration of slavery was in the lower South, it hardly quashed all dissent in the region. Yeoman farmers and other common whites in hill country, mountain, and wiregrass regions proved vigilant in their efforts to make sure that the slaveholders' paternalism was limited to slaves and other appropriate dependents. They insisted that it not become an ideology used to control other white men. Persistent critics of paternalism, such as members of the South Carolina Association, who thought paternalism lacked the toughness and realism to manage slavery safely and effectively, continued to be heard, but they enjoyed less influence than before. Even within the paternalist camp disagreements emerged over whether or not slavery should be seen as perpetual or as a positive good or remain viewed as a temporary but necessary evil that defied remedy.

Moreover, despite its broad acceptance in the lower South, this ideological reconfiguration of slavery found gaining traction across the upper South a hit-or-miss proposition. To be sure, it gained footholds in heavy slaveholding areas of the upper South, but across the region the idea of an ideological reconfiguration of slavery remained less influential than the idea of a gradual demographic reconfiguration accompanied, where necessary, by an ideological whitening that limited all privileges of citizenship to white men. The upper South, as a whole, still thought of slavery, as it had at the republic's founding, as a problem that could and would likely be solved eventually by bringing slavery to a very slow and gradual end. To talk of slavery as a "social blessing," as some in the lower South did, or as a problem that could be effectively ameliorated with enough paternalism, enough teaching of Christianity to the slaves, and enough practice of Christianity by masters, sounded radical and defective to many whites in the upper South. On balance, the upper South remained more inclined to find its answer to the slavery question in the internal slave trade, sending slaves out of their region to supply demand from the lower South. In a sense, upper South whites still thought of answering the slavery question sale by sale; increasingly, paternalist voices in the lower South thought about answering it soul by soul, as conversions transformed the hearts of masters and slaves alike, rendering the institution a mere shadow of its former self.

CONCLUSION

By the late 1830s, the upper and lower South had each decided that their respective answers to the slavery question lay in different ways of reconfiguring the institution. Each region wanted to make it easier to manage the problems they saw as endemic to slave society. Each also sought a better position from which to defend their views on slavery to a critical world. In both the upper and lower South, these Jacksonian-era reconfigurations of slavery, though hardly static, would remain ones the respective regions would work to implement for as long as slavery existed in the United States. In the upper South, that reconfiguration was a demographic one. The idea of a demographic reconfiguration of slavery emphasized the gradual whitening of the region and depended heavily on continued lower South demand for slaves and an active internal slave trade. The upper South's idea of a demographic reconfiguration of slavery was sharply contested internally. The principal contretemps arose between those who agreed with lower South whites on an ideological reconfiguration of slavery that accepted the institution as paternalistic and possibly perpetual and the advocates of whitening who continued to view slavery as a temporary evil that could be tolerated for a time but not touted as a model republican social order. In most of the upper South, the advocates of demographic reconfiguration generally prevailed in the contest, but their victory was hardly uniform across the region.

The lower South's reconfiguration was ideological in nature, and it revolved around the embrace of race as the chief justification for slavery, the acceptance of white egalitarianism as the ethos of the region's political culture, and the triumph of paternalism as the lower South's prevailing ideology of slaveholding. The hegemony of the lower South's successful ideological reconfiguration of slavery was arguably more sweeping and emphatic than that of whitening in the upper South, but it was hardly without its lingering critics. Its chief opposition remained those critics of paternalism who remained unconvinced that it effectively controlled slaves, though some white plain folk worried that slaveholder paternalism might creep into relationships between independent white household heads and infringe on their cherished autonomy. Moreover, paternalism's triumph as an ideology for justifying slavery was never matched by its level of acceptance by masters as a method of managing slaves. In some ways, paternalism as a defense of slavery was most undermined not by its vociferous opponents, but by the many indifferent slaveholders who never even tried to practice it. Additionally, other forms of dissent from the new ideological consensus also persisted. Few lower South whites accepted slavery in the abstract as desirable, and some dissenters thought the dominant ideological reconfiguration adopted by the region put too positive a spin on slavery. A healthy minority of lower South whites remained unconvinced that slavery was a positive good or a social blessing. Yet by the late 1830s, only a few lower South whites thought a whitening of their region remotely possible; in fact, the viability of the upper South's whitening strategy depended on the lower South's willingness to grow blacker.

But consensus need not mean unanimity, and a policy majority need not even be a consensus. In the end, the demographic reconfiguration of slavery in the upper South and the ideological reconfiguration of slavery in the lower South represented the best answers the respective regions could give to the slavery question (or questions), and these answers, different and sometimes conflicting as they were, did much to explain how upper and lower South whites understood their position with regard to slavery, and how they saw themselves as citizens of the United States right down to secession and Civil War.

Even at a distance of nearly 150 years from its inception, the American Civil War still stands as the pivotal event in the nation's history. The story of the development of these answers to the slavery question lays a foundation for understanding why so many whites in the Old South gave their all to defend their positions just a quarter century later. In the final analysis, these tortured efforts to answer the slavery question explain nothing less than how and why whites in the Old South created the self-images they fought to preserve in the American Civil War.

ACKNOWLEDGMENTS

This book has been a labor of love for the author—a long and arduous labor of love to be sure, but a labor of love nonetheless. If anything, I enjoyed "working" on the book so much that finishing it became a matter of secondary to the pursuit of the elusive notion of "getting it right"—a fiction at best and a white whale–like obsession at worst. But if the project never ceased to be a labor of love for the author, it has certainly been, at times, an imposition on colleagues, friends, and, most of all, family, all of whom have shared the sacrifice without necessarily fully sharing the author's abiding affection for the task. All of those who have either helped or sacrificed have earned my sincere gratitude and deep appreciation. A few, but certainly not all, are singled out for explicit thanks in the paragraphs that follow.

Among the many who have helped are library and manuscript archivists across the Southeast, including those at the Library of Virginia and the Virginia Historical Society in Richmond, the Southern Historical Collection at the University of North Carolina at Chapel Hill, the Manuscripts Division of Perkins Library at Duke University, the Manuscripts Division of the Library of Congress in our nation's capital, the Manuscript Division of Lower Mississippi and Louisiana Collection at LSU, the Archives and Library Division of the Mississippi Department of Archives and History in Jackson, the Georgia Archives, the Manuscripts, Archives and Rare Books division of the Woodruff Library at Emory University, the Tennessee State Library and Archives in Nashville, and other repositories where I spent shorter periods of time. Closer to home, the staffs of the South Carolina Historical Society in Charleston, the South Carolina Department of Archives and History, and South Caroliniana Library in Columbia earned special thanks with their dedicated service and continued support. Dr. Rodger Stroup proved a master at running the South Carolina Department of Archives and History on budgets than ran from lean to meager. Dr. Allen Stokes, Director of the South Caroliniana Library and long-time friend, deserves a special tribute for his contributions to my research and appreciation for sources over the course of my entire career.

Additionally, over the many years I worked on this project, I have benefitted from the dedicated work of a number of talented research assistants. In the project's early stages, Kim Kellison, then a doctoral student at USC and now a faculty member at Baylor University, helped with early newspaper research, and Trenton Hizer, also a doctoral student at the time and now an archivist at the Library of Virginia, contributed valuable work with pamphlets and manuscripts. Since joining the staff at the Library of Virginia, Dr. Hizer has remained a valuable advisor and resource on Virginia sources of all types. Veronica Bruce McConnell also helped with newspaper and manuscript work during a critical period. In recent years, another doctoral student at USC, Sara Eye Burrows, not only provided invaluable help with manuscript, archival and inter-library loan research but also helped obtain copies of material from other repositories, sought permissions for use of sources, and helped prepare the manuscript for submission and publication generally, all while completing her own dissertation.

My colleagues in the Department of History at the University of South Carolina also deserve special thanks for their support and encouragement. Retired colleagues Tom Terrill and Robert Weir heard more about the project in the early stages than they cared to and each offered a number of valuable suggestions. A special thank you goes out to longtime department chair Professor Patrick Maney, who not only made the department a terrific place to work during his nine years as chair but also gave my project generous support. I finished the manuscript and prepared it for publication after becoming department chair in 2007, and I want to thank Dean Mary Anne Fitzpatrick of the College of Arts and Sciences and the entire staff of the Department of History for making it possible for me to do so. Larry Glickman read the introduction to the volume and offered immensely useful comments on it, and he offered a number of valuable suggestions about other book-related matters, including the title. Outside my department, David Carlton of Vanderbilt University and Peter Coclanis of UNC–Chapel Hill remain valuable advisors on all matters of scholarship, and each tolerated me as an extended house guest at crucial points in my research for this book. Critical to the completion of the manuscript was an National Endowment for the Humanities Research Fellowship in 2001-2002 and an sabbatical leave form University of South Carolina in the Spring 2007. Susan Ferber, my acquisitions editor at Oxford University Press, showed just the right blend of patience and persistence and has been perceptive in many matters once the manuscript approached completion. Sue Warga's fine copy-editing saved me from numerous errors, and Joellyn Ausanka's experience and wisdom guided me through the production process.

I lost both of my parents during the latter stages of work on this book, my father in 2005 and my mother in 2007. Gracious livers of long and productive lives, their support and encouragement steadied me in difficult times as it always had. My father modeled patience and discernment while tirelessly offering encouraging words, and my mother lived as though the opportunity to work was its own reward, an example I will never forget. Their loss leaves me even more appreciative of the support offered by my remaining family, and, as a small expression of my gratitude, this book is dedicated to Janet, Travis, and Sonya, who endured and enjoyed the ups and downs of its making along with the author, showing love, affection, understanding and concern in their respective ways all the while, and, in the manner suggested by Saint Augustine, using words when necessary. In the best Faulknerian sense, they have not only endured but prevailed. For Travis and Sonya, I hope my work has modeled perseverance and a commitment to finding the right words that they might find encouragement in. And I trust that Janet knows how much I value the investment she has made in the work—and its author. I know the final product is inadequate compensation for all they have endured, but I hope the daily richness of our life together is its own reward.

Lacy K. Ford
COLUMBIA, SC
MARCH 2009

ABBREVIATIONS

BHC	Baptist Historical Collection, Furman University, Greenville, South Carolina
DU	Manuscripts Division, Perkins Library, Duke University, Durham, North Carolina
FU	Special Collections, James B. Duke Library, Furman University, Greenville, South Carolina
HNOC	Historic New Orleans Collection, Williams Research Center, New Orleans, Louisiana
HSP	Historical Society of Pennsylvania, Philadelphia, Pennsylvania
LC	Library of Congress, Washington, D.C.
LSU	Louisiana and Lower Mississippi Valley Collection, Louisiana State University, Baton Rouge, Louisiana
LV	Library of Virginia, Richmond, Virginia
MDAH	Mississippi Department of Archives and History, Jackson, Mississippi
MHS	Maryland Historical Society, Baltimore, Maryland
NA	Archives of the United States, Washington, D.C., and College Park, Maryland
SCDAH	South Carolina Department of Archives and History, Columbia, South Carolina
SCHS	South Carolina Historical Society, Charleston, South Carolina
SCL	South Caroliniana Library, University of South Carolina, Columbia, South Carolina
SHC	Southern Historical Collection, University of North Carolina at Chapel Hill
TSLA	Tennessee State Library and Archives, Nashville, Tennessee
TU	Howard-Tilton Memorial Library, Tulane University, New Orleans, Louisiana
UVA	Alderman Library, University of Virginia, Charlottesville, Virginia
VHS	Virginia Historical Society, Richmond, Virginia
W&M	Earl Swan Collection, College of William and Mary, Williamsburg, Virginia

NOTES

INTRODUCTION

1 Samuel Johnson, "Taxation No Tyranny: An Answer to the Resolution and Address of the American Congress," in *The Works of Samuel Johnson* (Troy, NY: Parfreats and Company, 1913), 14:99–144.

2 Portions of this summary of my argument are drawn from Lacy Ford, "Reconfiguring the Old South: 'Solving' the Problem of Slavery, 1787–1838," *Journal of American History* 95 (June 2008): 95–122.

3 For overviews of this literature, see Eric Foner, "The Causes of the American Civil War: Recent Interpretations and New Directions," *Civil War History* 20 (September 1974): 197–214; Don Fehrenbacher, "The New Political History and the Coming of the Civil War," *Pacific Historical Review* 54 (May 1985): 117–42; Kenneth M. Stampp, "Race, Slavery, and the Republican Party in the 1850s," in his *The Imperiled Union* (New York: Oxford University Press, 1980), 105–35; William W. Freehling, "The Divided South, Democracy's Limitations, and the Causes of the Peculiarly North American Civil War," in his *The Reintegration of American History* (New York: Oxford University Press, 1994), 176–219; Lacy Ford, "Introduction: A Civil War in the Age of Capital," in *A Companion to Civil War and Reconstruction*, ed. Lacy Ford (Malden, MA: Blackwell, 2005), 1–22.

4 A fine example of a recent comprehensive study that avoids narrowing its focus to the late antebellum era is Michael O'Brien, *Conjectures of Order: Intellectual Life and the American South, 1810–1860*, 2 vols. (New York: Cambridge University Press, 2005). Recent works tackling the issue of the formation of the Old South from the perspective of a particular issue, locale, or subregion include Eva Sheppard Wolf, *Race and Liberty in the New Nation: Emancipation in Virginia From the Revolution to Nat Turner's Rebellion* (Baton Rouge: Louisiana State University Press, 2006); Matthew Mason, *Slavery and Politics in the Early American Republic* (Chapel Hill: University of North Carolina Press, 2006); Tom Downey, *Planting A Capitalist South: Masters, Merchants and Manufacturers in the Southern Interior, 1790–1860* (Baton Rouge: Louisiana State University Press, 2006); Adam Rothman, *Slave Country: American Expansion and the Origins of the Deep South* (Cambridge, MA: Harvard University Press, 2005); Kirsten E. Wood, *Masterful Women: Slaveholding Widows from the American Revolution Through the Civil War* (Chapel Hill:

University of North Carolina Press, 2004); Robert H. Gudmestad, *A Troublesome Commerce: The Transformation of the Interstate Slave Trade* (Baton Rouge: Louisiana State University Press, 2003); Edward E. Baptist, *Creating an Old South: Middle Florida's Plantation Frontier Before the Civil War* (Chapel Hill: University of North Carolina Press, 2002); Walter Johnson, *Soul by Soul: Life Inside the Antebellum Slave Market* (Cambridge, MA: Harvard University Press, 1999); Daniel S. Dupre, *Transforming the Cotton Frontier: Madison County, Alabama, 1800–1840* (Baton Rouge: Louisiana State University Press, 1997); Christopher Morris, *Becoming Southern: The Evolution of a Way of Life, Warren County and Vicksburg, Mississippi, 1770–1860* (New York: Oxford University Press, 1995).

5 See William W. Freehling, *The Road to Disunion: Secessionists at Bay, 1776–1854* (New York: Oxford University Press, 1990).

6 Erskine Clark, *Dwelling Places: A Plantation Epic* (New Haven: Yale University Press, 2005); Lacy K. Ford, "A Paternalist's Progress: Insurgency, Orthodoxy and Reversal in the Old South: Review of Erskine Clark's *Dwelling Place: A Plantation Epic*," *Reviews in American History* 35 (March 2007): 46–56.

7 Willie Lee Rose, "The Domestication of Domestic Slavery," in William W. Freehling, ed., *Slavery and Freedom* (New York: Oxford University Press, 1982), 18–36; Jeffrey Robert Young, *Domesticating Slavery: The Master Class in Georgia and South Carolina, 1670–1837* (Chapel Hill: University of North Carolina Press, 1999), 123–60.

8 The Southside area of Virginia is that portion of the state lying south of the James River but east of the Blue Ridge mountains.

9 Historians have recently labeled this newly coherent set of ideas as "racial modernism." See James Brewer Stewart, "The Emergence of Racial Modernity and the Rise of the White North, 1790–1840," *Journal of the Early Republic* 18 (Summer 1998): 181–217; Lacy K. Ford Jr., "'Making the White Man's Country' White: Race, Slavery and State Building the Jacksonian South," *Journal of the Early Republic* 19 (Winter 1999): 713–37.

10 See, for example, Susan Wyly-Jones, "The 1835 Anti-Abolition Meetings in the South: A New Look at the Controversy over the Abolition Postal Campaign," *Civil War History* 47 (December 2001): 289–300.

11 The ongoing controversy among historians over the Vesey plot played only a secondary role in my decision to focus on the scare and the varied white reactions to it. For an introduction to this controversy, see Michael P. Johnson, "Denmark Vesey and His Co-Conspirators, Part I, *William and Mary Quarterly* 58 (October 2001): 915–76, and Robert Gross, ed., "Forum: The Making of a Slave Conspiracy II," *William and Mary Quarterly* 59 (January 2002): 135–202.

ONE. OWNING SLAVES, DISOWNING SLAVERY

1 George Washington to John Francis Mercer, September 9, 1786, in *The Papers of George Washington: Confederation Series*, ed. W. W. Abbot, Dorothy Twohig, et al. (Charlottesville: University Press of Virginia, 1992–97), 4:43–44.

2 See Max Farrand, ed., *The Records of the Federal Convention of 1787* (New Haven: Yale University Press, 1911), 2:371 (for Charles C. Pinckney quote) and 2:373 (for Rutledge quote). On Rutledge, see James Haw, *John and Edward Rutledge of South Carolina* (Athens: University of Georgia Press, 1997); on Charles Cotesworth Pinckney, see Marvin R. Zahniser, *Charles Cotesworth Pinckney: Founding Father* (Chapel Hill: University of North Carolina Press, 1967).

3 See James Madison to Thomas Jefferson, October 24, 1787, in *The Papers of James Madison*, ed. Robert Rutland et al. (Chicago: University of Chicago Press, 1977), 10:206–19, at 214.

4 On this point, see Paul Finkelman, "Slavery and the Constitutional Convention: Making A Covenant With Death," in Richard Beeman, Stephen Botein, and Edward C. Carter II, eds., *Beyond Confederation: Origins of the Constitution and American National Identity* (Chapel Hill: University of North Carolina Press, 1987), 188–225, and Jack N. Rakove, *Original Meanings: Politics and Ideas in the Making of the Constitution* (New York: Knopf, 1996), 83–93. Rakove suggests that the original report on these subjects issued by the standing committee claimed so much for the South in order that "later modification of its recommendations could be portrayed as a compromise of the part of the South." On the large question of the upper South's position on slavery and the slave trade compared to that of the lower South, see William W. Freehling, *The Road to Disunion: Secessionists at Bay, 1776–1854* (New York: Oxford University Press, 1990), esp. 120–31.

5 Farrand, ed., *The Records of the Federal Convention of 1787*, 2:415–16.

6 *Notes of Debates in the Federal Convention of 1787 Reported by James Madison* (New York: W. W. Norton, 1987), 503–4.

7 Ibid. On Mason, see Robert Rutland, *George Mason, Reluctant Statesman* (Baton Rouge: Louisiana State University Press, 1980, reprint ed.).

8 Clarence E. Carter and John Porter Bloom, eds., *The Territorial Papers of the United States* (Washington: Government Printing Office, 1934–69), 4:3–19; Walter Clark, ed., *The State Records of North Carolina* (Goldsboro, NC: 1886–1905), 24:561–63.

9 Don E. Fehrenbacher, *The Slaveholding Republic: An Account of the United States Government's Relations to Slavery*, comp. and ed. Ward M. McAfee (New York: Oxford University Press, 2001), 253–63.

10 For an overview of the congressional debate over these petitions, see William C. DuGiacomantonio, "'For the Gratification of a Volunteering Society': Antislavery and Pressure Politics in the First Federal Congress," *Journal of the Early Republic* 15 (Summer 1995): 169–97, and Richard S. Newman, "Prelude to the Gag Rule: Southern Reaction to Antislavery Petitions in the First Federal Congress," *Journal of the Early Republic* 16 (Winter 1996): 571–99.

11 See Eileen Daney Carzo, ed., *Texts of Documents, Administration of George Washington, 1789–1797* (Wilmington, DE: M. Glazier, 1985), 3:422–29; *Annals of Congress,* 1st Congress, 2nd Session, 1182–98.

12 See *Annals of Congress,* 1st Congress, 2nd Session, 1188, 1198.

13 Ibid., 1199, 1204.

14 Donald Robinson, *Slavery in the Structure of American Politics, 1765–1820* (New York: Harcourt, Brace and Jovanovich, 1971), 299–312; *Annals of Congress,* 1st Congress, 2nd Session, 1189, 1203–1205, 1453–1473.

15 *Virginia Herald and Fredericksburg Advertiser*, April 1, 1790; *Annals of Congress,* 1st Congress, 2nd Session, 1453–74.

16 Edward Carrington to James Madison, April 7, 1790, Adam Stephen to James Madison, April 5, 1790, James Madison to Robert Pleasants, October 30, 1791, in *The Papers of James Madison*, ed. William T. Hutchinson, William M. E. Rachal, et al. (Chicago: University of Chicago Press, 1962–91), 13:142, 13:176, 14:91–92.

17 Robinson, *Slavery in the Structure of American Politics*, 309–16.

18 On these points, see the important work of Sylvia Frey, *Water from the Rock: Black Resistance in a Revolutionary Age* (Princeton, NJ: Princeton University Press, 1991), 81–142, and "Between

Slavery and Freedom: Virginia Blacks in the American Revolution," *Journal of Southern History* 49 (August 1983): 375–98. See also Gerald W. Mullin, *Flight and Rebellion: Slave Resistance in Eighteenth-Century Virginia* (New York: Oxford University Press, 1972), esp. 124–39. For a comprehensive examination of these issues focusing on the African American perspective, see Douglas R. Egerton, *Death or Liberty: African Americans and Revolutionary America* (New York: Oxford University Press, 2009). Egerton's book appeared while this manuscript was in press, and hence too late to influence my interpretation.

19 [George Washington], *The Will of General George Washington: To Which Is Added, a Schedule of His Property Directed to Be Sold* (Alexandria, VA, 1800); Washington quote is also found in Helen Hill, *George Mason: Constitutionalist* (Cambridge, MA: Harvard University Press, 1938), 287; see also Egerton, *Death or Liberty*, 146. For a perceptive study of Washington's views on slavery, see Henry Wiencek, *An Imperfect God: George Washington, His Slaves, and Slavery* (New York: Farrar, Straus and Giroux, 2003).

20 Richard Henry Lee, "Address to the House of Burgesses to the King in Opposition to the Slave Trade," April 1, 1772, in William J. Van Schreeven et al., eds., *Revolutionary Virginia: The Road to Independence* (Charlottesville: University Press of Virginia, 1973–83), 1:85–88; on Lee, see Oliver Chitwood, *Richard Henry Lee: Statesman of the Revolution* (Morgantown : West Virginia University Library, 1967), esp. 17–21.

21 William Wirt Henry, *Patrick Henry: Life, Correspondence and Speeches* (1891; reprint, New York: Burt Franklin, 1969), 2:152–53.

22 "Scheme for Replevying Goods," in *The Papers of George Mason*, ed. Robert A. Rutland et al. (Chapel Hill: University of North Carolina Press, 1970), 1:61; see also Jeff Broadwater, *George Mason: Forgotten Founder* (Chapel Hill: University of North Carolina Press, 2006), 34–38.

23 Madison, "Notes for the National Gazette Essays, c. 19 December 1791 to 3 March 1792," in *The Papers of James Madison*, ed. Hutchinson, Rachal, et al., 14:160–64; see also Lacy K. Ford, "Inventing the Concurrent Majority: Madison, Calhoun and the Problem of Majoritarianism in American Political Thought," *Journal of Southern History* 60 (February 1994): 19–58.

24 For two instructive introductions to Jefferson's thought on slavery and its place in the large society of the upper South written a quarter century apart, see Paul Finkelman, "Jefferson and Slavery: 'Treason Against the Hopes of the World,'" in Peter S. Onuf, ed., *Jefferson's Legacies* (Charlottesville: University of Virginia Press, 1993), 181–224, and Winthrop Jordan, *White over Black: American Attitudes Toward the Negro, 1550–1812* (Chapel Hill: University of North Carolina Press, 1968), 429–81. The literature on Jefferson is vast; for an introduction, see Peter Onuf, "The Scholars' Jefferson," *William and Mary Quarterly* 50 (October 1993): 671–99.

25 Thomas Jefferson, *Notes on the State of Virginia,* ed. William Peden (Chapel Hill: University of North Carolina Press, 1954), 155–56.

26 Joseph Ellis, "Jefferson: Post DNA," *William and Mary Quarterly* 62 (January 2000): 125–38; Annette Gordon-Reed, *Thomas Jefferson and Sally Hemings: An American Controversy* (Charlottesville: University of Virginia Press, 1997). This argument draws heavily on Lacy Ford, "Reconfiguring the Old South: 'Solving' the Problem of Slavery, 1787–1838," *Journal of American History* 95 (June 2008): 95–122.

27 Jefferson, *Notes*, 162–63.

28 On this point, see Rhys Isaac, *The Transformation of Virginia, 1740–1790* (Chapel Hill: University of North Carolina Press, 1982); Mechal Sobel, *The World They Made Together: Black and

White Values in Eighteenth-Century Virginia (Princeton, NJ: Princeton University Press, 1987); Cynthia Lynn Lyerly, *Methodism and the Southern Mind, 1770–1810* (New York: Oxford University Press, 1998); James D. Essig, *The Bonds of Wickedness: American Evangelicals Against Slavery, 1770–1808* (Philadelphia: Temple University Press, 1982); Jay Worrell, *The Friendly Virginians: America's First Quakers* (Athens: University of Georgia Press, 1994).

29 Benjamin Henry Latrobe, *The Virginia Journals of Benjamin Henry Latrobe, 1795–1798*, ed. Edward C. Carter II (New Haven: Yale University Press, 1977), 191–92; W. Harrison Daniel, "Virginia Baptists and the Negro in the Early Republic," *Virginia Magazine of History and Biography* 80 (1972): 60–69, esp. 62–63; Luther P. Jackson, "Religious Development of the Negro in Virginia from 1760 to 1860," *Journal of Negro History* 16 (January 1931): 168–239; Mechal Sobel, *Trabelin' On: The Slave Journey to an Afro-Baptist Faith* (Princeton, NJ: Princeton University Press, 1988), 206.

30 Donald M. Mathews, *Slavery and Methodism: A Chapter in American Morality, 1790–1845* (Princeton, NJ: Princeton University Press, 1965), 7–9.

31 Thomas Coke, *Extracts of the Journals of the Rev. Dr. Coke's Three Visits to America* (London, 1790), 33–36.

32 Jesse Lee, *A Short History of the Methodists, in the United States of America: Beginning in 1766 and Continued till 1809* (Baltimore, 1810), 70–83.

33 Coke, *Extracts of the Journals*, 37–40.

34 Lee, *A Short History of the Methodists*, 102.

35 Lyerly, *Methodism and the Southern Mind*, 119–45.

36 Daniel, "Virginia Baptists and the Negro in the Early Republic," 66.

37 Donald R. Hickey, "America's Response to the Slave Revolt in Haiti, 1791–1806," *Journal of the Early Republic* 2 (Winter 1982): 361–79; Timothy M. Matthewson, "George Washington's Policy Toward the Haitian Revolution," *Diplomatic History* 3 (1979): 321–36.

38 George Washington to John Vaughn, December 27, 1791, in *The Writings of George Washington*, ed. John C. Fitzpatrick (Washington, DC: Government Printing Office, 1931–44), 31:453.

39 Thomas Jefferson to James Monroe, July 14, 1793, in *The Papers of Thomas Jefferson*, ed. Julian Boyd et al. (Princeton, NJ: Princeton University Press, 1950–), 26:503.

40 Lt. Gov. James Wood (of Virginia) to Governor William Moultrie (of South Carolina), c. August 1793, Governor's Messages, #577, Records of the General Assembly, SCDAH.; Governor Henry Lee to Colonel Robert Goode, May 17, 1792, Executive Letter Book, LV.

41 John Randolph's Deposition, July 21, 1793, in H. W. Flourney, ed., *Calendar of Virginia State Papers* (Richmond: 1975–93), 6:452–53; for the original, see Deposition of John Randolph, July 22, 1793, Executive Papers, Box 80, 21–30 August Folder, LV.

42 Robert G. Harper to his constituents, March 20, 1799, in *Papers of James A. Bayard, 1796–1815*, ed. Elizabeth Donnan (Washington, DC: Annual Report of the American Historical Association of 1913, 1915), 2:90.

43 Allen Kulikoff, *Tobacco and Slaves: The Development of Southern Cultures in the Chesapeake, 1680–1800* (Chapel Hill: University of North Carolina Press, 1986), esp. 317–436.

44 On this point, see Edmund Morgan's magnificent *American Slavery, American Freedom: The Ordeal of Colonial Virginia* (New York: Norton, 1975).

45 On South Carolina, see Peter A. Coclanis, "Distant Thunder: The Creation of a World Market in Rice and the Transformations It Wrought," *American Historical Review* 98 (October 1993): 1050–78.

46 On this point, see Richard Dunn, "After Tobacco: The Slave Labor Pattern on a Large Chesapeake Grain-and-Livestock Plantation in the Early Nineteenth Century," in John J. McCusker and Kenneth Morgan, eds., *The Early Modern Atlantic Economy* (New York: Cambridge University Press, 2000), 344–63.

47 Demographic calculations in this and all subsequent paragraphs are made from data found in the following sources: U. S. Bureau of the Census, *Negro Population of the United States, 1790–1815* (Washington, DC, 1918), 51; U.S. Bureau of the Census, *Population of the United States in 1860* (Washington, DC, 1864), 592–602; Ira Berlin, *Slaves Without Masters* (New York: Pantheon, 1974), 23, 46–47, 136–37, 396–403.

48 My understanding of slavery in early national Delaware has been shaped by Patience Essah, *A House Divided: Slavery and Emancipation in Delaware, 1638–1865* (Charlottesville: University Press of Virginia, 1996). On these points, see 7, 25.

49 Only about 7 percent of Maryland's black population was free in 1790, compared to 30 percent in Delaware, the regional high, and 4 percent in Virginia. Clearly any effort to end slavery or to "whiten" Maryland faced a bigger challenges than a similar effort in Delaware. Despite its focus on a later period, William J. Evitts, *A Matter of Allegiances: Maryland from 1850 to 1861* (Baltimore: Johns Hopkins University Press, 1974), 1–23, is excellent on Maryland geography and its influence on the state's economy.

50 My understanding of slavery in early national Maryland has been shaped by T. Stephen Whitman, *The Price of Freedom: Slavery and Manumission in Baltimore and Early National Maryland* (Lexington: University of Kentucky Press, 1997).

51 In addition to the sources cited in note 46, see Alison Goodyear Freehling, *Drift Toward Dissolution: The Virginia Slavery Debate of 1831–32* (Baton Rouge: Louisiana State University Press, 1982), 11–35; Freehling, *The Road to Disunion*, 30–31, 152–67.

52 After 1810, the two states veered off on different tracks in terms of racial demography. Kentucky never again had as many slaves (111,000) as it had in 1810, and its proportion of slaves generally declined over the antebellum decades. In Tennessee, however, the slave population nearly doubled between 1810 and 1820 and increased dramatically in every antebellum decade thereafter, though slaves never accounted for more than 20 percent of Tennessee's population. See Berlin, *Slaves Without Masters*, 23, 46–47, 136–37, 396–403.

53 Paul G. E. Clemens, *The Atlantic Economy and Colonial Maryland's Eastern Shore: From Tobacco to Grain* (Ithaca, NY: Cornell University Press, 1980), esp. 165–205; Carville V. Earle, "A Staple Interpretation of Slavery and Free Labor," *Geography Review* 68 (January 1978): 51–65; Barbara J. Fields, *Slavery and Freedom on the Middle Ground: Maryland During the Nineteenth Century* (New Haven: Yale University Press, 1985), 4–6; Essah, *A House Divided*, 69–74.

54 Essah, *A House Divided*, 41–52.

55 *Laws of the State of Delaware*, 2:884–88.

56 *Laws of the State of Delaware*, 2:941–44.

57 Essah, *A House Divided*, 40–41.

58 *Laws of the State of Delaware*, 2:884–88.

59 Essah, *A House Divided*, 86–109.

60 *Laws of the State of Delaware*, 2:1321–5.

61 Essah, *A House Divided*, 104–7; Truitt quoted in (Delaware) *House Journal*, January 5, 1810; *Laws of the State of Delaware*, 4:337–40.

62 Berlin, *Slaves Without Masters*, 23, 46–47, 136–37, 396–403; Essah, *A House Divided*, 7–8, 25–26, 39, 77–79.

63 Essah, *A House Divided*, 93–118.

64 Berlin, *Slaves Without Masters*, 29–31; Whitman, *The Price of Freedom*, 67; *Laws of Maryland, 1790*, chapter 9.

65 [John S. Tyson], *Life of Elisha Tyson, Philanthropist* (Baltimore, 1925), 25.

66 Whitman, *The Price of Freedom*, 51–52.

67 Term slaves were slaves promised manumission at some future date but still obligated to their owner for a specified period. See Stephen Whitman, "Diverse Good Causes: Manumission and the Transformation of Urban Slavery," *Social Science History* 19 (Autumn 1995): 333–70; see also Whitman, *The Price of Freedom*, 93–118.

68 According to Whitman's *The Price of Freedom*, esp. 8–60, demand for slave labor in Baltimore also increased because slave labor proved surprisingly adaptable to urban needs. Slave artisans and mechanics proved much more valuable in the city than in the countryside, and Baltimore employers used slaves in the city's infant industries, such as chemicals and textiles. Plus the city's new elite also found slaves useful as household servants.

69 Whitman, *The Price of Freedom*, 10–32; Berlin, *Slaves Without Masters*, 23, 46–47, 136–37, 396–403.

70 Whitman, *The Price of Freedom*, 10–11, 65–67, 96–97; Tadman, *Speculators and Slaves*, 12; quotation found in Jeffrey R. Brackett, *The Negro in Maryland: A Study in the Institution of Slavery* (Baltimore: Johns Hopkins University Studies in Historical and Political Science, 1889), 58–61. The Maryland law on slave imports always allowed slaveholders who wanted to settle in Maryland to bring their slaves with them. Over time, the Maryland legislature approved several additional exceptions to the ban. Maryland residents could file a declaration that they were bringing slaves into the state for their own use rather than for sale or hire. Additionally, during the early 1790s, the Maryland legislature permitted slaveholders fleeing the rebellion in Saint Domingue to bring their slaves into the state, and later it allowed New York masters to move to Maryland with their slaves after the Empire State passed its post-nati emancipation law. See Whitman, *The Price of Freedom*, 10–11.

71 Ira Berlin, *Many Thousands Gone: The First Two Centuries of Slavery in North America* (Cambridge, MA: Belknap Press, 1980), 265; Jean B. Russo, "A Model Planter: Edward Lloyd IV of Maryland, 1770–1796," *William and Mary Quarterly* 49 (January 1992): 62–88.

72 Michael Tadman, "The Hidden History of Slave Trading in Antebellum South Carolina; John Springs III and Other 'Gentlemen Dealing in Slaves,'" *South Carolina Historical Magazine* 97 (January 1996): 6–29; see also Lacy K. Ford, "The Tale of Two Entrepreneurs in the Old South: John Springs III and Hiram Hutchison of the South Carolina Upcountry," *South Carolina Historical Magazine* 95 (July 1994): 198–224. Maryland newspaper quote is found in Berlin, *Many Thousands Gone*, 265.

73 Tadman, *Speculators and Slaves*, 12.

74 This dramatic increase of the free black population in Maryland can be attributed to private manumission and thus indirectly to both the relative stagnation of the tobacco economy and the simultaneous rise in demand for free labor in the burgeoning port city of Baltimore. To be sure, slavery thrived in early national Baltimore, where numerous artisans and craftsmen held slaves. In 1810, one-third of all Baltimore craftsmen owned at least one slave, and though the

incidence of slaveholding among craftsmen fell sharply during the next decade, more than 20 percent of all craftsmen remained slave owners in 1820. Thus in its initial stages, the expansion of the Baltimore economy merely drained skilled slaves (and domestic servants) from the surrounding countryside. The use of hired slaves in the city, however, ultimately gave way to a preference for free labor, even free black labor. After 1820, not only did the slave proportion of Maryland's population shrink but the actual number of slaves living in the state of Maryland declined. See Whitman, *The Price of Freedom*, 10 and passim.

75 Data in this and the two following paragraphs calculated from sources cited in note 46.

76 John Chester Miller, *The Wolf by the Ears: Thomas Jefferson and Slavery* (New York: Free Press, 1977), 22; Robert McColley, *Slavery in Jeffersonian Virginia* (Urbana: University of Illinois Press, 1964), 127–32; Robinson, *Slavery in the Structure of American Politics*, 88–93.

77 Thomas Jefferson to James Heaton, May 20, 1826, in Thomas Jefferson, *Writings*, ed. Merrill Peterson (New York: Literary Classics, 1984), 1516. Jefferson had originally intended to present his gradual emancipation proposal to a state constitutional convention that the Virginia Assembly declined to call.

78 Jefferson, *Autobiography*, in ibid., 44.

79 Jefferson, *Notes*, 163.

80 Jefferson's own preferences on the question of how colonization should proceed changed over time, but he also never doubted that an appropriate plan for colonization could be crafted if sufficient support developed. For Jefferson, it was not the impracticality of colonization that stymied the movement but its lack of popular support. See Peter S. Onuf, "'To Declare Then a Free and Independent People': Race, Slavery and National Identity in Jefferson's Thought," *Journal of the Early Republic* 18 (Spring 1998): 1–46, and "Every Generation Is an 'Independent Nation': Colonization, Miscegenation and the Fate of Jefferson's Children," *William and Mary Quarterly* 57 (January 2000): 153–70.

81 For example, see Petition of Barkly County, c. November 1785, General Assembly, Legislative Petitions, Miscellaneous Chronology, 1784–86, Box 291, Folder 46, and Petition of Frederick County, c. November 1785, General Assembly, Legislative Petitions, Miscellaneous Chronology, 1784–86, Box 81, Folder 10, LV.

82 Thomas Coke, *Extracts of the Journals of the Rev. Dr. Coke's Three Visits to America* (London, 1790), 45; Francis Asbury, *Journals and Letters*, ed. Elmer T. Clark (London: Epworth, 1958), 1:489.

83 A number of the petitions are published with an introduction in Fredrika Teute Schmidt and Barbara Ripel Wilhelm, "Early Proslavery Petitions in Virginia," *William and Mary Quarterly* 30 (January 1973): 133–46.

84 Ibid., 138–40.

85 Ibid., 140–43.

86 Ibid., 143–44; for an examination of the emergence of proslavery thought in Virginia during these years, see David D. Robson, "'An Important Question Answered': William Graham's Defense of Slavery in Post-Revolutionary Virginia," *William and Mary Quarterly* 37 (October 1980): 644–52.

87 William Warner Hening, *The Statutes at Large in Virginia* (Richmond, 1821–23), 9:268.

88 Gerald W. Mullin, *Flight and Rebellion: Slave Resistance in Eighteenth-Century Virginia* (New York: Oxford University Press, 1972), 126; Schmidt and Wilhelm, "Early Proslavery Petitions in Virginia," 140, 144.

89 Over the next two decades, the Virginia Assembly tweaked the law on a number of occasions but left it generally intact. In 1780, the Assembly revised the law to allow refugees from the British occupation of South Carolina and Georgia to bring their slaves to Virginia, though they could only stay for one year after hostilities ceased without forfeiting their slaves. Modifications in 1789 and 1790 merely gave slaveholders moving into the state as residents longer to register their slaves without penalty. With regard to the slave trade, Virginia's slave code of 1792 did little more than codify existing legislation on the subject. It permitted only whites taking up residence in Virginia to bring slaves into the state and it required those settlers to take an oath declaring that their slaves were not imported for the purpose of sale. A minor revision of the slave trade law in 1796 opened the smallest of loopholes in the ban by allowing Virginia residents to bring any slaves born in Virginia but later moved out of the state back to the Old Dominion if the master so desired. But even this tiny exception applied only to the original owner of the slaves in question. Any slave who had been sold after leaving Virginia could still not be reintroduced into the state. See McColley, *Slavery in Jeffersonian Virginia*, 163–72.

90 For an overview of modern approaches to the study of the southern backcountry and frontier, see Gregory Nobles, "Breaking into the Backcountry: New Approaches to the Early American Frontier, 1750–1800," *William and Mary Quarterly* 46 (October 1989): 641–70; Albert H. Tillson Jr., "The Southern Backcountry: A Survey of Current Research," *Virginia Magazine of History and Biography* 98 (July 1990): 387–422.

91 Stephen Aron, *How the West Was Lost: The Transformation of Kentucky from Daniel Boone to Henry Clay* (Baltimore: Johns Hopkins University Press, 1996), esp. 125–49; Ellen Eslinger, "The Shape of Slavery on the Kentucky Frontier, 1775–1800," *Register of the Kentucky Historical Society* 92 (Winter 1994): 1–23.

92 Lowell H. Harrison, *The Antislavery Movement in Kentucky* (Lexington: University Press of Kentucky, 1978), esp. 1–26.

93 Philanthropos [David Rice], *Slavery Inconsistent with Justice & Good Policy: Proved by a Speech Delivered in the Convention, Held at Danville, Kentucky* (Philadelphia, 1792); this pamphlet is also reprinted with minor omissions in McColley, *Slavery in Jeffersonian Virginia*, Documentary Supplement 2, 194–204. See also Vernon F. Martin, "Father Rice, the Preacher Who Followed the Frontier," *Filson Club Historical Quarterly* 29 (October 1955): 324–30.

94 Asa Earl Martin, *The Antislavery Movement in Kentucky Prior to 1850* (Louisville, KY: Filson Club, 1918), 11–17.

95 The Breckinridge quotation is found in Hazel Dicken-Garcia, *To Western Woods: The Breckinridge Family Moves to Kentucky in 1793* (Rutherford, NJ: Fairleigh-Dickinson University Press, 1991), 171. On Breckinridge's career, see Lowell H. Harrison, *John Breckinridge: Jeffersonian Republican* (Louisville: Filson Club, 1969), esp. 103–9.

96 Lowell H. Harrison, *Kentucky's Road to Statehood* (Lexington: University Press of Kentucky, 1992), 97–103; Joan Wells Coward, *Kentucky in the New Republic: The Process of Constitution Making* (Lexington: University Press of Kentucky, 1979), 37.

97 Harrison, *Kentucky's Road to Statehood*, 103–4.

98 Philanthropos, *Slavery Inconsistent with Justice.*

99 Ibid.

100 "To the Freemen of Kentucky," *Kentucky Gazette*, April 4, 1799; Harrison, *Kentucky's Road to Statehood*, 109–10; Samuel M. Wilson, ed., *Journal of the First Constitutional Convention*

of Kentucky, Held in Danville, Kentucky, April 2–19, 1792 (Lexington: State Bar Association of Kentucky, 1942). On the political thought of Nicholas, see Huntley Dupre, "The Political Ideas of George Nicholas," *Register of the Kentucky Historical Society* 39 (June 1941): 201–23.

101 George Nicholas to James Madison, May 2, 1792, in *The Papers of James Madison*, eds. Hutchinson, Rachal, et al., 14:296; see also Aron, *How the West Was Lost*, 90.

102 Martin, *The Antislavery Movement in Kentucky*, 16–17.

103 Hubbard Taylor to James Madison, April 16, 1792, in *The Papers of James Madison*, eds. Hutchinson, Rachal, et al., 14:289.

104 William Lewis to John Breckinridge, July 18, 1799, Breckinridge Family Papers, LC.

105 "Constitution of Kentucky—1792," in Francis Newton Thorpe, ed., *The Federal and State Constitutions, Colonial Charters, and Other Organic Laws of the States, Territories, and Colonies Now of Heretofore Forming the United States of America* (Washington, DC: Government Printing Office, 1909), 1264–77; Harrison, *Kentucky's Road to Statehood*, 115–30; Coward, *Kentucky in the New Republic*, 37–47; Chamberlain, "The Evolution of State Constitutions," 36–44.

106 John Robinson, *The Testimony and Practice of the Presbyterian Church in Reference to Slavery* (Cincinnati, 1852), 123–24; Martin, *The Antislavery Movement in Kentucky*, 22.

107 Robert Davidson, *The History of the Presbyterian Church in Kentucky* (New York, 1857), 336–37; Martin, *The Antislavery Movement in Kentucky*, 23.

108 But see also Jeffrey Brooke Allen, "The Origins of the Pro-Slavery Thought in Kentucky, 1792–1799," *Register of the Kentucky Historical Society* 77 (April 1979): 75–90 on the growing support for slavery in the new state.

109 *Kentucky Gazette*, April 4, 1799.

110 "No Convention," c. 1798, a pamphlet found in Breckinridge Family Papers, LC. This pamphlet is quoted extensively in Martin, *The Antislavery Movement in Kentucky*, 27. George Nicholas died unexpectedly just three days after the convention began, and John Breckinridge emerged as the principal shaper of the 1799 constitution.

111 Quotation found in Coward, *Kentucky in the New Republic*, 112. See also George Nicholas to John Breckinridge, February 16, 1799, Breckinridge Family Papers, LC.

112 John Breckinridge to Governor Isaac Shelby, March 11, 1798, Breckinridge Papers, LC. On Breckinridge's influence on Kentucky's 1799 constitution, see Lowell H. Harrison, "John Breckinridge and the Kentucky Constitution of 1799," *Register of the Kentucky Historical Society* 57 (July 1959): 209–33.

113 Chamberlain, "The Evolution of State Constitutions," 50–59; Aron, *How the West Was Lost*, 94–96; Coward, *Kentucky in the New Republic*, 48–86.

114 [Scaevola], "To the Electors of Fayette County," in *The Papers of Henry Clay*, ed. James F. Hopkins et al. (Lexington: University Press of Kentucky, 1959–91), 1:7. "Scaevola" was a pseudonym Clay used in writing letters during the pre-convention campaign to shape public opinion.

115 Aron, *How the West Was Lost*, 94–95; Chamberlain, "The Evolution of State Constitutions," 56–63; Coward, *Kentucky in the New Republic*, 115–27.

116 Aron, *How the West Was Lost*, 124–49.

117 Harrison, *The Antislavery Movement in Kentucky*, 25–27; J. H. Spencer, *A History of the Kentucky Baptists from 1789–1886* (Cincinnati: J. R. Baumes, 1886), 2:17. See also John Boles, *Religion in Antebellum Kentucky* (Lexington: University Press of Kentucky, 1976), 104–12.

118 David Barrow, *Involuntary, Absolute, Hereditary Slavery Examined on the Principles of Nature, Reason, Justice, Policy and Scripture* (Lexington, KY: Bradford, 1808); Spencer, *A History of the Kentucky Baptists,* 2:120; Martin, *The Antislavery Movement in Kentucky*, 38–39; Harrison, *The Antislavery Movement in Kentucky*, 26–28. Going much further than most early national-era emancipationists were willing to go, Barrow attacked white supremacy as well. The "talents or abilities" of blacks, Barrow declared, "are not inferior to the whites in any respect." But Barrow's surprising critique of white racism actually reduced the effectiveness of his bold witness against slavery, as his unorthodox views on race severely limited his audience in early national Kentucky. Historian John Boles has argued that by 1811 only 300 of Kentucky's 17,000 Baptists held antislavery views; see Boles, *Religion in Antebellum Kentucky*, 116–17.

119 The following discussion of slavery in early Tennessee draws heavily on the older but valuable insights of Chase C. Mooney, *Slavery in Tennessee* (Bloomington: Indiana University Press, 1957), esp. 1–29, 64–85; see also Stanley John Folmsbee, *Sectionalism and Internal Improvements in Tennessee, 1796–1845* (Knoxville: East Tennessee Historical Society, 1939), 1–19 on how Tennessee geography slowed the growth of slavery in the state until around 1810.

120 The first written source conveying this tradition is John Allison, *Dropped Stitches in Tennessee History* (Nashville: Marshall and Bruce, 1897), 80. See also James W. Patton, "Progress of Emancipation in Tennessee," *Journal of Negro History* 17 (1932): 67–102.

121 Asa E. Martin, "The Anti-Slavery Societies of Tennessee," *Tennessee Historical Magazine* 1 (1915): 261–80.

122 *Acts of Tennessee, 1801*, 27; see also Mooney, *Slavery in Tennessee*, 19–20.

123 Martin, "The Anti-Slavery Societies of Tennessee," 261.

124 Mooney, *Slavery in Tennessee*, 67–85.

125 The temporary, necessary evil concession made by upper South leaders, however, worried slaveholders in the lower South, who were becoming convinced that slavery was essential to their long-term economic well-being and wanted loyal political allies and trading partners in the upper South. On this point, see Freehling, *Road to Disunion*, 121–43.

126 James Madison, "Memorandum on an African Colony for Freed Slaves," in *The Papers of James Madison*, ed. Rachal Hutchinson et al., 12:437–38; James Madison, "Answers to Questions Concerning Slavery," c. 1823, in *The Writings of Madison*, ed. Gaillard Hunt (New York: G P. Putnam's Sons, 1900–10), 9:134; James Madison to Robert J. Evans, June 15, 1819, in *Letters and Other Writings of James Madison*, ed. William C. Rives and Philip R. Fendall (Philadelphia, 1865), 3:133–38; McCoy, *Last of the Fathers*, 253–322; see also Gaillard Hunt, "William Thornton and Negro Colonization," *Proceedings of the American Antiquarian Society* 30 (1920): 32–61.

127 For good overviews of Tucker's efforts on behalf of emancipation, see McColley, *Slavery in Jeffersonian Virginia*, 132–36; Freehling, *Drift Toward Dissolution*, 90–96; Phillip Hamilton, "Revolutionary Principles and Family Loyalties: Slavery's Transformation in the St. George Tucker Household of Early National Virginia," *William and Mary Quarterly* 60 (October 1998): 531–56.

128 St. George Tucker to Jeremy Belknap, January 24, 1795, in *Collections of the Massachusetts Historical Society*, 1877, 3:191–92.

129 St. George Tucker, *A Dissertation on Slavery: With a Proposal for the Gradual Abolition of It, in the State of Virginia* (Philadelphia, 1796).

130 Ibid., esp. 18–22.

131 St. George Tucker to Ludwell Lee, November 30, 1796, Ludwell Lee to St. George Tucker, December 5, 1796, and George K. Taylor to St. George Tucker, December 8, 1796, in Tucker-Coleman Collection, W&M. See also McColley, *Slavery in Jeffersonian Virginia*, 134–35.

132 St. George Tucker, "Queried Relating to Slavery in Massachusetts," in *Collections of the Massachusetts Historical Society*, 1877, 3:428.

133 See Douglas R. Egerton, *Gabriel's Rebellion: The Virginia Slave Conspiracies of 1800–1802* (Chapel Hill: University of North Carolina Press,1993); Testimony of Ben Woolfolk, "Trial of Nicholas King," in Flourney, ed., *Calendar of Virginia State Papers*, 9:161–62.

TWO. REBELLION AND REACTION

1 The three standard accounts of the Gabriel insurrection scare are Gerald W. Mullin, *Flight and Rebellion: Slave Resistance in Eighteenth-Century Virginia* (New York: Oxford University Press, 1972), esp. 140–63; Douglas R. Egerton, *Gabriel's Rebellion: The Virginia Slave Conspiracies of 1800–1802* (Chapel Hill: University of North Carolina Press, 1993); and James Sidbury, *Ploughshares into Swords: Race, Rebellion and Identity in Gabriel's Virginia, 1730–1810* (Cambridge: Cambridge University Press, 1997). For a recent update, see Douglas R. Egerton, *Death or Liberty: African Americans and Revolutionary America* (New York: Oxford University Press, 2009), 271–81.

2 The single most extensive set of published records of Gabriel's rebellion are the deposition and trial records collected in William Price Palmer and Henry W. Flourney, eds., *Calendar of Virginia State Papers* (Richmond, VA, 1875–93), 9:140–74; but see also the *Journal of the Senate of the Commonwealth of Virginia, 1800* (Richmond, VA: Thomas Nicolson, 1800), 26–33, and the transmission of materials copied at the instruction of Governor James Monroe and transmitted to the General Assembly, found in Executive Communications, December 5, 1800, General Assembly, House of Delegates, Office of the Speaker, Executive Communications, 1800–1803, Box 8, Folder 7, LV. Virtually all of the primary sources were developed by whites during the investigation and prosecutions that accompanied the scare, and thus they are subject to all of the caveats concerning such evidence that were so effectively raised with regard to similar evidence developed in the later Denmark Vesey investigation by Michael P. Johnson in "Denmark Vesey and His Co-Conspirators, Part I," *William and Mary Quarterly* 58 (October 2001): 915–76. These matters will be examined in more detail in a later chapter. For my purposes here, the question of whether or not the information given in postscare slave testimony, testimony given under duress, threat, physical punishment and torture, and testimony possibly designed to reduce one's own punishment by implicating others was truthful is less important than that many whites seemed to accept the information provided in such testimony as accurate and reacted accordingly.

3 Henrico County Court Order Book, number 9, 94–95, LV; see also Philip J. Schwarz, "Gabriel's Challenge: Slaves and Crime in Late Eighteenth Century Virginia," *Virginia Magazine of History and Biography* 90 (July 1982): 283–309, and Sidbury, *Ploughshares into Swords*, 55–56.

4 On this point, see Egerton, *Gabriel's Rebellion*, 50–58; Mullin, *Flight and Rebellion*, 150–63.

5 Trial of Gilbert, 22, and Trial of Samuel Byrd, 24, in Executive Communications, December 5, 1800, Box 8, Folder 7, LV.

6 Egerton, *Gabriel's Rebellion*, 58–64; for supportive evidence from the primary sources, see, for example, Witnesses Against John, the Property of Mary Jones of Hanover County, 11–12, in Executive Communications, December 5, 1800, Box 8, Folder 7, LV. See also Sidbury, *Ploughshares into Swords*, 99–102.

7 Egerton, *Gabriel's Rebellion*, 51–52; Sidbury, *Ploughshares into Swords*, 72–82.

8 My conclusions here are drawn from consideration of the sources cited in note 2.

9 Governor James Monroe to Virginia House of Delegates, Executive Communication, December 5, 1800, General Assembly, House of Delegates, Office of the Speaker, Executive Communications, 1800–1803, Box 8, Folder 7, LV.

10 See Mullin, *Flight and Rebellion*, 148–52; Egerton, *Gabriel's Rebellion*, 58–68; Governor James Monroe to Virginia House of Delegates, Executive Communication, December 5, 1800, General Assembly, House of Delegates, Office of the Speaker, Executive Communications, 1800–1803, Box 8, Folder 7, LV. For additional supporting evidence, see "Evidence Against the Negroes Tried, September 11," in Flourney, ed., *Calendar of Virginia State Papers*, 9:141–44.

11 "John's Case" and "The Trial of Ben Alias Ben Woolfolk, Belonging to P. Greyham," in Flourney, ed., *Calendar of Virginia State Papers*, 9:142, 171.

12 Evidence surfaced in depositions and slave testimony, including that of Ben Woolfolk, once a close associate of Gabriel's who emerged as one of the prosecution's key witnesses, that "two Frenchmen" played an integral role in planning the insurrection. See "Evidence Against Negroes Tried September 11," and "Confessions of Ben Alias Ben Woolfolk," in Flourney, ed., *Calendar of Virginia State Papers*, 9:141–42, 150–52. If true, such information was politically volatile, since Federalists had repeatedly argued that the Republicans' affinity for French Jacobinism encouraged slave unrest and promised to undermine slavery itself over the long term. Documented reports of French involvement in Gabriel's plot would have cut hard at the Republican base among Virginia slaveholders during the 1800 campaign and would have put Thomas Jefferson and his supporters on the defensive. Douglas Egerton argues that Monroe systematically corralled and suppressed any hard evidence suggesting French influence to prevent it from being used by Federalists to their political advantage. But if Monroe made such efforts, they hardly prevented the Federalists from hearing the testimony and spreading rumors about French involvement in the insurrection plot. This issue is crucial to Egerton's overarching interpretation that Gabriel's rebellion was inspired in part by the political rhetoric of the heated 1800 campaign and that the Federalists in particular tried to use the insurrection scare to convince voters that the Republicans flirted with notions of equality that would prove dangerous to a slaveholding society. For conflicting views on this point, see Douglas Egerton, "'As Much Right to Fight for Our Liberty as Any Men': Gabriel's Rebellion and the Election of 1800," *Journal of Southern History* 56 (May 1990): 191–214, his *Gabriel's Rebellion*, esp. 103–15, and Sidbury, *Ploughshares into Swords*, 133–35.

13 See Egerton, *Gabriel's Rebellion*, 69–73. Egerton's interpretation of the rebellion places the contact that Gabriel and his co-conspirators had with artisanal republicanism and its critique of merchants, especially during the election campaign of 1800, at the center of slave motivation. Thus he interprets the statement about black rebels dining with white merchants as a celebration of the achievement of equality of artisans and merchants as the fulfillment of artisanal radicalism. My review of the evidence suggests that ideas of artisan republicanism were only one set of oppositional ideas among the slave rebels and not one that appeared to enjoy any

particular pride of place among the rebels. The concept of rebels dining with merchants also follows biblical notions of a "Great Reversal" in which the last become first and the first become last. In this instance the last (slaves) vanquish the first (powerful merchants) and then sit at table with them. On the variety of oppositional traditions, including both artisanal republicanism, evangelical Christianity, and the ideologies of the French and American revolutions, see Sidbury, *Ploughshares into Swords*, 55–94.

14 James Callender to Thomas Jefferson, September 13, 1800, Jefferson Papers, LC. Callender, a Republican pamphleteer, was jailed in Richmond by the Adams administration on charges of sedition at the time the rebellion plot was discovered.

15 Egerton, *Gabriel's Rebellion*, 69; see also "Evidence Against Negroes Tried September 11" and "The Trial of Gabriel," in Flourney, ed., *Calendar of Virginia State Papers*, 9:143, 164–65.

16 Mosby Sheppard to James Monroe, August 30, 1800, in Executive Communication, December 5, 1800, General Assembly, House of Delegates, Office of the Speaker, Executive Communications, 1800–1803, Box 8, Folder 7, 1, LV.

17 William Mosby to James Monroe, November 10, 1800, in Executive Communication, December 5, 1800, General Assembly, House of Delegates, Office of the Speaker, Executive Communications, 1800–1803, Box 8, Folder 7, 2, LV.

18 Governor James Monroe to Virginia House of Delegates, Executive Communication, December 5, 1800, General Assembly, House of Delegates, Office of the Speaker, Executive Communications, 1800–1803, Box 8, Folder 7, LV. Monroe's active counterinsurgency mobilization certainly alerted area whites that an insurrection scare was afoot before any news reports were published.

19 "Trial of Nicholas' King," in Flourney, ed., *Calendar of Virginia State Papers*, 9:161–63. This testimony was given by Mary Martin, a shopkeeper.

20 Egerton, *Gabriel's Rebellion*, 79, 103–7; *Virginia Herald* (Fredericksburg), September 16, 1800.

21 James Monroe to Thomas Jefferson, September 15, 1800, Jefferson Papers, LC.

22 Thomas Jefferson to James Monroe, September 20, 1800, James Monroe Papers, LC.

23 John Randolph to Joseph Nicholson, September 26, 1800, Nicholson Papers, LC.

24 Letter to Editor, September 20, 1800, in the *Norfolk Herald*, October 18, 1800.

25 Minor quoted in Ruth C. Fitzgerald, *A Different Story: A Black History of Fredericksburg, Stafford, and Spotsylvania, Virginia* (Fredericksburg, VA: Unicorn Press, 1979), 65.

26 Joseph Jones to James Monroe, September 9, 1800, Executive Papers, LV.

27 Egerton, *Gabriel's Rebellion*, 107–11; *Norfolk Herald*, October 11, 1800. Monroe had earlier been advised by those who held Gabriel in custody that the chief insurrectionist had informed them that he would "give your Excellency a full information about the conspiracy" but "will confess to no one else." See Colonel Thomas Newton to Governor James Monroe, September 24, 1800, in Flourney, ed., *Calendar of Virginia State Papers* 9:155–56. Monroe apparently calculated that he had nothing to gain by granting a face-to-face interview with the accused leader of a slave rebellion. The surviving record leaves no evidence that such a meeting ever occurred.

28 James T. Callender to Samuel Pleasants, October 1, 1800, in *Virginia Argus*, October 3, 1800; (Philadelphia) *Aurora*, September 24 and 26, 1800. The *Aurora* was edited by the accomplished Jeffersonian publicist William Duane.

29 Quoted in William Cabell Bruce, *John Randolph of Roanoke* (New York: G. P. Putnam's Sons, 1922), 2:250.

30 Governor James Monroe to Virginia House of Delegates, Executive Communication, December 5, 1800, General Assembly, House of Delegates, Office of the Speaker, Executive Communications, 1800–1803, Box 8, Folder 7, LV.
31 Ibid.
32 *Virginia Gazette and General Advertiser*, December 11, 1800, 1–2.
33 (Fredericksburg) *Virginia Herald*, September 23, 1800, 2–3.
34 Winthrop Jordan, *White over Black: American Attitudes Toward the Negro, 1550–1812* (Chapel Hill: University of North Carolina Press, 1968), 560–65; Sidbury, *Ploughshares into Swords*, 132–38.
35 [George Tucker], *Letter to a Member of the General Assembly of Virginia, on the Subject of the Late Conspiracy of the Slaves with a Proposal for Their Colonization*, 2nd ed. (Richmond, VA: H. Pace, 1801).
36 George Tucker to St. George Tucker, March 7, 1801, Tucker-Coleman Papers, WM.
37 *Journal of the House of Delegates, 1800–1801*, 61; Thomas Brooke to Levin Powell, December 22, 1800, Powell Papers, LC.
38 John Randolph to Joseph Nicholson, September 26, 1800, Nicholson Papers, LC.
39 Egerton, *Gabriel's Rebellion*, 147–51.
40 *Journal of the House of Delegates, 1800–1801*, 47–48.
41 Samuel Shepard, ed., *The Statutes at Large of Virginia, from October Session 1792, to December Session, 1806, Inclusive* (Richmond: Samuel Shepard, 1836), 2:279–80; *Journal of the House of Delegates, 1800–1801*, 61; *Journal of the Senate of Virginia, 1800–1801*, 60.
42 *Journal of the House of Delegates, 1800–1801*, 47–48; Egerton, *Gabriel's Rebellion*, 148–54.
43 James Monroe to Thomas Jefferson, June 15, 1801, in Philip Slaughter, *The Virginian History of African Colonization* (Richmond: Macfarlane and Fergusson, 1855), 2–3.
44 Thomas Jefferson to James Monroe, November 24, 1801, in Slaughter, *The Virginian History of African Colonization*, 3–4.
45 Ibid.
46 Jefferson asked that all communications about the matter remain confidential. James Monroe to Thomas Jefferson, December 8 and 21, 1801, Thomas Jefferson Papers, LC; James Monroe to the Virginia General Assembly, December 21, 1801, Executive Letterbook, LV.
47 Douglas Egerton, "'Fly Across the River': The Easter Slave Conspiracy of 1802," *North Carolina Historical Review* 68 (April 1991): 87–110; Egerton, *Gabriel's Rebellion*, 119–46. For a different point of view, see Thomas C. Parramore, "Aborted Takeoff: A Critique of "Fly Across the River,'" *North Carolina Historical Review* 68 (April 1991): 111–21; but see also Egerton's response, "A Rejoinder," *North Carolina Historical Review* 68 (April 1991): 122–24. See also Jeffrey Crow, "Slave Rebelliousness and Social Conflict in North Carolina, 1775–1802," *William and Mary Quarterly* 37 (January 1980): 79–102.
48 John Scott to James Monroe, April 23, 1802, Executive Papers, LV.
49 Egerton, *Gabriel's Rebellion*, 126–31.
50 William Prentis to James Monroe, January 4 and 5, 1802, Testimony of Willis Pillar at Trial of Jones' Joe, January 7, 1802, and Richard Jones to William Prentis, January 2, 1802, and William Martin to James Monroe, January 2, 1802, all in Executive Papers, LV.
51 Egerton, *Gabriel's Rebellion*, 134–46; for examples of Monroe's sentiments, see James Monroe to John Cowper, May 12, 1802, James Monroe to Thomas Newton, May 2, 1802, and his "Circular—To the County Courts," April 16, 1802, Executive Letterbook, LV.

52 For the resolutions, see Slaughter, *The Virginian History of African Colonization*, 5; see also *Journal of the House of Delegates in Virginia, 1802*, 71; James Monroe to Thomas Jefferson, February 13, 1802, Jefferson Papers, LC.

53 On this point see Egerton, *Gabriel's Rebellion*, 148–56, esp. n. 21.

54 James Monroe to Thomas Jefferson, February 13, 1801, Jefferson Papers, LC.

55 Thomas Jefferson to James Monroe, June 2, 1802, Jefferson Papers, LC.

56 Thomas Jefferson to Rufus King, July 13, 1802, Rufus King to Thomas Jefferson, December 18, 1802, Jefferson Papers, LC; Christopher Gore to Thomas Jefferson, October 10, 1802, Executive Papers, LV. See also Thomas Jefferson to John Lynch, January 21, 1811, Thomas Jefferson Papers, LC.

57 Rufus King to William Wilberforce, January 8, 1803, Rufus King to Henry Thornton, April 30, 1803, and Rufus King to Thomas Jefferson, May 12, 1803, Jefferson Papers, LC.

58 See James Monroe to Thomas Jefferson, June 11, 1802, Jefferson Papers, LC; Egerton, *Gabriel's Rebellion*, 158–59. In his important analysis of this issue, Egerton argues that first Monroe and then Jefferson cooled on the idea of pursuing a colony because it appeared probable that any slaves accepted by Sierra Leone, or any other nation on the African coast, would become free after transport. Neither wanted to make capital crime a path to emancipation for slaves. In my view, Jefferson saw this issue as one of a series of complications but not a problem fatal to the endeavor. At this point in their careers both Jefferson and Monroe remained seriously interested in launching a colonization project for the long-term benefit of Virginia, though initiating such a project was not their top priority.

59 This legislative resolution is reprinted in Slaughter, *The Virginian History of Colonization*, 6.

60 Thomas Jefferson to Governor John Page, December 27, 1804, Jefferson Papers, LC. This letter is also published in Slaughter, *The Virginian History of Colonization*, 5–6. See also Philip J. Schwarz, "The Transportation of Slaves from Virginia, 1801–1805," *Slavery and Abolition* 7 (December 1986): 215–40.

61 The colony had been established under the authority of the British (who did not shy from the identity of imperial power) and the colony was already in operation. Drew R. McCoy, *The Elusive Republic: Political Economy in Jeffersonian America* (Chapel Hill: University of North Carolina Press, 1980), 280–81.

62 For Egerton's view, see *Gabriel's Rebellion*, 158–62; see also William Cohen, "Thomas Jefferson and the Problem of Slavery," *Journal of American History* 56 (December 1969): 503–26; McCoy, *The Elusive Republic,* 196–208; Peter S. Onuf, "Every Generation Is an 'Independent Nation': Colonization, Miscegenation and the Fate of Jefferson's Children," *William and Mary Quarterly* 57 (January 2000): 153–70; William G. Merkel, "To See Oneself as a Target of a Justified Revolution: Thomas Jefferson and Gabriel's Uprising," *American Nineteenth Century History* 4 (2003): 1–31.

63 *Virginia Argus*, January 17, 1806, 2.

64 Ibid., 3.

65 Ibid., January 17, 1806, 2.

66 Ibid., 3.

67 Samuel Shepard, ed., *The Statutes at Large of Virginia, from October Session 1792, to December Session, 1806, Inclusive* (Richmond: Samuel Shepard, 1836), 3:251–53. For analyses of the 1806 law, see Alison Goodyear Freehling, *Drift Toward Dissolution: The Virginia Slavery Debate of 1831–32* (Baton Rouge: Louisiana State University Press, 1982), 116–19; Jordan, *White over Black*, 574–77.

68 John H. Russell, *The Free Negro in Virginia, 1619–1865* (Baltimore: Johns Hopkins University Studies in Historical and Political Sciences, 1913), 71; *Maryland Laws, 1806*, 66; Berlin, *Slaves Without Masters*, 92–93; T. Stephen Whitman, *The Price of Freedom: Slavery and Manumission in Baltimore and Early National Maryland* (Lexington: University of Kentucky Press, 1997), 144.

69 John Hope Franklin, *The Free Negro in North Carolina, 1790–1860* (Chapel Hill: University of North Carolina, 1943), 41–45.

70 Charles Pettigrew to Ebenezer Pettigrew, May 19, 1802, in Sarah M. Lemmon, ed., *The Pettigrew Papers* (Raleigh; North Carolina Department of Archives and History, 1971), 1:285–86.

71 Shepard, ed., *The Statutes at Large of Virginia*, 3:108.

72 *Virginia Argus*, February 15, 1804; Shepard, ed., *The Statutes at Large of Virginia*, 3:124. Robert McColley, *Slavery in Jeffersonian Virginia* (Urbana: University of Illinois Press, 1964), 104–5. The provisions requiring that an ordained white minister preside over services and instruction effectively ensured that Quakers could not sponsor or lead legal meetings, since the Quakers had no ordained clergy.

73 Shepard, ed., *The Statutes at Large of Virginia*, 3:124; John H. Russell, *The Free Negro in Virginia, 1619–1865* (Baltimore: Johns Hopkins University Press, 1913), 141.

74 Loren Schweninger, "The Underside of Slavery: The Internal Economy, Self-Hire, and Quasi-Freedom in Virginia, 1765–1785," *Slavery and Abolition* 12 (September 1991): 1–22; Sidbury, *Ploughshares into Swords*, 187–209; Sarah S. Hughes, "Slaves for Hire: The Allocation of Black Labor in Elizabeth City County, Virginia, 1782–1810," *William and Mary Quarterly* 35 (April 1978): 260–89; Lois Green Carr and Lorena Walsh, "Economic Diversification and Labor Organization in the Chesapeake, 1650–1820," in Stephen Innes, ed., *Work and Labor in Early America* (Chapel Hill: University of North Carolina Press, 1988), 144–88.

75 Editor of *Richmond Virginian*, c. 1808, quoted in Egerton, *Gabriel's Rebellion*, 165–66.

76 *Journal of the House of Delegates of Virginia, 1808*, 85; Egerton, *Gabriel's Rebellion*, 166

77 May 21, 1808, manuscript version of "Travels in America, 1806–1809: The Journal of Alexander Dick," 180, UVA.

78 Peggy Nicholas to Wilson Cary Nicholas, December 21, 1808, Wilson Carey Nicholas Papers, UVA.

79 On the general perception of free blacks, see Ira Berlin, *Slaves Without Masters: The Free Negro in the Antebellum South* (New York: Oxford University Press, 1974), esp. 79–107; for specific Virginia references, see Charles F. Mercer to Alexander Stevenson, November 3, 1823, Benjamin Bland Papers, VHS; and Charles F. Mercer to William Gaston, January 1, 1828, William Gaston Papers, SHC.

80 Jefferson, *Notes on the State of Virginia*, 132–39.

81 St. George Tucker, "Queries Relating to Slavery in Massachusetts," in *Collections of the Massachusetts Historical Society* 3 (1877): 405–8.

82 James Madison, "Answers to Questions Concerning Slavery," c. 1823, in *Writings of Madison*, ed. Gaillard Hunt (New York: G. P. Putnam's Sons, 1900–10), 9:134.

83 Charles Fenton Mercer to John Hartwell Cocke, April 19, 1818, John Hartwell Cocke Papers, Alderman Library, University of Virginia.

84 John Taylor, *Arator; Being a Series of Agricultural Essays, Practical and Political: in Sixty-four Numbers*, 6th ed. (Petersburg, VA: John M. Carter, 1818), 48. On Taylor, see Robert Shalhope, *John Taylor of Caroline: Pastoral Republican* (Columbia: University of South Carolina Press, 1980); O'Brien, *Conjectures of Order*, 2:881–88.

85 Matthew Mason, "The Battle of the Slaveholding Liberators: Great Britain, The United States and Slavery in the Early Nineteenth Century," *William and Mary Quarterly* 59 (May 2002): 665–96; Frank A. Cassell, "Slaves of the Chesapeake Bay Area and the War of 1812," *Journal of Negro History* 57 (April 1972): 144–55; Christopher T. George, "Mirage of Freedom: African Americans in the War of 1812," *Maryland Historical Magazine* 91 (December 1996): 427–50.

86 "Confession of Tom," in Flourney, ed., *Calendar of Virginia State Papers*, 10:120–23.

87 Wilson Cary Nicholas to William Branch Giles, January 13, 1813, Wilson Cary Nicholas Papers, LC; Charles K. Mallory to James Barbour, February 13, 1813, and James Monroe to James Barbour, March 31, 1813, in Flourney, *Calendar of Virginia State Papers*, 10:192–93. See also John C. A. Stagg, *Mr. Madison's War* (Princeton, NJ: Princeton University Press, 1983), 381–412.

88 "Indemnities Due Under the Award of the Emperor of Russia for Slaves and Other Private Property Carried Away by the British Forces in Violation of the Treaty of Ghent," in United States Congress, *American State Papers; Documents, Legislative and Executive: Foreign Relations* (Washington, D.C.: Government Printing Office, 1832–61), 5:800–18.

89 Proclamation of Alexander Cochrane, 2 April 1814, in William R. Manning, ed., *Diplomatic Correspondence of the United States: Canadian Relations, 1784–1860* (Washington, DC: Carnegie Endowment, 1940), 1:647–52.

90 Robert Gleig, *A Subaltern in America: Comprising His Narrative of the Campaigns of the British Army, at Baltimore, Washington, etc., etc. During the Late War* (Philadelphia: Carey and Hart, 1833), 24; Roger Norman Buckley, *Slaves in Red Coats: The British West India Regiments, 1795–1815* (New Haven, CT: Yale University Press, 1979), 1–142.

91 John Coalter to Joseph C. Cabell, 28 April 1814, Cabell Family Papers, UVA.

92 Thomas Jefferson to Edward Coles, August 25, 1814, in *The Writings of Thomas Jefferson*, ed. Paul Leicester Ford (New York: G. P. Putnam's Sons, 1899), 9:477–79.

93 On Mercer, see Douglas Egerton, *Charles Fenton Mercer and the Trial of National Conservatism* (Oxford: University Press of Mississippi, 1989), esp. 65–131.

94 Charles Fenton Mercer, *An Address to the American Colonization Society at Their 36th Annual Meeting* (Geneva, 1854); Charles Fenton Mercer to John H. Cocke, April 19, 1818, Cocke Collection, UVA.

95 Charles Mercer's interest in colonization was more conservative than humanitarian. To be sure, Mercer readily admitted that "slavery is wrong" and denounced the institution as the "blackest of all blots and foulest of deformities." But Mercer also argued that "freeing the slaves now would do more harm than good." He regularly insisted that colonization had "nothing…to do with domestic slavery" but only with the removal of free blacks. The Virginian's views on free blacks were strikingly harsh but not atypical. Mercer casually asserted that "more than half" of all free black women were "prostitutes" and more than half of all free back males were "rogues." Colonization, he insisted, would free the state from a group of people who were "every day polluting and corrupting public morals." Egerton, *Charles Fenton Mercer*, 107–12.

96 P. J. Staudenraus, *The African Colonization Movement, 1816–1865* (New York :Columbia University Press, 1961), 23–35, 69–116; see also Douglas B. Egerton, "'Its Origin Is Not a Little Curious': A New Look At the American Colonization Society," *Journal of the Early Republic* 5 (Winter 1985): 463–80; David M. Streifford, "The American Colonization Society: An Application of Republican Ideology to Early Antebellum Reform," *Journal of Southern History* (May 1979): 201–20

97 The best overall analysis of the American Colonization Society remains P. J. Staudenraus, *The American Colonization Movement, 1816–1865* (New York: Columbia University Press, 1961). On points made in this paragraph, see esp. 23–35 and 69–116.

98 Robert G. Harper, *A Letter from Gen. Harper, of Maryland, to Elias B. Caldwell, Esq., Secretary of the American Society for Colonizing the Free People of Colour, in the United States, with Their Own Consent* (Baltimore, 1818); but see also Christopher Phillips, "The Dear Name of Home: Resistance to Colonization in Antebellum Baltimore," *Maryland Historical Magazine* 91 (1996): 481–504.

99 Adams, who eyed Crawford as a potential presidential rival, privately admitted that he thought the whole proposal merely a popularity-seeking gimmick concocted by the Georgian. Staudenraus, *The African Colonization Movement,* 70–74; William H. Hoyt, *The Papers of Archibald D. Murphey* (Raleigh, NC: E. M. Uzzell, 1914), 2:61–62; *Thirty-Sixth Annual Report of the American Colonization Society* (Washington, DC, 1853), 38–43.

100 *Memoirs of John Quincy Adams*, ed. Charles Francis Adams (Philadelphia: J. B. Lippincott, 1874–77), 4:321–22, 355–56; Edward S. Delaplaine, *Francis Scott Key: Life and Times* (New York: Biography Press, 1937), 203–4; Benjamin F. Hall, *Official Opinions of the Attorneys General of the United States* (Washington, DC: W. H. & O. H. Morrison, 1873–), 1:314–20; John Pendleton Kennedy, *Memoirs of the Life of William Wirt: Attorney General of the United States* (Philadelphia; Lea and Blanchard, 1849); Staudenraus, *The African Colonization Movement, 1816–1865,* 51–53; Harry Ammon, *James Monroe: The Quest for National Identity* (New York: McGraw-Hill, 1971), 521–25. On relations between Adams and Crawford in this period, see Paul C. Nagel, *John Quincy Adams: A Public Life, A Private Life* (New York: Knopf, 1997), 241–67; Chase C. Mooney, *William H. Crawford, 1772–1834* (Lexington: University of Kentucky Press, 1974); and E. Wayne Cutler, "William H. Crawford: A Contextual Biography," Ph.D. dissertation, University of Texas, 1971. Calhoun's overall view of the colonization movement receives a pithy summary from Irving Bartlett, *John C. Calhoun: A Biography* (New York: W. W. Norton, 1993), 221. Based on available evidence, Calhoun kept remarkably quiet about the colonization movement while in the Monroe cabinet. Not even John Quincy Adams' fulsome diary reveals any significant expression of opinion on the subject by Calhoun even though the two cabinet secretaries privately discussed the issue of slavery on several occasions.

101 Egerton, *Mercer*, 109; Charles Fenton Mercer to John H. Cocke, April 19, 1818, Cocke Collection, UVA.

102 Freehling, *The Road to Disunion*, esp. 150–61, offers a judicious analysis that has influenced my thinking on these subjects.

103 For insightful introductions to the concept of diffusion, see Freehling, *Road to Disunion*, 150–57; McColley, *Slavery in Jeffersonian Virginia,*173–175; and McCoy, *The Last of the Fathers,* 265–74. On the importance of the emerging cotton boom in the lower South, see John Hebron Moore, *The Emergence of the Cotton Kingdom in the Old Southwest: Mississippi, 1770–1860* (Baton Rouge: Louisiana State University Press, 1988); Joyce E. Chaplin, "Creating a Cotton South in Georgia and South Carolina, 1760–1815," *Journal of Southern History* 57 (May 1991): 171–200; and Lacy Ford, *Origins of Southern Radicalism: The South Carolina Upcountry, 1800–1860* (New York: Oxford University Press, 1988), 1–43.

104 *Annals of Congress*, 5th Congress, 2nd Session, 1310.

105 Ibid., 1309–12.

106 Everett S. Brown, ed., "Documents: The Senate Debate on the Breckinridge Bill for the Government of Louisiana, 1804," *American Historical Review* 22 (January 1917): 340–64. The Breckinridge quotations can be found on pages 354 and 345. The debate over slavery in Louisiana is covered in more detail in chapter 4.

107 On the latter point, see Matthew Mason, *Slavery and Politics in the Early American Republic* (Chapel Hill: University of North Carolina Press, 2006), 177–212.

108 *Annals of Congress*, 15th Congress, 2nd Session, 1188–91.

109 *Annals of Congress*, 16th Congress, 1st Session, 1391.

110 Thomas Jefferson to John Holmes, April 22, 1820, in *The Writings of Thomas Jefferson*, ed. Ford, 10:157–58.

111 James Madison to James Monroe, February 23, 1820, and James Madison to Marquis de Lafayette, November 25, 1820, in *The Writings of James Madison*, ed. Gaillard Hunt (New York: G. P. Putnam's Sons, 1910), 9:23–26, 35–41.

112 See McCoy, *The Last of the Fathers*, 265–76.

113 On these demographic patterns, see Allen Kulikoff, "Uprooted Peoples: Black Migrants in the Age of the American Revolution, 1790–1820, " in Ira Berlin and Ronald Huffman, eds., *Slavery and Freedom in the Age of the American Revolution* (Charlottesville: University Press of Virginia, 1983), 143–71.

114 Thomas Dew, "Abolition of Negro Slavery," *American Quarterly Review* 12 (1832): 189–265. A few months later, the essay was reprinted in pamphlet form as *Review of the Debate in the Virginia Legislature of 1831 and 1832* (Richmond: T. H. White, 1832). A modern print of the original essay can be found in Drew G. Faust, *The Ideology of Slavery: Proslavery Thought in the Antebellum South, 1830–1860* (Baton Rouge: Louisiana State University Press, 1981), 21–78.

115 Tadman, *Speculators and Slaves*, 12; Berlin, *Slaves Without Masters*, esp. 396–97. North Carolina also "exported" just over 10,000 slaves during this era. Kentucky and Tennessee continued to acquire slaves through 1820, though Kentucky politicians had emerged as leading diffusionists, suggesting that Kentucky expected to become a slave-exporting state at some point, which it did after 1820. Tennessee remained a slave-importing state until the 1850s, when the opening of lucrative new Texas markets drew off slaves from western Tennessee.

116 On the concept of "disowning slavery" and how the process worked during gradual emancipation in New England, see Joanne Pope Melish, *Disowning Slavery: Gradual Emancipation and Race in New England, 1780–1860* (Ithaca: Cornell University Press, 1998).

THREE. OPENING THE SLAVE TRADE

1 Joseph Clay to James Jackson, February 16, 1784, in Elizabeth Donnan, ed., *Documents Illustrative of the Slave Trade to America* (Washington, DC: Carnegie Institution, 1935), 4:630–31.

2 Robert Olwell, *Masters, Slaves and Subjects: The Culture of Power in the South Carolina Low Country, 1740–1790* (Ithaca: Cornell University Press, 1998), 221–70; Sylvia Frey, *Water from the Rock: Black Resistance in a Revolutionary Age* (Princeton, NJ: Princeton University Press, 1991), 81–142; Betty Wood, *Women's Work, Men's Work: The Informal Slave Economies ofLowcountry Georgia* (Athens: University of Georgia Press, 1995), and *Gender, Race and Rank in a Revolutionary Age: The Georgia Lowcountry, 1750–1820* (Athens: University of Georgia Press, 2000).

3 The Constitution specified that the federal government could not prohibit the foreign slave trade for twenty years after ratification, leaving the question up to the states during that period. See Paul Finkelman, "Slavery at the Constitutional Convention: Making a Covenant with Death," in Stephen Botein, Richard Beeman, and Edward C. Carter, eds., *Beyond Confederation: Origins of the Constitution and American National Identity* (Chapel Hill: University of North Carolina Press, 1987), 188–225, and Finkelman's *Imperfect Union: Slavery, Federalism and Comity* (Chapel Hill: University of North Carolina Press, 1981), esp. 20–45; Jack N. Rakove, *Original Meanings: Politics and Ideas in the Making of the Constitution* (New York: Alfred A. Knopf, 1996), 85–88.

4 Patrick Brady, "The Slave Trade and Sectionalism in South Carolina, 1887–1808," *Journal of Southern History* 38 (November 1971): 601–20. Charles Cotesworth Pinckney's vote against closing the slave trade in 1787 remains only partially explained. Throughout the legislative session, Pinckney expressed serious concern about the indebtedness of the state's citizens. As a result, he was a strong supporter of legislation to meliorate the state's private debt crisis. It was precisely this concern over individual indebtedness and debtor unrest that led many legislators to support closing the trade. But the older Pinckney broke ranks with his allies to vote against closing the slave trade. Rawlin Lowndes, a friend and political opponent of Pinckney, later claimed that Pinckney saw keeping the slave trade open a matter of principle for South Carolina and would never vote to close the trade regardless of circumstances. See Jonathan Eliot, ed., *The Debates in the Several State Conventions on the Adoption of the Federal Constitution* (Philadelphia, 1836), 4:272–73; Marvin R. Zahniser, *Charles Cotesworth Pinckney: Founding Father* (Chapel Hill: University of North Carolina Press, 1967), 81–82.

5 Thomas Jefferson to Edward Rutledge, July 14, 1787, in *The Writings of Thomas Jefferson*, ed. Paul L. Ford (New York: G. P. Putnam's Sons, 1892–99), 4:410.

6 Not even Virginia or Massachusetts sent a more distinguished delegation to the Constitutional Convention in Philadelphia. John Rutledge, a former governor and president of the national Congress, stood at the heart of the Rutledge-Pinckney alliance, which proved staunch defenders of Lowcountry interests and political power, consistently opposing greater representation from inland areas, and of the faction that later led the early Federalist party in South Carolina. Charles Cotesworth Pinckney, son of the famous indigo innovator Eliza Lucas Pinckney and her husband, Charles, matriculated at Oxford and studied law at London's Middle Temple. As a young lawyer, Charles Cotesworth Pinckney struck even casual acquaintances as a "man of brilliant natural powers." By the time of his death in 1825, Pinckney owned more than 300 slaves and maintained a personal library of 1,600 volumes. Along with the Rutledges, Charles Cotesworth Pinckney emerged as a leader of one of Charleston's prominent Federalist factions in the 1790s. Charles Pinckney, a younger cousin of Charles Cotesworth Pinckney, was only thirty years old when selected to serve as a delegate, but he had already earned a reputation for brilliance in South Carolina. He would later serve four terms as governor of South Carolina and was virtually a regular member of the state legislature. He earned the name "Blackguard Charlie" when he split with other family members and left the Federalist Party in 1800 to support Jefferson. After joining the Republicans, Pinckney became South Carolina's foremost example of the aristocrat as champion of the common people. Though he lived lavishly and cultivated the image the self-indulgent patrician, Pinckney also aggressively courted popular support among Charleston's artisans ands workers. His Republican affiliation and flamboyant campaign style drew sharp criticism form Federalists, who branded him a

"demagogue." Finally, Pierce Butler, an Irish immigrant who arrived in Charleston in 1767, was the only South Carolina delegate not directly tied to the Charleston elite at the time of the 1787 convention. Butler had married into the wealthy Middleton family, over the objection of most Middleton patriarchs, and through that marriage acquired substantial plantation interests in Beaufort. One established as planter, Butler began a long career of large-scale speculation in backcountry property. Butler's speculative endeavors brought him into close contact with many backcountry leaders, and while a strong supporter of the1787 Constitution, Butler emerged as a leader of the Jeffersonian opposition during the 1790s and worked hard to build Republican loyalty among backcountry politicians. Despite their later differences, all four South Carolina delegates supported the idea of a stronger national government in 1787. To an extent, all four delegates supported the idea of a strong national government because they saw it as a needed protector of slavery rather than a threat to it. See Ernest M. Lander Jr., "The South Carolinians at the Philadelphia Convention, 1787," *South Carolina Historical Magazine* 57 (July 1956): 134–55; Jerome J. Nadelhoft, "South Carolina: A Conservative Revolution," in Patrick T. Conley and John P. Kaminski, eds., *The Constitution and the States: The Role of the Original Thirteen in Framing and Adoption of the Federal Constitution* (Madison, WI: Madison House, 1988), 156–84. On Rutledge, see James Haw, *John and Edward Rutledge of South Carolina* (Athens: University of Georgia Press, 1997); on Charles Cotesworth Pinckney, see Zahniser, *Charles Cotesworth Pinckney*; on Charles Pinckney, see Marty D. Matthews, *Forgotten Founder: The Life and Times of Charles Pinckney* (Columbia: University of South Carolina Press, 2004); on Butler, see John M. Reynolds, "The Republicanism of Pierce Butler: South Carolina Framer of the Federal Constitution," master's thesis, University of South Carolina, 2004; and Lewright Sikes, *The Public Life of Pierce Butler: South Carolina Statesmen* (Washington: University Press of America, 1979).

7 Patrick Brady, "The Slave Trade and Sectionalism in South Carolina, 1887–1808," 601–20; Zahniser, *Charles Cotesworth Pinckney: Founding Father*, 81–87. On the social unrest that accompanied the debt relief movement, including Shays-style efforts to prevent the courts from holding sessions, see Robert A. Becker, "Salus Populi Suprema Lex: Public and South Carolina Debtor Relief Laws, 1783–1788," *South Carolina Historical Magazine* 80 (January 1979): 65–75; Robert A. Becker, ed., "John F. Grimké's Eyewitness Account of the Camden Court Riot, April 27–28, 1785," *South Carolina Historical Magazine* 83 (July 1982): 209–13; Jerome J. Nadelhoft, *The Disorders of War: The Revolution in South Carolina* (Orono: University of Maine at Orono Press, 1981), 155–68.

8 Charleston *Morning Post*, March 23, 1787, in Donnan, ed., *Documents Illustrative of the Slave Trade to America*, 4:493. Gillon, a merchant, planter, and land speculator with large backcountry holdings, often championed artisanal and backcountry causes against the wishes of the Federalist elite; however, in 1787 he was still burdened by large debts from his wartime mercantile activity.

9 Journal of the South Carolina House of Representatives, March 17 and 22, 1787, and January 23, 1788, SCDAH. The proviso closing the slave trade was part of a larger bill providing debtors with a measure of relief by stipulating that debts could be collected only in three yearly installments.

10 Brady, "The Slave Trade and Sectionalism in South Carolina, 1887–1808," 602–6.

11 Rebecca Starr, *A School for Politics: Commercial Lobbying and Political Culture in Early South Carolina* (Baltimore: Johns Hopkins University Press, 1998), 85–107; Eliot, ed., *Debates*, 4:263–316. For a more complete account of the South Carolina delegation's fight to gain constitutional protection for the international slave trade, see chapter 1.

12 Elliot, *Debates*, IV, 253–317, quote on 273. See also Carl J. Vipperman, *The Rise of Rawlins Lowndes, 1721–1800* (Columbia: University of South Carolina Press, 1978), 240–57. Ironically, Lowndes had joined the three of four Convention delegate in closing the state's slave trade in 1787 while serving in the South Carolina Assembly.

13 Donnan, ed., *Documents Illustrative of the Slave Trade to America*, 4:493; George C. Rogers Jr., *Evolution of a Federalist: William Loughton Smith of Charleston* (Columbia: University of South Carolina Press, 1962), 161.

14 Brady, "The Slave Trade and Sectionalism in South Carolina," 609; Rachel Klein, *Unification of a Slave State: The Rise of the Planter Class in the South Carolina Backcountry, 1760–1808* (Chapel Hill: University of North Carolina Press, 1990), 125–35.

15 Journal of the South Carolina Senate, December 9 and 10, 1797, SCDAH; George D. Terry, "A Study of the Impact of the French Revolution and the Insurrections in Saint Domingue upon South Carolina, 1790–1805," master's thesis, University of South Carolina, 1975.

16 Charles Pinckney to George Washington, September 12, 1791, quoted in Rogers, *Evolution of a Federalist*, 249.

17 During the 1790s, the South Carolina legislature passed a series of biennial bans of the foreign slave trade. To keep the ban in place, the legislature had to renew it every two years. The internal or domestic slave trade remained closed between 1792 and 1804. Brady, "The Slave Trade and Sectionalism in South Carolina," 608–10; Mark D. Kaplanoff, "Making the South Solid: Politics and the Structure of Society in South Carolina, 1790–1815," Ph.D. dissertation, Cambridge University, 1979, 52–55, 59–62; see also Winthrop Jordan, *White over Black: American Attitudes Toward the Negro, 1550–1812* (Chapel Hill: University of North Carolina Press, 1968), 380–91.

18 Ralph Izard to Edward Rutledge, September 28, 1792, Izard Papers, Dreer Collection, Members of the Old Congress, vol. III, HSP. Izard owned multiple plantations throughout the South Carolina Lowcountry, including four rice plantations in the Pee Dee and a town home in Charleston. In 1795, he owned more than 11,000 acres and more than 460 slaves; see N.Louise Bailey, Mary L. Morgan, and Carolyn R. Taylor, eds., *Biographical Directory of the South Carolina Senate, 1776–1985* (Columbia: University of South Carolina Press, 1986), 2:795–97. For a good overview of the impact of the French Revolution and the successful slave revolt in Saint-Domingue, see Klein, *Unification of a Slave State*, 203–37. See also Mark D. Kaplanoff, "Making the South Solid," 52–55.

19 Ralph Izard to Mathias Hutchinson, November 20, 1794, Izard Papers, SCL.

20 Pierce Butler to John Holmes, November 5, 1793, Pierce Butler Letterbook, SCL.

21 Terry, "A Study of the Impact of the French Revolution and the Insurrections in Saint Domingue upon South Carolina, 1790–1805," esp. 95–131.

22 Harriott L. Pinckney to Mrs. Frances Pinckney, November 24, 1797, Thomas Pinckney Papers, SCL; J. Allison to Jacob Read, December 5, 1797, Read Papers, DU; and Edward Rutledge to John Rutledge Jr., November 21, 1797, John Rutledge Jr. Papers, DU.

23 *Annals of the Fifth Congress*, 129–53. Despite his Federalist leanings, Harper's land speculation brought him into close contact with prominent interior planters, including Wade Hampton and Pierce Butler, both of whom he joined in land speculations schemes at one time or another. See Joseph W. Cox, *Champion of Southern Federalism: Robert Goodloe Harper of South Carolina* (Port Washington, NY: Kennikat Press, 1972), 125–27.

24 Governor Charles Pinckney to South Carolina Senate, November 28, 1798, Governor's Messages, #721, Record Group S165009, SCDAH.

25 Trial of Slaves Accused of Attempted Murder of Their Master, 1798, John Ewing Colhoun Papers, SCL. John Ewing Colhoun was an older cousin of John C. Calhoun and part of the loose Republican coalition of Upcountry planters pieced together initially by Pierce Butler.

26 Ruth Scarborough, *The Opposition to Slavery in Georgia Prior to 1860* (reprint, New York: Negro Universities Press, 1968), 107–11; Ralph Betts Flanders, *Plantation Slavery in Georgia* (Chapel Hill: University of North Carolina Press, 1933), 37–39, 182–83.

27 Kaplanoff, "Making the South Solid," 55.

28 John Drayton to Governor James Monroe, September 27, 1800, in Governor's Messages, #768, November 25, 1800, Record Group S165009, SCDAH.

29 General Orders, September 27, 1800, Paul Hamilton to Governor John Drayton, October 17, 1800, and William Hayne to Governor John Drayton, October 20, 1800, in Governor's Messages, #768, November 25, 1800, Record Group S165009, SCDAH.

30 James Monroe to John Drayton, October 21, 1800, in ibid.

31 Message of John Drayton, November 25, 1800, in ibid.

32 Read, a United States Senator, was an influential Federalist with strong ties to British and northern commercial interests. On the large role played by Read in the direction of South Carolina's Federalist Party in the 1790s, see Rogers, *Evolution of a Federalist*, esp. 115–16.

33 Jacob Read to Governor to John Drayton, July 18, 1800, in Governor's Messages, #768, November 25, 1800, Record Group S165009, SCDAH.

34 Ibid.

35 Message of John Drayton, Governor's Messages #768, November 25, 1800, Record Group S165009, SCDAH.

36 "The Address of the General Conference of the Methodist Episcopal Church to all their Brethren and Friends in the United States," May 20, 1800, in Message of John Drayton, November 25, 1800, Governor's Messages, #768, Record Group S165009, SCDAH

37 Message of John Drayton, November 25, 1800, Governor's Messages, #768, Record Group S165009, SCDAH.

38 Jacob Read to Governor to John Drayton, July 18, 1800, in Governor's Messages, #768, November 25, 1800, Record Group S165009, SCDAH.

39 Message of John Drayton, Governor's Messages #768, November 25, 1800, Record Group S165009, SCDAH. Drayton perceived the conduct of free blacks as every bit as much a problem as slave control. The governor complained that free blacks in Charleston "are assuming some of the rights of citizenship" (chiefly taking cases to court), and he urged the legislature to end the privilege in short order. Drayton, the son of William Henry Drayton of Drayton Hall in St. Andrew's Parish, studied law in Charleston under Charles Cotesworth Pinckney and emerged as a leading early-nineteenth-century southern intellectual. He owned a rice plantation at Georgetown as well as land along the North Santee. In addition to serving as governor, Drayton represented the city of Charleston in both the state House and Senate. In 1812, he was appointed to the federal bench by President James Madison. In addition to his legal and political work, Drayton earned a reputation as a writer. His writings on botany, history, and education and his aptitude for watercolors earned him a position in the German Royal Society of Sciences in 1804. Bailey, Morgan, and Taylor, eds., *Biographical Directory of the South Carolina Senate, 1776–1985*, 2:419–21.

40 Jacob Read to Governor to John Drayton, July 18, 1800, in Governor's Messages, #768, November 25, 1800, Record Group S165009, SCDAH.

41 David J. McCord, ed., *The Statutes at Large of South Carolina* (Columbia: A. S. Johnston, 1840), 7:440–43.

42 Message of John Drayton, November 25, 1800, Governor's Messages, #768, Record Group S165009, SCDAH; See also Henry William DeSaussure to John Rutledge Jr., February 17, 1802, and July 12, 1803, John Rutledge Jr. Papers, SHC.

43 McCord, ed., *The Statutes at Large of South Carolina*, 7:436–46. See also Journal of the South Carolina House of Representatives, 1800, November 11 to December 20, and Journal of the South Carolina Senate, 1800, November 24 to December 20, SCDAH. On the Stono rebellion, see Mark M. Smith, ed., *Stono: Documenting A Slave Rebellion* (Columbia: University of South Carolina Press, 2005); Peter H. Wood, *Black Majority: Negroes in Colonial South Carolina from 1670 through the Stono Rebellion* (New York: Knopf, 1974), 308–26; Mark M. Smith, "Remembering Mary, Shaping Slave Revolt: Reconsidering the Stono Rebellion," *Journal of Southern History* 67 (August 2001): 513–34; John K. Thornton, "African Dimensions of the Stono Rebellion," *American Historical Review* 96 (October 1991): 1101–13; Edward A. Pearson, "'A Countryside Full of Flames': A Reconsideration of the Stono Rebellion and Slave Rebelliousness in the Early Eighteenth-Century South Carolina Lowcountry," *Slavery and Abolition* 17 (August 1996): 22–50.

44 McCord, ed., *The Statutes at Large of South Carolina*, 436–40.

45 Ibid.

46 Paul Hamilton to Governor John Drayton, October 17, 1800, and William Hayne to Governor John Drayton, October 20, 1800, in Governor's Messages, #768, November 25, 1800, Record Group S165009, SCDAH; McCord, ed., *The Statutes at Large of South Carolina*, 436–46.

47 McCord, ed., *The Statutes at Large of South Carolina*, 442–43.

48 Division Orders Issued by Governor James Jackson of Georgia, September 11, 1802, in Message of Governor John Drayton, December 3, 1802, Governor's Messages, #846, Record Group S165009, SCDAH. The above enclosure was forwarded to Drayton by Daniel Huger, the governor's private secretary, who was dispatched to Savannah to inquire.

49 Howard A. Ohline, "Georgetown, South Carolina: Racial Anxieties and Militant Behavior, 1802," *South Carolina Historical Magazine* 73 (July 1972): 130–40 presents a good brief overview of this scare. See also Message of Governor John Drayton to the Speaker and Members of the House of Representatives, December 3, 1802, Governor's Messages, #846, Record Group S165009, SCDAH.

50 Horry owned three rice plantations near Winyah Bay area, one on the Santee and more than 100 slaves. He also owned a town home in Columbia, where he resided in later years. In 1801, a new election district was carved out of Georgetown and named after Horry. In the twentieth century, a portion of Horry County, the so-called Grand Stand area around Myrtle Beach, developed as a national vacation attraction that brings hundreds of thousands of visitors to the coast annually. Inland portions of the Horry district, part of the state's declining tobacco belt, remain among the state's poorest areas. Ward owned a Waccamaw rice plantation and was the father of Joshua John Ward, 1800–1853, who owned ten plantations, including Brookgreen, and more than 1,000 slaves, mostly in the Georgetown area, in 1850. See Bailey, Morgan, and Taylor, eds., *Biographical Directory of the South Carolina Senate*, 753–55.

51 Message #1 of Governor John Drayton, November 23, 1802, Governor's Messages, #836, Record Group S165009, SCDAH; Ohline, "Georgetown, South Carolina: Racial Anxieties and Militant Behavior, 1802," 130–40.

52 See Petition of Members of the Charleston Baptist Association..., October 31, 1801, Legislative Petitions, Records of the South Carolina General Assembly, 1801, Record Group S165015, #00123, and Petition of Members of the Charleston Baptist Association..., c. 1802, Legislative Petitions, Records of the South Carolina General Assembly, 1802, Record Group S165015, #00181, SCDAH. The 1801 petition was handwritten and signed by Furman and six other Baptist ministers. The 1802 petition, an slightly abbreviated version the petition of the previous year, was printed and signed by almost thirty "Members of the Charleston Baptist Association, representing thirty congregations of Christian citizens of South Carolina."

53 Petition of the Inhabitants of Chester District Asking a Revision in the Law Which Impairs the Giving of Religious Instruction to Slaves and Free Persons of Colour, c. 1801, Legislative Petitions, Records of the South Carolina General Assembly, 1801, Record Group S165015, #00122, SCDAH.

54 Petition of Members of the Charleston Baptist Association..., October 31, 1801, Legislative Petitions, Records of the South Carolina General Assembly, 1801, Record Group S165015, #00123, SCDAH.

55 Petition of Members of the Charleston Baptist Association..., c. 1802, Legislative Petitions, Records of the South Carolina General Assembly, 1802, Record Group S165015, #00181, SCDAH.

56 Lacy K. Ford, *Origins of Southern Radicalism: The South Carolina Upcountry, 1800–1860* (New York: Oxford University Press, 1988), 19–37; Klein, *Unification of a Slave State*, 269–302.

57 The revisions prevailed narrowly (9–7) among middle district representatives and lost among parish representatives (20–29). House Journal, November 29, 1803, SCDAH. My analysis on this point follows that of Klein, *Unification of a Slave State*, 290–91.

58 Howell M. Henry, *Police Control of the Slave in South Carolina* (reprint, New York: Negro Universities Press, 1968), 134–35. Ultimately, white interference with biracial religious gatherings became a subject regulated by the courts. See chapter 6.

59 Presentment of the Edgefield District Grand Jury, 1802, Grand Jury Presentments, Records of the South Carolina General Assembly, 1802, Record Group S165010, #00006, SCDAH.

60 Presentment of the Edgefield District Grand Jury, October 1802, Grand Jury Presentments, Records of the South Carolina General Assembly, 1802, Record Group S165010, #00004, SCDAH.

61 Inhabitants of Abbeville District, Petition Asking for the Repeal of the Acts Barring the Importation of Negroes into the State..., October 23, 1802, Legislative Petitions, Records of the South Carolina General Assembly, 1802, Record Group S165015, #00129, and Inhabitants of Abbeville District, Petition Asking for the Repeal of the Acts Barring the Importation of Negroes into the State..., c. 1802, Legislative Petitions, Records of the South Carolina General Assembly, 1802, Record Group S165015, #01567, SCDAH.

62 Marjorie Mendenhall, "A History of Agriculture in South Carolina, 1790–1860," Ph.D. dissertation, University of North Carolina at Chapel Hill, 1940, 105–8; Ronald E. Bridwell, "The South's Wealthiest Planter: Wade Hampton I of South Carolina, 1754–1835," Ph.D. dissertation, University of South Carolina, 1980, 397–504; Mark D. Kaplanoff, "Making the South Solid: Politics and the Structure of Society in South Carolina, 1790–1815," Ph.D. dissertation, Cambridge University, 1979, 9–13; Joyce E. Chaplin, "Creating a Cotton South in Georgia and South Carolina, 1760–1815," *Journal of Southern History* 57 (May 1991): 171–200; Lacy Ford, *Origins of Southern Radicalism: The South Carolina Upcountry, 1800–1860* (New York:

Oxford University Press, 1988), 1–19. See also Wade Hampton to John Chesnut, August 25, 1800, Williams-Chesnut-Manning Papers, SCL.

63 David Ramsay, *The History of South Carolina* (Charleston, SC: David Longworth, 1809), 2:120–21, 131–91, 230–46. For more on Ramsay, see Arthur H. Shaffer, *To Be an American: David Ramsay and the Making of the American Consciousness* (Columbia: University of South Carolina Press, 1991).

64 John Drayton, *A View of South Carolina as Respects Her Natural and Civil Concerns* (Charleston, SC: W. P. Young, 1802), 135–68.

65 Thomas Dryden Spratt, "Recollections of His Family" [c. 1875], Spratt Family Papers, SCL. In these quotations, James Spratt's son, Thomas D. Spratt, is reflecting on his father's life and times. See Ford, *Origins of Southern Radicalism*, 19.

66 On these points, see Chaplin, "Creating a Cotton South"; Lacy Ford, *Origins of Southern Radicalism*, 1–43; John Hebron Moore, *The Emergence of the Cotton Kingdom in the Old Southwest: Mississippi, 1770–1860* (Baton Rouge: Louisiana State University Press, 1988); James David Miller, *South by Southwest: Planter Emigration and Identity in the Slave South* (Charlottesville: University Press of Virginia, 2002); Edward Baptist, *Creating an Old South: Middle Florida's Plantation Frontier Before the Civil War* (Chapel Hill: University of North Carolina Press, 2002); Daniel Dupre, *Transforming the Cotton Frontier: Madison County, Alabama, 1800–1840* (Baton Rouge: Louisiana State University Press, 1997); Randolph B. Campbell, *An Empire for Slavery: The Peculiar Institution in Texas, 1821–1865* (Baton Rouge: Louisiana State University Press, 1989).

67 Memorial to Congress, October 23, 1797, in Clarence Edwin Carter, *The Territorial Papers of the United States* (Washington, DC: Government Printing Office, 1940), 5:221–23.

68 Adam Rothman, *Slave Country: American Expansion and the Origins of the Deep South* (Cambridge, MA: Harvard University Press, 2005), 45–54, esp. 51; David J. Libby, *Slavery and the Mississippi Frontier, 1720–1835* (Jackson: University Press of Mississippi, 2004), 37–59; John Hebron Moore, "Two Cotton Kingdoms," *Agricultural History* 60 (Fall 1986): 1–16.

69 See Ira Berlin, *Many Thousands Gone: The First Two Centuries of Slavery in North America* (Cambridge: Harvard University Press, 1998), esp. 358–65; *Generations of Captivity: A History of African American Slaves* (Cambridge, MA: Harvard University Press, 2003), esp. 161–44; and "Time, Space, and the Evolution of Afro-American Society in British Mainland North America," *American Historical Review* 85 (February 1980): 44–78.

70 See Lacy Ford, "Reconsidering the Internal Slave Trade: Paternalism, Markets and the Character of the Old South," in Walter Johnson, ed., *Internal Passages: The Domestic Slave Trade in the United States*, 143–64; Adam Rothman, "The Domestication of the Slave Trade in the United States," in Johnson, ed., *Internal Passages*, 32–54.

71 John Drayton, *A View of South Carolina*, 146; Charleston *City Gazette*, November 9, 1803.

72 House Journal, Papers of the General Assembly, December 17, 1802, 134, SCDAH; Senate Journal, Papers of the General Assembly, December 11–18, 1802, 162, 166, 217, 219–22, 230, SCDAH.

73 See Peter J. Kastor, *The Nation's Crucible: The Louisiana Purchase and the Creation of America* (New Haven: Yale University Press, 2004), 19–52.

74 This argument has been most persuasively advanced by Jed Handelsman Shugerman, "The Louisiana Purchase and South Carolina's Reopening of the Slave Trade in 1803," *Journal of the Early Republic* 22 (Summer 2002): 263–90.

75 *Charleston Courier*, December 2, 1803; Thomas Sumter, Jr. to James Monroe, December 11, 1803, James Monroe Papers, LC (microfilm of original held at New York Public Library).

76 *Charleston Courier*, December 5, 1803; Governor James Richardson to the House of Representatives, 1803, in Donnan, ed., *Documents Illustrative of the Slave Trade to America*, 4:500–1. John Drayton, Richardson's predecessor as governor from 1800 to 1802, had also conceded that the prohibition of the importation of slaves had proven hard to enforce and that slave smuggling became widespread during his tenure. While governor, Drayton had repeatedly recommended tighter control over the state's black population, both slave and free, though he had never broached the idea of reopening the slave trade. But in 1803, Drayton, no longer governor but once again serving as a legislator, abruptly reversed his position and supported reopening the African slave trade. John Drayton, *A View of South Carolina*, 145; Message of John Drayton, November 25, 1800, Governor's Messages, #768, and Message #1 of Governor John Drayton, November 23, 1802, Governor's Messages, #836, in Record Group S165009, SCDAH.

77 *Charleston Courier*, December 26, 1803, reporting remarks made on December 6, 1803. Portions of this debate are also reprinted in Donnan, ed., *Documents Illustrative of the Slave Trade to America*, 4:502. During the early 1800s, William Smith amassed a large tract of land in the southwestern corner of York district and increased the number of slaves he held from ten to seventy between 1800 to 1810. He also owned a home in the courthouse town of Yorkville, where he practiced law. Through the connections he made in Yorkville, he built a political network throughout the district. Over his lifetime, Smith also built a fortune through sprawling cotton plantations in South Carolina, Alabama and Louisiana. He moved to Alabama in the 1830s and died there in 1840 at the age of seventy-eight. See Bailey, Morgan, and Taylor, eds., *Biographical Directory of the South Carolina Senate, 1776–1985*, 3:1517–9.

78 South Carolina General Assembly, House Journal, 1803, 70, SCDAH.

79 South Carolina General Assembly, House Journal, 1803, 12, 17–18, SCDAH.

80 South Carolina General Assembly, House Journal, 1803, 121–22, SCDAH.

81 South Carolina General Assembly, House Journal, 1803, 124–47, SCDAH.

82 Analysis based on votes recorded in South Carolina General Assembly, House Journal, 1803, 124–47, SCDAH, and Walter B. Edgar, *Biographical Directory of the South Carolina House of Representatives* (Columbia: University of South Carolina Press, 1974), 1:259–63.

83 See South Carolina General Assembly, House Journal, December 17, 1803, 147–51, SCDAH. The key vote, recorded on pages 149–51, was on the second reading of the reopening bill. On page 149, the House Journal reported the result of this vote as 55–46, but on pages 150–51 the official recording of the ayes and nays clearly shows that the roll call result was 55–47. Hence I have used the latter numbers in my analysis of voting patterns. In his "The Louisiana Purchase and South Carolina's Reopening of the Slave Trade in 1803," 279, Jed Shugerman characterizes the vote as 55–46. Shugerman cites the House Journal, 150–51, as his source even though those pages clearly record a 55–47 vote. In his "Making the South Solid," 328, Mark Kaplanoff correctly refers to the vote as 55–47.

84 My definitions of Lowcountry and interior here are based on the two broad distinctions made by the state's 1790 constitution for tax purposes. It divided the state into two broad divisions, lower and upper, and set up separate treasurers for the two divisions. The lower division treasury remained in Charleston; the upper division treasury was located in the new state capital of Columbia. In the early 1800s, the lower division or Lowcountry included all of the state's political subdivisions designated as parishes, except Orange, plus the election districts of Horry,

Marion and Williamsburg. (Most of the geopolitical subdivisions in the lower division retained the colonial name of "parish." After 1790, interior subdivisions were called "districts." So the political subdivisions known as "counties" across most of the nation were called either "parishes" or "districts" in antebellum South Carolina.) By this definition, the Lowcountry began at the coast and extended about sixty miles inland. The interior (or upper division) included not only all of the districts on or above the fall line, but districts on the inner coastal plain such as Barnwell (Winton), Clarendon, Claremont (Sumter), Darlington, and Marlboro. Hence the term *interior* as used here includes districts below the fall line but above the outer coastal plain as well as districts on or above the fall line. Later analysis will define Upcountry more precisely as that portion of the interior lying at or above the state's fall line. In this particular instance, the inner coastal plain districts split evenly on the issue and hence did not shape the "interior" vote significantly. See Bailey, Morgan, and Taylor, eds., *Biographical Directory of the South Carolina Senate, 1776–1985*, 3:2012 for a map of these divisions and districts.

85 While sectional patterns in the vote on reopening the slave trade were noticeable, separate roll call analyses, conducted by Patrick Brady and Mark Kaplanoff, of legislative voting patterns for 1803 reveal that when compared to other key issues of the session the legislature's vote on the slave trade was decidedly less sectional in nature than many other votes, emphasizing that cross-sectional coalition building was important to the success of the reopening movement. The same vote which reopened the foreign slave trade also reopened the domestic or interstate trade. My analysis is based on House Journal, November 21–December 17, 1803, Records of the General Assembly, 1803, 12, 17–18, 54, 64, 70, 121–22, 124–27, 147–51, 168, 172, 187, 192, 225, SDAH; and Edgar, *Biographical Directory*, 1, 259–63. See also Kaplanoff, "Making the South Solid," 62–65, 326–29; and Brady, "The Slave Trade and Sectionalism in South Carolina," 612–14. On Senate action, see Senate Journal, Records of the General Assembly, November 21–December 17, 1803, 35, 53, 84, 148, 153, 156–59, SCDAH. The significant minority of representatives from Charleston and its immediate hinterland who voted to reopen the slave trade were likely driven by the hope that the slave trade itself would prove a boon to Charleston merchants and shipping interests, though a few probably looked to the expansion of cotton production along the Cooper and Santee rivers.

86 Recent scholarship emphasizing the importance of the opportunity to resell imported slaves to the new Louisiana territory rightly corrects an older view emphasizing only demand from the South Carolina interior, but this scholarship nonetheless paints a portrait in need of still further refinement. See esp. Shugerman, "The Louisiana Purchase and South Carolina's Reopening of the Slave Trade," 263–90, but see also Brady, "The Slave Trade and Sectionalism in South Carolina," 601–20, and Klein, *Unification of a Slave State*, 246–57.

87 For Lowndes quote, see *Annals of Congress*, 8th Congress, 1st Session, 991–93. In their public arguments, however, advocates of reopening the trade mentioned only the need for slaves in South Carolina's interior and the near impossibility of enforcing the prohibition on the trade as reasons justifying the reopening. But their reticence was probably born of a desire to keep the reopening an entirely state question, carefully avoiding offering any invitation to federal scrutiny or legislation on the matter until after the reopening was a fait accompli.

88 My argument here runs counter to the view that South Carolina's reopening of the foreign slave trade was part of a concerted strategy of slaveholder imperialism forcefully expressed in Shugerman, "The Louisiana Purchase and South Carolina's Reopening of the Slave Trade," 288–90.

89 Adam Rothman, *Slave Country: American Expansion and the Origins of the Deep South* (Cambridge, MA: Harvard University Press, 2005), 24–35; Libby, *Slavery and the Mississippi Frontier*, 3–36; Jack D. L. Holmes, "Cotton Gins in the Spanish Natchez District, 1795–1800," *Journal of Mississippi History* 31 (August 1969): 159–71; Moore, "Two Cotton Kingdoms," 1–16. South Carolina supporters of reopening the African slave trade probably expected that the federal government would apply the same policy to the slave trade in Louisiana that it had in Mississippi: prohibiting the foreign trade while allowing the interstate or domestic trade. They then made the rest of their political and economic calculations accordingly. But the development of federal policy toward the slave trade in Louisiana proved more complicated and uncertain precisely because South Carolina had reopened the foreign slave trade.

90 Isaac Briggs to President Thomas Jefferson, March 1, 1804, in Carter, *The Territorial Papers of the United States*, 9:146–49. On Briggs' background, see Rothman, *Slave Country*, 42–44.

91 Rothman, *Slave Country*, 83–95. See also James Dorman, "The Persistent Specter: Slave Rebellion in Territorial Louisiana," *Louisiana History* 18 (Fall 1977): 389–404; Paul F. Lachance, "The Politics of Fear: French Louisianians and the Slave Trade, 1786–1809," *Plantation Society* 1 (June 1979): 162–97.

92 William Claiborne to Thomas Jefferson, July 10, 1806, in *Official Letter Books of W. C. C. Claiborne, 1801–1816*, ed. Dunbar Rowland (Jackson, MS: State Department of Archives and History, 1917), 3:361–65.

93 William C. C. Claiborne to James Madison Thomas Jefferson, May 8, 1804, in *Official Letter Books*, ed. Rowland, 2:134.

94 *Annals of Congress*, 8th Congress, 1st Session, 994–98, 999–1002, 1011–4, 1016–8. Northerners disagreed, however, over the excise tax.

95 Ibid., 991–93.

96 Ibid., 1003–7.

97 Ibid., 1003–4.

98 Ibid., 1012.

99 Ibid., 1012–4, 1028–35.

100 Lewis Kerr to Isaac Briggs, March 24, 1804, Briggs-Stabler Papers, Baldwin Library, Maryland Historical Society, Baltimore, Maryland.

101 William Plumer, *William Plumer's Memorandum of Proceedings in the United States Senate, 1803–1807*, ed. Everett Somerville Brown (New York: Macmillan, 1923), 130.

102 Ibid., 113.

103 Everett S. Brown, ed., "Documents: The Senate Debate on the Breckinridge Bill for the Government of Louisiana, 1804," *American Historical Review* 22 (January 1917): 340–64. The Breckenridge quotation can be found on 345; the first Franklin quotation can be found on 354 and the second on 345; the White quotation is on 347 and the Jackson quote on 349. The exception to the general pattern of upper South opposition to the foreign slave trade was Maryland senator Samuel Smith. The lone upper South senator who supported allowing Louisiana to import slaves from overseas, Smith believed that the people of Louisiana "wish for African slaves, and we ought to let them have a supply." Smith granted that Congress had the "constitutional right to prohibit slavery in that country," but he doubted "as to the policy of it." See Brown, "Documents: The Senate Debate on the Breckinridge Bill…, 1804," 348.

104 Plumer, *William Plumer's Memorandum*, 114.

105 Brown, ed., "Documents: The Senate Debate on the Breckinridge Bill…, 1804," 340–64. The Dayton quote is on 345, the John Smith quote is from 346–47, the Samuel White quotation is on 347, the Hillhouse quotation is on 346, the second John Smith quote is on 345, and the Jackson quote is on 349. Dayton's interest in the lower Mississippi territory eventually landed him in trouble; in 1807 he was arrested for his suspected involvement in the Aaron Burr conspiracy. However, Dayton was later released and never stood trial.

106 *Annals of Congress*, 1804, 240; Brown, ed., "Documents: The Senate Debate on the Breckinridge Bill…, 1804," 340–64; Rothman, *Slave Country*, 29.

107 Brown, ed., "Documents: The Senate Debate on the Breckinridge Bill…, 1804," 340–64. The Israel Smith quote is on 348; the Franklin quote is on 350. Still, an overwhelming majority of senators who spoke on the floor conceded the truth of New Jersey senator Dayton's assertion that "South Carolina now has right to import slaves" and that the constitution prevented Congress from ending South Carolina's participation in the overseas trade until 1808. Dayton's observation can be found in ibid., 352.

108 Ibid.; the Franklin and Breckinridge quotations are on 354.

109 Ibid.; the John Smith quote is found on 353.

110 Wright's position is expressed in Plumer, *William Plumer's Memorandum*, 131–32.

111 *Annals of Congress*, 242. Only two of the eleven votes for the emancipation of imported slaves came from senators representing slaveholding states (by John Brown of Kentucky and William Wells of Delaware), while eight of the seventeen votes against emancipation came from southern senators. Nine votes against the motion came from free-state senators, including John Quincy Adams and Timothy Pickering of Massachusetts.

112 Plumer, *William Plumer's Memorandum*, 124–34; *Annals of Congress*, 1804, 241–44.

113 *United States Statutes at Large*, 8th Congress, 1st Session, 283–89; Rothman, *Slave Country*, 30–31.

114 *Annals of Congress*, 1804, 241–44.

115 Brown, ed., "Documents: The Senate Debate on the Breckinridge Bill…, 1804," 340–64. See 350 for the Jackson quote, 354 for the Nicholas quote, and 350–51 for the Israel Smith quote.

116 For a broad overview of this congressional legislation, see Don E. Fehrenbacher, *The Slaveholding Republic: An Account of the United States Government's Relations to Slavery* (New York: Oxford University Press, 2001), 259–63; Donald L. Robinson, *Slavery in the Structure of American Politics, 1765–1820* (New York: Harcourt Brace Jovanovich, 1970), 396–400.

FOUR. EXTENDING SLAVERY

1 Peter J. Kastor, *The Nation's Crucible: The Louisiana Purchase and the Creation of America* (New Haven: Yale University Press, 2004), esp. 87–88; R. Randall Couch, "William Charles Cole Claiborne: An Historiographical Review," *Louisiana History* 36 (Fall 1995): 453–65; Joseph T. Hatfield, *William Claiborne: Jeffersonian Centurion in the American Southwest* (Lafayette: University of Southwestern Louisiana, 1976). Wilkinson proved a loose cannon. He used his small military force judiciously in establishing American authority in Louisiana but stretched his role as military commander in search of political influence. He worked closely with Aaron Burr for a time before publicly backing away from Burr's plans once the latter's western ambitions were exposed. Over time, the cautious Claiborne's relations with the adventurous and

ambitious Wilkinson grew strained, though Claiborne found Wilkinson's troops valuable in bringing Louisiana under American control.

2 William Claiborne to James Madison, March 16, 1804, in *Official Letter Books of W. C. C. Claiborne, 1801–1816*, ed. Dunbar Rowland (Jackson, MS: State Department of Archives and History, 1917), 2:42–48, esp. 46.

3 John Watkins to William C. C. Claiborne, February 2, 1804, in *Official Letter Books,* 2:3–13, quotation on 10.

4 William Claiborne to James Madison, March 10, 1804, in ibid., 25–26.

5 Ibid. This document can also be found in Governor William C. Claiborne to James Madison, March 10, 1804, in Elizabeth Donnan, ed., *Documents Illustrative of the Slave Trade to America* (Washington, DC: Carnegie Institution, 1935), 4:662, note 1 to document 440.

6 John Craig Hammond, "'They Are Very Much Interested in Obtaining an Unlimited Slavery': Rethinking the Expansion of Slavery in the Louisiana Purchase Territories, 1803–1805," *Journal of the Early Republic* 23 (Fall 2003): 353–80; Donald L. Robinson, *Slavery in the Structure of American Politics, 1765–1829* (New York: Harcourt Brace Jovanovich, 1971), 396–400; James Scanlon, "A Sudden Conceit: Jefferson and the Louisiana Bill of 1804," *Louisiana History* 9 (Spring 1968): 139–62.

7 William Claiborne to James Madison, March 16, 1804, in *Official Letter Books,* 2:42–48.

8 William Claiborne to James Madison, March 31, 1804, in ibid., 2:76–77.

9 Governor William C. Claiborne to James Madison, May 8, 1804, in Donnan, ed., *Documents Illustrative of the Slave Trade to America*, 4:662–63.

10 Dubreuil quoted in Adam Rothman,, *Slave Country: American Expansion and the Origins of the Deep South* (Cambridge, MA: Harvard University Press, 2005), 31.

11 Annals of Congress, 8th Congress, 2nd Session, 1598–608; quotation is found on 1606. On Livingston, see William B. Hatcher, *Edward Livingston: Jeffersonian Republican and Jacksonian Democrat* (Baton Rouge: Louisiana State University Press, 1940).

12 William C. C. Claiborne to President Thomas Jefferson, April 15, 1804, in Clarence Edwin Carter, *The Territorial Papers of the United States* (Washington, DC: Government Printing Office, 1940), 9:221–23.

13 William Claiborne to James Madison, June 22, 1804, in *Official Letter Books*, 2:216–17.

14 Governor William C. Claiborne to James Madison, July 12, 1804, in Donnan, ed., *Documents Illustrative of the Slave Trade to America*, 4:663.

15 Kastor, *The Nation's Crucible*, 55–75.

16 John Watkins to William C. C. Claiborne, February 2, 1804, in *Official Letter Books,* 2:3–13, esp. 6.

17 William Claiborne to Mayor Boré, March 19, 1804, in *Official Letter Books,* 2:50–51.

18 William Claiborne to James Madison, July 12, 1804, in *Official Letter Books,* 2:245–46.

19 William Claiborne to James Madison, October 16, 1804, in ibid., 2:352–60, quotations taken from 358–59. Claiborne worked hard to monitor the African slave trade, which remained legal until October 1. He thought that with the ban pending, great "exertions" would be made to import as many slaves as possible, leading to the arrival of "the refuse negroes of the English Islands" and "even some brigands of St. Domingo." Claiborne tightened security at the embarkation points at Balize and Plaquemine in an effort to "exclude those slaves" who were "accustomed to blood and devastation" and whose "counsel & communication with our present Black population may be pregnant with much future mischief."

20 Petition of the Inhabitants & Colonists of Louisiana to His Excellency William Claiborne, September 17, 1804, in Carter, *Territorial Papers*, 9:297.

21 William Claiborne to Thomas Jefferson, September 18, 1804, in Carter, *Territorial Papers*, 9:298.

22 Petition of the Inhabitants & Colonists of Louisiana to His Excellency William Claiborne, September 17, 1804, in Carter, *Territorial Papers*, 9:297.

23 William Claiborne to Thomas Jefferson, September 18, 1804, in Carter, *Territorial Papers*, 9:298; William Claiborne to James Madison, September 20, 1804, and Claiborne's General Orders, September 22, 1804, in *Official Letter Books*, 2:337–38, 339–40.

24 William Claiborne to President Thomas Jefferson, November 25, 1804, in Carter, *Territorial Papers*, 9:338–41, quotation on 340.

25 Jed Handelsman Shugerman, "The Louisiana Purchase and South Carolina's Reopening of the Slave Trade in 1803," *Journal of the Early Republic* 22 (Summer 2002): 263–90; Hammond, "Rethinking the Expansion of Slavery in the Louisiana Purchase Territories, 1803–1805," 353–80.

26 House Journal, December 17, 1803, Records of the General Assembly, 1803, 147–51, SCDAH; Edgar, *Biographical Directory of the South Carolina House of Representatives*, 1:264–67. Governor James Richardson, who had suggested the reopening of the trade in his annual message to the legislature in 1803, made no mention of the subject in his 1804 message. See Governor's Messages, November 28, 1804, SCDAH.

27 South Carolina Senate Journal, December 8, 1804, 92–94; N. Louise Bailey, Mary L. Morgan, and Carolyn R. Taylor, eds. *Biographical Directory of the South Carolina Senate, 1776–1985* (Columbia, S.C.: University of South Carolina Press, 1986), 3:1830–1.

28 William Claiborne to James Madison, July 31, 1804, in *Official Letter Books*, 3:35–36.

29 Paul F. Lachance, "The Politics of Fear: French Louisianians and the Slave Trade, 1786–1809," *Plantation Society* 2 (June 1979): 162–97.

30 John Watkins to Secretary John Graham, September 6, 1805, in Carter, *Territorial Papers*, 9:500–4.

31 Ibid.

32 James Brown to Albert Gallatin, December 11, 1805, in Carter, *Territorial Papers*, 9:545–48. As U.S. attorney, Brown was uncertain whether the act legalized the importation only of slaves who had entered the United States before 1798 (a provision of the 1804 law) or of all slaves legally imported into the Untied States regardless of their date of entry.

33 Gwendolyn Midlo Hall, "Louisiana Slave Database, 1719–1820," in Gwendolyn Midlo Hall, ed., *Databases for the Study of Afro-Louisiana History and Genealogy, 1699–1860* (Baton Rouge: Louisiana State University Press, 2000); Shugerman, "The Louisiana Purchase and South Carolina's Reopening of the Slave Trade in 1803," 281–83; Lachance, "The Politics of Fear," 171–81; Tadman, *Speculators and Slaves: Masters, Traders and Slaves in the Old South* (Madison: University of Wisconsin Press, 1989), 226–27.

34 Henry William DeSaussure to Ezekiel Pickens, September 10, 1805, in Henry William DeSaussure Papers, SCL.

35 "Reminiscences of Ebenezer S. Thomas, 1803," in Donnan, ed., *Documents Illustrative of the Slave Trade to America*, 4:503; see also Ebenezer S. Thomas, *Reminiscences of the Last Sixty-Five Years* (Hartford, 1840), 2:35–36.

36 Message of Governor Paul Hamilton, November 25, 1805, Governor's Messages, Papers of the General Assembly of South Carolina, 1805, #92101-02, SCDAH.

37 "Diary of Edward Hooker, 1805–1808," in *American Historical Association Annual Report* 1 (1896): 881–82.

38 House Journal, December 3, 1805, Papers of the South Carolina General Assembly, 1805, 73, SCDAH.

39 "Diary of Edward Hooker, 1805–1808," 867–70.

40 Ibid., 878–80.

41 Analysis of the key senate vote is based on South Carolina Senate Journal, 1805, 172–77; vote is recorded on 176–77. See also Bailey, Morgan, and Taylor, eds., *Biographical Directory of the South Carolina Senate*, 3:1830–831.

42 Marion quoted in *Annals of Congress*, 9th Congress, 1st Session, 348.

43 *Charleston Courier*, December 17, 1806. The *Courier*'s legislative correspondent reported House passage of the prohibition with "only two dissenting voices."

44 South Carolina Senate Journal, 1806, 34, 100, 184–85, SCDAH; vote is recorded on 184–85. See also Bailey, Morgan, and Taylor, eds., *Biographical Directory of the South Carolina Senate*, 3:1832–3.

45 Ibid. Joseph Calhoun had voted in favor of the trade in 1804 and 1805; see materials cited in notes 37 and 51. It is also possible that if an arrangement concerning the vote had been privately negotiated in advance, then that arrangement might have provided less sectional division in the final vote than in previous years.

46 Henry V. Ames, *The Proposed Amendments to the Constitution of the United States During the First Century of Its History* (Washington, DC: Government Printing Office, 1897), 2:208–9, 326–28.

47 *Raleigh Register*, July 26, 1806.

48 *Charleston Courier*, July 10, 1806; see also editorials in the same newspaper printed on January 22 and July 12, 1806.

49 James D. Richardson, ed., *A Compilation of Messages and Papers of the Presidents* (Washington, DC, 1897–1914), 1:396.

50 Matthew Mason, "Slavery Overshadowed: Congress Debates Prohibiting the Atlantic Slave Trade to the United States, 1806–07," *Journal of the Early Republic* 20 (Spring 2000): 59–81.

51 *Annals of Congress*, 1806, 9th Congress, 2nd Session, 221, 174, 266, 173 (quotations found in order on pages cited).

52 Mason, "Slavery Overshadowed," 67–68.

53 *Annals of Congress*, 1806, 9th Congress, 2nd Session, 626–27.

54 Ibid., 636.

55 Ibid., 238.

56 Ibid., 240.

57 Mason, "Slavery Overshadowed," 77–81.

58 Wade Hampton to Thomas Sumter, March 15, 1808, appeared in the Charleston *City Gazette*, April 15, 1808. It is also quoted at length in John Harold Wolfe, *Jeffersonian Democracy in South Carolina* (Chapel Hill: University of North Carolina Press, 1940), 222.

59 James A. McMillin, *The Final Victims: Foreign Slave Trade to North America, 1783–1810* (Columbia: University of South Carolina Press, 2004), 30–48, estimates that just over fifty thousand slaves were imported through South Carolina during the years in which the trade was reopened. McMillin's carefully crafted estimates are based on admittedly incomplete newspaper and port records. South Carolina senator William Smith estimated in 1820 that forty thousand slaves had been imported during the same years, but, as McMillin points out, Smith based his estimate solely on information provided by the Charleston Customs House at the

senator's request. Surviving newspaper and manuscript evidence suggests that Customs officials were not always diligent in tracking vessels involved in the slave trade, and thus their information led to an undercount of slaves imported. Moreover, the information provided to Smith apparently ignored entirely slaves imported through South Carolina's two lesser ports, Beaufort and Georgetown.

60 Charles Ball, *The Narrative of Charles Ball*, ed. Isaac Fisher (New York, 1837), 286, 28–29.

61 *Annals of Congress*, 1821, 17th Congress, 2nd Session, 1135–8; *Annals of Congress*, 16th Congress, 1st session, 259–75.

62 Rothman, *Slave Country*, 85–89.

63 Governor William C. C. Claiborne to James Madison, July 12, 1804, in Donnan, ed., *Documents Illustrative of the Slave Trade to America*, 4:663. For evidence regarding Louisiana planter sentiment, see [Pierre-Louis Berquin-Duvallon], *Travels in Louisiana and the Floridas in the Year 1802, Giving a Correct Picture of Those Countries*, trans. John Davis (New York: I. Riley and Co., 1806), 81.

64 Everett S. Brown, ed., "Documents: The Senate Debate on the Breckinridge Bill for the Government of Louisiana, 1804," *American Historical Review* 22 (January 1917): 340–64, esp. 353.

65 Kastor, *The Nation's Crucible*, 115–20; Paul F. Lachance, "The Politics of Fear: French Louisianians and the Slave Trade, 1786–1809," *Plantation Society* 2 (June 1979): 162–97; on the foreign French, see Tregle, *Louisiana in the Age of Jackson* (Baton Rouge: Louisiana State University Press, 1999), esp. 26–33.

66 William Claiborne to Robert Smith, May 10, 1809, in *Official Letter Books*, 4:363–66.

67 William Claiborne to William Savage, November 10, 1809, in *Official Letter Books*, 5:3–5.

68 James Sterrett to Nathaniel Evans, June 24, 1809, Nathaniel Evans Papers, LSU.

69 William Claiborne to Robert Smith, July 29, 1809, in *Official Letter Books*, 4:392.

70 Paul F. Lachance, "The Foreign French," in Arnold R. Hirsch and Joseph Logsdon, eds., *Creole New Orleans: Race and Americanization* (Baton Rouge: Louisiana State University Press, 1992), 105; Kastor, *The Nation's Crucible*, 115; Paul Lachance, "The 1809 Immigration of Saint-Domingue Refugees to New Orleans: Reception, Integration and Impact," *Louisiana History* 19 (Spring 1988): 109–41.

71 William Robertson to Secretary of State James Madison, May 24, 1809, in Carter, *Territorial Papers*, 9:841.

72 The best account of the German Coast rebellion is Rothman, *Slave Country*, 106–17. See also Kastor, *The Nation's Crucible*, 127–31; Joe Gray Taylor, *Negro Slavery in Louisiana* (Baton Rouge: Louisiana Historical Association, 1963), 212–13; James Dorman, "The Persistent Specter: Slave Rebellion in Territorial Louisiana," *Louisiana History* 18 (Fall 1977): 389–404; Thomas Marshall Thompson, "National Newspaper and Legislative Reactions to Louisiana's Deslondes Slave Revolt of 1811," *Louisiana History* 33 (Spring 1992): 5–29. The rebellion was the largest in terms of slave participants; Nat Turner's revolt in 1831 resulted in many more casualties.

73 Manuel Andry to Governor William Claiborne, January 11, 1811, in Carter, *Territorial Papers*, 9:917–19.

74 Captain John Shaw to Secretary of the Navy Paul Hamilton, January 18, 1811, Letters Received by the Secretary of the Navy from Captains, Record Group 45, Microfilm Copy M125, 19:35, National Archives.

75 William Claiborne to Secretary of State Robert Smith, January 9, 1811, in *Official Letter Books*, 5:95–96.

76 Wade Hampton to the Secretary of War, January 16, 1811, in Carter, *Territorial Papers*, 9:917–19.

77 Ibid. For a complete description of Hampton's role in suppressing the rebellion, see Ronald E. Bridwell, "The South's Wealthiest Planter: Wade Hampton I of South Carolina, 1754–1835," Ph.D. dissertation, University of South Carolina, 1980, 575–79.

78 Manuel Andry to William Claiborne, January 11, 1811, in Carter, *Territorial Papers*, 9:915–16; Rothman, *Slave Country*, 106–17.

79 Wade Hampton to William Claiborne, January 12, 1811, in Carter, *Territorial Papers*, 9:916–17; this letter was also reprinted in *Louisiana Gazette*, January 14, 1811.

80 Wade Hampton to the Secretary of War, January 16, 1811, in Carter, *Territorial Papers*, 9:917–19.

81 William Claiborne to Major Bullingney, January 9, 1811; Claiborne's Circular to the Several Colonels of Regiments and the Several Parish Judges on the Coast, January 10, 1811; Claiborne to Major St. Armand and Colonel Manuel Andry, January 14, 1811; Claiborne to Mr. Dubourg, January 14, 1811, in *Official Letter Books*, 5:95–101.

82 William Claiborne to Secretary of State Robert Smith, January 14, 1811, in *Official Letter Books*, 5:100.

83 William Claiborne to Secretary of State, January 14 and 20, 1811; Claiborne to Colonel Manuel Andry, January 13, 1811; Claiborne to Major St. Armand and Colonel Manuel Andry, January 14, 1811, in *Official Letter Books*, 5:96, 97, 99, 111; *Louisiana Gazette*, January 21 and 22, February 12 and 18, 1811.

84 William Claiborne to Mr. Dubourg, January 14, 1811; Claiborne to Major St. Amand, January 20, 1811, in *Official Letter Books*, 5:99, 109–10.

85 William Claiborne to John N. Destrehan, January 16, 1811, in *Official Letter Books*, 5:100–1.

86 Manuel Andry to William Claiborne, January 11, 1811, in Carter, *Territorial Papers*, 9:915–16.

87 Rothman, *Slave Country*, 111–12; Kastor, *The Nation's Crucible*, 129–30.

88 "Summary of Trial Proceedings of Those Accused of Participating in the Slave Uprising of January 9, 1811," *Louisiana History* 18 (Fall 1977): 472–73.

89 *Louisiana Gazette*, January 21, 1811.

90 Rothman, *Slave Country*, 114; "Summary of Trial Proceedings of Those Accused of Participating in the Slave Uprising of January 9, 1811," 472–73.

91 "Summary of Trial Proceedings of Those Accused of Participating in the Slave Uprising of January 9, 1811," 472–73.

92 Samuel Hambleton to John Porter, January 25, 1811, David Dixon Porter Papers, LC.

93 See Albert Thrasher, *On to New Orleans! Louisiana's Heroic 1811 Slave Revolt* (New Orleans: Cypress University Press, 1995), 229–47; Rothman, *Slave Country*, 114–15.

94 Samuel Hambleton to David Porter, January 25, 1811, David Dixon Porter Papers, LC.

95 John Shaw to William Hamilton, January 18, 1811, John Shaw Papers, LC; Edward Palfrey to John Gorham Palfrey, January 23, 1811, in Hannah Palfrey Ayer, ed., *A Legacy of New England: Letters of the Palfrey Family* (Portland, ME: Athoensen Press, 1950), 1:19.

96 David Porter to Samuel Hambleton, February 23, 1811, David Dixon Porter Papers, LC.

97 Anonymous traveler quoted in Rothman, *Slave Country*, 115; see Anonymous, "Trip to New Orleans 1811," 34, Miscellaneous Manuscript Collections, #1797, LC.

98 Lubin F. Laurent, "A History of the St. John the Baptist Parish," 68–72, Louisiana Room, Louisiana State University Library.

99 Rothman, *Slave Country*, 106–8.

100 On this point, see Tommy R. Young, "The United States Army and the Institution of Slavery in Louisiana, 1803–1815," *Louisiana Studies* 13 (Fall 1974): 201–22.

101 Adam Rothman, "The Expansion of Slavery in the Deep South, 1790–1820," Ph.D. dissertation, Columbia University, 2000, 106–8. Rothman does not advance this argument in his excellent book, which is a substantial revision of this dissertation.

102 Rothman, *Slave Country*, 110.

103 On this point, see Dorman, "The Persistent Specter," 393–95; Rothman, *Slave Country*, 16–22, 75–76, 106–17.

104 Rothman, *Slave Country*, 110–12, quotation on 112.

105 Hugh M. Hamill, Jr., *The Hidalgo Revolt: Prelude to Mexican Independence* (Gainesville: University of Florida Press, 1966); John Tutino, *From Insurrection to Revolution in Mexico: Social Bases of Agrarian Violence, 1750–1940* (Princeton: Princeton University Press, 1986); Felix D. Almaraz Jr., *Tragic Cavalier: Governor Manuel Salcedo of Texas, 1808–1813* (Austin: University of Texas Press, 1971).

106 Andrew McMichael, "The Kemper 'Rebellion': Filibustering and Resident Anglo-American Loyalty in Spanish West Florida," *Louisiana History* 43 (2002): 133–65; Isaac Joslin Cox, *The West Florida Controversy, 1789–1813: A Case Study in American Diplomacy* (Baltimore: Johns Hopkins University Press, 1918).

107 Wade Hampton to William Claiborne, January 12, 1811, in Carter, *Territorial Papers*, 9:916–17.

108 W. C. C. Claiborne to Robert Smith, January 14, 1811, in *Official Letterbooks*, 5:100.

109 William Claiborne to Joint Session of Orleans Territorial Legislature, January 29, 1811, in *Official Letterbooks*, 5:123.

110 Answer of the Legislative Council to Governor Claiborne's Speech, January 31, 1811, and Answer of the House of Representatives to Governor Claiborne's Speech, n.d., in *Official Letterbooks*, 5:127–29, 129–31. See also James Dorman, "The Persistent Specter," 399–400; and Taylor, *Negro Slavery in Louisiana*, 214.

111 Bridwell, "Wade Hampton I of South Carolina," 387–405; *Niles Weekly Register*, 3rd ser., 25 (1823): 126; see also Christopher Fitzsimmons to Wade Hampton I, March 15, 1811, Fitzsimmons Letterbook, SCL.

112 William S. Hamilton to John Hamilton, April 12, 1811, William Hamilton Papers, SHC.

113 *Niles Weekly Register*, 3rd series, 32 (1827): 101; *Niles Weekly Register*, 4th series, 38 (1829): 18.

114 William S. Hamilton to John Hamilton, April 15, 1811, William Hamilton Papers, SHC.

115 On this point, see Junius P. Rodriguez, "Always 'En Garde': The Effects of Slave Insurrection upon the Louisiana Mentality, 1811–1815," *Louisiana History* 33 (Fall 1992): 399–416: Rothman, *Slave Country*, 116–17.

116 *Annals of Congress*, December 12, 1811, 480.

117 Rothman, *Slave Country*, 119–23.

118 *Annals of Congress*, December 12, 1811, 480.

119 Andrew Jackson to William Claiborne, January 5, 1813, in *The Papers of Andrew Jackson*, ed. Sam B. Smith et al. (Knoxville: University of Tennessee Press, 1980–), 2:352.

120 "Resolutions of the City of Washington," July 28, 1812, in Carter, *Territorial Papers*, 5:303.

121 James Moore to David Hutchison, July 26, 1812, Hutchison Family Papers, SCL.

122 David Holmes to James Wilkinson, October 19, 1812, in Carter, *Territorial Papers*, 6:328–29.

123 James Moore to David Hutchison, July 26, 1812, Hutchison Family Papers, SCL.

124 James Moore to David Hutchison, August 28, 1814, Hutchison Family Papers, SCL.

125 Andrew Jackson to William Claiborne, July 21, 1814, in *Correspondence of Andrew Jackson*, ed. John Spencer Bassett (Washington, DC: Carnegie Institution of Washington, 1926–35), 2:10.

126 William Claiborne to Andrew Jackson, September 20, 1814, in *Papers of Andrew Jackson*, 3:143.

127 Jacques Villeré to Eligius Fromentin, October 19, 1814, Villeré Papers, Williams Research Center, Historic New Orleans Collection, New Orleans. The original letter is in French and the English translation is provided by the Williams Research Center.

128 Kastor, *The Nation's Crucible*, 167–80.

129 Sean Wilentz, *The Rise of American Democracy: Jefferson to Lincoln* (New York and London: W. W. Norton and Co., 2005), 173–75.

130 Andrew Jackson to Waters Allen, December 23, 1814, in *Papers of Andrew Jackson*, 3:216.

131 Wilentz, *Rise of American Democracy*, 174–75.

132 "Representation from the Members of the Legislature of the County of Attakapas, January 1815," reel 16, Andrew Jackson Papers (microfilm), LC.

133 Andrew Jackson to Robert Hays, February 9, 1815, in *Correspondence of Andrew Jackson*, 2:162.

FIVE. PATERNALISM EMERGES

1 The literature on the expansion of slavery into the old Southwest is extensive, but five modern studies stand out: Adam Rothman, *Slave Country: American Expansion and the Origins of the Deep South* (Cambridge, MA: Harvard University Press, 2005); James David Miller, *South by Southwest: Planter Emigration and Identity in the Slave South* (Charlottesville: University Press of Virginia, 2002); Edward E. Baptist, *Creating an Old South: Middle Florida's Plantation Frontier Before the Civil War* (Chapel Hill: University of North Carolina Press, 2002); Daniel S. Dupre, *Transforming the Cotton Frontier, Madison County, Alabama, 1800–1840* (Baton Rouge: Louisiana State University Press, 1997); and John Hebron Moore, *The Emergence of the Cotton Kingdom in the Old Southwest: Mississippi, 1770–1860* (Baton Rouge: Louisiana State University Press, 1988).

2 The best discussion of this prevailing pattern is William W. Freehling, *The Road to Disunion: Secessionists at Bay, 1776–1854* (New York: Oxford University Press, 1990), 119–286.

3 In addition to the primary sources, my thoughts on the lower South's search for an ideological reconfiguration of slavery, and on the evolution of the southern proslavery argument generally, have been influenced by Larry E. Tise, *Proslavery: A History of the Defense of Slavery in America, 1800–1840* (Athens: University of Georgia Press, 1987), esp. 286–362. My argument differs from Tise's in a number of respects, but particularly in dating the beginnings of the ideological reconfiguration in the lower South to an earlier period than does Tise.

4 Willie Lee Rose, "The Domestication of Domestic Slavery," in *Slavery and Freedom*, ed. William W. Freehling (New York: Oxford University Press, 1982), 18–36. This important essay was first presented as a public lecture at Yale in 1973. After Professor Rose suffered a severe stroke in 1978, the essay was published for the first time in a collection of Rose's essays edited

by William W. Freehling, then Rose's colleague at Johns Hopkins University. In this essay, Rose called for historians to pay more attention to change over time in the study of slavery and slaveholding. Over time, variations in slavery and slave management practices across time and space have appeared and effectively reshaped the study of slavery. For leading examples, see Ira Berlin, *Many Thousands Gone: The First Two Centuries of Slavery in North America* (Cambridge, MA: Harvard University Press, 1998), esp. 358–65; Ira Berlin, *Generations of Captivity: A History of African American Slaves* (Cambridge, MA: Harvard University Press, 2003); and Ira Berlin, "Time, Space, and the Evolution of Afro-American Society in British Mainland North America," *American Historical Review* 85 (February 1980): 44–78. Mark M. Smith, *Mastered by the Clock: Time, Slavery and Freedom in the American South* (Chapel Hill: University of North Carolina Press, 1997) emphasized the importance of change over time in slave management practices in his pioneering study of time discipline on southern plantations. This volume attempts to expand Rose's insight through an extended analysis of the evolution of white attitudes and slaveholder ideology over time.

5 Jeffrey Robert Young, *Domesticating Slavery: The Master Class in Georgia and South Carolina, 1670–1837* (Chapel Hill: University of North Carolina Press, 1999), esp. 123–60. In giving a label to the set of ideas he described, Young eschewed the term *paternalism* because of its historiographical baggage in favor of the term *corporate individualism*. For Young, the ideology of corporate individualism held that a household model must be used to define social relations beyond the boundaries of the traditional household. Familial discipline and affection must prevail in master-slave relations as well as in those of the nuclear family. Control remained with the head of the corporate household. In this book, I have chosen to use the term *paternalism*, after due consideration of alternatives, because I believe that it offers the best shorthand description of the qualities I am including under the label. *Paternalism* also has the added advantage of being the term that most closely reflects the concept of slavery as a domestic institution, slave-labor production as a expansive version of the household mode of production, and slave management as that of managing an extended household, all concepts aggressively advanced by nineteenth-century slaveholders in their justification of slavery. The ideology of paternalism and the concept of domesticity emerged as increasingly important to slaveholders' self-definition as well as to their ideological defense of slaveholding. For practical purposes, what I call paternalism and what Young calls corporate individualism are essentially the same set of ideas and assumptions.

6 Rose, "The Domestication of Domestic Slavery," 23–23, 27–28, 34–35.

7 For examples of this literature, see Joyce E. Chaplin, "Slavery and the Principle of Humanity: A Modern Idea in the Early Lower South," *Journal of Social History* 24 (December 1990): 299–315; Joyce E. Chaplin, *An Anxious Pursuit: Agricultural Innovation and Modernity in the Lower South, 1730–1815* (Chapel Hill: University of North Carolina Press, 1993), esp. 53–58, 124–28; Alan Gallay, "The Origins Of Slaveholders' Paternalism: George Whitfield, the Bryan Family, and the Great Awakening in the South," *Journal of Southern History* 53 (August 1987): 369–94; Allan Gallay, *The Formation of a Planter Elite: Jonathan Bryan and the Southern Colonial Frontier* (Athens: University of Georgia Press, 1989).

8 Chaplin, *An Anxious Pursuit*, 53–58.

9 Berlin, *Many Thousands Gone*, 142–227; Daniel C. Littlefield, "Plantations, Paternalism and Profitability: Factors Affecting African Demography in the Old British Empire," *Journal of Southern History* 47 (May 1981): 167–82.

10 Lacy Ford, *Origins of Southern Radicalism: The South Carolina Upcountry, 1800–1860* (New York: Oxford University Press, 1988), 1–43; Rachel Klein, *Unification of a Slave State: The Rise of the Planter Class in the South Carolina Backcountry, 1760–1808* (Chapel Hill: University of North Carolina Press, 1990), 246–59; Joyce E. Chaplin, "Creating a Cotton South in Georgia and South Carolina, 1760–1815," *Journal of Southern History* 57 (May 1991): 171–200.

11 Robert Olwell, *Masters, Slaves and Subjects: The Culture of Power in the South Carolina Low Country, 1740–1790* (Ithaca, NY: Cornell University Press, 1998), 221–70; Sylvia R. Frey, *Water from the Rock: Black Resistance in a Revolutionary Age* (Princeton, NJ: Princeton University Press, 1991), 81–171; Philip D. Morgan, "Black Society in the Lowcountry, 1760–1810," in Ira Berlin and Ronald Hoffman, eds., *Slavery and Freedom in the Age of the American Revolution* (Charlottesville: University of Virginia Press, 1983), 83–141; Philip D. Morgan, *Slave Counterpoint: Black Culture in the Eighteenth-Century Chesapeake and Lowcountry* (Chapel Hill: University of North Carolina Press, 1998), esp. 665–68; Jerome J. Nadelhaft, *The Disorders of War: The Revolution in South Carolina* (Orono: University of Maine Press, 1981), 45–85.

12 Joyce E. Chaplin, "Tidal Cultivation and the Problem of Slavery in South Carolina and Georgia, 1760–1815," *William and Mary Quarterly* 49 (January 1992): 29–61.

13 *Minutes of the Charleston Baptist Association*, November 2, 1799, Baptist Historical Collection, FU.

14 Ford, *Origins of Southern Radicalism,* 19–25; Christine Leigh Heyrman, *Southern Cross: The Beginnings of the Bible Belt* (New York: Knopf, 1998), esp. 117–60.

15 Mark D. Kaplanoff, "Making the South Solid: Politics and the Structure of Society in South Carolina, 1790–1815," Ph.D. dissertation, Cambridge University, 1979, 59.

16 Young, *Domesticating Slavery*, 123–24.

17 Olwell, *Masters, Slaves and Subjects*, 282–83.

18 James Oakes, "Review Essay: Slaves Without Contexts," *Journal of the Early Republic* 19 (Spring 1999): 103–9. In this essay review of Berlin's *Many Thousands Gone*, Oakes notes that the modern historiography of slavery too often invokes the concept of paternalism without giving it a clear definition and without specific reference to its historical context. I am trying to avoid this pitfall by herein being explicit about my definition of paternalism and explaining why I think it flourished in a particular historical context.

19 Rose, "The Domestication of Domestic Slavery," 27–39; Freehling, *The Road to Disunion,* esp. 59–97; William W. Freehling, "Unlimited Paternalism's Problems: The Transforming Moment on My Road to Understanding Disunion," in *The Reintegration of American History: Slavery and the Civil War* (New York: Oxford University Press, 1994), 105–37; Ira Berlin, *Many Thousands Gone: The First Two Centuries of Slavery in North America* (Cambridge: Harvard University Press, 1998), esp. 1–14; Young, *Domesticating Slavery,* 123–60; George M. Fredrickson, *The Black Image in the White Mind: The Debate on Afro-American Character and Destiny, 1817–1914* (New York: Harper and Row, 1971), 51–64. For a thoughtful analysis of how the use of the concept of paternalism evolved over time in the historiography of the Old South, see Mark M. Smith, *Debating Slavery: Economy and Society in the Antebellum South* (Cambridge, UK: Cambridge University Press, 1998), 16–30.

20 The definition of paternalism offered here is my own, and it is based on my reading or an array of primary and secondary sources. The origins and influence of paternalism have been much debated by scholars for many decades. In recent historiography, this ideal of slave mastery has carried many names (see, for an example, note 18 above). The label *paternalism* has proven a durable,

if at times controversial, one. But whatever the name given, the set of ideas referred to generally consist of, or are at least similar to, those I am grouping under the term *paternalism* in this study. The term *paternalism* admittedly carries some baggage, not least because of its use by Ulrich B. Phillips as part of his Progressive-era characterization of slavery as a benign or even benevolent institution. Phillips used the idea of slaveholder paternalism to buttress his white supremacist apologia for the Old South. Phillips argued that southern slaveholders embraced paternalism at the sacrifice of economic efficiency and hence left their region ill-prepared for the competitive rigors of the postbellum free-labor economy. Phillips' critique of paternalism was not that it marginalized blacks as inferiors but that Old South paternalism had created a historic drag on the emerging New South economy. African American scholars never accepted Phillips' argument and to bolster their point pointed to the harshness of slavery and the bitterly racist attitudes it fostered among whites. In his sweeping reassessment of slavery during the 1950s, Kenneth Stampp argued forcefully that the paternalism Phillips touted proved a sham in practice. Beneath paternalist rhetoric, whites pursued their own interests and treated slaves as they saw fit. The articulation of a paternalist ideology, Stampp concluded, served to obscure the facts that "slaveholders were more often ambitious entrepreneurs than selfless philanthropists and that "southern slavery was not so much a patriarchal institution as a practical labor system." See Ulrich B. Phillips, *American Negro Slavery: A Survey of the Supply, Employment and Control of Negro Labor as Determined by the Plantation Regime* (New York: D. Appleton, 1918), and Kenneth M. Stampp, *The Peculiar Institution: Slavery in the Ante-bellum South* (New York: A. A. Knopf, 1956).

21 The standard statement of the modern understanding of paternalism is Eugene D. Genovese, *Roll, Jordan, Roll: The World the Slaves Made* (New York: Pantheon, 1974), esp. 3–10, 658–65. In an impressive of work, Genovese redefined the concept of paternalism, as introduced by Phillips and demolished by Stampp. Drawing of the work of Italian Marxist Antonio Gramsci, Genovese defined paternalism as a complex "dialectic of accommodation and resistance" through which masters established hegemony over slaves but which allowed slaves to resist the masters' efforts to impose their will unilaterally. Though their resistance slaves defined paternalism in their own way and "refused that surrender of will which constituted the ideological foundations" of paternalism as masters understood it. The hegemonic system of slavery, characterized by an intricate "web of paternalistic relationships," allowed masters to define themselves as paternalists but allowed slaves to "transform their acquiescence in paternalism into a rejection of slavery itself." For Genovese, the ideology of paternalism grew out of the very nature of labor control in a slave society rather than from a specific set of ideas, such as those of Christian stewardship. Paternalism hinged not on treatment of slaves or character of masters but on the perpetual negotiations between master and slave over working and living conditions. Genovese insisted that slaves used the ongoing negotiations to win accommodations that allowed family, religious, and cultural life to develop within slave communities; these resources helped them resist the imposition of slaveholder hegemony from above. The invisible institutions of slave life and culture mitigated the hegemony of the South's peculiar institution. On these point Genovese's theoretically sophisticated work sparked debate among historians, but his interpretation of paternalism itself emerged as hegemonic among historians of slavery for at least a generation, if not longer.

22 Undated letter of William Moultrie, c. 1800, Moultrie Papers, SCL. Born in 1730, Moultrie earned a measure of military acclaim as he led the American effort to turn away the British navy at Fort Sullivan on Sullivan's Island in 1776. For his bravery, the Continental Congress

renamed the fort in his honor. An accomplished politician as well as military leader, Moultrie led the cause of county court creation during his first term as governor during the 1780s. During his second term as governor during the 1790s, he incurred the wrath of the Washington administration for giving a hearty welcome to Citizen Genet when the controversial French republican visited Charleston.

23 John B. Boles, *The Great Revival, 1787–1805: The Origins of the Southern Evangelical Mind* (Lexington: University Press of Kentucky, 1972); Donald G. Mathews, "The Second Great Awakening as an Organizing Process, 1780–1830," *American Quarterly* 21 (Spring 1969): 23–43; Young, *Domesticating Slavery*, 146–48; Ford, *Origins of Southern Radicalism*, 29–33; Lacy Ford, "Reconsidering the Internal Slave Trade: Paternalism, Markets and the Character of the Old South," in Walter Johnson, ed., *Internal Passages: The Domestic Slave Trade in the United States* (New Haven: Yale University Press, 2004), 143–64.

24 William Freehling, "Denmark Vesey's Antipaternalistic Reality," in *The Reintegration of American History: Slavery and the Civil War* (New York: Oxford University Press, 1994), 34–58; Littlefield, "Plantations, Paternalism and Profitability," 167–82.

25 William Johnson, *Nugae Georgicae: An Essay Delivered to the Literary and Philosophical Society of Charleston, South Carolina, October 14, 1815* (Charleston, SC: J. Hoff, 1815), 3–40, quotations from 35–37.

26 Daniel C. Littlefield, "'Abundance of Negroes of That Nation': The Significance of African Ethnicity in Colonial South Carolina," in David R. Chesnut and Clyde N. Wilson, ed., *The Meaning of South Carolina History: Essays in Honor of George C, Rogers, Jr.* (Columbia: University of South Carolina Press, 1991), 19–38, notes that South Carolina slaveholders preferred country-born slaves to African natives; Michael P. Johnson, "Runaway Slaves and Slave Communities in South Carolina, 1799–1830," *William and Mary Quarterly* 38 (July 1981): 418–41, argued that the influx of African slaves into South Carolina when the state reopened the foreign slave trade between 1804 and 1807 energized collective resistance in South Carolina, confirming a long-standing South Atlantic slaveholder belief that country-born slaves were less rebellious. On Louisiana slaveholder preference for African or Caribbean slaves, see Jed Handelsman Shugerman, "The Louisiana Purchase and South Carolina's Reopening of the Slave Trade in 1803," *Journal of the Early Republic* 22 (Summer 2002): 263–90; Rothman, *Slave Country*, 83–92.

27 Johnson, *Nugae Georgicae*, 35.

28 Adam Rothman, "The Domestication of the Slave Trade in the United States," in Walter Johnson, ed., *Internal Passages: The Domestic Slave Trade in the United States* (New Haven: Yale University Press, 2004), 32–54.

29 Willie Lee Rose chastised historians for consistently "undervaluing the Christian religion" in its impact on slaveholders and slaves alike, and urged them instead to seek to "recapture its [Christianity's] dominance" in the nineteenth century South. See Rose, "The Domestication of Domestic Slavery," 31.

30 For an overview, see Donald Mathews, *Religion in the Old South* (Princeton, NJ: Princeton University Press, 1977), 136–84. See also Heyrman, *Southern Cross*, 92–94; Ford, *Origins of Southern Radicalism*, 21–24.

31 Johnson, *Nugae Georgicae*, 35–37.

32 Manuscript essay, "On Slavery," n.d., Botsford Papers, FU. The undated manuscript on which this paragraph is based was almost certainly written by Botsford early in 1812 as an answer to

an inquiry concerning life and working conditions on a Lowcountry rice plantation. In a letter to a fellow minister and friend, Botsford mentions having recently written the manuscript; see Edmund Botsford to John Roberts, February 28, 1812, Edmund Botsford Papers, FU.

33 Young, *Domesticating Slavery*, 124. Young maintains—rightly, in my view—that the ideological foundation slaveholders developed for slavery called for the "social subordination of women and slaves" while protecting "the liberties of white men."

34 For a related arguments on point, see Stephanie McCurry, *Masters of Small Worlds: Yeoman Households, Gender Relations, and the Political Culture of the Antebellum South Carolina Low Country* (New York: Oxford University Press, 1995), and Michael P. Johnson, "Planters and Patriarchy: Charleston, 1800–1860," *Journal of Southern History* 46 (February 1980): 45–72.

35 "Speech of Freeman Walker," January 19, 1820, *Annals of Congress*, 16th Congress, 1st session, 159–75; "Speech of Richard Johnson," February 1, 1820, *Annals of Congress*, 16th Congress, 1st session, 345–60; "Speech of William Smith," January 26, 1820, *History of Congress*, 16th Congress, 2nd session, 259–75, esp. 270.

36 Richard Furman, *Exposition of the Views of the Baptists Relative to the Coloured Population of the United States in a Communication to the Governor of South Carolina* (Charleston, SC: A. E. Miller, 1823).

37 "Further Remarks in Debate on His Fifth Resolution," January 10, 1838, in *The Papers of John C. Calhoun*, ed. Clyde N. Wilson et al. (Columbia: University of South Carolina Press, 1998), 14:80–86.

38 On Furman, see James A. Rogers, *Richard Furman: Life and Legacy* (Macon, GA: Mercer University Press, 1985).

39 Margaret Watson, *Greenwood County Sketches* (Greenwood, SC: Attic Press, 1970), 5; see also Ford, *Origins of Southern Radicalism*, 20.

40 Records of the Baptist Church at Welsh Neck, August 2 and September 5, 1779, SCL; on Winchester, see Edwin Martin Stone, *Biography of the Reverend Elhanan Winchester* (Boston, 1836).

41 Records of the Baptist Church at Welsh Neck, March 2, 1782, SCL; Charles D. Mallary, *Memoirs of Elder Botsford* (Charleston, SC: W. Riley, 1832), 44–45.

42 John Asplund, *The Baptist Annual Register* (London: n.p., 1792), 104–6.

43 Francis Asbury, *The Journals and Letters of Francis Asbury*, ed. Elmer T. Clark et al. (Nashville: Abingdon Press, 1958), 2:41.

44 John B. Boles, "The Great Revival," in Charles Reagan Wilson and William Ferris, eds., *The Encyclopedia of Southern Culture* (Chapel Hill: University of North Carolina Press, 1989), 319–20, makes these points succinctly.

45 Mathews, "The Second Great Awakening as an Organizing Process, 1780–1830," *American Quarterly* 21 (Spring 1969): 23–43.

46 "Testimony of Reverend Jonathan McGready, May 28, 1802," in George Howe, *Presbyterian Church in South Carolina* (Columbia, SC: Duffie and Chapman, 1870–83), 2:107–9.

47 "A Letter from Dr. Furman of Charleston to Dr. Rippon of London," in David Benedict, *A General History of the Baptist Denomination* (New York: L. Colby, 1848), 2:167–71. This letter is also printed in Howe, *The Presbyterian Church in South Carolina*, 2:109–13.

48 The Methodists' success in winning converts owed to their preaching of the Armenian doctrine of unlimited free grace, the idea that the triune God offers salvation through Christ for all who believe. This approach contrasted with the avowed Calvinism of Presbyterians and most

Baptists, who believed that God offered salvation only to members of an elect of unknown and unknowable size. See Donald G. Mathews, *Slavery and Methodism: A Chapter in American Morality, 1780–1845* (Princeton, NJ: Princeton University Press, 1965), 3–61.

49 Cynthia Lynn Lyerly, *Methodism and the Southern Mind, 1770–1810* (New York: Oxford University Press, 1998), 47–72; Mathews, *Slavery and Methodism*, 3–29; Abel M. Chreitzberg, *Early Methodism in the Carolinas* (Nashville: Publishing House of the Methodist Episcopal Church, 2897), 48–89; Albert D. Betts, *History of South Carolina Methodism* (Columbia, SC: Advocate Press, 1952), 159–67; James D. Essig, *The Bonds of Wickedness: American Evangelicals Against Slavery, 1776–1808* (Philadelphia: Temple University Press, 1982), 97–157.

50 Richard Furman to Edmund Botsford, October 10, 1802, Furman Papers, FU.

51 Edmund Botsford to John M. Roberts, February 28, 1812, Botsford Papers, FU.

52 Edmund Botsford to John M. Roberts, August 7, 1802, Botsford Papers, FU.

53 Edmund Botsford to John M. Roberts, November 24, 1802, Botsford Papers, FU.

54 Richard Furman to Edmund Botsford, October 10, 1802, Richard Furman Papers, FU.

55 Edmund Botsford to John M. Roberts, August 7, 1802, Botsford Papers, FU; in this letter Botsford reports on Furman's opinions of the revivals expressed in a letter from Furman to Botsford. The letter from Furman to Botsford has not been found.

56 Edmund Botsford to Richard Furman, October 15, 1808, Botsford Papers, FU.

57 Edmund Botsford to Richard Furman, May 26, 1812, Botsford Papers, FU.

58 Richard Furman to Dr. William Rogers, March 18, 1816, and Richard Furman to Iveson Brooks, March 23, 1820, Furman Papers, SCL.

59 Edmund Botsford to Richard Furman, May 26, 1812, Botsford Papers, FU.

60 "A History of Bethesda Presbyterian Church," 79–87, in Bethesda Presbyterian Church Records, SCL; Leah Townsend, *South Carolina Baptists* (Florence, SC: Florence Printing Company, 1925), 301.

61 Edmund Botsford to [?], November 1, 1809, Botsford Papers, SCL.

62 Ford, *Origins of Southern Radicalism*, 24.

63 Benedict, *General History of the Baptist Denomination*, 2:172.

64 Larry E. Tise, *Proslavery: A History of the Defense of Slavery in America, 1701–1840* (Athens: University of Georgia Press, 1987), esp. 286–307; Drew G. Faust, *The Ideology of Slavery: Proslavery Thought in the Antebellum South, 1830–1860* (Baton Rouge: Louisiana State University Press, 1981), 1–20; Fredrickson, *The Black Image in the White Mind*, 71–96.

65 Edmund Botsford, *Sambo and Toney: A Dialogue in Three Parts* (Georgetown, SC: Francis M. Baxter, 1808).

66 For Botsford's description of his preparation and intentions, see Edmund Botsford to Richard Furman, October 15, 1808, Botsford Papers, FU. For a thoughtful commentary on Botsford writing process, see Michael O'Brien, *Conjectures of Order: Intellectual Life and the American South, 1810–1860* (New York: Cambridge University Press, 2005), 1:412–13.

67 Edmund Botsford to Richard Furman, February 20, 1809, Botsford Papers, FU.

68 Edmund Botsford to Richard Furman, c. 1809, Botsford Papers, FU.

69 Edmund Botsford to Richard Furman, October 25, 1814, Botsford Papers, FU.

70 Botsford, *Sambo and Toney*, 4–11.

71 Ibid., 4–11, 15–18.

72 Ibid., 23–24.

73 Ibid., 43–45.
74 Ibid., 38–45.
75 Ibid., 29.
76 See Edmund Botsford to Richard Furman, October 15, 1808, Botsford Papers, FU.
77 [Botsford], "On Slavery."
78 See Walter Johnson, "A Nettlesome Classic Turns Twenty-Five," *Common-Place* 1 (July 2001): 1–8, at www.common-place.org. In this silver-anniversary review of Eugene Genovese's *Roll, Jordan, Roll,* Johnson maintains that paternalism flourished in part because "efforts between 1831 and 1861 of a group of slaveholding reformers to stave off the growing antislavery movement in parts of the upper South and the nation at large." I agree with Johnson on this point, and would advance a more general observation that the operation of slavery as Genovese described in his classic volume largely applies to the late antebellum era. Thus Genovese's is a discussion of paternalism as an ideology at the zenith of its influence, not in its formative years. See also Genovese, *Roll, Jordan, Roll,* esp. 70–75.
79 Young, *Domesticating Slavery,* 124.
80 The best overall treatment of entrenched opposition to evangelical values from the persistence of non-Christian traditional ethical codes treatment is Bertram Wyatt-Brown, *Southern Honor: Ethics and Behavior in the Old South* (New York: Oxford University Press, 1982), 101–5.
81 On the centrality of force to traditional notions of slave control, see Norrece T. Jones Jr., *Born a Child of Freedom, Yet a Slave: Mechanisms of Control and Strategies of Resistance in South Carolina* (Hanover: University Press of New England, 1990), esp. 11–36; and Betty Wood, "Prisons, Workhouses, and the Control of Slave Labor in the Lowcountry Georgia, 1763–1815," *Slavery and Abolition* 8 (September 1987): 247–81.
82 Among others, Rose, "The Domestication of Domestic Slavery," 25–27, emphasizes that once the slave trade closed and the slave population grew increasingly American-born, the idea of slavery as a domestic institution grew more practical. See also Littlefield, "Plantations, Paternalism and Profitability," 167–82.
83 The standard account of the Stono Rebellion is Peter Wood, *Black Majority: Negroes in South Carolina from 1670 Through the Stono Rebellion* (New York: Knopf, 1974), 308–26; but see also Mark M. Smith, "Remembering Mary, Shaping Revolt: Reconsidering the Stono Rebellion," *Journal of Southern History* 67 (August 2001): 513–34, and John K. Thornton, "African Dimensions of the Stono Rebellion," *American Historical Review* 96 (October 1991):1101–13. On slave resistance during the Revolutionary era, see Frey, *Water from the Rock,* 45–242; Morgan, *Slave Counterpoint,* esp. 257–317; Olwell, *Masters, Slaves and Subjects,* 221–70. On white tardiness in accepting the full humanity of slaves, see Chaplin, "Slavery and the Principle of Humanity," 299–315.
84 Charles Joyner, *Down by the Riverside* (Urbana: University of Illinois Press, 1984), 127–40; Erskine Clark, *Dwelling Places: A Plantation Epic* (New Haven: Yale University Press, 2005); esp. 1–151.
85 Betty Wood, "'White Society' and the 'Informal' Slave Economies of Lowcountry Georgia, c. 1763–1830," *Slavery and Abolition* 11 (December 1990): 313–31; Betty Wood, *Women's Work, Men's Work: The Informal Slave Economies of Lowcountry Georgia* (Athens: University of Georgia Press, 1995), 80–121; Morgan, *Slave Counterpoint,* 204–12, 346–53; Morgan, "Black Society in the Lowcountry, 1760–1810," 83–141.

86 Peter A. Coclanis, "How the Lowcountry Was Taken to Task: Slave Labor Organization in Coastal South Carolina and Georgia," in Robert L. Paquette and Louis Ferleger, eds., *Slavery, Secession, and Southern History* (Charlottesville: University Press of Virginia, 2000), 59–78, and "Slavery, African-American Agency and the World We Have Lost," *Georgia Historical Quarterly* 79 (Winter 1995): 873–84; Joyner, *Down by the Riverside*, 43–81; Philip Morgan, "Work and Culture: The Task System and the World of Lowcountry Blacks, 1700–1880," *William and Mary Quarterly* 39 (October 1982): 563–99; Morgan, *Slave Counterpoint*, 204–43, 358–76; Olwell, *Masters, Slaves and Subjects*, 213–14; Chaplin, *Anxious Pursuits*, 117–28. On the role played by free blacks under this accommodation, see Michael P. Johnson and James L. Roark, *Black Masters: A Free Family of Color in the Old South* (New York: Norton, 1984), 32–41; Marina Wikramanayake, *A World in a Shadow: The Free Black in Antebellum South Carolina* (Columbia: University of South Carolina Press, 1973), esp. 5–30.

87 Robert Olwell, *Masters, Slaves and Subjects*, esp. 141–80, details the degree of autonomy and mobility often enjoyed by skilled slaves and slave marketers allowed to participate in the market economy and earn money as well as the threat this measure of autonomy posed to slave control during the Revolutionary era.

88 On the general concern that evangelicals were soft or unmanly and the evangelical efforts to dispel such concerns, see Heyrman, *Southern Cross*, 206–52.

89 Richard Furman to Dorothea M. Furman, November 15, 1816, Furman Papers, FU.

90 Johnson, *Nugae Georgicae*, 35–38.

91 For example, see the lengthy argument by a Charleston editor after the Vesey scare: Edwin C. Holland, *A Refutation of the Calumnies Circulated Against the Southern and Western States*...(Charleston, SC: A. E. Miller, 1822), esp. 11–12.

92 Janet Duitsman Cornelius, "*'When I Can Read My Title Clear': Literacy, Slavery, and Religion in the Antebellum South* (Columbia: University of South Carolina Press, 1991), 11–58.

93 Draft letter of the Board of Managers of the Charleston Bible Society to Governor Thomas Bennett Jr., September 23, 1822, Charleston Bible Society Records, SCHS. On Furman as the actual author of this letter, see Robert Paquette and Douglas Egerton in their fine article "Of Facts and Fables: New Light on the Denmark Vesey Affair," *South Carolina Historical Magazine* 105 (January 2004): 8–35, esp. 11–16.

94 Jacob Read to Charles Pinckney, June 18, 1807, Pinckney Papers, SCL.

95 Ralph Izard Jr. to Alice Izard, December 18, 1808, Ralph Izard Papers, LC.

96 Hugh McCauley to Isaac Ball, June 2, 1814, Ball Family Papers, SCL.

97 Charles Cotesworth Pinckney to Jedediah Morse, December 1, 1810, Gratz Collection, HSP.

98 These figures are those developed and presented John Scott Strickland, "Across Time and Space: Conversion, Community and Cultural Change Among South Carolina Slaves," Ph.D. dissertation, University of North Carolina at Chapel Hill, 1985, 209–77. Calculated from thorough examinations of primary sources, including local church and denominational records, these are the best such statistics available. My thinking in this portion of the chapter has been profoundly influenced by Strickland's research and argument and our conversations on the subject some years ago.

99 "A Register of the Members of the Baptist Church at Charleston, S.C., Under the Pastoral Charge of Reverend Basil Manly (1830)," FU.

100 Strickland, "Across Time and Space," 232–34; "A Register of the Names of the Members of the Baptist Church at Charleston, S.C. under the Pastoral Charge of Reverend Basil Manly

(1830)," Baptist Historical Collection, FU; *Proceedings of the 1845 Meeting on the Religious Instruction of the Slaves* (Charleston, 1845).

101 Strickland, "Across Time and Space," 233–37.

102 *Journals and Letters of Francis Asbury*, 2:70.

103 William Hammett Journal, May 2, 1793, SCL.

104 *Journals of the General Conference of the Methodist Episcopal Church* (Columbia, 1834), 44–45.

105 *Journals and Letters of Francis Asbury*, 11:70; William Wightman, *The Life of William Capers* (Nashville: Southern Methodist Publishing House, 1859), 138–40.

106 Francis Asbury Mood, *Methodism in Charleston*, (Charleston, 1859), 130–32.

107 Trinity Methodist Church Records, SCHS.

108 *Journals and Letters of Francis Asbury*, 11:45–46.

109 Asplund, *Baptist Annual Register*, 104–6.

110 Records of Philadelphia Baptist Church, May 1806, April 1807, SCL; Records of Big Creek Baptist Church, November 2, 1823, SCL.

111 Edmund Botsford to Richard Furman, May 26, 1812, Botsford Papers, FU.

112 Manuscript pamphlet of the Baptist Church at Charleston, July 1819, SCL.

113 Records of the Cheraw Baptist Church, December 11, 1821, SCL; Records of the Mechanicsville Baptist Church, April 6 and May 12, 1821, SCL.

114 Howell M. Henry, *The Police Control of the Slave in South Carolina* (1914; reprint, New York: Negro Universities Press, 1968), 164–66.

115 Botsford, *Sambo and Toney*, 42.

116 Edmund Botsford to Richard Furman, October 15, 1808, Botsford Papers, FU.

117 Ibid.; Edmund Botsford to Richard Furman, February 20, 1809, Botsford Papers, FU.

118 Edmund Botsford to Richard Furman, May 26, 1812, Botsford Papers, FU.

119 George M. Fredrickson, "The Long Trek to Freedom," *New York Review of Books*, July 12, 2005, 40–42; quotation on 41.

SIX. PATERNALISM CONTESTED

1 *Annals of Congress*, December 12, 1811, col. 480; Adam Rothman, *Slave Country: American Expansion and the Origins of the Deep South* (Cambridge, MA: Harvard University Press, 2005), 119–62.

2 David R. Williams served in the War of 1812 as a brigadier general on the Canadian front, though he was disappointed when President Madison did not give him an important command in the war against the Creeks; James Hamilton started the war as a lieutenant but left as a major, serving mostly under the command of General George Izard; Joel Poinsett, who considered himself an expert in military tactics, spent most of the war as Madison's special agent in South America, where he involved himself more deeply in the military affairs of revolutionary movements in the hemisphere than one sent to negotiate commercial treaties should have. Poinsett was captured by the British when he attempted to return to the Unites States during the war and was forced to remain in Buenos Aires until the war was over. Arguably all three men expected to earn a larger reputation for military prowess during the war that they actually achieved. See Harvey Toliver Cook, *The Life and Legacy of David Rogerson Williams* (New York, 1816), 98–137; Robert Tinkler, *James Hamilton of South Carolina* (Baton Rouge: Louisiana State University Press, 2004), 29–31; J. Fred Rippy, *Joel Poinsett: Versatile American* (Durham: Duke University Press, 1935), 35–60.

3 Message of Governor David R. Williams to Senate and House of Representatives, November 25, 1816, Governor's Messages, #1191, SCDAH.

4 Williams was a native of the Cheraw area who was educated in Rhode Island. On his return to South Carolina he developed extensive planting and manufacturing interest in and around Society Hill, along the Pee Dee River, in Darlington District. An unusually well-diversified planter, Williams built a cotton mill where he used the labor of slave children. He also operated a saw mill, a cotton gin, and a shoe factory at various points in his life. He served as governor from November 1814 into December 1816. When he died in 1830, Williams owned nearly three hundred slaves, but his interest in economic diversity had led to him to strongly oppose emerging nullification sentiment. See Cook, *Life and Legacy of David Rogerson Williams*, 131; N. Louise Bailey, Mary L. Morgan, and Carolyn R. Taylor, eds., *Biographical Directory of the South Carolina Senate, 1776–1985* (Columbia: University of South Carolina Press, 1986), 3:1730–3.

5 Letter from Francis G. Deliesseline to Edwin Clifford Holland, c. 1822, printed in Holland's *A Refutation of the Calumnies Circulated Against the Southern and Western States Respecting the Institutions and Existence of Slavery Among Them* (Charleston, SC: A. E. Miller, 1822), 75–77. Deliesseline was a resident of Camden at the time of the insurrection.

6 C. Vann Woodward, ed., *Mary Chesnut's Civil War* (New Haven: Yale University Press, 1981), 815. James Chesnut Sr. lived a long and prosperous life in Kershaw County. He died in 1866 at the age of eighty-seven. By 1860, he owned three plantations (including his main residence, Mulberry), more than seventeen thousand acres, and nearly 450 slaves in Kershaw county. Writing in the 1860s, Mary Chestnut also called him "one of the last of the lordly planters who ruled this Southern world." See Bailey, Morgan, and Taylor, eds., *Biographical Directory of the South Carolina Senate*, 1:297–98.

7 Message of Governor David R. Williams to Senate and House of Representatives, November 25, 1816, Governor's Messages, #1191, SCDAH; Letter from Francis G. Deliesseline to Edwin Clifford Holland, c. 1822, printed in Holland's *A Refutation*, 75–77.

8 *Camden Gazette*, July 4, 1816; Rachel Blanding to Hannah Lewis, July 4, 1816, Blanding Papers, SCL; Letter from Francis G. Deliesseline to Edwin Clifford Holland, c. 1822, printed in Holland's *A Refutation*, 75–77; Thomas J. Kirkland and Robert M. Kennedy, *Historic Camden* (Columbia: State of South Carolina, 1903–26), 2:187–95.

9 *Camden Gazette*, July 4, 1816; Rachel Blanding to Hannah Lewis, July 4, 1816, Blanding Papers, SCL.

10 The five freeholders were Benjamin Bingham, Joseph Brevard, Burwell Boykin, Thomas Whitesides, and Benjamin Carter. All of the testimony quoted in this paragraph can be found in the following manuscript records: *State of South Carolina vs. Negro March and Negro Jack*, Court of Magistrates and Freeholders Trial Papers, #20, Kershaw District, SCDAH; *State of South Carolina vs. Negroes Abram, Renty, and Cato*, Court of Magistrates and Freeholders Trial Papers, #22, Kershaw District, SCDAH. Notations internal to the documents cited in this note indicate, as does the handwriting of the recorder, that the bulk, if not all, of the "testimony" taken in these cases and reported in these was given to the Camden Town Council during its investigation of the alleged insurrection plot on July 2, and not to the Magistrates and Freeholders Court convened by July 3, even though the testimony is archived in the court's trial records. The presence of this examinations in the official trial papers suggests that they may have been used at trial. If the court took additional testimony, it is not currently found in

SCDAH files, and I have not been able to locate it. Nevertheless, the testimony given to the town council during its investigation is revealing. The town council consisted of town intendant Abram Blanding and wardens R. W. Carter, John Reed, William Langley, and Wyatt Starke.

11 *State of South Carolina vs. Negro March and Negro Jack*, Court of Magistrates and Freeholders Trial Papers, #20, Kershaw District, SCDAH; *State of South Carolina vs. Negroes Abram, Renty, and Cato*, Court of Magistrates and Freeholders Trial Papers, #22, Kershaw District, SCDAH. Additionally, another slave, Stephen, was convicted but pardoned, and Big Frank was imprisoned for a year and sent out of the country. Nine slaves were questioned but discharged. See the letter from Francis G. Deliesseline to Edwin Clifford Holland, c. 1822, printed in Holland's *A Refutation*, 75–77.

12 Charleston *Southern Patriot and Commercial Advertiser*, July 8, 1816.

13 Charleston *Southern Patriot and Commercial Advertiser*, July 10, 1816.

14 Rachel Blanding to Hannah Lewis, July 25, 1816, Blanding Family Papers, SCL.

15 Ibid.

16 Message of Governor David R. Williams to Senate and House of Representatives, November 25, 1816, Governor's Messages, #1191, SCDAH. By this time, Camden whites understood the aborted insurrection of 1816 as one scripted in advance by erstwhile slave rebels. The plot was revealed when a slave informant tipped off whites in key leadership positions. Acting on the tip, white authorities mobilized quickly. They arrested suspects fingered by the slave informant. While in custody these suspects were subjected to regular and persistent punishments. Some of the accused kept their own counsel, while others admitted guilt; still others begin to identify other conspirators in an effort either to save themselves or to escape further punishment in jail. Somewhat formal proceedings held by white authorities gathered what they deemed "testimony," though all such testimony was coerced to some degree. These "courts" then imposed sentences on the accused. Executions were generally carried out quickly, as information about the narrowly escaped disaster leaked throughout the surrounding community, which demanded quick retribution. Ultimately the investigators and the courts came in for public praise from high authorities, but other citizens worried that some of those involved in the alleged insurrection had escaped detection. It was a script replayed on a larger stage, and much greater drama, before a national audience just a few years later in Charleston. For an account of another similarly "scripted" insurrection plot, see Eric W. Plaag, "New York's 1741 Slave Rebellion in a Climate of Fear and Anxiety," *New York History* 84 (Summer 2003): 275–99.

17 Charleston *Times*, July 17, 1816.

18 Letter from Francis G. Deliesseline to Edwin Clifford Holland, c. 1822, printed in Holland's *A Refutation*, 75–77.

19 *Camden Gazette*, July 11, 1816.

20 Janet Duitsman Cornelius, *"When I Can Read My Title Clear:" Literacy, Slavery and Religion in the Antebellum South* (Columbia: University of South Carolina Press, 1991), 11–36; Edmund Botsford, *Sambo and Toney: A Dialogue in Three Parts* (Georgetown, SC: Francis M. Baxter, 1808), 38–45.

21 Letter from Francis G. Deliesseline to Edwin Clifford Holland, c. 1822, printed in Holland's *A Refutation*, 75–77.

22 *Camden Gazette*, July 11, 1816. A week later editor Langley published the fact that the slaves involved in the alleged insurrection who "were professors of religion did not belong exclusively

to one church." See *Camden Gazette*, July 18, 1816. On Langley, see Kirkland and Kennedy, *Historic Camden*, 187, 300.

23 *Camden Gazette*, July 11 and 18, 1816.

24 Marina Wikramanayake, *A World in a Shadow: The Free Black in Antebellum South Carolina* (Columbia: University of South Carolina Press, 1973), 122–23; David J. McCord, ed., *The Statutes at Large of South Carolina* (Columbia, SC: A. S. Johnston, 1840), 7:442–49.

25 Howell M. Henry, *The Police Control of the Slave in South Carolina* (New York: Negro Universities Press, 1914), 134–38.

26 *Bell v. Graham*, in *Nott and McCord's Reports* (1818), 278–82; see also Fairfield County Court of Common Pleas, Judgment Roll, #1389, Fall 1818.

27 Ibid.

28 Francis A. Mood, *Methodism in Charleston* (Nashville: Stephenson and Evans, 1856), 131–33; Christopher Leevy Johnson, "'I Wouldn't Take Nothing for My Journey Now': A Journey to an Afro-Methodist Faith in the South Carolina Lowcountry Before the Civil War," M.A. thesis, University of South Carolina, 2000, 37–51.

29 Wikramanayake, *A World in a Shadow*, 119–28.

30 Daniel A. Payne, *The History of the African Methodist Episcopal Church* (New York: Johnson, 1968), 27–30; Johnson, "'I Wouldn't Take Nothing for My Journey Now,'" 46–47.

31 Charleston *City Gazette*, December 4, 1817; *Charleston Courier*, June 9, 1818; Charleston *Southern Patriot*, June 10, 1818.

32 Payne, *The History of the African Methodist Episcopal Church*, 44–45; Daniel A. Payne, *Recollections of Seventy Years* (New York: Arno Press, 1969), 11–40, 100–8, 161–65; Daniel A. Payne, "Organization Essential to Success for the Quarto-Centennial of African Methodism in the South" (Philadelphia, 1890), 39–40, in *Sermons and Addresses of Daniel Payne, 1853–1891*, ed. Charles Killian (New York: Arno Press, 1972).

33 Wikramanayake, *A World in a Shadow*, 124–25. Wikramanayake wrongly dates this development to 1817, however. The legislative petitions cited in the three notes below clearly contain internal evidence dating the matter to 1820.

34 Petition of Inhabitants of Edisto Island Advocating Curbing Certain Rights of Free Blacks, Persons of Color and Slaves as Well as Citing the Activities of Abolition Societies in Charleston, c. 1820, Legislative Petitions, Records of the South Carolina General Assembly, n. d., Record Group S165015, #01870, SCDAH.

35 Petition of Inhabitants of Charleston Advocating a Curtailment of Certain Rights Granted to Free Blacks, Persons of Color and Slaves as Well as Citing the Activities of Abolition Societies, October 10, 1820, Legislative Petitions, Records of the South Carolina General Assembly, 1820, Record Group S165015, #00143, SCDAH.

36 Petition of Sundry Free Persons of Color, Attached to the African Methodist Episcopal Church in Charleston Called Zion, Asking Permission to Worship on Charleston Neck, with the Endorsement of Various Protestant Pastors of the Area [c. 1820], Legislative Petitions, Records of the South Carolina General Assembly, n.d., Record Group S165015, #01893, SCDAH. Palmer, pastor of the architecturally unique "Circular" church in Charleston, proved an enduring, if relatively quiet, supporter of colonization (see ch. 8).

37 "On the Condition of Blacks in This Country," *Panoplist and Missionary Herald* 16 (November 1820): 482.

38 Charleston Delegation, Report and Supporting Papers on the Petition of Certain Free Persons of Color, Having Seceded from a Particular Methodist Church, Asking Permission to Wor-

ship in a Building Erected by Them in the Suburbs of Charleston, December 2, 1820, Reports of Legislative Committees, Records of the South Carolina General Assembly, 1820, Record Group S165005, #00228, SCDAH.

39 Johnson, "'I Wouldn't Take Nothing for My Journey Now,'" 46–47. Together these congregations were known as the Bethel Circuit.

40 Petition of Inhabitants of Edisto Island Advocating Curbing Certain Rights of Free Blacks, Persons of Color and Slaves as Well as Citing the Activities of Abolition Societies in Charleston, c. 1820, Legislative Petitions, Records of the South Carolina General Assembly, n.d., Record Group S165015, #01870, SCDAH.

41 Petition of Inhabitants of Charleston Advocating a Curtailment of Certain Rights Granted to Free Blacks, Persons of Color and Slaves as Well as Citing the Activities of Abolition Societies, October 10, 1820, Legislative Petitions, Records of the South Carolina General Assembly, 1820, Record Group S165015, #00143, SCDAH.

42 "On the Condition of Blacks in This Country," *Panoplist and Missionary Herald* 16 (November 1820), 482–83.

43 John G. Jones, *A Concise History of the Introduction of Protestantism into Mississippi and the Southwest* (St. Louis: P. M. Pinckard, 1866), 102–10; Margaret DesChamps Moore, "Religion in Mississippi in 1860," *Journal of Mississippi History* 22 (October 1960): 223–38.

44 Randy J. Sparks, *On Jordan's Stormy Banks: Evangelicalism in Mississippi, 1773–1876* (Athens: University of Georgia Press, 1994), 60–70; see also Z. T. Leavell and T. J. Bailey, *A Complete History of Mississippi Baptists: From the Earliest Times* (Jackson: Mississippi Baptist Publishing Co., 1904), 1:75, 129, and Mississippi Baptist Association, *Republication of the Minutes of the Mississippi Baptist Association, from Its Organization in 1806 to the Present Time* (New Orleans: Hinton, 1849), 21–87.

45 Sparks, *On Jordan's Stormy Banks*, 70; J. F. H. Claiborne, *Mississippi, as a Province, Territory and State* (Jackson, MS: Power and Barksdale, 1880), 145–46.

46 William Winans Autobiography, 10, Cain Archives, Millsaps College, Jackson, Mississippi; Ray Holder, *William Winans: Methodist Leader in Antebellum Mississippi* (Jackson: University Press of Mississippi, 1976).

47 Sparks, *On Jordan's Stormy Banks*, 70; Richard A. McLemore, *A History of Mississippi* (Hattiesburg: University and College Publishers of Mississippi, 1974), 1:234–54.

48 Claiborne, *Mississippi*, 361; Edwin A. Miles, *Jacksonian Democracy in Mississippi* (Chapel Hill: University of North Carolina Press, 1960), 44–45.

49 Mack Swearingen, *The Early Life of George Poindexter: A Story of the First Southwest* (New Orleans: Tulane University Press, 1934), 28–29 and passim.

50 Percy Lee Rainwater, "Notes on Southern Personalities," *Journal of Southern History* 4 (May 1938): 226.

51 Allen Nevins, *Ordeal of the Union* (New York: Scribner, 1947), 1:540–41; Sparks, *On Jordan's Stormy Banks*, 70; Claiborne, *Mississippi*, 391; Winans Autobiography, 166–72, Cain Archives.

52 "Laws of the State of Mississippi (1822)," in William Sumner Jenkins, ed., *Records of the States of the United States* (Washington, DC: Library of Congress, 1949), 184.

53 Charles Sydnor, *Slavery in Mississippi* (New York: D. Appleton, 1933), 55–56; Swearingen, *Early Life*, 28–29 and passim; Mississippi Baptist Association, *Republication of the Minutes*, 167–68.

54 Rachel Klein, *Unification of a Slave State: The Rise of the Planter Class in the South Carolina Backcountry, 1760–1808* (Chapel Hill: University of North Carolina Press, 1990), 290–91.

55 Statistics used herein calculated from Ira Berlin, *Slaves Without Masters* (New York: Pantheon, 1974), 46–47, 136–37, 396–403.

56 Presentment of the York District Grand Jury, October 29, 1816, Grand Jury Presentments, Records of the South Carolina General Assembly, 1816, Record Group S165010, #00025, SCDAH.

57 Presentment of the Fairfield District Grand Jury, November 1816, Grand Jury Presentments, Records of the South Carolina General Assembly, 1816, Record Group S165010, #00012, SCDAH.

58 Presentment of the Richland District Grand Jury, 1816, Grand Jury Presentments, Records of the South Carolina General Assembly, 1816, Record Group S165010, #00019, SCDAH.

59 Presentment of the Lexington District Grand Jury, 1816, Grand Jury Presentments, Records of the South Carolina General Assembly, 1816, Record Group S165010, #00018, SCDAH.

60 Presentment of the Spartanburg District Grand Jury, November 11, 1816, Grand Jury Presentments, Records of the South Carolina General Assembly, 1816, Record Group S165010, #00021, SCDAH.

61 Presentment of the Kershaw District Grand Jury, November 19, 1816, Grand Jury Presentments, Records of the South Carolina General Assembly, 1816, Record Group S165010, #00015, SCDAH.

62 Message of Governor David R. Williams to Senate and House of Representatives, November 25, 1816, Governor's Messages, #1191, SCDAH.

63 *Charleston Courier*, December 13, 18, and 25, 1816.

64 *Camden Gazette*, December 12, 1816.

65 Presentment of the Spartanburg District Grand Jury, November 1817, Grand Jury Presentments, Records of the South Carolina General Assembly, 1817, Record Group S165010, #00014, SCDAH.

66 Message No. 1 of Governor Andrew Pickens to Both Branches of the Legislature of the State, November 28, 1817, Governor's Messages, #1213, SCDAH.

67 *Augusta Herald*, December 9, 1817, excerpted in *Charleston Courier*, December 15, 1817.

68 Charleston *City Gazette*, December 23, 1817; *South Carolina Statutes at Large*, eds. Thomas Cooper and David J. McCord (Columbia, SC: A. H. Johnston, 1836–41), 7: 455–58.

69 Presentment of the York District Grand Jury, October 1818, Grand Jury Presentments, Records of the South Carolina General Assembly, 1818, Record Group S165010, #00018, and Presentment of the Chester District Grand Jury, November 1818, Grand Jury Presentments, Records of the South Carolina General Assembly, 1818, Record Group S165010, #00004, SCDAH.

70 Message No. 1, from His Excellency the Governor [Andrew Pickens] to the Legislature of South Carolina, November 24, 1818, Governors Messages, #1236, SCDAH.

71 *Charleston Courier*, December 12, 1818.

72 Charleston *City Gazette*, December 8, 9, and 12, 1818,

73 The House roll call is reported in the *South Carolina State Gazette*, December 8, 1818. Voting analysis calculated from data derived from House Journal, Records of the General Assembly, 1818, 16, 26, 33–37, 85, 198–99; Senate Journal, Records of the General Assembly, 1818, 28, 36–37, 46, 78–80, 116, 125–26, 194–95; Bailey, Morgan, and Taylor, eds., *Biographical Directory of the South Carolina Senate, 1776–1985*, 3:1844–5 and passim; Walter B. Edgar, *Biographical Directory of the South Carolina House of Representatives* (Columbia: University of South Carolina Press, 1974), 1:296–300.

74 *Charleston Courier*, December 12, 1818. McCreary, a Baptist who owned nine slaves when he died in 1833, was a fifth-term senator. Clendenin, a lawyer, was serving his second term in the Senate at the time of this vote, and he served five more consecutive terms thereafter. See Bailey, Morgan, and Taylor, eds., *Biographical Directory of the South Carolina Senate, 1776–1985*, 1:308–9, 2:978–79. While a distinct geographic pattern emerged within the Lowcountry on this issue, no clear pattern emerged in the Upcountry.

75 Message of the Governor [Thomas Bennett] to the Senate and House of Representatives of the State of South Carolina, November 27, 1821, Governor's Messages, #1296, SCDAH.

76 L. Q. C. Lamar, *Compilation of the Laws of Georgia* (Augusta, 1821), 608.

77 *Acts of Georgia*, 1817, 139–43; Winfield Collins, *The Domestic Slave Trade of the Southern States* (New York: Broadway, 1904), 42.

78 *Augusta Chronicle*, October 11, 1817, quoted in U. B. Phillips, *Georgia and States Rights* (Yellow Springs, OH: Antioch Press, 1968 [1902].), 157.

79 "Message of Governor William Rabun," November 3, 1818, *Journal of the [Georgia] Senate*, 1818, 8.

80 Lamar, *Compilation*, 817.

81 For an overview of Georgia's efforts to regulate the domestic slave trade, see Ruth Scarborough, *The Opposition to Slavery in Georgia Prior to 1860* (1933; reprint, New York: Negro Universities Press, 1968), 113–20.

82 *Harry et al. v. Decker and Hopkins*, 1 Mississippi, 1818: 36; *Annals of Congress, 15th Congress, 2nd Session*, 388; see also Charles Sydnor, *Slavery in Mississippi* (New York: D. Appleton, 1933), esp. 239–41.

83 Winbourne Magruder Drake, "The Framing of Mississippi's First Constitution," *Journal of Mississippi History* 29 (April 1956): 79–110; Sydnor, *Slavery in Mississippi*, 162–65; Edwin A. Miles, *Jacksonian Democracy in Mississippi* (Chapel Hill: University of North Carolina Press, 1960), 41–42; Oscar B. Chamberlain, "The Evolution of State Constitutions in the Antebellum United States: Michigan, Kentucky, and Mississippi," Ph.D. dissertation, University of South Carolina, 1996, 89–123.

84 Berlin, *Slaves Without Masters*, 36, 45, 21–58; Joe Gray Taylor, *Negro Slavery in Louisiana* (Baton Rouge: Louisiana Historical Association, 1963), 21–58.

85 Only 571 free blacks lived in Alabama in 1820 and only 458 lived in Mississippi. Georgia, an older state, had more free blacks (1,763) that Alabama and Mississippi combined, but, in terms of proportion, the Georgia free black population still accounted for only about 0.5 percent of the state's relatively robust population of nearly 190,000 in 1820. See Berlin, *Slaves Without Masters*, 23, 46–47, 136–37, 396–403.

86 On this subject, see Michael P. Johnson and James L. Roark, *Black Masters: A Free Family of Color in the Old South* (New York: W. W. Norton, 1984), esp. 3–106; Bernard E. Powers, *Black Charlestonians: A Social History, 1822–1885* (Fayetteville: University of Arkansas Press, 1994), 36–73; Robert L. Harris Jr., "Charleston Free Afro-American Elite: The Brown Fellowship Society and the Humane Brotherhood," *South Carolina Historical Magazine* 82 (October 1981): 289–310; Joel Williamson, *New People: Miscegenation and Mulattoes in the United States* (New York: Free Press, 1980), 14–24; Wikramanayake, *A World in a Shadow*, esp. 77–81; Berlin, *Slaves Without Masters*, 179–81; Joseph G. Tregle, *Louisiana in the Age of Jackson* (Baton Rouge: Louisiana State University Press, 1999), 35–37; H. E. Sterkx, *The Free Negro in Ante-bellum Louisiana* (Rutherford, NJ: Fairleigh Dickinson University Press, 1972), 91–159.

87 A. S. Clayton, *A Compilation of the Laws of Georgia Enacted Between 1800 and 1810* (Augusta, 1813), 27, 369, 462–63, 665–66; T. R. R. Cobb, *Digest of the Statute Law of Georgia in Force Prior to 1851* (Athens, 1851), 1125; Lamar, *Compilation*, 801, 811; see also Ruth Scarborough, *The Opposition to Slavery In Georgia Prior to 1860* (New York: Negro University Press, 1933), 175–78.

88 For an overview of these developments, see Berlin, *Slaves Without Masters*, 92–99; Lamar, *Compilation*, 801–13; O. H. Prince, *Digest of Laws of Georgia Enacted Previous to 1820* (Milledgeville, 1822), 466. Later court decisions allowed manumission through will and testament if the freed slaves were required to leave the state. See Ralph Betts Flanders, *Plantation Slavery in Georgia* (Chapel Hill: University of North Carolina Press, 1933), 248–53.

89 Wikramanayake, *A World in a Shadow*, 21–30; Message to the Senate and House of Representatives of the State of South Carolina, November 27, 1820, Governor's Messages, 581–86, SCDAH.

90 McCord, ed., *The Statutes at Large of South Carolina*, 7:459–60.

91 *Snow v. Callum*, 1797, in Helen Catteral, ed., *Judicial Cases Concerning American Slavery and the Negro* (Washington, DC: Carnegie Institution, 1928–37), 2:279; John Belton O'Neall, ed., *The Negro Law of South Carolina* (Columbia, SC: J. G. Bowman, 1848), 11; Wikramanayake, *A World in a Shadow*, 34–35; Henry, *The Police Control of the Slave in South Carolina*, 168–69; McCord, ed., *The Statutes at Large of South Carolina*, 7:436–43.

92 Wikramanayake, *A World in a Shadow*, 35–37.

93 See *Charleston Courier*, December 12 and 18, 1821.

94 This section draws heavily on Adam Rothman, *Slave Country: American Expansion and the Origins of the Deep South* (Cambridge, MA: Harvard University Press, 2005), esp. 24–35; Sterkx, *The Free Negro in Ante-bellum Louisiana*, 91–159; Taylor, *Negro Slavery in Louisiana*, 21–58; Garry B. Mills, *The Forgotten People: Cane River's Creoles of Color* (Baton Rouge: Louisiana State University Press, 1977), 192–217; Ira Berlin, *Slaves Without Masters*, 108–32, and Tregle, *Louisiana in the Age of Jackson*, 27–32.

95 Rothman, *Slave Country*, 37–54; Sterkx, *The Free Negro in Ante-bellum Louisiana*, 91–95.

96 John Watkins to John Graham, September 6, 1805, in Clarence E. Carter, ed., *The Territorial Papers of the United States*, vol. 9: *The Territory of Orleans, 1803–1812* (Washington, DC: Government Printing Office, 1940), 503.

97 Statement of Stephen to Governor William Claiborne, January 23, 1806, in Carter, ed., *The Territorial Papers of the United States*, vol. 9: The *Territory of Orleans, 1803–1812*, 575–76.

98 *Laws of the Territory of Orleans* (1806), 1st Legislature, 1st Session, 128, and 1st Legislature, 2nd Session, 180–82.

99 Sterkx, *The Free Negro in Ante-bellum Louisiana*, 94–96.

100 William C. C. Claiborne to Robert Smith, May 20, 1809, in *Official Letter Books of W. C. C. Claiborne*, ed. Dunbar Rowland (Jackson, MS: State Department of Archives and History, 1917), 4:363–64.

101 Claiborne to William Savage, November 10, 1809, in *Official Letter Books of W. C. C. Claiborne*, 5:3–6.

102 *Third Census of the United States, 1810*, 82.

103 Berlin, *Slaves Without Masters*, 123.

104 Francis Newton Thorpe, ed., *The Federal and State Constitutions, Colonial Charters, and Other Organic Laws of the States, Territories, and Colonies Now or Heretofore Forming the United States of America* (Washington, DC: Government Printing Office, 1909), 3: 1378–429.

105 Berlin, *Slaves Without Masters*, 119–32.

106 Quoted in Roland C. McConnell, *Negro Troops of Antebellum Louisiana: A History of the Battalion of Free Men of Color* (Baton Rouge: Louisiana State University Press, 1968), 78.

107 Berlin, *Slaves Without Masters*, 128–32.

108 *Laws of Louisiana* (1816–17), 3rd Legislature, 1st Session, 44–48.

109 During the rest of the 1820s, the Mississippi legislature routinely rejected more petitions for manumission than it approved. See Charles S. Sydnor, "The Free Negro in Mississippi," *American Historical Review* 32 (July 1927): 769–88. Alabama, with a free black population as small as that of Mississippi and concentrated heavily in Mobile, took little or no action to tighten its regulation of free blacks until after the Denmark Vesey insurrection. See James B. Sellers, *Slavery in Alabama* (Tuscaloosa: University of Alabama Press, 1950), 361–98.

110 "Speech of Freeman Walker," January 19, 1820, *Annals of Congress*, 16th Congress, 1st session, 159–75.

111 "Speech of Nathaniel Macon," January 20, 1820, *Annals of Congress*, 16th Congress, 1st session, 219–32.

112 "Speech of Richard Johnson," February 1, 1820, *Annals of Congress*, 16th Congress, 1st session, 345–60.

113 "Speech of Freeman Walker," 174; "Speech of Richard Johnson," 346.

114 "Speech of Charles Pinckney," February 14, 1820, *History of Congress*, 16th Congress, 1st session, 1310–30. For a comprehensive discussion of the position Pinckney took in the Missouri debates, see Mark D. Kaplanoff, "Charles Pinckney and the American Republican Tradition," in Michael O'Brien and David Moltke-Hansen, eds., *Intellectual Life in Antebellum Charleston* (Knoxville: University of Tennessee Press, 1986), 85–122.

115 "Speech of William Smith," January 26, 1820, *History of Congress*, 16th Congress, 2nd session, 259–75; see also "Speech of William Smith," December 8, 1820, *History of Congress*, 16th Congress, 2nd session, 51–77.

116 "Speech of William Smith," January 26, 1820, esp. 270.

117 Ibid. For a discussion of Smith's position during the Missouri Compromise, see Caroline P. Smith, "South Carolina Radical: The Political Career of William Smith" (master's thesis, Auburn University, 1971), 72–133; see the replies to William Smith's January 1820 speech found in *History of Congress* 16th Congress, 2nd Session, 275–99.

SEVEN. THE SCARE

1 The historiography of the Denmark Vesey insurrection scare is vast, rich, and in recent years increasingly contested. The bulk of this literature and the specific historiographical controversies at issue will be cited in various notes throughout this chapter. John Lofton's *Insurrection in South Carolina: The Turbulent World of Denmark Vesey* (Yellow Springs, OH: Antioch Press, 1964) remains a valuable account of the insurrection, and much of the material in this paragraph is drawn from that volume, 144–81. Recent efforts to supplant Lofton's account as the master narrative of the insurrection include Douglas Egerton, *He Shall Go Out Free: The Lives of Denmark Vesey* (Madison, WI: Madison House, 1999), a scholarly work, and David Robertson, *Denmark Vesey* (New York: A. A. Knopf, 1999), a more popular treatment. The recent historiographical controversy over the nature of the Denmark Vesey scare and the reasons for it, and over the scope and even the existence of the plot itself, has stimulated historians to scrutinize more

closely the evidence concerning the alleged insurrection plot. For Michael P. Johnson's provocative and impressive argument suggesting that historians have ignored evidence that white authorities exaggerated the scope of the plot and its prospects for success, and seriously misdiagnosed the possible causes of any slave unrest in Charleston in 1822, see his "Denmark Vesey and His Co-Conspirators, Part I," *William and Mary Quarterly* 58 (October 2001): 915–76. In the next issue of the same journal, a number of scholars responded to Johnson's argument; see Robert Gross, ed., "Forum: The Making of a Slave Conspiracy II," *William and Mary Quarterly* 59 (January 2002): 135–202. This issue includes essays by Edward Pearson, Douglas Egerton, David Robertson, Philip D. Morgan, Thomas J. Davis, Winthrop D. Jordan, James Sidbury, and Robert L. Paquette, and a reply by Michael P. Johnson. The most persistent and method critics of Johnson's bold new interpretation have been Douglas Egerton and Robert Paquette. See Douglas R. Egerton, "'Why They Did Not Preach Up This Thing': Denmark Vesey and Revolutionary Theology," *South Carolina Historical Magazine* 100 (October 1999): 298–318; Robert L. Paquette and Douglas R. Egerton, "Of Facts and Fables: New Light on the Denmark Vesey Affair," *South Carolina Historical Magazine* 105 (January 2004): 8–35; and Robert L. Paquette, "From Rebellion to Revisionism: The Continuing Debate About the Denmark Vesey Affair," *Journal of the Historical Society* 4 (Fall 2004): 291–334. Johnson's critique of interpretations of the Vesey scare elaborated on an earlier article, Richard C. Wade, "The Vesey Plot: A Reconsideration," *Journal of Southern History* 30 (May 1964): 143–61. Wade argued that anxious whites had mistaken loose talk about rebellion for a well-thought-out insurrection plot. Wade's argument was perhaps most forcefully challenged by William W. Freehling, "Denmark Vesey's Peculiar Reality," in Robert H. Abzug and Stephen E. Maizlish, eds., *New Perspectives on Race and Slavery in America: Essays in Honor of Kenneth M. Stampp* (Lexington: University Press of Kentucky, 1986), 25–50.

2 The narrative in the early paragraphs of this chapter is based, unless otherwise noted, on the earliest and best primary sources we have on the Denmark Vesey insurrection scare. These sources offer abundant detail concerning some aspects of the alleged plot and the subsequent white reaction. However, each of these primary sources was composed or complied by white authorities shortly after the events described or discussed in them and each source had an intended audience. In every case, a desire to shape the perceptions of that audience likely influenced the shaping of the accounts left behind. Also in each case, these valuable primary sources provide better evidence of what white authorities thought, or wanted others to think, about the alleged insurrection plot than as evidence about what actually happened in Charleston during the summer of 1822. These sources are: Document B: Evidence, Governor's Messages, no. 1328, series no. S165009, Records of the General Assembly, SCDAH; "Circular Letter of Governor Thomas Bennett, 10 August 1822," *National Intelligencer*, August 24, 1822, 2; [James Hamilton], *An Account of the Late Intended Insurrection Among a Portion of the Blacks of the City* (Charleston, SC: A. E. Miller, 1822); Lionel H. Kennedy and Thomas Parker, *An Official Report of the Trials of Sundry Negroes Charged with an Attempt to Raise an Insurrection in the State of South Carolina; Preceded by an Introduction and Narrative; and in an Appendix, a Report on the Trials of Four White Persons, on Indictments for Attempting to Excite the Slaves to Insurrection* (Charleston, SC: James R. Schenk, 1822); Message #2 of Governor Thomas Bennett to the Senate and House of Representatives of the State of South Carolina, November 28, 1822, St 828, SCDAH. These sources and their strengths and limitations will be discussed further in later notes.

3 Kennedy and Parker, *An Official Report*, 33–34.

4 Hamilton, *An Account of the Late Intended Insurrection*, 3–7; Kennedy and Parker, *An Official Report*, 34–36.
5 Hamilton, *An Account of the Late Intended Insurrection*, 6–7; Kennedy and Parker, *An Official Report*, 35–36. The "invulnerable" slave accused by William Paul was the African-born conjurer known as Gullah Jack Pritchard, who is discussed later in this chapter.
6 Hamilton, *An Account of the Late Intended Insurrection*, 8–9; Kennedy and Parker, *An Official Report*, 36.
7 Hamilton, *An Account of the Late Intended Insurrection*, 10–12.
8 *Reminiscences of William Hasell Wilson, 1811–1902*, ed. Elizabeth B. Pharo (Philadelphia: Patterson and White, 1937), 6. As an adult, Wilson became chief engineer of the powerful Pennsylvania Railroad. See Theodore Jervey, *Robert Y. Hayne and His Times* (New York: Macmillan, 1909), 131–32.
9 Kennedy and Parker, *An Official Report*, 36–37; Hamilton, *An Account of the Late Intended Insurrection*, 10–11.
10 The public received virtually no official word about the insurrection scare and the concomitant investigation until June 29, and thereafter received only sketchy press reports of the severe punishments meted out to alleged leaders of the thwarted insurrection until the investigation and subsequent "trials" ended in August. For the first press account, see Charleston *Gazette*, June 29, 1822.
11 *Reminiscences of William Hasell Wilson*, 6.
12 E. M. Starr to Cedric Wildman, July 19, 1822, Zalmon Wildman Papers, SCL.
13 Kennedy and Parker, *An Official Report*, 32–38. While the *Official Report* has its liabilities as a source, the report contains, if nothing else, the information the Vesey court wanted the public to have regarding the insurrection scare.
14 Hamilton, *An Account of the Late Intended Insurrection*, 11.
15 Message #2 of Governor Thomas Bennett to the Senate and House of Representatives of the State of South Carolina, November 28, 1822, St 828, SCDAH.
16 Later in his lifetime, the wealthy Hamilton invested heavily if not always wisely in an array of banking, railroad, and insurance ventures as well as in western lands. Ultimately his speculation in Texas lands and risky loans he made to the Republic of Texas pushed him into financial embarrassment and virtual bankruptcy by the early 1840s. He spent the final years of his life (he died in 1857) trying to recoup his losses and repay friends and family a portion of the money he owed them. See Robert Tinkler, *James Hamilton of South Carolina* (Baton Rouge: Louisiana State University Press, 2004), esp. 9–27; Virginia Louise Glenn, "James Hamilton, Jr. of South Carolina," Ph.D. dissertation, University of North Carolina, 1964, 1–15; William W. Freehling, *Prelude to Civil War: The Nullification Controversy in South Carolina, 1816–1836* (New York: Harper and Row, 1966), 149–52.
17 Elizabeth Lynch's half brother, Thomas Lynch III, signed the Declaration of Independence, and her father, Thomas Lynch Jr., was a member of the First and Second Continental Congresses until incapacitated by a brain hemorrhage. See Tinkler, *James Hamilton*, 12.
18 Tinkler, *James Hamilton*, 28–42; Glenn, "James Hamilton, Jr. of South Carolina," 16–42.
19 Ibid.
20 The biographical information on members of the Magistrates and Freeholders Court has been compiled from a number of sources. Foremost among those sources are N. Louise Bailey, Mary L. Morgan, and Carolyn R. Taylor, eds., *Biographical Directory of the South Carolina Senate, 1776–1985* (Columbia: University of South Carolina Press, 1986), 1:371–73, 2:1314–5. James

Legare resigned from the court due to health problems on July 19, 1822. His replacement, prominent planter-lawyer Henry Deas, fit the general profile of other court members. A native of Edinburgh, Deas studied at Princeton and was admitted to the South Carolina bar in 1791. During the 1790s he served as a solicitor on the state's southern circuit. But Deas ultimately relied more on planting than law for his income. Over the course of his lifetime, Deas owned at lest seven plantations, and at his death in 1847 he owned ninety-four slaves. He resided primarily in a house in Charleston and on one of his North Santee plantations. He was a brother in-law of Elias Horry. Like others active in the Vesey investigation, Deas supported the Federalist Party early in his career but drifted toward active support for nullification by the early 1830s. Deas was also active in the civic life of Charleston, serving on the city's library board, on the board of the College of Charleston, and as free school commissioner. From 1827 to 1834 he served as president of the confrontational South Carolina Association, an organization that took it upon itself to enforce laws regulating slaves and free blacks in Charleston after the Vesey scare. He was first elected to the state senate in 1824 and served continuously until 1835. From 1828 to 1835 he served as president of the Senate. Like others on or associated with the Court, Deas earned a political popularity during the crisis that served him well in later years. On the larger phenomenon of the migration of South Carolina Federalists to the nullification camp, see George C. Rogers Jr., "South Carolina Federalists and the Origins of the Nullification Movement," *South Carolina Historical Magazine* 71 (January 1970): 17–32.

21 Hamilton, *An Account of the Late Intended Insurrection*, 17–18; Johnson, "Denmark Vesey and His Co-Conspirators, Part I," 922–25; Document B: Evidence, 55–80.

22 Ibid.

23 James Hamilton apparently sent a letter dated July 3, 1822, to his counterpart in Savannah, Mayor Charles Harris. Hamilton apparently wanted to keep Harris abreast of developments in Charleston in the interest of the safety and security of Savannah, a commercial competitor but a similarly situated black-belt port city. In a letter on July 6, Martha Richardson, residing in the Savannah home of her brother-in-law, Major John Screven, a Lowcountry rice planter, told her nephew James Proctor Screven that Harris, then mayor of Savannah, had arrived at the Screven home carrying a letter written by intendant James Hamilton. According to Richardson's reporting, Hamilton dated his letter by its content, noting at one point that six of the accused were "yesterday executed." Vesey and five others were executed publicly on July 2. See Martha Proctor Richardson to James Proctor Screven, July 6, 1822, Arnold-Screven Papers, SHC.

24 Ironically, the most information historians have on Denmark Vesey, from a source dated close to the time of his execution, comes from the leader of the investigation, James Hamilton, and the court that sentenced him to death. See Hamilton, *An Account of the Late Intended Insurrection*, 16–17, 29–30, and Kennedy and Parker, *An Official Report*, 11–18. The information published about Vesey in these accounts is certainly the information Hamilton and the court wanted the Charleston public to know about Vesey, but a careful reading of the sources suggests that, at the least, it is no less accurate than other information given about the alleged leader of the aborted insurrection. For a judicious assessment of what historians know and do not know about Vesey, see Johnson, "Denmark Vesey and His Co-Conspirators, Part I," 915–20. See also Lofton, *Insurrection in South Carolina*, 26–74. Egerton, *He Shall Go Out Free* offers an intriguing overview of Vesey's life, though Egerton interprets undocumented aspects of Vesey's life rather freely.

25 Charleston *Gazette*, June 29, 1822.

26 John Potter to Langdon Cheves, June 29 and July 20, 1822, Langdon Cheves Papers, SCHS.

27 Johnson, "Denmark Vesey and His Co-Conspirators, Part I," 951; Document B: Evidence, 143. One of the unanswered questions about the investigations is why alleged ringleaders such as Vesey and Gell remained at large for nearly a month after the first witness was examined.

28 [William Johnson], "Communication: Melancholy Effect of Popular Excitement," *Charleston Courier*, June 21, 1822.

29 Ibid.

30 Donald G. Morgan, *Justice William Johnson, The First Dissenter: The Career and Constitutional Philosophy of a Jeffersonian Judge* (Columbia: University of South Carolina Press, 1954), 126–46; John Potter to Langdon Cheves, June 29, 1822, Langdon Cheves Papers, SCHS. An edited version of all of Potter's letters appears in Robert S. Starobin, ed., *Denmark Vesey: The Slave Conspiracy of 1822* (Englewood Cliffs, NJ: Prentice-Hall, 1970), 74–79.

31 *Charleston Courier*, June 29, 1821.

32 Ibid.

33 William Johnson, *To the Public of Charleston* (Charleston: C. C. Sebring, 1822).

34 Ibid., 5–6.

35 Ibid., 5–11.

36 Ibid., 10–13.

37 Anna Hayes Johnson to her cousin, June 23, 1822, Ernest Haywood Papers, SHC. An edited version of Anna Johnson's letters appears in Starobin, ed., *Denmark Vesey*, 72–74.

38 *Charleston Courier*, June 29, 1822.

39 *Charleston Courier*, July 1, 1822.

40 Ibid.

41 Charleston *Southern Patriot*, July 12, 1822.

42 Henry W. DeSaussure to Joel R. Poinsett, July 6, 1822, Joel R. Poinsett Papers, HSP.

43 Anna Hayes Johnson to her cousin, June 23, 1822, Ernest Haywood Papers, SHC.

44 Martha Proctor Richardson to James Proctor Screven, July 6, 1822, Arnold-Screven Papers, SHC. Richardson apparently wrote with Hamilton's July 3 letter, or a copy of it, in front of her and quoted at length from it. See note 23 for a full explanation of Hamilton's letter.

45 On Bennett's pre-gubernatorial career, see Bailey, Morgan, and Taylor, eds., *Biographical Directory of the South Carolina Senate, 1776–1985*, 2:128–30; Craig Miller Bennett, "Family Records of Governor Thomas Bennett, Jr.," *South Carolina Historical Magazine* 51 (January 1950): 51–61, esp. 51–54.

46 Bennett recounted most of these details in his gubernatorial message to the legislature six months later. See Message #2 of Governor Thomas Bennett to the Senate and House of Representatives of the State of South Carolina, November 28, 1822, St 828, SCDAH. See also, Morgan, *Justice William Johnson*, 138–40.

47 Johnson, "Denmark Vesey and His Co-Conspirators, Part I," 935–39. Paquette and Egerton, "Of Facts and Fables," 23–29, emphasizes that even if owners were not always allowed to visit their slaves, members of the Charleston clergy were allowed to visit imprisoned blacks frequently.

48 Kennedy and Parker, *An Official Report*, 17–22; see also Document B: Evidence, 143–44.

49 Governor Thomas Bennett to Attorney General Robert Y. Hayne, July 1, 1822, Governor's Messages, 1814–1822, St 828, #1266, Document D, SCDAH.

50 Robert Y. Hayne, Office of the Attorney General, to Governor Thomas Bennett, July 3, 1822, Governor's Messages, 1814–1822, St 828, #1268–1274, Document E, SCDAH.

51 Again, see note 23. For the secondhand reporting of Hamilton's observations, see Martha Proctor Richardson to James Proctor Screven, July 6, 1822, Arnold-Screven Papers, SHC.

52 Ibid.

53 Ibid.

54 Ibid.

55 At least four blacks almost certainly testified between July 2 and July 9, when the court was not in session, and other witnesses may have testified during these curious "recess" sessions. See Johnson, "Denmark Vesey and His Co-Conspirators," 932.

56 *Charleston Courier*, July 1 and 10, 1822; Charleston *Southern Patriot*, July 12, 1822.

57 Document B: Evidence, 80–88.

58 Hamilton, *An Account of the Late Intended Insurrection*, 16–24; Kennedy and Parker, *An Official Report*, 37–40; Johnson, "Denmark Vesey and His Co-Conspirators," 939–53; Lofton, *Insurrection in South Carolina*, 162–72.

59 Hamilton, *An Account of the Late Intended Insurrection*, 13–27; Kennedy and Parker, *An Official Report*, 32–40.

60 John Potter to Langdon Cheves, July 10, 1822, Langdon Cheves Papers, SCHS.

61 Kennedy and Parker, *An Official Report*, 39–40; Hamilton, *An Account of the Late Intended Insurrection*, 19–21; Johnson, "Denmark Vesey and His Co-Conspirators," 945–53.

62 Kennedy and Parker, *An Official Report*, 66–73.

63 Johnson, "Denmark Vesey and His Co-Conspirators, Part I," 944–58; see also Document B: Evidence, 88–232.

64 *Charleston Courier*, July 29, 1822. On Saturday, August 3, a second Magistrates and Freeholders Court convened to conduct the trials of twelve additional slaves and two free blacks. One of the slaves, William Garner, who had fled the city and been captured near Columbia and returned to Charleston for trial, was sentenced to death; seven other slaves were found guilty and sentenced to "transportation" out of the state as soon as it could be arranged and imprisonment in the workhouse until such arrangements were made. Four slaves and the two free blacks charged were found not guilty. The second court adjourned sine die on Thursday, August 8, 1822, ending the long series of "trials" conducted and punishments meted out as a result of the Denmark Vesey scare. On the activity of the second court, see *Charleston Courier*, August 9, 1822, and Document B: Evidence, 233–54.

65 *Charleston Mercury*, July 29, 1822.

66 *Charleston Mercury*, August 19, 1822.

67 The court actually judged Charles Drayton, the slave of former governor John Drayton, as "not a leader" but a person who "had taken so active a part in the business, as to be perhaps as much known in it as the leaders were." John Oliver Killen, *The Trial Record of Denmark Vesey* (Boston: Beacon Press, 1970), 38. Rolla, Ned, and Batteau were all slaves of Governor Thomas Bennett.

68 Killen, *The Trial Record of Denmark Vesey*, 24–30, 37–40, 41–131.

69 Lofton, *Insurrection in South Carolina*, 175; Charleston *City Gazette*, July 31, 1822. In the second court, the magistrate's were Charles M. Furman, a Charleston banker, and Jacob Axson, who often served as defense counsel during the second session of the first court. In addition to Joel Poinsett and Robert Y. Hayne, a congressman and attorney general, respectively, the freeholders were Thomas Rhett Smith, Thomas Roper, and John Gordon. See also Jervey, *Robert Y. Hayne*, 133.

70 Killen, *The Trial Record of Denmark Vesey*, 132.
71 Kennedy and Parker, *An Official Report*, 131–35; *Charleston Courier*, July 29 and 30, August 9, 1822.
72 Anna Hayes Johnson to Elizabeth Haywood, July 18, 1822, Ernest Haywood Papers, SHC.
73 Anna Hayes Johnson to Elizabeth Haywood, June 23, 1822, and Anna Hayes Johnson to Elizabeth Haywood, July 18, 1822, Ernest Haywood Papers, SHC.
74 Anna Hayes Johnson to Elizabeth Haywood, July 24, 1822, Ernest Haywood Papers, SHC.
75 John Potter to Langdon Cheves, July 10, 1822, Langdon Cheves Papers, SCHS.
76 John Potter to Langdon Cheves, July 16, 1822, Langdon Cheves Papers, SCHS.
77 Ibid. Freehling, "Denmark Vesey's Peculiar Reality," 38–39, argues that Haig's threat to poison wells, the only section of the manuscript transcript censored in the later published version, represented the "peculiar nightmare" of masters because it suggested that an "individual household assassin" could use the position of domestic trust to participate in collective action that might go unidentified until many lives had been lost. Certainly Charleston authorities took some care to avoid scaring whites or circulating incendiary ideas to literate blacks by not publishing this portion of Haig's testimony. My own view of the matter is that the possible poisoning of the wells suggested a deadly form of domestic resistance not easily prevented or remedied by the kinds of forceful action and restrictive legislation that Hamilton and his allies saw as the appropriate response to the insurrection scare. To highlight this dimension of slave resistance was to suggest that the authorities' proposed solutions were inadequate. Paternalists, on the other hand, argued that the best protection against such domestic treachery was precisely the kind of domestic loyalty they sought to inculcate, though the success of such efforts would always be less than perfect and leave the society vulnerable to such ideas. But paternalists could argue that their approach rendered coordinated poisoning on a widespread basis much less likely.
78 Martha Proctor Richardson to James Proctor Screven, August 7, 1822, Arnold-Screven Papers, SHC.
79 The importance prominent slaveholders placed on "interpreting" slave unrest to the larger community has been admirably analyzed in Michael Wayne, "An Old South Morality Play: Reconsidering the Social Underpinnings of the Proslavery Ideology," *Journal of American History* 77 (December 1990): 838–63.
80 *National Intelligencer*, August 24, 1822, 2. Two weeks later, another national publication, *Niles' Weekly Register*, also obtained and published Bennett's letter, introducing it with the same caveat. See *Niles' Weekly Register*, September 7, 1822, 9–11.
81 *National Intelligencer*, August 24, 1822, 2.
82 Ibid.
83 *National Intelligencer*, August 24, 1822, 2; Message #2 of Governor Thomas Bennett to the Senate and House of Representatives of the State of South Carolina, November 28, 1822, St 828, SCDAH.
84 Ibid.
85 Hamilton, *An Account of the Late Intended Insurrection*. Bennett's circular letter, dated August 10, 1822, certainly became public before Hamilton's account, and even the publication of Bennett's circular by the *National Intelligencer* on August 24, 1822, seems to have predated the publication of Hamilton's pamphlet. Hamilton's *Account* was likely in circulation before *Niles' Weekly Register* picked up Bennett's letter on September 7, 1822.

86 Hamilton, *An Account of the Late Intended Insurrection*, 30.
87 Johnson, "Denmark Vesey and His Co-Conspirators, Part I," 936–39.
88 Hamilton, *An Account of the Late Intended Insurrection*, 28–29.
89 "To the Public," in Hamilton, *An Account of the Late Intended Insurrection*, inside front cover.
90 Hamilton, *An Account of the Late Intended Insurrection*, 17, 28–29.
91 Ibid., esp. 29–30.
92 William W. Freehling, "Denmark Vesey's Antipaternalistic Reality," in *The Reintegration of American History: Slavery and the Civil War* (New York: Oxford University Press, 1994), 34–58. This argument closely parallels points first made by Freehling in "Denmark Vesey's Peculiar Reality," in Abzug and Maizlish, eds., *New Perspectives on Race and Slavery in America*, 25–50.
93 Hamilton, *An Account of the Late Intended Insurrection*, 29–30.
94 Ibid., 23–24.
95 Martha Richardson to James Proctor Screven, September 16, 1822, Arnold-Screven Papers, SHC. Richardson wrote on September 16 that the "trials have been published in a small pamphlet I have read." It seems more plausible that she read Hamilton's concise account. All evidence suggests that Kennedy and Parker's *Official Report* was not published until early November, though doubtless some prominent individuals, and especially the members of the court who approved the final version, had seen drafts at earlier times.
96 Kennedy and Parker, *An Official Report*.
97 Both Johnson, "Denmark Vesey and His Co-Conspirators, Part I," esp. 941–48, and Freehling, "Denmark Vesey's Antipaternalistic Reality," 56–57, note differences between the official public transcript of the trials published by Parker and Kennedy in October and the original manuscript source prepared by clerks during or very shortly after the trials, though they attribute different levels and kinds of interpretive significance to the discrepancies. Freehling found the published report a generally reliable transcription of the manuscript evidence with the exception of a decision to exclude from the published version testimony about the planned poisoning of wells. Johnson found the *Official Report* thoroughly "sanitized" by the court for public consumption and different from the surviving manuscript in many particulars.
98 Kennedy and Parker, *An Official Report*, esp. 1–5.
99 Johnson, "Denmark Vesey and His Co-Conspirators, Part I." I would draw essentially the same conclusions by comparing the claims advanced in Kennedy and Parker, *An Official Report,* and Hamilton, *An Account of the Late Intended Insurrection*, with the actual contents of Document B: Evidence.
100 Kennedy and Parker, *An Official Report*, 11–12.
101 Ibid., 11–17.
102 Ibid., 32–40; Johnson, "Denmark Vesey and His Co-Conspirators, Part I," esp. 948–60.
103 Kennedy and Parker, *An Official Report*, 40.
104 Ibid., 13–15.
105 Ibid., 17, 28–30; Hamilton, *An Account of the Late Intended Insurrection*, esp. 28–30.
106 Anna Hayes Johnson to Elizabeth Haywood, July 27, 1822, Ernest Haywood Papers, SHC.
107 *Charleston Courier*, November 15, 1822; *Charleston Mercury,* October 30, 1822; Charleston *City Gazette*, October 15, 1822. A full analysis of this debate follows in the next chapter.

EIGHT. ANALYZING THE SCARE

1 The chief case for the exaggeration of the plot is made persuasively in Michael P. Johnson, "Denmark Vesey and His Co-Conspirators, Part I," *William and Mary Quarterly* 58 (October 2001): 915–76. For responses to Johnson's argument, see Robert Gross, ed., "Forum: The Making of a Slave Conspiracy II," *William and Mary Quarterly* 59 (January 2002): 135–202. More detailed responses followed in Douglas R. Egerton, "'Why They Did Not Preach Up This Thing': Denmark Vesey and Revolutionary Theology," *South Carolina Historical Magazine* 100 (October 1999): 298–318; Robert L. Paquette and Douglas R. Egerton, "Of Facts and Fables: New Light on the Denmark Vesey Affair," *South Carolina Historical Magazine* 105 (January 2004): 8–35; and Robert L. Paquette, "From Rebellion to Revisionism: The Continuing Debate About the Denmark Vesey Affair," *Journal of the Historical Society* 4 (Fall 2004): 291–334.

2 Charleston *Southern Patriot*, July 19, 1822.

3 For examples, see the Charleston *Southern Patriot*, August 21, 1822, and the *Charleston Mercury*, August 19 and 20, 1822.

4 Henry W. DeSaussure to Joel Poinsett, July 6, 1822, Poinsett Papers, HSP.

5 *Charleston Mercury*, October 30, 1822.

6 Joel Poinsett to President James Monroe, August 22, 1822, James Monroe Papers, LC.

7 Charleston *Southern Patriot*, July 19, 1822; "Presentments of the Grand Jury, Charleston District," reported in the Charleston *Gazette*, October 15, 1822.

8 "Presentments of the Grand Jury, Charleston District," reported in the Charleston *Gazette*, October 15, 1822.

9 "An Observer" to *Charleston Courier*, July 10, 1822.

10 *Charleston Mercury*, December 4, 1822.

11 Ibid.

12 "Communication from 'An Old Inhabitant,'" Charleston *Southern Patriot*, July 5 and 19, 1822. For examples of concern over the threat dram shops presented to the control of slaves and free blacks, see the Charleston *Southern Patriot* July 19, 1822, and the Charleston *Courier*, January 31, 1823.

13 Charleston *Courier*, January 31, 1823.

14 Charleston *Courier*, November 13, 1922.

15 Ibid. These opinions were advanced in a letter drafted for the *Courier* and addressed to members of the legislature by "A Native Citizen."

16 Mabel C. Webber, "The Thomas Pinckney Family of South Carolina," *South Carolina Historical Magazine* 29 (January 1938): 15–25; Charles Cotesworth Pinckney, *Life of General Thomas Pinckney* (Boston: Houghton, Mifflin, 1895). The latter author was Thomas Pinckney's grandson.

17 [Thomas Pinckney], *Reflections, Occasioned by the Late Disturbances in Charleston. By Achates* (Charleston, SC: A. E. Miller, 1822), esp. 7–9.

18 Reported in *Charleston Mercury*, October 30, 1822.

19 Pinckney, *Reflections*, 10–19, 22–23.

20 Ibid., 12–15.

21 Ibid., 19–28.

22 See "Advertisement," inside front cover of Pinckney, *Reflections*.

23 On DeSaussure, see William Harper, *Memoirs on the Life and Character and Public Services of the Late Honorable Henry William DeSaussure, Prepared and Read at the Circular Church,*

15 February, 1841 (Charleston, SC: W. Riley, 1841); John Belton O'Neall, *Biographical Sketches of the Bench and Bar of South Carolina*, 2 vols. (Charleston, SC: S. G. Courtenay, 1859), 243–52; Benjamin F. Perry, *Reminiscences of Public Men* (Greenville, SC: Shannon, 1889), 59–62.

24 [Henry William DeSaussure], *A Series of Numbers Addressed to the Public on the Subject of the Slaves and the Free People of Color; First Published in the* South Carolina State Gazette *in the Months of September and October, 1822* (Columbia, SC: State Gazette Office, 1822). Given the closeness of their friendship and the similarity of their of the arguments, it is not only possible but probable that Pinckney and DeSaussure consulted each other in the preparation of their pamphlets, though I have found no hard evidence proving that they conferred. Nor is it possible to sort out who influenced whom on the subject. Both pamphlets appeared in November 1822. The newspaper articles upon which the DeSaussure pamphlet was complied appeared in September and October in a Columbia weekly, the *South Carolina State Gazette*, on September 11, 18, 12, October, 1, 8, 15, and 22.

25 DeSaussure, *A Series of Numbers*, 20–22.

26 Ibid., 20–21.

27 Ibid., 21–22.

28 Ibid., 20–22. DeSaussure pronounced the idea of colonizing a large number of slaves "an enormous and overwhelming expense" and a process that would inflict "great suffering, miseries, and destruction" upon the colonized ex-slaves during their journey back to Africa, where, DeSaussure confidently predicted, they would probably face "utter annihilation on their arrival" (22).

29 Martha Proctor Richardson to James Proctor Screven, September 16, 1822, Arnold-Screven Papers, SHC. In this letter to her nephew, Richardson extracts a portion of a letter she had received from DeSaussure.

30 Pinckney, *Reflections*, 20–27; DeSaussure, *A Series of Numbers*, 15–22; Erskine Clark, *Our Southern Zion: A History of Calvinism in the South Carolina Low Country* (Tuscaloosa: University of Alabama Press, 1996); Larry E. Tise, *Proslavery: A History of the Defense of Slavery in America, 1701–1840* (Athens: University of Georgia Press, 1987), 286–307.

31 On the concept of a "favored" or "key" slave, see the new introduction to the paperback edition of Michael Tadman, *Speculators and Slaves: Masters, Traders, and Slaves in the Old South* (Madison: University of Wisconsin Press, 1996), xix–xxxvii, and Michael Tadman, "The Interregional Slave Trade in the History and Myth-making of the U. S, South," in Walter Johnson, ed., *The Chattel Principle: Internal Slave Trades in the Americas* (New Haven: Yale University Press, 2004), 117–42.

32 Richard Wade, *Slavery in the Cities: The South, 1820–1860* (New York: Oxford University Press, 1964), esp. 143–79.

33 Jacob Read to Charles Pinckney, June 18, 1807, Pinckney Papers, SCL.

34 "Memorial of the Citizens of Charleston," in U. B. Phillips, *Plantation and Frontier Documents* (Cleveland, OH: A. H. Clarke, 1909), 2:103–16. This memorial is also reprinted in Robert S. Starobin, ed., *Denmark Vesey: The Slave Conspiracy of 1822* (Englewood Cliffs, NJ: Prentice-Hall, 1970), 103–16.

35 Edwin C. Holland, *A Refutation of the Calumnies Circulated Against the Southern and Western States*...(Charleston, SC: A. E. Miller, 1822), 11–12.

36 Benjamin Elliott, "To Our Northern Brethren," in Holland, *A Refutation of the Calumnies*, 79–82.

37 Robert Turnbull to Edwin Holland, c. 1822, in Holland, *A Refutation of the Calumnies*, 51–56. Turnbull readily admitted that his remarks applied chiefly to slaves on the Sea Islands and in the Lowcountry rather than as a generic commentary on slavery.

38 Holland, *A Refutation of the Calumnies*, 11–13, 61, 83–86. Apart from the flaws of Christian paternalism, Holland thought all the other causes of the Vesey plot readily amenable to remedy. Holland identified these "auxiliary" causes as well-publicized antislavery sentiment in the North, the latitude given free blacks, and the autonomy informally granted slave artisans.

39 "Memorial of the Citizens of Charleston to the Senate and House of Representatives of the State of South Carolina," in U. B. Phillips, *Plantation and Frontier Documents*, 2:103–16.

40 Ibid. The familiar litany of proposed remedies recited in this memorial eventually emerged as the core of the legislative agenda advanced by the Charleston delegation when the state legislature met in late November, suggesting the involvement of leading Charleston politicians, and perhaps even Hamilton himself, in drafting the memorial.

41 Ibid.

42 On Furman's stature in his field, see James A. Rogers, *Richard Furman: Life and Legacy* (Macon, GA: Mercer University Press, 1985); Winston C. Babb and Lynn E. May Jr., "Richard Furman," *Encyclopedia of Southern Baptists* (Nashville, TN: Broadman Press, 1958–82.)

43 George Howe, *History of the Presbyterian Church in South Carolina* (Columbia, SC: Duffie and Chapman, 1870–83), 2:194–96; Clark, *Our Southern Zion: A History of Calvinism in the South Carolina Lowcountry, 1790–1890* (Tuscaloosa: University of Alabama Press, 1996),142–44; George N. Edwards, *A History of the Independent or Congregation Church of Charleston, South Carolina, Commonly Known as the Circular Church* (Boston: Pilgrim Press, 1947), 65–71.

44 A South Carolinian [Frederick Dalcho], *Practical Considerations Founded on the Scriptures Relative to the Slave Population of South Carolina* (Charleston, SC: A. E. Miller, 1823), 37.

45 Albert Sydney Thomas, *The Episcopal Church in South Carolina or a Historical Account of the Protestant Episcopal Church in South Carolina, 1820–1857, Being a Continuation of Dalcho's Account* (Columbia, SC: R. L. Bryan, 1957), 14, 233–34, 241–61.

46 Howe, *History of the Presbyterian Church*, 2:53–58, 326.

47 Lester D. Stephens, *Science, Race and Religion in the American South: John Bachman and The Charleston Circle of Naturalists, 1815–1895* (Chapel Hill: University of North Carolina Press, 2000).

48 Frank Saunders and George A. Rogers, "Bishop John England of Charleston: Catholic Spokesman and Southern Intellectual," *Journal of the Early Republic* 13 (Fall 1993): 301–22; John Francis Devanny, "Bishop John England and the Rhetoric of Republicanism," master's thesis, University of South Carolina, 1995; Peter Clarke, *A Free Church in a Free Society: The Ecclesiology of John England, Bishop of Charleston, 1820–1842, A Nineteenth-Century Missionary Bishop in the Southern United States* (Hartsville, SC: Center for John England Studies, 1982).

49 For examples of the newspaper's discussion of slavery, see, for examples, Charleston *Southern Intelligencer*, June 22 and July 13, 1822. The *Southern Intelligencer* was a cooperative and leading ministers and denominations in the Charleston area. The newspaper had a decidedly Presbyterian tone, but the Congregationalist Palmer clearly shaped its content as well.

50 Differently put, the editors accused Hamilton of an inability to correctly identify evil, at least as Presbyterians understood the problem of evil theologically. Bennett, on other hand, likely just thought Hamilton was evil. See the Charleston *Southern Intelligencer*, July 13, 1822.

51 Benjamin M. Palmer, *Religion Profitable: With a Special Reference to the Case of Servants* (Charleston, SC: J. R. Schenk, 1822), 16.

52 Mary Thomas Lamboll Beach to Elizabeth Gilchrist, October 7, 1822, Mary Thomas Lamboll Beach Papers, SCHS.

53 Charleston *Southern Intelligencer*, November 16, 1822.

54 The too-long overlooked work of the Charleston Bible Society has been adeptly rediscovered by Robert Paquette and Douglas Egerton in their fine article "Of Facts and Fables: New Light on the Denmark Vesey Affair," *South Carolina Historical Magazine* 105 (January 2004): 8–35, especially 11–16.

55 On the creation of the Bible Society and fleeting glimpses of its activities, see Marvin R. Zahniser, *Charles Cotesworth Pinckney: Founding Father* (Chapel Hill: University of North Carolina Press, 1967), 272–74; Rogers, *Richard Furman*, 71; *The Constitution of the Bible Society of Charleston, and the First Report of Its Managers*...(Charleston, SC: J. Hoff, 1811); *Report of the Charleston Bible Society, Made at Its Twelfth Anniversary, 17th June 1822* (Charleston, SC: J. R. Schenk, 1822).

56 Clark, *Our Southern Zion*, 105–21, 142–64; George Howe, *History of the Presbyterian Church*, 2:51–58, 326. Arthur Buist remained at First (Scots) Presbyterian in Charleston until 1832, when he resigned due to ill health. His father, George Buist, served First Scots from 1805 until his death in 1818 at age thirty-nine. The elder Buist also ran a highly respected school for boys while pastor of First Scots. George Buist's pastorate represented something of a golden age for First Scots, and during these years Buist and his congregation "planted" a new church that became Second Presbyterian. Less is known about Artemus Boies, who served as pastor of Second Presbyterian during the Vesey scare. Boies, however, knew both Arthur Buist and Congregationalist Benjamin Palmer.

57 On Legare, see N. Louise Bailey and Elizabeth Ivey Cooper, *Biographical Directory of the South Carolina House of Representatives, 1775–1790* (Columbia: University of South Carolina Press, 1981), 3:426–27. On Grimke, see Adrienne Koch, "Two Charlestonians in Pursuit of Truth: The Grimké Brothers," *South Carolina Historical Magazine* 69 (July 1968): 159–70.

58 Paquette and Egerton, "Of Facts and Fables: New Light on the Denmark Vesey Affair," 13–16, note 18. Paquette and Egerton performed some excellent historical detective work to discover this letter in the Charleston Bible Society Records, SCHS. The first four pages of the draft letter, written in Furman's hand and dated September 1822, exist in the Richard Furman Papers, FU. The last four pages, also written in Furman's hand and dated c. 1822, can be found in the Furman Papers, SCL. The nine-page draft in the Charleston Bible Society records is not written in Furman's hand. The Bible Society's letter, with Furman obviously its primary author, is edited and published, along with Bennett's eventual reply, in Paquette and Egerton, "Appendix: Letters on the Vesey Affair," *South Carolina Historical Magazine* 105 (January 2004): 36–48.

59 The city's religious press was active in calling for a day of Thanksgiving throughout the late summer and fall. At least two weeks before the Bible Society's letter to Bennett, Charleston's *Southern Intelligencer* published a petition from "Many Citizens" to the city council urging the designations of such a day. See *Southern Intelligencer*, September 7 and October 5, 1822.

60 See Mary Beach to Elizabeth Gilchrist, July 5, 1822, Mary Lamboll Thomas Beach Papers, SCHS; Confession of Bacchus Hammet, n.d., William Hammet Papers, DU; Paquette and Egerton, "Of Facts and Fables: New Light on the Denmark Vesey Affair," 23–27.

61 Draft letter of the Board of Managers of the Charleston Bible Society to Governor Thomas Bennett Jr., September 23, 1822, Charleston Bible Society Records, SCHS. This letter is published in Paquette and Egerton, "Appendix: Letters on the Vesey Affair," 36–43.

62 Ibid.

63 Ibid.

64 Governor Thomas Bennett Jr. to the Board of Managers of the Charleston Bible Society, October 1, 1822, Charleston Bible Society Records, SCHS. This letter is published in Paquette and Egerton, "Appendix: Letters on the Vesey Affair," 43–48.

65 Ibid.

66 Rogers, *Furman*, 223–25.

67 In December, Furman, by this time president of the South Carolina Baptist Convention, had expanded the nine-page letter he drafted for the Charleston Bible Society in September into a twenty-page essay (one quickly published in Charleston and circulated as a pamphlet). In this pamphlet, Furman offers essentially the same commentary on the Vesey affair as he had in the September letter. Most of the new material included in the pamphlet lay in a much-expanded discussion of the biblical justification of slavery and an elongated explanation of how Christian paternalism provided the practical answer to questions about the proper Christian relationship between master and slave. Again, see Rogers, *Furman*, 223–25.

68 Rogers, *Richard Furman*, 223–27.

69 For the pamphlet form, see Richard Furman, *Exposition of the Views of the Baptists Relative to the Coloured Population of the United States in a Communication to the Governor of South Carolina* (Charleston, SC: A. E. Miller, 1823).

70 Furman, *Exposition*, esp. 15.

71 Ibid., 7–13. Here Furman began to argue that neither masters nor slaves could assume that slavery itself might constitute a violation of Christian teaching, but instead must accept slavery as established by "Divine government" rather than the sins of a broken world. In doing so, Furman began to advance an argument that the church's radical and reforming spirit applied only in the "spiritual" realm and not to the established "order of things" in the material and secular world, and marked an early beginning for the ultimate retreat of the southern church into the doctrine of spirituality, a retreat that would establish the southern white church as a tacit guardian of powerful secular interests, such as that of slaveholders, rather than offering a prophetic challenge to the existing social order. On the doctrine of spirituality, see Ernest Trice Thompson, *The Spirituality of the Church: A Distinctive Doctrine of the Presbyterian Church* (Richmond: John Knox, 1961); Jack P. Maddex, "From Theocracy to Spirituality: The Southern Presbyterian Reversal on Church and State," *Journal of Presbyterian History* 54 (Winter 1976): 438–57; James Oscar Farmer Jr., *James Henley Thornwell and the Metaphysical Confederacy* (Macon, GA: Mercer University Press, 1986), 256–60.

72 Furman, *Exposition*, esp. 16–19.

73 Ibid., 16–17.

74 Ibid., 17–19.

75 Ibid., 10–11.

76 Ibid., 12.

77 Dalcho, *Practical Considerations*.

78 On Dalcho's life and career, see George Walton Williams, "The Rev. Frederick Dalcho, MD," *Historical Magazine of the Protestant Episcopal Church* 26 (December 1957), esp. 1–14.

79 Dalcho, *Practical Considerations*, 3.
80 Ibid., 37–38.
81 Ibid., 7–8.
82 Ibid., 7.
83 Ibid., 26–28.
84 Ibid., 35–37.
85 Ibid., 30–32.
86 Ibid., 31–33.
87 Ibid., 4–5,
88 Ibid., 30–31.
89 Ibid., 6.
90 William Johnson to Thomas Jefferson, December 10, 1822, Jefferson Papers, LC. See also Donald G. Morgan, *Justice William Johnson, The First Dissenter: The Career and Constitutional Philosophy of a Jeffersonian Judge* (Columbia: University of South Carolina Press, 1954), 137–39.

NINE. REACTING TO THE SCARE

1 Robert Tinkler, *James Hamilton of South Carolina* (Baton Rouge: Louisiana State University Press, 2004), 42–49, offers a good account of the intrepid Hamilton's whirlwind of activity during these important months. Also see Virginia Louise Glenn, "James Hamilton, Jr. of South Carolina," Ph.D. dissertation, University of North Carolina, 1964, 16–32, 44–47.
2 *Charleston Mercury*, October 22, 1822.
3 *Charleston Mercury*, October 19, 1822.
4 Lowndes resigned his seat in May 1822 and died of tuberculosis in late October 1822, while on a voyage to Europe to regain his health. *Charleston Courier*, June 11, 1822; Carl J. Vipperman, *William Lowndes and the Transition of Southern Politics, 1782–1822* (Chapel Hill: University of North Carolina Press, 1989), 261–64.
5 James Hamilton to Langdon Cheves, October 10, 1822, Langdon Cheves I Papers, SCHS; Tinkler, *James Hamilton*, 46.
6 Charleston *Gazette*, November 18, 1822.
7 Stephen Elliott to William Elliott, November 13, 1822, Elliott-Gonzales Papers, SHC; James Hamilton to Langdon Cheves, November 30, 1822, Langdon Cheves Papers, SCHS; James Hamilton to William Elliott, November 22, 1822, Elliott-Gonzales Papers, SHC. Hamilton received 740 votes to runner-up Screven's 389 and also-ran Elliott's 175. See the *Charleston Courier*, December 17, 1822.
8 For a description of Hamilton's later prowess as a political organizer, see James Brewer Stewart, "'A Great Talking and Eating Machine': Patriarchy, Mobilization and the Dynamics of Nullification in South Carolina," *Civil War History* 37 (September 1981): 197–220.
9 Tinkler, *James Hamilton*, 47–48; Glenn, "James Hamilton," 138–215.
10 For a good brief overview of Bennett's messages and the South Carolina legislature's action concerning matters related to the Denmark Vesey scare during its 1822 session, see John Lofton, *Insurrection in South Carolina: The Turbulent World of Denmark Vesey* (Yellow Springs, Ohio: Antioch Press, 1964), 190–97.
11 Message #1 of Governor Thomas Bennett to the Senate and House of Representatives of South Carolina, November 26, 1822, Governor's Messages, 1814–1822, 1316–01 to 1360–20, SCDAH.

12 Message #2 of Governor Thomas Bennett to the Senate and House of Representatives of the State of South Carolina, November 28, 1822, St828, SCDAH. Governors often sent more than one lengthy message to the legislature during a single session.

13 Ibid.

14 Ibid.

15 Ibid. Not that all interior legislators opposed an active state government, but those who favored it wanted it to focus on measures designed to foster the expansion of the cotton economy above the fall line. At the same time, the cost of the internal improvements effort had given rise to a strong "economy" faction in state government, a faction led by Upcountry legislators and holding significant support in the region. See Lacy K. Ford, *Origins of Southern Radicalism: The South Carolina Upcountry, 1800–1860* (New York: Oxford University Press, 1988), 16–18.

16 Message #2 of Governor Thomas Bennett to the Senate and House of Representatives of the State of South Carolina, November 28, 1822, St828, SCDAH.

17 Ibid.

18 Ibid. Including this controversial plea among his list of legislative recommendations also guaranteed that the legislature would probably not consider Bennett's overall recommendations as a body, though they did consider a number of them individually.

19 Message #2 of Governor Thomas Bennett to the Senate and House of Representatives of the State of South Carolina, November 28, 1822, St828, SCDAH.

20 Charleston *Gazette*, December 4, 1822.

21 Charleston *Mercury*, December 4, 1822.

22 Charleston *Gazette*, December 4, 1822.

23 Charleston *Mercury*, December 11, 1822.

24 South Carolina General Assembly, House Journal, 1822, 58, 100, 105, SCDAH; see also the Charleston *Mercury*, December 11, 1822.

25 See South Carolina General Assembly, House Journal, 1822, 122–23, SCDAH for the roll call vote. Analysis made using the above House Journal and Walter B. Edgar, *Biographical Directory of the South Carolina House of Representatives* (Columbia: University of South Carolina Press, 1974), vol. 1, esp. 306–9.

26 South Carolina General Assembly, House Journal, 1822, 123, SCDAH. For information on Pinckney and O'Neall, see George C. Rogers, "Henry Laurens Pinckney—Thoughts on His Career," in James B. Meriwether, ed., *South Carolina Journals and Journalists* (Spartanburg, SC: Reprint Company, 1975), 163–75, and Thomas H. Pope, *The History of Newberry County, South Carolina* (Columbia: University of South Carolina Press, 1973), 40–146.

27 South Carolina General Assembly, House Journal, 1822, 151–54, SCDAH. The special committee (of which Hamilton was a member) appointed to review the legislation recommended striking the legislative permission clause, perhaps as a means of improving chances of the passage for other portions of the bill, but Hamilton voted against striking the clause requiring legislative permission on the House floor.

28 Ibid., 152–54.

29 Ibid., 165–66.

30 Ibid., 180.

31 Ibid., 203–51. No roll call votes on this legislation were recorded by the Senate.

32 "An Act for the Better Regulation and Government of Free Negroes and Persons of Color; and for Other Purposes," *South Carolina Statutes at Large*, eds. Thomas Cooper and David J.

McCord (Columbia, SC: A. H. Johnston, 1836–41), 7:461–62; Charleston *Mercury*, December 11, 1822. Additionally, the legislature also funded the Charleston delegation's request for an appropriation $100,000 to build an arsenal or "citadel" to enhance the city's ability to protect itself against insurrection and invasion.

33 Tinkler, *James Hamilton*, 47–48. Surviving documents offer no definitive explanation for Hamilton's failure to include in his legislative agenda calls for tighter restriction of the religious instruction of slaves and for tough new laws against teaching slaves to read.

34 The standard work on the operation of the politics of slavery is William J. Cooper Jr., *The South and the Politics of Slavery, 1828–1856* (Baton Rouge: Louisiana State University Press, 1978), though Cooper's work focuses on a later period and on the how the politics of slavery shaped the South's participation in national politics. On Hamilton's increasing attachment to the politics of slavery, see Tinkler, *James Hamilton*, 50–77.

35 Philip M. Hamer, "Great Britain, the United States, and the Negro Seaman Acts, 1822–1848," *Journal of Southern History* 1 (February 1935): 3–28; *Niles Weekly Register*, March 15, 1823, 31–32.

36 Hamer, "Great Britain, the United States, and the Negro Seaman Acts," p. 5; *The Argument of Benjamin Faneuil Hunt, in the Case of the Person Claiming to Be a British Seaman, Under the 3rd Section of the State Act of December 1822, in Relation to Negroes, Etc., Before Judge Johnson, Circuit Judge of the United States for the 6th Circuit* (Charleston, SC: A. E. Miller, 1823).

37 The best information indicating that Adams discussed the matter with both Hamilton and Poinsett and based his recommendation to the British on Poinsett's assurances is found in *The Opinion of the Honorable William Johnson, Delivered on the 7th of August, 1823, in the Case of the Arrest of the British Seaman Under the 3d Section of the State Act, Entitled "An Act for the Better Regulation of Free Negroes and Persons of Color, and for Other Purposes, Passed in December Last* (Charleston, 1823). On the cessation of enforcement, see William W. Freehling, *Prelude to Civil War: The Nullification Controversy in South Carolina, 1816–1836* (New York: Harper and Row, 1965), 112.

38 The first notice calling a meeting of the South Carolina Association appeared in the *Charleston Courier*, July 14, 1823. A later article explained that the South Carolina Association would hold an organizational meeting in St. Andrews Hall on July 24; see the *Charleston Courier*, July 24, 1823. A full history of the South Carolina Association, an important breeding ground for states' rights radicalism in South Carolina, remains unwritten. For a good brief introduction to the organization, see Alan F. January, "The South Carolina Association: An Agency for Race Control in Antebellum Charleston," *South Carolina Historical Magazine* 78 (July 1977): 191–201.

39 *Charleston Courier*, July 26, 28, 1823; see also January, "The South Carolina Association," 193.

40 Freehling, *Prelude to Civil War*, 113.

41 See the *Charleston Courier*, August 5 and 14, 1823, for criticism of the Association. Supportive responses appeared in the Charleston *Courier*, August 15, 1823, Charleston *Mercury*, July 29, October 20, November 5 and 6, 1823, and the Charleston *City Gazette*, July 20, 1823.

42 "Vindex," *Charleston Courier*, August 15, 1823; *Charleston Courier*, August 25, 26, 28, and September 10, 1823.

43 "A Member," *Charleston Courier*, July 24, 1823.

44 Officers of the Edisto Island Auxiliary Association, Petition Asking for an Act of Incorporation in Order to Pursue Their Purpose of Aiding the Constituted Authorities in Regulating the

Colored Population, November 18, 1823, Legislative Petitions, 1823, #151, in Records of the General Assembly, Record Group S165015, SCDAH.

45 "Memorial of the South Carolina Association," [November] 1823, Legislative Petitions, n.d., #1415, Records of the General Assembly, Record Group S165015, SCDAH. For similar requests from nearby areas, see Members of the Black Swamp Association, Petition for an Act of Incorporation for Their Group in Order to Better Enforce the Laws for Governing and Managing Negroes and Free Persons of Colour, December 9, 1823, Legislative Petitions, 1823, #147, and Officers of the Edisto Island Auxiliary Association, Petition Asking for an Act of Incorporation.

46 The best overall discussion of the Elkison case is Donald G. Morgan, *Justice William Johnson, the First Dissenter: The Career and Constitutional Philosophy of a Jeffersonian Judge* (Columbia: University of South Carolina Press, 1954), 190–206; see also Hamer, "Great Britain, the United States, and the Negro Seaman Acts," 5–8.

47 *The Argument of Benjamin Faneuil Hunt*; Morgan, *Justice William Johnson*, 192–94.

48 Letter of William Johnson in *Charleston Mercury*, August 21, 1823.

49 *Elkison v. Deliesseline*, no. 4366, in *Federal Cases, Circuit and District Courts, 1789–1880* (St. Paul: West Publishing, 1894–97), 8:493–98.

50 William Johnson to Thomas Jefferson, August 11, 1823, Jefferson Papers, LC.

51 *Memoirs of John Quincy Adams*, ed. Charles Francis Adams (Philadelphia: J. B. Lippincott, 1874–77), 6:176.

52 *The Opinion of the Honorable William Johnson*.

53 The best analysis of the newspaper debate between Johnson and his critics is Donald G Morgan, "Justice William Johnson on the Treaty-Making Power," *George Washington Law Review* 22 (1953–54): 187–215. The Charleston *Southern Patriot* refrained from publishing articles on the subject, but charges and countercharges filled the columns of the *Charleston Mercury*, the *Charleston Courier*, and the Charleston *City Gazette*. The "Caroliniensis" essays were later collected and published as [Robert J. Turnbull and Isaac E. Holmes], *Caroliniensis* (Charleston, SC: A. E. Miller, 1824). John B. Irving, a Lowcountry physician and rice planter, identified Holmes and Turnbull as the authors of the "Caroliniensis" essays in his memoir. See *A Day on Cooper River by John B. Irving, M.D.*, Louisa Cheves Stoney, ed. (Columbia, SC: R. L. Bryan, 1932), 63. Irving himself served as recording secretary of the association in 1828 and wrote with firsthand knowledge of the authorship of the essays. Morgan, "Justice William Johnson," 196, carefully establishes Johnson as the author of "Philonimus."

54 *Caroliniensis*, 37–42; quotations from 41, 40.

55 *Gibbons v. Ogden*, 9 Wheat 1 (1824); quotation at 227.

56 "Philonimus" to "Caroliniensis," no. 8, *Charleston Mercury*, September 15, 1823.

57 "Memorial of the South Carolina Association," 1823; see also *Charleston Mercury*, August 22 and September 19, 1822.

58 William Johnson to John Quincy Adams, July 3,1824, in "Free Colored Seamen," House Committee Reports, 27th Congress, 3rd Session, no. 80 (January 20, 1843), 14.

59 John Marshall to Joseph Story, September 26, 1823, in Warren, *The Supreme Court in United States History* (Boston: Little, Brown, 1922–26), 1:626; *The Papers of John Marshall*, ed. Herbert Johnson et al. (Chapel Hill: University of North Carolina Press, 1974–98), 9:338–39.

60 Hamer, "Great Britain, the United States, and the Negro Seaman Acts," 8–9.

61 *Acts of the State of South Carolina, 1823* (Columbia, 1824), 59–63; Hamer, "Great Britain, the United States, and the Negro Seaman Acts," 9. Johnson had ridiculed the enslavement provision in his *Elkison* decision, arguing that in the context of a larger effort to isolate South Carolina slaves, it was counterproductive to introduce new slaves with deep knowledge of foreign ports due to their experience as seamen. Apparently the legislature agreed.

62 These developments are all detailed by Hamer, "Great Britain, the United States, and the Negro Seaman Acts," 10–12.

63 Freehling, *Prelude to Civil War*, 114–15.

64 Charleston *Southern Patriot*, December 7, 1824.

65 *Charleston Courier*, December 7, 1823.

66 Whitemarsh Seabrook, *A Concise View of the Critical Situation and Future Prospects of the Slave-holding States* (Charleston, SC: A. E. Miller, 1825), 7.

67 Herbert V. Ames, ed., *State Documents on Federal Relations* (Philadelphia: University of Pennsylvania Press, 1900–6), 5:207.; Charleston *Southern Patriot*, December 15, 1824.

68 Robert Y. Hayne to C. C. Pinckney Jr., December 21, 1824, transcribed in full in Theodore Jervey, *Robert Y, Hayne and His Time* (New York: Macmillan, 1909), 180–81.

69 *Charleston Courier*, December 22, 1824.

70 *Charleston Mercury*, December 8, 1824.

71 January, "The South Carolina Association," 197–201; Hamer, "Great Britain, the United States, and the Negro Seaman Acts," 11–16; Freehling, *Prelude to Civil War*, 115–16.

72 Seabrook, *A Concise View*, 6–8.

73 On the creation of the Charleston Chamber of Commerce, see Members of the Charleston Chamber of Commerce, Petition and Supporting Papers Asking for an Act of Incorporation, November 18, 1823, Legislative Petitions, 1823, #45, Records of the General Assembly, Record Group S165015, SCDAH.

74 Members of the Charleston Chamber of Commerce and Inhabitants of the City, Petition for Modifications of Acts Concerning Ingress of Persons of Color from Any Vessels Entering the Ports of the State, November 18, 1826, Legislative Petitions, #34, 1826, and Charleston Chamber of Commerce, Petition and Supporting Papers Asking That the Laws Regulating Free Blacks or Slaves Employed as Cooks or Stewards on Vessels Entering Charleston Be Altered, November 19, 1830, Legislative Petitions, 1830, #124, Records of the General Assembly, Record Group S165015, SCDAH.

75 Members of the Charleston Chamber of Commerce and Inhabitants of the City, Petition for Modifications of Acts Concerning Ingress of Persons of Color from Any Vessels Entering the Ports of the State.

76 Ibid.

77 Ibid.

78 Petition of Members of the South Carolina Association, Asking to Be Incorporated for the Purpose of Helping and Supporting the Authorities in Enforcement of Slave Regulations, Legislative Petitions, n.d., #4757, and Committee Report Concerning Petition of the South Carolina Association, December 11, 1828, both found in Records of the General Assembly, Record Group S165015, SCDAH. The repository's finding aids incorrectly date the association's request for incorporation as circa 1825.

79 William Johnson to Thomas Jefferson, August 11, 1823, Jefferson Papers, LC.

80 William Johnson to Thomas Jefferson, December 10, 1822, Jefferson Papers, LC.

81 Thomas Jefferson to William Johnson, March 4, 1823, in *Works of Thomas Jefferson*, ed. Paul Leicester Ford (New York: Putnam, 1905), 7:279. In his reply, Jefferson chided Johnson for the creeping nationalism that both the retired president and James Madison saw in justice's decisions.

82 William Johnson to Thomas Jefferson, April 11, 1823, *South Carolina Historical Magazine* 1 (1900): 207–10.

83 William Johnson to Thomas Jefferson, August 11, 1823, Jefferson Papers, LC.

84 Morgan, *Justice William Johnson*, esp. 190–229.

85 "A Member," *Charleston Courier*, July 24, 1823.

86 On the anti-antislavery movement in the United States as a whole, see Larry E. Tise, *Proslavery: A History of the Defense of Slavery, 1701–1840* (Athens: University of Georgia Press, 1987), esp. 204–7.

87 On Walker, see Peter P. Hinks, *To Awaken My Afflicted Brethren: David Walker and the Problem of Antebellum Slave Resistance* (University Park: Pennsylvania State University Press, 1997). For an examination of one lower South state's reaction, see Hasan Crockett, "The Incendiary Pamphlet: David Walker's Appeal in Georgia," *Journal of Negro History* 86 (2001): 305–18.

88 As John Hope Franklin explained years ago, virtually all legislative initiatives designed to impose tighter controls on slaves and free blacks in North Carolina during the 1820s failed due to the opposition of predominantly white western counties. See John Hope Franklin, *The Free Negro in North Carolina, 1790–1860* (Chapel Hill: University of North Carolina Press, 1943), 62–72.

89 Ruth Scarborough, *Opposition to Slavery in Georgia Prior to 1860* (New York: Negro Universities Press, 1968), 107–23.

90 James B. Sellers, *Slavery in Alabama* (Tuscaloosa: University of Alabama Press, 1950), 140–94; J. Mills Thornton III, *Politics and Power in a Slave Society: Alabama, 1800–1860* (Baton Rouge: Louisiana State University Press, 1978), 319–20.

91 Joe Gray Taylor, *Negro Slavery in Louisiana* (Baton Rouge: Louisiana State University Press, 1963), 21–58; Herman E. Sterkx, *The Free Negro in Ante-bellum Louisiana* (Rutherford, NJ: Fairleigh Dickenson University Press, 1972), 285–315; Alexander Barrow to William S. Hamilton, January 25, 1830, William S. Hamilton Papers, LSU.

92 Winbourne McGruder Drake, "The Framing of Mississippi's First State Constitution," *Journal of Mississippi* 29 (April 1956): 79–110; Charles Sydnor, *Slavery in Mississippi* (New York: D. Appleton, 1933), 161–72; Charles Sydnor, "The Free Negro in Mississippi," *American Historical Review* 32 (July 1927): 769–88; Edwin A. Miles, *Jacksonian Democracy in Mississippi* (Chapel Hill: University of North Carolina Press, 1960), 41–42; Oscar B. Chamberlain, "The Evolution of State Constitutions in the Antebellum United States: Michigan, Kentucky, and Mississippi," Ph.D. dissertation, University of South Carolina, 1996, 89–123.

TEN. DISCOURSES OF COLONIZATION

1 In addition to these three discourses, a fourth discourse occasionally appeared in the mix. It occurred within the lower South between the radical opponents of colonizationists and those lower South whites who continued to see colonization as an appropriate method for reducing the already small number of free blacks living in the region. This discussion was much less vigorous and surfaced less often than the other three. It was also an increasingly one-sided discussion where opponents of colonization dominated the conversation during most of the 1820s. Echoes of this less audible debate appear from time to time in this chapter but will not

be given as much attention as the other three. This discourse will be treated at greater length when it emerges with more vigor in the lower South in connection with the Nat Turner insurrection.

2 The best overall analysis of the American Colonization Society remains P. J. Staudenraus, *The African Colonization Movement, 1816–1865* (New York: Columbia University Press, 1961). Eric Burin, *Slavery and the Peculiar Solution: A History of the American Colonization Society* (Gainesville: University Press of Florida, 2005) offers a more recent overview of the ACS that surpasses Staudenraus' in its emphasis on the role of local activists and the response of slaves to the movement. An earlier history of the movement, Early Lee Fox, *The American Colonization Society, 1817–1840* (Baltimore: Johns Hopkins University Press, 1919) remains helpful. Two nineteenth-century accounts of colonization contain valuable information: Archibald Alexander, *A History of Colonization on the Western Coast of Africa* (Philadelphia: William S. Martein, 1846) and Philip Slaughter, *The Virginian History of Colonization* (Richmond: Macfarlane and Ferguson, 1855). For the impact of the Missouri debates on sectional feelings, see Glover Moore, *The Missouri Controversy, 1819–1821* (Lexington: University Press of Kentucky, 1953); Richard H. Brown, "The Missouri Crisis, Slavery, and the Politics of Jacksonianism," *South Atlantic Quarterly* 65 (Winter 1966): 55–72; and William W. Freehling, *Prelude to Civil War: The Nullification Controversy in South Carolina, 1816–1836* (New York: Harper and Row, 1965), 89–133. Marie Tyler-McGraw, *An African Republic: Black and White Virginians in the Making of Liberia* (Chapel Hill: University of North Carolina Press, 2007).

3 On the sometimes toxic mix of racism and humanitarian sentiment involved in the formation of the American Colonization Society and the key role of prominent slaveholders in the organizing process, see Douglas R. Egerton, "'Its Origin Is Not a Little Curious': A New Look At the American Colonization Society," *Journal of the Early Republic* 5 (Winter 1985): 463–89, and also Egerton's *Charles Fenton Mercer and the Trial of National Conservatism* (Jackson: University Press of Mississippi, 1989), esp. 161–96. The effort to identify the driving force behind white support for colonization still generates considerable historiographical disagreement. Staudenraus, *The African Colonization Movement,* presents most of the movement's founders as individuals motivated by both sincere if flawed humanitarian concerns and a measure of self-interest. The standard presentation of the interpretation that the colonization movement was driven largely by racial concerns remains Merton L. Dillon, "The Failure of American Abolitionists," *Journal of Southern History* 25 (May 1959): 159–77. Other motives have also been identified; see also Frankie Hutton, "Economic Considerations in the American Colonization Society's Early Effort to Emigrate Free Blacks to Liberia, 1816–36," *Journal of Negro History* 68 (Autumn 1983): 176–89. Taken as a whole, the recent literature suggests the colonization movement was indeed a broad-based coalition that held under its umbrella colonizationists acting from a wide variety of motives that sometimes were diametrically opposed. For an insight into the limits of mainstream religious philanthropy, see Andrew E. Murray, "Bright Delusion: Presbyterians and African Colonization," *Journal of Presbyterian History* 58 (Fall 1980): 224–37. For a case study of the prominent role of southern Protestant clergymen in the region's uneven colonization efforts in a later period, see Timothy F. Reilly, "The Louisiana Colonization Society and the Protestant Missionary, 1830–1860," *Louisiana History* 43 (Fall 2002): 433–77.

4 The general if gradual tendency for the reform or "uplift" movements of the early nineteenth century to embrace the emerging white supremacy ideology is cogently argued by James B. Stewart, "The Emergence of Racial Modernity and the Rise of the White North,

1790–1840," *Journal of the Early Republic* 18 (Summer 1998): 181–217. For additional perspectives, see the comments on Stewart's argument by Jean L. Soderlund, James O. Horton, and Ronald G. Walters in the same issue. See also James Brewer Stewart, "Modernizing Difference: The Political Meanings of Color in the Free States, 1776–1840," *Journal of the Early Republic* 19 (Winter 1999): 691–712.

5 On northern free black opposition to colonization, and the Philadelphia protest in particular, see Leon F. Litwack, *North of Slavery: The Negro in the Free States* (Chicago: University of Chicago Press, 1961), esp. 24–27; see also Leonard Curry, *The Free Black in Urban America, 1800–1850* (Chicago: University of Chicago Press, 1981), and Julie Winch, *A Gentleman of Color: The Life of James Forten* (New York: Oxford University Press, 2002), 177–206, and her *Philadelphia's Black Elite: Activism, Accommodation and the Struggle for Autonomy, 1787–1848* (Philadelphia: Temple University Press, 1988). Recent illuminating studies include James O. Horton and Lois E. Horton, *In Hope of Liberty: Community and Protest Among Northern Free Blacks, 1700–1860* (New York: Oxford University Press, 1997); Gary B. Nash, *Forging Freedom: The Formation of Philadelphia's Free Black Community, 1720–1840* (Cambridge, MA: Harvard University Press, 1988); Gary Nash and Jean Soderlund, *Freedom by Degrees: Emancipation in Pennsylvania and Its Aftermath* (New York: Oxford University Press, 1991); Carol V. R. George, *Segregated Sabbaths: Richard Allen and the Emergence of Independent Black Churches, 1760–1840* (New York: Oxford University Press, 1973).

6 On Jefferson's notion for separate "independence" for whites and blacks, see Peter S. Onuf, "'To Declare Them a Free and Independent People': Race, Slavery, and National Identity in Jefferson's Thought," *Journal of the Early Republic* 18 (Spring 1998):1–46.

7 *Report of the Senate Committee on Foreign Relations, April 18, 1828*, 20th Congress, 1st Session, Senate Document No. 178 (Washington, DC, 1828), 1–15; quotation on pages 14–15. This report was drafted by Virginia senator Littleton Waller Tazewell, a conservative delegate to the Virginian Constitutional Convention of 1829–30 and later a supporter of Calhoun and nullification.

8 *Seventh Annual Report of the American Colonization Society*, 1824, 9–12.

9 Staudenraus, *The African Colonization Movement*, 169–70.

10 Herman V. Ames, ed., *State Documents on Federal Relations: The States and the United States* (Philadelphia: University of Pennsylvania Press, 1900–6), 5: 203–4, 207–8, 210; *African Repository and Colonial Journal*, 1 (July 1825): 154.

11 [John Pendleton Kennedy], *African Colonization*, 27th Congress, 3rd Session, House Committee Report no. 283, serial 428, Washington, DC, 1843), 926–33; Ames, ed., *State Documents on Federal Relations*, 207–8.

12 Ames, ed., *State Documents on Federal Relations*, 207–8.

13 *Register of Debates*, 18 Congress, 2nd Session, I, 623. Longtime Federalist Rufus King had previously "belittled" the efforts of the ACS, thinking they highlighted the miserable plight of slaves in the South without offering meaningful relief. See Robert Ernst, *Rufus King, American Federalist* (Chapel Hill: University of North Carolina Press, 1968), 391–94.

14 *Register of Debates*, 18 Congress, 2nd Session, I, 696.

15 Ames, ed., *State Documents on Federal Relations*, 208–9.

16 For biographical information on Seabrook, see N. Louise Bailey, Mary L. Morgan, and Carolyn R. Taylor, eds. *Biographical Directory of the South Carolina Senate, 1776–1985* (Columbia: University of South Carolina Press, 1986), 2:1434–6.

17 Whitemarsh Seabrook, *A Concise View of the Critical Situation and Future Prospects of the Slave-holding States* (Charleston, SC: A. E. Miller, 1825). For biographical information on Seabrook, see Bailey, Morgan, and Taylor, eds., *Biographical Directory of the South Carolina Senate*, 2:1434–6.

18 Seabrook, *A Concise View*, 4; Seabrook's characterization of the colonization movement's criticism of slavery drew heavily on, and at some points quoted directly (but without attribution) from, the argument made by Baltimore physician and colonizationist Dr. Eli Ayers, published as "Extract from Dr. Ayers' Communications," in *The Seventh Annual Report of the American Society for the Colonization of the Free People of Colour*, 64–104; see esp. 90–91.

19 Seabrook, *A Concise View*, 6–7.

20 Ibid., 13–14.

21 Ibid., 6–7.

22 The most recent and penetrating analysis of the proslavery argument and its position in the intellectual life of the Old South is Michael O'Brien, *Conjectures of Order: Intellectual Life and the Old South, 1810–1860* (Cambridge: Cambridge University Press, 2004), esp. 2:938–92. See also Larry E. Tise, *Proslavery: A History of the Defense of Slavery, 1701–1840* (Athens: University of Georgia Press, 1987).

23 Edward Brown, *Notes on the Origin and Necessity of Slavery* (Charleston, SC: A. E. Miller, 1826). On the tendency for southern slaveholders to see mastery of dependents as essential to independence, see Stephanie McCurry, "The Two Faces of Republicanism: Gender and Proslavery Politics in Antebellum South Carolina," *Journal of American History* 78 (March 1992): 1245–64, and *Masters of Small Worlds: Yeoman Households, Gender Relations, and the Political Culture of the Antebellum South Carolina Lowcountry* (New York: Oxford University Press, 1995).

24 Brown, *Notes*, 42–43. Following close on the heels of Seabrook's anticolonization tirade, and echoing some of the religious arguments advanced by Lowcountry religious leaders Furman and Dalcho in the immediate aftermath of the Vesey scare, Brown's pamphlet not only contributed to the emerging South Carolina tirade against the colonization movement but also highlighted the small boomlet of literature justifying the lower South's position on slavery that emanated from Charleston and its immediate environs in the years between the Vesey scare and the nullification crisis. The historian's search for the precise beginning of the proslavery argument is a futile one, if for no other reason than that the argument developed in minds, on the stump, on the floor of Congress, and from a plethora of pulpits well before it received systematic treatment in books, pamphlets, and published sermons. But Brown's pamphlet was among the first to express few if any reservations about using slavery as the permanent basis for the South's social system. Brown's pamphlet, though it still emphasized the "necessity" rather than desirability of slavery, claimed slavery brought many economic benefits to the South and the nation, and even to the cause of human progress. Moreover, Brown offered no scenario for phasing out slavery for any reason other than the loss of economic viability. Such defenses of slavery hardly advanced an aggressive "positive good" argument, but Brown had shifted away from a simple defense of the morality of holding slaves toward advancing a case for the superiority of slave labor in certain situations. Any "country to be free from the burden of slavery must possess a population sufficiently large to find a supply equal to the demand for labour," Brown insisted. The northern states had emancipated their slaves, Brown argued, not from philanthropy nor from concern for civil equality but because slaves were becoming an economic burden. See Brown, *Notes*, esp. 28–38.

25 Benjamin Morgan Palmer to Ralph R. Gurley, September 8, 1827, American Colonization Society Papers, Library of Congress (microfilm), Washington, DC.

26 Nash published these essays under the pseudonym Caius Gracchus in the *Richmond Enquirer* on August 13, 1825, August 19, 1825, August 26, 1825, October 11, 1825, January 21, 1826, and April 14, 1826. He also contributed an essay under a slight different pseudonym, Philo-Gracchus, on December 10, 1825. Caius Gracchus is identified as Nash by nineteenth-century Virginia historian Hugh Blair Grigsby in a note on the cover of a pamphlet collection he owned. Initially, however, Grigsby apparently thought the author was William Branch Giles, leader of the coalescing states' rights Jacksonian faction in Virginia politics. See *Controversy Between Caius Gracchus and Opimius in Reference to the American Society for the Colonization of the Free People of Colour of the United States* (Georgetown, DC: James C. Dunn, 1827), found in the VHS. See also "Review," *African Repository and Colonial Journal* 3 (March 1827): 3–48.

27 *Richmond Enquirer*, August 19, 1825.

28 Ibid., October 11, 1825.

29 Ibid., August 26, 1825.

30 Ibid. Nash candidly admitted that southern slaveholders loved wealth and zealously defended property rights in slaves, which they saw as the key to wealth. Any threat to property rights in slaves faced not only determined resistance from slaveholders but also significant and perhaps insurmountable constitutional obstacles.

31 Under the pseudonym Opimius, Fairfax County's William Fitzhugh wrote a series of essays countering Nash and defending the American Colonization Society. These essays appeared in the Richmond Enquirer on October 25, 1825, November 11, 1825, November 18, 1825, November 25, 1825, February 28, 1826, March 4, 1826, June 2, 1826, and August 18, 1826. Opimius is identified as William Fitzhugh by Hugh Blair Grigsby in a note on a pamphlet cover, though Grigsby apparently first presumed that Opimius was *Richmond Whig* editor and colonization advocate John Hampden Pleasants. Fitzhugh's portion of the exchange was covered thoroughly as "Review: Controversy Between Caius Gracchus and Opimius...," *African Repository and Colonial Journal* 3 (March 1827): 3–18, and "Review: Controversy Between Caius Gracchus and Opimius...," *African Repository and Colonial Journal* 3 (April 1827): 33–48. The entire exchange between "Opimius" and "Caius Gracchus" was published in pamphlet form in 1827, see *Controversy Between Caius Gracchus and Opimius in Reference to the American Society for the Colonization of the Free People of Colour of the United States* (Georgetown, DC: James C. Dunn, 1827). For biographical information on Fitzhugh, see Robert P. Sutton, *From Revolution to Secession: Constitution Making in the Old Dominion* (Charlottesville: University of Virginia Press, 1989), 166.

32 *Richmond Enquirer*, November 18, 1825. See "Review: Controversy Between Caius Gracchus and Opimius," 16–17.

33 Ibid.

34 John French to Ralph R. Gurley, December 9, 1826, ACS Papers, LC (microfilm).

35 Jesse B. Harrison, "The Colonization Society Vindicated to Virginia," *African Repository and Colonial Journal* 3 (September 1827): 193–208; quotations from 196–97 and 201–2.

36 Ibid., 202–3, 207–8.

37 Asa Earl Martin, *The Anti-Slavery Movement in Kentucky Prior to 1850* (Louisville, KY: Standard Printing Company, 1918), 52–53; Lowell H. Harrison, *The Antislavery Movement in Kentucky* (Lexington: University Press of Kentucky, 1978), 28–33; John B. Boles, *Religion in Antebellum Kentucky* (Lexington: University Press of Kentucky, 1976), 118–20.

38 Woodville *Republican*, August 4, 11, and 18, 1827. For an overview of colonization activity in Mississippi, see Charles Sydnor, *Slavery in Mississippi* (New York: D. Appleton, 1933), 203–38. Key members of the Natchez elite remained confident that free blacks could be removed without setting the region on a slippery slope toward abolition. Dr. Jon Ker, a prominent Natchez physician and planter and a key supporter of colonization, privately observed that "all men of sound judgment and sober reflection" agreed that "as to slaves, neither the Society nor our Government can in the remotest degree meddle with them." Ker quoted in Franklin L. Riley, "A Contribution to the History of the Colonization Movement in Mississippi," in *Publications of the Mississippi Historical Society* 9 (1906): 349.

39 James Birney to Ralph Gurley, December 1832, in *Letters of James Gillespie Birney, 1831–1857*, ed. Dwight Dumond (London: Appleton, 1938) 1:20–21.

40 *Acts of Georgia, 1827*, 194–203; Ruth Scarborough, *Opposition to Slavery in Georgia Prior to 1860* (1933; reprint, New York: Negro Universities Press, 1968), 218–20.

41 Staudenraus, *The African Colonization Movement*, 174–75.

42 John H. Kennedy to R. R. Gurley, November 27, 1827, Lyman D. Brewster to R. R. Gurley, June 26, 1828, and John Latrobe to R. R. Gurley, January 27, 1827, ACS Papers, LC (microfilm).

43 William Atkinson to Ralph R. Gurley, July 4, 1827, ACS Papers, LC (microfilm).

44 Memorial of the American Colonization Society for Colonizing the Free People of Color of the United States: January 29, 1827, 19th Congress, 2nd Session, House Document no. 64, serial 151, 4–5.

45 Resolutions of the Legislature of Georgia in Relation to the American Colonization Society: February 4, 1828, 20th Congress, 1st Session, Senate Document no. 81, serial 165, 5–11.

46 "Auxiliary Societies: Resolutions of the Jackson County (Geo.) Auxiliary Colonization Society," *African Repository and Colonial Journal* 3 (February 1828): 369–70.

47 *Register of Debates in Congress*, 19th Congress, 2nd Session, 290–95.

48 Ibid., 296.

49 [Robert J. Turnbull], *The Crisis: or Essay of the Usurpations of the Federal Government, by Brutus* (Charleston, 1827), esp. 7, 126–38.

50 Ibid., 131–32.

51 William Atkinson to R. R. Gurley, July 4, 1827, ACS Papers, LC.

52 James Nousse to R. R. Gurley, December 29, 1827, ACS Papers, LC.

53 For examples, see Jesse Burton Harrison to R. R. Gurley, February 25, 1828, John Thompson Brown to R. R. Gurley, November 20, 1827, Benjamin M. Palmer to R. R. Gurley, June 8, 1827, William Winans to R. R. Gurley, July 20, 1827, Stephen Foster to R. R. Gurley, June 11, 1827, and John Ehringham to R. R. Gurley, June 23, 1827, ACS Papers, LC.

54 W. H. Robbins to R. R. Gurley, October 13, 1827, ACS Papers, LC.

55 "Letter from the Secretary of the Society to Joel Early, Esq. of Greensborough, Georgia," *African Repository and Colonial Journal* 3 (December 1827): 289–96; "Auxiliary Societies: Resolutions of the Jackson County (Geo.) Auxiliary Colonization Society," 369–70. For recent scholarship suggesting that Gurley's characterization of northern colonizationist sentiment as antiabolitionist contained a very substantial degree of accuracy, see Eric Burin, "Rethinking Northern White Support for the African Colonization Movement: The Pennsylvania Colonization Society as an Agent of Emancipation," *Pennsylvania Magazine of History and Biography* 127 (April 2003): 197–229.

56 William Atkinson to Ralph R. Gurley, July 4, 1827, R. A. Toler to Gurley, August 9, 1827, John Ehringham to R. R. Gurley, June 23, 1827, Jesse Burton Harrison to R. R. Gurley, February 25, 1828, ACS Papers, LC.

57 Harrison's views were presented in two forms. See Jesse Burton Harrison, "The Colonization Society Vindicated to Virginia," *African Repository and Colonial Journal* 3 (September 1827): 193–208; and "Report of the Board of Managers of the Lynchburg Auxiliary Society," *African Repository and Colonial Journal* 4 (August 1828): 172–79.

58 Jesse Burton Harrison, "The Colonization Society Vindicated to Virginia," *African Repository and Colonial Journal* 3 (September 1827): 193–208.

59 Ibid., esp. 207–8.

60 "Report of the Board of Managers of the Lynchburg Auxiliary Society," 172–79.

61 "Extract from a Defense of the Society," *African Repository and Colonial Journal* 3 (August 1827): 174–79. The essay by "Virginius" first appeared in the *National Intelligencer* on June 14, 1827.

62 Lyman Brewster to R. R. Gurley, June 26, 1828, ACS Papers, LC.

63 Report of Mr. Tazewell in the Senate of the United States, April 28, 1828, 20th Congress, 1st Session (1828), at 178, 1–15.

64 Ibid., 14–15.

65 Entries of June 6, 1828, and October 23, 1829, Hugh Blair Grigsby Diary, VHS.

66 Lyman D. Brewster to R. R. Gurley, June 26, 1828, ACS Papers, LC.

67 William Atkinson to R. R. Gurley, December 2, 1828, ACS Papers, LC.

68 Ibid.

69 Alison G. Freehling, *Drift to Dissolution: The Virginia Slave Debate of 1831–32* (Baton Rouge: Louisiana State University Press, 1982), 120–21; Staudenraus, *The African Colonization Movement*, 178; Slaughter, *The Virginian History of African Colonization*, 18–19.

70 Henry M. Kerr to R. R. Gurley, July 23, 1829, and Lyman Brewster to R. R. Gurley, June 26, 1828, ACS Papers, LC.

71 I. J. Roberts to R. R. Gurley, February 24, 1829, and Benjamin M. Palmer to R. R. Gurley, May 23, 1829, ACS Papers, LC.

72 William H. Craven to R. R. Gurley, September 2, 1829, ACS Papers, LC.

73 Joseph Davis to R. R. Gurley, July 7, 1829, ACS Papers, LC.

74 "Communication: Mr. Tazewell's Report," *African Repository and Colonial Journal* 3 (January 1828): 330–49.

75 Benjamin M. Palmer to R. R. Gurley, September 8, 1827, ACS Papers, LC.

76 "Address: Delivered Before a Society in North Carolina, Auxiliary to the Society at Washington, for Colonizing the Free People of Colour on the Coast of Africa," *African Repository and Colonial Journal* 3 (May 1827): 65–75.

77 "Memorial of the Auxiliary Society of Powhatan. For Colonizing in Africa the Free People of Colour of the United State," *African Repository and Colonial Journal* 5 (March 1829): 15–23.

78 "Address of William M. Rives to the Lynchburg Colonization Society on the First of August," *African Repository and Colonial Journal* 5 (October 1829): 234–42.

79 "Virginia Legislature: Report of the Committee, to Whom Were Referred Sundry Memorials on the Subject of Colonizing the Free People of Colour of Virginia," *African Repository and Colonial Journal* 5 (April 1829): 50–55.

80 "Review: An Address Delivered Before the Hawkins County Colonization Society, Tennessee, by John A. McKinney, Esq., July 4, 1830," *African Repository and Colonial Journal* 6 (October 1830): 225–35.

81 Ibid.

82 Charles Cotesworth Pinckney, *An Address Delivered in Charleston Before the Agricultural Society of South Carolina at Its Anniversary Meeting*... (Charleston, SC: A. E. Miller, 1829), 1–24, esp. 8–9. The author of this address was the namesake and nephew of the older Charles Cotesworth Pinckney, a founder who attended the Constitutional Convention of 1787 and ran twice as an unsuccessful Federalist nominee for president of the United States (1804 and 1808). The elder Charles Cotesworth Pinckney, a founding member of the Charleston Bible Society, supported the ACS at its founding but grew disillusioned in the early 1820s and denounced its efforts before his death in 1825. The younger Charles Cotesworth Pinckney was born in 1789 and died in 1865 in the upcountry district of Abbeville, likely as a wartime refugee; the younger Pinckney's son and namesake became a prominent Episcopal minister in South Carolina. See Mabel L. Webber, "The Thomas Pinckney Family of South Carolina," *South Carolina Historical Magazine* 39 (January 1938): 15–35. On this point, see also Tise, *Proslavery*, 387. On the elder Pinckney, see Marvin R. Zahniser, *Charles Cotesworth Pinckney: Founding Father* (Chapel Hill: University of North Carolina Press, 1967), 277–78. On the character and hospitality of the elder Charles Cotesworth Pinckney, see P. J. Staudenraus, ed., "Letters from South Carolina, 1821–22," *South Carolina Historical Magazine* 58 (October 1957): 209–17. On the elder Pinckney's involvement with the Charleston Bible Society, see Robert L. Paquette and Douglas Egerton, "Of Facts and Fables: New Light on the Denmark Vesey Affair," *South Carolina Historical Magazine* 105 (January 2004): 8–35.

83 Pinckney, *An Address Delivered in Charleston Before the Agricultural Society of South Carolina*" 10.

84 "Review of Mr. Pinckney's Address," *African Repository and Colonial Journal* 5 (January 1830): 328–36. The statement about Virginia slaveholders' willingness to manumit their slaves if colonization was guaranteed was first made by Jesse Burton Harrison in 1828; see "Annual Meeting of the American Colonization Society," *African Repository and Colonial Journal* 3 (January 1828): 321–37, quotation on 335. The statement was repeated in *African Repository and Colonial Journal* 4 (December 1828): 305. Historiographical debate over how the free blacks colonized by the ACS reacted to their new Liberian circumstances continues in recent work. Howard Temperley, "African American Aspirations and the Settlement of Liberia," *Slavery and Abolition* 21 (2000): 67–92, maintains that the black Americans sent to Liberia failed to integrate successfully with native Africans and generally did not embrace African culture. Gabriel Guarino, "'Here We Live Under Our Own Vine and Palm Tree': The Syncretism of African and American Worldviews of Americo-Liberian Ex-slaves," *Liberian Journal Studies* 27 (2002): 18–27, challenges this view, suggesting that many American blacks embraced indigenous African practices. Lott Cary, an ex-slave from Virginia who went to Liberia, criticized "native African forces of disorder" in letters back to Virginia in which he sought to encourage more Virginia free blacks to emigrate; see John Salliant, "'Circular Addressed to the Colored Brethren and Friends in America': A Unpublished Essay by Lott Cary, Sent from Liberia to Virginia, 1827," *Virginia Magazine of History and Biography* 104 (1996): 481–504.

85 Staudenraus, *The African Colonization Movement*, 150–168; Burin, *Slavery and the Peculiar Solution*, 57–78, 141–59.

86 Ralph R. Gurley to James McDowell, September 9, 1828, McDowell Papers, SHC.

87 Rough Draft of Address to the Colonization Society, August 11, 1827, McDowell Papers, SHC.

88 Resolutions to be Proposed to Colonization Society, c. 1825, McDowell Papers, SHC.

89 [James McDowell], "Address of the Rockbridge Col. Society," *African Repository and Colonial Journal* 4 (November 1828): 273–281. No author is identified by the *Repository*, but the essay is a very slight revision of a draft found in McDowell's papers; see Rough Draft of Address to the Colonization Society, August 11, 1827, McDowell Papers, SHC.

90 Rough Draft of Address to the Colonization Society, August 11, 1827, McDowell Papers, SHC.

91 "Address of the Rockbridge Col. Society."

92 "Annual Meeting of the American Colonization Society," *African Repository and Colonial Journal* 3 (February 1828): 353–61. Moderate northerners active in the ACS joined Key, McDowell, and Gurley in trying to convince wary southerners that the society's northern members were not all abolitionist wolves clothed as colonizationist sheep. Connecticut's Thomas Storrs assured the South that there was "no opinion generally prevailing" in the "Northern States" favoring "Immediate, absolute and universal emancipation." Indeed, Storrs maintained, such a "contemporaneous emancipation" would "only bring a common calamity on all the states, and the most severe misery on those who were to be thrown upon society under the most abject, helpless, and deplorable circumstances." But Storrs tempered his insistence that the northern states would reject immediate abolition with his equally passionate plea that "no part of the Union" should become an advocate for perpetual slavery.

93 "An Address: Delivered to the Colonization Society of Kentucky, at Frankfurt, December 17, 1829, by the Honorable Henry Clay, at the Request of the Board of Managers," *African Repository and Colonial Journal* 6 (March 1830): 1–25.

94 Ibid.

95 Ibid.

96 "Annual Meeting of the American Colonization Society," *African Repository and Colonial Journal* 3 (January 1828): 331–37, quotation on 335.

ELEVEN. RUMORS AND INSURRECTION

1 William Blackfoord to R. R. Gurley, October 21, 1829, ACS Papers, LC.

2 "Intelligence: Slavery in Virginia," *African Repository and Colonial Journal* 5 (September 1829): 221.

3 Hugh Blair Grigsby to John Tazewell, February 3, 1829, Tazewell Family Papers, LV.

4 John N. Tazewell to Hugh Blair Grigsby, February 7, 1829, Hugh Blair Grigsby Papers, VHS.

5 Benjamin Brand to R. R. Gurley, August 18, 1829, and Thomas Hunt to R. R. Gurley, September 5, 1829, ACS Papers, LC (microfilm); "Intelligence: Slavery in Virginia," *African Repository*, 221.

6 John Hope Franklin, *The Free Negro in North Carolina, 1790–1860* (Chapel Hill: University of North Carolina Press, 1943), 64.

7 For a good brief overview on the impact of Walker's pamphlet on the slaveholding states, see Clement Eaton, "A Dangerous Pamphlet in the Old South," *Journal of Southern History* 2 (August 1936): 323–34.

8 Two excellent modern editions of Walker's pamphlet are available. See *David Walker's Appeal*, ed. Sean Wilentz (New York: Hill and Wang, 1995), and *David Walker's Appeal to the Coloured Citizens of the World*, ed. Peter P. Hinks (University Park: Pennsylvania State University Press, 2000). Copies of the three original editions of the pamphlet are rare.

9 *David Walker's Appeal*, ed. Wilentz, 75.

10 Ibid., 43.

11 Ibid., 64–65.

12 Ibid., 25. Both quotations are found on this page.

13 Peter P. Hinks, *To Awaken My Afflicted Brethren: David Walker ad the Problem of Antebellum Slave Resistance* (University: Pennsylvania State University Press, 1997) has become the standard modern scholarly analysis of Walker. See esp. 1–62.

14 *David Walker's Appeal*, ed. Wilentz, xix; Hinks, *To Awaken My Afflicted Brethren*, 11, 269–70.

15 My own interpretation of Walker is heavily influenced by Sean Wilentz, *The Rise of American Democracy: Jefferson to Lincoln* (New York: W. W. Norton, 2005), 330–35.

16 Eaton, "A Dangerous Pamphlet in the Old South," 323–34.

17 Hasan Crockett, "The Incendiary Pamphlet: David Walker's Appeal in Georgia," *Journal of Negro History* 86 (Summer 2001): 305–18.

18 Herbert Aptheker, *One Continual Cry: David Walker's Appeal to the Colored Citizens of the World, 1829–1830*...(New York: Humanities Press, 1965), 46.

19 See George Gilmer to William T. Williams, December 21, 1829, in Letter Book of Governors of Georgia, 1829–30, 10–11, Georgia Department of Archives and History, Morrow, Georgia.

20 Milledgeville *Southern Recorder*, January 16, 1830.

21 Milledgeville *Federal Union*, July 17 and August 7, 1830.

22 Milledgeville *Southern Recorder*, October 23, 1830.

23 Milledgeville *Federal Union*, July 17, 1830.

24 William H. Pease and Jane H. Pease, "Walker's Appeal Comes to Charleston: A Note and Documents," *Journal of Negro History* 59 (July 1974): 287–92.

25 Charleston *City Gazette*, March 3, 1830.

26 *Baton Rouge Gazette*, March 20, 1830.

27 *Laws of Louisiana* (1830), 9th Legislature, 2nd Session, 90–94; see also Herman Sterkx, *The Free Negro in Ante-bellum Louisiana*, 98–99.

28 Baton Rouge *Gazette*, April 17, 1830.

29 *Laws of Louisiana* (1831), 10th Legislature, 1st Session, 98.

30 Sterkx, *The Free Negro in Ante-bellum Louisiana*, 101–2.

31 *Woodville Republican*, August 4, 1827.

32 For example, see William Winans to R. R. Gurley, March 30, 1827, and July 20, 1827, ACS Papers, LC (microfilm).

33 Natchez *Natchez*, September 25, 1830.

34 Dr. John Ker to Major Isaac Thomas, June 25, 1831, in Franklin L. Riley, "A Contribution to the History of the Colonization Movement in Mississippi," in *Publications of the Mississippi Historical Society* 9 (1906): 348.

35 Franklin, *The Free Negro in North Carolina*, 64–70.

36 From the *North Carolina Journal*, reprinted in Milledgeville *Federal Union*, September 11, 1830.

37 Owen's message emerged in part as a response to a letter from a Wilmington magistrate. See James F. McKee to Governor John Owen, August 7, 1830, reprinted in *David Walker's Appeal*

to the Coloured Citizens of the World, ed. Hinks, 104–6. See also Franklin, *The Free Negro in North Carolina*, 67.

38 Franklin, *The Free Negro in North Carolina*, 67–70; *Laws of North Carolina, 1823–1831*, 10–18, 29–30.

39 Raleigh *Register*, April 28, 1831.

40 Benjamin Brand to R. R. Gurley, August 18, 1829, ACS Papers, LC (microfilm)

41 William B. Giles to Linn Banks, January 7, 1830, Executive Communications, Box 37, LV; Alison Goodyear Freehling, *Drift Toward Dissolution: The Virginia Slavery Debate of 1831–32* (Baton Rouge: Louisiana State University Press, 1982), 82–83.

42 *Niles' Weekly Register*, February 27,1830, 4.

43 Eaton, "A Dangerous Pamphlet in the Old South," 329–30; Herbert Aptheker, *Nat Turner's Slave Rebellion* (New York: Humanities Press, 1966), 37–42; *Acts Passed at a General Assembly of the Commonwealth of Virginia* (Richmond, 1831), 107–8. See also William G. Shade, *Democratizing the Old Dominion: Virginia and the Second Party System, 1824–1861* (Charlottesville: University of Virginia Press, 1996), 212.

44 Tomlinson Fort to Edward Everett, February 15, 1830, Tomlinson Fort Papers, EU.

45 For the standard overview of Turner's rebellion, see Stephen B. Oates, *The Fires of Jubilee: Nat Turner's Fierce Rebellion* (New York: New American Library, 1975). Still useful is Aptheker, *Nat Turner's Slave Rebellion* and even William Sidney Drewry, *The Southampton Insurrection* (Washington: Neale, 1900). But perhaps the best single account of Turner's insurrection can be found in Thomas Parramore, *Southampton County, Virginia* (Charlottesville: University Press of Virginia, 1978). Freehling, *Drift to Dissolution*, 1–10, and William W. Freehling, *The Road to Disunion: Secessionists at Bay, 1776–1854* (New York: Oxford University Press, 1990), 178–81, offer excellent brief interpretations of the Turner revolt. Several valuable collections of documents related to the insurrection have been compiled and published. See Henry Irvine Tragle, ed., *The Southampton Slave Revolt of 1831: A Compilation of Source Material* (Amherst: University of Massachusetts Press, 1971); Eric Foner, ed., *Nat Turner* (Englewood Cliffs, NJ: Prentice-Hall, 1971; and Kenneth S. Greenberg, ed., *The Confessions of Nat Turner and Related Documents* (Boston: Bedford/St. Martin's, 1996). For purposes of this narrative and analysis, I have relied most heavily on the last volume. Two enormously helpful volumes, both of which have influenced my interpretation significantly, have appeared in the past decade; see Kenneth S. Greenberg, ed., *Nat Turner: A Slave Rebellion in History and Memory* (New York: Oxford University Press, 2003), and Scot French, *The Rebellious Slave: Nat Turner in American Memory* (Boston: Houghton Mifflin, 2004). The former is a valuable collection of scholarly essays on Turner and the rebellion. The latter is an important study of how historical memory has treated Turner and his rebellion from the time of its occurrence down to the present day. In addition to the sources cited specifically in the notes below, my narrative and analysis presented in this chapter are based on the works cited in this note.

46 W. G. Parker to Governor John Floyd, September 14, 1831, Executive Papers, LV; Kenneth S. Greenberg, "Name, Face and Body," in Greenberg, ed., *Nat Turner: A Slave Rebellion in History and Memory*, 3–23.

47 Thomas R. Gray, *The Confession, Trial and Execution of Nat Turner, the Negro Insurrectionist* (Petersburg, VA: John. B. Ege, 1881), 7–11. For a recently published edition, see Greenberg, ed., *The Confessions of Nat Turner*, 44–48.

48 Kenneth Greenberg, "The Confessions of Nat Turner: Text and Context," in Greenberg, ed., *The Confessions of Nat Turner*, 3–14.
49 Gray, *The Confession, Trial and Execution of Nat Turner*, 12–13; *Fayetteville Journal*, August 31, 1831; *Norfolk and Portsmouth Herald*, August 29, 1831.
50 Thomas C. Parramore, "Covenant in Jerusalem," in Greenberg, ed., *Nat Turner: A Slave Rebellion in History and Memory*, 58–76, esp. 58–59. In this essay, Parramore presents the best brief account of Nat Turner's insurrection.
51 See, for example, Herbert Aptheker, "The Event," in Greenberg, ed., *Nat Turner: A Slave Rebellion in History and Memory*, 45–57; French, *The Rebellious Slave*, 33–277; Parramore, "Covenant in Jerusalem," 62.
52 Gray, *The Confession, Trial and Execution of Nat Turner*, 12–13.
53 Ibid., 13.
54 Ibid., 15.
55 Southampton County Minute Book, 1830–35, 72–131B, LV; Parramore, "Covenant in Jerusalem," 59–61; Gray, *The Confession, Trial and Execution of Nat Turner*, 12–15. Rumors of a cache of weapons in Jerusalem were apparently false.
56 Freehling, *Drift Toward Dissolution*, 4–5.
57 Gray, *The Confession, Trial and Execution of Nat Turner*, 15–16; *Norfolk and Portsmouth Herald*, August 26, 1831.
58 Gray, *The Confession, Trial and Execution of Nat Turner*, 16–17.
59 Richmond *Constitutional Whig*, September 5, 1831.
60 Gray, *The Confession, Trial and Execution of Nat Turner*, 17–18.
61 Richmond *Enquirer*, August 30, 1831.
62 Gay Neale, *Brunswick County, Virginia, 1720–1975* (Clarksville, VA: Brunswick County Bicentennial Committee, 1975), 206; New York *Daily Advertiser*, August 29, 1831, *Halifax Roanoke Advocate*, October 13, 1831.
63 Richmond *Constitutional Whig*, September 3, 1831.
64 John Hill Wheeler, *Historical Sketches of North Carolina, from 1584 to 1851* (Philadelphia: Lippincott, Grambo, 1851), 210.
65 *New York General Advertiser*, September 1, 1831, quoted in Parramore, "Covenant in Jerusalem," 69.
66 Richmond *Constitutional Whig*, August 29 and September 3, 1831. On Pleasants, see F. N. Boney, "Rivers of Ink, a Stream of Blood: The Tragic Career of John Hampden Pleasants," *Virginia Cavalcade* 18 (Summer 1968).
67 Boney, "Rivers of Ink," 73.
68 Parramore, "Covenant in Jerusalem," 70.
69 For a complete record of these trials, see the Southampton County Minute Book, 1830–35, 72–131B, LV; see also Greenberg, "The Confessions of Nat Turner: Text and Context," 18–23.
70 For a good overview of the events in Sussex that piqued my interest in that aspect of the Turner rebellion, see Scot French, *The Rebellious Slave*, 37–45.
71 Sussex County Order Book, 1827–15, 249–56, Sussex County Records, reel 26, LV.
72 Ibid.
73 Ibid.
74 Richmond *Enquirer*, September 30, 1831.
75 Freehling, *Drift Toward Dissolution*, 6.

76 William O. Goode and E. B. Hicks to John Floyd, n.d., in *The Speech of James McDowell, Jr. (of Rockbridge) in the House of Delegates of Virginia, on the Slave Question* (Richmond, 1832), 27.
77 Benjamin Cabell to Governor John Floyd, September 20, 1831, Executive Papers, LV.
78 N. E. Sutton to Governor John Floyd, September 21, 1831, Executive Papers, LV.
79 Jane Randolph to Sarah Nicholas, n.d., Edgehill-Randolph Papers, UVA.
80 Robert P. Waller to George Blow, September 21, 1831, Blow Family Papers, VHS.
81 John Rutherfoord to William C. Rives, November 6, 1831, William C. Rives Papers, LC.
82 Robert P. Waller to George Blow, September 21, 1831, Blow Family Papers, VHS.
83 George W. Mumford to Sarah Mumford, September 10, 1831, Mumford-Ellis Papers, DU.
84 Richmond *Constitutional Whig*, August 29, 1831.
85 Gray, *The Confession, Trial and Execution of Nat Turner*, 17–18. Richmond *Enquirer*, November 8, 1831; Richmond *Constitutional Whig*, November 3, 1831.
86 Richmond *Enquirer*, November 8, 1831.
87 Ibid.
88 Norfolk *American Beacon*, November 8, 1831.
89 Parramore, "Covenant in Jerusalem," 73.
90 David F. Allmendinger Jr., "The Construction of *The Confessions of Nat Turner*," in Greenberg, ed., *Nat Turner: A Slave Rebellion in History and Memory*, 24–42. This essay and other work reminds us that *The Confessions of Nat Turner* tells readers what Gray wanted to tell them. For works that raise questions about the authenticity of Gray's rendering of Turner's confession, see Seymour L. Gross and Eileen Bender, "History, Politics and Literature: The Myth of Nat Turner," *American Quarterly* 23 (October 1971): 487–518, and Mary Kemp Davis, *Nat Turner Before the Bar of Justice: Fictional Treatments of the Southampton Slave Insurrection* (Baton Rouge: Louisiana State University Press, 1999), esp. 63–76.
91 Ibid. Sam Francis, one of Nat's six original confidants, apparently told investigators very little about the insurrection, but Gray seems to have believed Francis' assertion that there had been nothing "like a general concert among the slaves." Jack Reese claimed that he was forced to follow Turner by his brother-in-law, Hark Travis, one of Nat's top lieutenants. Gray's third client, Moses Moore, a fifteen-year-old slave on the Travis farm, joined Turner's band, perhaps involuntarily, when the insurgents left the Travis place. The teenage Moore testified against twelve defendants, more than any other witness, and his testimony proved so valuable that white authorities commuted his sentence for his efforts.
92 Allmendinger, "The Construction of *The Confessions of Nat Turner*," 31–35, makes a persuasive case that Gray was the author of this letter, written on September 17 and published in the Richmond *Constitutional Whig*, September 26, 1831. Daniel S. Fabricant, "Thomas R. Gray and William Styron: Finally, a Critical Look at the 1831 Confessions of Nat Turner," *American Journal of Legal History* 37 (July 1993): 332–61, argues that Gray was also the author of a letter that appeared in the Richmond *Enquirer*, November 8, 1831.
93 Gray, *The Confession, Trial and Execution of Nat Turner*, 16–19.
94 Ibid.
95 Southampton County Minute Book, 1830–35, 123, LV.
96 Richmond *Constitutional Whig*, November 11, 1831; Norfolk *Herald*, November 14, 1831.
97 See Vincent Harding, "Symptoms of Liberty and Blackhead Signposts: David Walker and Nat Turner," in Greenberg, ed., *Nat Turner: A Slave Rebellion in History and Memory*, 79–102.

98 Virginia governor John Floyd disagreed, arguing that the plot was more extensive. Compare Gray, *The Confession, Trial and Execution of Nat Turner,* 7–20, with John Floyd to James Hamilton, November 19, 1831, John Floyd Papers, LC.

99 Richmond *Constitutional Whig*, September 26, 1831. This letter from Thomas R. Gray to the *Constitutional Whig* was also reprinted in the Norfolk *American Beacon*, October 1, 1831.

100 Michael Wayne, "An Old South Morality Play: Reconsidering the Social Underpinnings of the Proslavery Ideology," *Journal of American History* 77 (December 1990): 838–63; on this point, see also Christopher Morris, "The Articulation of Two Worlds: The Master-Slave Relationship Reconsidered," *Journal of American History* 85 (December 1998): 982–1007.

101 Lynchburg *Virginian*, November 21, 1831. It is hard to see why Gray had a special stake in minimizing the scope and significance of Turner's insurrection. The 1830 census showed him owning no slaves, and while he doubtless hoped to acquire slaves as his wealth increased, his short-term opportunity lay in playing up interest in the Turner insurrection rather than playing it down. On the larger political context in which the revolt occurred, see Freehling, *Drift to Dissolution*, esp. 36–81.

102 James Sidbury, "Reading, Revelation and Rebellion: The Textual Communities of Gabriel, Denmark Vesey and Nat Turner," in Greenberg, ed., *Nat Turner: A Slave Rebellion in History and Memory*, 119–33.

103 "Citizens" to Governor John Floyd, August 28, 1831, Executive Papers, LV.

104 Mary Lee to Mrs. M. L. Custis, c. 1831, Lee Family Papers, LC.

105 N. E. Sutton to Governor John Floyd, September 21, 1831, Executive Papers, LV.

106 John Floyd to James Hamilton, November 19, 1831, John Floyd Papers, LC.

107 See the contents of John Floyd's Slave and Free Negro Letter Book, c. 1831, Executive Papers, LV.

108 John Floyd to James Hamilton, November 19, 1831, John Floyd Papers, LC.

109 Freehling, *The Road to Disunion*, 178–81. To be sure, the alleged Vesey plot threatened to rally slave domestics against their masters and their masters' families in some instances, but in the main the plot was allegedly concocted by largely autonomous slaves and free blacks who planned to overthrow local authority in Charleston and seize control of the city, if only briefly.

110 Richmond *Constitutional Whig*, August 29, 1831.

111 Thomas Ritchie to William C. Rives, October 12, 1831, William C. Rives Papers, LC.

112 Robert Pollard to William C. Rives, January 30, 1832, William C. Rives Papers, LC.

113 J. W. Paine to James McDowell, January 16, 1832, McDowell Papers, SHC.

114 Draft of remarks, n.d., c. 1831, Box #68, McDowell Papers, SHC. The notes for McDowell's draft were fleshed out into the *Speech of James McDowell, Jr. (of Rockbridge) in the House of Delegates of Virginia, on the Slave Question*... (Richmond, 1832).

115 A Copy of the Records of the Church of Christ at Raccoon Swamp Meeting House, esp. 64–65, LV. The original from which this copy was made can be found at the Virginia Baptist Historical Society, University of Richmond, Richmond, Virginia.

116 *Minutes of the Virginia Portsmouth Baptist Association Held at Dams Church, Surry County, Virginia, May 26–28, 1832* (Norfolk: Shields and Asburn, 1832), 14, 25–27.

117 *Minutes of the Virginia Portsmouth Baptist Association, Held at Tanner's Creek Church, Norfolk County, Virginia, May 25–27* (Norfolk: Shields and Asburn, 1833), 14–15.

118 *Minutes of the Virginia Portsmouth Baptist Association, Held at Beaver Dam's Church, Isle of Wight County, May 24–27, 1834* (Norfolk: Shields and Asburn, 1834), 10–11; *Minutes of the*

Virginia Portsmouth Baptist Association Held at Sappony Church, Sussex County, May 23–25, 1835 (Norfolk: Shields and Asburn, 1835), 10–11.

119 *Minutes of the Virginia Portsmouth Baptist Association Held at Sappony Church, Sussex County, May 23–25, 1835* (Norfolk: Shields and Asburn, 1835), 10.

120 Report of Sussex County Court, February 1835, to Governor Littleton Tazewell, Executive Papers, LV.

121 James S. French to Governor Littleton Tazewell, February 14, 1835, Executive Papers, LV.

122 Ibid.

123 Petition from the Citizens of Sussex County to the Governor and Council of the State of Virginia, February 1835, Executive Papers, LV.

124 Ibid.

125 French, *The Rebellious Slave*, 63–64; Sussex County Order Book, 1827–35, 460, Sussex County records, LV.

TWELVE. THE UPPER SOUTH DEBATES SLAVERY AND COLONIZATION

1 Copy of letter from John Marshall to R. R. Gurley, December 14, 1831, Faulkner Family Papers, VHS.

2 Copy of letter from James Madison to R. R. Gurley, December 29, 1831, Faulkner Family Papers, VHS. This letter can also be found in *The Writings of James Madison*, ed. Gaillard Hunt (New York: G. P. Putnam and Sons, 1910), 9:468–70.

3 Charles Fenton Mercer to Charles J. Faulkner, February 12, 1832, Faulkner Family Papers, VHS.

4 William C. Rives to John Rutherfoord Papers, February 8, 1832, John Rutherfoord Papers, DU. On Rives' increasing agreement with Madison in this era, see Drew R. McCoy, *The Last of the Fathers: James Madison and the Republican Legacy* (Cambridge: Cambridge University Press, 1989), 332–38.

5 Thomas Ritchie to William C. Rives, October 12, 1831, William C. Rives Papers, LC. On Ritchie's political clout, see Joseph H, Harrison, "Oligarchs and Democrats: The Richmond Junto," *Virginian Magazine of History and Biography* 78 (April 1970): 184–98. For a work that questions the influence and coherence of the alleged junto, see F. Thornton Miller, "The Secret and All-Powerful Club—or Myth," *Virginia Magazine of History and Biography* 99 (July 1991): 63–80.

6 John Floyd to James Hamilton, November 19, 1831, John Floyd Papers, LC.

7 Entry of November 21, 1831, in Charles Ambler, *The Life and Diary of John Floyd: Governor of Virginia, an Apostle of Secession, and the Father of the Oregon Country* (Richmond: Richmond Press, 1918), 89–91.

8 William W. Freehling, *The Road to Disunion: Secessionists at Bay, 1776–1854* (New York: Oxford University Press, 1990), 183, suggests the likelihood of a forceful but now lost reply from Hamilton spelling out lower-South-style objections to Floyd's ideas. Kenneth Greenberg, ed., *The Confessions of Nat Turner and Related Documents* (Boston: Bedford/St. Martin's, 1996), 109, agrees with Freehling's assessment. Nat Turner's biographer, Stephen Oates, suggests in his *The Fires of Jubilee: Nat Turner's Fierce Slave Rebellion* (New York: Harper and Row, 1975), 137, that it was John C. Calhoun himself, who visited Richmond in the winter of 1831–32, who dissuaded Floyd from pursuing his proposed course. Trenton Eynon Hizer, "'Virginia Is Now Divided': Politics in the Old Dominion, 1830–1833," Ph.D. dissertation, University of South Carolina, 1997, 308–12, assesses these arguments and concludes Floyd could have made

his own decision to pull back based on his assessment of what was politically possible once the legislature convened without any prompting from either Hamilton or Calhoun. Indirect evidence from Floyd's diary implies that he still hoped to make gradual emancipation at the legislative session but recognized that raising it in his annual message was not the best strategy. See Ambler, *The Life and Diary of John Floyd*, 171.

9 *Journal of the House of Delegates of the Commonwealth of Virginia, Begun and Held at the Capital, in the City of Richmond, on Monday the Fifth Day of December, 1831* (Richmond: Thomas Ritchie, 1831), 9–10.

10 Entry of December 26, 1831, in Ambler, *The Life and Diary of John Floyd*, 172.

11 *Norfolk and Portsmouth Herald*, December 9, 1831. The limited support for gradual emancipation that existed in eastern Virginia came from cities and towns such as Norfolk, Portsmouth, and Petersburg, places with strong ties to the larger commercial economy.

12 For an intriguing and thoughtful analysis of the Virginia Convention debates, and especially their place in the larger intellectual context of the antebellum South, see Micael O'Brien, *Conjectures of Order: Intellectual Life and the American South, 1810–1860* (New York: Cambridge University Press, 2005), 2:798–816.

13 Valuable secondary accounts of the convention include: Alison Goodyear Freehling, *Drift Toward Dissolution: The Virginia Slavery Debate of 1831–32* (Baton Rouge: Louisiana State University Press, 1982), 36–81; Dickson D. Bruce, *The Rhetoric of Conservatism: The Virginia Convention of 1829–1830 and the Conservative Tradition in the South* (San Marino, CA: Huntington Library, 1982); McCoy, *The Last of the Fathers*, 240–52; Freehling, *The Road to Disunion*, 1:162–77; Hizer, "'Virginia Is Now Divided,'" 167–220. See also Merrill D. Peterson, ed., *Democracy, Liberty and Property: The State Constitutional Conventions of the 1820s* (Indianapolis: Bobbs-Merrill, 1966); Don E. Fehrenbacher, *Constitutions and Constitutionalism in the Slaveholding South* (Athens: University of Georgia Press, 1989); Fletcher M. Green, *Constitutional Development in the South Atlantic States: A Study in the Evolution of Democracy* (Chapel Hill: University of North Carolina Press, 1939), especially 62–65; and Laura J. Scalia, *America's Jeffersonian Experiment: Remaking State Constitutions, 1820–1850* (DeKalb: Northern Illinois University Press, 1999). The convention debates were published in full in *Proceedings and Debates of the Virginia State Convention of 1829–1830* (Richmond: Ritchie and Cook, 1830). They are more readily available in a modern two-volume reprint edition, see *Proceedings and Debates of the Virginia State Convention of 1829–1830* (New York: Da Capo Press, 1971).

14 In the subsequent April 1830 ratification election, voters approved the new constitution by more than ten thousand votes, largely because the popularity of the liberalized suffrage requirement. Over 90 percent of all votes cast in the Piedmont favored adoption of the new constitution, while 86 percent of Tidewater voters approved. In the Valley, where many of the newly enfranchised voters lived, over 64 percent of all voters approved the new constitution. But west of the Alleghenies, over 80 percent of all voters cast ballots against adoption. Freehling, *Drift to Dissolution*, 48–49, 76–81; Hizer, "'Virginia Is Now Divided,'" 252–65; Freehling, *The Road to Disunion*, 1:169–77.

15 Hizer, "'Virginia Is Now Divided,'" 322–27; Freehling, *Drift to Dissolution*, 265–69; Ira Berlin, *Slaves Without Masters: The Free Negro in the Antebellum South* (New York: Pantheon, 1974), 136–37, 396–403.

16 *Journal of the House of Delegates, 1831–1832*, 29; *Richmond Enquirer*, December 15 and 17, 1831. For a good analysis of the petition competition, see Eva Sheppard Wolf, *Race and Liberty in*

the *New Nation: Emancipation in Virginia from the Revolution to Nat Turner's Rebellion* (Baton Rouge: Louisiana State University Press, 2006), 198– 206; Quaker petition quoted on 199.

17 *Richmond Enquirer*, December 17, 1831.

18 Ibid.

19 *Richmond Enquirer*, December 15 and 17, 1831.

20 Hizer, "'Virginia Is Now Divided,'" 311–17.

21 *Richmond Enquirer*, January 7, 1832.

22 Richmond *Constitutional Whig*, January 10, 1832.

23 *Richmond Enquirer*, January 7, 1832.

24 Freehling, *Drift Toward Dissolution*,

25 *Richmond Enquirer*, January 12, 1832.

26 There are a number of valuable accounts of Virginia's great legislative debate over slavery and colonization. See Joseph C. Robert, *The Road from Monticello: A Study of the Virginia Slave Debate of 1832* (Durham, NC: Duke University Press, 1941); Dickson D. Bruce, *The Rhetoric of Conservatism: The Virginia Convention of 1829–1830 and the Conservative Tradition in the South* (San Marino, CA: Huntington Library, 1982); Freehling, *Drift Toward Dissolution*, 122–95; Freehling, *The Road to Disunion*, 1:178–96; Hizer, "'Virginia Is Now Divided,'" 322–79; William G. Shade, *Democratizing the Old Dominion: Virginia and the Second Party System, 1824–1861* (Charlottesville: University Press of Virginia, 1996), especially 191–224; Wolf, *Race and Liberty in the New Nation*, 196–234.

27 *Richmond Enquirer*, January 12, 1832; Freehling, *Drift Toward Dissolution*, 129.

28 Walter Holladay to Robert Powell, February 9, 1832, Holladay Family Papers, VHS; see also Richard Parker to Littleton W. Tazewell, February 6, 1832, Tazewell Family Papers, LV.

29 Diary entry of January 12, 1832, in Ambler, *The Life and Diary of John Floyd*, 174.

30 *Richmond Enquirer*, January 19, 1832.

31 Ibid.

32 Ibid.

33 *Richmond Enquirer*, January 16, 1832; see also *The Speech of Charles James Faulkner (of Berkeley) in the House of Delegates of Virginia, on the Policy of the State with Respect to Her Slave Population* (Richmond: Thomas W. White, 1832).

34 *Richmond Enquirer*, January 16, 1832; see also *The Speech of Thomas Marshall (of Fauquier) in the House of Delegates of Virginia, on the Policy of the State with Respect to Her Colored Population* (Richmond: Thomas W. White, 1832).

35 *Richmond Enquirer*, January 21, 1832. Gholson delivered his speech on January 12, 1832.

36 Ibid.

37 *Richmond Enquirer*, January 14, 1832; see also *The Speech of William H. Brodnax (of Dinwiddie) in the House of Delegates of Virginia, on the Policy of the State with Respect to Its Colored Population* (Richmond: Thomas W. White, 1832), 3–21.

38 Ibid. Brodnax thought Randolph's post-nati plan forced slaveholders to lose property value and hence amounted to a threat to private property rights, and the Southsider objected to any notion that nonslaveholders should be allowed to vote on plans of emancipation.

39 *The Speech of William H. Brodnax (of Dinwiddie) in the House of Delegates of Virginia, on the Policy of the State with Respect to Its Colored Population* (Richmond: Thomas W. White, 1832), 21–40.

40 *Richmond Enquirer*, January 24, 1832.

41 *Richmond Enquirer*, January 16 and 31, 1832.

42 *Richmond Enquirer*, January 17, 1832.

43 Ibid.

44 Ibid.; *Journal of the House of Delegates of the Commonwealth of Virginia*, 99.

45 *Richmond Enquirer*, February 4, 1832.

46 *Richmond Enquirer*, January 19 and February 11, 1832.

47 *Richmond Enquirer*, January 19, 1832; see also *The Speech of John Thompson Brown, in the House of Delegates of Virginia, on the Abolition of Slavery* (Richmond: Chas H. Wynne, 1860).

48 Richmond *Constitutional Whig*, March 28, 1832. Goode's remarks were also published in Robert, *The Road from Monticello*, 105–7.

49 *Richmond Enquirer*, February 14 and 16, 1832.

50 *The Speech of Henry Berry (of Jefferson) in the House of Delegates of Virginia, on the Abolition of Slavery* (Richmond: Thomas W. White, 1832).

51 *Speech of James M'Dowell, Jr. (of Rockbridge) in the House of Delegates of Virginia, on the Slave Question* (Richmond: Thomas W. White, 1832). See also Notes on "Great Slavery Debate," in Folder 74, McDowell Papers, SHC.

52 *The Speech of Philip Bolling (of Buckingham) in the House of Delegates of Virginia, on the Policy of the State with Respect to Its Colored Population* (Richmond: Thomas W. White, 1832).

53 Richmond *Constitutional Whig*, February 11, 1832; see also *The Speech of Thomas Jefferson Randolph, in the House of Delegates of Virginia, on the Abolition. of Slavery* (Richmond: Samuel Shepard and Co., 1832).

54 *The Speech of Phillip Bolling (of Buckingham)*, 9–19.

55 Information needed for vote analysis and analysis itself can be found in *Journal of the House of Delegates of the Commonwealth of Virginia*, 109–11; Robert, *The Road from Monticello*, 29–32, 113–18; Freehling, *Drift to Dissolution*, 159–60, 272–78. See also Freehling, *Road to Disunion*, 1:187–89; Shade, *Democratizing the Old Dominion*, 199–203.

56 Ibid.

57 Freehling, *Drift Toward Dissolution*, 160–61. Accomack, an Eastern Shore county, also presented an exception to general eastern support of the status quo regarding slavery. A stronghold of mechanics and fisherman, Accomack had the smallest slave population (28 percent) in the Tidewater.

58 Freehling, *Drift Toward Dissolution*, 158–69.

59 *Journal of the House of Delegates of the Commonwealth of Virginia*, 109–11.

60 Thomas Jefferson Randolph to Jane Randolph, January 29, 1829, Edgehill-Randolph Papers, UVA.

61 Richmond *Constitutional Whig*, January 26 and 28, 1832.

62 Lawrence Dade to Daniel F. Slaughter, March 13, 1832, Daniel F. Slaughter Papers, DU.

63 Thomas Smith to William P. Smith, February 25, 1832, William P. Smith Papers, DU.

64 Robert Pollard to William C. Rives, January 30, 1832, William C. Rives Papers, LC.

65 Robert Powell to Walter Holladay, March 13, 1832, Holladay Family Papers, VHS.

66 John Rutherfoord to William C. Rives, c. July 1832, John Rutherfoord Papers, DU.

67 Thomas Ritchie, February 16, 1832, William C. Rives Papers, LC.

68 Richmond *Constitutional Whig*, January 31, 1832.

69 *Lynchburg Virginian*, February 2, 1832.

70 Charles S. Carter to R. R. Gurley, December 22, 1831, ACS Papers.

71 The debate can be followed in *Richmond Enquirer*, February 14, 1832. See also, Freehling, *Drift to Dissolution*, 177–90.

72 Freehling, *Drift to Dissolution*, 190–92; Richmond *Constitutional Whig*, March 13, 1832.

73 *Journal of the House of Delegates for the Commonwealth of Virginia, 1832–1833* (Richmond, 1833), 226–28; Henry Brodnax to R. R. Gurley, February 14, 1833, ACS Papers, LC; Freehling, *Drift to Dissolution*, 216–22.

74 [Benjamin Watkins Leigh], *The Letter of Appomatox to the People of Virginia: Exhibiting a Connected View of the Recent Proceedings in the House of Delegates on the Subject of the Abolition of Slavery* (Richmond: Thomas W. White, 1832). After letters to newspapers taking issue with Leigh, the eastern lawyer published a follow-up article, clarifying his initial positions. See Appomatox [Leigh], "Postscript," in *Richmond Enquirer*, February 28, 1832.

75 [Leigh], *The Letter of Appomatox*, 3–7.

76 Ibid., 27–30.

77 Ibid., 12–13.

78 Ibid., 14–15.

79 Ibid., 15–17.

80 Ibid., 24–27.

81 Thomas R. Dew's work was first published as the "Abolition of Negro Slavery" in *American Quarterly Review* 12 (1832): 189–265. Shortly thereafter it was republished in pamphlet form as *Review of the Debate in the Virginia Legislature of 1831 and 1832* (Richmond: T. W. White, 1832). Two decades later the essay found its way into a major collection of proslavery essays that circulated widely in the South, *The Pro-slavery Argument as Maintained by the Most Distinguished Writers of the Southern States* (Charleston: Walker, Richards, 1852), 287–490. The most accessible modern version is Thomas R. Dew, "Abolition of Negro Slavery," in Drew Gilpin Faust, ed., *The Ideology of Slavery : Proslavery Thought in the Antebellum South, 1830–1860* (Baton Rouge: Louisiana State University Press, 1981), 21–77. My citations are to this 1981 version because of its accessibility.

82 Dew, "Abolition of Negro Slavery," in Faust, ed., *The Ideology of Slavery*; see also Kenneth M. Stampp, "An Analysis of Thomas R. Dew's *Review of the Debate in the Virginia Legislature*," *Journal of Negro History* 27 (October 1942): 380–87. For a recent assessment of Dew's thought, see O'Brien, *Conjectures of Order*, 2:888–97, 942–49.

83 Dew, "Abolition of Negro Slavery," in Faust, ed., *The Ideology of Slavery*, 24–27.

84 Ibid., 28–50.

85 Ibid., 55–61.

86 Ibid., 63–67.

87 Ibid., 72–77.

88 James Madison to Thomas R. Dew, February 23, 1833, in *The Writings of James Madison*, 9:498–502. While the boom in the lower South hurt Virginia, Madison reasoned, it added "more to the growth and prosperity of the whole [nation] than it subtracts from a part of the community."

89 The ACS covered its other flank by convincing Southside moderate William Brodnax to seek legislative funding for a gradual removal of free blacks. William Brodnax to Ralph R. Gurley, February 14, 1833, American Colonization Society Papers, LC.

90 This essay was first published as Jesse Burton Harrison, "Abolition Question," *American Quarterly Review* (December 1832): 1–48. Shortly thereafter it appeared in two parts in the ACS journal. See Jesse Burton Harrison, "Review: The Slavery Question in Virginia," *African Repository and Colonial Journal* 9 (March and April 1833): 1–15, 33–51. Over seventy years later, Harrison's essay was again published as "The Question of Slavery in Virginia," in Francis Burton Harrison, ed., *Aris Sonis Focisque: The Harrisons of Skimino* (n.p., 1910). For biographical information on Harrison, see Michael O'Brien, *All Clever Men, Who Make Their Way: Critical Discourse in the Old South* (Fayetteville: University of Arkansas Press), 55–57. On Harrison's education and training, see O'Brien, *Conjectures of Order,* 1:136–40.

91 Harrison, "Review: The Slavery Question in Virginia," *African Repository and Colonial Journal* 9 (March 1833): 4–7.

92 Harrison, "Review: The Slavery Question in Virginia," *African Repository and Colonial Journal* 9 (April 1833): 42–50.

93 Ibid., 49–50.

94 This point is noted indirectly in Freehling, *The Road to Disunion*, 1:190–95.

95 Berlin, *Slaves Without Masters*, 136–37, 396–401; Freehling, *The Road to Disunion*, 1:207–8.

96 Patience Essah, *A House Divided: Slavery and Emancipation in Delaware, 1638–1865* (Charlottesville: University Press of Virginia, 1996), 117–19, is very useful on these points. See also James Newton, "Delaware's Reaction to the Nat Turner Rebellion," *Negro History Bulletin* 38 (1974).

97 Quoted in Essah, *A House Divided*, 117.

98 Ibid., 118; Delaware *House Journal*, January 3, 1832.

99 *Laws of the State of Delaware* 8:208–10.

100 Quoted in Essah, *A House Divided*, 117.

101 Oscar B. Chamberlain, "The Evolution of State Constitutions in the Antebellum United States: Michigan, Kentucky and Mississippi," Ph.D. dissertation, University of South Carolina, 1996, 22–63. In 1830, Kentucky was just beginning to emerge as a net exporter of slaves, having exported less than one thousand slaves more than it imported during the 1820s, but during the 1830s, Kentucky exported almost twenty thousand slaves, and from 1830 to 1860, Kentucky would export more than seventy thousand slaves. See Michael Tadman, *Speculators and Slaves: Masters, Traders, and Slaves in the Old South* (Madison: University of Wisconsin Press, 1989), 12.

102 Lowell H. Harrison, *The Antislavery Movement in Kentucky* (Lexington: University Press of Kentucky, 1978), 40–41; Asa Earl Martin, *The Anti-Slavery Movement in Kentucky Prior to 1850* (Louisville: Standard Printing Company, 1918), 88–97.

103 Harrison, *The Antislavery Movement in Kentucky,* 46–49.

104 Ibid., 48; Martin, *The Anti-Slavery Movement in Kentucky*, 95–96.

105 For a good overview of the colonization movement in Kentucky, see Jeffrey Allen Brooke, "Did Southern Colonizationists Oppose Slavery? Kentucky 1816–1850 as a Test Case," *Register of the Kentucky Historical Society* 75 (April 1977): 92–111. But see also J. Winston Coleman Jr, "The Kentucky Colonization Society," *Register of the Kentucky Historical Society* 39 (January 1941): 3–5; and Harrison, *The Antislavery Movement in Kentucky,* 30–31.

106 *African Repository and Colonial Journal* 6 (May 1830): 80.

107 Ibid., 57.

108 Coleman, "The Kentucky Colonization Society," 3–5; Harrison, *The Antislavery Movement in Kentucky,* 35.

109 On Birney, see Betty Fladeland, *James G. Birney: From Slaveholder to Abolitionist* (Ithaca, NY: Cornell University Press, 1955). See also William Birney, *James G. Birney and His Times* (New York, 1890); Harrison, *The Antislavery Movement in Kentucky*, 38–46.

110 Berlin, *Slaves Without Masters*, 136–37.

111 My discussion of Maryland's response to the Nat Turner insurrection is heavily influenced by that of William Freehling in *The Road to Disunion*, 1:197–210.

112 *Maryland Gazette*, March 22, 1832.

113 See *Journal of the Proceedings of the House of Delegates for the State of Maryland, Dec. Session, 1831*, 524–26. On the malapportionment of the Maryland legislature, see William J. Evitts, *A Matter of Allegiances: Maryland from 1850 to 1861* (Baltimore: Johns Hopkins Press, 1974), 31–42; on the vote, see Freehling, *The Road to Disunion*, 1:204.

114 Berlin, *Slaves Without Masters*, 202–12; Whitman, *The Price of Freedom*, 98, 138.

115 *Maryland Gazette*, March 29, 1832.

116 Freehling, *The Road to Disunion*, 1:204–5.

117 Ibid., 205; *Maryland Gazette*, March 22, 1832.

118 Penelope Campbell, *Maryland in Africa: The Maryland State Colonization Society, 1831–1857* (Urbana: University of Illinois Press, 1971), 15–58.

119 Freehling, *The Road to Disunion*, 1:206–7.

120 Campbell, *Maryland in Africa*, 211–37.

THIRTEEN. TENNESSEE DEBATES SLAVERY

1 See http://fisher.lib.virginia.edu/collections/stats/histcensus. The best overviews of Tennessee's response to Turner are Jonathan M. Atkins, *Parties, Politics and the Sectional Conflict in Tennessee, 1832–1861* (Knoxville: University of Tennessee Press, 1997), 18–21, and Chase C. Mooney, *Slavery in Tennessee* (Bloomington: Indiana University Press, 1957), 8–28.

2 *Acts of Tennessee, 1831*, section 13; Mooney, *Slavery in Tennessee*, 7–28.

3 J. Merton England, "The Free Negro in Ante-bellum Tennessee," *Journal of Southern History* 9 (February 1943): 37–58; Atkins, *Parties, Politics and the Sectional Conflict*, 19; Mooney, *Slavery in Tennessee*, 19. This ban remained in effect for eleven years, when a revision allowed county court judges to make exceptions.

4 Mooney, *Slavery in Tennessee*, 20.

5 *Nashville Republican*, September 22, 1833.

6 *Nashville Republican*, October 29, 1833.

7 Ibid.

8 Ibid.

9 Ibid.

10 Mooney, *Slavery in Tennessee*, 21.

11 On Tennessee geography and its impact on the demography of slavery in the state, see Stanley John Folmsbee, *Sectionalism and Internal Improvements in Tennessee, 1796–1845* (Knoxville: East Tennessee Historical Society, 1939), 1–19. Information on population calculated from data found in the following sources: U.S. Bureau of the Census, *Negro Population of the United States, 1790–1815* (Washington, DC, 1918), 51; *Population of the United States in 1860*, 592–602; Berlin, *Slaves Without Masters*, 23, 46–47, 136–37, 396–403; and http://fisher.lib.virginia.edu/collections/stats/histcensus.

12 Gordon E. Finnie, "The Antislavery Movement in the Upper South Before 1840," *Journal of Southern History* 35 (August 1969): 319–42; James W. Patton, "The Progress of Emancipation in Tennessee, 1796–1860," *Journal of Negro History* 17 (January 1932): 67–102; Asa Earl Martin, "The Anti-Slavery Societies of Tennessee," *Tennessee Historical Magazine* 1 (1915): 1–20.

13 Stephen B. Weeks, *Southern Quakers and Slavery* (Baltimore: Johns Hopkins Press, 1899), 236; Asa Earl Martin, "The Anti-Slavery Societies of Tennessee," 262–64.

14 Martin, "The Anti-Slavery Societies of Tennessee," 266; Mooney, *Slavery in Tennessee*, 66; Ruth A. Ketring, *Charles Osburn in the Anti-Slavery Movement* (Columbus: Ohio State Archaeological and Historical Society, 1937), 36–37.

15 Mooney, *Slavery in Tennessee*, 67–68. The committee report of the petitions is quoted at length in Mooney.

16 Laurence B. Goodheart, "Tennessee's Anti-slavery Movement Reconsidered: The Example of Elihu Embree," *Tennessee Historical Quarterly* 41 (Fall 1982): 224–38; Asa Earl Martin, "Pioneer Anti-Slavery Press," *Mississippi Valley Historical Review* 2 (March 1916): 509–28; Elihu Embree, *The Emancipator* (reprint), 7.

17 Merton L. Dillon, *Benjamin Lundy and the Struggle for Negro Freedom* (Urbana: University of Illinois Press, 1966); Mooney, *Slavery in Tennessee*, 68–69.

18 Martin, "The Anti-Slavery Societies of Tennessee," 270.

19 Ibid., 270–71; *The Genius of Universal Emancipation* 8 (1828): 93–94.

20 Caitlin A. Fitz, "The Tennessee Antislavery Movement and the Market Revolution, 1815–1835," *Civil War History* 52 (March 2006): 5–40.

21 Ibid., 9–14.

22 Patton, "The Progress of Emancipation in Tennessee, 1796–1860," 68; Fitz, "The Tennessee Antislavery Movement," 16–17; James Brewer Stewart, "Evangelicalism and the Radical Strain in Southern Antislavery Thought During the 1820s," *Journal of Southern History* 39 (August 1973): 379–96.

23 There is still no modern comprehensive study of Tennessee's 1834 constitutional convention. For good brief overviews, see Paul Bergeron, *Antebellum Politics in Tennessee* (Lexington: University Press of Kentucky, 1982), 38–41; and Robert Cassell, "Newton Cannon and the Constitutional Convention of 1834," *Tennessee Historical Quarterly* 25 (1956): 224–42. Older but still useful is Joshua W. Caldwell, *Studies in the Constitutional History of Tennessee* (Cincinnati, 1895). Fletcher M. Green's classic *Constitutional Development in the South Atlantic States, 1776–1860: A Study in the Evolution of Democracy* (Chapel Hill: University of North Carolina Press, 1930), remains the best introduction to the democratizing trend, however variegated, of Jacksonian-era southern state constitutions, but Green's study is confined to the seaboard states.

24 Bergeron, *Antebellum Politics in Tennessee*, 38; Cassell, "Newton Cannon and the Constitutional Convention of 1834," 227.

25 Bergeron, *Antebellum Politics in Tennessee*, 38–39; Cassell, "Newton Cannon and the Constitutional Convention of 1834," 228–29.

26 See Fitz, "The Tennessee Antislavery Movement," 16–25.

27 Legislative Petition Collection, 38–1834, TSLA.

28 Ibid.

29 Legislative Petition Collection, 32–1834, TSLA; *Knoxville Register*, November 30, 1831.

30 William B. Campbell to David Campbell, August 8, 1833, Campbell Family Papers, DU.

31 William B. Campbell to David Campbell, March 15, 1834, Campbell Family Papers, DU.

32 An excellent overview of the convention's actions issues is Chase C. Mooney, "The Question of Slavery and the Free Negro in the Tennessee Constitutional Convention of 1834," *Journal of Southern History* 12 (November 1956): 487–509. See also Mooney, *Slavery in Tennessee*, 76–82.

33 Mooney, "The Question of Slavery and the Free Negro," 488–89; Fitz, "The Tennessee Antislavery Movement," 18–23.

34 Fitz, "The Tennessee Antislavery Movement," 24; Mooney, "The Question of Slavery and the Free Negro," 489.

35 *Journal of the Convention of the State of Tennessee* (Nashville: S. H. Laughlin and J. F. Henderson, 1834), 15.

36 Ibid., 28–30; *Nashville Republican and State Gazette*, May 31, 1834.

37 *Journal of the Convention*, 70

38 *Nashville Republican and State Gazette*, June 10, 1834.

39 Ibid.

40 Ibid.

41 Ibid.

42 Analysis in this paragraph is based on information found in *Nashville Republican and State Gazette*, June 10, 1834; Bergeron, *Antebellum Politics in Tennessee*, 20; Folmsbee, *Sectionalism and Internal Improvements in Tennessee*, 1–8; *Journal of the Convention*, 3–4, 71.

43 *Journal of the Convention*, 71–72.

44 *Nashville Republican and State Gazette*, June 10, 1834; Mooney, "The Question of Slavery and the Free Negro," 492; *Journal of the Convention*, 72.

45 *Journal of the Convention*, 87–93. The entire McKinney committee report was "spread" on these pages of the convention journal.

46 Ibid, 87–89.

47 Ibid., 88–89.

48 Ibid., 90–91.

49 Ibid.

50 Ibid., 92.

51 Ibid., 92–93.

52 Ibid., 94.

53 *Nashville Republican and State Gazette*, June 26, 1834; *Journal of the Convention*, 98–100.

54 Ibid.

55 *Journal of the Convention*, 98–99; *Nashville Republican and State Gazette*, June 26, 1834.

56 Ibid.

57 *Nashville Republican and State Gazette*, July 10, 1834. Cahal's remarks are printed in full in this issue.

58 *Nashville Republican and State Gazette*, June 26, 1834.

59 Ibid.

60 *Journal of the Convention*, 99–100.

61 *Journal of the Convention*, 102–4; *Nashville Republican and State Gazette*, June 28, 1834.

62 *Journal of the Convention*, 106; see also sources cited in notes 12 and 44.

63 *Journal of the Convention*, 125–31; *Nashville Republican and State Gazette*, July 15, 1834.

64 *Nashville Republican and State Gazette*, July 24, 1834.

65 Ibid.

66 *Nashville Republican and State Gazette*, September 9, 1834. McKinney's remarks, published by the Nashville newspaper in September, were delivered to the convention in July, but the date of these remarks is noted by neither the newspaper nor the convention journal.

67 *Nashville Republican and State Gazette*, September 9, 1834.

68 *Nashville Republican and State Gazette*, July 24, 1834.

69 *Journal of the Convention*, 146–51.

70 Ibid.

71 Ibid., 71.

72 *Nashville Republican and State Gazette*, August 5, 1834.

73 Analysis in this paragraph is based on *Nashville Republican and State Gazette*, August 5, 1834; *Journal of the Convention*, 200–1; Bergeron, *Antebellum Politics in Tennessee*, 20, 40–41; Folmsbee, *Sectionalism and Internal Improvements in Tennessee*, 1–8; ; Cassell, "Newton Cannon and the Constitutional Convention of 1834," 239; Fitz, "The Tennessee Antislavery Movement," 26–37; Mooney, "The Question of Slavery and the Free Negro," 502–3.

74 Ibid.

75 Calculations and analysis in this paragraph are based on the sources cited in note 73 above and the population data available at population calculated from data available at http://fisher.lib.virginia.edu/collections/stats/histcensus/.

76 *Journal of the Convention*, 222–28.

77 Ibid.

78 Ira Berlin, *Slaves Without Masters: The Free Negro in the Antebellum South* (New York: Pantheon, 1974), 136–37, 396–403.

79 *Nashville Republican and State Gazette*, September 28, 1833.

80 For an overview, see Mooney, "The Question of Slavery and the Free Negro," 503–9.

81 Francis N. Thorpe, *Federal and State Constitutions, Colonial Charters and Other Organic Laws of the States, Territories and Colonies*... (Washington, DC, 1909), 6:3426–44.

82 *Nashville Republican and State Gazette*, July 1 and 15, 1834; Atkins, *Parties, Politics and the Sectional Conflict*, 22; Bergeron, *Antebellum Politics in Tennessee*, 2.

83 Mooney, "The Question of Slavery and the Free Negro," 503.

84 *Journal of the Convention*, 37.

85 *Nashville Republican and State Gazette*, June 28, 1834.

86 *Nashville Republican and State Gazette*, July 1, 1834.

87 Ibid.

88 *Journal of the Convention*, 107–8.

89 *Nashville Republican and State Gazette*, July 1, 1834. In addition to the Marr-Blount resolutions, the convention considered an addition to Carter's proposal of from the previous day. Carter proposed adding language specifically denying voting rights to free blacks who were eligible to vote at the time of the ratification of the 1834 constitution and turning the issue of determining color to the state courts. Carter's addition to his pervious motion was approved on a voice vote and the convention moved on to other issues.

90 *Nashville Republican and State Gazette*, July 15, 1834.

91 *Nashville Republican and State Gazette*, July 5, 1834.

92 *Nashville Republican and State Gazette*, July 10, 1834.

93 *Nashville Republican and State Gazette*, July 5, 1834

94 *Nashville Republican and State Gazette*, July 29, 1834.

95 *Journal of the Convention*, 208–9. John McKinney succeeded in getting the only caveat to the white-males-only clause when the convention approved his amendment stating that "no person shall be disqualified from voting in an election on account of who is now, by the laws of this State, a component witness in a court of justice against a white man." Since, as a general rule, only whites could testify against other whites in court, this proviso seemed unnecessary, but in Tennessee, following a practice carried over from territorial days, men who were fifteen-sixteenths white were allowed to testify against whites. This exception prevented the disfranchisement of a tiny number of who had one great-grandparent who was not white. While the evidentiary record is largely silent on the question, it is probable that this exception was included to avoid disfranchising those men who had a native American great-grandparent. A significant proportion of these men likely could have passed for white anyway. See Thorpe, *Federal and State Constitutions*, 6:3434, and Mooney, "The Question of Slavery and the Free Negro," 506.

96 Analysis based on *Journal of the Convention*, 3–4, 208–9; Bergeron, *Antebellum Politics in Tennessee*, 20; Folmsbee, *Sectionalism and Internal Improvements in Tennessee*, 1–8.

97 *Nashville Republican and State Gazette*, July 10, 1834.

98 Ibid.

99 *Nashville Republican and State Gazette*, July 5, 1834.

100 *Nashville Republican and State Gazette*, July 15, 1834; see also *Journal of the Convention*, 107.

101 On herrenvolk democracy, see George M. Fredrickson, *The Black Image in the White Mind: The Debate on Afro-American Character and Destiny, 1817–1914* (New York: Harper and Row, 1971), 61–70, 93–94. For an introduction to the egalitarian republican formulation, see William W. Freehling, *The Road to Disunion: Secessionists at Bay, 1776–1854* (New York: Oxford University Press, 1990), 162–77.

102 On this point, see Lacy K. Ford, "The Popular Ideology of the Old South's Plain Folk: The Limits of Egalitarianism in a Slaveholding Society," in Samuel Hyde, ed., *Plain Folk of the South Reconsidered* (Baton Rouge: Louisiana State University Press, 1997), 205–27; Atkins, *Parties, Politics and the Sectional Conflict*, 4–5; Bergeron, *Antebellum Politics in Tennessee*, 38–39; Cassell, "Newton Cannon and the Constitutional Convention of 1834," 239–42.

103 Ford, "The Popular Ideology of the Old South's Plain Folk," 224–26.

104 On this tendency across the antebellum South, see Lacy Ford, "Making the 'White Man's Country' White: Race, Slavery and State-Building in the Jacksonian South," *Journal of the Early Republic* 19 (Winter 1999): 713–37. On this point in a national context, see James Brewer Stewart, "Modernizing 'Difference': The Political Meanings of Color in the Free States, 1776–1840," *Journal of the Early Republic* 19 (Winter 1999): 691–712. For a similar point regarding gender, see Stephanie McCurry, "The Two Faces of Republicanism: Gender and Proslavery Politics in Antebellum South Carolina," *Journal of American History* 78 (March 1991): 1245–64.

105 *Nashville Whig*, quoted in Mooney, *Slavery in Tennessee*, 82.

FOURTEEN. ENDING FREE BLACK SUFFRAGE IN NORTH CAROLINA

1 William Pettigrew to Ebenezer Pettigrew, September 3, 1831, Pettigrew Family Papers, SHC.

2 The best overview of the impact of Turner's insurrection on North Carolina remains John Hope Franklin, *The Free Negro in North Carolina, 1790–1860* (Chapel Hill: University of North Carolina Press, 1943), 70–72. See also *Raleigh Register*, September 15 and 22, 1831.

3 John C. Latta to Robert C. Caldwell, September 14, 1831, David Franklin Caldwell Papers, SHC; Fayetteville *Carolina Observer*, September 21, 1831; *Raleigh Register*, September 15 and 22, 1831. See also Harry L. Watson, *Jacksonian Politics and Community Conflict: The Emergence of the Second American Party System in Cumberland County, North Carolina* (Baton Rouge: Louisiana State University Press, 1981), 153.

4 Thomas E. Jeffrey, *State Parties and National Politics: North Carolina, 1815–1861* (Athens: University of Georgia Press, 1989), 77.

5 Franklin, *The Free Negro in North Carolina,* 64–76.

6 Lewis Williams to William Gaston, December 21, 1831, William Gaston Papers, SHC; see also Jeffrey, *State Parties and National Politics*, 112.

7 See http://fisher.lib.virginia.edu/collections/stats/histcensus; Jeffrey, *State Parties and National Politics*, 282; John C. Inscoe, *Mountain Masters, Slavery and the Secession Crisis in Western North Carolina* (Knoxville: University of Tenessee Press, 1989); John C. Inscoe, "Mountain Masters: Slaveholding in Western North Carolina," *North Carolina Historical Review* 61 (April 1984): 143–73; J. Carlyle Sitterson, *The Secession Movement in North Carolina* (Chapel Hill: University of North Carolina Press, 1939), 5–19.

8 The best introduction to constitutional reform in North Carolina is still Harold J. Counihan, "The North Carolina Constitutional Convention of 1835: A Study in Jacksonian Democracy," *North Carolina Historical Review* 46 (October 1969): 335–64; see also Fletcher M. Green's classic *Constitutional Development in the South Atlantic States, 1776–1860: A Study in the Evolution of Democracy* (Chapel Hill: University of North Carolina Press, 1930), 224–33. On the internal improvements issue, see Thomas Jeffrey, "National Issues, Local Interests, and the Transformation of Antebellum North Carolina Politics," *Journal of Southern History* 59 (1982): 24–48, and Thomas Jeffrey, "Internal Improvements and Political Parties in North Carolina, 1836–1861," *North Carolina Historical Review* 55 (April 1978): 111–56.

9 For an overview of these debates, see Franklin, *The Free Negro in North Carolina*,, 108–20; see also Thorpe, *Federal and State Constitutions*, 4:2787–94. A few counties apparently resorted to extralegal means to prevent or restrict free black voting despite the wording of the state constitution.

10 Judge Buxton of Fayetteville, quoted in Stephen B. Weeks, "The History of Negro Suffrage in the South," *Political Science Quarterly* 9 (1894): 676.

11 The New Bern petition is quoted at length in Franklin, *The Free Negro in North Carolina,* 108.

12 Louis D. Henry to William Gaston, December 30, 1831, William Gaston Papers, SHC.

13 John H. Bryan to Ebenezer Pettigrew, July 27, 1832, Pettigrew Family Papers, SHC; Franklin, *The Free Negro in North Carolina,* 107–9.

14 Daniel M. McFarland, "Rip Van Winkle: Political Evolution in North Carolina, 1815–1835," Ph.D. dissertation, University of Pennsylvania, 1954, 60–61. See also James H. Broussard, *The Southern Federalists, 1800–1816* (Baton Rouge: Louisiana State University Press, 1978), 226–28; Jeffrey, *State Parties and National Politics*, 53.

15 Salisbury *Western Carolinian*, June 20, 1820.

16 *Proceedings of the Friends of Convention at a Meeting Held in Raleigh, December 1822* (Raleigh, 1822), esp. 3; *To the Freemen of Orange County* (n.p., 1823), 4–6. On the disproportionate influence of Caswell County on antebellum North Carolina politics, see William S. Powell, *When the Past Refused to Die: A History of Caswell County, 1777–1977* (Durham, NC: Moore, 1977).

17 *Journal of a Convention Assembled at the City of Raleigh on the 10th of November, 1823* (Raleigh: J. Gales and Son, 1823); *The Proposed New Constitution of the State of North Carolina* (Raleigh: J. Gales and Son, 1823); McFarland, "Rip Van Winkle: Political Evolution in North Carolina," 151–52; Jeffrey, *State Parties and National Politics*, 54–55.

18 Jeffrey, *State Parties and National Politics*, 55–56.

19 Salisbury *Western Carolinian*, May 25, 1825; *Proceedings and Debates of the Convention of North Carolina Called to Amend the Constitution of the State* (Raleigh, NC: Joseph Gales, 1836), 117–18.

20 Jeffrey, *State Parties and National Politics*, 56–57; McFarland, "Rip Van Winkle: Political Evolution in North Carolina," 329–31.

21 Speech of William Long, in *Debate in the Legislature of North Carolina on a Proposed Appropriation for Re-Building the Capitol and on the Convention Question* (Raleigh: J Gales and Sons, 1832), 25–26.

22 Speech of John Daniel, in ibid., 55–56.

23 William Gaston to Robert Donaldson, December 9, 1831, William Gaston Papers, SHC.

24 Harry L. Watson, "Squire Oldway and His Friends: Opposition to Internal Improvements in Antebellum North Carolina," *North Carolina Historical Review* 54 (April 1977): 105–19.

25 McFarland, "Rip Van Winkle: Political Evolution in North Carolina," 377–400; Watson, *Jacksonian Politics and Community Conflict*, 199; Counihan, "North Carolina, 1815–1836: State and Local Perspectives on the Age of Jackson," Ph.D. dissertation, University of North Carolina, 1971, 65–69, 121–28.

26 Jeffrey, *State Parties and National Politics*, 57–59; Counihan, "North Carolina, 1815–1836," 135–36; McFarland, "Rip Van Winkle: Political Evolution in North Carolina," 366–67.

27 *The Papers of William A. Graham*, ed. J. G. De Roulhac Hamilton and Max R. Williams (Raleigh, NC: Division of Archives and History, 1957–), 1:303.

28 For example, see *Raleigh Register*, January 14, February 25, and March 25, 1834; *Western Carolinian*, quoted in the *Raleigh Register*, February 4, 1834; Salisbury *Carolina Watchman*, in the *Raleigh Register*, July 29, 1834; *Raleigh Register*, April 29, 1834.

29 *Raleigh Register*, June 17, 1834.

30 Jonathan Seawell Jones to Daniel M. Barringer, November 7, 1834, Daniel M. Barringer Papers, SHC.

31 William H. Haywood Jr., *To the People of Wake County* (*Raleigh*, 1834).

32 Jeffrey, *State Parties and National Politics*, 62; McFarland, "Rip Van Winkle: Political Evolution in North Carolina," 432–34; Counihan, "North Carolina, 1815–1836," 138–41.

33 "To the People of North Carolina," *Raleigh Register*, March 25, 1834. See also *Raleigh Register*, April 29, 1834.

34 "To the People of North Carolina."

35 David Swain to William Gaston, October 11, 1834, William Gaston Papers, SHC; "Governor's Message" in *Raleigh Register*, November 25, 1834.

36 *Raleigh Register*, December 30, 1834, and January 6, 1835.

37 Jeffrey, *State Parties and National Politics*, 62.

38 Counihan, "The North Carolina Constitutional Convention of 1835," 336–37; *Raleigh Register*, January 20, 1835; *North Carolina Standard*, February 13, 1835.

39 Counihan, "The North Carolina Constitutional Convention of 1835," 337–38.

40 *Raleigh Register*, January 27, 1835.

41 *Raleigh Register*, March 31, 1835.

42 Form the *Oxford Examiner*, reprinted in the *Raleigh Register*, February 3, 1835.

43 *North Carolina Standard*, January 9, 1835.

44 *North Carolina Standard*, March 20, 1835.

45 *Raleigh Register*, April 21, 1835; *North Carolina Standard*, May 29, 1835; Counihan, "The North Carolina Constitutional Convention of 1835," 339–40.

46 *North Carolina Standard*, June 12, 1835.

47 *Raleigh Register*, June 2, 1835.

48 For an exception, see *Raleigh Register*, July 29, 1834. This pro-convention, pro-reform letter to the Whig press, from "A Freeman of Wake," addressed the pros and cons of free black voting at some length before recommending colonization as the best solution to the state's free black "problem."

49 *North Carolina Standard*, June 19, 1835. This issue also carries extensive coverage of this first round of debate over free black suffrage.

50 *Proceedings and Debates of the Convention of North Carolina Called to Amend the Constitution of the State* (Raleigh, NC: Joseph Gales, 1836), 60–61.

51 William C. Allen, *A History of Halifax County* (reprint; Greenville, SC: Southern Historical Press, 1993).

52 Ibid.

53 *Proceedings and Debates of the Convention of North Carolina*, 60–61.

54 Ibid., 61. Edwards was part of the cluster of politicians representing the interests of Roanoke River planters, often referred to as the "Warren Junto." Edwards replaced his kinsman Macon in the United States House in 1815 (when the latter was elected to the Senate) and served five consecutive terms. During his time in Congress, Edwards shared a mess with a celebrated group of Old Republicans that included Macon, John Randolph of Roanoke, H. G. Burton, and T. H. Hall. Though not as doctrinaire as Macon or Randolph, Edwards supported economy in government and strict construction of the Constitution, and he developed a keen eye for perceived threats to slavery; he supported the republican caucus nomination of William Crawford for president in 1824. Like Macon, he readily took up the Jackson banner later and emerged as a key southern supporter of Martin Van Buren. See William S. Powell, ed., *Dictionary of North Carolina Biography* (Chapel Hill: University of North Carolina Press, 1979–96), 2:141.

55 Ibid., 61–62; see also *North Carolina Standard*, June 19, 1835.

56 *Proceedings and Debates of the Convention of North Carolina*, 62–69.

57 Ibid.; see also Nathaniel Macon to John H. Bryan, April 20, 1832, William S. Bryan Papers, SHC. Privately, the proto-Whig Bryan admitted the he found the Old Republican Macon "entirely too radical in his notions" on most issues. See James W. Bryan to John H, Bryan, June 25, 1835, Bryan Family Papers, SHC.

58 Ibid.

59 *Proceedings and Debates of the Convention of North Carolina*, 69–70.

60 Ibid., 70–71. Branch was forced out of Jackson's cabinet during its "reorganization" during the controversy over the social reception given Margaret "Peggy" Eaton by cabinet families. On Branch's career, see William S. Hoffman, "John Branch and the Origins of the Whig Party in North Carolina," *North Carolina Historical Review* 35 (July 1958): 299–315.

61 *Proceedings and Debates of the Convention of North Carolina*, 71.

62 Ibid, 71–72.

63 Ibid., 72.

64 Ibid. The roll call on this vote was not recorded.

65 Ibid., 72–73. Shober married Anna Hanes, whose family was also prominent among North Carolina Moravians. The Haneses later expanded their mercantile success into the production and sale of plug tobacco (later sold to competitor Richard Joshua Reynolds) and the development of textile mills in the Piedmont.

66 Ibid., 73.

67 Ibid., 73–74.

68 Ibid., 74–75.

69 Powell, ed., *Dictionary of North Carolina Biography*, 4:188. Chatham County was nearly one-third slave in 1830.

70 *Proceedings and Debates of the Convention of North Carolina*, 75–79.

71 Ibid.

72 Ibid., 80.

73 Ibid., 79.

74 Ibid., 80. Morehead, a leading Whig and strong champion of economic diversification, would later serve two terms as governor and become president of the North Carolina Railroad.

75 Toomer's remarks are found in *Proceedings and Debates of the Convention of North Carolina*, 80. This crucial roll call vote is recorded on 80–81.

76 Calculations in this paragraph and later paragraphs made by author on basis of information found in *Proceedings and Debates of the Convention of North Carolina*, 1–3, 80–81; *North Carolina Standard*, June 19, 1835.

77 For ascertaining party affiliation of delegates I have followed Counihan, "The North Carolina Constitutional Convention of 1835," 340–41, unless Counihan's conclusions are directly contradicted by evidence found in other sources cited through these notes. See also *Proceedings and Debates of the Convention of North Carolina*, 1–3, 80–81; *North Carolina Standard*, June 19, 1835.

78 *Proceedings and Debates of the Convention of North Carolina*, 351–52. Delegate James W. Bryan, Gaston's friend and brother-in-law, claimed that Gaston "is listened to with profound attention" at the convention and that he served as a calming and moderating influence on delegates. See James W. Bryan to John H. Bryan, June 7, 1835, Bryan Family Papers, SHC.

79 *Proceedings and Debates of the Convention of North Carolina*, 354.

80 Ibid., 353–54, 355.

81 Ibid., 352–53. King, however, admitted to concern over the fact that allowing free black voting on too generous terms might "invite" the in-migration of "unworthy" free blacks seeking to "exercise that right with impunity."

82 Ibid., 355.

83 Ibid., 356.

84 Ibid. Carson, a self-educated mountain farmer, won election to Congress in 1824 as a Jackson supporter. In Congress, Carson became a trusted friend of James K. Polk, Sam Houston, and Warren R. Davis, a pro-Calhoun congressman from South Carolina. Through Davis, Carson took a strongly pro-Calhoun course in opposition to John Quincy Adams, against tariffs, and, ultimately, in favor of nullification in 1832. His pro-nullification stand cost Carson his House seat to challenger James Graham in 1833. But Burke county remained loyal to Carson and elected him to the 1835 convention. Carson's brother, James Carson, represented nearby Rutherford County at the convention, and James joined his brother as part of the minority of mountain

delegates who favored total disfranchisement. See Powell, ed., *Dictionary of North Carolina Biography,* 1:210.

85 *Proceedings and Debates of the Convention of North Carolina,* 356.

86 Ibid., 357.

87 Ibid.

88 Ibid., 357–58.

89 Eastern delegates still overwhelmingly favored complete disfranchisement of free blacks, voting 45–26 to defeat the amendment. Conversely, western delegates supported Gaston's proposal, 28–19. The partisan tendency of the vote on the Gaston amendment also roughly paralleled those of the June vote. Democrats opposed the Gaston amendment 19–14. Eastern Democrats, however, voted most solidly, 14–7, to uphold total disfranchisement, while western Democrats actually favored the Gaston amendment by a margin of 7–5. Whigs split almost evenly on the amendment, voting 29–28 to reject it. Eastern Whigs opposed the amendment 19–13, but western Whigs supported allowing free blacks with substantial property to vote, 15–10. Reversing their stance from a month earlier, independent delegates rejected the Gaston amendment, 16–12. Calculations made from data found in *Proceedings and Debates of the Convention of North Carolina,* 357–58, and in the other sources cited in notes 76 and 77. Evidence is scarce on the question of why Gaston's amendment attracted slightly fewer votes that the number originally cast against black disfranchisement in June. But at least two plausible interpretations suggest themselves. First, some Piedmont and mountain delegates who were generally opposed to all but the most minimal freehold or taxpaying requirements for voting may have voted against Gaston's amendment on the grounds that his $500 property requirements was too high. Second, a few western delegates, knowing the general shape of the proposed amendments by late July, may have decided to accept the disfranchisement of free blacks, an amendment desired by the majority of eastern delegates, in order to facilitate the overall approval of the proposed constitutional revisions.

90 Ibid., 356.

91 Lacy Ford, *Origins of Southern Radicalism: The South Carolina Upcountry, 1800–1860* (New York: Oxford University Press, 1988), 103–8; see also William A. Schaper, "Sectionalism and Representation in South Carolina," *Annual Report of the American Historical Association for the Year 1900* (Washington, DC: Government Printing Office, 1902), 245–460.

92 The elimination of borough representation (the representation of certain towns over and above the county representation) resulted at least in part from a lingering eastern thirst for revenge against those who had called the convention in the first place. Anti-reform eastern delegates resented the alliance forged in the 1834 legislature between borough representatives (who almost uniformly supported internal improvements) and western constitutional reformers (who also yearned for internal improvements) to eke the convention bill out of a long intransigent legislature. See Counihan, "The North Carolina Constitutional Convention of 1835," 344–46; Jeffrey, *State Parties and National Politics,* 62; James W. Bryan to John H. Bryan, June 25, 1835, Bryan Family Papers, SHC.

93 All newspapers quoted in *Raleigh Register,* August 4, 1835.

94 *North Carolina Standard,* July 17, 1835.

95 *Raleigh Register,* September 29, 1835.

96 Fayetteville *Carolina Observer,* June 16, 1835.

97 *Newbern Spectator* quoted in *Raleigh Register,* September 29, 1835.

98 *North Carolina Standard,* July 17, 1835.

99 Counihan, "The North Carolina Constitutional Convention of 1835," 361.
100 James W. Bryan to John H. Bryan, June 25, 1835, Bryan Family Papers, SHC.
101 In North Carolina, the liberalization of the suffrage for whites applied only to elections for the House of Commons, governor, and local elections. North Carolina retained the freehold requirement for voting for state senators until the 1850s, when this question became fodder for another constitutional reform movement. See Jeffrey, *State Parties and National Politics*, 62–63; Thomas E. Jeffrey, "Beyond 'Free Suffrage': North Carolina Parties and the Convention Movement of the 1850s," *North Carolina Historical Review* 62 (October 1985): 387–419.
102 Franklin, *The Free Negro in North Carolina,* 116–20; Thorpe, *Federal and State Constitutions,* 4:2787–94.
103 *North Carolina Standard,* July 10, 1835.
104 *Raleigh Register,* July 14, 1835.
105 *Raleigh Register,* June 26 and August 18, 1840; *North Carolina Standard,* September 9, 1840.
106 Powell, ed., *Dictionary of North Carolina Biography,* 2:87–88.
107 *Asheville News,* May 11 and 25, 1854.
108 *Proceedings and Debates of the Convention of North Carolina,* 356.
109 *Asheville News,* May 11, 1854.
110 *Fayetteville Argus* reprinted in *Greensborough Patriot,* May 20, 1854.
111 *Greensborough Patriot,* December 2, 1854.
112 *Autobiography of Asa Biggs,* ed. Robert D. W. Conner (Raleigh: Edwards and Broughton, 1918); also see Biggs autobiography at http://docsouth.unc.edu/fpn/biggs/biggs.html.
113 *Proceedings and Debates of the Convention of North Carolina,* 80–81, 357–58; see also *North Carolina Standard,* June 19 and July 17, 1835.
114 Franklin, *The Free Negro in North Carolina,* 120.
115 *State of North Carolina v. Newsom,* 27 North Carolina 183. On this decision, see Franklin, *The Free Negro in North Carolina,* 77–78.
116 For an earlier version of this argument, see Lacy K. Ford, "Making the 'White Man's Country' White: Race and State Constitutions in the Jacksonian South," *Journal of the Early Republic* 19 (Winter 1999): 713–37. On the content of racial modernism and its expanding influence in the Jacksonian era, see James Brewer Stewart, "The Emergence of Racial Modernity and the Rise of the White North," *Journal of the Early Republic* 18 (Summer 1998): 181–217. See also the comments by Jean L. Sunderland, James Oliver Horton, and Ronald G. Walters along with Stewart's response in the same issue, 218–36.
117 See also James Brewer Stewart, "Modernizing 'Difference': The Political Meanings of Color in the Free States, 1776–1840." *Journal of the Early Republic* 19 (Winter 1999): 691–712. The growing southern attachment to paternalism as an ideology will be discussed in the next chapter. The partisan divide on racial modernity was largely a matter of degree rather than kind. It was not that all white Democrats or white egalitarians abandoned all concern about uplift (or that all Whigs retained it), but that defining racial difference mattered more to most Democrats while uplift remained more central to Whigs than Democrats.
118 While Tennessee exported only about six thousand more slaves than it imported between 1830 and 1860 and did not become a net exporter until the 1850s, North Carolina exported over 95,000 slaves, more than every state except Virginia and South Carolina, during those same years and had become a net exporter as early as 1800. See Michael Tadman, *Speculators and Slaves: Masters, Traders and Slaves in the Old South* (Madison: University of Wisconsin Press, 1989).

FIFTEEN. REACTION IN THE LOWER SOUTH

1 *Baton-Rouge Gazette*, March 20, 1830.

2 Herman E. Sterkx, *The Free Negro in Ante-bellum Louisiana* (Rutherford, NJ: Farleigh Dickinson Press, 1972), 98–99. By both number and proportion, Louisiana had the largest free colored population in the lower South by a wide margin. In fact, free people of color accounted for 13 percent of the state's nonwhite population in 1830.

3 Joe Gray Taylor, *Negro Slavery in Louisiana* (New York: Negro Universities Press, 1969), 41–48.

4 *Baton-Rouge Gazette*, April 17, 1830.

5 *Laws of Louisiana* (1831), 10th Legislature, 1st Session, 98.

6 Sterkx, *The Free Negro in Ante-bellum Louisiana*, 121–24.

7 Rachel O'Connor to David Weeks, October 13, 1831, David Weeks and Family Papers, LSU.

8 John M. Sacher, *A Perfect War of Politics: Parties, Politicians, and Democracy in Louisiana, 1824–1861* (Baton Rouge: Louisiana State University Press, 2003), 58, 75.

9 Lacy Ford, "Reconsidering the Internal Slave Trade: Paternalism, Markets and the Character of the Old South," in Walter Johnson, ed., *The Chattel Principle: Internal Slave Trades in the Americas* (New Haven: Yale University Press, 2004), 143–64, esp. 156–57; Taylor, *Negro Slavery in Louisiana,* 21–48; Sterkx, *The Free Negro in Ante-bellum Louisiana*, 285–315.

10 E. G. W. Butler to Thomas Butler, May 5, 1830, Butler Family Papers, LSU.

11 Thomas A. Scott to William S. Hamilton, February 8, 1830, Hamilton Papers, LSU.

12 Alexander Barrow to William S. Hamilton, January 25, 1830, Hamilton Papers, LSU.

13 *Acts of the Extra Session of the Tenth Legislature of the State of Louisiana, 1831* (New Orleans, 1831), esp. 4–10.

14 J. S. Johnston to Thomas Butler, March 12, 1832, Butler Family Papers, LSU.

15 Taylor, *Negro Slavery in Louisiana,* 43–46.

16 W. E. Paxton, *A History of the Baptists of Louisiana from the Earliest Times to the Present* (St. Louis: C. R. Barnes, 1888), 149–50.

17 *Natchez Gazette*, October 26, 1831.

18 Stephen Duncan to Thomas Butler, September 4, 1831, Butler Papers, LSU.

19 Vicksburg *Advocate and Register*, September 16, 1831.

20 Natchez *Natchez*, March 16, 1832.

21 Ibid. In state with a free black population of less than five hundred, the licensing process was not unenforceable and it appears that most free blacks were in fact licensed to stay, but the passage of the law in 1831 suggests the heightened security concerns, especially in and around Natchez,in the immediate aftermath of Turner's revolt.

22 Vicksburg *Advocate and Register*, December 23, 1831.

23 Vicksburg *Advocate and Register*, January 6, 1832.

24 Vicksburg *Advocate and Register*, December 23, 1831, and January 6, 1832.

25 Ford, "Reconsidering the Internal Slave Trade," 157–59.

26 Brandon quoted in Charles Sydnor, *Slavery in Mississippi* (London: D. Appleton, 1933), 161–62. Winburne McGruder Drake, "The Framing of Mississippi's First State Constitution," *Journal of Mississippi* 29 (April 1956): 79–110; Sydnor, *Slavery in Mississippi*, 161–65; Charles Sydnor, "The Free Negro in Mississippi," *American Historical Review* 32 (July 1927): 769–88; Edwin A. Miles, *Jacksonian Democracy in Mississippi* (Chapel Hill: University of North Carolina Press, 1960), 41–42.

27 Jonathan Stewart to Duncan McLaurin, June 30, 1831, Duncan McLaurin Papers, DU.
28 Natchez *Natchez*, November 9, 1832.
29 Winburne McGruder Drake, "The Mississippi Constitution of 1832," *Journal of Southern History* 23 (August 1957): 354–70; Natchez *Courier*, November 9, 1832.
30 Ford, "Reconsidering the Internal Slave Trade," 157–59.
31 Natchez *Courier*, August 23, 1833.
32 Natchez *Courier*, August 23, November 9 and 13, 1833.
33 Sydnor, *Slavery in Mississippi*, 161–71.
34 Ibid.
35 *Groves v. Slaughter*, 40 United States 449 (1841).
36 *Woodville Republican*, February 15, 1845; Sydnor, *Slavery in Mississippi*, 168–70.
37 James B. Sellers, *Slavery in Alabama* (Tuscaloosa: University of Alabama Press, 1950), 140–94; J. Mills Thornton III, *Politics and Power in a Slave Society: Alabama, 1800–1860* (Baton Rouge: Louisiana State University Press, 1978), 319–20.
38 Clay quoted in Sellers, *Slavery in Alabama*, 375.
39 *African Repository and Colonial Journal* 9 (August 1833): 171–74; Huntsville *Democrat*, October 3, 1833.
40 Milledgeville *Southern Recorder*, October 6, 1831.
41 Ibid., September 18, 1831.
42 Milledgeville *Federal Union*, January 12, 1832.
43 Ruth Scarborough, *Opposition to Slavery in Georgia Prior to 1860* (reprint; New York: Negro Universities Press, 1968), 107–23; Gilmer quoted on 118–19.
44 Ruth Scarborough, *The Opposition to Slavery in Georgia Prior to 1860* (New York: Negro Universities Press, reprint 1968, copyright, 1933), 18–20.
45 *African Repository and Colonial Journal* 8:124–25.
46 William W. Freehling, *Prelude to Civil War: The Nullification Crisis in South Carolina, 1816–1836* (New York: Harper and Row, 1965), 62–63; *Charleston Mercury*, October 4 and December 9, 1831.
47 Samuel Townes to George Townes, October 8, 1831, Townes Family Papers, SCL.
48 Presentment of the Fairfield District Grand Jury, November 1831, Grand Jury Presentments, Records of the South Carolina General Assembly, 1831, Record Group S165010, #00005, SCDAH.
49 Presentment of the Kershaw District Grand Jury, October 1831, Grand Jury Presentments, Records of the South Carolina General Assembly, 1831, Record Group S165010, #00011, SCDAH.
50 Presentment of the Richland District Grand Jury, October 1831, Grand Jury Presentments, Records of the South Carolina General Assembly, 1831, Record Group S165010, #00023, SCDAH.
51 Presentment of the Georgetown District Grand Jury, c. 1831, Grand Jury Presentments, Records of the South Carolina General Assembly, 1831, Record Group S165010, #00010, SCDAH.
52 Report of the Committee on the Colored Population, December 12, 1831, Reports of Committees of the South Carolina General Assembly, 1831, Records of the South Carolina General Assembly, 1831, Record Group S165010, SCDAH.
53 Tadman, *Speculators and Slaves*, 12.

54 John Floyd to James Hamilton, November 19, 1831, John Floyd Papers, LC.

55 Presentment of the Sumter District Grand Jury, November 1829, Grand Jury Presentments, Records of the South Carolina General Assembly, 1829, Record Group S165010, #00017, SCDAH.

56 Presentment of the Richland District Grand Jury, October 1831, Grand Jury Presentments, Records of the South Carolina General Assembly, 1831, Record Group S165010, #00023, SCDAH.

57 Presentment of the Kershaw District Grand Jury, October 1831, Grand Jury Presentments, Records of the South Carolina General Assembly, 1831, Record Group S165010, #00011, SCDAH.

58 For example, see Whitemarsh Seabrook, *A Concise View of the Critical Situation and Future Prospects of the Slave-holding States in Relation to the Coloured Population, Read Before the Agricultural Society of St. Johns, Colleton on the 14th of September, 1825* (Charleston: A. E. Miller, 1825). Two fine works by Janet Duitsman Cornelius on slave literacy and white opposition to it that have shaped my thinking on the issue include *When I Can Read My Title Clear: Literacy, Slavery, and Religion in the Antebellum South* (Columbia: University of South Carolina Press, 1991), esp. 37–58, and *Slave Missions and the Black Church in the Antebellum South* (Columbia: University of South Carolina Press, 1999).

59 On Pinckney, see George C. Rogers Jr., "Henry Laurens Pinckney: Thoughts on His Career," in James B. Meriwether, ed., *South Carolina Journals and Journalists* (Spartanburg, SC: Reprint Company, 1975), 163–75.

60 House Journal, 1831, 94, 140, 143, 145–46, 186–87, 205; Senate Journal, 1831, 53, 65, 138. The house also demanded that the senate remove security provisions that required plantation owners to employ one white for every twenty-eight male slaves and make that white available for patrol duty.

61 Erskine Clarke, *Dwelling Place: A Plantation Epic* (New Haven: Yale University Press, 2005), 107–9.

62 Minutes of the Synod of South Carolina and Georgia, December 3, 1831, Presbyterian Historical Society, Montreat, North Carolina.; *The Charleston Observer*, March 29, 1834.

63 A. D. Sims, *A View of Slavery, Moral and Political* (Charleston: A. E. Miller, 1834).

64 Thomas S. Clay, *Detail of a Plan for the Moral Improvement of Negroes on Plantation, Read Before the Georgia Presbytery* (n.p., 1833); Clarke, *Dwelling Place*, 142–43.

65 *Charleston Observer*, November 2, 1833.

66 Presentment of the Richland District Grand Jury, 1833, Grand Jury Presentments, Records of the South Carolina General Assembly, 1833, Record Group S165010, #00007, SCDAH.

67 Petition of M. H. DeLeon, Intendant of Columbia, on Behalf of the Town Council for Stronger Laws to Prohibit the Teaching of Slaves to Read and Write, c. 1833, Petitions to the General Assembly, Records of the South Carolina General Assembly, 1833, Record Group S165015, #02829, SCDAH.

68 House Journal, 1833, 54; Senate Journal, 11, 16, 29–30. SCDAH.

69 House Journal, 1833, 96–98, SCDAH.

70 Senate Journal, 1833, 104, 115, SCDAH.

71 For biographical information on Warren, see N. Louise Bailey, Mary L. Morgan, and Carolyn R. Taylor, eds., *Biographical Directory of the South Carolina Senate, 1776–1985* (Columbia: University of South Carolina Press, 1986), 3:1685–7.

72 For the roll call, see Senate Journal, 1833, 115, SCDAH.

73 Whitemarsh Seabrook, *Essay on the Management of Slaves, and Especially on Their Religious Instruction, Read Before the Agricultural Society of St. John's Colleton* (Charleston: A. F. Miller, 1834).
74 Ibid.
75 Ibid., 13–26.
76 Ibid., 15–16.
77 Ibid., esp. 22–26.
78 Petition of Sundry Ministers in St. Philip's and St. Michael's Parishes . . . Including Minutes of the Meeting of Said Ministers . . . , c. 1834, Petitions to the General Assembly, Records of the South Carolina General Assembly, 1834, Record Group S165015, #01803, SCDAH.
79 Ibid.
80 Ibid.
81 Ibid.
82 Senate Journal, 1834, 111, 124, 145, SCDAH.
83 House Journal, 1834, 15, 28, 59, 71, 91, 107, SCDAH.
84 Peter Guilday, *The Life and Times of John England, 1786–1842* (New York: America Press 1927), 2:176–83.
85 Daniel Payne, *Recollections of Seventy Years* (Nashville: Publishing House of the AME Sunday School Union, 1888), 34–38.
86 Robert Lathan, *History of the Associate Reformed Synod of the South. . . .* (Harrisburg, PA: Author, 1882).
87 Lowry Ware, *A Place Called Due West: The Home of Erskine College* (Columbia, SC: R. L. Bryan, 1997), 30–67: and his *Old Abbeville: Scenes from the Past of a Town Where Old Time Things Are Not Forgotten* (Columbia, SC, 1992), 25–31, 75–83.
88 Edward R. Laurens, *A Letter to the Honorable Whitemarsh Seabrook of St. John's Colleton in Explanation and Defence of an Act to Amend the Law in Relation to Slaves and Free Persons of Color* (Charleston: Observer Office Press, 1835).
89 Nathaniel Bowen, *A Pastoral Letter on the Religious Instruction of Slaves of Members of the Protestant Episcopal Church in the State of South Carolina, Prepared at the Request of the Churches of the Diocese . . .* (Charleston: A. E. Miller, 1835).
90 Ibid., 3–4.
91 Ibid., 8–26.
92 Ibid., 13.
93 Ibid., 8–26.
94 See Clarke, *Dwelling Place*, esp. 1–110. My analysis herein is based heavily on Lacy K. Ford, "A Paternalist's Progress: Insurgency, Orthodoxy and Reversal in the Old South," *Reviews in American History* 35 (March 2007): 46–56.
95 Charles C. Jones to Mary Jones, July 22, 1829, Charles C. Jones Papers, TU.
96 Charles C. Jones to Mary Jones, July 9, 1829, and May 18, 1830, Charles C. Jones Papers, TU.
97 Charles C. Jones to Mary Jones, May 18, 1830, Charles C. Jones Papers, TU.
98 Mary Jones to Charles C. Jones, November 24, 1829, Charles C. Jones Papers, TU.
99 *Charleston Observer*, August 24, 1833.
100 Clarke, *Dwelling Place*, esp. 152–66.
101 On this point, see Willie Lee Rose, "The Domestication of Domestic Slavery," in William W. Freehling, ed., *Slavery and Freedom* (New York: Oxford University Press, 1982), 18–36;

Jeffrey Robert Young, *Domesticating Slavery: The Master Class in Georgia and South Carolina, 1670–1837* (Chapel Hill: University of North Carolina Press, 1999), esp. 123–60; Bertram Wyatt-Brown, "Modernizing Southern Slavery: The Proslavery Argument Reinterpreted," in J. Morgan Kousser and James M. McPherson, eds., *Region, Race and Reconstruction: Essays in Honor of C. Vann Woodward* (New York: Oxford University Press, 1982), 27–49.

102 On this visit, see Clarke, *Dwelling Place*, 167–79.

103 Charles C. Jones to William Plumer, June 28, 1834, PHS.

104 Clarke, *Dwelling Place*, 170–71.

105 Charles C. Jones to Mary Jones, November 5, 1835, Charles C. Jones Papers, TU.

106 Charles C. Jones to Mary Jones, November 5 and 6, 1835, Charles C. Jones Papers, TU.

107 Charles C. Jones to Mary Jones, November 5, 1835, Charles C. Jones Papers, TU.

108 Clarke, *Dwelling Place*, 169–74.

109 Charles C. Jones to Mary Jones, November 5, 1835, Charles C. Jones Papers, TU.

110 Ibid.

111 Ibid.

SIXTEEN. ABOLITION POISON AND SOUTHERN ANTIDOTES

1 For overviews of the mail campaign, see Richard R. John, *Spreading the News: The American Postal System from Franklin to Morse* (Cambridge: Harvard University Press, 1995), 257–80; Mitchell Snay, *Gospel of Disunion: Religion and Separatism in the Antebellum South* (Chapel Hill: University of North Carolina Press, 1997), 19–52; William W. Freehling, *Prelude to Civil War: The Nullification Crisis in South Carolina, 1816–1836* (New York: Harper and Row, 1965), 340–48; and Bertram Wyatt-Brown, "The Abolition Postal Campaign of 1835," *Journal of Negro History* 50 (October 1965): 227–38.

2 Leonard L. Richards, *"Gentlemen of Property and Standing": Anti-Abolition Mobs in Jacksonian America* (New York: Oxford University Press, 1970); David L. Grimsted, *American Mobbing, 1828–1861: Toward Civil War* (New York: Oxford University Press, 1998).

3 *North Carolina Standard*, August 13, 1835.

4 For a comprehensive overview of the southern reaction, see Susan Wyly-Jones, "The 1835 Anti-Abolition Meetings in the South: A New Look at the Controversy over the Abolition Postal Campaign," *Civil War History* 47 (December 2001): 289–309.

5 Charleston *Southern Patriot*, July 29, 1835.

6 The most thorough account of the crisis in Charleston is John, *Spreading the News*, 257–67. The incident as seen by Huger can be tracked through the primary documents published in Frank Otto Gatell, ed., "Postmaster Huger and the Incendiary Publications," *South Carolina Historical Magazine* 64 (October 1963): 193–201.

7 Alfred Huger to Samuel Gouverneur, August 1, 1835, in Gatell, ed., "Postmaster Huger and the Incendiary Publications," 194–95; *Charleston Mercury*, July 31, 1835; Alfred Huger to Amos Kendall, published in *Richmond Enquirer*, August 25, 1835; C. S. Hamilton to L. H. Hamilton, July 30, 1835, in Harvey S. Teal, ed., "Attacks on the Charleston, South Carolina Post Office," *La Posta: A Journal of American Postal History* 17 (1986): 54–56.

8 Alfred Huger to Samuel Gouverneur, August 1, 1835, in Gatell, ed., "Postmaster Huger and the Incendiary Publications," 194–95.

9 *Charleston Mercury*, August 11, 1835; John, *Spreading the News*, 263–68.

10 Alfred Huger to Samuel Gouverneur, August 6, 1835, in Gatell, ed., "Postmaster Huger and the Incendiary Publications," 196–97.
11 Andrew Jackson to Amos Kendall, August 9, 1835, in *Correspondence of Andrew Jackson*, ed. John Spencer Bassett (Washington, DC: Carnegie Institution, 1926–35), 5:360.
12 See Amos Kendall's open letter to Alfred Huger, dated August 5, 1835, in the *Richmond Enquirer*, August 11, 1835.
13 Robert I. Gage to James M. Gage, August 31, 1835, James M. Gage Papers, SHC.
14 *Charleston Mercury*, August 11, 1835.
15 Alfred Huger to Samuel Gouverneur, August 15, 1835, in Gatell, ed., "Postmaster Huger and the Incendiary Publications," 199–200.
16 Milledgeville *Southern Recorder*, August 4, 1835.
17 *North Carolina Standard*, August 20, 1835.
18 *Richmond Enquirer*, reprinted in the Raleigh *North Carolina Standard*, August 13, 1835.
19 *Nashville Republican*, August 4, 1835.
20 Wyly-Jones, "The 1835 Anti-Abolition Meetings in the South," 291–95.
21 A report on the Virginia meeting can be found in the *Nashville Republican*, August 27, 1835.
22 *North Carolina Standard*, September 17, 1835.
23 *North Carolina Standard*, October 8, 1835.
24 *North Carolina Standard*, September 10, 1835.
25 Charlotte *North Carolina Journal*, August 28, 1835.
26 Milledgeville *Southern Recorder*, September 8, 1835.
27 Milledgeville *Southern Recorder*, December 11, 1835.
28 Milledgeville *Southern Recorder*, November 20, 1835.
29 Augusta *Chronicle*, September 19, 1835.
30 Milledgeville *Southern Recorder*, December 11, 1835.
31 Edmund Bellinger, *A Speech on the Subject of Slavery: Delivered 7th September 1835 at a Public Meeting of the Citizens of Barnwell District, South Carolina* (Charleston: Dan J. Dowling, 1835).
32 *Charleston Mercury*, October 5, September 18, 1835.
33 *Camden Journal*, September 19, 1835.
34 Pendleton *Messenger*, September 11, 1835.
35 "Report and Resolutions of a Public Meeting at Pendleton, September 9, 1835," in *The Papers of John C. Calhoun*, edited by Robert L. Meriwether (Columbia: University of South Carolina Press, 1959–), 12:548–54; see also Pendleton *Messenger*, September 11, 1835.
36 Ibid.
37 For good overall accounts of this insurrection scare, see Edwin A. Miles, "The Mississippi Slave Insurrection Scare of 1835," *Journal of Negro History* 42 (January 1957): 48–60; Laurence Shore, "Making Mississippi Safe for Slavery: The Insurrection Panic of 1835," in Orville Vernon Burton and Robert C. McMath, eds., *Class, Conflict and Consensus: Antebellum Southern Community Studies* (Westport, CT: Greenwood Press, 1982), 96–127; Christopher Morris, "An Event in Community Organization: The Mississippi Slave Insurrection Scare of 1835," *Journal of Social History* 22 (Autumn 1988): 93–111; and Daniel S. Dupre, *Transforming the Cotton Frontier: Madison County, Alabama, 1800–1840* (Baton Rouge: Louisiana State University Press, 1997), 224–37. For a larger perspective of fear of slave and free black activity along the Mississippi River, see Thomas C. Buchanan, *Black Life on the Mississippi: Slaves, Free Blacks and the Western Steamboat World* (Chapel Hill: University of North Carolina Press, 2004).

38 Miles, "The Mississippi Slave Insurrection Scare of 1835," 49–50; New Orleans City Council, *Report of a Conspiracy to Incite a Rebellion Throughout the Slave States* (n.p., 1835), 2–9.
39 Ibid.
40 Jackson *Mississippian*, March 14, 1834.
41 *North Carolina Standard*, October 22, 1835; Miles, "The Mississippi Slave Insurrection Scare of 1835," 49–50.
42 *North Carolina Standard*, August 6, 1835.
43 Milledgeville *Southern Recorder*, August 4, 1835.
44 Henry S. Foote, *Casket of Reminiscences* (Washington, DC: Chronicle Publishing, 1874), 251.
45 J. F. H. Claiborne, *Life and Correspondence of John A. Quitman*... (New York: Harper & Brothers, 1860), 1:138.
46 Jackson *Mississippian*, quoted in Miles, "The Mississippi Slave Insurrection Scare of 1835," 56–57.
47 *United States Telegraph*, September 24, 1835.
48 John M. Sacher, *A Perfect War of Politics: Parties, Politicians, and Democracy in Louisiana, 1824–1861* (Baton Rouge: Louisiana State University Press, 2003), 76.
49 Rachel O'Connor to A. T. Conrad, August 3 and 24, 1835, and Rachel O'Connor to Frances. S. Weeks, September 7, 1835, David Weeks Collection, LSU.
50 New Orleans City Council, *Report of a Conspiracy to Incite a Rebellion Throughout the Slave States* (n.p., 1835), 1–3.
51 Dupre, *Transforming the Cotton Frontier*, 231–37.
52 Huntsville *Southern Advocate*, July 21, 1835.
53 Huntsville *Southern Advocate*, September 1, 1835.
54 Huntsville *Southern Advocate*, September 1 and 15, October 6, 1835.
55 *Niles' Register*, October 3, 1835; James B. Sellers, *Slavery in Alabama* (Tuscaloosa: University of Alabama Press, 1950), 368–69.
56 Milledgeville *Southern Recorder*, November 10, 1835.
57 Milledgeville *Southern Recorder*, November 27, 1835.
58 *North Carolina Standard*, November 10, 1835.
59 *Raleigh Register*, January 5, 1836.
60 *Camden Journal*, November 28, 1835.
61 *Charleston Mercury*, December 19, 1835.
62 John C. Calhoun to Francis Pickens, July 17, 1835, in *The Papers of John C Calhoun*, 12:542–44.
63 John C. Calhoun to Duff Green, August 30, 1835, in *The Papers of John C. Calhoun*, 12:547–48.
64 Quoted in Freehling, *Prelude to Civil War*, 346.
65 Freehling, *Prelude to Civil War*, 346–47.
66 Report from the Committee on Incendiary Publications, February 4, 1836, in *The Papers of John C Calhoun*, 13:54–67.
67 William W. Freehling, *The Road to Disunion: Secessionists at Bay, 1776–1854* (New York: Oxford University Press, 1990), 308–10.
68 Sean Wilentz, *The Rise of American Democracy: Jefferson to Lincoln* (New York: W. W. Norton, 2005), 411.

69 Freehling, *Prelude to Civil War*, 348.
70 Quoted in Wilentz, *The Rise of American Democracy*, 412.
71 Andrew Jackson to Amos Kendall, August 9, 1835, in *Correspondence of Andrew Jackson*, 5:360.
72 Speech on Abolition Petitions, March 9, 1836, in *The Papers of John C. Calhoun*, 13:91–110.
73 John C. Calhoun to Augustin S. Clayton and Others, August 5, 1836, in *The Papers of John C. Calhoun*, 13:262–65.
74 For an overview, see Freehling, *The Road to Disunion*, 1:310–66.
75 *Register of Debates, 24th Congress, 1st Session*, December 16, 1835: 1961.
76 *Register of Debates, 24th Congress, 1st Session*, January 21, 1836: 2242–3.
77 Edward W. Johnston to James H. Hammond, February 28 and March 9, 1836, James Henry Hammond Papers, LC (microfilm, SCL).
78 First Remarks on Receiving Abolition Petitions, January 7, 1836, in *The Papers of John C. Calhoun*, 13:22–25.
79 See Freehling, *The Road to Disunion*, 1:322–36.
80 Ibid., 326–27.
81 *Register of Debates, 24th Congress, 1st Session*, March 14, 1836: 810.
82 George W. Owens to Martin Van Buren, May 16, 1836, Martin Van Buren Papers, LC.
83 John Forsyth to Martin Van Buren, August 5, 1836, in William Allen Butler, *A Retrospect of Forty Years, 1825–1865* (New York: Charles Scribner's Sons, 1911), 78–79.
84 Martin Van Buren to Nathaniel Macon, February 13, 1836, quoted in Donald B. Cole, *Martin Van Buren and the American Political System* (Princeton: Princeton University Press, 1984), 270.
85 Freehling, *The Road to Disunion*, 1:329–36.
86 On Pinckney, see George C. Rogers Jr., "Henry Laurens Pinckney: Thoughts on His Career," in James B. Meriwether, ed., *South Carolina Journals and Journalists* (Spartanburg. SC: Reprint Company, 1975), 163–75.
87 Lacy K. Ford, *Origins of South Radicalism: The South Carolina Upcountry, 1800–1860* (New York: Oxford University Press, 1988), 155–57.
88 James H. Hammond to M. C. Hammond, February 21, 1836, James Henry Hammond Papers, SCL.
89 Robert Y. Hayne to James H. Hammond, January 18, 1836, James Henry Hammond Papers, LC (microfilm, SCL).
90 Henry L. Pinckney, *Address to the Electors of Charleston District, South Carolina, on the Subject of the Abolition of Slavery* (Washington, DC, 1836); *Register of Debates, 24th Congress, 1st Session*, February 8, 1836: 2491.
91 Ford, *Origins of South Radicalism*, 156–58.
92 James M. Smylie, *Review of a Letter from the Presbytery of Chillicothe to the Presbytery of Mississippi* (Woodville, MI: William A. Norris, 1836).
93 *Charleston Observer*, September 26, 1835; Charles Colcock Jones, *The Religious Instruction of the Negroes in the United States* (Savannah, GA: Thomas Purse, 1842), 77–80; Ralph Flanders, *Plantation Slavery in Georgia* (Chapel Hill: University of North Carolina Press, 1933), 172–80.
94 Erskine Clarke, *Dwelling Place: A Plantation Epic* (New Haven: Yale University Press, 2005), 172.

SEVENTEEN. THE IDEOLOGICAL RECONFIGURATION OF SLAVERY IN THE LOWER SOUTH

1 Susan Wyly-Jones, "The 1835 Anti-Abolition Meetings in the South: A New Look at the Controversy over the Abolition Postal Campaign," *Civil War History* 47 (December 2001): 289–309.

2 See Thomas L. Haskell, "Capitalism and the Origins of Humanitarian Sensibility, Parts I and II," *American Historical Review* 90 (April and June 1985): 339–61, 457–566. On this point, the question of whether or not the rise of humanitarianism was an outgrowth of the market revolution and the immediate abolition movement a product of that humanitarianism, as Haskell has argued, is not as important as the fact that a number of white southerners recognized the attack as grounded in humanitarianism, whatever its origins, and felt that an in-kind reply was essential.

3 Register of Debates, 24th Congress, 2nd Session (February 1, 1836): 2248–66.

4 John C. Calhoun, "Further Remarks in Debate of His Fifth Resolution," in *The Papers of John C. Calhoun*, ed. Clyde N. Wilson (Columbia: University of South Carolina Press, 1981), 14:80–86, quotations from 85–86.

5 Mitchell Snay, *Gospel of Disunion: Religion and Separatism in the Antebellum South* (New York: Cambridge University Press, 1993).

6 Larry Tise, *Proslavery: A History of the Defense of Slavery in America, 1701–1840* (Athens: University of Georgia Press, 1987), 323–62.

7 William W. Freehling, *The Road to Disunion: Secessionists Triumphant, 1854–1861* (New York: Oxford University Press, 2007).

8 Lacy K. Ford, "Making the 'White Man's Country' White: Race and State Constitutions in the Jacksonian South," *Journal of the Early Republic* 19 (Winter 1999): 713–37.

9 Michael O'Brien, *Conjectures of Order: Intellectual Life and the American South, 1810–1860* (New York: Cambridge University Press, 2005), 1:215–53.

10 Edmund Bellinger, *A Speech on the Subject of Slavery: Delivered 7 September 1835 at a Public Meeting of the Citizens of Barnwell District, South Carolina* (Charleston: Dan J. Dowling, 1835).

11 Register of Debates, 24th Congress, 2nd Session (February 1, 1836): 2248–66; William Harper, *Memoir on Slavery, Read Before the Society for the Advancement of Learning of South Carolina at Its Annual Meeting in Columbia, 1837* (Charleston: J. Burges, 1838).

12 John C. Calhoun, "Further Remarks in Debate of His Fifth Resolution," in *The Papers of John C. Calhoun*, 14:85–86.

13 Lumpkin quoted in Ralph Betts Flanders, *Plantation Slavery in Georgia* (Chapel Hill: University of North Carolina Press, 1933), 252.

14 James M. Smylie, *Review of a Letter From the Presbytery of Chillicothe to the Presbytery of Mississippi* (Woodville, MI: William A. Norris, 1836).

15 Daniel Whitaker, *Sidney's Letters to William E. Channing* (Charleston: Edward C. Counsell, 1837).

16 Thomas C. Thornton, *An Inquiry into the History of Slavery* (Washington, DC: W. M. Morrison, 1841).

17 Lacy K. Ford, "The Popular Ideology of the Old South's Plain Folk: The Limits of Egalitarianism in a Slaveholding Society," in Samuel Hyde, ed., *Plain Folk of the South Reconsidered* (Baton Rouge: Louisiana State University Press, 1997), 205–27.

18 Robert Barnwell Rhett, *Address to the People of Beaufort and Colleton Districts upon the Subject of Abolition, January 15, 1838* (n.p., 1838), 3–13; James Henry Hammond, *Two Letters on Slavery*

in the United States Addressed to Thomas Clarkson, Esq. (Columbia, SC: Allen and McCarter, 1845).

19 James Henry Hammond, "Hammond's Letters on Slavery," in *The Pro-Slavery Argument* (Charleston: Walker and Richards, 1852).

20 Theophilus Fisk, *The Bulwark of Freedom: An Oration Delivered at the Universalist Church in the City of Charleston, S.C., June 28, 1836* (Charleston: Office of the Southern Evangelist, 1836).

21 Basil Manly, "Duties of Masters and Servants, n.d.," Basil Manly Sermons, Archives and Special Collections, Southern Baptist Theological Seminary, Louisville, Kentucky.

22 Thornton, *An Inquiry into the History of Slavery.*

23 Abel Upshur, "Domestic Slavery," *Southern Literary Messenger* (October 1839): 677–87.

24 Ibid.

25 Thomas Cooper, *The Crisis: Being an Inquiry into the Measures Proper to be Adopted by the Southern States in Reference to the Proceedings of the Abolitionists* (Charleston: Dan J. Dowling, 1835).

26 James H. Thornwell, *The Rights and Duties of Masters: A Sermon Preached at the Dedication of a Church, Erected in Charleston, S.C., for the Benefit and Instruction of the Coloured Population* (Charleston: Walker and James, 1850).

27 *Laurensville Herald*, June 25, 1858.

28 Chester *Standard*, May 16, 1856.

29 Arthur Simkins, *Address Before the State Agricultural Society of South Carolina* (Edgefield, SC: Advertiser Office, 1855), esp. 1–2.

30 Speech of William King Easley, c. 1850, William King Easley Papers, SCL.

31 Address of O. Reed Broyles, c. 1849, O. R. Broyles Papers, DU.

32 Draft Speech of Benjamin Herndon Rice, c. 1860, Walllace, Rice, and Duncan Papers, SCL.

33 William Henry Trescot, *The Position and Course of the South* (Charleston: Walker and James, 1850), esp. 9–11, 60; and Trescot, "Oration Before the South Carolina Historical Society, 1859," *Russell's Magazine* 3 (July 1859): 289–307.

34 Erskine Clarke, *Dwelling Place: A Plantation Epic* (New Haven: Yale University Press, 2005), 167–79.

35 "Report and Resolutions of a Public Meeting at Pendleton, 9 September 1835," in *The Papers of John C. Calhoun*, edited by Robert L. Meriwether (Columbia: University of South Carolina Press, 1959–), 12:548–54.

36 Hammond, *Two Letters on Slavery.*

37 William Rufus Bailey, *The Issue, Presented in a Series of Letters on Slavery* (New York: John S. Taylor, 1837), esp. 56–64.

38 Richard Fuller and Francis Wayland, *Domestic Slavery Considered as a Scriptural Institution: In a Correspondence Between the Rev. Richard Fuller of Beaufort, S.C. and the Rev. Francis Weyland of Providence, R.I.* (New York: Lewis Colby, 1845), 138.

39 Thornwell, *The Rights and Duties of Masters.*

40 For an a fine overall treatment of Mississippi, see Randy J. Sparks, *On Jordan's Stormy Banks: Evangelicalism in Mississippi, 1773–1876* (Athens: University of Georgia Press, 1994), esp. 115–31.

41 Smylie, *Review of a Letter From the Presbytery of Chillicothe to the Presbytery of Mississippi.*

42 Quoted in Mitchell Snay, "American Thought and Southern Distinctiveness: The Southern Clergy and the Sanctification of Slavery," *Civil War History* 35 (December 1989): 322.

43 Basil Manly, "Duties of Masters and Servants," Basil Manly Sermons, SBTS.

44 Thornton, *An Inquiry into the History of Slavery.*

45 Timothy Flint, *Recollections of the Last Ten Years* (Boston: Cummings, Hilliard, 1826), 342–43.

46 John G. Jones, *A Concise History of the Introduction of Protestantism into Mississippi and the Southwest* (St. Louis: P. M. Pinckard, 1866), 240.

47 Sparks, *On Jordan's Stormy Banks,* 117; Jones, *A Complete History of Methodism as Connected with the Mississippi Conference* (Baton Rouge: Claitor's Book Store, 1966 [1887–1908]), 2:488; John G. Jones Autobiography and Journal, MDAH.

48 William Winans Autobiography, 10, 164–72; William Winans to Gerrit Smith, *Liberty (Mississippi) Advocate,* March 31, 1838.

49 "On the Emancipation of Slaves," c. 1821, Basil Manly Papers, SCL.

50 See A. James Fuller, *Chaplain to the Confederacy: Basil Manly and Baptist Life in the Old South* (Baton Rouge: Louisiana State University Press, 2000).

51 Randy J. Sparks, "Mississippi's Apostle of Slavery: James Smylie and the Biblical Defense of Slavery," *Journal of Mississippi History* 51 (May 1989): 89–106.

52 Jones, *A Concise History,* 240–41; Sparks, "Mississippi's Apostle of Slavery," 97–98.

53 Smylie quoted in Sparks, *On Jordan's Stormy Banks,* 120.

54 *Christian Herald,* October 1, 1836.

55 Smylie quoted in Sparks, *On Jordan's Stormy Banks,* 120.

56 Crystal Springs Methodist Circuit, Methodist Quarterly Conference Records, August 1844, MDAH; William Winans to Daniel de Vinne, 31 August 1841, Winans Papers, Cain Archives, Millsaps College.

57 Smylie, *Review of a Letter from the Presbytery of Chillicothe to the Presbytery of Mississippi,* 74.

58 Jonathan P. Stewart to Duncan McLaurin, November 30, 1848, Duncan McLaurin Papers, DU.

59 Thornton, *An Inquiry into the History of Slavery*; Fuller and Wayland, *Domestic Slavery Considered as a Scriptural Institution*; and Basil Manly, "Duties of Masters and Servants," Basil Manly Sermons, SBTS.

60 George Freeman, *The Rights and Duties of Slaveholders: Two Discourses Delivered on Sunday, November 27, 1836 in Christ Church, Raleigh, North Carolina* (Charleston: A. E. Miller, 1837).

61 Hammond, *Two Letters on Slavery.*

62 Bailey, *The Issue.*

63 Fuller and Wayland, *Domestic Slavery Considered as a Scriptural Institution.*

64 Edmund Bellinger, *A Speech on the Subject of Slavery.*

65 Thornwell, *The Rights and Duties of Masters.*

66 William W. Freehling, "James Henley Thornwell's Mysterious Antislavery Moment," *Journal of Southern History* 57 (1991): 383–406.

67 Bailey, *The Issue.*

68 Fuller and Wayland, *Domestic Slavery Considered as a Scriptural Institution.*

69 Thornton, *An Inquiry into the History of Slavery.*

70 Thornwell, *The Rights and Duties of Masters.*

71 The discussion draws heavily on my presentation in Lacy Ford, "Reconfiguring the Old South: 'Solving' the Problem of Slavery, 1787–1838," *Journal of American History* 95 (June 2008): 95–122. See also Susan Wyly-Jones, "The 1835 Anti-Abolition Meetings in the South," 289–309; Lacy Ford, "Inventing the Concurrent Majority: Madison, Calhoun and the Problem of Majoritarianism in American Political Thought," *Journal of Southern History* 60 (February 1994): 19–58, and "Prophet with Posthumous Honor: John C. Calhoun and the Southern

Political Tradition," in Charles Eagles, ed., *Is There a Southern Political Tradition?* (Jackson: University Press of Mississippi, 1996), 3–25, 207–11.

72 For the full exchange, see *Register of Debates*, 24th Congress, 2nd Session, cols. 717–24. For a perceptive overview of Rives' career, see McCoy, *Last of the Fathers*, 323–69.

73 Ashworth's argument on this point is found in his "The Relationship Between Capitalism and Humanitarianism," *American Historical Review* 92 (October 1997): 813–28, and "Free Labor, Wage Labor, and the Slave Power: Republicanism and the Republican Party in the 1850s," in Melvyn Stokes and Stephen Conway, eds., *The Market Revolution in America: Social, Political and Religious Expressions* (Charlottesville: University Press of Virginia, 1996):128–46. On the importance of its critique of slavery to the rise of the free-labor ideology in the North, see Eric Foner, *Free Soil, Free Labor and Free Men: The Ideology of the Republican Party Before the Civil War* (New York: Oxford University Press, 1970), 40–72; Eric Foner, "Free Labor and Nineteenth Century Political Ideology," in Stokes and Conway, eds., *The Market Revolution in America*, 99–127.

74 John C. Calhoun, "Further Remarks in Debate of His Fifth Resolution," in *The Papers of John C. Calhoun*, ed. Clyde N. Wilson (Columbia: University of South Carolina Press, 1981), 14:80–86, quotations taken from 85–86..

75 Harry L. Watson, "Slavery and Development in a Dual Economy: The South and the Market Revolution," in Stokes and Conway, eds., *The Market Revolution in America*, 43–73, offers an excellent analysis of the progress of the market revolution in the South. For an argument that the market revolution largely bypassed the South, a position I reject, see Douglas R. Egerton, "Markets Without a Market Revolution: Southern Planters and Capitalism," *Journal of the Early Republic* 16 (Summer 1996): 237–56. My argument in this paragraph differs from Ashworth's chiefly on the point of his unexamined assumption that traditional economic systems had long viewed "society as the family writ large" and that only with the rise of wage labor did social thinkers come to view the family as a "refuge" from society at large. I am arguing that it was the emergence of paternalism as a way of understanding slavery, not a set of social assumptions dating from precapitalist time immemorial, that allowed southern thinkers to understand slavery as a domestic institution and to see their society as one of extended households writ large. As such, an understanding matured among southern thinkers, religious and political, the quest for an ideological reconfiguration of slavery as the foundation for white independence and opportunity rather than as a temporary and necessary evil gained momentum in the region. My view of how white southerners increasingly saw slavery as a domestic institution parallels the view set forward in Young, *Domesticating Slavery*, esp. 123–92.

76 For the full exchange, see *Register of Debates*, 24th Congress, 2nd Session, cols. 717–24. For a perceptive overview of Rives' career, see McCoy, *Last of the Fathers*, 323–69.

77 *Register of Debates*, 24th Congress, 2nd Session, cols. 720–23.

78 Ford, "The Popular Ideology of the Old South's Plain Folk."

79 Peter S. Onuf, "'To Declare Them a Free and Independent People': Race, Slavery and National Identity in Jefferson's Thought," *Journal of the Early Republic* 18 (Spring 1998): 1–46.

80 For an analysis of Calhoun's thought on slavery as the economic foundation of a white republic, see Lacy K. Ford Jr., "Republican Ideology in a Slave Society: The Political Economy of John C. Calhoun," *Journal of Southern History* 54 (August 1988): 405–24. For a recent reassessment of Calhoun's thinking along similar lines, see O'Brien, *Conjectures of Order*, 2:848–66, 914–37.

81 *Proceedings of the Meeting in Charleston, S.C., May 13–15 on the Religious Instruction of the Negroes Together with the Report of the Committee and the Address to the Public* (Charleston: B. Jenkins, 1845), 3–5.

82 Ibid., 15; for an overview of the meeting, see Clarke, *Dwelling Place*, 247–52.

83 *Proceedings of the Meeting in Charleston, S.C.*, 13–18.

84 *Charleston Observer*, May 24, 1845.

85 *Proceedings of the Meeting in Charleston, S.C.*, 13–18.

86 Ibid., 5–7.

87 Ibid., 7–8.

88 Ibid., 8–9.

89 Ibid., 9–10.

90 Ibid., 19–71.

91 Ibid., 20–22, 23–26, 33–34.

92 Ibid., 26–28, 37–38.

93 Ibid., 35–36, 42, 46–47, 50–51.

94 Ibid., 56–58.

95 Ibid., 71–72.

INDEX